ACCOUNTING FOR FUNDAMENTALISMS

THE FUNDAMENTALISM PROJECT

—————————— VOLUME ——————————

4

ACCOUNTING FOR FUNDAMENTALISMS

The Dynamic Character of Movements

EDITED BY
Martin E. Marty and R. Scott Appleby

Sponsored by
The American Academy of Arts and Sciences

The University of Chicago Press
Chicago and London

MARTIN E. MARTY and R. SCOTT APPLEBY direct the Fundamentalism Project. Marty, the Fairfax M. Cone Distinguished Service Professor of the History of Modern Christianity at the University of Chicago, is senior editor of *Christian Century* and the author of numerous books, including the multi-volume *Modern American Religion,* also published by the University of Chicago Press. Appleby directs the Cushwa Center for the Study of American Catholicism at the University of Notre Dame, where he is associate professor of history. He is the author of *"Church and Age Unite!" The Modernist Impulse in American Catholicism.*

The collection of essays in this volume is based on a project conducted under the auspices of the American Academy of Arts and Sciences and supported by a grant from the John D. and Catherine T. MacArthur Foundation. The opinions expressed are those of the individual authors only, and do not necessarily reflect the views of the American Academy or the supporting foundation.

The University of Chicago Press, Chicago 60637
The University of Chicago Press, Ltd., London
© 1994 by The University of Chicago
All rights reserved. Published 1994
Printed in the United States of America

03 02 01 00 99 98 97 96 95 94   5 4 3 2 1

ISBN (cloth): 0-226-50885-4

Library of Congress Cataloging in Publication Data

Accounting for fundamentalisms : the dynamic character of movements / edited by Martin E. Marty and R. Scott Appleby ; sponsored by the American Academy of Arts and Sciences.
    p.   cm.—(The Fundamentalism project ; v. 4)
    Includes bibliographical references and index.
    1. Religious fundamentalism.   I. Marty, Martin E., 1928–
II. Appleby, R. Scott, 1956–   III. American Academy of Arts and Sciences.   IV. Series.
BL238.F83   1991 vol. 4
291'.09'04 s—dc20
[291'.09'04]   93-36621
                                                        CIP

∞ The paper used in this publication meets the minimum requirements of the American National Standard for Information Sciences—Permanence of Paper for Printed Library Materials, ANSI Z39.48–1984

CONTENTS

Part 4   Accounting for South Asian Fundamentalisms

Conclusion

ACKNOWLEDGMENTS

We thank first the advisers who began planning and conceptualizing this volume in meetings at the House of the American Academy of Arts and Sciences in Cambridge, Massachusetts. M. H. Abrams, Nancy T. Ammerman, T. N. Madan, Robert Fryken-berg, Stephen Graubard, Samuel Heilman, James Piscatori, Emmanuel Sivan, and Tu Wei-Ming participated in those sessions on May 6 and 7, 1990.

Also contributing in significant ways to the process of identifying and recruiting scholars and clarifying the themes for this volume were Gabriel Almond, James Barr, Daniel Brumberg, Calvin Goldscheider, Arthur Green, Bruce Lawrence, Frank Lech-ner, Franklin Presler, and M. Nazif Shahrani. Many other scholars contributed to this volume through written responses and criticisms of particular essays after they were presented during a public conference; those not mentioned by name here are ac-knowledged by the authors in the endnotes.

We owe a special debt of gratitude to Joel Orlen, executive officer of the American Academy of Arts and Sciences, for his leadership and encouragement in advancing the project from stage to stage.

We thank University of Chicago professors W. Clark Gilpin, dean of the Divinity School, and Frank Reynolds, director of the Institute for the Advanced Study of Religion, for providing intellectual stimulus, office space, and the semi-annual use of Swift Lecture Hall.

Alan Thomas of the University of Chicago Press made valuable recommendations and supervised the various phases of volume review and production with his usual high level of professionalism. Randolph M. Petilos, Jennie Lightner, and Kathy Gohl also contributed to the editorial process in significant ways.

Our industrious colleagues on the Fundamentalism Project staff make possible the appearance of these volumes after relatively brief intervals. Patricia Mitchell coordi-nated various phases of this volume's production and worked closely with the Press in preparing it for publication. By her energetic attention to detail and irrepressible enthusiasm, Barbara Lockwood once again proved herself an extraordinarily effective office manager, in whose debt the editors happily remain.

INTRODUCTION

Martin E. Marty and R. Scott Appleby

Accounting for Fundamentalisms: The Dynamic Character of Movements is the fourth volume in a series examining organized religious reaction to secular modernity in the twentieth century.

The first volume in the series, *Fundamentalisms Observed,* presented fourteen detailed studies of movements within Christianity, Judaism, Islam, Hinduism, Sikhism, Buddhism, and Confucianism which, despite the substantive differences among them in terms of doctrine, cosmology, social composition, size, organization, and scope of influence, share certain general traits. In those studies, "fundamentalism," the term used to refer to these shared traits,[1] connoted a tendency, a habit of mind, found within religious communities and paradigmatically embodied in certain representative individuals and movements. Fundamentalism appears as a strategy, or set of strategies, by which beleaguered believers attempt to preserve their distinctive identity as a people or group. Feeling this identity to be at risk, fundamentalists fortify it by a selective retrieval of doctrines, beliefs, and practices from a sacred past. These retrieved "fundamentals" are refined, modified, and sanctioned in a spirit of shrewd pragmatism: they are to fend off outsiders who threaten to draw the believers into a syncretistic, areligious, or irreligious cultural milieu. Moreover, these fundamentals are accompanied in the new religious portfolio by unprecedented claims and doctrinal innovations. By the strength of these innovations, the retrieved and updated fundamentals are meant to regain the same charismatic intensity today by which they forged communal identity from the formative religious experiences long ago.

In this sense contemporary fundamentalism is at once both derivative and vitally original. In their efforts to reclaim the efficacy of religious life, fundamentalists have much in common with other religious revivalists of past centuries. But fundamentalism intends neither an artificial imposition of archaic practices and lifestyles nor a simple return to a golden era, a sacred past, a bygone time of origins—although nostalgia for such an era is a hallmark of fundamentalist rhetoric. Instead, religious identity thus renewed becomes the exclusive and absolute basis for a re-created political and social order that is oriented to the future rather than the past. By selecting elements of tradition and modernity, fundamentalists seek to remake the world in the service of a dual commitment to the unfolding eschatological drama (by returning all

1

things in submission to the divine) and to self-preservation (by neutralizing the threatening Other). Such an endeavor often requires charismatic and authoritarian leadership, depends upon a disciplined inner core of adherents, and promotes a rigorous sociomoral code for all followers. Fundamentalists set and maintain boundaries, identify and mythologize their enemies, seek converts, and create and sustain an array of institutions in pursuit of a comprehensive reconstruction of society.

The second and third volumes in the series were published simultaneously in 1993 as companion pieces, for they explored the extent of influence or "impact" of fundamentalist movements, from the early twentieth century to the year 1990, in six "zones" or spheres of human existence. *Fundamentalisms and Society* described fundamentalist worldviews and the impact of Islamic, Christian, and Jewish fundamentalisms on scientific research and the application of technology in societies in North America and the Middle East. It also analyzed fundamentalist prescriptions for family life and the role of women in the United States, Latin America, Egypt, Iran, Pakistan and Japan. Finally, the volume examined fundamentalist educational systems and communications networks in the United States, Guatemala, Israel, Iran, and India. *Fundamentalisms and the State* was more comprehensive, examining fundamentalist (or fundamentalist-like) inroads in politics and lawmaking, fundamentalist economic policies, and militant fundamentalists' use of violence as a political tool. Case studies included Christian fundamentalists in the United States and Northern Ireland; Muslim fundamentalists in Iran, Egypt, Pakistan, Saudi Arabia, Sudan, and Turkey; Jewish fundamentalists in Israel; and Hindu, Sikh, and Buddhist "fundamentalists" in South Asia.

The two-part study of fundamentalist influence yielded many conclusions too complex to summarize here, but it demonstrated repeatedly that, because the state regulates many aspects of social existence and establishes the basic political and cultural conditions within which social life occurs, fundamentalists inevitably become involved in modern political life, even when they attempt to preserve their separateness from secular society. In so doing they participate in a common discourse about modernization, development, political structures, and economic planning. Fundamentalists may nuance and modify the terms of that discourse—they may successfully or unsuccessfully try to redirect or reinvent aspects of it—but they are contained within it and find any hope of even a partial return to a pristine premodern world, much less the construction of a purely Islamic or Christian or Jewish modern society or polity, well out of reach.

When they play politics to influence the policies of the state, fundamentalisms are thus necessarily involved in some measure of compromise and accommodation. Political involvement may alter the original exclusivist, dogmatic, and confrontational mode of the fundamentalist to such a degree that the word "fundamentalism" or its cognates may no longer seem to apply. In the attempts to create alternative social and educational institutions, however, the arena of fundamentalist concern is more narrowly circumscribed for maximum effect and minimum compromise. Authors of *Fundamentalisms and Society* use words like "pragmatist" or "accommodationist" to describe their subjects less frequently than do authors of *Fundamentalisms and the*

State. The authors of *Fundamentalisms and Society* discuss fundamentalist strategies designed to challenge the state selectively rather than to destroy or remake it through the proximate means of a national election, a coup, or a popular revolution. An intense preoccupation of fundamentalists with individual conduct and interpersonal relations has had significant consequences for women in their relationship to men and to children, and for children in terms of their education and upbringing. The chapters on women, family, and education document intense and persistent efforts on the part of fundamentalists to secure what they describe as a traditional social and religious order.

Indeed, with a few important exceptions, fundamentalists have enjoyed the greater success in reclaiming the intimate zones of life in their own religious communities than in remaking the political or economic order according to the revealed norms of the traditional religion. Yet they persist in making forays into the outside world; they persist in activism designed either to protect or expand the borders of their enclave or to transform some aspect of the environment which threatens to undermine their hold on values and lifestyles they find essential to their identity.

Accounting for Fundamentalisms picks up the story at this point by examining the conditions under which a fundamentalist religious group, movement, or organization changes its ideological and behavioral patterns, as a result of internal developments as well as engagement with people and forces outside the group or movement. Each author was asked, in writing about the movement he or she knows best, to examine the relationship, over time, between the *organizational characteristics of fundamentalist movements* (their various structures, sizes and social compositions, recruitment processes, modes of governance or decision-making, and means of retaining members and mobilizing resources) and their *changing worldviews, ideologies, and programs* (the "fields of discourse" they construct through the reinterpretation of symbols and ethical traditions, through the stories they tell of themselves, of the world, and of their aims, etc.). How may we account for the various attitudes, ideologies, and behaviors of fundamentalist movements toward the outside world? Drawing upon the same religious tradition, why do certain fundamentalist movements act aggressively against outsiders, while others are integrationist or accommodationist, still others passive or separatist in relation to the surrounding community and culture?

In choosing cases to examine within religious traditions, then, the teams of scholars that contributed sections of the volume were particularly attentive to the various modes of action adopted by a movement over the span of its recent (twentieth century) history. Movements that fall within the family of comparative "fundamentalisms" have organized themselves for action "over against" a dominant political, social, and/or religious culture; but many have also at some juncture adopted programs of withdrawal and isolation from society. Others retreat from a stance that could be called radical fundamentalism—marked by a movement's insistence on retaining its separateness by aggressive action or protective withdrawal—and willingly become assimilated to some degree into a larger political, social, and/or cultural milieu. The following chapters examine these various modes of fundamentalist movement behavior, and attempt to account for the changes by examining the external environment as well as the internal dynamics of the movement in question. In other words, the explanation of a particular fundamentalist movement is to be found in the interaction between the external environment and the organizational characteristics, worldview, and historical experience of the movement itself. This interaction, in turn, yields the dynamic relationship within the movement between worldview/program and the organizational structures and processes that serve to advance or give expression to the worldview and to implement the program.

Despite the specificity of these guidelines, they have not served as a procrustean bed confining the expansive talents of the various experts contributing to the volume. Each author has followed his or her own interpretation of these guidelines, using them to enhance rather than restrict the presentation of the significant ideological and organizational shifts of the movement in question. In examining changes over time, for example, some authors thought in terms of decades, others in years or even months. The essays on the Jewish haredi fundamentalist movements, for example, take the long perspective, tracing the development of the haredi ideology and organization from the late nineteenth century (but they do tend to contrast two identifiable phases), while Jean-François Legrain's analysis of the dynamic nature of the (much younger) Islamic movement of Palestinian resistance, Hamas, focuses on the state of the movement immediately before and after the Gulf War of 1990–91.

The volume is intended as a major resource for students, commentators, and policy analysts who seek to understand the conditions under which movements are themselves transformed by their protest against the established order. Each of the four sections of the volume was coordinated by an associate editor, a scholar of that particular type of fundamentalism, who helped the general editors select and recruit the authors, formulate the guidelines presented above, and shape the individual essays according to these guidelines. Thus Nancy T. Ammerman, Samuel C. Heilman, James Piscatori, and Robert Frykenberg were our close collaborators in preparing this volume. Each of these scholars has also provided a synthetic essay summarizing and analyzing the themes and findings of the various studies in each section of the volume.

Together the essays in the present volume form part of the basis for the next volume in the series, *Fundamentalisms Compared,* which will take a synoptic view of the previous scholarly and journalistic research on the topic in order to construct an explanatory model of global, antisecular, religious resurgence. In that volume, comparativists and theorists will also review the various usages of the word "fundamentalism" and debate whether or not one (Western, originally Protestant Christian) term, even when emptied of its original connotations and used as a broad comparative construct, is sufficient to encompass the "family resemblances" noted by scholars studying these phenomena. Those scholars may conclude that "fundamentalism" is simply too laden with pejorative or imperialist connotations to be employed by responsible commentators; or, they may determine that the term does in fact describe the central substantive similarity among the various movements, namely, the process of selective retrieval, embellishment, and/or construction of "essentials" or "fundamentals" of a religious tradition for the purposes of halting the erosion of traditional society and fighting back against the encroachments of secular modernity. In any case, the Fundamentalism Project directors and advisory committee decided at the outset of the endeavor, in 1988, to postpone delivering final verdicts on the use of the term until the bulk of the research and writing had provided the comparativists with ample grist for their theoretical mills. Thus most (but not all) of the scholars contributing to the present volume, as in previous volumes of the series, do use the term "fundamentalism" generally to describe the movement in question, but they do so with several qualifications in mind and with the assurance that we editors will inform readers that the term is used here in a tentative and exploratory rather than an absolute way.

The present volume does not engage in direct comparison across traditions, although the reader of the entire volume, or even of more than one section, will readily notice the recurrence of certain key "triggers" of fundamentalist activism across religious traditions and geographical regions. Several themes recur in the twenty-eight chapters that follow; three of these themes merit special mention in an introduction orienting readers to the accomplishments and limitations of the volume.

First, it is not clear that every entity examined as a "fundamentalism" is primarily a "movement." In fact there are fundamentalist or fundamentalist-like groups, organizations, and movements examined herein. Robert Frykenberg, in introducing the chapters on South Asian fundamentalisms, observes this distinction by arguing that the Jamaat-i-Islami, which has in its lifetime undergone a shift from a popular movement to a fundamentalist political organization, might be less influential in the long run than the Tablighi Jamaat, which is clearly a movement in every sense of the word—it is fluid, popular, dynamic, driven by a singular vision rather than by bureaucratic inertia or by routinized organizational requirements.

In this distinction lies a telling question to be posed to fundamentalisms that attempt to remain oppositional, exclusivist, and antisecularist but that also organize themselves for effective participation in political processes: Is it possible for a fundamentalist *movement* to be sustained over a long period of time, especially after the death of its charismatic leader (see the essays on Habad Hasidism in this volume by Friedman and Ravitzky) or after it wins some measure of influence and political success and earns a niche in the existing order (see the Ammerman and Wuthnow essays on Christian fundamentalism in this volume)? Or are fundamentalist movements that seek political power destined to become organizations or pressure groups? If so, how does this transformation affect the character of the fundamentalist impulse by which the entity originated—its religious idealism, for example, or its absolutist mentality?

In the concluding chapter, sociologist Rhys H. Williams sets the discussions of particular "movements" in the context of recent work on organizational theory and the sociology of social movements. He utilizes the concept of social movement organizations (SMOs) as a way of comparing the diverse expressions of fundamentalist activism examined in the volume. Readers who prefer to frame their study of the rich empirical material and analysis of the individual chapters may wish to turn to Williams' chapter first before plunging into the particular cases.

A second theme recurring in these studies is that fundamentalism is a reaction to secular modernity, but it is not necessarily reactionary. Rather than portraying fundamentalist SMOs as impelled primarily by people losing their established place in society, the authors of several case studies establish the fact that the fundamentalist

activists often are *newly* empowered people using whatever methods, ideas, and languages they have available. The distinction between SMO leaders and "rank and file"
members is perhaps less important than the distinction between the charismatic and/
or authoritarian preacher or imam or guru, who serves as the religious inspiration
and moral guide of the movement, and the operational leaders and followers, who are
charged with implementing his moral code and spiritual (or religio-nationalist) vision.
The latter group, the functionaries of the SMO, tend to be drawn heavily from among
student populations and unemployed or underemployed youth. They may inherit the
mantle of the prophet, but fundamentalists are also concerned with carving out a
niche for themselves in the social order. The "language of return" to a sacred past is
particularly useful for groups in these situations, since it provides a legitimacy that
their social statuses may not automatically provide.

This leads to a third general theme found in the following essays: the ironic and
striking fluidity and adaptability of movements that presume themselves to be defending timeless, fixed, and immutable "fundamentals." Everywhere the external environment—no less than the internal dynamics generated by resource needs, the
requirements of mobilization, and ideological-organizational shifts over time—poses
continuing challenges to the self-definition of fundamentalists. These changing circumstances dictate that the fundamentalist SMOs transform themselves in order to
meet the various requirements of survival, state oppression or manipulation, or, in
some cases, success in the political arena.

In short, it seems that in order to defend tradition, fundamentalists must constantly reinterpret it or select from among its diverse teachings and behavioral norms
the appropriate prescription for the particular needs of the moment. In some cases,
as in Egyptian Islamic radicalism or the three-tiered Hindu nationalist revival, the
"movement"—actually, a constellation of SMOs, some autonomous and discrete,
others overlapping—operates at different levels simultaneously, resourcing different
traditions to ground an array of strategies in the long conflict with the secular government. In other settings, as in the case of militant Iraqi Shi'ism or political Islam in
Algeria, the internal dynamics of the movement are almost entirely triggered by fluctuations in the external environment, especially the policies of the state.

Given that the following essays were completed in 1992 and early 1993, it is worth
noting that the rapid dynamism of the movements under consideration, as they interact with the sociopolitical environment, guarantees that they will have changed again,
perhaps several times, in the year or so required to produce a book from this manuscript. Already, in early 1993, the tentative process of "normalization" between the
Mubarak government and the radical Islamist movements of Egypt, described by Gehad Auda in this volume, seems endangered by a new cycle of government repression
and radical activism; already, in early 1993, Algerian Islam was reportedly reconsti-
tuting itself after the FLN crackdown discussed by Hugh Roberts; already, in the
aftermath of the 6 December 1992 destruction of the Babri Masjid in Ayodhya and
the ensuing communal riots and outlawing of Hindu militant organizations, the organizational strategies and rhetoric of India's Hindu, Sikh, Muslim, and Christian
activists have been profoundly altered.

Well aware of the rapidly changing fortunes of fundamentalist movements, whose dynamism is the basic premise of this volume, the contributors to *Accounting for Fundamentalisms* do not attempt to predict the future or present the latest developments (which by now are old news) as conclusive. Rather, the contributing scholars provide the type of analysis that will help readers to understand and account for new developments in years to come. Shortly after David Stoll consigned his essay on Guatemalan evangelicals to the press, for example, that country's born again president, Jorge Serrano Elías, suspended basic constitutional rights, dissolved the Congress and the Supreme Court, and claimed almost dictatorial powers in response to a political crisis—a surprising series of moves that alienated most Guatemalans, as well as the international community, and led, two weeks later, to Serrano's overthrow. These developments reflected a confluence of factors, including the inherent political and economic instability of Guatemalan society, a condition which Stoll discusses at length in accounting for the niche occupied by Pentecostals in Guatemalan society, as well as the (highly unpredictable) individual freedom of the main actor in the drama, Mr. Serrano—personal freedom being an "independent variable" which neither Stoll nor any other social scientist (much less ordinary human beings) can hope to "account for," but which nonetheless plays a decisive role in religious and political behavior as in other arenas of human conduct. Neither is Ousmane Kane's analysis of Nigeria's Izala movement rendered any less useful to analysts and students of fundamentalism by the fact that, six months after Kane completed the essay, the country's president, General Ibrahim Babangida, voided the results of the long-awaited national elections of June 1993, throwing Nigeria into a convulsion of riots and political crises that left no major social actor unaffected—including the Islamic fundamentalists.

The following pages suggest that fundamentalist movements are not entirely unlike other religious or ideological activists, but they face an additional challenge of having to justify ideological shifts, and the programmatic changes accompanying them, to members who base their loyalty in part upon the assumption of both consistency and immutability in the fundamental doctrines and goals of the movement. Susan Harding, among other contributors, explores this tension between professed and operative beliefs in her analysis of the shift in North American Christian fundamentalism's apocalyptic ideology from a strict premillennial dispensationalism, which framed a program of radical separatism from the mainstream of American political and cultural life, to an unspoken postmillennialism which allowed Christian activists to organize for effective political participation in anticipation of Jesus' Second Coming in glory.

The first three sections of this volume are organized according to a single religious tradition and the various forms or movements of fundamentalism within it (Christianity, Judaism, Islam), while the fourth section is organized according to a region, South Asia. This decision was not arbitrary; it was made after considerable discussion and debate about the nature of fundamentalisms and the presence of a unique set of circumstances in South Asia in which at least four religious traditions have produced "fundamentalist-like" movements or groups in the last thirty to fifty years. We might have simply labeled the section "Hinduism," but it is clear that the rise of Hindu nationalism was an important "trigger" for the formation of countermovements in Islam, Sikhism, Buddhism, and Christianity within the same region and during the same historical era. To "account for" Hindu "fundamentalism" without also "accounting for" the dynamics of these other virulent forms of fundamentalism would have been to tell only a part of the story.

The topics discussed in this volume elicit great passion both from fundamentalists and from those who would oppose them or even seek merely to understand them. The authors, many of whom hail from the nations or religious traditions about which they are writing, are nonetheless resolutely "of the Western academy." The editors asked them to put in brackets their own presuppositions, an approach that does not mean they successfully leave them behind, but that they become aware of them, take them into consideration, and do some compensating for them. The goal in every case is to come up with essays in which the people described therein would recognize themselves in the portrait, even if they would almost inevitably disagree with the conclusions and evaluations of these nonfundamentalist authors.

The fact that nonfundamentalists do the writing guarantees that this volume, and the entire project, reflects a particular orientation to foundational questions and produces conclusions in keeping with that orientation. What are the sources of truth? What are the appropriate criteria for evaluating data and judging success or failure? From the perspective of a nonfundamentalist, fundamentalisms are often scandalous. They appear to stand in the way of individual self-determination, to violate basic human rights, and to impede material advancement, progress, and prosperity. But this is precisely the point of fundamentalisms: they and their God are not to be judged according to human standards. One cannot evaluate social behavior along strictly humanistic lines; behavior is good if it conforms to God's will. Thus, the reasoning goes, critics who do not share the ethical and philosophical assumptions of fundamentalists cannot hope to do them justice.

In mentioning this important matter of various perspectives on a controversial subject such as fundamentalism, it is important to state clearly that the positions or interpretations put forth in this collection of essays are those of the individual authors and do not necessarily reflect the views of the American Academy of Arts and Sciences. In undertaking this project, the principal purpose of the Academy is to bring together scholars with the best credentials in the several areas and cultures under study, and to ask them to present as inclusive and fair a presentation as possible. We are confident that the readers of the present volume will conclude that this purpose has been well served.

Notes

1. What the editors wrote in their introduction to *Fundamentalisms Observed* is also true of the present volume: Let it be said at the outset that the directors of the project have assured all authors herein that in this introduction and in all that follows, they will

make it emphatically clear that "fundamentalism" is not always the first choice or even a congenial choice at all for some of the movements here discussed. Most of the essayists take some pains to say why they are uneasy with the term, and they say so often, with evident awareness that some of their colleagues who specialize in the same topics will criticize their assent to use the term. We have asked them to keep their apologias brief, since we would elaborate here. Among the reasons for insistence on a single term are these:

First, "fundamentalism" is here to stay, since it serves to create a distinction over against cognate but not fully appropriate words such as "traditionalism," "conservatism," or "orthodoxy" and "orthopraxis." If the term were to be rejected, the public would have to find some other word if it is to make sense of a set of global phenomena which urgently bids to be understood. However diverse the expressions are, they present themselves as movements that demand comparison even as they deserve fair separate treatment so that their special integrities will appear in bold relief. Second, when they must communicate across cultures, journalists, public officials, scholars, and publics in the parts of the world where these books have their first audience have settled on this term. Rather than seek an idiosyncratic and finally precious alternative, it seemed better for the team of scholars to try to inform inquiry with the word that is here to stay and to correct misuses.

With those two reasons goes a third: all words have to come from somewhere and will be more appropriate in some contexts than in others. Words which have appeared in these paragraphs—"modern," "religious," "liberal," and "secular"—are examples. It is urgent in all cases that these terms be used in such ways that they do justice to the particularities of separate realities, something which we are confident readers will find the present authors responsibly undertaking to do. Fourth, having spent four of the five years set aside for research and study comparing "fundamentalism" to alternatives, we have come to two conclusions. No other coordinating term was found to be as intelligible or serviceable. And attempts of particular essayists to provide distinctive but in the end confusing accurate alternatives led to the conclusion that they were describing something similar to what are here called fundamentalisms. The prefix "ultra-" or the word "extremist" did not connote enough. When scholars made suggestions for replacements such as "revolutionary neo-traditionalist Islamic (or Jewish, or Christian, or whatever) radicalism" and were then asked to define these alternatives, they came to describe pretty much what the other authors were calling "fundamentalism."

We early came to an agreement, then, that the authors could take some pains to mention any uneasinesses they had with the term, with the assurance that we editors would ask readers constantly to think of what we here call "fundamentalisms" as being equal to "fundamentalist-like" movements. It will be appropriate in virtually every case to picture individual quotation marks surrounding the term and then proceed with the inquiry and the reading. If people cannot agree on cross-cultural terms like the chosen one, "fundamentalism," they are also not likely to agree on all features of its definition. Readers of these essays will find, however, that the authors have certain elements of definition in mind, without which they would not know what to seek. Ludwig Wittgenstein's concept of "family resemblances" seems appropriate.

1

Accounting for Christian Fundamentalisms

The Dynamics of Christian Fundamentalism: An Introduction

Nancy T. Ammerman

In the volumes that have preceded this one in the Fundamentalism Project, a vast array of fundamentalist-like movements has been described, and their activities in the world have been analyzed. We have seen traditionalist movements from North America to East Asia emerging in cultures that vary from the most newly "developing" to the "postmodern." We have observed the social labor of believers adapting old ideas to new situations and new situations to the dictates of their faith. These are movements that seek to remake the world—to shape the families and schools, economies and polities in which we live. And yet they are also movements made by the very worlds they seek to remake. As they interact with the cultures and institutions around them, their own ideas about themselves and their mission evolve.

This volume brings us to the task of examining that interaction between fundamentalisms and the social world, attempting to see the regularities and patterns in it. We approach the task by way of comparison. What can we learn by looking at similar movements in different contexts? or by looking at different movements in the same context? Which processes of mobilization and world construction are similar enough to shed light across cultures and movements? And which movements show us by their differences where the bounds of definition must be located? Much of what we know about the social world is, of course, known by comparison. We recognize the shape of one object by noting its differences from another, create a name for this because we see it is different from that. In the sections that follow, we look—by comparison—for the ways in which this thing we have named "fundamentalism" can be recognized.

Fundamentalism is perhaps most familiar to us in its original North American Protestant guise. Arising in the United States around the turn of this century, it set out a defense of orthodox beliefs about the Bible, a defense of traditional virtues and ways of life. Although these beliefs and practices were widely shared in the United States throughout the nineteenth century, by the beginning of the twentieth century they were seen as changing and under threat. Declaring themselves ready to "do battle royal for the fundamentals of the faith,"[1] believers took on, during the 1920s, both their own denominations and the nation's schools. They organized campaigns against religious liberalism in the churches and the teaching of evolution in the schools. But in both arenas, fundamentalists lost their crusades for institutional and rhetorical control. Modern voices gained hegemony.[2]

Despite their apparent defeat in those campaigns, fundamentalists proved resilient and innovative in the years ahead. They built an extensive institutional infrastructure, concentrating their energies on evangelism and missions, education and publishing. They maintained a vibrant subculture in the midst of the modern world, a way of life both very modern and defiantly antimodern. The fundamentalist story about the world and the fundamentalist way of living in the world remained plausible for a sizable segment of the U.S. population even while the writers of history books were assuming fundamentalism had disappeared.

Then in the mid-1970s, fundamentalists again began to occupy the public arena in the United States. Led by such television preachers as Jerry Falwell and Pat Robertson, fundamentalists shed their reticence about political action. They held giant rallies and registered voters, organized their own Christian schools and elected state legislators. Rather than wait for an apocalyptic end to history, they were determined to change the way history is written. Building on the infrastructure already in place, fundamentalists seemed to regain a place in the cultural and political landscape of the country. Assessing the sources of this renewed public activism is one of the tasks of this section. We look for the ways in which the activist vision of recent years is different from fundamentalism's earlier quieter periods, paying special attention to the dynamic nature of the relationship between belief and culture.

Both during the apparently "inactive" interim and in this renewed period of activism, one of the channels for fundamentalist energy has been overseas mission work. Missionaries have spread their message out over the world, continuing the Protestant "errand to the world" begun in the nineteenth century,[3] but giving it the particular flavor born in the fundamentalist cultural struggles of the 1920s. By the 1970s, in Latin America, mission work (and a variety of changes that made the culture more open to their efforts)[4] had begun to result in a burgeoning evangelical population. Some converts had ties to strict fundamentalist mission agencies, others to less hardline "evangelical" groups, others to "mainline" missions of long standing. But the fastest growing groups were Pentecostal and charismatic in nature, mostly Protestant, but Catholic as well.[5]

As a result, the doctrines and lifestyles of North American fundamentalists were being transported into new cultures, becoming intertwined with the cultures and politics of those societies in controversial new ways. Latin American converts in city and countryside became teetotaling Bible readers, witnessing to the power of being "born again." The ideas they preach sound like "gringo" fundamentalism, and their ascetic way of life seems to duplicate U.S. taboos. This Latin extension of fundamentalist mission work, then, offers us a chance to see how a vastly different context interacts with beliefs and practices held in common across the borders. As I argue in the conclusion of this section, beliefs and practices rightly called "fundamentalism" in the United States are more properly called "innovation" south of the Rio Grande.

More properly called fundamentalist—but in still another cultural context—were the traditionalist movements arising within Catholicism during this same period. In Italy, the traditional dominance of the Catholic Church has, within the last generation, noticeably eroded. Constitutional changes deprived the Church of its privileged status, and cultural changes removed the Church from the center of public discourse. Still, many Italians found their lives most meaningfully integrated by the rigorous Catholic discipline and activity of their local *scuole di communità*, a branch of Comunione e Liberazione. They eagerly pursued a Catholic way of life that encompassed economic, political, cultural, and personal domains, remaking both individual and community life in the process. Looking at the Italian Catholic experience offers another important contrast. The beliefs and practices are different, as is the political context, but there are structural and rhetorical similarities that keep this case within the fundamentalist family.

Protestant activists in the United States, Protestant innovators in Latin America, and Catholic traditionalists in Italy—these are the cases that frame our questions. In each case, we look at the kind of story the movement tells about the world, listening for the way in which it "selectively retrieves" elements from the society's tradition, while reweaving those elements into new habits of life and mind. We listen as well for the way in which those stories stand in contrast to and in dialogue with the social world inhabited by each movement. Fundamentalists, we find, are keenly observant culture critics. The stories that tell them who they are also tell them who they are not, setting out both a vision of future triumph and a litany of the world's woes. And as with all good stories, the plot is malleable enough to adapt to changing audiences and new circumstances.

Fundamentalist ideas do not, of course, exist in the cultural stratosphere. They are generated and supported in concrete social institutions. In each of our cases, we look for characteristic modes of institution building. We examine the scope and form of the organizations each movement has sought to build. We look for the way fundamentalism transforms personal and familial lives and the necessity for placing those lives inside a creative social space where the transformation can continue. While such institutionalizing does not distinguish fundamentalism from any other social movement, *as* a social movement, fundamentalism must establish its own distinctive social forms.

Sometimes those social forms have existed largely out of public sight, leaving the world of economy and state unchallenged. But sometimes fundamentalism assumes an activist form, seeking to remake the institutional and cultural world beyond its own subcultural borders. Such activism arises in response both to the movement's own resources and connections and to the demands and structures of the world outside. Its forms and strategies are shaped both by the group's ideology and by the particular political traditions and structures within which it works. As we compare Ecuador, Guatemala, the United States, and Italy, we may be able to see the extent to which fundamentalism itself shapes the form of the activity, as well as how that activity pours fundamentalist content into a mold shaped by the culture's particular political economy.

We begin our comparison of the dynamics of Christian fundamentalist movements with an orienting essay by Robert Wuthnow and Matthew P. Lawson. They offer us a sociological framework for understanding the dynamics of fundamentalist movements. These authors focus primarily on the recent activism of U.S. Protestant fundamentalists, making some comparisons to various European and Latin American cases. They offer us a theory of "cultural articulation," arguing that understanding fundamentalism's durability requires understanding the particular "fit" it has established between ideas and social structure. They ask about the conditions under which fundamentalism arises, the relationship between those movements and their environments, and the factors that make survival most likely.

Chapter 3 is a more specialized look at recent fundamentalist activism in the United States. Susan Harding's analysis tells us not so much about *why* fundamentalist activism gained momentum but about *how* the movement itself was transformed. By closely examining changes in apocalyptic discourse—talk about the end times—she shows how fundamentalists carved out a rhetorical space as active cultural critics and how their reading of the past and future challenged "conventional" readings. In developing new ways of telling stories about God's action in cosmic history, she argues, new forms of human action became possible.

This same sort of close analysis of the interaction between culture and ideology, between discourse and action, is present in chapter 4 by Tod D. Swanson. By listening to testimonies and going to the evangelical *conferencias* of Quichua Indians in Ecuador, Swanson found the old indigenous cultural patterns among the new. He also shows us how old patterns paved the way for change, and how new religious patterns made various economic and political behaviors more likely. We begin, in his essay, to see how the converts of fundamentalist missionaries are both similar and dissimilar from their North American counterparts.

The mix of North American influence and indigenous political circumstances in Guatemala is taken up by David Stoll in chapter 5. The growth of Protestantism in Guatemala, and the sixteen-month reign of a "born-again dictator" (Ríos Montt) have thrust apparently quiescent evangelicals toward the public arena. That arena is, however, infested with corruption and raw military power. Stoll looks for the ways converted businessmen, politicians, and military officers are changing their own lives and wonders whether those individual changes will have any effect on the intransigent political and economic problems of the country.

What we see in each of these essays are conservative religious groups offering a critique of the culture in which they live and setting forth a vision of change. How they frame those critiques is variable, however—some assume shared but threatened traditions, for instance, while others proclaim a new vision. Also variable are the opportunities and constraints that make each vision more or less believable and workable.

In the final case, chapter 6, Dario Zadra takes us inside Comunione e Liberazione, an international movement based in Italy. An examination of this movement allows

us to see the effects of a society where the Catholic Church has enjoyed official establishment status. We see similarities to the U.S. case and differences from the Latin
ones. We look for the words and actions that give reality to the movement's argument
that society should be resacralized. Instead of defending the inerrancy of the Bible,
Catholic traditionalists are defending the authority of the pope and the legitimate
place of the Church at the center of society. Nevertheless, they seem to share with
other fundamentalists a concern with creating a space in which traditions can be sustained and made relevant.

Each writer describes the internal social dynamics out of which ideas and leaders
and institutions emerge, along with the external social dynamics that create opportunities and constraints for these movements. Harding and Swanson pay special attention to internal dynamics, especially how language and action take shape. Wuthnow
and Lawson, along with Stoll, concentrate more on the external forces with which
movements must contend, although they note various internal factors as well. Zadra
looks at the full range of internal and external dynamics in Comunione e Liberazione,
examining both the way it orders and critiques the world and the way it organizes to
seek change.

In the final chapter in part 1, I draw together what we have observed, sketching
out the commonalities and highlighting the differences. Many of the factors we see in
these pages are common social dynamics at work whenever groups of people—religious or secular—seek to interpret and act within a cultural and institutional world
only partially of their own making. The social dynamics of Christian fundamentalism
are both generic "social dynamics," common to all social movements and forces, and
strategies shaped particularly by their own special view of the world.

Notes

1. Curtis Lee Laws in the *Watchman Ex-
aminer,* quoted in G. Marsden, *Fundamentalism and American Culture* (New York:
Oxford University Press, 1980), p. 158.

2. For a discussion of the struggle for
rhetorical hegemony, see Susan Harding,
"Observing the Observers," in N. T. Ammerman, ed., *Southern Baptists Observed*
(Knoxville: University of Tennessee Press,
1993).

3. See W. R. Hutchison, *Errand to the
World: American Protestant Thought and Foreign Missions* (Chicago: University of Chicago Press, 1987). See also Joel A.
Carpenter, "Fundamentalist Institutions and

the Rise of Evangelical Protestantism,
1929–1942," *Church History* 49, no. 1
(1980): 62–75.

4. Daniel Levine offered a helpful exposition of the conditions for Protestant gains
in Latin America in "Protestants and Catholics in Latin America: A Family Portrait"
(Paper presented to the public conference of
the Fundamentalism Project, November
1991).

5. For a discussion of figures on church
membership in Latin America, see David
Stoll, *Is Latin America Turning Protestant?*
(Berkeley: University of California Press,
1990).

2

Sources of Christian Fundamentalism in the United States

Robert Wuthnow and Matthew P. Lawson

$\mathbf{A}$s a distinct social movement, fundamentalism in the United States came into being only about a century ago.[1] It emerged at a time when progress, social evolution, modernism, and liberalism were all hailed as the wave of the future. In academic circles, fundamentalism was generally dismissed as a backwater reaction, hopelessly naive in its intellectual assumptions and overly dogmatic in its theological outlook. Few thought it could long survive. Yet survive it has, leaving many unanswered questions in its wake. Why has fundamentalism remained a vibrant force in American society despite advances in science, technology, higher education, and other developments once thought to have diminished its appeal? What are the social and cultural factors empowering it? Why have some of its followers turned toward militant social activism while others remain quiescent? Are the conditions nurturing fundamentalism similar to those in other advanced industrial societies? How do they differ from the conditions promoting fundamentalism in developing societies?

Such questions are not dissimilar from the ones social scientists ask about other interesting features of their world. But in the case of fundamentalism, the answers given have also become part of normative evaluations of the movement itself. If it could be shown that, in the past, fundamentalism was a function of an authoritarian personality style, for example, then it becomes possible not only to dismiss its theological claims but to associate it with fascism, bigotry, and racism. Or, to come closer to the present, if it could be said that fundamentalism grows because it wheedled its way into power, cleverly disguising its militant, hegemonic intentions, then it could be likened to the dangerous, potentially violent political movements occurring in other parts of the world. Questions about the sources of fundamentalism, therefore, imply an evaluative stance toward it as well.[2] This is because accounts are themselves subject to a process of social construction: they do not simply provide a way of organizing bedrock empirical data; they reflect the values and assumptions that scholars bring to their data.[3] For this reason the present chapter is also oriented toward the issue of how to *think* about fundamentalism in the United States. Other studies (including chapters in this volume and in previous volumes in this series) have amply described the history of the fundamentalist movement and have examined many of its specific characteristics. But the issue remains of how to understand its social roots—how to account for it—and how this understanding may then figure into our evaluation of it. To see this point more concretely, a useful starting place is to consider some prominent examples of how fundamentalism has been accounted for in the scholarly literature.

"The strength and persistence of fundamentalism," Henry Steele Commager wrote in 1950, "is one of the curiosities of the history of American thought." He found it puzzling that a nation "so optimistic and self-confident" could also be home to a religious orientation that "insisted on the depravity of man." He could not understand how people who were distrustful of authority could trust the counsels of fundamentalist preachers. Equally puzzling, he wrote, was that "a people so inclined to independence should take their religious ideas at second hand" and that "a people so scientific minded should resolutely ignore the impact of science in the realm of religion." Moved by these peculiarities, Commager thus sought to account for them. Perhaps scientific discoveries were modifying our understanding of truth so rapidly that some in our midst needed to cling to the security of timeless dogma. Perhaps they knew the Scriptures could not withstand too much scrutiny, so they argued more stridently for blind faith in divine revelation. Perhaps, he suggested, they were like white supremacists in the American South, who proclaimed racist ideology because their way of life was rapidly coming to an end. Plausible, too, was the possibility that fundamentalists were at heart hypocritical: presenting an outward show of spirituality but not taking their faith seriously enough to question it and let it be informed by the trials of personal experience. Fundamentalism, Commager charged, was superficial, a faith of comforting slogans about biblical inerrancy which could never be put into practice. It was, therefore, a view that encouraged histrionics, querulous and negative preaching, backwater political maneuvering, and occasional outbreaks of militancy, but it could not survive as a vibrant force in American life; indeed, Commager found that by midcentury it was already in serious decline.[4]

Nearly half a century later, predictions of fundamentalism's demise have of course proven to be dramatically premature. The strength and persistence that puzzled Commager remain its presenting features. Now, as then, it runs against the grain of modern society, taking issue with scientists' explanations of the universe, disputing moral relativism in public life, and doggedly insisting on the inerrant truth of the Bible. If some of its original fervor has been channeled into the quieter streams of moderate evangelicalism, it has nevertheless witnessed renewed energy in the past two decades, capturing the administrative center of the nation's largest Protestant denomination, fueling an ultraconservative movement within the Republican party, training thousands of college and seminary students, and founding megachurches by the score.[5] So important has fundamentalism remained that it may be only a small overstatement to suggest that it has placed an indelible stamp on religion in the twentieth century. Certainly it is true, as R. Laurence Moore asserts, that "one would scarcely know how to discuss contemporary American Christianity without using the word 'Fundamentalism.'"[6] And if its relevance to scholarly discussions is given, its impact on the beliefs and practices of American society has been considerable as well. According to one national survey, 9 percent of the adult U.S. population identify themselves as "fundamentalists."[7] Other survey evidence suggests that the core tenets of fundamentalism may be held even more widely; for example, 44 percent of the adult public believe life after death is gained only through Jesus Christ, 30 percent describe themselves as "born again," 28 percent agree that "everything in the Bible should be taken literally, word for word," and 27 percent deny that the Bible "may contain historical or scientific errors."[8]

Still regarding it as a curiosity, scholars have thus continued to seek explanations for the persistence of fundamentalism. A decade after Commager's analysis, historian Richard Hofstadter, in his Pulitzer Prize-winning *Anti-Intellectualism in American Life,* offered what would become one of the most influential accounts of fundamentalism, writing that it represented a thorough-going and militant reaction to the prevailing forces of modernity. It was rooted, he wrote, in "a militant type of mind" found in individuals who "live by hatred as a kind of creed." Setting his interpretation in a sweeping panorama of history, Hofstadter described the militant fundamentalist as a person who was insecure in his faith (as in his livelihood), and who therefore clung tenaciously to a few simple truths, all of which were becoming increasingly incompatible with the liberalizing and secularizing forces in American religion and in the culture more generally.[9]

Hofstadter's argument has been echoed in the accounts offered by a number of other scholars. Joseph R. Gusfield's study of the American temperance movement, for example, drew specifically from Hoftstadter, but added social class as an important consideration. He argued that fundamentalism is part of the "rear guard with which small-town America and commercial capitalism fight their losing battle against a nationalized culture and an industrial economy of mass organizations." Fundamentalism, Gusfield claimed, was a losing battle, but one nevertheless understandable because the moral values of the old middle class were in fact being displaced by the more cosmopolitan assumptions of a new middle class.[10] A similar theme also became evident in theoretical interpretations. In *The Homeless Mind*, for example, Peter Berger, Brigitte Berger, and Hansfried Kellner present a far-reaching analysis of the effects of modernization on human consciousness, arguing that the growing role of bureaucracy, technology, and pluralism has led inevitably to "discontent" as well as to greater material comfort. Fundamentalism, they imply, is like nationalism in the political sphere: it is a reaction to modernity that tries, largely within the private realm, to reconstruct meaning in an otherwise chaotic universe.[11] More recently, a similar line of interpretation has been advanced by sociologist James Davison Hunter, who proposes that "an empirical and conceptual basis for a general theory of fundamentalism" lies in regarding it basically as a religious community that "derives its identity principally from a posture of resistance to the modern world order."[12]

Recent efforts to account for fundamentalism have also been influenced by the shifting perspectives generated from careful studies of the fundamentalist movement itself and from studies of a wider variety of social movements. Much of this work has been descriptive, but accounts of the sources of fundamentalism have also been put forth. In his highly influential study of fundamentalism between 1870 and 1925, George M. Marsden suggests that the movement was nurtured by all of the following: a cultural crisis following World War I, rural-urban differences, increasing ethnic diversity, migration, alienation, a desire for roots, and generational factors. Marsden emphasizes, however, that none of these factors provide a satisfactory account of the movement, that its origins were complex, that they lay importantly in theological disputes themselves, and that easily measurable factors should not be given prominence in scholarly interpretations for this reason alone. His analysis also suggests that leadership and theological training played a vital role in the origins of fundamentalism; that certain ideas (such as dispensationalism and premillennialism) had a life of their own that seemed not to depend very much on external social conditions; and that the movement was nevertheless given shape by politicians, liberal religious leaders, and the mass media, especially in conjunction with the Scopes trial in 1925.[13] Studies of contemporary fundamentalism have often emphasized similar arguments. Especially evident is an emphasis on internal factors rather than wider societal conditions. Dean M. Kelley's widely read book *Why Conservative Churches Are Growing,* for example, stresses the importance of authority structures within congregations which can enforce strict norms, promote consensus on basic beliefs, and draw people into intimate social relationships. Kelley ranks fundamentalist churches higher than liberal or moderate churches on these factors. In his view, moral and doctrinal strictness enjoys a natural advantage in competing for adherents because such strictness is consistent with strong organization, zealous commitment, and generous donations.[14] In her ethnographic study of a fundamentalist congregation, Nancy Tatom Ammerman also emphasizes that the sources of fundamentalism's persistence in the modern world lie in a social process. A stance of resistance toward modernity, she suggests, is simply a starting point, a kind of legacy toward which some Americans may be attracted for any number of reasons. But this legacy is perpetuated only through an on-going process that provides order and legitimates moral discipline. The community is thus essential to the maintenance of fundamentalism. The community supplies friends, draws people together by giving them tasks to perform, enhances their self-esteem, and provides them with workable rules for everyday life. Fundamentalism perpetuates itself by molding the lived experience of the believer to the point that this experience is the same as that idealized in the language of the community itself.[15] Studies of fundamentalists' increasing involvement in American political life have of necessity dealt with factors beyond the local congregation, but have also stressed the importance of leadership, organizational channels, financial resources, alliances, and rhetorical skills.[16]

Even a preliminary overview such as this shows that efforts to account for fundamentalism in the United States are quite varied, pointing not to a single source or causal interpretation but to an array of contributing factors and competing explanations. The diversity is partly attributable to the fact any phenomenon as important as fundamentalism does indeed derive from multiple sources. But it should also be evident from these examples that competing interpretations derive from different theoretical perspectives and imply different evaluations of fundamentalism itself. Commager's account, for example, betrays little patience with fundamentalism. His view, like that of Hofstadter and Berger, reflects an emphasis on long-term cultural change. In contrast, Ammerman's study takes greater care in attempting to view the fundamentalists' world from the inside. Its account stems less from a grand view of history than from a theory of community. Both of these perspectives are valuable, the one helping us to understand the large picture, the context, and the other the internal dynamics and processes on which the persistence of fundamentalism depends. An adequate account of fundamentalism must, however, find a way to bring these different perspectives together. Without such integration, the proponents of different accounts will simply talk past one another, proposing alternative perspectives but failing to provide a way to decide among them, except on the basis of personal taste.

In this chapter, we develop an argument about the main kinds of social factors that need to be examined in order to understand the social location and role of fundamentalism in American society. This is done by extending previous work emphasizing the role of *resources* in the social environment. In applying this approach, we seek to impose order on the sources of Christian fundamentalism without taking a reductionistic stance toward the movement itself. In other words, we distance the argument from much in the scholarly tradition which tries to account for fundamentalism by demonstrating it to be a reflection of social factors somehow more basic or foundational, such as the struggle between social classes or the authority relations of sovereign groups. At the same time, we argue that an understanding of Christian fundamentalism must ultimately pay attention to its interaction with the social context in which it occurs, and that this interaction exercises an influence over the character of fundamentalism that, while scarcely causal, determinant, or unidirectional, is nevertheless real. In general terms, then, the approach is sociological, emphasizing the *social* sources of fundamentalism but leaving room for other factors as well.

Theory of Cultural Articulation

A theory of cultural articulation provides a framework well suited for considering the social sources of Christian fundamentalism in the United States.[17] This theory has been advanced as a perspective for understanding the social sources of major cultural changes brought about by ideological movements (such as the Protestant Reformation, the Enlightenment, and European socialism). According to the theory, ideological movements succeed or fail, locate themselves in particular social spaces, and acquire distinctive form and content through a process of articulation with their social environments. Articulation implies an appropriate fit or match between ideology and social structure such that sufficient resources can be attained to perpetuate the ideology, *but* it implies a level of disarticulation as well which prevents the movement's ideas from becoming entirely dependent on its social environment. Understanding the articulation between ideology and social structure thus requires paying attention to a complex set of variables specifying relevant attributes of the social environment, dynamics of the constellations of movements or "communities of discourse" that serve as ideological carriers, and the internal structuring of ideology itself. Each set of variables is further specified: attributes of the social environment are specified as environmental conditions, institutional contexts, and action sequences; movement dynamics as processes of ideological production (or variation), selection, and institutionalization (or retention); and ideological structure as social horizons, discursive fields, and figural actors. Examining the attributes of these variables is thus the means of analyzing the relationships among particular components and processes that contribute to the shaping of an ideological movement. In combination, they afford sensitivity both to the wider social context in which a movement arises and to the more immediate processes by which a movement shapes and sustains itself. The meaning of these variables is elaborated as fundamentalism is considered in the sections that follow.

The suitability of this framework as an approach for understanding the social sources of fundamentalism is suggested by the following considerations. Fundamentalism may be regarded as an ideology in both the general and more specialized meaning of this term, that is, it is essentially about ideas. The "fundamentals" from which the movement drew its name at the start of the twentieth century were ideas about the certainty of God's existence, the inerrancy of the Bible, the end times, and the necessity of personal salvation. Contrasting cases (not emphasizing ideas) would be movements concerned principally with the distribution of power or other resources, for example, a movement to colonize a newly discovered geographic region, to foment a coup d'état, or to sell hula hoops.

Ideas are of course part of any movement, but the promulgation of ideas or truths for their own sake is a feature more prominent in some than in others. In the more specialized sense of the term, an ideology is not a distinct set of beliefs, but an analytic dimension of beliefs, values, gestures, and other symbols which pertains to the ordering of social relations. Fundamentalism, in this sense, has an ideological dimension because its core beliefs are concerned not simply with doctrinal verities, but with how believers should live. In short, fundamentalism makes moral claims. It suggests, for example, that believers should separate themselves from unbelievers, that certain standards of sexual behavior and marital fidelity should be upheld, and that energy should be expended supporting the community of fellow believers. Again, it is perhaps the case that all bodies of belief and knowledge have an ideological dimension, but for some this dimension is more important than for others. For example, science makes moral claims on researchers to be honest and to communicate their findings with fellow scientists, but a scientific idea itself (such as the theory of quasars) may be largely devoid of moral claims.

It is this ideological dimension (or, for short, ideology) that raises the question of articulation in the first place. For, if ideas make claims about social relationships, then the structure of resources in the social environment and the character of social relationships envisioned in the ideology itself inevitably come together to a greater or lesser degree. It also goes without saying that fundamentalism is a movement or constellation of movements, which means simply that it exists in real space and in historical time. It is not simply an imagined or hypothetical idea, such as a thought in a person's mind, but involves the practices of individuals and, moreover, involves them collectively. Fundamentalists are a community of discourse in that they produce ideas and talk with one another about these ideas. They are bound together by the exchange of these ideas and by attempts to put them into practice. The boundaries of this community are, however, not clearly delineated, but determined by the questions being asked by the observer. Thus, for some analytic purposes, the relevant community of discourse is restricted to those who believe in a few fundamentals themselves (for example, a congregation), while for other purposes it may be important to consider a larger group, some of whom may hold additional beliefs or who may provide partners for disagreement. Substantively, fundamentalists and evangelicals have often been at pains to distance themselves from each other, for example, yet at least two national empirical studies have shown that self-identified "evangelicals" and self-identified "fundamentalists" are scarcely distinguishable on many demographic characteristics and social attitudes (although they do disagree on some doctrinal issues).[18] The fluidity of the boundaries of the fundamentalist community is, as we shall see, an important factor in understanding its success in modern society.

If fundamentalism can be regarded as an ideological movement, it is now possible to say more clearly why the theory of cultural articulation is preferable to the two standard approaches (and two more specialized applications of these approaches) found in the literature. These are the sociology of knowledge and social movement theory, and their specialized applications, respectively, are adaptation theory and resource mobilization theory. Sociology of knowledge theory has been concerned with understanding the social sources of ideas.[19] Applied to the study of religious beliefs, such as fundamentalism, this approach emphasizes modernization as a prevailing feature of social structure and argues that religious beliefs generally adapt to this situation.[20] Thus, religion becomes more secular in modern society, although exceptions may be granted, such as the backlash or reactionary movements of which fundamentalism is presumably an example. Articulation theory is preferrable to this approach because it does not attribute ultimate causality to social structure,[21] but instead emphasizes the partial fitting together of the two. Moreover, articulation theory is less deterministic, recognizing the partial autonomy of ideas from social structure as well as the multiplicity of processes involved. Unlike modernization theory, it identifies more of the intervening factors, rather than drawing such a direct link between broad conditions and individual consciousness.[22] Religious leaders and their followers thus acquire greater importance as agents in charge of their own movements, thereby allowing the theological and ecclesiological debates that Marsden emphasizes, for example, to be considered without dismissing the factors that Commager or Gusfield emphasize.

The second approach (social movement theory) and its more specialized application (resource mobilization theory) have also been concerned with the social shaping of ideas. The central argument in this approach is that ideas are produced, and thus depend on social movements to produce new ones, and these movements in turn enjoy relative degrees of success depending on their leaders to mobilize support, raise cash, make alliances, and so on. If sociology of knowledge theory is too determinant, social movement theory is often not determinant enough. In the extreme, it places an inordinate emphasis on the internal dynamics of movement organizations themselves. This also means that the wider field of competing movements may be neglected. Articulation theory is preferable because it takes into explicit consideration the limiting conditions imposed by the wider social environment, but recognizes that this environment consists of other movements. It thus argues for considering the range of variation among these movements, how they compete, and the factors leading them to occupy different social niches. It allows the discursive practices within fundamentalist congregations, such as those emphasized by Ammerman, for example, to be recognized, but also stresses that these practices are possible only because institutional space is available in the first place, and because symbolic demarcations set congregations off from competing religious claimants. It is also preferable to versions of resource mobilization theory (and of cultural production theory) which focus less attention on the form and content of ideas themselves.[23]

With this preliminary introduction to the theoretical framework, the discussion now proceeds to the ways in which this perspective helps in understanding fundamentalism. Some of the specific dimensions of variation among each set of variables identified above are discussed with reference to how they have influenced the development of fundamentalism in the United States. The discussion is then divided into three main sections. The first section, concerned with the wider setting of American fundamentalism, pays attention to the environmental conditions under which it occurs. Some observations are made about the demographic, economic, educational, spatial, cultural, political, and religious factors composing this wider environment. Such factors supply the potential resources—the raw materials—from which the fundamentalist movement has arisen: the people, leaders, outlooks, tolerance, means of communication, grievances, and so on. In the United States a complex interplay among many of these factors has done much to reinvigorate fundamentalism in the past quarter century. In addition, attention is paid to the more specific institutional contexts of fundamentalism: how leaders are able to utilize and shape the resources they find in their environment. Shifting to this level reveals that the movement itself plays an active role in its own formation, including the action sequences that develop over time. Here, the variety within the fundamentalist movement becomes more evident.[24] To systematize the ways in which fundamentalism's interaction with its environment figures in its development, the second section considers the ways in which variation has been encouraged, both within American fundamentalism and in the broader array of competing religious and social movements in this country. Some social conditions have not so much resulted directly in fundamentalism as in a widening of the opportunities for religious movements of all kinds to emerge. Given this wide variation, it makes sense to ask why some movements are selected in various places and among various subpopulations. And finally, how has fundamentalism institutionalized itself, giving it a more stable and powerful role in relation to its environment?

In emphasizing variation, selection, and institutionalization, the discussion suggests that fundamentalism cannot be understood adequately by focusing directly on it as a single social movement. Instead, it must be considered as part of a wider field of competing movements. It exists in dynamic tension with its various detractors and competitors. Struggling with them to gain and preserve its resources, it necessarily is shaped by the contours of its social environment. If the first two sections focus more on social and institutional factors that may shape fundamentalism, the third section shifts the vantage point, asking from within the worldview of the movement itself how it symbolizes its social context, gains control over its own discourse in the process, and then discursively reconfigures its world in a way that generates action. Specific issues here include the tensions that fundamentalism sets in place between itself and the wider society and the models of behavior it holds up as ideals to its members. These issues are discussed more briefly than those in the other two sections, but they provide a necessary complement to those sections as well as an important conceptual link with the approaches taken in the other chapters on Christian fundamentalism.

The discussion is historically specific, focusing mainly on the United States since World War II and considering the politically active varieties of fundamentalism associated with such leaders as the Reverend Jerry Falwell and broadcaster Pat Robertson in relation to other (politically passive) fundamentalisms among contemporary Protestants and Roman Catholics. It defers to others who have attempted to provide abstract, situationally free definitions of fundamentalism.[25] It recognizes that much of the present interest in fundamentalism has arisen from substantive, rather than grand theoretical, concerns. In the United States, recent expressions of fundamentalism have typically included such identifying marks as belief in the literal and inerrant divine truth of the written Bible, an emphasis on distinct individual conversion experiences and efforts to encourage others to have such experiences, perforce a strong distinction between believers and nonbelievers, and in many instances a view of divine intervention in and guidance of human history as expressed in dispensational, premillennial, and apocalyptic doctrines.[26] Apart from this core of common beliefs, contemporary fundamentalists vary widely in their specific denominational and theological traditions. One of the most significant of these variations concerns views of the charismatic gifts, such as speaking in tongues and the internal cleansing power of the holy spirit. Fundamentalists are also to be distinguished from evangelicals, the latter typically placing less emphasis on literal readings of the Bible and drawing less sharp distinctions between themselves and adherents of other faiths. But the specific tenets of fundamentalism, shown in the last section of the chapter, are also relational, taking on meaning from the cultural contexts in which they occur and defining themselves in opposition to these contexts. To show how the North American case differs from, or is similar to, other cases, the discussion (drawing on secondary sources) pays some attention to fundamentalist movements in Western Europe and Latin America.[27]

In discussing this framework, we need not retell the story of American fundamentalism itself. That story has been told in other chapters and books. Readers interested in the specific details of who did what, when, and why should look elsewhere. The aim of this chapter is to identify the relevant factors in an effort to understand the social role of fundamentalism and to compare it with other social movements or with comparable religious movements in other societies. Taking this stance has been dictated partly by the division of labor inherent in a multivolume series such as this. But it also grows out of previous work and reflects an orientation toward the study of religion which is worth considering in its own right. One of the important tasks of the sociologist is to do what the historian is often reluctant to do, namely, to think broadly about the wider context in which a particular phenomenon takes place. If all sociological interpretation is a hermeneutic exercise, then one mode of understanding must be to draw these broader connections. In the case of American fundamentalism, these have already been drawn implicitly in the vast literature on modernization and secularization. Some of the recent literature has rightly argued that the persistence of fundamentalism reveals the inadequacy of those frameworks. But to understand fundamentalism, as some of this literature does, simply in terms of astute leaders or as a product of a religious "market" is not illuminating either. A more complex model is required that emphasizes the ways in which religion *articulates with* its social environment. Fundamentalism, indeed, has articulated markedly well. Its environment has been more conducive to its success that has generally been recognized.

The Environment of Christian Fundamentalism

One distinction we can draw between environmental conditions and institutional contexts is that the former are the less proximate, general characteristics of the society in which fundamentalism is being examined, while the latter refer to more immediate organized situations in which fundamentalism is located. Environmental conditions are the more macroscopic of the two, subsuming what are often referred to as the characteristics of social structure, but also used here quite explicitly to include what some would call culture. Factors such as the overall stage of economic development of a society, on the one hand, or the degree of value rationality or ethnic heterogeneity, on the other hand, would fall within this definition of environmental conditions. The dimensions of variation in environmental conditions that are most likely to influence the character of ideological movements in general are whether the environment is relatively resource rich or resource poor, whether it is relatively homogeneous or heterogeneous, and whether it is temporally stable or unstable. Each of these variables can be specified further by type of resource or by subsections of the environment; for example, a society may be resource rich in terms of economic productivity, but resource poor in terms of political freedoms. Which aspects of the environment are relevant to consider is thus a function of the ideological movement to be understood. In the case of fundamentalism, salient characteristics of the U.S. environment include resource richness, heterogeneity, and relative instability. Richness is evident both in levels of economic affluence and in political freedoms that guarantee the right of religious expression. Heterogeneity includes ethnic, religious, racial, and regional diversity. Relative instability derives from the fact that political and economic conditions in the twentieth century have generally been orderly, but that factors capable of influencing fundamentalists have also been outside their control and at times unstable (for example, the Great Depression cut off valuable economic resources, making it harder for fundamentalists to organize, while recent judicial decisions have produced uncertainty for fundamentalists seeking to promote parochial schools or religious broadcasting networks).[28] Formal analysis of ideological systems gives reason to believe that fundamentalist systems, characterized by relatively few core beliefs that can also be disconnected from one another, are particularly suited to heterogeneous, relatively unstable environments.[29]

Institutional contexts pertain to questions of organization and leadership, especially within the domain of religion itself. In the United States, fundamentalism in the early part of the twentieth century was confined largely to northern branches of the Presbyterian and Baptist churches. While both these denominations were influenced by the broader environmental conditions in which they existed, fundamentalism was also more directly shaped by the availability of resources in them and by struggles over these resources. For example, the fact that both had publishing houses, colleges, and mission boards and that trained clergy were capable of leading in the struggle over these resources meant that the fundamentalist movement ceased being a mere battle over ideas and acquired organization and structure.[30] In the period since World War II, fundamentalism of course has remained largely within a *religious* institutional context. Quantitative data on the formation of sectarian schisms, for example, show that most fundamentalist denominations have arisen from such schisms, and that schisms in general are influenced by levels of membership, church polity, leadership issues, and theological disputes.[31] Fundamentalists who have, however, launched colleges, television stations, theme parks, and political campaigns have allowed other institutional settings to become relevant to their operations. This broadening has made it somewhat more difficult for contemporary fundamentalists to control their own discourse. Nevertheless, it is also true that fundamentalism would attract far less interest at present were it not for the resources at stake within the Southern Baptist Convention.[32]

The distinction between environment and institution is important because it points out two kinds of factors that have potential to account for the sources of fundamentalism. Environmental conditions draw attention to factors that serve as potential constraints or opportunities for fundamentalism ("potential" can be taken to mean "other things being equal"). Institutional contexts draw attention to mediating conditions,[33] which refer to an intermediate level of social organization that translates potential constraints and opportunities into "resources." A resource, then, is something in the immediate context of a movement that it can use to pursue its aims. Students of social movement resources generally emphasize leadership, constituents, allies, finances, facilities, and less tangible resources such as slogans and unifying beliefs, and they pay special attention to whether or not these resources are available for mobilization at strategic times.[34] Liebman's work on the religious right, for example, has emphasized how fundamentalist clergy, and institutional networks among these clergy, provided the leadership necessary for the Moral Majority to become a national movement in the late 1970s,[35] and Guth and Ammerman have documented similar roles among Southern Baptist clergy.[36] More recent work also suggests the importance of taking into account variations within particular institutions that may be attributable to differential levels of power or freedom to act. For example, variations within the Catholic hierarchy in ideological orientation may be explainable in terms of these differentials.[37]

Environments and institutions afford comparative analyses, as a hypothetical comparison between two societies, both of which enjoy a relatively high level of economic prosperity, illustrates. According to some theories,[38] this prosperity may constrain fundamentalism from appearing because people enjoying prosperity should be content with their present life rather than seeking comfort in beliefs about an afterlife. Institutional contexts, though, reveal that the same level of prosperity in the two societies can have radically different implications, depending on how that prosperity is arrogated and organized. In one society, prosperity may be channeled into established religious institutions, while in the other society prosperity may be directed toward concert halls, museums, parks, conspicuous consumption, or government welfare programs. In the first, religious institutions are a considerable factor: if some religious leaders or followers become dissatisfied with the way money is being spent or churches governed, they may form a countermovement aimed at reforming religion itself. In the second case, religious institutions have fewer resources at their disposal, so a reform movement may be more concerned with art policies and welfare spending than religious issues. Other things being equal, fundamentalism would be more likely in the first society than in the second, even though both societies are equally prosperous.

This example in fact describes one of the characteristics that distinguishes the United States from many other advanced industrial societies. For historic reasons, more of the fruits of economic growth have been channeled into religious institutions in the United States than in many other societies. Particularly during the nineteenth century, when a number of societies in Western Europe were experiencing rapid industrialization, governments with strong control over religion were reluctant to allocate money for construction of church buildings or the training of clergy, preferring to expend these resources on such secular capital construction outlays as railways, on military programs, or even on nascent social welfare policies.[39] In contrast, the U.S. Constitution forbade such tampering with religion, placing responsibility for its fortunes in the hands of local citizens, who built churches with alacrity.[40] As a result, religious institutions entered the twentieth century in the United States in a much stronger position than in virtually any other country.[41] And in this context fundamentalism grew more than in societies where religious institutions were weaker, partly because individuals at the grass roots were conditioned to attend church and to think that religion could provide answers to their problems, but also because ample numbers of seminaries and theologians were able to perpetuate and augment the ideas on which fundamentalism was founded.[42] During the first two decades of the twentieth century, American religion actually experienced growth as a result of increased competition between Protestants and Roman Catholics and among Protestants themselves; religious leaders of varying persuasions—leaders of the Social Gospel movement,[43] for example, as much as fundamentalists—were seeking ways of revitalizing traditional morality and making it more relevant to contemporary social conditions; urbanization and economic growth were adding numbers to the clergy;[44] and a few theologians in such places as Princeton and Chicago had sufficient prestige and autonomy that they were able to draw esoteric ideas (such as Darbyism and scientific creationism) together and give them much greater prominence in American religion. In recent decades, fundamentalism has grown more visible again, not so much (as its leaders might say) because of the secularity of American society but because of the society's wealth of religious resources.[45]

Similar arguments can be made that help make sense of variations in the strength of fundamentalism in other societies. For example, the strength of militant Protestant and Catholic orthodoxies in Northern Ireland, or the rise of conservative Catholic movements in Italy, or the growth of Protestant Pentecostalism in Latin America can to some extent be understood in terms of the historic strength of institutional religion in those societies. Religion provided a richer institutional context in which reform movements could emerge in societies such as those of France, Germany, or Sweden, where historic relations with government inhibited the strength of established religious institutions.[46] Compared with most European and Latin American societies, religion in the United States is also more heterogeneous. Thus, fundamentalist sects were able not only to draw on a *general* climate of religiosity, but to secure resources from *specific* denominations and traditions: independent Baptists from the Baptist tradition, Nazarenes and Holiness churches from the Methodist tradition, Orthodox Presbyterians from the Presbyterian tradition, and so on. As a result, fundamentalism has been more internally diverse in the United States than might have otherwise been the case, causing it to lack unity, but also to be the source (through missionary efforts) of much of the sectarian diversity among Protestant fundamentalists in other countries as well. This example also suggests that other environmental conditions need to be considered.

One condition is the role of government. In three societies in which religion in general has remained strong until fairly recently—the United States, the Netherlands, and Northern Ireland—a Protestant majority has dominated but a significant Roman Catholic population exists as well. Indeed, this interfaith competition has contributed to the overall vitality of religious institutions in these societies.[47] But the role of government has resulted in quite different opportunities for fundamentalist movements to emerge. In the United States, Protestant hegemony has been maintained by asserting a strict wall of separation between church and state, which among other things has prevented public monies from being used to support Catholic schools. Fundamentalists have been able to draw on this tradition to argue against government interference in other realms, from regulations affecting their own parochial schools to the use of tax money for abortions. In the Netherlands, Protestant-Catholic relations are guided by active government intervention. Tax monies are used to underwrite church programs, including Protestant and Catholic schools, which form the basis for a "pillarized" system of socioreligious institutions. There is room for a free church movement, but less legitimacy and opportunity for fundamentalists to form large-scale institutions of their own. In Northern Ireland the relations between Protestants and Catholics have been governed by an external force—the British government. Militant fundamentalist Protestantism and Catholicism have emerged with a strong antigovernment bias that nevertheless looks to policy-makers to implement their demands.[48]

As these examples suggest, fundamentalism is often like a third party in politics. If dominant religious institutions are tied closely to government and receive sufficient resources to carry out their work, there may be little room for a third force to develop. But if the dominant institutions support an unpopular government or are themselves in opposition to government, third parties may be able to develop a niche of their own. The analogy should not be pushed too far, of course, for religious institutions differ from political parties. There are, however, precedents indicating the validity of the idea. For example, historian Mary Fulbrook has shown that pietist beliefs in the eighteenth century took quite different forms in England, Prussia, and Württemburg because of the patterns between established religious institutions and government.[49]

These predisposing conditions aside, fundamentalists also appear to have an increasing tendency to view politics as a legitimate activity. Fundamentalism in many Latin American and European countries, as in the United States, is associated with political parties or with opposition movements that seek to influence electoral, legislative, and judicial outcomes. This development is especially important in view of the fact that, in the past, fundamentalism disdained political involvement. Many contemporary varieties do so as well. Until the early 1970s, for example, fundamentalists in the United States generally viewed the political domain with distrust, preferring to pray rather than mount public campaigns or vote.[50] Yet at present fundamentalism appears to be distinguished by political militancy. This shift can be accounted for by the fact that the state has become a more prominent feature of the social environment. To achieve their ends, fundamentalists feel they must influence the political process. Even in societies that guarantee separation of church and state, the latter has grown in ways that intrude on the "voluntary space" in which religion has functioned.[51] From safety regulations governing public assemblies to the ways in which old-age insurance and funding for day-care centers are provided, the state is an actor whose claims must be taken into account. It is precisely in these free spaces, historically, that the smaller sects of which contemporary fundamentalism is reminiscent flourished.[52] They, unlike established faiths that entered into mutually beneficial arrangements with the state, depended on the state's coercive powers being held in abeyance. Where it was not (and when symbolic gestures were made by the state that suggested intrusions), fundamentalist groups were likely to feel beleaguered. Certainly, a large number of the issues around which fundamentalists in the United States have organized since the 1960s (school prayer, parochial schools, the regulation of religious broadcasting) have been of this type.

But fundamentalist militancy has not emerged in recent decades because of state expansion alone. The period since World War II has witnessed unparalleled state expansion—in outlays for national defense and public education, in entitlement programs and transfer payments, and in numbers of federal employees—and yet some of this expansion has pinched the purses of individual fundamentalists, just as it has nonfundamentalists, but without generating negative responses (national defense is an example). Other forms of expansion have touched fundamentalist churches more directly, for example, regulations requiring the marking of fire exits, ramps for the disabled, more careful reporting of pastors' salaries, and so on. These regulations have perhaps prompted greater awareness of Big Brother, but have resulted in few overt protests. Fundamentalists have responded to situations they believed involved moral issues—abortion, homosexuality, and the right to pray in public schools, among others. Thus, it has not so much been government expansion in general but penetration into the moral sphere which has prompted fundamentalist reactions. It is no accident that Jerry Falwell called his movement Moral Majority, and that religious conservatives are especially likely to perceive moral decay as a grave social and political issue. In a 1992 survey of the U.S. labor force, for example, 68 percent of self-identified religious conservatives (compared to only 40 percent of religious liberals) said "moral corruption" was an extremely serious problem in American society.[53]

The political environment in which contemporary fundamentalism has reappeared also includes processes in the political economy of the world system[54] which have promoted a more general shift toward cultural conservatism, or at least instability in political loyalties which has been conducive to the growth of conservative movements.[55] In the United States and Western Europe, heightened economic competition in the world system and a slowdown of growth in Gross National Product have resulted in fiscally conservative regimes coming into power. By coupling calls for reductions in social programs with appeals to individual morality, these regimes have been able to enlist the support of fundamentalist groups, which in turn have gained some political clout as a result.[56] This support appears to have come from white-collar and middle-class fundamentalists whose economic fortunes depend more on keeping tax rates low by reducing government spending than on the social welfare programs that poorer fundamentalists might desire.[57] Not only in the United States but in Great Britain and Canada, conservative religion and conservative morality have joined forces with the conservative economics of some political candidates. Fundamentalist politics have thus formed in opposition to various sociomoral orientations of the modern state, but in support of economic policies favorable to the middle class.

In the developing countries of Latin America and other parts of the world, the consequences have been quite different, producing fundamentalism but of a different hue.[58] Shrinkage in global economic fortunes has led to extremes of human suffering and domestic political instability. In unstable political and economic situations, fundamentalists have encouraged their followers to take whatever personal control of their lives they could and not to worry so much about the larger context. Thus as the world seemed to fall apart around them, fundamentalists felt empowered and comforted. Core nations were sometimes less able or willing to take aggressive action to prevent political and economic instability, and indigenous class factions that depended on an expanding export economy were sometimes weakened by budgetary crises, foreign debt, and fluctuations in trade. In the face of this instability, class factions both in and out of power sometimes looked to fundamentalist groups with faithful constituencies for support. In Guatemala, as David Stoll has shown in chapter 5 of this volume, Ríos Montt appealed to fundamentalists for support in his struggle against radical guerrillas, and in Nicaragua the Sandinistas appealed to both liberationist Catholics and Protestant fundamentalists for support in the first years after overthrowing the Somoza regime.[59]

Perhaps the most puzzling feature of the social environment in which contemporary Christian fundamentalism has appeared is the relatively high levels of education that exist in modern societies generally and often among fundamentalists themselves. If fundamentalism were truly a function of simplemindedness and lack of exposure to modern ideas, as is alleged,[60] then it should have diminished as a result of growth in higher education. Especially during the past third of a century, college attendance has risen dramatically in the United States and in most other advanced industrial societies.[61] And yet fundamentalism seems not to have diminished. One possibility of course is that it has diminished in fact, but not in appearance because the remaining minority has grown more vocal, stirring, as it were, to make their wishes known with their last breath. That fundamentalism is almost dead is certainly an overstatement, but there may be some truth to the assertion that it is diminishing. In the United States, for example, surveys asking about biblical literalism have shown a decline in the proportion of the population who hold this belief.[62] Still it seems puzzling that fundamentalism fares so well in the face of an ever more educated population.

Even though a growing proportion of the population may have attained higher levels of education and the absolute stock of knowledge available in a given society may have grown, the relationship of various segments of the population to that knowledge must be considered. Thus, the average person knows much more about history, the arts, other cultures, and the outer reaches of the universe than at any time in the past. But some people still know much more about these topics than others do. An engineer in Duluth, for example, may know a great deal about the mechanics of this trade and yet feel there is an alien world out there, located in the big cities and in universities and literary circles, about which he knows little.[63] His religious views may be shaped less by the fact that he actually knows a lot than by the fact that he feels like he doesn't. Furthermore, he realizes that he knows his own subject matter well, is intelligent, has an advanced degree, and works in a well-paying profession. Thus, he is unlikely just to parrot what he hears coming out of the big cities and the art councils and the think tanks. Instead, he may feel that his experiences and knowledge of the world support his views over theirs. His fundamentalism reassures him in this belief and provides, through trust in the veracity of the Bible, an authoritative and more encompassing point of view. In broader terms, educational expansion in the United States has thus upgraded the overall level of technical and cultural knowledge, but has nevertheless left a great deal of variation, even among the better educated, and some of this group will continue to find fundamentalism an appealing view of the world.[64]

To conclude this section, it is well to note how counterintuitive these arguments may appear against the background of prevailing conventional wisdom, especially that drawn from theories of modernization and secularization. Over the past quarter century the United States has undergone significant economic, political, and educational expansion. Conventional wisdom suggests that all these developments would inhibit the occurrence of a strong fundamentalist movement: rising incomes should make people more content with the secular world, government expansion should make them better able to realize their purposes through normal political channels, and educational upgrading should reduce the ignorance from which fundamentalism presumably springs. None of these predictions has been borne out. Conventional wisdom would then reply that fundamentalism might still be expected as a backlash against such modernizing forces.[65] But if so, why would it occur among the well-off, the politically involved, and the better educated? The present arguments suggest that social reality is more complex than conventional wisdom acknowledges. Fundamentalism has not been a direct psychological response to changing environmental conditions. Instead, these conditions have created new opportunities—niches—which fundamentalists have been able to use to their advantage.

The Dynamics of Christian Fundamentalism

The problem with focusing on the environmental conditions and institutional contexts in which fundamentalism arises is that these factors imply stasis, whereas the notion of something *arising* suggests the need for a more dynamic understanding. This problem can be circumvented by conceiving of the social environment in transitional terms, such as economic "growth" rather than economic "prosperity." Nevertheless, the fact remains that fundamentalism is itself a dynamic process, a movement that unfolds over time. As it unfolds, it also changes its relations to its environment. The environment may create niches, but then fundamentalists and other movements compete actively with one another to occupy these niches, and in the process, religious ideologies articulate with social structure.

To capture social movement dynamics, some investigators have tried to identify typical phases through which all movements must go.[66] There is, for example, an early phase of assembling in which people gather to express their grievances;[67] later, a leader emerges and helps frame these grievances as specific demands; eventually the leader may die, causing the movement to face problems of succession. Such models can be useful for understanding a well-defined movement, such as the Free Speech Movement that began in Berkeley, California, in 1964, or the Moral Majority movement that Jerry Falwell brought into being in the late 1970s.[68] But fundamentalism is a broader social phenomenon, a result of many specific movements and organizations, and firmly rooted in established cultural traditions.[69] It is an internally diverse movement, divided into factions of independent Baptists, Pentecostalists, small sects, and Bible churches, all separated by important doctrinal positions (and by the doctrine of separatism itself), and its boundaries sometimes melt imperceptibly into the larger population that identifies itself as "evangelical" or simply as "religiously conservative."[70] Usually it does not go through such neatly identified stages. To understand its dynamics, then, it must be viewed in a larger context.

For this purpose, it is helpful to draw theoretical inspiration from the work of population ecologists who have been concerned with ways in which loosely scattered aggregates of species, individuals, social characteristics, and even organizations adjust to their environments. In this literature, three conceptual moments are generally identified: production, selection, and retention.[71] Production is the phase in which new movements and countermovements come into being, thus enlarging the overall range of variation in available belief systems. Selection is the process by which these various movements seek out distinct niches in the social environment, adapting to its differential resources, and thereby resulting in some movements' ability to flourish better than others. Retention is the phase in which movements gain greater control over their own resources and thus become institutionalized as stable features of the social environment itself. Although these processes are sometimes depicted as the work of blind forces in the larger society, they depend on the day-to-day decisions of movement leaders and the willingness of their followers to commit time and energy to these movements. Especially important is the fact that religious movements are always in competition with other movements—other fundamentalist groups, nonfundamentalist religious movements, and secular organizations attempting to make claims on individuals' time and energy.[72] Particularly useful examples of this competition can be found in Brazil and other parts of Latin America. There, fundamentalist movements of different stripes compete for resources with Catholic Base Communities, Catholic traditionalism, and a variety of spiritualist religions. Each offers a sense of community and a religious response, albeit quite varied, to a broad range of social concerns.[73]

One way to gain a better grasp of the social sources of fundamentalism in the United States, therefore, is to look at the general uncertainty in the moral order of society since the 1960s.[74] Starting in that decade, if not earlier, expectations about moral commitments and the moral communities sustaining those commitments became increasingly ambiguous. Young people went away to college, developed different occupational expectations from their parents, lost ties with their communities of origin, and confronted a variety of new challenges in ethics and lifestyles.[75] From the beginning, the splashier movements that experimented with political radicalism and countercultural lifestyles were opposed by ultraconservative religious and political movements. New belief patterns were produced, in short, greatly enlarging the options from which young people could choose.[76] In addition, the 1960s were a time when ecumenical movements that had been initiated shortly after World War II came to fruition, especially in prompting mergers among mainline Protestant denominations. In response to these impending mergers, a noticeable increase in the level of schisms appeared in this period, and some of these schisms consisted of new fundamentalist groups.[77] More generally, the established niches in which religious groups had settled during the preceding century[78] were being reconfigured by changing conceptions of race, by increased geographic mixing of Protestants and Catholics, and by the gradual assimilation of ethnic groups.[79]

Thus the changing economic and political conditions considered in the last section not only contributed new resources and opportunities, they also generated uncertainty. Old rules lost the resources needed for reinforcement. New rules were largely up for grabs. For fundamentalists, and for potential converts to fundamentalism, these uncertainties were enormously important. Rising levels of education seemed to generate moral relativism and place greater burdens on the individual to decide what was ultimately true and morally right. New freedoms in sexual conduct ran against the values many people had been taught from early childhood. Of special consequence for religious conservatives was the fact that the evangelical movement, established in the 1940s, was now beginning, by its own design, to provide an attractive alternative to the more separatist and doctrinaire fundamentalists.[80] Also of consequence were uncertainties about the freedoms of television ministries or colleges that fundamentalists had been founding. Government regulations, antidiscrimination laws, and the lure of new scholarship programs all created new uncertainties.[81] Most of these developments had obvious implications for Protestant fundamentalists. Comparable developments, however, were creating uncertainties in the Roman Catholic and Jewish communities as well. In the former, the Second Vatican Council and the reshaping of ethnic neighborhoods were especially important;[82] in the latter, changes in ethnic identification wrought by increasing rates of interfaith marriage, changing gender roles, and a new round of conflict in the Middle East were crucial developments.[83] More generally, how to live was the issue, as the emphasis on lifestyle experimentation in the 1960s indicated. This period was not particularly auspicious for fundamentalists, especially in view of the more liberal religious and political movements that were attracting far more visible attention. But it was out of this uncertain time that fundamentalists began to hone their new sense of concern for the moral order.

The selection process began almost at once and extended during the 1970s and 1980s. Many of the fringe movements that appeared on the religious scene in those years gradually failed. Some did so as a result of idealism that made it difficult for collective decisions to be made or for viable economic bases to be established.[84] Among the more conservative Christian groups, many also failed, but were often absorbed into established churches. Over a longer period, the human costs associated with experimentation with drugs and sex also took their toll. Resisting the status quo by dropping out and turning to drugs cost much in economic stability and health. Movements that cautioned against such activities, yet retained a stance in opposition to aspects of the status quo, offered an important alternative. Likewise the questioning of traditional gender roles by feminists encouraged conservative countermovements that offered alternative answers to the same questions.[85] The net result of this selective process was that a number of fundamentalist movements were left in relatively strong shape.

The exact manner in which social movements are produced and selected depends greatly on the degree of heterogeneity already present in a society.[86] As a general rule, the likelihood of fundamentalism being present at all is increased by higher levels of heterogeneity, whereas the likelihood of fundamentalism becoming a powerful and unified movement is greater where some, but limited heterogeneity exists. The reason heterogeneity heightens the likelihood of fundamentalism's presence is that distinct social niches are more readily available for it to occupy. In the United States, regional, ethnic, and religious diversity all contribute to the likelihood that fundamentalism can find at least limited niches to occupy—for example, Orthodoxy in Jewish communities around New York City, militant Catholic fundamentalism in isolated ethnic enclaves around Philadelphia, or fundamentalist Baptist offshoots in the Midwest and South. Likewise the religious and ethnic heterogeneity in Brazil and Mexico allows a variety of fundamentalist groups to flourish, while countries such as the staunchly Catholic Colombia and the highly secular Venezuela are much less hospitable to fundamentalism.[87] But for fundamentalism to solidify as a major national movement, the boundaries defining some of these niches must either shrink in importance or be drawn along the same lines as other social divisions. Fundamentalism has been able to gain national prominence in places such as Guatemala or the southern United States, for example, because whole regions could provide unified constituencies as localistic, familial, tribal, or political divisions diminished in importance.

In this regard, it is worth speculating that the re-emergence of fundamentalism in the United States in the 1970s and 1980s was nurtured by the persistence of one "ethnic" enclave—the southern (largely Baptist) Bible Belt[88]—and by the decline of others. As the South acquired a new economic base during these years,[89] many of its churches and meetinghouses gained new resources as well as a sense of entitlement in national political affairs.[90] Their constituents played an identifiable role in politics, much in the same way the Celtic fringe (according to Michel Hechter's well-known analysis) did in British politics a century earlier.[91]

The ethnic enclaves that diminished were the smaller conservative sects that had emerged from earlier waves of immigration, such as the Dutch Calvinists and Scottish Presbyterians.[92] As migration and intermarriage broke up these enclaves, some of their members probably shifted religious loyalties to larger fundamentalist bodies, such as fundamentalist Baptist churches or Assemblies of God churches. In a broader sense, denominational barriers eroded significantly during the period after World War II, and this erosion contributed to the emergence of a division in American religion between religious liberals and conservatives.[93] It may have helped solidify the fundamentalist wing within the broader conservative spectrum as well.

Retention of their beliefs has also been accomplished with considerable success by American fundamentalists. One of the most significant ways in which fundamentalism institutionalizes itself, giving itself power over its own destiny, is by identifying a stock of specialized knowledge over which it is the sole or chief arbiter. Students of elite culture have in recent years emphasized the concept of "cultural capital,"[94] a name for the advantages that go with attending Exeter and Yale and being able to read items correctly from a French menu and discuss the latest Broadway play. These things are all like money in the bank, a kind of capital investment from which people can draw to get ahead in life. But fundamentalists have their own forms of cultural capital. It may consist of resources that to the outsider seem unimportant—being able to recite Bible verses from memory, knowing all the stanzas of "Amazing Grace" by heart, saying Amen at the appropriate time, praying a long spontaneous prayer in public with considerable fervor and sincerity, or having been acquainted with a family who went to Africa as missionaries. Such capital gives fundamentalists power and prestige within their own community.

These are valuable forms of cultural capital in fundamentalism, even though they may not be respected in the outside world, because they are commodities the fundamentalist community can produce and certify without the resources in scarce supply in the wider world. Fundamentalism is, in this sense, a variety of what Clifford Geertz has called "local knowledge."[95] It exists in local settings and depends largely on the interaction of the group to be understood. It is not so much a medium of exchange that can be used in universalistic transactions (like money) but a vehicle of restricted exchange, a carrier of meanings that do not easily permeate external boundaries. They reaffirm the group, giving it resources over which others cannot easily gain control. Fundamentalists, in emphasizing separatism from the outside world, have often been in a good position to maintain this control over their own ideas and beliefs. The founding of fundamentalist elementary and secondary schools has been one way of accomplishing this task.[96] Another way has been the founding of fundamentalist colleges with strict codes of belief, dress, and moral conduct.[97]

The challenge fundamentalism has faced in recent years in advanced societies has come mainly from its attempts to "go public," as it were. Fundamentalists have long believed the world was created in seven days. But when those beliefs cease to be the result of local teachings and are presented in the same terms as those used in universalistic scientific publications, then they are more easily turned over to the credentialing agencies of the larger society. This challenge from the wider society is perhaps one reason why Pentecostal varieties of fundamentalism appear to be growing more rapidly than their more cognitively or doctrinally oriented counterparts. Rather than attempting to formulate doctrines and moral statements according to rational or scientific principles, Pentecostal churches are more likely to emphasize the inherent non-rationality of faith, its basis in personal emotional experiences, and a feeling of unity and mutuality among the body of believers. Here, participation generates its own resources, as warmth and caring feed on themselves. External authorities, especially those representing the cold, uncaring worlds of bureaucracies, corporations, big government, and rationalistic universities, can make few compelling claims against the resources of these churches.

This localizing and insulating aspect of fundamentalism is especially important in underdeveloped societies and in the less developed segments of advanced societies. Where resources are scarce, the capacity to control them becomes all the more important. Especially when competing with more established religious institutions, fundamentalism often has an advantage in such situations. In Latin America, for example, Protestant missions were largely unable to make inroads in gaining converts from Catholicism until local bodies, from congregations to denominations, were able to control their own resources independent of international concerns. In this arena fundamentalist congregations, using local lay preachers and generating high levels of commitment to the local body, were able to develop into mutual aid societies offering emotional and physical support to members in need. The Catholic Church and other externally controlled religious organizations traditionally focused their resources on schools, hospitals, and charitable organizations which could not respond in the same way to needs at the local level.[98]

In the United States, greater affluence means that fundamentalists themselves are more likely to be exposed to the wider culture (e.g., through travel or purchases of consumer goods); occupational demands may force fundamentalists to mix regularly with nonfundamentalists (a consequence of women being incorporated into the labor force);[99] and of course the mass media make it more difficult for fundamentalists to isolate themselves, especially in recent years. Scandals involving conservative television preachers have eroded confidence in clergy more generally, perhaps having some negative effects among fundamentalists themselves. Fundamentalists in politics, it appears, have in the 1992 national election opted for a strategy designed not to attract media attention (as Jerry Falwell and Pat Robertson did in the 1980s), but to avoid such attention by focusing on local elections, running so-called stealth candidates (whose religious affinities are not disclosed), and even by timing rallies to avoid local media coverage.[100]

Fundamentalism then in recent decades has been in competition with other religious and secular movements, all of which were in their own ways responding to the moral uncertainty in American society. In this competition, fundamentalists have enjoyed certain advantages, partly because heterogeneity of the environment gave them protected niches to occupy, and partly because of their own strategic use of resources. They have developed their own forms of cultural capital and have been able to retain control over the interpretation of this capital. At the same time, there has been a basic tension between using these resources for the internal benefit of their own community and exposing them to the critical winds that prevail in the more universalistic arenas of American politics.

The Culture of Christian Fundamentalism

The various conditions and processes of fundamentalism just described help us to understand its social sources, yet further analysis is required to obtain a better sense of how social conditions and ideas articulate. Fundamentalism is, after all, a distinctive set of beliefs and practices, a language, a discursive style, a way of talking, of communicating something important to oneself and to one's fellow believers about the sacred, about how to live, and even about how to act out one's values in broader social settings. Accounts of it are vacuous if they do not take these characteristics into consideration.

Like any religious orientation, fundamentalism is not so much about prospering or growing or governing, although it may be those things too, but about living, and knowing how to live, so that life has meaning and value.[101] Accordingly, fundamentalism is concerned with the symbols and concepts and languages that give meaning to life. Indeed, its distinguishing feature is the assumption that life has meaning only in relation to certain of these frameworks, especially the historic role of Jesus in atoning for the sinfulness of humankind, the authority of the Bible as God's unique and inerrant revelation of divine truth, and the importance of following certain moral prescriptions for behavior and belief that are taken as pleasing to, or in keeping with, the divine will. To say that fundamentalism holds itself to be the unique framework in which life has meaning is to imply that it also sets itself over against various other frameworks that are false, errant, deceptive, and capable of leading people astray. Especially in a religiously pluralistic society such as ours, this "setting against" is likely to stand out. It means, for one thing, that fundamentalism also contains its own picture of society, and indeed of history (especially in dispensationalist and premillennial orientations), a picture that tells its members how to think about people outside the faith, how to think about morality and politics, and how to interpret current events in light of historical trends.[102] It also means that this social horizon, perhaps to a degree more evident than in most other systems of belief, is a framework in which *polarities* abound. The believer exists in a world of right and wrong, good and evil, light and darkness, mammon and God, flesh and spirit, demons and angels, worldly temptations and heavenly salvation. Fundamentalism argues for a restricted or focused meaning of biblical truth in opposition to more elaborated or unfocused meanings. Even its form provides a deliberate contrast with nonfundamentalist language, for example, by moving from complexity to simplicity, and by employing rhetorical devices, such as redundancy, that reinforce single interpretations.[103] Fundamentalists, it should also be observed, are assisted in maintaining these polarities by liberal religionists who use fundamentalism as a foil, repeating (and further simplifying) its claims in order to make their own arguments.[104]

Fundamentalists are of course enjoined to seek the light and shun the darkness, to keep themselves pure, and to avoid consorting with unbelievers. But to understand fundamentalism in this way only is to miss its essence. Few people of any faith (or of no faith at all) would deny wanting to side with goodness as opposed to evil. Nor is it accurate to say that the fundamentalist wishes more acutely than most to "love good and abhor evil." The difference lies not so much in the fact that fundamentalists conceive of polarities but in the way in which these polarities are understood—as sharply opposing contrasts. And they are associated with a number of distinct cultural connotations. If the sharpness of polarities in fundamentalist thought is sometimes taken as a cognitive style,[105] the cultural connotations associated with these polarities are nevertheless matters of social construction. To take an obvious example, during the 1950s and 1960s, communism served as a favorite symbol of evil among fundamentalists (and even today it is possible to receive direct mail solicitations from fundamentalist preachers calling for mass campaigns of vilification against individual college professors who espouse Marxist perspectives).[106] But earlier in the century, urban life and often the Roman Catholic Church or Jews served the same purpose.[107] And in the twenty-first century, fundamentalist hatred is likely to shift toward other targets, such as Muslims, environmentalists, homosexuals, the New Age movement, or politicians of certain parties.[108] It is unlikely that fundamentalists take these oppositional stances purely out of irrational hatred. Instead, fundamentalist discourse constructs the symbolic worlds in which its adherents live. It does so partly by responding to the real environment in which it finds itself: fundamentalists did not have to invent communism as an object of hatred; it was already there, and they were not the only ones to hate it.[109] But fundamentalism does engage in a creative act when it constructs these objects. It selects some features of its environment, attaches negative valences to them, and ignores others.

This selective, constructed world is the "social horizon" of the fundamentalist. It, rather than the social environment in the more external way in which it has been described in previous sections, is the world in which the fundamentalist lives.[110] It is a world constructed and maintained in discourse. It depends on the conversations and Bible studies and sermons and church dinners in which the fundamentalist participates. But it also articulates with the external world (that is, with the social horizons in which nonfundamentalists live). It gives the fundamentalist an understanding of what is going on in the world and why it is happening. Thus, fundamentalists are themselves social analysts. Like social scientists, as they try to understand the social conditions that led fundamentalists into national prominence, they too attempt to diagnose the social characteristics of their world. Their diagnoses and those of social scientists do not always coincide, of course, but there is a degree of articulation between the events happening in the social environment and how fundamentalists choose to talk about it. The moral uncertainty referred to earlier was not a product entirely of their invention; they merely helped put it on the national agenda. The same was true of the fiscal conservatism that began to influence American politics in the 1980s. Fundamentalists responded positively to these appeals, but also reinterpreted them, turning them into moral capital.

Were it only that fundamentalism constructs a social horizon in which to live, it would be difficult to distinguish their beliefs from others,' except by reciting the specific arguments they have made about the apocalypse, communism, AIDS, pornography, or homosexuality. But fundamentalism, as observed, imposes a basic polarity on its social horizon. It is, in this sense, a form of cultural criticism.[111] It selects much from the secular world to vilify, declares that world polluted and uninhabitable, and identifies a life that is more worthy of pursuing. This is what some have referred to when they say fundamentalism is essentially antimodern, or that it poses a counterdiscourse to the discourse of modernity.[112] Fundamentalism defines itself in polar opposition to modernity. And, compared with more complex forms of cultural criticism, it often does little more than negate secular society, while presenting itself as a utopian alternative.[113] But this view needs to be qualified in two important respects. First, fundamentalism does not reject modernity entirely; it rejects it selectively. A North American fundamentalist, like an Ecuadorian fundamentalist, may lash out against alcoholism, and yet feel comfortable taking sleeping pills, drinking coffee, or working for a multinational corporation that damages the environment and the health of its workers. To say that fundamentalists are simply antimodern misses the extensive degree to which they are also modern. Second, fundamentalist discourse does not define its basic polarity simply as a past-versus-future orientation, as some observers imply.[114] Fundamentalists do not see the train of civilization moving along the tracks into the future and call for putting the engine in reverse. Instead, they envision switching points along the track and call for the train to move in one direction into the future instead of another.

Care must also be taken in suggesting that fundamentalism poses as a counterdiscourse, for that implies a dominant discourse that simply exists apart from fundamentalist constructions. Fundamentalism is not a monolithic counterdiscourse consisting of principles and ideals that differ from external discourse. Rather, it is internally a dialogic construction.[115] It consists of an internal conversation between its own view of Christian fundamentals and its own view of something opposed to these fundamentals. It does not simply respond to modernity; it caricatures modernity, redefining it in a way that heightens the contrast between its evils and the good life provided by a belief in Christ. Seeing fundamentalism as a form of cultural criticism, rather than dismissing it as a form of mental retardation, allows its creativity and vitality to be recognized. But, in defending the creativity of fundamentalism, its simplicity must not be neglected either, like the anthropologist who tries to turn primitives into sophisticated scientists. The reason fundamentalism often appears simpleminded is that it, like all forms of cultural criticism, is designed to motivate people toward taking some action. It is not a purely intellectual (or anti-intellectual) exercise concerned with spinning out theories of society; it is a call for action, a plea for a changed lifestyle.[116] To invoke this plea, it often adopts a rhetorical style that moves from the complex to the simple, from the chaotic to the commonsensical.[117] It accuses its opponents of making life more complicated than it needs to be, arguing instead that one merely needs to find the simple truth. And yet the truth it seeks is anything but simple. This is where the critics of fundamentalism, who charge that it only provides ridiculous certainty in the face of true complexity, fail to understand it. Just as a Marxist vision of the perfect classless society can produce libraries filled with complex discussion and debate, so fundamentalism envisions a lifestyle that takes at least a lifetime to figure out. The apocalypse (as Susan Harding's chapter demonstrates) might be taken as a case in point.

The other feature of fundamentalist culture which is sometimes misunderstood is that it does not set up a polarity between good and evil only to identify itself with the light and distance itself from the darkness. This tendency toward self-righteousness is what nonfundamentalists frequently find objectionable. And fundamentalism is no more free of it than any other truth-seeking belief system. But the point that critics and naive adherents both ignore is that the emphasis in these phrases is not so much on right and truth as on seeking. The fundamentalist riles opponents by asserting not only that there is a better life but also that he or she knows what this life is. In doing so, the fundamentalist seems to side with the good. But closer inspection of fundamentalist discourse shows that the believer is also a seeker, a pilgrim, someone who is striving after the good, but never (at least in this life) having attained it with perfection.[118] Evangelist Pat Robertson disturbs the secular consciousness when he declares that God told him personally to run for the presidency; but even Robertson poses as a seeker, someone who does not understand the will of God but is willing to follow it to see where it leads. Such an orientation does not mean that the fundamentalist takes a more relativistic stance toward opposing religious views, but it is associated with taking those views into account and with learning from them.[119]

This brings the discussion, then, to the final feature of fundamentalist culture—the figural actor—that must be understood in trying to account for its social sources. The seeker, the image of the pilgrim set upon a journey in faith, is also a cultural construction. It is, to be sure, a function largely of the polar theological or moral discourse in which it is framed. But it also draws on material from the surrounding social environment. If Jesus or the Good Samaritan or some other biblical figure serves as a "type" in the technical sense of the word in which fundamentalists use it,[120] that type nevertheless takes on some of the admired characteristics of its culture and negatively illustrates others. For example, in a society such as ours which values knowledge, the model Christian—even for the fundamentalist—often becomes someone who knows the Bible, studies it dutifully, and faithfully takes notes during the Sunday service. Or, as has been observed,[121] the fundamentalist image of Jesus in American society may reflect the therapeutic motif by stressing the intimacy and warmth of the Christ.

Conclusion

The foregoing has identified a number of factors that have contributed to the rise, persistence, and relative success of fundamentalism in the United States. As a way of drawing the various parts of our argument together, a summary of how these factors have made the fundamentalist movement possible and how they have shaped it is in order. These conclusions necessitate a different view of fundamentalism than is present in some of the literature.

Fundamentalism, it has been argued, is a reflection of the overall strength of American religion, not its weakness. Modernization theory suggests the opposite. It associates fundamentalism with prevailing decline in religious commitment, viewing it more as a backlash phenomenon. Other arguments take a similar view, but suggest, for example, that fundamentalism may be strongest where other faith-expressions are weakest.[122] The present claim is that the fundamentalism movement benefitted from the fact that a place like Princeton Theological Seminary was there to encourage theological scholarship; that trained theologians could start Westminister Theological Seminary or Dallas Theological Seminary; that church buildings often could be purchased cheaply by fundamentalists when other denominations moved their operations to the suburbs; that wealthy laity would fund publication of fundamentalist pamphlets; and that many other churches were providing basic religious instruction to children who would later convert to fundamentalism. These resources, of course, increased the likelihood that people with no religious training might be attracted to fundamentalism. A church on nearly every corner and neighbors interested in recruiting new members made it more likely for the typical factory worker, farmer, housewife, or computer operator to turn to fundamentalism than, as in other societies, to political parties, labor unions, or other associations. The *perception* of religious strength is also an important consideration. Although fundamentalists are commonly characterized as dour pessimists, this depiction is only partially accurate. They may indeed be critical of secular morality and of liberal churches. But one source of fundamentalism's persistence is its own conviction that it will prevail, and this conviction is sometimes bolstered by an optimistic appraisal of the broader religious mood. Thus in recent years, fundamentalist writings frequently have cited Gallup polls and church-growth statistics to show that religious commitment in the United States is strong, and perhaps growing, and to suggest that fundamentalism is the wave of the future.[123]

The present discussion has also led to the counterintuitive idea that in the United States, government has been more the friend of fundamentalism than its enemy. Many fundamentalists of course would not see it this way. Nor would social scientists bent on showing government to be a serious source of secularization. But government has actually served American fundamentalism quite well. In maintaining basic political order, it has minimized the attention most people pay to politics, thereby freeing up much of their leisure energy to be devoted to watching television or attending religious services. The one time political order came close to breaking down (the late 1960s) was in fact the time fundamentalists probably had the most difficulty capturing public attention. Separation of church and state has been the friend of fundamentalism as well. A single state church might well have legislated fundamentalists out of existence. In addition, the wall of separation itself has provided a symbolic barrier against which fundamentalists could play. Court decisions that threatened to alter this boundary, say, by moving religion out of publicly funded schoolrooms, or by imposing new standards on religious broadcasting, were thus occasions for fundamentalists to mobilize. In addition, fundamentalists have become more politically active since the mid-1970s because government has also become more of a determinant of social resources during this period. This, then, is another instance of needing to know something about the wider environment in order to understand fundamentalism itself. Were fundamentalism viewed as an isolated social movement, observers would perhaps conclude that it was trying to seize power for itself, that it was becoming dangerously militant, and that the society was on the verge of being returned to totalitarianism. But the wider view shows that political action committees advocating numerous agendas have actually become more numerous and powerful during this period, and that government now reaches more deeply into the pockets of most citizens than ever before and regulates a growing share of their everyday life. It is thus not surprising that fundamentalism has adjusted to this development. Not to have done so would have been as surprising as the church paying no attention to the plague in the late Middle Ages.

Rising levels of education are another important factor to which U.S. fundamentalists have had to adjust. Seeing education as a threat to the worldview of fundamentalists is fairly common. Seeing it as a potential resource is less obvious because modernization theory has too often been concerned with the direct effects of new ideas on individuals' religious beliefs. Social movement theorists have focused on the psychological dynamics of individual believers as well. And those who have focused on organizational dynamics have not emphasized the role of broader trends, such as rising levels of education. The perspective outlined here suggests that these increases have indeed been important, and they have influenced fundamentalism not so much by undermining the beliefs of individuals but by providing new resources. Higher education in the short run at least provides fundamentalist churches with new power and with improved means of voicing their message. Rising levels of education among fundamentalists themselves is an important development.[124] It provides trained leadership, and it places fundamentalist churches squarely within the networks of the new middle class, where they can influence its neighborhoods through Bible studies, prayer fellowships, and personal friendships. Symbolically, fundamentalism gains respectability. But higher education is probably beginning to change the nature of spirituality among fundamentalists as well. For example, some fundamentalists show enormous interest in creation science,[125] in rational methods of disciplining their children,[126] in improving the technical quality of public schooling, and in logical deductive proofs of the existence of God or the validity of the Bible. Fundamentalism has always been a response to the more educated culture of the twentieth century rather than a simple rejection of it.[127] From the beginning, it tried to defend its principles on the basis of more scholarship, not less, and on the basis of greater study and reflection rather than intuition or revelation alone.

Implicit in the foregoing is also a broader conception of American society that challenges some assumptions of modernization theory itself. Neither the persistence of American religion in general nor the resurgence of fundamentalism in particular is easily reconciled with views of modern society that emphasize only secularization, the advances of science, or the increasing uniformity of social life produced by government, education, or industrialization. Even refinements pointing out differential levels of exposure to modernity add little in explanatory power. Other characteristics of modernization, however, need to be recognized. One is that modernization has been disruptive as well as progressive. It has created widespread ambivalence. Fundamentalists and nonfundamentalists alike have decried the loss of community, the demise of hallowed traditions, and the seeming inauthenticity of the modern self. Modernization has also proceeded unevenly, not simply leaving some groups behind but putting them at a permanent disadvantage (for example, in poorly paid jobs in the rising service industries). Fundamentalism flourished in African-American, Latino, and working-class white Anglo communities, not despite modernization but because of it. At the same time, modernization has contributed its own resources. Urbanization, for example, created neighborhoods, greater opportunities for short-distance travel, and easier communication, all of which created more heterogeneous niches into which fundamentalist churches could move. Industrialization, of course, diminished the economic role of the farm, the small town, and the shopkeeper, as Gusfield observes, but the moral logic of these traditional roles did not cease to be relevant. Indeed, recent research shows much continuity.[128] The same emphasis on schedules, for example, that made railways successful in the nineteenth century contributed to the development of automobile assembly lines and air transportation in the twentieth century. Fundamentalists who believed in hard work, strict moral discipline, and clear rules of personal conduct could adjust well to the new environment. New developments in theological criticism may have been largely irrelevant because daily experience, especially when confirmed in close-knit religious congregations, continued to match many of the practical injunctions fundamentalists found in their Bibles.[129] In these ways at least, the wider environment was not unconducive to fundamentalism.

The discussion of the dynamics of fundamentalism, focusing on processes of production, selection, and institutionalization, need not be repeated, except to emphasize that fundamentalism has had to adjust in the past three decades to a period of major social resettling. Prior to World War II, when scholars such as H. Richard Niebuhr and H. Paul Douglass tried to create a social map of American religion, they were able to do so largely with reference to region, immigration, race, and social class. What has become evident since World War II is a reshuffling of all these identities. Old niches, filled by ethnically identified denominations, have altered significantly, and in the process, individual converts have become available for fundamentalist recruitment. One example that illustrates this process well concerns a church in Michigan which gravitated toward fundamentalism in the 1980s. The church, founded by Scottish Presbyterians, had been in existence for more than a hundred years. During much of that time, its sponsoring denomination had clung fiercely to ethnic traditions. Through intermarriage, clustering in semi-isolated farming communities, and distinctive religious practices (such as closed communion), its members had maintained its identity for a long period. But the 1960s took most of its youth away from the farms, first to secular colleges or to the military, and then to jobs in the suburbs. Membership in the denomination declined steadily. Some new churches were founded, opting largely for a broader evangelical theology that diminished the ethnic customs and heritage. And a few, such as the one in Michigan, veered farther to the theological and political right. By the end of the 1980s, it had embraced the Christian Reconstructionist movement,[130] become militantly involved in the pro-life movement, and committed itself more firmly than ever before to the inerrancy of the Bible and the need for personal salvation. This example indicates that the social sources of fundamentalism at the individual or congregation level are likely to be quite varied. A particular pastor can make an enormous difference.[131] Even reading a particular book, or a unique episode in the life of the church, can be decisive. Yet the breakup of ethnic communities and the spinoff of their members into various mainline, evangelical, or fundamentalist churches has been a general pattern.

Implied in this depiction of cultural change is of course the reality of competition among religious organizations. Fundamentalists have done well at institutionalizing themselves and retaining control over their own ideas and practices. For the most part, they have not tried to advance scientific theories, run business organizations, or formulate government policy; they have focused their energies on being churches. The fact that until recently they were largely ignored by the mass media was to their advantage. If journalists did not understand them, it was at least clear to their membership that journalists' views did not then matter. Preaching a powerful sermon, praying a powerful prayer, feeling the movement of the Holy Spirit, being able to recite Bible verses, knowing who D. L. Moody was, or having the latest version of the Scofield Bible—these were the markers of being a valued member of the community.

We have also emphasized that fundamentalist discourse should be taken seriously in any effort to understand its social role and implications. A brief chapter, devoted largely to other tasks, is of course not the place to present an exegesis of this discourse. It is nevertheless important to recognize the polarity that characterizes much of fundamentalist discourse. Its critics are largely correct in accusing it of painting the world

in absolutes, of viewing things as right or wrong, of drawing sharp distinctions between the saved and the heathen, and of paying much attention to the struggles between good and evil and between truth and heresy. Fundamentalists have their own
view of society—their own *sociology,* as it were—and this view is likely to include deep
criticisms of secular institutions, concern about the downward trajectory of morality,
and a clear vision of what must be done for the society to redeem itself. Fundamentalism thrives on the opposition it generates. It thrives on the fact that there are deeper
and more complex truths to be discovered, even within its own heritage. It is a community of discourse that needs to talk in militant terms, more so than it actually needs
to behave in militant ways. Its strident language attracts attention from the outside
world, and in the process helps its members distance themselves from that world.

Finally, there is a normative lesson to be learned from all this as well. If accounting for fundamentalism helps in understanding it coldly, analytically, and intellectually, it must also be recognized that fundamentalism is not as foreign to modern
culture as it or its critics like to make out. For the critic, it may be most helpful to
understand that fundamentalism is more sophisticated in its own right and less a
reaction to the dominant culture than generally supposed. For the fundamentalist, it
should be important to see that guidelines for moral behavior are not being taken
literally from holy writ. Literalism notwithstanding, fundamentalism is very much a
matter of cultural interpretation.

Notes

1. Although some of the theological ideas
of fundamentalism are much older, historians generally prefer to identify the term
"fundamentalism" with a distinct movement
in the United States that began around the
start of the twentieth century and gained expression in a series of pamphlets called *The
Fundamentals: A Testimony to Truth,* published between 1910 and 1915. See Mark A.
Noll, *A History of Christianity in the United
States and Canada* (Grand Rapids, Mich.:
Eerdmans, 1992), pp. 376–86; and, for a
brief definition of fundamentalist theology,
Raymond F. Collins, "Fundamentalism," in
Alan Richardson and John Bowden, eds.,
*The Westminster Dictionary of Christian
Theology* (Philadelphia: Westminster Press,
1983), pp. 223–24.

2. Adding to the confusion is the fact that
social scientists have been guided by differing conceptual models, variously emphasizing contrasts between sects and churches,
the role of deprivation in the rise of religious

movements, and tensions between religious
conservatives and liberals; these models are
reviewed in Matthew P. Lawson, "Sects and
Churches, Evangelicals and Liberals: Shades
of Max Weber in the Sociology of Religion,
1904–1990" (Manuscript, Department of
Sociology, Princeton University, 1992).

3. This view of accounts is amplified in
Marvin B. Scott and Stanford M. Lyman,
"Accounts," *American Sociological Review* 33
(1968): 33–47.

4. Henry Steele Commager, *The American Mind: An Interpretation of American
Thought and Character since the 1880s*
(New Haven: Yale University Press, 1950),
pp. 178–83.

5. These and other accomplishments of
the movement are summarized in Ed Dobson, *The Fundamentalist Phenomenon: The
Resurgence of Conservative Christianity*
(Garden City, N.J.: Doubleday, 1981), esp.
chap. 1; on the founding of megachurches,
see Elmer L. Towns, *America's Fastest Grow-*

ing Churches (Nashville: Impact Books, 1972).

6. R. Laurence Moore, *Religious Outsiders and the Making of Americans* (New York: Oxford University Press, 1986), p. 150.

7. John C. Green, James L. Guth, Lyman A. Kellstedt, and Corwin E. Smidt, "National Survey of American Evangelicals: Preliminary Report" (Manuscript, Ray C. Bliss Institute of Applied Politics, University of Akron, 1992); based on an extensive survey of more than four thousand randomly selected respondents.

8. The first two responses are from the Akron survey; the latter two from a 1992 survey of more than two thousand adults in the U.S. labor force conducted by Robert Wuthnow.

9. Richard Hofstadter, *Anti-Intellectualism in American Life* (New York: Knopf, 1962), pp. 117–29.

10. Joseph R. Gusfield, *Symbolic Crusade: Status Politics and the American Temperance Movement* (Urbana: University of Illinois Press, 1963), pp. 9–11.

11. Peter Berger, Brigitte Berger, and Hansfried Kellner, *The Homeless Mind: Modernization and Consciousness* (New York: Random House, 1973), esp. chap. 8.

12. James Davison Hunter, "Fundamentalism in Its Global Contours," in Norman J. Cohen, ed., *The Fundamentalist Phenomenon: A View from Within; A Response from Without* (Grand Rapids, Mich.: Eerdmans, 1990), pp. 56–72.

13. George M. Marsden, *Fundamentalism and American Culture: The Shaping of Twentieth-Century Evangelicalism, 1870–1925* (New York: Oxford University Press, 1980), esp. chaps. 22–25.

14. Dean M. Kelley, *Why Conservative Churches Are Growing,* rev. ed. (New York: Harper and Row, 1977).

15. Nancy T. Ammerman, *Bible Believers: Fundamentalists in the Modern World* (New Brunswick, N.J.: Rutgers University Press, 1987).

16. Much of this literature is referenced in subsequent notes.

17. Robert Wuthnow, *Communities of Discourse: Ideology and Social Structure in the Reformation, the Enlightenment, and European Socialism* (Cambridge: Harvard University Press, 1989). Readers should consult this volume for greater detail than can be presented in the present chapter about the theory of cultural articulation and to see how it applies to major episodes of cultural change. Parts of the theory especially relevant to the present discussion can also be found in Wuthnow, *Meaning and Moral Order: Explorations in Cultural Analysis* (Berkeley: University of California Press, 1987); idem, "Sociology of Religion," in Neil J. Smelser, ed., *Handbook of Sociology* (Beverly Hills, Calif.: Sage, 1988), pp. 473–509; idem, "Infrastructure and Superstructure: Revisions in Marxist Sociology of Culture," in Richard Münch and Neil J. Smelser, eds., *Theory of Culture* (Berkeley: University of California Press, 1992), pp. 145–70; and idem, *Producing the Sacred: An Essay on Public Religion* (Urbana: University of Illinois Press, 1994). The present chapter draws substantively on the discussion of religious conservatism in Wuthnow, *The Restructuring of American Religion: Society and Faith since World War II* (Princeton: Princeton University Press, 1988); the theory of cultural articulation is implicit in the framework of that volume as well.

18. In the 1992 survey by Green et al., "National Survey of American Evangelicals," 11 percent of the public identified themselves as evangelicals, in addition to the 9 percent who claimed they were fundamentalists, but the two gave similar responses to a number of political questions. In a 1982 national survey of evangelicals, those who identified themselves as fundamentalists did not differ on most demographic factors from those who identified themselves as evangelicals; see Stuart Rothenberg and Frank Newport, *The Evangelical Voter: Religion and Politics in America* (Washington, D.C.: Institute for Government and Politics, Free Congress Research and Education Foundation, 1984).

19. Standard sources include Karl Mannheim, *Ideology and Utopia* (New York: Harcourt, Brace, 1936); Peter L. Berger and

Thomas Luckmann, *The Social Construction of Reality: A Treatise in the Sociology of Knowledge* (Garden City, N.Y.: Doubleday, 1966); and Kenneth Thompson, *Beliefs and Ideology* (London: Tavistock, 1986).

20. For example, Peter L. Berger, *The Sacred Canopy* (Garden City, N.Y.: Doubleday, 1967); Thomas Luckmann, *The Invisible Religion* (London: Macmillan, 1966); Robert N. Bellah, *Beyond Belief* (New York: Harper and Row, 1970); James Davison Hunter, *American Evangelicalism* (New Brunswick, N.J.: Rutgers University Press, 1983).

21. Social structural determination varies but is evident in most theories of modernization, for example, in Berger's concern with the effects of structural diversity and in Bellah's concern with institutional differentiation in his theory of religious evolution.

22. A parallel argument is made in N. J. Demerath III and Rhys H. Williams, "Secularization in a Community Context: Tensions of Religion and Politics in a New England City," *Journal for the Scientific Study of Religion* 31 (1992): 189–206.

23. For example, Laurence R. Iannaccone, "Religious Practice: A Human Capital Approach," *Journal for the Scientific Study of Religion* 29 (1990): 297–314; and Richard A. Peterson, ed., *The Production of Culture* (Beverly Hills, Calif.: Sage, 1976); discussions that draw clearer connections between productive factors and ideas themselves include Terry Eagleton, *Criticism and Ideology* (London: Verso, 1976); and M. M. Bakhtin and P. M. Medvedev, *The Formal Method in Literary Scholarship: A Critical Introduction to Sociological Poetics* (Cambridge: Harvard University Press, 1985).

24. Chapter 7 by Nancy Ammerman in this volume summarizes and extends our observations in this chapter about organizational variety.

25. See for example, Frank Lechner, "Fundamentalism Revisited: A Sociological Analysis," in Thomas Robbins and Rick Anthony, eds., *In Gods We Trust*, 2d ed. (New Brunswick, N.J.: Transaction, 1990), pp. 77–97.

26. On the defining characteristics of fundamentalism in the United States, see Nancy T. Ammerman, "North American Protestant Fundamentalism," in Martin E. Marty and R. Scott Appleby, eds., *Fundamentalisms Observed* (Chicago: University of Chicago Press, 1990), chap. 1; for historical background see Marsden, *Fundamentalism and American Culture*.

27. Although it was the original intention of the architects of this volume that the present chapter would draw together and compare the social conditions discussed by the authors of the other chapters on Christian fundamentalism, a different strategy evolved. Those chapters, written by scholars with firsthand exposure to the movements at issue, focus more on internal dynamics of the movements themselves than on wider conditions. For that reason, this chapter pays greater attention to the United States than might otherwise have been the case and discusses fundamentalism in Europe and Latin America only insofar as those countries help in understanding fundamentalism better in the United States. In several of these chapters the authors also take a stance against the idea of fundamentalism having "sources" that can be of value in "accounting" for them, preferring instead to emphasize the internal dynamics and processes by which movements construct their own realities. To complement this perspective, the present chapter focuses more on the macroscopic conditions under which Christian fundamentalism has arisen than on its microscopic dimensions.

28. These episodes are discussed in Wuthnow, *Restructuring of American Religion*, chap. 8.

29. This argument is developed in Wuthnow, *Meaning and Moral Order*, chap. 6.

30. On these struggles, see Marsden, *Fundamentalism and American Culture*.

31. Robert C. Liebman, John Sutton, and Robert Wuthnow, "Exploring the Social Sources of Denominationalism: Schisms in American Protestant Denominations, 1890–1980," *American Sociological Review* 53 (June 1988): 343–52.

32. Nancy T. Ammerman, *Baptist Battles: Social Change and Religious Conflict in the Southern Baptist Convention* (New Brunswick, N.J.: Rutgers University Press, 1990); Robert A. Baker, *The Southern Baptist Convention and Its People* (Nashville: Broadman Press, 1974).

33. Distinguishing environmental conditions from institutional contexts does not of course rule out consideration of the fact that the broader environment in modern societies is also increasingly "institutionalized," a fact emphasized in so-called neo-institutional approaches to organizations; for example, George M. Thomas, John W. Meyer, Francisco O. Ramirez, and John Boli, *Institutional Structure: Constituting State, Society, and the Individual* (Beverly Hill, Calif.: Sage, 1987); Walter W. Powell and Paul J. DiMaggio, eds., *The New Institutionalism in Organizational Analysis* (Chicago: University of Chicago Press, 1991).

34. Charles Tilly, *From Mobilization to Revolution* (Reading, Mass.: Addison-Wesley, 1978); Roberta Ash, *Social Movements in America* (Chicago: Markham, 1972); David R. Cameron, "Toward a Theory of Political Mobilization," *Journal of Politics* 36 (1974): 138–71; Rosabeth Moss Kanter, *Commitment and Community: Communes and Utopias in Sociological Perspective* (Cambridge: Harvard University Press, 1972); William A. Gamson, *Power and Discontent* (Homewood, Ill.: Dorsey, 1968); idem, *The Strategy of Social Protest* (Homewood, Ill.: Dorsey, 1975).

35. Robert C. Liebman, "Mobilizing the Moral Majority," in Robert C. Liebman and Robert Wuthnow, eds., *The New Christian Right: Mobilization and Legitimation* (New York: Aldine, 1983), pp. 49–73.

36. James L. Guth, "Southern Baptist Clergy: Vanguard of the Christian Right?" in Liebman and Wuthnow, *The New Christian Right,* chap. 6; Ammerman, *Baptist Battles.*

37. Gene Burns, *Frontiers of Catholicism* (Berkeley: University of California Press, 1992).

38. Weber's emphasis on the needs of the disprivileged for salvation is the classic example; see Max Weber, *The Sociology of Religion,* trans. E. Fischoff (1922; Boston: Beacon, 1964). Fundamentalism has been associated more recently with various kinds of deprivation or disorganization, for example, H. Richard Niebuhr, *The Social Sources of Denominationalism* (New York: Harper, 1929); Gary Schwartz, *Sect Ideology and Social Status* (Chicago: University of Chicago Press, 1970); Rodney Stark and William Sims Bainbridge, *The Future of Religion: Secularization, Revival and Cult Formation* (Berkeley: University of California Press, 1985).

39. Wuthnow, *Communities of Discourse,* chaps. 11 and 12.

40. Wuthnow, *Restructuring of American Religion;* Roger Finke and Rodney Stark, *The Churching of America, 1776–1990* (New Brunswick, N.J.: Rutgers University Press, 1992).

41. See Kenneth D. Wald, *Religion and Politics in the United States* (New York: St. Martin's Press, 1987), chap. 1, for more recent comparative figures.

42. Ernest Sandeen, *The Roots of Fundamentalism: British and American Millenarianism, 1800–1930* (Chicago: University of Chicago Press, 1970), stresses the theological heritage of fundamentalism, but fails to emphasize the social resources necessary to carry on this work.

43. This point is emphasized in Daniel Sack, "The Social Gospel as a Nostalgic Movement" (Paper presented at the Religion and Culture Workshop, Princeton University, 1992); see also Robert T. Handy, ed., *The Social Gospel in America, 1870–1920: Gladden, Ely, Rauschenbusch* (New York: Oxford University Press, 1966); and for an interpretation of the more general mood of the period that differs from Henry Steele Commager's, see Robert M. Crunden, *Ministers of Reform: The Progressives' Achievement in American Civilization, 1889–1920* (New York: Basic Books, 1982).

44. Clifford J. Clarke, "The Bible Belt Thesis: An Empirical Test of the Hypothesis of Clergy Overrepresentation, 1890–1930," *Journal for the Scientific Study of Religion* 29 (1990): 210–25.

45. George Gallup, Jr., *Religion in America, 1992* (Princeton: Princeton Religion Research Center, 1992), indicates relative religious strength in recent decades; see also Andrew M. Greeley, *Social Change in American Religion* (Cambridge: Harvard University Press, 1990).

46. On the relative likelihood of religious motivations to appear in personal discourse in the United States and France, see the interesting evidence in Michele Lamont, *Money, Morals, and Manners* (Chicago: University of Chicago Press, 1992).

47. Empirical evidence supporting this relationship for the United States is presented in Kevin J. Christiano, *Religious Diversity and Social Change: American Cities, 1890–1906* (Cambridge: Cambridge University Press, 1987.)

48. The foregoing analysis draws conceptually from the general framework of church and state relations presented in David Martin, *A General Theory of Secularization* (New York: Harper and Row, 1975).

49. Mary Fulbrook, *Piety and Politics* (Cambridge: Cambridge University Press, 1985).

50. Robert Wuthnow, "The Political Rebirth of American Evangelicals," in Liebman and Wuthnow, *The New Christian Right,* chap. 9.

51. On the effects of state growth and market expansion in advanced industrial societies, see Robert Wuthnow, ed., *Between States and Markets: The Voluntary Sector in Comparative Perspective* (Princeton: Princeton University Press, 1991).

52. Following in the line of Max Weber and James Luther Adams, this argument is developed in Max L. Stackhouse, "The Space for Voluntary Associations," in Robert Wuthnow and Virginia A. Hodgkinson, eds., *Faith and Philanthropy* (San Francisco: Jossey-Bass, 1990), chap. 2.

53. Robert Wuthnow, "Economic Values Survey," a survey conducted among 2,013 randomly selected members of the U.S. labor force in 1992; questions and results are to be published in a forthcoming book.

54. Robert Wuthnow, *Rediscovering the Sacred: Perspectives on Religion in Contemporary Society* (Grand Rapids, Mich.: Eerdmans, 1992), chap. 7.

55. For the United States, see Jerome L. Himmelstein, *To the Right: The Transformation of American Conservatism* (Berkeley: University of California, 1990); on Western Europe, see John W. P. Veugelers, "Ideologies of Far Right Parties in Contemporary France and Britain" (Manuscript, Department of Sociology, Princeton University, 1992).

56. David Harrington Watt, "United States: Cultural Challenges to the Voluntary Sector," in Wuthnow, *Between States and Markets,* chap. 9; James Davison Hunter, *Culture Wars* (New York: Basic Books, 1991).

57. David Harrell suggests that status issues contribute to the political agendas of newly middle-class fundamentalists; Harrell, "The Roots of the Moral Majority: Fundamentalism Revisited," in Kenneth Aman, ed., *Border Regions of Faith: An Anthology of Religion and Social Change* (Maryknoll, N.J.: Orbis, 1987). Comparing the characteristics of members of Christian right-wing organizations in two periods, Clyde Wilcox found that the activist leaders were of relatively high status and education; Wilcox, "America's Radical Right Revisited: A Comparison of the Activists in Christian Right Organizations from the 1960s and the 1980s," *Sociological Analysis* 48, no. 1 (January 1987): 46–57.

58. See especially Pablo A. Deiros, "Protestant Fundamentalism in Latin America," in Marty and Appleby, *Fundamentalisms Observed,* chap. 3.

59. The case of Nicaragua is discussed in David Stoll, *Is Latin America Turning Protestant?* (Berkeley: University of California Press, 1990).

60. Hofstadter, *Anti-Intellectualism in American Life;* John Shelby Spong, *Rescuing the Bible from Fundamentalism: A Bishop Rethinks the Meaning of Scripture* (San Francisco: Harper San Francisco, 1991).

61. Wuthnow, *Restructuring of American Religion,* chap. 7.

62. George Gallup, Jr., "Fifty Years of

Gallup Surveys on Religion," *Gallup Report* 236 (1985): 1–14.

63. This example, not completely fictional, is consistent with in-depth interviews the authors have conducted during the past few years. Further support is provided by research currently in progress on Christians in higher education by John Schmalzbauer, Department of Sociology, Princeton University.

64. In George Marsden, "Preachers of Paradox: The Religious New Right in Historical Perspective," in Mary Douglas and Steven M. Tipton, eds., *Religion and America* (Boston: Beacon 1983), p. 163, Marsden points out the association of fundamentalism with the technological strand in American culture in which "truth is a matter of true and precise propositions that, when properly classified, will work. Fundamentalism fits this mentality because it is a form of Christianity with no loose ends, ambiguities or historical developments." He goes on to cite evidence that the leaders of the creation science movement work in the fields of applied sciences and engineering. For other reports on the educational attainments of fundamentalists, see Nancy T. Ammerman's "Southern Baptists and the New Christian Right," *Review of Religious Research* 32, no. 3 (1991): 213–36; and Ronald Burton, Stephen Johnson and Joseph Tamney, "Education and Fundamentalism," *Review of Religious Research* 30, no. 4 (1989): 344–59.

65. For example, Berger, Berger, and Kellner, *The Homeless Mind*. In fairness, Berger has probably shifted his own views on this subject; see Peter L. Berger, *A Far Glory* (New York: Free Press, 1992).

66. The classic example is Weber's discussion of prophecy and the routinization of charisma in *The Sociology of Religion*. Anthony F. C. Wallace's discussion of revitalization movements is more recent and more elaborate; Wallace, "Revitalization Movements," *American Anthropologist* 58, no. 2 (1956): 264–81. It has been applied to the recent evangelical revival by William McLoughlin, *Revivals, Awakenings and Reform* (Chicago: University of Chicago Press, 1978).

67. Clark McPhail and David L. Miller, "The Assembling Process: A Theoretical and Empirical Examination," *American Sociological Review* 38 (1973): 721–35.

68. See, for example, Liebman, "Mobilizing the Moral Majority."

69. See Marsden, *Fundamentalism and American Culture,* and Hunter, *American Evangelicalism.*

70. On these varieties, Ammerman, "North American Protestant Fundamentalism"; and especially Donald W. Dayton and Robert K. Johnston, eds., *The Variety of American Evangelicalism* (Knoxville: University of Tennessee Press, 1991). Assessments of empirical studies are made difficult because some investigators have been interested in fundamentalism narrowly defined, others in evangelicalism, or in religious conservatism, and still others in the variety of religious sects.

71. While these concepts bear a resemblance to the phases of individual movements identified by the researchers cited above, our level of analysis is different; we are concerned to explain how many movements can arise from different parent stocks in response to similar environmental opportunities and constraints. Population ecology models have been fruitfully applied to organizational development; see Howard Aldrich, *Organizations and Environments* (Englewood Cliffs, N.J.: Prentice Hall, 1979); and Michael T. Hannon and John Freeman, "The Population Ecology of Organizations," *American Journal of Sociology* 82, no. 5 (1977): 929–64. For a fuller discussion of their application to meaning systems, see Wuthnow, *Meaning and Moral Order.* The contrast between what is here similar to an "environmental conditioning" perspective and "random variation" and "emergent systems" perspectives is described in Elaine Romanelli, "The Evolution of New Organizational Forms," *Annual Review of Sociology* 17 (1991): 79–103.

72. Competition has of course been much emphasized in the study of American reli-

gion; for example, Peter L. Berger, "A Market Model for the Analysis of Ecumenicity," *Social Research* 30 (1963): 70–79; and R. Stephen Warner, "Work in Progress: Toward a New Paradigm in the Sociology of Religion," *American Journal of Sociology* 98 (1993): 344–76. Most of even the latest work, however, relies too heavily on the metaphor of "markets" without either trying to understand more fully the characteristics of markets or taking into account the problem of articulation between ideologies and their social environments.

73. John Burdick, in "Gossip and Secrecy: Women's Articulation of Domestic Conflict in Three Religions of Urban Brazil," *Sociological Analysis* 51, no. 2 (1990): 153–70, examines how women select among different religious groups with different styles for handling particular issues.

74. On the concept of uncertainty, see Wuthnow, *Meaning and Moral Order,* chap. 5; Michael T. Hannan, "Uncertainty, Diversity and Organizational Change," in Neil J. Smelser and D. R. Gerstein, eds., *Social Change and Behavioral Sciences* (Washington, D.C.: National Academy of Sciences, 1986), pp. 73–94; and Michael T. Hannan and John Freeman, *Organizational Ecology* (Cambridge, Mass.: Ballinger, 1989).

75. This argument is developed at greater length in Wuthnow, *Restructuring of American Religion,* chaps. 7–8.

76. See Steven Tipton, *Getting Saved from the Sixties: Moral Meaning and Conversion in Cultural Change* (Berkeley: University of California Press, 1982); Charles Y. Glock and Robert N. Bellah, eds., *The New Religious Consciousness* (Berkeley: University of California Press, 1976); and Robert Wuthnow, *The Consciousness Reformation* (Berkeley: University of California Press, 1976).

77. Liebman, Sutton, and Wuthnow, "Exploring the Social Sources of Denominationalism."

78. Niebuhr, *Social Sources of Denominationalism.*

79. Further discussion of these changes in found in Wuthnow, *Restructuring of American Religion;* and Wuthnow, *Christianity in the 21st Century.*

80. George M. Marsden, *Understanding Fundamentalism and Evangelicalism* (Grand Rapids, Mich.: Eerdmans, 1991).

81. Dean M. Kelley, "The Rationale for the Involvement of Religion in the Body Politic," in James E. Wood, Jr. and Derik Davis, eds., *The Role of Religion in the Making of Public Policy* (Waco, Tex.: J. Dawson Institute of Church-State Studies, Baylor University, 1991), chap. 6; Dennis N. Voskuil, "The Power of the Air: Evangelicals and the Rise of Religious Broadcasting," in Quentin J. Schultze, ed., *American Evangelicals and the Mass Media* (Grand Rapids, Mich.: Zondervan, 1990), chap. 3.

82. Andrew M. Greeley, *The American Catholic: A Social Portrait* (New York: Basic Books, 1977); J. Jacques Thierry, *Opus Dei: A Close-up* (New York: Cortland, 1975); Jonathan Rieder, *Canarsie* (Cambridge: Harvard University Press, 1985); Kenneth Briggs, *Holy Siege* (San Francisco: Harper San Francisco, 1992); and William D. Dinges and James Hitchcock, "Roman Catholic Traditionalism and Activist Conservatism in the United States," in Marty and Appleby, *Fundamentalisms Observed,* chap. 2.

83. Steven M. Cohen, *American Modernity and Jewish Identity* (New York: Tavistock, 1983); idem, *American Assimilation or Jewish Revival?* (Bloomington: Indiana University Press, 1988); Lynn Davidman, *Tradition in a Rootless World: Women Turn to Orthodox Judaism* (Berkeley: University of California Press, 1991); Samuel C. Heilman and Steven M. Cohen, *Cosmopolitans and Parochials: Modern Orthodox Jews in America* (Chicago: University of Chicago Press, 1989).

84. One study in the vast literature on new religious movements which discusses these factors is Benjamin Zablocki, *Alienation and Charisma: A Study of Contemporary American Communes* (New York: Free Press, 1980).

85. Susan Rose reports that many of the

women in a charismatic community she studied had participated in the feminist movement. Though they acknowledged their husbands as the leaders of the household, in practice, power was not so clearly delineated. Rose, "Women Warriors: The Negotiation of Gender in a Charismatic Community," *Sociological Analysis* 48, no. 3 (1987): 245–58. Similarly in Colombia, Elizabeth Brusco found that conversion plays an active role in changing gender roles in the household, giving women an outside means of influencing their husband. Brusco, "The Household Basis of Evangelical Religion and the Reformation of Machismo in Colombia" (Ph.D. diss., University of Michigan, 1986). Salvatore Cucchiari has found similar effects in Sicily. Cucchiari, "Between Shame and Sanctification: Patriarchy and Its Transformation in Sicilian Pentecostalism," *American Ethnologist* 17, no. 4 (1990): 687–707.

86. Wuthnow, *Meaning and Moral Order,* pp. 187–93.

87. Deiros, "Protestant Fundamentalism in Latin America."

88. Charles R. Wilson, ed., *Religion in the South* (Jackson: University of Missippi Press, 1985).

89. J. C. McKinney and L. B. Bourque, "The Changing South: National Incorporation of a Region," *American Sociological Review* 36 (1971): 399–412.

90. S. T. Henderson, "Social Action in a Conservative Environment: The CLC and the Southern Baptist Churches," *Foundations* 23 (1980): 245–51; Ammerman, *Baptist Battles.*

91. Michael Hechter, *Internal Colonialism: The Celtic Fringe in Britain's National Development* (Berkeley: University of California Press, 1981). David Martin maintains a similar view about the importance of "peripheral" regions in fostering and perpetuating revivalistic Christianity. See Martin, *Tongues of Fire: The Explosion of Protestantism in Latin America* (Oxford: Basil Blackwell, 1990).

92. Donald Luidens, Daniel Olson, and R. Stephen Warner supplied helpful information.

93. Wuthnow, *Restructuring of American Religion.*

94. For references, see Michele Lamont and Annette Laureau, "Cultural Capital: Allusions, Gaps and Glissandos in Recent Theoretical Developments," *Sociological Theory* 6, no. 2 (1988): 153–68.

95. Clifford Geertz, *Local Knowledge* (New York: Basic Books, 1983).

96. Melinda Bollar Wagner, *God's Schools: Choice and Compromise in American Society* (New Brunswick, N.J.: Rutgers University Press, 1990); Alan Peshkin, *God's Choice: The Total World of a Fundamentalist Christian School* (Chicago: University of Chicago Press, 1986).

97. Research currently in progress by C. Gray Wheeler and John Schmalzbauer (Department of Sociology, Princeton University) examines these codes in a sample of more than 160 Protestant, Catholic, and secular colleges.

98. See Stoll, *Is Latin America Turning Protestant?*

99. Ammerman, *Bible Believers;* Lawson, "Catholic Charismatics" (Paper presented at the Religion and Culture Workshop, Princeton University, 1992).

100. This information is drawn from a variety of unpublished sources, including symposia on the 1992 election held at Princeton University, the Educational Testing Service, and the Brookings Institution.

101. See Ammerman, *Bible Believers.*

102. Insightful material on the social horizons of contemporary fundamentalist leaders is presented in Martin E. Marty and R. Scott Appleby, *The Glory and the Power: The Fundamentalist Challenge to the Modern World* (Boston: Beacon, 1992).

103. The most sophisticated analysis of this rhetoric is Marsha Witten, "The Restriction of Meaning in Religious Discourse: Centripetal Devices in a Fundamentalist Christian Sermon," in Robert Wuthnow, ed., *Vocabularies of Public Life: Empirical Essays in Symbolic Structure* (London: Routledge, 1992), chap. 1; see also Witten's forthcoming book from Princeton University Press.

104. Liberals' reactions to fundamentalists are examined in Wuthnow, *Christianity in the 21st Century.*

105. See Hunter, *American Evangelicalism.*

106. For example, a direct mail solicitation from Ron Robison, dated October 1990, calling for the ouster of a female professor at the University of Massachusetts.

107. Marsden, *Fundamentalism and American Culture.*

108. Neonazism, neofascism, and other right-wing extremist movements should not be confused with fundamentalism; the fundamentalist opposition to Muslims, New Age groups, and the like is, however, evident in various publications and in talking with individual members of fundamentalist churches.

109. This is the part of the articulation process that involves absorption of the external social world into the social horizon of the ideology itself.

110. A vivid example of constructing and living in such a horizon is presented in Susan Harding, "The Gospel of Giving: The Narrative Construction of a Sacrificial Economy," in Wuthnow, *Vocabularies of Public Life,* chap. 2.

111. "Criticism" is used here in the special sense developed in Wuthnow, *Communities of Discourse.*

112. Much has been written about fundamentalism's relationship to modernity. Discussions may be found in Hunter, *American Evangelicalism;* Bruce B. Lawrence, *Defenders of God: The Fundamentalist Revolt against the Modern Age* (San Francisco: Harper and Row, 1989); and Frank Lechner, "Fundamentalism and Sociocultural Revitalization in America: A Sociological Interpretation," *Sociological Analysis* 46 (1985): 243–59.

113. In *Communities of Discourse,* Wuthnow shows, for example, how leaders of the Protestant Reformation did more, especially in setting up polarities, but also in identifying workable strategies within these horizons.

114. See, for example, Hofstadter, *Anti-Intellectualism in American Life;* Ralph Clark Chandler, "The New Religious Right: Worshipping a Past That Never Was," *Christianity and Crisis* 42 (1982): 21–32.

115. M. M. Bakhtin, *The Dialogic Imagination,* trans. Caryl Emerson and Michael Holquist (Austin: University of Texas Press, 1981).

116. L. J. Lorentzen, "Evangelical Life-Style Concerns Expressed in Political Action," *Sociological Analysis* 41 (1980): 144–54.

117. For examples from fundamentalist sermons, see Robert Wuthnow, "Religious Discourse as Public Rhetoric," *Communication Research* 15 (June 1988): 318–38; see also Wuthnow, *Rediscovering the Sacred,* chap. 3.

118. This orientation has been emphasized empirically in Batson's work on the "quest orientation"; see C. Daniel Batson, "Measuring Religion as Quest," *Journal for the Scientific Study of Religion* 30 (1991): 416–29, 430–47; and Brian A. Kojetin, Danny N. McIntosh, Robert A. Bridges, and Bernard Spilka, "Quest: Constructive Search or Religious Conflict?" *Journal for the Scientific Study of Religion* 26 (1987): 111–15.

119. Sam G. McFarland and James C. Warren, Jr., "Religious Orientations and Selective Exposure among Fundamentalist Christians," *Journal for the Scientific Study of Religion* 31 (1992): 163–74.

120. Edward Taylor, *Upon the Types of the Old Testament,* ed. Charles W. Mignon (Lincoln: University of Nebraska Press, 1989).

121. See Merideth McGuire, *Ritual Healing in Suburban America* (New Brunswick, N.J.: Rutgers University Press, 1988).

122. Stark and Bainbridge, *The Future of Religion.*

123. For example, Dobson, *The Fundamentalist Phenomenon,* chap. 1; and Tim LaHaye, *The Battle for the Mind* (Old Tappan, N.J.: Fleming H. Revell, 1980), chaps. 9–10.

124. Empirical evidence is discussed in Wuthnow, *Restructuring of American Religion.* Research conducted since the mid-

1980s shows that education differentials between self-identified religious conservatives and liberals have diminished considerably in importance; Robert Wuthnow, *Acts of Compassion* (Princeton: Princeton University Press, 1991), chap. 5; Wuthnow, *Christianity in the 21st Century,* pt. 3. Research focusing on denominational affiliations shows that fundamentalist and evangelical members have gained substantially in educational levels over the past two decades, but have still not risen to the same level as mainline Protestants or Roman Catholics; John Schmalzbauer, research in progress, Department of Sociology, Princeton University.

125. Ronald L. Numbers, *The Creationists* (New York: Knopf, 1992).

126. Wagner, *God's Schools.*

127. Marsden, *Fundamentalism and American Culture.*

128. For example, James R. Beniger, *The Control Revolution* (Cambridge: Harvard University Press, 1988); and Frank Dobbin, "Metaphors of Industrial Rationality: The Social Construction of Electronics Policy in the United States and France," in Wuthnow, *Vocabularies of Public Life,* chap. 10.

129. Ammerman, *Bible Believers.*

130. For a description of the Reconstructionist movement, see Ammerman, "North American Protestant Fundamentalism," pp. 49–51.

131. In an evangelical context, at least, this point is evident in R. Stephen Warner, *New Wine in Old Wineskins* (Berkeley: University of California Press, 1988).

3

Imagining the Last Days: The Politics of Apocalyptic Language

Susan Harding

For many born-again Christians, current events and the daily news are composed of "signs of the times," Bible-based signs that the world is approaching the end of human history. We are living in the Last Days, or the End Times. The Great Tribulation is soon to follow, perhaps has begun already, and will end horrifically for unbelievers in the Battle of Armageddon, and gloriously for true believers in the Second Coming of Jesus Christ. Christ's return begins his millennial rule on earth, hence, these Christian apocalyptic narratives are called "premillennialist." Thoroughly pessimistic about the course of current history, they contrast with "postmillennial" stories which foresee Christ's return at the end of an essentially progressive millennium of human rule. While postmillennial visions prevailed among American Protestants during the most of the nineteenth century, they withered away after the Civil War, and today most Bible-believing Protestants in America are premillennialists of one sort or another.[1]

The Branch Davidians who built an armed compound in Waco, Texas, provoking the Bureau of Alcohol, Tobacco, and Firearms into a deadly confrontation in the spring of 1993, were acting out a kind of "historic premillennialism."[2] In historic premillennial scenarios, the present is the very last moment of human history, of both the Last Days and the Great Tribulation, a highly combustible moment in which all as-yet-unfulfilled Bible prophecies are being fulfilled. These apocalyptic stories cast their speakers, "the remnant," the only true Christians, as actors in the precise events that bring on Armageddon and the Second Coming. Historic premillennialists are not necessarily violent, but they invariably *enact* their apocalyptic stories in some way or another. Thus, it is relatively easy to see their stories as "political" in the sense of producing a people who act out the history their peculiar apocalyptic posits.

It is more difficult to see the apocalyptic narratives of the born-again Christians who produced the New Christian Right during the 1980s as "political" in the same sense. Most born-again Christians are not "historic" but "futurist" premillennialists. They are futurist in that they divide the end of history into two distinct periods: the present, or the Last Days, in which Bible prophecies are *not* being fulfilled, and the future, the Great Tribulation, in which they *are* fulfilled. The prevailing futurist scheme among born-again Christians, called "dispensationalism," specifically denies all true Christians any role in the final fulfillment of Bible prophecies by "rapturing" them off the earth for the Tribulation—they cannot, by definition, directly enact Bible prophecies in the way, say, David Koresh could. Still, they too *enact* their apocalyptics. Their End Time stories are formative and constitutive, and thus are "political" in the sense of creating a particular *lived* reality.[3]

While the Branch Davidians were a tiny band of apocalyptic believers, dispensational premillennialists are not. Doctrinal dispensational believers—largely fundamentalists and Pentecostals—may number ten to fifteen million. Furthermore, the watershed of unconscious and semiconscious belief—of what I call narrative belief—may extend to another ten to fifteen million, largely charismatic, Christians. In a word, dispensationalism, broadly defined, is the way most Bible-believing Christians in America read current history and the daily news.[4] Nor are they a desperate lot, driven into their apocalyptic visions by a peculiar need for certitude and consolation: born-again Christians in America today now have approximately the same class, educational, and occupational profile as the population as whole, and so, roughly, do those among them who practice some form of dispensational apocalypticism.

In this chapter, I first discuss what I mean by the "politics" of dispensationalist narratives in more detail and show how the spread of more or less orthodox dispensationalist reading practices among American Christians after the 1860s *marginalized* them by placing them outside current history. Then I show how major dispensationalist preachers collectively revised those narratives in the 1980s in ways that *demarginalized* American Christians by inventing a major historical role for them in the Last Days. Finally, I provide a glimpse of how fundamentalist Christians are imagining the 1990s.

Dispensational Politics

What difference does apocalyptic belief make? President George Bush frequently consulted dispensationalist preacher Billy Graham during the Persian Gulf Crisis, including the day he ordered the bombing of Baghdad and started the war. Did Graham tell Bush that he, Bush, in executing this war, might be unfolding events that were part of God's plan for history? If Bush believed something of that sort, did it matter? Did the (apparent) fact that Ronald Reagan believed the dispensational scheme of the future affect his actions as president? His secretary of the interior, James Watts, publicly declared The End was near, and he turned nature over to business at an alarming pace. Did he do that, as many supposed, because he knew this era of human dominion was almost over and there was no point in protecting the environment? Did born-again Christians support the Persian Gulf War because of their peculiar millennial vision? Did that vision cause or significantly contribute to their political mobilization in the 1980s?

These are questions apocalyptic outsiders ask. Essentially, they want to know, is this particular sort of apocalyptic thought dangerous, or is it harmless? Is it politically consequential, or is it "just religion?" Is it "just rhetoric?"

The answers provided by scholars and journalists vary widely, depending mostly on what they count as "dispensational belief" and as "politics." Timothy Weber, for example, in his definitive history of dispensational premillennialism in America, *Living in the Shadow of the Second Coming,* focused narrowly on doctrinal believers. They were in the forefront of right-wing Christian activism during the 1980s, but Weber argued that their political activities were not a consequence of, did not follow from, their dispensational doctrines. As he put it, "American premillennialism was and is primarily a *religious* movement. Although it has some social and political consequences, premillennialism's paramount appeal is to personal and religious sentiments."[5]

Most scholars and journalists, and, for that matter, dispensational preachers and writers, agree with Weber. Even mentioning politics in the vicinity of Bible prophecy is suspect. Elmer Towns preached a three-part series on "Iraq and Bible Prophecy" at Thomas Road Baptist Church in the fall of 1990. Several times he concluded segments by saying, "but that's politics, and I'm not talking about politics here," thereby marking the rest of his speech as "not politics." Jeffrey Hadden asked Jerry Falwell and Pat Robertson if eschatology (the doctrine of "final things" or "Last Days") was "a significant variable in explaining the political engagement of the New Christian Right." They said no, and he cited them on behalf of his argument to that effect.[6]

Scholars and preachers agree that dispensational premillennialism is apolitical because they share cultural presuppositions about language and politics, about the nature and relationship of language and action, belief and behavior, religion and politics. Doctrines and beliefs may be said to cause, or at least influence, behavior when that behavior conforms in a literal way to previously articulated statements. If doctrines literally counsel against "politics" and if believers deny any connection between particular beliefs and behavior, then doctrines are apolitical and particular beliefs may not be said to cause behavior. Such presuppositions derive from the nineteenth- and early twentieth-century intellectual and professional movements that separated religion and politics to the benefit of emerging secular elites. By now, however, those presuppositions actually work to the advantage of religious movements by blocking critical thought about how *all* religious discourses, including dispensationalism, are political and efficacious.

Frances FitzGerald and Paul Boyer, who do not agree with the conventional notion that dispensationalism is apolitical, ground their arguments in somewhat broader definitions of "dispensational belief" and "politics." In "The American Millennium," FitzGerald argued that U.S. foreign policy debates since World War II have been deeply, if unconsciously, shaped by popular premillennial visions. In her view, premillennial ideas, including the specifically dispensational narrative framework, structured the ways in which the entire foreign policy establishment, including U.S. presidents, thought about issues, crises, imperatives, enemies, victories, and defeats.[7]

Paul Boyer, in his recent study of "prophecy belief" in American culture, *When Time Shall Be No More,* made a similar argument about Bible-believing Americans in general, and, at least in times of crisis, about Americans in general. Exposed to Bible prophecy by "popularizers," millions of Americans "view world events and trends, at least in part, through the refracting lens of prophetic belief," which thus shapes "the American public's response to a wide range of international and domestic issues."[8]

The problem with all these answers, and the questions behind them, is that they depend on analytic distinctions—between religion and politics, belief and behavior, language and action, the Bible and history, prophecy and current events—that are specifically resisted within Bible-believing Christendom. Dispensationalism, viewed from the perspective of apocalyptic insiders, is not so much a system, or set, of *religious beliefs* as it is a narrative mode of *knowing history.* Dispensationist readings of current events such as the Persian Gulf War are not merely religiously correct interpretations, as if that war, those events, existed outside those interpretations; dispensationalist readings *are* those current events for many Americans. The readings are, among other things, radically supernatural claims about reality and history, and, as such, they *are* also a kind of political action. In this perspective, the point is not to explain why some Americans succumb to such readings, nor is it to investigate their political consequences. The relevant question is: What is the politics of those apocalyptic readings?

Go to any one of the thousands of Baptist, Brethren, charismatic, Pentecostal, and nondenominational churches in America that profess premillennial dispensationalism and listen to sermons and Bible studies on the End Times, the Tribulation, and the Millennium. Listen to the cornucopia of apocalyptic audio tapes; read prophetic articles and journals; browse through the brimming racks of books on prophecy in your local Christian bookstore; take a look at the videos "documenting" the Rapture and the Tribulation. Then talk to any of a wide variety of Bible-believing Christians about how God is dealing with America now. Ask them what the Bible says about the AIDS crisis, the New Age movement, Satanic cults and demonic principalities, and the current epidemic of abortion, pornography, homosexuality, divorce, crime, and drugs. Ask them about Israel, about what God has in store for Israel. Ask them about the Persian Gulf War. Ask them what the election of Bill Clinton means for America.

If you listen to their sermons and read their publications on unfulfilled Bible prophecies, you will hear them talk about current events. If you ask them about current events, you will hear them talk about those events in terms framed by Bible prophecy. Dispensationalism is not always political in the sense of advocating specific actions that count as political in American culture, but it *is* always political. It is political insofar as it constitutes not only current events for many born-again believers, but also their understanding of and place in history itself. Dispensationalism is a kind of narrative politics that contests hegemonic secular ("modern") voices of journalists and academics—whose theories of history are also political—for control over the definition and meaning of current events and of "history" more broadly.

Whether the tense is biblical, present, or post-Rapture, dispensational discourse produces a point of view from which history is narrated. It constitutes those on behalf of whom history is directed ("we") and those to whom history happens ("they"). Bible prophecy presents itself as a set of fixed doctrines or specific beliefs, but it is spoken as a complex, shifting, flexible, pervasive interpretive field, a wide range of narrative figures and frames, a living metanarrative that maps out history, geopolitics, current events, historical forces and trajectories, the telos of history, its agents, its benefactors, and its victims—all from "a biblical point of view."

Reading dispensationalism in this theoretical vein—as narrative, not doctrine; as discourse that constitutes reality, not language that (erroneously) represents reality— steers attention away from cause and effect questions about why people do things and why they believe things, and toward questions of figuration and contestation: Who are the historical actors fashioned by dispensational discourse? On whose behalf is history designed; to whom does history happen? Innovations and variations in dispensational discourse become clues to internal conflicts, to changing definitions of historical events and actors, to continuing debates with rival metanarratives, and to shifting lines of power and authority. The point is not to look for the "political effects" of such discursive reinscriptions, but to understand them *as political* because they constitute the subjects and objects, the meaning and purpose, the motives and goals, of historical action.

A Mad Rhetoric

Orthodox dispensational premillennial visions are "futurist." They not only separate human history from the millennium but also separate the period of tribulation from human history: the Last Days are followed by the Tribulation, which is followed by the Millennium. Current history—the Last Days or End Times—ends when the Rapture occurs, that is, when Christ appears and lifts his Bride, the (true) Church, up into Heaven. Then the Tribulation begins, a period of seven years when all unfulfilled Bible prophesies are fulfilled and God and Satan, Christ and Antichrist, come to blows on a genocidal scale in Israel. The Tribulation culminates in the bloody Battle of Armageddon when Christ returns with his army of (true) Christians to usher in his millennial reign. In this scheme, Christians have no role in unfolding the events that bring about the millennium: nothing they (or anyone else) does can change the date of the Rapture, which only God knows, having set the date at the beginning of time. Nor do they have any role in the prophesied events that actually usher in the millennium, having been raptured, removed from earth for the duration of the Tribulation. Unlike Christians in both postmillennial and historic premillennial narratives, dispensational Christians, and futurist premillennial Christians in general, are not cast as central actors in human history.

The "orthodox" elaboration of dispensationalism, the one brought to this country from Great Britain by John Nelson Darby in the mid-nineteenth century, spread through various networks of conservative preachers in Brethren, Baptist, Methodist, and Holiness denominations during the late nineteenth century. During the twentieth century, orthodox dispensationalism was codified and popularized in study Bibles and

Bible institutes, and reproduced by the leading dispensational training school, the Dallas Theological Seminary. Dispensational premillennialism was invented in the nineteenth century, but not out of whole cloth; it reworked well-worn premillennial dreams that were circulating widely in Britain and the United States in the wake of the French Revolution. And it took on the task of asserting and protecting the veracity of Bible prophecies in the face of higher criticism with exceptional vigor.[9]

In particular, by positing a pretribulational Rapture and by arguing that its date is not known and cannot be known, dispensationalists placed all fulfillment of unfulfilled Bible prophecies in the future and drew an incontrovertible line between Now and Then. As long as (true) Christians are on earth, unfulfilled Bible prophecies, strictly speaking, are not coming true. God will fulfill unfulfilled prophecies, which apply only to the fate of Jews and Israel, during the Tribulation. Meanwhile, in this, the Church Age, speculations about how current events might be preparing the way for Tribulation prophecies are just that, speculations. *Strictly speaking, the Bible is silent about current history, about Christians in current history, and about America.* Thus, the dispensationalist scheme exempts believers from having to prove what higher critics argued they had to prove if the Bible was "really true," namely, that unfulfilled Bible prophecies have come true or are coming true. Indeed, the scheme—in particular, the pretribulational Rapture which is so soon, but absolutely not now—asserts the incontrovertible veracity of the Bible by assuring believers that Bible prophesies are perpetually *about* to come true.

Higher critical readings of the Bible not only undermined its transcendent authority during the seventeenth, eighteenth, and nineteenth centuries, but they opened up ground for the development of modern scientific and historical discourses—"modern" meaning here secular, that is, accounts of nature and history in which God played no part—discourses which gradually quarantined and displaced religion as a public arbiter of reality. Bible believers continuously contested, and continue to contest, higher critical moves and their degradation of the truth of the Bible in the form of official doctrines, popular polemics, cultural critiques, and counterdiscourses—among them, dispensationalism.

Modern metanarratives of history, also invented during the nineteenth century, included world history, social evolution, and Marxist theories—grand totalizing schemes of human history arranged into a sequence of epochs or stages or modes of production. Dispensationalism occupies the same terrain, the same metanarrative landscape, and also divides history into stages (called "dispensations"). The similarity ends there, however, and the contrasts begin.

Modern biblical critics submitted the Bible to history and found the Bible wanting; dispensationalists submit history to the Bible and find history wanting. Modern historians expelled deities from history; dispensationalists entrench God and Satan and the conflict between them as the very pattern of history. The interpretive strategies deployed by dispensationalists as they biblicize history and current events are the very ones most repugnant to the modern, "critical" eye and ear—biblical proof-texting, typologizing, and erratic literalizing (some passages read "plainly," others according to bizarre, obscure codes). And dispensationalists specifically "literalize" the biblical texts modern readers find most disturbing—the most incredible and the most vio-lent—namely, the apocalyptic texts, which invariably foretell a dreadful death to any and all who reject their absolute truth.

Dispensationalists refuse the progressive telos of modern history and its implicit assumption that human nature is good and educable. Instead, they pronounce history, overall and in each of its stages, irreversibly regressive, precisely because human beings are by nature sinful. The logic of dispensational history is not an unfolding of "ratio-nal" forces but rather a timeless struggle between good and evil that dwarfs human comprehension. The "rise of the West," "the development of capitalism," and "the expansion of American hegemony" are not central stories in world history. History instead is centered in the Middle East and narrated as the relentless fulfillment of biblical prophecies organized around reemergent biblical empires plunging into war, all ultimately in pursuit of the apple of God's eye, Israel and the Jews, with whom God has some unfinished business.

All historical discourses constitute subjects—persons from whose point of view his-tory is narrated and directed—as well as objects—historical events, periods, forces, and figures. Dispensationalism casts the subjects of "modern" theories of history, namely, enlightened men and women, as, at best, hapless agents of Satan, at worst, villains with demonic designs. It casts Bible-believing Christians, on the other hand, as tem-porary victims and the ultimate heroes of history. In dispensationalist accounts, Chris-tians emerge as the subjects of current history, albeit subjects who are removed and waiting, while modern men and women become historical objects whose behavior requires study and explanation.

Features such as these render dispensationalism a kind of madness from the modern point of view, and that, I argue, makes dispensationalism compelling from a Bible-believing point of view. Dispensational premillennialism is a willfully "mad rhetoric," and speaking it (being spoken by it) is a political act, a constant dis-sent, disruption, and critique of modern thought, and, specifically, of modern histori-cal discourses that constitute hegemonic knowledge about world events, past and present.

Orthodox Agency

A tour of Israel with Jerry Falwell's Old-Time Gospel Hour Tours seems not unlike a tour of Greece with a secular tourist agency. Familiar landscapes and events and actors from history "come alive," and what was a two-dimensional story about the past, about "the origin of civilization," pops vividly into three dimensions. One feels and sees oneself walking within history; history, somatized, becomes somehow "more real." But the two tours are also absolutely unlike each other, for Jerry Falwell's Holy Land tourists also find themselves inside the future, walking its landscape, knowing its actors, foreseeing its events. They walk within the scenes of Christ's First Coming two thousand years ago and of his Second Coming, which they know will be soon. They know they will be with him, among his troops, as he returns to rule on earth for the Kingdom Age. So real, immediate, specific, and unarguable is the future they foresee that the Old-Time Gospel Hour tour guide and teacher Harold Willmington buried a Protestant Bible wrapped in plastic in one of the caves in the Valley of Petra for the Jews who will hide there after the "destruction of the Jews" begins during the Tribulation.[10]

Willmington recalled that W. E. Blackstone, a nineteenth-century scholar of Bible prophecy, "felt that someday the terrified survivors of the Antichrist's bloodbath will welcome the opportunity to read God's Word," so he hid thousands of copies of the New Testament in the caves of Petra.[11] Willmington and Blackstone knew, on the basis of Scripture, that those Edomite caves would be the "special hiding place" where "one-third of Israel will remain true to God" during the Tribulation (Zech. 13:9, 14:5; Isa. 63:1; Dan. 11:41). Willmington was more modest than Blackstone, leaving the remnant just one large Bible, but he was no less certain of the future. In the Bible he inscribed this note: "Attention to all of Hebrew background: This Bible has been placed here on October 14, 1974, by the students and Dean of the Thomas Road Bible Institute in Lynchburg, Va., U.S.A. We respectfully urge its finder to prayerfully and publicly read the following Bible chapters. They are: Daniel 7 and 11; Matthew 24; II Thessalonians 2; Revelation 12 and 13."[12]

No dispensational doctrine, no preacher, instructed Harold Willmington to bury a Bible in the caves of the Valley of Petra. Nor did Willmington bury it there because he imagined current events to be related to future events in some causal fashion. Whatever Harold Willmington did in 1974, whatever he or anyone else does at any time before the Rapture, Jews in the Tribulation will hear the Gospel and be converted in the Valley of Petra before the Battle of Armageddon. It is not only this unequivocal *knowledge* of the future that makes dispensationalism heady. It is also the particular relationship between what happens now and what happens then, and it is through this relationship that dispensationalism effects action, if obliquely, on the plane of human history. Dispensational discourse constitutes Christians as historical agents who operate according to a typological theory of historical causality and agency.

Typology remains the reigning mode of reading the relationship between past and future events in dispensationalist reading communities. Simply put, what comes before prefigures, or "typifies," what comes after. What comes after fulfills, or completes, what came before. New Testament figures, above all Jesus Christ, fulfill Old Testament figures such as Adam, Abraham, Isaac, and Moses. Most generally, the New Testament, read typologically, establishes a point of view from which to read the Old Testament. Likewise, Tribulation events, as foretold in both testaments, establish a point of view from which to read current history, and that record, the testament of current history, is being written, or, rather, *enacted* now.

To the secular ear, these are literary, not historical, terms because the Bible is not a history book. To the born-again ear, the relationship between the foreshadowed and its fulfillment is not a symbolic or allegorical one. Typological readings are not mere filaments of interpretation tying stories about events together in some folk Imaginary. Event and story have not been torn asunder in orthodox Protestant discourse. Biblical stories do not represent history, they *are* history, past and future. Nor are "storied events" that prefigure and fulfill each other connected merely by the historical tissue of cause and effect, for much might intervene between the two to change the outcome. The historical tissues connecting biblically storied events are the sinews of divine design, and nothing interrupts God's plan, by definition. Former events do not bring about later ones, but rather reveal, in advance, God's plan. Christians through their actions today cannot alter God's plan, but they may be enacting it. Their actions may prefigure, or "typify," the events of the Second Coming of the Lord. Thus, dispensational Christians read history backward: Future events, which are fixed and known, determine—if only in the sense of enabling Christians to imagine—the shape, the content, and the significance of present events and actions.

Revivalists understood dispensationalism's typological springs of action perfectly. Beginning with Dwight L. Moody in the late nineteenth century, they fashioned its vision of the future into one of the most powerful evangelistic tools in their kit.[13] Not wanting to be here for the Tribulation and knowing that it could begin at any minute has convinced many malingering souls to receive Christ. And knowing the Bible foretells the spread of the Gospel to the four corners of the world before Christ comes again has constituted them as world-class missionaries. Old-fashioned dispensational futurists like Harold Willmington are locked out of forthcoming struggles in Israel by the Rapture, which will situate them on high, seated beside Jesus in Heaven, to watch the Tribulation unfold below. Apart from getting saved, living piously and evangelizing, nothing they do now matters. Yet they may, each in their own small way, hope themselves into, if not will themselves into, God's plan for the Last Days. So Harold Willmington, in the thrall of his extraordinary foreknowledge of Tribulation geopolitics, buried a Bible in the Valley of Petra on a tour of Israel.

Heterodox Asides

Not all dispensationalists are so orthodox, and even orthodoxy is a complex, flexible, shifting, polymorphous field of reading practices. There are long-standing disputes about the exact timing of the Rapture, speculations, for example, that it will occur during, not before, the Tribulation.[14] Many biblical literalists (including those holding the former fort of biblical inerrancy, Princeton Theological Seminary) thought the Rapture and many other dispensational exegeses of Bible texts were scandalously unliteral and positively errant readings. Arguments among conservative Protestants about the validity of dispensationalism may have contributed to the doctrine's relatively low profile in the fundamentalist movement of the 1920s and may also have partially motivated the dispensational repudiation of "politics."[15]

Within the camp of dispensationalists, controversies raged. Two events anchored dispensational orthodoxy: the publication of C. I. Scofield's definitive dispensational study Bible in 1909 and the founding of Dallas Theological Seminary by a group of dispensationalist "party-liners" in 1924; but the millennial seas were hardly calmed. The holiness and Pentecostal movements of the late nineteenth and early twentieth century appropriated dispensational ideas piecemeal, patched them together with other theological pieces, and proclaimed that the outbreaks of supernatural gifts after 1906 (especially speaking in tongues) were "signs" that Christ was en route, was already arriving in this Latter Rain of miracles. Another set of heterodoxies developed around the timing of the Rapture—perhaps Christ would rapture the Church midway during the Tribulation, or at the end of it, in the same instant He returned to rule his Kingdom on earth.[16] In either case, Christians would be on earth during the Tribulation. This meant that Tribulation might have already begun; accordingly, Christians, and America, might be agents in bringing about Christ's Second Coming. The orthodox position articulated by Dallas Theological Seminary theologians and preachers, meanwhile, held firm to the pretribulational timing of the Rapture.

Dispensationalist narrators sometimes note or lament these divisions and "differences of opinion," but they scarcely acknowledge the arena of widest (and wildest) interpretive variation, namely, the reading of "signs of the times." Within certain broad limits, the dialogue between current events and biblical imagery is each dispensational narrator's zone of free play. Orthodox speculation is constrained by futurism, that is, by the conviction that all Bible prophecies are fulfilled only after the Rapture. In this view, if Bible prophecies were being fulfilled in current events, Christians would not be here to witness them. But dispensational observers prognosticate nevertheless; they find "signs" that prophecies are about to be fulfilled in current events. Sometimes they speak of those signs as prophecies. Sometimes events occur that seem very nearly to fulfill prophecies. This is where the free play begins.

Both world wars and the Russian Revolution occasioned vast and varied debates about how God's plan was unfolding, but the biggest outpourings occurred after 1948, when the state of Israel was founded, and after 1967, when the Israelis "unified" Jerusalem in the Six Day War. Those events resembled specific and pivotal Bible prophecies which orthodox dispensational spokesmen expected to be fulfilled after Christ raptured believers. Dallas Theological Seminary spokesmen held that events in Israel only incompletely fulfilled prophecies—they would be completed fully after the Rapture. But the line between "signs" and "prophecies," between pre-Rapture and post-Rapture events, was harder than ever to locate.

The heterogeneity, instability, and partiality of dispensational narrative framings of current events undermine the absolute "futurism" of Bible prophecies. Everyone "knows for certain" that no Bible prophecy can be fulfilled before the Rapture. But what if events scheduled to occur after the Rapture seem to occur before it? Much of the variation in dispensational discourse emerges around questions such as these. Such questions and their answers in effect open up "historic premillennial cracks" within dispensational premillennialism. These scenarios suggest that God has more in store for Christians (even Americans) than had hitherto been gathered, that Christians may be more directly implicated in Bible prophecies than had been previously supposed, and that Christians figure, ever so slightly perhaps, in events that bring Christ back finally to staunch the dreadful downhill slide of history.

The old-fashioned dispensationalist scheme is still spoken in sermons on the Rapture, the Tribulation, and the Second Coming, in self-declared pretribulational, premillennial churches (see ads in the Yellow Pages), and in books by (older) Dallas Theological Seminary professors. But believers are routinely exposed to an undifferentiated array of variations—in other sermons by their preachers, in other books (the prophecy sections in most Christian bookstores contain a hodgepodge of millennial texts), on television, audio and video tapes, in conversations among Christian friends from other churches.[17] Finally, dispensationalism frames born-again readings of "the news" in implicit ways, and its presuppositions may be sutured into other discourses, so that some born-again, even some non-born-again, believers may speak dispensationalism (as Molière's bourgeois gentleman spoke prose) without knowing it.[18] By now, given the volume and pace of Christian publishing and broadcasting and the absence of anything like a code of "intellectual property" (indeed, there is a license among preachers to "borrow" material without restraint or citation), today's innovation in Bible prophecy may be tommorrow's cliché.[19]

Historic premillennial subtexts, side stories, and trajectories always characterized dispensationalism—it, as a living narrative tradition, never was the purely futurist premillennial discourse it presented itself to be. But these speculations did not congeal into a serious reinscription of Christians in history until the 1980s. Until that decade, dispensational narratives remorselessly cast Christians in the wings of public life in America. During that decade, major popular dispensational preachers and writers, heterodox and orthodox, fashioned bold new narrative frames that not only cast Christians onto history's center stage but momentarily reversed the course of human history, opening up a veritable "postmillennial window" in the End Times.

Opening a Postmillennial Window

Although future events—the trials of the Tribulation period—are known and fixed according to Bible prophecy, dispensational "histories of the future" vary enormously and change with an ease that is remarkable only to outsiders.[20] What is consistent is the implicit dispensational instruction to "read history backward," to interpret the significance of present events as "signs" that tribulational prophecies are always already coming true, that future events are unfolding now. Dispensationalism thus landscapes the terrain of current history with events, figures, organizations, and trends that foreshadow the cataclysmic future known and fixed by God.

Before the 1980s, dispensationally framed sermons, writings, journals, films, tapes, and conferences, insofar as they addressed current history at all, were almost entirely devoted to analyzing global events for any sign of the gathering storms that would culminate in "the war to end all wars" in Israel. Earthquakes, typhoons, famines, wars; arch-villainous leaders, and men who preached world unity and peace; global communications, the space age, and the computer revolution; rapid population growth, the rise and collapse of great economic systems; the Common Market, the Cold War and the end of the Cold War; shifting political alliances and borders in Africa, Asia, Europe, and, above all, the Middle East—all these world-scale events and many, many more were seen as fashioning the future leaders and armies that will converge in the Valley of Megiddo.

What about America? What about domestic events? Christians, American and otherwise, following Matthew 28:19, had one duty, one task, to complete in current history: *Go ye therefore, and teach all nations, baptizing them in the name of the Father, and of the Son, and of the Holy Ghost.* In short, save souls. Aside from this, their Great Commission, Christians at home, in America, could only wait, live holy lives, support Israel, and read domestic events as "signs of the times." Local signs of impending doom included any evidence of growth or development in education, technology, communications and transportation, population, material well-being, liberal theology, secularization, ecumenicism, atheism, witchcraft, Satanism, astrology, communism, crime, drug use, and divorce. The outcome of these domestic trends was straightforwardly the demise of America as an economic and political power in the Last Days. America might not even survive the Rapture as a nation, and most certainly had no role in the events of the Tribulation.

Dispensational preachers and writers plying political agendas in the 1980s did not contradict, much less overturn, this dispensational scheme of things, but they opened it up to one degree or another of postmillennial dreaming. Major national preachers and writers, including Hal Lindsey, Tim LaHaye, Billy Graham, and Jerry Falwell, sorted out a new kind of time with the End Times, a potentially progressive period in what was otherwise a hopelessly regressive era. The Tribulation, as ever, was a time when God would judge the Jews according to immutable Bible prophecy, but the outlines of another, pretribulational, judgment, one not foretold in Bible prophecy, also came clear. Before the Rapture, during the Last Days, God would judge *Christians,* and his judgment was reversible. If Christians responded to God's call through holy living and *political action,* God would spare them. Thus were Christians constituted by dispensational preachers and writers as political agents in and of the present.

Hal Lindsey, by far the most popular dispensational writer in the 1970s, made a relatively slight but nonetheless dramatic adjustment. *The Late Great Planet Earth,* published in 1970, reportedly sold eighteen million copies and was described by the *New York Times* as the "number one non-fiction best-seller of the decade."[21] *Late Great Planet Earth,* in line with other mainstream dispensational writing and preaching in the 1970s, aggressively constituted born-again Christians as a marginal people, and America as a marginal nation, in its vision of the End Times. In *The 1980s: Countdown to Armageddon,* published in 1980, Lindsey made a shift that was not in itself postmillennialist but was a slippery slope insofar as it converged with the innovations of other writers and preachers. Lindsey argued that if Christians got "involved in preserving this country," it was possible that America would remain a world power through the Last Days. Christians should live as if Jesus could come today, and "that means that we must actively take on the responsibility of being a citizen and a member of God's family. We need to get active electing officials who will not only reflect the Bible's morality in government, but will shape domestic and foreign policies to protect our country and our way of life."[22] Lindsey did not build a reputation as a political writer, but his altered vision was a piece of the political placement of born-again Christians in historical time during the 1980s.

A few of the leading politically vocal preachers and writers took off in explicitly postmillennial or posttribulational directions.[23] But most stayed within a relatively orthodox dispensational fold, and some, like LaHaye, Graham, and Falwell, played out implicitly postmillennial scenarios in far bolder terms than Lindsey.

During the 1970s, preacher and best-selling author Tim LaHaye never as much as intimated that American Christians had anything else to do with their lives on this earth but pray, live right, and save souls. In 1980, on the other hand, in his widely read book *The Battle for the Mind,* he began to construct a more elaborate End Time history. LaHaye read domestic "signs of the times" as the effects of the "liberal humanist" effort to take over the country, an effort that amounted to a "pre-Tribulation tribulation" which could "destroy America." However, it was not too late to save America. The Great Tribulation, he said, "is predestined and will surely come to pass. But the pre-Tribulation tribulation—that is, the tribulation that will engulf this country if liberal humanists are permitted to take total control of our government—is neither predestined nor necessary. But it will deluge the entire land in the next few years, unless Christians are willing to become much more assertive in defense of morality and decency than they have been during the past three decades."[24] LaHaye urged Christians to pray and witness, as usual, and also to help the victims of humanism (unwed mothers, divorced partners, children being raised by single parents), to join the national drive to register Christian voters, to campaign for pro-moral candidates, to expose amoral candidates and incumbents, to educate themselves and their friends, to run for public office, to join pro-moral organizations, to speak out and write vigorously on moral issues, and to contribute money and work for pro-moral causes.

Billy Graham, in *Approaching Hoofbeats: The Four Horsemen of the Apocalypse,* published in 1984, also identified the present time as a kind of pre-Tribulation tribulation, but for very different political ends (which proves Timothy Weber's point that a specifically right-wing agenda does not follow from dispensationalism).[25] The Four Horsemen Graham discerned were not signs of the true Tribulation, which he still figured as irreversible, but instead signs of a forthcoming judgment of God, "an Armageddon," which was *conditional.* The signs, the Horsemen, were familiar in their broad strokes—deception, war, famine, and plagues—but Graham's precise rendering of each sign was as liberal as it was conservative, and the Jesus whom he promised would soon liberate us, rang of the social gospel as much as the gospel of personal salvation. Indeed, in his rendering of war, Billy Graham was positively radical, targeting the nuclear arms race, declaring it "sin" and "not God's will," imaging "total cosmocide," arguing *"war is not necessary,"* and calling on Christians to work for peace, an end to the nuclear arms race, and nuclear disarmament.[26]

Jerry Falwell, perhaps more than any other dispensational-yet-political preacher during the 1980s, implicitly argued against the grain of dispensational orthodoxy. He was the leading spokesman for the New Christian Right, and the head of its flagship organization, the Moral Majority, which, insofar as it was a grass-roots organization, rode piggyback on preexisting networks of doctrinally pretribulational dispensational premillennialist churches.[27] In his speech, his writings, and his actions during the 1980s, Falwell constructed grounds for political action where before he had argued against such grounds, enabling himself to say that Christian political activism mattered, that it was necessary, even that it would be efficacious, that Christians *could* and *should* change history. More than any of the other preachers, Falwell converted, or rather diverted, dispensationalism from a rationale for separation from the world into a rhetoric of urgent engagement with the world.

Falwell argued that the "moral crises" that led him to organize the Moral Majority were simultaneously irreversible and reversible. They were "signs of the times," indications that Christ is coming very soon, *and* matters that (American) Christians must take into their hands and try to do something about.

> Is there hope for our country? I think so. I believe as we trust in God and pray, as we Christians lead the battle to outlaw abortion, which is murder on demand, as we take our stand against pornography, against the drug traffic, as we take our stand against the breakdown of the traditional family in America, the promotion of homosexual marriages, as we stand up for strong national defense so that this country can survive and our children and our children's children will know the America we've known. As we pray and preach and lead, Christian friends, I think there is hope that God may one more time bless America. . . . I believe that between now and the Rapture of the Church, America can have a reprieve. God can bless the country and before the Rapture I believe we can stay a free nation. . . . I believe that we can pray and that God is able to deliver us out of tribulations.[28]

World history is hopelessly regressive, careening pell-mell into Satan's maw, and it may seem as if America is plummeting down the same dark tunnel, but not necessarily, not if Christians act now.

Here is Falwell's signature innovation in the dispensational reinscriptions of the 1980s: *In order to do the only thing* dispensational orthodoxy prescribed them to do in the End Times, namely, spread the Gospel to the four corners of the world, Christians *must do more than* spread the Gospel to the four corners of the world. Falwell reversed the political valence of the Great Commission prescription so that, instead of counseling against politics, it enjoined political action. He argued that, unless born-again Christians acted politically, they would lose their "freedom" (religious and political), which was what enabled them to spread the good news at home and abroad, that is, to fulfill Bible prophecy. Here is how he put it before an audience of students at Moody Bible Institute in 1984:

> On the Christian campuses all over America kids are not only winning souls and loving the Bible and loving Christ, they're becoming good citizens. They are getting registered to vote, they are getting informed. They are determining that we are no longer going to lose by default. . . . We're going to do some-

thing, we're going to have revival, and we're going to have restoration, and the rebuilding of this great nation, so that out of a society and an environment of freedom we might evangelize the world in our generation, and before the Rapture, take a multitude on to Heaven with us.[29]

The exact terms in which Falwell framed the conflict varied quite a bit during the 1980s, but throughout his politically virulent years he deployed his postmillennially adjusted dispensational lens and logics to render, to fashion and refashion, the historical moment, himself, his opponents, his allies and audience, and their mission.

The core of the New Christian Right was composed of dispensational premillennialists—and their leaders, their spokesmen, the men who spoke them into political existence. Preachers and other movement leaders figured and framed Christians, constituting their identity and agency as political actors. These preachers figured and framed their opponents, and what counted as problematic, symptomatic, emblematic, and ameliorative in terms of the dispensational metanarrative. Although right-wing born-again Protestants hardly overthrew "modernity" or cast "secular humanists" out of power in American society at large, they succeeded in reenfranchising themselves politically and culturally and staked a claim to national hegemony in the 1980s. Their theorization of the "pre-Tribulation tribulation" neither reflected nor effected the shift in the hegemonic scales. It *was* the shift, discursively speaking, insofar as it renarrated the pattern of history and the place of born-again believers in that history.

Cracks in the Window

We cannot foresee how dispensational frames and figures will mutate as the third millennium approaches. We only know that it matters how those apocalyptic scenarios shift, and, that if we listen carefully to the shifts, to their details and the nuances, we may learn how born-again Christians are resituating themselves as agents in and of history. We may read their politics and perhaps, too, perceive the present and the future from their point of view.

Contemporary dispensationalists caught up in the "little tribulation" unfolding before the Rapture have a wider range of actions open to them than they had before the 1980s. Their definition of "holy living" has been broadened to include all sorts of political, cultural, economic, and moral actions that may stave off God's conditional judgment on America. But the "postmillennial window" they opened was in fact just a window; it could be shut at any time. It did not alter the basic structure of history, of either the End Times or the Great Tribulation, and most born-again Christians continue to operate according to a specifically "not-modern" dispensational causal logic, one more divine than human. Their prayers and activities on behalf of "saving America" may stay God's hand, but they may not, and either way, the world is going to hell. Moreover, their moral campaigns also foreshadow and partake of the ultimate struggles between the forces of God and Satan during the Great Tribulation. Christians were thus perched precariously by the 1980s reinscriptions within a bifocal vision of present history; both Satan and God are winning, and Christians are double historical agents.

The Persian Gulf War, for example, quickened millennial dreams among many born-again Christians. In December 1990, as the nation was poised on the brink of war, Zondervan Publishing House reportedly printed a million copies of an updated version of *Armageddon, Oil and the Middle East Crisis,* by John Walvoord.[30] Over 600,000 copies had reportedly sold by early February, and Billy Graham was distributing another 300,000 copies free.[31] *The Blood of the Moon: The Roots of the Middle East Crisis* (1991), *Global Peace and the Rise of the Anti-Christ* (1990), *The Rise of Babylon: Sign of the End Times* (1991), and other biblical interpretations of events in the Middle East also sold briskly. Prophetic newsletters *(Omega Letter, Midnight Call)* expanded their direct-mail campaigns in order to tap newly awakened readers. Local preachers delivered sermons and conducted Bible studies on "Iraq in Bible Prophecy," "The Persian Gulf War from God's Perspective," "The Middle East Crisis: A Step toward Armageddon?" and "Making Sense of This End Time Madness." Televangelists also preached on the apocalyptic portent of the Gulf Crisis and their ratings went up.[32] Weekly stories and editorials in Christian magazines located events in the Gulf in biblically based schemes. All over the country, born-again Christians pondered the Persian Gulf War in terms of Bible prophecy.

Within the prevailing scheme of dispensational premillennialism, believers wondered: Is this Armageddon? Is Saddam Hussein the Antichrist? Is his rebuilding of Babylon a fulfillment of Bible prophecy?[33] Generally, they thought not. The Bible says these events will occur only after the Rapture, the much anticipated moment, "the twinkling of an eye," in which Christ appears in the sky, "catches up" all believers, and carries them off to heaven. On the other hand, current events in the Middle East are surely "signs" that the blessed moment is near, that Christ is coming soon for his bride, the (true) Church. The Bible did not predict the Persian Gulf War, but the war and other events were preparing the way for Bible prophecies to come true. They were unequivocal evidence and proof that God is in control of history, that his plan is unfolding.

The Rev. Jerry Falwell put it this way the Sunday before the ground war began, in his sermon at Thomas Road Baptist Church (later nationally broadcast and sold as a video cassette to his Old-Time Gospel Hour audience):

> The ground war is looming on the horizon, maybe as I speak it may have begun. Multinational forces present in the Middle East, the threat of nerve gas, chemical warfare, even nuclear war missiles, all of these are the ingredients of a doomsday or armageddon. But let me tell you something: the Scriptures say that an armageddon cannot take place until Jesus comes and catches away his bride, the Church. We will not be here for Armageddon.
>
> If Jesus were to come today, and we were caught up, then would begin seven years of Tribulation upon the earth at the end of which God would have judged the earth, and then hundreds of millions of troops will come down upon Israel and the Lord Jesus Himself will lead the charge against them. The

blood will flow in the streets up to the bridles of the horses for two hundred miles.

And then that is not the end. Then while the dead are buried over a seven-month period of time during the Kingdom Age that has just begun, our Lord Jesus with the Saints will sit down upon the Throne of David in Jerusalem and for one thousand years will rule in perfect peace upon the earth. That is what is yet to come.

No one is going to destroy this earth, by the way, with nuclear power or anything else because, should the Lord come today, God still has one thousand and seven years of use for this planet. The seven-year Tribulation period, the thousand-year Kingdom Age. So nobody is going to destroy the earth. Saddam Hussein, Qaddafi, Yassir Arafat, Assad, or any of those butchers. Mark it down. It's a fact. The Soviets? No. God has the plan. He is King of Kings, Lord of Lords, and whether they like it or not, the king's heart, even Hussein's, though he may not know it, the king's heart is in the hands of the Lord, and as the rivers of water, He, God, turns it whither so ever He will.[34]

While Jerry Falwell, along with most of his colleagues, read the events of the Persian Gulf War in orthodox premillennial dispensationalist terms, his rendering of subsequent domestic political events took a strikingly heterodox turn. God backed America in the Gulf, but Satan was on the loose at home, most manifestly in the Democratic National Convention and the election of Bill Clinton as president of the United States. For months after the election, my mailbox bristled with letters from "Jerry," mostly about Clinton's campaign to destroy both the military and America by letting "the gays" take over. In February 1993, he preached a sermon called "America Declares War against God," which concluded with the usual appeal to spiritual, moral and political action in order "to save America." But in his depiction of current events under Bill Clinton, "the country's first New Age president," Falwell deployed overtly Tribulational imagery, that is, the language of irreversible cataclysm. In effect, Falwell broke the orthodox taboo against imagining the Last Days in terms reserved for the Tribulation and thus conflated Then and Now.

Falwell first listed a string of presidentially ordained "American tragedies" of 1993—executive orders allowing abortion counseling in federally funded clinics, abortions in military hospitals, medical research on fetal tissue, the eventual importation of RU-486 ("chemical warfare against the unborn"), the eventual end of the ban on gays in the military, and the official endorsement of homosexuality as a lifestyle in America for the first time in its history. Then Falwell said:

My heart fluttered as I watched all this happening [at the Inaugural Ball]. I listened as Barbara Streisand and Whoopi Gouldberg . . . Goldberg, and Michael Jackson and Chevy Chase and the Hollywood Establishment danced in ecstasy at this total releasing of immorality and vulgarity and indecency and anti-moral values on the American society. The network TV anchors were beside themselves.

I want you to open your Bibles to the Book of the Revelations, the last

Book of the Bible. Look at chapter 16, verses 16 through 21. " . . . And he gathered them" (God gathered them) "together in a place called in the Hebrew Armageddon" (the last great battle). "And the seventh angel poured out his vial into the air, and there came a great voice out of the temple of heaven, from the throne, saying, It is done. And there were voices and thunders, and light-nings; and there was a great earthquake. . . . And the great city was divided into three parts, and the cities of the nations fell. . . . And every island fled away, and the mountains were not found. And there fell upon men a great hail out of heaven, every stone about the weight of a talent" (and notice the re-sponse of men during the Tribulation to all this wrath and judgment): "and men blasphemed God" (sounds like today) "because of the plague of hail; for the plague thereof was exceedingly great."

Now turn to chapter 17, verse 14: "These shall make war with the Lamb" (capital L. Who is the Lamb? That's the Lord Jesus Christ. These shall make war with the Lamb), "and the Lamb shall overcome them: for he is Lord of Lords, and King of Kings: and they that are with him are called, and chosen, and faithful."

I believe that today America is making war with the Lamb. We have de-clared war against God.[35]

These figurings directly from the Book of Revelation do not make Falwell a historic premillennialist any more than those of the 1980s made him a postmillennialist, but they show him in motion, reconfiguring himself, his people, his enemies, history, and their place in history. At the very least, it seems the Reverend Falwell is splicing his 1980s "postmillennial window" with a pattern of "historic premillennialist cracks."

Indeed, the 1990s installments of Christian apocalypticism, combined with the 1980s chapter, redirect the trajectory of the whole apocalyptic book—that is, these recent developments alter the telos of modernity itself. If there is a world coming to an end in this moment of multiple apocalyptic outbreaks, it is the modern, liberal, secular world in which orthodox religious communities have become politically do-mesticated, barren, or, most fantastic of all, a vanishing breed. And if that world, rather than the orthodox religious communities it attempted to suppress, is vanish-ing, then those of us habitually outside specifically apocalyptic communities—commu-nities who *know* the future in ways we cannot—will often find ourselves waiting, watching, listening.

Thus have Israeli Intelligence agents become avid observers and auditors of the various groups of dispensational Christians who occupy Jerusalem.[36] Dispensational Christians know the Temple will be rebuilt during the Tribulation and that its recon-struction might begin before the Rapture. Because they know the Temple will be rebuilt, they also know that one of the most holy places in the Muslim faith, the Dome of the Rock, which now stands on the site of the old Temple, will be destroyed. They do not know when these events will occur, or how, only that they will occur, and some Christians in Jerusalem have come to understand that they may be implicated in God's plan to rebuild the Temple and in the destruction of the mosque that neces-sarily precedes it. So Israeli Intelligence listens, lest any of the dispensational Christians who are in Israel "realize" that God has chosen them to blow up the Dome of the Rock.

Likewise, the Bureau of Alcohol, Tobacco, and Firearms stormed David Koresh's compound on 28 February 1993, in hopes of abolishing him, his group, and his kind. It was the Bureau's Persian Gulf War, its Desert Storm, as it turned out, in more ways than one—a spectacle intended to display the immense power and legitimacy of the U.S. government, but one that ended by demonstrating nothing so much as the government's powerlessness, its blindness, its inability to govern the course of events. David Koresh, like Saddam Hussein, survived and carried on while the assembled forces of the world waited outside, stalemated.

The televangelical scandals of 1987–88, featuring Jim and Tammy Faye Bakker, Jimmy Swaggart, Ted Koppel, and Jerry Falwell, were a similar moment of fantastic closure from the modern point of view. Outsiders and critics hoped that the sordid revelations about the Bakkers and Swaggart would put an end to the New Christian Right, that pesky little chapter in modernity's otherwise steady unfolding toward ever more secularity and reason. Instead, the televangelical scandals turned out to be the beginning of yet another pesky little chapter, one that was still being written, or acted out, at all levels of the 1992 campaigns and elections, and will keep unfolding during the 1990s.

Acknowledgments

In addition to primary and secondary sources, my reading of dispensational discourse is based on ethnographic fieldwork in Jerry Falwell's Thomas Road Baptist Church community carried out during 1982–87. For enabling this essay in varied ways, I thank Nancy Ammerman, Scott Appleby, Martin Marty, Patricia Mitchell, and my anthropology colleagues at the University of California at Santa Cruz. I am especially indebted to the work and encouragement of Frances FitzGerald and Timothy Weber on this subject.

Notes

1. On millennial movements elsewhere in the world, see Norman Cohn, *The Pursuit of the Millennium* (New York: Oxford University Press, 1970); Michael Adas, *Prophets of Rebellion* (Chapel Hill: University of North Carolina Press, 1979); Christopher Hill, *The World Turned upside Down* (New York: Viking Press, 1972); Barbara Tuchman, *Bible and Sword* (New York: Funk and Wagnalls, 1956); and Karen E. Fields, *Revival and Rebellion in Colonial Central Africa* (Princeton, N.J.: Princeton University Press, 1985). On earlier millennial movements in

the United States, see A. F. C. Wallace, *The Death and Rebirth of the Seneca* (New York: Vintage Books, 1972); Paul Johnson, *A Shopkeepers' Millennium* (New York: Hill and Wang, 1978); Michael Barkun, *Crucible of the Millennium* (Syracuse, N.Y.: Syracuse University Press, 1986); and Ernest Lee Tuveson, *Redeemer Nation* (Chicago: University of Chicago Press, 1968).

2. The Branch Davidians, also known as the Koreshians, descended from a community founded in Waco by dissident Seventh Day Adventists in the 1930s. The Seventh

Day Adventist church, in turn, descended from the most notorious performance of "historic premillennialism" in U.S. history, namely, the Millerite movement of the 1830s and 1840s centered in upstate New York. According to Whitney Cross, William Miller and his fellow itinerant preachers convinced well over fifty thousand people, and a million or more Americans were "skeptically expectant," that "time would run out" and Christ would come again on 22 October 1844. In the wake of his failure to come as expected on that day, a number of groups formed around reinterpretations of "the signs of the times," including the Seventh Day Adventists. See Whitney R. Cross, *The Burned-Over District* (New York: Harper and Row, 1965), pp. 287–321.

3. While professional observers of millennial movements elsewhere in the world and in the United States before 1900 usually portray them as politically virulent, most who comment on contemporary dispensationalism consider it apolitical or politically inconsequential. For example, see Timothy P. Weber, *Living in the Shadow of the Second Coming* (Chicago: University of Chicago Press, 1987); and Dwight Wilson, *Armageddon Now!* (Inst. Christian, 1991). Exceptions are works by Frances FitzGerald and Paul Boyer and, of course, Ernest R. Sandeen, *The Roots of Fundamentalism* (Chicago: University of Chicago Press, 1970), who argued that the fundamentalist controversies of the late nineteenth and early twentieth centuries were deeply motivated by dispensational dreams.

4. See Wilson, *Armageddon Now!* p. 12; Weber, *Living in the Shadow of the Second Coming*, p. 274; and Paul Boyer, *When Time Shall Be No More* (Cambridge, Mass.: Belknap Press of Harvard University Press, 1992), pp. 2–4.
Weber provides a list of the denominations doctrinally committed to dispensationalism or composed of large numbers of doctrinal believers. The Bible Baptist Fellowship, the General Association of Regular Baptist Churches, the Conservative Baptist Association of America, the Baptist General Conference, the Evangelical Free Church of America, the Independent Fundamental Churches of America, Plymouth Brethren, Grace Brethren, the Bible Presbyterian church, and the Baptist Missionary Association are "predominantly premillennialist denominations." In addition, Weber notes, many independent and Bible churches are dispensationalist, as are most Pentecostal denominations, including the Assemblies of God, and there are large and vocal factions of premillennialists in nonpremillennialist denominations, including the Southern Baptist Convention. *Living in the Shadow of the Second Coming*, p. 274.
Boyer also distinguishes between doctrinal believers and "believers who may be hazy about the details of biblical eschatology [the doctrine of 'last things'], but who nevertheless believe that the Bible provides clues to future events. . . . This group, comprising many millions of Americans, is susceptible to popularizers who confidently weave Bible passages into highly imaginative end-time scenarios, or promulgate particular schemes of prophetic interpretation." *When Time Shall Be No More*, pp. 2–3.

5. Weber, *Living in the Shadow of the Second Coming*, p. 229.

6. Jeffrey K. Hadden, "Religious Broadcasting and the Mobilization of the New Christian Right," in Jeffrey K. Hadden and Anson Shupe, eds., *Secularization and Fundamentalism Reconsidered* (New York: Paragon, 1989), pp. 249–50.

7. Frances FitzGerald, "The American Millennium," *The New Yorker*, 11 November 1985, pp. 105–96.

8. Boyer, *When Time Shall Be No More*, pp. xii, 2–4.

9. See George M. Marsden, *Fundamentalism and American Culture* (Oxford: Oxford University Press, 1980); also see Weber, *Living in the Shadow*.

10. Willmington wrote about his gift to the future in his commentary on the Book of Revelation in H. L. Willmington, *Willmington's Guide to the Bible* (Tyndale, 1981), pp. 562–63; and Elmer Towns, dean of Liberty Seminary, mentioned it in his sermon "Iraq in Bible Prophecy" during the Persian Gulf War.

11. Willmington, *Willmington's Guide to the Bible*, p. 563.

12. Ibid.

13. Weber, *Living in the Shadow of the Second Coming*, pp. 9 and 32ff.

14. Ibid., pp. 240–41.

15. Curtis Lee Laws, who invented the term "fundamentalist" in 1920 to describe those who would "do battle royal for the fundamentals of the faith" against theological modernism, stated that he chose that term instead of "premillennialist" because "the group does contain those who differ radically with one another on the whole millennial question." Laws, *Moody Bible Institute Monthly*, September 1922, p. 15. Competing dispensationalist orthodoxies have perennially caused fundamentalists grief. (Looking forward, asking Jerry Falwell if his politics are motivated by eschatology is like asking him, "Are you illegitimate, are you divisive, are you irrational?" in the eyes not just of outsiders, but of many of his co-believers.)

16. Weber noted, in *Living in the Shadow of the Second Coming*, p. 240: "Though posttribulational premillennialism was evident in the early prophetic conferences, by the turn of the century its advocates had been successfully prevented from voicing their views in dispensationalist-controlled periodicals and were rarely invited to speak at prophetic conferences. Dispensationalists so effectively overcame the other view that many dispensationalists today erroneously believe that posttribulationalism is new and dispensationalism is the oldest premillennialist position." Weber makes clear that the posttribulational position is in fact the older one (p. 21).

17. Ibid., p. 216. Weber points out that many of the major televangelists (Jerry Falwell, Jim Bakker, Oral Roberts, Rex Humbard, Billy Graham, Jimmy Swaggart) were dispensationalists of some sort and that the 1970s witnessed the first generation of full-length "prophecy films" (*A Thief in the Night, A Distant Thunder, Image of the Beast, The Rapture, The Road to Armageddon*, and so on).

18. Frank Peretti projected future struggles between Miltonesque demons and angels in small-town America in two riveting and best-selling novels published in the 1980s (*Piercing the Darkness* and *This Present Darkness*). Though unorthodoxically and implicitly, both novels were partially landscaped according to a dispensational reading of Bible prophecies.

19. For extensive discussions of the shifting "signs of the times" in this century, see Wilson, *Armageddon Now!*; Weber, *Living in the Shadow of the Second Coming*; and Boyer, *When Time Shall Be No More*. George M. Marsden, *Reforming Fundamentalism: Fuller Seminary and the New Evangelicalism*, describes the wobbling of Arno Gaeblien (in the journal *Our Hope*) and Wilbur Smith in this regard (pp. 71, 73). Wilbur Smith, for example, asserted the impossibility of equating current events/persons with prophecies, yet "found a remarkable number of prophetic statements that seemed to refer to the present era" (p. 73).

20. The future is perfectly known and fixed to God, and the Bible is his perfect record, but human knowledge and interpretation are fallible, therefore stories change, constantly.

21. Other books by Hal Lindsey include *The Rapture, There's a New World Coming, Satan Is Alive and Well on Planet Earth, Terminal Generation, The 1980s: Countdown to Armageddon, The Promise*, and *Combat Faith*. Books by other mainstream dispensational authors (Tim LaHaye, John Walvoord) also gained large readerships, but none on the scale of Lindsey's. Although some observers think there was a prophecy boom beginning in the 1970s, it probably makes more sense to think of the dispensational audience as growing gradually after World War II, fueled as much by the increasing level of education among born-again Christians (which did not specify what they read but advanced reading habits generally) as by the steadily growing circulation of books, pamphlets, movies, and crusaders (foremost among them, Billy Graham) articulating dispensational themes.

22. Lindsey, *The 1980s* (Bantam, 1983), p. 157.

23. Post-tribulationalism was revived after World War II by a host of evangelical scholars critical of dispensational biblical hermeneutics. The popular revival came later, was less explicit, and overlapped in many of its moves with the pre-Tribulation tribulation pretribulationalists [!]. The position was popularized by Jim McKeever (*Christians Will Go Through the Tribulation* [Omega Publications, 1978]) and, more obliquely, by Pat Roberston (and Bob Slosser, *The Secret Kingdom* [Bantam, 1984]; and *America's Dates with Destiny* [Nashville: Nelson, 1986]). See Weber, *Living in the Shadow of the Second Coming,* pp. 222–24, 241; on Robertson's position, see David E. Harrell, *Pat Robertson* (San Francisco: Harper and Row, 1987), pp. 143–49. The major post-millennial elaboration within the New Christian Right was Kingdom Now theology (a.k.a. Dominion Theology and Christian Reconstructionism) associated with Rousas John Rushdoony and Gary North.

24. Tim LaHaye, *The Battle for the Mind,* pp. 218–19.

25. Weber, *Living in the Shadow of the Second Coming,* p. 226.

26. Billy Graham, *Approaching Hoofbeats: The Four Horsemen of the Apocalypse,* pp. 137, 129, 128. Graham, in fact, was not stepping out on a limb here, but rather taking up an appeal made as early as the late 1940s by such evangelical theologians as Carl Henry and Harold Ockenga. Cf. Marsden, *Reforming Fundamentalism,* p. 76.

27. The network was composed of churches in the Baptist Bible Fellowship (some three thousand of them with membership rolls of 1.5 million), plus hundreds of fellow-traveler churches and preachers (such as Charles Stanley and W. A. Criswell's Southern Baptist churches).

28. Jerry Falwell, "1980 Bible Prophecy Update," Old-Time Gospel Hour audio tape.

29. Jerry Falwell, "Founder's Week Sermon," 1 February 1984, Moody Bible Institute audio tape, FW84–5.

30. *New York Times,* 2 February 1991. *The National and International Religion Report,* 28 January 1991, reported Zondervan had 550,000 copies in print.

31. *New York Times,* 2 February 1991. *The National and International Religion Report,* 28 January 1991, reported that the Billy Graham Evangelistic Association distributed 400,000 copies.

32. *New York Times,* 2 February 1991.

33. No specific Bible passage anticipates the rebuilding of Babylon. Rather, dispensationalists deduce its rebuilding from various Old and New Testament chapters (especially Isa. 13 and Rev. 17–18) which predict the absolute and violent destruction of Babylon. Historical Babylon was never so destroyed, therefore Babylon must be rebuilt in order to be so destroyed.

34. Jerry Falwell, "The Middle East Crisis and Armageddon," Old-Time Gospel Hour video tape, 1991.

35. Jerry Falwell, "America Declares War against God," Old-Time Gospel Hour sermon, 1993.

36. Emmanuel Sivan, pers. com.

CHAPTER 4

Refusing to Drink with the Mountains: Traditional Andean Meanings in Evangelical Practice

Tod D. Swanson

As I arrived in the Ecuadorian Puruhá community of El Troje just at dusk I could hear the familiar falsetto voices rising to the rhythms of a San Juanito band. Crowds in *anacos* and ponchos were sharing food and drink in front of a whitewashed church. One might have guessed that a traditional Andean fiesta was in progress. But something was not quite right. The women coming out to greet me offered me soft drinks instead of rum or *chicha* (barley or maize beer), and as I began to make out the lyrics I could hear that their content was Protestant. In fact, it was not a traditional fiesta but an evangelical *conferencia*. These particular native people had been converted by the Gospel Missionary Union, a Christian fundamentalist organization from North America.

The basic question I hope to answer in this chapter is this: Behind their native dress and Andean tunes, are these converts basically clones of the missionaries who converted them? In the 1946 *Handbook of South American Indians,* George Kubler declared authoritatively that Andean religion had died out in the eighteenth century when the Quechua people became essentially Catholic.[1] That notion dominated scholarly thought until the 1970s, when a whole series of new studies rediscovered native religion within Andean Catholicism. But just when the anthropologists were rediscovering Andean religion, it started slipping through their fingers. In alarming numbers Andean Indians were becoming Protestants.

Surprisingly, many social scientists have taken it for granted that native converts simply adopt the worldview and conservative lifestyle of the North American Christian fundamentalists who convert them. If that is the case, then the economic and political consequences of conversion are predictable. It is this predicted outcome that has caused hope for some, but alarm for others, interested in the future of native South Americans. British sociologist David Martin, for example, suggests that the

Protestant conversion of Latin America could create an environment conducive to economic advancement along the lines proposed by Max Weber in *The Protestant Ethic and the Spirit of Capitalism*.[2] Scholars less sanguine about the free market often share similar premises. The liberationist bishop of Riobamba, Leonidas Proaño, warned that the conversion of his Puruhá flock would instill disruptive capitalist values in their society. But what if these basic assumptions are wrong? What if native converts are adopting the fundamentalist message for their own Andean reasons and adapting it to fit traditional Andean assumptions about life, including economic life? In these circumstances, the consequences of fundamentalist missions are much less predictable.

In this chapter I examine the dynamic transformation of the fundamentalist message which occurs as it is preached and appropriated across cultural boundaries. I probe the label "evangelical" in the same way that the scholars of the 1970s looked beneath the surface of "popular Catholicism." If the Catholic conversion of native Andeans has been found to cover developments in more substantial continuity with traditional religion, perhaps the same might be true for evangelical conversion.

To explore this possibility I look closely at religious change among the Ecuadorian Puruhá, a native people who live on the high tundra-like *páramo* of Chimborazo Province, where they raise barley, potatoes, and sheep. They are speakers of Quichua, or Inga as they call it, the language spread northward into Ecuador during the Inca expansion of the late fifteenth century. Until the 1960s the Puruhá were staunchly resistant to Protestant missions, but then, for reasons not well understood, mass conversions swept the páramo even in areas with little direct missionary contact. The conversion of the Puruhá has become controversial, at once the cause of celebration by evangelical strategists and the subject of dire warnings by those who fear the effects of missions on native people. I use their case to argue quite different conclusions.

In recording Puruhá testimonies I was initially impressed with how the language of drinking and not drinking dominated their discourse. "The way of life that we had with the priests in the fiestas was only drunkenness," one man told me. "We have had a change of heart; what has changed is especially the drunkenness."[3] Not surprisingly it was this rejection of drinking that, to many outsiders, seemed to mark Puruhá evangelicalism as an imported, non-Indian movement. While teetotaling is one of the most distinctive marks of North American fundamentalism, in native Andean religion chicha and *trago* (sugarcane rum) are omnipresent sacramental fluids. Surely a religion that breaks with rum drinking, these observers argue, has broken with the very core of Andean religion.

But there are other analogies besides fundamentalism for understanding a Native American embrace of prohibition. On the Navajo, Hopi, and Papago reservations in Arizona, for example, sobriety is deeply tied to new forms of Indian religion (such as the Native American Church), to Indian power and Indian eschatologies. Amid the flyers tacked up outside the post office in Second Mesa, one is likely to find one for the Miss Hopi Sobriety contest. In some cases prohibition was borrowed from the preaching of Protestant missionaries, but it has now become a symbol of Indian resistance which has meaning within native eschatologies. I wondered if the same might be true for the Puruhá Quichua.

In this chapter I use the Puruhá break with alcohol as a symbol for other characteristics of the fundamentalist lifestyle adopted by the native converts. Because drinking and not drinking are central to both evangelical and traditional religious discourse
in the Andes, they may serve as a lens through which to interpret larger issues of
religious and economic change in the wake of fundamentalist missions. To do so,
however, I must begin by discussing the meaning of alcohol in Andean religion.

A Fluid Contest: The Meaning of Alcohol in Andean Religion

The meaning of alcohol in Puruhá religion is clearest in the curing rites of the *jambiri*,
or medicine people. These healers see themselves as kinsmen, usually *compadres* or
consorts of the mountain deities—Mt. Chimborazo, Mt. Carihuayrazu, and so forth—
that ring the horizon. Their power to heal comes directly from "drinking with" these
compadre mountains. Because so many Puruhá Quichua are now Protestant, I was
unable to observe a traditional Puruhá curing ceremony there. However, I did attend
closely related Quichua curing ceremonies in the Calderon area (150 miles north of
the Puruhá) in which some of the patients were Puruhá. In the ceremonies I attended,
a patient offered tobacco and rum to the healers, whom they addressed as "compadre"
or "comadre." The healers then offered the rum and tobacco to their own mountain
compadres, blowing the rum over stone icons of the mountains. "So that they may
give us power, joy," Compadre José Manuel told me, "it is our custom to gather
together all of our mountains when we begin to cure. That is why we have to say [to
them], '[Mt.] Imbabura, [Mt.] Pichincha, *salud, salud!* [cheers!]'" That is why we have
to say, 'Let us drink together! *Upiashun!*'"[4]

At first it seemed that the shaman drank with mountains simply to close the deal,
much like a businessman might drink with a powerful banker from whom he wants
favors. But rum has deeper religious meanings in the Andes. Rum is offered because
rum is the symbolic equivalent of blood, and blood in turn is the carrier of a religious
power called *suerte*. In Spanish, suerte means luck, but as used by Quichuas suerte is
a personal power to win contests and attract business, and it is present in the life fluids
or winds pulsing through the body. This notion of suerte is crucial not only to traditional Andean assumptions about health, but also to assumptions about the nature of
economics. An increase in suerte brings increased health and prosperity. A loss of
suerte brings illness and poverty. In Andean cosmology, suerte circulates along lines
of *compadrasco* from mountains to human beings and back again. Because the quantity
of suerte is limited, the quest for this religious power is competitive. One kin group
can increase their suerte only by decreasing the suerte of another.

When a sick person asks for a cure, the healer, I'll call him José Chimbolema, feels
her pulse. If it is weak he says something like, "Comadre Rosita, envious people have
taken the earth from your footprints and two bottles of rum to a witch to ruin your
suerte. Because of that, that *cerro bravo* [killer mountain] Mother Tungurahua has 'hit'
you with a *huayra* [dry wind]. In that wind the powerful breath of Mt. Tungurahua
has sucked out your blood and stolen your suerte, comadre." "With good reason,"

says Comadre Rosita, "with good reason I wondered why that Maruja Guamán followed me back from the market last Thursday. For no reason she envies the few potatoes I sell. I bet she took the earth from my footprints to that witch Pedro Vega."[5]

To cure these ills the power of Comadre Rosita's blood containing her suerte must be won back from Maruja Guamán and from the rival shaman, Pedro Vega, by drinking with the mountains. To accomplish this the healer, an experienced contestant, enters into a drinking and blowing contest with the mountains. In the Puruhá area, these mountains would probably be Tungurahua and Chimborazo. The healer sprays rum onto the icons of the mountains, or he spews it in the direction of the mountains, and he drinks it on behalf of the mountains. If Compadre José's suerte is strong enough, he will win suerte from the mountains on Comadre Rosita's behalf. But if his suerte is weak, then the mountains will steal what suerte he had through the medium of alcohol.

It may seem like Compadre José and his network are drinking only with Chimborazo and Tungurahua, but indirectly they are also engaged in a drinking contest with the rival shaman. Somewhere across the *huaycu* (canyon), Pedro Vega is also drinking with Chimborazo and Tungurahua, trying to cure his patients by draining the suerte of José and his patients. Through the drink, one of them will increase his suerte, while the other will be drained of suerte. If he is more powerful, Compadre José will find that drinking clears his head so that he can hear Chimborazo telling him how to blow and giving him powerful breath to sing. Meanwhile across the huaycu, Pedro Vega may be having a very different experience. He finds that the more he drinks with Chimborazo, the more the rum merely dulls his senses, so that his singing becomes blurred and he seems unable to cure his patients. His suerte is being drained away and his patient will weaken. This is because, in exchange for the rum offered by Compadre José, Chimborazo is cycling the missing fluids back into Comadre Rosita's body, draining them from Pedro Vega and his patients. To actualize this return, Compadre José soaks her body with the second bottle of rum and gives her more rum to drink. As the person's health returns, their pulse and body fluids may even be compared to strong rum.

The role of rum in fiestas can be understood by analogy to curing services like this one. Like the curing service, the fiesta is a means for transferring suerte between rival communities who drink together with the mountains. At the root of the fiesta structure in the Ecuadorian Andes are paired higher- and lower-altitude neighborhoods loosely linked through ties of ritual kinship called *compadrasco*. At the time of the harvest lower on Chimborazo, the higher-altitude compadres are invited down to work, drink, and share in the produce. Later the lower-altitude compadres will be invited to celebrate the harvest higher up on Chimborazo.

In a ritual act called the *mugu*, the fiesta sponsor offers a cup of rum to a compadre. And as Federico Aguiló put it, "to offer a drink to a compadre" triggers "a chain of mutual offerings that lasts until the most complete drunkenness is reached."[6] As the two *comunas* drink together, they enter into an open religious state similar to that which occurs in the curing service—a state in which suerte can be transferred from one comuna to another through competitive displays. Activated by rum, the suerte in the blood and breath of the *comuneros* is displayed in powerful singing, speaking, and dancing. Dancing down roads and around in circles, young women raise their voices in a powerful falsetto song. Accompanying them are young men who display the power of their *own breath* by blowing tunefully across a *rondador* or, more recently, a harmonica. Distinctive colors of dress mark the exact place on the mountains from which the dancers come, and the superior weave of the garments displays the suerte of that place. The comuna whose drunken dancing makes the most powerful showing draws the suerte of the rival community to itself.

In pre-Columbian times, to drink in these fiestas was to drink with Chimborazo, to dance with Chimborazo, to enter into a contest with Chimborazo in order to increase the suerte of the competing communities. But when the agricultural fiestas were correlated with the Christian year, the Puruhá drank and danced not only with the mountains, but also with Nuestro Señor and with the saints. At Christmas, compadres drank together with the Christ Child; in Holy Week, they drank to accompany Christ in his suffering, and to mourn him at his wake.

While on one level the fiesta worked as a competition between Indian comunas, it was always also an exchange of suerte with the white world. Each year on Corpus Christi or San Juan, a procession of dancing Puruhá presented a portion of the harvest to the white hacienda owner and the white priest. These offerings of Puruhá suerte (song, voice, breath, food) challenged the white world to reciprocate. In accepting the harvest the *hacendado* would, in turn, formally toast his Indians (sometimes with wine) and offer them a case of rum. The priest responded with a Mass, and his drinking of the wine on behalf of the native parishioners was imagined to be similar to the shaman's drinking of rum on the patient's behalf. Both actions were understood as reciprocal transfers of white suerte to the Indian world.

The white priests and hacendados may not have realized it, but in performing these actions they were involved in a religious drinking contest with their Indians, mediated by Mt. Chimborazo. Earlier in the year, as Puruhá compadres danced and drank barley chicha together while waiting for this harvest to mature, they sang the following traditional song and probably others like it:

> Lord Chimborazo, Lord Chimborazo,
> Do not send your snow, your hail;
> Do not soak my wheat, my grain.
> It is not mine Lord Chimborazo. May the master never beat me,
>   never in my life.
> We Indian people drink [poor] barley beer,
> And the master who does no work drinks [expensive] wine.

By accusing Chimborazo of unfairly giving wine, a drink with more powerful suerte, to the whites, this song-prayer implicitly asks Chimborazo to right the imbalance later on when the whites drink wine with him. And it asks that the Indians not be beaten for too meager a harvest when they have to present it to the whites. By singing such songs over the harvest, the Puruhá in effect entered into a drinking contest for suerte not only with Chimborazo but with the white world. And by doing so, they hoped to win in the transfer of suerte that would happen later on when the harvest was offered to the priest and the hacendado.

To progress through a fiesta, testing one's power to drink to the limit against white and Indian compadres, was like going through a curing session with a healer. In theory, at least, the economic power in one's life fluids became heartier. The suerte won from other comunas or from the white world in this way was never merely secular, however. It was a blessing, understood as the quite physical presence of Christ's power or the saint's power in the blood and breath of the blessed person.

Although suerte can be won through fiesta drinking, drunkenness is also a spiritually dangerous state in which soul substance can be lost. Several people told me that after drinking heavily at a fiesta and then dancing across the fields in the night, they had awakened with their legs dangling over the edge of a precipice. The mountain's presence in the rum had tried to lure them over a cliff, where they might spill out all of their blood into the canyon (a mountain artery). Like other Andean peoples, the Puruhá think that a dancer's suerte drains out into the precise place on the mountain trail where he passes out. In fact, Puruhá medicine men from the community of Cacha actually have a special rite for recovering the lost soul substance from the very spot where the dancer passes out. In such cases, the drunk's vitality is not just lost into the earth. If it is not recovered, it is taken into the mountain and then transferred to rivals—to the white world or other winning fiesta drinkers who thereby increase their own suerte. On several occasions I have heard healers tell patients that the loss of suerte is due to their inability to control drinking. If such persons continue to drink, they may render themselves vulnerable to a definitive defeat by more powerful drinkers such as whites. To win their suerte back such patients must stop drinking.

The Religious Meaning of the *Fiesta Tiempo* in Puruhá Testimonies

The Puruhá were confident that by drinking with Nuestro Señor and the saints in the fiestas, they circulated fluid blessing between themselves and the saints. But at least by the late 1960s that vision of the fiesta stood in stark contrast to reality. Across the highlands of Ecuador drinking patterns were changing. Homemade native brews were being replaced by commercial brews with dangerously high alcohol levels. And the fiestas that should have led to prosperity were becoming deadly.

María Muzo de Tasiguano, a Llano Grande Quichua woman from an area where drinking is still heavy, describes the change poignantly. Back in her girlhood, she says, "Chicha was made from germinated maize, and that chicha was delicious, thick, like now they drink beer, but it was not as intoxicating. . . . People drank rum, yes, but from one liter of rum they got six bottles. They mixed it with water and sugar, and they drank it calmly; they never got sick." In her mind the year 1964 marked the beginning of the end—a final defeat of Indian culture by the changing liquor policies of the white world.

That our way of life came to be lost is not the fault of the evangelical church. It was lost because of the godless government. . . . Doctor Velasco Ibarra [then president of Ecuador] outlawed it. He completely prevented the making of chicha. Some government agents came . . . to break our *maltas* [earthen vessels] with the chicha in it, to pour it out for us on the ground. They came to mistreat the people . . . and now from the year 1964 on, they didn't let them drink chicha. Now they have them drinking beer and contraband rum and all. And the people are dying. And the men that drink! How many men have now died from drinking those things? And that is why I say that the ancestors' time was more wholesome [*sano*]. They had their fiestas, yes, but it was more wholesome than now. Now . . . all the young men are ruined. The young men drink beer, they get drunk, they go and violate the girls, they grab them and ruin them.

One hundred and fifty miles away, similar developments were unraveling the fabric of Puruhá society. Already by the 1950s Puruhá drinking had become indiscriminate. In 1966 Eileen Maynard wrote of the mestizos living in the Puruhá area around Lake Colta:

Their main source of revenue . . . derives from the sale of cheap cane liquor *(aguardiente)*, and the fabrication and sale of a fermented corn beer *(chicha)*. In order to attract Indian customers, they brew a *chicha* potent enough to produce almost instantaneous intoxication. Ideally the main ingredient of *chicha* is corn, but the commercial beverage contains a minimum of corn and a maximum of unrefined sugar. To produce the necessary "kick," two toxic ingredients are added, ammonia and the flowers of the *huantu* tree (*Datura sanguinea*).[7]

As the Puruhá's dependence on commercial brews increased, their indebtedness to local whites reached unbearable levels. As evangelical Puruhá remember the *fiesta tiempo* in their testimonies, local priests increased the number of fiestas and fiesta sponsors (called *priostes*). Every Friday night throughout the year leading up to a fiesta, a prioste had to gather together the prospective dance retinue, along with numerous compadres, and take them down into town. A white tavern owner, who might also be a compadre, would then turn over a suite of rooms to the prioste as if it were his own home. After the prioste was drunk, the tavern owner continued supplying as much food and liquor as the retinue could consume throughout the weekend. When the prioste sobered up on Monday afternoon, he was presented with the debt which he had to acknowledge. By the 1960s nearly all Puruhá resources were in hock to the white world, and many Puruhá were dying from alcohol-related maladies. Their suerte had literally run out.

It was in this context that North American missionaries from the fundamentalist Gospel Missionary Union (GMU) began to tell the Puruhá that even though they were baptized Catholics, their drunken indebted lives evidenced the absence of Christ in their hearts. Because their present testimonies look back through a generation of change, it is no longer possible to know with certainty the thought processes of Puruhá who converted to Protestantism thirty years ago. But in light of the meaning of alcohol in traditional fiestas and curing rites, it is possible to reconstruct their motives with a high degree of probability.

According to GMU accounts, missionary preaching usually occurred in the context of medical visits, and it was some time after the curing of physical ailments that the first religious breakthroughs came. A brief look at one of these accounts (this one by Margaret McGivney) is sufficient to grasp the religious significance missionary medicine must have had for the Puruhá at this juncture in their history: "One Christmas morning Dora Regier and I were beginning to prepare our Christmas dinner . . . when there was a knock at the door. A man had come from a community two hour's journey across the mountain seeking help for a woman who had fallen off a cliff while returning home from town. She had been to a baptism and had gotten drunk during the feasting. . . . With a prayer to the Lord for help, I began to clean out the wound and sew up the gash." When the two missionary women finally got home that night, they were immediately summoned to help another woman who had also fallen off a cliff: "Early in the morning we again gathered up our medical supplies and went over to see this woman. We found that she had been dancing along the road while she was drunk. She had danced right off a cliff, fallen about twenty feet and landed on her head."[8] On the surface these events seem routine. Two drunk women accidentally fell into canyons and were patched up by missionary nurses. But for the Puruhá the significance of such events must have been profound.

First, the date of the fiesta is Christmas, so at the time of the accidents the victims were drinking with the Niño Jesús, hoping to win a blessing. In their drunkenness, both women fell into canyons, and one of them is even said to have "danced right off the cliff." As we have seen, falling over a canyon is one of the most stereotyped ways in which a mountain is believed to take the suerte of a person. Therefore their near encounters with death had a clear religious meaning. It was unmistakably in contest with the mountains, and through the medium of alcohol that these women were lured to their accidents. If they were hoping to win the blessing of the Christ Child through these activities, then it would have been the blessing of the Christ Child in their blood and breath that would have been taken from them in the fall, had they died as a result of their accidents.

These two cases are particularly suited to my argument, but they are not atypical. My father was a missionary doctor in another part of Ecuador during roughly the same period (the early 1960s), and I recall that during the time of the fiestas he usually worked on accident victims of this kind late into the night. As we have seen, Puruhá jambiri had specific rites for recovering the patient's suerte from the place on the mountain where the drunken person fell. Because native medicine men warned that being attended by missionary personnel would further ruin a patient's suerte, Indian people involved in fiesta accidents like these would usually come to the missionaries only after a jambiri such as Compadre José Chimbolema had failed to cure them. By the time the missionaries saw them, patients like these had doubly lost their blessing, first when they drank with the saints and danced off the cliff, and second when the jambiri drank with the mountains on their behalf and lost. For Indian people, the loss of suerte is a religious loss, somewhat analogous to what missionaries might mean by the loss of salvation.

The way in which the GMU missionaries cured these "lost causes" must have been particularly significant to the Puruhá. Healing was always accompanied by a Gospel witness in which the Indians were informed of their lostness and offered a contrasting portrait of the saved life. In GMU memoirs drunkenness figures prominently as both a spiritual symptom of "lostness" and a physical symptom accompanying Puruhá illness. It is therefore almost certain that in witnessing to the patients, missionaries linked the physical consequences of drunkenness (broken body, death, indebtedness) to the absence of Christ. The missionaries also had a pretty good idea of who was to blame for the absence of Christ in Puruhá hearts. It was those Catholic priests who kept the Indians from the Bible and made them celebrate the feasts of wooden "idols" (the saints).

After describing the present lostness of the Indian people, missionaries then offered a contrasting portrait of the blessings that would come from conversion. In her account of the medical visit, the GMU nurse Margaret McGivney actually contrasted the drunken fall of the Puruhá women to her own success in crossing the same canyons on the way home: "We were still some distance from home when darkness over took us. I am sure that the Lord had his hand over us as we crossed and walked alongside the deep ravines."[9] Witnessing of this kind was combined with teaching Gospel songs to the patient and the patient's family.

GMU missionaries probably did not fully understand what alcohol meant for the Puruhá. Yet their message made sense in Puruhá terms. Why did fiestas that should have led to prosperity lead only to poverty and death for the Puruhá? Obviously the missionaries were right. It was because they had drunk with the priests and lost. Like mountains who win blood from drunks in fiestas, the priests and the liquor merchants had conspired to take the power of Christ from the Puruhá by keeping them drunk. In contrast, the missionary healers wanted to give Christ's blessing to the Indian people in the form of health. And their medicine was strong enough to win back the lost suerte from the mountains and from the priests. The Gospel songs that accompanied healing would have been understood as the *taquina,* or curing songs, of the missionary healer. Learning to sing them was a powerful way of regaining the blessing of Christ which had been lost. If Margaret McGivney was divinely protected from falling into canyons, then the suerte of Christ imparted by the missionaries would also protect Puruhá converts in their own contests with the mountains.

In this context, Puruhá conversion is not best understood as the abandonment of a worldview. In fact, José Manuel Guamán, the Puruhá president of the Evangelical Indian Federation of Ecuador, told me that many evangelicals still think God circulates blessings through Mt. Chimborazo: "Up to the present time the majority of our people believe that . . . it is because of Chimborazo that the grains are no longer fruitful or that there will be some economic crisis . . . but this belief no longer goes beyond belief in a [biblical] Creator." Rather, conversion should be understood as a new move in the old play of religious power between the Puruhá and the white world. Awakening to the fact that they did not really have the power of Christ because of what they saw as the fiesta conspiracy, the Puruhá gave up drinking and became evangelicals.

GMU doctor Donald Dilworth's description of the conversion of El Troje exemplifies the formal change of allegiance that occurred in many Puruhá comunas following a series of missionary medical visits: "The first sign of the great change was apparent when the four [Mullu] brothers came to [the GMU station at] Colta declaring they wanted to build a church. . . . They had not attended a drunken fiesta for a year. . . . The older brother had been a leader. All would still work in a *minga* for community projects, but they would no longer carry the 'saint' through the field when it failed to rain."[10] The Catholic chapel was the only analogy the Mullu brothers had for understanding what the new evangelical chapel might mean. In asking for the evangelical chapel, therefore, they must have intended something similar to their understanding of a Catholic chapel but with certain specific differences. For example, because the eldest Mullu brother was an *alcalde* (an elder in the fiesta system), his authority to ask for the new chapel clearly rested on the suerte won through drinking contests in the old Catholic chapel. His intent, therefore, could not have been to abandon the religious exchange of suerte altogether, but only to alter it. If the Mullu brothers were not rejecting the contest for suerte itself, it can only have been drinking with the priests as an effective means of winning suerte that was being rejected. The purpose of requesting the new chapel must have been, first, to replace the Hispanic priests with North American missionaries as mediators of the blessing exchange and, second, to replace drunken fiestas with similar rites that excluded drinking.

For the people of El Troje, the fiesta had clearly gone from being a show of Puruhá power to a display of the absence or loss of that power. No longer intelligible as a display of health, it became a display of bewitchment and death. In short it was a display of white power and Indian bondage. When I met Matías, one of those original Mullu brothers, he was wearing the white poncho of an evangelical deacon, a garment that mirrored the albs once worn only by priests. One of Mullu's neighbors told me what was to be gained by exchanging the old title of alcalde for that of deacon: "Well, in earlier times . . . the alcaldes that we had [were] . . . not like a mayor in the city, but rather it was those who had to put on the fiesta, and those who had to do what the priest ordered. The priest used to say [to the fiesta sponsors], 'All right, now you have to go out and collect the tithe of the harvest,' and so they did it." In 1990 Deacon Mullu was still not drinking, and as far as he was concerned, the power lost to the priests had been recovered. Throughout Puruhá country there were now over five hundred independent congregations, led not by alcaldes or priests but by deacons like himself.

Conferencia as Counter-Fiesta

The conferencia, described in the opening lines of this chapter, replaced the fiesta as the central rite of evangelical Puruhá religion. Like Puruhá evangelicalism as a whole, the conferencia cannot be understood on its own but as one side in a rapidly changing contest for blessing. By interpreting the conferencia in this light I hope to portray the distinctively Indian character of the evangelical movement in Chimborazo.

At the core of the fiesta rivalry inherited by the conferencia was the opposition between alcaldes, who had by definition brought blessing to their communities by sponsoring fiestas, and people called *ashcos,* or "dogs," who declined that duty. Because they refused to sponsor fiestas, *ashco longos* were believed to have actually drained suerte from their communities. "If the person had already made two or three fiestas, then that person was important. Then they said to him, 'You are now an important person,' and they gave him a place, they gave him preference. If they didn't put on any fiesta they would say, 'This one is like a dog, this one is worthless.'" For traditional people, ashco was the worst possible insult. It denoted persons who were ostracized from the community because they were too miserly to reciprocate the hospitality of compadres.

The question posed by conversion (and later answered by the conferencia) was how to position evangelicals within this alcalde/ashco polarity. The Mullu brothers, for example, were clearly not ashcos before their conversion (one of them had already reached the highest level of fiesta sponsorship), but when they broke with fiesta drinking they effectively broke with the network of compadres through which suerte circulates. And thus from the perspective of traditionalists they placed themselves in the category of ashco longos.

Not surprisingly the rest of the community rose up against the early converts, saying things like "How could you do something like that? That is not good. [Now] you have to go live with the gringos. Why do you have to change your religion?" The Mullu brothers were badly beaten, and one of them, Matías Mullu, was thrown into a canyon and left for dead. As with the earlier examples of the women who fell into the canyon during fiesta dancing and drinking, throwing Matías Mullu into the canyon had a marked religious meaning. Mullu recovered from his injuries, even though the men who threw him into the canyon had intended him to die as an ashco—like a dog, outlawed by the community, his blood fed back into the mountains through the canyon.

Because they had inadvertently fallen into the status of ashco, converts like the Mullus were in especially desperate need of compadres. But precisely because they had broken with drinking, they could no longer gain them through the fiesta system. Recognizing the centrality of the fiesta in Indian life, missionaries deliberately introduced adaptations of North American Bible conferences as "Christian" substitutes. The *conferencias,* however, quickly took on a life of their own. In the early conferencias, evangelical comunas closer to the missions hosted sympathetic or newly converted compadres from comunas higher in the páramo. When the compadres arrived, the hosting evangelicals were particularly anxious to lay to rest the charge of ashco longo. Although they could not offer or respond to a compadre's past hospitality with the traditional toast of "Upiashun! Let us drink together!" they could swamp their guests with food and soft drinks. To offer this hospitality, they dressed in their most beautiful clothes. They sang with powerful sami, and speaking eloquently, they attributed their newfound power to the break with trago and to the presence of Christ in their hearts. In this context the "Bible conferences" introduced by the missionaries became counter-fiestas, that is, stylized answers to the challenge of ashco implicit in the fiestas sponsored by traditional rivals. When the evangelical comunas succeeded in displaying the power of their suerte, the visiting compadres were won over to the evangelical side. The ties of compadrasco were strengthened in the new fictive kinship of evangelical brotherhood and sisterhood. Later these higher-altitude comunas would reciprocate by sponsoring conferencias of their own. Sponsoring these exchanges of conferencias were evangelical deacons like Matías Mullu. By doing so they brought blessing to their communities, answering the charges of ashco and turning them back on their rivals.

In the wake of Vatican II, however, attacks on the evangelicals took new directions to which the conferencias were forced to respond. Mentored (in its early stages) by liberationist priests, a powerful pan-Indian movement arose across Ecuador which sought to renew pride in traditional Indian culture. In this new context the meaning of ashco longo was increasingly combined with *tzala tucushca,* another insult which means "turned white." Tzala tucushcas were ashcos who declined to dance in fiestas not so much because they were poor, but because they were ashamed to be recognized publicly as Indians. Even if they did return hospitality, evangelicals in particular were accused of being tzala tucushcas and were blamed as a group for the widespread loss of Indian pride in the fiesta.

Father Federico Aguiló, one of the supporters of the pan-Indian movement, described the loss of the Puruhá fiesta complex with great sadness: "Today the memory barely exists of the musical competitions . . . in which boys improvised their songs. . . . [The] rondador, the *pingullo,* and the flute [*quena*], . . . [which] have been the mark of a Puruhá-Quichua creativity [are being] swept [away] by the transistor radio [and in particular by evangelical Quichua broadcasts on the radio]. Interest in music continues to be pressing, but only in listening, without any great possibility of native creativity."[11] Since more and more Indian youths were refusing to participate in traditional fiestas, either out of shame or because of evangelical conversion, the old charge of ashco longo was extended to include the exchange of Indian culture for white or North American culture through conversion.

To counter this loss of Indian culture, traditional dance hierarchies in Catholic communities across Ecuador were evolving into pow-wow-like dance competitions that consciously displayed Indian pride. In the context of these fiestas the combined charge of tzala tucushca/ashco was renewed against the evangelicals. Like opposing dance hierarchies, the conferencias and the new pow-wow/fiestas began to rival each other as modern displays of Indian suerte. To compete, each had to outshine its rivals not only in the traditional exchanges of hospitality, dress, and music, but also in modern political and economic symbols of power and in the self-consciously Indian modernity of its youth. When I approached the large revival-style tent erected in a field in Gatazo, for example, the local deacons (who seemed much like sober alcaldes) immediately invited me into the cooking facilities set up outside. I was made to sit down with visiting deacons from another comuna, and together we were swamped with consecutive bowls of food. No white food vendors, missionaries, priests, or hacendados were present. Three whole slaughtered bulls hung from the rafters. Enormous cauldrons of potato soup were cooking. When we had consumed all the food we could, the deacons offered us one glass of Coca-Cola after another in much the same way that traditional elders offer trago. The elders contrasted themselves with whites and people from other comunas who still drank. One of the deacons told about a recent bus trip in which he was so surrounded by drunks that he was afraid of becoming intoxicated by the fumes:

> Now we have had a change in our heart. Now we are thinking people. We think of our kids, something our parents didn't do. Now almost all of us [the Puruhá people] have stopped losing our money . . . in the cantinas [bars]. So that now when we go to a city to work, we come back with food. We buy clothes, at least we fix up our little home in a manner worthy of human habitation. Our fathers did not think like that. For them, it was only drink, drink, every day. [It was] to sponsor fiestas, and because of those fiestas they were called great in their gatherings, in the gatherings of our fathers.

These particular testimonies were directed partly at me and the tape recorder, but they give some idea of the kind of testimonies that might be given to sympathetic or recently converted compadres. At one level the language of such testimonies sounds like ordinary evangelical language about the blessings that come from having Christ in the heart—the joy of gathering together with Christian brothers and sisters contrasted to the drunken waste of the "world." But to anyone familiar with Puruhá religion, the language of the conferencia has other levels of meaning which resonate with the Andean world. Unlike North American testimonies, Puruhá testimonies frequently have a corporate character in which the "before" refers not just to some point in an individual biography, but to a point in Puruhá history, the *time of fiesta* drunkenness. In contrasting the present time of conferencias to the time of the fiestas, narrators implicitly reverse the polarity between alcalde/prioste and ashco. According to the testimonies, it turns out that the priostes "who were called great in the gatherings of our fathers" were not respected deposits of suerte, after all, but something very much like ashcos. As they were mere drunks and dupes of the whites, they lost so much suerte that they could not even care for their own children. In contrast, the well-dressed evangelical hosts who were once called ashco longos now offer overwhelming amounts of food and Coca-Colas to visiting comunas. They don't live in a doghouse like those old priostes, and they don't abandon their children or compadres either. As anyone can see from the conferencia itself, they are blessed people whose economic clout has increased considerably. But so far, this impressive display of wealth and hospitality would not have answered the charge of tzala tucushca. What if their well-nurtured children cared nothing about Indian identity?

When I had eaten too much but not enough to satisfy my hosts, I broke away from the cooking rooms and entered the big revival tent (which the deacons had assured me was not owned by missionaries). As I made my way through the crowd, a group of thirteen-year-olds headed by a daring girl I'll call María Elena Mullu motioned me to sit with them. Despite the fact that their faces were carefully made up with eyeliner and lipstick, they wore traditional anacos and long straight hair. As I scanned the young Puruhá people who crowded into the tent, I noticed that most of them wore traditional anacos and ponchos. The girls seemed to be resisting the pressure to cut or curl their hair in non-Indian styles. A handful of straw landed on my neck. Behind me were three boys from another comuna, wearing what looked like designer jeans under their red ponchos. Obviously one of them had intended the straw for María Elena Mullu. An elder walked by wearing a white poncho and carrying a stick he used to tap people who were sleeping or misbehaving. María Elena waited until he had passed and then threw a stick at the boys from Troje Alto.

The mere fact that large numbers of chic young people like María Elena Mullu dress in markedly Indian ways, and go to conferencias to be seen and to impress other young people might seem unremarkable. But it is the young people of her age-group who are most likely to be ashamed of Indian culture. In many parts of Ecuador, any display of chic is almost by definition a rejection of Indian identity. María Muzo de Tasiguano, a Llano Grande Quichua grandmother from outside the Puruhá area, expressed the concerns of many older people well: "[The young] don't want to know anything about the Indian nation. Now they don't want to speak [their language]. Many señorita persons don't want anyone to know that they are Indians. I have not changed my dress. I have not changed it. I speak in my language with those who speak, with those who don't speak it, I speak Spanish. And so it is that in these times the community is being ruined." In a country where there is strong pressure to pass as white, the large number of young people who attend conferencias in traditional dress and speak to each other in Quichua works as a conspicuous display of modern Indian identity.

Like the rival fiestas, the conferencias are also displays of traditional music. In fact the service in progress seemed mostly an endless singing contest. Dressed in their bright anacos, groups of *panicuna* "sisters" from comuna after comuna were awaiting their turn to display their vocal powers. While they waited, they shared food and joked with musicians from other comunas. As the evening wore on, local deacons introduced one group after another by the comuna from which they came. José Naula, a son of one of the first converts in El Troje, expressed the goal of evangelical Puruhá music like this: "Music makes me move so that I can live. I should express my own community without speaking badly of anyone." Despite his position as director of the Quichua-language broadcasts of the World Radio Missionary Fellowship (probably the same broadcasts Father Federico Aguiló blamed for taking away the creative impulse of fiesta music), Naula's criterion for good music has a certain traditional character to it. The music that displayed the most powerful suerte was traditionally that which expressed the singers' own comuna without any envy of the rival comunas. From a certain angle the conferencia singers could claim to display these criteria well. Although they no doubt knew popular Caribbean *cumbias* from the radio, even young evangelical women sang in the falsetto Puruhá style. And even if the lyrics were evangelical, they were not exactly foreign because the words had been composed to express the experience of the Puruhá converts themselves.

In contrast to this singing without envy, Naula charged the musical groups of the rival liberationist Indian movement with envious singing manipulated from outside: "There are persons who are manipulated," he said, "in these last years they are rising up with traditional music, especially in Imbabura. In Imbabura I have heard some singing groups say, 'we are going to have liberation, out with the Yanquis.' I don't like that word. I do not like to speak against a pastor, nor against a country, nor against a whole religion. . . . How good it is to sing, but with good words." The conferencia would go on like that for three more days. The local deacons informed me that two other similar conferencias were in progress at the same time in other Puruhá communities, and that they too were attracting large numbers of young people.

In interpreting the power to attract these young people as a competitive display of Puruhá suerte, I do not claim to have told the whole story. Many of the questions posed by Puruhá conversion need to be answered from the outside by the social sciences. David Stoll, for example, has shed a great deal of light on the Puruhá by placing them in the context of international politics and competition among multinational development agencies such as World Vision.[12] My question, however, has been different: How are broader developments in the hacienda economy, the liquor market, evangelical missions, and the Catholic Church intelligible from within the religious imagination of the Puruhá? And consequently, how does evangelical conversion make sense to them as a development within these traditional institutions?

No outsider can really get inside the indigenous perspective, but I have used Puruhá testimonies and research on Andean religion in Ecuador to try to imagine conversion as a move from inside Puruhá history. I have argued that, from the inside, the competition between conferencia and pan-Indian fiesta can be understood as a modern version of the old conflict over suerte. Who now represents the power of Puruhá suerte and who are the ashcos? At stake in the conflict is the legitimate representation of Indian modernity. The Confederation of Indian Nationalities of Ecuador (CONAIE), umbrella group for the pan-Indian movement, claims the right to represent the 40 percent of Ecuador's population they recognize as Indian. With that claim goes the right to negotiate with the many monied private organizations, businesses, and foreign and national governments interested in the resources of the Indians. In recognition of its right to represent all Ecuadorian Indian peoples, CONAIE demands that all outside funding for Indian groups be channeled through them. The Federation of Evangelical Indians of Ecuador led by Puruhá evangelicals, however, claims as much as a quarter of the Indian population and disputes CONAIE's right to represent them.

Behind the conflict over money and clout are related yet conflicting conclusions about the sources of returning Indian suerte. Leaders of the pan-Indian movement who grew up after Vatican II tend to view the Catholic Church not as a competitor but as an ally in their quest for Indian power. As they see it, it is the hacienda owners, as heirs of the conquerors, who are the main enemy. Fundamentalist missionaries tend to be seen as part of a larger U.S./hacienda-owner plot to destroy the power of the Indian people by destroying their identity—turning them away from the traditional dances, shamanism, and so forth. Consequently, evangelical Indians can look like tzala tucushcas who have sold out their people to U.S. interests. Their present prosperity (shored up by World Vision and other development agencies) seems suspiciously like a U.S. payoff for abandoning their culture.

From the evangelicals' perspective, in contrast, a crucial connection exists between not drinking and the return of Indian power. The worst thieves of Indian suerte, as they see it, were the priests (supposedly allied with the liquor merchants) who forced Indian people to sponsor the fiestas. Consequently it is from the white priests that the blessing now returning to the Puruhá is being drained off. Viewed from the evangelical comunas of Chimborazo, the far-reaching changes in the Catholic Church after Vatican II seem to have strictly local causes. The success of the Puruhá evangelical movement forced their old enemies the priests and their following of Catholic Indians to change tactics. When they saw that they were losing the Indians, the priests copied the evangelicals, began distributing Bibles, and got on the bandwagon of Indian liberation. "The Catholics lost the respect of the Indian people," one Puruhá leader told me, "now once again they want to be given a place [of authority]. So there is a fight between evangelicals and Catholics. We evangelicals are not manipulated. The Catholics want to dominate the world."

In this polarized environment, evangelical Puruhá are suspicious of Catholic priests no matter what they do. Perhaps the best example was the evangelical response to the late Archbishop Leonidas Proaño, a saintly champion of Indian rights. When I interviewed him in 1983, Proaño was particularly concerned with the effects of liquor on the Indian communities. And he told me that when he drove past the evangelical communities, tears came to his eyes because it reminded him of how past failings of the Catholic church had led to needless splits in the Indian people. One would think that with bishops like Proaño, evangelicals might return to the Catholic fold, but Basilio Malán, an evangelical leader from Pulucate, described their response to Proaño's overtures like this:

> One time I had an audience with Bishop Proaño in Riobamba, so that he could ask me why I defended Wycliffe [Bible translators]. I said, "Wycliffe hasn't done any work around here, we don't know them." And so they accused us of having left our culture. A brother said, "Well, Señor Obispo Proaño, would you like to see us back in the condition our parents were in before us? Their poor feet scarred and a little hat sewed over old ones? Do you want to see us like that? Why don't you want to see us now as transformed people? Or don't we have the right to dress with dignity?' So he said, 'Well, yes, but you have changed your culture." So I said to him, "We speak Quichua. Here is my wife, she has not lost her language, the dress that we wear, the *bayeta*, the anaco." I explained all this to him. "We'll talk more about this later," he said, but we never had another meeting.

Because they do not join in the ban on liquor, and because they are often allied with progressive priests like Proaño, even the most dedicated leaders of the pan-Indian movement can seem more like tzala tucushcas selling out their people than like the legitimate winners of Indian suerte they claim to be. In the polarized climate of rivalry, CONAIE's claim to be recognized as the only representative of Ecuadorian Indians seems suspiciously like the old claim of the Catholic missions to be the legal representatives of Indians. And their demand that all development funding be channeled through the national Indian organizations looks like another priestly attempt to regain control of the Indian suerte that was won from them in conversion.

In contrast to the leaders of the pan-Indian movement, evangelicals see themselves as legitimate Indian authorities because it was through their break with drinking and the priests that their fortunes improved. Like the old-time priostes, they are the ones who won back the blessing for their communities. They deny that North American funding organizations such as World Vision are bribing them to abandon their culture. Rather, they see the organizations as vehicles by which economic legitimacy is delivered into the Puruhá communities.

Just as CONAIE's bid to represent Indian identity is made through large public displays of Indian culture and power, so the evangelical claim is made in the conferencia. By rehearsing the story of the Puruhá break with priests and trago, while displaying the modern suerte-like power that has come to them through accepting Christ, the conferencias could be said to solidify relations with the divine sources of power in a manner that attracts still more power, or "blessing." As such, the conferencias work like fiestas to raise the economic pulse of the evangelical Puruhá and to establish their claim as the legitimate representatives of a Puruhá modernity.

Conclusion

This chapter has examined the dynamic transformation of the fundamentalist message as it crosses cultural boundaries. Evangelical Christians are committed, of course, to the idea that it is the *same* Christ who lives in both missionary and evangelical Indian hearts. For them, all of the differences I have explored in this chapter are matters of external packaging. But taking the Puruhá Quichua case as a widely accepted example of conversion, I have argued that when entire Indian communities convert, they do so for traditional religious reasons which they continue to hold even after conversion. The continuities that underlie these reasons are not superficial. They go to the core of religious identity.

My argument is based in part on the logic of testimony. Typically, testimonies have a before-and-after structure in which the after *seems* like a complete break with the before: "I once was lost but now am found, was blind but now I see." Actually, however, there is such strong continuity between the two that the before determines the meaning of the after. To limit the chapter, I have focused narrowly on the comparative meaning of drinking and not drinking, of the fiesta and conferencia. I chose these symbols not because they were the only symbols. Other prominent symbols shared by traditional and evangelical Puruhá might have worked equally well. But these are sufficient to make my point. In Puruhá Quichua testimonies, the before refers to the drunken powerlessness of an earlier age dominated by the fiesta, the *fiesta tiempo*. In contrast the present age could be called the *conferencia tiempo,* because it is in the conferencia that the powerful Indian modernity of the converted life is most clearly displayed. Because the conferencia is a kind of dry fiesta, or counter-fiesta, its meaning must be sought within the religious meaning of alcohol in the fiesta itself.

By comparing fiesta and conferencia, I have argued that some of the most basic religious assumptions underlying evangelical Puruhá piety are shared more with traditional Andean religion than with North American evangelicalism. For both, history is a contest over the economic/religious power traditionally called suerte or *bendición*. This blessing, circulating between groups, is closely associated with Chimborazo and with the fertility of the earth. It resides in the blood and breath. It brings health and prosperity. And it underlies fictive kinship ties between higher- and lower-altitude communities. Because rituals are a competitive display of blessing or suerte, rivalry between groups remains at the heart of religious identity.

Interpreted within this context the Puruhá *conferencia* is not a North American "Bible conference," but a development within the Puruhá complex of rival fiestas which evolved by analogy to those bible conferences. Like the fiesta, it is an occasional festive encounter between comunas in which each comuna competes for blessing through singing and overwhelming hospitality. The major difference between the conferencia and the fiesta is the absence of alcohol in the conferencia. But even this difference is based on similarity. For both, alcohol is the medium of gaining and losing blessing or suerte. And it is within this common field of meaning that abstention makes sense as a winning move.

My conclusion that Puruhá evangelicalism is best understood as an internal development within Andean religion is not meant to question the integrity of Puruhá Quichua conversions or to challenge their understanding of the Bible. Rather, it is a question of what conversion is. I assume that what evangelicals mean by conversion—a complete break with a past religion to become a new creature—is not possible because religious change works through continuities in difference.

Large-scale Puruha "conversion" was possible only because the traditional meaning of alcohol in Andean religion was successfully carried over into evangelical usage. But with that carryover came core aspects of Andean religious identity. Religious identity is not like a house that one can move in and out of. To say that an Indian people has been converted by the preaching of fundamentalist missionaries does not therefore mean that they have moved out of a traditionally Indian home and into a fundamentalist structure imported from the United States.

Most scholars tend to view the impact of missionaries from the outside: North Americans endowed with zeal and funds enter Indian areas with the intent of extending their own ethos. Because they are economically and politically stronger, these latter-day religious conquistadors achieve their purpose. Conversion is conquest. In questioning the adequacy of this scenario, my intent has not been to defend the missionary enterprise. Relatively speaking, missionaries do have tremendous economic power, and they do intend to destroy native religions—a creative cultural heritage that has evolved over centuries of interaction with the Andean environment. But interpreting missionaries as religious conquerors too often assumes passivity on the part of the Indian people, that they were mere patients acted upon by the powerful forces of a foreign culture.

My intent has been to give the Puruhá their due as agents of history. American fundamentalist preaching encountered the Puruhá very late in their history, when they had already long made Christianity their own and when the contest for power with the white world was far advanced. The Puruhá were not simply conquered by foreign money and foreign ideas. Rather, fundamentalist preaching was understood by analogy to the preexisting symbols of Puruhá Christianity. Conversion was a religious response made with some integrity from within that preexisting world. Given the limited options available to them, it was also a strategic move that made sense within the economic contest for suerte. A teetotaling Puruhá may look like a teetotaling Baptist, but it is really a similarity in difference. In the Puruha context, teetotaling is not only a mark of the born-again Christian, but also of ethnic resurgence. It marks a people who in the future may align themselves with ethnically Indian special interests and not necessarily with the conservative agenda of an international Christian right. Teetotaling is also a strategic move in the contest for suerte intelligible within specifically Andean notions of economy. It therefore may not be an indication of a wider Puritan-like thriftiness contributing to the accumulation of capital. Instead, in their conferencias, evangelical Puruhá may continue to consume and display their wealth much as other Andean people do in fiestas.

Notes

1. George Kubler, "The Quechua in the Colonial World," in Julian H. Seward, ed., *The Andean Civilizations,* vol. 2 of *Handbook of South American Indians* (Washington, D.C.: Bureau of American Ethnology, 1946), p. 403.

2. See David Martin, *Tongues of Fire: The Explosion of Protestantism in Latin America* (Cambridge, Mass.: Basil Blackwell, 1990).

3. The quotes are from my fieldwork notes of 1990. All translations are my own. Funding for the fieldwork came from the Arizona State University Humanities Research Award and from the American Academy of Arts and Sciences.

4. Because many Puruhá jambiri cure in private, I was unable to observe firsthand a Puruhá Quichua healing session, but I attended similar healing services in the Calde-

rón area some 150 miles north of the Puruhá in which some of the patients were Puruhá. My sketch of Puruhá healing is based on these closely related services, combined with secondhand reports by Puruhá informants and a reading of the available literature.

5. The encounter between Comadre Rosita, José Chimbolema, and Pedro Vega is a composite sketch created out of various cases that I actually observed in the Calderon area.

6. Federico Aguiló, *El hombre del Chimborazo* (Quito: Ediciones Abya-Yala, 1987), p. 158. The translation is my own.

7. Eileen Maynard, ed., *The Indians of Colta: Essays on the Colta Lake Zone, Chimborazo (Ecuador)* (Ithaca, N.Y.: Cornell University Press, 1966), p. 13.

8. These accounts are found in Ben J. Nickel, *Along the Quichua Trail* (Smithville, Mo.: Gospel Missionary Union), pp. 82–83.

9. Ibid., p. 84.

10. Donald R. Dilworth, "Historical, Ethnological and Sociological Factors in the Evangelization of the Quichuas of Ecuador"

(M.A. thesis, Fuller Theological Seminary, 1967).

11. Aguiló, *El hombre del Chimborazo*, pp. 174–75.

12. See David Stoll, *Is Latin America Turning Protestant? The Politics of Evangelical Growth* (Berkeley: University of California Press, 1990).

"Jesus Is Lord of Guatemala": Evangelical Reform in a Death-Squad State

David Stoll

The vision came when an upper-class evangelical church relocated next to an old colonial aqueduct. The crumbling Spanish brickwork of the aqueduct crosses Guatemala City along the top of a serpentine earthwork left behind by a departed Mayan civilization. As soon as the church started building, government archaeologists leaped to the defense of the pre-Colombian site. But before the church's laborers stopped, they are said to have dug up the head of a snake carved in stone. The leaders of El Shaddai Church interpreted the suddenly revealed archaeology of their new location as a sign: the Lord had brought them face to face with his vision for Guatemala.

Three hundred years before Christ, Pastor Haroldo Caballeros announced, the serpent mound had been built to dedicate the entire country to Satan. Ever since that offering to the plumed serpent, the Mesoamerican god Quetzalcoatl, Guatemala and all of Latin America had been cursed. Why else would a continent so rich in resources and faith be among the poorest and most indebted of the earth? Why else would a country so green and blessed by God be so afflicted with violence and poverty? But now this curse of centuries could be lifted, Caballeros said. It is probably no coincidence that the name of his church, El Shaddai, means "the Almighty" in Hebrew: this was a vision not just for saving souls, but for seizing a country's destiny. Caballeros preached like a polished courtroom advocate—his former profession—and was attracting influential people to El Shaddai, including a man about to be elected president of the country.

Funded by a well-heeled congregation, Caballeros mounted a national prayer campaign to take the vision for overcoming the serpent's curse to every evangelical pastor in the country. Fifty thousand prayer warriors were needed to battle the territorial demons controlling Guatemala, Caballeros declared. God wanted to open up the skies and rain down his blessings. He wanted to bring a revival with so many signs, prodigies, and wonders that every tongue would confess that Jesus is Lord of Guatemala. Uplifted by an army of prayer, the church would rise up like a giant. It would prophesy over Guatemala, liberate it, and turn the curse into a blessing.

More than a little vision was needed to see 1990 as a year of blessing for Guatemala. As Caballeros took his prayer campaign to the provinces, business leaders in the capital were uttering wounded cries. At a meeting of the Full Gospel Business Men's Fellowship, in a luxurious hotel a few blocks from the serpent mound, another member of the elite began his testimony by lamenting the sudden fall of the national currency against the U.S. dollar. His father had been one of Guatemala's most feared military presidents, under whose administration death squads became rampant. Young René[1] thought that he too would become president, but that was before surviving an assassination attempt and learning to sleep with a machine gun under his bed. He too had belonged to Guatemala's far right, René told the Full Gospel businessmen. But now he and a Catholic priest he had persecuted were working side by side to evangelize the country. (This was so despite the fact that Full Gospel is considered a Protestant organization, in a country where the Catholic Church warns its flocks against Protestant wolves in sheep's clothing.) Instead of becoming president of Guatemala, René had become the first president of this chapter of the Full Gospel Business Men, which was far better. Meanwhile, unfortunately, his country's debt crisis was getting worse. It was not right, he told the assembled Christian businessmen, that an economy revolving around the dollar should lose a quarter of its purchasing power in one week. It was not right that the walls protecting this New Jerusalem of the Americas be thrown down like that.

As René called on God to have mercy on his country, his repentant tone raised the question of whether self-reform was afoot in Guatemala's ruling class. Since 1954, when the United States toppled a government threatening North American investments, men like René had successfully defended their interests against reform and revolution. When guerrillas organized peasants in the eastern part of the country in the mid-1960s, then in the western highlands in the late 1970s, men like René had led devastating counterinsurgency campaigns. Now the Guatemalan army was the country's master, even after turning over the presidential palace to civilians. Repression was so effective that opposition forces seemed to have little popular support, even after the buying power of the average person had plummeted and hunger was rampant. The most popular recipe for advancement was leaving for the United States.

One of the few popular movements which thrived in this climate of fear and deprivation was born-again Christianity. Imported from the United States in the nineteenth century, evangelical Protestantism has gradually become less dependent on foreign patronage.[2] One sign of taking its own direction is the popularity of Pentecostal forms of worship, that is, baptism in the Holy Spirit, as manifested by speaking in tongues, faith healing, and prophecy. Even though the original missions opposed such practices, Pentecostals have become a large majority of Guatemalan Protestants. Their churches are growing so rapidly that, by 1990, Protestant leaders claimed 30 to 35 percent of a traditionally Catholic population.[3] Although the majority of Guatemalans still identify themselves as Catholic, the number active in church life has been outstripped by the number of active Protestants. It is common for several times as many people to be meeting in new cinder-block chapels as in the imposing colonial church in the plaza. Moreover, Guatemala is only the most striking instance of the evangelical, mainly Pentecostal, growth taking place all over Latin America.

Like brethren in other Central American countries, Guatemalan Protestants usually refer to themselves as *evangélicos*. Although few call themselves *fundamentalistas,* their devotion to the Bible, to being "born again," and to evangelism identify them in important ways with North American fundamentalists. Like their missionary mentors from the United States, they believe in strict abstention from alcohol and other vices, uphold the "fundamentals" of the faith, and trace their spiritual genealogy to the fundamentalist revolt against the mainline North American denominations early in the century.[4]

Yet the change in cultural context, from Anglo to Hispanic America, has stretched the usual associations of the fundamentalist moniker. While U.S. fundamentalists want to restore the traditional religious values which they believe made their country great, Guatemalan believers do not clamor to return to their own religious and cultural roots. In Guatemala, such antecedents would have to be found not in Protestantism, but in the Mayan civilizations destroyed by the Spanish Conquest or the Catholicism imported from Spain in the sixteenth century. Instead of returning to their roots, evangelical leaders want to tear them up. Blaming Guatemala's backwardness on its Hispanic Catholic heritage, they want to remake themselves and their country in the image of another society which they idealize along fundamentalist lines—the United States. Despite all the conservative associations of the term "fundamentalist," these believers dream of a cultural revolution, a new outbreak of the Protestant Reformation which, this time, will penetrate the Hispanic pale. A movement that secular observers dismiss as a hopeless crusade to return to the past, or as a negation of the ability of human beings to shape their own future, is to believers a crusade to adopt a new cultural heritage and construct a godly future.

Evangelical churches in Latin America have, for the most part, been movements of the self-improving stratum of the lower classes. Researchers have concentrated on evangelicals in villages and poor urban neighborhoods. They have wielded concepts like migration, acculturation, and modernization to describe the adjustment of marginal populations to larger social forces. The resulting studies suggest the ability of evangelical Christianity to empower individuals, reform families, and elevate community morals.[5] But until recently, evangelical movements were relatively small except in Chile and Brazil, and they had not influenced the Hispanic elites of the region. Consequently, what has not been asked is whether born-again religion can effect social change on a larger scale. Now that born-again Christianity is breaking through its previous ceiling in the middle class, disseminating higher in the social scale, and broadening its vision, its success raises new questions. What will it look like when practiced by elites? Will upper-class evangelicals behave any differently than upper-class Catholics? How are the aspirations of evangelical elites constrained by the political economies in which they find themselves? Can evangelical practices change those political and economic systems?

If evangelical reform is visible anywhere, it should be in Guatemala, where the percentage of evangelicals is the highest in Latin America and elite churches have become more prominent than in other countries. Indeed, two of the last four heads of state have been evangelicals, an unprecedented turn of events in a region where elites have been almost exclusively Catholic. To ask how born-again religion could affect the social system, in 1990 I interviewed twenty-five evangelical leaders about the ways their movement is changing how power is exercised in Guatemala. When they told me that the Gospel prevented men from coming home drunk and abusing their families, I asked, "What about the army? What about political parties, the state bureaucracy, and business?" If Protestantism helps peasants control their drinking habits, can it persuade lawyers and colonels to obey the law?

The Protestant Challenge to Catholic Hegemony

Evangelical churches have grown steadily in Guatemala for decades, but not until the 1970s did they become omnipresent in the social landscape. Only in the next decade did they begin to look like a potential source of political and cultural hegemony, as symbolized in the figure of a born-again dictator. Significantly, the early 1980s were the same years in which the revolutionary movements of Central America were at their height. In Guatemala, the army was on the point of losing control of the western highlands when, in March 1982, junior officers staged a reform coup against their corrupt high command.

Unknown to the conspirators, the retired general they installed as head of the new government had, not long before, joined an evangelical sect based in California. General Efraín Ríos Montt did not just promise to end government abuses and restore order, as the heads of military juntas usually do: he also declared he had been put in power by God. He halted death-squad kidnappings in the capital, cleaned up civil administration, and harangued Guatemalans to change their sinful ways. In the countryside, unfortunately, the army continued its rampage against peasants suspected of supporting the guerrillas. According to Amnesty International, 2,186 men, women, and children were killed in rural Guatemala during Ríos Montt's first fourteen weeks in office.[6]

Banned political parties, the Catholic Church, and the Left denounced Ríos as a tyrant who was plunging the country into a holy war. Internationally he became known as the born-again butcher. Paradoxically, for many Guatemalans Ríos Montt's sixteen months in office were a return to relative stability compared to the random massacres of the previous regime. In the 1990 presidential race, to the horror of establishment politicians who regarded him as unpredictable and dangerous, the ex-dictator became the most popular candidate. Only a constitutional ban prevented him from being elected.

Under Ríos Montt, the Catholic hierarchy warned that evangelical growth was a political strategy to dominate the country. Most Catholic clergy in Guatemala conceded the right of parishioners to join dissenting churches. But as more evangelicals defined their faith as a basis for political action, their new activism threatened Catholic claims to be the national church.[7] At one time the Catholic Church wielded considerable power in Guatemala. The very bulk of its installations, surpassing anything else on the traditional landscape, suggests their importance. The huge old churches in Indian towns were set up to overawe a peasant population conquered by the Spanish Empire. Particularly in these towns, which once made up most of the population, Catholic clergy could be more influential than a colonial or republican government. When dreams of modernization stirred the Guatemalan elite in the nineteenth century, the Catholic Church stood in the way with its hold on rural land, labor, and popular ideology. Modernizers had to break clerical authority, a process which began in the civil wars of the nineteenth century and continues today.

Just as telling have been internal weaknesses in the Catholic Church.[8] Priests were always in short supply, but the system itself was unable to respond to new spiritual needs when the colonial order broke up. As traditional agrarian communities diversified, so did the requirements of the people in them: while some sought solace in communal traditions, others wished for the kind of discipline associated with religious sects. Even though Catholic missionaries responded with great creativity—through new pastoral organizations, development projects, and political organizing—they were unable to respond to everyone's needs.[9] In particular, they were not able to satisfy a growing hunger for conversionist religion, the emotional, transformative kind of faith which has helped so many people adjust to the social dislocations of capitalism.

Brought in by a supportive Liberal state and a wide-open market economy, the evangelical missionaries and their converts ended the Catholic monopoly. The evangelical style of leadership was more egalitarian than Catholic authority: while the traditional Church jealously guarded clerical prerogatives, old-fashioned sectarianism—the splitting of one church from another in endless personal and doctrinal quarrels—opened up the leadership of evangelical churches to anyone who had the charisma to exercise it. While Catholics struggled to sacramentalize huge parish populations, new Protestant groups focused all their energy on recruiting the most spiritually restless, in a competitive drive to build up followings.

These disadvantages were still somewhat hidden, and the Catholic Church still a central institution in many Indian towns, when what priests refer to as "apocalypse" struck. The Church was still considered a conservative institution when, in the 1960s, the army's accelerating domination of political life began to radicalize clerics and lay leaders. By the late 1970s, even conservative priests began to speak out about the atrocities committed in counterinsurgency campaigns. Enraged by the resulting human rights reports, the army accused the Catholic clergy of collaborating with the guerrillas and, over a three-year period, killed more than a dozen priests and hundreds of lay leaders. The position taken by Guatemala's evangelical leaders was quite a contrast: they stood by silently, praying for divine intervention. They rarely expressed sympathy for the many Catholic pastoral agents murdered by security forces. Instead, they were more likely to justify the persecution by repeating army propaganda about priests storing guns in rectories. Although unheroic, their posture sheltered members from reprisals and became a powerful draw for Guatemalans seeking sanctuary from the army's wrath.[10]

For Catholics who had been persecuted by the army, a born-again military president seemed to promise more of the same. The outspoken general used his skill with evangelical rhetoric to provide a new moral justification for the army's rhetoric of extermination against alleged guerrilla collaborators, forcing the Catholic Church to maintain a costly oppositional stance.[11] But for evangelicals, the sudden appearance of a military strongman speaking their language and promising to end government abuses was a miraculous answer to prayer.

Even though the shift to Protestantism cannot be attributed specifically to Ríos Montt, everything about his regime dramatized the loss of Catholic authority. His closest advisers in the national palace were elders from the congregation he had joined, the Eureka, California-based Church of the Word. Supporters launched a prayer campaign, based on the Book of Nehemiah, to "rebuild the walls of Jerusalem." The evangelist Luis Palau arrived to celebrate the Protestant centenary in Guatemala and, with Ríos standing beside him, proclaimed that it could become the first reformed country in Latin America. A born-again dictator had dramatized underlying shifts in Guatemalan society which were eroding the traditional position of the Catholic Church. He drew attention to evangelicals and defined their political role in a controversial new way. What had appeared to be a quiescent mass of the poor and lower middle class, apolitical and otherworldly in attitude, began to look like a movement with a vision for running the country.

Evangelical Organization in a Catholic Society

Born-again religion in Latin America is spilling beyond conventional boundaries and reaching into the upper class. Researchers accustomed to looking at Latin American evangelicals in terms of distinct social organizations such as congregations, sects, denominations, and parachurch agencies are finding that increasing numbers of people touched by the movement do not fit the image of a fervent, active member of an evangelical church. If we look at the lived experience of Latin Americans who have been influenced by evangelical Protestantism, rather than their degree of adherence to church doctrine, such experiences spill far beyond the boundaries of evangelical social organizations. If we look at the families, social networks, life careers, and personal interpretations of people who claim born-again experiences, their declarations of faith begin to look more like experiments, and the precise boundaries of doctrine blur into the ceaseless negotiations of social life.

With their rhetoric of separation, of being "in but not of the world," the leaders of evangelical churches make much of their own distinctiveness. If we focus on institutional beliefs, claims, and practices, it is easy to conclude that many evangelical churches seek to avoid the wider society and withdraw into an ecstatic social world. The popularity of Pentecostal forms of worship has heightened the perception of a sectarian movement apart. But when John Page studied the personal networks of

Pentecostals in Brazil, he found that their metaphors of withdrawal from "the world" simply do not reflect their interactions with the rest of society—without which they would be hard put to attract as many other people as they do.[12]

As for the experimental character of evangelical experience, it is evident from the transitory nature of affiliation. Many members pass through a series of churches, eventually become inactive, and may or may not continue to identify themselves as evangelicals. When church-growth researcher Jean Kessler asked a representative sample of Costa Ricans "Have you been an evangelical at any time in your life?" almost twice as many answered yes as currently identified themselves as such.[13] A comparable survey has yet to be done in Guatemala, but now that Protestantism is fashionable, so is dropping out of church life: the number of nominal evangelicals is growing rapidly, as is the number of Guatemalans straddling the fence with identities such as "I'm a Christian."

Evangelical influence has begun to permeate the culture in ways that do not require specific church memberships. Disregarding warnings from their hierarchy,[14] Catholics increasingly explain themselves in pietistic terms borrowed from the Protestant movement. A taxi driver says he's Catholic and then defines it—"we sing hymns too"—by comparison with evangelicals. "Catholics and evangelicals are going to unite because the two are heading for the same objective, no?" he concludes. "I'm half evangelical," another taxi driver says. "I don't go to church but all my family does." In a park crowded with idle men, one says he's a bit of both Catholic and evangelical, then denies that he's an evangelical, insists that he is a Catholic, and explains his faith in quasi-evangelical terms. Above all, he has given up smoking, drinking, and philandering for the undernourished pregnant woman resting beside him. "Guatemala is a beautiful country but Guatemalans are bad," he keeps repeating like a litany. "Throughout the republic, thousands apologize for not being evangelical," a national leader told me.

One example of how evangelical mores are infiltrating a Catholic society, and how evangelical institutions from the United States can be reinterpreted in a foreign context, is the Full Gospel Business Men's Fellowship. Founded in southern California, Full Gospel is a U.S.-based international network of men's clubs dedicated to fellowship in the Holy Spirit. In the 1980s, it expanded rapidly in Central America. By witnessing to business and political elites, Full Gospel hoped to bring peace to the war-torn region. By 1990 there were 150 chapters in Central America, with 59 of them and several thousand members in Guatemala alone. Meetings are held in restaurants and hotels, with rows of men in business suits sitting down to lunch like the Rotary Club, only to break into a hymn or suddenly jump up and start hugging each other. The climactic event is the testimony of a reformed male—a repentant philanderer, drunk, tax cheat, or worse—who confesses his sins and tells how the Lord changed his life.

The style is clearly evangelical. Full Gospel was started by Pentecostals from the United States, and many of the members there belong to the Assemblies of God. Yet Full Gospel denies being an evangelical organization. Instead, spokesmen say it is organized around testimonies of life transformation, not Bible teaching or preaching.

It does not require new members to make a declaration for Christ, let alone submit to adult baptism—both necessary to join an evangelical church. Instead, Full Gospel proclaims disinterest in where members go to church, and in Guatemala a majority of the members are Catholic. In fact, leadership is firmly in the hands of upper-class Catholics who are said to discriminate against fellow Catholics leaving for evangelical churches.

How could an evangelical organization be captured by Catholics? How could the dividing line between evangelical and Catholic, so emphasized by most church leaders in Guatemala, become so unclear? The men running Full Gospel are products of a religious revival which has brought Pentecostal practices into the Catholic Church in many countries. The charismatic movement dates to the 1960s in the United States, when speaking in tongues, faith healing, and prophecy broke out in the Catholic Church as well as in mainline Protestant denominations. Like their Pentecostal mentors, the charismatics interpreted their experiences as an outpouring of the Holy Spirit. In Guatemala, where many Catholics were also attracted by Pentecostal practices, the resulting charismatic renewal became particularly visible in wealthy neighborhoods of Guatemala City during the 1970s. Full Gospel played a special role, as did less well-known groups like Gospel Outreach of Eureka, California. Unlike local Pentecostal leaders inured to sectarian battle, the North Americans did not demand that Catholic seekers immediately redefine themselves as *evangélicos,* thereby enabling the renewal to reach a wider audience.

The distinction between *católico* and *evangélico* began to blur, with born-again religious experience preached inside parts of the Catholic Church. The renewal became a middle ground where upper-class Catholics could have a born-again experience without taking the socially disprestigious step of declaring themselves evangelicals. Enough charismatics have eventually joined evangelical churches that, from the point of view of many Catholic clergy, the movement is a slippery slope downward into Protestantism. To keep charismatics inside the Catholic Church, the hierarchy has encouraged them to venerate symbols of Catholic authority such as the Virgin Mary, drawing a clear boundary against mariolatry-repudiating evangelicals. From a Protestant point of view, the charismatic renewal has become a clerical tactic to slow the defection of Catholics to evangelical churches. Full Gospel is so undemanding of Catholic members who continue to smoke cigarettes, wear crucifixes, and honor the Virgin Mary that dissidents eventually started a new network to uphold evangelical distinctives, the Hombres Cristianos (Christian Men). Even the name of the new group suggests the popularity of obscuring the Catholic-Protestant boundary.

Enough charismatic Catholics have turned evangelical to contribute to a new style in Guatemalan Protestantism, the "charismatic" or "neo-Pentecostal" churches. The most well known is the Church of the Word which Ríos Montt joined, via the charismatic renewal, a few years before coming to power. Neo-Pentecostals tend to be more urban, literate, prosperous, and higher in the social scale than traditional Pentecostals.[15] Unlike most Guatemalan evangelicals, who are poor and getting poorer, neo-Pentecostals come mainly from managerial and upper classes which continue to batten on agribusiness exports to the United States, a regressive tax system, and sundry monopolistic structures concentrating income in their hands. In contrast to most Guatemalans, they tend to have money to spend in the U.S.-style shopping malls going up along the capital's traffic arteries. On Sunday mornings, parked cars ring their churches. Because of rapid growth, neo-Pentecostal congregations often meet in unconventional places such as convention halls, hotels, and circus tents. A thousand or more people at a service is not unusual. These are superchurches, of the kind popular in the U.S. Sun Belt, led by masters of ceremonies who choreograph services as smoothly as if they were television shows. Neo-Pentecostal churches are known for their warmth as well as glitz, however, thanks to their well-organized networks of "house churches." These smaller-scale worship groups and Bible studies meet in homes and neighborhoods. If you don't like one home worship group, you can always try another, or move on to the latest superchurch to become fashionable, as did many members of the Word Church who left for El Shaddai in the late 1980s.

The location of neo-Pentecostals in the privileged class makes them receptive to the North American religious right, whose messages have been transmitted in increasing volume over the subsidiaries of electronic evangelists like Pat Robertson and Jimmy Swaggart.[16] Indeed, one of the reasons upper-class Catholics have become interested in the born-again message is their reaction to the social teachings of the Catholic Church and the leftward politicization of part of the clergy.[17] Neo-Pentecostals are particularly attracted to the "prosperity" or "health-and-wealth" gospel popularized by such media.[18] This palatable doctrine that God wants Christians to enjoy the good things in life implies that poverty and misfortune reflect a lack of faith. While the health-and-wealth gospel retains the evangelical language of sin and repentance, it promises that personal transformation will be rewarded by affluence—quite a contrast to the humble rewards of self-restraint and survival sought by lower-class evangelicals. What appeals to neo-Pentecostals is a gospel of personal possibility in a situation that still offers them, unlike most Guatemalans, the chance for U.S.-style middle-class consumption and upward mobility.

At first sight, this is not a Christianity that agonizes over social obligations beyond the congregation and family. Most neo-Pentecostals belong to the social classes whose privileges the Guatemalan state protects, not the classes it represses. Like traditional evangelicals, most neo-Pentecostal pastors teach that the purpose of the church is confined to saving souls. But neo-Pentecostal congregations have so many connections with national institutions that they have created the impression that evangelicals as a group are moving from political withdrawal to engagement. Ríos Montt's brief rule in 1982–83 was simply the most visible sign of their emergence and connections. Born-again religion has percolated upward into social strata whose members habitually engage in politics, hence they are receptive to the admonitions of evangelical theologians for "social responsibility." The emergence of congregations in wealthy neighborhoods, together with upward mobility in older denominations, has created a new stratum of evangelical professionals eager to project their principles into society and politics. As a result, even "health-and-wealth" Christians can start to look like reformers.

Despite all the attention to flamboyant elite churches, evangelicals are still underrepresented in the upper strata compared to the lower. In the capital, elite evangelicals cluster in less than a dozen churches, including Word, Elim, Christian Fraternity, El Shaddai, and Shekinah—which have drawn on the charismatic renewal or split off from other churches that did. Even in the most prestigious churches, the upper class (owners of substantial firms or properties) is outnumbered by the upper-middle class (such as managers and professionals) and lower-middle class (such as taxi drivers and schoolteachers). The Full Gospel network is considerably diluted in this sense: while chapters meeting in luxury hotels are clearly upper class, those in the passé hotels of the old city center are made up of mid-level civil servants and owners of small businesses.

Of the Guatemalan elite, that is, owners of plantations or firms, only a small percentage has turned evangelical to date. One missionary estimated that even if 30 percent of the country as a whole is evangelical, as few as 5 percent of the elite might be. Evangelicals do not appear as a recognizable interest group in the powerful business lobbies known as the Comité Coordinador de Asociaciones Agrícolas, Comerciales, Industriales y Financieras (CACIF). But they are best represented among owners of "modern" businesses based on the importation of foreign technology. Evangelicals are least well represented in the more conservative wing of the bourgeosie. These are the owners of plantations, who grow coffee and other exports, and whose requirements for labor control did much to create the institution of the death squad. Plantation owners include many army officers, active and retired, and they are the dominant wing of the Guatemalan elite. Despite testimonies like René's quoted at the beginning of this chapter, the evangelical gospel seems to have made less impression on them than on the rest of Guatemalan society.

The Power of Prayer

The ideology of empowerment has become popular in elite churches. Wherever I went in search of evangelical impact on the Guatemalan social order, one name kept cropping up—Paul Yonggi Cho of South Korea, whose occasional visits to Guatemala have inspired many pastors there. Prophet of the megachurch, Cho has organized in Seoul what is said to be the largest congregation in the world. Worshiping with half a million people under the same organizational roof does not appeal to everyone, but for neo-Pentecostals, who have been shaped in so many ways by the church-growth movement, bigger is usually better. Yet it is not just the size of Cho's church which has impressed Guatemalan evangelicals, but Cho's country as well. Until recently poor and oppressed, it has suddenly leaped into the ranks of the industrial countries. The analogy to Guatemala is clear, or so believers hope, because Paul Yonggi Cho preaches the power of prayer. If South Korea has achieved its economic miracle through prayer, perhaps Guatemala can do the same.[19]

What neo-Pentecostals call "prayer warfare" or "spiritual warfare" may seem strangely triumphalistic in a situation such as Guatemala's. Projecting their hopes and fears in the language of millennialism, many fundamentalists continue to voice pessimistic scenarios in which an ever more sinful world rushes downward to destruction, redeemable only by the physical return of Christ. Yet eschatological gloom has not precluded wildly optimistic scenarios for national redemption, from some of the same prognosticators. During the early 1980s, such interpretations became so popular in the North American fundamentalist movement that they became known as "dominion theology"—the central tenet being that the Lord has given Christians dominion over the earth and wants them to exercise it.

In Guatemala, the usual pessimism still reigns in lower-class churches, which are experiencing the full cost of economic crisis, and doomsday is still available in upper-class churches for events provoking sufficient anxiety. But better-off Christians have increasingly been drawn to visions of dominion, encouraged by visiting evangelists insulated from the day-to-day costs and compromises of living in Guatemala. Like millennialism in any time and place, dominion theology gives believers a place in the divine plan, a sense of themselves as actors, of being someone who can make a difference, and it positions them for social and political action in the cosmic drama.[20] The rhetoric of empowerment has been most attractive to members of the elite and hopeful new professionals from the middle class, people wishing to affirm their social position and assert a new ideology of control against the many threats they face.

For evangelicals accustomed to living under a repressive political system that offers few possibilities for constructive action, the language of activism is prayer. To a non-believer like myself, prayer sounds like passivity and resignation. But asking the Lord to intervene in an impossible situation is not inaction, a North American missionary corrected me. According to him, "You have to get back to providence, to the Book of Daniel, for example, and trying to move the hand of God. . . . The more Christians pray, the greater power which angelic forces have over demonic forces. Satan is the prince of this world. . . . He took territory away from God which we now have to reclaim."

Significantly, neo-Pentecostals are making much of demons that, based on biblical precedents, control particular areas.[21] Spiritual warfare against territorial demons provides a graphic frame of reference for believers struggling to exert their influence over communities and nations. As I pressed for a nonprovidential chain of causality, a pastor explained helpfully: "If God controls the universe and I pray to him, he can work in several ways. He can change the hearts of people, for example. There is a great quantity of Christians who do not live as such. They don't pay their taxes, they don't stop at traffic lights, they don't reject bribes. What would this country be like if they started behaving like Christians?" Certainly prayer could mobilize whoever was praying, and that could affect their social attitudes.[22]

Evangelicals are groping for ways to translate a reformation in personal morality into a reformation in public morality. The rhetoric of such prayer campaigns as "Jesus is Lord of Guatemala"—about curses and demons, prayer warfare and opening up the skies so that God can rain down his blessings—provides a new moral language to interpret Guatemala's crisis, identify underlying causes, and suggest ways to deal with them. On the analogy of casting demons out of a person, these Christians want to cast demons out of a country. Social exorcism is a language with considerable appeal in a folk Catholic society whose spiritual world is basically animistic. The struggle of prayer warriors to "bind" demons is also a struggle to "bind" the powers of corruption, violence, and poverty.

For lack of a better term for spiritual mobilization as a basis for reforming society, let us call it "moralization." Moralization starts with the traditional evangelical belief in the power of personal moral transformation, of individuals being "born again." To change society you have to start by changing the hearts of individuals, evangelical leaders argue. Change enough individuals, they believe, and you will change society. More honest officials will inhabit the government, Christian military officers will end egregious human rights violations, businessmen and workers will treat each other with greater respect.

But facing a desperate national situation, the manifest power of the state, and destructive conflicts between entrenched political interests, moralization also becomes an ideology for taking control. To the old formula of personal transformation, upper- and upper-middle-class evangelicals are adding a new managerial vision in which Christians take command of society and reform it from on high. The vision is not necessarily plausible; indeed, it seems in stark contradiction to the pragmatics of survival. Nonetheless, let us explore how evangelicals are trying to moralize Guatemalan society from the bottom up and the top down, in sundry ways. These include encouraging men to be responsible to their families, changing other basic social attitudes, serving as "salt and light" in subordinate positions in business, government, and the army, and taking command of the state through electoral politics.

Evangelicals as Salt and Light

When I asked evangelical leaders how their movement is changing the way power is exercised in Guatemala, most found it difficult to answer in the social and political terms I was seeking, except for two with academic training similar to my own. Instead, they answered in terms that seemed most real and evident to them: testimonies of conversion—their own or others—illustrating the power of the gospel to effect personal transformation. Yet such testimonies speak directly to social and cultural issues, the most common of which is how men treat their families. Confessions of machismo also proved the most consistent theme in the dozen or so testimonies of the Full Gospel Business Men's Fellowship I heard.

The story of a salesman I will call Arturo Rivera, a man in his early forties with an innocent face, seems to scour every corner of immorality. His early success working for a transnational corporation was based on getting government buyers drunk, taking them to prostitutes, and blackmailing them into ordering from him. His own drinking made him an "assassin by motor" and, after twenty-seven accidents, completely uninsurable. Finally he was brought to ruin: living in a dwelling with a dirt floor in an outlying barrio, smoking marijuana to escape his feelings of despair, blaming wife and children for his lack of self-control. The turning point came when the dreaded *judiciales* (government kidnappers) arrived, to collect him in payment for his countless debts. To stall the death squad, his abused wife risked her life so he could escape out the back. Suppressing tears at this point, Arturo concluded with how Jesus had changed his life and reconciled him with his family.

A civil servant I will call Alfonso Palacios, forty-eight, described an idyllic childhood in the eastern part of the country. Then the snake in paradise: "The Latin American male is generally a macho, but above all where I come from." Young Alfonso learned to drink, patronize brothels, and brawl. Liquor held little power over him; his great weakness was picking quarrels with other men—hard to believe from his smooth, tranquil face—and with his spouse. Imitating how his father behaved toward his mother, he treated his wife like *basura* (trash) and was proud of it. When she asked to talk with him, he would lose his temper and abuse her. But this life was intolerable, Alfonso continued, because there was no peace in his heart. After coming to the Lord, he could communicate with his wife and children, learned a new approach to traffic accidents, and no longer experienced guns being held to his ear.

Such testimonies do not necessarily tell us how men are actually behaving toward their families, subordinates, and peers. We have no family, congregation, or workplace ethnography for corroboration, nor any statistical comparison of evangelical and non-evangelical behavior. Just because it has become popular to confess in public does not necessarily mean that one's behavior has changed. But there are reasons to take these stories seriously. It is common for wives (including Arturo's, for the record) to vouch that their spouses have improved. The desire of men to make such confessions—at variance with traditional models of masculinity and not easy to make, judging from the weeping—suggests a definite shift in social mores. If so, it should affect not just how men act out their masculinity but the wider system of gender roles, how children are socialized, and conceivably how authority is exercised in the society as a whole.[23]

Even as pietism influences the population, Guatemala's public institutions continue to suffer a lack of credibility. Nothing works the way it is supposed to; nothing is what it seems. From behind the scenes, an all-powerful army has continued to define what is permissible for the civilian governments elected since 1985. While the minister of defense talks democracy, thinly disguised army death squads kidnap dissidents. Understandably, most Guatemalans continue to avoid oppositional politics like the plague—while the politics of opportunism, embraced by the country's civilian political parties, once again flourishes. So long as civilian politicians do not offend the most powerful interests in Guatemalan society, they are allowed to compete for political office and the rewards of corruption. Meanwhile, basic issues like military accountability, land reform, and taxation of the wealthy continue to be off limits.

Hence the habitual silence of evangelicals on issues Guatemalans term *delicado*—the ones that could get them killed. "Evangelicals don't want to denounce the army, or even the police and the authorities in general, or go to court, for fear of reprisals," said one well-known leader. "It's very delicate. And not only for evangelicals. For Catholics, too. The Catholics only do it through their bishops. It is the principal problem Guatemalans face—fear of reprisals. That if they denounce abuses, they will be driven off, robbed, killed." Out in the churches of the poor and the lower-middle class, most evangelicals are not given to optimistic visions about reforming Guatemala. Such talk is still suspect even in some of the most sophisticated, well-connected urban churches. "We believe that the kingdom of heaven is something which cannot be implanted because it is a kingdom which is not seen," explained a spokesman for the influential Elim Church, where caution reigned. "If the church tries to change established human structures, it becomes humanistic and falls within the terrain of the theology of liberation, of trying to impose the kingdom."

In a movement drawn primarily from the lower and middle classes, in a society with narrow latitude for innovative political leadership, most evangelicals are "in between" rather than "in charge," and will remain so into the forseeable future. What difference can they make? Instead of the grandiose rhetoric of prayer warfare, evangelical leaders are more likely to talk about their followers as salt of the earth, or the leaven which makes bread rise, or as beacons of light.

In the government bureaucracy, many evangelicals have reached middle- and upper-level posts. Presumably they are well placed to serve as salt or leaven. But in institutional systems lubricated by the *mordida* (the "bite" or bribe), in which an appointee who fails to enrich himself is considered a fool or a threat, how do born-again Christians maintain their integrity, let alone encourage morality in government? One high-level administrator told me how he had been able to use a personal relationship with President Vinicio Cerezo (1986–91) to turn down the hordes of job seekers and grafters sent over by Cerezo's party functionaries. But most evangelical functionaries in the Cerezo administration had less leverage and were forced to make excuses for themselves, a missionary reported. Such as "Yes, what can we do about it?" "We're doing what we can," or "If we complain, we're out on the street." "If a person wants to stand firm and not accept a bribe, they fire him," a national leader acknowledged. "That's why many evangelicals accept bribes."

"The evangelical ought to put up a fight against the system of bribes," said the pastor of a church consisting of middle-class doctors, accountants, and engineers. "But it's very difficult. As pastor, I don't have the right to demand a moral stand. Yes, to struggle a bit, but not to the death. Every Christian has to struggle alone and at his own risk, because he can end up without a job in a country with high unemployment." The pastor told the story of a customs official in his congregation who refused to accept a substantial bribe, to allow the private airplane of a well-known family to bypass customs. Soon his life was being threatened, he lost his job and was reduced to selling in the street. Such problems are "daily bread" for pastors of middle-class congregations like his own. "They're in-between," he said of his members.

Evangelical businessmen face similar dilemmas. Obliged to obtain countless permits from government offices, how do they survive without paying bribes? "I don't give bribes but I do make friends," one explained. "Friendships are what is needed. The Christian has to look out for himself by establishing friendships within the government." If he had a problem with the Interior Ministry, the businessman explained, he would go to the corresponding cabinet minister—who happened to attend the Full Gospel Business Men's Fellowship. When passports were needed, he obtained a letter from a congressman permitting him to jump past a long line of suffering applicants. When he refused to pay more than U.S. $1000 in bribes to obtain a telephone, a friend working for the utility had to pay a smaller bribe on his behalf—an ethical distinction which hardly affects how the system works.

Because of the level of patronage and corruption in the state apparatus, evangelicals have a special incentive to set up their own social agencies. The tradition of organizing educational institutions, media enterprises, and relief projects dates to the first foreign missions. During the late 1960s the older Protestant churches began their own agricultural and community development projects in Mayan communities, as well as legal and medical services to the squatter settlements spilling down the ravines behind middle-class neighborhoods. By the late 1980s a wider range of churches was undertaking such projects. While these efforts continue to emphasize personal salvation, they also represent an attempt to devise alternative institutions as a way of changing the system.

Evangelicals were projecting their agenda into vacuums left by the government's bankrupt and demoralized social institutions, sometimes with the backing of U.S. organizations like Prison Fellowship. In the case of juvenile offenders, according to the research institute AVANCSO, evangelical volunteers offer a supportive new social group as well as contacts for gaining a foothold in law-abiding society. They pluck converts out of state institutions and promote the family as the vehicle for reintegration into society. The result tends to be more convincing than what secular social workers have to offer. Evangelicals are helping people in crisis change their lives through one of the few resources at their disposal, religious faith.[24] "We take a message of restoration to all those persons who are not incorporated into the productive life of society," a leader at Elim told me with supreme confidence. "We can rehabilitate every person who takes the decision to restore their souls."

The sternest test of evangelical reform in Guatemala is the most powerful and feared institution in national life, the army. Owing to the intense conformity of military life, evangelicals seemed almost nonexistent in the officer corps prior to Ríos Montt. The general himself was an outsider: when junior officers gave him his moment of glory in 1982, it took the colonels in charge of army bases just sixteen months to replace him with a more conventional military figurehead. Under Ríos, nonetheless, it became customary for base commanders to allow evangelists, often North Americans, to preach to their men and distribute Bibles. By the late 1980s, officers could be found scattered through middle- and upper-class churches. According to the evangelical chaplain for the army's service academy, he was surprised to learn that as many as half of the four hundred cadets identified themselves as evangelical.

Yet believers within the officer corps have to comport themselves with great caution. Unsympathetic senior officers and peers interpret the refusal to get drunk and to philander as a reproach to their own unreformed ways. When a lieutenant published his testimony after Ríos Montt's fall, he was immediately discharged for threatening the institution. Colonels and generals seem to "come out" as evangelicals only after retiring, as if an active witness contradicts the demands of military hierarchy. There are no organized prayer groups in the army, a retired colonel explained, because that would create an impermissible "class within a class."

The four evangelical officers and the chaplain I interviewed all insisted that army commanders did not fear that moral scruples would prevent converts from carrying out orders. Instead, they stressed the duty of subalterns to obey orders. When I pressed them on the subject of human rights, two of the officers mentioned Old

Testament precedents for slaughtering old men, women, and children along with combatants. They went on to narrate anecdotes about providential deliverance from moral dilemmas.[25]

The Government of God

As the foregoing review of evangelicals' practice indicates, it is still not easy to find ways in which born-again Christians are changing the exercise of power in Guatemalan society above the family level. Unable to affect how the army and the state wield power, their main accomplishment continues to be constructing their own alternative system, that is, recruiting multitudes of people into new social groups that insist their purpose is strictly religious. Even if the behavior of individuals and families is changing, it has yet to translate into institutional change, except to further undermine the traditional counterweight to state power in Guatemala, the Catholic Church, at a time when nothing has evolved to replace it—not an evangelical leadership with weight in national affairs, let alone a civil society practicing respect for democratic rights and obligations.

Until recently, evangelicals in Guatemala were a small, powerless minority who tended to avoid politics. If born-again religion ever reformed society as a whole, such change was expected to come only slowly and incrementally, as the result of masses of individual conversions. Then the dramatic example of Ríos Montt awakened evangelical leaders to a controversial new scenario. Perhaps their rapidly growing strength meant that change could be mandated from on high in the presidential palace, by an evangelical president.

The rapid demise of the Ríos Montt experiment underlined the need for caution. After less than a year and a half, the general was removed from the national palace by an army command offended at his holier-than-thou attitudes. Fearing persecution by the Catholic hierarchy and the army, influential pastors retreated to the careful demarcation of political and religious spheres. While members could become politically active as individuals, evangelical churches as institutions should not. To clarify the line of separation, members who became activists or candidates were supposed to resign any church offices they might hold.[26]

Even after evangelicals constituted one-third of the population, the majority of their leaders continued to focus on building up their congregations. Despite considerable mentoring from the North American religious right, these men were all too aware that the Guatemalan context was very different from the North American one. Expanding their scope of action into the political arena meant running more risks than they cared to take. What brought the evangelical movement into politics was less pastoral activism[27] or North American influence than the movement's extension upward on the class scale. As evangelical churches attracted more of the sort of people who customarily jockeyed for power—businessmen, professionals, and military officers—the movement itself changed.

For all the discredit into which the political system has fallen, the aspiring upper-middle level of society still mobilizes around the myriad political parties, as vehicles to compete for advantage in the next regime. Three months before the 1990 election, my interviews with evangelical lawyers and retired military officers unexpectedly turned into interviews with hopeful future deputies, and my quest for social vision bumped into their own political hopes. The head of a state enterprise proved to be a presidential candidate. At one point he threw back his head and warbled at me in tongues, then outlined his platform. It was based on Deuteronomy 28 ("Thou shalt lend unto many nations, and thou shalt not borrow"), and he referred to it as the government of God.

Evangelical politics in Guatemala point toward two different styles of authority. Ríos Montt exemplified the dream of the strongman in power, enforcing change from the top down. For his supporters, many of whom were Catholic, his status as a military man was at least as important as his religion, as summed up in the widespread belief that here was a *militar recto,* a just military man. The hopes invested in the figure of the general dated back further than the country's Protestant churches. Ríos was instantly recognizable as the nineteenth-century *caudillo,* the man on horseback who saves the nation.[28] He represented a traditional (and Catholic) style of authority, yet he talked like an evangelist, preaching that Guatemalans could save themselves and their country through moral exertion. In particular, he was attempting to translate the military virtues so abhorred by many foreign observers—obedience, discipline, devotion to authority—into a new culture of civic responsibility premised on a different kind of authority, the law. "Guatemala is not the police, the captain, the mayor, or the congressman," he told crowds during the 1990 election. "Guatemala is you! The mayor may think he is the authority. The captain may think he is the authority. The policeman may think he is the authority. But authority is he who obeys the law! Even if he has a pistol or a machine gun, this is not authority!"[29]

As a general accustomed to rule by fiat, Ríos was not a very consistent example of the virtues he was preaching. To the discomfort of many, including Protestants concerned about church-state separation, his fervent moralism sounded like a fundamentalist theocracy. Nor did the military chain of command he envisioned from God through himself to the nation sit well with the prevailing style of evangelical leadership, that is, the mutual deference of independent church leaders with no claims to authority over each other. In a sense, Ríos Montt's authoritarianism was a step backward for a movement that, owing to its decentralized form of organization, pointed toward a civil society where authority was based on checks and balances. This was the second style to which evangelical religion pointed—a kind of participation evident in many evangelical churches, but one that had yet to be practiced on the level of national politics.

Revealingly, it took the stern, imposing figure of Ríos Montt to galvanize evangelicals for electoral competition. The quietism of evangelicals had, as their numbers increased, become a loud silence, as if they were an incipient political formation for Guatemalans rejecting the established parties. But they were not a ready-made constituency, as born-again politicians learned when the country returned from a military to a civilian regime. The evangelical contender for the 1985 election was Jorge Serrano Elías, a businessman reformer whom Ríos had appointed to preside over his advisory Council of State. To ward off charges of an evangelical power grab, Serrano's managers denied that they were mounting a religious campaign; but they were mainly evangelicals themselves, and they tried to organize through pastors. The results were disappointing: even though Serrano placed a respectable third—ahead of all the traditional right-wing parties—evangelicals failed to materialize as a bloc, and he obtained only 13.8 percent of the vote. Like the rest of the electorate, the majority of evangelical voters chose the Christian Democrats, a centrist party that originated in the Catholic reform politics of the 1960s and had suffered considerably from army repression.

Although an appealing candidate, Serrano was completely overshadowed in the next presidential campaign by his former chief—until Ríos Montt was thrown out of the race by a constitutional proviso against candidates previously brought to power by coup d'états. President Serrano—elected in January 1991 to serve until 1996—offered a different translation of born-again religion into the public sphere. As a politician, he represented businessmen who placed a high priority on peace and stability as the necessary basis for carrying out neoliberal reforms of Guatemala's state and economy. Serrano was a far more conciliatory figure than Ríos, a consensus builder rather than an authoritarian, who took care to emphasize that he did not govern as a representative of the evangelical church. His mother's family were Maronite Christians from Syria, part of an immigrant business community accustomed to making up for its lack of a power base by making deals.

Prior to election, Serrano demonstrated his negotiating skills by participating in a semi-official "national dialogue" between various sectors of Guatemalan society and the revolutionary movement. Once in office, he was able to bring a reluctant army to the negotiating table with the guerrillas. But he was not about to confront the army over its murder of dissidents. When he raised the issue of "impunity," that is, the unaccountability of the powerful before the law, he was rewarded with an increase in death-squad activity. Typical as well was Serrano's success in stabilizing the national currency against the dollar. While skillful management was part of the reason, another was Guatemala's conversion into a haven for laundering illegal drug profits—the only plausible explanation for an explosion of luxury construction in the capital, even though, for most of the population, the economy continued in recession.[30] Like other reformers being elected across Latin America, he faced an international debt crisis pounding the majority of the population into the ground, elites unwilling to make concessions, and a political system too compromised to extract even minimal compromises and reforms.

Prayer Warfare and Social Reform

Most evangelical leaders still assume that Latin America can follow U.S. models. Based on their own born-again experiences, in which they rose into the middle class (or managed to stay in it) by avoiding costly vices, they believe that the most fruitful response to social evils is to convince more individuals to change their lives. As for structural injustice, making the exercise of authority more honest and responsible is their answer, not forcing radical structural changes. If enough people follow the rules, evangelical leaders believe, existing institutions will function the way they are supposed to, with a broader distribution of rewards and more respect for civil liberties.

What this means in terms of church politics is suggested by the position espoused by the main evangelical association, in national reconciliation talks with the guerrilla movement. At a 1990 encounter, the representatives of the Evangelical Alliance of Guatemala explained that it was not their duty to examine the historical, social, and economic causes of Guatemala's civil war (which would involve confronting the army over its domination of national life). Instead, they said, evangelical churches were accomplishing a silent form of social work which was transforming Guatemalan society from the ground up.[31]

What does this ameliorative approach offer for reforming the institutions of power in Guatemalan society? Could a new language for talking about the problem of authority change how that authority is exercised? Evangelicals claim that, eventually, it can. To quote Ríos Montt:

> I don't propose an economic program but rather an ethical and moral one. Our problem is disorder. We have to put order into our lives. We need law, order, and discipline. Not Fascism or Nazism, just order and discipline. Restoring order is not a question of administrative measures. It's a matter of setting a moral example. What's important is that the people understand that we know what the law is and that we will apply it. Democracy isn't letting people do whatever they want. Democracy means freedom with responsibility. Democracy means fulfilling your duties.[32]

"In prayer to raise up a nation," an evangelical social worker explains, "breaking spiritual bonds implies having an attitude more open to the changes which are necessary. . . . Then social changes can occur more easily." For example, evangelicals claim, prayer can attack the historical curse of the Spanish Conquest which has done so much to keep Guatemala poor and backward. How so? "You have to understand this country in terms of the Conquest," a businessman told me. "The mentality of the conqueror and the conquered is the great tragedy of this country. It has divided the country in two"—between Indians and the non-Indian Ladinos who discriminate against them. Latin Americans have long blamed their problems on *la mancha indígena* (literally, "the Indian stain")—their failure to exterminate the indigenous population as effectively as did the Anglo settlers of North America. The evangelical businessman have a different perspective on the problem: Christians have the responsibility to teach Ladinos and Indians to treat each other like brothers, and prayer will generate the spiritual dynamism to do so.

Can born-again practice affect the political culture of Guatemala and encourage more equitable social relations? The most detailed argument for such possibilities has been made by the sociologist David Martin. Drawing historical parallels with Protestantism in Europe and North America, Martin describes how evangelicals set up a private, protected sphere—the congregation—that becomes a "free social space" or "protective social capsule" for generating more egalitarian social relations and forms of authority.[33] The resulting reforms can become a model for changes in the wider society, as occurred in nineteenth-century England when the morality of dissenting churches infiltrated the Anglican establishment, or as Pentecostal experience has infiltrated the Catholic Church through the charismatic renewal. Martin's colleague Peter Berger goes further, calling Latin American Protestantism a nascent "revolution-in-the-making" of the bourgeois variety, with the potential to build "democratic capitalism" in Latin America. Under the influence of Protestantism, Latin America is finally to imitate the pluralistic norms and broad economies of the Protestant heartland in Western Europe and the United States.[34]

Evangelical leaders themselves are making hopeful analogies to South Korea, whose huge, disciplined evangelical churches presumably explain its successful industrialization. But compare South Korea with the other boom economies of the East Asian rim, in Taiwan and Singapore where Christianity is largely absent, and Protestantism can hardly be seen as the key variable. In the case of Guatemala's evangelical elite, prayer warfare against curses and demons could provide a language that actually inspires reform, or it could become a quasi-magical rationale for failing to deal with the structural reasons for national backwardness such as the failure to control the extreme right, push through basic administrative reforms, and broaden the country's internal market.

The reformist bourgeoisie remains an elusive category in Guatemalan society. According to researcher Marcie Mersky, three political tendencies predominate in the Guatemalan upper class. The first is the "old guard," who do not believe in the rule of law and oppose political modernization. Such unrepentant reactionaries are outnumbered by what Mersky calls the "majority tendency," who support a return to constitutional government but only on the army's terms. While this second tendency in the Guatemalan bourgeoisie gives lip service to democracy, its loyalties remain with the national security state which the army maintains behind the façade of changing regimes. A third sector of the bourgeoisie, "the new modernizing right," centers around new industries and nontraditional exports. It opposes coups d'état, makes a more convincing show of revulsion against death squads, and actively seeks a wider social consensus based on free enterprise. Such neoliberal reformers were exemplified by President Jorge Serrano in the early 1990s, but whether they represented upper-class evangelicals as a whole is open to question.[35]

Evangelical growth may be a prelude to modernization in Latin America. But the Guatemalan case is hardly analogous to earlier situations of Protestant-inspired change and reform. The Guatemalan context puts severe restraints on the ability of aspiring reformers even to speak out, let alone accomplish anything. Like other Latin Americans, Guatemalans are also being caught in deeper and more disadvantageous forms of dependency on the global capitalist economy. With the country becoming a free trade arena for transnational giants, competitive forces are likely to undermine the kind of small-scale entrepreneurialism which Protestantism is supposed to promote but which in fact is already well established in Latin America.[36]

Evangelicals are also facing new obstacles in the extremely strong, contradictory messages of consumerism which emanate from the United States even more powerfully than Protestantism does. In the Quiché Maya town of Sacapulas, I found Assemblies of God elders, men in their thirties and forties from an upwardly mobile generation of schoolteachers and civil servants, worshiping in a handsome new temple which was almost empty. Afterward, they lamented that their younger siblings and children were converting instead to the town's new satellite dish. Jesus Christ had been very popular with the town's youth in the 1970s; now their successors were more interested in rock music and video.[37] Sociologist Timothy Evans distinguishes between the early stage of modernization, which entailed building infrastructure for an export-oriented world economy, and the contemporary stage (some would call it "post-modern"), with its "intense development of modern means of mass-communication (especially television)" and "wholesale dissatisfaction with the quality of life chances and life styles available to the people."[38]

Any argument for Protestant social reform depends on the faith (or at least on the values associated with it) passing to the next generation. But to the extent that modern capitalist economies commercialize images of sex and violence and encourage habits of instant self-gratification, the resulting patterns could undermine the reproduction of born-again churches and their ability to serve as a vehicle for cultural change. The "health-and-wealth" gospel is an attempt to resolve this contradiction by promising that believers will receive the rewards of modern consumption. But it may not be a very stable solution, as the poverty of the majority of Guatemalan evangelicals is increasing rather than decreasing.

With evangelical growth, the spectacle of Ríos Montt, and the election of Jorge Serrano as a guide, born-again Protestants seemed to be establishing a precarious spiritual hegemony in Guatemala. While the Catholic Church will continue to be an important institution, evangelical assumptions are increasingly defining how Guatemalans understand themselves and their world. No matter how deeply Guatemala plunges into poverty and chaos, the personal discipline encouraged by evangelical churches will have survival value compared to traditional folk Catholicism. What remains doubtful is whether evangelicals will be able to deal with the underlying inequalities and institutionalized violence which have brought Guatemala to its present state.

Notes

1. Not his real name.

2. For an account of Guatemalan Protestantism as a national movement, see Virginia Garrard Burnett, "A History of Protestantism in Guatemala" (Ph.D. diss., Tulane University, 1986).

3. According to O.C. (Overseas Crusades) Ministries, 31.6 percent of the Gua-

temalan population was evangelical by July 1987, not counting Mormons and Jehovah's Witnesses. Roy A. Wingerd, Jr., "Primer reporte general del Credimiento y Distribución de la Iglesia Evangélica de Guatemala de diciembre 1980 a julio 1987," 12 January 1988, pp. 6, 8. For lack of census and survey data in Guatemala, even carefully calculated claims are projections based on (a) the membership which each denomination claims; (b) a multiplier (often rather large, in this case 3.5) to account for unbaptized children and neophytes; and (c) growth rates of reported members for past years, in this case averaging 11.8 percent. The result can be quite misleading. For example, O.C. Ministries predicted that by the end of 1990, Guatemala would be 45 percent evangelical. But available survey data corroborate that Guatemala is unusually Protestant. In mid-1990 a Catholic sociologist found that 30 percent of a random sample of 352 people around Quezaltenango said they were evangelical, while another 5 percent identified themselves as Mormons, Seventh Day Adventists, or Jehovah's Witnesses. Timothy E. Evans, "Percentage of Non-Catholics in a Representative Sample of the Guatemalan Population" (Paper presented to the Latin American Studies Association, Washington, D.C., 4 April 1991).

4. The Central American Mission, still one of the most influential evangelical institutions in Guatemala, was founded by C. I. Scofield, author of the famous Scofield Reference Bible, which defined correct doctrine for several generations of North American fundamentalists. Through the mission's influential seminary and radio station, it has popularized the distinctive fundamentalist eschatology of dispensationalism far beyond the boundaries of its own churches, including such nonfundamentalist "historical" denominations as the Presbyterians. Dennis Smith, "The Gospel according to the United States: Evangelical Broadcasting in Central America," in Quentin Schultze, ed., *American Evangelicals and the Mass Media* (Grand Rapids, Mich.: Zondervan Books, 1990).

5. For Guatemala, see June Nash, "Protestantism in an Indian Village in the Western Highlands of Guatemala," *Alpha Kappa Delta*, Winter 1960, pp. 49–53; and idem, "Protestant Groups and Coping with Urban Life in Guatemala City," *American Journal of Sociology* 73 (May 1968): 753–67. David Martin surveys many such studies in *Tongues of Fire: The Explosion of Protestantism in Latin America* (London: Basil Blackwell, 1990).

At the same time, Protestantism can be associated with new kinds of class stratification. This is particularly evident in indigenous communities where sectarianism erodes social cohesion and undermines previously strong defenses against the outside world. For a case study of Protestantism which is associated with the breakdown of communal authority and the sale of productive land to the tourist industry, in a Cakchiquel Maya town on Lake Atitlán, see Duncan Earle, "Authority, Social Conflict, and the Rise of Protestants: Religious Conversion in a Mayan Village," *Social Compass* (forthcoming). For an analysis of Protestantism both as a moral revolution and as a process of class stratification in another Cakchiquel Maya context, see Sheldon Annis, *God and Production in a Guatemalan Town* (Austin: University of Texas Press, 1987).

6. "Guatemala: The Human Rights Record, 1987" (London: Amnesty International Publications, 1987), pp. 161–68. Not all these killings can be attributed to the army, but local testimony bears out the claim that the army was responsible for the majority of massacres during the period. Indeed, judging from my interviews in the Ixil area of El Quiché Department, numerous army massacres were never reported to human rights agencies, so the actual number of deaths could be significantly higher. For more detailed accounts of Ríos Montt, with differing assessments of his responsibility for human rights violations, see Joseph Anfuso and David Sczepanski, *He Gives, He Takes Away,* republished as *Servant or Dictator?* (Eureka, Calif.: Radiance Publications, 1983). Also David Stoll, *Is Latin America Turning Protestant? The Politics of Evangelical Growth* (Berkeley: University of California Press, 1990); and idem, "Why They Like Ríos Montt," *NACLA Report on the Americas* 24, no. 4 (January 1991): 4–7.

7. Constitutionally, the Catholic Church has been disestablished in Guatemala since 1871. But the Catholic hierarchy argues that Catholicism is essential to national identity. Evangelicals continue to perceive official favoritism toward it.

8. A recent account of the crisis of the

Catholic Church in Guatemala is Jose Luís Chea, *Guatemala: La cruz fragmentada* (Sabanilla, San Jose, Costa Rica: Editorial Departamento Ecuménico de Investigaciones y Facultad Latinoamericana de Ciencias Sociales, 1988).

9. When parish priests inveighed against costly, inebriated fiestas honoring saints, to the satisfaction of peasants redirecting their surplus from communal rituals to personal accumulation, it offended traditionalists. When Catholic priests tried to placate the traditionalists by blessing traditional ceremonies, it offended parishioners intent on breaking with the old ways and encouraged their exit to fledgling Protestant churches.

10. Virginia Garrard Burnett, draft manuscript.

11. Catholics continue to point out instances in which the army manipulates evangelicals against them. In Chunimá, Chichicastenango, in 1990, Catholics refusing to serve in the army's civil patrols were attacked by evangelicals still in the patrols and under pressure from the army. In the Ixcán region, refugees returning from Mexico to accept the government's amnesty were heavily Protestant, with most of the Catholic refugees remaining in Mexico because they refused to trust the army. As a result, evangelical returnees were being assigned cooperative land which used to belong to Catholics. Even at the height of the violence, however, religion was just one of the many kinds of conflict prompting neighbors to take vengeance on each other. The usual relationship was toleration, with mutual recrimination from competing leaders rather than rank and file, who were too busy keeping food on the table to waste energy over religious differences.

12. John Page, "Brasil Para Cristo: The Cultural Construction of Pentecostal Networks in Brazil" (Ph.D diss., New York University, 1984).

13. Of 1,276 adults, 8.9 percent said they were evangelical and another 1.6 percent identified themselves as Mormons or Jehovah's Witnesses, two unorthodox groups whose behavior is sufficiently similar to be often lumped together with evangélicos. Another 8 percent of the sample said they had been evangelical at another time in their lives but not now, suggesting a desertion factor of almost half. Of this latter group of ex-evangelicals, nearly two-thirds identified themselves as Catholic, another third said they had no religion, and the remainder became Mormons, Witnesses, or Jews. Jean B. A. Kessler, "A Summary of the Costa Rican Evangelical Crisis: August, 1989," IDEA/Church Growth Studies Program, Pasadena, California, July 1990, pp. 2, 5–6.

14. The most detailed indictment has been a pastoral letter from Archbishop Próspero Penados del Barrio, "La Iglesia Católica en Guatemala, signo de verdad y esperanza," published in the daily newspaper *La Hora* on 18 January (pp. 16, 22) and 19 January (pp. 16, 22) 1989.

15. For an analysis of the differences between the two, see Smith, "The Gospel according to the United States," pp. 294–95.

16. For a detailed look at evangelical media in Guatemala, see Susan Rose and Quentin Schultze, "The Evangelical Awakening in Guatemala: Fundamentalist Impact on Education and Media," in Martin E. Marty and R. Scott Appleby, eds., *Fundamentalisms and Society: Reclaiming the Sciences, the Family, and Education* (Chicago: University of Chicago Press, 1992).

17. Dennis Smith, "Coming of Age: A Reflection on Pentecostals, Politics and Popular Religion in Guatemala," *Pneuma* (forthcoming).

18. For a description of the prosperity message and the growth of neo-Pentecostal churches in South Africa, see E. S. Morran and L. Schlemmer, *Faith for the Fearful: An Investigation into New Churches in the Greater Durban Area* (Durban: University of Natal, 1984).

19. Cho is such a strict premillennialist that he may not make this claim himself, but the equation was being made by Guatemalan evangelical leaders I interviewed in 1990.

20. For further details on dominion theology, see Stoll, *Is Latin America Turn-*

ing Protestant? and H. Wayne House and Thomas D. Ice, *Dominion Theology: Blessing or Curse?* (Portland, Ore.: Multnomah Press, 1989).

21. For representative interpretations, see John Dawson, *Taking Our Cities for God: How to Break Spiritual Strongholds* (Altamonte Springs, Fla.: Creation House, 1990); and James Robison, *Winning the Real War: Overcoming the Power of Darkness* (Altamonte Springs, Fla.: Creation House, 1991).

22. "Intercession is spiritual defiance of what is, in the name of what God has promised. Intercession visualizes an alternative future to the one apparently fated by the momentum of the current contradictory forces.... It creates an island of relative freedom in a world gripped by unholy necessity." Walter Wink, "Prayer and the Powers," *Sojourners,* October 1990.

23. My point is speculative, but groundwork on the topic has been laid by Elizabeth Brusco, "The Household Basis of Evangelical Religion and the Reformation of Machismo in Colombia" (Ph.D diss., City University of New York, 1986).

24. Asociación para el Avance de las Ciencias Sociales en Guatemala, "Por si mismos: Un estudio preliminar de las 'maras' en la Ciudad de Guatemala," in *Cuadernos de Investigacion,* no. 4 (Guatemala City, 1989), pp. 44–53.

25. One told the following story. A lieutenant in the Salvadoran army fell into an ambush and was taken prisoner by guerrillas. Wounded and in danger of execution, he offered his life to the Lord. After being liberated by his army comrades, he found they did not appreciate his witness, which led to further tests of faith. In battle he was ordered to take the most dangerous positions. When his Christian testimony won over an entire town, he was suspected of making a deal with the guerrillas. Preaching in a church that had been infiltrated, he picked the guerrillas out of the crowd with a question from a Bible quiz. Within ten minutes his message had the guerrillas on their knees, tearful and repentant. Next, even though he had given his guerrilla converts

amnesty, an order arrived to execute them. Under suspicion for collaborating with the enemy, he appealed the order up the chain of command. At last he came face to face with a general. On hearing his story, the general ripped up the order, having just accepted Christ at a banquet of the Full Gospel Business Men's Fellowship.

26. Hopes for organizing a political party with a direct line from God continued to percolate. What more sophisticated leaders wanted to avoid was illustrated by the pastor from Quezaltenango who said he had been told to run for president by an angel. The angel healed him of cancer and ordered him to reorganize the long-defunct Liberal Progressive party, associated with a dictator who was overthrown in 1944. *Hechos* (Guatemala City), 14 January 1990, p. 14.

27. Guatemala's first two evangelical presidents have both collided with pastors and fellow elders over their political plans. In the case of Ríos Montt, the Church of the Word discouraged him from running for president in 1981 but enthusiastically supported his dictatorship the following year. Anfuso and Sczepanski, *He Gives, He Takes Away.* As for Serrano Elías, he was forced to leave the Elim Church following his unsuccessful run for president in 1985.

28. The military strongman was a product of national independence in the early nineteenth century, when authoritarian rule from far-off Spain was replaced by a local elite who tried to institute republican norms. Soon political factions were raising armies against each other, only to let power slip into the hands of warlords. The resulting pattern of misrule has continued down to the present. During constitutional interludes, civilian authority becomes associated with corruption and disorder to such an extent that popular sentiment coalesces around military dictators employing the rhetoric of law and order.

29. Recorded by author in Nebaj, Department of El Quiché, 1 September 1990.

30. "Drug Trafficking Increases in Guatemala," *Latin America Press,* 23 April 1992, p. 5.

31. Marco Tulio Cajas, "La guerra es

inmoral: Queremos la paz," *Hechos* (Guatemala City), November 1990, pp. 39–40. The talks were also attended by the Conference of Evangelical Churches of Guatemala (CIEDEG), which supports the same kind of social critique as the Catholic Church, and is affiliated with ecumenical groups in the United States and Europe but represents far fewer denominations than the Evangelical Alliance.

32. Quoted in Marc Cooper, "The Last Rattle on the Snake," *Village Voice,* 24 July 1990, pp. 35–40.

33. Martin, *Tongues of Fire,* pp. 268, 279, 284.

34. Ibid., p. ix. For different interpretations of the Protestant analogy, see Michael Dodson and Laura Nuzzi O'Shaughnessy, *Nicaragua's Other Revolution: Religious Faith and Political Struggle* (Chapel Hill: University of North Carolina Press, 1990); and Jean Pierre Bastian, *Breve historia del Protestantismo en América Latina* (Mexico City: Casa Unida de Publicaciones, 1986).

35. A fourth tendency, and the smallest according to Merskey, believes that long-term stability requires the redistribution of income to increase the purchasing power of the lower classes. Marcie Mersky, "Empresarios y transicion politica in Guatemala" (Paper for the project Modalidades de los Procesos de Democratización in Centro América, sponsored by the government of Norway and coordinated by Consejo Superior de Universidades de Centro America, 1988), pp. 16–19.

36. Rose and Schulze, "The Evangelical Awakening."

37. Cf. Timothy Evans on the long-established Church of God in San Francisco El Alto, Totonicapán, which also seemed to experience a high rate of nominalism. "I don't like the old folks' ways," said one youth who belonged to the church but did not attend services. "I'd rather go to the disco." Evans, "Religious Conversion in Quezaltenango, Guatemala" (Ph.D diss., University of Pittsburgh, 1990), p. 246.

38. Ibid., p. 292.

Comunione e Liberazione:
A Fundamentalist Idea of Power

Dario Zadra

The movement Comunione e Liberazione (CL) began in Milan, Italy, in 1956. The founder, Luigi Giussani, is a Catholic theologian and priest who remains the uncontested leader of the movement. Giussani's vision is of a revitalized society, with the living actual presence of Jesus Christ as the central source of inspiration for culture, economy, politics, and all of life. His vision is embodied in the diverse economic, cultural, and political organizations that make up the movement, and it is taught in the Scuola di comunità centers which are the heart of the religiously based community Giussani hopes to build.

The movement has spread to thirty countries, including the United States, and has strong organizations in Brazil, Uganda, Germany, Spain, and Switzerland. These national movements are directly influenced by the main Italian model, however, and maintain similar modes of internal and external relations. All have the same president, and all rely on the Italian periodicals of CL (translated into six languages) for their main channel of information. My discussion refers primarily to the movement in Italy, where CL has become a significant cultural and political presence, both in numbers and organization.

The vitality of the movement may be recognized in the strength with which its members place religion at the center of a new worldview and in their evangelistic efforts at transforming the relationship between modern society and religion. The members of CL are convinced that their movement marks the beginning of a renewal of Christianity, for they are certain that the movement gives new expression to the central "fact" affirmed by Christians, that Jesus Christ lived and continues to live. "There is a New Start when the Beginning—the living actual presence of Jesus Christ—again happens as an event of life in the present."[1] CL has come into being, its members believe, because God's grace has occurred in their lives. Thus the movement carries its own intrinsic moral authority (*autorevolezza*), an authority that comes from the transcendent, miraculous experience of grace. Accordingly, while they insist that salvation must come through fidelity to the tradition of the "true Church," they are not "primitivists" seeking a rejection of present institutions and a return to the original sources of Christianity. The contemporary acceptance of the actual presence of Jesus Christ is the central event from which all else comes.[2]

The theology and organization of Comunione e Liberazione developed primarily during the period between 1960 and 1980, when Italy was undergoing rapid social and cultural change. For a time the political situation threatened to collapse into civil war. Unsettling for religious and political life alike, the social turmoil weakened Italian culture, customs, and traditional ways of life. It also engendered a variety of reactions. During this period a large number of new movements reflected and also inspired new forms of social and individual life.

The secularization process preceding this period was long and difficult for the Italian Church. The Church had been a major force in the old Italian regime; but since the eighteenth century, various movements have struggled for democratic reform and political unity in Italian society, a process in which the Church lost much of its cultural and political influence. With time, the strains on the power of the Church increased. Cities and industrial centers grew, and new social and political movements arose, resulting in the religious and political estrangement of most of the working class. The Church finally found its bastion in the people living in the country and small towns. But retreat to the countryside exacted a heavy price: the Church became increasingly defensive and closed. By ancient tradition the Church had been an urban reality; now it presented itself as a minority culture and developed an idealized form of religiosity which laid stress on individual interiority. During the long period of fascism the hierarchy of the Church acquiesced to the regime. Only after the end of the Second World War were people in the Church able to confront afresh the relation of the Christian tradition to the modern political and cultural situation in Italy.

In the post-war period a succession of Catholic movements, including the Movimento di Azione Cattolica, the Movimento dei Laureati Cattolici, the Associazioni Cristiane Lavoratori Italiani, and the Comunità Mariane, aimed at various sorts of social reform. These Catholic movements revived the influence of bishops and pastors in fields of activity that had been ceded over the years to secular institutions. The movements were preoccupied with asking why the Church had failed to understand the cultural and sociopolitical transformations of the last centuries and why the Church had become a force without direction. According to many of the bishops, the Church considered itself besieged by modernity; only a defensive position seemed possible.

The direction of Comunione e Liberazione, however, was quite different. Rather than concern itself with the past, the movement looked toward a new reconstruction of society. Rather than seek compromise with modernity, it issued unequivocal condemnations. Comunione e Liberazione proposed a new form of ecclesial imagination and gave life to a new idea of cultural and political organization in the cities. This resonated with the quasi-revolutionary optimism expressed in Italian social movements of the 1960s and 1970s. Convinced as it was that society had come to a critical and defining stage, CL formulated anew the terms of the position of the Church in society. To the defensiveness of the bishops, CL counterposed a new church—young, optimistic, without the scars of history. By claiming anew the living presence of Jesus Christ as the religious center of the Church, CL adopted an attitude of conquest of the cultural and political arena, guided by a radical criticism of modernity and of the state.

CL condemned the modern world as the source of nearly every political and social ill of recent history. Those who advocate modern ideas about state and culture, ideas built on human initiative and centered on human values rather than on the living presence of Jesus Christ, have been and are considered to be the enemies of CL. Other Catholic movements have also offered new approaches to the position of the Church in society and culture. They too were urban, cultivated, and theologically informed. But these other movements were convinced defenders of the public and secular character of the state and of culture. They considered the condition of individual liberty and responsibility to be the foundation for a sound Church and a sound society. Although such liberal views were common to many Christians in Italy, they proved unable to attract significant support either from the Church hierarchy or from the large organizations of Catholic laypersons.

Thus CL, which openly rejected the secular character of the state, emerged as the religious movement in Italy that most successfully voices a theological critique of modernity and advances an ambitious religious-political project for Italian society. The theological language of CL draws on images that the Italian Catholic Church has itself cultivated over the years, especially the image of a "Church expelled" from Italian society, an image that goes back to the events that brought the papal state to an end. Comunione e Liberazione, therefore, enjoys important support from the Church's hierarchy and appears poised for continued growth.

The Dynamics of Comunione e Liberazione

Central Ideas

The core of CL's worldview stems from two main ideas—that Christ is the saving event in human history, and that religious authority is a fundamental element of the human condition.

The question of power and legitimate authority in Comunione e Liberazione does not start with the premise that freedom of the individual is the primary source of the creativity of human life. Comunione e Liberazione begins with the following premises: the individual's life is defined by the central events of his or her history, the individual lives through society, and society's authority is defined by its normative center. For participants in CL, *the* central event in life is a saving encounter with the communion embodied in the Church. Moreover, society's normative center is located in the religious fact celebrated in that saving encounter. In other words, the Christ event should be at the center of the social history through which individuals live their lives.

Following from these premises, CL holds that the Church provides the principle of authority in society, the principle by which the moral quality of freedom is to be judged. Persons are only free as they live in connection with the central event of Christ; they are only individuals in so far as they live in a society with this event as its moral foundation.

From this postulate derives the determining role played by the principle of power in Comunione e Liberazione. Power is at once individual and social. Because the Church is the expression of the constitutive reality of the event of salvation in history, the Church's religious authority must define history and society. Because the individual's life is to be oriented to that same reality, religious sensibilities have authority over reason or desire. Power is thus located in religious sensibilities and religious institutions, and religious authority holds together the vast range of action spawned by the movement. By claiming religious authority, CL also claims the power to reconstruct society on these premises.

Thus for CL, "authority" is the very principle of orthodoxy. According to Giussani, authority is the way the event of Christ, an event necessary for human salvation, is translated into history. Although most Christian theologies begin by granting a special authority to the life and work of Christ, in CL the authoritative character of the event of salvation is directly translated into the authority of the Church, which guides and binds human conscience. Authority is expressed by the pope or by the moral authority of the founder of the movement or by other persons within the movement who serve as interpreters of CL's distinct religious view. Indeed, the movement defines itself as *Scuola di comunità*, the communal life through which the Church is brought into being.

The idea of translating the authoritative Christ event into present human history takes concrete form in the educational method and the criterion of community building adopted by the movement. "Comunione e Liberazione is nothing but the endeavor of introducing in a pedagogical way the concrete structure of authority of the Church."[3] Specifically, members learn to recognize the event of grace in their own religious sense and experience by imitating a person who already lives the values of the movement.[4]

In this system of thought, the value of human existence emerges not from the individual in isolation but from those relationships that bring individuals into a community. More precisely, value is believed to emerge from the dynamics of the encounter that creates community (language reminiscent of Durkheim's notion that collective vigor and religious faith coincide).[5] Through the present experience of Christ as a person, a "saving condition of community" is created.[6] The Church is the society of salvation originated by faith in Christ. In the Church (especially as experienced through the movement), a redeemed human existence is visible.

Giussani begins his ecclesiology—his ideas about the nature of the Church—with his dogmatic identification of the Roman Catholic Church with the saving event. But he does not stop there. His ideas also include the organic, cosmic, experience of communion with the Church that comes from Eastern Orthodoxy (especially the Russian concept of *sobornost*—the belief that "living in communion" creates a specific knowledge of faith). Giussani also draws heavily from American Protestant thought. In Giussani's "system," the theologies of Johann Adam Moehler and Karl Adam exist alongside those of John Henry Newman; Karl Barth filters in through Reinhold Niebuhr and Paul Tillich; Henri De Lubac coexists with G. K. Chesterton, and Maurice Blondel with Jerome Hamer. Lines of thought taken from orthodox theology are developed together with others absorbed from American revivalism.[7] Giussani is not primarily a scholar or a theologian, but an apologist. His strength is his enthusiastic belief that Christianity can resolve the contemporary crisis of religious conscience.[8] This profound conviction allows Giussani to bring together inconsistent theological starting points: the charismatic character which is assigned both to the historical event of Christ and to the saving encounter with a believing person; a faith which is defined through authority as well as through "authoritativeness"; and an explicit scholastic theology and philosophy used to sustain his argument about the embodiment of salvation in the Roman Catholic Church.

From the beginning, Giussani's ideas about the centrality of the Christ event have been both spiritual and social. The believer was to encounter not an idea but a person, Christ, and that saving encounter was to be made possible by the actual encounter with one who has already known Christ and can be the believer's moral guide. This person-to-person transmission of the faith is, of course, reminiscent of Protestant evangelicals, but it is couched in the language of Catholic sacramentalism. As members of CL encounter the movement, they encounter an actual social reality that claims its authority and salvific power in the founding event of Christ. The authority of that event, they argue, is recognized not through reason but through the faculty of religious sense (*sentimento religioso*).[9] This religious sensibility is made evident to the individual by the perception of his or her moral incompleteness, by intellectual curiosity and wonder, and by a "spiritual hunger" that is satisfied only in an encounter with Christ through an encounter with the movement. This simple theological formula is the dominant and recurrent motif heard from leaders and members alike.

In interviewing both young people who are involved with CL and the leadership of the movement, I have observed that the movement's theological and anthropological positions have a strong and wide-ranging appeal to traditional loyalties and religious beliefs present in Italian society. But CL is different from a traditionalist movement. Its beliefs and practices offer a new religious and countercultural way of looking at modern society and culture. CL boldly claims that the Church embodies authoritative truth that is binding on society at large. By claiming the presence of Christ, the Church also claims divine authority—a kind of inerrancy, not of the biblical text (as in Protestant fundamentalism) but of the Church. The conscience of the individual is shaped by and beholden to the Church, and the Church ought be considered the living and legitimate paradigm of society. This authoritative claim carries with it a direct attack against a set of ideological enemies. The need for religious authority is built on a premise of original sin; thus CL identifies and attacks "Pelagianism." Since "Arianism" does not underline adequately the divinity of Christ, it too is assailed. CL accuses Protestantism of undermining the authority of the pope, and attacks Humanism for its lack of a sense of transcendence.[10]

Thus CL condemns modernity as a cultural and political form of life that has freed itself from any sovereign religious principle. Modernity has subjugated both religion and society to the criterion of reason and to the principle of freedom. CL places itself squarely against this project, claiming that modernity has produced an illegitimate form of power. CL affirms anew the autonomy of religion from reason and religious society's authority over individual choice or responsibility. On that foundation, CL proclaims the legitimacy of direct religious action in the cultural and political field.

The theological ideas that guide Comunione e Liberazione have developed as the focus and membership of the movement have evolved. In the early days of the movement, Giussani was animated by the desire to bring the young students of Milan to an explicit and public affirmation of Christ as the saving event for the individual and society. Then called Gioventù Studentesca (GS), the movement was seen primarily as a social environment supportive of the students' religious faith.[11] Giussani's program was not different in intent from that of other religious associations of the time, especially Catholic Action. But where others lacked vision and religious enthusiasm, GS was optimistic and aggressive.[12] Giussani was convinced that existing Catholic habits of mind and culture were inadequate and narrow and ultimately incapable of assuring the permanence of Christianity in Italian society. The inevitable result of this moral depression was that Catholics had submitted to a secularized view of life and lost their religious sensibility. It was this modern submission to secularity—nowhere more apparent than in universities—that Giussani sought to criticize and overcome.

Giussani did not, however, ask his young followers to give up every aspect of the modern world. He has never opposed technological or scientific modernization. The members of the movement maintain that they are perfectly at home in the modern scientific technological urban world and within the political world. (They have more than an average instinct for politics.) Their objection is, rather, to the spirit of modernity—in particular, its insistence on a freedom of conscience that excludes the religious attitude at its very root—and to the institution of the modern state. Modernity, according to Giussani, excludes the very concept of Christian existence because one of the epistemological criteria of modernity is to consider "man as measure of all things."[13]

Comunione e Liberazione's critique of modernity is, then, fundamentally theological. The attitude that considers man as measure of all things is just the opposite of the religious spirit. According to Giussani, the religious spirit begins to be active in people's lives when they come to accept in faith an event that happened independently of their consciousness, two thousand years ago. "It is the perception of this event which revives and strengthens the elemental sense of dependence and the nucleus of original evidence to which we give the name of religious sense."[14] This event introduces a new, active reality in the world. "What is in fact Christianity if not the event of a new man who, with a new character, becomes a new protagonist on the scene of the world."[15] Here Giussani seems to echo Pope Paul VI's statement that "the Christian identity in history is primarily a Fact, the Fact of a new reality, of a new creature which is the Church, 'an ethnic entity sui generis' which converges in its wholeness toward Christ."[16] By denying these facts, modernity, according to CL, is atheistic and divested of any viable spiritual value. Having started with the Enlightenment affirmation of a self without God, modernity has ended as a prisoner to its own dependence on knowledge, its own expectation of progress, its own insistence on freedom.

Comunione e Liberazione's theological critique of modernity is also, at its root, a political statement and critique:

> Man appears to us in the present epoch to be damned to struggle between the alternatives of presumption and cynicism for the very reason of considering himself the measure of all things. But there is a common denomination for these two positions, namely, that the modern man, to live and to guarantee a minimum of order, has to give to the State a power which is exorbitant, quasi-divine. The State, either in the absolutist Hegelian form or in the radical social one, ends by summoning and interpreting all the motivations of estimation, honor, hope and guidance of today's men. Consequently the Christian finds himself in the situation of affirming his right to exist—either as possibility or as significance—vis à vis a State which is a no lesser enemy to him than was the Roman empire to the Christians of the first centuries. From a certain point of view, the state is an even greater enemy to him now than it ever was to them then. . . . Power, not in its ontology and therefore in its structural ethical value, but in its present historical-political reality, shows a radical hostility against the religious sense. It is this hostility that I intend to contest. [This present political] power, through the instrument of invasion of conscience which it possesses—first of all the mass media—cannot but try to influence as much as possible the people with values and attitudes which will allow the state to continue the status quo and so to perpetuate its dominion. I do not imply that such dynamics are always deprived of purposes which are both ethical and humanly constructive. I affirm only that these intentions do not find in the religious sense either a self-limitation of the power, or an opening to the help of a even greater factor, namely, faith. But an atheist state cannot exist. If the state does not make reference to a principle which transcends it and which therefore places limits on it, the State by its own nature tends to claim a divine dimension. This is the root of the modern idolatry of the state.[17]

According to CL the evidence of modernity's flaws can be seen in the violent nature of the modern political system and in the threat of its collapse. A system like communism seems inevitable once the modern premises are put in place. This judgment passed on the modern state does not make exceptions for the Western political systems ruled by democratic parties. The reason is that "even democracy, when it refuses the religious reference, becomes an illusory morality."[18] CL has been harshly critical of the Christian Democratic party, which enjoyed ruling majorities throughout the post-war period in Italy. The Christian Democrats, according to CL, failed to recognize that the modern state brings with it unacceptable cultural and political principles. Furthermore, the party failed to transform its political hegemony into cultural hegemony and simply succumbed to the secularized culture. In the judgment of CL, the result of this theological and cultural ineptitude has been the fall of Italian society into a profound secularization, evidenced by its acceptance of divorce and abortion and its promotion of that practical form of Western atheism known as consumerism.

Whatever the historical accuracy of this reading of modernity, this summary judgment has its attraction. It combines the sharp directness of an uncompromising ideology—standing against all the evil identified in modernity—with the emotional strength of a mythic historiography. In Comunione e Liberazione's telling of the story, this evil world may be saved by the redemptive activity of their own movement. Modernity serves as the counterfigure against which the movement struggles, the idea over against which they define themselves. Inside the movement, the event of Christ and submission to religious authorities are central; outside the movement, modernity shoves aside all religious sensibilities. To a culture defined as atheistic and to a world power considered totalitarian, CL opposes a world of human beings made free by their faith in the event of Christ and by the authority of the Church.

Membership and Activities

Comunione e Liberazione is successful in large part because it is diverse and flexible in its forms of membership. The movement actually consists of a number of different groups. A large number of persons take part in the Scuole di Comunità (Schools of Community). Others join the Fraternità or the religious association of the Memores Domini, while many more participate in the enterprises of the Compagnia delle Opere.

The term Movimento di Comunione e Liberazione stands, first and foremost, for those 100,000 to 120,000 persons who participate weekly in the Scuole, the main local institutions of the movement. These groups are the center of CL's activities in the parish.[19] Most of the participants—male and female in equal proportion—are between fifteen and twenty-five years of age. They are usually middle-class students from urban areas. Each group is led by adult members of CL and by a priest.

The Scuola has two main activities, namely, the "school of theology" and what is called Il Raggio (The Spoke, as in the spoke of a wheel). This activity most clearly defines the nature of the Scuola di Comunità. Il Raggio is a group discussion of a concrete cultural or social problem, or of a need in the community. The term *raggio* implies that each individual member is asked to bring concerns to the group. The discussion involves the members in active Christian interpretation of needs in their society and directs them toward finding practical solutions to these problems. Il Raggio is neither group therapy nor mere subjective expression. It provides, rather, a forum for redefining perceived needs and acting individually and collectively on those needs in society at large. Through this discussion and action, participants in the Scuole create "Christian community."

The Scuole di Comunità offer their young participants opportunities to learn the interpretations and the actions that give life to CL's theological belief in Christ as the origin and center of individual and social life.[20] For them, this belief is defined by spiritual submission to religious authority in all of life and by a call to personal initiative and activism in the world. The members of CL often refer to each other as *militanti* ("activists").

Since about 1980 CL has also tried to appeal to working-class young people through the efforts of the CL subdivision Giovani Lavoratori (Young Workers) and with special Solidarity Centers. These centers offer help to young working-class persons who wish to find a job or to develop technical skills. Despite this outreach to the working class, the movement has not cut across class lines to a significant degree; the initiative CL/Giovani Lavoratori has not modified the demographic, social, and cultural characteristics of the movement, which began in high schools, colleges and universities, and continues to develop its language and methods with the needs and the values of that social group in mind. The primary change in the demographics of CL is simply the ageing of its original members and the growing number who are work in professional occupations. In short, CL remains solidly middle class and urban.

Comunione e Liberazione also includes a large association of persons called La Fraternità, a lay secular association recognized in 1983 by the Catholic Church as a *persona juridica,* a canonically constituted entity within the jurisdiction of the Church. Individuals become members of La Fraternità simply by agreeing for an unspecified time (of their choosing) to live by the rules of the order. The purpose of the Fraternità is to promote an ecclesial community of life among its members and to support the activities of the movement as a whole. In 1991 the Fraternità had twenty thousand members, mostly between twenty-eight and thirty-five years of age. Although the Fraternità is considered the "mature fruit" of the movement in terms of way of life, and although it is a large, active resource for the movement, it is not identical either in terms of personnel or status in church law with the movement as a whole.

A third association which comes under the term Movimento CL is Memores Domini. Its members are bound for life by vows of poverty, celibacy, and obedience. No precise membership number is available.[21]

While Memores Domini requires high levels of commitment for life, CL also offers activities that require only minimal commitment, drawing in large numbers of people for short periods and special events. Among the most visible of CL's national activities are large annual gatherings such as the Meeting of Peace (at Rimini) and the Meeting of the Mediterranean. The Rimini gathering is a major cultural event in Italy, with the main productions televised nationally (including a 1991 specially commissioned play by Eugene Ionesco). The meeting features major political and cultural figures from throughout Europe[22] and attracts approximately 150,000 people.

Taken together, the CL activities can be quite demanding for its members. Each contributes monthly a proportion of his or her income (the exact amount is discretionary) to the international missions and the national organizations of the movement. Beyond this contribution, each member spends approximately a thousand dollars a year attending meetings and retreats. They give of their time as well. They participate in the weekly activities of the Scuola di Communità, in the Sunday liturgy in their parishes, and many meet daily for common prayer. In addition, they participate in the social enterprises of the group. In the course of the year each member spends approximately one month participating in the national activities of the movement. A substantial part of the members' free time is thus occupied with activities related to Comunione e Liberazione.

If the first distinctive aspect of CL is its specific ecclesial method of creating Church community, the second distinctive aspect is the Opere (the Works). The title Le Opere refers to activities and institutions born from the creative spirit of the movement. They include a large number of cultural, social, political and economic enterprises that have grown out of the cultural and civic environments in which the members feel called to work. These enterprises are therefore described as having a theological status within CL, for it is through these activities that the movement is to create a new religiously based society. Members create schools, workshops, and businesses which are religiously inspired, culturally and socially "united around the recognition of the Christian truth."[23] If CL is going to be a way of living the Christian faith, the Opere provide a form of "operative friendship" among the members and a way in which their vision of a renewed Church is fulfilled. According to CL, the Opere are the building blocks of a new Christian society, or the points of force from which CL may push toward the advent of that new society, while also creating a setting in which individual economic, political, and cultural motivations are reshaped.

In addition to building solidarity and reshaping individual character, the Works are also economically and politically effective. They bolster the finances of the movement and provide a greater capacity to exert political influence. The Compagnia delle Opere appears particularly effective in the development of areas of service often left unattended, especially areas related to the needs of young people and the need for improved working environments. Its president in 1991, Giorgio Vittadini, described their appeal this way: "The economists argue that the economic development of the next years will depend upon a factor which is forgotten because often it does not appear to be fundamental for the success of a business, big or small: human capital. We do not have any doubt about it. We know, also because we do not have large capital, how valuable human resources are in building an economic enterprise."[24]

Institutional Form

Many movements have developed in the Catholic world of post-war Italy, movements that provide the ideological and organizational backdrop against which Comunione e Liberazione has grown.[25] According to recent studies, 85 percent of the adult Italian population identify themselves as Catholic,[26] and 10 percent—approximately 4 million people—claim to belong to a religious group, association, or movement.[27] These religious associations, groups, and movements cover a large variety of interests. Some have as their primary goal the private religious and spiritual concerns of their members,[28] others are dedicated to voluntary charitable works,[29] others are committed to missionary activity.[30] These groups differ in their organizational form as much as they differ in their aims. Some, such as the pro-life movement, are clearly specialized. Others, like Azione Cattolica Italiana (Italian Catholic Action), have a more comprehensive religious goal. To achieve its general purpose, Azione Cattolica is organized bureaucratically into various branches—by age (children, youth, adults), by sex, by profession (teachers, artisans, nurses, etc.)—all connected through a central organization and dependent on the Bishops' Conference. Other Catholic organizations are directly dependent upon the local bishop rather than the national conference, while some are dependent upon the Vatican itself (Opus Dei, Focolarini, etc.) and are therefore international in scope. Comunione e Liberazione is organizationally a mixed picture: it is an association recognized by the pope as having an autonomous international status, but it has at the same time a direct connection with each diocesan bishop and local parish organization. Its own organizational divisions follow parish and diocesan lines. In the case of conflict with the local bishop, however, the movement remains protected by papal jurisdiction. In other words, CL has an organization independent from the bishops, although it remains bound with them to a general agreement of purposes and method.[31] Its organizational connections to the Catholic hierarchy are flexible enough to allow the activities of the movement a wide range of legitimacy.

The movement is also very flexible in its encouragement of local initiative. The activities of the Opere, for instance, come from within the movement but are institutionally independent; they are seen as the responsibility of the people who originated them. They are also formally independent of control by diocese, parish, or other levels of Church hierarchy. Nevertheless, they are coordinated by two main institutions of CL, namely, Compagnia delle Opere (CO), and the political arm, Movimento Popolare (MP). The presidents of these two institutions are members ex officio of the National Council of Comunione e Liberazione.

The Compagnia delle Opere, a nonprofit organization founded in 1986, was originally intended to promote cooperation and assistance among companies, cooperatives, and institutions so as to better utilize resources and energies, and to promote the employment of young and unemployed persons. The organization is not a stockholding company. Rather, it is a system of communication and a network of solidarity among its member institutions and businesses. It has developed a cross-functional means of coordination which results in its organization looking more like a spider's web than a hierarchical unified system. It provides for the exchange of information, contacts, and legal advice. The main Milan office of CO is organized like a service center, with departments for sales, finance, marketing and communication, foreign development, employment and training, and for the start-up and development of companies. The CO has thirty-two branch offices located in Italy as well as an office in Brussels and another in Warsaw.

The main organ of communication within the movement is *Litterae Communionis,* the official monthly magazine. This publication, professionally produced on a par with major national periodicals, is widely read among movement members. The national secretariat in Milan provides press services and communication for the movement and organizes the main national activities.

The movement is held together, in large part, by the ideas propagated by its founder, ideas largely contained in a popular series of books and disseminated through the movement's highly effective planning and communication apparatus. While each local CL group is organizationally and financially independent, ideology and organizational policy are highly centralized around the charismatic founder, Luigi Giussani, who, with his Council, directs national activities from the headquarters in Milan. The related international organizations—the Fraternità and the Memores Domini—are also headquartered in Milan and are represented on the Council as well. The small group of regional organizers, leaders of national activities, and representatives of Fraternità, the Compagnia delle Opere, and of the Movimento Popolare have the primary task of providing theological and practical inspiration and effective administration so that the movement can grow. Whether they are accomplishing this task is judged entirely by the president (Giussani) and the small group of key leaders who surround him. Authority and approval are highly centralized through informal links to the primary charismatic leader of the movement. CL's ecclesiological choice is decidedly for a charismatic concept of authority and an organic society with a clear center of unity.

The Changing CL Dynamic

By 1968 the original ideas of CL about the spiritual and social dimensions of the Christ event were being transformed by the explosion of the Italian youth political movements. Many youths of Gioventù Studentesca began to connect what they had experienced in the movement with the possibility of revolutionary political action in favor of the poor and against the institutional violence of the modern state. In fact, in 1968–69 the majority of the members of GS left to join the student movement, and later many of them enlisted in radical Marxist movements.

In the 1970s, after a period of disorientation, the remnant of GS developed a new formulation of its own goal and nature. It was then that they took the name Comunione e Liberazione. The goals of the movement became more clearly religious and the structure more ecclesial, and they clarified their own political ethos. At the university CL had had to face the Marxist movements (which at the time ruled the field); in that confrontation it became explicit that CL would reject violence and that its foundation would be the Christ event, not ordinary political rationality.

This theological development did not mean, however, that the movement became less political. In 1974 CL had to bear the brunt of the effort to abrogate Italian legislation on divorce. This proved to be a watershed event, the occasion of a third awakening of CL, an awakening that made it decisively and more explicitly political. After its birth in the 1950s and its second awakening during the student movements of the 1960s, CL entered the 1970s still mainly located on university campuses. But in 1974 CL found itself in a larger arena, alone among the Catholic political and social movements in giving unconditional testimony to the idea of Christianity in Italy. The ordeal of the national referendum on divorce served both to test the total obedience of CL to the Church's authority (which had invited CL to become a protagonist in the fight against divorce), and to demonstrate the novelty of CL's training among the Catholic movements of the Italian Church. From that moment on, CL saw itself in the forefront of the battle between the friends and enemies of the Church, as the new legitimate Catholic voice for a cultural and political alternative to the triumph of laicism. The style of CL became more combative on the economic and political fronts, with both the Compagnia delle Opere and the Movimento Popolare having significant national effects.[32]

The events of 1974 gave new political meaning to Giussani's theological system.

The movement claimed religious authority as the guide for both individual conscience and the state, especially on matters that pertained to morality, faith, education, family legislation, and the like. Now its religious action was geared toward implementing a concrete social and political program. CL thus became a historic sociopolitical experiment that took the Christian faith as the legitimate criterion of political action and evaluation. Catholic Christianity became the explicit motivation for political claims and direct political action in Italy, with the goal of creating a new society around the recognition of the Christian truth. Such a transformation of society would de facto reduce the role of the state and affirm the creative role of religious social solidarity. The primary political principle would be the sort of creative human freedom found only in submission to religious authority, thus assuring the Church her rightful position in society.

Since the Church is an original and essential source of saving power, it is necessary, in Comunione e Liberazione's view, that the Church not be separated from the public form of power. Only the Church can legitimately establish normative structures which rule human existence. To negate this, to deny the order of legitimacy established by God, is tantamount to a profession of atheism, the practical atheism that characterizes modernity. This idea of Christianity does not accept a constitutional political system that allows for a public principle of power totally separated from the religious normative way of life. At the root of CL's project is an ancient concept that places Christianity and the Church at the center of public life.[33] The internal logic of their theological system can allow no alternatives.

Modernization has always been accompanied by a variety of responses. But in Italy, as in other societies with Catholic traditions, modernization is also charged with a tension that comes from the disestablishment of the Catholic Church and the move toward a pluralistic society and a democratic polity. For centuries the Church had been privileged by the assumption, often legally formalized, that the Catholic view, as it was specifically defined by the papacy, had a rightful cultural hegemony. Faced with this cultural and political loss, modernity was seen as a siege against the Church. The siege mentality has inspired a segment of the Italian Catholic world to condemn both modern politics and theological or ecclesial innovation.

In Italy, the defensive approach toward modernity was strong enough to determine the social and political life of the whole country. The result was 150 years of tension between Church and state—from the loss of the papal state, to the Church's long-standing prohibition against political participation by the faithful, and to its lenient response to fascism. Through the papal decree "Non expedit" of 1868, Catholics were prohibited, for about five decades after the end of the papal state, from taking any direct role in politics, either as voters or candidates. The Vatican sought thereby to weaken the liberal parties and the monarchy. When the monarchy, under pressure from the socialists, finally sought Catholic support, the Vatican's hope was that the result would be the reinstatement of a Catholic nation and the temporal power of the pope.[34]

It is against a background of repeated attempts to reinstate Church influence that CL's breakthrough in 1974 must be understood. The papal decree "Non expedit" was one political adaptation to the loss of the Church's power and influence caused by the formation of the modern secular state. For a time earlier in this century, many in the Church apparently hoped fascism would or could redress the imbalance between Church and modern state.[35] Since World War II the primary political response of the Church has been to try to unify all Catholics into one party, thereby reinstating indirect church influence. Comunione e Liberazione is different. They seek a more radical redefinition of political power. For them, the only legitimate power derives from connection with the saving reality of Christ and the Church. All of their actions are, therefore, considered to be political actions. Whether bringing concerns to the Scuole or creating new Opere, they are working toward redefining society. CL has no qualms about power. The founder of the movement says: "The Christian does not have uneasy feelings about power. On the contrary, the Christian should desire power to make less difficult the way that each man has to enter into to bring about his destiny."[36]

The Dynamics of Success

The strength of this religious movement is measured not primarily by the number of its adherents (although CL is significant in size), but by the persuasiveness of its worldview in shaping the individual member's interpretation of his or her experiences. Institutionally, the strength of the movement depends on its success in bringing about a new method of communal life and in developing, from that communal perspective, a new manner of thinking about life as a whole. Comunione e Liberazione has spread in Italy due to its success in projecting an image, favorably received by many young people, of a community with an unambiguous worldview and method of living and a plain, frank style of confronting society with religious assurance and generosity.[37] Its clear orthodoxy and its community of religious solidarity have appealed to many.

The movement is also successful because it has developed structures of membership that are well adapted to the particular demographic groups to which it appeals. Membership statistics, in fact, are not a very useful measure of CL's growth. Because a significant proportion of CL's participants and contributors are men and women at the beginning of their adult and professional lives, there is an inherent instability in the CL population. CL has responded to this by creating flexible forms of membership that allow for such coming and going.

The Scuole di comunità, for instance, do not have an official form of membership. They depend on the capacity of each local Scuola to attract new individuals to compensate for the constant flow of members away from active participation. The wide variety of activities available in the Opere provides diverse and flexible opportunities for involvement. And the method of Il Raggio allows each Scuola to shift its focus as the needs of its members and the world change daily. These may range from the constitutional crises in Italy, to the political changes in Russia or the Persian Gulf War, from papal policy or reforms in the university, to the homeless or abortion. At the local level, the movement is spread widely over many interests. It is held together as a whole by a solid, distinct, and largely unseen leadership in Milan.

The leadership of CL has deliberately designed the institutional form of CL as a movement, refusing to install the official forms of membership which are common in other Catholic organizations. CL is fluid, its organizational boundaries permeable by design, freeing it from the institutional ties that would impose the agenda of the Church hierarchy.

CL is not dominated by an elite class of members who have taken permanent religious vows (a situation common to religious orders in the Catholic Church and to the new "secular institutes" such as Opus Dei, which has been a personal prelature since 1986). In the case of CL the fact of belonging to the Fraternità or Memores Domini does not entail any privilege or special right to leadership in the movement (although leaders *are* often drawn from Fraternità). Members of Memores Domini may have taken vows which are similar to those of the religious orders and institutes, but they are not considered the central nucleus of the movement, nor is the aim of the movement to sustain the development of the Memores Domini.

Such flexibility carries, of course, certain risks for the movement. Recognition of these risks can be seen in certain new elements in CL's rhetoric in the early 1990s. There were new calls for strengthening the psychological and religious sense of belonging among members, emphasizing that without the movement the individual member could not stand firm in faith and would put God to the test. Each individual member was invited to identify with the movement, and there were efforts more closely to interconnect the various parts of the movement.[38]

CL's emphasis on authority also creates a much more corporate and active practice of the life of faith. For CL, religious education comes chiefly through membership in a society, a society in which members are challenged to become actively involved—as a community—with the needs of the larger community. Giussani complains that other youth organizations leave their members with an opaque view of the relation between religion and social life and a dispersed sense of powerlessness rather than a collective sense of power.

As the young members of CL identify specific needs in the community and act on them, they are thrown into society with a real measure of responsibility and made to believe that the religious tradition and the community are entrusted to them. The positive relationships they develop within the movement are then contrasted with the negative situation of the society as a whole. CL does not form theologians or scholars or religious specialists. Its religious formation is meant to be mental training for action in social life. Each member is challenged to make what CL stands for the central vocation in his or her life, putting the salvation event into practice. Exuberant self-confidence in action is accompanied by an equally exuberant certitude in thought.

Living under the principle of religious authority, in communion with the salvation found in Christ and the Church, propels the members of Comunione e Liberazione outward with a will to bring Christianity to life. For this reason solidarity and active leadership are the primary practical principles for the life of the movement, both wrapped with the title of "faith." Members experience a strongly felt urgency to act, an urgency dictated by a clear identification with the movement, by the immediate needs discovered in the society, by the active presence of well-identified enemies, and by a clear competitive will to outdo those enemies.[39] Thus the movement is not simply a way of life of the individual Christian. It is the place where individuals become

Church and the Church comes into being within society. Hence the great appeal the movement has for its members—they find a community in which to belong and significant work through which they anticipate transforming society. They are constantly reminded by the movement leadership that society is in need of a profound change and that any change must be religious to be real. Militanti in Comunione e Liberazione are eager to help bring that change about.

The Impact of Comunione e Liberazione

CL has a most ambitious goal: it aims to defend and reaffirm the fundamental claim of the Church to be the measure and origin of society, to reorient Italian society as a whole toward Catholic Christianity. The significance of this project emerges from the magnitude of the aim and from the methods of organization that CL brings to it. These methods have been acquired by the movement over many years, formed as CL has confronted the crises of its own development. The features of the movement now most apparent were developed in the 1970s and early 1980s. In its earliest days, the movement was primarily an alternative to the Catholic cultural and social conformism of the high school students of Milan. In the 1960s the original idea was reshaped in a close confrontation with the student movement, emerging with a clear rejection of social messianism. But the crises of the 1970s demonstrated the utility and possibilities for a broader national implementation of Giussani's idea of Christianity in Italy.

In the 1980s the movement showed signs of solid organizational growth. While continuing its activity in high schools and universities, and while extending the network of Scuole di Comunità and Opere, CL assumed a larger national profile. The development of CL's style and national range of influence was certainly in part a mature outcome emerging from the core of the movement (especially from the aging of the Fraternità and the quality professional and economic support the movement received from it). But clearly this new national initiative reflected the ideological confidence of CL and their evident organizational capacity.

The movement does not consider itself to be the whole Church, but to represent the essential characteristics and claims of the Church. It does not claim to be the only instrument for realizing the new Christianity, but it does claim to be the most coherent and active force seeking this vision. In the face of what CL considers the resignation and myopia of most Catholic lay persons, the movement has actively engaged in "the project of Christianity" in Italy, resisting hosts of "enemies," including the modern state. Comunione e Liberazione's aims are both ideological and practical, theological and political. The movement seeks to bring a religious view to the critique of modernity while also reversing the legitimacy of the present order of cultural and political power.

Economic and Public Works

CL's attempt to reorient Italian society is located in part in the large and diverse panoply of charitable, economic, cultural, financial, and educational endeavors (about four thousand member companies and institutions) that constitute the Opere. These have their impact at both the local and national levels. Among those that have been organized into national networks are the Centri di Solidarietà, which assist the homeless and drug addicts; Centers for Health Care and for the study of health care legislation in areas not covered by the government health care system; Centri Didattici e di Sviluppo Scolastico, which provide teaching materials to primary schools and teachers, largely in humanities subjects such as history and literature; Sindacato delle Famiglie, which acts as a parliamentary lobby for legislation affecting the family; and Cooperative Universitarie, which provides student housing, cafeterias, and student centers in the major universities. Financing for these large-scale university services comes directly from the government. The movement also has professional centers that offer technical architectural and environmental impact studies for private and public, city and regional, development projects. In addition, the *associazioni professionali* bring together professionals such as engineers, doctors, lawyers, and scientists for religious study and philanthropic work.

Cultural Works

In addition to active impact in the economic realm, CL is also concerned with the larger realm of culture. Comunione e Liberazione combines two distinct traditions of debate about modernity, one explicitly political, the other cultural. In concert with two hundred years of arguments by romantics, conservatives, and Marxists, CL opposes the idea that the state is the necessary agent of human perfection. Rather, one finds in culture, or in the institutions which express it, the necessary agent of the critical and comprehensive consciousness of the person. But this discussion is given a special twist by CL. They argue that the main cultural agent in society should be the Church. The state should exist only as an instrumental agent, adjunct to the Church and society. And because the Church should be the main agent of the culture, they are critical of the present condition of Italian culture; a reformed culture will be necessary if it is to fulfill its proper role. Italian culture has given secular and atheistic values primacy and has put itself at the service of a "new power" that is financial, international, and antireligious.

To accomplish this cultural reform, CL encompasses several professionally organized and institutionally sophisticated initiatives under the umbrella of Le Opere. The AIC, Italian Association of Cultural Centers, was established in 1983 to contribute to the cultural, social, and artistic progress and development of Italian society. Since 1988 ISTRA, a research institute for social change, has organized the International Academy of Science and Culture which promotes ties with foreign universities and institutes. Jaca Books is a large and respected academic publishing house, based in Milan. *Il Sabato* is a highly combative weekly political and cultural magazine, with a subscription list of over a hundred thousand, and a circulation of about three hundred thousand. The periodical *30 Giorni* is a monthly published in six languages which offers detailed information about the Church. The Christian Study Center of Russia was established in Milan thirty years ago to support the cause of human rights in the Soviet Union. In recent years, the center has taken on the role of mediator for independent groups and Christian communities in the former Soviet Union. It produces a bimonthly journal, *L'Altra Europa* (The other Europe), and has a book department, La Casa di Matrona, which publishes translations in Italian of Russian philosophical, literary, and theological works as well as texts in Russian for distribution in the former Soviet Union.

In the language of the publications of CL, especially in *Litterae Communionis, 30 Giorni,* and *Il Sabato,* one can find the echo of both political and cultural discussions. The style of CL's publications is dogmatic, sometimes aiming more to confirm the reader than to persuade the unpersuaded. Writers are not likely to offer alternative interpretations or contrary evidence. Friends of the movement are glorified, while enemies are denounced unforgivingly. Still, the wit of these publications is lively, sharp, and paradoxical. These widely read periodicals actively place the relations among Church, society, and state in Italy at the center of the political agenda.

Political Works: Il Movimento Popolare

As we have seen, Comunione e Liberazione's line of thought privileges the idea of an organic society against the centralized form of the state. CL pursues these political goals through Il Movimento Popolare, the political expression of the Compagnia delle Opere. Movimento Popolare was constituted in 1976 with the statutory purpose of supporting those individuals and groups who would promote the Catholic tradition (in the specific sense that this is represented by the Compagnia delle Opere) in local and national political institutions and in a wide variety of cultural organizations.[40] It has been connected to the Christian Democrats, although it is not a political party. It has become, instead, an independent power broker and an effective voice in the creation of public opinion. Il Movimento Popolare nominates and campaigns for the election of candidates who favor the Compagnia delle Opere and its initiatives. CL proved a very effective electoral machine at every level of the electoral process and became more influential in the Christian Democrat party in the early 1990s. In every major local and national election, Movimento Popolare was successful in electing its representatives, thereby assuring itself of significant political influence.

The political program of Il Movimento Popolare can be summed up in their slogan "less state, more society." This formulation of the opposition between state and society has had a long history in Italian political life going back to the popular movements organized by Catholics in the nineteenth century. The original connotations of "less state, more society" were the demand for greater popular participation over against the intrusion of the state and for a limited constitutional role in Italian society for the Catholic Church.

After World War II, and especially with the Second Vatican Council, Catholic opinion underwent a profound philosophical change in favor of separation between church and state and toward a pluralist view of society and culture. In the view of the founders of CL, this change has led to an undermining of the Church's constitutional position in areas of family life, morals, and education. CL has actually accused the Christian Democrat party of seeking political power even at the cost of legitimating the secular state's positions on abortion and divorce, while ignoring the de-Christianization of society. The party has failed, CL believes, to offer Catholic interpretations and alternatives and to work to assure a Catholic cultural hegemony. Instead, the Christian party has become the instrument of the "new power," a force that is the enemy of the Church and the true enemy of CL.[41] CL has thus revived the old slogan "more society, less state," but for new reasons. Instead of the demand for greater pluralism and popular participation, the theology and political strategy of CL are aimed toward what they would not be reluctant to describe as a new type of Catholic hegemony.

CL's ideas about power and their goals in Italian society are unambiguously hegemonic, not because Giussani or CL wishes to deny to others the right to express cultural differences (which they do not), but because even cultural differences must be defined in terms of the salvation available only through the Church. Primary cultural power, then, belongs to the Church. The Church, through its various movements, is to become the archetypical form of society. This is not primarily a matter of the official position and role of religion. It is rather a new ethos which is socially expressed in an expansive form of solidarity and which is sustained from within by hierarchical authority.

Comunione e Liberazione and the Church

The movement has no sectarian or separatist tendencies. Instead, it presumes to reflect the Church as a whole and has made itself proof of the claim that the Church is a creative form of society. CL raises a strong antagonistic voice against any who differ with the main idea of Christianity, as defined within the movement. But Comunione e Liberazione gives complete loyalty to the Church, and especially to the present pope, John Paul II. Giussani instructed his followers that

> The only issue is how we can center everything on the word of the Pope even more clearly and intensively, heartily and generously. For this reason those who have authority [*autorevolezza*] in the Movement ought to be an example of true discipleship to the word of the Teacher. Which person God employs to educate his Church, from the point of view of the content of the truth, in a certain way is indifferent. Nevertheless, at the present moment of the Church, the human personality of the Pope is by itself pedagogically highly significant. The persons who carry the responsibility for our Movement have the grave duty to identify themselves with the human type that today guides the Church, to identify themselves with that human certainty made strong by faith which the Pope lives, with the urgency of assuring that Christ will become the key of every conviction about man and the world.[42]

There are certainly other contemporary Catholics in Italy who do not share CL's view of the Church or of the Church's role in the state. Many dread any growth of political religious forces, let alone their hegemonic power in a modern society. Many see pluralistic modern society as allowing a vital and creative presence to Christian religion, a creativity not bound by any direct link with political power.[43] It is this very opinion, nevertheless, that is anathema to an influential part of the Church hierarchy and to CL, both of which seek to assert the preeminence of the Church against the modern Italian state.[44]

What impact does CL have on religious opinion? The answer to this question must be tentative. Most religious opinion in Italy is seasoned by a complex tradition and by a diffuse religious skepticism. It is difficult to distinguish the real strength of CL from the "echo effect" that the movement tries to produce within the Catholic world. CL claims to speak for the very survival of the true Church and to act against the mortal enemies of the Church, within and without. Some would say there is a large element of tactical bluff mixed with exuberant self-assurance in the claim of the movement to speak for the Church and for its rights. Nevertheless, CL can point to approval from the hierarchy and significant support from the Vatican in backing the claim. Signs of approval, plus intense activity and considerable success, produce the "echo effect," which in turn gives the impression of much greater effectiveness and influence than is actually the case.

What has been clear is that CL's critique has had the capacity to change the terms in which its members—and the larger Italian Church—think about the relationship of the Church to the culture. At least since Vatican II, many in the Church had talked in terms of bringing the Church up to date in relation to the cultural and political changes that had occurred in modern society. The Church had accepted the ethical and political innovations of modernity, although the cultural values of modernity and the new political institutions had developed in large measure independent from the official policy of the Church. But recently, influenced by the rhetoric of CL, much Catholic opinion has turned toward condemnation of the ethics of modernity, condemnation especially of the separation of the Church from the larger society, a separation that is seen as responsible for the disastrous victories of the forces of modernity.

Comunione e Liberazione and Italian Politics

Is CL a religious movement first and a political force last, or vice versa? The ambiguity derives from the movement's refusal to accept the modern liberal separation of those terms. On the mental horizon of Giussani there seems to be only one solution to the problems of the present day. He places his only hope for a rightful politics in the active presence in the political world of persons with religious conscience, something Giussani thinks the Movimento Popolare of CL can do: "I do not hold a 'confessional state' to be the political ideal, but, rather, a State which is guided by men surely religious. . . . Such an ideal situation would become more feasible if its reactivation were trusted not to a single personality, though exceptional, but to a company of men profoundly religious: a true company of Jesus. Furthermore, the confessional state is never just. Even if there were only one person with a different conscience, that individual would deserve full respect and freedom."[45]

As we have seen, CL has been successful in placing "a company of men profoundly religious" into the political arena. But beyond these individual and collective efforts at direct participation, CL is also a force in the ideological battles that shape Italian politics. Religious movements like CL often embrace ideology as a major substitute for direct political power in the modern state. Ideology is a form of intervention in the political system which can amount to direct political action. In Italy the idea of a cultural-political hegemony has passed from one ideological group to another, in a play of counterattacks and a display of odium ideologicum. Ideological hate has been one of the most disruptive forces within Italian society, while at the same time serving as a most economical and readily available instrument of social, albeit sectarian, solidarity. One major disadvantage of appealing to the odium ideologicum in the political arena is, however, the difficulty of then working toward political compromise, that most fundamental expression of tolerance.

Ideological religious tension has continued to play a role in Italian politics, despite the collapse of the communist threat and despite the profound anti-ideological evolution of the Christian Democrats. This should not surprise us. The line of Catholic opinion of which CL is a vocal part seems determined to keep the level of ideological tension as high as possible as a motivation to action. After the collapse in 1989 of the Italian Communist party (PCI), a new-old enemy—*illuminismo* (Enlightenment thinking)—was identified by the Church. It was suddenly seen lurking behind previous enemies and actually suspected of being the cause of all movements contrary to the idea of Christianity. The list of enemies is now larger and more threatening than before—Masonry, Pelagianism, Arianism, Humanism, Protestantization. They are regularly called back to the scene to justify the call to arms against the secularization of the state and of life.

Conclusion

Comunione e Liberazione envisions the future as shaped by progress—not technological or humanistic progress, but "evangelization." Their view of personal and social history posits a saving event as the central normative fact, a fact that exists independent from human consciousness and responsibility. Yet it is also a fact that demands human response and participation. CL's emphasis on the necessity of a significant encounter with a person of faith is highly reminiscent of revivalist Protestant forms of evangelization.

Does this revivalist rhetoric and practice cast doubt on their traditional Catholic sacramentalism? On the contrary, CL is solidly communal and Catholic, alongside their experiential activism. This is no individualistic, "protestant" form of evangelization. As people encounter grace, they are challenged to respond in faith and obedience, to place religious motivation at the center of life, to submit to religious authority (especially in the person of the pope), and to act to bring their society into right relationship with the Church that embodies Christ's saving presence. CL offers the paradoxical combination of an evangelical ethos, firmly under the authority of the pope.

The complexity and ambiguity of Comunione e Liberazione's political and religious discourse offer a paradox of another sort. On the one hand, the revivalist spiritual and theological character is an authentic and strong source of energy for the movement. There is here a language and a form of organization that has awakened the imaginations of thousands of Italian young adults toward a new religious sensibility. They speak of reconstructing Italian society through the actions of thoroughly religious persons working in the political and cultural order. Religion, as the primary instrumentality of culture, would ascend naturally, as the role of the state would shrink.

On the other hand, the political rhetoric and vision of the movement seem to continue a long-standing political position in the Catholic world—that of returning the Roman Catholic Church to its traditional role of political power. Which of these inconsistent options will prevail depends on conditions external to the movement, namely, developments in Catholic theology, the support of the pope and the religious hierarchy, and the vicissitudes of Italian politics. Even as the members of Comunione e Liberazione seek to remake their society, they are remade by it.

Notes

1. *Quattro testimoni di Gesu' Cristo* (interviews), a supplement to *Il Sabato*, no. 48 (30 November 1991): 7.

2. In these affirmations are echoes of both traditional Catholic doctrine and the Barthian emphasis on the historical uniqueness of Christianity.

3. *Da quale vita nasce Comunione e Liberazione*, a supplement to *Litterae Communionis*, nos. 7–8 (1979), p. 18 (*Dqv* in future references). The substance of authority is further explained there as "the great hypothesis inside which one puts himself at work."

4. *Dqv*, p. 17.

5. Emile Durkheim, *Elementary Forms of the Religious Life* (New York: Macmillan, 1965).

6. The following passages are quoted from the 1985 edition of Luigi Giussani, *La coscienza religiosa nell'uomo moderno* (Milan: Jaca Book, 1985): "The power of an individual is measured by the intensity of his self-consciousness, that is, by the perception he has of the values which define his personality. . . . These values flow into the Ego from the lived history to which the Ego itself belongs. . . . The fundamental geniality of a subject amounts to the strength of his consciousness of belonging. For this reason the people of God becomes a new cultural

horizon for each subject that belongs to it" (p. 71). From these premises derive both the reason and the method of the Scuole di Comunità of the movement: "The education to faith is education to a cultural competence. Should not, therefore, the first purpose of a Christian school be to develop the consciousness of belonging in the pupil?"

7. An autobiographical guide to the theological development of Luigi Giussani is offered in *Dqv*, pp. 11–15; in Luigi Giussani, *Il Movimento di Comunione e Liberazione: Coversazioni con Robi Ronza* (Milan: Jaca Book, 1987), pp. 175–79 (*MCL* in future references); and in "Conversazione con Luigi Giussani," *Annuario Teologico 1984* (Milan: Istra, 1984), pp. 131–37. See also Giussani's early work, *Teologia protestante americana* (Venegono: La Scuola Cattolica, 1969).

8. Giussani defines theology as the "enthusiasm of faith." A theology not sustained by such a character lacks religious sense. *MCL*, p. 177.

9. See Luigi Giussani, *Tracce di esperienza cristiana* (Milan: Jaca Book, 1984); idem, *Il senso religioso* (Milan: Jaca Book, 1986).

10. See S. Abbruzzese, *Comunione e Liberazione* (Paris: Editions du Cerf, 1989); E. Pace, "Fondamentalismo italiano: Il caso di Comunione e Liberazione," in Pace, *Il re-*

gime della verita': Il fondamentalismo religioso contemporaneo (Bologna: Il Mulino, 1990), pp. 87–103; L. Accattoli, "Il movimento popolare: Forza e limiti di un messianismo politico," in P. Corbetta and R. Leonardi, eds., *Politica in Italia* (Bologna: Il Mulino, 1988), pp. 293–313; G. Postal, "Le occasioni perdute," *Il Popolo,* 21 March 1991.

11. *MCL,* pp. 20–24.

12. *MCL,* pp. 12–20, 181.

13. "Il 'potere' del laico, cioe' del Cristiano: Intervista a Monsignor Luigi Giussani a cura di Angelo Scola," *Come 2000 anni fa,* a supplement to *Il Sabato,* no. 31 (5 August 1989): 12.

14. Ibid., p. 17.

15. Ibid., p. 11.

16. Antonio Socci and Roberto Fontolan, *Tredici anni della nostra storia,* a supplement to *Il Sabato,* no. 13 (26 March 1988): 50.

17. *Come 2000 anni fa,* pp. 13–14, 21–22.

18. Ibid., p. 22.

19. The parish priest is not recognized as having any special authority toward CL, except when the priest himself is a member of the movement.

20. The works of the founder are the core of CL's canonical texts. They are studied in great depth, one each year. The most significant are *Tracce di esperienza cristiana* (1984), *Alla ricerca del volto umano* (1984), *La coscienza religiosa nell'uomo moderno* (1985), *Il senso religioso* (1986), and *Sulla rivelazione* (1987). All are published by Jaca Book, Milan.

21. Luigi Giussani, "Memores Domini," *30 Giorni,* May 1989; *MCL,* pp. 172–75.

22. For example, the 1990 Meeting of Peace was visited by Lech Walesa; Hans Dietrich Genscher, the German foreign minister; Jan Carnogursky, the vice-president of Yugoslavia; and Giulio Andreotti, the Italian prime minister and a close supporter of CL from its beginnings.

23. S. Quinzio, "Giussani: CL e la politica," *La Stampa,* 20 September 1989.

24. *Corriere delle Opere* (Milan) 5, nos. 7–8 (1990).

25. The formation and structure of the Catholic movements in Italy during the initial development of CL are delineated by several studies. See, for example, "Associazioni, movimenti, comunita' di base," in Alberto Abelli, et al., *Chiesa in Italia, 1975–1978* (Brescia: Queriniana, 1978), pp. 129–78; A. Favale, ed., *Movimenti ecclesiali contemporanei* (Rome: Las, 1982); S. Burgalassi, "Religiosita' e comunita' ecclesiastica in Italia," in S. Burgalassi, et al., *Comunita' locale ed ecumenismo* (Rome: Ave, 1973), pp. 75–125. For an updated map of the Catholic movements in Italy, see Franco Garelli, *Religione e Chiesa in Italia* (Bologna: Il Mulino, 1991), pp. 237–71.

26. There is vast literature on the subject of religious conformity in Italy. Vincenzo Cesareo, ed., *L'icona tecnologica: Immagini del progresso, struttura sociale e diffusione delle innovazioni in Italia* (Turin: Fondazione Agnelli, 1989); G. Calvi, ed., *Indagine sociale italiana. Rapporto 1986* (Milan: Angeli, 1987); J. Stoetzel, *I valori del tempo presente: Un'inchiesta europea* (Turin: Sei, 1984); Silvano Burgalassi, *Le cristianità nascoste. Dove va la cristianità italiana?* (Bologna: Edizioni Dehoniane, 1970); Roberto Cipriani, *La religione diffusa* (Rome: Borla, 1988); Giuseppe Brunetta and Antonio Longo, eds., *Italia cattolica, fede e pratica religiosa negli anni Novanta* (Florence: Vallecchi Editore, 1991). On the development of non-Catholic religious movements in Italy, see A. N. Terrin, *Nuove religioni: Alla ricerca della Terra Promessa* (Brescia: Morcelliana, 1985); G. Filoramo, *I nuovi movimenti religiosi: Metamorfosi del sacro* (Bari: Laterza, 1986); J.-F. Mayer, *Le nuove sette* (Genova: Marietti, 1987); M. Castiglione, *I testimoni di Geova: Ideologia religiosa e consenso sociale* (Turin: Claudiana, 1981); G. Ambrosio, "Le piccole religioni per la societa' complessa: Sette e nuovi movimenti religiosi in Italia," *Il Regno,* March 1985, pp. 135–38; A. Penna and S. Ronchi, *Il protestantesimo: La sfida degli evangelici in Italia e nel mondo* (Milan: Feltrinelli, 1981); B. Bouchard and R. Turinetto, *L'"altra chiesa" in Italia: Gli evangelici* (Turin: Claudiana, 1976).

27. These data may be found in Cesareo, *L'icona tecnologica*. These figures are similar to those of a previous study (1985) done by the University of Trent and published in H. Schadee, "Consumi valori e ceti sociali," *Polis*, no. 3 (1989). In that research 9.4 percent of people aged fifteen to sixty-five said they belonged to a religious association, movement, or group. Twenty-five percent of the age group eighteen to sixty-four stated that in the past they had belonged to a religious association or movement. See also Franco Garelli, *Religione e chiesa in Italia* (Bologna: Il Mulino, 1991), p. 238. The large occurrence of Catholic movements and associations in Italy should be coupled with the well-established diocesan organization of the Church. The Italian territory is subdivided into 224 dioceses, partitioned into 26,000 parishes (one per 2,200 people). The religious organization is directed by 37,300 diocesan priests, 134,000 nuns, and 27,800 priests belonging to religious orders.

28. This is the case, for example, of the movements of the Focolarini, Neocathecumens, Comunities of Christian Life, Pro Sanctitate, Cursillos, Equipe Notre Dame, and Christian Renewal.

29. For a survey of the vast movement of religious voluntary service see G. Sarpellon, "Censimento delle istituzioni assistenziali collegate con la chiesa," in G. C. Milanesi, ed., *Chiesa ed emarginazione in Italia* (Bologne: Dehoniane, 1979); G. Sarpellon, et al., *Stato e chiesa di fronte al problema dell'assistenza* (Rome: Edimez, 1982).

30. For example, Lega Missionaria, Mani tese, Laicato missionario, and Gioventù Missionaria.

31. A 1989 incident concerning *Il Sabato* may typify the case. *Il Sabato* is a weekly national magazine which belongs to the financial institution IET (Instituto Editoriale Internazionale) and is published by EDIT. IET and EDIT are two of the opere created around and by the movement. Ideologically *Il Sabato* has always reflected closely the political and cultural views of the movement. But in 1989, after a public show of displeasure by a large number of Italian bishops toward the political and rhetorical style of the

weekly, Giussani declared that *Il Sabato* would no longer be considered an official publication of CL. It has continued its editorial policy with a similar editorial board and with the same direct ties with the Movimento Popolare.

32. CL has since tried to portray itself as the Catholic voice in the Catholic institutions, for example, in the Azione Cattolica and in the Catholic University of Milan, as well as in the Christian Democratic party.

33. *MCL*, pp. 150–55.

34. See Gaetano Salvemini, *Il partito popolare e la questione romana* (Florence: La Voce, 1922), pp. 9–11. This state of mind is reflected well in a quote taken from the *Civiltà Cattolica* of May 1886 "Italy is divided in three parts: the 'legal,' which goes under the name of *sabaudista* and covers every type and color of liberalism, the democratic included; the 'socialist,' which brings together the radicals as well as the republican, the socialists of the various schools which are hand in hand with the anarchists; the 'Catholic,' which is solidly with the Pope, for whom it advocates independence. The 'legal,' if left alone, is progressively losing the ground under her feet; it does not have enough strength to win the 'socialist.' Therefore, for its own sake, it begs for help from the 'Catholic.' On the other hand the 'Catholics' think that the value of saving the social order of Italy is different from the worth of saving its political order. In the first case it is the "real Italy" which is reinforced, in the second it is the 'legal Italy.' But which duty forces the Catholics to save the legal Italy? Although Socialism in Italy is growing and is expanding, it is still far from the chance of victory. . . . It would be a great error if the Catholics, under the pretext of avoiding a triumph of the socialist in the remote future, were to strengthen with their help the hateful tyranny of liberalism. Let the dead of liberalism bury their dead" (quoted by Salvemini, *Il partito popolare e la questione romana*, p. 7).

35. On this subject see the important work by Pietro Scoppola and Francesco Traniello, eds., *I catolici tra fascismo e democrazia* (Bologna: Il Mulino, 1975).

36. *Come 2000 anni fa,* p. 12.

37. *Dqv,* esp. pp. 3–5 on reasons for the development of the movement. This image projected by the movement appears to be a significant reason for belonging to CL. It figures clearly in almost all the interviews I have conducted with young members.

38. See the partial report of the meeting of the International Council of Comunione e Liberazione (August 1991), "Corresponsabilità," *Litterae Communionis,* November 1991, pp. 31–35.

39. *MCL,* p. 21.

40. The main figure in the Movimento Popolare is Roberto Formigoni currently the vice-president of the European Parliament.

41. Augusto del Noce, a philosopher who has achieved major intellectual authority within the Movimento Popolare, wrote: "In these days an idea of Gramsci is often referred to which can be shared also by someone who has opposite political views: namely, that it is not possible to reach political hegemony without first having achieved cultural hegemony. One can further develop this idea in these terms: a force which does hold political power but relinquishes cultural hegemony to other forces cannot but administer cultural power in favor of those forces; furthermore, were such forces not simply different but also antithetical to it, its seeming holding of political power would inexorably damage the expressed principles which had at the start promoted it. This is what has happened in Italy during the forty years of political hegemony of the Christian Democrats. Such a complete secularization had not been accomplished by the Jacobins, or the Freemasons, or the communists. There must be a reason for this. It is the one that I have just stated." Augusto del Noce, "Introduction" in *Tredici anni della nostra storia.* The substance of this evaluation was already anticipated in the judgment that Giussani in 1976 had given of the Italian religious situation, in *MCL,* p. 107. In Giussani's view, the Catholics had forfeited their cultural politics for a secularized and immanentist interpretation of life.

42. *Dqv,* pp. 19–20.

43. The transformation which the idea of a historical Christian project has undergone in Italy between the 1930s and the 1980s has been discussed in Romolo Pietrobelli, ed., *L'idea di un progetto storico dagli anni '30 agli anni '80* (Rome: Edizioni Studium, 1982).

44. Francesco Traniello, *Citta dell'uomo: Cattolici, partito e stato nella storia d'Italia* (Bologna: Il Mulino, 1990); Pietro Scoppola and Francesco Traniello, eds., *I cattolici tra fascismo e democrazia* (Bologna: Il Mulino, 1975); Sandro Magister, *La politica vaticana e l'Italia, 1943–1978* (Rome: Editori Riuniti, 1979); Giuseppe De Rita, *Chiesa e società in Italia* (Rome: Ave, 1985); G. Martina, *La chiesa in Italia negli ultimi trent'anni* (Rome: Studium, 1977).

45. *Come 2000 anni fa,* p. 23.

CHAPTER 7

Accounting for Christian Fundamentalisms: Social Dynamics and Rhetorical Strategies

Nancy T. Ammerman

The Christian believers we have seen in these pages are actively involved in shaping and being shaped by the social world in which they find themselves. They are people who have confronted a wide array of challenges and devised stories and strategies with which to meet those challenges. The story they tell is a story of defending vital truths, and the strategy they have developed protects their own social and rhetorical space and extends it wherever possible. They are an evangelistic people, anxious to share what they have found, anxious for others to experience the grace they claim; but they are pragmatic evangelists, constantly assessing where the fields are most ready for planting and harvest and where the ground is too beaten down or rocky to plow. In the pages that follow, I pull together what we have learned about the social dynamics of Christian fundamentalism.

The seed fundamentalists wish to sow is a powerful story about the nature and destiny of the world and the ways individuals, communities, and nations should live in that world. This world is in the hands of an almighty God, they say, a God who created it from nothing and will eventually bring human history to a close. In that basic theistic presupposition they may not differ markedly from many other people of faith. Where they do differ from nonfundamentalists is in their conviction that they have a clear and detailed picture of the beginning and typological pictures of the end, along with a clear blueprint of the rules for right living in the present. All are contained in knowable form in the pages of holy Scripture (and, in the case of Catholics, in the traditions and authorities of the Church). Their sense of certainty may never, as Robert Wuthnow and Matthew P. Lawson point out in chapter 2, be a sense of having arrived. But it is a sense of having the right road map, of having directions that are backed by divine wisdom and by divinely authorized human custodians of truth.

The fundamentalist sense of certain and knowable truth is a conviction that demands response and that makes a difference—in the mind of the believer, an eternal difference. Outside of the grace of the Church, or outside of the biblically revealed way, everyone is doomed to eternal damnation, and societies are doomed to chaos. Within God's way, a transformed, successful, and happy life is possible. The contrast between salvation and damnation is very clear and is rehearsed in the testimonies they give. Fundamentalist believers cannot be content to "hide their light under a bushel," practicing a divinely ordered life in seclusion. At the very least, they seek to convert their individual friends, neighbors, and family members. In a world that is sinful and dying, they seek to offer the words of life. In the words of Wuthnow and Lawson, their "simple" answers are "a call for action, a plea for a changed lifestyle."

This conviction that the world is best knowable and livable through the lens of divine revelation is coupled with the fundamentalists' conviction that their revelation is one that radically reframes all of life. All other knowledge, all other rules for living are placed in submission to the images of the world found in the sacred texts and traditions. All other authorities and credentials are de-legitimated, or at least put in their place. Claims based on science, legal precedent, even employee handbooks have to be measured against the claims of Scripture and tradition. And so creationists are sure that the earth is not millions of years old; Operation Rescue's Randall Terry dares to assert a higher law that calls him to save the lives of babies about to be aborted;[1] and Christian students defiantly pray and read their Bibles in the public schools they attend. They are no more willing to recognize multiple moral authorities in the various institutions in which they live than they are to recognize multiple moral authorities in the various cultures that occupy our diverse world. Theirs is a rhetoric of purity and totality as well as a rhetoric of certainty. It asserts a "de-differentiated" world in which all spheres of life are knit together by divine will.[2]

Fundamentalist Myths: Visions of Past and Future

Fundamentalism is also a rhetoric of purposefulness that links past and future, beginning and end, in ways that shape the present. In the face of a "modern" world that must choose between "natural selection" and complete uncertainty for an account of its beginning, fundamentalists of the Christian sort offer an account that is orderly and purposeful. Their God created the world, and their God will bring it to an immanent conclusion, offering rewards to the just and punishment to the damned. That in itself, however, is not so remarkable; religious groups of all sorts are likely to give some sort of sacred meaning to history. Fundamentalist accounts are remarkable for their rejection of plural and subjective readings of history and for their attempt to overcome the removal of some parts of history (the secular, political, or public) from the scope of sacred renderings. Comunione e Liberazione sees itself as an agent of God in the restoration of the Church's place in Italian society, utterly rejecting the separation of church and state that has characterized liberal democracy. And as Susan Harding points out in chapter 3, the "history" practiced by North American Protestant fundamentalists places God at the center. They act as if divine action is fully explanatory—as much in the affairs of nations as in those of persons and families and churches. It stands therefore in marked contrast to the "history" practiced by the academy, where there is no room for sacred activity.

These rhetorical strategies of claiming a clear, certain, and all-encompassing truth, truth that separates saved from damned and gives purpose to the future, are necessary marks of fundamentalist movements; but they might also be found in other, religious and secular world-transforming movements. One could say the same about Bagwhan Shree Rajneesh or even about the role of the state in a Marxist-Leninist society. They too are sure they have a singular path toward the future. What distinguishes a fundamentalist movement is the anchorage of its vision in a "golden past" and a longed-for future, both found blueprinted in a religious text. Moreover, the particular religious text on which fundamentalists base their vision is one that has already played a significant role in shaping the sense of "peoplehood" present in their society. *Fundamentalist movements are organized efforts to shape the future of a people in light of a past that is seen through the lens of sacred texts and authorities traditionally available in the culture.*

This definition poses serious difficulties when it encounters the activities of evangelicals and Pentecostals in Latin America. It is hard to argue that Latin American evangelicals are the keepers of a lost tradition. While one *can* plausibly argue that the dominant religious tradition in the United States was once evangelical, a tradition today's fundamentalists claim to want to renew, such an assertion is not possible in the Latin American case. Latin American evangelicals are not trying to renew the Catholic Church and return it to its place at the center of culture. On the contrary, they want people to leave the Catholic Church. If we are looking for renewal and reform *within* the dominant religious tradition, we might look toward the base communities instead. Evangelicals, on the other hand, are likely to encounter conflicts with Catholicism and to be seen as a dangerous challenge to Catholic hegemony, in David Stoll's words (chap. 5). Evangelicals consciously reject much, if not all, of the Catholic heritage (even though they draw, often unconsciously, on the traditions and worship styles of both Catholicism and before). In fact, the basic polarity in much of Latin American Protestant rhetoric seems to be the Catholic-evangelical contrast.

People whose religious language and lifestyle might look like fundamentalism in North America represent a substantially new religious tradition in areas south of the Rio Grande, and new religious movements have different constituencies and dynamics from movements within traditions.[3] Latin American evangelicals draw on *both* the traditions of the Yankees and their own indigenous symbols to create a new synthesis, something neither exclusively homegrown nor exclusively imported, neither a clear derivation from "tradition" nor a completely new movement. While there may be a number of similarities between these religious innovators and North American innovators drawing on similar biblical and theological roots, we should recognize the differences their differing contexts may produce. These differences, I contend, are sufficient to make the term "fundamentalist" unsuitable in the Latin American case. They may be conservative, evangelical, even linked to specific North American fundamentalist groups—but relative to their own culture they are not fundamentalist.

One of the things these Latin American movements *do* have in common with the North American and European cases examined in this section is their attempt to redefine the central characteristics of their own peoplehood. These are movements that contain at least some elements of public activism. As such they promulgate more than just a picture of transformed individual lives or disciplined, caring congregations. An activist message is also a message about the life of a people—usually a people defined by their nationhood, but sometimes (as in the case of Ulster, for instance) defined by their ethnicity.[4] The fundamentalist message is not only about being an individual believer, but also about being a believing nation.

We hear it in U.S. fundamentalists' vision of America returning to godly ways, fulfilling the Great Commission, and protecting Israel. We hear it in the Pentecostal pastor who proclaims that Jesus wants to be Lord of Guatemala. His is a vision of Guatemalan peoplehood which competes with the vision promulgated by the Catholic Church, which has always seen itself as the preserver and definer of what it means to be Guatemalan. We see the same struggle for religious and national definition in Comunione e Liberazione's claims about the legitimate role of the Church in shaping all of Italian society. And we notice the way in which evangelical communities lay claim to defining a new Indian identity for converts in Ecuador, again coming into conflict with Indian movements that take Catholicism as a necessary core identity.

In the U.S. and Italian cases, fundamentalists make claims to being the legitimate keepers of the nation's traditions. Italian Catholics argue in word and deed against the separation of the Church from its former role in government and daily life. U.S. fundamentalists talk about the Christian intentions of the Founding Fathers, picturing the U.S. Constitution as a sacred document built on biblical principles and granting political liberties as a sacred trust. Former Reagan administration aide Oliver North spoke to Southern Baptist pastors in 1991, reminding them of the nation's desperate need for revival and of the believer's accountability for the nation's moral character. When he spoke of the Christian's mission, there simply were no neat distinctions between the task of saving eternal souls and reforming government at every level. Since the nation was founded on biblical principles, Christians have a special responsibility for its preservation and guidance.

> In the opening words of our Constitution, it speaks of the "blessings of liberty"; blessings are not things given by man unto himself; they're not given by governments to their people; they're given by God Almighty. Our forefathers understood that. . . . Jefferson bases the entire thesis of this country on the basis that life, liberty, and the pursuit of happiness are gifts from Almighty God. [That] also assumes the involvement of a godly people in the governance of this nation, and we have a desperate need for that kind of involvement today [applause]. . . . It's the responsibility of Christians to get others involved in the [political] process and in so doing lead this nation back to God.

Faye Ginsberg quotes Randall Terry as calling for "a nation where once again the Judeo-Christian ethic is the foundation for our politics, our judicial system, and our public morality; a nation not floating in the uncertain sea of humanism, but a country whose unmoving bedrock is Higher Laws."[5]

There is much more than political theory here. This is a mythic telling of the American story which combines nostalgia for a dimly remembered simple and pious past with discontent over the current state of affairs. At the same 1991 Southern Baptist pastors conference, legendary fundamentalist pastor W. A. Criswell spoke of "the secret of the greatness of America" in elaborately woven stories of past heroes, military victories, waving flags, and "humble Georgia farmers" who gather their families each night around the "sacred book" and prayer. What is created in such stories is a powerful mythic image of a pristine state from which we have fallen and to which we must return, a movement of history that demands the heroic participation of the faithful.

Latin American evangelicals have no such easy recourse to widely shared national traditions. Yet even here we find converts reaching back into the symbols of their own history to find stories that prefigure their current efforts to rebuild and renew. The current chaos in Guatemala is foreseen in a divine curse delivered centuries ago, a curse evangelicals have the power to lift. Their new vision is framed in terms of transforming the cursed land into the blessed nation God always intended. And Puruhá evangelicals can explain their reversal of fortune and hopes for the future with stories and actions that build on ancient ways of claiming power. Like their North American counterparts, they find legitimacy for their vision of renewal in explicit and implicit symbols and traditions recognized as central to the culture. Unlike their North American counterparts, however, they find that the evangelical part of their new identity is *not* part of the culture and must be transformed to make it really "native." In Latin America, evangelicals are hoping to forge newly *redeemed* national identities, not newly restored ones.

What we have seen in each of these movements, then, is a sacred story about past and future which lays claim to the present. The fundamentalist sense of history is, in fact, less linear than the progressivist historical mind instilled by the Enlightenment. Fundamentalists are more willing to make leaps of imagination across centuries, likening what happened to Jesus to what they experience today or seeing what is expected to happen after the Rapture in what they watch on the news. The Puruhá see the chaos and conflict around them as the end of an old age, while at the same time they—by their conversion—are already living in a new age. We see this creative reading of history/future most clearly in the dispensational rhetoric of Jerry Falwell and other fundamentalist political activists in the recent North American Protestant tradition. As Harding argues, their telling of the future shifted during the 1980s, even as they were reshaping their action in the present. In a dynamic conversation between present events and visions of the future, between possible action and necessary action, these apocalyptic preachers spoke a movement into being.

All social movements create and promulgate a particular vision of the future. The distinguishing mark of a *fundamentalist* social movement is the relationship it claims between past and future. The mobilizing stories at the heart of fundamentalist movements are stories that link a renewed future with renewed adherence to the sacred texts and authorities formerly dominant in that society.

Fundamentalists as Culture Critics

The words fundamentalists speak hold out a vision of a transformed future that stands in marked contrast to the decadence of the present age. Fundamentalists look at the world in which they live and see immorality, violence, corruption, and sin. It has fallen far short of what God would have it be. In the United States, the list of social ills includes divorce and the "breakdown of the traditional family." It also includes a variety of other family-related issues—from gay rights to pornography to sex education and abortion. The present age is ignoring God's laws, living only for the pleasure of the moment, and reaping a harvest of illness and despair as a result. Among God's people, by contrast, children obey their parents, fathers take seriously their responsibilities as head of the household and provider, and mothers embrace their vital role as nurturer of the next generation of Christians.

The need for strong, bold, and godly family men is paralleled at the national level by the need for a strong military. On the same day that Southern Baptist pastors heard W. A. Criswell, they also heard evangelist Jack Graham interweave images of spiritual and political warfare, describing the biblical figure John the Baptist as "launched from the hand of God like a Patriot missile," a "one-man Desert Storm" who helped usher in the messianic age. Fundamentalists are sure that the American system of democracy and free enterprise is not only worth protecting but also worth spreading. Leaders who shy away from exercising power and critics who question the legitimacy of such actions are dangerous cancers eating away at the national soul, robbing us of our ability to act on behalf of what we know to be right. Like Comunione e Liberazione, U.S. fundamentalists have no qualms about the use of power in pursuit of a more godly world. Today's nation, like today's family, is floundering for the lack of righteously exercised power.

In Guatemala and Ecuador, the list of ills is slightly different. Guatemalan evangelicals rail against guerrillas, decry economic woes and the debt crisis, and condemn the evils of machismo. They invoke contrasting visions of a future that is blessed, prosperous, and peaceful, and they give eyewitness accounts of the way individual lives and families have changed. As David Stoll reports, it is sobriety and attention to his family that a converted Guatemalan businessman is most likely to cite as evidence of God's activity in the world.

The evangelical Puruhá center their critique of the world on alcohol consumption. In chapter 4, Tod D. Swanson reports that their testimonies are likely to be laced with references to drinking (before) and abstinence (after). Their identity as an evangelical Indian people was forged in their conflicts with unconverted friends and family over rum. The old system evangelicals describe was one that had robbed them of their power, transferring it to priests and liquor merchants, leaving them subject to debt and illness. Drunken fiestas with revelers falling to their deaths in canyons, coupled with economic enslavement to the local merchants who profited by this system, have now been replaced by Christian fiestas (conferencias) of a different sort, gatherings that sustain rather than threaten families, economies, and health.

In Italy, Comunione e Liberazione concentrates its energies on condemning the evils of modernity—especially as found in the modern state. By making "man the measure of all things," the modern way of thinking has blasphemed God. By refusing to grant the Church a legitimate place at the center of society, the modern state is inherently atheistic and doomed to chaos and failure. Abortion, divorce, and political turmoil are but the visible signs of the evils of modern society.

Wuthnow and Lawson point out that fundamentalist movements paint the world in black and white, creating radical polarities between good and evil. But they do not manufacture the evil they see; they merely name it, highlight it, caricature it. Theirs is a keen reading of the actual threatening forces present in their society. It is not surprising, then, that fundamentalist movements seem to arise at times when the definitions of good and evil are in the process of being renegotiated, when long-standing implicit polarities have been called into question. When fundamentalism first arose a century ago in the United States, social and intellectual dislocations were rampant.[6] As Harding observes, the intellectual world was in the process of reframing the "historical metanarratives," placing "progress" and "enlightenment" in charge of an inevitably unfolding future, and relegating the sacred to a dim past. By the 1960s, intellectual and social changes were again rocking the nation, with social and demographic changes especially noticeable in the "New South."[7] The entire culture seemed uncertain about how to behave. And within that cultural chaos, American Catholics were also absorbing the redefinitions of tradition created by Vatican II.[8] Both Protestants and Catholics found themselves offended and outraged that others who claimed to be Christian could accept such radically altered rules for living and worshiping. Both were also assessing what began to seem like a growing and aggressive secularity in the highest levels of culture and in an ever-expanding state.

In that same era, the situation for Catholics in Italy included, as Dario Zadra points out in chapter 6, the radical youth movements and political chaos that seemed to threaten the very foundation of Italian society. The 1974 referendum on divorce was merely the most visible symbol of moral decay. Comunione e Liberazione, in response, focused first on the very heart of the chaos—university campuses. Even in times of little cultural upheaval, students represent a classic case of persons in social, cultural, geographic, and moral transition. As the CL students have aged, they and the movement have branched out into virtually every area of Italian economy, politics, and culture, offering a highly integrated way of life organized around religious sensibilities and religious authority, but fully participating in the urban, technological world.

As societies are dislodged from stable traditional ways of life, some groups find those traditions useful as a rallying point as they reorganize life in a changing and seemingly chaotic world. So long as the tradition is in place, there is no need to organize to defend it. But when the external boundaries and the internal structures of the communities that have sustained the traditions can no longer make them matters of habit and assumption, one of the responses is likely to be a fundamentalist movement that seeks to restate those traditions in ways that take account of the new circumstances.

The situation of rapid change and moral ambiguity is, in fact, fertile ground for all sorts of religious and political movements. When fundamentalists create new narratives in response to wars and shifting national alliances and boundaries, they may be doing nothing more than other groups are doing at the same time. We all must make new sense of the world when it changes. Sociologist Ann Swidler has described these circumstances as "unsettled" times and points out that they produce vigorous ideological entrepreneurship.[9] And, as Rodney Stark has theorized, *any* new movement that succeeds in such an environment is likely to claim and to exhibit at least some continuity with preexisting religious traditions. Some familiar symbols, practices, or authorities are kept, even if reinterpreted.[10] What distinguishes a fundamentalist movement from the others, then, is the centrality of tradition in its rhetoric and practice. These are the movements that make unambiguous claims to continuity with past practices and truths. They do not claim to have transformed tradition or to have reformed it. They claim, rather, that tradition—if lived as they say it should be—can transform the person, the community, indeed the society. Having created a history premised on continuity between past golden age and future glorious triumph, their rhetoric about the present takes on transformative power, pressing the present toward conformity with those past/future visions. Their claims about "tradition" are never merely about the past. They must retain enough of the elements in their culture's telling of its history to be plausible. But a mere call to the past would have no transformative power. Rather, in their linking of past to future, and in their rejection of a progressive view of history, they ironically claim the power of this future/past in the present.

These definitional distinctions again pose problems in the Latin American case. Both North American Protestant and Italian Catholic movements can make such claims to continuity with dominant cultural traditions; Latin American Protestants cannot. Like their European and North American counterparts, they *have* arisen out of "unsettled times." In Ecuador, evangelical missionaries found the soil ready for their seed when, in the 1950s and 1960s, the fiesta culture reached a critical point, resulting in communities and families unable to sustain themselves under the heavy burden of drink and debt. In Guatemala, the military and economic turmoil of the past decade and a half seems to have opened a door for evangelicals as well. David Martin's survey of research on Latin American evangelicals leads him to conclude that conversion seems most likely in the times and places where some dislocation of the traditional communities and hierarchies has taken place. Protestantism, he says, "emerges at a certain point in the opening up of a society, particularly among people above the lowest level of indigence and with some independent resources of mind or money or skill."[11] But a slightly opened society allows a variety of movements to grow, and what distinguishes Protestantism in that context is its creation of *new* ways of life, not its defense of old ones.

What fundamentalists have in common with new religious movements, then, are their origins in unsettled times and their insistence that the current cultural situation is unacceptable. In both explicit and implicit ways, the story they tell is a story that stands in criticism of the culture. They assess the habits and institutions and ideas of the world around them and find them wanting. They explicitly list the aspects of the culture they find unacceptable. But their very telling of a different kind of story about who we are and where we are going also constitutes, according to Harding, an implicit criticism of the culture's dominant ideas and of the institutions that perpetuate those ideas. Theirs is a defiant "That's *not* the way it is."

Simply voicing this critique is itself a political act. It refuses legitimacy to the institutions that perpetuate the culture in its current decadent state. But, as Harding observes, the way the story is told can open and close windows of activity. In *Bible Believers* I argued that the question has never been whether fundamentalists would be active in shaping their world. The question is rather how they define, at any given moment, what constitutes the world in which they are to be active.[12] In some times and places, that world has barely extended beyond immediate family and small congregation. In other times and places, the call to follow God takes the believer into marketplace, school, government, and foreign affairs. A favorite scripture among North American fundamentalists is 2 Chronicles 7:14, "If my people, which are called by my name, shall humble themselves and pray and seek my face and turn from their wicked ways; then will I hear from heaven, and will forgive their sin, and will heal their land." In some times and places that scripture is preached as a call to repentance and revival in the church. At most, the church is seen as a kind of redeeming remnant whose righteousness may save the nation from God's wrath. At other times and places, that scripture is preached as a call to national repentance, a last chance to avert U.S. decline. In the first version of the story, "my people" is heard as a reference to the true believers who inhabit the church. In the second version, "my people" is the nation, much as it was for the Hebrews to whom the plea was first addressed. The first version of the story expresses the intentions of a pious remnant, people who criticize the corruption of their age and who resist it by their own defiant piety and belief. The second version expresses the determination of a people seeking to bring about the cultural repentance that will avert disaster. The first version directs attention inward; the second outward. It is all the same story, but the meanings attached to its characters and plots change as it is told and retold in response to the changing panorama of daily events.

Social Supports for Fundamentalism

In the chapters in this section (as indeed in the entire volume), the authors have tried to assess the social contexts and resources that are the conversation partners for fundamentalist movements. The chapter by Wuthnow and Lawson talks about the external conditions—from the degree of heterogeneity to economic stability and governmental regulation—that make the success of fundamentalism in a competitive ideological environment more likely. And Harding's essay points out how new forms of discourse can make possible new forms of action. In many instances, the necessary conditions for movement success are not unique to fundamentalism; they are simply the essential ingredients for any movement's survival. In other instances, the particular form these social processes take is shaped by their fundamentalist character.

All new movements, for instance, must have effective leadership; fundamentalist movements, because of their insistence on singular truth, are likely to establish leadership structures that are strictly hierarchical in form. Nonfundamentalist movements, in contrast, may adopt more democratic forms. They may also celebrate their very newness with fluid ideological and organizational practices that change with the whims of the leaders and the contingencies of the moment. In contrast, by tying their rhetoric to "tradition," fundamentalist movements are more inclined toward (at least the appearance of) stability in their ideas and structures. In addition, new movements face certain challenges of legitimacy not usually faced by fundamentalist movements. Fundamentalists can usually be assured of legal protections and a certain level of community acceptance that is not automatically afforded a new movement. The creation of a fundamentalist movement is a dynamic social process in which the raw materials of culture and discontent are shaped by the particular ideological and social resources of the movement itself.

Perhaps the most hostile environment for the growth of fundamentalism is, as Wuthnow and Lawson point out, one in which the society is relatively homogeneous and stable. There is little in the way of cultural space for critique and diversity. Where religious homogeneity is also tied to a strong or repressive state and to the dominant social classes in the society, dissidence may be just under the surface, but it is quite unlikely to be expressed. It is only as the power of the Catholic Church has weakened in much of Latin America, for instance, that evangelicals have been able to see the fruits of a century of missionary labors.[13] And in North America, if Will Herberg was right about the postwar dominance of a cultural "Protestant-Catholic-Jew" melting pot, the generation between 1940 and 1965 may have entertained too much cultural consensus to allow much room for the critiques voiced by fundamentalists. People were simply too satisfied and shared too many religious assumptions.

In contrast, where neither the state nor the society is hospitable to religiosity, fundamentalism is no more likely to grow than is any other form of faith. Here, France is perhaps the classic example.

In contexts that are relatively hostile to their growth, fundamentalist movements—where they arise at all—are likely to emphasize the building of congregations and homes that can nurture and sustain the faithful. We have already seen the emphasis placed on families by all these movements. Unwholesome and destructive families are the stuff out of which fundamentalists build their caricature of "the world." High rates of marital disruption, uncertain gender roles, even ambiguities in sexual identity are challenges facing everyone. Fundamentalists read those statistics, however, and offer them up as evidence of a way of life that must be rejected, a way of life that stands in contrast to the care and stability promised to the faithful. In Italy, changes in divorce and abortion laws are the most vivid evidence, in the rhetoric of Comunione e Liberazione, of the need to restore the Church's influence.

To offer such a critique, fundamentalist communities must direct a good deal of energy toward creating and supporting viable families. Part of that energy goes toward promulgating and reinforcing the habits of personal morality and piety which seem almost inevitably to strengthen the bonds of family life. Stoll and Swanson (along with David Martin) emphasize what happens when men give up their participation in a machismo culture dominated by alcohol. The economic, physical, and psychic strains posed by excessive consumption are eliminated, as are the attendant "temptations of the flesh." The result is men who are more often present in the family, squander less money on outside pursuits, and are rewarded for concentrating their energies on providing economic and emotional care for their families.

The restoration of patriarchy in household and public life is the ideal, rhetorically extolled and modeled by the leaders of these fundamentalist communities. Ginsberg has noted the aggressive "male" style of Operation Rescue leaders.[14] And Southern Baptist pastors have been reminded often, of late, that theirs must be the "bold-not-bland" leadership of a "man's man" (as the evangelist Bailey Smith put it).[15] The need for strong and bold men who will take charge is often contrasted to a picture of the weak man who is too easily influenced by women and gives up his rightful authority. The most enthusiastic applause received by W. A. Criswell at the 1991 pastors' conference was for his mocking imitation of "sissy effeminate preachers." As Deberg has shown, Criswell's comments would have put him at home among North American fundamentalists in the earlier part of the twentieth century. They, too, expended a good deal of homiletical breath on the question of proper authoritative roles for men.[16]

What has become increasingly clear to observers of a variety of fundamentalist, evangelical, Pentecostal, and Orthodox Jewish communities, however, is that the rhetoric of patriarchy and submission serves primarily as a normative counterweight to the individualistic and hedonistic ways of the larger society.[17] The rhetorical contrast is between a secular world where people put personal pleasure ahead of family responsibility and a religious community where individuals accept their rightful and God-given roles and responsibilities. Between those two ideological poles, actual fundamentalist families negotiate an everyday routine that encompasses as much discussion and compromise as male dominance—and more male "nurturance" than male aggression. While final decisions and primary economic responsibility may rest with husbands, wives know that their mates are supposed to place the needs of the family ahead of personal (male) desires. Drawing on the work of Elizabeth Brusco, Martin asserts that evangelical religion in Colombia provides "an ideology which can be used by women to domesticate men."[18] And many women are willing to submit to the authority of the caring and responsible men created by fundamentalist conversions.

Emphasizing the responsibility of husbands for their families would, of course, mean little if the community were not able to engender the skills, habits, contacts, and resources that make economic survival possible. In the U.S. congregation I studied, families were engaged in a variety of self- and mutual-aid practices that gave reality to the ideals being preached.[19] Most of the families needed two incomes, but many of the wives earned the extra they needed by working in the church's preschool or academy—jobs that kept them close to their children. Others cared for each other's children, worked flexible schedules, and helped each other find part-time jobs. Members and others in the wider fundamentalist community made calls to friends in personnel offices and hired each other when the occasion presented itself.

Family concerns, then, are intertwined with economic ones. David Martin's review of various studies of Latin American Protestants leaves the strong impression that families are helped not only by their newfound habits of sobriety, but also by the tangible economic skills and connections shared by converts at all economic levels.[20] To build the kind of families fundamentalists espouse requires attention to economic concerns, usually in very pragmatic, local, and ad hoc ways. As Laurence Iannaccone has pointed out, there is little that could pass for systematic, academic-style, fundamentalist economic thought,[21] but that does not mean fundamentalists do not think about economics. Sometimes, as Stoll observes about Guatemala, the "health and wealth," "name it and claim it" gospel of prosperity serves both as an explanation for and an incentive toward economic success for the already advantaged in a struggling capitalist system. But even there, the practice of "claiming the blessings" may look like the same pragmatic mutual aid I observed in the northeastern United States. Indeed, as Stoll observes, in the midst of a dysfunctional social service system, evangelicals have been actively setting up their own parallel structures. Here they can avoid the bribes and corruption of the "official" system and fill some of the gaps left by governments and economies that do not work.

Even more strikingly, the *suerte* (or blessing) that Swanson notes among evangelical converts seems to translate into prosperity that is generated in mutual aid and celebrated in communal activities. He is not convinced that Quichua prosperity is the precursor of full-fledged capitalism, only that these converts have learned ways of prospering within a larger capitalist system. Comunione e Liberazione, on the other hand, is nothing if not capitalist. Central to what it means to join this movement is participation in Le Opere, the far-flung economic enterprises of the group. These enterprises fill gaps in the available services in the economy and give attention to the human dimensions of work. Their resacralization of economic activity has both religious and economic consequences. In each case, we find the faithful looking out for the well-being of fellow believers, working together to prosper for the good of the community and its families.

Fundamentalist action in the world, then, always consists in strategies aimed at strengthening families, actions that often also entail pragmatic economic efforts. But none of these actions in the world would be possible without the basic social unit in which fundamentalism exists—the congregation (a role taken in Comunione e Liberazione by the *scuole di communità*). Sometimes these units are little larger than extended families, but whether it is fifty who gather or five thousand, fundamentalist congregations seek to provide the sort of "extended family" ties of nurture and emotional support which make them very powerful social units. Here people without families find both fictive kin and actual partners. Here people who have left behind the neighbors who celebrated births and deaths with them gain a new "village" of neighbors. It is no accident that believers so often refer to each other as "brother" and "sister," for the relationships they build in the congregation are often familylike in their intensity. From shared meals to shared projects to matchmaking, the congregation performs the rituals and functions of the traditional community. When fundamentalists evoke images of an alien modern society full of strangers who do not care for each other, they often contrast that alien world to an earlier era; but the lived contrast to a world of strangers is their own re-created community.

Whether it is the scuola di comunità of CL or the weekly luncheon of Full Gospel or the network of churches and publishers which created and carried the 1980s revisions of North American apocalypticism, each movement must carve out some protected space in which to do the most basic social work of conversing and dreaming and exhorting, playing and mourning, condemning and celebrating. If fundamentalism is a "discursive style, a way of talking" (to use the words of Wuthnow and Lawson), it must have arenas in which its idiom is spoken, in which its sacred stories about the self and the world are rehearsed. So fundamentalists gather in congregations and in "parachurch" meetings, seeking as many opportunities as possible for telling their story.

The Quichua images Swanson described are particularly potent recognitions of the centrality of speech in the life of the community. For these Indians, wind is a carrier of power. They are reassured that they have regained their suerte by their enthusiastic and powerful singing. Their control of their own lives is symbolized by their control of the spoken and sung word. And the strength of their communities is tested and kept alive by their competitions with other evangelical communities. It is in speaking and singing that they know they are truly alive.

The words and practices generated in these communities are the stuff from which fundamentalism is made. They are the "cultural capital" that can be invested in individual status distinctions, rewarding, as Wuthnow and Lawson observe, those who master the community's valued knowledge and establishing a system of value that stands over against the values of "the world." These same valued words and stories can also be used, as Harding observes, as a means for expanding and transforming the community's knowledge. By means of their own words and practices, not by way of outside intervention, the community can speak new actions and responses into being.

Perhaps it is the power of the discourse of communities which lends urgency to the evangelical crusade to recruit "prayer warriors" in Guatemala. To pray is to speak to God in terms the community has defined as the appropriate language and subject matter for divine address. Whether publicly voiced or privately practiced, praying is an exercise in speaking about the world in God's terms. While it may seem passive to the skeptical observer, it keeps alive a critical consciousness. It reinforces the contrast between the way things are and the way God would wish them to be. It provides a rhetorical exercise in what Peter Berger labeled "ecstasis," standing outside everyday reality, experiencing the sacred in a way that relativizes the mundane.[22]

At the very least, then, a fundamentalist movement must have a place to pray. No matter how beleaguered and small, it is the congregation that is the minimal arena for social action. When no other avenues are open, fundamentalists gather to lament the sad state of the world and speak about their visions of a radically transformed future. Sometimes, as Wuthnow and Lawson point out, both the policies of the state and the religious homogeneity of the society may confine fundamentalist activity to this small sphere. Stoll notes as well that certain kinds of political activity are simply too dangerous within the Guatemalan context of unchecked military power. Where fundamentalist visions of a new society are met with overwhelming external odds, the cultural work of the movement is likely to be internal, simply preserving and nurturing individuals, families, and congregations.

Where the space for dissident religious activity is somewhat larger, fundamentalists are likely to create an expanded range of religious institutions. As we have already noted, following Wuthnow and Lawson, the size and strength of this religious space may be affected by long-standing cultural traditions and policies of the state. Some societies simply direct more of their economic and cultural capital toward religion than do others, and fundamentalists can share in that bounty or scarcity.

Where fundamentalists have the resources, their religious visions may be sustained in a variety of activities, with distinct but overlapping networks of compatriots. They "fellowship" at prayer breakfasts and gospel lunches. They attend youth rallies and evangelistic crusades. They subscribe to evangelical magazines and watch charismatic preachers on television. Their kids go to camps and sporting events, and wives gather with other women to talk about health and wholeness. The spread of the new apocalypticism Harding describes—through books and tapes and television, as well as through churches and conferences and Holy Land tours—is testimony to the infrastructure now in place among North American fundamentalists. Latin American evangelicals are sustained by hundreds of local radio personalities and increasing numbers of Christian schools, in addition to the radio and television broadcasts that come in from the North. Participants in Comunione e Liberazione can draw on periodicals and publishers, cultural events, professional associations, and the enormous range of their routine economic, political, and religious activity. As the resources of fundamentalist movements grow and the cultural space for such activity expands, believers create an increasing array of materials and activities to sustain and enrich the life of their communities.

In the early stages of such religious openness and ferment, we may find the rather amorphous evangelical milieu of a Guatemala. Charismatic Catholic prayer meetings and Full Gospel (Protestant) lunches may be frequented by the same converts, either concurrently or in serial fashion, as the population shops about among various religious visions of reform. In later stages, the institutional lines may become more clearly drawn, connecting some activities naturally with others and distinguishing that set of organizations from its competitors. Such advanced institutional lines of demarcation could be seen, for instance, in the conflict generated by fundamentalist Jerry Falwell's intervention in the Pentecostal ministry of Jim and Tammy Bakker. Neither constituency—fundamentalists or Pentecostals—was happy. Nevertheless, even in the highly developed institutional milieu of the United States, other situations draw the lines less clearly, and many local believers still move rather casually across boundaries their leaders would draw more emphatically.

As fundamentalists create such an expanding array of institutions, they are both further insulated from the surrounding society and inevitably drawn toward it. Their institutions are at once alternatives and mirrors. Adopting the pattern of the larger culture—from business associations to women's clubs to theme parks (to take the U.S. example)—they fill these "secular" structures with "sacred" contents. They can be at once "in the world but not of it."

In these circumstances, the very strength of their movement may propel believers outward into their neighborhoods and workplaces as witnesses. A fundamentalist surrounded by a panoply of products and services and activities has an attractive alternative to offer her unsaved neighbors. She is supplied with ample resources (from books and tracts to training sessions and recruiting activities) to support her evangelistic efforts, and the way of life to which she invites friends and family can easily compete with other institutional and cultural sectors of the society to which that person might be attracted. As the believer is evangelizing, she is, on the one hand, drawn into increasing encounters outside the protected environment of the home and congregation. On the other hand, the very nature of the encounter reinforces her sense of distinctness. As she seeks to convince another of the need to be saved, she is reassured of her own salvation.

Conditions for Fundamentalist Activism

The dynamic relationship between the society outside the movement and the innovations of the movement itself can be seen in a number of ways, then. It can be seen in the interplay between external social conditions and the readings of those conditions by fundamentalists. It can be seen in the complex relationship between demographic shifts that increase the number of dislocated people and the norms and practices of fundamentalist communities—which in turn may alter the familial and economic landscape. It can also be seen in the push from internal institutional strength outward into the environment.

Even where fundamentalism is struggling and virtually invisible, it still nurtures its critique of culture, sometimes implicitly, sometimes explicitly. A variety of circumstances may conspire, however, to take this vision outside the confines of the families and congregations where it lies dormant. Growing institutional strength may mean a growing constituency. But even that growing constituency may remain relatively uninvolved in matters outside their religious domain until dynamic new leaders arise from within to challenge their complacency. These leaders speak the story in a new way, creating thereby, as Harding argues, new ways to envision oneself and one's world. No matter how chaotic or morally ambiguous the world, active response is unlikely so long as believers envision themselves an embattled minority awaiting the End. To name themselves the Moral Majority and to claim this time before the End as a time for God to work miracles is quite another story. It is a story that emerged from a number of writers during the 1970s and 1980s, but it was given its most forceful voice by televangelists Falwell and Robertson, along with, to a lesser extent, Swaggert and the Bakkers. Here the movement generated from within the new leadership resources it needed for transforming itself from internal maintenance to external activism.

Fundamentalists were helped, of course, not only by the strength of these leadership personalities, but also by their use of the broadcast media that carried the messages. They even learned how to stage "media events" and produce quotable "sound bites," using the secular media to carry "news" of their movement.[23] North American fundamentalists had been using radio and television from the beginning. They saw it

as an extension of the urban mass revivals they had been hosting since the late nineteenth century. Beginning in the 1920s, they created and paid for radio programs and
eventually built stations and networks—this during an era when more "mainline"
churches got free air time from many stations. When the free time disappeared in the
early 1960s, evangelicals of all sorts had an infrastructure in place, ready to dominate
the airwaves.[24]

At the same time, powerful evangelical radio stations were being set up in Latin
America. At first almost all the programming was produced by North American missionaries; but as indigenous churches grew, so did broadcasting with a real local flavor, programs that were exciting and dramatic, and usually broadcast live. As new
technologies made more specialized programming possible, more Christian messages
were made available. These media do not create evangelical movements, but they do,
in the words of Rose and Schultze, "amplify and shape" them. In Central America,
radio allows evangelicals to "witness to their faith via the spoken word to a culture
that loves conversation and discussion, with the apparent authority of the voice of a
real person presenting the word of God."[25] The availability of broadcast media is one
of the resources that has enabled fundamentalists to compete so successfully for a
larger niche in the cultural ecology.

They were also aided, as Wuthnow and Lawson observe, by their own increasing
levels of education and skill. In describing Catholic traditionalists, William Dinges
and James Hitchcock point out that organizing a movement requires people accustomed to going to meetings, administering labor, producing written materials, and
so forth.[26] One does not have to be a member of the intellectual elite to have gained
enough verbal and organizational skills to feel confident tackling public issues. In the
generation after World War II, fundamentalists moved to cities and went to college
along with the rest of the U.S. population. In the process they gained both the exposure to alien ways of life which fueled their cultural critique and the skills with
which to spread their critical message.

Another of the external forces that may have aided fundamentalists during the
1970s and 1980s was, according to Wuthnow and Lawson, the shifts in the global
economy which moved especially Great Britain, Canada, and the United States toward economic conservatism. Fundamentalists were able to join forces with politicians calling for reduced social programs, gaining "a modicum of political clout as a
result." Meanwhile, that same global economy was producing the suffering and dislocation in Latin America which provided a context, as noted above, for the growth
of new evangelical communities.

Fundamentalists in the United States were eager to support policies that reduced
social spending, in part because they themselves now occupied the middle class (as
Wuthnow and Lawson rightly point out). But they were also eager to limit the size
of government because the expansion of the state in the post–World War II period
(and especially since 1960) had begun to be perceived as a threat to their way of life.
As legislation, regulation, and court decisions moved increasingly into family-related
domains, fundamentalists saw the state condoning immorality and punishing traditional families. It was not so much that they wanted a smaller state that would leave

families alone; rather the expansion of the state had warned them of policy directions they saw as dangerous.

They were also warned of their differences with U.S. cultural leadership by their struggles over schooling. By the late 1960s, many American fundamentalists had come to believe that public schools had become untenable as nurturers for their children or for the Christian society of which believers dreamed. Schools had become too pluralistic, too committed to "human rights," too secular. The response by fundamentalists was twofold. The first strategy was to create alternatives. The growth and character of the Christian School movement have been documented in a number of excellent studies and need not be rehearsed.[27] What is important here is the extent to which the establishment of schools not only increased the institutional strength of fundamentalism, but also brought fundamentalists into a more "public" arena.[28] In these schools, believers developed and passed on their dreams not only for Christian churches and homes, but also for a Christian America, run on biblical principles. They instilled, therefore, a broader, more public vision in their teachers and students. But the schools themselves also occupied public space. Here institution-building fundamentalists encountered the long arm of the state in the form of everything from building codes to teacher certification. They soon learned that these institutions would not be isolated enclaves, but agents through which believers would begin to assert themselves against the state.

The other fundamentalist response to "secular humanism" in the public schools was to fight to change the schools themselves. During the 1970s, as the movement gained a broader understanding of its mission and power, it began to organize in support of a variety of changes in public education. Among the most visible on the national scene was a call for a constitutional amendment to allow prayer in schools, thus reversing the 1963 Supreme Court decision that had ruled public school religious exercises out of bounds. Various state legislatures attempted their own versions, but each was quickly declared equally unconstitutional. As the southeastern United States began to receive large numbers of immigrants from non–Bible Belt territory, offended newcomers were often the occasion for discontinuing school religious observances that had survived into the 1980s. The public institutions of the land held firm on the principle of a strict "wall of separation," while fundamentalists increasingly suspected that a few secular humanists were conspiring to keep God out of public schools and indeed excluded from all public life.

By the end of the 1980s, one of the liveliest areas of fundamentalist political activism was largely invisible to the eyes of the national media. Hundreds of local parents were forming textbook review committees and getting elected to school boards. Visible activists in Texas and California were organizing to pressure publishers and to testify at hearings. Success in those two huge textbook markets inevitably had repercussions throughout the nation.[29] Other parents inspected school libraries and objected to the teaching of sex education in their districts. Having begun to recognize the education of their children as something they were unwilling to leave to an unbridled state, fundamentalists found themselves involved in political issues ranging from "equal access" for after-hours student religious groups to tax-supported voucher systems that would allow "parental choice." Having ventured into education, they had walked into the public domain.

Given the weakness of the public educational system of Guatemala, Christian schools there have encountered no such state reluctance. As Rose and Schultze described the situation, accreditation is apparently easy to get, and any system that relieves the government of the obligation to spend money on education is probably welcome. There is also little reason for the state to fear the ideology being promulgated in these institutions; students are taught that failure is the fruit of laziness and sin, and that the chief purveyor of evil in the world is communism. Rose and Schultze noted that almost all of the schools are locally run, but some use North American curricular packages—especially Accelerated Christian Education (ACE). Because students at various levels can largely work on their own, this particular system is gaining acceptance by schools on meager budgets with few trained teachers.[30] It remains to be seen whether Guatemalans will eventually put their own indigenous cultural stamp on these North American materials—as they have with North American broadcasting and other evangelical institutions. At this point the resources of North American experience in education are being utilized in support of the movement, and those resources carry with them a vision of Guatemalan peoplehood that is shaped north of the Rio Grande by U.S. fundamentalists. As the indigenous movement gains its own strength, it may no longer need these external resources; but at the moment, in these formative years, messages from the North are helping to shape "Christian education" in Guatemala.

Nowhere is "Christian education" so public as in the activities of Comunione e Liberazione's scuole di communità. The image of the spoke evokes the connection between the center of faith and the involvement of that faith in economic, political, and cultural affairs. The concerns reframed by the group's discussion are never fully reinterpreted until a collective response of faith has been formulated. The very form of education chosen by Luigi Giussani instills in his young followers a sense of responsibility for the whole polity, a commitment to bringing religious concerns back into the center of public life.

Leaders with a new vision of Christian peoplehood, media through which to communicate their message, schools to nurture the coming generation, and an economic and political climate that makes conservatism popular—all are resources on which fundamentalists can draw in any attempt to remake their societies. But remaking a society also requires explicitly political organization and activity. It requires a willingness to register and vote, to address one's concerns to legislators, perhaps to form a political party or support a coup d'état.

As U.S. fundamentalists began to question the family, school, and even arts policies of liberal government agencies, they began to discover just how different the humanist vision of America was from their own. They discovered that they could not take for granted in government, media, or educational leaders any affirmation of the nation's Jewish and Christian roots or any sense that morality should be guided by something beyond individual choice. In hindsight it is hard to disentangle which came first—their discovery of the culture's problems or their formulation of an alternative vision—but it is clear that during the 1970s and 1980s, U.S. fundamentalists were actively arguing against the size and direction of all levels of government. Donald Heinz discerned early in the movement that what we are observing was a clash of symbol systems.[31] As a secular version of the American myth was emerging, fundamentalists were challenged to reformulate their own. External challenges and internal resources combined to produce a newly invigorated assertion of the fundamentalist sense of what it meant to be an American.

The result was a flurry of political organizing. North American fundamentalists not only spoke differently about their role in the world; they also began to build the organizational structures that would carry and sustain their message. They built around the television ministries vast direct-mail fund-raising and lobbying efforts. They went into local churches to register voters. They organized dozens of special interest groups and political action committees, from the Religious Roundtable to the American Coalition for Traditional Values.[32] Inside the Republican party, conservative religionists became a formidable force.[33] Some among their number even took up residence in Washington, D.C. to coordinate letter-writing campaigns and to buttonhole legislators. The turn from internal movement maintenance to external political action is perhaps seen most vividly in the transformation of the Southern Baptist Christian Life Commission after fundamentalists took control of it in the late 1980s. Rather than simply producing educational materials for churches as they had under "moderate" leadership, the agency opened a Washington office and began to work on Capitol Hill, communicating the conservative desires of their constituency directly to Congress.

In other political systems, the activism of fundamentalists takes different organizational forms. None of the other nations in this comparison has the same sort of well-defined two-party system or the long history of stable democracy as does the United States. The multiparty systems elsewhere open up the possibility for a distinctly fundamentalist political party, although none has apparently emerged. CL has operated as a power broker within the Christian Democratic party of Italy, much as fundamentalists operate within the Republican party in the United States

The most volatile fundamentalist entanglement in politics is clearly that in Guatemala. At the same time that neo-Pentecostals were claiming to be "merely religious," one of their own became dictator, surrounding himself with fellow believers. Stoll argues that Ríos Montt's regime redefined evangelicals as a political force. They have not yet, however, found effective political forms of organization to counter the state bureaucracy's "politics of opportunism" and the rampant killing and corruption of an unchecked military. On the one hand they create egalitarian communities that may nurture the skills of democracy. But on the other hand they preach a moral revival of law and order imposed from above. And there are contradictory political tendencies even within the movement. So long as they stay away from explicit political critiques and activities, their power is likely to remain fractured, subject to the manipulation of those who *do* wield power.

In the United States, the power of fundamentalists to effect political change is also limited, primarily by the prevailing liberal interpretations of the Establishment Clause of the First Amendment. Legal opinion for several decades has held that because no religion may be favored over another, religion must be kept out of the public sphere entirely. As John Garvey has shown,[34] fundamentalist efforts to introduce "creation science" and "moments of silence" have tried to build on the very principles of freedom and equality they share with liberals. On these grounds, they have had some success in what Garvey calls their "defensive" agenda—their efforts to protect their schools, churches, and homes from excessive regulation. However, since fundamentalists do not accept the separation of the world into public (where religious neutrality is the rule) and private (where free exercise is the rule), their overarching desire to use the law to guide citizens toward right living (what Garvey calls their "offensive" agenda) has met with much less success. Even when decisions have gone their way, the legal reasoning has been on religiously neutral grounds. Even if fundamentalists believe that the U.S. system of government was built on scriptural principles and ought to continue to support these principles, most of the nation either disagrees with their premise or with the fundamentalist reading of which biblical principles ought apply. In a stable electoral democracy, the weight of legal tradition, constitutional precedent, and majority vote have conspired to limit fundamentalist political success.

As fundamentalists have entered the political arena, they have had to operate within the constraints imposed there. In the United States, those constraints include an established two-party system and a constitutionally guarded tradition of keeping religion at arm's length from official government entanglement. In Guatemala, the constraints include everything from the pervasive system of bribes to the threat of death at the hands of the military. Each society provides fertile ground for the fundamentalist message, some opportunities for expansion and activism, and constraints imposed by everything from economic and demographic deficits to legal precedents.

As fundamentalist movements constantly assess the failings of their present surroundings, they may evoke visions of past and future glories that offer explanation and hope to many. By placing life into a mythic context, people can claim their special role in creating the future. They can also create congregations and reform family life. They can, with enough resources, even establish a pervasive system of alternative institutions in which public and private are rewoven for those living in them. But there are enormous obstacles—both lack of resources and external constraints and limitations—that stand between fundamentalists and the transformation of whole societies.

Notes

1. See Faye Ginsberg, "Saving America's Souls: Operation Rescue's Crusade against Abortion," in Martin E. Marty and R. Scott Appleby, eds., *Fundamentalisms and the State: Remaking Polities, Economies, and Militance* (Chicago: University of Chicago Press, 1993), pp. 557–88.

2. Frank Lechner, "Fundamentalism and Sociocultural Revitalization in America," *Sociological Analysis* 46 (1985): 243–59.

3. See R. Stark, "How New Religions Succeed," in D. Bromley and P. Hammond, eds., *The Future for New Religious Movements* (Macon, Ga.: Mercer University Press, 1987).

4. On the case of fundamentalist Prot-

estants in Northern Ireland, see Steve Bruce, "Fundamentalism, Ethnicity, and Enclave: Ulster Protestants and American Fundamentalists," in Marty and Appleby, *Fundamentalisms and the State,* pp. 50–67. What U.S. fundamentalists find so attractive about Ian Paisley is not only his political and religious conservatism, but also his unabashed wedding of his religious vision to his political one.

5. Ginsburg, "Saving America's Souls," p. 568.

6. The historical background of North American fundamentalism is treated in G. Marsden, *Fundamentalism and American Culture* (New York: Oxford University Press, 1980); and in N. Ammerman, "North American Protestant Fundamentalism," in Martin E. Marty and R. Scott Appleby, eds., *Fundamentalisms Observed* (Chicago: University of Chicago Press, 1991), pp. 1–65.

7. Wuthnow and Lawson point out the significance of changes in the South to the fundamentalist resurgence in the United States. See also N. Ammerman, *Baptist Battles: Social Change and Religious Conflict in the Southern Baptist Convention* (New Brunswick, N.J.: Rutgers University Press, 1990).

8. See W. D. Dinges and J. Hitchcock, "Roman Catholic Traditionalism and Activist Conservatism in the United States," in Marty and Appleby, *Fundamentalisms Observed,* pp. 66–141.

9. A. Swidler, "Culture in Action: Symbols and Strategies," *American Sociological Review* 51 (1986): 273–86.

10. Stark, "How New Religions Succeed."

11. D. Martin, *Tongues of Fire* (London: Basil Blackwell, 1990), p. 202.

12. N. Ammerman, *Bible Believers* (New Brunswick, N.J.: Rutgers University Press, 1987).

13. Stoll makes this point about the breakup of Catholic hegemony in Guatemala, as does Martin, *Tongues of Fire,* p. 59.

14. Ginsburg, "Saving America's Souls."

15. Southern Baptist Convention Pastors Conference, Atlanta, Ga., June 1991.

16. B. Deberg, *Ungodly Women* (Philadelphia: Fortress, 1990).

17. S. Rose, "Women Warriors: The Negotiation of Gender Roles in an Evangelical Community," *Sociological Analysis* 48 (1987): 245–58; M. J. Neitz, *Charisma and Community* (New Brunswick, N.J.: Transaction, 1987); E. Brusco, "The Household Basis of Evangelical Religion and the Reformation of Machismo in Columbia." (Ph.D. diss., City University of New York, 1986); D. Kaufmann, *Rachel's Daughters* (New Brunswick, N.J.: Rutgers University Press, 1991); Martin, *Tongues of Fire;* Ammerman, *Bible Believers,* and others.

18. Martin, *Tongues of Fire,* p. 181.

19. Ammerman, *Bible Believers,* chap. 8. A particularly vivid example can be seen in the congregation portrayed in "Born Again," a PBS broadcast (James Ault, producer).

20. Martin, *Tongues of Fire,* chap. 11.

21. L. Iannaccone, "Heirs to the Protestant Ethic? The Economics of American Fundamentalists," in Marty and Appleby, *Fundamentalisms and the State,* pp. 342–66.

22. P. Berger, *The Sacred Canopy* (New York: Anchor Books, 1967), pp. 43, 98–100.

23. J. Hadden and A. Shupe, *Televangelism: Power and Politics on God's Frontier* (New York: Henry Holt, 1988).

24. R. Frankl, *Televangelism* (Carbondale: Southern Illinois University Press, 1986).

25. S. Rose and Q. Schultze, "The Evangelical Awakening in Guatemala: Fundamentalist Impact on Education and Media," in Martin E. Marty and R. Scott Appleby, eds., *Fundamentalisms and Society: Remaking the Sciences, the Family, and Education* (Chicago: University of Chicago Press, 1993), p. 434.

26. Dinges and Hitchcock, "Roman Catholic Traditionalism," pp. 111–15.

27. A. Peshkin, *God's Choice* (Chicago: University of Chicago Press, 1986); and S. Rose, *Keeping Them out of the Hands of Satan* (New York: Routledge, 1988).

28. This is suggested by Susan Rose in

"The Impact of Fundamentalism on Education," in Marty and Appleby, *Fundamentalisms and Society,* pp. 452–89.

29. Ibid., pp. 470–73.

30. Rose and Schultze, "The Evangelical Awakening."

31. D. Heinz, "Clashing Symbols: The New Christian Right as Countermythology," *Archives de Sciences Sociales des Religions* 30 (1985): 153–73.

32. A. Hertzke, *Representing God in Washington* (Knoxville: University of Tennessee Press, 1988).

33. J. C. Green and J. L. Guth, "The Christian Right in the Republican Party," *Journal of Politics* 50 (1988): 150–65.

34. J. Garvey, "Christian Fundamentalism and American Law," in Marty and Appleby, *Fundamentalisms and the State,* pp. 28–49.

2

Accounting for Jewish Fundamentalisms

Quiescent and Active Fundamentalisms: The Jewish Cases

Samuel C. Heilman

The premise of the chapters that follow, as indeed for all those in this volume, is that religious fundamentalism, a term historically associated with versions of American Protestantism and more recently also used to describe varieties of Islam, has generic characteristics that apply to a multiplicity of religious contexts. Hence not only Christianity and Islam but also Hinduism, Buddhism, Judaism, and other religions may be found to have "fundamentalist" variants. Commonly, we consider fundamentalist religion assertive and uncompromising in its attachment to what its adherents view as the authentic and, hence, fundamental tenets of the faith. Conservative in outlook, fundamentalisms embrace tradition and appear to eschew even relatively limited changes in that tradition, even and perhaps especially when the tenor of the times seems to demand accommodations. They assert that they alone comprehend the meaning of history, understand the significance of the present moment, and see how past and future are connected.

One might argue that what ties all fundamentalisms together is their believers' conviction (correct or not) that their religion as they practice it is part of an unbroken tradition beginning with the earliest prophets and practitioners of the faith and continuing into the contemporary present, linking all those who came before as well as those who shall come after and who remain true to the faith, in one great chain of religious being. Fundamentalists regard themselves as the true heirs of the ancients.

Sometimes, but not always, a body of texts acts as the media or legacy of this cherished tradition, while a series of practices or norms serves as the framework supporting it. But texts are, of course, subject to emendations and deletions, to say nothing of reinterpretation, and the events of history and social change often alter and reframe practices or undermine norms. To fundamentalists, these changes are threatening for they call into question a sense of continuity so central to their faith. And thus, often, fundamentalists find themselves either ignoring or denying change—or at the very least reinterpreting it away. This, of course, makes them dependent on authoritative interpreters of these texts, people—rabbis, preachers, imams, and the like—who can read history into and out of Scripture and put real events into a fundamentalist frame or context.

For those who have kept faith with the tradition, if tomorrow somehow appears to break with such endless repetition of the everlasting and sacred past, this appearance is illusion, since all real change has been prophesied and, hence, prefigured in the past and is therefore not really new after all. For those religions that speak of an end of days, the eschatological tomorrow comes as no surprise to the fundamentalists among them. They expect (and often see signs of) the Messiah and the end of history. They conceive the present and future in terms of the past. In a sense, fundamentalist believers are resolutely ahistorical, considering the differences between yesterday and today immaterial and ontologically insignificant. They prefer to look at life as part of endless repetitions of fundamental archetypes. To fundamentalists, "there is nothing new under the sun." That is why no matter what, "the old-time religion is good enough."

In a sense, fundamentalists who thus "keep the faith" fight back—culturally, ideologically, and socially—against the assumptions and patterns of life that are taken for granted in contemporary secular society and culture, refusing fully to embrace or celebrate them.[1] They keep their distance and refuse to endorse the legitimacy of any culture that opposes what they perceive as fundamental truths. Such an antithetical culture is one that is secular and affirmatively modern. It is base, therefore grossly popular, barbarous, crude, and essentially profane. It produces a society that respects no sacred order and ignores the possibility of redemption. But all sorts of religiously serious Jews can share these feelings and attitudes. Those, however, who can see the essential antagonism of these two cultural domains *and* who feel the need to fight back constitute the fundamentalists.

Many of those who in nineteenth-century Europe were originally called Orthodox Jews had the ideological prerequisites to qualify as fundamentalists by the terms of this broad definition.[2] This is especially true of those among them who went further, who consciously kept their distance from the Western cultures and secular societies which surrounded them and who resolutely stressed their opposition to the trends of cultural assimilation, who remained in the black coats of mourning over the Jewish exile from their Holy Land while others took on the bright colors of assimilation, who stayed in the traditional yeshivas reviewing only Talmud while others went to the universities to explore other sorts of wisdom, who were punctilious and rigid in their attachment to the most stringent demands of religious ritual and custom while others embraced religious reform or at least compromise, and who defined an alternative order to the contemporary one. These people have come to be called *haredim*.[3]

Similarly, those religious Jews who saw an overwhelmingly religious meaning in the national return to their ancient homeland and the conquest and resettlement of tribal lands, who perceived these events of recent Jewish history as the fulfillment of biblical prophesies and harbingers of messianic days, also had the ideological prerequisites. Among the latter, those who took steps to turn such signs into recipes for action to help bring about that end of days also qualify as fundamentalists. These include the Gush Emunim (Bloc of the Faithful), and others who have come to be called *haredim leumiyim* (nationalist Orthodox), who redefined Zionism and the program for Jewish national renewal in strictly religious terms. Among them are Habad Hasidim, who also see signs of and seek to hasten the end, expecting the imminent arrival of the Messiah. As fundamentalists, all these groups see today with a vision of yesterday and a prefigured tomorrow, although—as the chapters in this section demonstrate—each does so in a distinctive and paradigmatic way.

We can categorize in numerous ways these Jews whom we loosely call "fundamentalist." We could divide them in terms of political orientation, separating those who choose to operate within the context of modern Zionism and those who do not. Alternatively, we could talk about historical and ideological distinctions, distinguishing between Hasidim, Misnagdim, and Mizrachistim Jews who differed about how to express their orthodoxy and attachment to religious Judaism.[4] We could even differentiate on the basis of lifestyle and appearance, contrasting those who wear black coats, hats, and beards with those who don knit skull caps and the attire of the twentieth century. Each of these differences represents important distinctions among those Jews who fit the fundamentalist mold.

But these distinctions are particularistic; they are most meaningful only within the context of Jewish life. While drawing them would provide rich ethnographic texture to any portrait of Jewish fundamentalism, such an effort would make it difficult to fit the Jewish variant into this volume and the series in general that seeks to provide students of fundamentalism with "family resemblances." For that end, a more generic way of categorizing is necessary. We have, therefore, selected a modified binary model to organize the chapters in part 2. In this model, fundamentalists in general and the Jewish cases in particular are divided formally into polar types: one characterized by quiescent resistance, and the other by active fighting back against a culture and way of life they consider dangerous and ultimately sacrilegious. And there is a third syncretistic type: those groups that fluctuate between quiescent and active fundamentalism. The chapters in this section explore and exemplify these distinctions.

Quiescent Fundamentalism: The Case of the B'nai Yeshiva

The quiescent aspect of fundamentalism, simply stated, is an unyielding refusal to be moved from an attachment to a perceived tradition coupled with a structured resistance to contemporary culture and values, a resolute unwillingness to be absorbed by or to absorb them. The first element may be called *traditionalism;* the second, *contra-acculturation.*

Traditionalism is a contemporary attitude that nurtures a positive and continuing emphasis on the advantages and benefits of maintaining the tradition, precisely at a time when others look forward to the new as superior. This is not the same as remaining ignorant of modernity; that is only possible for traditionals, who can conceive of no other way to live, who automatically accept and habitually carry on unchangingly what has been handed down to them (that, after all, is what "tradition" means). While being a *traditional* is a matter of destiny rather than choice and is only possible today, if at all, in a few obscure or sheltered corners of the world, *traditionalism* is a matter of personal choice, a contemporary option requiring a special effort and an outlay of cultural energy or resources.[5] Strictly speaking, traditionalism is *not* fundamentalism, but it is a necessary correlate to it.

When, however, people move beyond traditionalist championing of the past but create the conditions to resist alternatives to it, they take the first steps toward fundamentalism. Contra-acculturation is such a step. In his original definition, Melville Herskovits designated contra-acculturation as a two-part process of cultural resistance: "to stress the values in aboriginal ways of life, and to move aggressively . . . toward the restoration of those ways."[6] To be sure, both steps of contra-acculturation are abetted by pluralism, a condition that legitimates more than one way to live one's life, and are paradoxically only imaginable in what Peter Berger has called "the situation of modernity," a time when individuals are freed from custom and habit and reliance on the unquestioned wisdom of yesterday to select and fight for their own way of life.[7]

Of the two steps that Herskovits defines, the first is clearly the more quiescent one. Here the "stress" of which he speaks may take the form of moving toward a kind of cultural isolation, creating a cultural enclave, a semi-autonomous region in which a particular way of life is sustained whose norms, values, patterns of behavior, and even language are different from those in the larger host society. Commonly, these fundamentalists limit themselves to living and protecting an exemplary and exclusively traditionalist life, believing that thereby they can at once fulfill their obligations, take a stand against other ways of life, and also attract followers from among those who may have abandoned the tradition or else who know nothing about it (though with regard to this last point, they are often reluctant to reach out to missionize even among Jews lest they import the very culture from which they have withdrawn).

In the Jewish case, the following statement by a contemporary haredi, which celebrates attachment to Jewish tradition and Orthodox practice—"Torah and Mitzvah," in the words of the writer—articulates this stand:

> Let Torah and Mitzvah alone be our home, our fatherland and our fountainhead. Let the art of obedience be our consummate skill, G-d's dominion our yoke, G-d's burden our pride and joy, G-d's state our aspiration, binding and immovable.
>
> Let us all become total Jews, all of us subjects and citizens of the total Kingdom of G-d, natives of the Torah state, fellow soldiers in the army of G-d. Let each one of us stand firm in his position, gallant and valiant; let there be no more half-heartedness or fragmentation. Let us march forward, proud and strong in our heroic retreat back to the will of G-d. . . .
>
> You, our brothers, you, the straightforward, stillstraight, unbroken, but also you, the seekers and ponderers, and even you, the doubters, pseudo-Jews, the party hacks, pragmatists, celebrated and admired—give ear. . . . However un-

sympathetic and "holier-than-thou" it may seem, only the ancient, unadulterated Jewish heritage with its honest motto *Moshe emess v'Toraso emess* [Moses is true and his Torah is true] can be accepted as Jewish. We can have it no other way! Anything else that goes by this designation is nothing but delusion, error, illusion and intoxication with which we can never come to terms. . . . His kingdom on earth will flourish only if we are loyal and true to His will.[8]

While the essential message here is not so much one of negating the modern secular world but rather of affirming the traditionalist one, the fundamentalist warning to the world comes through—that any other way "is nothing but delusion, error, illusion and intoxication." And yet the writer feels "endangered on all sides" from that world and therefore spends much energy building high the ramparts that will keep it out.

Then begins the process of structuring life in that enclave, reestablishing customs and creating frameworks within which traditionalism will flourish. This process, the second step of Herskovits's definition, is what Peter Berger and others have called "world-building" activity. Yet it is a "building" that turns most of its attentions inward toward building the fortress.[9] Certainly this activity is not absolutely static, for it requires a host of actions and constant vigilance to structure a protected enclave, particularly when surrounded by contemporary society as the haredim are in the places where they have made their homes—predominantly the cities of the West and the modern state of Israel.

Yet in comparison with other sorts of fundamentalism which are far more active in "fighting back" against the dominant culture, this group appears quiescent, comparatively passive, or at least hardly active only condemning as an afterthought the outside world that tries to enter through the membrane separating the enclave from it.

Concretely then, quiescent Jewish fundamentalism has largely focused its energies on remaining apart from the contaminations of contemporary culture (the "heroic retreat") and living the "ancient, unadulterated Jewish heritage." For these Jews, such contact as there is with those who do not share their worldview and ethos is considered at most instrumental yet never culturally valued. Quiescently fundamentalist Jews turn away from contemporary Gentile culture and its acculturating Jewish imitators not only to separate themselves from its threats but also to reconfirm ancient rituals and faith. To some this demands speaking a distinctive Jewish argot (Yiddish or Hebrew) or having autonomous schools for their children which stress Jewish separatism and rejection of contemporary culture and values. To others it means simply ignoring alternative cultures, especially those they view as "pseudo-Jewish." In Israel this is defined as Zionist culture; in America it is often such movements as Reform, Conservative, or even modern Orthodoxy which claim to have made accommodations to and accepted the legitimacy of the demands of the world beyond the Jewish one. In all cases, it means living life in a haredi ghetto as much as possible. Sometimes this ghetto is the yeshiva, the academy of Jewish learning, and its neighborhood; other times it is in the court of the Hasidic rabbi *(rebbe)*.

In the chapters 9 and 10, Haym Soloveitchik and Charles Selengut focus on an important segment of this quiescently fundamentalist Jewish community: the people who constitute the world of the yeshiva, or *b'nai* (sons of the) *yeshiva* or *b'nai Torah,* as they frequently call themselves these days.[10] Seeing themselves as part of an unbroken chain linked to an oral tradition that began at the dawn of Jewish peoplehood and was nurtured in the great talmudic academies of the Babylonian exile but more recently shaped in the yeshivas of nineteenth- and early twentieth-century Lithuania (as well as much of Eastern Europe and subsequently throughout the precincts of Orthodoxy) and currently is maintained in their successor institutions in Israel and the Diaspora, these b'nai Torah consider themselves among the true bearers of fundamental Judaism.

To b'nai Torah, their yeshivas were and continue to be the true fortresses for the preservation of Jewry and Judaism. They set themselves apart in them, an elite, almost priestly order, whose sole dedication is to Torah.[11] As David, the warrior of the Bible, was transformed through this ethos into a scholar-king and psalmist, so the Jews were transformed into People of the Book, and their leaders into teachers. Their cultural discourse was rooted in the study of sacred texts—predominantly the Talmud and other volumes that hermeneutically unpack the embedded meanings in Scripture and Jewish tradition. Yeshiva rabbi-teachers were seen as "vital links in the chain of Jewish historical knowledge."[12] In particular, the heads of the academies, the *roshey yeshiva,* were the Torah sages who served as religious leaders and models for the b'nai yeshiva.

Typical of the way these roshey yeshiva perceived their role is the comment reportedly made by Rabbi Joseph Dov Halevi Soloveitchik, one of the most prominent of roshey yeshiva in nineteenth-century Lithuania: "We are obligated to maintain the stronghold of the Torah, to initiate students and to hand over the Torah to the generations to come, but only in the way marked by our fathers, the light of generations."[13] These quiescent fundamentalists embraced the Torah as a frame of reference for how the world should be organized, yet they did not see themselves as having to act in history to bring about the changes necessary in the real world to assure this world order. They just expressed and affirmed it in their own lives and the lives of people they taught or guided.

In his discourse on the worldview of these Jews, Haym Soloveitchik demonstrates how the roshey yeshiva based their authority on a knowledge of the texts, which in turn evolved into a *da'as Torah,* a capacity to understand the intention of the texts (and their divine inspiration), which provided guidance for all that appeared new. Ironically, their prerogative to apply da'as Torah to a novel situation was predicated on their traditionalism and the realization that they had no responsibility to lead their followers "in paths and ways that are new."[14] The sages' reading of the texts tried to show that there was nothing new under the sun. The more the world appeared as an environment of endless metamorphosis—as it did in this century—the more an attachment to these texts (and their interpreters) as epitomized by the yeshiva became not only a way of stressing the tradition but also a relatively quiescent expression of an unwillingness to be swept up by this change.

Out of these institutions came rabbis who published responsa literature, the questions and answers that stretched Jewish law over all aspects of contemporary existence and made everything new seem to have a prefigured response in tradition. Nothing made the past seem more vital than these institutions and the people who identified with and through them. Thus, an institution and a pattern of life that was once simply an expression of an attachment to tradition became a means of quietly fighting back against contemporary social order. Certain Jewish customs associated with traditionalist Jewry were elevated to the level of Divine commandments.[15] A cultural enclave was fortified with customs, texts, their interpreters, and students.

After the cultural changes brought about by Jewish emancipation and enlightenment, the best place to put a yeshiva was in a location separate from general society.[16] Ideally, Jews would rarely leave the refuge of the yeshiva and cross the invisible but unmistakable borders separating their world from the outside. When they did, it was only for the most instrumental of needs—to make a living or to get something they could not get in their own domains. Selengut, in chapter 10, traces this practice to Volozhin and the yeshivas of Lithuania, but he shows that the theme was repeated in the United States, when the founders of the Lakewood Yeshiva, perhaps the premier American institution of this sort, chose a rural New Jersey town, away from the centers of Jewish urban settlement, for their home base.

As the outside world became increasingly open and attractive, the yeshiva and all it represented became both a metaphor and medium for cultural resistance. No longer simply an institution for the intellectual elite, scholars, and rabbis, it became the primary school and a world unto itself. Genuine Jewish life became identical with learning in the yeshiva. While originally and essentially an institution only for males, yeshivas for women (most prominently and first the Bais Ya'akov schools founded by Sara Schenierer in Krakow, Poland, early in this century but by now far more ubiquitous) became almost as common a feature of all b'nai Torah communities. And even when women did not attend their own schools, they defined themselves through their fathers, brothers, husbands, and sons who made their lives in and around the yeshiva.

To be sure, Israeli yeshivas did not by and large find themselves isolated sites. They were located in Jerusalem, where a city grew around them, and in B'nai B'rak (on the outskirts of Tel Aviv) and other urban centers. Thus yeshivas created their cultural enclaves in the very heart of the world that opposed them and their way of life, something that paradoxically necessitated a far more active resistance to the culture and society they disdained. Although there are other reasons, to which I return later, one is therefore not surprised that the fundamentalist struggle became more active in Israel than in America: when one community is isolated from another, it is easier to forget about the other; but when one sees the other always at the gates, struggle becomes critical. In the latter case, boundary setting is inescapable.

Soloveitchik implies that the yeshiva induced not a morality but an ethos whose main elements included a quiescent attachment to textual study and the notion of received rabbinic authority. Moreover, he explains, that leadership, when it went beyond the pages of the holy books, was "reactive rather programmatic," responding to specific situations that disturbed their way of life rather than mapping out a broad blueprint for coherent action. Two thousand years of being a people in exile, of being a barely tolerated minority and turning that into a virtue, Soloveitchik argues, did not make it possible for these Jews to articulate a plan for taking over the world or even their own destiny. And even when their numbers were swollen by the dislocations and trauma of this century, they remained framed by their consciousness of being in exile and a beleaguered minority.

People choose a quiescently fundamentalist stance for various reasons. Perhaps they find themselves in a place where others are perceived to be in cultural and instrumental control. In general, passivity is dominant when believers perceive themselves to be a vulnerable minority, when they see no hope and thus no reason to alter the cultural context in which they live. As Diaspora traditionalist Jews, b'nai yeshiva, wherever they have lived, remain conscious of themselves as a cultural minority group, which they express in an ideology of salvation that asserts that Jews are fundamentally helpless to alter their condition—only God can do that. As Soloveitchik puts it in chapter 9, for the b'nai yeshiva, "the Jewish posture is and ought to be quietism to bear until the final end"; as Selengut expresses it, in chapter 10, they believe "Israel's suffering cannot be avoided." While they may not approve of the world around them and try as much as possible to withdraw from it in practice and thus resist it in principle, they nevertheless take "its physical as well as its cultural environment as a given . . . , as facts of life to which they must learn to adjust."[17] This adjustment is minimalist in nature: Learn only as much of the vernacular and the ways of the outside world as is necessary to get by; do not change your ways except when necessary to avoid persecution or financial ruin; stay away from the *goyim* whenever and wherever possible; attend Jewish schools and live only among others like yourselves.[18] Answer to the authority of your own laws and only bow to the demands of the general social order when unavoidable. Concern yourselves only with parochial affairs. Give charity but only to your own causes.[19]

Not only Jews of the Diaspora who perceive themselves in exile and therefore basically defenseless and powerless take the relatively quiescent stance. There are Jews in Israel as well who sense themselves to be in "exile inside their land." They conceive of the contemporary state of Israel as essentially no different from any other culture governed by outsiders; to them most Israelis are recusant secularists and Jewish Gentiles. Here, therefore, as in all exiles, they see themselves ontologically powerless, and they see their best strategy for survival as one of passive and quiescent isolation from the mainstreams of culture. Isolation is insulation.

Rabbi Eliezer Schach, the current *rosh yeshiva* at the Ponovez Yeshiva in B'nai B'rak and an ideological leader among these people, puts it this way: "Jewry is inherently a people apart. Any Jews' attempt at assimilation is doomed to failure, for ultimately they will be rejected by the non-Jews. . . . Divine wisdom decreed this status for Jewry and it cannot be otherwise."[20]

Study of texts in a yeshiva is of course a perfect way of structuring life so that one can turn away from other concerns. Selengut argues that these b'nai yeshiva must be distinguished from Hasidim, who are also haredim. Unlike Hasidim who believe in *tikkun,* repair (both personal and cosmic) that can make the world better by active intervention that includes Torah study but goes well beyond it, b'nai Torah believe that their primary obligation is not to make the world better but simply to guarantee its existence by studying the Torah for whose merit it and they were created.[21] "The very act of creation," Selengut explains in his articulation of this exquisitely passive yeshiva attitude, "was taken by God to foster Torah study and in the event that Torah study should cease the universe would be immediately destroyed." Not only do b'nai yeshiva view their study as a means by which they display and reaffirm a faith in God, who reveals to them the texts they review. They also see this study as their fundamental raison d'être.

Nor do the b'nai Torah believe that the political activism of Zionists or even the religiously motivated acts of its advocates to bring about a better and fuller life for Jews are desirable. Indeed, as Soloveitchik explains, to these Jews the idea of the nation as supreme authority, as having sovereign will or engaging in political activity independent of Divine will, is anathema. To do anything more than to wait patiently for God to act and to study His Torah is to become caught up in messianic activity or false labors, neither of which will bear fruit (for only God can change history). Even worse, these activities will deter b'nai Torah from what they truly must do with the precious few years they have been given: reviewing the sacred texts and remaining within the framework of its legal boundaries. Aviezer Ravitsky and Menachem Friedman, in chapters 12 and 13, show that in early Habad Hasidism, which also emphasized study and was quiescent about messianism, the notion of hastening the Redemption and bringing about the end of history by a return to Zion were viewed as mistaken and even sacrilegious.

In this world of the b'nai yeshiva, moreover, there was an inversion of the outside values. From their perspective, work and success in the outside world was for a yeshiva boy a source of shame, or at best not worth talking about, while living on the dole in order to remain devoted to study was a mark of pride. The immortals of the yeshiva world were not those who made their mark in society at large; they were those interior giants who knew the itinerary and byways of halakha, Jewish law.

To outsiders, the quiescent group often appears less radical because its members choose not to take the offensive against the surrounding culture to satisfy the demands of their way of life. To members of the mainstream culture, these people often seem marginal, a curious residue from a world long left behind, irrelevant. But they are tolerable, even vaguely charming in the way that the past can in the light of nostalgia seem attractive. By themselves and keeping to themselves, quiescent fundamentalists are among the least threatening to their contemporary counterparts.

Again, there are important differences between Israel and America. Because the yeshivas in Israel are—to put it metaphorically—so much closer to the secular street than in America (where even ultra-Orthodox Brooklyn seems a world apart from secular Manhattan), and where the b'nai yeshiva have entered the national political arena where they jockey for scarce funds to support their institutions, teachers, and students, their very existence seems more threatening. When the cost of the yeshiva way of life becomes onerous as it has lately in Israel, the charm of the b'nai Torah disappears in the eyes of the host society. The secular society, which in the early days of the state was willing to support the world of yeshivas when its students were few, is now less willing to spend the huge sums necessary to sustain a flourishing system of unemployed b'nai Torah who depend on stipends from the institutions of learning, which in turn depend on funds from the taxpayers. A yeshiva that gets money to enlarge its facility at the expense of some secular cause, whose students are exempted from the universal military draft, often is perceived by others as a slap in the public face. Americans, on the other hand, are less aware of or concerned with this yeshiva disinterest and disinvolvement with American life and culture.[22] They can still look with some detachment at that world and even see some charm in it.

If, in general, secular society has not been too much concerned with the more quiescent, bookish Jewish fundamentalists, so long as they remain in their institutions and concentrate on their texts and their rabbis' lessons, the opposite is not the case. The haredim are very much concerned with what they sense is just beyond their gates and worry lest it intrude upon them. The passivity of their withdrawal to a cultural enclave, they worry, will not always work. Thus, those who choose this way of life are always anxious (that is the literal meaning of "haredi") about its potential corruption by sinister alien—modern—forces. This is what makes them fundamentalists and not just traditionalists. Thus haredi fundamentalists in Jerusalem urge Jews not to vote in Israeli state elections; banish a bathhouse or swimming pool adjacent to a haredi neighborhood, where sexes are strictly segregated and the unclothed body is an iniquity; oppose a proposed football stadium in the holy city of Jerusalem because its doors will be open on the Sabbath and thus encourage sacrilegious desecration; demand the end of an archeological dig because it blasphemously disturbs the sacred rest of the departed by coming too close to an ancient Jewish cemetery and endangers the souls of Jews, both living and dead; or close a road to prohibited vehicular traffic on the Sabbath or burn down bus shelters containing advertising posters of scantily clad women. Yet all this "fighting back" is inherently quiescent for it emphasizes maintaining the purity of their own ethnic and cultural enclave.

Quiescent fundamentalism is inherently unstable because those who are passive, unmoving, are more likely to be manipulated and shoved around. Even when they structure their enclaves with all sorts of rituals and a hierarchy of authorities or surround themselves with high walls and sanctions to keep members from leaving, those who are passive are, by definition, less able to fight back against the pressures exerted from the outside. The more successful that contemporary society and culture become or seem to become in luring adherents away from the tradition, the greater the pressure to get beyond static attachments to the cultural enclave. Even the most quiescently fundamentalist find they feel pressure to fight back more aggressively in order to hold on to their members and their way of life. That pressure has been mounting during the last few generations as Jews have been swept into the open societies and cultures of the West. This has turned many traditionalists into fundamentalists. And each small victory has acted to encourage greater activity. Such victories include the stubborn survival of the world of the yeshiva and the growth of various Hasidic courts on the new soils of America and modern Israel (both once considered poisoned ground).[23]

Yet haredim by and large do not move beyond quiescent fundamentalism, for to do so, they believe, would be to get caught up in the whirlwind of contemporary existence. It would mean, ultimately, becoming like the enemy against whom they struggle. It would mean assimilating. Thus practically all haredi fundamentalism seeks to protect its cultural enclaves. This is epitomized by the signs posted on the borders of haredi neighborhoods warning outsiders to stay out or alter their behavior when entering the haredi precincts. Presumably these signs are meant to fight back against the outside and obviate the need for violence. In both their tone and ubiquitousness, they are imploring rather than threatening. Even when haredim become violent, when they throw stones against prohibited vehicular traffic on the Sabbath or protest a "sacrilegious" archeological dig at a burial site, these acts are carried out to keep others and other ways of life away from them more than to change the way that others live. Haredim become active but only in a very limited way.

Paradoxically, for fundamentalists of all sorts, the greatest perceived threats come not from those who are absolutely different but rather from the acculturated few who seem to have staked out a middle ground. The absolutely different represent an un-thinkable evil, but those who occupy a moderate middle ground and make it seem that one can be a little bit secular without abandoning Orthodox Judaism represent the insidious and thinkable alternative to the fundamentalist way of life. Deviation from the central core values is first toward the middle ground and only from there toward the periphery. Hence the fundamentalist struggles are more vigorous against reforming Jews than Gentiles and, among Jews, most puissant against those who claim to define Orthodoxy in modern terms.[24] To fundamentalists, compromises are the most threatening.

Haredim thus save their greatest contempt not for those altogether different from them—Gentiles or even Jews who have totally reformed Judaism (considered "hope-lessly beyond the pale")—but rather fight most against those who are partially Ortho-dox, who make their peace with contemporary culture and thereby lend legitimacy to acculturation and contemporary secular culture.[25] In America the modern Orthodox and in Israel the religious Zionists (first Mizrachistim and later the followers of Gush Emunim and the like) represent such enemies.

This is not to deny that haredi Jewish fundamentalists have been agitated by secu-lar Zionism and the reality of a modern Jewish state in the Land of Israel. On the contrary, modern Israel with its alternative visions of what it means to be a full-fledged Jew, its possibilities of Jewish national sovereignty and authority, its opportunity to shuck Jewish minority status and powerlessness, and its hints of humanly assisted messianic renewal (especially after 1967 and against-the-odds survival and territorial expansion), represents a great challenge to the old Jewish ways established in the Diaspora. To some it means the end of business as usual for Jews, and that is threat-ening to traditions of all sorts.

For the haredim who are quiescently fundamentalist, the ideal was perhaps most dramatically articulated in the slogan made famous by Rabbi Moses Sofer, known as the Hatam Sofer and a major rabbinical influence of the last generation, who asserted: "The new is prohibited by the Torah." This is traditionalism turned into a fundamen-talist slogan, but it is hardly a call to activism.

Active Fundamentalism

Active fundamentalists, as already suggested, are not absolutely different from those who are quiescent. Both require a resolute attachment to the tradition or religious heritage and a steadfast refusal to accept corruption of it by the realities of history. Both deny the inevitability of secularization and acculturation to modernity and see religion as the ultimate authority. Both are certain that their patterns of behavior and values are the only authentic expressions of Jewish existence. Both argue that it is therefore possible and necessary to stay the course and fight back against those who require significant changes. Both groups perceive themselves in the provinces of the saved, in a state of grace—*erlicher Yidn,* as they call themselves. Both remain punctilious in their attachment to Jewish ritual; both are Orthodox Jews.

Yet there are important differences between the groups. While passivity encourages withdrawal, activity engenders expansion, which in turn necessarily involves the active fundamentalists with the world beyond their borders.[26] Thus the activists go out to meet the cultural enemy and often strike preemptively against it, drawing lines well beyond the boundaries their more passive counterparts have set. They push forward their own domains, going on the offensive to defend themselves and their way of life and faith.

Fundamentalists move beyond passivity, into a more animated, radical, and activist fundamentalist stance, because they sense impending crisis. If they believe their way of life is in imminent danger of collapse, if they feel they are under attack, or if they feel the end of days is near, they will act to prop up the foundations of their world and become aggressive in counterattack or preparation for the messianic days. And because active fundamentalism is also inherently unstable, pulling its advocates along with its forward motion, these people often find themselves pulled not only outside the parameters of tradition but also into a dependence on ideologies and authorities that go beyond the exclusively religious. Accordingly, for those who have made passivity their ethos—the haredim—the sense of crisis must be extraordinarily intense to get them to move beyond quiescent fundamentalism, for they worry that activity and engagement in active kulturkampf will only sweep them into confrontations and culture contact that will ultimately undermine their effort to protect themselves and their way of life. A group whose primary program is to keep to themselves is loathe to go on the attack, for it is encounter with the other that worries them.

Convincing quiescent fundamentalists to become active is obviously not easy. It requires that radicals either (1) "uncover" issues that demonstrate to their potential or real followers the insidious and critical penetration of the corrosive forces of the other world, or (2) convince the faithful that a unique moment in history has arrived after which nothing will ever again be the same. That unique moment can be one in which either the counterforces seem particularly weakened or hope for radical change seems especially promising. To create the first condition, fundamentalists must find elements of the opposing culture seeping in everywhere. Even potential dangers must be confronted. Such fundamentalists see problems in all sorts of places: a legal system, political democracy, the lyrics of a popular song, personal grooming, a style of clothes,

advertising, or even the way their institutions of learning are financed—the possibilities are incalculable because culture is so pervasive. But this approach to life makes
them, as Soloveitchik puts it, "reactive rather than programmatic," especially when the
matters in question are "precisely those areas where the texts provide no guidance."

To some extent this sort of fundamentalism emerges from an acute sense of contention and competition for the hearts and minds of believers and from a conviction
that the forces of contemporary culture are powerful and omnipresent and therefore
the best defense is an offensive that attacks the counterlife even before it has a chance
to erode the tradition. Thus fundamentalists attack even the tiniest intrusions. They
try to change the world before it changes them. They look to affect legislation and
change the lifestyles around them. Those who adopt the radical stance of fundamentalism seek actively to alter and negate the impact of the modern outside world. Their
confrontation with the counterworld is not implicit, a way of life, but aggressively
explicit, a political program. This they do because they are convinced their way of life
is in a state of crisis. Under these conditions, fundamentalists cross out of their enclaves and engage the other in battle lest their own boundaries be overrun and way of
life obliterated.

To these sorts of fundamentalists, only an active and contentious struggle against
the outside world can protect the past and the future. More than that, only through
such confrontation can people demonstrate to themselves and others how true they
are to the tradition. Those who lead the struggle in the haredi world are *shomrei
emunim,* or *shomrei hadass,* guardians of the faith and religion, and Neturei Karta,
defenders of the city of God. Once, this group was larger, but these days such active
fundamentalism among haredim is by and large the program of a relatively small band
of extreme haredi opponents of Zionism, who are also the self-appointed "soldiers"
of the Modesty Patrols which wander Jerusalem looking for new threats to their version of Judaism.[27] These active fundamentalists have been sapped by the fact that "the
only socializing institutions in haredi society are yeshivas which control their young
wards in monastery-like fashion" and thus do not allow them to be swept away by
activism, even the activism of the Neturei Karta.[28] Thus these active fundamentalist
haredi groups have steadily lost followers among the haredim who choose the yeshiva
life with its essentially quiescently fundamentalist attitude of withdrawal. In large
measure the haredi world today is a society that sees itself overwhelmingly made up
of yeshiva students and their families; it consists mainly of traditionalists and quiescent fundamentalists.

To be sure, haredim in Israel are still far more vigorous in their efforts to "fight
back" against the dominant culture than, for example, those in the United States.
Although still a minority group, they are a militant and uncompromising minority.
My own experiences with the group in both Israel and the United States illustrate the
difference graphically. After over a year of anthropological research among Jerusalem
haredim, where it was common to see shops with posted signs instructing would-be
customers that separate shopping hours for men and women were in effect so that
undesirable contact between the sexes might not occur[29] and where broadsides on
store windows warned those in "immodest dress" that they would not be tolerated or

served (such "immodest" dressers were usually tourists), I came back to New York City and did some shopping in one of the many electronic stores run by Hasidim. At first glance, the bearded and earlocked salespeople in New York looked to be twins of those I had seen in Jerusalem, but they were *not* twins in action. With my Jerusalem mind-set, I was struck that on the doors of Forty-Seventh Street Photo in midtown Manhattan, one of the largest of such establishments, there were of course no signs warning the immodest away, and it was unthinkable that such an operation would have separate shopping hours for men and women. While the New York store was closed on Sabbaths and Jewish holy days and all its salespeople were Satmar Hasidim or the like, the store was open to all sorts of trade. As I walked in I was again struck by the sight of a Satmar Hasid serving and talking to an obviously non-Hasidic woman with a very revealing decolletage. He seemed totally oblivious to and undisturbed by this sight—something his Jerusalem counterpart would never have countenanced. Moreover, when the New Yorker unhesitatingly handed his customer her receipt, he closed the encounter with the quintessentially American "Have a nice day." His Israeli twin would never have uttered such a "secular" or contemporary phrase. The latter would have turned away from such customers. Indeed, a young man such as I found behind the counter in New York would have been inside the yeshiva studying Talmud in Jerusalem, leaving store-keeping to older men or those past the age of corruption. And unlike the New Yorker, the haredi shopkeeper would have had an open volume of some sacred text nearby for perusal when the customers were not at the counter. Thus, from the perspective of the haredi in Israel, his counterpart in New York has lost much of the struggle of contra-acculturation. Indeed, those haredim in Israel who are not ready to fight back in an aggressively fundamentalistic way have started going to America, where compromise is possible.[30]

As far as the American counterpart is concerned, only at home, in his cultural enclave (or if he gets on a plane and goes to Israel), can he truly express his haredi self. But of course that means the American has already compartmentalized himself: he has fallen into the very trap that the first Jews who ventured out of the ghetto fell into; he has become "a man in the street (his place of business) and a Jew at home (his home community)." To the Israeli haredi, that kind of unfortunate compromise has not yet happened, although the Neturei Karta and its supporters might argue that even in Israel, those who remain quiescent have already lost the battle.

But the Neturei Karta and its supporters are not the only Orthodox Jews who take an actively fundamentalist stand. Another group, which Eliezer Don-Yehiya discusses in chapter 11, constitutes an alternative that is far more programmatic in its fighting back. These people claim to possess a blueprint for their version of true Jewish identity. They also act because they believe a crisis is at hand and because they are convinced they must turn the world into a place that will respond to the needs of the day. Even more, they are a group convinced that this is a unique moment in Jewish history: the beginning of the Redemption. This, they argue, is a time when the counterforces are weak and the nation of Israel is prepared to change the secular course it has followed.

The activist group Don-Yehiya examines comprises those who have come out of the "nationalist yeshivas" in Israel, particularly those affiliated with the views of the

Mercaz Harav institution founded and led by Rabbi Abraham Isaac Kook, first chief rabbi of Palestine, and his son Zvi Yehuda. This yeshiva, and many of its graduates who went on to become roshey yeshiva and religious (as opposed to secular) Zionist activists among the Gush Emunim, represents a fountainhead of Orthodox Jewish activism which has taken the battle out of the institution and into both the political arena and mass culture of contemporary Jewish life, especially in Israel. Don-Yehiya argues that although it was an educational institution and hence a place of isolation and learning—and as such naturally a site that embodied quiescent fundamentalism—Mercaz Harav, because of its embrace of modern Zionism, absorbed much of the adaptive activism of a contemporary social movement. Its students and teachers became caught up in the ideals of Zionism that eschewed the passive powerlessness of exile and waiting for redemption and presented an alternative program of Jewish liberation. Yet as Orthodox b'nai Torah, the Mercaz Harav people placed religious Judaism at the center of their concerns and infused their support of Zionism with it. The synthesis of these two, hastened by a sense of the religious significance of the contemporary events of Jewish history—especially the founding of the modern Jewish state in the Holy Land in 1948 and its extension and miraculous survival against all odds in 1967 and again in 1973—gave birth to a religious activism. This activism broadened the reach of religion to include Zionism and take it over, and it deepened Zionism so that it was not simply a secular, nationalist movement but seen by the Mercaz Harav people as part of the Divine and biblical promise of redemption. Yet, as Don-Yehiya explains, the religious Zionists were always wary of being caught up by the secular elements of the movement they embraced and tried continually to endow it with religious meaning.

The outcome of this synthesis was to wrest control of Zionism from secularism, to ground it in sacred texts, to steer it by rabbinic and religious motives. And all this also would redeem those who had been caught up in it so that they would see their activity as religious and not simply political or nationalistic. This would hasten the end of days, returning the nation to ancient biblical glories and restoring the tradition to dominance. The people of Mercaz Harav were dazzled by the miracle of the return to Zion, both in its diminished form after partition and even more so by its enlarged form after 1967. This was *atchalta d'geula,* the beginning of the Redemption.

They created institutions of Jewish learning in which these ideas were expounded. Their prophets were first Rabbi Abraham Kook, the father, and later Rabbi Zvi Yehuda Kook, the son. Each provided religious explanations for the events of contemporary Jewish history. If Kook the Elder was abstract and mystical, Kook the Younger offered operational advice. The advice was to extract Zionism from the grip of secular culture, something that only religious activism could accomplish. The study of biblical texts concerned with the Land of Israel became paramount, not for purely educational reasons but as a program for action, a design for the future. And even ritual activities— Don-Yehiya offers an example of prominently displayed ritual fringes—were transformed into displays of Jewish sovereignty and renaissance. Once again the Jewish people were chosen. Once chased and persecuted, they now were sovereign, returned to their own divinely Promised Land, by the grace of God.

This particularism led to an emphasis on the matter of sovereignty over the entire

Land of Israel and a conviction that they need never again be persecuted by Gentiles but could militantly strike back at those who would displace them from their land. Arabs, other nations, even Jews who lacked true faith were enemies if they did not acknowledge the particularism/chosenness and the title to the land. They did not shun army service as did the haredim; instead, they saw the army as an instrument of God. The state was not sacrilege, as the haredim argued; it was God-given. Moreover, they saw their religion not as something that led to withdrawal and isolation but rather something that required all Jews—even unbelievers and secularists—to be persuaded that the Promises of God were being fulfilled. What was particularly compelling about these activist fundamentalists was that they suggested, via their zeal, that "those who accept their cultural environment as a given are those who don't take religion as seriously as they sometimes pretend."[31]

Unlike the haredim, these activists were not powerless exiles waiting for heavenly miracles. The network of yeshivas in the Mercaz Harav mold, many of them founded after 1967 and located in the conquered territories, became the institutions in which these views were articulated and inculcated. These were not haredi yeshivas that retreated from national life. On the contrary, they sought to capture the spirit of national life, to draw adherents from the general population, to enlighten religiously those who did not see the religious significance of events. This aim seemed achievable after the wars of 1967 and 1973, as people who normally did not turn to religion suddenly did so, albeit briefly. National will, as Don-Yehiya explains, was seen as equivalent to Divine will. To rebel against it was to revolt against the Kingdom of Heaven. In these days, a Jew could not rise up against a fellow Jew, certainly not in the way haredim did.

Activism became a pattern of their lives. It meant responding to the Divine signs of an imminent redemption. Yet because activist radical fundamentalists are not, as I have suggested, content to contest culture alone, many of these Jews saw as part of their task the forging of a national will that supported their vision of the new millennium. They began to harry their more passive co-believers (as well as unbelievers) and tried to turn them into activists whenever possible by appealing to their religious sympathies or anxieties as well as to their nationalist inclinations. These fundamentalists entered into the political dialogue and tried to affect both governmental policy and public opinion. They did not keep to themselves in a society apart but entered into mainstream society as *agents provocateurs* who sought to change culture and the body politic. As the rabbis among them saw it, the national will needed religious refinement, something a religious education and revival could bring about. Schools, youth movements, and even a special national radio station that played inspirational songs were the vehicles for this shaping of the national will. "What we need to do now," Rabbi Shlomo Aviner, head of the Ateret Cohanim Yeshiva in the Old City of Jerusalem and student of Rabbi Zvi Yehuda Kook, explained (as Don-Yehiya quotes him), "is to teach 'our light' to the nation of Israel."

At their peak, the members of Gush Emunim and graduates of Mercaz Harav did indeed briefly capture the imagination and conscience of many Orthodox Jews, including some haredim who admitted in private that they were impressed (and therefore threatened) by these believers. And they even caught a wave of triumphalism that swept across the entire nation. They seemed to steal the pioneer spirit that had once been at the heart of Israeli national character.

But ultimately they did not succeed in shaping the national will. Instead their activism led to dissension.[32] This first became apparent in the national conflict over withdrawal from Sinai. Later it was manifested in the widespread turmoil over the activities of the "Jewish underground," particularly those of the group that hoped to blow up the mosque on the Temple Mount and attacked the Islamic College as well as several Arab mayors in the territories. These events, coupled with the death of Rabbi Zvi Yehuda Kook and the subsequent absence of a unified ideological leadership, have undermined the active fundamentalists.

As a result, some radicals slipped beyond the boundaries of Judaism and began to base their activities on nonreligious sources of inspiration. In effect they no longer acted only within the parameters of religious fundamentalism. Don-Yehiya traces this development in his analysis of some underground leaders' explanations of their activities. Their behavior reflects the way activist fundamentalists run the risk of becoming caught up and carried away by what they fundamentally wish to avoid—contemporary culture. And contact runs the risk of integration since enemies have a nasty way of becoming images of one another. Activist fundamentalism runs the risk of becoming what Emmanuel Sivan calls "innovative traditionalism," a way of life that transcends and ultimately alters tradition under the guise of being part of it.[33]

In Don-Yehiya's analysis, Yehuda Etzion of the underground is an example of one who has made this leap beyond the boundaries of religious fundamentalism. He and his allies are radical nationalists with innovative ideas that often seem to owe more to ideologies emerging from the secular rather than the religiously fundamentalist world. They offer yet another radical political ideology aimed at arousing the masses, another effort at conversion. Their example cautions the quiescent traditionalists who know—at least intuitively—that these dangers exist, and it accounts for the tension in their relationship with their more radical, yet fervent, fundamentalist counterparts.

In other cases, nonreligious radicals, like Gershon Solomon and the Temple Mount Faithful, have taken over some of the goals of the believers. Yet for them, rebuilding a Holy Temple on the Temple Mount is no longer a religiously motivated act but one which stresses nationalist symbolism: "whoever controls the Temple Mount has rights over the land of Israel."[34] And it is to be spearheaded by those whose interest is not in matters of Divine Will or religious practice. The fundamentalist who was true to his Jewish Orthodoxy, even in his activist mode, always waited for rabbinic authorization, which was a way to interpret and thus know God's will; he did not decide purely on his own as do the Temple Mount Faithful. And he always remained punctilious about Jewish ritual. But these radicals acted and continue to operate without the rabbis or an attachment to faith, while they are lax and sometimes altogether ignorant of Jewish law and praxis. Their starting point is not religion but rather nationalism that slipped into the symbolic frame of religion. Yet they have failed to attract the religious to their brand of nationalism, nor have they found nationalists thus far ready to slip into their quasi-religious goals. They remain marginal both in numbers and influence.

As for those rabbis who did embrace militancy, they did so to protect "the honor of Israel." Citing Scripture (Lev. 19:16), "Thou shalt not stand idly over they broth-er's blood," and Talmud (Berachot 58a), "He who comes to kill you, kill him first," they explained militancy in Judeo-legal terms as Jewish "self-defense." Yet these expla-nations did not satisfy the nation. Don-Yehiya argues that the activist fundamentalists have continued to lose ground, lacking organization and unity. Indeed, he explains, they have lately returned to the quiescence and relative isolation of traditional yeshiva study. They have moments when they seem to become like quiescently fundamentalist haredim. Even service in the army is increasingly shunned as something that will disturb the intensive Torah study now perceived as requisite for preparing the ground for the End of Days. "To train the nation as to its proper path," Don-Yehiya tells us in the name of Rabbi Yitzhak Shilat of the Ma'ale Adumim Yeshiva, "and to bring about unity among its various parts requires 'great scholars . . . compleat in their Torah and deeds.'" The activists are becoming b'nai Torah. The move from political activism to spiritual regeneration in which time is spent in meditation over texts or exercises in interpretation of the mysteries of the Messiah is also a move from active to quiescent fundamentalism, an effort not to be swept away by the activism. It is the yeshiva transforming the activists. After all, a life around texts in the Jewish context with its emphasis on abnegation of individuality and stress on the authority of the sages ultimately does not lead to activism. Or at least that is the evidence in the Jewish cases.

While these people are far from fading away, they are no longer the vanguard. Still, they can explode into the headlines when they create a settlement in response to a crisis—for example, an ambush and terrorist attack on a settler—or when they are shaken to activity by a political change, such as the peace conference or national elec-tions. Yet these acts no longer set an agenda as they once did (in part, of course, be-cause settlements have become a part of government policy). Rather, such actions are more defensive or an act of public protest. Yet if a limited crisis leads to a sense of enduring crisis, such acts could take on a life of their own and nudge people into a new round of active fundamentalism.

Hovering between Quiescent and Active Fundamentalism: Habad or Lubavitch Hasidim

Those who hover between quiescent and active fundamentalism are persons who, although tending to the defensive posture of cultural resistance characteristic of qui-escent fundamentalism, find that under certain limited circumstances they must go on the offensive. When they do so, however, they always maintain a longing to return to their quiescence after the battle is past. To illustrate this condition, Aviezer Ravitsky and Menachem Friedman in chapters 12 and 13 have focused on the case of Habad or Lubavitch Hasidim.

One of the most ubiquitous and widely known of contemporary Hasidic sects, in part because of their current active outreach program that aims to bolster the religious loyalty and renew the faith and Jewish practices of those who have strayed from tradition, these Hasidim seem to hover between the quiescent and active mode of fundamentalism. Tracing their origins to the first group of disciples of the founder of Hasidim, Israel ben Eliezer, the Baal Shem Tov, Habad Hasidim have oscillated from being a sect concerned with study of and meditation on their founders' sacred texts and maintaining a tradition of religious practices that emerged from it (what Friedman calls the "particularist" element) to becoming paragons of outreach and missionary work among religiously wayward Jews as well as harbingers of the Messiah (what he refers to as the "universalist" element).

In his articulation of their case, Friedman describes this first in historical terms, writing of two periods and identities of these Hasidim: the Lubavitch phase, the era of the second, third, and fourth rebbes or charismatic leaders, when the sect was focused around particularistic/localist concerns and study of texts, necessarily inwardly turned and quiescent in their fundamentalism; and the Habad phase, the era of the fifth, sixth, and current seventh rebbe, when feeling itself threatened by the instability of Jewish existence, it emphasized a universal mission to Jews, and lately even to Gentiles, becoming active in its fundamentalism.

Similarly, in his exposition of Habad ideology, Ravitsky speaks of its two sides: the first a "radically conservative posture" that "rejects such concepts as liberalism, pluralism, and universal human equality"; the second "a dynamic and activist attitude" that is "consciously expanding the boundaries of its religious involvement," acting to bring about *tikkun* and its repair of the world, a repair that even has of late come to include an effort to mold the consciousness and behavior of Gentiles. Friedman and Ravitsky provide us not only with an understanding of the dynamics of Lubavitch/ Habad, and the historical conditions accounting for them, but demonstrate how a group can move freely across the spectrum of fundamentalism.

Motivated by messianic and religious goals, these Hasidim began with a traditionalist concern for plumbing their own sources, making study something that went "beyond the scholarly class into the lives of the simplest men and women of the Jewish community."[35] They became contra-acculturationist and quiescent in their fundamentalism when they built their yeshivas and created their cultural enclaves. But the particular events of their history, one of forced migration throughout Eastern Europe and later to America, compelled them to make their message more universal as they struggled to attract and hold adherents. Combined with the trauma of recent Jewish history—persecution, wandering, and cultural change—and often thrust into the maelstrom of change, Habad found itself forced to missionize among Jews. In this activist mold it created the so-called *Temimim*, the *tzivos Hashem*, soldiers in "an army of God" with "mitzvah [Jewish commandment] tanks" whose "commando units" were out to bring God and his commandments to the Jewish (and now Gentile) people wherever they were: in airports, on street corners, and in the heart of the secular world.

The result was a history which embodied a Hasidic parable of a king who sent his son far away "in order that he should have more delight when the son returned," but who then discovered that the son did not return and instead forgot his royal origins. "The king sent a message to him—but he refused to come back. Then a wise minister discovered the secret of how to make the prince return." That minister "changed his garments and his language, to be like the son. He came close to him, on his level, and brought him back to his father."[36]

Nowhere did this second side emerge as fully as in the pluralist marketplace of ideas that contemporary Western society has become. With a literature and a charismatic leader as well as enthusiastic Hasidim who saw themselves on missions for the rebbe, and for the Messiah, Habad was able to do battle with the forces that undermined it and bring back sons to their "father."

In other words, Lubavitch began as a group whose character was essentially haredi. Their concern was with Lubavitch, their cultural enclave. Left alone, they might have evolved like other haredim, quiescent in their fundamentalism. And indeed, one side of Lubavitch is just that: content to keep to itself, to remain in Crown Heights near the headquarters of the movement at 770 Eastern Parkway or in their village in Israel, Kefar Habad. These are the Lubavitchers who want nothing to do with the non-Lubavitch elements of Crown Heights in Brooklyn or the secular state in Israel which surrounds their enclaves. They want to study their Tanya, the writings of their Hasidic master, and practice their ways. These are the Lubavitchers who refused entry to a group of female teachers from Hebrew University who came to visit one of their Jerusalem schools and wanted to get inside a classroom.[37]

But the other side, the Habad side, is reaching out, pushed by a feeling of crisis and urgency that comes from a realization that the current rebbe is a man near ninety and lacking any obvious heir. They light Hanukkah menorahs on city hall greens and reach out to the unaffiliated and assimilated, hoping that when these return to the ways of God, the Messiah will find it proper to come; they are also activated by what many among them—not so differently from the Mercaz Harav people—see as the beginning of an era of redemption. They sense that this is a unique moment in history and that they must act before it is too late. Indeed, in the aftermath of the Gulf War, the collapse of the Iron Curtain, and the "epoch-making ingathering of hundreds of thousands of suppressed and stricken exiles, converging on the Holy Land from undreamed-of directions," Habad published a full-page ad in the *New York Times* announcing to all readers that "The Time for Your Redemption Has Arrived!"[38] And when Michael Specter, a *New York Times* reporter preparing a story on Habad, was about to leave for Israel and asked the rebbe what message he had for his followers there, the rebbe whispered to tell them "the messiah is coming very soon."[39]

With thousands of supporters and a wide network of emissaries, Habad has been buoyed by its victories (including an unprecedented political victory in its support for the Agudat Israel party in the Israeli elections for the Twelfth Knesset), by its survival and growth, and by what it perceived to be evidence of Divine favor and the promise of imminent redemption. This encouraged an activism that fed on itself and pulled the sect out of its particularistic concerns and quietism. First, they went after religious Jews and then after all sorts of Jews. Now finally, as both Ravitsky and Friedman document, as the imminence of redemption has overwhelmed them, increasingly they try to effect spiritual change among others as well.

Still, the two sides of the sect remain in their separate compartments. There are those activities directed strictly to Lubavitchers, texts and gatherings open and meaningful only to them. There are the Habad schools for their young. These represent the quiescent fundamentalist side. Then there are the elements of outreach in which every Habad Hasid is seen as a messenger of the rebbe and God. Or put differently, there is the Lubavitch side, focused around 770 Eastern Parkway in Brooklyn, headquarters of the movement and seat of the current rebbe, Menachem Mendel Schneerson. And there is the Habad side, which (in Ravitsky's words) "knows no limits" and is ready to go to "every place and every person" to spread the word and defend the faith.

Which of these two aspects will predominate depends on the events that occur outside Lubavitch/Habad as much as on decisions made by the Hasidim themselves. But as a group they are torn between the two possibilities. Thus, one group erects billboards announcing the Messiah is immanent while another group of the very same Hasidim say that their rebbe and they are concerned about this activist messianism. Lubavitch and Habad, the quiescent and the active fundamentalism, embody both the haredi and the messianic religious Zionist. But it is a body that keeps changing form and character.

A barometer of the relations with the society outside, this group demonstrates how much of what we call fundamentalism is dependent on the course of events in the world surrounding them, how much is reaction rather than initiative. And perhaps that is the most important lesson all these chapters offer. To chart the growth or diminution of fundamentalism, its activity and passivity, one needs always to see it in its social and historical contexts.

Conclusion

While these three cases do not exhaust the possibilities for Jewish fundamentalism, nevertheless they disclose its general pattern—a fundamentalism that remains convinced of its correctness even as it swings between the quiescent and active. It may at one moment express itself as an abiding traditionalism and orthodoxy and at another rise up in militant confrontation with the forces that oppose it. Yet even the most exercised activists, those who contend with the onslaughts of an opposing culture and change or who struggle to bring about what they sense to be the imminent End of Days and messianic Redemption, pull back when the moment of crisis is past or the end does not come as planned. In a sense the Lubavitch/Habad model is the ideal type.

Until now, active fundamentalism has shown itself to be not only volatile but limited. In part this is because Jewish fundamentalists—even when they are active—seek to change the world without being changed by it. Moreover, the fundamentalist connection with a Jewish tradition is also limiting in that the tradition is dominated by rabbis and a set of sacred texts which, while offering a code of everyday behavior, are far more recondite and ambiguous when it comes to providing a plan of political action and social change. For generations, the Jews, both b'nai Torah and other traditionalists, have focused their concern with those texts on matters that point to the past or elements that deal with quotidian ritual existence, leaving nation building and messianism in the realm of the extracurricular. If, in these days, they seem at times caught up with the extracurricular, history suggests that in the end the People of the Book will return to the shelter of the study hall and the quiescent existence it embraces. Yet if the windows to that study hall remain open to the world outside, which beckons and disturbs those inside, the activists will continue to have their days in the sun.

Notes

1. See Martin E. Marty and R. Scott Appleby, "The Fundamentalism Project: A User's Guide," and Samuel C. Heilman and Menachem Friedman, "Religious Fundamentalism and Religious Jews: The Case of the Haredim," both in Marty and Appleby, eds., *Fundmentalisms Observed* (Chicago: University of Chicago Press, 1991).

2. See Jacob Katz, "Orthodoxy in Historical Perspective," *Studies in Contemporary Jewry* 2 (1986): 3–17; Moshe Samet, "The Beginnings of Orthodoxy," *Modern Judaism* 8 (1989): 249–69; Michael K. Silber, "The Emergence of Ultra-Orthodoxy: The Invention of a Tradition," in Jack Wertheimer, ed., *The Uses of Tradition: Jewish Continuity in the Modern Era* (Cambridge: Harvard University Press, 1992); and Samuel Heilman, *Defenders of the Faith: Inside Ultra-Orthodox Jewry* (New York: Schocken Books, 1992).

3. On the meaning and history of haredim, see Heilman and Friedman, "Religious Fundamentalism and Religious Jews," and Heilman, *Defenders of the Faith.*

4. See Heilman and Friedman, "Religious Fundamentalism and Religious Jews." Briefly, Hasidim emphasized pietism and mysticism, Misnagdim stressed a rigorous attachment to Jewish law and textual study, and Mizrachistim focused their religion on the goal of return to the spiritual center in the ancient homeland in the Land of Israel.

5. As Claude Lévi-Strauss found as he traveled way up the Amazon River, past what he believed were the boundaries of modern civilization, one could discover "shreds of Voltaire and Anatole France which impregnated the national culture even

in the depths of the bush." Lévi-Strauss, *Tristes tropiques,* trans. John Weightman and Doreen Weightman (New York: Washington Square Press, 1955), p. 19.

6. Melville Herskovits, *Man and His Works* (New York: A. A. Knopf, 1948), p. 531.

7. Peter L. Berger, *The Sacred Canopy* (New York: Doubleday, 1967), pp. 48–49.

8. Shimon Schwab, "The Great Awakening," in *Selected Writings* (Lakewood, N.J.: C.I.S. Publications, 1988), pp. 160, 162; originally published in *Mitteilungen,* April–May 1978.

9. Peter L. Berger and Thomas Luckman, *The Social Construction of Reality* (Garden City, N.J.: Doubleday, 1966), p. 103.

10. Strictly speaking we may think of b'nai yeshiva as referring to those who are still in the schools, and b'nai Torah as referring to those who, although graduated, still identify with the ethos, values, and lifestyles associated with the yeshiva. See Heilman, *Defenders of the Faith.*

11. For a discussion of the move from priestly to scholarly order, from Temple cult to People of the Book, see Samuel C. Heilman, *The People of the Book: Drama, Fellowship, and Religion* (Chicago: University of Chicago Press, 1987), pp. 1–8.

12. Nachman Bulman, "Introduction" in Moshe Domhey, *My Uncle the Netziv* (New York: Mesorah Publications, 1988). This volume is an English abridged edition of *Mekor Barukh* by Barukh Epstein.

13. Soloveitchik's remark is repeated by Israel Meir Kagan, the Hafez Hayyim,

quoted in Shmuel Graineman, *Sefer Hafez Hayyim 'al ha-Torah,* 2d ed. (B'nai B'rak, 1953), p. 253; translation mine.

14. Graineman, *Sefer Hafez Hayyim-'al ha-Torah.*

15. See Silber, "The Emergence of Ultra-Orthodoxy," p. 16, quoting a nineteenth-century haredi rabbi who asserts that "every Jewish custom is equal to the ten commandments."

16. For a fuller discussion of these trends, see Heilman and Friedman, "Religious Fundamentalism and Religious Jews."

17. Charles Liebman, "Religious Trends among Jews in the United States and Israel and Changing Images of Israel" (Paper presented at the Hebrew University of Jerusalem, December 1989), pp. 2–3.

18. For a description of what is viewed by many as the paradigmatic battle to separate the yeshiva world from contact with secular studies and all they symbolize and portend, see Jacob J. Schacter's exhaustive review of the events that led to the closing of the great yeshiva in Volozhin, Lithuania, in 1892. Schacter, "Haskalah, Secular Studies and the Close of the Yeshiva in Volozhin in 1892," *Torah U-Madda Journal* 2, pp. 76–133.

19. "Orthodox Jews are more likely to give to Orthodox charitable institutions, and the more Orthodox are likely to give more to those institutions. In broad terms, we suggest that as traditionalism increases, so too does charitable support for Orthodox institutions." Samuel C. Heilman and Steven M. Cohen, *Cosmopolitans and Parochials: Modern Orthodox Jews in America* (Chicago: University of Chicago Press, 1989), p. 134. See also Samuel C. Heilman, "Tzedakah: Orthodox Jews and Charitable Giving," in Barry A. Kosmin and Paul Ritterband, eds., *Contemporary Jewish Philanthropy in America* (Lanham, Md.: Rowman and Littlefield, 1991), pp. 133–44.

20. Rabbi Eliezer Schach, from an address given before the Agudat Israel leadership conference in January 1982, and translated and quoted in the *Jewish Observer,* February 1982, p. 5.

21. The argument for the social activism inherent in Hasidism is made in Naftali Loewenthal, *Communicating the Infinite: The Emergence of the Habad School* (Chicago: University of Chicago Press, 1990), pp. 37–38.

22. There is, however, rising resentment from some of the people in the neighborhood; blacks who share Brooklyn with their ultra-Orthodox neighbors often resent the fact that they seem invisible to the Jews and are treated with studied contempt. And, of course, fellow Jews in America have a hard time accepting the disinvolvement and disinterest they perceive in the b'nai yeshiva's attitude toward them.

23. For a case study, see Heilman, *Defenders of the Faith,* and also idem, "The Ninth Siyum Ha Shas at Madison Square Garden: Contra-Acculturation in American Jewish Life," in Norman Cohen and Robert Seltzer, *The Jews in America* (New York: New York University Press, forthcoming).

24. See Heilman and Cohen, *Cosmopolitans and Parochials,* and Heilman, *Defenders of the Faith.* For a historical example, see the the debate over Moses Mendelssohn's *Judaism,* reviewed in Silber, "The Emergence of Ultra-Orthodoxy," p. 27 and n. 90.

25. See Silber, "The Emergence of Ultra-Orthodoxy," p. 10, who uses these words to describe this attitude among the earliest of the ultra-Orthodox.

26. I am indebted to Charles Liebman for this insight and for his close reading and other helpful comments on an earlier draft of this chapter.

27. For a fuller discussion of these two groups see, Heilman and Friedman, "Religious Fundamentalism and Religious Jews," and Heilman, *Defenders of the Faith.* And for earlier efforts, see Silber, "The Emergence of Ultra-Orthodoxy."

28. Menachem Friedman, *The Haredi (Ultra-Orthodox) Society: Sources, Trends and Processes* (in Hebrew) (Jerusalem: Jerusalem Institute for Israel Studies, 1992), p. 99; translation mine.

29. This is, of course, one of the key ways the haredim distinguish themselves from what they consider the lax and sexually promiscuous secular/Gentile world.

30. See comments by Menachem Fried-man in an interview with Shachar Ilan in *Ha'aretz,* 10 January 1992.

31. Liebman, "Religious Trends among Jews in the United States and Israel," p. 7.

32. For the learned, dissension was anathema. Talmudic tradition teaches that internal Jewish dissension, baseless hatred, had led to the destruction of the Holy Temple and the Jewish exile. Rabbi Kook the Elder had always counseled that the only remedy was an undifferentiated love of every Jew for his fellow Jew. Only this attitude would bring the Redemption. Hence the emergence of strife and hatred among Jews over the activism of the Mercaz Harav was an ominous sign not only for practical but for theological and historical reasons.

33. Emmanuel Sivan, "Jewish and Islamic Fundamentalism: Common Approaches" (Paper presented at the conference Changing Patterns of Belief: From New Religious Movements to Fundamentalism, Queens College, City University of New York, 25 April 1990), n.p.

34. Eliezer Don-Yehiya quoting Gerson Solomon.

35. Loewenthal, *Communicating the Infinite,* p. 90.

36. Ibid., pp. 21–22.

37. The event occurred 12 January 1992 during a seminar in which I was involved and where the aim was to see haredi education. Although arrangements had been made in advance, the school decided that the classroom should remain a protected setting from which outsiders were excluded.

38. *New York Times,* 19 June 1991, p. A19.

39. Michael Specter, pers. comm., 17 January 1992.

CHAPTER 9

Migration, Acculturation, and the New Role of Texts in the Haredi World

Haym Soloveitchik

For PLS

The New Role

To speak of the new role of texts in the haredi world is to raise a natural question: What is new in this role and why confine it to the haredi world? Has not traditional Jewish society always been regulated by the normative written word, the halakha? Have not scholars, for well over a millennium, pored over the Talmud and its commentaries, its novellae and halakhic codes to provide Jews with guidance in their daily round of observances? Is not Jewish religiosity proudly legalistic and exegesis its classic mode of expression? Did not their "portable homeland," their indwelling in their sacred texts, sustain the Jewish people throughout its long exile?

The answer is yes. However, as the halakha is a sweepingly comprehensive regula of daily life—covering not only prayer and divine service, but equally food, drink, dress, sexual relations between man and wife, the rhythms of work and patterns of rest—it constitutes a way of life. And a way of life is not learned but rather absorbed. Its transmission is mimetic, imbibed from parents and friends, and patterned on conduct regularly observed in home and street, synagogue and school.

Did these mimetic norms—the culturally prescriptive—conform with the legal ones? The answer is, at times, yes; at times, no. And the significance of the no may become apparent from an example. Many know, most have heard of, kosher food, more specifically the kosher kitchen with its rigid separation of milk and meat—the separate dishes for milk and for meat, separate sinks, dish racks, towels, tablecloths, even separate cupboards. Indeed this stringent binary structure is the very heart of the

Jewish kitchen. Actually little of this has a basis in Jewish law. Strictly speaking there is no need for separate sinks, for separate dish towels, or cupboards. In fact, if the food is served cold, there is no need for separate dishware altogether. The simple fact is that the traditional Jewish kitchen, transmitted from mother to daughter over generations, has been immeasurably and unrecognizably amplified beyond all halakhic requirements. Its classic contours are the product not of legal exegesis, but of the housewife's religious intuition imparted in kitchen apprenticeship.

An augmented tradition is one thing, a diminished one may well be another. So the question naturally arises: Did this mimetic tradition have an acknowledged position even when it went against the written law? I say "acknowledged" because the question is not simply did it continue in practice (though this, too, is of significance), but was it accepted as legitimate? Was it even formally legitimized? Often yes; and, once again, a concrete example best brings the matter home. There is an injunction against "winnowing on Sabbath."[1] This gives us no pause. Who among us is out in the field winnowing? However, we do eat fish, and in eating fish we must, if we are not to choke, separate the bones from the meat. Yet in so doing we are separating the chaff (bones) from the wheat (meat). The upshot is that all Jews who ate fish on Sabbath (and Jews have been eating fish on the Sabbath for at least two thousand years) have violated the Sabbath. This seems absurd, but the truth of the matter is that it is very difficult to provide a cogent justification for separating bones from fish. In the late nineteenth century, a scholar took up this problem and gave some very unpersuasive answers. It is difficult to imagine he was unaware of their inadequacies. Rather, his underlying assumption was that it *was* permissible. There must be *some* valid explanation for the practice, if not necessarily his. Otherwise thousands of well-intending, observant Jews have inconceivably desecrated the Sabbath for centuries. His attitude was neither unique nor novel. A similar disposition is reflected throughout the multivolume *Arukh ha-Shulhan,* the late-nineteenth-century reformulation of *The Code of Jewish Law.*[2] Indeed, this was the classic Ashkenazic (North European) position for centuries, one which saw the practice of the people as an expression of halakhic truth. It is no exaggeration to say that the Ashkenazic community saw the law as manifested in two forms: the canonized written corpus (the Talmud and codes) and the regnant practices of the people. Custom was a correlative datum of the halakhic system. And, on frequent occasions, the written word was reread in light of traditional behavior.[3]

This dual tradition of the intellectual and the mimetic, law as taught and law as practiced, which stretched back for centuries, begins to break down in the twilight years of the author of the *Arukh ha-Shulhan,* in the closing decades of the nineteenth century. The change is strikingly attested to in the famous code of the next generation, the *Mishnah Berurah.*[4] This influential work reflects no such reflexive justification of established religious practice, which is not to say that it condemns received practice. Its author was hardly a revolutionary. His instincts were conservative and strongly inclined him toward some post-facto justification. The difference between his posture and that of his predecessor, the author of the *Arukh ha-Shulhan,* is that he surveys the entire literature and then shows that the practice is plausibly justifiable in terms of that literature. His interpretations, while not necessarily persuasive, always stay within the bounds of the reasonable. And the legal coordinates upon which the *Mishnah Berurah* plots the issue are the written literature and the written literature alone. With sufficient erudition and inclination, received practice can almost invariably be charted on these axes, but it has no longer an inherent validity of its own.[5]

Common practice in the *Mishnah Berurah* has lost its independent validity and needs to be squared with the written word. Nevertheless, the practices there evaluated are what someone writing a commentary on *The Code of Jewish Law* would normally discuss. General practice as such is not under scrutiny, is not under investigation in the *Mishnah Berurah*. It is very much so in the haredi community of today.

One of the most striking phenomena of the contemporary haredi community is the explosion of halakhic works on practical observance. I do not refer to the stream of works on Sabbath laws, as these can be explained simply as attempts to determine the status, that is, the permissibility of use, of many new artifacts of modern technology, similar to the spate of recent works on the definition of death and organ transplants. I refer rather to the publications on *tallit* and *tefillin* (prayer shawls and phylacteries), works on the daily round of prayers and blessings in synagogue and home, tomes on High Holiday and Passover observance, books and pamphlets on every imaginable topic. The vast halakhic corpus is being scoured, new doctrines discovered and elicited, old ones given new prominence, and the results collated and published. Abruptly and within a generation, a rich literature of religious observance has been created, and it is one about articles used by Jews and performances they have been engaged in for thousands of years. These books, moreover, are avidly purchased and on a mass scale; sales are in the thousands, occasionally in the tens of thousands. It would be surprising if such popularity were not some indicia of adoption. Intellectual curiosity per se is rarely that widespread. Much of the traditional religious practice has been undergoing massive reevaluation, and by popular demand or, at the very least, by unsolicited popular consent. In Jerusalem and Stamford Hill, London, in Borough Park, New York, and B'nai B'rak, Israel, religious observance is being both amplified and raised to new, rigorous heights.

This transformation has, furthermore, taken place in the inner sanctum of the haredi world and has left nothing untouched. For example, on Passover evening one is obliged to consume unleavened bread (*matzot*). One is also required by Jewish law to consume a certain minimal amount (*shiur*)—a quantity here equal to the size of an olive. Jews have been practicing the Passover seder for at least two thousand years, and no one paid very much attention to what that minimal amount was. One knew it automatically, for one had seen it eaten at one's parents' table on innumerable Passover eves; one simply did as one's parents had done. Around the year 1940, a famous Talmudist, the Hazon Ish, published an essay in which he vigorously questioned whether scholars had not seriously underestimated the size of an olive in talmudic times. He then insisted on a minimal standard about twice the size of the commonly accepted one.[6] Within a decade his doctrine began to seep down into popular practice, and by now has become almost de rigeur in haredi circles.[7]

This development takes on significance when placed in historical perspective. The problem of "minimal requisite quantities" (*shiurim*) has been known since the mid-eighteenth century, when scholars in both central and Eastern Europe discovered that the shiurim commonly employed with regard to solid food do not square with the liquid-volume shiurim we know in other aspects of Jewish law.[8] The ineluctable conclusion was that the standard requisite quantity of solid food consumption should be roughly doubled. Though the men who raised this issue were some of the most famous Talmudists of the modern era, whose works have been, and remain, the staples of rabbinic study to this day, their words nevertheless fell on deaf ears and were without any impact, even in the most scholarly and religiously meticulous circles.[9] It was perfectly clear to all concerned that Jews had been eating matzot for thousands of years and that no textual analysis could affect in any way a millennia-old tradition. The problem was theoretically interesting, but practically irrelevant.

And then a dramatic shift occurs. A theoretical position that had been around for close to two centuries suddenly begins in the 1950s to assume practical significance and within a decade becomes authoritative. From then on, traditional conduct, no matter how venerable, how elementary, or how closely remembered, yields to the demands of theoretical knowledge. Established practice can no longer hold its own against the demands of the written word.

Significantly, this loss by the home of its standing as religious authenticator has taken place, not simply among the modern Orthodox, but, first, indeed foremost, among the haredim, and in their innermost recess—the home. The zealously sheltered hearth of the haredi world can no longer validate religious practice. The authenticity of tradition is now in question in the ultra-Orthodox world itself.

This development is related to the salient events of Ashkenazic Jewish history of the past century. In the multi-ethnic, corporate states of central and Eastern Europe, nationalities lived for hundreds of years side by side, each with its own language, its own religion, its way of dress and diet. Living together, these groups had much in common, yet at the same time they remained distinctly apart. Each had, with its own way of life, its own code of conduct, which was transmitted formally in the school, informally in the home and street (these are the acculturating agencies), each complementing and reinforcing one another. Equally significant, each way of life seemed inevitable to its members. Crossing over, while theoretically possible, was inconceivable, especially when it entailed a change of religion.

These societies were traditional, taking their values and code of conduct as a given, acting unselfconsciously, unaware that life could be lived differently. This is best epitomized in the title of one of the four tomes of the famous *Code of Jewish Law* (*The Shulhan Arukh*). The volume treating religious law is called *Orah Hayyim* (The way of life). And aptly so. In the enclaves of Eastern Europe, going to *shul* (synagogue) in the morning, putting on a *tallit katan* (fringed garment), and wearing sidelocks were for centuries the way of life of the Jew. These acts were done with the same naturalness and sense of inevitability as we experience in putting on those two strange Western garments, socks and ties. Clothes are a second skin.[10]

The old ways came, in the closing years of the nineteenth century and the early ones of the twentieth, under the successive ideological assaults of the socialist and communist movements, as well as that of Zionism. In the cities there was the added struggle with secularism, all the more acute as the ground there had been eroded over the past half century by a growing movement of Enlightenment. The defections, especially in urban areas, were massive; traditional life was severely shaken though not shattered. How much of this life would have emerged unaltered from the emergent movements of modernity in Eastern Europe we shall never know because the Holocaust, among other things, wrote finis to a culture. There was, however, little chance that the old ways would be preserved by the "surviving remnant," the relatives and neighbors of those who perished, who earlier had embarked for America and Israel. These massive waves of migration had wrenched these people suddenly from a familiar life and an accustomed environment, and thrust them into a strange country where even stranger manners prevailed. Simple conformity to a habitual pattern could not be adequate, for the problems of life were now new and different.[11] What was left of traditional Jewry regrouped in two camps: those who partially acculturated to the society that enveloped them, and those who decisively turned their back on it, whom we have called haredim, for lack of a better term. They, of course, would define themselves simply as Jews—Jews resolutely upholding the ways of their fathers.

They are that indeed. Resolve, however, is possible only in a choice, and ways of life that are upheld are no longer a given. Borough Park and Bnai Brak, while demographically far larger than any *shtetl*, are, as we shall see, enclaves rather than cultures. Alternatives now exist, and adherence is voluntary. A traditional society has been transformed into an orthodox one,[12] and religious conduct is less the product of social custom than of conscious, reflective behavior. If the tallit katan is worn not as a matter of course but as a matter of belief, it has then become a ritual object. A ritual can no more be approximated than an incantation can be summarized. Its essence lies in its accuracy. It is that accuracy the haredim are seeking. The flood of works on halakhic prerequisites and correct religious performance accurately reflects the ritualization of what had previously been routine acts and everyday objects. It mirrors the ritualization of what had been simply components of the given world and parts of the repertoire of daily living. A way of life has become a *regula,* and behavior, once governed by habit, is now governed by rule.

If accuracy is now sought, indeed deemed critical, it can be found only in texts. For in the realm of religious practice (unlike that of civil affairs), custom, no matter how long-standing and vividly remembered, has little standing over and against the normative written word. To be sure, custom may impose an added stringency, but, when otherwise at variance with the generally agreed interpretation of the written law, almost invariably it must yield.[13] Custom *is* potent, but its true power is informal. It derives from the ability of habit to neutralize the implications of book knowledge. Anything learned from study that conflicts with accustomed practice cannot really be right, as things simply cannot be different than they are.[14] Once that inconceivability is lost, usage loses much of its force. Even undiminished usage would be hard-pressed to answer the new questions being asked. For habit is unthinking and takes little notice of detail. (How many people could, for example, answer accurately: "How many inches wide is your tie or belt?") When interrogated, habit replies in approximations, a matter of discredit in the new religious atmosphere.

There is a very strong tendency in haredi circles, both lay and rabbinic, toward stringency.[15] No doubt this inclination is partly due to any sect's need for self-differentiation; nor would I gainsay the existence of religious one-upmanship. It would be unwise, however, to view this development simply as a posture toward outsiders. The development is also immanent. Habit is static; theoretical knowledge is dynamic and consequential, as ideas naturally tend to press forward to their full logical conclusions. "Only the extremes are logical," remarked Samuel Butler, "but they are absurd." No doubt. What is logical, however, is more readily agreed upon than what is absurd. When the mean is perceived as unconscionable compromise, the extreme may appear as eminently reasonable.

It is one thing to fine-tune an existing practice on the basis of "newly" read books; it is wholly another to construct practice anew on the exclusive basis of books. One confronts in Jewish law, as in any other legal system, a wide variety of differing positions on any given issue. If one is concerned to do things properly (and these "things" are, after all, God's will), the only course is to attempt to comply simultaneously with as many opinions as possible. Otherwise one risks invalidation. Hence the policy of "maximum position compliance," so characteristic of contemporary jurisprudence, which in turn leads to yet further stringency.

This reconstruction of practice is further complicated by the ingrained limitations of language. Words are good for description, even better for analysis, but pathetically inadequate for teaching how to do something. (Try learning, for example, how to tie shoelaces from written instructions.) One learns best by being shown, that is to say, mimetically. When conduct *is* learned from texts, conflicting views about its performance literally proliferate and the simplest gesture becomes acutely complicated.[16]

Fundamentally, all the above—stringency, "maximum position compliance," and the proliferation of complications and demands—simply reflect the essential change in the nature of religious performance that occurs in a text culture. Books cannot demonstrate conduct; they can only state its requirements. One then seeks to act in a way that meets those demands. Performance is no longer, as in a traditional society, replication of what one has seen, but implementation of what one knows. Seeking now to mirror the norm, religious observance is subordinated to it. In a text culture, behavior becomes a function of the ideas it consciously seeks to realize.[17]

No longer independent, religious performance then loses its inherited, fixed character. Indeed, during the transitional period (and for sometime after), there is a de-stabilization of practice, as the traditional inventory of religious objects and repertoire of religious acts are weighed and progressively found wanting. For many of those raised in the old order, the result is baffling, at times infuriating, as they discover that habits of a lifetime no longer suffice. Increasingly, they sense that their religious past, not to speak of that of their parents and teachers, is being implicitly challenged, and, on occasion, not just implicitly. But for most, for the natives of the emergent text culture and its naturalized citizens alike, the vision of perfect accord between precept and practice beckons to a brave new world; and, as ideas are dynamic and consequential, the vision also beckons to an expanding one and one of unprecedented consistency. The eager agenda of the haredi community has, understandably, now become the translation of the ever-increasing knowledge of the Divine norm into the practice of the Divine service.

So large an endeavor and so ambitious an aspiration are never without implications.[18] Translation entails, first, grasping an idea in its manifold fullness and then executing it in practice. This gives rise to a performative spirituality not unlike that of the arts, with all its unabating tension. What is at stake here, however, is not fidelity to a personal vision, but to what is perceived as the Divine Will. Though the intensity of the strain may differ between religion and art, the nature of the tension is the same, for it springs from the same limitations in human comprehension and implementation. Knowledge rarely yields finality. Initially, thought does indeed narrow the range of interpretation by detecting weaknesses in apparent options, but almost invariably it ends by presenting the inquirer with a number of equally possible understandings, each making a comparable claim to fidelity. Performance, however, demands choice, insistent and continuous. Whatever the decisions, their implementation is then beset by the haunting disparity between vision and realization, reach and grasp.

A tireless quest for absolute accuracy, for "perfect fit"—faultless congruence between conception and performance—is the hallmark of contemporary haredi religiosity. The search is dedicated and unremitting; yet it invariably falls short of success. For spiritual life is an attempt, as a great pianist once put it, to play music that is better than it can be played. Such an endeavor may finally become so heavy with strain that it can no longer take wing, or people may simply weary of repeated failure, no matter how inspired. The eager toil of one age usually appears futile to the next, and the performative aspiration, so widespread now, may soon give way to one of a wholly different kind, even accompanied by the derision that so often attends the discarding of an ideal. Yet this Sisyphean spirituality will never wholly disappear, for there will always be those who hear the written notes and who find in absolute fidelity the most sublime freedom.

In all probability, so arduous an enterprise would not have taken so wide a hold had it not also answered some profound need. "The spirit blows where it listeth" is often true of individuals, rarely of groups. The process we have described began, roughly, in the mid-1950s,[19] gathered force noticeably in the next decade, and by the mid-1970s was well on its way to being, if it had not already become, the dominant mode of religiosity. The shift of authority to text, though born of migration, did not then occur among the immigrants themselves but among their children or their children's children.[20] This is true even of the post-Holocaust immigration. Haredi communities had received a small but significant infusion after World War II, which had strengthened their numbers and steeled their resolution. Unlike their predecessors, these newcomers came not as immigrants but as refugees, in groups rather than individually.[21] However, equally unlike their predecessors, they did not hail from the self-contained shtetl or the culturally isolated ghettos of Poland and the Pale. Few from those territories escaped the Holocaust. These refugees came from the more urbanized areas of central Europe, especially Hungary, and their arrival in America was not their first encounter with the contemporary world.[22] The rise of the text culture occurred only after a sustained exposure to modernity, in homes some twice removed from the shtetl.

This exposure finally made itself felt, as the century passed its halfway mark, not in willful accommodation, but in unconscious acculturation, as large (though, not all) segments of the haredi enclave increasingly adopted the consumer culture and its implicit values, above all the legitimacy of pursuing material gratification. Much of haredi community took on an increasingly middle-class lifestyle.[23] The frumpy dress of women generally disappeared as did their patently artificial wigs. Married women continued, of course, to cover their hair, as tradition demanded, but the wigs were now fashionably elegant as were also their dresses, which were, to be sure, appropriately modest, but now attractively so. Elegant boutiques flourished in Borough Park. Ethnic food gave way to culinary pluralism, and French, Italian, Oriental, and Far Eastern restaurants blossomed under the strictest rabbinic supervision, as did now kosher cruises. Dining out, once reserved for special occasions, became common. Rock music sung with "kosher" lyrics was heard at the weddings of the most religious.[24] There had been no "kosher" jazz or "kosher" swing, for music is evocative, and what was elicited by the contemporary beat was felt by haredim to be alien to a "Jewish rejoicing" (*yidishe simche*). This was no longer the case. The body syncopated to the beat of rock, and the emotional receptivities that the contemporary rhythm engendered were now felt to be consonant with the spirit of "Jewish rejoicing." Indeed, "Hasidic" rock concerts, though decried, were not unheard of. The extended family of the old country (*mishpokhe*) gave way considerably to the nuclear one. Personal gratification, here and now, and individual attainment became increasingly accepted values. Family lineage (*yikhes*) still played an important role in marriage and communal affairs, but personal career achievement increasingly played an equal, if not greater, one. Divorce, once rare in haredi circles, became all too familiar. The divorce rate, of course, was far lower than that of the surrounding society, but the numbers were believed sufficiently large and the phenomenon sufficiently new to cause consternation.[25]

Even haredi accomplishments had their untoward consequences. The smooth incorporation of religious practice into a middle-class lifestyle meant that observance now differentiated less. Apart from their formal requirements, religious observances also engender ways of living. Eating only kosher food, for example, precludes going out to lunch, vacationing where one wishes, and dining out regularly as a form of entertainment. The proliferation of kosher eateries and the availability of literally thousands of kosher products in the consumer market opened the way to such pursuits,[26] so the religious way of life became, in one more regard, less distinguishable from others. The facilitation of religious practice that occurred in every aspect of daily life was a tribute to the adaptability of the haredim and to their new mastery of their environment; it also diminished some of the millennia-old impact of observance.

Not only did the same amount of practice now yield a smaller sum of difference, but also the amount of practice itself was far less than before. A mimetic tradition mirrors rather than discriminates. Without criteria to evaluate practice, a mimetic tradition generally cannot distinguish between central and peripheral, or even between religious demands and folkways. And the last two tended to be deeply intertwined in Eastern Europe, as ritual, which was seen to have a physical efficacy, was mobilized to ward off the threatening forces that stalked man's every step in a world precariously balanced between the powers of good and the powers of evil (*sitra ahara*). The rituals of defense, drawn from the most diverse sources, were religiously inflected, for the Jew knew that what lay in wait for him was a *shed* and not, as the peasant thought, some goblin, and that these agents of the *sitra ahara* could be defeated only by the proven weapons of traditional lore. Prophylactic ritual flourished because it served the roles of both religion and science. Its rites were thoroughly intertwined with normative ones and, to most, indistinguishable from one another. Joined in the struggle for health, for example, were amulets, blessings, incantations, and prayers.[27] In the world now inhabited by the haredim, however, the material environment is controlled by a neutral technology, and the animistic, value-driven cosmos replaced by a mechanistic and indifferent one. Modernity has thus defoliated most of these ritual practices and stripped the remaining ones of their significance. People still gather on the eve of circumcision, but as an occasion of rejoicing, not as a nightwatch (*wachnacht*) to forestall Lillith from spiriting away the infant.[28] A Jewish hospital differs from a Catholic one in the symbols on its walls and in the personal religion of its staff, but not in the procedures of health care. As religion ceased to be called upon to control directly the natural world, many vital areas of activity lost their religious coloration, and, with it, their differentiating force.

It would be strange indeed if this diminution of otherness did not evoke some response in the haredi world. They were "a nation apart," and had lived and died for that apartness. Their deepest instincts called for difference, and those instincts were not to be denied. Problems of meaningful survival were not new to the haredim, and they were not long in evolving the following response:

> If customary observances differentiated less, more observances were obviously called for. Indeed, they always had been called for, as the normative texts clearly show, but those calls had gone unheeded because of the power of habit and the heavy hand of custom. The inner differences of pulse and palate may well have been leveled, and the distinctive Jewish ideals of appearance and attractiveness may equally have been lost. This was deplorable, and indeed the religious leaders had long railed against the growing pursuit of happiness.[29] But small wonder, for people had failed to take stock in the New World. They had turned to habit and folklore for guidance rather than to study, and despite the best of intentions, their observances had been fractional. Even that fraction had been less than it seemed, for superstition had been confused with law and, on occasion, even supplanted it. Religious life must be constructed anew and according to the groundplan embedded in the canonized literature and in that literature alone. While this reconstruction was going on, the struggle for the inner recesses of the believer would continue as before, only now it would be bolstered

by the intensification of religious practice. And there was hope for the outcome, for the moralists (*hakmei ha-mussar*) had always insisted that "the outer affects the inner," that constantly repeated deeds finally affect the personality. As for the so-called stringency, some of it was simply a misperception based on the casual attitude of the past, much only legal prudence. As for the remainder—if there was one—that too was for the good, for there could not be too much observance when dwelling amid the fleshpots of Egypt.

An outside spectator, on the other hand, might have said that as large spheres of human activity were emptied of religious meaning and difference, an intensification of that difference in the remaining spheres was only natural. Moreover, the more pervasive the influence of the milieu, the more natural the need of a chosen people to reassert its distinctiveness and to mark ever more sharply its identity borders. As the inner differences erode, the outer ones must be increased and intensified, for, progressively, they provide more and more of the crucial otherness. In addition, the more stable and comprehensive the code of conduct, the less psychologically threatening the subtler inroads of the environment. The narrowing of the cultural divide has thrust a double burden on religious observance, as ritual must now do on its own what ritual joined with ethnicity had done before. Religious practice, that spectator might have added, had always served to separate Jews from their neighbors; however, it had not borne alone that burden. It was now being called on to do so, for little else distinguished Jew from Gentile, or haredi from non-haredi, for that matter.

But then there is always a dissimilarity between what is obvious to the participant and what is clear to the observer.

Both haredi and observer, however, would agree that it was the mooring of religion in sacred texts that enabled the reassertion of haredi difference. And for those who sought to be different and had something about which to be genuinely different,[30] the 1960s in the United States were good years, as were the ones that followed. The establishment lost much of its social and cultural authority.[31] Anglo-conformance now appeared far more as a demeaning affectation than part of the civilizing process by which the lower orders slowly adopted the refinements of their betters. The "melting pot" now seemed a ploy of cultural hegemony and was out; difference, even a defiant heterogeneity, was in. Nor did haredim lose by the widespread disenchantment with modernity and with the culture that had brought it to pass.[32]

Not that the collapse of the WASP hegemony led to the haredi resurgence; rather, the changed circumstances reduced the social and psychological costs of distinctiveness, and the new atmosphere made the choices of their parents seem ever more problematic. What had appeared at the time as reasonable adjustments now appeared as superfluous ones, some even verging on compromise.[33] This only strengthened the new generation's quiet resolve that in the future things would be different, which, together with a respectful silence and a slightly bemused deference, often accompanies the changing of the guard in a traditional society, or in one that still takes its reverence seriously. To the children and grandchildren of the uprooted, the mandate was clear, indeed, had been long prefigured. Judaism had to return now, after the exile from

Eastern Europe and its destruction, as it had returned once before, after the Exile and destruction of the Second Temple, to its foundational texts, to an indwelling in, what the Talmud termed, "the four cubits of the halakhah." [34]

As wholly other as the haredim feel themselves to be from their godless brethren, and as different as they indeed are in their ways, nevertheless, they are, historically, part of the larger American Jewish community; and their reassertion of difference was one facet of that community's wider response to the conjunction of third-generation acculturation with the civil rights movement and the decline of the WASP ascendancy. The rapid emergence of the text culture among the haredim in the late 1960s and 1970s, and its current triumph should be viewed alongside two parallel developments: the sudden centrality, even cult, of the Holocaust, an event that, prior to the late 1960s, had been notably absent in American Jewish consciousness; [35] and the dramatic rise in intermarriage that occurred during these same years. The incidence of intermarriage, which until the mid-1950s had been extraordinarily low and stable for close to half a century (4 percent to 6 percent), quadrupled by 1968 to some 23 percent, and within twenty years approached, if not passed, the 50 percent mark. [36]

Most children of immigrants had decisively turned their backs on the old ways of their parents. Many had even attended faithfully the chapel of Acceptance, over whose portals they saw inscribed "Incognito Ergo Sum," and which, like most mottoes, was both a summons and a promise. [37] Whether that promise was more real than illusory may never be entirely known, for only rarely could the summons be fully met. Most Jews had imbibed in their immigrant parents' home far too many culturally distinctive characteristics for them to be indistinguishable from the rest, not to speak of being joined with other ethnic groups in so intimate an enterprise as marriage. For the second generation, this sense of otherness was reinforced by the social and career exclusions they experienced at home and the growing crescendo of persecution they witnessed abroad.

In the late 1950s and the 1960s, however, otherness collapsed from both within and without. A third generation raised in American homes came of age just at the time when the civil rights and Black Power movements were discrediting racism in many circles. With these uprisings, America discovered it had been born, indeed had long lived, in sin, and the establishment's sudden awareness of its centuries-long unawareness shook its confidence in its own monopoly of virtue, a necessary illusion of any ruling class. Its agony and confusion over foreign policy, long an area of special establishment accomplishment, induced a further loss of nerve. The center ceased to hold; meanwhile ethnic barriers were crumbling among the grandchildren of immigrants, as were the enforced solidarities of discrimination. This was especially true on college campuses, where young Jews were found in inordinate numbers. Many now saw no bar to intermarriage. Others sought their uniqueness outside themselves, in the unspeakable deeds of the Nazis. What had been previously known as "the destruction of European Jewry" became simply "the Holocaust," a word that now resonated with new and singular meaning. Admittedly, the astonishing victory of the Six Day War may have had to occur before Jews could dwell on their past victimization without fearing that it might be seen as a congenital defect. And perhaps only a new generation, unburdened by the complicity of silence, could bear aloft the memory of a frightful and premonitory past. But what is memorable, even inviolable, is not necessarily unique. The sudden, passionate insistence that the suffering of one's own people was sui generis and incomparable to that of any other nation in the long and lamentable catalog of human cruelty betokens, among other things, an urgent need for a distinction that must be met, but cannot be satisfied from within, from any inner resource. Finding one's inimitability in the unique horrors others have committed against oneself may seem a strange form of distinction, but not if there remains a powerful urge to feel different at a time when one has become indistinguishable from the rest.

One can respond to a loss of identity borders by intermingling, by finding another source of distinctness, or by re-creating the old differences anew. And much of American Jewish history of the past generation has been the intertwined tale of these conflicting reactions. People respond to situations according to their temperament and background. At the time, they appear divided by the different positions they adopt, as indeed they deeply are. In retrospect, however, they also appear united by the shared burden of the need for response and by their common confinement to the solutions that lie then at hand.

Just as the haredi response of difference should be seen horizontally, as part of wider, contemporary developments, so too should its acculturation be viewed vertically, plotted on the long curve of the history of Jewish spirituality. The growing embourgeoisement of the haredi community, repercussive as it was in itself, was also a final phase of a major transformation of values which had been in the making for close to a century, namely, the gradual disappearance of the ascetic ideal that had held sway over Jewish spirituality for close to a millennium.[38] While there was sharp division in traditional Jewish thought over the stronger asceticism of mortification of the flesh, the milder one of distrust of the body was widespread, if not universal.[39] The soul's control over the flesh was held to be, at most, tenuous, and without constant exercises in self-denial, there was little chance of the human soul triumphing over the constant, carnal pull. Certain needs and propensities had indeed been sanctioned and, in the instance of marital relations, even mandated by the Law. Sanction and mandate, however, do not mean indulgence, and the scope of what was seen as indulgence was broad indeed.[40] Natural cravings, if not closely monitored, could turn easily into uncontrolled desires, and while they need not be negated, they should be reduced to a minimum. To be sure, states of joy were encouraged by some, appropriate moments of rejoicing advocated by all; but joy, unlike pleasure, is preeminently a state of mind, for unlike pleasure, it reflects not simply the satisfaction of a natural impulse, but of a coming together of such a satisfaction with the experience of a value. Through a millennium of ethical (*mussar*) writings runs a ceaseless warfare between will and instinct, as does the pessimistic feeling that the "crooked timber of humanity" will never quite be made straight.

Little of all this is to be found in the moral literature of the past half century.[41] There is, to be sure, much criticism of hedonism; restraint in all desires is advocated, as is a deemphasis of material well-being. However, what is preached is "plain living and high thinking," rather than any war on basic instinct. The thousand-year struggle of the soul with the flesh has finally come to a close.

The legitimacy of physical instinct is the end product of the haredi encounter with modernity which began in the latter half of the nineteenth century as the emergent movements of the Enlightenment, Zionism, and socialism made themselves felt in Eastern Europe, and the current, widespread acceptance of physical gratification reflects the slow but fundamental infiltration of the surrounding society's this-worldly orientation. This metamorphosis, in turn, shifts the front of religion's incessant struggle with the nature of things: the spiritual challenge becomes less to escape the confines of the body than to elude the air that is breathed. In a culturally sealed and supportive environment, the relentless challenge to the religious vision comes from within, from man's bodily desires. In an open but culturally antagonistic environment, the impulses from without pose a far greater danger than do those from within. On the simplest level, the risk is the easy proffer of mindless temptation; on the deeper level, the risk is cultural contamination. The move from a self-contained world to a partially acculturated one engenders a transformation of the religious aspiration, as the quest becomes not so much to overcome the stirrings of the flesh as to win some inner deliverance from osmosis with the environment. Purity, as ever, is the goal. However, in a community that chooses, or must choose, not flight from the world, as the monasteries once did and the Amish do, but life within the larger setting, the aspiration is less to chasteness of thought than to chasteness of outlook.

Religion has been described as "another world to live in," and of nothing is this more true than of the enclave, with its inevitable quest for unalloyed belief and unblemished religiosity. The other world in which the haredim seek now to dwell, and whose impress they wish to bear, is less the world of their fathers than that of their "portable homeland," their sacred texts, which alone remain unblighted by the contagion of their surroundings.

But could the world emerging from these sacred texts be seen as different from that of their fathers, whose ways the haredim strove so vigorously to uphold? Such a perception would have undermined the entire enterprise of reconstruction. Memory now came to their aid as did, unwittingly, the Holocaust. The world of their fathers left no history, for like any traditional society, it saw itself as always having been what it was, and when little has changed there is little to tell, much less to explain. Of that world, there were now only the memories of the uprooted and the echo of those memories among their children; and memories are pliant, for recollection comforts as much as it recounts. Memories are our teddy bears no less than our informants, treasured fragments of an idealized past that we clutch for reassurance in the face of an unfamiliar present. The strangest and most unsettling aspect of the world in which the haredim now found themselves was its relentless mandate for change. Memory filtered and transmuted, and the past of haredi recollection soon took on a striking similarity to the emerging present.[42] Nor was there, after the Holocaust, an ambiguous reality to challenge their picture of its past. The cataclysmic events of the 1940s gave a unique intensity to the reconstruction of the haredim because no one else was left to preserve the flame; the same events also gave them free reign to create a familiar past, of which the present was simply a faithful extension.

This new past was a creature of recollection among post-World War II immigrants, but not among their offspring. Nor could the memory of the parents now be transmitted by word of mouth, as in the past, for the children had acquired alien ways of knowing, even in the most sacred of all activities, the study of the Torah. Halakhic literature, indeed traditional Jewish literature generally, has no secondary sources, only primary ones. The object of study from childhood to old age was the classic texts—the Pentateuch, the Mishnah, and the Talmud.[43] For well over a millennium all literary activity had centered on commenting on and applying those texts;[44] every few centuries a code would be composed that stated the upshot of these ongoing discussions. Self-contained presentations of a topic, works introducing the reader to a subject and then explaining it in lay language, did not exist. There were few, if any, serious works that could be read independently, that is, without reference to another text which it glossed. Indeed, the use of such a work would have been deeply suspect, for its reader would be making claim to knowledge that he had not elicited from the primary texts. Knowledge was seen as an attainment, something that had been wrested personally from the sources. Information, on the other hand, was something merely obtained, passed like a commodity, from hand to hand, usually in response to a question.

Study of primary sources is a slow and inefficient way to acquire information, but in traditional Jewish society, the purpose of study (*lernen*) was not information or even knowledge but a lifelong exposure to the sacred texts and an ongoing dialogue with them.[45] *Lernen* was seen as both an intellectual endeavor and an act of devotion; its process *was* its purpose. The new generation, however, obtained its knowledge in business and in daily affairs from books, and these books imparted their information in a self-contained, straightforward, and accessible format. They saw no reason why knowledge of the Torah should not be equally available to them in so ready and serviceable a fashion. The traditional mode of "learning" could only gain by such a natural supplement. In response to this widespread feeling, the past twenty years produced a rapidly growing, secondary halakhic literature—not only guides and handbooks, but rich, extensive, topical presentations, many of high scholarly caliber.[46]

In Israel, such books are in modern Hebrew; in America and England, they are in English. This constitutes yet a greater break with the past. Since the late Middle Ages, Ashkenazic Jewish society was "diglossic," that is, employing both a "higher" and "lower" language. Yiddish was used for common speech and all oral instruction; Hebrew, for prayer and all learned writing, whether halakhic, ethical, or kabbalistic.[47] The only halakhic works published in Yiddish were religious primers, basic guides written ostensibly for women, in reality also for the semiliterate, but viewed by all as "women's fare."[48] Even Hasidic tales and aphorisms, concerned as the writers were to preserve every nuance of the holy man's Yiddish words, were nevertheless always transcribed into Hebrew.[49] Things have changed dramatically over the past twenty-five years. Admittedly the revival of the Hebrew language in Israel, with its attendant secularization, has diminished some of Hebrew's aura as the "sacred tongue." However, the emergence of a rich and sophisticated halakhic literature in English stems less from the fact that Hebrew has been desacralized than because English is now the mother tongue of Anglo-Saxon haredi society as is modern Hebrew to its Israeli counterpart. The contemporary Jewish community is linguistically acculturated, unlike the communities of Eastern Europe, 80 percent of which in Poland, for example, still gave Yiddish rather than Polish as its first language as late as 1931.[50] The flood of works on halakhic prerequisites and the dramatic appreciation of the level of religious observance are proud marks of the haredi resurgence. This flow and swift absorption are possible, however, only because the community has unwittingly adopted the alien ways of knowing of the society in which it is enmeshed and whose language it now intuitively speaks.

With this acculturation also came the discovery of the historicity of things. The secular education of many haredi was rudimentary but enough for them to know that the record of the past is found in books. Any doubt was put to rest by experience. One had to anticipate the future to get a better handle on it. The only way to do that was by knowing the past—one's medical past, the past performance of a stock, of a business, or of a politician. There could be little memory of such pasts, but there was information, written records, and from these documents, a "history" could be reconstructed. If all else had a history, they too had one. To be sure, theirs was not "History," in the upper case, the sacred, archetypal record of the Bible and Midrash, with its "eternal contemporaneity,"[51] but the more mundane sort, "history," in the lower case, replete with random figures and chance happenings. Hardly paradigmatic for posterity, still it was significant enough to its immediate successors to merit their pondering its lessons. So alongside the new genre of secondary halakhic works, there has appeared, in the past generation, a second genre equally unfamiliar to their fathers, that of "history," written accounts of bygone events and biographies of great Torah scholars of the recent past,[52] images of a nation's heritage that once would have been imparted by the vibrant voices of home and street but now must be conveyed, as so much else in the "new world," by means of book and formal instruction.

These works wear the guise of history, replete with names and dates and footnotes, but their purpose is that of memory—to sustain and nurture, to inform in such a way as to ease the task of coping. Didactic and ideological, this "history" filters out untoward facts and glosses over darker aspects of the past. Indeed, it often portrays events as they did not happen.[53] So does memory; memory, however, transmutes unconsciously, whereas the writing of history is a conscious act. But this intentional disregard of fact in ideological history is no different from what takes place generally in moral education, as most such instruction seems to entail a misrepresentation of a harsh reality. We teach a child, for example, that crime does not pay. Were this in fact so, theodicy would be no problem. Yet we do not feel that we are lying, for when values are being inculcated, the facts of experience—empirical truth—cease somehow to be "true."

For if a value is to win widespread acceptance, to evoke an answering echo of assent in the minds of many, it must be experienced by them, not simply as a higher calling, but as a demand that emerges from the nature of things. When we state that "honesty" is "good," we are also saying that, ultimately, this is what is best for man, what we call, at times, "true felicity," to distinguish it from mere "happiness." We believe that, were we to know all there is to know of the inner life of a Mafia don and that of an honest cobbler, we would see that honesty is, indeed, the best policy. The moral life makes claim to be the wise life, and the moral call, to most, is a summons to realism, to live one's life in accord with the deeper reality.[54] A statement of value is, in this way, a statement of fact, a pronouncement about the true nature of things.

When we say that crime doesn't pay, we are not lying; we are teaching the child the underlying reality that we believe in or intuit rather than the distorted one of our fragmentary experience. Just as moral instruction imparts the lessons of a reality deeper than the one actually perceived, so too must sacred history reflect, to the believer, the underlying realities of the past rather than the distortions arising from the contingencies of experience and the haphazardness of documentation.

And the underlying reality of Jewish history to the haredim has been the Covenant that they had sealed with the Lord long ago at Sinai and that alone can explain their miraculous continuance. There had been backsliding enough in their long and stiff-necked history, for which the foretold price had been paid with fearful regularity. But when they had lived rightly, they had done so by complying with that pact, living, as it were, "by the book"—abiding by the wise counsel of His sages and living by the lights of His sacred texts. How else *could* the People of the Book have lived?

So alongside its chiaroscuro portrait of the past—the unremitting struggle between the Sons of Light and Darkness—common to all sacred history, comes the distinctive haredi depiction of the society of yesteryear, the world of their fathers, as a model of text-based religiosity, of which their own is only a faithful extension. The past is cast in the mold of the present, and the current text-culture emerges, not as a product of the twin ruptures of migration and acculturation, but as simply an ongoing reflection of the unchanging essence of Jewish history. And before we discount out of hand this perception of the past, we would do well to remember that in the court of Jewish belief, and, perhaps, even in the longer arc of Jewish history, it is the mimetic society, "moving easy in harness," that must render up an account of itself.

I have discussed the disappearance of a way of life and the mimetic tradition. I believe, however, the transformations in the haredi enclave go much deeper and affect fundamental beliefs. Assessments of other peoples' inner convictions are always conjectural and, perhaps, should be done only in a language in which the subjunctive mood is still in vigorous use. I can best convey my impression—and I emphasize that it is no more than an *impression*—by sharing a personal experience.

In 1959, I came to Israel before the High Holidays. Having grown up in Boston and never having had an opportunity to pray in a haredi yeshiva, I spent the entire High Holiday period—from Rosh Hashanah to Yom Kippur—at the famous Ponevizher Yeshiva. The prayer there was long, intense, and uplifting, certainly far more powerful than anything I had previously experienced. And yet there was something missing, something I had experienced before, something I had perhaps taken for granted. Upon reflection, I realized that there was introspection, self-ascent, even moments of self-transcendence, but there was no fear in the thronged student body, most of whom were Israeli born.[55] Nor was that experience a solitary one. Over the subsequent thirty years, I have passed the High Holidays generally in America or Israel, and, occasionally, in England, attending services in haredi and non-haredi communities alike. I have yet to find that fear present, to any significant degree, among the native born in either circle. The ten-day period between Rosh Hashanah and Yom Kippur are now Holy Days, but they are not Yamim Noraim—"Days of Awe" or, more accurately, "Days of Dread"—as they have traditionally been called.

I grew up in a Jewishly nonobservant community and prayed in a synagogue where most of the older congregants neither observed the Sabbath nor even ate kosher. They all hailed from Eastern Europe, largely from *shtetlach,* like Shepetovka and Shnipishok. Most of their religious observance, however, had been washed away in the sea-change, and the little left had further eroded in the "new country." Indeed, the only time the synagogue was ever full was during the High Holidays. Even then the service was hardly edifying. Most didn't know what they were saying and, bored, wandered in and out. Yet at the closing service of Yom Kippur, the Ne'ilah, the synagogue filled and a hush set in upon the crowd. The tension was palpable and tears were shed.

What had been instilled in these people in their earliest childhood, and what they never quite shook off, was that every person was judged on Yom Kippur, and, as the sun was setting, the final decision was being rendered (in the words of the famous prayer) "who for life, who for death, / who for tranquility, who for unrest."[56] These people did not cry from religiosity but from self-interest, from an instinctive fear for their lives.[57] Their tears were courtroom tears, with whatever degree of sincerity such tears have. What was absent among the students in Ponevezh and in other contemporary services—and, lest I be thought to be exempting myself from this assessment, absent in my own religious life too—was that primal fear of Divine judgment, simple and direct.[58]

Be these personal impressions as they may,[59] the palpable presence of God, His direct involvement in everyday life, *was* a fact of life in the Eastern European shtetl. Let us remember Tevye's conversations with God portrayed by Sholom Aleichem.[60] There is, of course, humor in the colloquial intimacy and in the precise way the most minute annoyances of daily life are laid, package-like, at God's doorstep. The humor, however, is that of parody, the exaggeration of the commonly known. The author's assumption is that his readers themselves share, after some fashion, Tevye's sense of God's responsibility for man's quotidian fate. If they didn't, Tevya would not be humorous; he would be crazy.

Tevya's outlook was not unique to the shtetl, or to Jews in Eastern Europe; it was simply one variation of an age-old cosmology that dominated Europe for millennia which saw the universe as being directly governed by a divine Sovereign.[61] If regularity exists in the world, that is simply because the Sovereign's will is constant, as one expects the will of a great sovereign to be. He could, of course, at any moment change His mind, and things contrary to our expectations would then occur, what we call "miracles." However, the recurrent and the "miraculous" alike are, to the same degree, the direct and unmediated consequence of His wish. The difference between them is not of kind but rather of frequency. Frequency, of course, is a very great practical difference, and it well merits, indeed demands of daily language, a difference in terms. However, this verbal distinction never obscures for a moment their underlying identity.

As all that occurs is an immediate consequence of His will, events have a purpose and occur because of that purpose. Rationality, or, as they would have had it, wisdom, does not consist in detecting unvarying sequences in ever more accurately observed events and seeing in the first occurrence the "cause" of the second. Wisdom, rather, consists in discovering His intent in these happenings, for that intent is their cause, and only by grasping their cause could events be anticipated or controlled. In the workings of such a world, God is not an ultimate cause; He is a direct, natural force, and safety lies in contact with that force. Prayer has then a physical efficacy, and sin is "a fearful imprudence." Not that one thinks much about sin in the bustle of daily life, but when a day of reckoning does come around, only the foolhardy are without fear.

Such a Divine force can be distant and inscrutable, as in some strains of Protestantism, or it can be intimate and familial, as in certain forms of Catholicism. In Eastern Europe it tended toward intimacy, whether in the strong Marian strain of Polish Catholicism or in the much supplicated household icon, the center of family piety, in Greek Orthodox devotion. And much of the traditional literature of the Jews, especially as it filtered into common consciousness through the Commentaries of Rashi, or richly amplified Yiddish translation of the Pentateuch,[62] contained a humanization of the deity which invited intimacy. God visits Abraham on his sickbed; He consoles Isaac upon the death of his father. He is swayed by the arguments of Elijah or the matriarchs, indeed by any heartfelt prayer, and decisions on the destiny of nations and the fate of individuals, the length of the day and the size of the moon are made and unmade by apt supplications at the opportune moment.[63] The humor of Sholom Aleichem lay not in the dialogues with God, but in having a "dairyman" rather than the Ba'al Shem Tov conduct them. The parody lay not in the remonstrances but in their subject matter.[64]

The world to which the uprooted came, and in which their children were raised, was that of modern science, which had reduced nature to "an irreversible series of equations," to an immutable nexus of cause and effect, which suffices on its own to explain the workings of the world. Not that most, or even any, had so much as a glimmer of these equations, but the formulas of the "new country" had created a technology which they saw, with their own eyes, transforming their lives beyond all dreams. And it is hard to deny the reality of the hand that brings new gifts with startling regularity.

There are, understandably, few Tevyas today, even in haredi circles. To be sure, there are occasions in the lives of most when the reversals are so sudden, or the stakes so high and the contingencies so many, that the unbeliever prays for luck, and the believer, more readily and often, calls for His help. Such moments are only too real, but they are not the stuff of daily life. And while there are always those whose spirituality is one apart from that of their time, nevertheless, I think it safe to say that the perception of God as a *daily, natural* force is no longer present to a significant degree in any sector of modern Jewry, even the most religious. Indeed, I would go so far as to suggest that specific Divine Providence, though passionately believed as a theological principle—and I do not for a moment question the depth of that conviction—is no longer experienced as a simple reality. With the shrinkage of God's palpable hand in human affairs has come a marked loss of His immediate presence, with its primal fear and nurturing comfort. With this distancing, the haredi world has been irrevocably separated from the spirituality of its fathers, indeed, from the religious mood of intimate anthropomorphism that had cut across all the religious divides of the Old World.

It is this rupture in the traditional religious sensibilities that underlies some of the loss of confidence in haredi circles. Zealous to continue traditional Judaism unimpaired, they seek to ground their new emerging spirituality less on a now unattainable intimacy with Him than on an intimacy with His Will, avidly eliciting Its intricate demands and saturating their daily lives with Its exactions. Having lost the touch of His presence, they now seek solace in the pressure of His yoke.

Though born of migration and acculturation, and further fueled by religious crisis, the current grounding of religion in written norms is well suited to, indeed, in a sense, is sustained by, the society in which the haredim now find themselves. Religion is a move against the grain of the tangible, but only for the very few can it be entirely that. As deeply as any ideology may stand apart from, even in stark opposition to, its contemporary environment, if this outlook is to be shared beyond the narrow confines of a few *âmes d'élites*, who need no supportive experience to confirm them in their convictions, its beliefs must in some way conform, or at least somehow correspond, to the world of people and things that is daily experienced.

The God envisaged throughout Eastern Europe—omnipotent, unfettered, and acting on the world as He willed—was well suited to, indeed, was, in a sense, an idealized enlargement of the absolute autocracy that then held sway. The intimacy with Him who was paradoxically both King and Father had deep roots in each religious tradition. At the same time, it corresponded to the royal image current in the world around them: the Emperor as "little father" or "affectionate father,"[65] sometimes harsh but always just, and ready to reconsider his judgments if good cause could be shown; all-powerful yet caring, and open to personal supplication if his attention could somehow be obtained. The old religiosity of prescriptive custom fitted in equally well with—indeed, could be seen as a natural extension of—the broader Eastern European pattern of authority, of compliance with accustomed ways and submission to long-standing prerogative. Authority came with age in the old country. The present received its empowerment from the past, so it seemed only right and natural to do things the way they always had been done.

The world now experienced by the haredim, by us all, is rule-oriented and, in the broadest sense of the term, rational. Modern society is governed by regulations, mostly written, and interpreted by experts accounting for their decisions in an ostensibly reasoned fashion. The sacred world of the haredim and the secular one that envelops them function similarly. While sharing, of course, no common source, they do share a similar manner of operation. As men, moreover, now submit to rule rather than to custom, haredim and modern man also share a common mode of legitimacy, that is, they have a like perception of what makes a just and compelling claim to men's allegiance, a corresponding belief in the kind of yoke people ought and do, in fact, willingly bear. And as the world now is currently governed by legislative rulers rather than personal ones, as in the past, so too do contemporary haredim, encountering now His precepts far more readily than His presence, experience God less as personal sovereign than as lawgiver. Religion can endure under almost all circumstances, even grow under most, but it flourishes more easily when the inner and outer worlds, the world as believed and the world as experienced, reflect and reinforce one another,[66] as did the mimetic religiosity in a traditional society, and as does now, to a lesser but still very real extent, the text-based religiosity with a legislative God in a modern, bureaucratic society.

The shift of authority to texts and their enshrinement as the sole source of authenticity have had far-reaching effects. Not only has this shift contributed to the policy of religious stringency and altered the nature of religious performance, but it has also transformed the character and purpose of religious education, redistributed political power in non-Hasidic circles, and defined anew the scope of the religious in the political arena.

A religiosity rooted in texts is a religiosity transmitted in schools, which was hardly the case in the old and deeply settled communities of the past. There the school had been second to the home in the inculcation of values. Basic schooling (*heder*) had provided its students with the rudimentary knowledge and skills necessary to participate in the Jewish way of life, while reinforcing and occasionally refining the norms instilled in the family circle. The advanced instruction (*yeshiva*) given a small elite was predominantly academic, cultivating intellectual virtuosity and providing its students with the expertise necessary for running of a society governed by halakha. Admittedly, underlying all study was the distinctive Jewish conviction that knowledge gave values greater resonance, and that in that all-consuming intellectual quest that was called love of "learning," as in mundane love to which it was compared, the self was submerged and one fused with that toward which one strained: understanding, the truth, the Torah.[67] And indeed, more was demanded of those who knew more. Useful as this cultural expectation may have been in tempering both behavior and character and in moderating, perhaps, the prerogatives of a clergy, it only intensified the emphasis on study in the traditional education. The affective powers of knowledge were held to be so great that the need of schooling to concentrate on its acquisition seemed ever more essential.

Now, however, the school bears most of the burden of imprinting Jewish identity.[68] For the shift from culture to enclave which occurred in the wake of migration means precisely the shrinkage of the religious agency of home and street and the sharp contraction of their role in cultural transmission. As the neighborhood will not and the family cannot adequately instill fealty to a way of life different from the one that envelops them, formal education has now become indispensable for imbuing a religious outlook and habituating religious observance.[69] The time spent by all in school has also been immeasurably lengthened, for convictions must be ingrained and made intimate, proprieties of behavior need to be imprinted by the deliberate enterprise of teaching, and for the impress to be durable, the individual must be kept in the mold during his formative years. So youth, and early manhood too, are now spent within the "walls of the yeshivah," for formal education has become preeminently an apprenticeship in the Jewish way of life.

How essential this education has become may be seen in the numerous Hasidic yeshivot now in existence, almost all of recent origin. For close to two hundred years, Hasidism had looked askance at the institution of yeshivot, viewing them not only as competing sources of authority to that of the Hasidic rabbi (*rebbe*), but also as simply far less effective in inculcating religiosity than the Hasidic home and local Hasidic synagogue, not to speak of the court of the rebbe himself. To be sure, several dynasties with a more intellectual bent had founded their own yeshivot.[70] These, however, were the exception and not the rule. Moreover, these institutions addressed a tiny, elite body only, and their role in the religious life of the community was peripheral. Within the past thirty years, Hasidic yeshivot have become a commonplace and attendance is widespread, as Hasidim have decisively realized that in the world in which they must currently live, even the court of the holy man may well fail without the sustained religious apprenticeship of the school.

This apprenticeship is long and uncompromising, but it has proven surprisingly attractive. No doubt the draft exemption in Israel provides strong inducement, but this leaves unexplained the same resurgence of the yeshiva in the United States and England. The new affluence of the haredim unquestionably plays a major role in maintaining the new and growing network of schools. Wealth, however, enables many things, and massive support of higher, non-career-oriented education need not necessarily be one of them. The yeshiva has won its widespread support and young men now flock to its gates primarily because it has become the necessary avenue to religious perspective and behavior, but also because it holds forth a religious life lived without the neglects and abridgments of the mundane environment. Resolutely set off from society yet living in closest proximity to ideals to which the larger community aspires, the yeshiva has, to some, all the incandescence of an essentialized world. Institutions of realization, such as monasteries, kibbutzim, or yeshivot, where the values of a society are most uncompromisingly translated into daily life, often prove attuned to youth's recurrent quest for the authentic. When the tides of the time do flow in their direction, their insulation from life appears less a mark of artificiality than a foretaste of the millennium, when life will finally be lived free from the pressures of a wholly contingent reality. Such institutions, it should be added, have generally exercised an influence on society wholly disproportionate to their numbers.

If religion is now transmitted to the next generation by institutional education, small wonder that the influence of the educators has increased dramatically, especially the sway of the scholar, the one most deeply versed in the sacred texts. For the text is now the guarantor of instruction, as the written word is both the source and the touchstone of religious authenticity. This, in turn, has entailed a shift in political power in non-Hasidic circles.[71] Authority long associated in Eastern Europe with the city rabbi, who functioned as a quasi-religious mayor, has now passed, and dramatically so, to Talmudic sages, generally, the heads of Talmudic academies—*roshei yeshiva*. Admittedly the traditional European rabbinate, urban, compact, and centralized, had no chance of surviving in America or Israel. It was ill suited to the United States with its sprawling suburbs and grass-roots, federal structure of authority. It was no less redundant in Israel, where the state now provides all the vital religious and social services previously supplied by the community (*kahal*), of which the rabbi was the head. However, the power lost by the rabbinate did not have to accrue necessarily to the roshei yeshiva. It is their standing as the masters of the book par excellence that has given them their newly found authority. In Eastern Europe of the last century, the rosh yeshiva was the equivalent of a head of an advanced institute, distinguished and respected, but without communal influence.[72] He was appointed because of his mastery of the book, and to the book and school he was then confined. This mastery now bestows on him the mantle of leadership.

And that mantle has become immeasurably enlarged, as the void created by the loss of a way of life (the *orah hayyim*), the shrinkage of a culture, manifests itself. Social and political issues of the first rank are now regularly determined by the decisions of Torah sages. Lest I be thought exaggerating, the formation of the 1990 coalition government in Israel hinged on the haredi parties. For months, Shamir and Peres openly courted various Talmudic scholars and vied publicly for their blessings. Indeed, the decision to enter the Likud coalition lay in the hands of a ninety-five-year-old sage, and, when he made public his views, his speech was nationally televised—understandably, as it was of national consequence.[73]

Admittedly this need for direction and imprimatur is partly the product of the melding of Hasidic and mitnagdic (non-Hasidic) ways of life, as the two joined forces against modernity. The Hasidim have adopted the mode of Talmudic study and some of the ideology of mitnagdim. In turn, the mitnagdim have adopted some of the dress of the Hasidim and something of the authority figure who provides guidance in the tangled problems of life.[74] This blending of religious styles is, to be sure, part of the story, but the crisis of confidence in haredi circles is no less a part.

This new deference is surprising, as political issues generally lie beyond the realm of law, certainly of Jewish law (*halakha*), which is almost exclusively private law. When political issues do fall within its sphere, many of the determinative elements—attainability of goals, competing priorities, trade-offs, costs—are not easily reducible to legal categories. Yet the political sphere has now come, and dramatically so, within the religious orbit.

Political reactions are not innate. Opinions on public issues are formed by values and ways of looking at things. In other words they are cultural. What had been lost, however, in migration was precisely a "culture." A way of life is not simply a habitual manner of conduct, but also, indeed above all, a coherent one. It encompasses the web of perceptions and values that determines the way the world is assessed and the posture one assumes toward it. Feeling now bereft, however, of its traditional culture, intuiting something akin to assimilation in a deep, if not obvious, way, the haredi community has lost confidence in its own reflexes and reactions. Sensing some shift in its operative values, it is no longer sure its intuitions and judgments are what some of its contemporaries have aptly termed "Torah-true."[75] It turns then to the only sources of authenticity, the masters of the book, and falls back on their instincts and their assessments for guidance. Revealingly, it calls these assessments *da'as Torah*— the "Torah-view" or "Torah-opinion."[76]

One could hardly overemphasize the extent of the transformation. The lay communal leadership had always reserved political and social areas for itself. Even in the periods of maximum rabbinic influence, as in sixteenth-century Poland, political leadership was firmly in the hands of laymen.[77] Indeed, as there is no sacerdotal power in post-Exilic Judaism, the structure of authority in the Jewish community is such that the rabbinate has social prerogative and deference, but little actual power, unless the lay leadership allows it to partake in it. Lacking the confidence to decide, that leadership now shares its power with rabbinic authority to an extent that would have astonished preceding generations.

Losing confidence in one's own authenticity means losing confidence in one's entitlement to power, that is, delegitimation, and a monopoly on authenticity becomes a monopoly on governance. It is the contraction of a once widely diffused legitimacy into a single sphere, and the change in the nature of authority that this shrinkage entails, that is the political tale told by the shift from culture to enclave.

Authority was broadly distributed in traditional Jewish society, for the Torah, the source of meaning and order, manifested itself in numerous forms and spoke through various figures. It was expressed, for example, in the home, where domestic religion was imparted, and in the synagogue (*shul*), where one learned the intricacies of the daily Divine service, and it was schooled in the venerated local traditions and in the communal study hall (*beth midrash*), where the widest variety of "learning" groups met under different local mentors, to engage in what was, or what they considered to be, "study of the Torah" (*lernen*).[78] These and other institutions were linked but separate domains. Each had its own keepers and custodians, who, in authoritative accents, informed men and women what their duties were and how they should go about performing them.

The move from a corporate state to a democratic one, and from a deeply ethnic to an open society, meant a shift from a self-contained world to one where significant ways of thinking and acting received some of their impress from the mold of the environment. This acculturation diluted the religious message of home and synagogue, compromised their authenticity, and, finally, delegitimated them. Only the texts remained untainted, and to them alone was submission owed. As few texts are self-explanatory, submission meant obedience to their interpreters. The compartmentalization of religion, typical of modern society, shrinks religion's former scope dramatically and often weakens its fiber. But where belief still runs strong, this constriction of religion means its increasing concentration in a single realm and a dramatic enhancement of the authority of the guardians of that realm. The broad sway of their current prerogatives stems from the shrinkage of the other agencies of religion, and it is the deterioration of these long-standing counterweights that gives this newly found authority its overbearing potential.

Thus modernity has, in its own way, done to the non-Hasidic world what the Hasidic ideal of religious ecstasy had done to large tracts of traditional Jewish society in the eighteenth century.[79] This consuming aspiration marginalized synagogue, school, and family alike, for they could, at most, instill this pious ambition, but scarcely show the path to its achievement. This only the holy man, the *zaddik,* could do. It also delegitimated the rabbi and the traditional communal structure, whose authority and purposes were unlinked to this aspiration. Then, in the eighteenth century, the intensification of one institution depreciated the authority of the others; now, the devaluation of other institutions has appreciated the power of the remaining one. The end result is the same: a dramatic centralization of a previously diffused authority. This centralization is now all the more effective because modern communications—telephone, newspaper, and cassette—enable the center to have ongoing contact with its periphery as never before.[80]

This concentration of authority has also altered its nature. Some nimbus attends all figures of authority, for if one did not feel they represented some higher order, why else submit? Yet, when authority is broadly distributed among father and mother, elders and teachers, deference to them is part of the soft submission to daily circumstance. There are, moreover, as many parents as there are families, and every village and hamlet has it own mentors. Their numbers are too large and the figures far too familiar for them to be numinous.

Concentration of authority in the hands of the master Talmudists shrinks drastically the numbers and creates distance. Such men are few and solitary. Moreover, they now increasingly validate the religious life of the many, as acculturation undermines not only authority but also identity. Even partial acculturation is a frightening prospect for a chosen people, especially for one that was bidden "never to walk in the ways of the Gentiles" and, faithful to that mandate, had long "dwelt alone." The deepest need of the enclave, threatened with a loss of meaningful existence, is authentication. Those who answer that need, who can provide the people with the necessary imprimatur, are empowered as never before. A divinity had always hedged great scholars in the past. Now, however, they validate religious life rather than simply embody it, and their existence is a necessity, not simply a blessing. To a community of progressively derivative identity, these guarantors of meaning appear unique and wholly other, "as if some chaste and potent spirit inhabited them like a tabernacle." Though grounded in verifiable, intellectual excellence, their authority has become ever more charismatic. Proof of that spiritual singularity, of their religious election, is now provided by the growing accounts of their supernatural power. The non-Hasidic culture, in which the mockery of the miraculous doings of holy men had been, in the past, a comic leitmotif,[81] has currently begun to weave its own web of wonder stories around the figures of the Talmudic sage.[82]

The increasing fusion of the roles of rosh yeshiva and Hasidic rabbi is, then, not simply a blending of religious styles, as noted before, but flows also from a growing identity in the nature of their authority. For the haredim sense that in the modern world, which they now must partially inhabit, unblemished knowledge of the Divine mandate is vouchsafed to few, and that religious authenticity is now as rare and as peremptory as was once the gift for Divine communion in the old, enclosed world, in which they had long lived.

Political Implications

What significance do these shifts in authority and transformations in spirituality have for the polity? Will these changes lead the haredim in Israel, where their power has grown progressively, to become activists, to seek to impose their will on the godless, to purge the present state of its impurities and restore it to its pristine condition?

The new emergent religiosity is, without question, one of ever-increasing demands, but these are the maximalist demands made of the religious, not the minimalist requirements made of the wayward. The aspiration is, furthermore, inward turning and elitist—to self rather than to community, to religious virtuosity and not to rudimentary conformance. The emergent monopoly of authenticity has concentrated unprecedented authority in the hands of the masters of the book. The political use to which they will put their new and growing power will depend on whether they have a blueprint for action, whether they view the state as a proper instrument of Divine purpose, and whether they are willing to use force to impose their will on the godless.

Activism means not simply legislation, but enforcement, for, otherwise, the law is stillborn. Enforcement of religious norms in a modern secular society means the use of violence, as large segments of the population, possibly even its majority, must be cowed into obedience. Nothing in the religious transformations outlined above should alter the long-standing traditions of nonviolence, which arose, perhaps, from the Jews' troubled sojourn among the Gentiles but, once formed, contributed to the manner in which deviancy was treated within the Jewish community itself.

Power presumes numbers, force needs critical mass, and Jews never possessed that mass. Exile means to be a minority, and thus adopting the "virtu" of majority and its modus operandi is not only wrong but suicidal. The traditional Jewish posture toward the outside world has been, of necessity, one of quietism, to bear until the final end.

As a downtrodden position must be made emotionally tolerable and capable of being rationalized, it would be surprising if protracted powerlessness did not induce values. In Christianity this may have generated the morality of turning the other cheek;[83] in Judaism it induced not a morality but an ethos, an aversion to violence and bloodshed together with a perception that warrior virtues were incompatible with the Jewish way of life. This was not pacifism in any way, but simply a matter of antithetical values. This ethos is already apparent in the Talmudic image of David: the warrior of the biblical narrative has been transformed into the scholar-king and psalmist.[84] Though antimilitarism and nonviolence are "generalized sentiments" in traditional Jewish society rather than principles, these sentiments are deep and long-standing. They are postures and values of some two millennia and are not easily overturned, certainly not in a society that seeks above all else to be traditional, to cleave to the ways of their fathers.

Political activism in the state would, furthermore, have to be in character with the traditions of coercion, which, in the Eastern European setting, was overwhelmingly private rather than public, with no celebration of power. In the choice between the denial of deviancy or the dramatization of its repression, states tend to dramatization, small communities to denial. The traditional Jewish communities practiced the quiet suppression of the small town rather than the public pageantry of gallows and stockade, preferring to sustain the inconceivability of deviance rather than to instill fear of its punishment. Only when an issue had rent the fabric of the community, as did, for example, Sabbatianism, and uniform conformity was no longer entertainable, did punishment take on an expressive function. Generally, however, the communities were sufficiently small and homogeneous that they felt little need to further impress their values on their members or to publicly express communal outrage by any ritual of violence. This broad-based conformity has long been lost, and any attempt to impose the once ubiquitous religious norms upon large bodies of secular Jews would require creating an atmosphere of public fear, entailing large-scale and dramatic public punishment. Such a campaign is possible, perhaps, in a Shi'ite tradition, but hardly in the haredi one.

Given this quietistic tradition, it is not surprising that what passes for haredi violence is, in reality, defensive actions against intrusions on its turf, not offensive initiatives seeking to impose its norms on others. What occasionally appears as offensive violence, such as burning down bus stops that display, to their mind, immodest advertisements, is actually a disagreement with the surrounding society as to what constitutes the haredi perimeter or the scope of its legitimate *cordon sanitaire*.

Unlike the Diaspora communities throughout history, the State of Israel does, indeed, possess the critical mass necessary for power. However, identification with the state by the haredim, either as an instrument of His will or as an entity to be restored to its "ancient" purity, as in Muslim countries, is highly unlikely. The "state" is irremediably alien and antithetical, not simply because of the militantly atheistic past of its architects and founders, but primarily because of the absolutist claims of nationalism. As religion declined, the emotions and allegiances formerly "affixed to the supernatural" were, during the nineteenth century, transposed onto "the new terrestrial religion of nationalism." The idea of the nation as supreme authority replacing pope or prince, owing obedience to no power outside it, admitting to the existence of no one above it, or the notion of the will of the people, which in a sovereign manner creates its own institutions and values, throws down a gauntlet to religion, as does the notion of a secular national identity making claim to an individual's total and ultimate allegiance. Unlike most other Eastern European minority nationalisms, which, in their formative stages, were welcomed by religious authorities, indeed, enjoyed their active patronage and participation,[85] Jewish nationalism was perceived by the religious leadership early on not as supporting religious identity, but as seeking to supplant it. It offered an alternative particularism, a "zealous separateness" unlinked to God but no less absolute in its claims. Looming as a surrogate religion, it was vehemently denounced.[86] The denunciations may well be forgotten over the course of time, as will be the anti-religious animosity of its founding fathers, but the essential incompatibility of nationalism with religion cannot easily be forgotten.

Even if this incompatibility should somehow be reconciled, or the statist claims abated, the nation-state remains irremediably alien to traditional Judaism. Rabbinic Judaism knows in theory a Davidic monarchy,[87] in practice only a post-Exilic Judaism. Indeed, for the past millennium it has known only a polycentric Diaspora Judaism comprising widely dispersed, autonomous local communities.[88] As for the modern democratic state and national sovereignty, it knows them not at all. Indeed, they are not capable of being expressed in traditional halakhic, or even Rabbinic, categories. And this drawback is greater than one might imagine. For a fundamental haredi belief is that all of Jewish history has been foreseen and prefigured in the sacred texts, and all that has God's sanction has, at the very least, been adumbrated in the canonized literature. (Indeed, to secular Jews, it is this consistent and almost exclusive use of classical language and categories with regard to current affairs that imparts the surrealistic quality to the publicly televised speeches of the Talmudic sages.)[89] It would be difficult to attach any importance to a cause or invoke the name of a polity so foreign to traditional Judaism that not only is it not intimated by any of the sources, but it cannot even be articulated in their timeless and all-encompassing vocabulary.[90]

The state is irredeemably alien, and, not surprisingly, it has been founded and run by atheists. It has no role to haredim in God's scheme of things, except perhaps as a mulch cow. God's ways are mysterious, and He may well have created for this heretical age an idol, made in the Gentile image, to whom other unbelievers now make abundant gifts. As these atheists, by the rules of their own ungodly game, need now the support of the haredim, they can and should be mulcted for concessions, to strengthen God's true kingdom on earth—the enclaves of the righteous remnant in Bnai Brak or Har Nof, Jerusalem. The haredim will function as a pressure group in the future, as they have in their lengthy past. For to them there is no essential difference between a Jewish state in Israel and a Gentile one in Exile. There may be a state *in* Israel, but it is not, nor ever can it ever be, the state *of* Israel.

Nor do the haredim pose the danger of a righteous minority enforcing God's will in an admittedly alien state, for they have no blueprint for running society. Significantly, no group has ever advocated the full application of Jewish law in the State of Israel, having it replace the "Gentile" law currently in effect. The current inability of halakha, still purely private and totally preindustrial, to regulate contemporary society is clearly perceived and acted on by all, religious Zionists and haredim alike, though, for obvious reasons, it is never articulated. To be sure, a system that took in good stride the shift from the agricultural society of biblical and Talmudic times to the mercantile one of the Middle Ages and early modern period would in all probability encompass the transition to an industrial economy and a sovereign state—in good time, but not in the foreseeable future. Law grows primarily by precedent, which means it grows slowly. The Talmudic sages are only too well aware of the inability of contemporary Jewish law to regulate, after close to a half century of sovereignty, even such basic functions as police, army, or public health—to name just a few of the areas the halakha would have to begin to address in any attempt to run the state. Jurists, more than others, know the limitations of their system and tend to be conservative and incrementalist in its expansion. Talmudic jurists are no different.

The shift of authority to texts has, if anything, widened dramatically the gaping lacunae in halakha in the area of public law. Possessing autonomy in the corporate states of the ancien régime, traditional Jewish society had known well self-governance and had, for centuries, dealt continuously with many of the basic problems of political life. Alongside the classic texts there was a rich tradition of polity. Admittedly it was on a minor and communal scale. However, it was very much there and could well now have served as a point of departure for a wider political theory. These conventions of governance, however, were part of the mimetic tradition, the many ways that communal affairs had actually been handled over the course of centuries. And while these maxims and regulations are to be found abundantly, if somewhat sporadically and with much local color, in the legal (responsa) literature, little of this is part of the binding canonical corpus. Those texts to which so much authority has recently shifted know little of, and concern themselves even less with, the issues of state and polity.

As for the new, extensive power now vested in the *roshei-yeshivah* (termed *da'as Torah*), it has arisen to provide the guidance, in personal and political affairs, that had been previously afforded by the self-understood prescriptions and ingrained reflexes of a traditional society. Reflexes are rarely programmatic, and self-understood prescriptions can scarcely address such radically new situations as the nation-state and the running of an industrial society.

This new leadership understandably then tends to be reactive rather than programmatic. It responds to specific situations; it does not possess any blueprint for social action. The *roshei yeshivah* have no domestic program, only domestic interests, strengthening the burgeoning enclaves of "the saving remnant." They have no foreign policy, but simply a general posture toward Gentiles, the traditional one of soft voice and low profile, and the constant reminder to the "nationalists" that the *goyyim* are many and the Jews are few. For this reason the haredim are, and always have been, convenient coalition partners, for they have narrow interests without any broader policy. They are, as Ben-Gurion put it, "the cheapest" political partners, for all those to whom foreign or domestic issues are the primary concern.

The haredim have no such concerns, could have no such concerns, for they have been covenanted by the Lord long ago, chosen for His purposes, and assigned their task. Now, as before, their fate rests on the fulfillment of that pact. The past century has witnessed the fall of empires and the rise of new states, including one in the Holy Land, but His covenant with the righteous remnant is no more altered by these events than by any other of the last two millennia. Fundamentalism has aptly been described as "the righteous remnant turned vanguard." Having long stepped out of history, the haredim view themselves as anchored unchangeably in a moment of time. They are, as we have seen, being transformed even as they are encamped. In encampment, however, there is no vanguard.

Acknowledgments

The haredi community described here is that of European or American origin. This chapter does not include or refer to religious Jewry from Muslim countries, commonly called *Sefaredim,* primarily because, unlike their Western brethren, their encounter with modernity is very recent. The chapter focuses on the contemporary communities of Israel, England, and America, each the product of migration. Contrast is made with the traditional community of Eastern Europe of the past century. A number of the traits and some of the outlook described here first made their appearance, albeit in an inflected form, among the religious elite of Eastern Europe, in the waning years of the nineteenth century and early decades of the twentieth, as their long and deeply settled communities encountered the emergent movements of modernity. This process intensified in the interwar period, in the wake of the successive dislocations of World War I and the Russian Revolution. No transformation is without roots and antecedents, and the current text culture is no exception. However, a nuanced filiation of each characteristic of contemporary haredi society lies beyond the scope of this study.

Anyone who distinguishes between a traditional society and an orthodox one is drawing on the categories of Jacob Katz. In general, the debt owed to Katz by all discussions of tradition and modernity in Jewish history exceeds what can be registered by bibliographical notation.

The ideas advanced here were first presented in lecture at the Gruss Center in Jerusalem of Yeshivah University in March 1984, and at a conference of the Kotler Center for the Study of Contemporary Judaism of Bar-Ilan University in the summer of 1986. I do not believe that I would have dared venture into an area well over five hundred years removed from that of my expertise had I not known that the leading authority on haredi society, Menachem Friedman, agreed with my basic ideas. Dr. Friedman's article "Life Tradition and Book Tradition in the Development of Ultraorthodox Judaism" appeared in Harvey E. Goldberg, ed., *Judaism from Within and from Without: Anthropological Studies* (Albany: State University of New York Press, 1987), pp. 235–55. Working far from my habitat, I was very fortunate in my friends and critics. Arnold Band, Yisrael Bartal, David Berger, Saul Berman, Marion Bodian, Mordecai Breuer, Richard Cohen, David Ebner, Emmanuel Etkes, David Fishman, Rivka (Dida) Frankel, Avraham Gan-Zvi, Zvi Gitelman, Judah Goldin, Jeffrey Gurock, Lillian and Oscar Handlin, Samuel Heilman, Wolfgang Iser, Jacob Katz, Steven Katz, Benjamin Kedar, Norman Lamm, Nehamah Leibowitz, Yeshayahu Leibowitz, Sid Z. Leiman, Leo Levin, Charles Liebman, Aviezer Ravitzky, Tamar and Yaakov Ross, Sol Roth, Anita Shapira, David Shatz, Margalit and Shmuel Shilo, Michael Silber, Emmanuel Sivan, Chana and Daniel Sperber, Prudence Steiner, Aviva and Shlomo Sternberg, Yaakov Sussman, Chaim I. Waxman, Leon Wieseltier, and Maurice Wohlgelernter all read and commented on the various drafts. Todd Endelman and Zvi Gitelman provided me with bibliographic guidance in the respective fields of acculturation and Eastern European nationalism. A special debt is owed Charles Berlin, the Judaica librarian of the Harvard College Library. Perceiving, long before scholars, the significance of both music and the recorded spoken word for the study of haredi society, he systematically assembled the only such cassette collection in existence. I am especially grateful to the Jerusalem–Constance Center for Literary Studies and its directors, Sanford Budick and Wolfgang Iser, who enabled me to present this study for discussion at their annual conference in Jerusalem in the late summer of 1991. Had I followed all the wise counsel I received, the final product would have been far better. For a presentation of some subsidiary themes with full documentation, see my essay "Transformations in Contemporary Orthodoxy," *Tradition,* forthcoming.

Notes

1. Strictly speaking this act of separation is classified as "selection" (*borer*). However, as there is no actual difference between borer and *zoreh,* I have, for simplicity's sake, used "winnowing," which is self-explanatory to the English reader. See "Laws of Sabbath," in *Code of Maimonides,* vol. III: *Book of Seasons* (New Haven: Yale University Press, 1961), VIII: 11.

2. Yehiel Michael Epstein, *Arukh ha-Shulhan.* The work was first published 1903–9 (see n.4), but has frequently been photo offset.

3. H. Soloveitchik, "Religious Law and Change: The Medieval Ashkenazic Example," *AJS Review* 12 (1987): 205–13.

4. Israel Meir ha-Kohen, *Mishnah Berurah.* This six-volume work, which has frequently been photo offset, was initially published over the span of eleven years, 1896–1907, and would appear to be contemporaneous with the *Arukh ha-Shulhan.* Bibliographically, this is correct; culturally, nothing could be further from the truth. Though born only nine years apart, their temperaments and life experiences were such that they belonged to different ages. The *Arukh ha-Shulkhan* stands firmly in a traditional society, unassaulted and undisturbed by secular movements, in which Rabbinic Judaism still "moved easy in harness." R. Israel Meir Ha-Kohen, better known as the Hafetz Hayyim, stood, throughout his long life (1838–1933), in the forefront of the battle against Enlightenment and the

growing forces of socialism and Zionism in Eastern Europe. (For simplicity's sake, I described this work in the text as a "code." Strictly speaking, it is a commentary to a code.)

5. Contrast the differing treatments of the *Arukh ha-Shulkhan* and the *Mishnah Berurah* at Orah Hayyim 345 : 7; 539 : 15 (in the *Arukh ha-Shulhan*) 5 (in the *Mishnah Berurah*); 668 : 1; 560 : 1; 321 : 9 (in *Arukh ha-Shulhan*) 12 (in the *Mishnah Berurah*). See also the revelatory remarks of the *Arukh ha-Shulkhan* at 552 : 11. For an example of differing arguments, even when in basic agreement as to the final position, compare 202 : 15 (in *Arukh ha-Shulhan*) with 272 : 6 (in *Mishnah Berurah*). This generalization, like all others, will serve only to distort if pushed too far. The Mishnah Berurah, on occasion, attempts to justify common practice rather unpersuasively, as in the instance of eating fish on Sabbath (319 : 4). See A. Y. Karelitz, *Hazon Ish, Orah Hayyim* (Bnei Brak: n.p., 1973), 53 : 4. Nor did the Arukh ha-Shulhan defend every common practice; see, for example, *Orah Hayyim* 551 : 23.

6. The essay is now readily available in A. Y. Karelitz, *Hazon Ish, Orah Hayyim, Mo'ed* (Bnei-Brak: n.p. 1957), sec. 39 (*Kuntras ha-Shiurim*). The author is universally known by his nom de plume, Hazon Ish. In view of the forum in which this essay appears and the audiences addressed, I have presented the famous upshot of his argument rather than the argument itself.

7. Menachem Friedman, "Life Tradition and Book Tradition in the Development of Ultraorthodox Judaism," in Harvey E. Goldberg, ed., *Judaism Viewed from Within and from Without* (Albany: State University of New York Press, 1987), pp. 235–38. See also David Singer, "Thumbs and Eggs," *Moment* 3 (September 1978): 37–38.

8. Ezekiel Landau, *Tzion le-Nefesh Hayyah (Tzlah)* (Prague, 1782) to *Pesahim* fol. 116b; The opinion of R. Elijah of Vilno (the GRA) is reported in the *Ma'aseh Rav* (Zolkiew, 1808).

9. The scholarly elite lived their life, no less than did the common folk, according to the mimetic tradition. They may well have tried to observe more scrupulously certain aspects of that tradition and to fine-tune some of its details, but the fabric of Jewish life was the same for the scholar and the layman. This distinguishes the mimetic tradition from the "Little Tradition" formulated by Redfield. See Robert Redfield, *The Little Community and Peasant Society and Culture* (Chicago: University of Chicago Press, 1960). The distinction in traditional Jewish society was not between popular and elite religion, but between religion as received and practiced and as found (or implied) in the theoretical literature.

10. I am presenting the traditional society solely as a foil of my analysis of the contemporary condition, presenting only those facets necessary for my argument. No world is homogeneous when seen from within; it admits of such a description only when viewed comparatively, as here. Haredi society is composed of Jews of Russian, Lithuanian, Polish, Galician, and Hungarian origin. In their contemporary form, they have, I believe, common characteristics. However, when one traces their past in a single paragraph, telescoping is inevitable. The dates given are those that roughly approximate the Eastern European process. The Central European (i.e., Hungarian) encounter with modernity has its own time frame. Experiencing modernity without migration, Hungarian Orthodoxy displayed, often in an inflected form, several of the characteristics of current haredi society. The

tendency to stringency appeared there early, though one feels that it was a response more to the allowances of the Reform than to the processes described here. Similarly, the return to texts expressed itself not in a reconstruction of religious practice, as the received ones remained much entrenched, but in a total submission to the text of the *Shulkhan Arukh,* a work which hitherto had been of great, but not binding, authority (see n.22). On Hungary, see Michael Silber, "The Historical Experience of German Jewry and Its Impact on the Haskalah and Reform in Hungary," in Jacob Katz, ed., *Towards Modernity: The European Model* (New Brunswick: Transaction Books, 1987), pp. 107–59, and the same author's outstanding essay, "The Emergence of Ultra-Orthodoxy: The Invention of a Tradition," in Jack Wertheimer, ed., *The Use of Tradition: Jewish Continuity in the Modern Era* (New York: Jewish Theological Seminary, 1993), pp. 43–85, and Jacob Katz's forthcoming work on Orthodoxy and Reform in Hungary to be published by the Magnes Press, Jerusalem. The *shtetl* to the end remained culturally isolated and cut off from the surrounding Gentile society. See Ben Cion Pinchik, *Shtetl Jews under Soviet Rule: Eastern Poland on the Eve of the Holocaust* (Oxford: Blackwell, 1990), pp. 12–20; Celia Heller, *On the Edge of Destruction: The Jews in Poland between the Two World Wars* (New York: Columbia University Press, 1977), pp. 7–20.

11. In these two sentences I have borrowed and rearranged phrases from Oscar Handlin, *The Uprooted,* 2nd. ed. (Boston: Little Brown, 1973), pp. 5–6.

12. Jacob Katz, "Orthodoxy in Historical Perspective," *Studies in Contemporary Jewry,* vol. II, ed. P. Y. Medding (Bloomington: Indiana University Press, 1986), pp. 3–17.

13. For a survey of the legal status of custom, see M. Elon, ed., *The Principles of Jewish Law* (Jerusalem: Keter Publishing House, 1975), s.v. Minhag. (As consent is the controlling factor in most areas of civil law, common usage is usually taken as a self-understood, mutually agreed upon condition.)

14. The traditional kitchen provides the best example of the neutralizing effect of tradition, especially since the mimetic tradition continued there long after it had been lost in most other areas of Jewish life. Were the average housewife (*bale-boste*) informed that her manner of running the kitchen ran contrary to the *Code of Jewish Law (Shulhan Arukh)*, her reaction would have been a dismissive "Nonsense!" She would have been confronted with the alternative, either that she, her mother, and her grandmother had, for decades, been feeding their families non-kosher food (*treifes*) or that the *Code* was wrong (or, put more delicately, someone's understanding of that text was wrong). As the former was inconceivable, the latter was clearly the case. This, of course, might pose problems for scholars; however, that was their problem not hers. Neither could she be prevailed upon to alter her ways, nor would an experienced rabbi even try to prevail upon her to do so. There is an old saying among scholars: "A *yidishe bale-boste* (a Jewish housewife) takes instruction from her mother only."

15. Chaim I. Waxman, "Towards a Sociology of Pesak," *Tradition* 25 (1991): 15–19, and the literature cited at nn.15–17. I find it difficult to view the *ba'al teshuvah* (newly religious) movement as instrumental in the recent empowerment of texts, though the construction of religious life on the basis of texts is most noticeable with them, as they have no home tradition whatsoever. First, the process begins in haredi circles well before any such movement came into existence. Second, the impact of *ba'alei teshuvah* on such haredi bastions as Benei-Brak, Borough Park, and Stamford Hill, not to speak of such elitist institutions as the yeshiva, is less than negligible. It would be a mistake to equate their occasional prominence in the modern Orthodox world, especially in outlying communities, with the deferential and wholly backseat role that they play in the haredi order. Third, the *ba'al teshuvah* movement is significant phenomenologically, not demographically. On this movement, see M. Herbert Danzger, *Returning to Tradition: The Contemporary Revival of Orthodox Judaism* (New Haven: Yale University Press, 1989).

16. Hasidim, arriving in groups rather than as individuals, and clustering centripetally around the court of the rebbe, generally maintained the mimetic observance a generation or so longer than their non-Hasidic counterparts. However, the past fifteen to twenty years has witnessed the absorption of the younger generation into the dominant text culture.

17. See also Michael Oakeshott, *Rationalism in Politics and Other Essays* (Indianapolis: Liberty Press, 1991), p. 474. The entire essay, "The Tower of Babel," is relevant to our larger theme, as is the one announced in the title.

18. I am addressing the intensification of ritual, not the nature of ritual, in a highly performative religion, such as Judaism.

19. I make this observation on the basis of personal experience and conversations with members of the haredi community. The note of newness is noticeable in the 1954 statement of Moshe Scheinfeld, quoted in Menachem Friedman, "Haredim Confront the Modern City," in P. Medding, ed., *Studies in Contemporary Jewry*, vol. 2 (Bloomington: Indiana University Press, 1986), pp. 81–82. For the exact text, see Chaim I. Waxman, "Towards a Sociology of Pesak," in Moshe Z. Sokol, ed., *Rabbinic Authority and Personal Autonomy* (Northvale, N.J.: Jacob Aronson, 1992), p. 225, n.17.

20. Haredim in America are at most third generation, as there was no haredi presence or group formation in the period of 1880–1920. See also Egon Mayer, *From Suburb to Shtetl: The Jews of Boro Park* (Philadelphia: Temple University Press, 1970), pp. 47–51, and Samuel C. Heilman and Steven M. Cohen, *Cosmopolitans and Parochials* (Chicago: University of Chicago Press, 1989), pp. 191–92.

21. I owe this observation to Samuel Heilman.

22. Mayer, *From Suburb to Shtetl*, p. 55. Eastern European Jewry encountered modernity with migration; Hungarian Jewry first encountered modernity in the nine-

teenth century and migration only in the mid-twentieth. As noted in n.10, central Europe had its own time frame. In this essay I have dealt, primarily, with the Eastern European experience, while attempting to make some references to and allowances for the Hungarian one.

23. Mayer, *From Suburb to Shtetl,* chap. IV, and his remarks at pp. 138–39. My presentation in this section is of the factors operative in the American haredi community. The same forces are at work, in my opinion, in the Israeli one. However, as Israeli society began first to know affluence only in the seventies and as the haredim there constitute a far larger percentage of the general population than they do in America, the Israeli acculturation is less advanced, and there are forces still resisting the consumer culture. But acculturation there is, as any acquaintance with haredim will evince. See Samuel C. Heilman and Menachem Friedman, "Religious Fundamentalism and Religious Jews: The Case of Haredim," in Martin E. Marty and R. Scott Appleby, eds., *Fundamentalisms Observed* (Chicago: University of Chicago Press, 1991), pp. 207–44.

24. The first record of the "neo-nigunim" was that of Shlomo Carlebach, *Haneshamah Loch,* cut in 1959. His compositions, though innovative, were not rock. His numerous successors adopted soft rock wholeheartedly. By the seventies, this music had reached floodtide and has continued on unabated. See Mordechai Schiller, "Chassidus in Song—Not for the Record," *Jewish Observer* (March 1975), p. 21. Bodily response to syncopation seems a natural reaction. We do not syncopate, however, to Indian or Japanese music. Syncopation, which is experienced as a primal, almost involuntary, response to a felt correspondence between an outside beat and the natural rhythm of the body, is in reality culturally acquired. Precisely because it seems elemental, is it so significant an indicia of acculturation.

25. See the newspaper articles cited by Mayer, *From Suburb to Shtetl,* p. 171 n.30, and see Chaim I. Waxman, *American Jews in Transition* (Philadelphia: Temple University Press, 1983), pp. 164–65, and Samuel C.

Heilman, *Defenders of the Faith* (New York: Schoken Books, 1992), p. 123.

26. I was unable to obtain reliable statistics on the number of products currently under the kashrut supervision of the haredim. To give the reader some idea of the order of magnitude involved, the Union of Orthodox Congregations, the largest kashrut body of modern Orthodoxy, has some sixty to eighty thousand (!) products under its supervision. (So I have been informed by sources both in that organization and in the Rabbinical Council of America. The number 16,000 given in anon, "Food, Food, a Matter of Taste," *Jewish Observer* [April 1987], pp. 37–39, is apparently a misprint for 60,000.)

27. See, for example, Sylvia-Ann Goldberg, *Les deux rives du Yabbok: La maladie et la mort dans le judaïsme ashkénaze: Prague XVIᵉ–XIXᵉ siècle* (Paris: Cerf, 1989). During most of this period, the practices in Central and Eastern Europe were much the same.

28. On *wachnacht,* see Herman Pollack, *Jewish Folkways in German Lands* (Cambridge: MIT Press, 1971), pp. 19–20; and Elliot Hurwitz, "The Eve of Circumcision: A Chapter in the History of Jewish Nightlife," *Journal of Social History* 23 (1989): 46–69, esp. n.9.

29. See Heilman, *Defenders of the Faith,* pp. 98–100, 248–52. I am not acquainted with a single haredi leader who has not bemoaned the growing embourgeoisement of the haredim.

30. I say "something about which to be genuinely different," for much that goes under the name of "new ethnicity" appears, to my untutored eye, to have been aptly characterized by Gans as "symbolic ethnicity." See Herbert Gans, "Symbolic Ethnicity: The Future of Ethnic Groups and Culture in America," *Ethnic and Racial Studies* 2 (January 1979): pp. 1–20. Characterize it as you will, haredi distinctness is far more substantive than that of most ethnic groups in the United States and has a far more assured future.

31. This holds true, mutatis mutandis, of Israel; see above, n. 23.

32. On the background of this "swing to the right" in the general Jewish community, see Heilman and Cohen, *Cosmopolitans and Parochials,* pp. 183–93. For the broader American scene, see, for example, the works of Glock and Bellah cited in their notes ad loc.

33. To give a small, but characteristic, example. The previous generation had accepted as a matter of course the use, in documents, publications, even letterheads, of English name forms, such as Moses, Nathan, Jacob, and the like. The members of the current generation decline to allow a hegemonic majority to appropriate their names and return it to them in an altered state. They sign Moshe, Nosson, or Yakov, as any survey of the authors of books cited in these footnotes will evince.

34. *Berakhot* 8a: "Since the day the Temple was destroyed the Holy One, blessed be He, has nothing in this world, but the four cubits of Halakhah."

35. Nathan Glazer, *American Judaism,* rev. ed. (Chicago: University of Chicago Press, 1972), pp. 171–72.

36. O. U. Schmelz and Segio Della-Pergola, "The Demographic Consequences of U.S. Jewish Population Trends," *American Jewish Yearbook* (1975): 142–43; Sidney Goldstein, "Profile of American Jewry," *American Jewish Yearbook* (1992): 124–28. The precise number is subject to some disagreement. However, there is little question of the overall magnitude.

37. "Incognito ergo sum" is not a phrase of my own minting, but one I once heard in my college days.

38. I have written "close to a millennium," as there is considerable controversy as to the nature—indeed, as to the very existence—of asceticism in Rabbinic Judaism. The various positions are discussed in Steven D. Fraade, "Ascetic Aspects of Ancient Judaism," in Arthur Green, ed., *Jewish Spirituality: From the Bible through the Middle Ages* (New York: Crossroads Publishing, 1987), pp. 253–88.

39. There is, unfortunately, no single work on medieval Jewish asceticism. Linked as it is with the purpose of human existence,

its ubiquity is not surprising in a world steeped in Neoplatonic thought which had its eye fixed steadily on the afterlife. The religious impulse continued on long after the original philosophical component had disappeared. The ascetic ideal begins with what is, perhaps, the most influential ethical work in Jewish thought, Bahya Ibn Paquda's *Hovot ha-Levavot* (Duties of the Heart), translated from Arabic into Hebrew by R. Yehudah Ibn Tibbon, with an English translation by Moses Hyamson (reprint; Jerusalem: Feldheim, 1978). The ideal wends its way through such influential works as *Sefer Hassidim, Sha'arei Teshuvah, Sefer Haredim, Reshit Hokhmah, Shevet Mussar, Mesillat Yesharim,* down to the writings of R. Israel Salanter in the late nineteenth century. On *Hovot ha-Levavot,* see Alan Lazaroff, "Bahya's Asceticism against Its Rabbinic and Islamic Background," *Journal of Jewish Studies* 9 (1970): 11–38. On R. Israel Salanter, see Emmanuel Etkes, *Rabbi Israel Salanter and the Mussar Movement* (Philadelphia: Jewish Publication Society, 1993), pp. 1–108. Much material on the later Middle Ages is to be found in Yaakov Elman, *Teshuvah be-Lev ve-Kabbalat Yissurim* (Jerusalem: Magnes Press, 1993).

40. See, for example, the formulations of the *Shulkhan Arukh* on conjugal relations in *Orah Hayyim,* 240:8–9. An English translation is available in *Mishnah Berurah, an English Translation of the Shulchan Aruch and Mishnah Berurah* (Jerusalem: Pisga Foundation/Feldheim Publishers, 1989), vol. II(C), pp. 435, 437. Maimonides' position, expressed in the *Guide,* that sexual activity was shameful, indeed bestial, was rejected in view of the religious imperative of marriage and procreation. However, sexual relations beyond the minimum required by the Law, or with any intent other than that of fulfilling the Law or of a theurgic nature, were decried by most writers. A brief but convenient survey is George Vajda, "Continence, mariage et vie mystique selon le doctrine du judaïsme," *Mystique et continence: Travaux scientifiques du VIIᵉ congrés international d'Avon. Etudes carmelitaines* (Brughes: Desclée, Debrouwer, 1952), pp. 82–92. On the scope of the religious imperative of

procreation, see Jeremy Cohen, *Be Fruitful and Increase, Fill the Earth and Master It: The Ancient and Medieval Career of a Biblical Text* (Ithaca, N.Y.: Cornell University Press, 1989), chaps. 3, 4. For the extent to which the ascetic ideal compromised the most basic family obligations, including the most elementary conjugal ones, even among the most religiously scrupulous, see Emmanuel Etkes, "Marriage and Torah Study among *Lomdim* in Lithuania in the Nineteenth Century," in David C. Kraemer, ed., *The Jewish Family: Metaphor and Memory* (New York: Oxford University Press, 1989), pp. 153–78 (esp. pp. 170–73). See also J. Katz, *Tradition and Crisis* (New York: Free Press of Glencoe, 1961), p. 243.

41. This is a tentative conclusion only, as I have not made an exhaustive study of contemporary ethical literature. Asceticism is noticeably absent from the writings of two of the most influential figures of our times, R. Eliyahu Dessler and R. A. Y. Karelitz, commonly known as the Hazon Ish. Nor have I found it, except in the most attenuated form, in a random sample of thirty-odd works of contemporary *mussar*, whether in English or Hebrew, by writers famous or little known. The contrast between these writers, many of whom are the spiritual heirs of the mussar movement, and the writings of that movement itself is striking. See Eliyahu E. Dessler, *Mikhtav me-Eliyahu*, 4 vols. (reprint; Jerusalem: n.p., 1987). The passage in vol. 3, pp. 152–53, is the exception that proves the rule. A. Y. Karelitz, *Sefer ha-Emunah ve-ha-Bittahon* (Jerusalem: n.p., 1954); idem, *Kovetz Iggrot*, 3 vols. (Bnei-Brak: n.p., 1990).

42. My remarks are based on personal acquaintance. I am unaware of any study of haredi recollections of the "old country" in the decades following the Holocaust.

43. Mark Zborowski, "The Place of Book Learning in Traditional Jewish Culture," in Margaret Mead and Martha Wolfenstein, eds., *Childhood in Contemporary Cultures* (Chicago: University of Chicago Press, 1965), pp. 130–33; Max Grunwald, "Das Lernen," *Jahrbuch für jüdische Volkskunde* 26–27 (1924–25): 98–110; Samuel C. Heil-

man, *The People of the Book* (Chicago: University of Chicago Press, 1983), pp. 1–8.

44. Creativity took the form of exegesis. See Gershom Scholem, "Revelation and Tradition as Religious Categories in Judaism," in idem, *The Messianic Idea in Judaism* (New York: Schocken Books, 1972), pp. 289–90.

45. See above, n.43, and Benjamin Harshav, *The Meaning of Yiddish* (Berkeley: University of California Press, 1990), pp. 16–24, esp. pp. 18–20.

46. See, for example, David I. Sheinkopf, *Issues in Jewish Dietary Laws: Gelatin, Kitniyyot, and Their Derivatives* (Hoboken, N.J.: Ktav, 1988); Chaim B. Goldberg, *Mourning in Halachah* (New York: Mesorah Publications, 1991); and J. David Bleich's series Contemporary Halakhic Problems (New York and Hoboken, N.J.: Ktav, 1977–81). The first large-scale halakhic presentation in English known to me was Shimon D. Eider, *The Halachos of Shabbos* (Lakewood, N.J.: S. D. Eider, 1970).

47. Max Weinreich, *History of the Yiddish Language* (Chicago: University of Chicago Press, 1980), pp. 247–57.

48. Khone Shmeruk, *Sifrut Yiddish be-Polin* (Jerusalem: Magnes, 1981), pp. 52–56; idem, *Sifrut Yiddish, Perakim le-Toldotehah* (Tel Aviv: Mif'alim Universita'im le-Hotza'ah le-Or, 1978), pp. 9–24, 37. See also *Teshuvot Maharil he-Hadashot* (Jerusalem: Machon Yerushalayim, 1977), no. 93.

49. Shmeruk, *Sifrut Yiddish, Perakim le-Toldotehah*, pp. 20–21 and n.16. So deep ran the perceived necessity of Hebrew that works originally composed in Yiddish would be translated and printed in Hebrew. The printed Hebrew text would then be translated back into Yiddish, and this translation would be published. A book that was originally published in Yiddish was perceived as not really existing; Hebrew books alone existed, and translations could only be made of existing works. See also Sara Zfatman, *Nissuei Adam ve-Shedah* (Jerusalem: Akademon, 1988), pp. 21–24.

50. Ezra Mendelsohn, *The Jews of Central Europe between the World Wars* (Bloomington: Indiana University Press, 1983), pp. 29–32. For Lithuania, see pp. 233–35, 227;

Latvia, pp. 250–52; Rumania, pp. 180–83.

51. See Yosef Hayim Yerushalmi, *Zakhor: Jewish History and Jewish Memory* (Seattle: University of Washington Press, 1982), pp. 5–52.

52. See, for example, Aaron Sorasky, *Reb Elchonon: The Life and Ideals of Rabbi Elchonon Bunim Wasserman of Baranovich* (New York: Mesorah Publications, 1982); Shimon Finkelman, *Reb Chaim Ozer: The Life and Ideals of Rabbi Chaim Ozer Grodzenski of Vilna* (New York: Mesorah Publications, 1987); and Yaakov M. Rapoport; *The Light from Dvinsk: Rav Meir Simcha, the Ohr Samayech* (Southfield, Mich.: Targum Press, 1990).

53. The line between the writing of history as it must have happened and the re-writing of history as it should have happened is fine indeed, as is often the line between believer and committed partisan. A good example, though a "right wing" and not a haredi one, of ideological history in English is Berl Wein, *Triumph of Survival: The Story of the Jewish People in the Modern Period* (Monsey: Sha'ar Press, 1990). See Monty N. Penkower's review in *Ten Daat* 6 (1992): 45–46. A haredi instance is the recent and much publicized withdrawal from print, by a famous yeshiva, of a translation of a well-known, early-twentieth-century autobiography (*Mekor Barukh*), because its accounts do not square with the current image of the past. See Jacob J. Schachter, "Haskalah, Secular Studies and the Close of the Yeshiva in Volozhin in 1892," *Torah U-Mada Journal* 2 (1990): 76–133. (See, further, nn.1 and 5 for examples of intentional censuring by the translator himself.)

54. These remarks are psychological rather than philosophic: not what makes the moral act, obedience or insight, but how is the sense of the dictate's rightness instilled? What evokes the inner assent to its mandate? More broadly, see Clifford Geertz, "Ethos, World View, and the Analysis of Cultural Symbols," in Geertz, *The Interpretation of Cultures* (New York: Basic Books, 1973), pp. 126–41, and the idem, *Islam Observed* (Chicago: University of Chicago Press, 1968), pp. 35–55.

55. Needless to say, some of the older congregants, including, of course, the roshei yeshivah, were Eastern European born, and the fear that had been instilled in their youth was palpable.

56. I have borrowed the vivid lines of the *u-netanah tokef* prayer only to convey the atmosphere of *neilah*. The prayer itself is recited earlier in the afternoon, in the *musaf* service. (The borrowing is apt, for the only other time that the synagogue filled up was at the recitation of the starkly personal and anthropomorphic *u-netanah tokef*, the Jewish equivalent, or, more accurately, antecedent of *dies irae*.)

57. For an *analogous* instance of the persistence in Eastern European immigrants of early notions of causation and punishment, see Barbara Meyerhoff's account of the efficacy of curses in *Number Our Days* (New York: Dutton, 1979), esp. pp. 164, 183.

58. I shared this impression with my father in 1969 and discovered that he was of a similar mind, indeed, had given expression to something much akin to this in a speech a few years before. See J. B. Soloveitchik, *Al ha-Teshuvah* (Jerusalem: Histadrut ha-Tzionit ha-Olamit, 1975), p. 199.

59. The issue is not whether my assessment of Boston and Ponivezh is correct, but whether the cosmology of Bnei Brak differs from that of the *shtetl*, and whether such a shift has engendered a change in the sensed intimacy with God and immediacy of His presence.

60. Sholom Aleichem, *Tevye the Dairyman and the Railroad Stories*, trans. with an introduction by Hillel Halkin (New York: Schocken Books, 1987). This work served as the basis for the Broadway play "Fiddler on the Roof."

61. See, for example, Keith Thomas, *Religion and the Decline of Magic* (London: Weidenfeld and Nicolson, 1971); David D. Hall, *Worlds of Wonder, Days of Judgment* (Cambridge, Mass.: Harvard University Press, 1989); W. I. Thomas and Florian Znaniecki, *The Polish Peasant in Europe and America,* vol. I (Boston: Badger, 1918), pp. 205–306.

62. *Rashi's Commentary to the Pentateuch,*

translated and annotated by M. Rosenbaum and A. M. Silberman, 5 vols. (reprint; Jerusalem: Silberman Family, 1973). The *Tzenah Re'enah* is far more than simply an amplified translation of the Pentateuch, but rather a *vade mecum* to the entire Midrashic world. Between 1622 and 1900 it was reprinted no less than 173 times (Shmeruk, *Sifrut Yiddish: Perakim le-Toldotehah*, p. 115), and its cumulative impact upon the mentality of Eastern European Jewry and its spirituality cannot be exaggerated.

63. The above works drew upon the dominant Rabbinic conception of God, on which see G. E. Moore, *Judaism* (Cambridge, Mass.: Harvard University Press, 1927), vol. I, pp. 357–442; Solomon Schechter, *Aspects of Rabbinic Theology* (reprint; New York: Schocken Books, 1961), pp. 21–56.

64. Much source material on this theme is now to be conveniently found in Anson Laytner, *Arguing with God: A Jewish Tradition* (Northvale, N.J.: Jason Aronson, Inc., 1990).

65. See Steven Field, *Rebels in the Name of the Tsar* (Boston: Unwin Hyman, 1989), pp. 1–29, esp. 9–17.

66. See the works of Clifford Geertz, cited in n.54.

67. I am indebted to Robert Redfield's essay "The Genius of the University" for the analogy and, for all purposes, also the very phrasing. The passage is found in *The Social Uses of Social Science: The Papers of Robert Redfield*, vol. 2 (Chicago: University of Chicago Press, 1963), pp. 244–45. (I altered the verbs, as I felt that "submerged" was more apt than "lost.")

68. Mayer, *From Suburb to Shtetl*, pp. 96–106 ("The Family as Audience"), and see Friedman, "Life Tradition and Book Tradition," pp. 241–50.

69. See Heilman, *Defenders of the Faith*, chap. 15.

70. Notably the dynasties of Ger (Gora Kalwaria), Sochaczew, and Alexandrów. Lubavitch established a yeshiva toward the end of the nineteenth century.

71. The political and religious power of the *rebbe* (Hasidic rabbi) remains intact, al-

though, unless I am very much mistaken, the growth of Hasidic yeshivot will ultimately take its political toll, not in the delegitimation of the rebbe's political power, but in the restriction of his competency in halakhic matters, with all of its far-reaching implications.

72. The nineteenth century is the proper foil for the twentieth-century developments described here. In prior centuries, yeshivot had been municipal institutions. The founding of the yeshiva of Volozhin in 1803 established the yeshiva as a regional institution. See Shaul Stampfer, "Shalosh Yeshivot Lita'iyot be-Me'ah ha-Tesha-Esreh" (Ph.D. diss., Hebrew University, Jerusalem, 1981), pp. 1–8; and, more generally, Jacob Katz, "Jewish Civilization as Reflected in the Yeshivot," *Journal of World History* 10 (1966–67): 674–704. (The Hungarian pattern was somewhat different; however, as stated in n.10, our discussion follows the lines of development in Eastern rather than Central Europe.)

73. Charles S. Liebman, "Jewish Fundamentalism and the Israeli Polity," in Martin E. Marty and R. Scott Appleby, eds., *Fundamentalisms and the State* (Chicago: University of Chicago Press, 1992), pp. 83–87.

74. Heilman, *Defenders of the Faith*, pp. 255–57, and more generally pp. 21–24.

75. This was a creative mistranslation of the German "Thoratreu" ("faithful to the Torah"), used by the neo-orthodoxy of Germany. It was first used by modern orthodoxy but subsequently attained far greater currency among what is called "right-wing" (though not "haredi") orthodoxy. See Jenna W. Joselit, *New York's Jewish Jews: The Orthodox Community in the Interwar Years* (Bloomington: Indiana University Press, 1990), p. 4.

76. Heilman, *Defenders of the Faith*, p. 25, and the article of Gerson Bacon "Da'at Torah ve-Hevlei Mashiah," *Tarbitz* 52 (1983): 497–508. For the understandable haredi reaction, see Yaakov Feitman, "Daas Torah—An Analysis," *Jewish Observer* (May 1992), pp. 12–27. Talmudic authorities did, indeed, take stands on political issues in the past. What is new in the contemporary scene is the unprecedented frequency and scope of

these stands, and the authority currently ceded to them. For a fuller discussion of other views of *da'as Torah,* see our article in the forthcoming issue of *Tradition. Da'as Torah* may not be wholly as strange as it first appears. America too believes that issues as broad as racial integration and as intimate as birth control can best be decided by nine sages steeped in the normative texts of the society and rendering their opinions in its legal idiom. And a Jewish historian might note that America, equally, has no mimetic tradition, either of peasantry or aristocracy—nor of clergy, for that matter. Perhaps, a nation that saw its birth in one text and was bonded by another, and has throughout its history amalgamated its ceaseless flow of immigrants by fealty, yet again, to a text, has something in common with contemporary haredi society.

77. Edward A. Fram, "Jewish Law and Social and Economic Realities in Sixteenth and Seventeenth Century Poland" (Ph.D. diss., Columbia University, 1991).

78. For the multiform nature of *lernen,* see Samuel C. Heilman, *The People of The Book* (Chicago: University of Chicago Press, 1983).

79. See Katz, *Tradition and Crisis,* pp. 231–44. I have used ecstatic religiosity for expositional purposes only. I am taking no stand on what unique aspect of the Hasidic zaddik delegitimized the traditional religious structure: his virtuosity in religious ecstasy or his standing as the axis-mundi, the channel through which the Divine force nurtures the world. See Arthur Green, "Typologies of Leadership and the Hasidic Zaddiq," in Arthur Green, ed., *Jewish Spirituality: From the Sixteenth Century to the Present* (London: Routledge and Keegan Paul, 1987), pp. 127–56, and notes ad loc.

80. I am indebted to Michael Silber for this last point.

81. A. A. Droyanov, *Otzar ha–Bedihah ve–ha–Hiddud,* vol. I (Tel Aviv: Devir, 1939), chap. 6. This collection is of the gentler humor. The more mordant jokes still await compilation. (I am not referring to literary satire, of which there was no lack, but to popular humor, which is probative of our point.)

82. For examples in English, see Shimon Finkelman, *The Chazon Ish: The Life and Ideals of Rabbi Avraham Yeshayah Karelitz* (New York: Mesorah Publications, 1984), pp. 203–12; idem, *Reb Moshe: The Life and Ideals of Hagaon Rabbi Moshe Feinstein* (New York: Mesorah Publications, 1986), pp. 237–49.

83. Friedrich Nietzsche, *The Genealogy of Morals* (New York: Vintage, 1967), I: 7–11.

84. Compare the biblical description in Samuel I, II with the portrait that emerges from Louis Ginzberg's *The Legends of the Jews,* vol. IV (Philadelphia: Jewish Publication Society, 1913), pp. 81–121, and notes ad loc. in vol. VI (Philadelphia: Jewish Publication Society, 1928), pp. 245–76, and notes ad loc.

85. Miroslav Hroch, *Social Preconditions of National Revival in Europe: A Comparative Analysis of the Social Composition of Patriotic Groups among the Smaller Nations* (Cambridge: Cambridge University Press, 1985), pp. 139–45.

86. The most explicit formulation is that R. Shalom Ber, the Rabbi of Lubavitch, in 1903. The text has been translated into English in Jerahmeel I. I. Domb, *The Transformation: The Case for the Neturei Karta* (London: Choma Press, 5718/58), pp. 223–33. See Aviezer Ravitzki, "Exile in the Holy Land: The Dilemma of Haredi Jewry," *Studies in Contemporary Jewry,* vol. V: *Israel: State and Society,* ed. P. Y. Medding (Bloomington: Indiana University Press, 1989), pp. 89–125, and his article in this volume.

87. See "Laws of Kings," *Code of Maimonides,* vol. 14: *Book of Judges* (New Haven: Yale University Press, 1949).

88. The Jewish community in Christian Spain is an exception to this statement, but this essay deals with the Ashkenazic communities. Poland from the late sixteenth to the mid-eighteenth century had a supercommunal structure, but there was full local autonomy in the running of day-to-day affairs. Be that as it may, nothing in Spain or Poland has prepared the halakha for the sovereign, national state.

89. Surrealistic to the modern mind but not to one raised on the political sermons of the seventeenth and eighteenth centuries. See, for example, Ellis Sandoz, ed., *Political Sermons of the American Founding Era, 1730–1805* (Indianapolis: Liberty Press, 1991).

90. The now famous statement of Rabbi A. I. Kook, written in 1916 and published posthumously in 1937 (*Mishpat Kohen* [Jerusalem, 1937], 144:13–15), was an attempt to give state enactments halakhic force, not to invest the state with any aura of Davidic or Sanhedraic authority. This personal position was, furthermore, unsupported by any *legal* source, only a passage from a *sermon* of a great medieval halakhist. *Derashot ha-Ran* (Jerusalem: n.p., 1974), no. 11. Indeed, the most that a generation of avid research for halakhic precedents for state authority has come up with has been that passage and an undocumented statement by a medieval Provencal Talmudist, R. Menahem ha-Meiri, which first saw the light of day in 1929, namely, *Beit ha-Behirah al Sanhedrin* (Frankfurt a. Main: Hermon, 1929), at 53a. Even on the basis of these sources, there are difficulties in finding halakhic sanction for state legislation, as a strong argument can be made that for such sanction to obtain, the members of the legislative body must be committed to the binding nature of the halakha. See A. Y. Karelitz, *Hazon Ish, Hoshen Mishpat* (Bnei Brak: n.p., 1990), Sanhedrin 16:4. For a brief survey in English of these issues, see Chaim Povarsky, "Legislative Power in the Jewish Legal System," *Touro College, Institute of Jewish Law: Jewish Law Report,* June 1991, pp. 1–14.

CHAPTER 10

By Torah Alone:
Yeshiva Fundamentalism in Jewish Life

Charles Selengut

On 26 March 1990, at the opening session of the recently formed Degel Ha Torah party convention in Tel Aviv's Yad Eliyahu sports stadium, Rabbi Eliezer Schach, the ninety-four-year-old spiritual head of the party and the dean of Israel's largest and most prestigious yeshiva, Yeshivas Ponovitz in B'nai B'rak, declared before a crowd of over ten thousand students and followers, representatives of the core voters of the party: "Our parliamentarians are well versed in secular matters but they have no connection with Jewish learning and tradition. They don't even know what Shabbat is, what Yom Kippur is. . . . They know nothing about the Jewish religion, and these are the people who will have to decide critical and essential matters facing the Jewish people. . . . When they meet in the Knesset they are not interested in strengthening Jewish religiosity. To the contrary they seek to pass laws that will destroy the Jewish religion."[1]

Schach's speech was carried on Israeli television, and in the United States excerpts were shown on national television news programs. The event was covered in some detail by the *New York Times* and was carefully analyzed to see which of the major Israeli parties engaged in a battle for parliamentary supremacy Schach would tell his followers to support. The speech, sufficiently ambiguous to permit both parties to initially claim his support, offered a "plague on both your houses' harangue."[2] Schach condemned both major parties for their secularism and non-observance of Jewish ritual and explained that Torah law must be at the center of Jewish life: religious faith and ritual observance, not the annexation of additional territory or shrewd diplomacy, will ensure the well-being of Israel and the continuity of Judaism.

Entering the stadium to the chants of the Psalmist's words, "Prolong the King's life, may his years be as many generations" (61:7), and addressing the male audience in a mixture of Hebrew, Aramaic, and Yiddish, the aged rabbi fascinated the Israeli public. Most Israelis and the overwhelming bulk of world Jewry were stunned by the sight of a traditionalist rabbi, attired in the rabbinical garb of nineteenth-century Lithuania, influencing the electoral process and calling for a complete return to traditional Jewish practice. According to Zionist ideology, traditional Judaism was supposed to disappear in a modern Jewish state.

Particularly disturbing to Israeli political insiders was Degel Ha Torah's refusal to recognize the legitimacy and Jewishness of the Israeli state. Degel Ha Torah partisans participated in the elections, campaigned for cabinet portfolios, and lobbied aggressively for governmental allocations for their educational and social institutions, but their rabbis forbid pledging allegiance to the state, its officials, and national symbols.[3]

B'nai Torah and Other Jews

The yeshiva Jews, in their own words, are *b'nai torah,* sons of Torah, or *b'nai yeshiva,* sons of yeshiva, who follow the traditions and practices of the Eastern European Litvishe (Yiddish for Lithuanian) yeshiva academies.[4] For b'nai torah, Torah study is the sine qua non of Judaism and the special bond between God and the Jews. The yeshiva ideal is the *talmid chochom,* the Torah scholar who has mastered Judaism's sacred texts, particularly the Talmud and its commentaries. The Litvishe tradition does not deny the importance of religious ritual and behavior—b'nai torah are meticulous observers of Jewish religious law—but it views Torah study as the essential religious obligation and behavior. Observance of other *mitzvos* (commandments) and a life of good deeds are helpful, but a life of ceaseless Torah study is essential to merit resurrection.[5]

Litvishe b'nai torah are often mistaken for Hasidim. Although there are nuanced differences in appearance which insiders can recognize, both groups seem to look alike. Males in both groups are bearded and earlocked, and dress in black or dark blue frock coats or suits, black hats, and white shirts. Women in both groups are modestly attired in long dresses. Married women in both groups must have their hair covered at all times, either with a kerchief or wig. Both Hasidim and b'nai torah are part of the ultra-Orthodox community of haredim. Haredim are united in their "refusal to endorse or legitimate Western culture . . . and their entire life is devoted to fortifying their own way of traditional Judaism."[6] In both Israel and the United States, they live in separate neighborhoods, have their own school systems, and generally do not socialize with anyone—Jew or Gentile—who is not a fellow believer. In spite of these similarities, there are continuing, and not insignificant, historical and theological differences between Hasidim and b'nai yeshiva.

B'nai torah are the heirs of the rabbinical and scholarly traditions of Rabbi Eliyahu, known as the Gaon of Vilna (1720–97), who has come to personify the b'nai torah ideal. An ascetic scholar reputed to have slept a mere four hours a night, devoting all his waking hours to Torah study and mastering all of its literature, the Gaon was revered by the masses and scholars alike. But he was also the symbolic leader of the misnagdim, those who opposed the developing Hasidic movement in the eighteenth century, which began as a pietistic revolt against the legalistic and intellectual religiosity of the rabbinical establishment. Rabbi Israel Baal Shem Tov (1700–1760), Hasidism's founder, taught that the simplest commandment, performed with *kavanah,* proper intention, is as worthy to God as the Torah study of a learned sage. Hasidim preach that God could be met not only in Torah study and ritual observance but in the mundane activities of eating, working, and social interaction.[7] The rabbinical establishment saw this and other deviations—dancing and drinking to religious ecstasy were also not uncommon in early Hasidism—as heresy. Misnagdim objected to what they saw as Hasidic denigration of Torah study and normative Jewish law in favor of undue emphasis on emotionality and religious fellowship as pathways to the Divine.

Although some of the early controversies abated after an initial period of severe conflict, recent events in Israel and the United States show that tensions exist, as the competition between the Hasidim-dominated Agudat Israel party and the supporters of Degel Ha Torah demonstrated. These tensions emerged with particular clarity at the Daf Yomi celebration (marking the completion of the seven-year round of Talmud study) held in New York City's Madison Square Garden in April 1990, attended by over twenty thousand people. Sponsored by the American Agudat Israel, the event was supposed to show American haredi unity, with speeches from famous Litvishe yeshiva deans *(roshey yeshiva)* and Hasidic rebbes to demonstrate that the political break between these two groups which had occurred during the Israeli elections had not extended to American shores. At the gathering, I sat among a group of Gur Hasidim, the main supporters of the Israel Agudat Israel party and the largest Hasidic sect in Israel. When Rabbi Elya Svei, a rosh yeshiva in Philadelphia and scion of misnagdim, rose to address the crowd, I turned to an elderly Hasid who was known to be a confidant of the Rebbe of Gur and said, "Rav Svei is a tremendous Talmud scholar. He is sure to become the spiritual head of the American Agudah movement." The Hasid did not disagree. "Perhaps," he said, "but you know he is a confidant of Rabbi Schach, and both speak evil about Habad Hasidim, calling them blasphemers." Both Habad and Gur Hasidim were allies in their support of Agudat Israel in the Israeli elections, while the misnagdim supported Degel Ha Torah. The elderly Hasid concluded: "These Litvishe roshey yeshiva are really against all Hasidim including Gur. The Litvishe still bear a grudge against us. They want to continue the old fight against Hasidism. They think they are the only good Jews." Another Hasid overhearing our conversation added: "The Litvishe are only interested in their yeshivas."

The Hasidim were objecting to what they perceived as the b'nai yeshiva emphasis on Torah scholarship alone and the denigration of the Hasidic ideal of the pious householder. As heirs of the mystical Lurianic kabbalistic tradition, Hasidim assert that all worldly activity—as well as study—can infuse holiness into the mundane world and transform human existence. Many Hasidic legends tell of God's positive response to the prayers of an unlettered but wholly sincere person, while the beseechments of a sophisticated but vain scholar remain unanswered. For Hasidim, every individual through communion with God and association with the charismatic rebbe can construct a religiously ordered life which will contribute to an ultimate messianic redemption.

To b'nai torah, Hasidism, despite its emphasis on piety and religious activity, is appropriate at best for those Jews unable or unwilling to immerse themselves in the demanding world of talmudic scholarship. One student at the Ponovezer yeshiva in B'nai B'rak explained: "Hasidim can be good Jews, but Hasidism is only appropriate for the poorly educated masses and for the *balabos* [layman] who wants to earn a good living and eat and drink with his friends." And, he concluded, "the future of Judaism depends on us alone, the b'nai torah who sacrifice everything for full-time Torah study." While they oppose Hasidim, the b'nai torah deny the legitimacy of liberal Jewish movements. They do not recognize the ordination of liberal rabbis, will not participate with them in religious ritual, nor will yeshiva rabbis or officials join together with liberal Jews in communal Jewish organizations. Individual liberal Jews are viewed as Jewishly unlettered and defined as unsuspecting victims of illegitimate "rabbis" who should know better and are to be held accountable for their violations of Torah law.

Finally, the modernist but still orthodox Judaism associated with Yeshiva University in New York City and the religious Zionist movement in Israel is also opposed. With their emphasis on reconciliation and synthesis between modern culture and traditionalism and stress on the evolutionary and adaptable nature of Jewish law, these Jews claim that being Orthodox need not restrict a faithful Jew from full access to the traditions of Western scholarship.[8] Moreover, the b'nai torah see a tremendous risk in accepting the modern orthodox model of a Jew who shows it is possible simultaneously to express fidelity to tradition and to non-Jewish society and culture. Dress code differences between the moderns and the b'nai torah have taken on significance in distinguishing the two groups. The modern Orthodox dress is conventional Western clothing with the addition of a *kippah srugah,* a knitted (as opposed to a black) skullcap as a religious head-covering for the men. Modern Orthodox women, too, do not generally follow the b'nai torah requirement for religious head-covering outside the synagogue. The b'nai yeshiva object to this acceptance of Western attire and view it as following in the ways of the Gentiles and throwing off the yoke of mourning for the losses of the Jewish past.

Lithuanian Yeshivas

"Yeshiva" comes from the Hebrew root word "to sit" and has a long association with places where men sat over Jewish sacred texts they studied. Many references to such academies of learning harken back to ancient Jewish experiences. These premodern yeshivas, often only small rooms in local synagogues, were usually administered by the local community and existed wherever there was a concentrated Jewish community. Frequently the communal rabbi served as dean of the local institution, and student scholars were supported by local communities and invited for meals and for Sabbath and holiday celebrations.

The Volozhin yeshiva, established in 1802 near Vilnius, Lithuania, by Rabbi Hayim Volozhiner, a student and confident of the Vilna Gaon, changed this model.

Its *novum* was its emphasis on the formalization, centralization, and rationalization of Talmud study. Moreover, what had been studied in apprenticeship to a scholar at a local yeshiva was now removed from its local setting to a central location where hundreds of students from all over Europe came to study common texts with scholars of international fame.

The Volozhin curriculum was not new, consisting almost entirely of Talmud and legal codes, subjects Jews had studied for ages. Rabbi Hayim, however, taught a talmudic methodology he had learned from his own teacher, the Gaon, stressing textual analysis and logical consistency. He and his students saw Talmud study as an act of piety and the highest form of Jewish spirituality. In addition, because he felt the dignity of yeshiva students was incompatible with the practice of taking their meals as handouts in local homes, he raised enough money to provide Volozhin students with room and board in a comfortable and dignified setting.[9] The Volozhin yeshiva became the prototype for all Litvishe yeshivas, and Rabbi Hayim, his talmudic scholarship, misnagdic piety, and emphasis on Torah study became the ideal for all future yeshiva deans.

Volozhin was followed by a host of similar schools established in the towns and hamlets of Eastern Europe: Mir, Telz, Kletsk, Slobodka, Lomza and Novogrudok. Some of the present-day yeshivas bear these town names and still maintain allegiance to the traditions of a particular yeshiva. Mir, for example, was known for incisive talmudic analysis constructing novel interpretations that would resolve centuries-old talmudic inconsistencies. Novogrudok emphasized *mussar,* ethical studies, stressing moral and spiritual improvement, and was thought by other yeshivas to be a bit unworldly or even otherworldly. Each school had its rosh yeshiva, whose lectures and personal style set the scholastic and spiritual tone of the school. Hours were long and admission was not easy. Only the truly gifted and committed would attend.

Throughout the last two centuries, yeshivas served as educational and socializing agencies for much of the leadership of traditional Judaism. Community rabbis, rabbinical judges, and religious decisors *(poskim)* were trained in these schools to take positions in the communal life of world Jewry.[10] Attending an elite yeshiva was often a form of upward mobility for a poor but bright boy. For a wealthy Jewish merchant, a son-in-law who was a Talmud scholar brought honor to the family.

The language of instruction and the lingua franca among students was Yiddish. The goal of these schools was to produce Torah scholars; secular studies were seen as taking time and energy away from their religious obligation to study. Although tinged with heresies, secular studies were thought by some to contain wisdom and insight into God's world and the human condition.[11] Extant reports and diaries show that it was not uncommon for yeshiva students and roshey yeshiva to study, surreptitiously or openly, the great works of Western philosophy, mathematics, and literature. Some highly traditionally Orthodox parents sent their offspring to yeshivas not only for the "official" Torah curriculum but in the hope that they would be exposed to "worldly" secular knowledge as well.[12]

Primarily, however, the Eastern European yeshivas were the training ground for a class of intellectual and religious "virtuosos." The religious life practiced in the yeshivas might be more intense, rituals performed with greater precision, and Torah study a full-time activity, but ordinary Jews and b'nai yeshiva shared a common religious worldview, theology, and lifestyle. The connection between the scholarly world of the yeshiva and traditionalist Jewish lay society continued until World War II.

The Holocaust contributed to the emergence of the new yeshiva fundamentalism. It had the twin effects of destroying many of the great European yeshivas as well as destroying for many Jews whatever confidence they may have had in the Christian world and Western civilization. "From a misplaced trust in the Gentile world," wrote Rabbi Yitzchok Hutner, the former rosh yeshiva of Yeshivas Rabbi Chaim Berlin in New York City and a past student of the Slobodka Yeshiva and University of Berlin, "the Jewish nation was cruelly brought to a repudiation of that trust. In a relatively short historical period, disappointment in the non-Jewish world was deeply imprinted upon the Jewish soul."[13] Even the limited Jewish openness to Western civilization had been wrong, as Germany, the nation which represented the pinnacle of that civilization to many assimilating Jews, led the destruction of European Jewry. The Holocaust was seen as God's divine rebuke for improper trust, for reliance and involvement in the Gentile world.[14] The response to the Holocaust—the Hebrew word *churban* is used in yeshiva circles to show connection with the "original" *churban*, the destruction of the Temples in Jerusalem—was to be akin to the earlier rabbinic responses to catastrophe: retreat from the Gentile world. "The Jewish condition has always been as a lone sheep among seventy wolves and the hatred of Israel is eternal," explains Rabbi Schach. "In every generation, Jewry has been sought for destruction and even in eras when things appear differently we should hold on to this knowledge because this is the tradition of our fathers and elders and this is the teaching of the holy rabbis. Only the secularists among us who have abandoned Torah ways are taken in by the pleasantries of Gentile nations but the truth of the matter is that every word they [Gentiles] speak is fraudulent and false."[15]

The Holocaust also paradoxically demonstrated the essential nature of the b'nai torah as a former student of Yeshivas Mir makes clear: "In a mysterious way, the Nazis knew what Jewish secularists want to deny, only the Torah and Torah study keeps us alive and if God forbid, Torah scholars are destroyed, Judaism itself would disappear. You won't read this in secular histories of the Holocaust but the Nazis were primarily after us the b'nai torah, b'nai yeshiva for they knew that if we disappear, there is absolutely no hope for the future of Judaism."[16] Thus the yeshiva world re-created itself after the Holocaust with a renewed sense of its own essentiality to Judaism and an unwillingness to do anything that would align it with the non-Jewish world. The breakdown of traditionalist culture in the 1960s and the growing acceptance of an ideology of moral relativity further reinforced the b'nai torah view that traditional Judaism—particularly in its emphasis on family life and sexual modesty—and contemporary culture were incompatible. B'nai torah, it was felt, had no choice but to fully reject what was in their eyes an immoral and degenerate modernism. The only thing to do was to go back to "the four ells of torah and halakha," to the *bais medrash*, the study hall, unencumbered by secular pursuits and isolated from non-Torah Jews.

The yeshiva world was transformed. From an elite position within traditionalist

Judaism, the yeshivas coalesced by the 1960s and 1970s into a sectarian movement at war with modernity and seeking to separate b'nai torah from all others. The yeshiva's historical relationship to the whole of Judaism yielded to a concern with the well-being of yeshivas and of b'nai torah alone. An earlier acceptance of traditional religious practices gave way to a new yeshiva ideology denying the religious validity of non-yeshiva Judaism, including other traditional forms. Ultimately there was a demand that only the roshey yeshiva be recognized as the authorities in Jewish law and practice. Thus the postwar yeshiva community "moved beyond traditionalism and toward what might be called active contra-acculturation or something akin to what today is called fundamentalism."[17]

Traditional Religion and Fundamentalism: The Case of Yeshiva Judaism

The yeshiva community constitutes a minority of world Jewry. Yet it is a global and international group with ongoing communication between yeshiva centers in Israel, the United States, and Europe. Its significance for contemporary Jewry is far greater than numbers alone indicate.[18]

Significant, perhaps critical, differences exist between the traditionalist Judaism of Eastern Europe and of contemporary b'nai torah fundamentalism. Traditional religions are based on the received practices and beliefs of the immediate religious environment, town, and family and passed on in mimetic fashion from one generation to another. They are "taken for granted."[19] Fundamentalisms are different. They are innovative, self-conscious movements, based on older and newer elements but presented as "the tradition," "old-time religion," and in the case of yeshiva Judaism, as *der emmeser mesorah,* "the authentic tradition," to give them legitimacy.[20] Fundamentalisms fight against the inherent diversity of religious traditions and seek to establish official "dogmas" which transform the diversity of tradition into a formalized series of articulated "fundamentals" of faith and/or practice which is now to be binding on all believers. The mosaic of traditionalism gives way to a fundamentalist unveiling of a singular religious truth.

Yeshiva Judaism is a case in point. Traditional Judaism, for example, asserts belief in divine revelation, maintains strict dietary laws *(kashrut),* mandates prohibitions on Sabbath work, and sets standards of sexual modesty.[21] Within the precincts of this world, however, there are different and occasionally conflicting definitions of divine revelation, the precise nature of kosher laws, the desecration of Sabbath, or even violations of modesty.[22] B'nai torah fundamentalism, however, challenges the legitimacy of even the limited pluralism associated with traditional Judaism. It asserts there is but one legitimate and authentic version of Jewish tradition, namely, the worldview developed and promulgated by the roshey yeshiva and religious decisors of the Litvishe yeshiva world alone. They assert that there is a single knowable "absolute truth."[23]

B'nai torah live in their own communities, intermarry only with other b'nai torah families, and do not recognize the religious authority of non-yeshiva rabbis. Deviations or disagreements with yeshiva doctrine are seen as a threat to Judaism, and it is not unusual for yeshiva rabbis to characterize differing interpretations—including tal-mudically based and Orthodox ones—as apostasy.[24] For b'nai torah, the rest of Jewry is seen as so far from a Torah life, their Judaism so compromised, and their mentalities so secularized that it is just a matter of time until they lose their Jewish identity and amalgamate with the Gentiles. In this situation, roshey yeshiva argue, why interact with such people, why put oneself in spiritual danger? B'nai torah see themselves as "defenders of God," as God's only hope for Judaism. If social isolation and turning inward will help b'nai torah retain their purity of purpose, so be it.

Beginning in the 1950s and accelerating in the following decades, the yeshiva leadership began a process of redefining and reinterpreting traditional Jewish doctrine and practice to give absolute authority in Jewish life to the rosh yeshiva. A process of gradual delegitimation of all other Judaisms began, and the center of Jewish life was now to be transferred from the community to the yeshiva, its teachers and students.[25] The parameters of the new yeshiva community were enlarged to include all who would accept the authority and worldview of the rosh yeshiva and live in yeshiva communities loyal to its theology and lifestyle. The term "yeshiva," historically asso-ciated with academic setting, now came to describe a new genre and mode of Jewish religious identification.

The bulk of yeshiva adherents are students or fellows of the yeshivas, but the move-ment also claims the allegiance of followers who, although not students, identify with the yeshiva movement, live in its communities, and work in auxiliary occupations as ritual meat-slaughterers, kosher food inspectors, scribes, and religious school admin-istrators and teachers. A third category of yeshiva followers, considerably less central in Israel, but a significant element in the American movement,[26] consists of people who work outside yeshiva communal life—as businessmen, manufacturers, computer specialists, and in the United States, a still smaller secularly educated group who work in the professions as attorneys, physicians, and accountants—but accept the religious authority of yeshiva rabbis. These people are a type of yeshiva laity, essential for their financial donations and political contacts but as laypeople marked by a substantially lower religious standing than the inner core of Talmud scholars or those who work in yeshiva-related endeavors.

Perhaps their central stronghold is the Israeli city of B'nai B'rak, adjacent to Tel Aviv, but considerable numbers of yeshiva Jews live in Jerusalem and other Israeli cities. In the United States, the most important centers are located in the New York metropolitan area, particularly Brooklyn, Queens and Rockland counties, and in Lakewood, New Jersey, Baltimore, Philadelphia, and Chicago. Enclaves of yeshiva Jews can also be found in England, France, Switzerland, and Belgium, with still smaller groups in Latin America and Australia. But whether in Lakewood, B'nai B'rak, or London, their primary allegiance is to the "yeshiva welt," the yeshiva world, and the rulings and happenings in one community are quickly communicated to the rest of the yeshiva world. Rabbis and representatives travel regularly to the various yeshiva communities, to collect or disburse funds and confer with their colleagues or to establish religious rulings and public policy followed by all b'nai torah. They also publish books of rabbinic responsa, Torah commentaries, and religious guides that serve as media of communication uniting the network of yeshiva Jews. Finally, because of their endogamy, many people in this world are united by ties of kinship.

The B'nai Torah Worldview

The core Jewish theological issue is the particularly Jewish understanding of theodicy—the attempt to reconcile a unitary omniscient God "with the imperfection of the world."[27] In Jewish theological writings, this central question was: How can the belief in Israel as God's chosen people be reconciled with the suffering of Israel and with the pariah status of Jews since the Babylonian Exile in 586 B.C.E.? The classical talmudic and rabbinic answer incorporated in the traditional holiday liturgy was "for our sins were we exiled from our land and distanced from out ancient soil."[28] Israel's suffering cannot be avoided.

As an alternative explanation, secular Zionism presented Jewish suffering as a consequence of diaspora life. A Jewish state, the Zionists claimed, would release Jewry from the indignities of pariah status and enable it to take its rightful place as a "nation among nations." Religious Zionism as well, while eschewing the humanistic cast of the secular ideology, acknowledges Jewish statehood as the dawning of a "new era" in Jewish history, the "beginnings of messianic redemption," and the end of diaspora existence. For these movements Jewish vulnerability can and ought be avoided through human action and political enterprise.[29]

To these optimistic interpretations, yeshiva Judaism demurs. For the yeshiva world the lessons of history and the faith of Israel affirm that Israel's suffering cannot be avoided. No political or social action can normalize Jewish life. The terrible error of modern Jews is their denial of the "unnaturalness" and "abnormality" of the Jewish people. What a pious Jew must do is wait, wait faithfully for divine redemption, the end of exile (*golus*), and world transformation through the coming of the Messiah, whose coming cannot be hastened by human actions.[30] The great illusion of Zionist ideology is the belief that a Jewish nation-state will do away with anti-Semitism. For yeshiva Judaism it is a patent religious truth that "Esau hates Jacob"—Jews are eternally persecuted by Gentiles.

Zionists, secularists, and nonbelievers want to delude themselves by trusting the occasional "kind words" of a presumably sympathetic world leader, but in fact, all are opposed to the well-being of Jews and Judaism. The situation in which contemporary Jews find themselves is inherently unpredictable and laden with danger. No political action, no military preparedness, no nation-state can change the essential and necessarily precarious condition of Jewish life. At most an uneasy truce or accommodation can be made with the non-Jews, while messianic waiting continues.

The continued state of golus existence, even in an Israeli nation-state with considerable military success, was emphasized in 1967 by Rabbi Shimon Schwab, who had been a prominent student at the Mir yeshiva in the 1930s. German-born and secularly educated, Schwab was the rabbi of the German-American Orthodox community Khal Adas Yeshurun and a leading English-language spokesperson for the yeshiva world.

Like many b'nai torah, he was fearful that the Israeli victories in the Six Day War would compromise the yeshiva emphasis on messianic passivity and the dutiful waiting for divine intervention. In spite of the Israeli control of Jerusalem's holy places, Rabbi Schwab declared: "As long as Mashiach [Messiah] has not come, the Golus continues. There is not a single word of the Prophets which has lost its external message. There is not one single sentence of our Sages which requires a new interpretation. Tragically so, it still is, as it was for 2000 years, namely 'For our sins were we exiled from out land.' True, messianic redemption is 'overdue' a thousand times. But as the messianic redemption has not come the Golus continues and *Kotel Ma'aravi* [the Western Wall] remains to be our Wailing Wall."[31]

The image of the self-reliant, activist, independent, native-born Israeli *sabra* is anathema to b'nai torah. The idea that political statehood can ensure collective Jewish security, the determination behind the slogan "Never again a holocaust," and the notion of progress toward a better human society are erroneous but still dangerous notions to yeshiva rabbis. At the December 1990 convention of the U.S. Agudat Israel organization, Rabbi Elya Svei virtually berated the five thousand attendees for what he evinced as sympathy—even among his ultra-Orthodox listeners—for the recently murdered Rabbi Meir Kahane. Kahane, who popularized the phrase "Never again" and urged Jews to respond to attacks on them with violence, had, in Svei's opinion, compromised Jewish faith: "'Never again'" is an antireligious, anti-Jewish slogan. If God wants to bring a Holocaust he will bring it. Ten thousand Kahanes would not have been able to stop it. We can tell God nothing!"[32]

Svei urged b'nai torah to reject "Gentile categories," including imagining that the exercise of military or political power will change the precarious Jewish condition before the coming of Messiah. To the contrary, argued Svei, attempting human solutions to the Jewish situation rather than relying on God only incurs increasing "divine wrath" and threatens Jews with additional punishments.

Jewry is not without potency, but Jewish might is not in national or military power but in spiritual force. For b'nai torah, as Rabbi Aaron Kotler, rosh yeshiva in Lakewood, explained: "Torah is the real life force of the nation of Israel. Torah is the reason of its existence and its place in the world. It is self-evident that the survival of the nation depends on its ties to Torah and Torah learning. It is well known that as torah learning weakened in various countries so did the existence of the nation of Israel. If the learning of Torah ceases, Israel would disappear—assimilation and profanation would result. The Torah learners keep the others alive."[33]

Yeshiva leaders have therefore warned that drafting b'nai torah into the Israeli armed forces, thereby forcing them to give up full-time study, would bring disaster to the Jewish state. To the contrary, "if the government knew how much yeshiva students protect the state's well-being through their study, they would put guards in the schools making sure that Torah study is never interrupted."[34]

In spite of their fundamental hostility to Gentiles and their distrust of them, b'nai torah leaders have evolved a peculiar stance that affirms their minority status and the passive dependence it fosters. When danger and persecution face Jewry, the proper response is not confrontation but *stadlanus,* respectful mediation with the authorities;

the Jewish posture is and ought be quietism—bearing suffering until the final end. Stadlanus is, in Rabbi Schach's words, "our survival plan throughout history." It entails acknowledging the legitimate and greater power of Gentile authorities and nations and approaching them out of the public eye with humility and self-abnegation in an effort to negotiate a settlement. This might mean pledging public support to a distasteful regime, paying ransom, or even carrying out the unsavory request of a powerful adversary. Stadlanus requires the public persona of the submissive powerless Jew approaching the Gentile authority to request a favor for himself or on behalf of the Jewish community. The Jewish petitioner cannot appear prideful or superior, for this antagonizes the Gentile, but though the Jew presents himself as a political and social inferior beseeching the Gentile for aid, inwardly the Jew "celebrates his moral superiority." The pious Jew has faith that at the end of time, his patience and humility will be vindicated when God returns his people to their rightful place of glory.[35] This is not an activist ideology.

In the yeshiva view, the 1991 Gulf War, for all the terror it brought upon Israel's population, served as a divine rebuke to the secular arrogance of contemporary Israel. God, as the official yeshiva paper *Yated Ne'eman* put it, was reminding Israel that its rightful role is not in waging war but in faith in the eternal protective power of God. During the bombing of Tel Aviv, no attack was mounted by the Israeli armed forces against the enemy for fear of offending the United States government, which requested that Israel not participate in the actual fighting. In a biting yeshiva polemic entitled, "And the Idols Are Destroyed," Rabbi Nosson Grossman, influential columnist for *Yated Ne'eman*, wrote:

> The essence of the Zionist dream concerned itself with the arrival of the Jewish nation to a secure place where the "new Jew" who took control of his destiny would live and this would mark the end of 2000 years of diaspora suffering. The Zionist slogan was "we take our destiny in our own hands." . . . They made bitter fun of the ghetto Jew who could be killed "like sheep to the slaughter." And now we find ourselves in the State of Israel where the army which defends it is unable to respond to the destruction of its cities. The leaders of the state find themselves adopting stadlanus which was the Jewish way for thousands of years in diaspora. We too have to accommodate to the interests of the Gentile nations. . . . The Israelis who scoffed at the *golus* Jews who ran from place to place for security now find themselves similarly running from city to city just like our ancestors who ran from the pogroms in Eastern Europe.[36]

By Torah Alone

What does the yeshiva world offer in place of activity? *Torah lishma*, study for "its own sake," is the central theological doctrine of yeshiva religiosity and culture. Based on a b'nai torah reading of scripture, particularly Joshua 1:8—"Let not this book of torah leave your mouth; you shall meditate upon it day and night"—b'nai torah maintain that Jews ought study Torah literally day and night. B'nai torah who engage in full-time study form a special cadre of religious scholars who are to be excluded from the responsibilities of earning a livelihood and are to be supported by the community at large.[37]

What is the great honor and opportunity of Torah study? Why do b'nai yeshiva forsake career, recreation, and cultural life for the sole pursuit of Torah? These issues are taken up in the work of Rabbi Aaron Kotler (1891–1962), by all accounts the most influential and authoritative postwar rosh yeshiva and a prime force in the establishment of contemporary yeshiva Judaism. Already a rosh yeshiva at an early age in Klesk, Poland, after emigrating to the United States in 1943 he founded Bais Medrash Gavohah in Lakewood, New Jersey. The first Litvishe yeshiva in the United States established solely for Torah study, it grants no degrees and permits no secular studies. Today it is an international yeshiva center with over fifteen hundred students, but then it was a rural farm community where Kotler felt his students would be removed from the negative influences of Jewish and secular America. Kotler argued that his students (and others like them) were the unrecognized protectors of human existence and Jewish well-being. In this view, God's very act of creation was taken to foster Torah study; in the event that Torah study should cease, "the universe would be immediately destroyed."[38] In Kotler's understanding, the essential purpose of creation and of the chosenness of Israel is for Jews to study Torah day and night. Only in the ceaseless daily labor of Torah study is the Jew true to his "essential being" in fulfilling God's most cherished commandment. This of course leaves little time for any other activity. It is a quiescent way to change the world.

The contemporary yeshiva world has elaborated and extended this Torah study philosophy, once only intended for the elite, the scholars, so that it is meant as a program for all. It is no longer elite but mass oriented. Whereas the early Litvishe yeshivas had severe entrance requirements, the contemporary yeshivas have a place for everyone. The earlier rarified intellectual spirituality of a small elite of advanced talmudic scholars has been transformed into a normative program for all of Jewry. Only particularly gifted students may gain admittance to the prestigious yeshivas like Ponovez or Mir, but there are dozens of other institutions of lower status open to ordinary or even underprepared students. Today, everyone—gifted or not, intellectually productive or not—is urged to remain life long in the yeshiva setting.[39]

In this ideological shift the Holocaust plays a role: the call to full-time study as a general norm emerged from the roshey yeshiva's almost palpable sense of remorse for the destruction of religious Jewry. "We have a responsibility to fill the gap left by the Holocaust"[40] is the way one American-born rosh yeshiva put it. Rabbi Kotler told his students that "in this era" after the destruction, Jews must make special efforts to study full time.[41] Such study is crucial, for it is the "modern" Jews in their abandonment of a life of Torah study and mitzvah observance for secular studies and hedonistic pleasures of the Gentile world who prolong Jewish pain and suffering. In the current view of yeshiva, it was the modern European Jews and their search for secularism, particularly the abandonment of yeshiva for university, which brought about the European Holocaust.

In spite of their insistence on the centrality of Torah study and the denigration of work and career, obtaining money and finding financial supporters for yeshiva students and their large families remain central concerns of the yeshiva world.[42] In order to encourage large financial donations, the roshey yeshiva have articulated a "theology of partnership" whereby wealthy non-b'nai torah supporters who contribute large sums are considered the spiritual equivalent of full-time Torah students and thereby receive similar eschatological rewards. And in a Weberian irony of unintended consequences, yeshiva culture sees talented and wealthy merchants and industrialists as uniquely blessed by God because they have the power to support yeshiva institutions.

Ideally, a *ben torah* studies life long. He begins in a *cheder*, a yeshiva elementary school, until age thirteen, the bar mitzvah age and the beginning of manhood, and then until around age sixteen attends a preparatory yeshiva where he studies scripture, Talmud, rabbinic commentaries, and law codes all day and evening. Students later enter the *yeshiva gedolah*, the senior yeshiva, where the famous teachers lecture. The yeshiva gedolah is a "total institution." The student eats and sleeps in the yeshiva and gives himself over to the authority of teachers, advisers, and rule makers—it is truly *in loco parentis*. These guides provide not only lessons in the texts but recipes for life, including ethics and rules of behavior proper for their world as well as guidance in marriage. Often the rosh yeshiva or his representative will arrange a match so that his student marries a young woman from among the families who can help him pursue a life of full-time Torah study.

After marriage, the student may attend a *kollel*, a yeshiva academy for married scholars. Some continue in the kollel, gradually moving up the pedagogic hierarchy until they become roshey yeshiva themselves, or, as is usually the case, there being more candidates than positions, kollel scholars continue their scholarship for years longer in the informal setting of these academies, where the only expectation is continued Torah study. Israelis, seeking to avoid the universal draft, are more likely than Americans to stay in the kollels until they are past the age of active service. (Yeshiva students are given a draft deferment, a practice that caused considerable debate during the 1992 Israeli elections.) Americans, with no such incentive, commonly leave earlier to support their wives and many children (birth control being eschewed and families being large). The Americans often seek employment in work allied to Torah studies, as cheder teachers or ritual slaughterers and kosher food supervisors, as directors of yeshiva organizations, as recruiters for yeshivas, and some as congregational rabbis in synagogues associated with the yeshiva world. Those who remain are given stipends by the yeshiva and kollel, accept charity, and receive a variety of governmental grants and welfare programs. Another source of income is the working kollel wife. The wife who cannot study is said to share in her husband's heavenly rewards by facilitating and supporting financially his kollel career. A working kollel wife is the norm in the yeshiva world.

In America perhaps as many as 30 percent eventually seek employment in such fields as computer programming, accounting, real estate sales and management, and other business ventures. These areas of employment are attractive career fields for American b'nai torah because they do not require a formal college degree. The American yeshiva community has established a number of adult institutions where courses for these occupations are given in the evening hours, after a full day of Torah study. The instructors are almost always observant religious Jews who are sensitive to b'nai torah needs. The American programs are usually funded by federal or state grants for adult employment retraining. Perhaps the largest and most popular of these institutes is COPE, the Computer Programming Training Center to Business and Industry administered by the American Agudat Israel Organization.

In the United States and Israel, however, insiders view one who leaves the yeshiva or kollel for outside employment and thus becomes a *balabos,* a lay householder, as a flop. He has, after all, abandoned eternity, a life of the spirit, for everyday work. Every yeshiva student I spoke to expressed this "fear" of ending up a balabos. One former American kollel member who left after a decade to study computer programming and was subsequently employed in a technical management position told me: "I guess I'm doing well, but I hate waking up in the morning and going to work. I feel I'm wasting my time. In the yeshiva I was involved in religious service. It is very hard to leave the yeshiva, but my in-laws really insisted that I earn enough to support my growing family."

This is the ideal. Yet secular Jews, along with large sectors of non-b'nai torah Orthodoxy in Israel and the United States, see in the *torah lishma* doctrine a particularly pernicious regimen which encourages b'nai torah to avoid their rightful family and civil responsibilities. Much of the growing civil and political conflict between yeshiva people and others in Israel is a direct consequence of the great financial burdens put on Israeli society by the growing number of b'nai torah whom the taxpayer supports through government grants.[43]

The Dynamics of Yeshiva Fundamentalism: Ideological Transformations

Beginning in the late 1950s, b'nai torah began to evince a more vocal and active separatism from other Jews. A guiding force behind the emerging yeshiva separatism was the charismatic Rabbi Kotler. Even by the vigorous yeshiva standards of Eastern Europe, Kotler was known as a *kana'i*—a zealot—and he was unalterably opposed to the accommodationist Judaism of the modernists and religious Zionists in Israel and the United States. He was convinced that any compromise of full-time study of Torah for anything but pure purposes would result in widespread assimilation. Furthermore, Kotler was opposed to any interaction with the liberal branches of Judaism because he felt such interaction legitimated the liberals' religious theology. After a series of meetings with other yeshiva heads in both America and the United States, he prevailed on them to state formally, publicly, and in writing their opposition to any official recognition of non-Orthodox Judaism. Thus in 1956 a rabbinical proclamation by eleven such yeshiva deans announced that "We have been asked by American rabbis and yeshiva graduates whether it is permissible to participate or be a member of the New York Board of Rabbis and similar groups in other communities, which are composed of reform and conservative 'rabbis.' . . . It had been ruled by the undersigned that it is forbidden by the law of our sacred torah to be a member or to participate in such an organization."[44] A yeshiva ideologue explained the ban this way:

> To the torah Jew, this very concept [pluralism] is repugnant. It is a basic tenet of Judaism that the Torah, in its entirety with interpretations and rules of exegesis and codification was divinely given. It is unchangeable. Consequently, orthodoxy totally rejects a movement that denies the G-dly origin of Torah and that allows itself the right to "amend Rabbinic law to meet the needs of the times." By definition, such a movement cannot be considered a legitimate expression of Judaism. And by maintaining membership in such mixed religious organizations as the Synagogue Council and various local rabbinical boards, orthodox rabbis and synagogues were, in effect, affirming the religious authenticity of their reform and conservative fellow members.[45]

All signers of the ban were European-educated and, with one exception, European-born rabbis who, in issuing the proclamation, bypassed the institutionalized U.S. rabbinate. While Orthodox rabbis in the United States rejected liberal theology, they strongly opposed the ban, acknowledging Reform and Conservative denominations as essential to the Jewish community. Bans and excommunication were identified with European extremism; tolerance, openness, and negotiation with one's religious adversaries with life in America. The emerging yeshiva fundamentalism, however, rejected religious pluralism and sought to delegitimate the religious leadership of the non-Orthodox rabbinate.

The denial of Jewish religious legitimacy for liberal Judaism was followed by a series of authoritative statements which claimed that, for Orthodoxy as well, yeshiva Judaism was the only legitimate Jewish tradition. Rabbi Hayim Dov Keller, an American, secularly educated rosh yeshiva in the Telshe yeshiva of Chicago, was chosen by the senior European yeshiva leaders to present a public denunciation of modern Orthodoxy in the English-language yeshiva journal *Jewish Observer*. Keller argued that the modern Orthodox attempt to integrate elements of modernity into the rabbinical tradition, in order to create a new Jewish orthodox synthesis, was contrary to all rabbinic traditions which, according to Keller and the European yeshiva rabbis, demanded that Judaism remain a self-contained religious system uncontaminated by religious or philosophical interchange. "The very concept of a synthesis of Western culture and Torah is a contradiction. By definition, Torah is the perfect will of God . . . to suggest that by itself something must be added to make it perfect is a negation of Torah."[46]

The critique of modern Orthodox theology was followed by a delegitimation of the religious decisions reached by the modernist rabbis. Rabbis and religious judges from the orthodox but modern Yeshiva University and State Rabbinate in Israel were said by b'nai torah leaders to be insufficiently pious to render religious decisions and interpretations. A case in point is Rabbi Schlomo Goren. The former chief rabbi of Israel was, from reports of former students, a frequent guest at his alma mater, Yeshivas Chevron, in Jerusalem during the 1950s. As his state involvement and somewhat messianic sympathies became public, he was forbidden to lecture in the yeshiva.

"Let's face it," a Ponovez Yeshiva graduate and yeshiva administrator in Israel told me about the b'nai torah opposition to secularly educated rabbis, "those who did not learn from the traditional Litvishe rosh yeshiva, those who never learned the secrets of Torah, those whose minds are filled with secular learning, with Plato and Kant, are not worthy to tell us a religious legal decision. To be a religious judge requires total involvement in Torah and this can only be gotten from study in the holy yeshivas." A Lakewood Yeshiva graduate explained the rejection of the modern Orthodox in this way: "They [the modern Orthodox] watch TV, go to the movies, their wives wear no head covering, they attend universities and run after the goyim." One area of difference was over the matter of the immutability of Jewish law, halakha. The modern Orthodox remained committed to their view that halakha could be made consonant with modernity, while b'nai torah saw modification of Jewish law as a compromise of religious truth. Rabbi Yissochor Frand, an American-born and influential b'nai torah ideologian, put it this way: "What was *assur* (forbidden) yesterday, remains *assur* today and what is *mutar* (permitted) today was always *mutar*. Halacha is absolute, halacha cannot be abolished, halacha cannot be fabricated. Halacha is not an amorphous area wherein changing social needs can be legislated."[47]

By no means was this view of halakha universal. As the historian Jacob Katz has argued, halakha always accommodated itself to social and economic circumstance. Nonetheless, the promulgation of a new doctrine of unchangeability enabled the b'nai torah community successfully to distance itself from their closest Orthodox modern competitors. After establishing "unchangeability" and "absolutism" as central religious norms, the yeshiva movement focused on matters of Jewish faith. Traditional Judaism had developed a body of basic beliefs and doctrines, but these tended to remain ambiguous, open to multiple legitimate interpretations. The tradition, for example, affirmed God's revelation of Torah and the divine nature of religious law, but just what revelation or divine law meant was never formally defined. What a believing Jew had to accept as supernatural or what degree of biblical literalism one had to subscribe to in order to remain a faithful Jew was never explicitly stated in the rabbinic tradition. The b'nai torah community, however, rejected the traditional open-endedness of Jewish theology and began a self-conscious effort to define the content of an emerging b'nai torah view of essentials of Jewish belief. Individuals or groups who rejected the new b'nai torah dogmas were to be labeled apostates.[48]

In a critical way, this very attempt at articulating the content of a traditional "taken for granted" Jewish faith culture based on collective behavior and communal values was itself a type of fundamentalism, that is, a Jewish effort to discover the "fundamentals" of faith which could then be set down as a series of propositional statements to which all Jews would have to assent.

Sociological Transformation

The ideological changes transforming b'nai torah life from traditionalism to fundamentalism were accompanied by new social patterns and religious practices calling for increased separatism and distinctiveness. Behaviors and practices permitted in the 1940s, 1950s, and early 1960s were redefined throughout the 1970s and 1980s as religiously inappropriate. Though not halakhically prohibited, they were nevertheless to be avoided by pious b'nai torah. Rabbi Moshe Feinstein (d. 1988), the rosh yeshiva of Yeshivas Tiferes Yerushalayim in New York City and the most authoritative religious decisor in the b'nai torah world, acknowledged that many of the new restrictions were not halakhically prescribed. Nonetheless he advised persons to conform to the new strictures.[49]

Added prohibitions and stricter rules were introduced in virtually all areas of life. Standard kosher meat preparations were replaced by a more demanding form of *glatt kosher,* which now became the required norm. Milk products, even kosher ones, were now replaced by special dairy *cholov yisroel* products, which meant an observant Jew had to be involved in the entire production. Religiously mixed neighborhoods were now to be avoided as yeshiva Jews were directed to live in b'nai torah neighborhoods. Those modern Orthodox synagogues with reduced physical barriers—not in accordance with b'nai torah standards—between men and women were declared inappropriate for prayer, much as an earlier generation had declared reform and conservative synagogues invalid. Televisions were banned in Orthodox homes in both Israel and the United States.[50] Although traditional law permits men and women to sit together and socialize at family and communal celebrations, new rules banning mixed seating and requiring physical partitions between males and females at all gatherings were made mandatory.

In time, the distinctions between religiously "inappropriate" behavior and the legally and halakhically forbidden behavior were lost. As a result, areas of acceptable yeshiva behavior in pre–World War II Europe or in the yeshiva life of the 1940s and 1950s came to be considered "nonreligious" and in some cases "against halakha." Individuals who continued in the earlier style were now to be excluded from yeshiva communities. In an interview, Rabbi Moshe Kaye, an executive of an American yeshiva organization who was ordained in Yeshivas Chaim Berlin in Brooklyn, was very much aware of the transformation:

> We used to be normal. We could wear colored shirts and just everyday clothes like everyone else. Only some hasidic boys wore black suits. Now you look at Lakewood, Ponovez, or Chaim Berlin and you won't see anything but white shirts and dark suits. We listened to pop music and knew what's going on. . . . I remember going to the movies regularly in high school. O.K., some particularly pious senior students might object, but everyone did it and we thought it's O.K. It was expected then that we would have some type of career— accounting, teaching, or sales—but now my own kids would not consider a secular career.

Rabbi Kaye's use of the word "normal" is not casual. During my meetings with him, he recalled with fondness his childhood and teenage years. Although he came from a very observant family, he looked and dressed "like everybody else." Both the schools and synagogues he attended in New York City during the 1950s welcomed b'nai torah and lesser observant Jews. The emphasis at the time, he explained, was on Klal Yisroel, the community of Israel, and though the more Jewishly learned and pious received higher status, all were accepted in the community. But life and the world are perceived to have changed. To remain a faithful ben torah now requires withdrawal and separation from contemporary society: "We have so many prohibitions," an editor for a yeshiva publication explained to me, "but don't forget the world changed, too. You can't go to the movies anymore. It's all *shmutz* [dirt], sex, and violence. And I am not sure we don't need new *chumros* [strict interpretive rules] today. Nonreligious people live like animals today. Sex and drugs, broken homes seem to be the rule. Maybe once you could be in the world but today you've got to avoid it."

The editor's remarks highlight a yeshiva perception that traditional religions and contemporary culture in the United States did share a common cultural core which the new ideologies of the 1960s cast asunder. The rise of a new sexual morality and the emphasis on gender equivalence destroyed the remaining links between orthodoxies of any sort and contemporary culture. For b'nai torah, the alienation of traditional religion from contemporary social norms meant that b'nai torah had now to separate themselves both externally, with distinctive dress and beards as religious obligations, and internally, by avoiding modern culture, art, music, and cinema. That is, they had to separate from the larger culture even in ways that traditional Orthodox Judaism did not require.

New prohibitions and stricter rules were introduced in an attempt to distinguish and eventually isolate b'nai torah from interaction with outsiders. Modesty rules particularly were expanded or given increased religious significance. These rules had always been part of Orthodox tradition, but the earlier yeshiva world in both the United States and Europe had been tolerant of nonconformity—some yeshiva wives did not wear headcoverings as is the technical rule for married women—but now even small violations of modesty norms are grounds for social ostracism. A director of a New York City Bais Ya'akov school, an institution for the daughters of b'nai torah, who was raised in small towns in the northeastern United States where her father had served as an Orthodox rabbi, explained the current situation:

> If we enroll a kid whose mother comes to school with an uncovered head or even with her bangs showing we get a lot of flack from our parents. They say "we pay a lot of money for a 'frummer' [pious] school where there are only yeshiva families and we don't want our kids exposed to a bad example." And I'll tell you they are right! If you see a woman without a full headcovering it means she is unprincipled. It means she thinks she can pick and choose her mitzvos [commandments]. . . . That means she probably violates other halakhos [religious rules]. How can you have anything to do with such a person?

In the United States, the new mood of self-confidence, due to the b'nai torah's survival in spite of predictions of its demise after World War II, led to the establishment or reorganization of b'nai torah schools to ensure that only children from yeshiva families would attend and that the ideology and curriculum would reflect the new b'nai torah ideas. These schools have become increasingly sectarian and religiously exclusive.

College attendance, never officially approved by the roshey yeshiva but tacitly tolerated in American yeshivas throughout the 1950s and 1960s, was banned in yeshiva schools in the 1970s. Colleges and universities were seen as the most pernicious carrier of modern Western values, striking at the heart of religious faith and morality. A leading b'nai torah scholar and counselor explained: "The student enters the school with natural truths, an aversion to wrongdoing and immorality, respect for authority of parents and government and the instinct toward charity and kindliness; and he graduates with the mad delusion that man is descended from the algae and that he possesses no free will or responsibility and that nothing is intrinsically right or wrong. Thus the diploma is actually a certificate which attests that the holder has been corrupted."[51]

The approach to all those outside the b'nai torah circle was to be one of *bitul,* negation and nihilation. Anything outside the Torah world was, in the words of Peter Berger, given a "negative ontological status" and not to be taken seriously.[52] Spiritual dangers and moral pollution were seen everywhere, not only in secular schools but in every facet of contemporary life. If contemporary Americans celebrate Thanksgiving, July Fourth, or other national days, then b'nai torah should avoid these celebrations like they avoid Christmas. Likewise theater, secular music, entertainment, current books, and even secular newspapers are to be avoided. Intellectual and humanistic traditions of Western civilization must be rejected. Western philosophical traditions, artistic sensibilities, and ethical conceptions have no relevance to the life of a ben torah. Western civilization is identified with secularism and ethical relativism, while Christianity is seen as the bearer of an anti-Jewish tradition that continues to nurture anti-Semitism.

Sacralization and Enchantment of Authority

The transformation of yeshiva from a religious elite to a sectarian movement with a new emphasis on halakhic unchangeability, social isolation, and the conscious delegitimation of all other Jewish movements itself required new legitimation, which was found in a revised and expanded view of yeshiva rabbinical authority. In Eastern European society, a rosh yeshiva was a scholar writing talmudic novellae, giving advanced lectures, and occasionally serving as a community religious consultant. In the yeshiva world of the last few decades, however, they have become eminences endowed with self-proclaimed, divinely inspired *da'as torah*—knowledge of the inner truths of Torah. They are the rightful authorities for providing guidance and making decisions on all political, religious, and personal issues facing Jews and Judaism. The decisions of these so-called Torah greats cannot rightfully be questioned by the faithful b'nai torah.

In this way, by identifying the opinions of the roshey yeshiva with divine will, yeshiva Judaism has successfully transformed an essentially pluralistic rabbinic tradition into a contemporary fundamentalism admitting but a singular religious truth. This new fundamentalism with the now widely accepted view of the gnostic insights of yeshiva rabbis is not without distinct sociological value in the often anomic marketplace of contemporary moral and ethical relativism. Following the pronouncements of b'nai torah leaders is to be in tune with eternity, while autonomous decision making without a rosh yeshiva's guidance is religious heresy and a consequence of the unbridled excesses of modern individualism. In a telling essay, a yeshiva ideologue in Israel explained that when b'nai torah participate in an election, it is not out of a civic duty or personal choice but because the rabbis have so instructed. "When they tell us to vote, it is a mitzvah and not an option. When they do not tell us to vote, it is an *issur* [prohibited act] and not an option."[53]

In the United States, these rabbis have counseled nonconfrontational politics and avoidance of public proclamations or demonstrations. In support of the yeshiva community's needs for housing, governmental aid to yeshiva schools, and help for local communities, they have urged quiet diplomacy based on personal contact with government officials and a close working relationship with the American Catholic hierarchy and various evangelical Protestant groups, whom the rabbis claim as b'nai torah's true ideological allies in an American wasteland of secularism and sexual immorality.

The authority of talmudically trained scholar rabbis is even invoked with regard to highly personal issues and situations: marriage and family life, change of job or residence, medical care, and interpersonal relations. Every ben torah has a story about how his personal rabbi helped him or his family in a time of difficulty, serving as a conduit to the divine.

The mainstream orthodox, including some senior b'nai torah who had been students in the pre-war yeshivas, objected to this radical expansion of rabbinical authority and to the b'nai torah leadership's involvement in politics and personal life. But by the mid-1970s, the clerical/scholarly elite of roshey yeshiva had successfully established itself as the central authority in traditionalist circles. From the mid-1950s onward, da'as torah was taught as an essential Jewish dogma in these schools, with the result that during the 1970s a large cohort of orthodox Jews, socialized into the new ideology, had reached adulthood and were ready to accept the b'nai torah leadership's claim to total authority. Also buttressing the expanding authority was the b'nai torah perception of the increasing dangers of modernity to religious belief and behavior. The roshey yeshiva, presenting themselves as bearers and defenders of traditionalist religious culture, were now seen as the necessary authorities to guide b'nai torah through the ever-present temptations of modern life.

Passive Apocalyptic Fundamentalism

The fundamentalism of the yeshiva does not lead to a religiously charged attempt at the recasting of Israeli society, where Jews are a majority, or in influencing American culture, where Jews are a small minority, into a yeshiva society governed by b'nai torah rules and values. In spite of their political rhetoric or their tenuous role as power brokers in Israeli politics, they make little attempt at mass proselytization. They do not seek to set governmental policy. Their politics is not an attempt at societal transformation but is aimed at the more modest attempt at obtaining economic and political support for the maintenance and eventual growth of their sectarian communities. Rabbi Schach put it plainly in an address in August 1990, when the Israeli yeshiva movement was still being courted by the major parties: "Fellow Jews, we must strengthen ourselves. We cannot change the world but we can improve ourselves. We can see to it that our children receive a Jewish education, that we send our sons to *chadorim* [private yeshiva elementary schools] that teach them *chumash* [Bible] and Rashi as was done throughout the generations. Go to *shul* [synagogue] to *daven* [pray] and take your son always with you. When you eat, make certain the food is kosher and the appropriate *brocha* [blessing] is said and see to it that your child does the same."[54]

Neither on that August 1990 occasion nor in any yeshiva proclamation is there a program for a general political takeover, nor is there a theological position asserting the rightful domination of religion over state. There are constant calls for repentance and a return to Orthodox practice and faith in yeshiva religiosity and leadership, but these proclamations do not challenge the separate spheres of religion and state. Specific governmental policies, practices, or guidelines may be challenged and bitterly attacked, especially rulings that appear to threaten the lifestyle of yeshiva followers. The essential status quo, the division of state and religion, however, is not condemned.

Yeshiva Judaism is unconcerned with societal transformation. For them a world without Torah is beyond redemption. The world is not denied as in the religions of otherworldly ascetic types. Rather, a faithful Jew accommodates to the realities of this life with the awareness that the sense world is but an anteroom to messianic eternity. Until the end, all a Jew can do is study Torah, do mitzvos, and wait with "full faith for the coming of Messiah."

Waiting is a central theme in yeshiva life—waiting with a firm conviction that all reform, conservative, reconstructionist, and other "non-observant" Jews will intermarry, assimilate, and disappear; waiting for the modern Orthodox to deny their modernity and come home to yeshiva; waiting for the Zionists to discover that statecraft cannot protect Jews from the ravages of anti-Semitism.[55]

Long-term waiting, however, results in anxiety, anger, and ambivalence. Yeshiva followers are fervent messianists, pray daily for the coming of Messiah, open and close all public gatherings with a prayer for messianic transformation, and endow religious rituals with messianic symbolism. Yet they are theologically constrained from doing anything to bring about this long-sought-for event. The repressed volcanic messianism in yeshiva life, made all the more powerful by the need to remain entirely passive, has led to increased bans and proclamations and even to character assassination against yeshiva adversaries, but it has not to this point resulted in mass violence.

The fundamentalism of yeshiva Judaism is passive, static, and apocalyptic. The world from this perspective cannot be made right; there is no steady progress to a better future. To the contrary, apocalyptic Jews "are totally impatient with the corrupt present, seeing it as a series of unprecedented calamities. . . . The end of days is viewed as a sudden revolutionary leap into an idealized future state when the believers will finally be rewarded for their years of suffering while oppressors . . . will be justly punished."[56] This firm but entirely passive messianism is at the core of yeshiva life and distinguishes it from other contemporary Judaisms both Orthodox and liberal. Zionist Orthodox Jews view the State of Israel as a sign of *atchalta d'geula*, the beginning of messianic redemption, which individuals hasten by working to create a just, merciful, and faithful society. In this view, human autonomy matters to God.[57] Ultra-nationalist Gush Emunim followers extend this and see a special place for Jewish political and military action in furthering the redemptive process. For some Orthodox ultranationalists, even violent actions may be undertaken to hasten the redemption.

The ultra-Orthodox Hasidim, followers of a mystical kabbalistic Judaism, have much in common with the yeshiva world.[58] But even within the enclosed and separatist haredi world, there are significant and growing differences between Hasidim and b'nai yeshiva. Hasidim wait for Messiah, too, but their doctrines concerning the importance of the community of Israel, *Klal Yisrael,* their religious emphasis on transforming all human activity into sacred service *(devekut),* and their desire for *tikkun ha'olam* (literally, mending the world) lead them to endow ordinary behavior and the larger Jewish community with sacred meanings and power. Hasidim are advocates of state legislation mandating religious observance, for only community-wide conformity to religious rules and moral codes can insure a just and human society open to messianic transformation. The Hasidic rebbes insist that the Hasidic Agudah party sponsor legislation banning abortion, prohibiting pork production, and requiring stricter public observance of Sabbath laws as a legitimate means of coercing a recalcitrant and secular Israeli society to conform to religious forms.

The yeshiva leadership, the Litvishe roshey yeshiva, demurs. In the yeshiva worldview, what Gentiles or non-Orthodox Jews do is of little consequence as long as yeshiva people are provided material means and freedom to continue their communal culture of Torah study in yeshiva and kollel. Prohibiting pork, demanding nationwide Shabbat observance, and urging limitations on abortions are just and good causes, but they do not address the central concerns, the lifeblood of Judaism, which is torah lishma. "For us," an administrator at the Ponovez Yeshiva with close ties to the Degel Ha Torah leadership told me in an interview, "the most important thing is *chinuch,* torah education. We need yeshivas, we need gedolim [Torah giants]; without yeshivas there are no gedolim and without gedolim, there is no Judaism. History proves that! We can't worry about the whole world. We are not in a position today to tell everybody what to do. So long as they [secularists, the Israeli government] leave us alone, we'll leave them alone. It is a *narrishkeit* [folly] for Hasidim to insist on these prohibitions. It is not going to make anybody religious and it could hurt the yeshivas."

Despite living in the United States and Israel in segregated enclaves, the Hasidim are theologically inspired to a concern for the larger community, for its healing and wholeness, and for a religious activism that is seen as preparatory to messianic transformation. A senior Hasid, a follower of the Rabbi of Gur, who accompanied me on a visit to the Gur community in Jerusalem, reported that "the rebbe couldn't sleep during the time the Hasidim were negotiating with the secular parties for increased religious legislation: the souls of the aborted fetuses came to him asking for life." Habad Hasidim were also active in the Agudah-sponsored legislation; their theological view is that a massive return to religious observance will usher in the Messiah.[59]

Yeshiva rabbis do not deny the importance of community or public religious observance, or even the need for religious legislation, but their theological insistence on the utter centrality of Torah study encourages a retreat from concern with the larger

Jewish community and discourages them from any other religious activism. Their political agenda and theological concerns are met so long as an alternative yeshiva society is successfully maintained. They can in this way remain within their passively apocalyptic fundamentalist enclaves.

In the United States, b'nai torah are aided by ethnic politics and engage in bloc voting. Local and state officials have generally been responsive to yeshiva needs for local zoning, kosher food supervision, and employee Sabbath observance. Nationally, too, ultra-Orthodox Jews continue to get a responsive hearing from conservative administrations. Unlike the bulk of the Jewish population, who are politically liberal and desire a continued emphasis on separation of church and state, b'nai torah, like their conservative allies, desire a religious presence in the public sphere—for example, prayer in the public schools, aid to religious education, and anti-abortion legislation and rulings—and these shared concerns make them a welcome presence to many conservative politicians and organizations.

Yeshiva Jews are angry. They are angry at secular and non-observant Jews because, in God's mysterious ways, b'nai torah suffer as a consequence of their fellow Jews' unfaithfulness. Forsaking career and money to live a modest material existence in order to study Torah, b'nai torah are rejected and castigated by those for whom they labor. The feeling in b'nai torah circles is that "We are the true heroes of Klal Yisroel, but secular-educated scientists and military experts get all the credit."

Secular Jews are angry, too. They see yeshiva Jews as living off the dole, shirking army service, and urging a return to what is for the secularists a dark and benighted era for Jews and Judaism. Geographical separation between the secular and yeshiva Jews helps defuse mutual hostility and maintain public civility, as does the shared memory of persecution and mass murder. These bases for civility may be lost to the next generation, however, which comes of age as the reality of the Holocaust recedes.[60]

Yeshiva Fundamentalism and Contemporary Religion

The b'nai torah community is far more important in contemporary Jewish life than its minority status indicates. Yeshiva families, like other ultra-Orthodox Jews, have a higher birthrate than other Jewish groups. It is estimated that each family produces between five to ten children. In contrast to secular Jews who have low birthrates and high levels of assimilation, yeshiva people center their whole life around Judaism. The power and influence of the ultra-Orthodox in both Israeli politics and religion and in American Jewish life are a consequence of their growing demographic and sociological presence among the highly committed and activist elements in world Jewry. Daniel Eleazar argues that while Orthodox Jews are a small minority among all people who are identified as Jews, they make up 50 percent to 70 percent of all who are identified as "religious in some way." "It is no wonder," Eleazar concludes, "that orthodoxy remains the dominant voice" in contemporary Jewish life "and claims the lion's share of public money directed to religious purposes."[61]

Yet there is another reason for the growing importance of yeshiva Judaism.

Modern Orthodox Judaism, the real competitor to the yeshiva, is itself undergoing a process of "yeshivization"[62] because the moderns send their children to schools where the teachers are often on the religious right (there being insufficient modern Orthodox who have chosen Jewish education as a career). Theological and halakhic pluralism, once the hallmark of the modernist camp, now gives way to increasingly fundamentalist and rigid interpretations of religious law and practice code.[63] Religious activism and identification with the State of Israel as a "religious phenomenon" and with the state as heralding the messianic era also recedes as staunch Zionist religious schools like Mercaz Harav encourage long-term deferment of army service in the interest of full-time Torah study. The philosophy of *torah u'maddah*—Torah studies and secular studies—is the Yeshiva University motto. It represents the creative attempt by the modernists to mold a synthesis of religion and scholarship. Yet it is under attack in modern Orthodox institutions as a compromise of the rabbinical tradition. As Gideon Aran puts it in another context, "after taking significant independent and innovative strides forward . . . [modern Orthodoxy] tends to return to the warm and safe bosom" of yeshiva Orthodoxy.[64] For Orthodoxy of any type, yeshiva still remains the critical frame of reference. In the final analysis it is the yeshiva rabbinical leaders who are the arbiters for Orthodoxy. Accordingly, we can expect modern Orthodoxy to take on many of the sectarian qualities of yeshiva life.

The attractions of yeshiva life are not to be overlooked. Yeshiva offers its adherents community and intimacy. Yeshiva institutions and neighborhoods stress personalism, and there is little bureaucratic formality. Everyone knows everybody else, is somehow related, or interacts as if they are. A norm of "fictive kinship" prevails where people are ritually and religiously obligated to help their "kinspeople" by taking care of a neighbor's children, inviting the needy to one's home, providing money for a destitute family, passing on clothing to the next family, and participating in each other's occasions of joy and grief.

The yeshiva world provides meaning and explanation for the "big questions": Why do I suffer? Where will I go when I die? What is the right action? How may I know it to be correct? Life in these communities provides protection against spiritual and moral "homelessness." Living amid the certainty of yeshiva life is a relief and release from the ambiguities of modernity. B'nai torah Judaism, like other fundamentalist religious systems, provides a totalistic system where all human activities are endowed with religious meaning.

Notes

1. Eliezer Schach, "We Are Agudah" (in Hebrew), in Schach, *And the Sun Shall Shine: The Emergence of Degel Hatorah* (B'nai B'rak: Machon, 1990), p. 136.

2. James M. Wall, "The Spiritual Leader as Power Broker," *Christian Century*, 18 April 1990, p. 138.

3. For an authoritative statement on the Degel Ha Torah attitude to the state, see Nosson Grossman, "Under Foreign Rule" (in Hebrew), in *Yated Ne'eman* (U.S. ed.), 31 May 1991, p. 3. Grossman explained that Degel Ha Torah "sees in the secular government a foreign rule, foreign and hostile. . . .

To our view there is no real difference between the situation of Jews in the diaspora under a gentile government and to the situation in this state [Israel]." According to Degel's rabbinical authorities participation in the Knesset is comparable to past Jewish participation in the parliaments of Poland, Hungary, and Rumania. The function of participation in those "Gentile parliaments" was not based on acceptance or love of country but on the practical need for Jews to obtain political leverage in order to protect their communal well-being. The same situation, claims Grossman, exists in the State of Israel.

Absent (at the party convention) was the blue and white flag of the State of Israel. "Absent was the singing of the national anthem, Hatikvah. Absent was the president whose presence usually graces such ceremonial occasions. As is well known it would have been beneath the dignity of the assembled to rise in his honor." *Jerusalem Post,* 30 March 1990, p. 4.

4. The appellation, "Litvishe," used in regard to yeshivas, does not refer to a geographic place only, but to a religious and educational genre. In this sense one speaks of Litvishe yeshivas in Poland, Russia, the United States, or the modern State of Israel. We generally use the Yiddish term rather than "Lithuanian," which is more associated with a political-national entity.

5. The doctrine of Torah study as a core religious activity is not entirely new. It is discussed in the Talmud, was codified in the Maimonidean law code, Mishnah Torah, and received its classical interpretation by Rabbi Hayim Volozhiner in his nineteenth-century work *Nefesh Ha'Hayim.*

6. For an excellent history of the emergence of the haredim, see Samuel C. Heilman and Menachem Friedman, "Religious Fundamentalism and Religious Jews: The Case of Haredim," in Martin E. Marty and R. Scott Appleby, eds., *Fundamentalisms Observed* (Chicago: University of Chicago Press, 1991), pp. 197–264.

7. For an anthology of Hasidic writings on spirituality, see Joseph Dan, *The Teaching of Hasidim* (New York: Behrman House, 1983).

8. Modern Orthodox Jews, unlike b'nai torah, see no prohibition against university study and enter the professions, university teaching, science, and law. See Samuel C. Heilman and Steven Cohen, *Cosmopolitans and Parochials: Modern Orthodox Jews in America* (Chicago: University of Chicago Press, 1989).

9. For a portrait of the Litvishe yeshivas, see Shaul Stampfer, "Three Lithuanian Yeshivas in the Nineteenth Century" (Ph.D. diss., Hebrew University, 1981).

10. The graduates of these schools served in rabbinical positions not only in Eastern Europe but in North America and Western Europe as well. A portion of the graduates, particularly at the turn of the century, later went into various types of business careers where they combined business and Torah. See Baruch Epstein, *Mekor Baruch* (Vilna, 1928) for a memoir and description of one such distinguished life.

11. For the complex and ambivalent attitude to secular studies in regard to the Volozhin yeshiva, see Jacob J. Schacter, "Haskalah, Secular Studies and the Close of the Yeshiva in Volozhin in 1882," *Torah U'Madda Journal,* vol. 2, pp. 76–133. See also David Mirsky, ed., *European Torah Institutions before the Destruction* (in Hebrew) (New York: Open Publishing, 1956). See also Oscar Fastman, "Trends in the American Yeshiva Today," *Tradition* (Fall 1967): 48–64.

12. Schacter, "Haskalah, Secular Studies and the Close of the Yeshiva," esp. pp. 94–96.

13. Yitzchok Hutner, "Holocaust—A Study of the Term and the Epoch It Is Meant to Describe," *Jewish Observer,* October 1977, p. 9.

14. Mordechai Gifter, Torah Perspectives (New York: Art Scroll Mesorah, 1986), pp. 106–11.

15. Eliezer Schach, *Michtavim U'mamorim,* vol. 1 (B'nai B'rak: Ponovitz Yeshiva, 1980), p. 8.

16. Rabbi Avigdor Miller, the famous yeshiva *mashgiach,* spiritual adviser and lecturer, explained that secularists and assimilating Jews were ultimately responsible for

the Holocaust but that Gentile hatred is directed at the outwardly pious and observant. "It is a truly queer phenomenon. The old type of Jew with his beard and long coat, more readily excites hatred in the gentile than does the assimilated Jew who is identical in appearance, garb, language and customs." Miller, *Rejoice O Youth* (Brooklyn, N.Y.: Balshon, 1962), p. 262. Miller and other yeshiva thinkers explain the suffering of the pious as a type of expiation for the transgressions of non-Torah observing Jews.

17. Heilman and Friedman, "Religious Fundamentalism and Religious Jews," p. 215.

18. Population figures for subgroups in the Jewish community are estimates, for there are no census figures for these groups. Based on Israeli election returns and published materials which give the total haredi population as 30 percent of world Jewry, I estimate yeshiva Jews to compose between one-third and one-half of the total haredi population.

19. Peter L. Berger and Thomas Luckmann, *The Social Construction of Reality* (New York: Doubleday, 1970).

20. For a discussion of the meanings of fundamentalism in international perspective, see Martin E. Marty and R. Scott Appleby, "Conclusion: An Interim Report on a Hypothetical Family," in Marty and Appleby, *Fundamentalisms Observed*, pp. 814–42.

21. For an introduction to traditional Jewish practice, see Hayim Donin, *To Be a Jew* (New York: Basic Books, 1972).

22. For an insightful study of the transformation from traditionalism to ultra-Orthodoxy, see Menachem Friedman, "Life Tradition and Book Tradition in the Development of Ultra Orthodox Judaism," in Harvey Goldberg, ed., *Judaism Viewed from Within and from Without* (Albany, N.Y.: State University of New York Press, 1987).

23. Marty and Appleby, "Conclusion: An Interim Report," p. 819.

24. See the strong attacks on the modernists Rabbis Emmanuel Rackman and Irving Greenberg, particularly in Avrohom Twersky, "A Rejoinder to Rabbi Lamm," *Jewish Observer*, Summer 1988, pp. 17–30.

25. For a sociological study of the phenomenon, see Menachem Friedman, "The Changing Role of the Community Rabbinate," *Jerusalem Quarterly* 25 (1986), pp. 79–99.

26. Israeli b'nai torah are limited in their employment opportunities even if they want to work because they have not completed military service, a prerequisite for most employment.

27. Max Weber, *The Sociology of Religion* (Boston: Beacon Press, 1963), p. 139. For the view of medieval and modern Jewish philosophy, see Julius Guttman, *Philosophies of Judaism* (New York: Schocken Books, 1963). The most prominent yeshiva scholar to address questions of Jewish suffering in a philosophical fashion is Yecheskel Levenstein, *Ohr Yecheskel*, vol. 3 (B'nai B'rak: Ginzberg, n.d.).

28. For the full text, see *Machzor Beis Yosef* (Brooklyn: Mesorah Art Scroll, 1988). "This is a cardinal principle of Jewish faith. History is not haphazard; Israel's exile and centuries long distress is a result of its sins" (p. 342).

29. For a contemporary theological presentation of this view, see David Hartman, *A Living Covenant: The Innovative Spirit in Traditional Judaism* (New York: Free Press, 1985).

30. See Levenstein, *Ohr Yecheskel*, vol. 3, p. 290. Levenstein, quoting scripture, Talmud, and Jewish philosophy, explains that Jewish suffering is part of the "necessary conditions that will bring Messiah." In this view, each generation's suffering is a contribution to the mysterious process of messianic transformation, which will come "suddenly" in an unexpected way. For a less philosophical presentation of this same position, see Eliezer Schach, "On Jewish Survival," *Jewish Observer*, February 1982, pp. 5–7.

31. Rav Shimon Schwab, *Selected Writings* (Lakewood, N.J.: CIS Publications, 1988), p. 115. For a recent restatement, see Nosson Grossman, "On Seeking the End of Time" (in Hebrew), *Yated Ne'eman* (U.S. ed.), 10 May 1991, p. 4.

32. Rabbi Svei's comments are an exact

quote from my field notes on the meeting, which were later corroborated. This essay and the quotes of yeshiva followers draw on my fieldwork in 1990–91, when I engaged in extensive participant observation, and conducted many field interviews and formal in-depth interviews with thirty yeshiva rabbis, students, and followers. I use pseudonyms for all respondents unless the words are those of leaders of the movement who are known to the public through their writings or official position.

33. Aaron Kotler, *Kesser Torah* (Lakewood, N.J.: Dershowitz, n.d.), p. 25.

34. Schlomo Wolbe, "The Yeshiva in our Era" (in Hebrew), *Mussaf Yated Ne'eman*, 25 August 1991, pp. 4–5. Yeshiva students receive long-term deferments from the Israeli army—a source of much conflict between secularists and b'nai torah as it is the source of tension between secularists and all haredim. These deferments, due to marriage and children turn out to be in most cases virtual exemptions.

35. Schach, "On Jewish Survival," p. 7.

36. Nosson Grossman, "And the Idols Are Destroyed" (in Hebrew), *Yated Ne'ema* (U.S. ed.), 8 February 1991, p. 25.

37. See Aaron Kotler, *Mishnas Rav Aaron* (Lakewood, N.J.: Machon Rav Aaron, 1980), pp. 27–29, for an authoritative statement on the philosophy of *torah lishma* and the Jewish community's obligation to support torah lishma scholarship.

38. Kotler, *Mishnas*, p. 57.

39. See for example, Schach, *Michtavim U'Mamorim*, vol. 2, pp. 15–16.

40. Rabbi David Steinwurtzel, during an address to a b'nai torah convention in August 1989 as reported in "Hundreds of B'nai Torah at Summer Convention," *Coalition*, September 1989, published by Agudat Israel of America, New York, N.Y.

41. Kotler, *Kesser Torah*, p. 25.

42. Funding is a major issue dividing secularist Israelis and yeshiva loyalists. B'nai torah seek larger and larger subsidies for their institutions—this is their primary "religious" demand. Secularists oppose what they see as handouts for those who do not

work and refuse to aid in the defense of the country. While the modern welfare state in the United States and Israel, which insures that every family—employed or not—has at least basic food and housing, is an important, perhaps, essential economic base upon which kollel society depends, it is too simple, in my view, to conclude that the kollel can only exist in a welfare state or that there is some causal relationship between them. There are at least two kollel academies in the United States, funded by a single industrialist or family.

43. As a sign of increasing tension between secularists and the Israeli ultra-Orthodox, acts of vandalism against synagogues in the yeshiva community of B'nai B'rak are increasing in number and frequency. See news articles in *Jerusalem Post*, 7–10 July 1991.

44. For the full text and background of the ban, see *The Struggle and the Splendor* (New York: Agudat Israel, 1982), p. 97. The ban, coordinated with yeshiva leaders in Israel who were interested in officially delegitimating these groups, set the ideological stage for later Israeli legislative consideration of the "Who is a Jew" bill in which an attempt was made to rule all non-Orthodox conversions to Judaism illegitimate.

45. Ibid., p. 98.

46. Hayim Dov Keller, "Modern Orthodoxy: An Analysis and a Response," *Jewish Observer*, June 1970, p. 6.

47. Yissochor Frand, "Where There's a Rabbinic Will There's a Halachic Way," *Jewish Observer*, October 1990, p. 8.

48. See, for example, Avrohom Twersky, "A Rejoinder to Rabbi Lamm," *Jewish Observer*, September 1988, pp. 17–30.

49. See, for example, Moshe Feinstein, *Igrot Moshe, Yore Deah* (New York: Moriah, 1973), p. 46.

50. These prohibitions, as with many others in the yeshiva and haredi communities, were not always formalized in legal responsa but enforced by social and economic sanctions. See Schach, *Michtavim U'Mamorim*, for the halakhic basis of these prohibitions.

51. Miller, *Rejoice O Youth*, p. 175. In my

interview with an American b'nai torah woman who graduated from a state university in the 1950s spoke for many yeshiva people: "Who can send a kid to college today? In our day you could still attend. People dressed with more modesty. You did not have the open sexuality you have today. Nowadays, professors speak outright pornography in class. The dormitories are mixed, and they are more like brothels."

52. Berger and Luckmann, *Social Construction,* p. 108.

53. "Voting," *Yated Ne'eman* (U.S. ed.), 26 April 1991, p. 10.

54. Eliezer Schach, "The Torah Jew, Child of Eternity," *Jewish Observer,* October 1990, p. 15.

55. I am indebted to Professor Tzvi Zahavy for bringing this phenomenon to my attention. See Tzvi Zahavy, "Of an Apocalyptic Tone Recently Adopted in Orthodox Judaism" (Occasional paper, no. 3, Dworsky Center for Jewish Studies, University of Minnesota).

56. Allen Segal, *Rebecca's Children* (Cambridge: Harvard University Press, 1987), p. 70.

57. For yeshiva theology, human actions matter, but the content of these approved religious actions are "preset" by God for execution by the pious. God does not desire human autonomy or innovation in the realm of religion but conformity to behavioral guidelines as delineated by the yeshiva authorities.

58. For an anthropological portrait of the ultra-Orthodox community, see Samuel Heilman, *Defenders of the Faith: Inside Ultra-Orthodox Jewry* (New York: Schocken, 1992).

59. In the aftermath of the 1991 Gulf War, representatives of various Hasidic communities, at the urging of Rabbi Menachem Schneerson, leader of the Habad Hasidim, signed a public proclamation calling on Jews to "sincerely realize that the Gulf War and its accompanying miracles mean the imminent arrival of *Mashiach* [Messiah]" and

calling for special study groups on such Messiah-related topics as Temple sacrifices and the resurrection of the dead. The proclamation urged that increased religious observances take place to bring "redemption closer." Among the signers were representatives of the Hasidic communities of Belz, Gur, and Vizhnitz. See an English version of the proclamation in *Jewish Week,* 3–9 May 1991, p. 20, and the full Hebrew text in *Algemeiner Journal,* 3 May 1991, p. 7. No yeshiva personality was associated with this proclamation. Privately, bnai torah viewed this type of messianic fervor as apostasy.

60. Some activists in both camps would deny that b'nai torah or the haredim in general and secularists are brothers. The b'nai torah leader Rabbi Eliezer Schach explained that if a government does not support yeshivas and "gedolim are not honored, that government doesn't deserve out taxes." See Schach, *And the Sun Shall Shine,* p. 214. See news articles in *Hadashot,* 7–10 July 1991, for the secularist view on "The Haredi Plague." See also Charles Liebman, ed., *Religious and Secular: Conflict and Accommodation between Jews and Israel* (Jerusalem: Keter, 1990).

61. Daniel J. Eleazar, "How Strong Is Orthodox Judaism—Really," *Jewish Action* 50 (2): 64. Eleazar offers an interesting analysis of the changing position of Orthodoxy and ultra-Orthodoxy within Judaism.

62. The parallel phenomenon in Hinduism is "Sanskritization," where lower castes take on the religious norms and behaviors of the upper-class, high-born Brahmins.

63. An example of the growing emphasis on "strict" interpretation is seen in the recent responsa of the distinguished Yeshiva University–trained and current faculty member Rabbi Herschel Schachter, "Go Follow the Tracks of Sheep" (in Hebrew), *Beit Yitzchak,* no. 17 (1985): 118–34.

64. Gideon Aran, "Jewish Zionist Fundamentalism: The Bloc of the Faithful in Israel," in Marty and Appleby, eds., *Fundamentalisms Observed,* pp. 265–344.

CHAPTER 11

The Book and the Sword:
The Nationalist Yeshivot and Political
Radicalism in Israel

Eliezer Don-Yehiya

Astriking change has occurred in popular understanding of the relationship between religion and nationalist political radicalism in Israeli society. The religious tradition, originally understood as politically passive and politically moderate in both content and style, is now associated with radical nationalism. This chapter demonstrates that the changing influence of religion on the Israeli political system owes its origins to changes in religious education. Of special importance is the growing influence of a *new* type of educational institution, the nationalist yeshiva (plural: yeshivot).[1] Yeshivot, whether modern or traditional, constitute the intellectual and social foundations of religious fundamentalism. Fundamentalism is a worldview that perceives religion, in theory and practice, as the exclusive source of authority and guidance in all areas of personal and social life. Fundamentalism is a peculiarly modern phenomenon because it is a response that seeks to preserve the integrity of religious values in the face of challenges of unprecedented magnitude in the history of religion—the challenges of modernization and secularization. Orthodoxy also asserts the sanctity and continued validity of the religious tradition in conditions of modernization. However, not all orthodox groups are necessarily fundamentalists, as in practice some of them are willing to compromise on the centrality of religion or on the strict adherence to religious traditions while adapting values and practices from modern culture. Fundamentalists are distinguished from such groups by their uncompromising stance on religion and its relation to modern society and culture.

Prior to the establishment of the State of Israel and during its early years of existence, fundamentalist orientations were confined to non-Zionist haredim, characterized by a traditional passive approach to political matters.[2] The religious Zionists, on the other hand, embraced a politically activist posture but eschewed nationalist radicalism as well as religious fundamentalism. They favored policies of religious and political moderation.[3]

Changes in this orientation became increasingly noticeable after the 1967 war. Religious Jews began to play a central role in radical national movements. They were also involved in violent political activities, of which the Jewish underground, described below, was the most outstanding. In addition, religious groups that had heretofore favored moderate political positions were radicalized. This process has been accompanied by a growing tendency among the politically radicalized religious Zionists to adopt fundamentalist patterns of religious outlook and behavior similar to those of the haredim. However, even in contemporary Israeli society, religious fundamentalism and political radicalism are not necessarily mutually reinforcing tendencies. Thus, the fundamentalist haredim continue to oppose nationalist political radicalism, and many political radicals of the right-wing parties are not religious. Furthermore, while most Israeli religious Jews oppose the surrender of territory captured in the Six Day War, many do so mainly for security reasons, not on the basis of messianic claims grounded in a religious-fundamentalist worldview.

The concern here is with the radical fundamentalists, distinguishable by virtue of the fact that their political values as well as their tactics are rooted in their interpretation of religion. Such fundamentalists draw their inspiration from the nationalist yeshivot, and especially from the Mercaz Harav yeshiva and institutions associated with it. Many are teachers, students, or graduates of these yeshivot.

These circles played a central role in the establishment of Gush Emunim in 1974.[4] They led it in its earliest phase, and many continue to influence it to this day. But the yeshivot and Gush Emunim never completely overlapped. Despite the decisive role of religiously observant Jews in the leadership of Gush Emunim, a fair proportion of its members and many of its sympathizers are secularists. Furthermore, not all of the movement's religious members identify with the messianic worldview that characterizes the Mercaz Harav graduates.[5] On the other hand, among groups that center around the nationalist yeshivot, one finds increasing reservations about radical political activity. In other words, Gush Emunim is not a pure fundamentalist movement, even though a large portion of its leaders and members are found within the Israeli fundamentalist camp. It is the nationalist yeshivot that provide the primary intellectual and organizational foundation for religious nationalist fundamentalism in Israel.

New versus Traditional Yeshivot

What are the basic characteristics of the new type of yeshiva system, and how has it contributed to strengthening fundamentalist and radical tendencies in Israeli society? In some ways, the new yeshivot have much in common with the traditional yeshiva system. The latter is the main base of that form of fundamentalism which favors policies of passivity and moderation, especially with regard to non-Jews. By its very nature, the yeshiva—of both the traditional and modern type—is far more than an educational institution because it projects an all-inclusive framework for life by asserting that religion, really *its* interpretation of religion, must dictate all of one's values and the totality of one's behavior. Moreover, because of the sweep and content of yeshiva studies and the length of time students remain there, students are socialized to its values in most intense forms. These values are reinforced by the emphasis on Jewish law *(halakha)* as a total system of conduct that permeates the yeshiva.[6]

The yeshiva thus molds its students, while isolating them to a large extent from the external secular-modern world. It fosters the authority of the sacred intellectual sources to which the students devote themselves. Authority extends to those who interpret the sources: the yeshiva staff, and the heads of the yeshiva in particular.

Students of the new yeshivot also undergo an intense process of socialization. These yeshivot, like the traditional ones, affirm values and behavioral norms sanctified by the Jewish religious tradition. The ancient sacred texts, the well-springs of tradition, are also the exclusive subject matter for study here. How did yeshiva education that fed and nurtured a passive political approach within the haredi public become a factor encouraging radical political activism when it was transferred to the religious Zionist camp?

The answer rests on differences in the development of the two types of yeshivot, their responses to the challenges of secularization and modernization, and the changes that took place in each. We may, in general, discern four ideal types of religious responses: isolation or withdrawal, adaptation, compartmentalization, and expansion.[7] The first and fourth responses represent different varieties of the fundamentalist approach. Both are characterized by a struggle to preserve the integrity of religious values and lifestyles in the face of social and cultural change. In the realm of post-Emancipation Judaism, both these approaches share the tendency to strengthen or expand the institution of the yeshiva, transforming it into a major instrument in the struggle against modern secular society.

The traditionalist haredim were the first to establish and strengthen a variety of organizational and educational institutions whose purpose was to unite and mobilize the religiously faithful and isolate them from the modern secular environment. Yeshivot became the central institutions in this enterprise. Isolationism or withdrawal was also expressed in the traditionalists' opposition to modern Zionism. Their antagonism to Zionism stemmed not only from opposition to political activism before the messianic age but from objection to any form of cooperation with Jewish secularists, especially within organizations led by secularists. In addition, Zionist ideology was perceived as an effort to substitute the symbols of land, language, and political autonomy for the Torah and commandments, which constituted, in their view, the sole basis for Jewish existence.[8] The yeshivot were the center of the haredi struggle against Zionism. Students were cautioned about and encouraged to strive against its serious dangers.

Religious Zionists, on the other hand, sought to adapt rather than reject or isolate themselves from secularization and modernization. But the characteristic strategy of these circles was compartmentalization. This approach distinguishes between behavioral realms guided by Jewish law and tradition and other behavioral realms which may be guided by considerations that are not rooted in sources of religious authority as long as they are not in conflict with them. In other words, even in those circles that continued to observe religious commands punctiliously, there was a decline in the centrality of religious values as a force that guides all areas of life.

Because the yeshiva was based on the principle of the centrality of religion as the *exclusive* source of authority and guidance—not something relating only to one compartment of life—it was difficult to adapt this institution to the approaches and behavioral patterns of nonfundamentalist religion found in the religious Zionist camp. Religious Zionist youth were educated in schools in which secular subjects comprised a significant part of the curriculum. Concern with the secular thrived in an atmosphere where religious laxity prevailed.

Within the Land of Israel, and until the 1950s, the only advanced yeshiva that proclaimed its identification with the Zionist enterprise and its sympathy toward general Jewish society was Mercaz Harav, founded by Rav Avraham Yitzhak Kook (1865–1935), the country's first chief rabbi. Rav Kook was among the most original and admired Jewish thinkers in the modern period, and his yeshiva represented a new type of response to Zionism and modernity, distinguishable from both the isolationist approach of the traditional yeshivot but also from the adaptationist and compartmentalist approaches prevalent in religious Zionist circles. This approach can be defined as *expansionism*, since it aspires to expand religious influence to every aspect of individual and social life, thereby providing religious meaning even to the process of modernization itself. According to Rav Kook and his students, Zionism and the State of Israel represent sacred expressions of messianic redemption. But their religious meaning must be uncovered and guided in accordance with religious principles. This approach, like that of the haredim, was unwilling to tolerate religious compromise in the face of secularism and modernization. It, too, therefore, tended to rely on the institution of the yeshiva as a major framework for direction and socialization. But fidelity to religious values, in accordance with this approach, did not demand withdrawal or isolation from the general Jewish society and the Zionist enterprise. Instead, religious values formed the basis for identification with this society and the Jewish national movement.

From the outset, Rav Kook's version of the expansionist approach contained the seeds of national political radicalism. Expanding the realm of the sacred and imposing it on modern nationalist values is liable to lead to an uncompromising struggle on behalf of nationalist goals, now perceived as an integral part of the *religious* world. However, in order for Rav Kook's doctrine to provide a source for a radical movement of political potential, his theoretical doctrine had to be translated into a politically operational doctrine. This was undertaken by his son, Rav Zvi Yehuda (1891–1982), who headed Mercaz Harav for an extended period and left a deep impression on it. In the aftermath of the Six Day War in 1967, Mercaz Harav became the major source of inspiration for the awakening of activist radical messianic currents in the religious Zionist public.

Mercaz Harav's contribution to the political radicalization of the religious Zionist camp was abetted by a process that was strengthened following the Six Day War but which began even earlier: the growth and rapid development of a comprehensive system of nationalist yeshivot, which like Mercaz Harav are characterized by a positive attitude toward Zionism and the State of Israel. Most of the newly established yeshivot are called "hesder yeshivot" and their students integrate army service with religious studies.[9]

The flourishing of nationalist yeshivot was made possible by the prior establishment and expansion of yeshiva high schools. These institutions, pioneered in 1940 by Rav Moshe Zvi Neria, a Mercaz graduate, were geared to youngsters from religious Zionist homes. Their curriculum combined secular and intense religious studies.[10] The establishment and expansion of the new educational institutions—secondary as well as advanced—are best accounted for by the response of religious Zionist circles to the fact that many youngsters raised in religious homes were abandoning religion. The sense of failure and weakness in the religious educational system prompted the establishment of new educational institutions in which the identification with Zionism and the modern state would be combined with intensive socialization into a traditional religious worldview. A necessary condition for the rapid growth of these institutions was the increased ability of parents to afford tuition fees which the new institutions, the secondary ones in particular, charged. Added to this was the willingness of the government to provide increased public funding for religious education at the secondary and advanced level.

Sources of Authority: Sacred Texts and Charismatic Leaders

The expansion of the nationalist yeshivot facilitated the penetration of a fundamentalist worldview into religious Zionist circles. This growing tendency within religious Zionism, especially among those who have studied in yeshivot or are influenced by them, is expressed by reliance on sacred texts as sources of authority and guidance in all areas of life, including the social and political realms. By its very nature, as an institution devoted to learning and analysis of religiously sanctified texts, the yeshiva demands unquestioning compliance with their authority. This is true of both the traditional and new yeshivot. They differ, however, in the manner in which they interpret the texts, in the emphasis they place on different types of text, and in the identity of the authoritative interpreters of the texts. These differences lead to contradictory conclusions, particularly in the political realm.

Religious Zionism, in its rejection of political quiescence and passive acceptance of the condition of *galut* (exile), and in its willingness to cooperate with non-observant Jews, deviates from the norms of traditional Jewish society. It seeks to justify such deviations by a re-interpretation of sacred sources. This attempt encountered numerous problems and difficulties. First, traditional circles relied not only on original sources, the Torah and the Talmud, as their authority, but also on a rich literature of secondary interpretation and rabbinic responsa which mediated between those original sources and daily life. Along with all this, living traditions of Jewish society, customs and folkways, also occupied a central role in determining what is or is not religiously legitimate. Hence, the attempt of religious Zionists to jump past the secondary interpreters and customs, to original sources, in order to legitimate their approach was itself a deviation from the accepted conventions of traditional Jewry. True, in response to secularism and modernization, haredi society has also increased its reliance on sacred text and accorded less importance to living and unwritten tradition.[11] However, this tendency finds expression primarily in the most narrowly defined areas of law and religion. With regard to contemporary political questions, haredi circles continue to rely on values and attitudes rooted in the traditional culture and on opinions of *g'doley Torah* (rabbinic Torah giants) whose orientation is politically quiescent and traditionalist. In contrast, among the new yeshivot, we find reliance on sacred texts as a source for adopting sociopolitical positions, even when they deviate from traditional norms. This reliance finds expression in the vast literature which deals with contemporary political questions from an halakhic perspective authored by teachers and students of the nationalist yeshivot.[12]

The problems associated with this new interpretation of sacred sources strengthened the pressing need of the religious Zionist public for a religious leadership who would legitimate the new interpretation. From the beginning of Zionism and to this day, the vast majority of religious leaders have been non-Zionist. Religious Zionism, therefore, required its own brand of leaders, prepared to formulate an original worldview based on a reinterpretation of traditional sources. Rav Kook was prepared to undertake this task, which required daring and originality, and this was one of the major factors accounting for his enormous importance within religious Zionism.

Historical Events as Religiopolitical Messages

One of the central tenets in Rav Kook's doctrine is the belief that historical events and processes reflect God's plan and, properly interpreted, instruct man on what he should do. This conception remains at the basis of the worldview of his disciples. While history is the arena in which God realizes his plan, according to the traditionalist view the master blueprints of history were determined in the biblical period. Subsequent events added nothing new, in principle.

The Mercaz Harav approach shares this appreciation of the central importance of biblical models but is distinguished in the special significance it attributes to contemporary events. These events are of religious import because they point to messianic redemption. As Yosef Hayim Yerushalmi notes, "only activist Messianism still has the capacity to revive and revert attention on current historical events and even lead to direct action on the historical plane."[13] However, the meaning of these events is not self-evident; they must be interpreted.

The messianic interpretation of contemporary events is connected to the Mercaz Harav conception of special divine messages intended for mankind. This conception provides legitimacy to deviation from traditional approaches and strengthens the need for new interpretations of traditional sacred texts. According to Rav Kook's approach, contemporary events are the framework through which texts are interpreted and political policies adopted. Perceiving historical events as the revelation of a divine plan does not lessen one's commitment to tradition or halakha, but adds a new dimension of religious authority—the voice of God revealed within historical processes. This perception further strengthens the fundamentalist dimension in the approach of Rav Kook and his students.

Attitudes toward Secularists and Secularism

In Rav Kook's dialectical approach, events of an apparently negative nature (Zionism led by heretics and secularists) are interpreted as the preparation or perhaps a test for events of a positive nature (the coming of messianic redemption). How was it possible, Rav Kook asked, for a secular movement to be the bearer of the very idea that paved the way to redemption? He resolved the problem by describing the expressions of secularism within Zionism and the Jewish community in general as a kind of outer, superficial, impermanent shell. As the process of redemption develops, the shell will crack and the inner spiritual light of the Zionist enterprise will be revealed as an expression of religious revival.

To uncover the sacred sources of the national revival and expose its religious significance, cooperation with secularists was necessary. This alliance would bring them closer to the observance of Torah and make them aware of the true religious meaning of their Zionism. Rav Kook shared with haredim a commitment to the centrality of religion and uncompromising adherence to its values. But from his perspective, this very commitment required that religious influence extend to all areas of public and private life, which entailed religious, social, and political activism as well as cooperation with secular forces building the Land of Israel.

In theory, Rav Kook's religious doctrines should have extended to all aspects of modern life, including modern Western culture. In fact, however, in Mercaz Harav the curriculum focused exclusively on the sacred sources of the religious tradition. Its students and teachers were already wary of the threatening influences of modern culture in general and the difficulty of imposing an expansionist approach upon it, that is, of interpreting it and reforming it in the spirit of Jewish values. Indeed, Kook's disciples tended, haredi-like, toward a policy of withdrawal from any cultural or intellectual expression not rooted in traditional Judaism. The difference between Mercaz Harav and haredi yeshivot, therefore, was confined to their attitudes toward Jewish nationalism and political activism. The haredi yeshivot and the circles associated with them isolated themselves from all expressions of secularism and modernity, Jewish as well as non-Jewish, including Zionism and its politically activist approach, while the Mercaz Harav people also isolated themselves where possible but engaged in Zionism and political activism.

The People, the Land of Israel, and the Nations of the World

Fear of the influence of modern values is associated with reservations and even hostility toward non-Jewish society out of which these values emerged. This fear is reflected in the emphasis placed by Mercaz Harav school on particularist elements within the Jewish tradition—elements especially salient in Rav Zvi Yehuda's approach. His attitude toward the nations of the world reflects the traditional image of them as avowed enemies of Israel, who persecute the Jewish people and plot its destruction. This image, derived from the historical experience of the Jews under conditions of oppression and humiliation during exile, was transferred by Rav Zvi Yehuda and his students to the realm of relationships between the State of Israel and the other nations.

It is interesting to compare this approach with that of classical Zionism, which viewed the oppression of Diaspora Jews as a consequence of their lack of territory and political sovereignty. Hence, with the renewal of political sovereignty, the Jewish people can emerge as equals in the family of nations. This notion is rejected by Rav Zvi Yehuda, who insists on the inherent contrast between the people of Israel and all other nations—a contrast not only preserved but even accentuated as the Jews leave galut (exile). Galut is characterized by Jewish dispersion on the one hand and mixing with non-Jews on the other. The return to Zion is characterized by separation from the Gentiles and reunification of Jews in their own land.

Rav Zvi Yehuda's approach reflects the influence of the Holocaust. In his view, the Holocaust testifies to the evil of the non-Jews and to the great gap and overwhelming enmity separating them from the Jews. It also confirms that the Land of Israel is the only place for the Jewish people and their Torah.[14] Moreover, just as the Holocaust was the ultimate expression of the humiliation and impotence of galut, the struggle for creation of the state immediately after the Holocaust and the continuing battle for its defense signal the return of power and national respect to the Jewish people.[15] Hence, there are many positive elements in the fact that Jews no longer confine themselves to spiritual matters but engage in warfare and possess the power of an autonomous state. Soon after the establishment of Israel, Rav Zvi Yehuda wrote: "With the perfection of our military system . . . the perfection of the essence of our rebirth is evident. We are no longer considered to be only 'The People of the Book.' Instead we are recognized as 'The People of God,' the holy people, for whom the Book and the sword descended together from heaven."[16] Rav Zvi Yehuda's views are an extreme version of the attitude of religious Zionists who argued that political passivity among the Jews was not a religious injunction but a consequence of the conditions of exile. Hence, as Jews returned to their land and established their independence, passivity would and should be abandoned.[17] (The contrasting approach of the haredim, who generally espouse a policy of political passivity with respect to the Gentiles, rests on the assumption that the theological condition of galut continues, despite establishment of the state.)[18]

Rav Zvi Yehuda's emphasis on the contrast between Jews and non-Jews leads to the conclusion that one ought not accord any trust to foreign states or consider their attitudes in any matter effecting Israeli policy. Foreign attitudes concerning the territorial dimension of the Arab-Israeli conflict deserve the least consideration. The Jewish people have exclusive rights to the entire Land of Israel, which is more than a territory the Jews require in order to sustain and defend themselves. A deep inner bond exists between the Jewish people and the Land of Israel which stems from the holiness of both. Maintaining the integrity of the Jewish people and the Torah depends on maintaining the integrity of the Land of Israel. They constitute an organic unity which cannot be separated.

Particularism and Political Activism

The particularism of Rav Zvi Yehuda and his disciples inclines them to favor militant policies in military-security matters. They have internalized negative images of foreign nations, religions, and cultures, but these images by themselves do not necessarily lead to political militancy. Haredi Jewry also harbors negative images of Gentile nations. The political radicalism of Mercaz Harav reflects the combined influence of the particularist approach toward non-Jews and political activism. This approach is distinct from that of the haredim, with their politically passive stance which enjoins any attempt to irritate the Gentiles or resort to violence in opposing them. But it is also distinct from "classical" religious Zionism, which combined political activism on behalf of nationalist goals with modern, Western, universalist values. Those circles that affirmed Zionism as a revolt against the currents of passivity, dependence, and impotence which characterized galut Jewry were nonetheless committed to achieving Zionist goals by peaceful means. Western values of rationalism and progress, which they internalized, led them to believe that through negotiation and diplomacy, both the Arabs as well as the nations of the West would recognize Zionist claims to the Land of Israel.

This is a convenient point to note, in broad outline, events and processes within Israeli society that strengthened the combination of traditional particularism and modern activism which is especially salient in the nationalist yeshivot. To some extent, these events and processes generated a spirit of activism within the haredi yeshiva world as well. But one of the major differences between the two types of yeshivot is that the isolationist or withdrawal strategy of the former is directed toward Jewish as well as non-Jewish society. Haredi students are protected from infancy against influences of modern Israeli culture and society. They are raised within the institutional confines of the "haredi counterculture." In contrast, students of the nationalist yeshivot are raised in relatively open environments, and even after they arrive at the yeshiva they continue to maintain contacts with other circles within Israeli society. The nationalist-yeshiva approach legitimates these associations in religious terms.

The growing awareness of the Holocaust in Israeli society played a major role in the reawakening of particularist and traditional conceptions regarding the hostility of Gentiles toward Jews. The memory of the Holocaust also enhanced the impact of the active political stance inherent in modern Zionism. Other events like the Israeli wars, as well as countless terrorist attacks against the populace, reenforced the Israeli perception of the Jewish people as besieged by enemies, with the rest of the world indifferent to its fate.

Another factor in the rise of particularist tendencies was the decline of secular

Zionist ideology, which had affirmed the integration of Zionism and universalist values.[19] This decline is associated with, though not entirely explained by, the mass immigration to Israel in the early years of statehood. A large proportion of these immigrants were Sephardi (oriental) Jews, whose orientations inclined them in a traditionalist-particularist direction.[20]

The strengthening of particularist and activist tendencies in Israeli society paved the way for an approach that merged both these tendencies "at high temperature." This merger, expressed in Rav Zvi Yehuda's doctrines, generated the political radicalism of the nationalist yeshivot. Their expansion, in turn, strengthened these tendencies within the broad religious public and indeed within Israeli society at large. They found additional strength in the rising influence of "radical messianism" after the Six Day War of 1967. That war stirred messianic enthusiasm within the religious public which Gush Emunim, especially the graduates of Mercaz Harav, translated into an ideological and practical political program.

Messianism and Political Radicalism

Messianism alone cannot explain the political radicalism of Mercaz Harav students, for it also plays a central role in haredi Judaism to this day.[21] Furthermore, messianic elements were always present in religious Zionism. They are found in the writings of Rabbis Zvi Hirsch Kalischer (1795–1874) and Yehuda Alkalai (1798–1874), who, in the middle of the nineteenth century, sought to associate Zionism with the messianic notion of divine redemption and thus mobilize support for a return of Jews to the Land of Israel.[22] After Israel was established, it was commonplace to refer to the state as "the beginning of our Redemption." Nevertheless, the religious Zionist eschewed politically radical positions in the first years of statehood.

Whereas the possibility or even the necessity of hastening redemption through the work of man was accepted by religious Zionism, the idea was never before understood to mean adoption of any means in pursuit of this goal. Moral considerations and the constraints and limitations of the environment were to be taken into account. The messianism of Rabbis Alkalai and Kalischer was based on the assumption that conditions now existed which would permit the return of Jews to Zion with the compliance and even assistance of the nations of the world. The two needed such an argument in order to answer their critics' charge that their activity violated the traditional Jewish approach, which forbade rebellion against the Gentiles. In the same spirit, religious Zionists in the British mandate period never seriously considered the idea that rebuilding the land and securing recognition of Jewish rights to the land justified violence. Later, most of the religious Zionists reconciled themselves with the partition of the Holy Land, dividing it between Jews and Arabs, although they considered the establishment of Israel as the beginning of messianic redemption.

The novelty of Mercaz Harav's approach was in *radicalizing* the messianic idea in terms of both goals and means. It is important to distinguish between two types of messianic ideologies or political movements: one type defines its goals in messianic terms, but selects its means on the basis of pragmatic considerations. In the other type, both goals and the means to achieve the goals are messianic. This second type of messianic movement is "radical messianism," and it inspires the nationalist yeshivot, though even most of their teachers and students eschew its more violent expression. To them, the State of Israel and its achievement in the military and political spheres are sacred and divine expressions of the process of redemption, and irreversible. The task of the entire Jewish people is to respond to the heavenly voice, which speaks through contemporary events, and to take an active part in the redemptive process until its completion. The means by which the goal of messianic redemption is achieved are not limited by any constraints, especially by any need for concern with the attitudes and interests of other nations or pressures which foreigners might exert. In nationalist yeshiva circles and Gush Emunim, one encounters the view that, since we live in the period of redemption, we can and ought to adopt policies and strategies of a radically new nature.

Radical messianism is a matter of some dispute today in these same circles. In a number of the new yeshivot, and particularly in Mercaz Harav, one now finds a tendency to withdraw from religiopolitical activism and to favor a religious fundamentalism closer to the haredi approach, with a major focus on educational activity. One of the factors influencing this process was the death of Rav Zvi Yehuda Kook in March 1982.

The Leadership of Rav Zvi Yehuda Kook

Students of Mercaz Harav and Rav Zvi Yehuda Kook exercised a profound influence on Gush Emunim. Yet Rav Zvi Yehuda was also admired as a spiritual leader by many who did not study in his yeshiva, even by some who were not religious. Admittedly, most of his admirers are unfamiliar with his doctrines first hand. His writing is difficult to understand, particularly for someone unaccustomed to a Jewish mystical style. However, his own pupils worked avidly to popularize his central ideas, which form the dominant motif in the literature of Gush Emunim and circles close to it.

Rav Zvi Yehuda's status as the editor, authoritative interpreter, and faithful heir to Rav Avraham Yitzhak Kook was an important factor in his own position as the preeminent leader. Unlike his father, he was neither an independent nor a profound thinker. His essays (mostly based on lectures) reflect practical conclusions derived from his father's doctrines. But his position was further strengthened by the ideas' radical content and his readiness to act upon them. In the words of Hanan Porat, Rav Zvi Yehuda was unique in that "there was nothing counterfeit about him."[23]

His death undermined radical political tendencies in the Israeli yeshiva world. The camp he headed was left without a spiritual authority acceptable to all its members, and its influence weakened markedly within the religious public and Israeli society in general. Even within Mercaz Harav yeshiva itself, no one emerged to fill his place as a leader and guide around whom the entire yeshiva could unite. Some looked to Rav Zvi Tau as such a person, claiming that Rav Zvi Yehuda himself had designated him spiritual heir. But Tau's opponents bested him in the controversy over who was to head Mercaz Harav. In 1993 this position is filled by Rav Avraham Shapira, who also served as chief rabbi of Israel, and Rav Shaul Yisraeli, among Rav A. Y. Kook's veteran pupils. These two aged sages are religious Zionists who oppose Israeli withdrawal from the territories. However, they do not translate their religious Zionism into political messianic activism. They do not encourage the mobilization of their students for political or settlement activity as Rav Zvi Yehuda commonly did.[24]

The crisis that emerged in the nationalist fundamentalist camp following the death of Rav Zvi Yehuda Kook worsened as a result of events that occurred shortly thereafter—Israeli withdrawal from Sinai and evacuation of the Jewish settlements along the Yamit strip in northern Sinai in April 1982. This crisis peaked two years later with the exposure of the Jewish underground. As a result Rav Zvi Yehuda's faithful disciples confronted a new and troubling reality, and sharp disputes erupted over the question of the appropriate response. These events have been widely documented so only a brief sketch of them is needed here. They have been selected as case studies not only because of their impact on further developments in the national fundamentalist camp but mainly because they highlight the interplay between fundamentalism and political radicalism within the nationalist yeshivot.

Crisis and Controversy: Withdrawal from Sinai

The activities to prevent Israel's withdrawal from Sinai constituted the peak of political involvement by nationalist yeshiva students,[25] yet they managed to raise a number of controversial questions within the nationalist religious camp. One question concerned a person's right to violate laws of the state or exercise force in resisting their implementation if they contravene the principle of a Greater Land of Israel or the unlimited right of Jews to settle anywhere on that land. In one respect, the question was as old as Gush Emunim. It formed the background to the struggle against returning territory to Egypt and Syria in the framework of a separation-of-forces agreement after the Yom Kippur War, and in the effort to establish Jewish settlements in the occupied territories against the wishes of the government. According to Rav Zvi Yehuda, any governmental decision leading to withdrawal from any portion of the Land of Israel or opposing the settling of the land lacked validity. Gush Emunim acted accordingly.[26]

Within nationalist religious circles, this decision was less controversial than it might at first seem. Until May 1977, the government of Israel was led by the Labor party, headed by Yitzhak Rabin. When first formed, the government commanded a bare majority in the Knesset. It depended on the votes of Arab members for its existence. The largest opposition party, the Likud, supported the struggle of Gush Emunim and its settlement campaigns. On this basis, Rav Zvi Yehuda and his students claimed that a government which does not command the support of a majority of the Jews of Israel does not represent the Jewish people and is certainly not authorized to surrender territory or prevent the establishment of Jewish settlements.

Even after the National Religious party joined the government, influential circles within the party, particularly among its "young guard," continued to support Gush Emunim and its settlement campaigns.[27] The government sought to avoid open confrontations with the movement and its mass of supporters, many of whom were recruited to settlement campaigns and protest activities from the benches of yeshivot. Consequently, the government often relaxed its opposition to the settlements once they were established. Expressions of public support for Gush Emunim and the success of its activity encouraged the feeling among its activists that they represented the real will of the people. They concluded that government opposition to their settlement activity lacked legitimacy. Furthermore, in violating government decisions, they were in fact helping the government reconsider their policies and arrive at decisions in accordance with the spirit of the nation.

The Likud's ascension to power aroused great enthusiasm in Mercaz Harav and Gush Emunim circles. However, as a result of Sadat's visit to Jerusalem in November of 1977, the Likud government under the leadership of Menachem Begin agreed to return all of the Sinai peninsula to Egypt and to evacuate the Jewish settlements located there. The center of Jewish settlement in this area was the town of Yamit. The treaty aroused rage and deep disappointment in the nationalist yeshivot.

These circles aligned themselves against the peace treaty and initiated a struggle to prevent the evacuation of Jewish settlements in Sinai. As the April 1982 deadline approached, students from nationalist yeshivot arrived in Yamit to encourage the settlers in the struggle. In many cases they brought their families with them and occupied the apartments the veteran settlers left. The nationalist yeshiva students also established two new settlements, thereby signaling their protest at the peace treaty. The hesder yeshiva in Yamit, headed by one of Rav Zvi Yehuda's outstanding disciples, played a central role in the activities to stop withdrawal from Sinai. Yet the uncompromising struggle against withdrawing from the Territories and uprooting Jewish settlements had to be weighed against the desire to avoid harming any Jew, especially Israeli soldiers, as the Israeli army was seen as a sacred symbol of Jewish sovereignty. The issue sharpened in the final stages of the withdrawal from Sinai, but with Rav Zvi Yehuda's death two months earlier, his students had no authoritative guide to direct them.

Three different approaches emerged among them: *extremists* were prepared to risk their lives and to utilize all means short of bloodshed to prevent the evacuation; *moderates* argued that in addition to prayer, efforts should focus on propaganda and persuasion in order to recruit public support and sway the government, but if these were insufficient, peaceful evacuation was demanded; and *those in-between* argued that opposition should persist but tactics were to be purely passive, with all displays of violence or instigation against the government or the army avoided. In the absence of a leader whose authority was acceptable to all factions, it was impossible to settle the controversy. Different parties acted on their own, and the subsequent confusion made it more difficult to recruit public support. The moderates argued that the struggle to stop withdrawal from Sinai was different from earlier struggles against government decisions because in those cases withdrawals were made by a government that did not enjoy majority support among Jews. However, the peace treaty, approved by a decisive majority of the Knesset, represented a transformation in public attitudes. Although the new policies might be flawed both religiously and politically, the struggle to change them must take place through persuasion, not violence. The most vigorous proponent of this position was Rav Tau, who told his students that when Rav Zvi Yehuda

> established Gush Emunim . . . the spirit of the people was elevated whereas the government was composed of weak persons concerned with their own affairs. He understood that the people were prepared for greater sacrifices than was the government . . . in other words the government was coercing the will of the people. It did not represent its wishes. . . . But since Begin returned from Egypt and one hundred forty thousand people assembled in a public square in Tel Aviv and danced because peace was at hand, Rav Zvi Yehuda determined the "the people are not with us" and, therefore, we must cease our efforts. The men of action of Gush Emunim didn't agree and our paths parted. There is no mandate for five thousand people [in Yamit] to coerce the Jewish people, to revolt against the spirit of the nation, and to erase that which was done publicly—this is a revolt against the kingship of God.[28]

Rav Tau's position is not based on a commitment to democracy. It reflects instead the importance he attributes to the "spirit of the nation," a popular concept in the literature of romantic nationalism that assumes religious significance in the doctrine of Rav Kook. The "spirit of the nation" is not always expressed in the attitudes and behavior of the majority of the public, but it is inscribed in the soul of the people. In Tau's opinion, force will alienate the public and create conditions that make the revelation of the nation's true spirit more difficult. His conclusion was that under existing conditions, the correct tactic is to concentrate on educational activities in order to bring about a revival of religionationalist consciousness.

The peace agreement challenged long-accepted religious conceptions regarding attitudes toward secular Zionism. The faithfulness of "secular" Jews to the Land of Israel legitimated the cooperation of Mercaz Harav circles and led them to perceive the "secularists" as agents fulfilling a divine mission. Yet their willingness to withdraw from territory of the Land of Israel and uproot Jewish settlements in accordance with the peace treaty challenged the entire basis upon which cooperation with the nonreligious rested.

Rav Shlomo Aviner, a devoted disciple of Rav Zvi Yehuda, was one of the first to notice the problem. He serves today as head of the Ateret Cohanim yeshiva and rabbi of Bet El, a settlement on the West Bank. Along with Tau, he is a figure of central influence within the Mercaz Harav community. According to Aviner, the peace accords are no more than a symptom of the severe crisis of secular Zionism.[29] Because Zionism lacks spiritual content, it cannot confront the difficulties involved in the process of redemption. The only way to overcome the crisis is to build a new movement on the wreckage of the "simple and superficial nationalism" represented by secular Zionism. The new movement will seek to nurture the spiritual dimension of national revival.[30] To do this requires great patience. "The true soldier is he who is armed with the weapon of patience . . . not brashness. Little by little we must save our nation from its spiritual woes."[31]

Critical of Gush Emunim, Aviner charges it has lost sight of its spiritual vision by virtue of its exclusive focus on practical activities. The spiritual vision must serve as the compass to guide practical activity. He concludes that attention must shift from political to intensive educational activities. "What we must now do is to teach our Lights [the doctrine of Rav Kook] to the people of Israel."[32]

The most prominent representative of the extreme position in the battle against the withdrawal from Sinai was Rav Yisrael Ariel, rabbi of Yamit, who called on Israeli soldiers to violate the order to evacuate the settlers. Ariel was the second-place candidate on the Kach list for the 1981 Knesset elections, just behind Kach leader Rabbi Meir Kahane.[33] Ariel subsequently left the movement. His position is a profoundly *activist fundamentalist* one. In his view, this-worldly activity expresses one's faith in the fullest and purest terms.[34] He rejects Aviner's effort to separate faith and education from action and to rank them according to priorities. In his opinion they are inextricably linked. Acts are not only the fruit of belief and education; they testify to belief, express belief, and educate to belief.

Ariel offers an additional argument that relates to the timing of redemption. It requires a high level of activity and no delay. Hesitation rather than impetuosity are the real threat. He also rejects considerations of public image. Only pure truth based on halakha can provide a guide to behavior. And even if one seeks to win support by persuasion, a policy of weakness and compromise will never influence the public. "Truth makes its way and by its power pierces all hearts, and the public adapts to truth even if it comes from the mouth of a few individuals."[35] The conflict between the Aviner and Ariel approaches emerged once more following the disclosure of the Jewish underground in April of 1984.

The Underground Affair and the Controversy in the Nationalist Yeshiva Camp

The connection between the Yamit affair and the Jewish underground is found in their common origin—the sense of crisis permeating Gush Emunim and nationalist yeshiva circles following the Camp David accords and the loss of the unified leadership of Rav Zvi Yehuda. Those who attacked the underground most bitterly, such as Aviner and Tau, were those who represented the moderate position in the Yamit affair. Expressions of public support for the underground after its members' arrest came primarily from the extreme opponents of the Sinai withdrawal, headed by Ariel. The underground included two factions with tenuous connections, distinguishable one from the other in terms of their motives and basic goals.[36] The group headed by Yehuda Etzion sought to blow up the Dome of the Rock mosque, which stood on the Temple Mount, the former location of the Jewish Temple. By so doing they believed they were preparing the way for redemption. A second group under the leadership of Menachem Livni sought to punish Arabs and thereby avenge the murder of Jews, especially Jewish settlers in the occupied territories. The event which triggered organized retaliation was a terrorist attack in Hebron in May 1980, in which six Jews, most of them students in a local hesder yeshiva (Kiryat Arba), were murdered. In response, the Jewish underground planted explosive devices in the cars of the Arab mayors who headed the Committee for National Guidance, a group which, according to settlers and their supporters, was a PLO front directing Arab terrorism in the territories. Two Arab mayors were seriously injured, and an Israeli army soldier who also happened to be a Druze was blinded while attempting to dismantle a third explosive device. In July 1983, Aharon Gross, a student in a satellite yeshiva of Mercaz Harav located in Hebron, was murdered. The underground responded with an attack on the Islamic College of Hebron, a center for anti-Israel activities. Three college students were killed in the attack and about thirty were wounded. Following additional Arab attacks, members of the underground decided on an act of mass violence. They rigged five buses with explosives timed to detonate while the buses were carrying Arab passengers in East Jerusalem. However, the Israeli General Security Services uncovered the plan and dismantled the devices before they exploded.

Members of the underground were arrested in April 1984 when the Security Services uncovered a plan to blow up the Dome of the Rock Mosque. Within both the nationalist yeshivot and Gush Emunim, critics charged the underground with violating the sacred principles of the sovereignty of Israel and national unity of the Jewish people. According to these critics, members of the underground demonstrated their own alienation from the Jewish people through their efforts to forcefully impose their will on the state and its institutions. Tau was particularly upset by the claim that Rabbis Levinger, Leor, and Waldman, former pupils of Rav Zvi Yehuda, had approved the activity of the underground. In Tau's words: "From our house of study, the same place from which ought to emanate an attitude of respect and sacred admiration for the state, comes . . . utter contempt and an effort to uproot the very institution of the state."[37]

Yehoshua Zukerman, another of Rav Zvi Yehuda's disciples and a senior teacher at Mercaz Harav, distinguished between permissible and forbidden acts of protest.[38] There is room, he argued, under special circumstances, for illegal acts, but only on condition that they do not arouse the hostility of the public and do not involve violence and deviation from the laws of morality, or force the government and public into a situation in which choices are forced upon them. Yoel Bin-Nun, a founder of Gush Emunim who taught at the Alon Shvut yeshiva, defined the behavior of the underground as the sin of "rebellion against the kingdom," which amounts to the dreadful sin of "rebellion against the kingdom of heaven."[39] He belittled the argument of underground activists and supporters who justified their challenge to the authority of the State of Israel on the basis of the claim that its secular institutions are without halakhic validity. This position, he said, is no different from that of the extreme haredim who distance themselves from the State of Israel and are unwilling to recognize its authority and its institutions. But haredim are at least consistent in their position. They reject the sovereignty of the state and the tools of its power, including the Israeli army. In contrast, the supporters of the underground advocate national sovereignty and power, but undermine the authority of the state which represents and protects them.

At the other end of the spectrum, Yisrael Ariel attacked those who condemned the Jewish underground. He distinguished between the concepts of "state" and "government." The State of Israel is indeed a sacred concept of the highest order, but the sanctity of the state does not adhere to all governmental institutions or require obedience to all its laws.[40] For a government to be recognized as a "kingdom of Israel," against which rebellion would be a severe sin, it must be appointed with the consent of the Torah giants and conduct itself in accordance with halakha. According to Ariel, Rav Zvi Yehuda "distinguished in clear terms between the state and the government. The state is holy. The government—not necessarily."[41] Ariel maintained that the very fact that Israel's system of government was democratic excluded it from the category of "the kingdom of Israel," because of the basic contradiction between democracy and Jewish law.[42]

The activities of the Temple Mount group raised additional problems, including the halakhic prohibition against setting foot on this most sanctified site of Judaism and the question of whether there are limits to the effort to achieve redemption. The plot to blow up the Dome of the Rock was subjected to the most severe criticism from rabbis and students of the nationalist yeshivot, particularly those identified with Mercaz Harav and its approach. Even those who condoned acts of vengeance against Arabs or expressed understanding had little to say on behalf of those involved in the Temple Mount plot.

Etzion and his friends in the Jewish underground are neither the first nor the last to respond to the fact that Israeli authorities have permitted the Temple Mount to remain under Muslim control. The best-known group seeking to restore control of the Temple Mount to Jewish hands is Temple Mount Faithful, led by Gershon Solomon. His struggle to "liberate the Temple Mount" from the supervision of Muslim authorities began immediately after the Six Day War. In a 1983 interview he described the strident opposition of Arabs to a Jewish presence on the Temple Mount as proof that they understand that "whoever controls the Temple Mount has rights over the Land of Israel."[43] Unlike Etzion and his friends, Solomon's group acts within the framework of the law. Nevertheless, they were the indirect cause of the mass riot of Muslims in the Temple Mount area during the Sukkot holidays of October 1990. The riot began after a rumor circulated that Solomon and his group intended to pray on the Temple Mount. The rumor persisted despite the fact that the police forbade Solomon and his group to ascend the Temple Mount, and they acquiesced. Israeli police dispersed the rioters, killing seventeen Arabs in the process.

The activity of the Temple Mount Faithful demonstrates that obsessive concern with the Temple Mount is not limited to fundamentalist religious circles. Some of those involved were totally non-observant Jews. Such individuals are ultranationalists to whom the Temple Mount is purely a national symbol. Their ideology has little to do with the doctrines of Rav Kook but is rooted in essays of Yisrael Eldad, a radical nationalist ideologue who contributes regularly to the Israeli press, and in the poetry of Uri Zvi Greenberg (1894–1981). Greenberg's poetry served as inspiration for the two violent anti-British Jewish underground organizations in the mandate period, the IZL (Irgun Tzvai Leumi, led by Menachem Begin) and the Lehi (Fighters for the Freedom of Israel, one of whose leaders was Eldad and another, former prime minister Yitzhak Shamir).

Etzion, like Solomon, was also inspired by Greenberg and the literature of the anti-British underground. However, Etzion, like the other members of the Jewish underground, was an observant Jew, raised and educated within the religious Zionist camp. He studied in a yeshiva high school and in the hesder yeshiva Har Etzion, in the settlement of Alon Shvut. He was an ardent follower of Rav Kook and a member of Gush Emunim. However, his worldview and tactics were formulated under the influence of Shabbetai Ben-Dov, a Lehi veteran who never studied in a yeshiva and who was not part of the Mercaz Harav approach. Ben-Dov's essays blend nationalist and religious themes into a radical messianic mixture.

It is unusual for a hesder yeshiva student to rely as heavily as Etzion does on a thinker outside the Orthodox religious camp. According to Etzion himself, this was the result of his own deviation from traditional conceptions. In the course of his own intellectual development, he grew increasingly critical of some central elements in the doctrines of the Rabbis Kook. Of all the underground members who were arrested, only Etzion offered an elaborate ideological explanation for his activity. He expressed this in his court testimony, in manuscripts submitted to the court, and in a series of articles published in the journal *Nekuda,* which he wrote while in prison.[44] Etzion denied any sanctity to the existing State of Israel. He espoused a radical-messianic approach which appropriates involvement in the process of redemption from God and transfers it to human beings. His approach is a clear deviation from religious orthodoxy. At its center rests the notion that national redemption is a broad and total goal, an immediate and most demanding task imposed on both the individual and the public. The plot to blow up the Dome of the Rock was based on the view that liberating the Temple Mount from an alien presence is a task of the Jewish people, a necessary part of their divine vocation to become, as the Torah enjoins, "a kingdom of priests and a holy people." This injunction provides meaning and value to Jewish existence. To fulfill this goal, the entire people must return to the entire land and exercise full sovereignty over it. In addition, a renewal of the kingdom of Israel must take place, which means establishing a state whose laws are based on the Torah, at whose center stands the Temple located on the Temple Mount, and where democracy does not rule.

According to Etzion, secular Zionism provided a partial corrective for traditional Judaism's sin of passivity, but it sought to base the life of the Jewish people on mundane existence. It lacked vision and goal. Religious Zionism tagged along. Rav Kook recognized that Zionism had deviated from the path of Israel's vocation, but he allowed the leadership of the people to remain in its hands. The main problem, however, was Rav Zvi Yehuda's approach, which sanctified the State of Israel in its present existence, thereby preventing criticism of the state despite its leaders' betrayal of the national vocation.

The novelty of Etzion's conception of redemption is clarified by comparing it to that of haredim on the one hand and religious Zionists on the other. According to the haredim, God alone is the Redeemer and Savior. All man can do is beg for His mercy, study sacred text, and perform good deeds in order to be worthy of salvation. According to the religious Zionists, redemption involves an interaction between the acts of God and the deeds of man. By contrast, in Etzion's approach, man alone fills the central role. Man must take full initiative and responsibility. One does not need heavenly permission or the consent of religious or political authorities to devote oneself to the task of redemption, nor is it conditional on social or political circumstances of any kind. The sense of mission alone compels man to utilize every means at his disposal to bring the process of redemption to fulfillment. He does not require or need to rely on divine intervention.

Etzion's perception of redemption is best understood by his response to critics who accused him of Shabbeteanism, a movement named after the false messiah Shabbetai Zvi, who led a seventeenth-century mass messianic movement among Jews.[45] His followers anticipated returning to the Land of Israel under his leadership. The deviations of the movement and its leader from religious law, the failure of the movement, and the exposure of its leader as a "false messiah" evoked keen disappointment among masses of Jews and not a few rabbis. Some even converted to other religions. Shabbetai Zvi and Shabbeteanism are names of opprobrium to this day among traditional Jews. In response to the charge that he had behaved as a false messiah, Etzion responded that Shabbetai Zvi's error had been in waiting for a miracle to transport him and his followers to the Holy Land. Instead, he should have developed a political program for returning the Jews to their homeland and renewing national sovereignty.[46]

The charge of false messianism which arose in a debate between Etzion and Yoel Bin-Nun, who had been Etzion's teacher at the yeshiva in Alon Shvut, reflects the difference between Etzion's approach to redemption and that of other Mercaz pupils. Etzion argued that if one were to "purify the Mount" in the face of strong opposition, violence was the only means; there was no alternative. Bin-Nun answered that purification will take place by "a meta-human sword," that is, through the miraculous intervention of heaven. Etzion turned the tables on Bin-Nun by comparing his approach to that of Shabbetai Zvi, who also requested miraculous assistance for performing of his mission.[47]

Etzion's view has been presented at some length in order to understand the intellectual roots of his plan, which might have drawn the State of Israel and the entire Middle East into a whirlpool of destruction and bloodshed. My summary conclusion is that Etzion and his colleagues, surprisingly enough, were neither halakhic fundamentalists nor messianic mystics. In fact, one of Etzion's co-conspirators, Dan Be'eri, severely criticized religious fundamentalism of the Merkaz Harav variety.

Not all the Temple Mount conspirators shared Etzion and Be'eri's view that blowing up the Dome of the Rock was a stage on the road to building the Temple and bringing about complete redemption. Some of them had no general conception of redemption, but they agreed to the plot because they were antagonistic to the existence of a mosque on the Temple Mount; they also believed this was a way to prevent withdrawal from Yamit. But they conditioned their continued participation on *permission from a rabbinic authority*. They subsequently abandoned the plan when the Sinai withdrawal was completed and they failed to secure rabbinic approval for the plan. Etzion and Be'eri understood redemption in a radical manner, and they were thus less troubled by the absence of any rabbinic sanction.

A third group, which included underground sympathizers rather than active members, argued that the plot was not inconsistent with the doctrines of the Rabbis Kook. This radical fundamentalist group, headed by Yisrael Ariel, undertook publication of the journal *Tzfia*. Yisrael Ariel sees no distinction between activity on behalf of the Land of Israel and the Temple Mount.[48] In his opinion, the religious injunction to build the Temple is an obligation incumbent upon Jews in all circumstances and is not conditioned on establishing the kingdom of Israel or spiritual preparation for redemption. Ariel denies that Rav Kook objected to practical activity in this regard. He infers from his statements that it is permissible to construct the Temple before the coming of the Messiah.[49] Ariel heads the Temple Institute, in which instruments and clothing are prepared for the temple service in accordance with procedures they believe were followed in the period of the Second Temple.

The Temple Mount affair reenforced the tendency of a majority of Mercaz Harav rabbis to insist on the necessity of being cautious with regard to redemption, leaving the matter of exact timing to God. Tau expressed this notion in his attack on Etzion's conception of redemption, which implies that "We . . . ourselves need to worry about redemption because there is something wrong with the rest of the people."[50] Rav Yair Dreyfus argued that we must overcome the "intemperate yearning for full and immediate redemption."[51] In the opinion of Rav Yehuda Shaviv, recognition of the sanctity of the Temple Mount requires the most cautious behavior in every matter associated with it. "A thousand mosques cannot make us forget the fact that at the peak of the mount, and only there, lies the site of our sanctuary . . . but we must also be aware that this site will only return to us through peaceful and straightforward means."[52]

Following exposure of the underground, Aviner published a lengthy series of statements and articles devoted to the topic of the Temple Mount. His central theme was that the Temple symbolizes "the ultimate return of the Jewish people to its land."[53] However, the task of building the Temple is a national enterprise, to be carried out in accordance with the wishes of the entire people as well as the state, and can only take place after the kingdom of Israel is restored in accordance with the Torah and the instructions of a prophet. Relying on the Rabbis Kook, Aviner states that "there is a sharp division between the issue of the Land of Israel and the issue of the Temple Mount. We yearn for the restoration of the Temple and we educate toward it; with regard to settling the land we are obliged to make every effort, to initiate and carry out whatever is in our power."[54]

Aviner distinguishes between the Temple Mount and other parts of Jerusalem. He established a nationalist yeshiva, Ateret Cohanim, which he heads, inside Jerusalem's Muslim quarter. This yeshiva operates a company that purchases buildings from Arabs in order to enlarge the Jewish settlement in the heart of the Muslim and Christian quarters of the Old City. All these activities, however controversial they may be, are carried out within the framework of the law. Students of Ateret Cohanim, with the assistance of Mercaz Harav students, were involved in the campaign to settle in the St. John's Hospice, which they call Neot David (the Oasis of David), in May 1990. Ateret Cohanim was involved in the Jewish settlement in the Arab village of Silwan in greater Jerusalem in November 1991. In this case, too, the settlers, most of whom are yeshiva students, entered apartments that had been bought from Arabs by the Ateret Kohanim company.

Acts of Retaliation: The Religious-Moral Dimension

The underground activity raised issues concerning the authority of the state and the obligation to obey its laws, as well as the nature of redemption and issues involved in rebuilding the Temple. The activity also raised or sharpened religiomoral problems with respect to the use of violence and terror. Relative to the dispute over the authority of the state and its laws, the religiomoral question was not accorded much consideration. True, the underground's critics touched on the issue, but it played a secondary role in their comments.

Some critics distinguished between various activities of the underground. They justified injury of the Arab mayors, claiming the attack was directed against people responsible for the murder of Jews. But they condemned the attack on the Islamic college and the attempt to sabotage the Arab buses, as these acts were intended to injure and kill indiscriminately, without distinguishing the innocent from the guilty.[55] The moral dimension found emphasis in Yoel Bin-Nun's criticism of "the idea of randomly wounding people, women and children."[56] He protested against "this slide into indiscriminate terror. An Arab is a person made in the image of God. Opposition to Arab sovereignty in the Land of Israel requires recognition of Arab rights as humans."[57]

In response, the underground's defenders represented the acts of retaliation as self-defense and a necessary deterrent since the government was unable to enforce law and order. An especially prominent motif in defense of the underground was the obligation to maintain the honor of Israel, which was humiliated if Jews remained impotent in the face of Arab attacks. The theme that a sovereign Jewish state must not respond like Diaspora Jewish communities was also stressed. The issue of morality was answered by some circles within the yeshiva world by citing such rabbinic epigrams as "Do not stand idly by while a friend's blood is shed," or "If someone comes to kill you, you are commanded to kill him first." Biblical precedents such as the murder of the inhabitants of Shechem by two sons of Jacob who revenged the violation of their sister, Dinah, were also cited.

Ariel was outspoken in condemning the arrest of the underground members, calling it a violation of the laws of the Torah.[58] He also demurred from those who defined the acts of the underground as murder. In his opinion, killing a Gentile is forbidden but it is not included in the prohibition of murder. That refers only to killing of

Jews.[59] The vast majority within the nationalist yeshivot did not support Ariel's extreme position. However, a considerable number expressed understanding of the underground members' motives, especially in the light of the government's inability or unwillingness to protect Jews from Arab attacks; they urged pardons for the underground members in prison but stopped short of justifying their actions. In this vein, sixteen rabbis, including heads of the hesder yeshivot at Kiryat Arba and at Kiryat Shmonah, Rabbis Dov Leor, Eliezer Waldman, and Tzfania Drori, circulated a petition within the Mercaz Harav community in June 1984 protesting against the criticism of the underground which had been voiced in Mercaz Harav circles.[60]

What emerges from all this is evidence of a transformation in the attitudes of Jewish religious leaders on questions of morality and political violence. In the years 1936 to 1939, the IZL, a Jewish underground organization, conducted acts of random vengeance against Arabs in response to acts of anti-Jewish terror by Arabs. A decisive majority of rabbis in the Land of Israel condemned these acts in unequivocal terms, stressing the stringent prohibition against killing innocent people.[61] The change of attitude indicates the strengthening of the activist-particularist tendency within broad circles of the Israeli religious community.

The underground affair sharpened the controversy within the nationalist religious camp concerning the appropriate response to Arab terror, a question that raised religious, moral, and political questions. These questions continue to trouble the community in the wake of the increase in violence with the outbreak of the Intifada in November 1987. Jews continue to conduct acts of violence against Arabs, generally in response to Arab terror, but such acts are usually the sporadic and unplanned work of individuals. Despite the exacerbation of the security situation since the Intifada, no serious effort has been made to organize retaliatory activity, certainly not on any ideological basis. To some extent this can be attributed to the "trauma of the underground" and to the sharp opposition it engendered from the very public it supposed would serve as a base of support. Nevertheless, the underground affair divided the nationalist religious community for a long time. Prolonging the controversy was an intensive effort to obtain a pardon for the underground prisoners. The decisive effect of that controversy was enhanced by the organizational weakness of the radical nationalist-religious circles.

Ideology and Organizational Dynamics:
The Nationalist Yeshivot and Gush Emunim

That segment of Israelis whose radical nationalism derives mainly from religious sources never had a distinct organizational foundation until the rise of Gush Emunim in the wake of the Yom Kippur War. But the movement has been severely weakened in recent years. In part, this is a consequence of events and processes discussed above. In addition, the major pressure group that speaks on behalf of the needs of Jewish settlers in the occupied territories comprises the residents themselves, organized in accordance with Israeli administrative procedures. It is questionable whether Gush Emunim, as of now, constitutes a distinct political movement. It lacks an authoritative leadership with the ability to arrive at decisions binding on members of the movement.

Gush Emunim never invested much effort in its own organization. It never developed a system of institutions at either the local or national level and never formulated procedures for appointments or decision making. The organizational weakness of Gush Emunim never troubled the movement's faithful as long as they were able to recruit supporters and activists for their activity on the basis of a common commitment to their operative goals and tactics. In the absence of an independent organizational structure, socialization and recruitment were carried out by institutions within the religious Zionist camp, especially the religious Zionist educational system led by the nationalist yeshivot. The absence of an authoritative leadership of its own was compensated for by the figure of Rav Zvi Yehuda, whom the organization claimed as its spiritual head. In the absence of its own ideological formulation, Gush Emunim adopted the doctrines of the Rabbis Kook.

Relying as it did on other institutions within religious Zionism, the movement devoted itself to propagating the concept of the Greater Land of Israel and settlement in the occupied territories. Until 1977, the government, led by the Labor party, was a convenient target for Gush Emunim's protest of official obstacles and hostility. This, too, united the membership and encouraged additional investment of effort. The years 1974 to 1977 were considered the movement's "years of glory." The 1977 Likud victory brought to power a party committed to the idea of the Greater Land of Israel and sympathetic to the settlement enterprise initiated and pioneered by Gush Emunim. But, in fact, government policy was not always compatible with the movement's policies. In those cases, there was less public sympathy for Gush Emunim.

The new government did offer generous support to those who moved into the Territories. New settlements were organized and their practical problems cared for by Amana, which functioned as an autonomous body of professionals. Growth in the number and size of settlements in the occupied territories generated the need for an organization to protect their interests in the areas of security, and social and economic life. These functions were assumed by the Council of Yesha (the Hebrew acronym for Judea, Samaria, and Gaza).

The settlers in the occupied territories are an increasingly heterogenous group from an intellectual and even a religious point of view. Many settled in the Territories not for ideological reasons but because homes were cheaper and the quality of the ex-urban or suburban life was deemed superior. Most of the residents are not religiously observant much less religious fundamentalists, especially in the larger settlements. In the smaller settlements, especially those deepest in the occupied territories and closest to dense Arab populations, most of the settlers are religious Jews, many of them graduates of the nationalist yeshivot.

Without a unified leadership and after the trauma of the underground, an attempt was made to reorganize Gush Emunim. This effort reflected the feeling that weaknesses at the organizational and leadership level had allowed for development of the underground.[62] The reorganization effort took place in the beginning of 1985 and sought to base the movement on a "substructure of broad public support and deep

Torah leadership."[63] This plan was in response to the charge that the original Gush Emunim leadership was elitist, but it was also a response to the growing gap between the activists on the one hand and the rabbis of the nationalist yeshivot.

The attempt to reunite the supporters of Gush Emunim and close the gap between the movement and the great majority of the rabbis associated with the nationalist yeshivot failed. The immediate cause stemmed from efforts to secure amnesty for the underground members. Criticism was not directed at the effort to obtain amnesty, but at the aggressive tone of the campaign and at transforming it into the movement's central activity. A few of the critics, including the Rabbis Yoel Bin-Nun and Menachem Fruman, announced their resignation from Gush Emunim. However, this act was really a formality; most nationalist yeshiva rabbis withdrew from any participation in Gush Emunim activity without announcing this publicly.

In the wake of growing criticism, Gush Emunim does not function as an organized movement based on broad public support or with leaders capable of reaching decisions and imposing decisions on its members and supporters. It is primarily a concept symbolizing firm commitment to a Greater Land of Israel and the settlement of Judea and Samaria. The decline of Gush Emunim is the organizational symptom of the weakening of radical political tendencies in the ranks of the nationalist yeshivot. This process occurs during the same period that has witnessed the growing involvement of those yeshivot in activities that inspire and foster fundamentalist forms of religious education and behavior. I elaborate on this development in the following section.

The Educational Strategy and Its Expression in the Nationalist Yeshivot

The withdrawal of national yeshivot circles from involvement in Gush Emunim's activities is linked to the growing tendency of those circles to stress education over politics as the main strategy for advancing their religious and nationalist goals. The decision to prefer the educational strategy was formulated during the struggle to prevent the withdrawal from Sinai. The underground affair further strengthened the commitment of many rabbis to replace the political struggle with education. Some of those who pioneered the new approach argued against the exclusive investment of energy in "the struggle for the Land of Israel," which meant neglecting other goals, particularly in the cultural-educational field. They applied their energy to propagating Torah and deepening the Jewish content of Israeli society. "The continuous and difficult struggle for settlements transformed us, the faithful to the Land of Israel," Rav Yitzhak Shilat wrote, "into obsessives for one cause . . . we neglected other fields . . . we must invest more in education."[64]

In 1990 Rav Tau described the vital importance of winning hearts through educational programs—the necessary prelude to practical activities in the social and political realm.[65] Such activities can only bear fruit, he believes, if there is a clear recognition of the aims and goals toward which they are directed. Rav Tau's approach constitutes an elaboration of the position he maintained during the Yamit struggle. Other educators in the Mercaz Harav camp, including Rabbis Aviner and Zukerman, share the same position. In a way, the emphasis on education is inherent in the very nature of the yeshiva. Thus, establishment and expansion of the nationalist yeshivot are in themselves significant parts of an educational strategy that preceded and facilitated the establishment of Gush Emunim. What is novel about Rav Tau's emphasis on education is that it forms a sort of counteraction to processes of political radicalization within the ranks of religious Zionism.

The nationalist yeshivot, especially those of the Mercaz Harav type, play a major role in the educational activities of the national-fundamentalist circles. The educational program of Mercaz Harav influenced other nationalist yeshivot as well as other educational institutions of the religious Zionist public. Nevertheless, some aspects of the Mercaz educational ideology were never accepted by the religious Zionist public or even in their entirety by other nationalist yeshivot. To understand the Mercaz approach we compare the method of study and educational atmosphere current within its walls and those of other newer yeshivot of its type with the method and atmosphere that prevail in a majority of other nationalist yeshivot of the hesder type.

In principle all the nationalist yeshivot affirm the goal of cultivating "sons of Torah faithful to the people of Israel."[66] However, in practice, most hesder yeshivot interpret this ideal differently than do yeshivot of the Mercaz Harav type, and their methods differ as well. In principle all nationalist yeshivot accord positive, even sacred, value to army service. (On this they differ from the haredi yeshivot, who have reservations about army service, and most of their students do not serve at all.) However, in practice most Mercaz students serve in the army about six months but devote at least nine or ten years to religious studies. By contrast, hesder students serve in the army at least eighteen months, and most of them do not study in the yeshiva more than about three and a half years. To be sure, Mercaz acknowledges the value of military service, but it insists that unless the yeshiva student devotes himself wholeheartedly to Torah study for a long and continuous period he will never become a Torah sage. The rationale given by Rav Aviner in the name of Rav Zvi Yehuda was that it is "impossible to compromise even one individual who might develop into a spiritual person . . . and what is the value of the army and all the wars if there are no educators for the people of Israel!?"[67]

Rav Zalman Melamed, head of the yeshiva in Bet El, argues that nurturing Torah giants is a matter of national priority which cannot be accomplished without lengthy, continuous, and intensive study free of distractions such as army service.[68] He also emphasizes the great importance of cultivating Torah giants within the nationalist religious camp. In a denigrating reference to haredi yeshivot, he adds, "We must not leave Torah study in the hands of those who are indifferent to or deny God's salvation."[69] In contrast, Rav Aharon Lichtenstein, head of the yeshiva in Alon Shvut, largest of the hesder yeshivot, believes that the shortened obligation of military service which Mercaz Harav and its associates accept is not compatible with the halakhic principle requiring citizens to do all in their power to prevent harm from occurring to others.[70]

In Mercaz yeshivot most of the students arrive with the aim of becoming a *ben Torah*.[71] They identify with the goals of the yeshiva and absorb its educational ideals, constituting a kind of different society, a religious scholar class. This is less true at hesder yeshivot, where study is now a norm in broad circles of religious Zionism. As a result, not everyone who enrolls in hesder comes prepared to devote himself to Torah study as a central goal in life.

Another difference is symbolized by attire and external appearance among these two kinds of yeshiva students. Hesder yeshivot students generally dress like other young adults in religious Zionist society. They are distinguishable from their non-religious peers by little more than a small crocheted yarmulke on their heads. In contrast, many Mercaz-type students grow beards, and the vast majority commonly wear large crocheted yarmulkes that cover almost the entire head. Many of them also prominently display their ritual fringes outside their shirts, a public expression of a higher standard of religious behavior. (Jews are commanded to wear fringes, but most who observe this commandment conceal them under their shirts—a practice that stems from Diaspora existence where such public displays were discouraged lest they stimulate anti-Semitism or xenophobia; the Mercaz people express their dismissal of these fears and their pride in Jewish sovereignty as well as religious fervor through these flying fringes.)

The nationalist yeshivot differ in their relationship to modern society and culture. Unlike the haredi yeshivot, where the focus is on Talmud and occasionally mystical or Hasidic writings, all the nationalist yeshivot, including Mercaz Harav, devote some time to studying Bible and Jewish thought. These subjects are not taught as academic courses, applying standard methods of scientific research, but rather as "sacred studies," in which the text is accepted as authoritative, subject only to the interpretation of traditional commentators. But scientific method in Jewish study is not condemned in most hesder yeshivot and in some instances even may be introduced by an instructor. However, in Mercaz Harav and its daughter yeshivot, reservations are expressed concerning the application of scientific research to any aspect of Jewish studies. They not only fear that the authority of traditional sources may be undermined, but they object to the application of critical analyses to the work of modern writers as well, especially to the work of Rav Kook, which possesses the status of sacred text in the Mercaz world.

An additional distinction is that the great majority of students of the Mercaz yeshivot eschew university studies, whereas many hesder graduates enroll in universities, majoring especially in such applied subjects as economics or law, which lead to high-paying jobs, despite the preferences of the hesder staff.[72]

Certainly hesder yeshivot are not all alike. The Alon Shvut and Ma'aleh Adumim yeshivot are reputed to be the most open to modern culture, although general studies are not part of the curriculum. On the other hand, orientations closer to the traditional Torah world are found in yeshivot such as Kerem B'Yavneh. Many of its graduates continue their yeshiva study after they have completed their hesder obligations and serve thereafter as teachers, rabbis, or rabbinical court judges.[73] On the other hand, Kerem B'Yavneh is less identified with the nationalist orientation of Mercaz Harav. Its leadership is closer to the haredi yeshiva world. Among the hesder yeshivot especially close to Mercaz Harav's orientation are Or Etzion, headed by Haim Druckman (among the founders of Gush Emunim and a former National Religious party Knesset member), and the yeshivot of HaGolan and Kiryat Arba. All their heads and most of their teachers are graduates of Mercaz Harav and educate their students in the spirit of the doctrines of the Rabbis Kook. Thus there is a continuum that runs from the haredi pole to the national religious one.

The Kiryat Arba yeshiva has adhered the most faithfully to radical political orientations that once characterized Mercaz itself. It was influenced in this direction by its heads: Rabbis Waldman and Leor, among the most militant leaders of nationalist yeshivot. The yeshiva's character was also influenced by its location on the outskirts of Hebron, a city in which the Jewish-Palestinian conflict has assumed its most intense form. A number of its students were murdered by Arab terrorists. Many of the yeshiva graduates settle in the occupied territories, and the yeshiva has been connected with a series of radical political activities.

The Alon Shvut yeshiva stands in contrast. This is largely attributable to the personalities of the two heads of the yeshiva, Rabbis Aharon Lichtenstein and Yehuda Amital, who are probably the most politically moderate of the rabbis of the nationalist yeshivot. Both were active in the establishment of Meimad, the most moderate and dovish of religious political parties competing in the 1988 Knesset elections. Amital, in fact, headed the Meimad list but failed to be elected, an indication of political currents within the religious Zionist world. To be sure, some of the staff and students of the Alon Shvut yeshiva hold extreme political views. A characteristic of the Alon Shvut and other hesder yeshivot is the variety of approaches to politics and modernity which is accorded legitimacy within its walls.

In summary, we can locate the various leaders of the Mercaz world along a continuum from radical to moderate. Among the most radical are Yisrael Ariel and, to a lesser degree, Moshe Levinger, Dov Leor, and Eliezer Waldman. At the other end of the continuum are rabbis such as Yoel Bin-Nun and Menachem Fruman, who preach moderation and self-restraint in relations with other sectors in Israeli Jewish society but also in relations with the Arabs. The majority of Mercaz rabbis and their followers support the centrist position of Rabbis Tau, Aviner, and Zukerman. They insist that Jews have exclusive right to exercise political sovereignty over the Land of Israel, whereas the Arabs only posses rights as individuals. They share with the more moderate group of rabbis opposition to any violation of the laws of the state or incitement against the government or the army. The central element of their approach is their emphasis on educational activity as a strategy for achieving their aims in the political as well as the spiritual sphere.

The number of students enrolled in hesder yeshivot exceeds the number enrolled in Mercaz-type yeshivot. (In 1993 there are about 3,500 students in fourteen hesder yeshivot, as compared to about 1,250 students in Mercaz Harav and its six daughter yeshivot.) Nevertheless, the impact of the latter on the religious Zionist public is far greater in part because it has established educational institutions for all age levels and staffed these institutions with its graduates. In addition, Mercaz people are found in disproportionately high numbers among the staff of other religious Zionist institutions, especially yeshiva high schools, where they transmit the spirit and doctrines they internalized during their own yeshiva studies. Finally, its graduates fill critical roles in religious institutions of all levels, as Torah scholars, rabbis, rabbinical court judges, and teachers.

The Fundamentalist Educational Program: The Educational Activities of Mercaz Harav

The Mercaz educational network—some critics refer to this combination of religious fundamentalism and ultranationalism as the "nationalist haredi"—includes, apart from Mercaz Harav itself and its six daughter yeshivot, many *kollelim* (yeshiva-like institutes for married men). In addition, there are kindergartens and elementary and secondary institutions which inculcate the Mercaz approach. In these institutions religious studies are emphasized at the expense of secular studies, and special attention is devoted to matters of faith and strict religious conduct, together with an emphasis on a nationalist worldview in the spirit of the doctrines of Rabbi Kook. The oldest of these institutions is Mercaz L'Tzeirim (Mercaz for Youngsters), founded in 1963 and located in the vicinity of its mother institution in Jerusalem. About two hundred high-school-age students are enrolled.

The elementary school system is called Noam. Its first school, founded in Jerusalem in 1972, is dedicated to "Love of Torah, observance of commandments, love of the people of Israel, and identification with the renewed kingdom of Israel . . . to encourage a pure Torah atmosphere . . . a total Jewish lifestyle and ethical quality." [74] There are Noam schools for girls as well as boys, and over eleven hundred students are registered in these schools in Jerusalem. Five kindergartens were also established in Jerusalem, and similar institutions exist in other cities. A further development is the establishment of a girls' high school, named Zvia after Rav Zvi Yehuda.

The development of the Mercaz network of educational institutions must be understood in the context of dissatisfaction with the conventional education provided by other religious Zionist schools, which operate under the aegis of the office for religious education in the Ministry of Education. The Mercaz circles accused those schools of tolerating a lukewarm religious atmosphere and excessive adaptation to modern culture, finding evidence in the weight the schools placed on secular studies, their employment of teachers deemed religiously unsuitable, and their neglect of standards of "modesty," especially mixing the sexes within the school and even within the classroom. These reservations were so strong that, before Noam was established, Mercaz circles in Jerusalem sometimes preferred sending their children to haredi schools. In two instances, Noam-type schools were actually incorporated into the haredi school system when it became apparent that there was no other system in which they could function. Choosing between a religious Zionist or haredi school continues to trouble parents in Mercaz circles who live where no Noam-type school is available. When queried on the matter, Rav Aviner refused to declare which type of school was better, saying that "each case has to be decided on its merits." [75]

Unlike the standard religious Zionist schools, Noam schools generally refuse to accept children from non-observant homes or those of limited Jewish educational achievements, preferring students whose parents are identified with Mercaz circles. Yet the selective, elitist nature of these institutions makes them attractive to many parents for whom their religious ideology matters less, which in turn has a certain moderating impact on the Noam schools. As the Noam case demonstrates, an educational program of a fundamentalist nature may possess a dynamic of its own by which the very success of the program can mute to a certain extent its fundamentalist intents.

Some of Mercaz Harav students and graduates established, in the neighborhood of their yeshiva, a school called Morasha (Legacy). Morasha places even greater emphasis than Noam on religious study, and secular studies are relegated to utter marginality. For example, English is not taught at Morasha. Rav Zvi Yehuda opposed teaching the language in religious institutions because it is perceived as a major symbol of the influence of Western-Christian culture.[76]

Morasha students are also distinctive in their external appearance. They tend to grow earlocks, display their ritual fringes outside their shirts, and don large yarmulkes. Their skull caps are crocheted rather than black; otherwise, they are indistinguishable in appearance from many haredi children. Morasha educators, however, note that they instruct students to love the people and the Land of Israel (a significant portion of time is devoted to social activity and touring the country), something they claim haredim do not do. The school places less emphasis on memorization of texts and more on educational experience. Morasha has its imitators, especially in the Judea and Samaria settlements.

Nationalist Haredism as a Lifestyle

The fundamentalist attitudes inherent in the Mercaz-type education are also reflected in the lifestyles of the nationalist haredim. A striking example is found in relations between the sexes. Orthodox Jewish tradition insists on modesty in dress and behavior and is wary of any proximity between men and women not married to one another. Haredi society has extended this prohibition to even the most innocent encounters.[77]

While religious Zionist society also rejected the sexual permissiveness of Western culture, it had adapted itself in part to Western behavioral norms in such matters as relations between the sexes and the status of women. Boys and girls studied and played together in its kindergartens and elementary schools and its B'nai Akiva youth movement. Mixed dancing and mixed swimming, though forbidden by halakha, were often quietly tolerated. Customs prevalent in traditional society—married women covering their hair, women dressing in skirts rather than pants and wearing long sleeves, men and women not shaking hands with each other, and separation of the sexes on social occasions such as weddings—were honored in the breach. Religious Zionists also permitted women to participate in public activities, and women were among the candidates for the Knesset on the National Religious Party list.

The expansion of the Mercaz type of yeshivot was a major factor in changing these attitudes and behaviors within the religious Zionist community. Mercaz supporters always emphasized the principle of separating the sexes and opposed deviations from the tradition.[78] Although Mercaz Harav exercised little influence during the British mandate period and the early years of statehood, after 1967 its influence on public life among the Jewish religious grew. First this influence was found only in political activity, but later, as the group narrowed its involvement in this area, its teachers and graduates became more involved in educational affairs and more concerned with the behavioral norms of the general religious public.

Rav Shlomo Aviner, leading spokesman for the Mercaz point of view, lectures and writes on social and educational topics involving matters of modesty and sexual relations. In a book published in 1991, he vigorously rejects mixing the sexes in B'nai Akiva or any other educational or cultural setting.[79] Citing the standard code of Jewish law that "man must maintain a very great distance between himself and women," Aviner suggests this code as a practical guide for conduct of relations between the sexes.[80] This position draws him into the struggle against contemporary behavioral patterns between the sexes, which are widespread even in religious Zionist society. As he explains: "there is no topic in which opposition between halakhic sages and the masses of Jewish faithful, who generally observe the commandments, is more extreme."[81] In line with these standards, in a number of B'nai Akiva branches, especially in the occupied territories, boys and girls carry on separate activity within the framework of the branch. This arrangement did not satisfy other Mercaz devotees, so they established their own even more religious haredi and nationalist youth movement called Ariel.

Aviner also objects to children engaging in cultural or leisure-time activity, such as playing the flute or listening to records, even recordings of religious songs. Children should only be directed to activity of inherent Jewish educational value. In answer to the argument that children need to enjoy themselves, he answers, "they can enjoy listening to stories about Torah giants."[82] Indeed, many Mercaz-type people, like their haredi counterparts, refrain from watching television, or attending movies or the theater.

They also have reservations about scientific research or works of literature and art. Scientific literature or history written by non-Jews is also inappropriate for children as well as adults. In Aviner's words: "We do not need the Gentiles. We have better sources, thank God. There are reliable works of history written by God-fearing authors . . . all decent, moral, philosophical, and intellectual knowledge found among the Gentiles was already included in the work of the intellectual geniuses of the Jewish people."[83] Statements such as these by Aviner hold special importance because they come in response to questions posed to him, in his capacity as prominent rabbi and educator by his followers. Ironically, Aviner holds a degree in engineering from the Sorbonne.[84] Interestingly, many nationalist haredi spokesmen were born abroad and acquired a secular education before they came to Israel and fell under the influence of Rav Zvi Yehuda.

Not surprisingly many representatives of the fundamentalist approach within religious Zionism were born abroad and posses Western educations. Those born abroad—in the heart of Western society and its modern culture—often come to Israel in reaction to their disillusionment with Western culture. Among religious Zionists, they are the most likely to undertake the struggle against Western influence, and they are also better equipped to wage this battle for they "know the enemy."

All these lifestyle tendencies are particularly noticeable in districts referred to as "Torah settlements." Here most inhabitants have no television sets in their homes. Here mixed social activities are strictly prohibited. Most of the families have many children, and settlers are indistinguishable from Mercaz Harav students in their external appearance. Another feature of these settlements is the status of the local rabbi, who has final authority on all matters that have halakhic aspects. The nationalist haredim are more stringent than the traditional haredim in some matters, especially those connected to the Land of Israel, insisting on the exclusive use of Hebrew dates. Many never go abroad, even on visits, except when sent to teach or encourage Jews to immigrate to Israel.

Critics, who include Gush Emunim supporters, accuse Mercaz educators of adopting a traditional haredi approach characterized by isolation, elitism, and sectarianism. This approach, they charge, divides the nation and weakens the influence of the religious public, especially those "faithful to the Land of Israel."[85] But spokesmen for Mercaz Harav justify their program by arguing that secular Zionism is in a state of *crisis* which cannot be overcome simply through political activity. Public willingness to support withdrawal from Yamit proves that Zionism, in its secular version, is a superficial ideology with no power of resistance or permanence. Therefore, a new ideology based on the eternal Torah of Israel must replace it, which requires intensive education to strengthen the nation spiritually. Only in this way will people appreciate the value of the Land of Israel and engage in the struggle on its behalf. Enhanced spirituality becomes a prologue to settlement and territorial expansion.

This rationale for Mercaz's educational emphasis raises a new question: If the purpose of education is to convince the general (secular) public to affirm religious values and recognize the sacred meaning of the Land of Israel, why do Mercaz circles concentrate their efforts on intensifying Torah education and religious observance *within* that segment of the population closest to them? And how do they expect to influence and transform the entire society by their system of elitist-fundamentalist education?

The answer, sometimes offered explicitly and certainly by implication, is that the educational strategy requires—particularly in the first stages—the development of a few specially qualified individuals capable of serving as exemplary figures and as a focus of spiritual influence and guidance for the masses. The desired goal is then to prepare a cadre of spiritual leaders who will influence, unite, guide, and ultimately mobilize the entire people for the fulfillment of national goals.

In the Mercaz view, the effort to influence the general society may be counterproductive if it is not based on the careful preparation of those who will eventually be involved in the enterprise. Those who try to influence outsiders are liable to be influenced themselves. The social isolation Mercaz encourages permits the members of this relatively closed society to influence, correct, and elevate others without being exposed to negative influences. It also creates a model society which might serve as an example to others. Finally, Mercaz apologists note that they have directed activities to the general public through workshops, public lectures, and seminars. The best-known effort is the new radio station, channel seven, which airs Hebrew songs from a ship anchored outside Israeli territorial waters. It also broadcasts informational programs of a propagandistic nature in the religious-nationalist spirit of Mercaz Harav.

Channel seven and other similar projects notwithstanding, the educational strategy of Merkaz Harav is somewhat paradoxical. While it speaks in the name of national unity and strives to educate and transform the entire society, in practice it tends to enhance isolationist tendencies within its own community of believers.

Summary and Conclusions

This chapter has described the unique nature of religious nationalist fundamentalism in the Mercaz Harav formulation, the problems engendered by this approach, and the means used to overcome them. Religious fundamentalism is generally characterized by intolerance toward outside society. Sometimes such an attitude generates a politically revolutionary radicalism that hopes to destroy the sinful society and its regime by use of force and replace it with a religiously pure state.[86] The passive approach of the Jewish tradition forecloses so radical a solution. The haredi public has adopted the withdrawal approach, which centers on creating a "counter-society," though one also finds that notion among Muslim fundamentalists.[87]

Jewish nationalist fundamentalism of the Mercaz Harav variety combines uncompromising fidelity to Jewish law and tradition with a basically positive attitude toward the existing national state and society. Indeed, religious sanctity is attributed to these entities despite their modern secular nature. The haredi criticism notwithstanding, there is no inconsistency in this attitude toward Zionism. Rav Kook's approach is not really tolerant, at least not in the way tolerance is understood in the West. It does not recognize the legitimacy of secular society or the subsequent secular state; it simply refuses to recognize their inherently secular nature.

This approach explains the apparent contradiction between the public ideology of Mercaz Harav circles and their actual behavior. Mercaz's positive attitude toward Zionism and the state is consistent with a rejection of its secular character. Rav Kook, his son, and their students combined their admiration for the achievements of Zionism and the state with a bitter criticism of its negative characteristics. They viewed their major role as uncovering the spiritual light *within* Zionism and transforming it into a force shaping Jewish society and the State of Israel.

Because Mercaz circles recognized Jewish national unity as a sacred value, they could not adopt the kinds of radical revolutionary activity employed by Islamic zealots. They even rejected the less radical tactics advocated by the Temple Mount group within the Jewish underground or Rabbi Meir Kahane's movement. The latter two groups and others like them differ from Mercaz circles because they combine political activism with sharp criticism of modern Zionism. They perceive Zionism as a secular movement lacking strong commitment to the Land of Israel. Like haredim, they accept Zionist secularism on its own terms and therefore reject it. Nevertheless, even the most politically radical groups within the Jewish underground were more accepting of the national state and society than Islamic zealots. Although the Jewish underground violated the law and undermined the authority of the state, it directed its violence against Arabs and Arab holy places, never against other Jews or the Jewish state.

The relative moderation of the most radical Jewish extremists stems from several factors. One is the impact of the civil war in Jerusalem prior to the destruction of the Second Temple in the year 70 C.E. From this traumatic event (documented and discussed in the Talmud) many religious Jews drew the conclusion that whatever the circumstances and whatever the cost, the shedding of Jewish blood by Jews must be avoided.[88] The Jews' continued perception that they shared a common historical experience of persecution and hostility strengthened this feeling, as did the Holocaust and the wars against Israel. This experience explains the fact that, despite the severity of the Yamit crisis, no Jewish blood was spilt. It also accounts for the restrained behavior of the government, which was a contributing factor in the relatively nonviolent resolution of the crisis. The policy implication is that given the conditions in contemporary Jewish Israeli society, a strategy of restraint is advisable for the government in situations like that of Yamit.

The democratic nature of Israeli society is also important. Where freedom of expression is absent and political organizations are limited by the state, education cannot substitute for revolutionary activity. In a democratic state, however, it can.

The intensive use of education within religious Zionist society has contributed to the dual, interrelated processes of religious radicalization and political de-radicalization. Initially the Mercaz approach combined political and religious radicalism. And contrary to notions prevalent in Israeli society prior to the Six Day War, that approach seemed to demonstrate that the two tendencies were compatible. In some respects, however, the relation between the two is rather strained.

Nominally, religious extremism and nationalist extremism continue to be reinforced by the insistence in Mercaz, and to a lesser degree in other nationalist yeshiva circles, on the principle of a Greater Land of Israel and objection to any compromise with the Arabs. According to Rav Aviner, Rav Zvi Yehuda was "extreme in everything, whether love of the Jewish people, love of the land, love of the state, love of Torah and its commandments."[89] But at the practical level, mobilizing all one's energy and resources for activity in one realm must come at the expense of activity in other realms. The Six Day War imparted enormous influence to the Mercaz Harav yeshiva, and directed its students' and sympathizers' energies to the realm of politics and settlement. Only when they withdrew from intensive political involvement could they direct their energies to the religious educational realm. By the same token, intense educational activity restrains intense dedication to political activity. The sacred books are all too absorbing.

Second, and of greater importance, is the fact that political activity necessitated cooperation with nonreligious elements. During the period of political activism, whether consciously or unconsciously, Rav Zvi Yehuda's disciples in Gush Emunim blunted their religious (as distinct from political) message lest it prove offensive to the non-religious. This policy is continued by the ultra-nationalist party Tehiya, which stresses the principle of cooperation between religious and secular Jews, especially in the political struggle. The terms of such an alliance preclude the religious from seeking to impose or even trying to convert the nonreligious to their point of view. This has led critics to charge the religious element in Tehiya with harboring a religiously compromising spirit.[90] Such a spirit is incompatible with religious fundamentalism—even that of the Mercaz Harav type. The growing force of such arguments likely played a major role in the failure of Tehiya in the 1992 Knesset elections.

Another important factor in the "fundamentalization" of religious Zionist circles is their relationship to the haredim. Religious Zionism was charged with constituting an unsuccessful compromise between the secular nationalism of modern Zionism and the religious authenticity of the traditional haredim. From the outset, those associated with the nationalist yeshivot strove to demonstrate that their religious beliefs and behavior were no less authentic or complete than those of the haredim. They insisted they were not compromising religious principles for their Zionist views but rather reinforcing them by adhering to Zionism.

The continued decline of secular Zionist ideology has released religious Zionists from the need to demonstrate that they are as Zionist as their nonreligious counterparts. But many religious Zionists feel that, with regard to religious observances, their community is still inferior to the haredi one—a feeling that can be counteracted by becoming more like haredim in this respect.

Alongside the religious Zionist tendency to imitate the haredim is their tendency to compete with them. Secondary yeshivot were forced to employ haredi teachers in the absence of qualified teachers from the religious Zionist sector with a sufficient yeshiva background. A considerable number of youngsters from religious Zionist homes were also obliged to continue their advanced Torah studies in haredi yeshivot, further contributing to the feeling that religious Zionists should have their own yeshivot at all levels to prevent a process of "haredization" of the religious Zionist public.

Influential figures in the nationalist yeshivot, however, particularly those of the Mercaz type, concluded that the process of institution building in itself is not enough. The haredim are in a dominant position in the Torah world—which includes the yeshivot, the rabbinate and the rabbinical courts—because the overwhelming majority of Torah giants are the product of haredi yeshivot. Hence, the only way to compete with the haredim in this very important sphere is to direct the nationalist yeshivot to the task of educating Torah giants—a task that requires the fullest devotion to the study of Torah as a life mission.

Political de-radicalization was also a response to antinomian fears that emerged following the revelation of the Temple Mount plot. This is not quite the same as Gershom Scholem's comment about the tension between the conservative halakha and the radical potential of messianism.[91] If man bears sole responsibility for bringing about redemption, political and halakhic restraints may disappear. This notion indeed characterized Yehuda Etzion's messianic conceptions which deviated from traditional

Judaism.[92] Messianism can, however, serve as a restraint to radical tendencies, even in activist circles, as long as messianists rely on God to share in the responsibility for achieving redemption. One lesson of Jewish history is that when messianic expectations are frustrated, messianism's radical potential subsides, which in turn tends to encourage the return to regular activities—including the study of Torah.

I conclude by pointing to the ambivalent and tense relationship between the institutional framework of the yeshiva and involvement in radical political activities. On the one hand, the nature of yeshivot as "total institutions" encourages a consistent and integral worldview characterized by unwillingness to compromise. Therefore, when the "struggle for the Land of Israel" became an educational objective of the nationalist yeshivot, the students participated enthusiastically. On the other hand, a continuous and intensive engagement in political activity may undermine the very orientation of the institution to isolate itself from the surrounding society. Yeshiva life by its very nature strengthens tendencies toward "pure religion" of a contemplative and quietistic sort. It encourages extremist tendencies in the religious realm because these are embedded in the very nature of religion as a system of faith and practice which claims absolute validity stemming from its transcendent origin.[93] But this same process also tends to moderate political activism.

All this suggests an abiding sense of ambivalence among the people of the nationalist yeshivot with regard to political activity. If the peace process stimulates action in some quarters, it may also stimulate a counterforce to moderate the action in these very same yeshiva circles. Or if the moderates are pulled into action by the activists, the former may serve to temper the actions of the latter.

My discussion suggests a major source of weakness in Israeli politically activist fundamentalism. It lacks an independent organizational base. Settlement activity was directed by Gush Emunim, but this organization, in which Mercaz Harav graduates played a key role, has never developed its own organizational substructure and never projected its own authoritative leadership. It depended upon the nationalist yeshivot and their leaders. The de-radicalization process has meant the return of the yeshivot to their original and natural task—educational institutions for the study of Torah. As a result, the fundamentalist political radicals are left without an effective organizational and leadership framework.

In March 1983, before the arrest of Jewish underground members, a group of armed hesder yeshiva students, led by Yisrael Ariel, penetrated the Temple Mount area. They sought to conduct a prayer service but also to demonstrate a Jewish presence. The police arrested them. The matter was raised in the Knesset and in the course of debate, Shlomo Lorincz of the haredi Agudat Yisrael party quoted the following exegetical text: "The book and the sword descended to the world entwined. If [there is] a sword—[there is] no book, and if [there is] a book—no sword." The haredi spokesman called on the rabbis and students of the nationalist yeshivot to "devote your time to study of Torah . . . and as for the matter of the Temple Mount, we can leave something for the Messiah."[94] It appears from our discussion that this recommendation was adopted, at least in part, by the majority of those connected to the nationalist yeshivot.

Notes

1. On the yeshivot and other types of religious educational institutions, see Michael Rosenak, "Jewish Fundamentalism in Israeli Education," in Martin E. Marty and R. Scott Appleby, eds., *Fundamentalisms and Society: Reclaiming the Sciences, the Family, and Education* (Chicago: University of Chicago Press, 1993), pp. 374–414.

2. On haredim, see Samuel C. Heilman and Menachem Friedman, "Religious Fundamentalism and Religious Jews: The Case of the Haredim," in Martin E. Marty and R. Scott Appleby, eds., *Fundamentalisms Observed* (Chicago: University of Chicago Press, 1991), pp. 197–264.

3. Eliezer Don-Yehiya, "Religion and Political Terrorism: Religious Jewry and the Retaliatory Acts in the 1936–1939 Events," *Hatzionut* 17 (1993): 155–90.

4. On Gush Emunim, see Ian S. Lustick, *For the Land and the Lord: Jewish Fundamentalism in Israel* (New York: Council on Foreign Relations, 1988); and Gideon Aran, "Jewish Zionist Fundamentalism: The Bloc of the Faithful in Israel," in Marty and Appleby, *Fundamentalisms Observed*, pp. 265–344.

5. Eliezer Don-Yehiya, "Jewish Messianism, Religious Zionism, and Israeli Politics: The Origins and Impact of Gush Emunim," *Middle Eastern Studies* 23 (April 1987): 215–34.

6. Charles S. Liebman, *Deceptive Images: Toward a Redefinition of American Judaism* (New Brunswick, N.J.: Transaction Books, 1989), p. 50.

7. On the various types of responses within religious Jewry toward modern culture and modern Jewish nationalism, see Charles Liebman and Eliezer Don-Yehiya, *Civil Religion in Israel: Traditional Judaism and Political Culture in the Jewish State* (Berkeley: University of California Press, 1983), chap. 7.

8. Eliezer Don-Yehiya, "Jewish Orthodoxy, Zionism, and the State of Israel," *The Jerusalem Quarterly* 31 (Spring 1984): 10–30.

9. Mordechai Bar-Lev, "The Hesder Yeshiva as an Agent of Social Change in Israel," *British Journal of Religious Education* 11 (1988): 38–46.

10. Mordechai Bar-Lev, "The Graduates of the Yeshiva High School in Eretz-Yisrael: Between Tradition and Innovation" (in Hebrew) (Ph.D. diss., Bar-Ilan University, Ramat Gan, 1977).

11. See Haym Soloveitchik, chap. 9, this volume.

12. A large portion of the articles in the Hebrew yearly *T'humim* are dedicated to this question. Eleven volumes have appeared to date. A large proportion of the editors and authors are graduates of the nationalist yeshivot.

13. Yosef Hayim Yerushalmi, *Zakhor: Jewish History and Jewish Memory* (Seattle: University of Washington Press, 1982), p. 24.

14. Zvi Yehuda Kook, "The Fortress of Holiness for Israel and Its Land," originally published in 1946 and reprinted in the collection of essays by Zvi Yehuda Kook, *L'Netivot Yisrael*, 3d ed. (in Hebrew) (Jerusalem: Hoshen Lev, 1989), vol. 1, pp. 61–63.

15. Zvi Yehuda Kook, "To Guard the People of Israel" (in Hebrew) in Kook, *L'Netivot Yisrael*, pp. 112–13. The essay was originally published in May 1948.

16. Ibid., p. 113.

17. Eliezer Don-Yehiya, "The Negation of Galut in Religious Zionism," *Modern Judaism* (May 1992): 129–55.

18. Aviezer Ravitzky, "Exile in the Holy Land: The Dilemma of Haredi Jewry," *Studies in Contemporary Jewry* 5 (1988): 89–125.

19. Liebman and Don-Yehiya, *Civil Religion in Israel*, chap. 3.

20. Eliezer Don-Yehiya, "Cooperation and Conflict between Political Camps: The Religious Camp and the Labor Movement and the Education Crisis in Israel" (in Hebrew) (Ph.D. diss., Hebrew University, Jerusalem, 1977).

21. The messianic activism that has been expressed most recently within Habad is also

based on the notion that divine redemption can be hastened by purely religious activity such as prayer, study of Torah, and performance of religious commandments and good deeds. Consequently, Habad messianism is different than the religiopolitical messianism of Mercaz Harav and/or religious Zionism in general.

22. Jacob Katz, *Jewish Nationalism: Essays and Studies* (in Hebrew) (Jerusalem: Hasifria Hazionit, 1979), pp. 263–356.

23. The quotation from Hanan Porat, NRP Knesset member and one of the founders of Gush Emunim, is from a speech he delivered at a conference on 31 March 1991 marking the one hundreth birthday of Rav Zvi Yehuda.

24. In a personal interview with Rav Yaacov Shapira, a member of the Mercaz board and the son of the head of the yeshiva, he said, "It is easier to get students to close their books [in order to mobilize for political activity] than to get them to return to their books."

25. On the withdrawal from Sinai and the struggle to prevent the withdrawal, see Gideon Aran, *The Land of Israel: Between Religion and Politics* (in Hebrew) (Jerusalem: Jerusalem Institute for Israel Studies, 1985); and Aliza Weisman, *HaPinuy* (Bet El: Sifriat Bet El, 1990).

26. The statements of Rav Zvi Yehuda are found in the appendix to Danny Rubinstein, *On the Lord's Side: Gush Emunim* (in Hebrew) (Tel Aviv: Hakibbutz Hameuchad, 1982); and in the periodical *Artzi* (in Hebrew) 1 (1982): 2–3.

27. Eliezer Don-Yehiya, "Stability and Change in a Camp Party: The National Religious Party and the Young Revolution" (in Hebrew), *Medina, Memshal V'Yahasim Beynleumiyim* 14 (1980): 25–52.

28. Quoted in Haggai Segal, *Ahim Y'karim: Korot Hamahteret Ha Yehudit* (Jerusalem: Keter, 1987), pp. 216–17. The quote does not appear in the English edition of *Dear Brothers: The West Bank and the Jewish Underground* (Woodmere, N.Y.: Beith-Shamai, 1988).

29. Shlomo Aviner, "The Killing of the Messiah, Son of Joseph," *Nekuda* (a Hebrew monthly), no. 11 (27 June 1980): 10–11.

30. Shlomo Aviner, "A Double Crises: The Body of Israeli Nationalism and Its Soul," *Nekuda*, no. 14 (15 August 1980): 12–13.

31. Aviner, "The Killing of the Messiah," p. 11.

32. Ibid.

33. The Kach movement has no real basis in the Israeli yeshiva world and therefore is not dealt with in this chapter.

34. Yisrael Ariel, "A Weakness of Ideology," *Nekuda*, no. 20 (5 December 1980): 8–9.

35. Ibid., p. 9.

36. On the underground, see Segal, *Ahim Y'karim*; Naomi Gal-Or, *The Jewish Underground: Our Terrorism* (in Hebrew) (Tel Aviv: Hakibbutz Hameuchad, 1990); Ehud Sprinzak, "Fundamentalism, Terrorism, and Democracy: The Case of the Gush Emunim Underground" (occasional paper, Wilson Center, Washington, D.C., 1986).

37. Quoted in Segal, *Ahim Y'karim*, p. 216.

38. Yechoshua Zukerman, "Faith in the State Prohibits Us from Creating a Balance of Terror," *Nekuda*, no. 73 (25 May 1984): 8.

39. Yoel Bin-Nun, "Yes, a Self Appraisal," *Nekuda*, no. 73 (25 May 1984): 13–14.

40. Yisrael Ariel, "Truly a Revolt against the Kingdom?" *Nekuda*, no. 73 (25 May 1984): 16.

41. Ibid., p. 17.

42. Yisrael Ariel, "Love That Injures," *Nekuda*, no. 79 (2 November 1984): 22–24.

43. Interview published in *Nekuda*, no. 62 (19 August 1983).

44. Yehuda Etzion, *Har HaBayit: Mismahhey Hagana B'Mishpat B'Nose Har HaBayit* (Published by Efraim Binyamin Kaspi, 1985). See also *Nekuda*, nos. 75, 93, and 94.

45. Gershom Scholem, *Sabbatai Sevi: The Mystical Messiah, 1626–1676* (London: Routledge and Kegan Paul, 1973).

46. Yehuda Etzion, "To Raise the Flag of Jerusalem," *Nekuda,* no. 93 (22 November 1985): 24.

47. Yehuda Etzion, "From the Flag of Jerusalem to the Movement of Redemption," *Nekuda,* no. 93 (22 November 1985): 28.

48. Yisrael Ariel, "When Will the Temple Be Built" (in Hebrew), *Tzfiya,* no. 2 (April 1985): 37–62.

49. Ibid., p. 56.

50. Quoted in Segal, *Ahim Y'karim,* p. 215.

51. Yair Dreyfus, "Light from within Darkness," *Nekuda,* no. 74 (21 June 1986): 17.

52. Yehuda Shaviv, "Who Will Climb the Mountain of God," *Nekuda,* no. 79 (2 November 1984): 21.

53. Shlomo Aviner, *Shalhevetya: Pirkei Kodesh Unikdash* (Bet-El: Sifriyat Hava, 1989),p. 13.

54. Ibid., p. 24.

55. Even Yehuda Etzion refused to take part in the attacks on the Islamic college and the Arab buses because they were acts of random vengeance against the Arab population. See "I Saw the Necessity to Prepare a Plan to Purify the Temple Mount" (in Hebrew) (A stenogram of Yehuda Etzion's opening remarks at his trial on 5 May), reprinted in *Nekuda,* no. 88 (24 June 1985): 24.

56. Bin-Nun, "Yes, a Self Appraisal!" p. 13.

57. Ibid., p. 14.

58. "About thirty God-fearing men, all punctilious in observing halakha, some of them sages, are held in jail. Why? Were they caught robbing a bank? Were they not motivated by the desire to fulfill religious commandments? Isn't the reason [for their action attributable to the fact that] Israeli security is negligent and indulgent of Arab terror?" Ariel, "Love That Injures," p. 24.

59 . Yisrael Ariel, "Things as They Are," *Tzfiya,* no. 1 (August 1984): 28–29.

60. The petition has also been published in "Friends, Heed Your Words," *Tzfiya,* no. 1 (August 1984): 41–42.

61. Don-Yehiya, "Religion and Political Terrorism."

62. Noam Arnon, "Don't Destroy, Don't Split," *Nekuda,* no. 89 (26 July 1985): 18–19.

63. Ibid.

64. Yitzhak Shilat, "Return to the Straight and Narrow," *Nekuda,* no. 89 (26 July 1985), p. 15.

65. Zvi Tau, *B'Shemen Raanan* (in Hebrew) (Jerusalem: n.p., 1990), pp. 399–403.

66. Rav Yitzhak Shilat of the Ma'aleh Adumim yeshiva writes that to guide the nation and unite its various segments, "great Torah sages . . . pure in their knowledge and deeds" who are also faithful to "the building of the nation in its land, materially and spiritually" are required. The development of such Torah giants "is the peak of the challenges that confront the hesder yeshivot." Yitzhak Shilat, "Hesder Yeshivot—Values and Religious Objectives" (in Hebrew), in *Maaley Asor: Sepher HeAsor L'Yeshivat Birkat Moshe, Ma'aleh Adumim* (Ma'aleh Adumim: Hotzaat Maaliyot, 1988), p. 44.

67. Shlomo Aviner, "Letters" (in Hebrew), *Iturey Kohanim* (1 January 1986): 1.

68. Zalman Baruch Melamed, "Torah Giants—That Is What the Nation Needs" (in Hebrew), *Techmim* (Elon Shvut: Zomet, 1987), vol. 7, pp. 330–34.

69. Ibid., p. 334.

70. Aharon Lichtenstein, "The Philosophy of Hesder" (in Hebrew), in *Techmim,* pp. 317–18.

71. See Charles Selengut, "By Torah Alone: Yeshiva Fundamentalism in Jewish Life," chap. 10, this volume.

72. See Yair Sheleg, "Hesder Yeshivot: Between Vision and Reality" *Nekuda,* no. 86 (26 April 1985): 12–15.

73. Yair Sheleg, "Settlers and Educators Are Wanted," *Nekuda,* no. 87 (24 May 1985): 13.

74. Pinhas Isaak, "'Noam' as a School and as an Educational System" (in Hebrew) (M.A. thesis, Bar-Ilan University, Ramat Gan, 1987), p. 12.

75. Shlomo Aviner, "A Zionist or Haredi School" (in Hebrew), *Iturey Kohanim* (28 August 1987): 28–29.

76. According to a personal interview with Rav Elisha Aviner, a graduate of Mercaz and head of the kollel in the Ma'aleh Adumim yeshiva. Rav Aviner is among the most active in the educational activities of the Mercaz circle. His children are enrolled in Morasha.

77. Moshe Samet, "Haredi Jewry in the Contemporary Era" (in Hebrew) *Mahalakhim* 1 (March 1969): 29–40. See also Samuel Heilman, *Defenders of the Faith* (New York: Schocken Books, 1992).

78. The Mercaz circle tends to ignore the related and important issue of women's role in public life because they acknowledge that any attempt to denounce women's achievements in this sphere will generate fierce opposition in the ranks of religious Zionism. In this respect the position of contemporary Mercaz differs not only from that of haredim but even from that of Rav Kook himself, who, during the mandate period, opposed granting women the right to vote. On Rav Kook's position, see Menachem Friedman, *Society and Religion: The Non-Zionist Orthodox in Eret-Israel, 1918–1936* (in Hebrew) (Jerusalem: Yad Izhak Ben-Zvi, 1977), chaps. 6–7.

79. Shlomo Aviner, *Hesed N'uraikh: Tnuat Noar V'Tzniut* (Bet El: Sifriat Hava, 1991).

80. Ibid., p. 34.

81. Ibid., p. 15.

82. Ibid.

83. Shlomo Aviner, "An Answer to A Question Regarding Study of Christian Sources" (in Hebrew), *Iturey Kohanim,* no. 56 (November 1989): 25.

84. The same institution conferred a similar degree on Rabbi Menachem M. Schneerson, the Lubavitcher rebbe.

85. Dan Be'eri, "Zionism More Than Ever," *Nekuda,* no. 95 (21 January 1986): 10.

86. In the Muslim formulation, this society is perceived as sinking in a swamp of ignorance and paganism *(jahiliyya)*. Emmanuel Sivan, *Radical Islam* (New Haven: Yale University Press, 1985), chap. 2.

87. Ibid., p. 83–86.

88. Rapoport argues that the terror campaigns (during the great revolt against the Romans) had a traumatic impact on Jewish consciousness, making it virtually impossible for the Jews to justify violence for political purposes until the middle of the twentieth century. David Rapoport, "Terror and the Messiah," in D. Rapoport and Y. Alexander, eds., *The Morality of Terror* (New York: Columbia University Press, 1988), p. 31.

89. Shlomo Aviner, *Torat Imkha Pirkei Hinuch* (Bet-El: Sifriyat Hava, 1991), p. 188.

90. Asher Cohen, "Political Partners: Relations between Religious and Non-Religious in One Political Party," in Charles S. Liebman, ed., *Religious and Secular: Conflict and Accommodation between Jews in Israel* (Jerusalem: Keter, 1990), pp. 131–50.

91. Gershom G. Scholem, *The Messianic Idea in Judaism* (New York: Schocken, 1971), pp. 17–24.

92. Etzion's approach even deviates from other expressions of *radical* messianism in Jewish history, for example, the messianism expressed during the great revolt against the Romans that climaxes the period of the second Temple. Basing his claim on Gershom Scholem, Rapoport states that the extremists among the rebels, the zealots and the sicariots, were characterized by "the certainty that God could be moved when the believer's action was sufficiently resolute and spectacular." Rapoport, "Terror and the Messiah," p. 28. In contrast, and contrary to the impression of many, Etzion's activity was not intended to "invite" divine intervention in the redemptive process.

93. Charles S. Liebman, "Extremism as a Religious Norm," *Journal for the Scientific Study of Religion* 22 (March 1983): 75–86.

94. *Divrey Haknesset* (in Hebrew) 96 (1983): 1826.

CHAPTER 12

The Contemporary Lubavitch Hasidic Movement: Between Conservatism and Messianism

Aviezer Ravitzky

Late in 1812, after the armies of Napoléon Bonaparte had invaded the kingdom of Russia, Rabbi Shneur Zalman of Lyady, the founder and formulator of the teachings of Habad Hasidism, prayed for the welfare of the Russian Empire and for the victory of Czar Alexander I. The Alter Rebbe likewise expressed a paradoxical vision concerning the anticipated results of this war for Russian Jewry: "I was shown [from heaven] that if Bonaparte would be victorious, the Jews would prosper and enjoy a more dignified position, but their hearts would become distant from their Father in Heaven." On the other hand, "If our master Alexander will be victorious, even though the Jews will be poorer and their status inferior, in their hearts they will be united and bound to their Father in Heaven."[1] In other words, the material benefits and civic privileges the Jews would likely enjoy under French rule were opposed to their best religious and spiritual interests. It would, therefore, be better for them to remain under the harsh yoke of the czar.[2]

Numerous examples from later Jewish experience in Western Europe, and particularly in the contemporary United States, confirm the observation of the rabbi of Lyady and justify his fears of the potential results of Jewish political emancipation and economic prosperity. Yet, interestingly enough, Habad Hasidism itself has been astonishingly successful in the modern world. It has harnessed this very situation to its own spiritual and institutional purposes in a manner unprecedented in its previous history. In fact, the contemporary center of Lubavitch Hasidism in the United States sends emissaries to all corners of the globe, and in particular has provided religious guidance and facilities to Jews in countries of oppression and persecution. More than any other ultra-Orthodox (haredi) group, Habad Hasidism has learned how to utilize the advantages of a prosperous society and the tools of modern technology for the dissemination of its teachings. While it is not the largest Hasidic court in contemporary Jewry, Habad surpasses others in its actual social presence and activity and in its impact on the outside world, both Jewish and non-Jewish. It explicitly recognizes the positive nature of the contemporary sociopolitical condition of the Jews within U.S. democracy, which it considers "a kingdom of kindness." In 1992, in an utterly unprecedented move, the rebbe and his disciples assumed direct responsibility for the ethical state of the non-Jewish population in the United States, calling on them to fulfill the seven Noachide commandments, namely, those religious obligations imposed upon every human being according to Jewish tradition. In so doing, Americans would be preparing themselves to greet the messianic redemption—the ultimate personal spiritual ascent and the final universal harmony—whose advent, according to Habad, is imminent.

In another paradox, the fifth master of the Habad dynasty, Rabbi Shalom Dov Baer Schneerson (the Maharshab), in 1904 articulated a harsh vision directed against a worldly political enterprise of the Jews themselves—namely, the recently arisen Zionist movement. R. Shalom Dov Baer anticipated the inevitable failure of this Jewish national pretension, which sought to take an activist initiative by organizing a collective immigration of the Jewish people to the Land of Israel even prior to the messianic era. The rebbe wrote: "The Zionist idea contains all manner of poison, which destroys and tears apart the soul. The Zionists will never succeed in gathering themselves together [in the Holy Land] by their own power. All their forces and many stratagems and strivings will be to no avail against the will of God. The counsel of the Lord will remain steadfast, for He alone will take us and gather us from the four corners of the earth."[3] Clearly the author perceived Zionism as an antimessianic undertaking and thus doomed to failure. This time, however, the actual historical development did not match the forecast of the rebbe.[4] Yet Habad Hasidism displays great vitality and energetic involvement within the contemporary State of Israel, the fruit of the Zionist enterprise. Their direct impress can be seen in many and varied walks of life, from broad educational activity to intensive political agitation and communal settlement.

In Israel, as in the United States, the young Hasidim periodically engage in public campaigns of religious influence and propaganda, beginning in the streets of the cities and ending in remote villages and army bases. They address the individual Jew, appealing to him or her to perform, on the spot, one of the commandments of the Torah (even if it merely be the recitation of Shema Yisrael), thereby renewing his or her direct personal connection with the Almighty. Simultaneously, they appeal to the broader community by means of the mass media, both print and electronic, as well as through advertisements and enormous billboards: "Prepare for the imminent coming of the Messiah!" They distribute leaflets, newsletters, pamphlets, and books in enormous quantities unparalleled by rival ideological groups. Moreover, they are energetically involved in the political life of the State of Israel. In 1988, their intense activity had a decisive role in the surprising success in the Knesset elections of the ultra-Orthodox Agudat Yisrael party, which doubled or tripled its electoral strength, while in 1990 its representatives played a central role in determining the fate of the parliamentary coalition and of the new government which emerged.

The outstanding feature of the contemporary Habad movement is hence its fervent, dynamic activism, which constantly seeks new stimuli and new peaks. Shortly after the establishment of the State of Israel, Habad Hasidism abandoned its traditional fear of secular activity and mundane labor in the Holy Land—a fear of "defiling . . . the Land by any form of material thing, stores, workshops and factories" (to quote the previous rebbe).[5] Instead, Habad established a rural settlement, Kfar Habad, as a physical base for its spiritual enterprise. Subsequently the Habad movement established many centers throughout the Land of Israel, from Kiryat Malachi in the south to Safed in the north.

Moreover, despite their full commitment to a traditional non-Zionist stance, contemporary Habad Hasidim repeatedly call on the government of Israel to adopt a clearcut hawkish policy, to oppose any territorial concessions, and to manifest a firm Jewish stance toward the nations of the world. They do not refrain from initiating "religious legislation" in the secular legislature, Israel's Knesset.

In other words, in Israel no less than in the United States, Habad Hasidim display an astonishing dynamism and ability to adjust. Modern reality provides Habad with a far-reaching and fruitful framework for the dissemination of its message, notwithstanding the fact that Habad Hasidim openly rejects many of the values and trends characterizing this reality. On the one hand, Habad Hasidism adheres to a consistent, radically conservative posture regarding matters of faith and religious norms: it clearly rejects such concepts as liberalism, pluralism, and universal human equality; it condemns any trace of modern epistemological skepticism; and it openly advocates fundamentalist positions on questions relating to religion and science. On the other hand, more than any other trend in contemporary haredi Jewry, Habad Hasidism displays a dynamic and activist attitude, approaching reality as a field of movement and change, consciously expanding the boundaries of its religious involvement. Should one therefore conclude that Habad's treatment of modern reality is purely instrumental and manipulative? Is the movement to be interpreted exclusively by way of analogy to parallel phenomena of religious radicalism in the Western world? Finally, what is the relationship between the traditional theological and ideological patterns of Habad Hasidism since its inception more than two hundred years ago and its present modes of thought and activity? Is the secret of the movement's success and its ability to adjust to the present situation rooted entirely in the sociological realm—in its organization and structure, and in the personal charisma of its spiritual leader? Or is it anchored as well in immanent theological elements, on the one hand, and in a later ideological evolution, on the other, which together haved paved the way for its present conquests?

In this chapter, I begin with some manifestations of continuity within Habad— those traditional theological patterns that have shaped its concrete encounter with the modern situation and its present social expansion. I then discuss certain ideological changes found in contemporary Habad, especially its acute and unprecedented messianic fervor, and conclude with a cautious look into the future.

Sacred and Profane in the Modern Reality

Since its beginnings, Habad thought has rejected any sharp dichotomy between sacred and profane, spirit and matter, God and the world. On the deepest level, everything that exists is a direct revelation of the infinite Divine Essence, which penetrates to every being and encompasses all reality. The Divine Immanence brings into existence and gives life to all; it is present everywhere in equal measure, down to the lowliest and most corporeal manifestations. R. Zalman of Lyady and his disciples carried these ideas further than other Hasidic trends and eventually developed a far-reaching acosmic conception: not only does all of reality reside ontologically within the Divine Being, but in truth, God Himself is the only true reality. Man's deceptive consciousness and his sensory illusions fool him into believing in the existence of a cosmic reality apart from the Divine Source.[6]

The highest goal of religious life was reinterpreted in this spirit: the service of God is intended to reveal the immanent Divine Presence and to realize it in every action and thought, in every place and time, thereby bringing man into close contact with the divine root of reality. Hence, all of being was conceived as an arena for the service of God, inviting human intervention and involvement: man is called on to discover divinity even on the lowest levels of reality, to "draw" godliness into the concrete particulars, and to expand the realm of religious activity into every domain of life. Parallel to this, any sacred use by man of one of the components of physical reality— be it mineral, vegetable, or sentient being—elevates that being to its sublime source within the divine realm. Consequently, no realm of human life or activity is bereft of a direct religious challenge.

Loyal to this conception, the present Lubavitcher rebbe, Rabbi Menachem Mendel Schneerson (b. 1902), insists that some of the regular Torah lessons be set specifically on weekdays, and not only on Sabbaths and festivals; similarly, he plays down the exclusive unique religious significance of the synagogue, as opposed to other locations, as even the latter are filled with sanctity and invite man to enter the divine realm. It is against this background that one must understand the rebbe's recurrent call to the Jews of the Diaspora to "create a Land of Israel here!"[7]—a call that evoked severe criticism from some radical Zionist rabbis.[8] The dimensions of "holiness of time" and "holiness of space" are themselves removed from time and space: the Jew is called on to encounter God and to realize the heights of religious tension in every situation and under all conditions. One line of thought in traditional Jewish eschatology indeed assures Israel that it will enjoy "an eternal Sabbath" (sanctity in time) just as the Land of Israel will in the future "spread out over all the lands" (sanctity of place).[9] The Habad Hasid is thus called on to anticipate this state of being in the very present reality, to "taste" (in their language)[10] in the here and now the ultimate future redemption.

Thus it should not surprise us that Rabbi Schneersohn's demand to broaden the scope of religious involvement and to sanctify the mundane is applied today to the new realms and horizons opened to modern man. In particular, one should not ignore the new scientific or technological discoveries without exploring their inner religious significance. For example, in 1980 the Satmar Hasidim severely attacked the Habad Hasidim for using the radio to broadcast lessons on the Tanya (the basic book of Habad Hasidism). The Satmar criticized the very idea of utilizing such an abominable vehicle—"an act of Satan"—which usually disseminates a message of heresy, for sacred things. Satmar thereby expressed its characteristic demonization of modernity. Tellingly, the Lubavitcher rebbe, who publicly supported broadcasting these lessons, did not respond with an instrumental argument describing radio as a neutral tool without any value significance. On the contrary, the radio waves are themselves "a tremendous power implanted by the Creator within nature so that, by means of an appropriate instrument, the voice of the speaker may be heard from one corner of the world to the other—at the very moment of speech," he claimed. "In radio, there is reflected a sublime spiritual matter."[11] The rebbe used a form of expression usually reserved (in religious language) for the divine realm: "Radio [waves], which transcend any measurement and any limitation of time and space in our world!"[12]

Other forces and manifestations of modern reality elicit a "new midrash" of this type—a monistic interpretation of reality that anchors the profane in the sacred, the corporeal in the spiritual, the finite in the infinite. The implication seems to be that "If there are fools who exploit these things for purposes other than that of sanctity, the Holy One, blessed be He, will not allow a good thing to go to waste by their doings."[13] Ironically, then, what makes it possible for Habad Hasidim to utilize the fruit of modernity and to "uplift" it is precisely their a priori negation of one of the salient features of the modern consciousness, namely, acknowledgment of the existence of a neutral saeculum.[14] Even were one to argue that this theory is ad hoc, propagated for utilitarian, pragmatic purposes, it is nevertheless elicited by traditional Habad patterns of thought.

Habad takes a suprisingly dualistic attitude toward the accomplishments of modern science. On the one hand, the Lubavitcher rebbe preaches a stubbornly and consistently fundamentalist view of the relationship between the literal meaning of the biblical text and scientific conceptions. Whenever any contradiction is found, the scriptural passage should be read in its clear, literal fashion.[15] Thus, the world was created 5,752 years ago; if fossil research suggests otherwise, or if calculations of the period of time required for light rays to have arrived at the earth from remote galaxies seem to indicate otherwise, one must assume that God originally "created fossils in their present state," and that "just as the stars were created, so were [simultaneously] the rays of light."[16] (A similar argument was raised at the end of the nineteenth century in the Christian polemic against Darwinism.)[17] Similarly, as implied by the literal meaning of Scripture, the sun revolves around the earth: the theory of relativity and the principle of equivalency may be invoked to counter contradictory categorical scientific statements.[18] In like fashion, the phenomenon of spontaneous generation of living things does exist (as stated in the Talmud)[19] and experimental zoology cannot prove otherwise, and so on. The doctrine of evolution "is liable to lead astray the imagination of uncritical people, to the point that they perceive it as a 'scientific' explanation of the mysteries of creation." Yet it is in fact without any real scientific basis: "The six days of creation are days, in the literal sense . . . each one of the species was created separately, *by itself,* not evolving from one another."[20] Any exegetical attempt to read the relevant verses differently is dismissed as mere apologetics, created by ignoramuses who understand neither the limitations of scientific research nor its conditional and hypothetical nature.[21] The rebbe has indeed made efficient use of his own academic, scientific education in order to develop these arguments in detail.

On the other hand, modern science gradually brings man closer to a recognition of cosmic monism and of the organic unity of reality. The inner connection drawn by physical science between matter and energy; the discovery of the centrality of psychosomatic interconnections in the human realm; the development of a model representing the orbital motion of electrons in the microcosmos, parallel to the orbital motion of heavenly bodies in the macrocosm—all these innovative concepts lead human consciousness toward the unified One. In the final analysis, the recognition of cosmic monism gradually elevates man to an awareness of acosmic monotheism, as "one cannot speak of the mutual influence of two existing things, when the only real Being is God, and the entire Creation is included in His unity."[22] Scientific reflection can thus raise one to the secret of mystical contemplation. The following reply was given by the Lubavitcher rebbe to a group of Orthodox Jewish scientists, concerning the "mutual influence between Torah and secular sciences":

> The very [dualistic] concept of monotheism cannot tolerate that concept of "mutual influence." He, may He be blessed, is present in all places and in every thing, and there is thus nothing which is not included in His Being. . . . Consequently, all of the true sciences are included within and stem from the Torah of God, while those "sciences" which are based upon falsehood are not sciences at all. . . . An inner relationship exists among electronics, acoustics, physics and mathematics. Einstein's great accomplishment was manifested in his success in finding the inner connection between energy and matter. Any separation between diferent branches of knowledge is thus inconceivable; acoustics, mathematics, philosophy, and religion all belong to one and the same unity.

Eventually, the "primary importance" of the sciences is only revealed

> when man "knows how to use them for the service of God and His Torah" [Tanya, chap. 8]. . . . This corporeal world, like the higher spiritual worlds, receives its vitality from the Torah; therefore, it ought to be exploited entirely for the purpose of profound understanding of the Torah. It is very dangerous and harmful to see the Torah—as is done by a certain professor in Jerusalem— as something separate from the world and distinct from everyday life. . . . This is an attempt to denigrate the Torah and to distort its meaning.[23]

This "certain professor in Jerusalem" is doubtless Yeshayahu Leibovitz,[24] the most radical and profound spokesman for the approach that sets a sharp division between the realms of religion and science; the rebbe of Lubavitch thus knew well whence to direct his criticism. To use here the language of sociology of religion,[25] Habad's approach is one of religious expansionism, as opposed to compartmentalization on the one hand, or complete rejection of modernity on the other.

Habad, the Jewish People, and the Other Nations

Let us now turn to the question of the religious-social mission of Habad Hasidim and the relation of this movement to the Jewish people, and toward mankind in general.

Were one to ask an articulate Habad Hasid about the number of adherents to his movement, he would probably answer, "Prima facie, all of the Jewish people are Habad Hasidim." Unlike other ultra-Orthodox groups, which primarily turn inward, seeking to build a loyal and well-defined bastion of Torah, the Habad group is turned outward, assuming responsibility for the collective soul of Israel and seeking to teach its path to the broad Jewish community. It sends its young emissaries on remote missions, "to the most distant ends, beyond which nothing could be further 'outside'"[26] (from both the geographical and spiritual viewpoints): from the central bus station in Tel Aviv to the Berkeley university campus, or to far-flung Jewish communities in the former Soviet Union and Morocco. Moreover, deviating from generally accepted norms, the Habad teacher expounds to his listeners mystical doctrines concerning the very Essence of the Godhead, and will publicly reveal the secrets of Kabbalah and Hasidism. He thereby removes many of the traditional barriers distinguishing between the exoteric and the esoteric, often bringing upon himself the wrath of religious leaders who adhere to other schools.

These features characterize Habad Hasidism even in its earliest days. In his own day, R. Shneur Zalman of Lyady was the only Hasidic teacher to formulate his doctrine of Hasidism in a systematic work, the Tanya. Here he expounded Hasidic doctrines regarding the Godhead, the human soul, and the service of God in accordance with a logical conceptual system, thereby making them available to a broader public. At the time, the revelation of these secrets, through publication in book form, aroused severe controversy.[27] As might be expected, his critics advocated limiting mystical contemplation to a select elite, and sought to guide the broad public to a simple faith and fear of God. However, R. Shneur Zalman remained adamant: "it is impossible to be God-fearing without contemplation."[28] The Alter Rebbe also devoted himself wholeheartedly to organizational activity, establishing new Hasidic centers. The social situation created as a result of this activity was described by one of his critics, R. Asher of Stolin, as follows: "There are thousands upon thousands, almost an entire country, who only speak in secrets of Torah and in allusions."[29] This portrait is drawn in exaggerated language, but even according to Habad tradition there were many who opposed the Rabbi of Lyady's declaration that "It is my definite opinion that one ought to teach the path to the many."[30] These dissenters were unable to tolerate this new order, which "sought out and revealed such an intense [spiritual] light to young people."[31]

These old traditions of Habad reappeared in each generation, shaping the consciousness of the rebbes and their disciples both with regard to the question of organizational activism and the dissemination of mystical secrets. As the previous rebbe, R. Joseph Isaac Schneerson, wrote concerning organizational matters: "We may assume that propagating is not without fruit. . . . Organization and the dissemination of its ideas have always occupied an important place in the Hasidic camp."[32] Or, as the present rebbe stated not long ago:

> One ought not to think that, because some people are on the "outside," on a lower level, one therefore ought to teach them only in accordance with their lower degree. [One should not think that] the more "elevated" matters of Hasidism, because they are so "precious," are irrelevant for those who are on the "outside" . . . [On the contrary,] we emphasize that study of the doctrines of Hasidism must be performed through the manner of spreading forth—disseminating them widely, to the very furthest place, without any contraction or limitations.[33]

The Hasid is called on to adhere to the ways of godliness—to disseminate and to "spread his fount outward" without limit. All are invited to share in the mystical secrets, without which true service of God is inconceivable.[34]

Indeed, today the spiritual and social mission imposed on Habad Hasidim is stressed with full urgency. This three-fold mission is directed first toward those observant Jews outside of the Habad camp, second toward those Jews who are removed from religious observance of Torah and mitzvot, and third toward the other nations of mankind. Let us examine these areas one by one.

In its earliest days, Hasidism already taught that the authentic religious leader enjoys an inward, essential connection with the members of his flock, and his soul encompasses the souls of all his Hasidim and unites them together. According to some doctrines, the soul of the tzaddik is connected in its root to the souls of the entire Congregation of Israel, wherever they may be. It is "composed" of all of them together and therefore embodies the inner spiritual structure of the whole people. The tzaddik thus serves as an intermediary between the individual Jew and his or her God, as "the influx of the Creator, blessed be He, is very great. It is thus impossible to receive his influx save by means of an intermediary."[35]

Contemporary Habad Hasidism preserves the original, radical formulation of this view. Thus the present rebbe is accustomed to speak of the "universal soul"[36] of his own teacher and predecessor, while his own disciples speak and write about him in even more superlative terms. For example, in a 1983 issue of the newsletter *Kfar Habad*, we read that the substantive connection of every Jew to the rebbe is "an existing fact that does not require the confirmation [of the individual], a fact stemming from the very place of the soul [of each person] as a small fragment of the Jewish soul organism, which the Rebbe—the brain—oversees." Denial of this inner connection by any Jew is "tantamount to denial of his very belonging to the Jewish people—Heaven forbid!"[37] By definition, this view recognizes neither the existence of non-Hasidic trends within Judaism, nor that of the numerous other Hasidic courts and rebbes: there are only those who are actual and conscious Habad Hasidim, and those who are potential, unaware Habad Hasidim. Both groups are objectively anchored in the same "universal soul." Rabbi Halperin, editor of *Kfar Habad*, wrote on the occasion of the rebbe's eightieth birthday (1982):

> It is incumbent upon us to light the torch of faith in the Moses of our generation.[38] . . . Specifically, during this era and in these days, it is obligatory to emphasize that faith in the Rebbe and connection to the Prince of the Generation is not merely one more detail of Divine service, however important a detail it may be. Faith in the leader of the generation is the primary and necessary condition for removing the entire Jewish people from the voracious mire, and to redeem them eternally. . . . For this reason, we should not, under any circumstances, respond with kid gloves to expressions of opposition to our father and shepherd.[39]

In other words, there is only one authentic Judaism[40] and one "Moses of this generation," and Habad Hasidim are the emissaries and disseminators of this truth. This, then, is their first mission.

Their second mission follows from the first: the adherents of Habad entirely reject the concept of a "secular Jew." Just as they reject the very separation between the sacred and the profane, they deny the distinction between a Jew who is "religious" and sanctified and one who is "secularized." Jewish religious identity is a matter of essence and substance; it is a given, objective fact. It is not based on ethnic, cultural, mental or historical factors, or even on the actual relationship of the individual to Torah and to *halakha* (Jewish law), but is rather a result of the divine nature of the Jewish soul. Thus when Rabbi Eliezer Schach, an opponent of Habad, recently challenged secularists and kibbutz members within Israel with the provocative question, "In what way are you Jewish?" the Lubavitcher rebbe cried out in protest, affirming the solid Jewish identity of each and every Jew, both far and near. The power of inner, objective Jewish merit is far greater than that of external, voluntary will; potential being, even if unconscious, is stronger than conscious actuality. The basic religious and social mission of Habad is thus intended to elevate the conscious choice of the individual to the level of one's inner Jewish chosenness, that is, to actualize one's inner given holiness.[41] In order to accomplish this aim, one must go out into the streets to persuade the Jew to place tefillin on his arm and to say Shema Yisrael. One does not sit passively, waiting for individual Jews to make a spontaneous, conscious decision, but one seeks him or her out, to restore them to their own nature and roots (even if only by performing a mizvah on a one-time basis). Thus the rebbe has taught: "The importance of a Jew does not stem from his own self, but from his attachment to and union with the Holy One, blessed be He. He is not an independent being; rather, all of his existence is the existence of the Holy One, blessed be He!"[42]

Again this monistic view, which considers all of Israel as one objective unity, clearly rejects any possibility of intra-Jewish religious pluralism. It similarly erects an ontological barrier between Jews and non-Jews, interpreting the singularity of the Jewish people as a metaphysical, innate trait of chosenness.

It is precisely against this background that we confront the third mission of the contemporary Habad Hasid, that directed exclusively toward the Gentiles. The chosen are not exempt from responsibility. On the contrary: in recent years the rebbe has increasingly emphasized that the encounter with the non-Jew also entails a religious challenge of the first order. His remarks concerning this subject reveal an attentiveness and sensitivity to new developments in the social and political condition of the Jews in the West.

It is well known that the Jewish religion is a particularistic one: it does not seek out members of other peoples in order to convert them to Judaism. Non-Jews may fulfill their obligation to the Creator by performing a limited number of religious and ethical demands (including, first and foremost, refraining from idolatry, bloodshed, and sexual license) and by establishing an appropriate social and legal order. Withal, in those times and places where Jews enjoy political power,[43] the halakha requires that one impose fulfillment of these universalistic obligations on the non-Jews. Indeed, the Lubavitcher rebbe openly demands that his followers tranform every encounter with the non-Jew, whether it be political or commercial, into an arena of persuasion by which their interlocuter would be brought closer to the observance of the Noachide commandments. In his words, the present situation of individual Jews grants them social and political opportunities unavailable to their persecuted ancestors, inviting them to expand the domain of direct religious responsibility to include other peoples and faiths![44] Habad Hasidim even elicited a positive declaration from President Ronald Reagan on the subject of the Noachide commandments, which they interpreted as additional confirmation that the time was ripe to take upon themselves this univ-ersalistic responsibility.

The rebbe has gone even further in this demand by claiming that the Jewish people are called on to prepare the nations of mankind for the forthcoming redemption. All Jews should prepare their non-Jewish counterparts to meet a world of peace, brother-hood, and universal faith. Jews are called on to convince non-Jews to act—right now—in a way "similar to the [anticipated perfection in messianic] times."[45] From now on, the prophetic vision of the End of Days must serve Jews as a guiding norm in their educational encounter with non-Jews. This directive clearly goes far beyond the origi-nal boundaries of the seven Noachide commandments, transcending the limits of their minimal demands within the historical realm into the utopian realm.

To the best of my knowledge, these concepts have no precedent in Jewish his-tory. They attract our attention in several respects: they reflect a clear consciousness of the new historical transformation—a consciousness not at all common in the ultra-Orthodox world; they illustrate the powerful messianic tension to be observed in contemporary Habad Hasidism; and they bear some similarity to trends on the con-temporary American scene. Likewise the Lubavitcher rebbe, unlike the overwhelming majority of Jewish religious leaders in the United States (including Orthodox lead-ers), supported introduction of a "moment of silence" in the U.S. public schools. The other leaders feared this innovation because it represented a breakdown in the wall of separation between church and state[46] (which presumably would be against Jewish interests), and because it had the potential for alienating Jewish pupils within the public schools. The rebbe, on the other hand, gave greater weight to the universal religious interest, as he understood it, wishing that every non-Jewish child confront his or her Creator each morning.

Acute Messianism

I have discussed the role played by traditional patterns of thought in shaping the present path of Habad Hasidism, both in terms of the broadening of the scope of religious involvement ("every path," "every place") and in terms of social expansion and conquest ("every person"). By way of contrast, I turn to manifestations of social and ideological change.

By far the most important change in the ethos and style of contemporary Habad, in contrast with earlier generations, is its placement of messianic concerns at the focus of religious consciousness and religious life. In this respect there has been a definite transformation: at the beginning of its path, Habad Hasidism advocated an approach of silence and the suppression of questions of collective historical messianic redemption, whereas today it is marked by clear expressions of concrete, acute messianic tension, unparalleled in latter-day Judaism. Moreover, the absolute certainty of the imminent coming of the Messiah has now become the supreme and decisive test of Jewish faith.

Generally speaking, the founders of Hasidism seldom addressed themselves to the messianic question, neutralizing *ab initio* any concrete messianic tension.[47] Hasidism treated any discussion of redemption in the social sphere, both national and universal, as marginal, concentrating most of its attention on the personal salvation of the individual, that is, on the mystical *tikkun* (correction) of the inner spiritual exile, here and now. Hasidism of course remained loyal to the traditional Jewish utopian vision, but it was not this vision that served as the impetus for the Hasidic religious revival or prompted it to shed new light upon the service of God. The tendency toward suppression of messianism is clearly reflected in the writings of the first teachers of the Habad school as well. Like their counterparts, they preferred to concern themselves with the inner redemption of the individual[48] rather than with the external, historical redemption of the community. At the same time, they stressed the constant divine presence which sustains the world, rather than the transcendent, singular messianic breakthrough anticipated in the future. The reader is thus hard put to find in the writings of the first four leaders of Habad any serious attempt to clarify the question of collective redemption.

This silence was partially broken at the beginning of the twentieth century by the fifth leader of Habad, R. Shalom Dov Baer Schneersohn (Maharshab), who addressed a number of theoretical questions concerning messianic redemption. The Zionist national awakening was the immediate cause for his open engagement with messianism. R. Shalom Dov Baer perceived Zionism as a pretentious attempt to force the End and to realize explicitly messianic goals (first and foremost, the ingathering of exiles) by human means; he therefore declared war against it. This struggle required him to pose an alternative model of authentic—heavenly, miraculous, and spiritual—messianism against the deceptive Zionist ambition. He attempted to provide the ideo-logical underpinnings for the traditional approach that requires the Jewish people to practice complete historical and political passivity until the coming of the divine re-demption.[49] Needless to say, he calls on the Jew to engage in intensive spiritual ac-tivity—and in particular, to spread the teachings of Hasidism—so as to bring nigh the redemption. However, "we must not heed them [the Zionists] in their call to achieve redemption through our own powers, for we are not permitted to hasten the End even by reciting too many prayers [*sic*],[50] much less so by corporeal strata-gems—that is, to set out from Exile by force."[51] Habad was hence called on to clarify the fundaments of the traditional belief in a national messianic redemption.

Only forty years later, the third stage in the development of the messianic approach within the Habad movement emerged—acute messianic tension. Such a tension was clearly manifested during the period of the Holocaust, when the previous rebbe, R. Joseph Isaac Schneerson, cried out in public for an "immediate redemption!" This may be seen as a classical example of catastrophic messianism: the leader led his flock during a period of indescribable suffering and experienced one exile after another. He witnessed the pogroms against the Jews of Russia at the beginning of the century, the Communist Revolution, and civil war; he was imprisoned, released, fled to Latvia and Poland, and, at the outbreak of World War II, was saved by his disciples and settled upon the alien soil of the United States. It is not surprising that he should have clearly seen the destruction of European Jewry as the height of the birthpangs of the Messiah:

> The troubles of Israel have now reached the most terrible degree; the people of Israel have undergone the birthpangs of the Messiah. . . . Therefore, the days of the redemption shall come immediately. This is the only true answer to the destruction of the world and to the anguish of the Jews. . . . Be ready for redemption soon, shortly, in our day! . . . The righteous redeemer is already at our window, and the time to prepare ourselves to receive his face is now very short![52]

The late rebbe thereby found his own way of endowing the Holocaust with a religious meaning: not a punishment for the sins of the past, as has been claimed by a number of ultra-Orthodox leaders, but the collapse of the present world order in anticipation of future redemption.

Rabbi Joseph Isaac came out with manifestos in the newspapers in three different languages, publicly heralding the approaching redemption as "a matter of fact" and "nearer than near." This declaration provided him an opportunity to call on the people to return to God fully and wholeheartedly in order to merit seeing the face of the Redeemer. Nothing is left for Israel, he said, but to "polish up the buttons of the royal garments" and thereafter "Immediate Repentance! Immediate Redemption!"

It was under the leadership of the present rebbe, R. Menachem Mendel Schneer-son, however, that this messianic tension reached its peak. Under his leadership, it has grown from year to year, indeed, from week to week. Every act and sermon, every "campaign" and call, is accompanied by clear messianic indications. The rebbe repeatedly tells his Hasidim that the Redeemer will appear to them, with his full glory and miracles, tomorrow, today, now!

> The King Messiah can come immediately, "in a twinkling of an eye." . . . And he certainly will come immediately. And as this is so, then clearly the King Messiah is already present in the world. . . . Moreover, he is present as a "great man" [a *gadol*] . . . a king from the house of David who meditates upon the Torah and performs its commandments, like David his ancestor."[53] Therefore, in our generation, there must be an extra emphasis upon everything connected with the faith in the coming of Messiah and the anticipation of his coming—a faith and anticipation which penetrate all of a person's reality, all the faculties of his soul.[54]

Here the rebbe creates an acute anticipation (perhaps in the belief that consciousness will shape reality?) of receiving the messianic revelation.[55] Likewise he appeals for spiritual intensity, for constant religious agitation: there is so much that can be accomplished and so little time left! "It is within the grasp of each of us to act so that the redemption will come quickly, not just tomorrow or after some time, but today, literally. . . . At this very moment one opens one's eyes and sees our righteous Messiah among us, in this very synagogue and in this very Study House, flesh and blood, soul and body."[56] This concrete, personal appearance of the Messiah is meant to bring about a total transformation—both historical and cosmic-metaphysical—"a new creation," the resurrection of the dead, and the restoration of the world in the kingdom of the Almighty. Who would not lend hand and heart to hasten this occurrence? However, unlike the messianic hope of the late rebbe, which sprang from a sense of crisis and catastrophe, the messianic tension of the 1990s is specifically connected with a feeling of well-being and optimism, of success and fulfillment. The birthpangs of the Messiah and their terrible travails have passed and are no more: "Trouble shall not rise up a second time" (Nahum 1:9).

On the eve of the Gulf War, the rebbe issued a call against the distribution of gas masks in the State of Israel. He promised his loyal disciples that God would protect and shelter the inhabitants of the Holy Land; indeed, many of his followers refused to accept the gas masks that were distributed by the Israeli army to all residents. The rebbe called on his Hasidim to visit Israel despite the approaching war and at the same time forbade its inhabitants to leave it. "It is obvious," he said during those difficult days, "that after the Holocaust, distress shall not rise up a second time—neither hide nor hair of it, heaven forbid! To the contrary: there will be only goodness and mercy, goodness which will be revealed to all the children of Israel, wherever they are. I stress—goodness that is sensed and manifest!"[57]

Similarly, the campaign to persuade non-Jews to fulfill the universal Noachide commandments and to prepare themselves for redemption was based on the claim that the current situation of Jews in the United States—"a kingdom of kindness"—presents each Jew with new possibilities unavailable to his or her persecuted ancestors from Asia or Europe. In the late 1980s and early 1990s, the fall of the communist empire, the disintegration of the Soviet Union, and the cessation of the armaments race between the superpowers were seen by the rebbe as constituting an explicit messianic sign, moving the nations of the world away from atheistic heresy and closer to observance of the Noachide commandments, while advancing the entire world toward fulfillment of the prophetic vision of peace—"they shall beat their swords into plowshares." Moreover, unlike his predecessor, R. Joseph Isaac, who made redemption solely dependent on repentance, the present rebbe foresees unconditional redemption. This, then, is the nature of the fourth, optimistic stage in the messianic development within the Habad movement.

This type of messianism, which has flourished under conditions of prosperity, success and conquest, must seek crest after crest, one climax after another. Otherwise, it cannot sustain the rising religious tension or renew the fervor of redemption. The previous, catastrophic type of messianism was supported by actual distress and suffering; it required no other incentive. A messianism of prosperity, however, constantly requires new stimuli and ever-growing audacity; it is not designed for patience or for protracted waiting, and certainly does not leave room for a "descent for the sake of ascent," for a downfall or crisis. This is in fact the story of the Habad movement today.

At the end of the 1980s, and even more so at the beginning of the 1990s, Habad Hasidim began to publish announcements in newspapers and on billboards openly proclaiming the imminence of the Messiah. The movement also published many pamphlets and newsletters on the subject of the Redemption. In his public sermons and talks, the rebbe himself repeatedly aroused this acute tension, intentionally placing the element of concrete messianic expectation in the focus of the religious consciousness of his Hasidim. At the end of Passover 5751 (April 1991), the Rebbe aroused an emotional storm by placing on the shoulders of his followers, of each man and woman, the direct responsibilty for the coming of the Messiah. To the astonishment of his Hasidim, he declared that he himself had exhausted all his efforts, all his spiritual powers, and that the final push was solely dependent on each individual and community. "Were you to pray and cry out in truth, then certainly, certainly, Messiah would already have come!" On Shabbat Pirlhas 5751 (6 July 1991), the rebbe inspired an even greater emotional frenzy when "he spoke of the coming of Messiah in sharp and clear terms, such as had never been heard before"[58]—to quote the Habad Hasidim themselves. He said:

> Certainly, without any doubt or shadow of a doubt, the time of redemption has already come. We have already seen concrete miracles witnessing that this is *the year in which King Messiah shall be be revealed,* leading to *the hour that the King Messiah* comes . . . and to the proclamation that, "behold this one [i.e., the King Messiah] comes" [Cant. 2:8]—*he has already come!* That is, we already stand upon the threshold of the days of Messiah, at the beginning of the Redemption, and immediately [there shall be] its continuation and completion.[59]

Since that day, even such declarations have become almost a matter of routine.

From the perspective of many individuals within Habad, the messianic tension is focused on the personality of the rebbe himself. He is spoken of in terms the Jewish tradition reserves for the Messiah alone, and some have taken this language to such extremes that in the past they have brought on the wrath of the rebbe.[60] However, all within Habad regard him as the most worthy "candidate" for the title, a kind of potential Messiah. Indeed, has not the rebbe himself said, they whisper privately, that "the King Messiah is already present in the world." Moreover, is he not present as a *gadol* (a great man)?[61] Nevertheless, the rebbe takes pains to base his authority and the source of his inspiration upon his predecessor, R. Joseph Isaac. To him, and to him alone, he ascribes the title Prince of our Generation. Likewise, the rebbe publicly expressed his displeasure when he realized that several of his Hasidim were gazing at him during prayer, rather than concentrating their hearts entirely on their Father in Heaven. Still, the messianic dynamic has a power and a logic of its own.[62]

We find in the contemporary Habad movement a collective messianic agitation utterly unlike anything that has preceded it; indeed, it would seem its like has not been seen in Jewish history since the seventeenth century. Needless to say, the Hasid, unlike the outsider, would deny any deviation from the traditional path of Habad. The earlier rebbes, he would claim, who knew themselves and their generation to be remote from the time of redemption, deliberately refrained from arousing messianic tension. "A long time yet before the time of Redemption," R. Shneur Zalman of Lyady said, "the Messianic outcry is not yet heard."[63] But this was not the case with the previous rebbe, who felt on his flesh the very birthpangs of Messiah. And the present rebbe, with his spiritual vision, himself perceives the rapid approach of the Messiah. They have been obliged "to cry out" and agitate every Jewish heart.

To express these developments in mystical language: in his day, R. Shneur Zalman of Lyady taught that "the Redeemer will only come after the completion of all the *beirurim* [the spiritual-cosmic process of 'selection' and 'correction' by returning the Divine 'sparks' to their source]."[64] His early heirs expressed themselves in like spirit.[65] On the other hand, the fifth rebbe, R. Shalom Dov Baer, said that "Now is the most final *beirur!*" and thus, "Ours is the generation of Messiah."[66] His son, R. Joseph Isaac, already saw the completion of the process of "selection" and "correction, " and thus publicly declared that "nothing is left but to polish up the buttons [of the royal garments]." Finally, the present rebbe explicitly said: "The service of the *beirurim* has been completed!"—that is, "All those [mystical] services needed to be performed in the time of the Exile have already been finished." In other words, the spiritual mission incumbent upon the Jewish people during the Exile has been completed and realized. If so, what possible reason can remain for the continuation of the Exile? And if it no longer has any reason, is not the path paved for the complete Redemption? "Thus," the rebbe said, "one may give thanks, and bless over the birth and revelation of the Messiah, *Sheheheyanu*—who has kept us alive and sustained us and brought us to *this day*."[67] In sum, what the outside observer perceives as historical and ideological transformations within Habad are seen by the believer as cosmic and metaphysical ones taking place in reality. The former are no more than the appropriate religious response to the latter.[68]

The messianic excitement within the Habad movement in the late 1980s and early 1990s is entirely detached from the State of Israel and its enterprises; needless to say, it has nothing in common with contemporary religious-Zionist messianism. True, the contemporary Habad movement has moved away considerably from its earlier militant struggle against the Jewish political and national revival, but even today it continues to reject the Zionist ethos. For example, the rebbe directs his followers to maintain each of the Jewish diasporas until the actual messianic revelation. Moreover, he continues to decry any religious tendency to relate to the State of Israel as the "beginning of redemption." Neither is the hawkish political stance the rebbe demands of the Israeli government—prohibiting any territorial withdrawal in favor of the Arabs—ideologically related to the position of any Zionist party.[69] Rabbi Aaron Dov Halperin, editor of *Kfar Habad,* explains this stance as "total opposition to Zionism and nationalism, coupled with a stringent prohibition against handing over a single inch of the territory that the Lord has granted us."[70] Habad political radicalism thus stems from different motivations. Officially it relies on a halakhic argument, proscribing Jews from turning over any portion of the Holy Land to non-Jews, at any time, as well as on a security argument, portraying the occupied territories as a necessary guarantee against enemy incursion into the area of Jewish settlement. However, on a deeper level, these political stances are directly connected with the acute *messianic* consciousness, which is, by its very nature, one of constant advance and conquest, not of retreat and withdrawal. It does not guide the believer toward compromise, but toward striving for wholeness and perfection, in both the temporal and the spiritual realm. The rebbe likewise calls on Jews to liberate themselves once and for all from the lowly stature that has characterized their relationship to other nations. The reality of Exile has shrunk and enslaved the Jewish soul, say the contemporary Lubavitchers; therefore, on the eve of Redemption, one needs to be freed of the exile mentality and to develop a new, proud, and erect stature.

On the face of it, these remarks suggest an interesting parallel to the classical Zionist idea of "negation of the Exile." For Habad, however, it is only the miraculous Redeemer who can bring Israel out of exile; the Jews are commanded only to prepare their hearts. In taking on this newly erect stature, the Jew is preparing to resist any non-Jew who tries to transgress against Jewish property. This resistance is not limited to the Land of Israel but is demanded as much in the Crown Heights neighborhood of Brooklyn (the rebbe forbade his followers to move out of their neighborhood, whose peaceful character seemed threatened by the intrusion of non-Jewish population) as in Gaza and Jericho.[71] The principle is one and the same, although of course in the Holy Land the validity of this principle is even greater and based on additional religious arguments.

Thus the circle has been closed in an ironic manner. The messianic swell in Habad Hasidism, which is self-sustaining and constantly searching for new heights, eventually brought many of the Hasidim to the conclusion that they must take the initiative of giving the messianic cart a final push by "helping" and encouraging the rebbe to reveal himself as Messiah—that is, to actualize his potential messiahhood through "coronation" by the public. Initially, some made cautious hints and restrained articulations. When the Rebbe did not protest, as he had in the past, people became more daring. During the winter of 1991, Hasidim began to distribute petitions among

Jewish communities, asking that people, in thousands and tens of thousands, declare in writing that they took upon themselves the kingship of "His holiness, the Rebbe, long may he live, the King Messiah." A group of Habad women even publicly turned to the rebbe, insisting that he no longer conceal his messianic mission—"that he be revealed to all eyes as the King Messiah, and immediately take us out of Exile!"[72] The traditional activism of Habad Hasidim, which now reached a stage of hyperactivism, was thus turned toward the rebbe himself, that is, toward as it were, the Messiah. No wonder their severe opponents in the ultra-Orthodox camp, the Lithuanian *misnagdim,* hurled against them one of the severest possible charges—that they were engaged in false messianism of the Zionist type, which sought to bring redemption by human efforts.

This is the irony: its opponents have come to regard Habad Hasidim, which at the turn of the century moved toward a theoretical examination of the messianic question as a negative response to Zionism, as a new and distorted manifestation of Zionist activism. Thus an official statement published by the circles of the mitnagdim declared that "This is a clear denial of the kingdom of heaven. . . . They have turned the Messiah, the desire of all Israel in all the generations, from the act of the Holy One blessed be He to an act of man." This is, in quintessence, "the Zionist outlook, which succeeded in penetrating also to Jews who observe mizvot: their idea that it is within the power of human beings to take themselves out of Exile and to achieve Redemption."

Needless to say, the objective observer can distinguish quite clearly between the historical activism of Zionism, which took place entirely within the earthly political plane, and the messianic activism of Habad, which is located entirely in the religious-spiritual plane. However, one cannot deny that even this latter messianic activism exposes the profound process of transformation which has taken place within Lubavitch. The fifth rebbe, R. Shalom Dov Baer Schneerson, explicitly wrote in 1899: "We must not heed them [i.e., the Zionists] in their call to achieve redemption through our own powers, for we are not permitted allowed to hasten the End even by reciting too many prayers concerning this!" Thus, Habad's opponents, cleverly basing their claim on the words of earlier Habad rebbes, argue that the contemporary activity and mindset of their Hasidic rivals revolves precisely around this type of "too many prayers" and "hastening the End."

In light of all that has been said, and especially in light of my claim that, since the seventeenth century, there has been no precedent in Jewish history to the present messianic agitation in Habad, one might wonder if this new phenomenon is a replay in smaller scale of the Sabbatian messianic hysteria that swept over the Jewish communities in 1666. I think not. First, Habad messianism is in no way connected with any violation of the bounds of Jewish religious law and has thus far not revealed any sign of religious antinomianism. On the contrary, the very laws and norms of the Torah constitute the laws and norms of the Redemption; the messianic process is completely subject to the halakhic criteria and guidelines set down by Maimonides in the final section of his Mishneh Torah. Moreover, this messianic arousal is not accompanied by any significant political or economic change in their way of life. The Hasidim draw a sharp distinction between their mystical consciousness and messianic fervor, on the one hand, and their pragmatic realism and practical shrewdness in everyday life, on the other. Unlike participants in other historical precedents, these Jews do not pack their belongings to greet the anticipated aliyah to the Land of Israel, nor do they sell their homes or cease their professional activities. *Olam ke-minhago noheg*—"the world goes on as always."

At the beginning of 1992, for example, the rebbe demanded that the government of Israel stand firm against any international pressure and refuse to grant autonomy to the Palestinian inhabitants of the West Bank and Gaza Strip. In his words, political or civil autonomy would likely bring about, over the course of years, the establishment of an independent, hostile Palestinian state. The naïve listener might well ask: What have we to do with gradual historical processes and long-range political considerations? Have we not just said that "this is the year in which the King Messiah shall be revealed" with wonders and miracles, that "immediately, Messiah comes," to redeem us from history and its travails? However, as we learn from other religious phenomena, only a clear distinction between the two realms—that of mystical religious consciousness and of practical, pragmatic life—enables believers to continue functioning within the real world. Indeed, this distinguishes them from visionary dreamers and moonstruck eccentrics. Believers pray to God to heal their children, but immediately turn to an expert physician. In contemporary Habad Hasidism, too, the faith is firmly messianic, but politics continue to be conducted in the world as it is, and business as usual proceeds in all the other areas of everyday life—work, trade, family, medicine, and so forth. The messianic future, as close as it may be, does not intrude into the present or threaten to upset it.

Habad Hasidism walks at the edge of the precipice, yet at this writing it has avoided the danger of falling into the abyss. The more urgent question, of course, is the extent to which Habad Hasidism can maintain this radical tension, draw upon constantly renewed stores of energy, and continue to ascend from height to height, without reaching a crisis.

Spiritual and Corporeal

An additional change manifest today in the life of Habad Hasidim, a pattern not found in original Habad ideology, is the all-inclusive, total role of the rebbe in shaping the concrete life and destiny of his Hasid.

R. Shneur Zalman of Lyady differed from the majority of contemporaneous Hasidic teachers in limiting the role of the Hasidic tzaddik to spiritual guidance and moulding the spiritual personality of the Jew. The tzaddik should not be expected to perform miracles or to aid his disciples in worldly matters; instead, it is his task to direct their paths in the service of God and toward closeness to Him. "Has there ever been in the past, or have you seen such a custom in any of the books of the earlier or later sages of Israel, that one ask [his rabbi] for counsel regarding corporeal matters?"

R. Shneur Zalman responded to his followers' request that he advise them in worldly matters.[73]

Contemporary scholars are divided as to whether the Rabbi of Lyady actually adhered to this theoretical principle, that is, whether he actually turned away all the appeals of his suffering followers.[74] However, they believe that unlike other Hasidic leaders, he made a tremendous effort to halt expectations of the rebbe's involvement in their material life. As the Alter Rebbe himself had heard from one of his own teachers, R. Menahem Mendel of Vitebsk, "The help of the bodies is beyond our power."[75]

Erosion of this principle occurred under the leadership of his successors. Habad traditions concerning Shneur Zalman's concept of religious leadership were faithful to the historical facts. For example, an important treatise composed during the last generation repeatedly reports that the Rabbi of Lyady refused to respond to the majority of requests concerning material needs and even ordered "to make it known and to publicize, that everybody who seeks advise in corporeal matters . . . will not be answered."[76] Yet the present social expansion of Habad Hasidism, combined with the strengthened charismatic position of the rebbe, further deepened the gap between the traditional, theoretical position and the actual practice. The dependence of the Hasidim on their rebbe regarding matters of livelihood and healing, business and matchmaking, society and politics, knows no limits; a loyal Hasid will make no significant decision without asking the blessing of the rebbe. Moreover, Hasidic oral tradition removes R. Shneur Zalman's remarks from their literal context. It is impossible, they say, to separate the physical and spiritual well-being of the Hasid, to distinguish between "earthly matters" and "heavenly matters." In any event, they emphasize, the Rabbi of Lyady qualified his remarks by implying that one may ask corporeal advice of those who are "true prophets . . . as there were aforetimes in Israel" (according to an oral communication from Rabbi Tuviah Blau).[77]

Conclusion

I began my discussion by asking whether the success of Habad Hasidism and the place it has carved for itself, both in the United States and in Israel, are rooted purely in sociological factors—its organization, structure, and charismatic leader—or whether they are also based on immanent conceptual elements, inherent in the traditional ideology and theology of this movement. I now conclude by formulating a dual answer to this question.

On the one hand, the Habad tendency to broaden the scope of religious involvement as far as possible, to include all those realms and horizons open to modern man, is deeply rooted in its traditional theological apprehension. It is this very apprehension which has enabled Habad, even today, to adjust itself to and conquer even the realm of the "secular." We have also seen that the typical activism, the "mission," and the social dynamism of contemporary Habad Hasidism are similarly rooted in its classical ideological elements. In other words, in terms of both aspects—"every place" and "every man"—the encounter between the new and the old has been a story of success and fecundity.

On the other hand, facing modern reality—confronting the historical activism of Zionism, and even more so, encountering a situation of freedom and prosperity—served as a radicalizing factor, shaping its messianic sensibility, which led it from one peak to another to the threshold of crisis. Habad Hasidism, which germinated and developed over the course of generations under conditions of hardship and oppression, eventually reached a state of intoxication once the surrounding environment became favorable. Similarly, the total personal dependency on the rebbe and his guidance, developed over the course of more than forty years, contributed in no small measure to this messianic development. The ninety-year-old rebbe is childless and has never openly prepared his own successor. Thus the inescapable threat of the end was gradually transformed and redeemed in Habad Hasidism consciousness into the long-awaited, ineluctable End.

Should this Hasidic group be required, at some point in the future, to exist without a messianic revelation and without the living presence of the charismatic tzaddik, it will likely be able to sustain the first two patterns, the models of ideological continuity described above ("every place" and "every person"). By contrast, the latter two patterns—the acute, concrete messianism and intense personal dependence—are likely to lose their force and even to be revealed as a subversive factor: it is unlikely that a charismatic heir of the stature of R. Menahem Mendel Schneersohn will emerge in the foreseeable future. There are spiritual and institutional interests of the highest order which will assure the continuity of the movement in one fashion or another, perhaps under collective leadership or under a "temporary" substitute (in the hope that a destructive battle of succession will thereby be averted). It is difficult to believe, however, that the movement will sustain its present powers of mass attraction or its present social impact. If it can no longer breathe the air of the peaks, it is doomed to exist on a different scope and with a different social coloration.

As I finished writing this chapter, the elderly rebbe was suddenly stricken by a severe illness. All pray for his speedy recovery and deliverance; yet the Hasidim have now been forced to halt and to tarry, in the absence of the flowing and fermenting prophetic voice—an unaccustomed, confusing wait for which they have not been prepared. They are now forced, for the first time, to stand up to a crisis and make personal and collective decisions by themselves, a heavy yoke from which they have been exempt for decades. A group of Habad rabbis in North America, who were no longer able to restrain themselves, published a "clear rabbinic ruling" declaring the messiahhood of the Lubavitcher rebbe! They anointed him as "a king of the Davidic dynasty" and concluded that the Divine oath should be applied to the rebbe: "His light shall never be extinguished, and that he shall live eternally—the life of the soul within the body" (14 April 1992).

This is in fact a prayer, a crying out, a rejection of the apparent state of affairs. It is an "activist" attempt to re-create the historical and metaphysical reality in a time of travail. Other Habad rabbis expressed their explicit opposition to this act, presumably not only for theological reasons. They realized that such a radical move would be likely to exacerbate the crisis—to deepen the fixation on the charismatic figure of the present leader—and thereby place obstacles in the way of the future renewal of the movement. In short, the future of Habad Hasidism, and the fate of this messianic model, which flourished under conditions of prosperity, has yet to be decided.

Is it not possible that the fears of the founding father, R. Shneur Zalman of Lyady, were justified regarding the far-reaching consequences for his community of emancipation, prosperity, and conquest?

Notes

1. H. M. Heilman, *Beit Rebbi* (Jerusalem, 1953), pp. 92–94.

2. This "paradox" thereafter appeared repeatedly, in various guises, among different Hasidic populations. According to a Hasidic tradition, when R. Menachem Mendel of Kotzk heard that "the government had decided to give the Jews equal rights, [he] burst into bitter tears." Yehezkel Rotenberg and Moshe Sheinfeld, *Ha-Rabbi mi-Kotsk veshishim gibborim saviv lo* (Tel Aviv, 1959), pt. 1, p. 71. "When Jews are dwelling in a foreign land, they should be aliens, not citizens." Shimon Federbusch, *Ha-Hasidut ve-Zion* (New York, 1963), p. 96. That is, Federbusch perceived that prosperity and equality severely diminish the Jewish consciousness of exile, upsetting the feeling of strangeness and separateness the Jew should cultivate in premessianic times in the lands of dispersion. For detailed sources and other examples, see Mendel Piakarcz, *Hasidut Polin* (Jerusalem, 1990), p. 269.

3. Shalom Dov Baer Schneersohn, *Iggerot ha-Qodesh* (New York, 1982), p. 130. Cf. Aviezer Ravitzky, "Exile in the Holy Land: The Dilemma of Haredi Jewry," in P. Y. Medding, ed., *Israel, State and Society, 1948–1988: Studies in Contemporary Jewry* (Oxford, 1989), vol. 5, pp. 113–14.

4. Of course one might argue that the rebbe here referred only to the total, messianic, ingathering of exiles of all of Israel. In any event, the rebbe was a staunch opponent—perhaps the staunchest—of the Zionist enterprise as such.

5. Moshe Goldstein, ed., *Tiqqun Olam* (Munkacs, 1936), p. 51.

6. Concerning the theology of Habad during its early generations, see Moshe Halamish, "The Theoretical Doctrine of R. Shneur Zalman of Lyady" (in Hebrew) (Ph.D. diss., Jerusalem, 1976); Rahel Elior, *The Paradoxical Ascent to God: The Kabbalistic Theosophy of Habad* (Albany, N.Y.,1992); idem, *Torat ha-Elohut ba-dor ha-sheni shel Hasidut Habad* (Jerusalem, 1982); idem, "HaBad: The Contemplative Ascent to God," in Arthur Green, ed., *Jewish Spirituality II*, vol. 14 of *World Spirituality* (New York, 1987), pp. 157–205; Louis Jacobs, *Seeker of Unity* (New York, 1966); Naftali Loewenthal, *Communicating the Infinite* (Chicago, 1990); Yoram Jacobson, "R. Shneur Zalman of Lyady's Doctrine of Creation" (in Hebrew), in *Eshel Be'er Sheva'l* (1976), pp. 307–68; Rivka Schatz, "Anti-Spiritualism in Hasidism" (in Hebrew), *Molad* 20, nos. 171–72 (1963): 516–20; Isaiah Tishby and Joseph Dan, "Hasidic Doctrine and Literature" (in Hebrew), *Ha-Enzeqlopedyah ha-'Ivrit* 17 (1965): 776–78; Amos Funkenstein, "Imitatio Dei and the Concept of Zimzum in Habad Teaching" (in Hebrew), in *Sefer ha-Yovel le-Raphael Mahler* (Tel Aviv, 1974), pp. 83–88.

7. This call was already proclaimed in the third generation of Habad Hasidism. The present rebbe is in the habit of issuing it from time to time. See, for example, the *Iggeret ha-Qodesh* which he sent prior to Rosh Hashanah 5751 (Fall 1990), published in

the Israeli press (e.g., in *Yedi 'ot Aharonot,* 17 September 1990). See M. M. Schneerson, *Sihot Qodesh—TShL"A* (Brooklyn, 1986), pt. 1, p. 63; idem, *Sha'arei Ge'ulail* (Jerusalem, 1991), pp. 168–74. But cf. Moshe Halamish, "R. Shneur Zalman of Lyady in the Land of Israel" (in Hebrew), *Hebrew Union College Annual* 61 (1990): i–xiii.

8. See Zvi Yehudah Kook, *Le-hilkhot Zibbur* (Jerusalem, 1987), p. 33

9. See Moshe Idel, "Some Conceptions of the Land of Israel in Medieval Jewish Thought," in Ruth Link-Selinger, ed., *A Straight Path: Studies in Medieval Philosophy and Culture in Honor of Arthur Hyman* (Washington, D.C., 1988), pp. 124–41; cf. *Yalqut Shim'oni* 2, sec. 503.

10. M. M. Schneersohn, *Sefer ha-Ma'amarim, TShM"V* (Brooklyn, 1986), p. 215.

11. In the rebbe's talk on *Parashat Mishpatim,* 5744 (1984), quoted in Joseph Weinberg, ed., *Shi'urim be-Sefer ha-Tanya* 3: vii. The idea that modern innovations reflect the strength and power of the Creator has long been known in Hasidic tradition. See also the rebbe's remarks concerning use of the telephone for disseminating Torah, in *Sihot Qodesh—TShL"A,* pp. 62–65.

12. See the remarks of the fifth rebbe of Habad, Shalom Dov Baer Schneerson, *Sefer ha-Ma'amarim—TR"S* (Brooklyn, 1985), p. 183.

13. *Shi'urim be-Sefer ha-Tanya* 3: xlii.

14. See Hermann Luebbe, *Saekularisierung, Geschichte eines ideenpolitishen Begriffs* (Freiburg, 1965); Jacob Katz, *Jews and Freemasons in Europe, 1723–1739* (Cambridge, Mass., 1970).

15. "Literally" *(kifshuto)* means as interpreted in earlier generations, first and foremost in Habad literature.

16. M. M. Schneerson, *Emunah u-Mada': Iggerot Qodesh* (Kfar Habad, 1974), pp. 93–99.

17. See Edmond Gosse, *Father and Son* (London, 1907), chaps. 5–16; Hava Lazarus-Yafeh, "Contemporary Fundamentalism—Judaism, Christianity, Islam," *Jerusalem Quarterly* 47 (1988): 33.

18. See M. M. Schneerson, *Hitva 'aduyot—TShM"V* (New York, 1986), III: 291; idem, *Emunah u-Mada'* Brooklyn, N.Y., 1986), pp. 103–6, 143; Y. Y. Havlin, ed., *Sha'arei Emunah* (based on the Rebbe's words) (Jerusalem, 1986), pp. 193–94.

19. Schneerson, *Emunah u-Mada',* pp. 131–33 .

20. See Havlin, *Sha'arei Emunah,* pp. 210–21 (emphasis in original). The methods of healing mentioned in the Talmud and in medieval halakhic literature likewise represent an eternal truth. See *Liqqutei Sihot* 23 (Brooklyn, 1984), pp. 33–41. However, in everyday life the rebbe advises his followers to obey their physicians "precisely" and "not to interfere with the instructions of a doctor." See *Iggerot Qodesh* 18 (Brooklyn, 1959), letter 6, p. 574.

21. Schneerson, *Emunah u-Mada',* pp. 7, 32, 46–49, 89–93, 131. Cf. Aryeh Carmell and Cyril Domb, *Challenge: Torah Views on Science and Its Problems* (Jerusalem, 1976), pp. 142–49.

22. Schneerson, *Hitva 'aduyot—TShM"V,* p. 291.

23. Schneerson, *Emunah u-Mada',* pp. 51, 136, 139–40, 146.

24. See Yeshayahu Leibovitz, *Yahadut, 'Am Yehudi u-Medinat Yisra'el* (Jerusalem, 1976), pp. 337–84.

25. Charles Liebman, *Deceptive Images* (Oxford, 1988), 43–60; idem, "Judaism and the Chaos of Modernity," in J. Neusner, ed., *Take Judaism for Example* (Chicago, 1983), pp. 143–64; Peter Berger, *The Heretical Imperative* (New York, 1979).

26. M. M. Schneerson, *Hitva 'aduyot—TShM"V,* pp. 136, 383; idem, *Sihot Qodesh—TShM"T* (Brooklyn, 1989), pt. 1, p. 132; idem, *Ma'ayenei ha-Yeshu'ah* (Brooklyn, 1988), p. 204: "to that outside, than which there is nothing further outside . . . to that lowly place, than which there is nothing lower." On the significance of the mission to other Jews, see idem, *Sefer ha-Shelihut* (Brooklyn, 1987); idem, *Sefer ha-Shelihut: TShM"A-TShN* (Brooklyn, 1991); idem, *Sefer ha-Shelihut—TShM"H* (Brooklyn, 1988), pt. 2, pp. 585–86.

27. See Mordecai Wilensky, "The Hasidic Settlement in Tiberias at the End of the Eighteenth Century" (in Hebrew), *Proceedings of the American Academy for Jewish Research* 48 (1981): i–xvii; Rahel Elior, "The Minsk Disputation" (in Hebrew), *Mehqerei Yerushalayim be-mahshevet Yisra'el* 4 (1982): 194; Emanuel Etkes, "R. Shneur Zalman of Lyady's Path as a Hasidic Leader" (in Hebrew), *Zion* 50 (1985): 324–54.

28. R. Shneur Zalman of Lyady, *Iggerot Qodesh* (New York, 1980), pp. 51, 124.

29. D. Z. Heilman, ed., *Iggerot Ba'al ha-Tanya u-venei doro* (Jerusalem, 1953), p. 185.

30. A. H. Glitzenstein, *Sefer ha-Toladot: Rabbi Shneur Zalman mi-Ladi* (Brooklyn, 1976), p. 3; Elior, "The Minsk Disputation," p. 193.

31. Elior, "The Minsk Disputation," pp. 217–18.

32. Ibid., p. 186.

33. Schneerson, *Hitva'aduyot—TShM"V,* pt. 3, p. 678; cf. idem, *Iggerot Qodesh* 9 (Brooklyn, 1954), letters 2622, 2684, 2854, 2887; 10 (1955), letters 2973, 3110; idem, *Devar Malkhut* 17, *Parashat Naso,* 5751 (1991), pp. 18–19; idem, *Quntres veha-hai yiten el libo* (Brooklyn, 1988), p. 76; idem, *Sefer ha-Ma'amarim* (Brooklyn, 1989), II: 101. For the theological basis of this idea, see, recently, idem, *Sefer ha-Ma'amarim: Bati le-gani* (Brooklyn, 1991), pt. 2, pp. 251–52.

34. See M. M. Schneerson, *Sihot Qodesh—TSh"M* (Brooklyn, 1986), I: 387–94; idem, *Liqqutei Sihot* 19 (Brooklyn, 1983), pp. 249–44; idem, *Sefer ha-Ma'amarim—TShM"V* (Brooklyn, 1986), p. 185.

35. R. Elimelekh of Lyzhensk, *No'am Elimelekh* (Jerusalem, 1960), p. 35. Cf. Yoram Jacobson, *Toratah shel ha-Hasidut* (Tel Aviv, 1985), pp. 138–42.

36. See, for example, Schneerson, *Hitva'aduyot—TShM"V* (Brooklyn, 1984), pt. 3, p. 89; idem, *Sihot Qodesh—TShM"T,* pp. 272–74.

37. Levi Levinson, *Kefar Habad,* 13 Tammuz 5743 (1983).

38. See the Tanya, chap. 42: "In every generation sparks of the soul of our teacher Moses, of blessed memory, descend, and they are embodied in the body and soul of the SaKefi of the generation"; cf. *Tiqqunei Zohar,* p. 112. The present rebbe said this concerning his predecessor (e.g., in *Sihot Qodesh—TShM"T,* p. 277), and appropriately, his followers say the same about him. See Yehezkel Sofer, "Moses Our Teacher of the '80's" (in Hebrew), *Kefar Habad,* 7 Nissan 5742 (1982).

39. Dov Halperin, *Kefar Habad,* 22 Adar 5742 (1982). See the severe attack on these positions by other schools within ultra-Orthodox Jewry, e.g., by the Satmar Hasidim: Mordecai Moshkowicz, *Quntres ha-Emet 'al Tenu'at Habad bi-shenot ha-80* (Brooklyn, n.d.); by the mitnagdim in Israel, loyal to Rabbi E. M. Schach: *Yated Ne'eman,* 4 Shevat 5787 (13 February 1987).

40. This authentic Judaism reached the height of its creative expression in the Hasidic movement, while Habad is in turn the authentic expression of this movement (the Baal Shem Tov, founder of Hasidism, is considered as the first leader of Habad).

41. See, for example, Schneerson, *Hitva'aduyot—TShM"V,* pt. 3, pp. 420, 431, 460, 486, 366.

42. Ibid., p. 515.

43. Maimonides, *Mishneh Torah: Hilkhot Melakhim* 8:10 .

44. Schneerson, *Hitva'aduyot—TShM"V,* pp. 63, 113, 525, 658; idem, *Emunah u-Mada',* pp. 32, 81. But cf. *Iggerot Qodesh* 19 (Brooklyn, 1959), letter 6474.

45. Schneerson, *Hitva'aduyot—TShM"V,* pp. 168, 184, 525.

46. Similarly, Reform Jewish leaders have recently protested Habad Hasidim's practive of placing Hanukkah menorahs on U.S. public buildings, seeing this too as a breach in the separation of church and state.

47. See Gershom Scholem, *The Messianic Idea in Judaism and Other Essays on Jewish Spirituality* (New York, 1971), pp. 176–202; idem, *Major Trends in Jewish Mysticism* (New York, 1941), pp. 328–30; Rivkah Schatz, *Hasidism as Mysticism* (Jerusalem-

Princeton, N.J., 1992), chap. 15; idem, "The Messianic Element in Hasidic Thought" (in Hebrew), *Molad* nos. 1/1 [24/211] (1967–68), pp. 105 ff. Cf. Isaiah Tishby, "The Messianic Idea and Messianic Tendencies in the Growth of Hasidism" (in Hebrew), *Zion* 32 (1967): 1–45.

48. See, for example, R. Shneur Zalman of Lyady, *Iggeret ha-Qodesh*, printed in standard editions of Tanya, [e.g., Kfar Habad, 1976], sect. 4: 210. But see also Tanya, chaps. 36–37, pp. 90–98.

49. See R. Shalom Dov Baer Schneersohn, *Torat Shalom* (Brooklyn, 1983), pp. 15, 72, 74; idem, *Ha-Ketav veha-Mikhtav* (New York, 1917); idem, *Quntres u-Ma'ayan mi-Bet ha-Shem* (New York, 1943), pp. 46–51; idem, *Iggerot Qodesh* (Brooklyn, 1982), I: 122, 130, 222, 292, 309–310; II: 337, 459, 490; S. D. Landau and Yosef Rabinowitz, eds., *Or la-Yesharim* (Warsaw, 1900), pp. 57–61; cf. Yosef Salmon, *Dat ve-Zionut* (Jerusalem, 1990), pp. 265–72.

50. This idea frequently appears in Hasidic literature. See also Rashi's commentary to Ketubot 111a, s.v., *she-lo yidhaqu*. On the other hand, see the remarks of R. Shalom Dov Baer in *Torat Shalom* (Brooklyn, 1983).

51. Landau and Rabinowitz, *Or la-Yesharim*, p. 57.

52. *Arba'ah Qol ha-Qore meha-Admo"r Shelit"a mi-Lyubavitch* (Jerusalem, 1943); *Ha-Qeri'ah ha-Qedoshah* 5701 (1941), nos. 9–11; 5702 (1942), no. 25; *Nezah Yisra'el* (Munich, August 1948); see also in the collections, *Sihot Qodesh—TSh"A* (Kfar Habad, 1981), p. 95; *Iggerot Qodesh* (Brooklyn, 1981), V: 377, 385, 408. Cf. Gershon Greenberg, "Redemption after the Holocaust according to Mahane Israel—Lubavitch, 1940–1945," *Modern Judaism* 12 (1992): 61–84.

53. Here he quotes Maimonides, *Mishneh Torah: Melakhim* 11:4.

54. Schneerson, *Hitva'aduyot—TShM""V,* III: 194. Cf. ibid., pp. 369, 450.

55. See, for example, M. M. Schneersohn, *Sefer Sihot—TShM"H* (Brooklyn, 1988), II: 533; idem, *Yein Malkhut* (Brooklyn, 1988), II: 517–18.

56. *Kefar Habad,* 10 Tamuz 5744 (1984). Cf. M. M. Schneersohn, *Sha'arei Ge'ulah* (Jerusalem, 1991), pp. 101–2.

57. M. M. Schneersohn, talk on 2 Tevet 5751 (19 January 1991), published in *Devar Malkhut, Parashat Va-era* (1991), n.p. Cf. idem, *Sefer ha-Ma'amarim—TShM"H* (Brooklyn, 1988), p. 171. These remarks were made in the context of a polemic with Rabbi E. M. Schach, leader of the Lithuanian or mitnagdic stream in Israel, who warned, on the eve of the Gulf War, of a new holocaust of punishment for abandoning religion and desecrating the Sabbath in Israel. See the reactions of those loyal to Rabbi Schach, published in *Yeted Ne'eman,* 18 Tevet 5751 (4 January 1991).

58. *Sihat ha-Shavu'a,* 238, *Devarim* 5751 (27 July 1991).

59. *Devar Malkhut* 24 (*Pinhas,* Q5731), p. 9. Emphases in the original.

60. See, for example, *Qovez Hiddushei Torah: ha-Melekh ha-Mashiah veha-ge'ulah ha-shelemah* (1983). Many Habad Hasidim deny authorship of this treatise, in which the rebbe is openly declared "the King Messiah."

61. Schneerson, *Hitva'aduyot—TShM"V,* III: 194; Maimonides, *Mishneh Torah: Melakhim 11:4.*

62. In many cases, the Hasidim only say of their rebbe what they have heard him say about his own predecessor.

63. R. Shneur Zalman of Lyady, *Torah Or* (Brooklyn, 1972).

64. R. Shneur Zalman of Lyady, *Ma'amarei Admo"r ha-Zaqen—TQS"H* (Brooklyn, 1980), p. 106. Cf. *Ma'amarei Admo"r ha-Zaqen ha-qezarim* (Brooklyn, 1981), p. 539; *Ma'amarei Admo"r ha-Zaqen—'Inyanim* (Brooklyn, 1983), p. 431.

65. For example: "Hence the Exile continues, for all the *beirurim* are not yet completed, " wrote the third rebbe of Habad, the Zemah Zedeq, "and when the *beirur* is complete, then the Messiah shall come," R. Menahem Mendel b. Baruch (Zemah Zedeq), *Or ha-Torah* (Brooklyn, 1972), VI: 1083. See also the remarks of his predecessor, the Mittler Rebbe, R. Dov Baer b.

Shneur Zalman, *Sha'arei Teshuvah* (Brooklyn, 1984), II: 45a; *Ma'amarei ha-Admo"r ha-Emza'i* (Brooklyn, 1986), p. 68a.

66. R. Shalom Dov Baer Schneersohn, *Torat Shalom* (Brooklyn, 1983), p. 74.

67. *Devar Malkhut* 13, *Parashat Emor* 5751 (1991), pp. 8–10; Shneur Zalman, *Shalarei Ge'ulah*, pp. 270–73 (emphasis in original).

68. See *Oro shel Mashiah* (Kefar Habad, 1991), pp. 5–13.

69. S. D. Wolpa, ed., *Da'at Torah be-'invenei ha-mazav be-erez ha-Qodesh* (Kiryat Gat, 1982); idem, *Shalom shalom ve-ein shalom* (Kiryat Gat, 1982); M. M. Schneersohn, *Hitva 'aduyot—TShM"V* (Brooklyn, 1982), I: 369–72; idem, *Hitva 'aduyot—TShM"G* (Brooklyn, 1983), p. 117, 243; idem, *Sefer ha-Ma'amarim—TShM"H* (Brooklyn, 1988), p. 33; idem, *Devar Malkhut* 21 (1991), p. 20.

70. *Kefar Habad*, 20 Adar I 5743 (1983).

71. See, for example, his remarks from 1979, published in *Liqqutei Sihot* 22 (Brooklyn, 1983), p. 334: "The painful question of the flight from neighborhoods populated by Jews [in New York City] . . .

and in a similar way [!] the painful and astonishing 'question' of the return of territories in the Holy Land."

72. See Yair Sheleg, "Ve-af al pi she-yitmahmehah," *Kol ha-'Ir*, 14 February 1992.

73. R. Shneur Zalman of Lyady, *Iggerot Qodesh* (Brooklyn, 1980), p. 56.

74. See Tishby and Dan, "Hasidic Doctrine and Literature," pp. 783–84; Moshe Halamish, "The Relation between Leader and Community in the Teaching of R. Shneur Zalman of Lyady," in Yehezkel Cohen, ed., *Hevrah ve-Historyah* (Jerusalem, 1980), pp. 79–92; Elior, "The Minsk Disputation"; Etkes, "R. Shneur Zalman's Path"; idem, "The Ascent of R. Shneur Zalman of Lyady to a Position of Leadership" (in Hebrew), *Tarbiz* 54 (1985): 435.

75. Menahem Mendel of Vitebsk, *Peri ha-Arez* (Jerusalem, 1974), p. 50.

76. See Elior, "The Minsk Disputation," p. 193.

77. Rabbi Tuviah Blau is the author of several books on Hasidim and one of the Habad leaders in Israel. I wish to thank Rabbi Blau for his interesting and illuminating conversation.

CHAPTER 13

Habad as Messianic Fundamentalism: From Local Particularism to Universal Jewish Mission

Menachem Friedman

Selective opposition to modernity and the hedonistic West is a key component of all groups termed "fundamentalist"; ironically, it is promulgated via modern technology, especially by the mass media. Radical fundamentalist groups are not only protest groups, however, for they believe that they alone possess the key to understanding history and hence also the ability to predict the future. Fundamentalists maintain that they understand all aspects, overt and covert, of modern realities. They contend that they can explain matters "as they really are" and not "as they appear to be," realizing what must be accomplished to restore the world to "normalcy." The basis for these claims differs from group to group and religion to religion: some rely on charismatic prophets, others on "appropriate" comprehension of Holy Writ, and so on.

Judaism, Islam, and Christianity share a foundation in sacred writings—the Torah, the Qur'an, and the New Testament, respectively—works accorded rich and complex interpretations. An extensive corpus of interpretative literature developed over numerous generations, these works not only provide the "correct" and "precise" meaning of the written word but also grant it contemporary significance. Sages explain the texts according to their simplest meaning and interpret the events of their own time by adapting the scriptural concepts to contemporary realities. The point of impact between "internal realities" derived from interpretation of sacred writings and current sociopolitical realities is also the point of conflict between fundamentalist groups and conventional orthodoxy. While the mainstream Orthodox avoid vague definitions of sociopolitical realities in terms of rediscovered internal truths, the fundamentalists increasingly propound an unambiguous view of the world and of their own function therein.

From this point of view, the Habad movement within Judaism, as it has developed over the past twenty years, constitutes a near-ideal type of fundamentalist religious movement whose internal interpretation of recent history is perceived as the stage preceding total and final Redemption. Habad decisively and unambiguously defines its involvement in politics and hyperactivity in religious life of Jewish society in Israel and in the Diaspora. Habad vigorously attempts to prove that its conception of reality and its active messianic anticipation are not only anchored in Jewish religious literature but constitute no innovation whatsoever in the normative religious sphere. Nevertheless, the following analysis of Habad's history and organizational structure demonstrates that in response to the religious dilemmas posed by the Jewish tragedy of the preceding generation, and the vital need to face the issue of continuity in the Habad dynasty, Habad developed a messianic-fundamentalist theology, focusing on a uniquely charismatic personality, Rabbi Menachem Mendel Schneerson, seventh in the Habad dynasty. The seventh Lubavitcher rebbe enjoys admiration, authority, and power unprecedented in Habad history, defying comparison with any other contemporary Jewish religious leader.

No other Jewish religious leader is as controversial as the Lubavitcher rebbe, whose emissaries, the Hasidim, appear to be everywhere—on university campuses in the United States, England, France, Australia, and South Africa, where they have established Habad Houses serving as community centers and student clubs. In such major urban areas as New York, London, Paris, Melbourne, and Tel Aviv, they attempt to convince Jewish passersby to place *tefillin* (phylacteries) on their heads and left arms. Jews residing far from major Western Jewish concentrations often discover that an emissary of the rebbe has arrived in their locality, offering Jewish education for their children and religious services for all. A small Jewish community may find a Habad House established in the neighborhood, attracting youngsters and adults alike. Jewish tourists in Katmandu on the eve of Passover learn that the rebbe's emissaries are preparing a Passover seder for them, while Jewish businessmen visiting Papua find Habad emissaries there to remind them of their Jewishness. The Jews of Russia, only recently liberated from the yoke of an atheistic ideology, are accompanied by Habad Hasidim, whom they consider representatives of authentic Jewish identity.

As high rates of assimilation arouse fears of extinction, Habad activities are generally appreciated and admired in the Jewish world. Many non-Orthodox Jews consider Habad's work as a primary means of ensuring continuity of Jewish identity and contribute considerable resources to finance such activity. Moreover, to many non-religious Jews, both in Israel and the Diaspora, Habad represents an authentic Jewish approach to love of one's fellow Jew, mutual assistance, open-mindedness, and tolerance, in stark contrast with the image of conventional Orthodoxy.

Nevertheless, Habad has always been the object of controversy, particularly in recent years. Its messianic element has become increasingly prominent, and most Habad Hasidim no longer hesitate to declare openly that their rebbe is none other than the Messiah who will soon reveal himself to all. Hence, as Aviezer Ravitsky mentions in chapter 12, it is hardly surprising that some Jewish leaders accuse Habad of diverging from the boundaries of the permissible and legitimate. Habad's lobbying for ratification in the Israeli Parliament of the "Who is a Jew" law, which would recognize as Jews only those born to a Jewish mother or converted by Orthodox rabbis, is perceived as a step toward delegitimation of Conservative and Reform Judaism in the United States. The initiative aroused a public and political storm in Israel and the United States alike.[1] Moreover, Habad's involvement in Israeli politics as an extreme right-wing group has undermined the movement's positive image.

Historical Background

The founder of Habad Hasidism is Rabbi Schneur Zalman (the Alter Rebbe, 1745–1813) of Lyady in White Russia. According to tradition, the Alter Rebbe is a descendant of Rabbi Judah Loewy (the Maharal of Prague, himself a direct descendant of King David). Rabbi Schneur Zalman was a disciple of the Maggid (Preacher) of Mezhirichi, successor of Rabbi Israel Baal Shem Tov, founder of the Hasidic movement. During the Maggid's time, Hasidim began to spread, becoming a mass movement which threatened the traditional way of life and the community establishment.[2] After the Maggid's death, his disciples dispersed throughout Poland, Lithuania, White Russia, Ukraine, and elsewhere, disseminating the teachings of their master. They became tzaddikim and led Hasidic sects in their respective places of residence. Most bequeathed their role to their sons after them, thereby instituting a dynastic leadership structure based on inherited charisma. From a sociological point of view, Hasidism effectively shattered the unity of traditional Jewish society, which was based primarily on the community as a religious-social unit (the *kehila kedosha* or "sacred community") representing the legitimate Jewish identity, reflected in a lifestyle based on halakha and customs institutionalized over generations. The formation of Hasidic sects based on unique religious norms and manifesting affinities for one dynasty or another created a new social reality in which several voluntary religious-social identities may coexist. This situation introduced a dimension of conflict and competition into Jewish life, primarily between Hasidim and non-Hasidim *(misnagdim)*[3] and also among the various Hasidic sects themselves. Such conflicts have been primarily of religious significance: each religious movement claims to represent the Divine Truth and feels compelled to convince all others of its veracity. However, certain political and economic factors were also involved.

The "missionary" principle, the compulsion prevailing in all fundamentalist religious movements to spread their message, is reflected in Hasidism in a legend about the Baal Shem Tov. In a letter to his brother-in-law, the Baal Shem Tov describes an event which occurred on Rosh Hashana in the year 5507 (1746): Through a mystical procedure called "spiritual exaltation," the soul of the Baal Shem Tov rose to the celestial spiritual world, ascending to the Hall of the Messiah. In response to the Baal Shem Tov's question: "When wilt thou come and redeem the People of Israel," the Messiah replied: "When you publicize your teachings and reveal them throughout the world, and when thy springs are dispersed abroad."[4] The Baal Shem Tov's vision links Redemption with the spread of Hasidism and its triumph over its detractors. Indeed, the missionary element was preserved in Habad more than in any other Hasidic sect;

the concept of "dispersing the springs" is of key significance in contemporary Habad Hasidism.

The rapid spread of Hasidism during and after its third generation of leaders—the disciples of the Maggid—despite harsh persecution in Poland, Ukraine, and other parts of Eastern and central Europe, changed the character of most Hasidic sects and their attitudes toward their respective environments. The transformation of Hasidism into a dominant social factor in most regions to which it spread, and its simultane-ous breakdown into dozens of "courts," each of a particularistic-local character with clearly delineated geographic "landscapes," dulled the sense of mission and the vision of "dispersing the springs" among non-Hasidic Jews. Thus, Gerer (Gur) Hasidism is identified with Kongres Polish Jewry, centered in Warsaw and environs, Belzer Hasid-ism with the Jews of Galizia, and Vizhnitzer Hasidism with the Jews of Bukovina, and so forth.

The various Hasidic courts often competed with one another for followers and sought to expand the boundaries of their influence. Such conflicts, however, were generally waged on a personal, social, or economic basis.[5] The particularistic-local character of the Hasidic sects, as reflected in outward appearance, spoken language dialect, and the order of prayers, determined the boundaries of their influence, even when compelled to leave the original "landscapes" in which they were founded and first developed. In this respect Habad Hasidism differed from all other Hasidic sects. Rabbi Schneur Zalman was recognized as the leader of White Russian Hasidim in 1788. His philosophy of Hasidism, the Tanya, was published in 1796 and became the basic sourcebook of Habad Hasidism for all generations. (The acronym Habad, the first letters of the Hebrew words *hochma, bina,* and *da'at*—wisdom, understanding, and knowledge—derives from the Tanya and relates the three attributes of the intel-lect of the Divine Spirit present within every Jew.)[6] The teachings of Rabbi Schneur Zalman were explained, developed, and embellished by his disciples and descendants over the years, so Habad Hasidism is based not only on the personal affinity of the Hasid and his rebbe, but also on intensive study of written religious literature. This dimension of identity and a sense of belonging places Habad on an intellectual plane and underscores its unique universal, achievement-oriented character among the vari-ous Hasidic movements.

Habad's unique character is primarily a result of its history within the geographic boundaries of its development. Unlike most other Hasidic sects, Habad had to con-tend with the challenge of opposition to Hasidism in general and to Habad in par-ticular. From the outset, Habad was at the center of the stormy battle waged against Hasidism by the traditional Jewish establishment. Concentrations of Habad Hasidim in White Russia were located close to the center of Hitnagdut in Lithuania. Rabbi Schneur Zalman, as the senior Hasidic leader, sought a face-to-face meeting with the leader of the misnagdim, Rabbi Eliyahu, the Gaon of Vilna.[7] But he was arrested twice by the Russian authorities in 1798 after being denounced by leaders of the struggle against Hasidism. His incarceration and release became a major theme in the consciousness, religious thought, and text of Habad Hasidim. The conflict between Habad and the misnagdim is, therefore, a basic and central component of Habad consciousness; the story of the imprisonment and release of the founding father of the movement arises annually as a point of departure for consolidating each Habad Hasid's sense of mission, of "dispersing the springs." Moreover, the social realities in early Habad concentrations differed from those of Poland and Ukraine, in which Hasidim won a decisive victory over mitnagdim. The constant struggle[8]—the need to protect young people from the influence of the mitnagdim and the hope of persuading them to join Habad—rendered the concept of mission a permanent factor in Habad consciousness and practice and prevented the movement's transformation into a just another particularistic-local Hasidic sect.

The Habad center in Lubavitch was established by Rabbi Dov Baer (1813), the son of Rabbi Schneur Zalman. This act marks the beginning of the Habad dynasty and the routinization of the charisma of the rebbe, the founding father, via its transmission to his descendants after him, as practiced in other Hasidic courts since the third generation of Hasidic movement leadership.[9] From this point, the terms Habad and Lubavitch are used interchangeably to identify Habad Hasidism, reflecting the tension between particularistic-local aspects (Lubavitch) and a consciousness of uniqueness and a sense of mission (Habad). In this respect, the history of Habad Hasidism may be divided into the era of the second, third and fourth rebbes (1812–82), marked by consolidation in the supportive environment of Lubavitch, and the era of the "presidency"—the fifth, sixth, and seventh rebbes (1883–), during which the stability of traditional religious Jewish existence was undermined and Habad Hasidism again felt threatened. Contemporary Habad/Lubavitcher Hasidism was shaped by the political and religious crises arising in the Jewish society of its home base in Russia, commencing with the 1880s, during the "presidency" of the fifth rebbe, Rabbi Shalom Dov Baer Schneerson.[10]

The turning point in Habad history is connected with the fifth Lubavitcher rebbe, Rabbi Dov Baer, and is largely a result of the religious, political, and economic crises affecting the Pale of Jewish settlement in Russia from the 1880s. Modernization, industrialization, and the development of railways seriously challenged the traditional economic structure. Furthermore, the rapid natural rate of increase of the Jewish population increased competition for the few traditional sources of income. Persecution and discrimination by the Russian regime and its ban on Jews living throughout most of the empire exacerbated the crises in traditional Jewish society. Secularization offered Jewish youth an opportunity to enter the general educational system, acquire a modern education, and learn a useful occupation. However, this option generally entailed abandoning the Jewish religion and lifestyle, which traditional religious authorities severely condemned. Notwithstanding such opposition, the economic crisis and the challenge of secularization and education attracted more and more young Jews to general education and undermined the grasp of the traditional religious leadership—rabbis and Hasidic rebbes—in Jewish society. This erosion from religion and tradition threatened the religious leadership's confidence; by the turn of the century, it posed a life-or-death challenge for traditional-religious Judaism, Hasidic and non-Hasidic alike. Moreover, the steadily worsening economic and political crisis impelled many people, primarily of the younger generation, to move from rural to urban regions and from Eastern Europe to Western Europe, North America, South Africa, and Australia. Consequently, traditional social supervisory frameworks began to crumble and parental moral authority diminished, especially since parents often became financially dependent on their children. This too attenuated the power of religion and tradition in shaping the Jewish lifestyle.

New elites arose in Eastern European Jewish society, posing an alternative to traditional Jewish identity and to recognition of halakha as its only legitimate expression. Some sought to accelerate the integration of Jews into the surrounding culture through cultural organizations or political parties. Others, however, perceived their goal as effecting an overall political-cultural change, whether by replacing the autocratic Russian Empire with a new, socialistic and egalitarian society or by establishing a new, secular, democratic, nationalistic Jewish society (Zionism). All such elites and organizations challenged the status of Orthodox Judaism and the religious leadership. Traditional rabbis and Hasidic rebbes became marginal as Jewish communities, especially in the major cities, became pluralistic. The Jewish religion was no longer the only source of Jewish identity, and a traditional-religious lifestyle was no longer a condition for legitimate Jewish identity.

The traditional religious authorities found it most difficult to adjust to the new religious and cultural realities. They would not legitimize a Jewish identity that did not incorporate unconditional commitment to halakha, but the situation did not allow for dissociation from these "non-Jewish" Jews,[11] posing a social and theological problem for the traditional religious leadership which is still of considerable significance to this day. Unwillingness to legitimize a Jewish identity not committed to halakha, coupled with an intensive erosion process, led to portraying the situation as a temporary aberration, accorded new meaning to the concept of repentance, and introduced new content to the Jewish religious mission.

Secularization and modernization primarily affected the Jews of Lithuania and White Russia. Lithuanian Jewry's response to the challenges shaking traditional Jewish society was the higher yeshiva—the talmudical academy—exemplified by Yeshiva of Volozhin. This significant development contained the embryo of postwar haredi Judaism.[12] In 1803, Rabbi Haim of Volozhin established a structurally and organizationally innovative institute of religious studies. Unlike the traditional yeshiva, which was generally a community institution, the Yeshiva of Volozhin transcended the community framework and was supported by individual contributions from the surrounding vicinity and elsewhere. Most students were not local residents, and the yeshiva had to attend to their material and spiritual needs. The Volozhin-type yeshiva was effectively a closed world of young men expected to devote all their time to Torah study, a quasi-monastic community of students severed from their home communities and isolated from the surrounding environment. The students, young men aged fifteen and older, were separated from their parents and family traditions, their lifestyle and conceptions reshaped via direct and unmediated confrontation with texts and the influence of teachers and mentors.

From the outset, the yeshiva was a response to the challenge of Hasidism.[13] It reinstated the ideal of Torah study as the only means of realizing communion with God and imparted a sense of togetherness resembling that of the Hasidic sects. However, as the threat of the Enlightenment and secularization increased, the Volozhin-type yeshivas established in the villages of Lithuania and White Russia began to nurture a new religious-intellectual elite, which contended that Torah study is the only way to cope with the challenge of secularization and modernization. Improvements in transportation and communications enabled the yeshivas to expand their fund-raising activities and to recruit students with intellectual potential who lived in villages far from the centers of Jewish religious culture. Talented young people who formerly had to remain within the limited framework of the small community could now play an active role in the centers of Jewish scholarly society.

Habad now found itself threatened by secularization and the Enlightenment on the one hand, and by the Volozhin-type yeshivas, which attracted the most gifted of Habad youth, on the other. Moreover, the yeshivas represented a traditional, universal Jewish idea, reuniting schism-ridden traditional Judaism, threatened by the Enlightenment and assimilation, with all its apparently obsolescent particularistic-local manifestations. All these developments took place against a background of persecution, pogroms, mass emigration to the West, and the first signs of revolutionary and national political organization. Habad found itself at the center of the social and spiritual ferment taking place in Jewish society. Rabbi Shalom Dov Ber Schneerson had to contend with all these difficult challenges.

Habad under the Maharshav's Leadership: The Mission to All Israel

Rabbi Shalom Dov Baer, the Maharshav, was born on 5 November 1860, the second son of Rabbi Shmuel, the fourth Lubavitcher rebbe. Rabbi Shalom was twenty-two when his father died, and only ten years later, on the Jewish New Year of 5654 (1893), he accepted the "yoke of presidency" after his elder brother Rabbi Zalman declined the post.[14] During the first few years of his "presidency," the Maharshav was preoccupied with consolidating Habad Hasidism. A prolific writer, he traveled frequently among his Hasidim and was active in the political sphere. He maintained contact with the leader of Lithuanian Jewry during this stormy era, and with Rabbi Haim Soloveichik of Brisk, the most outstanding representative of the Lithuanian, Volozhin-type yeshiva world. The Maharshav's travels and meetings with Jewish leaders expanded his personal horizons and provided him with a first-hand impression of the situation of traditional religious Jewry in general and of Habad Hasidim in particular. He was able to assess the extent of erosion and the attractive power of socialism and Zionism. To Habad Hasidim and others, these meetings and contacts with leading misnagdim denoted the restoration of unity among the traditional keepers of the faith in the face of common enemies—the Enlightenment, secularization, socialism, and Zionism. At the same time, however, the Maharshav addressed the threat to Habad's place in traditional-religious Jewish society posed by the new yeshivas and the attractive power of Torah scholars such as Rabbis Spector and Soloveichik, who symbolized traditional Judaism, even to young Habad Hasidim.

To meet the challenge head-on, the Maharshav established a Habad yeshiva in Lubavitch (15 September 1897), using the Lithuanian yeshiva as his frame of reference. The yeshiva was called Tomchei Temimim and its students were called Temimim.[15] The Maharshav's conception of the function of its students, as expressed in several of his addresses, was that the yeshiva students, the "pure ones," were to serve as soldiers in the rebbe's army; they would be dedicated "without concessions and without compromise" to their commander and to the war against the enemies of Hasidism, the enemies of Judaism, the enemies of God.

The dramatic changes in traditional Jewish society—secularization, erosion from religion and tradition, and the increasing power of the "enlightened" deviants—were to him a sign of the impending days of the Messiah. The Maharshav defined his own era as the Jubilee of the Footsteps of the Messiah, enabling him to explain to himself and his followers the harsh realities of secularization and erosion. According to tradition, just before the Messiah comes, "audacity" will increase and the "enemies of the Lord" will gather strength. The function of the "soldiers of the House of David," the Tomchei Temimim students, was to wage war against the enemies and "disperse the springs with dedication to Torah and fear of Heaven and worship of the heart, without concessions and without compromise, for they shall save Israel from the enemies of the Lord and those who vilify the Messiah."[16]

The Baal Shem Tov's vision acquired a new significance in the context of the modernization and secularization that involved traditional religious Judaism in an unprecedented struggle for survival. The "enemies of the Lord who vilify the Messiah" were the supporters of the Enlightenment, who sought to alter traditional educational patterns and encouraged Jews to provide their children with a modern education. The Maharshav also perceived the Zionist movement and the traditional enemies of Habad—the misnagdim—as threats. The Maharshav considered the various manifestations of Zionism to constitute a substantive antithesis of traditional Jewish identity, for he could only perceive the Zionist objective of establishing a Jewish state in the Land of Israel in its messianic context. In an address to his "pure ones," the Maharshav claimed that Zionism's message of redemption conflicts with the order of redemption for God's rebuilding of the Holy Temple in Jerusalem, which must precede the ingathering of the Jews to the Land of Israel. Moreover, the Messiah will rebuild the Temple only after the "dispersal of the springs," the springs of (Habad) Hasidism. It is no coincidence that the yeshiva was established less than a month after the First Zionist Congress in 1897. The popularity of Zionism and its leader, Herzl, was then at its peak in the Russian Pale of Settlement.

Although the Maharshav considered the Lithuanian rabbis his allies in the struggle against the Enlightenment, he never forgot that misnagdic Judaism constituted a threat to Habad Hasidism. The conflict with the misnagdim was not only a historical conflict but a daily one in the traditional Jewish villages of the Pale of Settlement. Moreover, the large Volozhin-type yeshivas constituted a challenge for village young people, attracting Habad youth as well. No doubt the establishment of the Tomchei

Temimim yeshiva was a response to this challenge. On one occasion the Maharshav declared that "our yeshiva was not founded for Torah [study] alone. Torah is not lacking, thank God. There are many yeshivas and Torah is not lacking, especially in this region," referring to the Lithuanian yeshivas. At Tomchei Temimim, the day would be devoted to the study of Hasidic philosophy alongside study of the Talmud and commentaries, which was the sole legitimate study of the Lithuanian yeshiva curriculum. When the Maharshav demanded that his students manifest "dedication to Torah and fear of Heaven and worship of the heart, without concessions and without compromise," he implied that they dare not model themselves after their Lithuanian counterparts, whom he believed tainted by the Enlightenment.[17]

The Maharshav formulated the principles of Habad's conception of the situation and its function therein: (1) the present era heralds the coming of the Messiah; (2) the Messiah's coming is contingent on "dispersing the springs" of Hasidism, that is, the philosophy of Habad, as expressed in the Tanya and other writings of Lubavitcher rebbes ("presidents"), among all Jews; (3) this is the main function of Habad—of the rebbe and his "pure" students. Thus, Habad necessarily became the bearer of a unique fundamentalist truth and a universal Jewish mission. Furthermore, the Maharshav based Habad on young people as a dynamic element. They are the rebbe's "soldiers" and must be totally devoted to him, thereby bringing the Messiah ("the House of David") closer. As indicated below, the present Lubavitcher rebbe's court also makes liberal use of military terminology.

The Maharshav's anti-Zionist conception differed from that of other traditional-religious circles. Among the latter, opposition to Zionism was based on the principle that a Jew must remain almost entirely passive in the messianic process, all details of which are shrouded in mystery. In contrast, the Maharshav's objections were based precisely on an active messianic stand, defining the present era as one which heralds the coming of the Messiah, a process whose details are indeed known and revealed. Moreover, messianic activism, according to the Habad conception, takes place almost exclusively on the religious-spiritual plane. This fundamentalist position is diametrically opposed not only to the Zionist ideal but also to Zionist activity. The favorable view adopted by anti-Zionist traditional-religious leaders toward Jewish settlement in the Land of Israel, however reserved it may have been, was deemed contrary to the messianic process by the Maharshav. Hence he also opposed the Agudat Israel movement, despite his initial approval, because of its involvement in urban and rural Jewish settlement in Palestine after World War I. Most leading religious authorities within Agudat Israel perceived such activity as part of Israel's return to its land, an essential component of the messianic process if the Creator indeed judges it a "favorable time" to send His Messiah. Habad, which considered the "dispersal of the springs" as a necessary precondition to the coming of the Messiah, could not accept this approach.

The development of motor transport and the improvement of postal and telegraphic communications utterly changed the scope of the Maharshav's world and that of Habad Hasidism. Large-scale migration brought many Habad Hasidim to the cities of Eastern and Western Europe and the United States, but improved communications facilitated continued contact with them through correspondence and dispatch of Hasidic doctrine *(da'ah)*. The Maharshav and his son and right-hand man, the Maharitz, were perhaps the first Hasidic leaders to understand the dialectic significance of modern technology in the development of Hasidism. Lubavitch became a center for maintaining extensive postal contact with Hasidim who had left their familiar geographic-particularistic surroundings and migrated to places so far away that in earlier days they might have lost contact with the rebbe. Moreover, Habad could dispatch not only letters and treatises, but also personnel. Yeshiva graduates (Temimim) were sent to communities of emigrants to serve as rabbis, teachers, and ritual slaughterers; they reported periodically to the center, indicating the necessary course of action to promote "dispersal of the springs." The ethnic-Ashkenazic barriers of Habad Hasidism were broken down by dispatching Temimim to Georgia, providing this Eastern European Jewish community with religious and educational services (as well as Habad "missionaries"). Habad was essentially the only Hasidic sect to break through these Ashkenazi–Eastern European barriers.

Yet one could hardly call the Habad of the Maharshav a striking success. Habad did not succeed in halting the erosion from tradition that plagued Jewish society ruthlessly up to World War II. The Habad court was unable to prevent even Lubavitch residents themselves from joining socialist and Zionist parties, as did their counterparts throughout the Pale of Settlement. Nevertheless, the Maharshav did succeed in laying the foundations for postwar Habad as a movement that succeeded in changing its particularistic-local character, in breaking through the traditional ethnic boundaries of Hasidism, and in discerning the dialectic elements of modern technology and applying them to ensure the continuity of traditional-religious Judaism.

World War I accelerated the processes of deterioration and erosion of religion and tradition among Jews living within the boundaries of the Russian Empire. On 24 October 1915, as the German army approached, the Maharshav left Lubavitch with his family, never to return. The "official" explanation places his departure from Lubavitch on the same symbolic-mystical plane as the Alter Rebbe's departure from Lyady during the Napoleonic Wars. The Alter Rebbe's departure was perceived as a mystical "act of war" by the rebbe against Napoléon, symbol of the Enlightenment and apostasy. The Maharshav continued his grandfather's tradition of war against the Enlightenment, leaving Lubavitch as part of his struggle against the Germans, who represented Western intellectualism. He apparently did not realize that a revolution in Russia would attempt to uproot religion and tradition with unprecedented determination, force, and means.

When the Bolshevik Revolution erupted, traditional-religious Judaism, including Habad Hasidism, was cut off from the Jewish world in one fell swoop. For Habad, the Soviet Revolution was a kind of Holocaust. The vast majority of Habad Hasidim lived in the Soviet Union. Even if they themselves tried to remain loyal to the faith of their fathers, the next generation largely abandoned it, willingly or otherwise. Even before the Nazi Holocaust, Habad had to cope with the holocaust perpetrated by the atheistic Bolsheviks on both the practical and theological planes. The Maharshav did not live to see the full extent of the tragedy inflicted on his Hasidim, first by the communists and then by the Nazis. He died in 1920 in Rostov, his mantle assumed by his only son, Rabbi Joseph Isaac Schneerson (the Maharitz).

Exile: Rabbi Joseph Isaac Schneerson, the Sixth Lubavitcher Rebbe

Rabbi Joseph Isaac Schneerson, the Maharitz, sixth in the Habad dynasty, was born on 21 June 1880. He had served as his father's right-hand man, primarily as the administrative director of the Tomchei Temimim yeshiva. It was his destiny to lead Habad during the Soviet Revolution and the horrendous era of the Holocaust. The State of Israel, which declared its independence two years before his death in 1950, also demanded a change in attitude. Rabbi Joseph Isaac was not a revolutionary like his father. However, having followed the Maharshav constantly, documenting virtually every moment of his life, he understood that the Jewish world had completely changed, necessitating reassessment of Habad's traditional views. Thus he laid the foundations for Habad as an active religious movement with a "missionary" character in a Jewish world whose traditional foundations had been almost entirely uprooted.

The communist regime, with the eager assistance of the Yevsektsiya, the party's Jewish Affairs Department, applied itself with revolutionary enthusiasm to uprooting religion from Jewish life.[18] Torah study at schools and yeshivas was considered a counterrevolutionary activity, and students and teachers were jailed and punished. Given the economic conditions then prevailing in the Soviet Union, any activity contrary to the regime's instructions entailed a tangible danger of starvation, not to mention incarceration and exile. Virtually all traditional religious frameworks succumbed to the threats of the revolutionary regime—an entirely new situation for traditional Jewry. The Yevsektsiya, the main factor in the war against Jewish religious institutions, comprised young Jews suffused with revolutionary enthusiasm and a burning hatred for religion, the majority of whom had grown up in traditional homes. In a certain sense, this was a civil war within Jewish society, in which the balance tipped clearly in favor of the revolution. Within a short time, nearly all Jewish schools and yeshivas were closed. Habad, under the leadership of the Maharitz, was essentially the only Jewish organization to maintain an underground network of religious schools. Habad thus succeeded where most traditional factors failed, primarily because it was better organized, had a more energetic leadership, and especially because young Tomchei Temimim students, in their total devotion to the rebbe, were willing to endanger themselves and maintain schools and yeshivas. Also, due to efforts by Habad Hasidim in the United States, the rebbe was the conduit for the transfer of funds from Western organizations and individuals to the Jews of the Soviet Union. These funds enabled the rebbe to finance his underground network even during the virtual famine that faced the Soviet Union after the blood-drenched civil war.

In this respect, post-revolutionary Habad became the representative of traditional Judaism throughout the Soviet Union. Henceforth, Habad was no longer restricted to defined particularistic-local boundaries. Its emissaries reached Jewish population concentrations throughout the region, disseminating Judaism as interpreted by Habad. Paradoxically, the imprisonment and exile of emissaries by the authorities helped spread Habad Hasidism among Jews of varying origins and traditions. The activities of the rebbe's emissaries in Georgia and in the ancient Jewish community of Bokhara constitute outstanding examples of this phenomenon.

In 1927, after monitoring the Maharitz's activities closely, the authorities decided to imprison him. However, thanks to pressure from Jewish organizations outside the Soviet Union, the rebbe was released and eventually allowed to leave the country with his family. His departure was undoubtedly a relief for the Yevsektsiya. The Habad Hasidim who remained behind did not exert any substantial influence, although their presence symbolized Jewish courage in the face of an overtly hostile regime. The rebbe himself went into "exile," first in Riga and then in Warsaw and Otwock, where he reestablished his yeshiva and restored the Habad center, maintaining wide-ranging contacts with the Habad "diaspora," especially in the United States.

The Maharitz's sojourn in Poland may be defined as "exile,"[19] although the concept must be perceived in a sociological sense rather than a historic-religious one. Warsaw was indeed a great Hasidic center, but not for Habad. The dominant Hasidic court in Warsaw was that of Gur. Hence from the 1920s, Habad Hasidism no longer relied on its autochthonous surroundings, but rather on a broader dispersal, particularly in the United States. Contacts between the various Habad groups and the center were maintained through letters and articles dispatched from the Habad court, and detailed reports sent to the rebbe by his emissaries in the "diaspora." Habad was the first Hasidic court to be organized in modern fashion. The rebbe's secretariat was responsible for contacts with Hasidim; it dispatched and received information and writings on Habad doctrine. While nearly all other Hasidic sects considered themselves linked with their traditional "boundaries," the Maharitz's secretariat in Warsaw reinforced its ties with Habad Hasidim in New York. While the traditional Hasidic courts considered the New World "beyond the Pale," the Maharitz himself paid an extended visit to the United States in 1929.

Organizational and communal realities in the United States posed a difficult problem for traditional Eastern European Jewry. Separation of church and state and the very nature of the United States as a country of immigration automatically thwarted any attempt at organizing a community on a local-geographic basis. Jews organized voluntarily in synagogues. Habad had to rely on modern organizational procedures to create a framework encompassing its Hasidim in major cities like New York and throughout the United States. Its purpose was to reinforce the particularistic Habad identity in the American melting pot and to conduct fund-raising campaigns to maintain the Habad court and yeshiva and to aid the Jews of the Soviet Union. In 1924 the rebbe established the American Association of Lubavitcher Hasidim, which became an economic and political tool of vital significance to the future of Habad Hasidism. When World War II broke out and Poland was overrun, the association undertook extensive diplomatic efforts to bring the rebbe and his family to the United States. In winter 1940 the Rebbe and most of his family left Warsaw for Riga by rail, from which they sailed to the United States, arriving on 19 March 1940.

If Hassidic Warsaw was exile for Rabbi Yosef Yitzhak, then New York was more so. In the process of transition from the old world to the new, most Jews abandoned their traditional religious lifestyle. Financial distress, separation from family, and dissolution of social supervisory frameworks facilitated the immigrants' adoption of their new surrounding culture. But the factors that encouraged Jewish immigrants to alter their lifestyle and especially to abandon their traditional outward appearance (beard, hat, long black coat) were generally social and not economic; traditional-looking Jews not only felt strange and different in New York but also were ridiculed. Thus the new generation of American Orthodox rabbis abandoned their traditional rabbinic garb and appeared clean-shaven and dressed in modern suits. Those who inquired about this phenomenon were told, "America is different."[20] This defense and adjustment mechanism accorded post facto legitimacy to diversion from tradition in America, just as German neo-Orthodoxy was considered an Orthodox way of life suitable for modern German Jews alone.

For the Maharitz, his own transition to the United States during the war and the Holocaust befalling his Hasidim in the Old World raised serious theological questions. At this stage, it appeared that the God of history was not the God of Habad. First, the Soviet Revolution had totally undermined the status of Habad in its birthplace and in the land where most of its Hasidim lived. Then World War II had brought the annihilation of traditional religious Judaism throughout Eastern Europe. Furthermore, the rebbe had had to flee once again, this time to that "different" America, modern and secular in character and nature. Habad theology was forced to contend with these difficult questions. The answers given by the rebbe constitute the basis of contemporary Habad Hasidism as a messianic fundamentalist movement.

On his arrival in the United States, the Maharitz declared that "America is no different." Habad's mission in the United States would be to express Jewish uniqueness to its fullest extent, even in the external, public sphere. To maintain a traditional beard in America is to declare: "I am a Jew"; to wear traditional Jewish clothing in New York is to avow in public: "I am not ashamed of being different." Beyond the declaration was a basic theological message: the Maharitz had not abandoned his Hasidim and fled to the United States. He did not come to save himself but to fulfill a religious mission vital to the future of the Jewish people. The concept of mission among the Jews of America (the "lower hemisphere" in Habad terminology)[21] thus became a central component in the Habad conception of redemption.

But America *was* different. A decisive majority of American Jews, including the Orthodox, perceived Habad as a curiosity. As soon as he arrived in New York, the Maharitz established a yeshiva, but its student body almost exclusively comprised young men from Poland and Russia, with virtually no American-born students. The Maharitz initiated various activities to spread Judaism among English speakers, but his success was only marginal. With the assistance of his son-in-law, Rabbi Menachem Mendel Schneerson, he established the Center for Educational Affairs, which offered an alternative and a supplement to state secular education. The results of these efforts, however, were none too impressive.

World War II came to an end, and the atrocities of the Holocaust were revealed to the world for the first time. Jewish refugees flooded Western Europe, seeking a place to live. Some Habad Hasidim succeeded in escaping the Soviet Union and sought a new home as well. Because of U.S. immigration quotas, most refugees ended up in Palestine. In 1948 the State of Israel was declared and the gates were opened wide to welcome the Remnant of Israel, including a significant number of Habad Hasidim. All these events clearly affected Habad as a whole. The Maharitz was the first rebbe to be involved in establishing a Habad agricultural settlement in Israel, Kfar Habad (1949). At the same time, a Habad yeshiva was established in Lod. This period marked a turning point in Habad history since, in the early 1920s, the Maharitz had strongly opposed any attempt to base the Jewish community in Palestine on agricultural settlement and industry;[22] even during the Holocaust, he had exhorted his Hasidim not to believe in the "false prophets [the Zionists] who promise deliverance and comfort" after the war.[23]

About that time the Maharitz became critically ill.[24] He attempted to encourage activity among the Jews of Morocco, but was unable to accomplish very much. The Maharitz died on 28 January 1950, and Habad Hasidism, already dealt a crushing blow by the Russian Revolution and the Holocaust, now faced a serious dilemma: Who would succeed the Maharitz as rebbe? Rabbi Joseph Isaac had had three daughters and no sons. His youngest daughter had perished with her family in the Holocaust. The eldest was married to Rabbi Shmaryahu Gourary (the Rashag), who accompanied his father-in-law throughout his life and headed the Habad yeshivas, while the middle daughter was married to Rabbi Menachem Mendel Schneerson (the Ramam), a direct descendant of the Zemah Zedek, the great-grandfather of the Maharitz. Prima facie, the Rashag appeared more deserving of the crown of leadership.[25] Nevertheless, the Ramam was chosen as rebbe. This was the most significant turning point in the annals of Habad.

After the Holocaust, haredi society had been dispersed throughout the modern Western world. Although Habad was better prepared to cope with this challenge than other haredi groups, the environment still posed a formidable threat. Habad also had to address the Holocaust and the significance of the State of Israel. Habad's historic view of Zionism was close to that of the most radical anti-Zionist sects, such as Munkatsh and Satmar.[26] In coping with these problems, the Ramam paved a new path which changed the character of Habad Hasidism.

The Ramam, the Seventh Lubavitcher Rebbe: Against All Odds

The life story of Rabbi Menahem Mendel Schneerson is full of internal contradictions. Born in Nikolayev, on the shores of the Black Sea, on 18 April 1902 (11 Nisan 5662—called "the clear day" by Habad Hasidim),[27] the Ramam obtained a general education and studied foreign languages, along with his religious studies.[28] In this his childhood was markedly different from that of other Jewish children from traditional homes, who were barred from obtaining a general education and certainly were not permitted to study foreign languages. His upbringing also differed from that of other sons of Hasidic rebbes, groomed to follow in their fathers' footsteps.[29]

These biographical details do not suit the heir of the Maharshav, who fought so passionately against the Enlightenment and its attempt to alter patterns of Jewish education in Eastern Europe. Menahem Mendel obtained a broad Torah education at his father's home and in traditional academies, but never attended a yeshiva, not even a Habad yeshiva. Little reliable information is available about his life during the first few years of Soviet rule. However, it appears that during this stormy period, he became close to the family of the Maharitz. Shortly after the Maharitz left Russia and settled in Riga, the Ramam arrived there as well. In Riga the rebbe's court was in a state of demoralization. The need to adjust to the new situation and increasing concern over the numerous Hasidim without leadership under Stalin's regime demanded recruitment of all forces for action.

But the Ramam did not stay at the court for long. By May 1928 he was already a student in Berlin, and had married Haya Mushka, the daughter of the Maharitz. When the Nazis rose to power, he moved to Paris, far from the Habad court and Hasidim, where he lived until 1941. Some biographers state that in Berlin he studied Jewish philosophy, while others claim he studied philosophy of science. Later, in Paris, he studied marine engineering at the Sorbonne. So not only did the Ramam acquire an academic education, but he did so in Berlin, capital of the Jewish Enlightenment that Habad had fought tooth and nail.[30] Afterward he studied in Paris, considered a wanton city by the faithful of Israel. "Official" biographies of the rebbe exert considerable effort coping with these "unpleasant" facts. Offering a mystical-kabbalistic explanation, they also strive to prove that while in Berlin and Paris, the Ramam maintained close contact with the Habad court and fulfilled vital functions for his father-in-law. At the same time, he spent days and nights studying Torah, both the exoteric (the Talmud and commentaries) and the esoteric (Kabbala), and led assimilated Jews back to Judaism.[31]

After the Maharitz arrived in the United States, he attempted to bring over his son-in-law and daughter. His success was partly due to the Ramam's professional training, which was of top-level military significance to the United States government in those days of fierce naval warfare. On 23 June 1941, the Ramam's ship docked at New York harbor.

While working for the U.S. Navy, the Ramam began assisting his father-in-law in his attempts to reach the American Jewish public, so eroded by secularization. He was appointed head of the Center for Educational Affairs, whose primary function was the publication and distribution of Habad religious literature and the establishment of schools. In this sphere, the Ramam maintained a distinct advantage over his brother-in-law, Rabbi Shmaryahu Gourary (the Rashag), who headed the Habad yeshiva; the former had first-hand familiarity with the modern secular world and also knew the language. The Ramam obviously impressed leaders of the U.S. Association of Habad Hasidim, which had begun to acquire major influence in the Habad court. It is precisely because "America is different" that the Ramam constituted the only hope for Habad's future in the "lower hemisphere." This alone was not sufficient, however. For many years, the Rashag had been his father-in-law's right-hand man, spending all his time at the court and yeshiva, which were essentially alien to the Ramam. The Ramam's general education was an advantage but also a drawback among the defenders of Habad tradition. Thus the Maharitz's demise pitted the two sons-in-law, the Rashag and the Ramam, against one another.

Habad historiography tends to conceal the story of this struggle for succession, but evidence gathered from internal Habad circles at the time underscores the confrontation between the two contenders. The struggle for accession to the position of Lubavitcher rebbe, the president of Habad, constitutes a point of departure for comprehending the subsequent development of the Ramam's own theology and politics.

According to one widely reported story, the Ramam manifested a new leadership quality—the ability to "speak" with the departed rebbe. The custom of visiting the graves of the righteous and the belief that their intercession can influence the Divine powers are deeply rooted in Jewish tradition in general and in Hasidic tradition in particular.[32] "Conversation" with the deceased, in the form of a written plea placed on the grave, is part of Hasidic practice. Therefore, the Ramam's custom of visiting his father-in-law's grave and praying for response to his own pleas and those of his Hasidim, which commenced immediately after the seven days of mourning, ostensibly constituted no innovation whatsoever. Nevertheless, the act described embodies an astounding breakthrough that accorded the Ramam the legitimacy and authority he so desperately required during those days of perplexity and turmoil.

The Raman said that in a spiritual sense, the Maharitz is still among his Hasidim: "For even today, the rebbe issues instructions, as he always did and always will."[33] In response to requests of Hasidim that he accept leadership formally, the Ramam said: "The rebbe responds even now. You need only ask." He concluded by indicating that "the rebbe will lead us to complete Redemption."[34] Thus the pilgrimage to the rebbe's grave is not merely a traditional act of visiting the graves of the righteous, but rather a reflection of a unique situation preceding the coming of the Messiah. On the substantive, internal plane, the Maharitz did not die the way others do. Apparently, all who wish to "speak" to the rebbe "need only ask." In a practical sense, however, this was the Ramam's unique gift. Throughout this period, the Ramam spoke of the Maharitz as if he were still the living rebbe, considering himself as an intermediary alone. He continued to visit the grave regularly, bringing the pleas of his Hasidim. To requests for a blessing, he always responded: "I will recall [it] at the grave."[35] In other words, I will raise the matter before the rebbe, the Maharitz.

Thus the death of the Maharitz is not seen as contradicting the belief that he will bring about messianic redemption: death is apparently a substantial component of the pangs of Messiah. However, so long as the rebbe does not rise from his grave before all, Redemption has not yet arrived. Moreover, so long as the rebbe, the Maharitz, still "lives" in New York, the Ramam cannot leave (for example, for the Land of Israel), as he must maintain perpetual contact with the ostensibly deceased rebbe—who in truth is alive.

On the first anniversary of the Maharitz's death, Rabbi Menachem Mendel Schneerson issued his first Da'ah—a Hasidic address which in Habad tradition symbolizes his assumption of the status of rebbe/president. Although the struggle of leadership had apparently come to an end, various substantive problems remained concerning the image and personal history of the Ramam, the Bolshevik Revolution in Russia, and the complex realities of the post-Holocaust period and the establishment of the State of Israel. As a haredi religious leader and inheritor of the Habad dynasty, the new Lubavitcher rebbe had to deal with these issues constantly.

The main question affecting the entire haredi lifestyle concerned the significance of the Holocaust and the establishment of the State of Israel. Habad sources offer a variety of explanations for the Holocaust, most of which do not deviate from conservative haredi thought. On the one hand, the sins of the Jews are the cause, with some hints that Zionism is the sin in question. On the other hand, the Holocaust is an unfathomable Divine mystery which certainly conforms with the pangs of Messiah.[36] However, it appears that the most substantive problem is that of the departure of the rebbe from his Hasidim and followers in Poland and Russia. Was the rebbe trying to rescue himself and his family, abandoning all the others to their fate? No Hasid can ask these questions and continue to believe in the rebbe, but no Hasid can leave these questions unanswered. For the Ramam, who had just inherited his father-in-law's position, these questions were connected with his own legitimacy as the leader of Habad Hasidism, and in the background was his nearly thirteen-year sojourn in Germany and France during the most important period for consolidation of his personality as a religious leader. Moreover, the Ramam had to address the establishment of the State of Israel and the Ingathering of the Exiles—processes utterly contradictory to the pronouncements of the Maharshav and Maharitz.

At one of the first events in which he participated as the new Lubavitcher rebbe, the Ramam uttered several remarks hinting at Habad's approach to these problems. In recounting the various incarnations of the Torah down through the ages, he explained the shifts in the geographic location of Jewish religious cultural centers: from the Land of Israel to Babylonia, from Babylonia to Spain, to Germany, Poland, Russia, and so forth. Now, claimed the rebbe, the Torah has reached the United States, the "lower hemisphere," that part of the world where the Torah was not given. Once the Torah's "mission" is completed, the time of Redemption will come. The groom understood that the Ingathering of the Exiles to the State of Israel, which so moved the Jewish world at that time (1950), was a reflection of the Redemption to which the rebbe referred. No, the rebbe responded, the Ingathering of the Exiles will be accomplished only by the Messiah. In the order of Redemption the Messiah's revelation necessarily precedes the Ingathering of the Exiles to the Land of Israel.[37]

From this point of view, the departure for the "lower hemisphere" by the Maharitz and the Ramam was not an escape from the Nazi horror, but rather part of the messianic process, the last stage of Exile. The Ramam went on to clarify that the establishment of the State of Israel, which enabled mass immigration of Jews from the East and West alike, was not part of the Redemption process, for had it been, the rebbe would already have immigrated to the Land of Israel. The Ramam's fate is thus necessarily intertwined with that of his father-in-law as active participants in Habad's mission to all Israel. "Lubavitch," the symbol of local particularism, is now abandoned in favor of "770" in New York, representing the rebbe's worldwide mission. The rebbe's home in Brooklyn becomes a center at which truly important events are taking place, affecting the destiny and future of the Jewish people.

On numerous occasions, the Ramam extensively and explicitly addressed the question of immigration to Israel before the coming of the Messiah, linking the phenomenon with Habad's traditional anti-Zionist stand. Those familiar with rabbinic homiletics will detect a harsh anti-Zionist and anti-State of Israel tone in the rebbe's address. Most such sermons were delivered in the 1950s, when Israel's educational policy was aimed at secularizing the children of new immigrants from Islamic countries. Nevertheless, the basic principles of Habad remain unchanged to this day, as reflected in the rebbe's exposition on the Sabbath of the Torah portion Vayehi (Gen. 47:28–50:26) on 24 December 1988, relating to the verse "And Jacob dwelled in the land of Egypt." A banner headline in the Yiddish newspaper *Allegemeiner Journal*, a quasi-official organ of Habad, proclaimed: "The Lubavitcher rebbe clarifies that genuine [Jewish] life is possible especially if one lives and works in Exile." The rebbe and his father-in-law, the president of our generation, will then go to the Land of Israel together, after the coming of the Messiah and the resurrection of the dead.

In summary, the destiny and peregrinations of Habad rebbes/presidents are not merely a collection of details but a substantive part of the redemption process, of preparing the world for the coming of the Messiah, of "dispersing the springs to the lower hemisphere." Thus it is no coincidence that the presidents of Habad came to the United States and not to the Land of Israel; in their view, until the Messiah comes, one may live a full Jewish life only in the Diaspora. A paradoxical theology enables the Ramam to combine Habad's fundamentalist-messianic conception with the complex realities of the Jewish people in the wake of the Holocaust and the establishment of the State of Israel, and with the complex and extraordinary story of his father-in-law and himself.

The Great Breakthrough: Habad's Universal Mission, Past and Present

During the Ramam's era, Habad enjoyed its greatest success in penetrating the boundaries of Orthodox Jewish society, despite the challenges posed by Western society and large-scale secularization and assimilation. This complex situation, characterized by the resurgence of haredi society—to which Habad belongs—and unprecedented integration and loss of national-religious identity, changed Habad's image and status in haredi society in particular and Jewish society in general.

The point of departure for understanding these changes is the concept of mission, as interpreted by Habad. The Habad mission was first institutionalized by the Maharshav. Subsequently, however, the Ramam developed the concept differently, in accordance with new socioeconomic realities. Today, the Habad mission can be realized only in a Western welfare state in which Jewish society enjoys a relatively high standard of living and maintains reciprocal relations between its haredi and non-haredi elements; the mission constitutes a substantial part of the haredi "scholar society"[38] that has been developing since the 1950s. This society is characterized by the unique socialization process its members undergo at yeshivas and *kollels* (higher religious academies), at which they spend about ten years of their lives after marriage. These institutions provide a framework for organizing and recruiting young people for religious-social purposes. The Habad mission, as formulated by the Ramam, is to ensure full exploitation of the opportunities inherent in the haredi "scholar society," on the one hand, and its reciprocal relations with non-Orthodox Jewish society on the other.

In this context, the term "reciprocal relations" refers to a series of mutual benefits in the moral-national and socioeconomic spheres. Haredi society had always relied on the financial support of non-haredi Jewish elements, but the changes taking place in Western Jewish society after World War II created ideal conditions for interchange between haredi society and non-haredi Jewry. Jews enjoyed unprecedented success in joining Western economic and cultural systems. Most young Jews began attending universities, where they experienced unmediated contact with open-minded, achievement-oriented Western culture and a society in which origins and religious identity were not a basis for discrimination and social rejection. Consequently, the rate of assimilation increased phenomenally, posing a tangible threat to the continuity of Jewish identity. Many Western Jewish circles have expressed deep distress over their inability to provide the younger generation—especially on college campuses—with any substantial Jewish identity. In contrast, haredi society in the West succeeded in consolidating its ranks, reducing erosion to negligible dimensions, which alleviated the sense of conflict and anxiety and introduced a feeling of self-confidence. Thus a new basis was established for reciprocal relations and dialogue between the non-haredi Jewish world and haredi society, both fighting side by side in the fateful battle for Jewish identity and continuity.

Superior preparation for meeting the new challenges differentiated Habad from other elements in haredi society. For most haredim, modern society is still perceived as threatening; it arouses a desire for seclusion, for closing ranks and preventing exposure of the younger generation to modernity. Habad is different in this respect. Habad is not oblivious to the risks posed by exposure to Western society and culture. However, the Ramam's Habad seeks to comprehend the complexity of modern society, its openness and its weaknesses. At the same time, it is prepared to develop tools for dialogue and reciprocal relations of a type that will not unduly endanger the religious-social identity of Habad Hasidim. Habad's readiness to respond to the challenge is inextricably bound with its history, its ideology of "dispersing the springs," its problems vis-à-vis haredi society and the image and character of the Ramam himself.

The chief mechanism enabling Habad to forge reciprocal relations with the broader, secular, liberal Jewish world may well be "compartmentalization." This term generally refers to a variety of techniques and principles by which the modern Orthodox Jew organizes his or her behavioral norms and professional and social life. In Habad's relations with the Jewish world in which it operates, compartmentalization refers to different levels of ideology and language as well as to behavioral norms.

Habad emissaries active on university campuses claim to represent historic Judaism. Their efforts to bring young Jews closer to an Orthodox way of life are explained in terms of national identity and the need to prevent assimilation as a national and not necessarily religious Jewish interest. On the internal level, that same activity is accepted as part of the messianic process of "dispersing the springs." Each such "compartment" demands another language and code of behavior. Only by compartmentalizing the different activity formats and differentiating among the various levels of explanation and legitimation could Habad maintain so complex a system of mutual relations with the secular Jewish world.

It is not always possible to preserve the boundaries of the different compartments. Internal crises, sparked by contradictions, have recently led to the disappearance of certain compartmental barriers. This phenomenon necessarily engenders increasing difficulties in the complex system of reciprocal relations which Habad maintains with the "other" Jewish world.

The Internal Basis of Mission

Under the Ramam's leadership, Habad's mission to non-Orthodox Jewry has become its crowning achievement. It is precisely because "America is different" that the Maharitz had to come there to "disperse the springs," thereby hastening the Messiah's coming. His heir and followers must continue this mission, bringing Hasidism to every Jew, even in the farthest and most remote locations. This concept recalls the Divine sparks dispersed in the valleys of impurity, as indicated in the Kabbala of the Ari of Safed.[39]

The emphasis on mission as the quintessential reflection of Hasidism has some basis in the history and philosophy of Habad. However, its current manifestation is a new phenomenon. It is reasonable to posit that the Ramam's personal history had much to do with the development of the Habad mission. After all, he undertook a mission to a place "so far that there can be nothing farther" (Berlin) and to one "so low that there can be nothing lower" (Paris). Today's emissary and his dispatcher—who was himself previously an emissary—are part of the same mission, devoted to the same ideal and seeking the same objective: bringing about the coming of the Messiah and the redemption of Israel.

The Mission's Structure and Organization

Habad's mission has a complex organizational structure. It is in no way dependent on local, personal initiatives; virtually all aspects thereof are governed at the center, at 770, by the rebbe himself. An examination of the numerous letters published by the Ramam reveals an astounding fact: the rebbe not only corresponds with thousands of his Hasidim, responding to all who appeal to him, but he writes to them at his own initiative, providing incentive and encouragement and reprimanding those whom he believes are negligent in their task of "dispersing the springs." He seeks to subjugate all, to exploit both institutionalized and personal influence for the benefit of the all-encompassing goal—bringing the Messiah through the dissemination of (Habad) Hasidism.

Administratively, the mission is managed by a special headquarters at 770, which is part of the Center for Educational Affairs, headed by Rabbi Haim Mordechai Isaac Chadkov until his death in April 1993. National and regional centers are situated throughout the world. In Israel the mission is run by the Young Habad Organization, based in Kfar Habad. In Paris an emissary of the rebbe, Binyamin Gorodetzky, is in charge of all emissaries in Europe and activities in Arab countries. Shmuel David Reitzik is the rebbe's emissary to the west coast of the United States, Nahman Sodek coordinates emissaries' activities in England, and Yitzhak David Groner is head of the Habad Center in Melbourne, Australia, and is responsible for activities in the Far East. These officials and countless others responsible for hundreds and thousands of male and female emissaries report regularly to the rebbe and obey his instructions and orders.

The mission assumes various forms, ranging from sporadic, one-time, incidental activities to assignment to a permanent mission, demanding the emissary's time twenty-four hours a day. The crowning achievement of the mission is the establishment and operation of a Habad House in a distant city with few Jews or at a university campus attended by Jews totally alienated from their Jewish identity. The rebbe is familiar with all emissaries and often selects them personally. Most are students of the kollel affiliated with the center at 770. Habad House directors are all married; their wives participate in the mission by keeping house, tendering hospitality, conducting lectures and lessons for women, and operating Habad kindergartens. Generally, the emissary receives a temporary allocation for his initial steps in the new location. Eventually, however, he must find his own sources of financing to develop and expand the enterprise.

A Habad House is an open house that supplies information on the Jewish religion and customs. The emissary must develop contacts with the local Jewish establishment, including suppliers of ritual items, such as matzot before Passover and the Four Species for Sukkot. He conducts lectures and classes in the Habad spirit, hosting outsiders and students on Sabbaths and holidays and tendering assistance to the needy. In principle, a Habad House is a system that engages in social work and "markets" Judaism in attractive packages. Concern, warmth, and involvement are the operating principles of the Habad House, which the rebbe appropriately calls "a house of Torah, prayer, and charity."[40] Habad Houses, initially established on major college campuses in the United States, emulated the characteristic student clubs and fraternities, but soon they spread to other locations as well. In Israel, for example, nearly every city and town has a Habad House. Habad's impressive success in developing and maintaining this extensive system constitutes a heavy burden on its human resources.

The Habad mission, especially insofar as Habad Houses are concerned, clearly mandates personal and family sacrifice. A young, recently married man must leave his hometown for "exile" in a strange city, where he is to raise his children, far from his extended family and the close friends with whom he was raised and educated. This mission also entails a considerable measure of personal anxiety, lest the emissary fail at his mission and be held accountable by the all-powerful and all-knowing rebbe. Numerous Habad publications on this subject reflect an effort to inculcate personal confidence among potential emissaries. In many expositions, primarily those addressing the inception of a mission, the rebbe orders the emissary to commence activities immediately on his arrival at his new destination, while still a total stranger. He does not allow the emissary one free moment to realize his loneliness and unfamiliarity, but directs him to contact local Jews and expose himself more publicly, thereby committing him to his status and function.[41] The religious-messianic significance of the emissary's function is emphasized as a means of encouragement and inspiration.

Besides encouraging and nurturing emissaries, the rebbe and his associates also "punish" candidates who decline the role after having been selected, as well as those whose families refuse to permit their departure. The Ramam's correspondence includes a letter in which the parents of a young man implored the rebbe not to send their son on a mission,[42] indicating that the young man's separation from his mother would adversely affect her health. The rebbe responded to their request, as he could not compel the young man to undertake the mission against his will. However, he indicated clearly that he considered this request a breach of discipline by someone whom he formally considered a member of his "troops." "I thought that he was *my* soldier," wrote the Ramam, "and that I could assign him. . . . However, it emerges that before he makes any decision, he must listen to his mother and family. Obviously, this is not the behavior of a soldier—to inquire about conditions and time periods and then to ask his family's opinion of the matter." Thus, according to the rebbe, the emissary's primary loyalty is to the rebbe, even if it contrasts with the wishes of his wife and/or mother. After receiving such a letter, the young man and his parents no longer had a place in the Habad community. Subsequent publication of this letter in a collection of the rebbe's correspondence served as a warning to other "soldiers" who might have considered "revolt."

Campaign Missions

The "total" missions, characterized by absolute submission to the rebbe's orders, are complemented by various "campaigns," which demand a kind of partial commitment. These campaigns, generally conducted by young people, constitute incidental departures from one's home, yeshiva, or kollel to the streets of the modern, secular city in an attempt to persuade noncommitted Jews to participate in a religious-traditional ceremony. The Tefillin Campaign is perhaps the most well known and evident among them. Habad Hasidim, generally two yeshiva or kollel students, set up a table with several pairs of tefillin in the main square of a large city or at other locations frequented by crowds. They approach male passersby, inquiring if they are Jewish. An affirmative response elicits an invitation to put on tefillin. The Hasidim place the tefillin on the person's arm and head and recite the appropriate blessings with him. They then remove the tefillin, concluding the ceremony.

The rebbe first ordered inception of the Tefillin Campaign shortly before the Six Day War (June 1967). Since then, Habad Hasidim have been taking to the streets and city centers of Tel Aviv, London, New York, and many other locations.

Why focus on tefillin, which entails a rather complex commandment from a halakhic point of view? According to the Shulhan Aruch,[43] one must be physically clean before putting on tefillin; furthermore, one's attention must not be diverted by secular matters. Obviously, such conditions cannot be met by passersby who are totally unfamiliar with the laws of tefillin. The rebbe and his Hasidim are obviously well aware of the laws stipulated. Nevertheless they believe that it is acceptable to risk transgressing the given strictures of the Shulhan Aruch to achieve a vastly more important goal, namely, confronting the uncommitted Jew with awareness of his unique Jewish identity.

From a social point of view, one may define tefillin as a total "other," as an entity entirely apart from the non-Jewish world. For the non-Jew, tefillin are completely "Jewish." When a passerby in the modern city identifies himself as a Jew to young Habad Hasidim, they immediately isolate him from the non-Jewish surroundings. At this point, no apparent change takes place: he still resembles all the other passersby. However, once they place tefillin on his arm and head, he is transformed from a "non-Jewish" Jew to a committed Jew whose Jewish identity has an unambiguous public manifestation. This is the starting point. To transform the uncommitted Jew into a person identified as a Jew to himself and to others, one must first confront him with his Jewish identity. This objective is achieved when the subject agrees to "abandon" his non-Jewish identity and to put on tefillin in public. Once he declares his Jewish identity so blatantly, there is a chance, however slight, that he may continue to do so by attending meetings and ultimately "repenting" and "enlisting" in Habad.

There is also another, "internal," explanation, connected with Habad's mystical-kabbalistic conceptions. Habad's Jewry-wide mission of "dispersing the springs" seeks to cleanse the Jewish soul, the source of holiness, from the dross of the non-Jewish environment. As such, Habad accords utmost importance to dispatching of emissaries to the ends of the earth, in search of Jews totally immersed in the non-Jewish environment. These Jews are to be "redeemed," that is, made aware of their Jewishness and of the significance and obligations of Jewish identity. This concept is based on the kabbalistic conception of "arousing the sparks of holiness dispersed in the valley of impurity"[44] as a condition for the coming of the Messiah and complete redemption. Hence placing tefillin on the arm and head of the unidentified Jew is the first step in purifying the Jew of his non-Jewishness, releasing the spark of holiness from the captivity of impurity.

These two explanations are not mutually contradictory, but rather complement one another. Both are of paramount significance in assessing Habad's status in the contemporary Jewish world. As explained above, Habad optimally exploits its mutual relations with secular Jewish society by compartmentalizing the external and internal planes. The Tefillin Campaign, however, penetrated the boundaries between the two compartments, as contradictions within the internal sphere mandated changes in other compartments as well. The Tefillin Campaign extracts the Jew from his non-Jewish surroundings, cleansing the holiness within him of all alien impurities, provided, of course, that the Jew in question is indeed Jewish according to halakha, that is, a person whose mother is Jewish or who is a legitimate convert. "Purification" of persons deemed Jewish by other criteria—but unacceptable according to halakha and Jewish tradition—will yield opposite, catastrophic results. It does not separate the Jew from the non-Jew, but rather drives in the non-Jewish element, tainting holiness with impurity. This does not bring the Messiah closer, but rather repels and distances him.

One may thus understand why Habad considers it significant and perhaps even essential to Jewish survival to resolve the issue of "Who is a Jew" by amending Israel's Law of Return to define Jewish identity exclusively according to halakha. Habad has rendered this issue a top priority of religious principle, sparking several coalition crises in Israel. It is precisely through such activity that Habad again broke through the barriers of compartmentalization, endangering its mutual relations with the liberal, non-haredi Jewish world that perceives Jewish identity differently.

The Ramam's campaigns effectively transform Habad into a recruited society, unparalleled in haredi society in general and among the Hasidic courts in particular. This change is of indubitable significance to Habad's history as well. In the Maharshav's time, only yeshiva students were recruited as "soldiers of the House of David." Today, however, every Habad Hasid, wherever he may be, is a "soldier" in the rebbe's army and an active emissary in fulfillment of the mission. When Hasidic sects had particularistic-local identities, they reconciled themselves to the realities of "the Exile." In Habad's case, however, the particularistic-local identity was never well consolidated; once it was shattered, Habad had to justify its existence on a mission to all Israel, that is, dispersal of the springs and hastening messianic Redemption. It thus necessarily developed a kind of fundamentalist activism and became an organized, recruited movement, unparalleled in Jewish history, partly because of the personality of its leader, the Ramam.

The Mission: Messianic Activism

The Ramam's public appearances over the past few years and the popular literature distributed by his Hasidim reflect an extreme personality cult, unparalleled in other Hasidic sects and even in past Habad history. Habad Hasidim themselves often indicate that the Ramam is different from all previous Lubavitcher Rebbes. One Habad leader explains this difference in terms of internal Habad concepts: The last generation before Redemption requires a "president" of the highest level, as his assignments are most difficult. He must pluck out all the sparks of holiness from the depths of impurity, "whiten the most difficult and complex stains," and epitomize and complete the work of all previous "presidents."[45]

This assessment reflects the paradoxical dynamics of Habad's development. Other Hasidic sects of particularistic-local character invariably express the opposite conception, wherein each rebbe is considered inferior to his predecessors. For Habad, however, the mission to all Jews, which is of overtly messianic significance, virtually demands belief that the rebbe is at the highest level. "The great miracle of our generation," writes one young Habad leader about his rebbe, "is the miracle of his leadership, unique among the generations. . . . The intensity of the miracle is essentially the wonder, the uniqueness which transcends all definitions and explanations. . . . Happy is the nation for whom this is so. Yea, happy is the people whose God is the Lord, and happy is the generation whose leader is the Rebbe."[46]

In one respect, this reaction is surprisingly subdued. Since the 1970s, various Habad publications have hinted that the rebbe himself is the Messiah. One such allusion may be found in the slogan the Rebbe himself coined. "We want the Messiah now, in substance!" The final word of the Hebrew slogan MAMASH clearly alludes to the messiahship of the rebbe, as it is an acronym of his name, Menachem Mendel Schneerson. Initially, the Hasidim were cautious, half-heartedly denying the connection, but their intentions gradually became clearer. Today, virtually all Habad Hasidim recognize the Ramam as the Messiah and no longer hesitate to express their views in public. A wave of messianic activism has swept over Habad: billboards and bumper stickers in Israel proclaim "Long live our master, our teacher and rebbe, the king Messiah!" and Hasidim are signing a petition to the rebbe, asking him to declare himself the Messiah.

Habad publications recounting the characteristics of the Messiah, according to fundamentalist sourcebooks,[47] emphasize the features also attributable to their leader, the Ramam. The basis for active messianism in Habad was already established in the days of the Maharshav. Subsequently, after the horrors of the Holocaust, the Maharitz declared that the purification process was nearly complete, with only marginal details remaining to rectify the world for the advent of the Messiah. The Ramam was preaching to the converted, transmitting his message with increasing clarity: the Messiah's time has come. Behold, he standeth behind our wall (see Song of Songs 2:9), and we need only exert one final effort for him to be here now, in substance.[48]

Somewhat paradoxically, this messianic conception is linked with Habad's extremely hawkish political views regarding the territories conquered by Israel in the Six Day War. The rebbe not only rejects relinquishment of territory out of hand but also opposes alternative solutions, such as the granting of autonomy to Arab residents of the Administered Territories. How does this position conform with the anti-Zionist history of Habad in general and that of the Ramam in particular? To attribute an anti-Zionist outlook to Habad today would appear to contradict not only the rebbe's hawkish views but also the involvement of Habad Hasidim in various aspects of Israeli life and their intensive links with key figures in Israeli politics. Some cabinet ministers and Knesset members were invited to meet with the rebbe when they visited New York; he conferred with them and blessed them.

Nevertheless, Habad was and remains anti-Zionist. Habad's position regarding the State of Israel is the standard Haredi approach: a Jewish state cannot be led by non-religious Jews; therefore, it is not legitimate. The state itself has no connection with Redemption; it is not the "inception of Redemption"—not only because it is secular in nature, but also because it is not part of the order of Redemption appearing in fundamentalistic texts. The state itself has no theological significance. Nevertheless, at the same time, one may claim that the present era is a messianic era: all extraction of good from bad has been completed. Therefore, one should not relinquish territories held by Jews, as this land was promised to the Jewish people and will be in their possession when the Messiah comes. Nevertheless, the state as such has no theological significance.

Messianic dynamics, by their very nature, must become increasingly active. Habad's overall historical circumstances and subjective realities rapidly brought matters to a climax in 1992, transforming Habad into a messianic, fundamentalist movement. The near-apocalyptic events of the past few years, such as the Six Day War, the collapse of communist regimes in Eastern Europe, and the Gulf War reinforce these messianic dynamics. The collapse of communism in Russia is obviously of key significance in the messianic process affecting Habad, particularly because the Soviet Revolution was Habad's principal enemy, forcing the rebbe to leave his Hasidim. It is as if the matter has been rectified and the circle has been closed, with victory ultimately belonging to Habad. Furthermore, the Gulf War, and not the War of Independence (1948), epitomizes the messianic era. This was a war in which Israel did not participate and in which Jews were not harmed. Moreover, the rebbe foresaw the war and its outcome: the victor was not the Israeli (Zionist) army but God Himself, who fought on our behalf and revealed His secrets to His prophet/Messiah.

If the messianic foundations of Habad Hasidism were already laid by the Maharshav and the Maharitz, what impelled the Ramam and his followers toward messianic activism and the belief that the rebbe himself is the Messiah? Apparently this development is a function of the paradoxical realities affecting Habad Hasidism.

Habad's influence within and outside the Jewish world has increased far beyond what might have been expected when the Ramam first assumed the position of rebbe. The movement's activities on academic campuses in the United States, England, and France and the work of emissaries in the former Soviet Empire have accorded it considerable prestige in the Jewish world. Behind this extensive activity is a superior bureaucratic organization, employing thousands of persons and imparting social and political strength to its leaders. This entire complex system is totally dependent on the charismatic personality of the Ramam.

The rebbe turned ninety-one on 14 April 1993. The fact that the rebbe has no children and has never groomed a successor from among his more distant relatives during his decades of "presidency" renders the issue of continuity of the Habad dynasty a threatening question. The messianic response is virtually the only one capable of allaying these fears and suspicions: according to Jewish tradition, in the days of the Messiah, the Angel of Death will no longer reign and the dead will be resurrected. To the Habad Hasidim, the rebbe's advanced age and the absence of an heir has become a somewhat paradoxical basis for messianic faith: if the rebbe has no heir, then he must have no need of one, for he is soon to reveal himself as the Messiah, whom death cannot conquer. It is no coincidence that the Ramam is the seventh in the dynasty of Lubavitcher rebbes, symbolizing the "Sabbath" of Redemption.

The spread of belief in the rebbe as Messiah is facilitated by the total absence of checks and balances in Habad Hasidism, as such systems are difficult to apply in groups with charismatic leaders. In other Hasidic sects, elders and family traditions tend to moderate any extreme demands by the rebbe. In Habad, however, these factors have been effectively neutralized. Because of the Lubavitcher rebbe's longevity and advanced age, none of the elder Hasidim who selected him or the friends who surrounded him in his youth are still alive. The rebbe himself lives alone, without family. There is no one to engage him in friendly conversation or utter a word of criticism. Many who surround him are financially dependent on him and consider him a super-human being. Is it any wonder they are tempted to believe he is the Messiah?

On 2 March 1993 the rebbe suffered a stroke which left him partially paralyzed, incapable of speech. Within Habad, the rebbe's condition had no adverse effect on the faith of his followers, but actually served to intensify their messianic propaganda. No longer do the rebbe's followers try to mask their belief, but actually confront him with their conviction that he is the messiah.

Internal processes can cause fissures in the compartmental barriers between inner realities and external mutual relations with others. Habad has enjoyed more popularity in non-haredi Israeli society than any other haredi group. It has established mutual relations with the Israeli establishment and the man in the street, based on its war against assimilation, the religious services it provides to the secular citizen, and its role as a representative of palatable "authentic" Judaism. Habad has penetrated every corner of Israeli society with smiling faces and a helping hand. Yet as internal messianic tension cracks the compartmental barriers, Habad's fundamentalist messianic conceptions break through, revealing a new, unfamiliar side to the movement. Habad has become a prime factor in the fragmentation of the haredi camp, inducing a schism in Agudat Israel.[49]

Now that messianic tension in Habad is reaching new peaks, will the movement be able to withstand the extreme messianic fervor engendered by the rebbe's demise? Can it maintain its "recruited" society in the Ramam's absence? Can Habad present its mission as an ideal once messianic tension subsides? Some claim that messianism in Habad is still under control. In comparison to previous messianic movements in Jewish history, especially that of Sabbetai Zevi,[50] in which messianic faith "penetrated" the financial sphere, with many Jews ceasing their daily economic activity in hope of the Messiah's revelation, Habad maintains messianic tension in the religious-spiritual sphere alone. Nevertheless, even if this distinction is correct, one should not take too lightly the significance of a crisis within Hasidism if and when the rebbe departs this world. Will Habad remain the same? Lacking a particularistic-local affinity, can it continue to exist without the bonding cement of the rebbe? In light of the above analysis, the answers to all such questions appear negative. Even if Habad does remain part of the Jewish scene, it will have become an entirely different sect.

Notes

1. M. Samet, "Who Is a Jew," *Jerusalem Quarterly* 36 (Summer 1985): 88–108.

2. See S. Dubnov, *History of Hasidism* (in Hebrew) (Tel Aviv: Dvir, 1930); G. Scholem, *Major Trends in Jewish Mysticism* (New York: Schocken, 1954), pp. 325–

50; M. Buber, *The Tales of Hasidism* (New York, 1947); S. Ettinger, "The Hassidic Movement—Reality and Ideals," in H. H. Ben-Sasson and S. Ettinger, eds., *Jewish Society through the Ages* (New York: Schocken, 1969), pp. 251–66; S. H. Dresner, *The*

Zaddik (London, 1960); "Hasidism," *Encyclopaedia Judaica,* vol. 7, pp. 1390–1432.

3. Literally "opponents"; also called Litvaks (Lithuanians) because the center of opposition to Hasidism was in the Jewish communities of Lithuania.

4. The letter was first published in Rabbi Yaakov Yosef Hacohen, *Ben-Porat Yosef* (A fruitful vine is Joseph) (in Hebrew) (Korets [White Russia], 1781). For a photocopy of the letter, see A. Kahane, *The Book of Hasidism,* 2d ed. (in Hebrew) (Warsaw, 1922), pp. 76–77; also G. Scholem, "The Historical Image of Rabbi Israel Baal Shem Tov," in *Dvarim BeGo* (Explications and implications) (Tel Aviv: Ofakim-Am Oved, 1975), pp. 309–11.

5. The history of Hasidism over the last few generations is full of such disputes: for example, Sanz versus Sadigura, Belz versus Munkatsh, or Alexander versus Gur.

6. Liqqutei Amarim, *Tanya,* trans. N. Mindel (New York: Kehot, 1962), chap. 3, pp. 30–33.

7. Elijah ben Salomon Zalman, the Vilna Gaon (1720–97), who led the opposition to Hasidism although he did not have an official function in the Vilna community.

8. Much of the Habad literature, especially that which describes the lives of Habad Hasidim in White Russia, describes daily conflicts with misnagdim. For example, see the description of the childhood of Rabbi Shmuel Bezalel (Rashbatz), teacher of the Maharitz, in *Kovetz HaTamim* (The pure anthology), (Warsaw: Association of Habad Yeshiva, Tammuz 5695 [July 1935], pp. 41–35. See also the Maharitz's analysis of opposition to Habad, ibid., p. 33.

9. Concerning internal tension surrounding the struggle for succession between the son of Rabbi Dov Ber and his disciple, Rabbi Aharon of Starashilia in the second generation of Habad Hasidism, see R. Elior, *The Theory of Godliness in the Second Generation of Habad Hasidism* (in Hebrew) (Jerusalem: Magnes Press, 1982), pp. 14–15.

10. The entire Habad dynasty to date:
R. Schneur Zalman (Alter Rebbe)
  (1745–1813)

R. Dov Baer Schneerson (Mittler Rebbe)
  (1773–1827)
R. Menahem Mendel Schneerson
  (Zemah-Zedek) (1789–1866)
R. Baruch Shalom (1804–69)
R. Joseph Isaac (1809–75)
R. Judah Leib (1811–66)
R. Hayyim Schneur Zalman
  (1814–80)
R. Israel Noah (1816–83)
R. Samuel (1834–82)
R. Shalom Dov-Baer (Mahashav)
  1866–1920
R. Joseph-Isaac (Maharitz) (1880–1950)
R. Menachem Mendel (Ramam) (1902–)

11. The most outstanding precedent is that of the Karaites, who did not accept the authority of the Talmud, the basis for traditional halakha, as equivalent to that of the Written Law. In most of the Jewish Diaspora, the Karaites were excluded from traditional Judaism.

12. See M. Friedman, "Haredim Confront the Modern City," in P. Medding, ed., *Studies in Contemporary Jewry* (Bloomington: University of Indiana Press, 1986), vol. 2, pp. 74–96; S. C. Heilman and M. Friedman, "Religious Fundamentalism and Religious Jews: The Case of the Haredim," in Martin E. Marty and R. Scott Appleby, eds., *Fundamentalisms Observed* (Chicago: University of Chicago Press, 1991), pp. 234–40.

13. See E. Etkes, "The Methods and Deeds of Rabbi Haim of Volozhin as a Reaction of the Mitnagdic Community to Hasidism," in *Proceedings of the American Academy for Jewish Research* (Hebrew section) (New York, 1972), pp. 1–45.

14. Although the official history of Habad ignores it, Rabbi Zalman served as rebbe for at least half a year, whereupon he resigned his position and moved to Vitebsk. See I. Z. Wolfson, "Megilat Vitebsk" (The scroll of Vitebsk), in *The Book of Vitebsk* (in Hebrew) (Tel Aviv, 1957), pp. 230–53.

15. The Hebrew word *tamim* means pure, complete, with no moral flaw. This may hint at the Maharshav's severe criticism of students at Lithuanian yeshivas.

16. The rebbe addressed his "soldiers" in

a quasi-military ceremony conducted at their yeshiva. See A. H. Glitzenstein, "Rabbi Shalom Dov Ber Schneerson of Lubavitch, the Maharshav," in *Sefer Hatoladot* (The book of generations) (in Hebrew) 2d ed. (Kfar Habad [Israel]: Kehot [KeHoS], 1976), pp. 227–36.

17. Although in his programmatic address, "He who goeth out to the war of the House of David" (see n. 18), the Maharshav determines that the main objective of the "pure ones," the yeshiva students, is to combat the Enlightenment, in many other remarks he appears to consider the primary function of the Habad yeshiva as coping with the threat of the Lithuanian yeshivas. Therefore, the Maharshav considered the value of learning Hasidic doctrine (da'ah) to exceed that of studying the Talmud and commentaries ("overt" studies); those of his pupils who did not accept his assessment were to leave the yeshiva. See Glitzenstein, *Sefer Hatoladot,* pp. 162–63. At the same time, he severely criticizes the behavior of rabbis who graduated the Lithuania yeshivas. Ibid., pp. 174, 176; see also Y. Mark, *In the Company of the Great [Scholars] of the Generation* (in Hebrew) (Gvil, Jerusalem, 1958), p. 198. For the position of the present rebbe, the Ramam, see. M. M. Schneerson, *Igroth Kodesh* (Sacred missives) (Kfar Habad: Kehot, 1990), vol. 8, p. 4, letter dated 28 Kislev 571 (5 December 1953).

18. The Yevsektsiya was established in the Soviet Union in 1918. For information on its activities directed against religion and tradition, see M. Altschuler, *The Yevsektsiya in the Soviet Union* (in Hebrew) (Tel Aviv: Sifriyat Hapoalim, 1980); Zvi Gitelman, *Jewish Nationality and Soviet Politics* (Princeton: Princeton University Press, 1972).

19. The sense of exile following departure from Lyubavichi was part of the internal Habad ethos. See the Maharitz's diary, 19 Av 5681 (23 August 1921), in *Kovetz HaTamim,* Nisan 5696 (March/April 1936), p. 32.

20. In Yiddish, "America is andersh [otherwise]." See *The Lubavitcher Rebbe, the Sacred Rebbe Rabbi Yosef Yitzhak* (in Yiddish) (Brooklyn: KeHoS, 1953), p. 14.

21. The Torah was given in the Eastern ("upper") Hemisphere and is to be dispersed throughout the world, including the Western ("lower") Hemisphere—America. See M. M. Schneerson, *Dvar Malchut* (Words of the Kingdom) (in Hebrew), 2 March 1991 (Ki Tissa 5751).

22. Y. Alfasi, *Hasidism and the Return to Zion* (in Hebrew) (Tel Aviv: Sifriyat Maariv, 1986), p. 87.

23. See M. M. Schneerson, ed., *HaYom Yom . . . Luah Or Zarua leHasidei Habad* (Today is . . . the Or Zarua Calendar for Habad Hasidim) (5703–4 [1952/53–1953/ 54]): *A Collection of Discussions and Writings of the Lubavitcher Rebbe, R. Yosef Yitzhak* (Kfar Habad: Kehot, 1990), p. 44.

24. The Maharitz suffered from multiple sclerosis and encephalitis and had difficulty speaking.

25. He was the older son-in-law and had accompanied his father-in-law throughout all his adventures in Soviet Russia and then in the United States. He headed the Habad yeshivas, a function similar to that which the Maharitz held before he became rebbe. Furthermore, he was raised as a traditional Habad rabbi, while his brother-in-law had never been a yeshiva student and had spent much time in Berlin and Paris, studying both religious subjects and marine engineering. See pp. 339–40.

26. Between the two world wars, Munktash was the most extremely anti-Zionist of the Hasidic sects; See *Encylopaedia Judaica,* vol. 12, pp. 513–14; vol. 14, pp. 1295– 96. Today, the Satmar sect is the most radically anti-Zionist. See S. Poll, *The Hasidic Community of Williamsburg* (New York: Schocken, 1962); I. Rubin, *Satmar: An Island in the City* (Chicago: Quadrangle, 1972).

27. The Ramam's family tree begins with Rabbi Menachem Mendel Schneerson, the Zemah Zedek, the third Lubavitcher rebbe. The Ramam was thus a direct descendant of the Zemah Zedek (after whom he was named) and therefore also a scion of the Alter Rebbe, Rabbi Schneur Zalman of Lyady. Habad biographers typically indicate that the Ramam was destined from birth to continue the dynasty. However, an examination of his life history evokes a different image.

28. See M. M. Laufer, *Yemei Melech* (The days of the king) (Kfar Habad: Otzar HaHasidim, 1989), pt. 1, pp. 137–39.

29. For example, the education of the Maharitz, father-in-law of the Ramam, was of course entirely different. He studied with one of the chief educators of Habad (the Rashbatz) and was under the constant supervision of his father, the Maharshav, who strenuously objected to any change in the traditional patterns of education and reacted with overt hatred to those who spread the Enlightenment. Incidentally, the Ramam's elder brother also studied general subjects and became a physicist, abandoning the religious way of life.

30. See above, pp. 334–35.

31. See Laufer, *Yemei Melech,* pp. 313–40, 373–92.

32. This custom is mentioned frequently in the Talmud, primarily regarding rainfall during a year of drought. See, for example, the Babylonian Talmud, Tractate Taanit 23b.

33. *Kfar Habad* (in Hebrew), 25 Shevat 5741 (30 January 1981).

34. Diary, 17 Tammuz 5710 (2 July 1950), published in *Kfar Habad,* 7 Adar I 5741 (11 February 1981).

35. See letters of Rabbi Menachem Mendel Schneerson, *Igroth Kodesh* (Sacred missives).

36. See the rebbe's letter of 25 Nisan 5740 (11 April 1980), published in *Kfar Habad,* 15 Sivan 5741 (17 June 1981); "Faith and Science" (in Hebrew), *Kfar Habad,* 1980, p. 116, in which the Jewish people in the Holocaust are likened to a patient whose doctors have decided to operate and amputate a limb. Those who do not understand medicine and perceive this incident without realizing the function of these doctors will believe that they are wicked, seeking to harm the patient.

37. See diary, 1 Adar 5711 (7 February 1951), published in *Kfar Habad* (in Hebrew) 25 Nisan 5741 (7 February 1951).

38. See n. 14.

39. See G. Scholem, "Isaac Luria and His School," in *Major Trends in Jewish Mysticism,* pp. 244–86.

40. Hebrew: GeMaCH, an acronym for *gemilut hasidim,* generally understood as helping the needy both materially and spiritually.

41. One outstanding example is that of the emissary Leib of Tustov, who was sent to Nancy and Metz in France. For a complete description, see *Kfar Habad,* 27 Tevet 5747 (20 January 1985), pp. 10–16.

42. See *Igroth Kodesh* 17 (Summer 1958) (Brooklyn: KeHoS, 1990), p. 52.

43. *Orah Hayyim,* sec. 38. The Shulhan Aruch is the basic codex of Jewish religious law.

44. Bukiet, "Mission and Hints."

45. See H. Glitzenstein, "The President of Our Generation" (in Hebew), *Kfar Habad,* 10 Nisan 5743 (24 March 1983).

46. A. D. Halperin, "Belief in the Messiah" (in Hebrew), *Kfar Habad,* 25 Shevat 5741 (30 January 1981).

47. Maimonides, *Mishneh Torah* (Laws of kings), chap. 11, law 4.

48. Halperin, "Belief in the Messiah."

49. Active messianism in Habad arouses powerful opposition in certain Haredi circles. Rabbi Eliezer Menachem Shach, head of the Ponivezh Yeshiva in Bnai Brak and leader of the Lithuanian components of Agudat Israel, came out with extraordinary severity against Habad and its rebbes. He called for severing all ties between Agudat Israel, which represents mainstream haredi Orthodoxy, and the Habad movement—an ultimatum rejected by the party's Hasidic components. On this background, Agudat Israel split before the elections to the Twelfth Knesset (1988), and Rabbi Shach established the Degel Ha Torah party. During a cabinet crisis in the National Unity Government (1990), the Ramam ordered his followers to support the Likud and would not allow establishment of a government headed by the Labor Alignment, notwithstanding the decision of Agudat Israel's Council of Torah Sages, the supreme religious authority of this party.

50. See G. Scholem, *Sabbetai-Svi: The Mystical Messiah, 1626–1676* (Princeton: Princeton University Press, 1973), pp. 461–77.

3

Accounting for Islamic Fundamentalisms

Accounting for Islamic Fundamentalisms

James Piscatori

The chapters that follow convey a sense of the richness of the contemporary Islamic scene. The Islamic movements in societies as diverse as Egypt, Algeria, Iraq, Nigeria, central Asia, and the West Bank and Gaza Strip are inescapably formed by the many social, cultural, and political experiences unique to their histories. The example of the Iraqi oppositional movements adds the further differentiating factor of Shi'i thought and practice. And yet, whether Sunni or Shi'i, Arab, African, or central Asian, several general patterns arise from the empirical details and shed light on how Islamic fundamentalist movements originate and evolve and what impact they possess.

The Formation of Islamist Movements

First, although a similar range of catalysts appears to be at work in the formation of the Islamist movements mentioned above, the most important stimulant may be derivative. The range of catalysts extends from social and economic disequilibrium, particularly that associated with rapid urbanization such as Ousmane Kane describes in the case of northern Nigeria (chap. 18), to opposition to state authority, the experience of colonialism, and the weight of dependency in the world economic system. In a sense, this range is only to be expected for it replicates patterns seen elsewhere in the studies of the Fundamentalism Project.[1]

More importantly, however, what we witness in the Islamist movements presented here is a second-order reaction. The formation of fundamentalist movements is thus not so much a reaction to the failures of modernization, though that acute sense of disappointment is obviously present; but, rather, a reaction to the failures of leaders—religious as well as political—to deal with these failures. In effect, second-generation movements have emerged—if not strictly chronologically second-generation, then at least programmatically. Gehad Auda's discussion of Egypt in chapter 15 indicates that radical Islamist sentiment is encouraged when national as well as local leaders respond ineptly or uncreatively to the increasing economic difficulties and deterioration in public services in Upper Egypt and the crowded suburbs of Cairo. In situating the rise of Islamist movements in Algeria squarely in the context of political crisis rather than social and economic deprivation, Hugh Roberts demonstrates in chapter 17 that the initial appeal of the Islamic Salvation Front (FIS) lay precisely in its ability to project itself as the real inheritor of the National Liberation Front (FLN) and its claim to national leadership. As Jean-François Legrain suggests in chapter 16, even in the case of Palestinian Islam, in which confrontation with Israel remains the special defining characteristic, opposition to the unsuccessful secular leadership of the Palestine Liberation Organization (PLO) has proved crucial to the formation of an Islamic movement which sees itself as the only alternative to both the occupation and PLO domination.

Second, and closely related to the first point, a fragmentation of religious authority has occurred in modern Muslim societies, and this has allowed a logic of Islamist proliferation whereby leaders and groups compete for authority. A complex attitude toward established religious leadership in particular is characteristic of Islamic movements. On the one hand, certain traditional religious leaders (ulama) like Shaykh 'Umar 'Abd al-Rahman, in unlikely exile from his native Egypt in the New Jersey suburbs of New York, continue to exercise considerable influence over adherents of radical groups, such as the Islamic Groups (al-jama'at al-islamiyya) in Egypt. Moreover, as Amatzia Baram demonstrates in chapter 20, the ulama provide the majority of the leadership in the anti-Ba'thist Supreme Assembly for the Islamic Revolution in Iraq (SAIRI) and are influential in its main contender, Hizb al-Da'wa al-Islamiyya, the Islamic Call party. Ulama such as these are responding to the inefficiencies and corruption of existing political leadership.

Yet on the other hand, the existing religious leadership has more often appeared to falter because of its intolerance of, even collusion with, the ideological competitors of reformist Islam (including the government). As Mark Saroyan (chap. 19) says of the ulama in the Soviet Union: to endow oneself with the right to proclaim something *jahili*, or pertaining to the "ignorance" associated with pre-Islamic times, was, in effect, to say there could be no Islam without the ulama. This claim was the ultimate in the self-generation of power, and it reflected in part a similar Marxist approach. Here the relationship to political power was a parallel one, since as long as the authority of the ulama was affirmed, so, too, was the authority of the state affirmed. The inchoate Islamic movements in central Asia are responding to the decades of such intimacy with the Soviet state which the Muslim Religious Boards practiced. In Nigeria, Izala, the Society for the Removal of Heresy and Reinstatement of Tradition, arose largely in opposition to a Sufi dominance accepted or encouraged by many of the ulama.

In the case of Egypt, the intermediary experience of an existing reformist or fundamentalist movement has proved formative. Both the modernizing policies of Gamal 'Abd al-Nasser and Anwar al-Sadat and the tame reactions of the Ikhwan al-Muslimin, the Muslim Brotherhood, paved the way for neo-Ikhwanist groups. In a sense, the

Brotherhood's leadership, whether or not formally ulama-trained at the venerable Islamic university of al-Azhar, delegitimized itself by cooperation with Sadat's regime and even participation in parliamentary elections in the more recent Mubarak era.

In such situations in which established religious leaders, especially the traditional ulama, appear to have become hopelessly compromised and the government untrustworthy, the field is left open to "new" intellectuals who appropriate to themselves the right to interpret Islam.[2] One example is Rashid al-Ghannushi, once a secondary school teacher who now heads the Islamic Tendency Movement (MTI) of Tunisia. Others discussed in this section include FIS's Abassi Madani, who with a Ph.D. in education from the University of London, also represents the influential new type of Muslim leader, as does the Izala's Usman Muhammad Imam ("U.M.I."), with his mixture of traditional and modern educational experiences.

The rise and proliferation of fundamentalist movements are thus related to the perception of a decline in legitimacy of the arbiters of Muslim opinion, whether these are the government, the ulama, or established reformist movements. Unable or unwilling to redress perceived injustices and inequalities, political and religious elites, even sometimes existing Islamist movements, come ineluctably to bear the hallmarks of failure. For younger, or at least relatively well educated and politically less accommodating activists, the rejection of such agents of failure must be resolute.

The Organization and Agenda of Islamic Fundamentalism

Third, Islamic fundamentalist movements, like the other fundamentalist movements discussed in this volume, are animated by judgment and censure, and this demarcation of the pure and impure affects fundamentalists' dealings both with nonfundamentalists and—significantly—with each other. A need for boundary setting, for affirming approval and disapproval, exists in such ideologically motivated movements.[3] Mubarak's Egypt has become *dar al-kufr* (land of unbelief), Saddam's Iraq is a jahili society, and Israel is the descendant of both the evil Banu Isra'il of ancient times and the treacherous Jews of Prophetic time depicted in the Qur'an.[4]

From the perspective of the outsider, Islam is constructed and reconstructed of such durable and pliable material that it is nearly pointless to assess deviation or orthodoxy—a point made in a different way by Rafiuddin Ahmed in chapter 24 on the Jama'at-i-Islami, which appears in part 4, of this volume. Yet from the perspective of the fundamentalist, the stakes are high: the faith must be protected from assault and preserved from heterodoxy. Da'wa in Iraq says that elimination of Saddam, "the enemy of religion and the Qur'an," is the preeminent duty of every Muslim, and, according to Islamic Jihad in the West Bank and Gaza, one obeys either "God and His Prophet," or "Mitzna, Mordechai, and Shomron [i.e., the Israeli occupiers]."[5]

This tendency to bifurcate the world and to deprive the faith of nuance often applies to competitive Muslim authorities and groups as much as it does to those perceived as un-Islamic or beyond the pale. As indicated above, rejection of existing religious elites is characteristic of contemporary Islamic fundamentalism, and hence "competition" naturally occurs among various Muslim actors, including among fundamentalist groups themselves. The contest between the Muslim Brotherhood in Egypt and more radical groups is indicative. In effect, struggle with groups or governments outside the Islamic circle is impeded or forestalled by the prior question: Which "Islam" will carry the banner in the war with its enemies? In Algeria, will it be FIS, or the local Hamas, or one of the other reformist parties? In the West Bank and Gaza, will it be Islamic Jihad or Hamas (the Movement of Islamic Resistance), the radical wing of the Muslim Brotherhood? In Iraq, will SAIRI finally displace Da'wa and Munazzamat al-'Amal al-Islami (Organization of Islamic Action) as the most coherent voice of opposition to Saddam Hussein?

But the related fundamentalist rhythms of censure and competition take on more complicated forms. Often a fundamentalist group imitates and adopts organizational structures and programs from its successful competitors, even when those competitors are pursuing a secular program. Baram, for example, illustrates how the Shi'i oppositional groups in Iraq have self-consciously and unhesitatingly borrowed the organizational and mobilizational insights of the Ba'th and Communist parties. Roberts explains that the FIS and FLN display parallel discourses: both purport to defend the nation; the FIS goal of an Islamic republic is the analogue of the FLN's goal of independence from the French; and the FIS's warnings to the army not to thwart the will of the people correlate to the FLN's admonition to the French during the revolution not to engage in further massacres.

At the same time, certain elements of the competitor's ideology may be "Islamized" and incorporated into the fundamentalist program. So effective has Hamas become in setting the agenda of the Intifada that the PLO has been moved to invoke an Islamic discourse in its own pronouncements. Indeed, it was noteworthy that at the Dakar summit of the Organization of the Islamic Conference in December 1991, only two leaders explicitly sounded Islamic themes concerning the fight against Israel—President Rafsanjani of Iran and the PLO's Yasser 'Arafat.[6]

The internal competition among fundamentalist groups themselves, moreover, determines to a significant degree the ideological shifts of the movement or group in question. Such interaction, however unwanted, may make it necessary for the fundamentalist ideology to be sharpened and even radicalized further in contrast to that of competitors. Legrain's discussion reveals the manner in which the Palestinian branch of the Muslim Brotherhood, preferring social welfare activism to armed struggle with Israel, responded to the Islamic Jihad's popular lead in espousing violence by broadening its own mission to include military engagement with the enemy.

Yet the impulse to set off the good from the evil, the orthodox from the deviant, rarely, if ever, involves physical migration from one territorial realm to another. Purity is only partly a spatial category, and movements of complete withdrawal *(hijra)* from the corrupted world seem notably absent in our configuration. Rather, purity appears to be experiential, a matter of conduct rather than place, of belief and lifestyle within the properly constituted community of like-minded people. The need for physical withdrawal and the creation of a morally secure distance is consequently reduced, and we do not see in these second-generation programmatic fundamentalist movements the kind of pointed desire for territorial and cultural withdrawal that we see, for example, in the chapters in the preceding section of this volume, in ultra-Orthodox Jewish fundamentalisms in Israel and elsewhere. As Auda explains, among certain Egyptian Islamists the mandate of moral isolation from the corruptions of society has had to be tempered by the equally unavoidable obligation to educate the public at large *(al-balagh al-ʿamm)*. The latter imperative has led to an ironic reliance on the publishing and media institutions of the very society condemned. In addition, the group Jamʿiyyat al-Takfir waʾl-Hijra (Society of Excommunication and Emigration) in Egypt, bitterly critical of the failings of Egyptian society, engaged in jihad rather than removal from the scene.

This engagement with the world is repeatedly seen in the social welfare activism of Islamist groups. Kane shows how the Izala controls a network of primary and secondary schools, which among other things meet the popular demand in northern Nigeria for the teaching of Arabic, and several hospitals and clinics. Legrain explains that the Muslim Brotherhood under Shaykh Ahmad Yasin solidified its base in the Gaza Strip through its operation of medical clinics, social and sporting clubs, and kindergartens. In Algeria in late October 1989 and in Egypt in October 1992, Islamist groups provided the most efficient organized assistance to earthquake victims. While government services proved inept or inadequate to the task, FIS in Algeria and a variety of Islamic groups in Egypt provided food, clothing, and temporary housing. Such activities have helped Islamists to attract adherents.

The search for purity among fundamentalists generates the imperative to proselytize and to convert, but, because of the fracturing of the Islamic movement that has been described, a kind of competitive *daʿwa,* a competitive call to Islam, comes into existence. Given the battle for the Muslim heart and mind that is unfolding, Muslims are the primary target of this proselytism. It follows that the composition of the various Islamist groups is in flux, and shifting memberships are often the result. In the case of Lebanon, Shiʿi activists are attracted alternately to AMAL (Afwaj al-Muqawama al-Lubnaniyya, the Lebanese Resistance Brigades) and Hizbullah (Party of God) and sometimes simultaneously to both Shiʿi movements.[7]

In the examples discussed in the chapters to follow, Hamas raids Jihad for members; SAIRI in Iraq overlaps with Daʿwa; Izala in Nigeria wins and loses members from competing Muslim groups. Such fluidity of membership is doubtless enhanced by the fact that, for the most part, recruits are drawn from a remarkably similar pool of individuals: young, male, urban, modern-educated, lower to middle class. Research into radical groups in Upper Egypt, such as al-Jamaʿa al-Islamiyya al-Jihadiyya and al-Shawqun suggests that the poor, unemployed, and uneducated are also being attracted. Boundary setting, coupled with competitive daʿwa, creates, therefore, a multiplicity of fundamentalist groups of shifting membership, which are nevertheless sufficiently mobilized to be fully engaged in the work of remaking the world.

A fourth general pattern emerges from the essays on Islamist movements: the relationship between ideology, or worldview, and organizational dynamics is not that of unequal partners—the latter simply deferring to and governed by the former. Boundary setting may imply ideology is the decisive factor in the equation, with changes in conduct, membership, or structure following changes in ideology. As we have seen in Egypt, the logical conclusion of *takfir,* a policy of invalidating the government and rival Islamist groups as "infidels," is a strategy of violence against both; it may also provide some attraction for the marginals of society, the *mustad'afun* (or "oppressed") of Iranian revolutionary discourse or "wretched of the earth" of Third Worldist discourse.

But the relationship between ideology and organization is not as straightforward as may have been supposed. Part of the reason lies in the obvious shifts of ideology which follow changes in the circumstances and fortunes of various groups. Baram demonstrates that, in the case of the Iraqi Shi'a, uncertain and overwhelmingly unfavorable conditions—an unsuccessful uprising against Saddam in March 1991, a fragmented Iraqi opposition, Saddam's continuation in power—encouraged the tentative beginnings of an argument that Islam is compatible with democracy. The subject of Islam and democracy is complex as well as controversial,[8] and there is no doubt that the Shi'a groups continue to affirm the absolute sovereignty of God and, in some cases, the importance of Khomeinist ideas like Rule of the Jurist *(wilayat al-faqih)*.[9] But the inference is unavoidable that, finding themselves in the position of having to cultivate links with both Western opponents of Saddam and nonreligious Iraqi oppositional movements, the fundamentalist movements have come to regard Western-style notions of popular political participation as appealing.

Because of inherent ideological ambiguities, the relationship between fundamentalist ideologies and movements is also more complex than often assumed. Auda points to the disadvantages or "paradoxical" results of ideological clarity. When, for example, the fundamentalist groups stress takfir or jihad, they run the risk of inspiring opposition—from a more accommodationist Muslim Brotherhood and, of course, from liberal non-Muslim sectors of the society—and hence imperiling their chances of mass support. On this specific point, the discernible rise in Egyptian fundamentalist activity in 1992–93 suggests that the jury is still out.

Yet this example serves to remind us that Islamic fundamentalist ideology, despite claims to purity and to prior rights of proselytism, is rarely an unchanging body of doctrine. Rather, as Legrain's example of Hamas in the West Bank and Gaza also demonstrates, it is something that evolves and changes with circumstances. As already noted, this organization felt constrained to adopt a Jihadist endorsement of violence against the Israelis. But, with an eye to the essentially nationalist nature of the struggle and the views of the many PLO partisans, it also made a concession in the direction of the PLO: nationalism (*al-wataniyya*), according to Hamas's covenant, is "a component of the faith [*juz' min al-'aqida*]."[10] In a similar manner, Kane demonstrates how the Izala is a movement that is "fundamentalist" in the sense of receiving inspiration from the reformist principles of Wahhabism, the movement that helped create the Saudi state, and is thus hostile to Sufi practices. Yet it is also modernist in its urban composition and orientations and thus discourages deferential traditional social practices. "Selective emancipation from tradition," in his useful phrase, is the consequence.

Saroyan's analysis of the changes in Islamic discourse in Soviet and post-Soviet central Asia also subtly illuminates the power of ideological ambiguity. In the days when Soviet rule was entrenched and the ideological supremacy of the Communist party bureaucracy relatively unchallenged, it might have been supposed that the Muslim establishment would need to espouse an ideology of subservience. In fact, according to Saroyan, the ulama constructed a kind of "counterdiscourse," which, precisely by arguing that Islam promoted many of the values of the model Soviet citizen, helped to provide for and protect Islam's place in the system rather than exclude or undermine it. Since the disintegration of the Soviet state, the ulama have neither fully rejected the old Soviet system in its entirety nor wholly exonerated themselves from past cooperation with the regime. The ideology is evolving and varies to some extent from republic to republic. Yet the very mixture of ideas, it must be observed, is scarcely unsuitable to the ulama's interests in a period when the challenge of new and rival Muslim groups has yet to crystallize.

A fifth general pattern points to the multiple transnational linkages that exist between a fundamentalist movement and groups or states outside its society. Although the Qur'an refers to Muslims as constituting one community of faith (*umma wahida*),[11] pan-Islamic political integration has always proven elusive. The abolition of the caliphate in March 1924 merely accentuated the competition among various Muslim leaders for supremacy.[12]

Since then, however, Muslim concerns and bonds larger than those related to one Muslim society have exercised some influence. The most obvious example relates to ideas that are shared and disseminated across national borders. Amatzia Baram's discussion of the Iraqi Shi'a makes clear how Ayatollah Khomeini's ideas on the Rule of the Jurist found favor in Iraq with Ayatollah Muhammad Baqir al-Sadr and, for several years, with Da'wa. Khomeini's political theory was formulated in exile in Najaf in Iraq, one of the major centers of Shi'i learning, and it was there that several overlapping political and ideological networks were created. Khomeini came under the protection of the politically activist Muhsin al-Hakim, whose sons were founders of Da'wa along with, among others, Muhammad Husayn Fadlallah, who later moved to Lebanon where he became the spiritual leader of Hizbullah.[13]

Ousmane Kane shows the importance of travel to and contact with the Wahhabi Saudis for the ideological formation of Shaykh Abubakar Gumi, the paramount Muslim official in northern Nigeria until his death in 1992. Owing mainly to the largesse of the Saudi-financed Muslim World League (Rabitat al-'Alam al-Islami),[14] many Nigerians have had the opportunity either to study in Saudi Arabia or to attend Saudi-influenced educational centers in Nigeria itself. In addition, Legrain points to Saudi financial support of Hamas, thereby perhaps accounting for Hamas' ambivalence during the Gulf Crisis in the wake of Saddam's invasion of Kuwait in August 1990. Hamas was loath to lose its popular base, but it was also cognizant of its lifeline to its Saudi backer.[15] Moreover, in the past, one wing of the FIS, incorporating the important leader 'Ali Ben Hadj, came under Saudi influence to some degree. Often referred to as Hanbalists after the school of law that prevails in Saudi Arabia, this group appeared reluctant to lean—as the FIS eventually did—in the direction of Saddam in the Gulf War.

As the Saudi example suggests, several Muslim states have proffered themselves as "patrons" of Islamic movements. Iran is the obvious competitor to Saudi Arabia, and studies have pointed to Iranian "export of the revolution"[16] to the Gulf (underground Shi'i groups in Bahrain, Kuwait, and eastern Saudi Arabia), Lebanon (Hizbullah), and since 1992, Sudan. Iranian support of the Shi'i groups in Iraq, especially SAIRI, has been important, but one should also bear in mind that, during the Shi'i uprising at the end of the Gulf War, the Iranians afforded little by way of concrete fraternal assistance. All the same, money, arms, technical and training assistance, and ideological inspiration cannot be seen as negligible. The Iranian presence in Sudan induced such anxiety for the Algerian government, which has feared Iranian subversion through Sudan, that it broke diplomatic relations with Iran at the end of March 1993.[17] One British newspaper reported that, in February 1993, at a meeting of Muslim groups from throughout the world, the Iranians announced their intention to support the Islamic Groups in their attempt to overthrow the Mubarak government; this was "the key to the creation of the Islamic umma."[18]

The chapters to follow do not point to a unified fundamentalist movement across the Islamic world, nor do they affirm the existence of a supreme command. As every volume of the Fundamentalism Project has plainly demonstrated, fundamentalisms are diverse and polymorphous and linked to the conditions of the particular societies that generate and sustain them. Islamic fundamentalism is no different, but the sharing of ideas and values and the similarities of leadership and external sources of support suggest that larger Muslim environments may sustain and transform homegrown fundamentalist movements.

The Contest for Power and Influence

The following chapters suggest a sixth and final observation. Indicators of transnational linkage need to be taken into our account, but because fragmentation of religious authority is the most notable aspect of modern political Islam, it must also be recognized that fundamentalisms possess an ambivalent relationship to power. Fundamentalist groups—sometimes led by the ulama, often by new intellectuals, and frequently by both—must constantly devise their policies in light of the needs and aspirations of a set of other actors: the government; Muslim patrons such as Saudi Arabia or Iran; competitor Islamist groups; and the mass of people who do not belong to the movement but whom it seeks to mobilize.

In a sense, all Islamist movements are engaged in the quest for political influence. The entire rationale of their existence is to change the society in which Muslims live so that they may more faithfully follow the dictates of Islam. A distinction is often asserted between those activists who seek to change society directly through political, possibly violent, means, and those who hope to do so gradually and indirectly by concentrating first on the content of individual Muslim hearts. The distinction is thus often and usefully drawn between *al-thawra al-islamiyya*, the Islamic Revolution, and *al-da'wa al-islamiyya*, the Islamic Call. The programs of the Jihad Organization in

Egypt and the Tablighi Jama'at,[19] a transnational da'wa group professing apoliticism, are doubtless different.

And yet the chapters to follow propose a qualification, suggesting that the line between the two realms of mission is not always so clearly drawn: Muslim activists often, though admittedly not all the time, pursue *simultaneously* the moral transformation of Muslims and the restructuring of society and government. Legrain's analysis demonstrates the ways in which the Muslim Brotherhood in the West Bank and Gaza has had to accept that its social program cannot succeed without direct participation in the struggle against the occupation. In Nigeria, Kane explains that the Izala, sponsored by several established politicians, does not in the main advocate a confrontational approach to Islamization. But its policies of attacking entrenched Sufi orders amounted to such a challenge to the social and political status quo. that the federal government denied official recognition from its founding in 1978 until after the rise to power of General Ibrahim Babangida in 1985.

Whatever Islamist political intentions may be, however, the ability of the government to co-opt, as well as repress, is enormous, and Hugh Roberts provides a cautionary tale for young fundamentalist movements. As they move from the arena of religiously inspired protest and reform to political engagement, they may be vulnerable to co-optation or manipulation by secular political veterans. According to Roberts, the FIS began as a genuinely religious movement (with only one ideologue, Abassi Madani, having any serious political experience) and was quickly overwhelmed by external forces for which it was unprepared. Not the least of these forces was the enduring military and political might of the tenacious power-brokers of the FLN who have ruled Algeria longer than most FIS activists have been alive. In this light, the dramatic rise of political Islam in Algeria seems accounted for more by the failure, and subsequent face-saving maneuvers, of wizened secular political hands than by a popular Islamic movement, which, in its organizational structural and political mechanisms, has been underdeveloped.

The details of Roberts's analysis may not be accepted by every observer of Algeria, but his theme of an unexpected relationship between fundamentalism and power resonates throughout the chapters to follow. In more general terms, the result of the complex relationships a fundamentalist movement maintains is by no means certain.

On the one hand, the fundamentalist group's interaction with the four actors mentioned above may lead to a recognition that ideological and strategic purity has only limited utility or is in fact counterproductive in the daily round of political exchanges and struggle. In Tunisia, various fundamentalist leaders have realized that, in the quest to implement their agenda and broaden their base, they must, to some extent, come to terms with the government and especially accept a working relationship with other Islamist groups. "Islamic pluralism" (*al-ta'dud al-islamiyya*)[20] is thus a challenge for fundamentalists, but it is also the practical alternative to unmitigated confrontation with the regime and with Muslim competitors.

Even in those societies in which the confrontation with the state is sharper and sustained—Egypt, Iraq, Algeria—forms of political accommodation have occurred as well. The explanation lies in part in the obvious near-monopoly of power by the government, but also in the fact that these movements—contrary to what often appears in the literature of fundamentalism—are not generally mass-based. The following chapters do not, for the most part, describe mass-based organizations but rather small cadre, elitist organizations. Lacking a broad base of support but hoping to achieve one and inevitably joined in a high-stakes competition with other Muslim groups, the fundamentalists frequently change tactics, if not also strategy. Uncompromising in rhetoric, often they compromise in fact. In Baram's terminology, pragmatism frequently prevails, and necessity constrains the true believer. As Kane demonstrates, the Saudi influence on the Izala generally has worked as a kind of restraint in Nigeria.

In a perhaps unanticipated way, such flexibility may give the state room to maneuver and push the political society along to some form of tentative stability. Whether "normalization," in Auda's term, is the result, there is no doubt that tacit bargaining routinely occurs between governments and Islamist oppositions. De facto rules of the game are formulated—in a market metaphor, "prices" are controlled. In the case of Egypt, precisely because the government has been aware of both the intense competition among Islamist groups and the existence of a sizable public opinion repelled by such events as the assassination of the intellectual Faraj Fuda in June 1992, it has appeared able, at least until mid-1992, to draw limits around the fundamentalist challenge.

Yet, on the other hand, fundamentalists' interaction with the various forces of society may serve to radicalize the process. Ishtiaq Ahmed, for example, believes that the inherent ambition of Muslim ideologues, even "modernists," to certify themselves as the spokesmen for an authentic Islam pushes the competition toward the extreme: "howsoever the modernists argue, their Islamic state would always be vulnerable to doctrinal pressure" and would lead to a "fundamentalist" state.[21] In the language of the market, the fundamentalist price may be bid upward as Islamists attempt to distance themselves from an un-Islamic government, compete with other groups, respond to the wishes of external patrons, or react to mass sentiment.

The Gulf Crisis of 1990–91 demonstrated in particular the power of the Muslim "street." In Jordan, Morocco, Algeria, and elsewhere throughout the Muslm world, ordinary men and women took to the streets to express either, positively, their support for Saddam or, negatively, their opposition to the Western-led military coalition arrayed against him. The Jordanian Muslim Brotherhood, mindful of its financial links with Gulf states such as Saudi Arabia and Kuwait, was at first hesitant to take an overtly critical stand on the coalition, but it soon adopted a tone more critical of the anti-Saddam forces and the Jordanian government. It had recognized the force of popular sentiment and the appeal of other organizations like Islamic Jihad-Bayt al-Muqaddas, whose leader had typically declared: "This is a battle between faith and atheism . . . the side of faith is led by Saddam . . . those who fight beside America today are doomed, for they have betrayed their nation and faith."[22]

The rivalries among fundamentalists are often crucial. In Algeria, in an attempt to certify its Islamic credentials and, at the same time, improve its position relative to Islamic competitors, the FIS has adopted less obliging rhetoric on the need for an

Islamic republic and the essential incompatibility of Islam and democracy. In a similar manner, Kane notes that the willingness of the Izala leadership to work with the government has spawned a "neo-Izala"—independent preachers and well-educated young people who were sympathetic to Saddam Hussein in the Gulf War and are critical of the United States and hostile to Israel.

An added dilemma exists for fundamentalists who are uncompromising in rhetoric but compromising in fact. Unwittingly, they may leave the ground open for less compromising and more radical fundamentalists—precisely the predicament of the Egyptian Muslim Brotherhood. The government may have hoped to promote it, and the Brotherhood may have so offered itself, as a "mechanism of mediation" between the state and radicals, as Auda says, but the result has been an Islamist scoring of points off an Ikhwan seemingly collaborationist. Caught thus between the Mubarak government and the more radical Islamic Groups which are gaining martyrs in daily violent clashes with the regime, the Brothers seek the intermediate path: refraining (along with most opposition parties) from participation in the elections for the People's Assembly in November 1990, but contesting—and winning—elections to professional associations of doctors, lawyers, and engineers.

In the process, the Brothers assert a measure of political influence even as they remain vulnerable to the charge of de facto collaboration with a corrupt and ostensibly un-Islamic system. The danger—and it is by no means certain what attitude the vast majority of Egyptians hold—is that anything short of total rejection of the state system will appear fatally compromising and hence impure. Therein would be the opportunity of the jama'at—and, of course, the security paradox of a regime, which already effectively confers a measure of legitimacy on these Groups the more it suppresses and uses torture against them.[23]

The Islamic tableau is nothing if not uncertain, however. The possibility of further radicalization looms, yet the limitations on these groups' influence may come precisely from the give-and-take of political contest, which encourages ideological transformations and tactical flexibility. Thus it may in the long run be reasonable to accept that many variants of Islamic fundamentalism exist and that one comprehensive, encompassing definition of the phenomenon is misleading. For one certain conclusion that emerges from the following chapters is the relative degree of ambiguity, in both ideology and structure, coherence and organization, that has characterized these various groups and movements.

Notes

1. See, for example, Nancy T. Ammerman, "North American Protestant Fundamentalism," pp. 12, 38–39; Samuel C. Heilman and Menachem Friedman, "Religious Fundamentalism and Religious Jews," pp. 199–200; and Daniel Gold, "Organized Hindu isms: From Vedic Truth to Hindu Nation," pp. 535–37, 575–80: in Martin E. Marty and R. Scott Appleby, eds., *Fundamentalisms Observed* (Chicago: University of Chicago Press, 1991).

2. For an important discussion of such

intellectuals, see Gilles Kepel and Yann Richard, eds., *Intellectuels et militants de l'Islam contemporain* (Intellectuals and militants in contemporary Islam) (Paris: Editions de Seuil, 1990).

3. See Martin E. Marty and R. Scott Appleby, "Conclusion: An Interim Report on a Hypothetical Family," in Marty and Appleby, *Fundamentalisms Observed*, pp. 821–22.

4. Qur'an, Sura VII, 166; Sura III, 14.

5. See, for example, Jihad statement (in Arabic), reproduced in Jean-François Legrain and Paul Chenard, eds., *Les voix du soulèvement palestinien* (Voices of the Palestinian uprising) (Cairo: Centre d'Etudes et de Documentation Economique Juridique et Sociale [CEDEJ], 1991), p. 11.

6. See, for example, BBC, *Summary of World Broadcasts*, ME/1252i (11 December 1991) and ME/1541 (13 December 1991). At 'Arafat's initiative, the summit was entitled the al-Quds al-Sharif (the noble Jerusalem) summit, and he and President Rafsanjani unsuccessfully fought against deletion of the word "jihad" in a resolution on Israel.

7. See James Piscatori, "The Shi'a of Lebanon and Hizbullah, the Party of God," in Christine Jennett and Randal G. Stewart, eds., *Politics of the Future: The Role of Social Movements* (Melbourne, Australia: Macmillan, 1989), pp. 306–9.

8. Muslim thinkers themselves have differed on the subject. The South Asian Abul A'la Maududi, for example, believed that Islam constituted a "theo-democracy," but that if democracy meant only the sovereignty of the people, it was antithetical to Islam: Maududi, "Political Theory of Islam," in John J. Donohue and John L. Esposito, eds., *Islam in Transition: Muslim Perspectives* (New York: Oxford University Press, 1982), pp. 253–54. Sayyid Qutb, the great theoretician of the Muslim Brotherhood in Egypt, regarded it as a jahili concept: Qutb, *Fi Zilal al-Qur'an* (In the shade of the Qur'an), as cited in Yvonne Y. Haddad, "Sayyid Qutb: Ideologue of Islamic Revival," in John L. Esposito, ed., *Voices of Resurgent Islam* (New York: Oxford Uni-

versity Press, 1983), p. 79. Rashid al-Ghannushi, the Tunisian Muslim leader, has endorsed the idea that Islam is inherently democratic: Ghannushi, *Fi al-Mubadi al-Islamiyya li-Dimuqratiyya wa'l-Usul al-Hukm al-Islamiyya* (On the Islami principles of democracy and the fundamentals of Islamic government) (n.p., 1410/1990); and idem, "Islam and Freedom Can Be Friends," *The Observer* (London), 19 January 1992, p. 18. Two interesting compilations which address the general question are: *Al-Hiwar al-Qawmi/al-Dini* (The nationalist and religious dialogue) (Beirut: Markaz Dirasat al-Wahda al-'Arabiyya, December 1989), esp. pp. 237–358; and 'Abdullah al-Nafisi, ed., *Al-Haraka al-Islamiyya: Ru'ya Mustaqbiliyya; Awraq fi'l-Naqd al-Dhati* (The Islamic movement: An examination of the future; Papers in self-criticism) (Cairo: Makatabat Madbuli, 1989). Among non-Muslims, Bernard Lewis has argued that, for Islamic fundamentalists, "democracy is obviously an irrelevance, and, unlike the communist totalitarians, they rarely use or even misuse the word"; Lewis, "Islam and Liberal Democracy," *The Atlantic*, February 1993, pp. 89–98, quotation at p. 91. And Amos Perlmutter has concluded that the two forces are mutually contradictory: Perlmutter, "Islam and Democracy Simply Aren't Compatible," *International Herald Tribune*, 21 January 1992, p. 6. Also see Martin Kramer, "Islam vs. Democracy," *Commentary*, January 1993, pp. 35–42.

9. For the definitive study of this concept, see Abdulaziz Abdulhussein Sachedina, *The Just Ruler in Shi'ite Islam: The Comprehensive Authority of the Jurist in Imamite Jurisprudence* (New York: Oxford University Press, 1988).

10. Article 12, *Mithaq Harakat al-Muqawama al-Islamiyya—Filistin (Hamas)* (Covenant of the movement of the Islamic resistance [Hamas]) (Palestine), 1 Muharram 1409/18 August 1988, p. 11.

11. Qur'an, Sura XLII, 8.

12. See Martin Kramer, *Islam Assembled: The Advent of the Muslim Congresses* (New York: Columbia University Press, 1985).

13. For information on these connec-

tions, see Chibli Mallat, *Shi'i Thought from the South of Lebanon,* Papers on Lebanon, no. 7 (Oxford: Centre for Lebanese Studies, 1988), pp. 9–15.

14. For information on this organization and related ones, see Reinhard Schulze, *Islamischer Internationalismus im 20, Jahrhundert* (Islamic internationalism in the twentieth century) (Leiden: E. J. Brill, 1990).

15. In addition to his chapter in this volume, see Jean-François Legrain, "A Defining Moment: Palestinian Islamic Fundamentalism," in James Piscatori, ed., *Islamic Fundamentalism and the Gulf Crisis* (Chicago: American Academy of Arts and Sciences, 1991), pp. 75–79.

16. See, for example, R. K. Ramazani, *Revolutionary Iran: Challenge and Response in the Middle East* (Baltimore: Johns Hopkins University Press, 1988); and idem, "Iran's Export of the Revolution: Politics, Ends and Means," in John L. Esposito, ed., *The Iranian Revolution: Its Global Impact* (Miami: Florida International University Press, 1990), pp. 40–62. Also see Farhang Rajaee, "Iranian Ideology and Worldview: The Cultural Export of the Revolution," in Esposito, *The Iranian Revolution,* pp. 63–80.

17. Christopher Walker, "Algiers Cuts Ties with Iran in Protest Over Extremist Violence," *The Times* (London), 29 March 1993, p. 13.

18. Safa Haeri and Andrew Hogg, "Iran's Mullahs Order Fundamentalists to Topple Mubarak," *Sunday Times* (London), 28 March 1993, p. 23.

19. For information on Tablighi Jama'at, see Mumtaz Ahmad, "Islamic Fundamentalism in South Asia: The Jamaat-i-Islami and the Tablighi Jamaat," in Marty and Appleby, *Fundamentalisms Observed,* pp. 457–530; also see Felice Dassetto, "The Tabligh Organization in Belgium," in Tomas Gerholm and Yngve Georg Lithman, eds., *The New Islamic Presence in Western Europe* (London: Mansell Publishing, 1988), pp. 159–73; and Anwarul Haq, *The Faith Movement of Mawlana Muhammad Ilyas* (London: George Allen and Unwin, 1972).

20. This is the term of Shaykh Jaballah, a leader of the Hizb al-Nahdah (Renaissance party), the name of the MTI since early 1989; *Summary of World Broadcasts,* ME/1242 A/7 (29 November 1991). The BBC translated the term as "multi-Islamism."

21. Ishtiaq Ahmed, *The Concept of an Islamic State: An Analysis of the Ideological Controversy in Pakistan* (London: Frances Pinter, 1987), p. 212.

22. Quoted in Beverly Milton-Edwards, "A Temporary Alliance with the Crown: The Islamic Response in Jordan," in Piscatori, *Islamic Fundamentalisms and the Gulf Crisis,* p. 99.

23. See, for example, Robert Fisk, "Egypt Fails to Curb Torture by Police," *The Independent* (London), 29 March 1993, p. 14.

CHAPTER 15

The "Normalization" of the Islamic Movement in Egypt from the 1970s to the Early 1990s

Gehad Auda

This chapter investigates the development of the Egyptian Islamic movement of the 1970s and 1980s. It looks at the movement "from within" in terms of ideology, organization, and membership, as well as its changes in relation to Egypt's democratization process. The argument advanced here is that the Islamic movement passed through two phases. In the first phase, during the 1970s, the movement was greatly influenced by radical ideas concerning the legitimacy of political authority, the definition of Muslim society, and the projection of force as the means for advancing the Islamic cause. In the second phase, during the 1980s, the Islamic movement came to influence the institutions and norms of Egyptian political life through a mixture of peaceful and violent means. During this phase, radical Islamic ideas loosened their grip on the political behavior of the believers.

The transition from the first phase to the second came as a result of "push" factors coming from Islamic radicalism and "pull" factors emanating from the political system. Ironically, the tendency of the radical Islamists to define the "other" eventually "pushed" the Islamic movement toward the mainstream because it led organizationally to internal incoherence and fragmentation of the radical forces, which in turn fostered a paradoxical relationship between ideology and behavior. During the 1980s and early 1990s, moreover, the Islamic movement was "pulled" toward the mainstream by the state's need to avoid political fragmentation, consolidate democratic change, and create a new national consensus. This chapter accounts for these factors and analyzes their dynamics.

Certain aspects of the Islamic movement as it operated within the context of state-society relations during the 1970s paved the way for the normalization of the movement during the 1980s. By normalization I mean a process through which measures of selective affinity and mutual though wary confidence ensue between two opponents.[1] Normalization does not indicate the absence of violence and malice on the part of each opponent toward the other. Rather, it signifies a qualitative change in the logic of their relations from mutual exclusiveness to relative accommodation. The concept of normalization is a structural-spatial one. It implies recognition by one opponent of the "political" existence of the other within specific boundaries. Through the normalization process a code of conduct emerges which determines realms of conflict, concessions, and cooperation. The crux of my inquiry is to analyze why and how President Hosni Mubarak's regime and the Islamic movement normalized their relations with each other during the 1980s.

The Nature and Limits of the Sunni Revolution

The Experience of the 1970s: The Essential Characteristics

By the end of the 1970s, observers of sociopolitical development and change in Egypt recognized three distinct meanings of the Islamic movement. The first referred to the increasing appeal of "Islamic ideology," that is, Islam as the source of political conduct and social life among the educated sector of the population.[2] The second indicated the rapid proliferation of groups that acted, mostly through violence, to apply Islamic ideology.[3] The third designated the rise, consolidation, and expansion of an Islamic social formation, that is, a constellation of institutions, ideas, practices, wealth, power, and relationships which served together to implement the ideological program.[4]

The Islamic movement in the 1970s was a sociopolitical expression of the contradiction and shortcomings of the modernization and transformation of state-society relations under Gamel Abdul Nasser (1952–70) and Anwar Sadat (1970–81).[5] Yet it was an organizationally unintegrated movement which cloaked diverse organizational formations.[6] These organizations were characterized by a low level of interorganizational cooperation and appeared as a manifestation of small-group politics within the context of increasingly popular social grievances.[7] Also, as a counterculture movement reflecting the revulsion of university students and the urban professional and semi-professional classes to the organization of modern life in Egypt, the Islamic current was an identity-seeking political movement composed of young radicals and older conservatives.[8]

The young radicals constituted the hard core of the movement.[9] They espoused ideas and concepts aimed at the total reconstruction of the state, society, and world along the lines of "pure" Islam. This task entailed re-creating the conditions that would make each of these spheres safe for Islam as it was perceived and conducted during the time of the Prophet and his four successors. The quest to restore the past through insulating themselves from society and assaulting the state made these youths radical fundamentalists.

As for the conservatives, they formed basically two groups. The first was, and still is, represented by the veterans of the Muslim Brotherhood (Jam'iyyat al-Ikhwan al-Muslimin). Their quest was reform based on the teachings of Islam, as mediated by Hasan al-Banna, with emphasis on the reconversion of individuals to Islam. We might call them hard conservatives. By contrast, the second group were soft conservatives, composed of al-Azhar shaykhs, Islamic traditionalists, and modern Islamists.[10] This group espoused a host of diverse ideas about how to make Islam influential in shaping the lives of Egyptians. What bound these conservatives together was the inclination to be affiliated with the state at large as well as their dependence on political-bureaucratic methods for propagating their ideas. Moreover, they, like the radicals, naturally maintained transnational links with other Islamists; all major organizations, in fact, sought followers outside as well as inside national boundaries.[11]

This chapter understands the dynamics of the Islamic movement as based on paradoxes. Emmanuel Sivan, following Weber, presents the paradox of medieval theology as the relevant text for modern politics.[12] Bassam Tibi, following Niklas Luhmann, supplies the paradox of indeterminacy of social transition in light of the fact that religion is determined.[13] Ali Dessouki, following a structural-functionalist view, emphasizes the paradox of political power in contrast to political representation.[14] Although these approaches are significant in understanding the dynamics of the relationship between the Islamic movement and its environment, none takes paradox per se as a conceptual lens. Therefore, none accounts for the internal paradoxes of the movement or analyzes them as an extension and reflection of the relationship the movement has with its external environment.

After its revival in the 1970s, the Islamic movement carried within it the seeds of three major paradoxes that eventually led to normalization with Mubarak's political regime during the 1980s. In order to understand these paradoxes, one must account for the organizational-ideological dimensions of the movement during the 1970s.

Ideological and Organizational Dimensions: Basic Concepts and Structures

During the 1960s, Islamic activists struggled with each other over three basic concepts: the call (*al-da'wa*), holy flight (*al-hijra*), and "excommunication" (*al-takfir*). The three concepts were central to the movement in the 1970s. Later in that decade, a fourth concept, violent struggle in the name of God (*al-jihad*), became prominent, leading to ideological and organizational divisions.

The concept of da'wa has been espoused by the Muslim Brotherhood since 1928. According to the writings of Hasan al-Banna, da'wa is the act of persuading the Muslim to abide by the tenets of Islamic law (Shari'a) and to apply them in everyday life. In al-Banna's understanding of Islam, once the individual professes the unity of God (*tawhid*) and the Prophecy of Muhammad, he is categorically a Muslim. This concept implies that the society and the state are categorically Islamic. Although the state and society are Islamic in principle, they include those who do not completely observe the Shari'a, for example, those who are neglectful of Islam (*sahaun*), hypocrites (*munafiqun*), wrong doers (*zalmaun*), transgressors (*taghun*), disobedients (*asaun*), those who trespass beyond bounds (*musrfaun*), and those who act heinously (*fasqaun*). Muslims of these types are the target of the da'wa of the Brotherhood. Classification of Muslims and the attempt to reconvert all the nonobservant Muslims are the main logic of da'wa. The Muslim Brothers emphasized that politics and governance are among the ordinances of the Islamic religion: man has inherited God's will on earth.

They conceptualized this type of inheritance as *istikhlaf*, whose purpose is to observe and apply God's precepts as revealed in the Qur'an and Sunna. Istikhlaf refers generally to the control of man over nature; according to the Brotherhood, however, it specifically indicates the building of an independent Islamic state and reforming individual lives according to Islamic norms.

The Brotherhood believes that da'wa is the main method for fulfilling the promise of istikhlaf. In this context, da'wa is predicated upon the Islamic ordinance of jihad. Da'wa is an evolutionary process that begins with reform of the individual and ends with Islamic mastery of the world. Thus da'wa proceeds in stages, from the forming of a Muslim home, through directing the society and liberating the country from what is un-Islamic, to the building of an international status for the Islamic community (*umma*). The process aims at changing the society and the world *from within* through interaction with the multiple realities of the society and the world, where the society is not completely Islamic and the world is un-Islamic. In this scheme, hijra and takfir do not have a place, and the violent form of jihad comes only as the last resort and under the specific conditions of colonialism. Embrace of the concepts of hijra and takfir represented a genuine Islamic reaction against Nasser's policies of control and modernization during the 1960s. The two concepts, taken together, assert the theoretical impossibility of the existence of different types of Muslims. There is only one type of Muslim—the individual who materially and spiritually acknowledges the sovereignty of God (*hakimiyya*).

Due to the writings of the Muslim Brotherhood ideologue Sayyid Qutb, who was imprisoned and later executed under Nasser, the concept of hijra came to play an influential role in shaping the Islamic ideology and movement.[15] Hijra is a program of action which gives witness to the totality of the sovereignty of God. This program is based on three interrelated descriptive concepts: the sovereignty of God (*hakimiyya*), the state of pre-Islamic ignorance (*jahiliyya*), and the struggle against jahiliyya (*jihad*). The underlying logic of these three concepts is a departure from the da'wa ideology, which seeks mainly to recall Muslims to observe the Shari'a. Qutb's ideology is not simply a behavior correction program, however, for it has an important structural element. It aims at re-creating Islamic life as a totality. Islamic life produces Muslims. (In da'wa, to the contrary, observant Muslims produce Islamic life.) Hijra aims at establishing the Islamic life which, for Qutb, is based on the sovereignty of God and thus characterized not only by the application of Shari'a, which is the ultimate realization of istikhlaf, but also, and perhaps more importantly, by the creation of a way of life that differs from Western modernity. Western modernity corrupts the possibility of witnessing to the sovereignty of God and, hence, makes it impossible for the individuals in the Islamic world to exist as Muslims.[16]

The concept of takfir was introduced by 'Ali Isma'il but articulated by Shukri Mustafa, who was arrested in 1965 on the allegation of being a Brotherhood member. In 1969, Shukri Mustafa declared that the head of the state security apparatus was an infidel; the government and the state were also branded as infidel. This was a new development in Islamic radicalization: the concept of takfir was never advocated by Qutb as a principal category of judgment. Although he rejected the modern state and society as belonging to the jahiliyya, he never condemned them as infidel (*kafir*). He condemned the political regime of Nasser as kafir because it consciously advocated and promoted jahiliyya. For Qutb, the distinction between the society and the political regime was crucial; because people in the society were oblivious to the jahiliyya in which they live, they could not be condemned as infidels. The political regime could, however, be condemned, because its leaders applied policies that consolidated this state of ignorance of Islam. According to Qutb, violent jihad might be pursued only against the political regime. The takfir concept broadly condemned as infidels the state, the political regime, and other activists in the Islamist movement who did not subscribe to the concept.

According to the writings of Shukri Mustafa, takfir is not a program of action like da'wa and hijra, but rather a position on issues.[17] It is an elaborate concept based on three rules of judgment. The first rule holds that the individual is a Muslim only if he fully observes all God's ordinances. Defining Islamic life in terms of ordinances was Mustafa's innovation. The logic of takfir argues that one of the major ordinances is the necessity of living within *jama'at al-muslimin* (the society of Muslims). Based on this rule, the principle of "making explicit and sure" emerges as the basis of the relationship between the Islamic society and outsiders (even individuals who claim to be Muslims). This principle holds that individuals outside the Islamic society cannot be judged as Muslims because they are not members of the society. But they cannot be judged as kuffar because they do not declare their infidelity. Hence, they should be recruited or invited to join the jama'a. If they reject the offer, they are not true Muslims.

The second rule of judgment is known as the contrast of ordinances. It holds that the ultimate purpose of Muslims is to establish Islamic government in the form of the caliphate. Muslims should, by this reasoning, suspend the performance of ordinances that might prove harmful to fulfilling of the ultimate goal. This rule is not in theoretical contradiction to the first rule, since it is only adhered to during the weak phase of Islamic society; it is, above all, a practical rule. Once the Islamic society becomes strong, every ordinance should be observed.

The third rule of judgment is of an ontological nature, with programmatic implications. Actions of the society of Muslims should be guided by precepts from the Qur'an and Sunna concerning the features and signs of the Day of Judgment. According to this apocalyptic vision, Mustafa believed in the necessity of total isolation because the Day of Judgment is preceded by the alienation of Islam from its people. The Islamic society should avoid all connections to the surrounding environment, and jihad is thus not a necessary condition for Islam to win the day. In addition, he saw the conflict between Christians and Muslims, not between Muslims and Jews, as one of the major signs of the Day of Judgment. Mustafa's hijra in this context is not similar to Qutb's: Qutb advocated "flight" for preparation and building strength; Mustafa asked his followers to embark on hijra for security, solitude, and waiting.

In addition to da'wa, hijra, and takfir, the concept of jihad was advocated by Salih Sirriya's message of faith (*risalat al-iman*) prior to 'Abd al-Salam Faraj's neglected ordinance (*al-farida al-gha'iba*).[18] Groups subscribing to this notion of jihad came together in 1980–81 and formed the Jihad Organization, a loose alliance that assassinated President Sadat in 1981. What makes the concept of jihad different in this presentation is an emphasis on the infidelity of the governing regimes and the immediate need for jihad. According to this concept, Muslim society is not the product of Muslim individuals, but of Islamic authority. Jihad is at the core of the quest for the application of the Shari'a, and from this perspective hijra is not permitted because it is seen as a desertion of jihad. Beyond this consensus, the main currents of jihad ideology diverge on whether it is acceptable to participate in peaceful conduct to change the orientations of those in authority.[19] In interpreting jihad, there has also been disagreement over the form of the Islamic government and political system. (For Salih Sirriya, the leader of Shabab Muhammad, Muhammad's Youth, there was no preordained Islamic system; for 'Umar 'Abd al-Rahman, a radical 'alim, or religious leader, in exile in the United States, the caliphal system is the only Islamic system; for Kamal al-Sa'id Habib of the Jihad Organization, the Islamic system should be a populist and developmental system as the reflection of the sovereignty of God.) By 1981 the concept of jihad came to be interpreted according to the caliphal system.

Organizational Dynamics

The main organizational concept of the radical Islamists is the jama'a. Although the term has become common, there have been and are a bewildering number of such societies or associations, which have entailed different structures, tasks, and practices according to different ideological articulations. The concepts of istikhlaf and da'wa imply two strategies: leadership (qiyyada) and educational/behavioral formation (tarbiyya). Meanwhile, the concept of takfir, particularly during the phase of weakness (istid'af), entails two different strategies: solitude and isolation (al-i'tikaf wa'l-i'tizal) and informing the public (al-balagh al-'amm). The concept of jihad, particularly in its Salafiyya version, requires the dual strategies of breaking away from the ruler and motivating the Muslims for jihad (al-khuruj 'ala'l-hakim wa'l-tahrid 'ala'l-jihad). How each set of strategies shaped specific structures, tasks, and practices under the state-society conditions of the 1970s is the main focus of this section.

The Muslim Brotherhood

During the first half of the 1970s, Muslim Brotherhood members were released from jail and sought to revive their organization. Leadership and recruitment problems arose as the Brotherhood tried to regain its pre–1952 political and cultural influence. There was a legacy of organizational rifts between the members of the Special Apparatus (al-Tanzim al-Khass) and the Brotherhood's formal leadership, that is, the general guide.[20] There was also the increasing radicalization of the young Islamists in the universities. In view of the long period of organizational discontinuity from 1953 to 1973, and the fact that their release from jail never implied their legal right to reorganize, the Muslim Brothers faced a serious challenge in reviving the organization.

In the Brotherhood, the term qiyyada refers to the leadership within the group itself. But the term may also refer to the leadership of the Islamic current inside Egypt or to the leadership of Islamic activism in the Muslim world. All these dimensions of leadership constituted a challenge in the 1970s, given the leadership struggle within the organization and the dubious nature of claims to Brotherhood leadership in Egypt and the Islamic world.

The Brotherhood adapted its structure to meet the challenge. First came emphasis on the international aspect of the organization as a way of asserting its leadership inside Egypt.[21] Hasan al-Hudaybi, the second general guide, held a meeting in 1973 which reconstituted the Shura (Consultative) Council and set up six membership committees in the Gulf region: three in Saudi Arabia and one each in Kuwait, Qatar, and the United Arab Emirates. These committees functioned mainly to ensure the Brotherhood's moral presence and secure allegiance to it, both among the Egyptians and the general populace of those countries. This proved instrumental in attracting strong financial backing for it. A second organizational adaptation was a policy favoring seniority of age and steadfastness during imprisonment as the criteria for selection of the general guide.[22] Conditions of illegality had prevented the Brotherhood from assembling the constitutive assembly to elect the general guide, and organizational compromises, in keeping with the new image it hoped to project as a peaceful political organization, would have given a stronger hand to remnants of the Special Apparatus. Moreover, the need to compete with radical Islamist organizations moved the Brotherhood to stress the history of its suffering and steadfastness under Nasser. 'Umar al-Tilmisani was selected as the third general guide in 1973. Finally, the organization decided to cooperate with the authorities by debating the young Islamic radicals in universities and attempting to curb the zealotry of some of its members.[23] This allowed the organization to shield itself from the scrutiny of the police and possible crackdowns, while leaving it free to present itself as the voice of political Islam. In the process, it penetrated the universities and attracted an increasing number of young members.

Although the basic Brotherhood tradition was to avoid involvement in any religious controversy, in the face of the proliferation of the radical Islamic interpretations of the Qur'an and Sunna, the group had to ponder and articulate its own Islamic views in order to prove its religious soundness. In this context, al-Hudaybi published an important work rebutting the radical concepts of hijra, takfir, jahiliyya, hakimiyya, and taghut,[24] and the Brotherhood's monthly magazine, *Al-Da'wa,* popularized its views on these issues.[25] The Brotherhood also moved to control university student unions and constitute al-Jama'a al-Islamiyya, or the Islamic Association, in the universities to represent its thinking.

The basic Ikhwanist tradition was the organizational integration of all membership sectors in one hegemonic organization. Given the illegality of the organization, however, and the innovation of university student representational structures—student unions—after 1952, the Brotherhood adopted a new organizational strategy. This strategy (which received some state assistance) entailed integrating the different Islamic societies in each university into one organization under the name al-Jama'a al-Islamiyya. On the ideological side, this group reflected Qutbian understandings, as in its invocation of the concept of God's governing authority *(hukm Allah)* in arguing against the notion of political parties.[26] Also, greater emphasis was placed on jihad as a violent corrective to that which is opposed to God. This emphasis induced further rifts in the movement and within certain Jama'a sections, particularly those in Upper Egypt. For example, the Jama'a expressed more enthusiasm for the Iranian Revolution than the Brotherhood. The tensions between the Upper Egypt sections and the Brotherhood culminated in the split of the Jama'a into two contending factions, each claiming the name of al-Jama'a al-Islamiyya. (For our purposes we call the Upper Egypt faction al-Jama'a al-Islamiyya al-Jihadiyya).

In the classical Ikhwanist structure, there are four types of membership: assistant member, affiliated member, working member, and *mujahid,* or combatant, member. In the Jama'a, however, there is only one type—the working membership. Whereas there is no title of *amir* (prince) in the Brotherhood structure, every university faculty has a jama'a which is headed by an amir. *Umara'* (pl. of amir) of the faculties constitute the Shura Council of the university, which also has an amir at its head. Umara' of the Egyptian universities constitute their Shura Council, headed by an amir chosen from among them. During the 1970s, Hilmi al-Jazzar held that post. The stronghold of the Jama'a has been the universities in metropolitan Cairo and in the Delta, with Cairo University the most important base.

Jama'at al-Muslimin

The Jama'at al-Muslimin, or Society of Muslims, first formed in Upper Egypt, in Asyut, after Shukri Mustafa's release from jail in 1971, was Shukri's own organizational invention. The organizational life of the society during the 1970s spanned only six to seven years. It had a simple autocratic leadership structure, and it was organized around a number of techniques designed to fulfill its goals of providing solitude and isolation for its members and informing the public about its beliefs. Securing isolation and solitude involved a selective change of lifestyle and hijra in which members of the society opted for a progressive de-linking between themselves and their immediate world as well as society at large. The logic of this strategy was to provide substitutes for work, family, and income. Thus the ideal male member of the society was married to a woman of the society, worked in manual labor, and received income from his own direct work. Hijra was understood as a process ending in physical migration from modern life. The society ordered some of its members to migrate to Yemen, Jordan, Saudi Arabia, and Libya to live in seclusion in the open spaces of these countries and to work and obtain money for support of the society.[27]

This approach to isolation and solitude (*al-i'tizal*) caused Mustafa to lose touch with segments of his membership, particularly those who had migrated to other countries. There was no organizational or ideological control over such migrants. Furthermore, the dynamics of i'tizal did not allow for exit from the organization or dissent. Mustafa applied harsh methods, including sometimes assassinating dissenting members, to ensure loyalty and compliance with the regulations of the society. This opened the way for double-crosses by disenchanted members. Finally, the society's belief that it was the only jama'a whose Islam was correct implied that other jama'at were infidels and should be avoided and fought. Accordingly the society found itself in a hostile environment of jama'at. The position of the society vis-à-vis the Muslim Brotherhood and Sirriya's Shabab Muhammad was a case in point.[28]

The second strategic goal of the Society of Muslims—informing the public (*al-*

balagh al-'amm)—was crucial for Shukri Mustafa's cause. If the public did not know about his cause, he would be unable to judge them infidels; therefore, the concept of takfir would be rendered practically irrelevant. However, because the only two ways of informing the public in Egyptian society are through publications and broadcasting, he was impelled to show flexibility and make some compromise with jahili society. For its own stability the state needed Mustafa and the Society of Muslims's efforts to prevent jihad, while the Society needed to be presented publicly in a favorable light and to gain the state's support in its dispute with other Islamic groups. This "matching interests" strategy ultimately led, however, to more state penetration of the Society and thus to its doom.[29]

Jihad Organization

The Jihad Organization of 1979–80 was a loosely integrated alliance among a number of organizations committed to the concept of jihad. It was the first time in the Islamic movement that the organizations espousing the same conceptual understanding of Islam came together in a united front. This unity was owed to the energy and ingenuity of Muhammad 'Abd al-Salam Faraj, who forged an alliance of the Jihad Organization that he had established in 1979 in Cairo and al-Jama'a al-Islamiyya al-Jihadiyya/Upper Egypt, headed by Karam Zuhdi and 'Umar 'Abd al-Rahman. The alliance included regionally based organizations and groups such as al-Tali'a al-Islamiyya (the Islamic Vanguards), established in al-Sharqiyya Governorate by Fathi 'Abd al-'Aziz al-Shuqaqi in 1979, and groups from 'Ali al-Maghrabi's Alexandria-based Jihad Organization. Also included were remnants and members of Sirriya's Shabab Muhammad, represented by such names as 'Atif Amir al-Jaysh; al-Rahal's Jihad Organization, which was headed at that time by Kamal al-Sa'id Habib; and 'Asam al-'Atar's faction of the Muslim Brotherhood. The alliance took on its specific organizational form during the summer of 1980, when Faraj and Zuhdi agreed to join forces against the political regime. The highest authority of this new organization resided in the Shura Council which included eleven members: five from Zuhdi's al-Jama'a al-Islamiyya and six from Faraj's Jihad. The organization was headed by 'Umar 'Abd al-Rahman as the general amir, but he only had the capacity to issue *fatawa* (religious judgments and interpretations).[30]

This type of leadership structure was new for radical Islamic groups. The amir was not the real commander, and the Shura Council was not formally headed by anyone. All its members were equal. The organization encompassed two real leadership structures. The first emanated from Faraj's Jihad Organization, while the second was related to Zuhdi's organization. Faraj's was organized along the principles of deconstruction[31] while Zuhdi's was organized along more cliquish lines. In Faraj's organization the real leadership was located in the middle levels of the organization, while in Zuhdi's leadership was dispersed and fragmented.

The mixture of these two sets of organizational principles ultimately made the alliance ineffective in launching successful collective action to topple the political regime and install an Islamic one. Indeed, combining the different organizational networks in one major organization stamped the Jihad Organization with fatal shortcomings. There were virtually no organizational mechanisms for achieving consensus on operational plans. Sadat's assassination was a case in point. The operational decision to assassinate Sadat was Faraj's alone, in the face of opposition from 'Abbud al-Zumur and other leading members of the Shura Council. The disagreement was not over the radical Islamic obligation to assassinate Sadat, but rather over whether Sadat's assassination should come within a larger framework of an Islamic revolution. There was no decision for assassination until eleven days before 6 October 1981. The decision was taken by Faraj in order to exploit the opportunity afforded by the participation of Khalid al-Islambuli, who was not a member but a sympathizer, in the military parade. For many members of the Jihad Organization the assassination came as a surprise, and most of them did not know what action to take when it occurred.[32]

Another shortcoming of the organizational structure was highlighted by the attempt to launch an Islamic revolution in the wake of Sadat's assassination. This revolution was to begin with a coup attempt against the local authorities in the city of Asyut. It was launched mainly by Zuhdi's organization. There was, however, no popular participation or support, revealing the limitation of the cliquish style of the Upper Egyptian segments of the movement. These Islamists allowed their behavior to be greatly influenced by organizational, social, and personal feuds and to be publicly portrayed and perceived as being in the tradition of Upper Egypt criminal gangs.

Three Paradoxes: The Dynamics of Normalization

The Islamic movement during the 1970s bred internal paradoxes which ultimately led to limitations on effectiveness and comprehensiveness. These paradoxes demonstrated the true nature and limitations of the Sunni revolution in Egypt.

The First Paradox: The Meaning of Being a Sunni

The term "Sunni" in Egypt refers to people who follow the religious practices of the Prophet Muhammad, the rightful Prophet of God. They recognize that the four caliphs after Muhammad were legitimate. Sunnis affirm that the Sunna is the second source of Islamic religion; it elucidates the meanings of the Qur'an in an ever-changing world.

The goal of Sunni Islam is twofold: to observe Islam as a religion, and to preserve it as an umma. In Islamic history the requirements for fulfilling these goals often contradict each other, and many Sunni thinkers have suggested schemes for eliminating or reducing the contradictions. In general, the major principle for reconciling the two sets of requirements is found in the concept of the least harm, that is, the pursuit of one goal should not deter the pursuit of the other goal. Thus the doctrine of *fitna* (dissension) is seen as the fatal fall that the Islamic umma should avoid at any cost. The doctrine of the least harm implies that the principle of *tamakkun* (empowerment) should guide any Sunni radical pursuit. Qutb's concept of hijra, for example, is rooted in the principle of tamakkun.

The Salafiyya—a broad movement historically linked with such "modernist" reformers as Rashid Rida and Muhammad 'Ali in the late nineteenth and early twentieth centuries—embraces the return to the basics of the religion. But this carries the threat of violating the Sunni principle of the least harm. Espousing jihad as the main concept of Islamic conduct, for example, seems to violate the principle of the least harm. In this sense the concepts of hijra, takfir, and jihad—which are often identified as elements of a Sunni revolution—are not Sunni in nature because the revolution is not based solely on the concept of tamakkun. It is rather a Salafiyya-type revolt. Thus the first paradox of the Islamic movement: the more the radical Islamists move toward a Salafiyya-style ideology and revolt, the more the Sunnis invoke their traditional emphasis on the inherent limitations of political opposition in order to preserve Islam. This paradox explains why al-Ahzar and major Sunni associations have not been susceptible to such concepts and, more importantly, why the persecution of the radical Islamists has never troubled the traditional Sunni authorities in Egypt.

Second Paradox: The Islamic Jama'a and the Masses

The essence of the second paradox is that the concept of the jama'a was designed to incorporate and mobilize Muslims. As conceived by the radical Islamists, however, it functioned in a manner that induced rifts, created fragmentation in the movement, and alienated the movement from the masses. In other words, the jama'a did not function as a vehicle for attracting more followers, building organic links with the masses, or unifying the movement.

In order to understand the dimensions of this paradox, one should keep in mind that the concept of jama'a is not theoretically similar to that of a cell or party or group. Any jama'a should rather strive to include *all* Muslims. But an Islamic jama'a is built in an elitist way and a cadre fashion. The record shows that every jama'a meant first to ensure the loyalty of its followers and members to its ideological line. In other words, every jama'a was conceived of as something different from the surrounding Islamic society, despite the claim that it aspired to represent and encompass every Muslim. Hence the paradox is as follows: the more every jama'a opens its boundaries to include Muslims at large, the more it loses its identity as something different from the Islamic mainstream of society. And the more the jama'a attempts to assert its peculiar identity in the face of the Islamic mainstream, the less able it is to include Muslims at large and hence to fulfill the Islamic promise of being an all-encompassing jama'a. Henceforth, the jama'at (pl. of jama'a) remain alienated from the masses.

Third Paradox: The Meaning of Jihad

The third paradox is complex. The radical ideology calls for exercising jihad as a direct action against every un-Islamic manifestation in society and the state, with emphasis on the use of violence against the state. Yet the action of jihad by radical Islamists renders them criminals, inspires chaos, and deepens their alienation from the masses because they have no well-developed political theory of jihad to inspire the collective action of Muslims. Instead, jihad degenerates into sporadic violence conducted by individuals.

According to the radical view, the duty of every Muslim individual is to conduct jihad on his own without waiting for a guiding leadership or relating it to specific conditions and capabilities. In this approach jihad is not thought to be a political means for political ends, and the individual Muslim is not thought to be engaging in political violence because jihad is not ordinarily conceived of as a process of political struggle. However, beating individuals, attacking stores, burning theaters, and assassinating individuals bring jihad—from the perspective of the state and law—under the category of criminal action. The dilemma of radical reason is that in its pursuit to eliminate jahiliyya, it eliminates people, and in doing so, it is inexorably branded as criminal. The violent actions of Jama'at al-Muslimin are a case in point. This conception of jihad destroys the movement from within and leads it to incite chaotic episodes in society. By disregarding the condition of leadership as necessary for planning jihad and by making it an individual duty, jihad becomes an individual's decision and consequently every individual pursues it as he sees fit. As the history of the Jihad Organization demonstrates, social chaos and the persistent failure of Islamic collective action are the natural outcomes of this conceptualization. Its sense of jihad did not appeal to the masses, but rather encouraged them to resort to the state for protection and safety.

This third paradox could thus be phrased as follows: the more the radical Islamists adopt a strategy of jihad, the less opportunity they have for changing society and the state along the lines of Islamic radical teachings and principles.

The Dynamics of Creating Political Actions

Sadat's assassination by the Jihad, followed by the state's success in curbing the hoped-for Islamic revolution, conveyed three significant lessons. First, it became clear that both forces, the regime and the Islamic movement, were strong enough to exercise impact on each other. Second, the state was more coherent in leadership and efficient in the use of force than the Jihad. Third, the task of combating religious fundamentalism was more likely to succeed through the war of ideas rather than through political manipulation, as was Sadat's style.

These three lessons set up new principles of interaction between the state and the Islamic movement at large. In the 1980s the regime under Mubarak and the Islamic movement at large recognized the limits of mutual manipulation and confrontation. Furthermore, the hard conservatives (i.e., the Muslim Brotherhood) and soft conservatives (i.e., the state religious apparatus—al-Azhar and the Ministry of Religious Endowments) provided a mechanism of mediation between the radicals and the state, and emerged as an alternative to the radicals in championing the Islamic cause. They also served, for the Mubarak regime, as a symbol of a new state legitimacy and strategy for democratic transition. In this new phase, the state also followed a strategy of selective violence against, and "reeducation" of, the radical fundamentalists.

Accommodation as a Normalization Tactic

A policy of mutual accommodation characterized the relations between the state and the Muslim Brotherhood. The Brotherhood accommodated the state in order to rehabilitate its position as the leading Islamic organization in the society and protect itself from being plunged into the crises created by the three paradoxes which stamped the Islamic movement by the end of the 1970s. In its turn, the state accommodated the Brotherhood in order to manipulate the Islamic radicals into moderation. Accommodation introduced subtle changes into the views and conduct of each toward the other and unexpectedly helped the state to reduce the power of the Brotherhood as an alternative political force.

The Muslim Brotherhood

For the Ikhwan, a new view of the state, society, and politics began to influence its conduct. The old view was articulated in 1937 in the demands presented by Hasan al-Banna to the leaders and kings of the Islamic world. These demands were divided into political and juridical affairs (e.g., calls for the eradication of partisan politics, reforming the law according to Shari'a principles, strengthening the army and building militias for jihad, and reforming governmental institutions and actions so as to incorporate Islamic teachings); into practical and social affairs (e.g., demands for reforming society according to Islamic teachings); and into economic affairs (e.g., demands to abolish *riba,* or usury, and encourage zakat, raise the standard of living of workers and farmers, protect the public from plundering private companies, and nationalize Egyptian economic institutions and activities). This older view was based on disdaining politics, seeing the state in the light of a simple and direct relationship between the ruler and the ruled, neglecting differences among Muslims or between Muslims and Copts, and locating political power in the hands of the ruler.[33]

The new view is best expressed by Ma'mun al-Hudaybi, the son of Hasan al-Hudaybi and the Brotherhood's leader in Parliament during the periods 1984–87 and 1987–90. Ma'mun al-Hudaybi sees the juridical authority of the state as independent; it should judge according to Islamic principles. With regard to the legislative authority, al-Hudaybi and the Brotherhood see the Parliament as an expression of the Islamic principle of *shura*—or consultation—that is, the Parliament should introduce legislation enforcing what is clearly and definitely mentioned in the Qur'an and debate what is not clearly and definitely mentioned as a rule of conduct in the Qur'an. The legislative authority in this view is instrumental in checking and balancing the executive authority. While the laws should observe the norms of the Qur'an, their implementation is the subject of ijtihad by religious scholars. Ma'mun sees electoral politics as the means for making the views of the Brotherhood influential in promulgating laws. Thus he prefers that executive authority be exercised according to the parliamentary model, that is, the government of the majority (in Egypt, the government is decidedly on the presidential model). As a part of the Egyptian nation, Ma'mun says, the Brotherhood is keen to mend fences with the executive authority, and he hopes that the government will accept it as representative of a segment of the population. Indeed, the government's continued denial of its political legitimacy is not a characteristic of a rational authority, which should be inclusionary and open to every current and force in the society. The state should exchange and appreciate the oppositions' opinions.[34]

According to Ma'mun, professional associations, student unions, voluntary associations, and clubs are representative of the population at large. He does not see them as primarily platforms for opposing the government. By controlling them the Ikhwan has enhanced its welfare and professional functions and ensures that these associations are not sources for conflict and instability. With regard to the radical Islamists, he notes that the Brotherhood follows a specific rule in dealing with them: cooperation when there is an agreement, appreciation and understanding when there is a disagreement. He draws a distinction between the "roots" (*usul*) and the "branches" (*al-furu'*) of Islam; disagreement is only possible over the latter, not the former. The Brotherhood can therefore absorb members with different views on subsidiary matters, Ma'mun claims, but does not seek relations with Islamic groups that espouse violence. For example, contrary to the views of more radical groups, the Copts should not be molested in their property, religion, or profession; the Brotherhood would only prohibit them from assuming government positions that are linked with the application of the Shari'a. Copts should be free to observe their religion in their personal affairs, that is, marriage, inheritance, food, and ceremonies.[35]

This new Ikhwanist view as presented by Ma'mun introduces the concept of politics into the Islamic movement's quest for applying the Shari'a. It understands the state structure as a complex one and recognizes the force of reality and political expediency as determinants of behavior. It does not represent a total discontinuity with the main teachings of the Brotherhood, but it is a new strategy which finds its premises in some of al-Banna's practices and al-Hudaybi's bent for legalism. Al-Tilmisani was the main champion of this view, which gathered momentum after 1981.

Motivated by this view, the Brotherhood plunged into all forms of legally organized politics after 1981. On the eve of the parliamentary elections in 1984, it joined forces with the New Wafd party. The Wafd won representation in the parliament as the only opposition party (a handful of representatives of the Action Party and the National Progressive Unionist party or NPUP were subsequently appointed by the president as MPs). The New Wafd won 58 seats in 1984, 12 of them occupied by Muslim Brothers, and this participation in electoral politics eased their relationship with the government.[36] This relationship further evolved when the Brothers remained distant from the three outbreaks of large-scale violence in 1986 and 1987 (by textile workers, security-police conscripts, and railroad workers). Moreover, under General Guides al-Tilmisani (who died in May 1986) and Muhammad Hamid Abu al-Nasr, a policy of active participation in the politics of professional associational life was set in motion. From 1987 to 1990, Brotherhood professionals were successful in controlling the elected majority of a great number of associations' boards. In the elections of the Engineers' Association in 1987, the Brothers gained 54 seats out of 61; in the bi-elections of the Medical Doctors' Association in 1988, they gained all 12 seats; in the bi-elections of the Commerce Graduates' Association in 1989, the Islamic list won a substantial segment of the votes; in 1990 the Islamic list won all the seats of the governing board of the Cairo University Professors' Club; and in 1990 the Islamic list won 10 seats out of 12 on the governing board of the Pharmacists' Association.[37]

The growing influence of the Brotherhood in the politics of associational life reflected its accommodation with the state. This accommodation found its driving force in the state's need to create a popular base against radical fundamentalists at a time of growing fiscal crisis and its consequent determination to fulfill its welfare functions, particularly with regard to the professionals of the middle classes. At the same time, the Muslim Brotherhood was driven to accommodation in order to renew its mass appeal and to seek fresh recruits from a new generation of young Muslims. The price paid by the state was to allow an ideologically hostile force to penetrate publicly the institutions of the professional middle class. The price the Brotherhood paid was to respect the state's need for political and social stability. This new social contract became the hallmark of Mubarak's style of democratization: unlike Nasser's and Sadat's approach to politics, which depended basically on a strong central leader, this aimed at consolidating the mainstream through creating consensus among political actors on the need to avoid involvement in destabilizing actions against the government.

The Muslim Brotherhood was one of the principal forces of the opposition which accepted this deal with the state. In effect, it agreed it would not politicize the socioeconomic hardships that accompanied economic reform, but would channel the quest for political reform and liberalization of the political system through state political institutions (to be defined to include political parties, professional associations, and Parliament) and not through demonstrations, violence, or strikes. It agreed, moreover, that its control of substantial influence in state political institutions would not lead it to try to transform these institutions into a power base hostile to the government, and that it would never seek political gains as a result of its control or influence over social resources.[38]

The record from 1984 to 1990 demonstrates that it played according to the rules. In the 1987 Parliament in which the Islamic alliance, composed of the Brotherhood and the Islamic Action party, won sixty seats, Brotherhood MPs developed a formula for public policy evaluation. This formula emphasized the primacy of public policies that are directly related to the psychological formation of the individual and the organization of the family. The Brotherhood members in Parliament were thus keen to pose questions to the ministers of education, information, and culture about their policies and to attack either the absence of Islamic content and orientation of the policy or its implementation when this was antagonistic to Islamic principles. For example, Brothers attacked the high school curriculum because it contained secular concepts about creation and individual choice; they criticized financial policy because it neglected the Islamic distinction between good and bad economic values and only emphasized striking a balance between demand and supply and rationalization of consumption.[39] They also called for linkage between the policy on foodstuff and the stability of the Egyptian family; for restoring the *waqf* (religious endowments) money under the control of the local governments to the Ministry of Religious Endowments to enhance the ministry's activities in the field of Islamic preaching; and for restraining the Ministry of Interior to refrain from attacking mosques (to root out radicals), because they are houses of God which should be safe from governmental interference.[40]

These Ikhwanist MPs insist that public policies ought to be directed to fulfilling general Islamic principles; satisfying socioeconomic target groups should be a secondary concern. For example, the adoption of Qur'anic criteria led them, during a discussion about the spread of crime and delinquency among the youth, to demand the universal imposition of Islamic dress on women as a way of mending the situation.[41] They also continue to remind the government, with its foreign policy of peace in the Middle East, that Jews are behind every harm to Islam and that jihad against them is an imperative.[42]

The Brotherhood's drive for accommodation was forced by its own organizational changes during the 1980s, such as the death of al-Tilmisani, which left the leadership structure in disarray. Because of the new tradition of appointing the general guide and not applying the original charter of the organization, which dictates methods of election, the need for consensus between the members of the pre–1952 leadership and the leading members who emerged after 1952 became crucial. As a consequence, the leadership was divided between three leaders: Muhammad Hamid Abu al-Nasr as the general guide, one of the remaining few original members of the Guidance Bureau under Hasan al-Banna; Ma'mun al-Hudaybi as the main Brotherhood speaker, one of the leaders of the generation that emerged during the prison years; and Mustafa Mashhur as the man in charge of its daily operation and one of the remaining leaders of the Special Apparatus. Thus the movement is composed of three generations of leadership. The older generation, who are reaching their seventies in the 1990s, worked with Hasan al-Banna and are considered the carriers of the original message. The second generation includes Ahmad Sayf al-Islam Hasan al-Banna, the son of Hasan al-Banna, and 'Abd al-Hamid al-Ghazali. This generation emerged during Nasser's reign and lent continuity to the whole organization after its ban during the 1950s. Their average age is forty-five to fifty-five. The younger generation includes 'Isam al-'Aryan and Hilmi al-Jazzar, men in their thirties and early forties, who renewed the Ikhwan's message during the 1970s.[43]

As a result of its involvement in every aspect of formal politics during the 1980s, the young generation acquired more prominence and influence in the structure of the organization. Sometimes this influence came at the expense of the old and middle generations, which signaled a change in the sources of leadership. Since 1929, loyalty to the organization and closeness to the general guide have been the main requirements for organizational leadership. Involvement in open politics added another requirement: the ability to win an election. This external requirement complicated the power game inside the Brotherhood for it expanded the influence of the younger generation and made some of them public celebrities. The need to curb the advancement of the younger generation was an operative factor—among others—behind the decision to boycott the parliamentary elections of 1990.

The State

The state under Mubarak emerged with a new sense of realism after Sadat's assassination and the radical Islamists' conspiracy against the state in 1981. The regime came to recognize that the Islamic movement is not monolithic, but is instead composed of many autonomous organizations and movements that have been and remain in competition with each other for new membership and influence over resources. The regime also appreciated the fact that the Muslim Brotherhood as an organization, particularly its leadership, had come to recognize the limits of seeking power through violence and penetration of the state apparatus. Further, the religious institutions of the state, particularly al-Azhar and the Ministry of Religious Endowments, had been discredited to a degree and were unable to control the arena of da'wa. The state therefore needed the help of a major force from *within* political Islam.

The aim of the state was not to destroy and eliminate political Islam or use it for fighting communism or leftist and secular political opposition in general. The state was, and is, aiming at moderating political tension for the purpose of creating conditions for economic reform. For moderation to succeed, the regime recognized, there must be critical confidence-building measures between it and the opposition—particularly the Islamic forces, because they pose the greatest threat to the regime's survival and legitimacy. Consequently, acknowledging its limited ability to penetrate the youth population, it opted for a tacit alliance with the Brothers because they would implement the Shari'a through nonviolent political means (without, of course, recognizing the legitimacy of the current institutional means for change.) For this tacit alliance to function in the interests of the regime, however, the regime had to contain the Brotherhood's religious appeal and thus had to induce greater activism in its religious institutions.

In other words, the regime sought to draw a distinction between the religious and the political influence of the Brotherhood, and in particular it hoped to exert more influence over the religious resocialization of youth. Toward this end, the High Committee for Islamic Da'wa, presided over by the grand shaykh of al-Azhar, was established by prime minister's decree on 15 February 1983.[44] The committee's responsibility was the promotion of da'wa inside and outside of the country. The minister of religious endowments is a member of the committee along with the ministers of education and information. Further, the regime upgraded the Endowment Ministry's financial resources and personnel. In 1987 the state increased the ministry's budget by LE 7 million and employed over three thousand preachers. The following year, Mubarak approved a plan for reducing the level of job dissatisfaction among the preachers in particular and in the ministry at large. This scheme was financed with LE 6 million from the government, part of which was used to establish new training centers to upgrade preaching skills.[45]

The High Committee for Islamic Da'wa sponsored, through the Ministry of Religious Endowments, a new, innovative organizational form of da'wa, *qawafil al-da'wa* (da'wa caravans), which consisted of a number of preachers from the ministry and the Azhar traveling to local mosques to engage youths in dialogue. According to the minister of religious endowments, by the end of 1988 the ministry had launched about seventy-two such missions.[46] In addition, the state reactivated the Higher Council for Islamic Affairs, which had been established in 1960 to propagate the state ideology. During the 1960s and 1970s, it remained aloof from the government's confrontation with the Brotherhood and the radical Islamists. During the 1980s it came under the authority of the Ministry of Religious Endowments (during the 1960s it was under the direct authority of President Nasser). Under the present Minister of Endowments, Muhammad Mahgub, a proposal was advanced to change the members of the council and to appoint activists in daʿwa. Muslim Brothers were suggested for this task, but they feared being identified with the state and rejected the offer. However, the council is active in promoting conferences and studies concerning daʿwa at large.[47]

The Limits of Accommodation

Accommodation between the state and the Ikhwan has proven over time to have its limitations. Each hoped that the accommodation process would allow it to sustain and consolidate its own course independent of the will of the other and of political changes. However, trouble arose with the deepening rift among state bureaucrats over the real aim and strategy of the Brotherhood, and over the reincarnation of the Labor party as an Islamic party, with which the Brotherhood has been in alliance since 1987.

The First Limitation: The State's Fear of Entrapment

The basic question for the state bureaucrats concerned the boundaries of accommodation. For these bureaucrats, particularly those in the Interior Ministry, the Ikhwan was simply an illegal anti-state political opposition. In this context, what Ikhwan activities could be seen as beneficial to the state? In fact Interior Ministry bureaucrats tended to see the organization as a very clever, enduring, uncompromising, violence-prone group. Allowing it access to the population and projecting it as legitimate would only enhance its power at the expense of the state; they thus feared that the state might be entrapped in the Brotherhood's web.

For the state religious apparatus the confusion and fear were even greater. The growing need of the state for a religious force that was popular and able to encounter the radical Islamists meant that al-Azhar shaykhs and bureaucrats of the Ministry of Religious Endowments might be rendered useless, thereby threatening their status with the regime; or, equally unacceptabe, they might be entrapped as agents of the Ikhwan's brand of daʿwa.

Despite the lines of understanding between the Brotherhood and the Ministry of the Interior which were established in the 1970s and early 1980s, the Ministry of the Interior was keen, particularly under the ministry of Zaki Badr (1986–90), to make Brothers feel themselves under surveillance by the police. During this period, particularly members of the young generation and their affiliates in the universities were exposed to detention, police harassment, and torture in prison.[48] The Interior Ministry never missed an opportunity to attack the Brotherhood publicly as a sly organization that only sought power and was never true to Islam. It attempted to prove that there was a covert deal between the Brotherhood and the radical Islamists, a division-of-labor scheme for destroying the state. Furthermore, it made great effort to restrict the Brothers' access to the public through confiscating their publications or banning their public meetings.

Meanwhile, al-Azhar and the Endowment Ministry bureaucrats were promoting their own brand of daʿwa, which upheld the state and its established religious institutions as Islamically justified. The Brotherhood disagreed with the establishment on a number of issues flowing from this basic difference. For example, it did not condemn violence against other Muslims on religious grounds, but rejected it as not preferable Islamically and unwise politically. Al-Tilmisani, the late general guide, considered the radical Islamists to be young victims of society who had gone wrong in understanding Islam and needed to accept the concept of *al-tarbiyya al-Islamiyya*, or Islamic education, as the only means for building an Islamic state. In 1989, however, the leading preachers of the state, headed by Shaykh Muhammad Mutawalli al-Sha'rawi and Shaykh al-Ghazali (both have an Azhari educational background), condemned the radicals on Islamic grounds for the use of violence against the state.[49]

Another example of the conflict between the religious apparatus of the state and the Brotherhood concerned the issue of riba or usury. The Brotherhood considered the profits on bank deposits as straightforward riba and encouraged the growth of financial organizations that do not deal in it. However, this stand threatened the ability of state banks to attract savings for economic reform, and in 1989 the state's mufti, Shaykh Muhammad al-Tantawi, declared that earnings from bank deposits were not a form of riba. Great names in Islamic da'wa who belong to the state religious apparatus defended this new position: for example, Shaykh 'Abd al-Mun'im al-Nimr, one of the leading religiously educated preachers, led the battle against the Islamic opposition. The state won the battle and thus gained the opportunity to strike at the Ikhwan's financial organizations.[50]

The Second Limitation: The Brotherhood's Delicate Balance

When the Brotherhood entered into a tacit alliance with the state, it came as part and parcel of a new strategy of building a delicate balance with the different forces in the political arena. The Brotherhood had to draw lines of understandings not only with the state, but also with the left, the Wafd, and Islamic radicals. Al-Tilmisani's efforts to rebuild the Ikhwan as a viable leading Islamic organization with influence in political life initiated this strategy, which proved reliable in protecting it from the state control. In 1981, for example, the jailing of Ikhwan leaders did not signify an attempt to destroy the organization and physically eliminate its leaders, as had been the case in 1954. Moreover, this strategy demonstrated its usefulness with regard to the radical Islamists. Notwithstanding the real tension and conflict between the radical Islamists and the Brotherhood, this strategy helped the Brotherhood avoid reliving the events of 1954 and 1965, when the deep conflict and public disagreement between it and the radical Islamists were manipulated by the state to destroy the Ikhwan's organization. In the eyes of the political forces of the left and the right, this strategy rendered the Brotherhood a legitimate political force representing a segment of the population—a great achievement in its history.

Before 1952, the Wafd and the other forces on the right and in the center had denied the Brotherhood any space in the political arena, and when Hasan al-Banna, the general guide and founder of the organization, was assassinated in cold blood in 1949 by the state, no political force took that as a threat to political life or grieved over him. The left kept silent during the state's persecution of the Ikhwan in 1954.[51]

For the Brotherhood, the strategic question of the 1980s was how to build lines of understanding with different and conflicting forces and at the same time maintain cohesion and credibility. It feared that constructing alliances with different forces would seduce it into making unwise commitments and fragment it. Neither did it wish to be perceived as playing both sides of the street. Nonetheless, during the period 1981–86 this strategy dominated the Brotherhood's organizational dynamics. The alliance with the New Wafd party on the eve of the 1984 parliamentary elections allowed it to participate in the Parliament for the first time in its political life. At the same time the leftist party, NPUP, advanced the idea of an alliance between the left and the Brotherhood and made it its daily business to defend jailed Brothers. During this period the Brotherhood used its influence with the state to have a number of Islamic activists released from jail, and in turn it played a role in calming the religiously agitated youth in various localities.

From 1987, however, the strategy of delicate balance began to produce liabilities for the Brotherhood. It was increasingly squeezed between the state and the opposition forces as a result of the latter's growing hostility over the slow speed of the democratization process and the state's strategy for economic reform. Moreover, the Brotherhood came under severe attack from radical Islamists because of its perceived passivity toward their torture in prisons and for bestowing a degree of legitimacy upon the state through participating in the parliamentary elections, despite the fact that the state does not apply the Shari'a or genuinely pursue the democratization process.[52]

As a result of this criticism the Ikhwan modified its strategy by leading the protest against the misuse of police authority, by active involvement with political opposition parties pressing for expansion of the democratization process and changes in the 1971 constitution, and by aggressive assertion of its primacy inside the Islamic movement.[53] These modifications made the Ikhwan more of an opposition force than an ally of the state, limited the positive effects of the strategy of delicate balance, and ultimately led to the Ikhwan's political demise as indicated by its nonparticipation in the parliamentary elections of 1990. With the general stand of the opposition against electoral participation binding the Brotherhood, it thus lost an important and legitimate platform. Because the state continued to prohibit the Brotherhood from forming a political party of its own, it became more vulnerable to its partner in the Islamic alliance, the Islamic Action party, which was becoming increasingly radical. In effect, the Brotherhood had opted for a central place in the Egyptian political arena but found itself marginalized and limited in impact by the early 1990s.

The Third Limitation: The State applying Soft Conservative Policies

The Muslim Brotherhood built its strategy on the premise that the polity is in need of a strong conservative shield against the radical fundamentalists in championing the cause of Islam. This premise was based on the assumption that the state elite is modernist in attitude and is not able politically and ideologically to represent the conservative mood of the middle classes, much less subdue the radical Islamists. Sadat's experience with the Islamic movement at large during the 1970s encouraged the Brotherhood to expect that the state's need of it would continue to grow. The political events during 1981 to 1988 indicated the correctness of the Brotherhood's understanding of the political dynamics in Egypt. In a nutshell, the Brotherhood sought to change in such a way as to deepen the state's need for the Brotherhood.[54]

This strategy faced the deep-seated suspicions of the state apparatus regarding the Brotherhood's real aims as well as the long Egyptian state tradition of political autonomy vis-à-vis its political allies. These shortcomings were consolidated by the shift of the Ikhwan to playing more of an oppositional role, particularly during the parliamentary elections of 1990 and the Gulf War of 1990–91.[55] Exploiting the Ikhwan's strategy, the state began to color the official state ideology with Islamic terminology and pose as the representative of the correct understanding of the Islamic religion. In this vein, the two major state-dominated political organizations—the state party, the National Democratic party (NDP), and the Parliament—emphasized in their official discourse their commitment to Islam and the Islamic state. Thus the sixth general assembly of the NDP, held in July 1992, produced a new document for political action, emphasizing that Egypt is not a secular state but an Islamic one, that Egypt believes in the values and norms of Islam, and that religious culture should be disseminated through different levels of the educational system.[56] In 1992 the speaker of the Parliament stressed that Egypt is a religious state. New laws were justified to the public on Islamic grounds, and leading members of the political elite made it their habit to utter religious statements, visit religious places, and address religious gatherings. The Ministry of Information, which is responsible for controlling the national television system, formulated new policy guidelines prohibiting movies, advertisements, or performances which might upset the Islamic feelings of the population. The Ministry of Education began to apply an unannounced policy of reforming the mixed school system along Islamic lines by transferring male teachers from girls' to boys' schools and restricting the establishment of any new mixed preparatory and secondary schools. This shift indicated that the state did not need the Brotherhood as a force for state legitimation.[57]

There was also clandestine dialogue between the local NDP leadership and the leading radical Islamists in the hope of finding common ground to control fundamentalist violence. This policy became standard with the coming of General 'Abd al-Halim Musa as the minister of interior in January 1990. The government's logic in seeking such communication favored straightforward appeasement: the government needed law and order, and the radical Islamists wanted to live in an Islamic environment. In return for the Muslim fundamentalists' promise to lessen the resort to violence, the state took measures to enforce the Islamization of the symbols of social life. In Upper Egypt, for example, five governorates prohibit the sale of liquor, although it is not generally prohibited by law. Moreover, the directors of public security in the provinces and the NDP's local party secretaries have been engaged in dialogue with the fundamentalists. The rule is that as long as the fundamentalists are quiet and orderly in conduct, their local social demands are satisfied. This policy of dialogue saw the editor-in chief of the NDP newspaper launch a major national campaign in July 1992 for a dialogue with the fundamentalists.[58] However, when the dialogue has given way to violence, as it has increasingly since mid-1992, the state's response has been counterviolence.

Within this framework of appeasement the state has attempted to craft a new measure for ideological combat with the radical fundamentalists—the use of erstwhile fundamentalists to convert the fundamentalists through debate. Although it has not been employed on a wide scale, this strategy has revealed the state's perhaps naive conviction that the best way to falsify the religious claims of the fundamentalists is through repentant "true believers," rather than through promotion of the Brotherhood's approach to Islam.

Violence as Part of Normalization

The policy of state violence against the Islamic movement, particularly its radical elements, is not new, but it has evolved through many phases. The policy is guided by the conviction that the Islamic movement is prone to violence against the state, unlike the other political opposition forces such as the Marxists and forces of the political right. Moreover, the policy is a response to the development of the patterns and techniques of Islamic violence. During the 1970s and 1980s state violence was the major state reaction against the Islamic jama'at. This policy of selective violence was not intended to annihilate the jama'at (as the policy under Nasser might have been construed), but rather to uproot its most aggressive elements, making them understand that their violence would be countered with a more crushing violence, and facilitating the ability of Muslims to leave the jama'at. The purpose was thus not to destroy the believers but to smooth the aggressive edge of the jama'at and check their conspiratorial nature against the state and society.

By the same token, the jama'at's violence functioned to constrain the Nasserist tradition of indiscriminate violence against the Islamic opposition. Violence between the state and the jama'at occurred within the framework of state appeasement of radical Islamists and the increasing localization and organizational fragmentation of the jama'at.[59] In this sense, state-jama'at violence and inter-jama'at violence functioned as a normalization dynamics.

The State

Since the 1970s the main institution charged with applying violence against Islamic jama'at has been the Ministry of Interior. Its policy was principally the product of an accumulation of responses and organizational innovation. The ministry had established a police special force in 1949 as a response to the Muslim Brotherhood's attack with automatic weapons on police troops. However, with the advent of the military regime of 1952, the ministry was no longer the spearhead against the Muslim Brotherhood. Up to 1967, the Military Police and Military Criminal Investigation Department, under the supervision of the office of the field marshal of the army, were in charge of encountering the radical Muslim Brotherhood. These two institutions pursued a policy of all-out violence against the Islamic movement.[60]

Prior to October 1977 and the rise of al-Nabawi Isma'il to the top of the Ministry, the Ministry of Interior created two structures which later proved useful against the

Islamic movement. The first was the Central Security Forces in August 1969, which came as a response to the failure of the regular police forces to check the mass demonstrations against the regime in February 1968. The ministry received training assistance from the military and from 1969 to 1973 the size of the forces increased from eight thousand to twenty-four thousand conscripts.[61] The second was the upgrading of the organizational status of the Public Investigation Department. Through Presidential Decree 544 of 1969, the department acquired organizational autonomy in its relationship with other departments in the ministry. Further, its name was changed to the Department of State Security (SSI) by Presidential Decree 841 of 1971. This change indicated the new tasks with which the SSI was charged. Since 1971, the SSI has been responsible to the minister of interior for monitoring and uncovering all political, social, and economic subversive elements, either national or foreign, and has been responsible for the security of outdoor activities of the president. This change was part of the demilitarization of the state under Sadat. Despite these organizational changes the ministry continued to view its role in resolving sociopolitical problems as complementary to the sociopolitical solutions provided by the regime.

When Hasan Abu Pasha became the minister of interior on 31 August 1982, the ministry began to act as a mechanism for uprooting the most aggressive and destabilizing political elements. Two new concepts in state policy followed from this shift. First, Abu Pasha introduced a distinction between two trends of the Islamic movement: moderates, those working openly through legal means; and extremists, those involved in clandestine activities. Second, Zaki Badr, who became the minister of interior on 27 February 1986, enlarged the concept of Islamic extremism to include actions aimed at changing the immediate environment through force. 'Abd al-Halim Musa, who became interior minister in January 1990, applied these two concepts in an active policy against the Jama'at which recognized the distinction, on the one hand, between the Muslim Brotherhood and the Jama'at, and, on the other, between Jama'at members who seek to change the immediate environment through force and those who do not. Musa also understood that Islamic radicalism motivated is not only by religious but also socioeconomic and political reasons. At the same time he emphasized publicly that police action was not directed against the Islamists' call to implement the Shari'a but against members of the Islamic movement who are inclined to use violence toward this end.

This policy dictated new organizational innovations such as placing more emphasis on information processing.[62] There was also a higher level of cooperation among the Ministry of Interior, the Ministry of Endowments, and the Ministry of Social Affairs. Under Abu Pasha, the Interior Ministry sponsored direct dialogue with radical elements in jails and throughout the country; Endowment Ministry shaykhs were involved in these dialogues. Under Zaki Badr, the Interior Ministry cooperated with the Ministry of Social Affairs to review regularly the activities of the religious voluntary associations and to provide money and opportunities for voluntary local associations in their efforts to enhance local living conditions. In addition, the Security Forces were reformed. Though the size of the forces was reduced by 15.5 percent, in the 1990s there has been more emphasis on efficiency. The dynamics of religious extremism among the youth have been carefully studied in an effort to build public opinion against it. The ministry has sponsored public forums, for example, which have attempted to build consensus among urban professionals and the middle classes against Islamic violence.[63]

Police action ordered by Musa aimed at dividing the Islamic movement. The Interior Ministry sought to undermine Islamic unity by distinguishing between the active fundamentalist groups and the passive ones. Yet in the early 1990s the ministry often targeted the wrong groups for surveillance and arrest. The attempted assassination of Abu Pasha is a case in point.[64] However, the ministry applied a double-track policy of selective mass arrests to break up the most salient clandestine Islamic organizations, while encouraging local security directors to accommodate the nonpolitical groups and thereby undermine any tendency toward radicalization.

As the riots in Asyut and elsewhere in 1992 and early 1993 clearly demonstrated, however, this policy contributed to the politicization of potentially passive groups, bred a selective alliance of interests between certain members of the local police leadership and the fundamentalists, and induced a conflict displacement between the Copts and the Islamic radicals instead of between the Islamic radicals and the political regime.

Another state security policy in the early 1990s led to frequent arrests (permitted by martial law) aimed at limiting the number of radical activists and preventing the radicalization of the moderates. However, the efforts of the Interior Ministry were constrained by the different policies of other ministries. Encouraging tourism, for example, entailed the creation of a culture of tourism which many radical and moderate fundamentalists alike considered un-Islamic and offensive.[65]

The Jama'at

In the 1980s and early 1990s four major Islamic associations or jama'at—al-Samawiyya, the Jihad Organization, al-Jama'a al-Islamiyya al-Jihadiyya, and al-Shawqun—projected violence against the state apparatus, against social conduct they believed to be un-Islamic, and against one another.[66] There were common features to this violence. Employed as a response to specific situations, actions, or conduct, the violence, though motivated by their fundamentalist beliefs, was not projected induscriminately and did not have a theory of its own.

Indeed, reduction of violence as the state moved from a policy tied to ideological concerns to a mechanism intended for co-optation and problem-solving was the legacy of the 1980s. During the 1970s, violence had been adopted by al-Jihad and abhorred by Jama'at al-Muslimin (al-Takfir wa'l-Hijra) for theoretical reasons not directly related to their fundamentalist understanding of Islam. The Jihad Organization, a broad alliance of smaller groups, understood violence as part of a larger action and strategy, the Islamic revolution. From this perspective violence would be justified if and only if it triggered the Islamic revolution,[67] and this understanding was the justification for restricting the exercise of violence to political authorities. As for Shukri Mustafa, violence was against his concept of de-linkage with society because violence involved interaction with society. Many of his followers still wonder how he slipped into kidnapping and murdering Shaykh Muhammad Husayn al-Dhahabi, a former minister of religious endowments, in the summer of 1977. Yet they believe that murder, paradoxically, confirmed the utility of Shukri's concept of hijra: deviation from the concept of physically abandoning society led to the destruction of the jama'a.

Violence perpetrated by these groups in the 1980s generally reflected a defensive posture more than an offensive strategy. (During the 1970s the Jihadist concept of violence had been part of a grand strategy to change the state and society.) The defensive posture of the jama'at was intended to abort the regime's efforts to isolate them geographically and financially and to change the environmental conditions of fundamentalism. Indeed, the organizational shift from an offensive to defensive posture owed its cause principally to the success of the Mubarak regime in breaking down the Jihad Organization and to the state's coordinated efforts against fundamentalists in local communities.

The exercise of violence during the 1980s and after was more sophisticated in operational planning and execution than fundamentalist violence in the 1970s. The fundamentalists had learned from the failure of the Islamic revolt in Asyut and its aftermath, which was thought to be partially the result of a low level of training among members of the jama'at.

Islamic Jihad members were provided with new opportunities for military training when they were recruited to fight against the Soviets in Afghanistan. Ironically, the regime did not object to young Jihad members and other jama'at activists fighting in Afghanistan, perhaps because it thought the flight of fundamentalists to Afghanistan would contribute to the reduction of their influence and number in Egypt and hence would increase the regime's potential for stability. The call and recruitment for Afghanistan were permitted in mosques before 1991. In 1992, military-style training was also provided for fundamentalists in camps in Sudan and for those Jihad members fighting in Bosnia. While the latter is permitted by the authorities, following the same logic of Afghanistan, the former is prohibited and opposed by the government on the ground that Egyptian fundamentalists trained in Sudan are threats to Egyptian national security. Hence, Islamic violence, particularly in Upper Egypt, was considered as related not only to regime stability but also to national security.[68]

Much of this training involved not only learning to plan and execute operations efficiently but also, and perhaps more importantly from the national security perspective, to handle sophisticated small arms. It is reported that the number of illegal weapons increased from 8,592 in 1987 to 13,000 in 1991. It is further estimated that the authorities uncovered and seized only 30 percent of the total number on the market and in the hands of the fundamentalists.[69] The fundamentalists' sophisticated weaponry training and use made Islamic violence during the 1980s and early 1990s categorically different from that of the 1970s. This led not only to a growing alliance between the jama'at and the private traders of weapons, and between the jama'at and outlaws, but also to a growing realignment of Islamic finances with the finances of drug trafficking, the black market, and money-laundering schemes.[70] Hence, violence not only served the cause of applying the Shari'a but also involved the fundamentalists in interests larger than the Islamic movement.

Violence was also employed by the legal Islamic opposition as a political asset in its contest against the regime. Many observers came to see the Islamic movement with its legal and illegal sections as one movement and to believe that it operates according to a division of roles: the illegal section exercises violence, and the legal one justifies it and seeks greater appeasement from the state in order to prevent more violence. This pattern was demonstrated in June 1992 in the assassination of Faraj Fuda, a secular publicist and advocate of a tough state stand against the Islamic movement. Although both the Islamic Action party and the Brotherhood condemned the assassination, they faulted the government for permitting secular intellectuals to air and advocate ideas antagonistic to Islamic feelings.[71] The government accepted at least part of the blame and increased its appeasement of the Islamic movement.

The violence perpetuated by the Islamic movement has also been justified indirectly by human rights groups, which explain it as a reaction to police brutality.[72] In short, Islamic violence has become a highly political issue between the government and the opposition; in turn, this conflict has rendered the opposition at large in Egypt a structural ally of the violence.

Al-Samawiyya

In 1965, when Shaykh 'Abdallah al-Samawi was affiliated with the Muslim Brotherhood, he went to jail as the result of the government sweep of Brotherhood members and sympathizers. While in jail he and Shukri Mustafa developed the doctrine of takfir. After his release in 1971, he returned to his home village in al-Fayyum in Upper Egypt and assembled a network of followers which became al-Samawiyya. His group's stronghold is in al-Fayyum and al-Minya. Before 1986, when he and members of his group were arrested and put on trial for allegedly legitimizing the burning of video clubs and churches in Cairo, al-Fayyum, and al-Minya, his name was linked both to Shukri Mustafa's Jama'at al-Muslimin and to the older brother, Muhammad, of Sadat's assassin, Khalid al-Islambuli. With Shukri Mustafa he accused society of living in jahiliyya, but broke with him over the issue of hijra, which he believed to be a misreading of both the Prophet's life and the development of Islam. Moreover, he disagreed with Mustafa over the permissibility of *taqiyya* (dissimulation or the false expression of one's belief) because, according to al-Samawi, it precludes and delays launching jihad.[73]

In the 1970s al-Samawi sought to establish an Islamic regime through jihad, but he was not included in the Jihad umbrella organization of 1981 and thus he escaped destruction. Al-Samawiyya is not an organization in any conventional sense: it is not hierarchical, a network, or cliquish. Rather, it is organized as a preacher with an audience. Perhaps this very organizational nature allowed al-Samawiyya to avoid proscription in 1992, since Shaykh al-Samawi credibly denied any organizational affiliation with the men who burned the video clubs and churches. Before the court he presented his thoughts on the Islamic movement in Egypt, and he argued that it should play a role on the international scene. This proposition implied a significant change because it entailed the relative acceptance of *dar al-harb* (un-Islamic countries)—although he continued to profess total antagonism to the Jews, Zionism, and

U.S. global hegemony. Al-Samawiyya contended that video clubs, which circulate indecent movies to lure Muslim youth from observance of their religion, are a Jewish/Zionist–Christian conspiracy. Mubarak's regime is un-Islamic for it fails to provide and maintain Islamic social justice, and the only cure for the spread of corruption and consumerism is application of the Shari'a.

In his diatribe before the judge, Shaykh al-Samawi accepted the traditional institution of al-Azhar and asked for an expansion of its role in government. He proposed that the president of Egypt should be elected from an assembly representing Muslims and be approved by the grand shaykh of al-Azhar. In this view, rulership is a partnership between the president and Shaykh al-Azhar. He recognized that the judiciary in Egypt is not infidel, and this separation of the judiciary from the state apparatus was a departure from his previous practice of accusing the whole state of being infidel. Most significant, however, was his contention that the Islamic rule of avoiding the greater harm prohibited him from urging the burning of video clubs. Even though the clubs are un-Islamic, burning them would only bring greater harm to Muslim lives in view of the government's new strategy of mass arrest. This logic represented a significant change: living in an un-Islamic state had become a lesser harm than subjecting Muslims to torture in jails and the indiscriminate arrest of families and relatives.

The Jihad Organization

After a foiled coup attempt in Asyut in 1981, the regime was successful in rounding up the leadership structure of the Jihad Organization. The only person who escaped the court sentence was Shaykh 'Umar 'Abd al-Rahman. Immediately, the alliance between the Jihadist Islamic Jama'a—what we have called al-Jama'a al-Islamiyya al-Jihadiyya—and the umbrella Jihad Organization disintegrated over the issue of electing the general amir of the organization. Al-Jama'a al-Islamiyya al-Jihadiyya with its stronghold in Upper Egypt wanted 'Abd al-Rahman to assume this position. Leaders of the Jihad Organization in Giza, Cairo, and Alexandria, however, proposed 'Abbud al-Zumur, who had been sentenced to life in prison. The issue was resolved peacefully, but a deep rift ensued in the alliance, with al-Jama'a al-Islamiyya al-Jihadiyya seceding. Another issue that engulfed the organization at the time was the appropriate strategy to use during a time of retreat. The Jihad Organization maintained its original position, wanting to continue clandestine activities, whereas the Jihadist Islamic Jama'a preferred open public activities. However, the Jihad Organization during the 1980s was crippled because its leaders were jailed.[74]

It seems that while in jail, Jihad leader 'Abbud al-Zumur maintained his principal views on the Islamic revolution, but he also objected to perpetuating violence that would involve greater harm to Muslims at large, and he showed a new readiness to accept a fatwa from al-Azhar ulama. This stance indicated a retreat from the original Jihad's advocacy of unconditional violence against the state and its condemnation of al-Azhar as un-Islamic. In addition, a Jihad group of lawyers publicly contested the election of the Lawyers' Association board in September 1992, possibly thereby indicating a departure from the clandestine activities of the Jihad and a newfound willingness to differentiate among state agencies. If true, this would represent an important intellectual development.

The Jihad Organization has suffered from the disintegration of its central command, however. As a result, small Jihadist jama'at have proliferated throughout the cities and towns of Egypt.[75] The structure of these small jama'at is simple and runs along cliquish lines of organization. The police have dealt with them according to the principle of "shoot to kill" because of their commitment to violence against the police. Some of these small jama'at were accused of assassinating Rif'at al-Mahgub, the speaker of Parliament, in 1990 and attacking some of the Copts' gold trading stores in Cairo and Upper Egypt.

Al-Jama'a al-Islamiyya al-Jihadiyya

The Jihadist Islamic Jama'a emerged during the 1980s as the champion of Islamic violence. Its members and cells have been implicated in the violent events of al-Fayyum, the hometown of 'Umar 'Abd al-Rahman, Bani-Su'aif, al-Minya, and Asyut. Its recruitment policies have been different from those of the umbrella Jihad Organization and the Brotherhood. The Jihadist Islamic Jama'a is a grass-roots organization emphasizing the recruitment of individuals on the margins of society—the unemployed, the poor, and the undereducated. Its membership profile includes a number of university graduates, but they are without work and mostly graduates of regional universities, not the universities of Cairo. They are integrated in their villages and neighborhoods. Most of the population in these areas, notwithstanding the violence, feel inclined to protect members of the Jama'a because of the populist attitude with which it conducts its activities. This attitude—which includes feuding with the Copts, an intense Islamic feeling of identity and dignity, and communal service—pits Jama'a members against the middle and upper classes in their neighborhoods. Under increasing siege by the authorities, members of the Jama'a have found themselves in alliance with outlaws (who, in the local culture, are looked on as victims of the social and government system) surrounding the poor and impoverished areas. According to a flyer in June 1992 celebrating the Islamic 'Id, this identification with the oppressed is understood in a global context; the group paints an image of the world in which Muslims are persecuted, especially in the United States, and in which some Muslims are in alliance with anti-Muslim forces.[76]

Members of al-Jama'a al-Islamiyya al-Jihadiyya have deployed crude violence in their communities, wielding primitive weapons, often shooting at random. However, they have also begun to use more sophisticated violence as a result of their increased training in Afghanistan and Sudan; the assassination of Faraj Fuda testifies to such a change.[77]

Al-Shawqun

The Shawqun organization, labeled a neo-Jihad organization by some observers, was founded by Shawqi al-Shaykh in al-Fayyum governorate. Al-Shaykh was a follower of 'Umar 'Abd al-Rahman and the son of a leading local member of the NDP. An engineer and irrigation inspector for the government, al-Shaykh joined the Jihad Organization with 'Abd al-Rahman, but in 1988 he split from the organization and accused 'Abd al-Rahman of leniency in spreading jihad and fighting the government. Violence was his way of spreading the word. 'Abd al-Rahman condemned him to death and considered him an infidel, but al-Shaykh in turn denounced 'Abd al-Rahman and condemned *him* to death.

From 1988 until the police shot him dead and rounded up his organization in 1990, al-Shaykh succeeded in building a strong organization and taking Khak village as its stronghold. Al-Shaykh's strategy of recruitment was simple and straightforward. He recruited only men reputed for power and wealth in their communities, and through them many followers joined.[78] His organization was divided into groups charged with administration, encompassing finance and food; with military training and the use of weapons; with meting out physical punishment; with application of the Shari'a; and with facilitating transportation.

Al-Shawqun was headed by rich men and it appeased rich families, yet the rank-and-file members of the organization were very poor and a mix of peasants, seasonal workers, fishermen, drivers, and people involved in rural, petty service delivery. Any person outside of the organization was considered an infidel and should be killed. Through the two years of its existence al-Shawqun was involved in violence against virtually everybody. Al-Shaykh's campaign of terror ended with his violent death in May 1990 and the arrest of most members of his organization. However, the group did not die easily: a week later a new organization was declared under the leadership of Ahmad Salim Khak, and it espoused the ideology of *takfir al-kafir* (pronouncing someone an infidel without giving him a chance to repent). This ideology promised more violence as it declared the police corps as forever infidel. Khak committed his group to kill one police officer for every group member killed by the police. Further, he has threatened every person who assists the state with robbery and murder. He has declared the village of Khak an independent Islamic *wilaya*, or governate. Predictably, he has asked his followers to seize the properties of the Copts because they are the enemy of Islam. Members of this new organization come from the lowest rank of the social structure; they are either the illiterate poor or work in petty rural services. This organization assassinated the head of the Fayyum Bureau of Monitoring Religious Extremism, and although the police have moved against it once again, it is still operating in 1993.

The Potential and Actual Limits of Violence

Violence between the state and radical Islamists has intensified since the mid-1980s and seems to be continuing, but two basic limitations on violence have seemed possible as a result of both the state drive for consolidating democratic openings and the changing membership of the radical Islamist groups.

The first limitation has been tied to the politicization process. Sadat's assassination by Islamic radicals indicated the failure of the regime to contain violence during a time of liberalization. Mubarak's regime faced a dilemma: How to manage political contestation and slow the process of redefining the legitimacy of the state—processes which resulted from liberalization—without eroding the autonomy of the state to pursue economic reform and decrease public spending? Also, how to maintain the executive privileges of the presidency with its special connection with the military? Sadat's exercise of violence aggravated the dilemma. The challenge for Mubarak's regime has been how to make state violence part of the rules of the game.

After Asyut's failed Islamic revolt, Mubarak's regime made efforts to differentiate between violence against the forces of legal opposition and violence against the Islamic radicals. Violence was not to be exercised against the opposition at large, but only in response to specific actions considered threatening to the stability of the regime. Within this principal framework of policy the Islamic movement has been increasingly seen as an aggregate movement and not a monolithic one.

Hence, state violence has differentiated between the legal opposition and the Islamic movement, and also functioned to disaggregate the Islamic movement. Toward this end, the democratic opening, or liberalization, has been confined to formal channels of political contestation and representation: elections, Parliament, and journalism. The actions of Islamic forces outside of these channels are being countered by state violence. This strategy has been based on the crucial assumption that participation through the formal channels would increase; therefore, violence against the groups outside the political institution would not increase the politicization of the populace at large.

Unfortunately, by the time of this writing—early 1993—the expansion of political participation has not been realized and thus the assumption has not been fulfilled. Active contestation among the political forces of the opposition has been constrained by the NDP-cum-state domination in writing the rules of the game, which has deprived the democratization process of real potential for expansion. Furthermore, the increasing economic and public services impoverishment of local communities, particularly in Upper Egypt and in the informal areas and inner-city neighborhoods of Giza and Cairo, has bred continuous discontent among the populace; around Giza and Cairo especially, the authorities have been uninformed and slow in response. Within this framework, state violence has faced increasing problems of justification and become a political issue between the opposition and the government, with growing rifts between state authorities and local representatives who are vulnerable to kinship and special interest connections. Popular general sympathy for fundamentalist violence aimed at the state security apparatus has been the characteristic outcome of this limitation. This sympathy is heightened when some Islamic radicals adapt their arguments and promote their cause in terms of social justice, standing against corruption. In short, state violence without the expansion of popular participation inevitably renders such violence a politicizing device and is thus counterproductive.

The second possible hope for limiting the arena of violence is found in the reaction against unlimited violence. During the 1970s violence was justified in religious terms. During the 1980s, however, the pattern of Islamic killing took the form of revenge and settling of accounts with the security apparatus, intellectuals, and state politicians.[79] The record suggests that Islamic violence turned during the 1980s to

Islamic terror, and this change was the outcome of the changing membership profile of Islamic radical organizations. Data show clearly the change from recruiting sons of the urban middle and upper middle classes to recruiting the marginals and those members of the lowest ranks of the social structure. Marginals, the poor, and the unemployed are more inclined to project the new type of Islamic violence than affiliates of the urban middle and upper-middle classes. Jama'at are more concentrated in the 1990s in the poor sections of Bani-Su'aif, al-Fayyum, al-Minya, Asyut, Giza, and Cairo, and as a consequence, violence is projected as a form of moral and material frustration.

Islamic terror has exposed the jama'at to a dilemma: on the one hand, their populist basis wins them support in the poorer segments of society. On the other hand, the increasing fragmentation of the jama'at themselves increases the tendency for inter-jama'at violence and aimless killing, which in turn scares away potential recruits from the middle and upper-middle classes. In short, more violence by Islamic radicals only means more killing and less potential for penetrating the dominant classes through recruitment. This in turn contributes structurally to the consolidation of a social force against radical Islamists.[80] At the same time, however, these same violent activities serve to enhance the radicals' legitimacy among the dissatisfied.

Conclusion

This chapter began by defining the concept of normalization as the recognition by opponents of the "political existence of each other within specific boundaries." Through the normalization process a code of conduct emerges which determines realms of conflict, concessions, and cooperation. From our investigation, we have seen the possibilities and limitations of structuring realms of conflict and cooperation between the various components of the Islamic movement and Mubarak's regime.

Yet has normalization occurred? On the ideological ground, the Egyptian state leadership has been using religion as a source of legitimacy, but one should note the elasticity of the official ideology of the regime. The Nasser and Sadat regimes moved back and forth from the left to the right and from secularism to religion in time of crises, national challenges, and reverses. In this sense, the move to declare Islam as the source of constraints on behavior and as the basis of legitimacy has been witnessed in each of the three regimes since the 1962 revolution.

Hence, the conflict between the Sadat and Mubarak regimes and the Islamic movement has been played out against a shared ideological background: the notion that Islam should be applied and Muslims should be virtuous. The difference—and it is a key one—is over the issue of power. The Mubarak regime has made immense efforts to combat the jama'at's ideological constructs which undermine its power, particularly the notions of takfir and hakimiyya. During the 1980s the state was successful in normalizing the jama'at on the issue of takfir, in return for which it increased references to Islam in its official ideology and projected itself as the defender of the Islamic cause. This change could be considered the Islamic movement normalizing the state, but from another perspective it could be seen as the state temporarily circumventing the ideological momentum of the Islamic movement.

In the early 1990s, Islamic political activism, whether conservative or radical, appears significant, although different in many ways from what occurred in the 1970s and 1980s. The most critical issue for the Mubarak regime remains, however, the monopoly of central power. The historical record under Nasser and Sadat clearly shows that defending such a monopoly is one of the major skills of the state. Mubarak has accepted the growing influence of the Islamic movement in Parliament (which in fact does not have any significant power in relation to the executive) and in the informal local power structure (which does not affect at all the central power dynamics in Egypt). However, because radical Islam rejects such state-defined rules of the game and retains populist appeal, the outcome of the regime's attempt to fragment the Islamic movement and co-opt it must be seen as far from clear.

Acknowledgments

A number of Egyptians assisted me in collecting the data necessary for the research. At the Center for Political and International Development Studies, which has the largest and most detailed data base on the Islamic movement in Egypt and some Arab countries, the researchers are ex-activists who greatly contributed to my understanding of the movement.

Notes

1. The concept of "normalization" is mainly understood as a process of confidence-building and developing areas of cooperation. See J. H. Herz, "Normalization in the International Relations," *Middle East Review* (Spring 1978): 10. Also see Paul Seabury and Angelo Codevilla, *War: Ends and Means* (New York: Basic Books), particularly part 3 on how wars end, pp. 243–76; and the special issue of *International Interactions* on pioneers of peace research, vol. 10, no. 2 (1983). Nicholas Onuf and Frank F. Klink, "Anarchy, Authority, Rule," *International Studies Quarterly* 33, no. 2 (June 1989): 149–73; and Henry Kissinger, *The White House Years* (London: George Weidenfeld and Nicolson, Ltd., 1979), particularly part 4, "From War to Peace." As it is formulated in this chapter, the concept indicates regulation of violence as a part of the confidence-building process.

Normalization here is further understood to carry with it a reactive risk. See Carol A. Heimer, *Reactive Risk and Rational Action* (Berkeley: University of California Press, 1985), particularly chap. 6; and Mary Douglas, *Risk and Blame: Essays in Cultural Theory* (London:Routledge, 1992).

2. See for example, Saad Eddin Ibrahim, "Anatomy of Egypt's Militant Islamic Groups," *International Journal of Middle East Studies* 12, no. 4 (December 1980): 423–53; also, Nazih Ayubi, "The Political Revival of Islam: The Case of Egypt," *International Journal of Middle East Studies* 12, no. 4 (December 1980): 481–99.

3. See, for example, Ali Hillal Dessouki, ed., *Islamic Resurgence in the Arab World* (New York: Praeger, 1982); and his "The Resurgence of Islamic Organizations in Egypt: An Interpretation," in Alexander S.

Cudsi and A. H. Dessouki, eds., *Islam and Power* (London: Croom Helm, 1981), pp. 107–18.

4. See, for example, Gehad Auda, "Islamic Movement and Resource Mobilization in Egypt: A Political Culture Perspective," in Larry Diamond, ed., *Political Culture and Democracy in Developing Countries* (Colorado: Lynne Rienner Publishers, 1993).

5. See Hrair Dekmejian, "The Anatomy of Islamic Revival: Legitimacy Crisis, Ethnic Conflict, and the Search for Islamic Alternatives," in Michael Curtis, ed., *Religion and Politics in the Middle East* (Colorado: Westview Press, 1981), pp. 31–42; in the same book, see Louis J. Cantori, "Religion and Politics in Egypt," pp. 77–90.

6. Saad Eddin Ibrahim, "Egypt's Islamic Activism in the 1980s," *Third World Quarterly,* April (1988): 632–57.

7. See Saad Eddin Ibrahim, "Anatomy of Egypt's Islamic Militant Groups"; John Esposito, ed., *Islam and Development* (Syracuse: Syracuse University Press, 1980); Hrair Dekmejian, "Islamic Revival: Catalysts, Categories, and Consequences," in Shireen Hunter, ed., *The Politics of Islamic Revivalism: Diversity and Unity* (Bloomington: Indiana University Press, 1988), pp. 3–19.

8. See Amira El-Azhary Sonbol, "Egypt," in Shireen Hunter, *The Politics of Islamic Revivalism,* pp. 23–38; Dessouki, *Islamic Resurgence.*

9. See Gilles Kepel, *The Prophet and Pharaoh: Muslim Extremism in Egypt,* trans. John Rothschild (London: Al-Saqi Books, 1985).

10. See Richard P. Mitchell, *The Society of Muslim Brothers* (London: Oxford University Press, 1969); for a Muslim Brotherhood perspective, see 'Abd al-Halim Mahmud, *Muslim Brotherhood: A View from Inside,* vol. 1: 1928–48 (in Arabic) (Alexanderia: Dar al-Da'wa, 1980). For a leftist perspective, see Rifa't al-Sa'id, *Hasan Al-Banna: When, How, and Why?* (in Arabic) (Cairo: Maktubat Madbuli, 1977). For a revisionist sympathetic historic account, see Tariq al-Bishiri, *Al-Haraka al-Siyasiyya fi Misr, 1945–1952* (The political movement in Egypt 1945–1952), 2d ed. (Cairo: Dar al-Shuruq, 1983). Not all al-Azhar shaykhs have been against the Brotherhood. Indeed, some of the prominent members were of al-Azhar background, such as Shaykh Muhammad al-Ghazali and Shaykh Ahmad al-Baquri. Al-Azhar opposed the Brotherhood due to the affiliation of some influential al-Azhar shaykhs before 1952 with political parties that had deep political distrust of it, such as the Wafd and Liberal Constitutionalists parties; the belief that the Brothers worked against the state (al-Azhar was part of the state before 1952 and more so after 1961); the involvement of a great number of al-Azhar shaykhs in Sufi orders which the Brotherhood did not respect; the involvement of a number of influential al-Azhar shaykhs in the activities of Islamic civil associations which the Brotherhood regarded as not furthering the Islamic cause; the strong view among leading sections of al-Azhar that the Brotherhood's da'wa simplifies Islam and disregards the doctrinal historic development of Islam; and the strong feeling that the Brotherhood seeks to dislodge al-Azhar from the leadership position of the Islamic current and the Muslims at large. See Zakariyya Sulayman al-Bayyumi, *al-Ikhwan al-Muslimin wa'l Jama'at al-Islamiyya fi'l-Hayat al-Siyasiyya al-Misriyya 1928–1948* (Muslim Brotherhood and Islamic groups in the Egyptian political life 1928–1948) (Cairo: Maktabat Wahaba, 1979), pp. 255–86, and Tariq al-Bishiri, *Al-Haraka al-Siyasiyya fi Misr.* In our context the term "modern Islamists" refers only to the conservative current because it is large in membership, attractive in appeal among the educated segment of the Islamic current at large and stronger in connections to many active Islamic institutions such as al-Azhar and political parties and forces. The conservative modern Islamists are more of a political reality while the radical modern Islamists are more of an intellectual phenomenon. The conservative modern Islamists distinguish themselves from the radical ones by emphasizing the civilizational dimension of religion and the recognition that the Shari'a must accommodate the conditions of modern life. The radical modern Islamists gives

primacy to modern conditions as the criteria by which to judge the relevance of the application of Islamic tradition and Shari'a. Radical modern Islamists include Faraj Fuda, who was assassinated by a fundamentalist Jama'a in 1992 for his views on Islam and its relevance to the modern life, Muhammad Sa'id al-Ashmawi, Hassan Hanafi, Muhamad Ahmad Khalif-Allah, and Husayn Ahmad Amin. Active leaders of the conservative modern Islamists include Fahmi Hudi; see his *Falsification of Consciousness* (in Arabic) (Cairo: Dar al-Shuruq, 1987) and *So That It Would Not Be Fitna* (in Arabic) (Cairo: Dar al-Shuruq, 1989); Muhammad 'Imara, see his *The Features of the Islamic Method* (in Arabic) (Cairo: Dar al-Shuruq, al-Azhar/The High Committee for Islamic Da'wa, 1991); Ahmad Kamal Abu al-Majid, see his *Neither Dialogue Nor Confrontation* (in Arabic) (Cairo: Dar al-Shuruq, 1989) and *A Modern Islamic View* (in Arabic) (Cairo: Dar al-Shuruq, 1991); Shaykh Muhammad al-Ghazali, *How Do We Deal With the Qur'an* (in Arabic) (Mansura: Dar al-Wafa', 1992); and *On Our Intellectual Tradition* (in Arabic) (Cairo: Dar al-Shuruq, 1991). Also the Grand Mufti Muhammad al-Sayyid al-Tantawi and some of the leaders of the Azhar, such as Shaykh At'ia Saqr, the head of the Fatwa Committee of al-Azhar, could be identified with this group.

11. On the importance of the religious drive, regardless of socioeconomic reasons or other situational motives, in explaining the widening scope of the new wave of Islamic revivalism across the Islamic countries, see John O. Voll, *Islam: Continuity and Change in the Modern World* (Colorado: Westview Press, 1982); Daniel Pipes, *In the Path of God: Islam and Political Power* (New York: Basic Books, 1983); and V. S. Naipaul, *Among the Believers* (London, 1981). However, there is a great debate among scholars over some derivatives of this proposition: whether Islam, on the one hand, and nationalism and the nation state, on the other, are compatible. James Piscatori provides an analysis on the compatibility of Islam and territorial pluralism in *Islam in a World of Nation-States* (Cambridge: Cambridge University Press, 1986), and "Islam

and International Order," in Hedley Bull and Adam Watson, eds., *The Expansion of International Society* (Oxford: Clarendon Press, 1984), pp. 309–21. This group of authors distinguishes between two important concepts: pan-Islam and transnational da'wa. Their argument essentially is directed toward refuting the proposition that the new current of Islamic revivalism is a pan-Islamic ideology. On the other hand, they recognize that the Islamic da'wa involves transnational relations in terms of organizations, values, and actions. Fred Halliday advances three types of the concept of internationalism: liberal, hegemonic, and revolutionary, in order to explain the current generic types of international politics: sectoral and individual reaction, asymmetrical integration of societies, and group ideology of international change. See his "Three Concepts of Internationalism," *International Affairs* 64, no. 2 (Spring 1988): 187–98. As for the transnational relations of the Islamic movement, see Bowyer Bell, "Contemporary Revolutionary Organizations," in Keohane and Nye, "Transnational Relations," p. 162n.11, and Gehad Auda, "An Uncertain Response: The Islamic Movement in Egypt," in James Piscatori, ed., *Islamic Fundamentalisms and the Gulf Crisis* (Chicago: The American Academy of Arts and Sciences, 1991), pp. 109–30. A great deal of evidence confirms the transnational relations of the current Islamic movement: see 'Abd al-Azim al-Mat'ani, *The Crime of the Century: The Story of the Occupation of the Sacred Mosque* (in Arabic) (Cairo: Dar al-Ansar, 1980).

12. Emmanuel Sivan, *Radical Islam: Medieval Theology and Modern Politics* (New Haven: Yale University Press, 1985).

13. Bassam Tibi, *The Crisis of Modern Islam: A Preindustrial Culture in the Scientific-Technological Age*, trans. Judith von Sivers (Salt Lake City: University of Utah Press, 1988).

14. Dessouki, *Islamic Resurgence*.

15. See Sylvia G. Haim, "Sayyid Qutb," in *Asian and African Studies* 16, no. 1 (March 1982): 147–56; Leonard Binder, *Islamic Liberalism: A Critique of Development*

Ideologies (Chicago: University of Chicago Press, 1988), pp. 170–205; Yvonne Yazbeck Haddad, "Sayyid Qutb: Ideologue of Islamic Revival," in John L. Esposito, ed., *Voices of Resurgent Islam* (New York: Oxford University Press, 1983); Muhammad Hafiz Diyyab, *Sayyid Qutb: Discourse and Ideology* (in Arabic) (Cairo: Dar al-Thaqafa al-Jadida, 1987); and Gehad Auda, "An Inquiry into the Dynamics of Sadat's Political Order" (Ph.D. diss., SUNY/Buffalo, 1984), pp. 71–81.

16. This argument is best presented by Qutb in his *Ma'alim fi'l Tariq* (Signposts) (Cairo: Dar al-Shuruq, 1982).

17. Shukri clearly specified his position on takfir before the military court in 1977. A complete record of his testimony is published in Rifa't Sayyid Ahmad, *The Militant Prophet: The Rejectionists* (in Arabic) (London: Riad al-Rayyes Books, 1991), pp. 53–109.

18. The concept of jihad has been further elaborated in four major documents: 'Umar 'Abd al-Rahman's *Mithaq al-Amal al-Islamiyya* (The charter of Islamic action) (Cairo: 1982), Tariq al-Zumur's *Falsafat al-Muwaja* (Philosophy of confrontation) (Cairo: 1985), Kamal al-Sa'id Habib's *al-Ihya' al-Islamiyya* (Islamic revival) (Cairo: 1986), and 'Abbud al-Zumur's *al-Minhaj* (The method), published in Muhammad Rajib, *'Abbud al-Zumur Speaks* (in Arabic) (Cairo: 1990).

19. Sirriya believed it is permissible as long as the individual is dedicated to the Islamic cause; parliamentary means of change is conceivable. Faraj rejected this on the grounds it is a form of lending an infidel authority assistance—which is prohibited in Islam.

20. For the functions of the special apparatus according to the Brotherhood's view and interpretation, see Ahmad 'Adil Kamal, *Muslim Brotherhood and the Special Apparatus* (in Arabic) (Cairo: Dar al-Zahra' li'l-'Alam al-Arabi, 1987), and Mahmud al-Sabagh, *The Truth about the Special Apparatus* (in Arabic) (Cairo: Dar al-I'tisam, 1989). The Muslim Brotherhood's special apparatus was implicated in many cases before the revolu-

tion of 1952 as the secret weapon of the Brotherhood to terrorize and assassinate their opposition. In addition, the special apparatus was its source of recruitment in fighting in Palestine in 1948. The issue of disbanding the special apparatus after al-Hudaybi's assumption of the position of the General Guide in 1950 was one of the major reasons for the group's organizational disarray. For a critical historical study of the special apparatus, see 'Abd al-'Azim Ramadan, *The Muslim Brotherhood and the Special Apparatus* (Cairo: Ruz al-Yusif, 1982).

21. This idea was related to me by one of the leaders of the Muslim Brotherhood who prefers to keep his name in confidence.

22. After al-Hudaybi's death in 1973, the issue of who would be the general guide was reopened. In order to avoid the Brotherhood's total organizational disarray, al-Hudaybi was selected and appointed by the Guidance Bureau (Maktab al-Irshad), which functions as the executive body.

23. 'Umar al-Tilmisani, *Remembrances, not Memoirs* (in Arabic) (Cairo: Dar al-Tiba' wa'l-Nashr al-Islamiyya, 1985), pp. 175–81.

24. Hasan Isma'il al-Hudaybi, *Du'at la Qudat* (Preachers, Not Judges) (Cairo: Dar al-Tiba' wa'l-Nashr al-Islamiyya, 1977). Also 'Abbas al-Sisi, an old veteran of the Brotherhood, recounts in his memoirs the battle against Jama'at al-Muslimin over the interpretation of the Qur'an and Sunna in his *From Slaughterhouse Back to al-Da'wa* (in Arabic) (Alexanderia: Dar al-Tiba' wa'l-Nashr wa'l-Sawtiyyat, 1988).

25. See different issues of *al-Da'wa* magazine during the 1970s. For a review and study of the function of the printed materials and journalism of the Brotherhood, see Muhammad Fathi 'Ali Shueir, *Printed Propaganda Materials of the Da'wa of the Muslim Brotherhood* (in Arabic) (Jidda: Dar al-Majma' li'l-Nashr wa'l-Tawzi', 1985), and Muhammad Mansur Mahmud Hibi, *Islamic Journalism in Egypt between Abdul Nasser and Sadat, 1952–1981* (Mansura: Dar al-Wafa' li'l-Tiba' wa'l-Nashr wa'l-Tawzi', 1990).

26. Badr Muhammad Badr, *al-Jama'a al-Islamiyya in Egypt's Universities: Facts and*

Documents (in Arabic) (Cairo: 1989), pp. 52–53.

27. Al-Tabaw' is a transitional phase which was aimed at gathering followers for final migration. The Society knew tabaw' in two occasions. The first when Mustafa ordered his followers at the beginning of his crusade to live in caves in Upper Egypt. The second occasion was when he agreed that some of his close members, including Safwat al-Zini, his confidant, should travel to the northern-eastern desert of Egypt in order to build a new village along Islamic principles.

28. See 'Abd al-Rahman Abu'l-Khayr, *Dhikriyati Ma'a Jama'at al-Muslimin* (My Memoirs with the Society of the Muslim) (Kuwait: Dar al-Buhuth al-Ilmiyya, 1980).

29. Ibid.

30. See papers of the State Security Police investigation of the case of the Jihad Organization. For the documents of the Jihad case before the High State Security Court in 1982 see, 'Abd al-'Aziz al-Sharqawi, *The Reasons of the Ruling in the Case of al-Jihad Organization* (in Arabic) (Cairo: 1985). Shawqi Khalid, *The Trail of a Pharaoh: The Secrets of the Trail of Sadat's Assassins* (in Arabic) (Cairo: Sina li'l-Nashr, 1986). In this case the court found 'Umar 'Abd al-Rahman not guilty because of his background. Because of his Azharite educational background he was not to be condemned for issuing a fatwa which rendered Sadat an infidel. According to al-Azhar rules, 'Umar 'Abd al-Rahman had—and has—the right to issue fatawa.

31. The term "deconstruction" is borrowed from the literature on local government and management. Deconstruction permits different units of the organization to enjoy autonomy; each has a wide margin of influence and governance, although each responds to the central level.

32. Personal interview with a member of 1982 Jihad Organization. Also see papers of the State Security Police investigation and al-Sharqawi, *Reasons*.

33. See Ibrahim al-Bayyumi Ghanim, *The Political Thought of Hasan al-Banna* (in Arabic) (Cairo: Dar al-Tawzi' wa'l-Nashr al-Islamiyya, 1992), pp. 348–52; for the fifty demands made by Hasan al-Banna in 1937, see 'Ali 'Abd al-Halim Mahmud, *Resocialization Methods of Muslim Brotherhood* (in Arabic) (Cairo: Dar al-Wafa', 1989), pp. 71–75.

34. Handwritten statement by Ma'mun al-Hudaybi in June 1990, in response to a set of questions related by the author asking for the Brotherhood's position on a number of issues.

35. Ibid.

36. Personal interview with a leading Brother who prefers his name be kept in confidence. This proposition is supported by an interview with a leading figure in the state security services.

37. For Doctors' Association, see the 1988 *Arab Strategic Report; al-Nur,* 13 April 1988; *al-Ahali,* 12 April 1988; *al-Akhbar,* 8 April 1988; *al-Ahram,* 13 April 1990; *al-Sha'b,* 17 April 1990; *al-Hayah,* 6 June 1991; and the *1990 Arab Strategic Report.* For Engineers Association, see *al-Sha'b,* 28 February 1989 and 5 March 1991; *al-Jumhuriyya,* 25 January 1991. For Pharmacists' Association, see *al-Akhbar,* 11 March 1988 and 25 March 1988; *al-Ahram,* 13 March 1990; *al-Wafd,* 19 March 1988 and 20 March 1988; and *al-Sha'b,* 20 March 1990. In 1992, the Brotherhhod, won more than half of the seats of the Board of the Lawyers' Association.

38. Gehad Auda, "Egypt's Uneasy Party Politics," *Journal of Democracy* 2, no. 2 (Spring 1991): 72–74.

39. Gehad Auda, "The Dominant Values and Culture as Criteria for Evaluation: A Study of Islamic Contributions," in al-Sayed Abdel Mutelb, ed., *Evaluating Public Policies* (in Arabic) (Cairo: Center for Political Research and Studies, 1989), pp. 257-58. For the general review of the experience of the Brothers in the parliament, see Muhammad al-Tawil, *The Muslim Brothers in the Parliament* (Cairo: al-Maktab al-Misri al-Hadith, 1992).

40. An account of the parliament secessions in *al-Ahram,* 24 February 1988, 26 June 1987, and 1 December 1987. These views were reiterated in an interview with 'Isam al-Aryan, a Brotherhood MP.

41. For an account of the parliament se-cession, see *al-Ahram,* 8 March 1988.

42. For an account of the parliament se-cession, see *al-Ahram,* 7 April 1988.

43. An interview with 'Isam al-Aryan.

44. Gehad Auda, "The Making of State Action: State Capacity and Islamic Political Organization under Mubarak" (Unpub-lished paper presented at the conference on "Dynamics of States and Societies in the Middle East," Cairo, 17–19 June 1989), p. 21.

45. *Al-Jumhuriyya,* 27 September 1987.

46. *Al-Ahram,* 6 March 1989.

47. Gehad Auda, "The Making of State Action."

48. See an account of the parliament se-cession of 19 February 1989, where Ikhwan MPs presented the interior minister with a number of questions concerning torture in prisons and political prisoners: *Liwa' al-Islam,* no. 1, 6 April 1989, and appendix.

49. This statement was made in a press conference and aired on the state-controlled television and published in the state-controlled newspapers. See *al-Akhbar,* 2 January 1989.

50. See Auda, "The Islamic Movement and Resource Mobilization"; 'Abd al-Rasul al-Zirqani, *Banks' Interest and Investment in Islam* (in Arabic) (Cairo: Dar al-Nashr li'l-Jama'at al-Misriyya, 1991); data bank of the Center for Political and International Devel-opment Studies. Shaykh al-Nimr died on 4 June 1991.

51. Different leftist historical accounts of the development of the relationship be-tween the Left and the 1952 leaders do not make this point of great concern in the relationship.

52. A number of leaflets of the radical Is-lamists indicated this orientation and per-ception particularly among the members of the Jihad Organization and al-Jama'a al-Islamiyya al-Jihadiyya of 'Umar 'Abd al-Rahman. See al-Jihad Organization, *al-Jihad Document and the Signposts of Revolu-tionary Action* (in Arabic); and the *Mithaq al-'Amal al-Islamiyya,* p. 66.

53. This aggressiveness is clearly shown in the argument of Mustafa Mashhur, a lead-ing member of the Brotherhood and one of its historic figures, during 1988 and 1989 which emphasized the unity of Islamic ac-tion in one country: see his, *The Unity of Islamic Action in the Country* (in Arabic) (Cairo: 1989). Also, this is seen in the Brotherhood's soft condemnation of the violent actions of the radicals against the state and the public life.

54. The logic of this strategy is found in two propositions: 1) the regime after Presi-dent Sadat suffers from a crisis of legitimacy and is in growing need of a popular/ideo-logical force for legitimization; and 2) the Muslim Brotherhood as a mobilizing mod-erate and conservative force is most suitable to play such role, particularly in view of the regime's capitalist policies of political and economic reform.

55. See Auda, "An Uncertain Response: The Islamic Movement in Egypt," in James Piscatori, ed., *Islamic Fundamentalism and the Gulf Crisis,* pp. 109–30.

56. The main document presented to the sixth general assembly of the NDP, the gov-erning party, in July 1992.

57. That is to say, that the state started to monopolize the representation of Islam in the society. The state and not the MB rep-resents Islam and the state's policies hence legitimize the state itself and the regime.

58. See Samir Rajib, *Huriti,* 27 July 1992, n. 128, p. 8. In Egypt it seems there are two trends in the government-controlled press on how to deal with Islamic funda-mentalists. The first trend is represented by *Ruz al-Yusif,* which asks the state not to have a dialogue with them and views them as destabilizing. Broadly speaking, it advo-cates semi-secular ideas. On the opposite end of the scale is *Huriti* which advocates a dialogue with fundamentalists for the pur-pose of co-opting them for the benefit of the state. Its strategy is to emphasize the re-ligiosity of the state and the president. The two magazines engaged in public debate over each other's strategy. See *Huriti,* 12 July 1992, n. 127, when Mu'min al-Haba',

the formal editor of *al-Nur,* a religiously soft fundamentalist magazine, wrote attacking *Ruz al-Yusif*'s defense of secularism.

59. Based upon observations from a field research for this chapter. These observations were supported by observations from field research conducted by the Center for Political and International Development Studies in Imbaba, Ayn Shams, Alexandria, Mallawi, and the cities of Bani-Su'aif and al-Fayyum.

60. Ahmad Ra'f, *Papers from the History of the Muslim Brotherhood: The Secret History of the Concentration Camp* (in Arabic) (Cairo: al-Mukhtar al-Islami, n.d.). ,For a Nasserist version of Nasser's policy toward the Ikhwan, see 'Abdullah Imam, *Abdul Nasser and the Muslim Brotherhood,* 2d ed. (in Arabic) (Cairo: Ruz al-Yusif Publications, 1986).

61. The National Center for Social and Criminological Researches, *The Comprehensive Social Survey of the Egyptian Society, 1952–1980: Volume 11 on Security* (in Arabic) (Cairo: 1985), p. 141.

62. Under Abu Pasha, a new organizationally autonomous department for information was established. See *al-Ahram,* 26 December 1986.

63. See for example the conference on social peace held by the Doctors' Association, the proceedings of which were published in *al-Ahram,* 11 and 12 January 1989.

64. The three persons who were arrested on 6 May 1987 and tortured for allegedly attempting to assassinate Abu Pasha but who were found innocent and released by the Minister of Interior, were Majdi Gharib Ahmad Fa'id, Faruq al-Sayyid Ashur, and Muhammad 'Abd al-Azim al-Bahari. The courts later confirmed their innocence.

65. The fundamentalist view on tourism is expressed by 'Umar 'Abd al-Rahman in an interview published in *al-Musawwar,* 4 December 1992, and 'Adil Hussayn, *al-Sha'b,* 25 September 1992 and 13 November 1992.

66. Needless to say, these were not the only Islamic jama'at which exercised vio-

lence but they were the ones who posed the greatest challenge to the authorities.

67. Perhaps this understanding accounts for the disagreement of Jihad's al-Zumur with 'Abd al-Salam Faraj and his disapproval at the very beginning of the plot to assassinate President Sadat. He only agreed when he was convinced that it might be the trigger for revolution.

68. See the statement of Musa before the Shura Council, 7 December 1992.

69. Ashraf Radi, "The Confrontation between the State and Islamic Jama'at in Egypt," *al-'Alam al-Yawm,* 4 July 1992.

70. Data collected by the program on Islamic fundamentalism, Center for Political and International Development Studies.

71. Ibid.

72. See, for example, the Egyptian Organization for Human Rights' report on 10 December 1992, *Torture in the Camps of the Central State Security Force* (in Arabic).

73. Data collected by the program on Islamic fundamentalism, Center for Political and International Development Studies.

74. It had been involved in the escape attempt of three of its military leaders from jail—known as the Isam al-Qamri case. Al-Qamri was a military officer who was recruited by Salim al-Rahal, and after al-Rahal's expulsion, joined 'Abbud al-Zumur in his Jihad Organization. However, this escape attempt ended with his being shot along with his fellows.

75. The Ahmad Yusif Jama'a in Bani-Su'aif, the Ayn Shams Jama'a, and the al-Sahel Jama'a are among the famous Jihadist small jama'at which are involved in local violence.

76. A flyer entitled, "Sufferings and Hopes" (in Arabic), distributed in June 1992.

77. Planning and execution were very sophisticated and resembled the Jihad conduct of using violence. Fuda was monitored for many days and his moves recorded and he was shot from a moving motorcycle; the killer escaped.

78. For example, he recruited Muham-

mad Yusif Khak who was from the largest and richest family in Khak village and whose father was an NDP parliament member, and uncle was the head man of the village. Khak became the second man in the organization.

79. This disappearance cannot be considered a contribution to the march of applying Shari'a. Faraj Fuda was killed for reasons of revenge for his attacks on the jama'at and Mahgub was killed by mistake, the Minister of Interior being the real aim because of his role in suppressing the Islamic movement. Hasan Abu Pasha , al-Nabawi Isma'il, and Zaki Badr are all are former Interior Ministers who have escaped death engineered by the Islamic radicals.

80. In September 1992, Islamic jama'at in Asyut accused local security forces, Copts, and wealthy families of conspiring against them.

Palestinian Islamisms: Patriotism as a Condition of Their Expansion

Jean-François Legrain

As the first assessments of Islamic activities of the 1980s and early 1990s appear, it becomes necessary to organize and analyze information regarding the Palestinian case in order to illustrate its specificity. By the end of the 1970s, Western observers of Islam had learned, finally, to talk about "*the* Islams" in the plural—the various forms the religion takes around the world—but some continue today to fall into the trap of speaking of "Islamism" or "Islamic fundamentalism" in the singular, as if it too were monolithic and easily categorized. In the 1990s, we are forced to acknowledge that "Islamic fundamentalism" must be rendered in the plural, not only between given countries, but, in most cases, within the same national and regional context.

In terms of general trends there is a difference, for example, between the phenomenon of "Islamization from above" (*Islamisation par le haut*), to use Gilles Kepel's term, or "revolutionary Islamism," to use Olivier Roy's term, on the one hand, and the phenomenon of "Islamization from below" (*Islamisation par le bas*), or "neo-fundamentalism," on the other.[1] In the first configuration, the priority is to overthrow the state through violent action (e.g., the Iranian model). In this program of action Islamization requires and is conditioned by the fall of tyrants. In the second configuration, Islamists set out to establish and organize "Islamized spaces" in society. They do so with the intent to obtain from the state (whose actual form is no longer radically contested) the acknowledgment of these spaces and their extension to the whole of society. Kepel and Roy insist on the chronological succession of the two phenomena; that is, once the Iranian Revolution was seen, by the mid-1980s, as having failed both to transform Iran fully according to an Islamic model and to export an Islamic revolution, there was disenchantment among the fundamentalist community with revolutionary Islamization. Islamic activists turned thereafter to programs of Islamization "from below," building an Islamic society "from the ground up," as it were. Of course this division is an ideal type and in reality was not replicated in precisely this way. But it serves to describe a general shift in attitudes among Islamic activist groups and organizations during the 1980s.

In the Palestinian case, the two Islamisms are easily identifiable. The movements of Islamic Jihad correspond to revolutionary Islamism and seek to throw off Israeli occupation to bring about a Palestinian state. For this trend the successful struggle for liberation constitutes the condition of a real re-Islamization of Palestine. By contrast, the different movements of the Muslim Brotherhood type reflect the model of re-Islamization from below. These groups have been interested in taking advantage of their quasi-immunity, a fruit of their abstention from the liberation fight, in order to pursue an authoritarian religious resocialization within the occupied territories.

The present study identifies the ideology, the behavior, the organizational structures, and the actors of each of these waves of Palestinian political Islam by comparing them before and after the onset of the Intifada in December 1987.

Before the Uprising: Palestinian Islamisms in Search of Partisans

During the first ten years of the Israeli occupation (1967–76) of the West Bank and Gaza Strip, Islam rarely constituted the primary principle of legitimization of the Palestinian struggle for liberation; rather, the fight was carried on almost exclusively in the name of pan-Arab or Palestinian nationalisms. The "official" Islam of the West Bank (including the administration of the *waqfs* [religious endowments] and the Shari'a courts) existed under the auspices of Jordan. The Supreme Islamic Council, established in Jerusalem after the 1967 war by the Palestinian notables hostile to the occupation, aligned itself with Jordan, and limited its activities to periodic publication of communiqués denouncing violations of the integrity of the Holy Places and repressive actions of the occupying force. In the Gaza Strip, the official administration of Islam proceeded under the auspices of autonomous associations, usually headed by graduates of the Egyptian al-Azhar University. In both cases, this Islamic leadership was content to restrict its activities to religious matters.

Authoritarian Re-Islamization without Political Legitimacy: The Muslim Brothers

At the end of the 1970s a movement claiming to uphold the tradition of the Muslim Brotherhood, connected to its Egyptian and Jordanian branches, and financially supported by Kuwait and Saudi Arabia, began to pursue the authoritarian re-Islamization of the society. In Gaza especially, but also sporadically on the West Bank, the presence of these Muslim Brothers was felt when they conducted violent raids on "places of perdition" (bars, cinemas) and against a number of unveiled women, whom they considered a scandalous cause of public debauchery.[2] Despite the radical nature of their discourse on the "Jewish entity," however, the Muslim Brotherhood did not openly confront the Israeli occupying forces during the decade that preceded the Intifada.[3] Rather, it limited its political activities to the struggle against the Palestinian Communist party in the name of fighting against atheism. Fatah, the main wing of the Palestine Liberation Organization (PLO), and Jordan were happy to encourage this Islamist attack on the "Left," and Israel too had an interest in encouraging divisions among the Palestinians. Exceptions to this general pattern occurred in 1984, when Shaykh Ahmad Yasin, founder of the most important network of Islamic associations in the Gaza Strip, and several of his associates were arrested and convicted for having founded an armed cell aimed at the destruction of Israel (although their arms had never been used).[4]

Although this decision not to engage in direct resistance with the Israelis cost them political legitimacy among many Palestinians, the Muslim Brothers managed to establish a large network of pious associations (entailing study of the Qur'an and the hadith) and of social and charitable societies (e.g., medical clinics, sports clubs, kindergartens) in the Gaza Strip. There Shaykh Yasin emerged as a charismatic and influential leader. His Islamic Assembly (al-Mujamma' al-Islami) infiltrated the majority of mosques and came to control the Islamic University through both administrators and students (regularly winning more than 75 percent of the vote). But on the West Bank, in spite of the spread of religious associations, the Brothers failed to establish a network or to find a charismatic leader. The majority of mosques escaped their control, and their only strongholds were in the universities, where they obtained roughly 40 percent of the votes in student elections.

Studying candidates slated in university elections gives a clear idea of the kind of people recruited by the Muslim Brothers.[5] On the West Bank, militant Islam was mostly a male phenomenon; only 3 percent of the Islamist candidates were women (as opposed to 13 percent of nationalist candidates). Although Muslim Brothers were representative of the general Muslim population in some respects, they were slightly more urban and less likely to live in refugee camps (only 2 percent as opposed to 8 percent of the general population). The Muslim Brothers were more urban than Fatah partisans, who were more likely than the general population to live in the camps, and they were more rural than the Marxist groups. The Islamist element was centered in the north, with the city of Nablus and the region of Tulkarm-Jenin as strongholds, and in the south, with Hebron and surrounding villages as strongholds. Like Fatah, but unlike the Marxist groups concentrated in the center region (Jerusalem, Ramallah, Bethlehem), the Islamists in the West Bank attracted a considerable number of students from Gaza. At the Islamic University of Gaza,[6] the Muslim Brothers consistently won the chairs of student councils, tallying up to 80 percent of the vote (men and women vote in different colleges). They lived in refugee camps in smaller proportions than did the general population (only 43 percent as opposed to 54 percent) and gathered mainly in the northern regions of the Gaza Strip: 74 percent of Muslim Brothers lived there compared to 52 percent of the general Muslim population. Only 4 percent of their candidates resided in the southern regions (Khan Yunis and Rafah). In contrast, Fatah was heavily represented in the south and underrepresented in the north, with the numbers of the Popular Front for the Liberation of Palestine (PFLP) reflecting the geographical distribution of the general population.

Such a sociological study, whose general lines are confirmed in the analysis of other samples (candidates slated at union or professional association elections), serves partially to dispel, at least in the Palestinian case, the conventional wisdom that the rise of Islamic radicalism is a barometer of the economic and social frustration of the most disadvantaged people in society. Most of the Palestinian refugees, unlike other *mustad'afun* (disadvantaged people) in the Muslim world, have maintained their allegiance to the different nationalist organizations of the PLO. In general terms, then, it may be said that, despite their intense activism in academic and university circles, the Islamists did not enjoy significant influence among *politisés*—politicized and activist people—before the mid-1980s because of their virtual refusal to enter the anti-Israeli resistance.

Armed Islam and Political Legitimacy without the Masses: The Islamic Jihad

It was only with the appearance of a second movement, rivaling the Muslim Brotherhood in the field of Islamic activism but fundamentally different in political behavior, that Islam became integral to the politics of the occupied territories. In the process, the Muslim Brotherhood itself was radically transformed. This second Islamist movement made jihad against Israel, in all its forms, including armed struggle, the central individual and immediate religious duty (*fard 'ayn*). The Islamic Jihad appeared publicly on the political arena in 1981, when students entered elections at the Islamic University of Gaza as *mustaqillun* (independent, but partisans of the jihad), standing against candidates from both the Muslim Brothers and the nationalist camp. The Jihad entered the military arena when an Israeli settler was stabbed and killed at Hebron by a commando unit led by Ibrahim Sirbil. The generic name "Islamic Jihad" was applied to the various groups embracing this principle, even though each had a different structure and "guide" at the helm. The movement was also diverse geographically, and its members and their activities ranged from the intellectual elite on the one hand to the military on the other.[7]

The new movement located its ideological roots in the Egyptian Jihad Organization, whose members had assassinated Egyptian president Anwar Sadat; in Sayyid Qutb, the Muslim Brotherhood intellectual who was executed by the Egyptian regime in 1966; and, although the Palestinian Jihad is Sunni and resolutely Palestinian, in 'Ali Shari'ati and the Islamic Revolution of Iran. The annihilation of Israel is, for Jihad, an obligatory condition of a profound and successful Islamization of society. Anti-Israeli radicalism is the theme of its discourse: the liberation of Palestine is fundamentally a religious question which concerns the entire Islamic community; the protection of Islam from the West's repeated attacks is the main challenge of this century; and, finally, since Israel constitutes the spearhead of this aggression, it is imperative to annihilate the Western menace by destroying the "Jewish entity."

Jihad developed in reaction to what they saw as the inefficient missionary efforts undertaken by the Muslim Brothers. Averting the attention of the believer from political and militant action and the priority of liberating Palestine, the Muslim Brothers' main program was judged ultimately damaging to Islam itself.

Unlike the Muslim Brothers, Jihad is not a mass movement but a nebulous circle of small groups organized loosely around and by "guides" and united by a common ideology. At Gaza, it arose primarily as a result of the activity of two men: Dr. Fathi Shqaqi, a physician in Rafah, who became the organizational leader, and 'Abd al-'Aziz

'Uda, a lecturer at the Islamic University, who became the spiritual guide. Both were in touch with Jihad study circles in Egypt and both supported the Islamic Revolution in Iran.[8] On the West Bank, Jihad cells were organized by Ibrahim Sirbil under the religious auspices of Shaykh As'ad Bayyud al-Tamimi (a resident of Amman); these cells were regrouped in the surroundings of Jerusalem (Abu Tor) and the region of Hebron.[9]

Palestinian Jihad activists were recruited from the ranks of the Muslim Brotherhood, from the religious wing of Fatah, as well as from the defunct National Liberation Forces, dismantled at the beginning of the 1970s. Many of these erstwhile NLF members rediscovered Islam while in jail, but were released in May 1985 as part of a prisoner exchange between Israel and the Popular Front for the Liberation of Palestine General Command of Ahmad Jibril.

Reviewing the student elections at the Islamic University of Gaza provides a limited sociological profile of the partisans of Jihad. As with the Muslim Brothers on the West Bank, the partisans of Jihad at Gaza enjoyed their highest level of popularity when they were the new force in the arena: in January 1983 they won 20 percent of the vote. Shortly thereafter they fell from this relative prominence, only to be revived with the groundswell of support just before the Intifada. As with the Muslim Brothers, the candidates of Jihad were almost exclusively men, with an over-representation of non-refugees (47 percent as opposed to 30 percent among the general population) and people living in the northern part of the Strip (77 percent as opposed to 52 percent among the general population). The Jihad candidates, then, accentuated the tendencies already observed in the Muslim Brothers.

The activism of the Jihad was an important stimulant to the Intifada, which occurred following the clashes of early October 1987 in Gaza between Jihad commandos and Israeli army forces. Some days before, the chief of the Israeli military police in the Gaza Strip had been stabbed by a Jihad activist. A series of Israeli countermeasures, including banning Shaykh 'Uda from Palestine, built such sympathy in the Palestinian population for the Jihad cause that it only required a relatively trivial incident—a collision between an Israeli truck and two Palestinian taxis carrying workers from Tel Aviv to Gaza—to lead finally to the radical questioning of the two-decades-old occupation, a process that ignited the fateful popular Palestinian resistance known as the Intifada.

The Intifada: The Fundamentalist Attempt to Seize Power

Virtually spontaneous when it began, the Intifada quickly organized itself through local and regional committees. In the case of PLO partisans, these committees reported to the Unified National Leadership of the Uprising (the UNLU or al-Qiyada al-Wataniyya al-Muwahhida li'l-Intifada). In the case of the Muslim Brotherhood, the committees reported to the Movement of Islamic Resistance, commonly known by its Arabic name and acronym Hamas. The different movements of Islamic Jihad remained outside of these command structures.[10]

Established at the beginning of January 1988 by bringing together the four largest nationalist organizations (the Fatah of Yassir Arafat, the PFLP of George Habache, the Democratic Front for the Liberation of Palestine of Nayef Hawatmeh, and the Palestinian Communist party), the UNLU immediately took charge of decisions concerning the appropriateness and timing of general strikes, demonstrations, and other forms of civil disobedience. This was done by the regular publication of numbered communiqués.[11] Its political program reaffirmed the principle that the PLO is the sole representative of the Palestinian people and demanded an international conference under United Nations auspices for creation of an independent state.

The Islamic Jihad: Fighting for Its Own Survival

Jihad became the first organized victim of massive Israeli repression. Virtually destroyed two or three months after the start of the uprising in early 1988, it reemerged at the end of 1988 in the form of periodic communiqués, symbolic monthly strikes, and the organization of a number of commando operations launched from outside of the West Bank and Gaza. It also claimed responsibility for numerous knife attacks against Israelis.

Having incited the uprising in the first place, the relatively small and fragile Jihad organization quickly found itself overwhelmed by the massive involvement of the entire population. The population included non-organized elements as well as forces structured in the different organizations of the PLO or engaged in the Muslim Brotherhood, which also decided to become involved in the Intifada after much hesitation.

Three main stages can be identified in the discourse and practice of the Jihad movement and the evolution of its relation to the PLO. During the first months of the uprising, the Jihad published periodic communiqués calling the people to mobilization; it decided to make popular unity its priority and thus de-emphasized its political differences with the PLO. The brigades of Jihad came to a common decision with them to abstain from the use of arms against Israeli positions. After two or three months of mobilizing the population by communiqués, however, Jihad suspended all publications due to the disorganization and fragmentation caused by Israeli army tactics designed to suppress the organization.[12]

The second phase of Jihad, in late 1988, was triggered by the meeting of the Palestinian National Council in Algiers and the official adoption by the PLO of United Nations resolutions 181, 242, and 338 as the basis for the settlement of the Palestinian question. In response, the Jihad decided to reorganize. In its recruiting efforts it highlighted its ideological and tactical differences with the PLO, though it did not seek, in this phase, to disrupt the UNLU timetable for acts of popular mobilization.

The third phase, which commenced in the autumn of 1989 after a few months of "silent" rebuilding, saw the open display of political differences and direct competition with the UNLU in setting the timetable and agenda of popular mobilization. In this phase Jihad cells inside the occupied territories and outside, across the Lebanese, Jordanian, and Egyptian borders, began again to organize military operations.

During these phases the Jihad did not adjust effectively to its own success. It had succeeded in inciting a popular uprising—a mass movement more or less dedicated to pursuing its immediate goal of overthrowing Israeli occupation and establishing a Palestinian state (although the specific character of that state remained unclear in the popular imagination)—but its own organization was not expansive enough to control or even direct a popular movement. It was, therefore, condemned to restrict itself to some occasional military operations serving the political interest of other groups such as Hamas, the PLO (as when Shaykh Tamimi agreed to participate in the Palestinian National Council in 1991), and Arab and Islamic states (Syria and Iran).

The Jihad current was also weakened by internal rivalries between the Shqaqi faction (Movement of Islamic Jihad in Palestine, whose headquarters are in South Lebanon and which is by far the most important faction) and the Tamimi faction (Movement of Islamic Jihad-Bayt al-Muqaddis, whose headquarters are in Amman). Even inside the Tamimi faction there was a subgroup led by Ibrahim Sirbil (Movement of Islamic Jihad-Kata'ib al-Aqsa) and another led by Ahmad Muhanna (Hizbullah-Filastin, whose headquarters are in South Lebanon and Syria). These internal rivalries and organizational limitations might have doomed the Islamic Jihad to relative insignificance, had not the massive deportation of Islamists by Israel in December 1992 provided a great boost to the Jihad's political credibility (about 60 of the 413 deportees were partisans of the Jihad). Following the attempted deportation, the mobilizations of Jihad became much more successful; for example, its monthly strike was much more widely observed in the occupied territories than had been the case previously.

The Muslim Brothers and the Acquisition of Political Legitimacy

The uprising challenged the Muslim Brothers by injecting a new dynamism into Palestinian society in the daily fight against the occupation. As a movement they responded in several stages, all the while maintaining a remarkable continuity in ideology.[13]

The first period stretches from December 1987 to February 1988, during which time the Muslim Brothers, as an organization, maintained their customary avoidance of direct engagement in the fight against Israel. Although Shaykh Yasin of the Muslim Brothers was the primary founder of Hamas, the movement published its three first communiqués (between 16 December 1987 and 11 February 1988) without mentioning its organizational links with the Muslim Brotherhood. These leaflets just called for reinforcement of the mobilization against the occupation and for the largest possible popular participation in the uprising. This delay in mentioning the Brotherhood was likely a calculated choice by the cautious Yasin. Eager to direct the unfolding of the events of the Intifada, he was nonetheless unsure that the uprising would last and form roots in the deepest strata of the Palestinian population. Thus at first he refused to reveal the structure and resources of the Brotherhood for fear of exposing it to Israeli repression.[14] Yasin's delay may also have been influenced by internal tensions in the Muslim Brotherhood between the partisans of a rapid and active engagement and the "old guard" defenders of traditional quietism.

The publication of the fourth communiqué, on 11 February 1988, inaugurated a new stage with the public adoption of the Movement of Islamic Resistance by the

Muslim Brothers as the "strong arm" of their association. The initials HMS (Harakat al-Muqawama al-Islamiyya) also appeared at that time, transformed in the next leaflet into the acronym Hamas ("zeal"), and was thereafter used to designate the group. From the moment the connection with the Muslim Brotherhood was officially acknowledged, Hamas functioned as a solidly structured organization. In the years since then, Hamas has utilized and coordinated the very networks that were independently established several years earlier by the Muslim Brotherhood.

One of these networks, according to the Israeli charge-sheet against Shaykh Yasin in 1989, is al-Majid ("the Glorious"), the original Muslim Brotherhood apparatus of information and internal security. Created in 1986 by Yahya al-Sinuwar and Khalid al-Hindi, both former presidents of the student council of the Islamic University of Gaza, al-Majid had the mission of collecting information about collaborators with the Israelis, drug traffickers, and "deviants." Under Shaykh Yasin's supervision, the al-Majid apparatus took the "appropriate measures" with respect to these *kuffar* (infidels), ranging from physical suppression to violent "warnings" such as clubbing. Al-Majid also had the mission of printing and distributing the publications of the Brotherhood, designed to inspire the religious sentiment of the population. These publications raised consciousness regarding the methods used by the Israeli security forces to entice Palestinian collaborators with hashish, wine, prostitutes, and films.

A second network, created in 1982 by Shaykh Yasin and named al-Mujahidun al-Filastiniyyun (the Palestinian Mujahidin), had originally been the military branch of the Muslim Brotherhood. By 1987, the Mujahidun was under the leadership of Salah Shahada, who was in charge of public relations at the Islamic University of Gaza. It had the mission of establishing military cells and prisoner committees, collecting information about the Israeli army, training recruits in military tactics, and organizing military operations.

This new stage, inaugurated with the official adoption of Hamas by the Muslim Brotherhood, was characterized by the publication in the communiqués of a precise timetable of mobilization for general strikes, fasting periods, and direct confrontations with the enemy. Hamas also strove to take control of organizing the uprising within the daily life of the population: it published warnings addressed to merchants and shopkeepers against exploiting the Palestinian populace caught up in the resistance movement; injunctions addressed to collaborators for a rapid repentance; and (repeating the UNLU recommendations) appeals for a return to agriculture and to the strengthening of the domestic economy. Hamas also worked to organize popular education around the mosques.

In terms of ideological content the Hamas communiqués were in direct continuity with earlier Muslim Brotherhood pronouncements and deviated little from the diatribes against passive Arab leaders and the Israeli occupiers which were formulated by the Jihad and the UNLU. Despite their fundamental political differences over the manner of solving the Palestinian question, Hamas and the PLO found themselves shoulder to shoulder in the street. This neighborly modus vivendi did not, however, lead to integration of the two leaderships into a single guiding structure for the Intifada. Following the example of Jihad during its own early period of popularity and organizational growth, Hamas, in these first two years of the Intifada, avoided under-lining its differences with the PLO, preferring to develop the theme of popular unity in order to increase the possibility of the general participation of an entire people in the fight against a common enemy.

At the end of this second stage, Hamas published its charter *(al-mithaq),* a forty page text divided into thirty-six articles, in which it synthesized its ideological and political positions. For the first time, the Palestinian Muslim Brothers clearly recog-nized that "patriotism [*wataniyya*] is an integral part of the profession of faith." As Palestine has been an Islamic waqf (endowment) since its Muslim conquest and will be until the Day of Judgment, jihad is a religious duty and the only way to victory. For Hamas, the people of Palestine have defended the soil while falling victim to Arab leaders who, in 1988 as in the 1936 revolt, were instruments of defeatism and servants of the West.

For the first time, the movement also enunciated its stand vis-à-vis the PLO. The charter sought to attenuate the disagreements: the text describes the PLO as "the closest of the closest to the Movement of the Islamic Resistance. Our fathers, mothers, and brothers are part of it; we share the same country, the same suffering, the same destiny, and the same enemy." One criticism, however, foreshadowed future rifts: Hamas strongly condemned the secularism which the PLO supposedly embraced as one of its cardinal principles.

Beginning in the summer of 1988, Hamas adopted a new strategy in the field which was designed to earn official recognition by the nationalists of its successful leadership in popular mobilization and, consequently, its possession of longed-for popular legitimacy. From this time, Hamas has positioned itself as the PLO's chief rival for supremacy in the Intifada. Numbering its leaflets, following the practice of the UNLU, Hamas gave a more important place to its daily calendar of mobilization. Furthermore, on 31 July 1988, when King Hussein of Jordan announced his decision to break administrative and legal relations with the occupied territories, Hamas seized the opportunity and immediately denied the PLO monopoly over the political heri-tage of Jordan.

On 2 August 1988, Hamas challenged the de facto primacy of the UNLU by publishing its own calendar of strikes and Intifada activities three days before the UNLU schedule. The UNLU responded in kind and tried to isolate the Muslim Brothers by calling its own strikes on the eve of those called by Hamas. In turn Hamas escalated the competition by expanding its field of activities, penetrating PLO strong-holds throughout the West Bank (with the exception of Jerusalem). Violent conflicts between the two organizations followed at Nablus, Ramallah, Hebron, and Bethle-hem. Eventually the will to preserve Palestinian unity transcended the dispute. Meet-ings at the highest level took place inside and outside the occupied territories and led to a compromise whereby the UNLU retained priority over publication of the time-table of mobilization—but only after consulting with Hamas leadership—and both parties committed themselves to respect each other's strikes.

Despite certain tensions, this newfound unity soon expressed itself in the field, sometimes even in the form of common organized paramilitary parades. Nevertheless,

Hamas continued to point out in its communiqués the vast difference between its vision and that of the PLO—the difference between an entirely liberated Palestine, a long-standing goal of the Muslim Brotherhood, and creation of a Palestinian state under the auspices of the international community—and therefore side by side with Israel—which the PLO had recently endorsed.

The difference was also displayed in relation to the American-Palestinian dialogue initiated in 1989, which was fiercely denounced by Muslim Brothers. But Hamas's radical refusal to negotiate the Palestinian cause did not spare the movement from losing itself in the ambiguities of pragmatic political behavior. In the context of an American-Israeli-Palestinian meeting in Egypt, for example, Shaykh Yasin, speaking from his prison cell on 23 September 1989, affirmed on Israeli television that he was willing to join a Palestinian delegation in negotiating with Israel, on the condition that the scope and framework of a peace plan be clearly defined.[15] Dr. Mahmud al-Zahhar, unofficial spokesman of Hamas in Gaza, asked that Hamas be allotted one-third of any Palestinian delegation that would negotiate at Cairo with the Israelis.[16] Although these overtures were repudiated in a later communiqué by the movement, they reveal the ambivalence in the Islamic camp regarding the most effective way to achieve leadership of the Palestinian resistance.

The Muslim Brothers finally split with the PLO over the question of refraining from direct military action, as endorsed by the UNLU. By way of contrast, Hamas organized a series of operations that included the kidnapping and execution of two Israeli soldiers in the spring of 1989.

Competition with the PLO and the quest for official recognition of Hamas' national role entered a new stage in the spring of 1990, when Hamas decided to request integration with the Palestinian National Council. In this context, Hamas's membership in the Council would allow the PLO to be recognized as a "national [*watani*] frame" which "includes all the individuals of the Palestinian people in the totality of their tendencies and leads them toward the complete and total liberation" (such a national frame must also include Hamas). Otherwise, the PLO might be seen as a "political orientation" (rejected by Hamas).[17] On 6 April 1990, Hamas sent a memorandum to the president of the Council[18] insisting that, in order to reflect accurately the changes produced by the uprising on the Palestinian stage, the National Council must reaffirm the inalienable unity of Palestine "from the sea to the river [Jordan] and from Negev to Ra's al-Naqura"; deny any legitimacy granted to the "Jewish entity"; repudiate all international resolutions (e.g., UN resolutions 181, 242, and 338) which contradict the Palestinian right on the whole of Palestine; ensure "the reaffirmation of the military option"; guarantee a representation in the council for each organization in proportion to its numbers in the field (by which standard Hamas demanded 40–50 percent representation); and, finally, abrogate "all the concessions and recognitions which contradict our right," including the 1988 resolutions of the Council.

These requests were rejected and sparked a public row with Fatah, leading to violent confrontations in the occupied territories and resulting in a number of wounded. The force of Hamas in the field and the necessity of maintaining "national unity" led to an agreement between the protagonists, with Hamas appearing once more as the winner. This reconciliation was officially ratified on 19 September 1990 by dissemination of a common communiqué on whose thirteen points Fatah and Hamas agreed. For the first time, the PLO agreed to Hamas's integration into all the prisoners' committees, which are virtual "schools of revolution" inside the Israeli detention camps and jails.[19]

The Gulf War and the general situation of the occupied territories during 1990, the third year of the uprising, allowed Hamas to gain even greater power. Finding themselves beaten down and their numbers decimated by violence,[20] and still without political power,[21] the Palestinians helplessly witnessed the en masse arrival of 160,000 Soviet Jews in 1990 and the reinforcement of the settler movement designed to "Judaize" the territories. In 1990, approximately 90,000 had settled in about 150 settlements in the West Bank and Gaza and 120,000 had settled in East-Jerusalem, where 150,000 Palestinians live. The "war of knives," set off in October 1990 (7 Israeli civilians were stabbed and more than 20 wounded in three months), reflected this widespread sense of despair just after the al-Aqsa Massacre (17 Palestinians killed by the army, 150 wounded on 8 October). Although in a number of cases these were isolated acts, they redounded to the notoriety of Hamas (and Islamic Jihad), which also claimed responsibility for several commando operations through the Jordanian front line.

Crushed by repression and desperately waiting for what looked like unpromising results of the diplomatic process, the Palestinian population by and large welcomed the Gulf Crisis of 1990–91, initiated by Saddam Hussein, as a detonator that would explode the increasingly unbearable status quo. The Palestinian resistance leadership found itself in the middle of two opposing tides. Both the PLO and Hamas were caught between the despair of their popular base expressed by the support given to Saddam and their long-term interests (for the PLO, this meant a diplomatic process obviously controlled by the United States; for the Muslim Brothers and Hamas, maintaining their financial and ideological ties with Kuwait and Saudi Arabia). Claiming the role of inter-Arab mediator, the executive committee of the PLO and its president Yassir Arafat refused explicitly to condemn the Iraqi invasion of Kuwait and leaned to Saddam's side in the crisis. Hamas first condemned the invasion of Kuwait, but nonetheless asked for positive response to certain Iraqi demands. Later, however, Hamas took refuge in a policy of silence designed to preserve its financing as well as its capacity for popular mobilization. When the war broke out, Hamas denounced the "new crusade" against Islam.[22]

Immediately after the war, in early 1991, the PLO was left temporarily paralyzed and deprived of all initiative: on the international stage, the anti-Iraqi camp, comprising both the United States and Arab states, made the PLO pay for the support it had given Saddam Hussein by excluding it from the diplomatic U.S.-brokered negotiations over the Arab-Israeli conflict. Deprived of its Arab financings, the PLO was in a weaker position than Hamas. The Islamic movement had shown, by its official silence, that it knew how to preserve the financial resources it derived from the Gulf. Fortified as a result of the legitimacy acquired by its involvement in the uprising and by the recognition of its place on the political stage by the UNLU, Hamas took advantage of the new weakness of the PLO. Hamas pursued its political activities with greater energy and resumed its traditional practices of authoritarian Islamization.

In almost all elections organized in the occupied territories after the end of the Gulf War, among associations of physicians, jurists, engineers, and the like, Hamas obtained 40–60 percent of the ballots, demonstrating the deeply rooted presence of the movement among the population. Thus Hamas proved itself capable of gathering together the "radicals," those partisans of the destruction of Israel and the entire Islamization of Palestinian society; the ordinary religious people, most of them from traditional sectors of the society; and, finally, ex-partisans of the PLO who were disappointed that PLO political concessions had not yet produced results and were intent on signifying their impatience and/or their despair.

The diplomatic process initiated by the United States after the Gulf War restored some of the lost credibility of the PLO, whose partisans reclaimed a representative role nobody could effectively challenge.[23] With its capital of popular support accumulated through five years of uprising and its now clear image of patriotic involvement, however, a more confident Hamas did not hesitate to make alliances with its ex-enemies, the Popular Front and other Marxist organizations, in common opposition to the Arab-Israeli negotiations. The 1992 opening of official liaison bureaus in Jordan, Syria, Sudan, Lebanon, and Iran, and the sending of mujahidin for military training[24] clearly indicated Hamas's willingness to rival the PLO on the international scene in order to take its place at the end of the process. (Hamas has no doubt about the inevitability of the failure of diplomacy as a way to solve the Palestinian question.)

Israel's deportation of hundreds of Hamas partisans in December 1992 gave the movement its first opportunity to meet officially with the highest level of PLO leadership to discuss Hamas's role in the national struggle. (These discussions continued in 1993 in Khartoum and Tunis.) By ordering the deportation, Israel unwittingly elevated Hamas to a lofty status as the latest symbol of the deepest strata of Palestinian identity—a people everyday threatened with deportation from its land—and linked this symbol with the renewed struggle against occupation. In the aftermath of the deportation fiasco, Islam and nationalism became more intertwined in the public mind than ever before, undermining the PLO's efforts to maintain its diplomatic and ideological hegemony. Hamas immediately capitalized on this public relations boon by organizing several military operations, winning local union elections, and enhancing its political and religious resources for popular mobilization.

Conclusion

By 1993, the sixth year of the Intifada, profound changes had occurred in the Palestinian political arena. The new bipolarization between PLO partisans, on the one hand, and the Muslim Brothers, on the other, constituted one of the major signs of this new balance of forces.

As elsewhere in the Islamic world, the two main trends in Islamism could still be observed at work in Palestine: revolutionary Islamism or "Islamization from above," advocated by the movements of Islamic Jihad, and the "Islamization from below" or "neofundamentalism" preferred by the Muslim Brothers. In a qualification of Kepel's and Roy's theses noted at the beginning of this chapter, however, the particulars of the Palestinian situation have affected the chronological succession of these two trends of Islamism as found elsewhere and eroded the very foundation of the Islamist criticisms of society. Within the context of the Israeli occupation and the absence of an independent Palestinian state, the nationalist discourse was able to control the mobilization of the masses for a longer period of time and was therefore able to postpone the expansion of the Islamist critique. As effective participation in the struggle for national liberation was seen by the vast majority of Palestinians as constituting a necessary condition for the acquisition of political legitimacy, Palestinian Islamism had no other choice but to appropriate the foundation of the legitimacy of its national rival—patriotism. Fighting Israel was the only way for the Muslim Brothers legitimately to enter the political arena while preserving their religious preoccupations. In Palestine, pietist Islamism had to transform itself into a "revolutionary Islamism" in order to be able to pursue its course of "Islamization from below."

In the Palestinian case, revolutionary Islamism has not been discredited, even if its objective—liberation of the whole of Palestine—has remained beyond reach. The Islamic Jihad's contribution to the early days of the Intifada gained for Islamic movements in general a measure of glory and legitimacy, thus affording them an opportunity to share a part of their ideals with the entire society. In spite of repression the movements of Islamic Jihad have not disappeared. They have maintained a significant mobilizing capacity, although this is limited by internal and personal quarrels between groups and leaders, by their factional mode of functioning, and by their image as agents for foreign states such as Iran and Syria.

Paradoxically, "revolutionary Islamism" maintains itself in large part through the renewal of the "pietist Islamism" movements that preceded it. In Palestine, "Islamization from below" began in the early 1980s. Until the uprising, the Muslim Brothers enjoyed the freedom to create their Islamized spaces in exchange for their refusal to join the anti-Israeli struggle. One of the priorities of the late 1980s and early 1990s for the Muslim Brothers was to enlarge these spaces at the expense of the nationalist camp. Such a goal, however, could be achieved only through acquisition of political legitimacy, which in turn required participation in the struggle for national liberation.

The Muslim Brothers, then, had to adopt as a tactic the order of priorities followed by the Islamic Jihad (no real Islamization without liberation) and, in the same way, had to compete in patriotism, the foundation of the PLO's legitimacy. In order to secure their "Islamization from below" for the long term, in other words, the Muslim Brothers, through Hamas, adopted the traits of "revolutionary Islamism" as the foundation of the national struggle, patriotism.

That the model of Islamic Jihad has functioned well in the field of politics is proven by the legitimacy acquired by Hamas. Despite the 1993 "breakthrough" in which Israel and the PLO reached an agreement for limited Palestinian autonomy in the Gaza Strip and Jericho, the Israeli occupation has not ended. Hamas, for the sake of Palestinian Islamism, has decided to combine the two models of Islamic revolution. Aware of the necessity to maintain the model of "Islamization from above," it continues its struggle against Israel. At the same time, it uses the national legitimacy acquired through this struggle to contest the PLO on the political level and to pursue and strengthen its traditional work of "Islamization from below." These efforts have only increased since Arafat's "treachery" of 13 September 1993 on the White House lawn.

Notes

1. Gilles Kepel, *La revanche de Dieu* (The revenge of God) (Paris: Le Seuil, 1990); Olivier Roy, *L'échec de l'Islam politique* (The failure of political Islam) (Paris: Le Seuil, 1992).

2. For this period preceding the Intifada and the Muslim Brothers, see Mohammed K. Shadid, "The Muslim Brotherhood in the West Bank and Gaza," *Third World Quarterly* 10, no. 2 (April 1988): 658–82. Also see Ziyad Abu 'Amr, *Al-Haraka al-Islamiyya fi'l-Diffa al-Gharbiyya wa Qita' Ghazza* (The Islamic movement in the West Bank and Gaza) (Acre: Dar al-Aswar, 1989).

3. The Muslim Brothers are in the process of rewriting the history of this period from the perspective of those participating in the liberation struggle. See *Al-Haqiqa al-Ghayba* (The masked reality), November 1987, 58 pp. (probably written by the Islamic Coalition of the Islamic University of Gaza); and *Fi'l-Dhikra al-Thaniyya li'l-Intilaqa; Hamas, Ishraqat Amal fi Sama Filastin* (On the occasion of the second anniversary of the uprising, Hamas, spark of hope in the sky of Palestine), 9 December 1989, 36 pp. (probably written by Hamas). For detailed bibliographic references, see Jean-François Legrain, "The Islamic Movement and the Intifada," in Jamal Nassar and Roger Heacock, eds., *Intifada: Palestine at the Crossroads* (New York: Praeger, 1990), pp. 175–90.

4. Shaykh Yasin was set free in May 1985, with the exchange of prisoners between Israel and the PFLP–GC (Popular Front for the Liberation of Palestine—General Command). Born in 1937, a refugee from the region of Ashkelon and living in Gaza, Shaykh Yasin is a former teacher. He is now almost completely paralyzed.

5. Jean-François Legrain, "Les élections étudiantes en Cisjordanie, 1978–1987" (The student elections on the West Bank, 1978–1987), *Egypte-Monde Arabe* (CEDEJ, Cairo), no. 4 (4th term, 1990): 87–128. The sample represents 702 candidacies.

6. My study is still in process and analyzes 306 candidacies presented between 1981 and 1987.

7. For more details, see Jean-François Legrain, "Les islamistes palestiniens à l'epreuve du soulèvement" (The Islamist Palestinians tested by the uprising), *Maghreb-Machrek*, no. 121 (July 1988): 5–42; Elie Rekhess, "The Iranian Impact on the Islamic Jihad Movement in the Gaza Strip" (Contribution to the colloquium The Iranian Revolution and the Muslim World, Tel Aviv University, 4–6 January 1988).

8. About the Movement of Islamic Jihad in Palestine of Shqaqi and 'Uda, see the introduction to *Min Manshurat Harakat al-Jihad al-Islami fi Filastin, Masirat al-Jihad al-Islami fi Filastin* (Conduct of Islamic Jihad in Palestine as seen by the communiqués of the Movement of Islamic Jihad in Palestine) (Beirut, 1989). Some of the leaflets in this collection had been already published in *Islam wa Filastin* (Islam and Palestine), a periodical of the movement, edited in France and published in the United States. This movement is also responsible for the periodical *Al-Mujahid*, published at Beirut, since the beginning of 1990.

9. About the Movement of Islamic Jihad Bayt al-Muqaddis (Jerusalem) and Kata'ib al-Aqsa (Battalions of al-Aqsa), see Shaykh As'ad al-Tamimi, *Zawal Isra'il, hatmiyya Qur'aniyya* (The disappearance of Israel, a Qur'anic ineluctability) (Amman, 1990); and Ibrahim Sirbil, *Harakat al-Jihad al-Islami wa'l-intifada* (The movement of Islamic Jihad and the uprising) (Amman: Dar al-Nisr, 1990).

10. Zeev Schiff and Ehud Yaari, *Intifada: The Palestinian Uprising—Israel's Third Front* (New York: Simon and Schuster, 1990); Nassar and Heacock, *Intifada.*

11. These communiqués have been published in English, in their PFLP version, in *No Voice Is Louder Than Voice of the Uprising* (Ibal publishing, 1989). Also see Jean-François Legrain, *Les voix du soulèvement palestinien: Edition critique des communiqués du Commandement National Unifié et du Mouvement de la Résistance Islamique, 1987–1988* (The voices of the Palestinian uprising: Scientific edition of the communiqués of the Unified National Leadership and of the Movement of Islamic Resistance), trans. in collaboration with Pierre Chenard (Cairo: Centre d'études et de documentation économique, juridique et sociale [CEDEJ], 1991).

12. Since October 1987 and on several occasions afterward, large operations were launched by the army in the spheres favorable to Jihad. Starting in spring 1988, the main leaders of the Palestinian "interior" (Shaykh 'Abd al-'Aziz 'Uda, Fathi Shqaqi, Ahmad Muhanna, and Sayyid Baraka) were deported, while Israel also attacked the military leaders of the "exterior" (three of them died when their car exploded at Limasso, Cyprus, in February 1988).

13. In the occupied territories, Hamas published its own version of its history, *Fi'l-Dhikra al-Thaniyya li'l-Intilaqa; Hamas.* See also the articles in *Filastin al-Muslima* (Muslim Palestine), published in Great Britain. For details on this period, see Jean-François Legrain, "Mobilisation islamiste et soulèvement palestinien, 1987–1988" (Islamist mobilization and Palestinian uprising, 1987–1988), in Gilles Kepel and Yann Richard, eds., *Intellectuels et militants de l'Islam contemporain* (Intellectuals and militants of contemporary Islam) (Paris: Le Seuil, 1990).

14. Yasin is now in jail for having founded Hamas, although this repression has brought notoriety and legitimacy to the Brotherhood.

15. *HaAretz,* 24 September 1989.

16. *Jerusalem Post,* 14 December 1989.

17. Interview with an anonymous leader of Hamas, in *Filastin al-Muslima,* May 1990, pp. 8–11.

18. The PNC (Palestinian National Council) has approximately 550 members (186 representatives of the occupied territories are forbidden by Israel to participate); only 5 Islamists belong to it ('Abd al-Rahman al-Hawrani and 'Abd Allah Abu 'Izza, who also belong to the Central Council of the PLO, and Amin Agha, Ahmad Salim Najm, and Hasan Ayish).

19. The text is reproduced in *Filastin al-Muslima,* October 1990.

20. Since 9 December 1987, more than 900 died and 70,000 were arrested out of a population of 1.5 million people in the occupied territories. Simultaneously the population experienced a fall of more than 35 percent in the standard of living.

21. The Israeli government of Yitzhak Shamir rejected all U.S. and Egyptian proposals for peace in the area, and on 20 June 1990 the United States broke off the dialogue it had begun with the PLO at the end of 1988.

22. For more details, see Jean-François Legrain, "Les Palestiniens de l'intérieur dans la crise du Golfe" (The Palestinians inside the occupied territories during the Gulf Crisis), in *Annuaire de l'Afrique du Nord 1990* (Paris: Centre National de la Recherche Scientifique [CNRS], 1993); and Jean François Legrain, "A Defining Moment: Palestinian Islamic Fundamentalism," in James Piscatori, ed., *Islamic Fundamentalisms and the Gulf Crisis* (Chicago: American Academy of Arts and Sciences, 1991).

23. Jean-François Legrain, "Apres 5 années d'intifada: Les Palestiniens de l'intérieur face à la conférence de paix" (After five years of uprising, Palestinians from inside the occupied territories facing the peace conference), *Esprit,* August–September 1992, pp. 152–63.

24. *Al-Watan al-Arabi* (The Arab nation), 23 October 1992.

CHAPTER 17

From Radical Mission to Equivocal Ambition: The Expansion and Manipulation of Algerian Islamism, 1979–1992

Hugh Roberts

Lorsque le pouvoir change, les médiations et les manipulations varient.
Bruno Étienne, L'Algérie, cultures et révolution

The dynamism of the Islamic fundamentalist movement in Algeria appears, at first glance, to have exceeded that of its counterparts elsewhere in the Muslim world outside Iran between October 1988 and January 1992. The period opened in Algeria with widespread riots, culminated in the legislative elections of December 1991, and was brought swiftly to an end with the resignation of President Chadli Benjedid.

During the 1988 riots, the Islamist movement demonstrated its ability to control and orient popular protest on the streets of Algeria's major cities, but its political (as distinct from spiritual) influence did not appear to go much beyond this stage. By autumn of 1989, however, the movement had given birth to an energetic political party, the Islamic Salvation Front (Al Jabha al-Islamiyya li-Inqadh, known in French as the Front Islamique du Salut or FIS), which displayed an impressive capacity for mobilization and organization beyond the immediate context of city streets in the way it took charge of large-scale relief operations following an earthquake at Tipasa, forty miles west of Algiers, on 29 October of that year.[1]

This activism led most observers to expect the FIS would fare well in the local and regional elections scheduled for June 1990, but nobody predicted the landslide the FIS actually achieved, winning 54 percent of the vote, and taking control of 856 of Algeria's 1,541 communal assemblies (Assemblées Populaires Communales or APC) and no less than 31 of Algeria's 48 provincial assemblies (Assemblées Populaires de Wilaya or APW).[2] During the Gulf Crisis of 1990–91, the FIS continued to display an impressive capacity for mobilization, organizing large demonstrations in support of Iraq; this capacity was further demonstrated in May 1991 when the FIS mobilized mass civil disobedience on the streets of Algiers in protest against a controversial electoral law. Finally, when the legislative elections were at last held in December

1991, the FIS once again surprised virtually all analysts by its performance; despite having suffered serious losses of leadership and cadres during the military clampdown of June-August 1991, the FIS was able to take 188 of the 232 seats won outright on the first ballot on 26 December and was clearly heading for a massive overall majority in the National Assembly (Assemblée Populaire Nationale or APN) once the second round of the election, to decide the remaining 198 seats, was held on 16 January. At this point, five days before the second ballot, the army induced President Chadli to resign and the electoral process was suspended. Algeria's new leaders set about suppressing the FIS once and for all.

Up until the dramatic denouement of the crisis in January 1992, many analysts were inclined to speak of Algeria as becoming "a second Iran." Nowhere else in the Arab world had a radical Islamist movement come so far so fast in bidding for national political power. The explanation for this remarkable dynamism of Algerian Islamism lies in the character and history of Algerian politics.

The Problem

The vitality of the Islamist movement in Algeria appears at first sight to have been produced by the FIS, which erupted from the margins into the center of the Algerian political arena and appeared rapidly to reach the threshold of state power. Because the FIS represented a remarkable mutation of the Isalmist movement, its character cannot be understood except in historical perspective.

This perspective, of course, depends on the period of time chosen. If we look at Algerian Islamism over the five-year period from January 1987 to January 1992, its dynamism appears in one light. If we look at the thirteen-year period of the Chadli presidency since 1979, its dynamism appears in a very different light. It is natural to assume that the longer of these two historical perspectives discloses the truer vision. Before demonstrating in what way this is so, let us first consider what the shorter perspective reveals.

On 3 January 1987, Algerian security forces cornered and killed Mustapha Bouyali, the leader of a small but vigorous Islamist guerrilla movement, in an ambush on the outskirts of Algiers. Bouyali had been on the run since 1982, and since August 1985 he had led the Armed Algerian Islamist Movement (Al-Haraka al-Islamiyya al-Jaza'iriyya el Musallaha, known in French as the Mouvement Islamiste Algérien Armé or MIAA).[3] Based in the Atlas Mountains to the south of Algiers, it had inflicted serious reverses on the security forces on several occasions. Bouyali's death appeared to mark the definitive end of the only serious instance of Islamist terrorism in independent Algeria and to symbolize the impasse in which the Islamist movement as a whole (of which Bouyali's group was atypical) found itself.

An impasse had been strongly suggested by the events of the previous November, when the city of Constantine, the administrative capital of eastern Algeria and the religious and cultural capital of the country as whole, had been shaken by what were, prior to 1988, the worst riots in the country's history since independence. The riots—

which quickly spread to other major towns in eastern Algeria, notably Setif—were entirely non-ideological in character. They had begun as orderly demonstrations by university students protesting poor food supplies, poor living conditions in student hostels, inadequate transport facilities, and overcrowding in lectures. High school pupils, protesting the government's new and highly selective educational policies, joined the demonstration, which developed into riots (in which unemployed youths soon joined) in response to the heavy-handed intervention of the security forces.[4] At no stage had the riots exhibited an Islamist character, despite the fact that Islamists had been among the students involved.[5]

In other words, the available evidence suggests that in late 1986 and early 1987, the Islamist movement did not hold the political initiative or pose a serious political threat to the state. As popular discontent grew in response to government austerity measures in the wake of the oil price collapse, this discontent seemed unlikely to express itself in an Islamist idiom, for it was a general popular reaction to deteriorating economic conditions rather than a particular minority's agitation of a controversial situation.

The transformation in the political fortunes of Algerian Islamism between January 1987 and December 1991 thus appears quite extraordinary. Moreover, the turning point does not seem to have been the riots of October 1988, for these too displayed an entirely non-ideological character during the first three days (4–6 October); it was only on the day of prayer, Friday, 7 October, that Islamists appeared on the streets and began to assert some authority over the rioters.[6] The thesis put out by government spokesmen, that the riots had been instigated by the Islamists, is unsupported by evidence, and it was subsequently generally admitted that the Islamists had merely jumped on the bandwagon.[7]

The evidence strongly suggests that President Chadli's decision to promulgate a new, pluralist constitution in February 1989, and the legalization of the FIS shortly afterward, marked the true turning point in the political fortunes of Algerian Islamism. This conclusion confronts us with two interesting enigmas.

First, why should the advent of pluralism have benefited the Islamist movement? Much of the literature on Islamic fundamentalism, especially that on the Iranian case, has emphasized that, in Muslim countries under dictatorial regimes, the lack of legal channels of expression ensures that the mosque is the main (if not the only) forum in which opposition to the authorities can be articulated, a state of affairs that naturally benefits Islamist movements by enabling them to establish a virtual monopoly of opposition discourse and leadership. This reasoning, moreover, appears to fit the Algerian case very well, at first glance, for the period 1980–82, when the Islamist movement grew rapidly under conditions of political dictatorship. By the same token, however, one would expect Islamist movements to lose ground, and other brands of political opposition to swell, once a dictatorial constitution was superseded by a pluralist one and the mosque ceased to be the only available forum for political dissent. The opposite happened in Algeria after February 1989. Why?

Second, the decisions of President Chadli to introduce a pluralist constitution and, subsequently, to legalize the FIS call for explanation. Had the massive riots of October 1988 been the work of the Islamists, one might explain the eventual decision to legalize the FIS as a purely pragmatic recognition of political reality on Chadli's part. But this was not the case. The riots revealed the marginal nature of the Islamists' influence until late in the process. They certainly did not bring irresistable pressure to bear on the Chadli regime to concede legal recognition to an Islamist party. Moreover, in legalizing the FIS in September 1989, the Chadli regime violated the spirit if not the letter of the new constitution and the law on political associations enacted by the National Assembly the previous July.

Article 40 of the constitution permitted the creation of "associations of a political character" but immediately qualified this: "This right, nonetheless, cannot be invoked in order to attack fundamental freedoms, national unity, the integrity of the territory, the independence of the country or the sovereignty of the people."[8] The FIS made clear from the start that its aim was to abolish the sovereignty of the people and replace it with the sovereignty of God. Its modus operandi involved frequent attacks on "fundamental freedoms" as these were defined in the same constitution.[9] The law on political associations defined the conditions on which such associations (including political parties) might be formed, and explicitly ruled out the formation of political associations based exclusively on religion; moreover, an amendment stipulating that no party might arrogate to itself the right to protect and defend Islam had been passed by the National Assembly by 120 to 52 votes.[10] Thus amended, the law gave Chadli the authority to refuse recognition to the FIS as a political party and so prevent it from entering the electoral arena, while allowing him to permit the FIS to operate as a strictly religious association. Yet he ignored the law and deliberately chose to legalize the FIS as a political party and therefore as an electoral challenger to the ruling National Liberation Front (FLN). Why?

Had the 1988 riots expressed a pent-up popular demand for democracy, or that similar pressure had developed within the FLN, one might explain the decision to introduce a pluralist constitution in February 1989 as a necessary response to this demand. But this was not the case. None of the numerous eyewitness accounts of the 1988 riots suggests that the rioters were demanding the democratization of the state, in the sense of replacing the single-party constitution with a multiparty one. And within the FLN there was certainly no enthusiasm for an end to that party's political monopoly. Moreover, the statements of government spokesmen in the weeks following the riots repeatedly fell short of affirming that a move toward political pluralism was in prospect,[11] and these statements provoked not the slightest sign of discontent, outside the politically weak intelligentsia.

In other words, Chadli introduced political pluralism without any serious public pressure to do so. He did not do so in order to inhibit the development of Islamist parties, for he went out of his way to legalize the FIS. Why, then, did he introduce the pluralist constitution in the first place?

The answers to these questions help explain the dynamism displayed by the Algerian Islamist movement between February 1989 and December 1991. It is clear that the formation of the FIS was a major turning point in the development of Algerian Islamism. Through the medium of the FIS the Islamist movement was able to expand dramatically from its initial bases on the margins of the political arena, in the universities and in those mosques not under state control, and invade virtually all spheres of Algerian public life.

The importance of this turning point becomes clearer in the course of our discussion of the major characteristics of Algerian Islamism before and after the foundation of the FIS in 1989. The dynamic development of the Islamist movement which the FIS represented cannot fully be understood, however, through a perspective that reaches back only as far as 1987.

The Context

Religious Life

Algeria is a profoundly Muslim country, and since independence, which prompted the precipitate departure of the overwhelming majority of the European community, its religious character has been enormously simplified. The Christian community has been reduced to a tiny minority, and the Jewish community has disappeared altogether.

Over 99 percent of Algerian Muslims are Sunnis, and the vast majority of these belong to the Malikite rite. (A small minority adhere to the Hanafite rite, a legacy of the Turkish period.) The non-Sunni element is constituted by the population of the seven cities of the Mzabis (the five cities of the Wadi Mzab proper, plus two satellite settlements nearby) in the center of the northern Algerian Sahara; this population, apart from recent immigrants from elsewhere, are Berber speakers and, more importantly, adherents of the Ibadi variant of Kharijism, and thus outside the fold of Sunni Islam. Despite their presence in a commercial diaspora in the cities of northern Algeria, the Mzabis are a marginal element in Algeria's religious life. The important religious diversity in Algeria is located within Sunni Islam itself.

Since the early decades of this century, the principal dichotomy within Algerian Islam has been between the puritanical and scripturalist Islam of the ulama and the charismatic Islam of the saints (*mrabtin,* or *marabouts* in French), descendants of the Prophet (*shurfa*), and the Sufi orders (*turuq*).[12] The cult of the saints has long been the dominant form of Islam of the Algerian countryside, and thus of the Algerian people as a whole, since the vast majority of Algerian Muslims were country dwellers prior to independence. But it has not been confined to the rural population, since many of the Sufi orders have had urban as well as rural lodges (*zawiyat*), and local patron saints or their shrines are found in Algiers, Constantine, and other large cities as well as in the countryside.

Maraboutic Islam, the Islam of the mrabtin and turuq, animated much of the Algerians' resistance to the French conquest from 1830 to 1871. Once this conquest had been consolidated, the incorporation of many saintly families into the colonial power structure as local notables and the subsidizing and manipulation of the turuq by the colonial authorities compromised them and ensured their quiescence. By the

1920s, maraboutic Islam was increasingly identified with the colonial order, and was a natural target on tacitly nationalist as well as overtly theological grounds for the movement of Islamic reform which had begun in Algeria in the wake of Muhammad 'Abduh's visit to the country in 1903.

The reform movement (*islah*) was inspired by the doctrines of 'Abduh and the other leaders of the Salafiyya movement in the Middle East (e.g., Jamal al-Din al-Afghani, Rashid Rida), and preached a purification of Islam through a return to the fundamentals of doctrine as contained in scripture.[13] In particular, it attacked the cult of the saints as an instance of the heresy of *shirk*, "associationism," "the view that saints and the dead and other beings or objects can through association with God partake of his sacredness."[14] This view was held to violate the fundamental tenet of Islam, the belief in the indivisible oneness (*tawhid*) of God.

From 1931 the reformers were organized in the Association of the Reformist Ulama, led by Shaykh Abdelhamid Ben Badis (1889–1940) of Constantine, and the cultural and religious action of Ben Badis and his colleagues transformed the religious field in Algeria and established the supremacy of a modernist, scripturalist, puritanical, and tacitly nationalist Islam at the expense of the old-time religion of the saints. The reformers exercised a powerful influence on the nationalist Parti du Peuple Algérien (PPA) of Messali Hadj. When an activist grouping within the PPA finally broke away to found the National Liberation Front (Jabhat al-Tahrir al-Wataniyya, Front de Libération Nationale or FLN) in 1954, they defined the purpose of their movement as "the restoration of the sovereign, democratic and social Algerian state *within the framework of Islamic principles*."[15] Following the allying of the Association to the FLN in 1956, its senior members were permanently represented within the FLN leadership.

It was entirely natural, therefore, that this reformist Islam should become the official Islam of the Algerian state at independence, with the Islam of the mrabtin and the turuq vigorously stigmatized (although primarily on modernist rather than theological grounds—that is, as superstition and charlatanism rather than heresy) by official spokesmen and the media.

The apotheosis of reformist Islam as the official religion of the independent state sowed one of the crucial seeds of the future Islamist opposition to this state. By making this Islam the official religion, and by providing it with state support, the regimes of Ben Bella and especially Boumediène consolidated their political control over the religious leadership and reduced the latter to paid servants of the state. In effect, the fledgling nation-state nationalized Islam much as it nationalized the press and the oil industry, and thereby subordinated the Islam of the reformers to the nationalist raison d'état. While the majority of the ulama were willing to accept this subordination to the nation-state, a minority vigorously refused to do so. The leading figures of this minority were Shaykh Abdellatif Soltani (1900–84) and Shaykh Ahmed Sahnoun (b. 1909), both of whom were to emerge in the 1970s and early 1980s as crucial leaders of the Islamist or fundamentalist movement.

The impulse to assert their independence from the state was evident in a society called Al-Qiyam (The Values) formed in January 1964. The intellectual leader of this society was Malek Bennabi (1905–73). The circle that formed around Bennabi produced many of the younger generation of Islamist leaders twenty years later.[16] Al-Qiyam was eventually suppressed by the Boumediène government in 1970, but this merely drove it underground, and the point of view it expressed was able to surface again without difficulty after Boumediène's death.

Economic and Social Change

Algerian society since independence has been living through the most profound upheaval in its history. This upheaval began before independence was achieved, in the colossal social disruption precipitated by the War of Independence.[17] Since 1962, a massive flight from the land has taken place, and the balance between rural and urban society has been dramatically altered.

Between 1965 and 1978, the rapid economic development which the Boumediène regime was able to promote enabled the state to accommodate popular aspirations to a considerable extent and thereby keep the social problems associated with rapid urbanization under a degree of control. In this context, the massive increase in Algeria's revenues from oil and gas enabled the government to create large numbers of jobs in new industries and services financed by these revenues, and thereby provide a substantial proportion of migrants to the cities with a social niche in the modern economy. In addition, the egalitarian policies of the Boumediène regime, the elements of price control and food subsidies, and the provision of welfare and of mass state education at primary and secondary levels, together with the extent to which the regime was able to limit the tendencies to corruption, facilitated the political incorporation of the urban poor. On the other hand, the expansion of the state's economic bureaucracy, especially at the expense of private landed property and commerce after 1971, constituted a major source of frustration for Algerian entrepreneurs, and, outside the *arabisant* intelligentsia in the universities, it was in this section of the population that Islamic propaganda against the regime's "socialism" first found a receptive audience.

The advent of the Chadli regime soon led to a major change in economic philosophy and policy, characterized by a retreat from socialism and a progressive liberalization of the economy, together with the abandonment of the elements of paternalistic and egalitarian welfarism in social policy.[18] After the early 1980s, the urban poor were no longer effectively incorporated within the political system, despite the fact that this category of the population was growing rapidly in absolute terms as a consequence of Algeria's unusually rapid demographic growth. Islamist agitation thus began to find an audience among the urban poor, whose alienation from the state deepened with the economic distress they experienced as a consequence of the austerity program made necessary by the fall in Algeria's revenues following the oil price collapse of 1986.

In general, the rapid economic and social change in Algeria since 1962 has destroyed the old structures of traditional society much faster than it has created new social structures in which to accommodate and integrate a population in flux. Those elements of the population belonging to social classes in the modern sense are in a minority. The majority of the population consists of uprooted peasants and tribesmen, living in a kind of sociological limbo in urban areas originally designed by Europeans for Europeans and which constitute a kind of bleak, bewildering, and dangerous wasteland for the majority of their inhabitants.

The Social and Moral Order

Prior to independence, the greater part of the Muslim population of Algeria lived in a social universe in which social structure and moral order were unified. This unity was found not only in the society of the Algerian village but also in that of urban Algeria, despite the element of disruption occasioned by the European presence. The upheaval during and immediately after the War of Independence threw the society into turmoil.

To a considerable extent, the society of the countryside—the extended family, the tribe, and the village community—was fundamentally destabilized by the flight from the land.[19] In the short and medium term, however, in the mountainous parts of the country, enough elements of the old social structure and way of life survived to enable the moral order also to survive.

In the cities it has been another story altogether. The remnants of traditional Muslim urban society have been swamped by rural migrants and thoroughly disoriented by the economic transformation since independence. Old urban elites whose position traditionally depended on the combination of commerce and landownership have for the most part found themselves bereft of both, and dependent for the preservation of their status on their representation within the administrative elite of the newly sovereign nation-state, and with little or no social or moral authority over the vast new urban plebs.[20]

As for rural migrants, their plight in the novel environment of the city has given rise to two contradictory tendencies: the tendency for the old values of the extended family and the village community to go by the board, and the tendency on the part of many migrants to try to re-create the kinship solidarities of the village as a source of solidarity and community in the anonymous urban world. Both tendencies have led to massive problems of the moral order. The first has been characteristically expressed in the crime indexes (especially juvenile delinquency) and prostitution, the second in the development of informal networks of solidarity in which individuals have found a makeshift sense of identity but whose operation has tended to sabotage the state's endeavors to create a modern social order. Such networks have been characteristically at odds with, and subversive of, the impersonal rationality of public administration and the modern notions of equity and impartial justice associated with them. They have lent themselves to the development of freemasonries and mafias of various kinds and to the proliferation of occult relationships typical of a "black market" economy.[21]

In addition, the catastrophic decline in the economic well-being and prospects of the urban poor over the last decade has added its own bitter twists to the moral chaos in which much of Algerian society has found itself. A large and steadily growing percentage of urban youth has been faced with the reality of endless unemployment combined with the implications of chronic overcrowding. A direct consequence is that an unprecedentedly high percentage of young men without jobs, a steady income, or the prospect of either have been unable to look forward to getting married and founding their own families.[22] Even the employed have had to face the implications of the acute housing shortage; the prospects of finding even a one-room apartment in which to embark on married life outside the parental home have been virtually nil. This situation has led to a social crisis of male sexuality among the younger generation in Algeria's cities. In turn this has ensured that the Islamist critique of Western conceptions of women, and the Islamists' insistence on the adoption of modest dress and segregation of the sexes in public places, will find a hearing.

The collapse of older moral certainties, the atomization of kinship groups, and the crisis of family life have provided extremely fertile ground for the development of a new puritanism, and the Islamist movement has been well situated to supply this.[23]

The Political Regime

The political framework within which the Algerian Islamist movement has developed has been furnished by the Algerian state. The state's nature cannot accurately be described as a one-party state nor as a military regime, although it has had formal elements of the first and substantial elements of the second. It cannot really be described as a dictatorship, or even as an authoritarian regime, except in a loose and somewhat misleading way. Three points about the Algerian state can be stated with certainty, however, and go a long way to defining its character.

First, it is a state in which the executive branch has enjoyed unquestioned supremacy over both the legislative branch and the judiciary. At no point since 1962 has the judiciary enjoyed substantial independence of the executive. The legislature was prorogued between 1965 and 1977. Before 1965 and since 1977 it has enjoyed only a small degree of independence from the executive. The National Assemblies elected in 1962 and 1964 under Ahmed Ben Bella were composed uniquely of candidates presented by the FLN, as were the National Assemblies elected under Boumediène in 1977 and Chadli in 1982 and 1987.[24] The FLN was not independent of the executive of the state, but merely one of the apparatuses of this executive, and was explicitly subordinate to the presidency after 1963.[25]

Second, it is a state in which, within the executive branch, political primacy is unquestionably enjoyed by the armed forces. It is the army—not the party or the police—which has been the principal locus and source of power. The army leadership set up the Provisional Government of the Algerian Republic (Gouvernement Provisoire de la République Algérienne or GPRA) in 1958; the general staff of the army under Boumediène rebelled against the GPRA in 1962 and brought Ahmed Ben Bella to power; and the army overthrew Ben Bella in 1965 and set up a Council of the Revolution under Boumediène's presidency to govern the country. A senior ranking colonel, Chadli Bendjedid, succeeded to the presidency after Boumediène's death. Again, it was the army that persuaded Chadli to resign in January 1992, set up a five-man High Committee of State to govern the country, and invited Mohammed Boudiaf to return from twenty-six years of exile in Morocco to preside over this body. The Party of the FLN has, in contrast, been essentially a politically lifeless facade for an executive that it has never directed or controlled.[26]

Third, the Algerian state is the creation of the historic FLN of the 1954–62 liberation war. The wartime FLN was not a political party, but a revolutionary nationalist movement that evolved from a loose coalition of guerrilla bands in 1954 into a complex state machine by 1962. The state machine consisted of an army (including both regular and guerrilla units as well as intelligence services), a legislature (the National Council of the Algerian Revolution, Conseil Nationale de la Révolution Algérienne or CNRA), and an executive branch consisting of an embryonic civil service, a diplomatic corps, an information service, and a police force directed by the GPRA, as well as apparatuses organizing Algerians inside the country (workers, businessmen, students, etc.)[27] and abroad (in France, Morocco, and Tunisia).[28]

The historic FLN became the Algerian state de jure in July 1962, in effect making the Algerian state the political heir of the historic FLN's complex legacy. Three aspects of this legacy particularly need to be borne in mind. First, the state is the heir to a national revolution determined to establish the sovereignty and unity of the Algerian nation, and as such this state has been oriented above all by the modernist ideology of nationalism,[29] derived from the European experience as mediated by French political traditions and influence.

Second, this state is the heir to a revolution that co-opted the earlier movement for Islamic reform, incorporated its leaders, and mobilized Algerians on the ground as Muslims.[30] The revolutionary leaders used Islam to give spiritual content to the notion of Algerian nationality and to transcend, in a common Muslim identity, the Arab-Berber dichotomy within the Algerian population. The War of Independence was popularly conceived as a *jihad* (holy struggle) by means of which Muslim Algeria at last freed itself from domination by a non-Muslim power and returned to the fold of the wider Muslim world, *dar al-Islam*.[31] The opposition between Arab nationalism and Islamic fervor, a dichotomy familiar to many Middle Eastern countries, never existed in Algerian popular nationalism.[32]

Third, the state is the creation of a movement that was based primarily in the countryside and especially the mountains, that is, on those elements of Algerian society—the tribes of the Atlas—whose social structures had best survived the colonial impact, and whose political traditions both sustained the guerrilla struggle and came to inform the internal political life of the movement itself. Long before 1962, therefore, the FLN was informally governed by traditional political norms, especially those of the village or tribal assembly, the *jama'a,* and riven by factional conflicts which were not the expression of ideological differences, but of competing parochial, tribal, and regional vested interests. What was true of the wartime FLN has remained true of the Algerian state since independence.[33]

These three aspects of the Algerian state—the supremacy of the executive, the primacy of the army, and the complex legacy of the revolution's synthesis of modernist nationalism, Islamic enthusiasm, and tribal political traditions—have had four important implications for the development of a radical Islamist movement in Algeria. First, because the supremacy of the executive has meant that law has been subject to raison d'état since 1962, it was inevitable that the question of the rule of law versus arbitrary government would become a central issue in Algerian politics. It is grist to the Islamists' mill, given the centrality of Islamic law, the Shari'a, to their project.[34]

Second, the primacy of the army has constrained the ability of successive Algerian governments to mobilize the consent of the governed, since the army has had a tacit veto on any mobilization tending to jeopardize its own institutional preeminence or material privileges.[35] Furthermore, the increasing professionalization of the army and the corresponding elimination from its leadership of men with a bona fide guerrilla past have relentlessly diminished the army's own capital of historic legitimacy; as a result, it has become progressively more difficult for the state to retain its grip on the populist strain in the Algerian political tradition. Because this strain has always had an Islamic dimension, the Islamist tendency in the opposition (as opposed to the left, the Berberists, or the liberal-democratic tendencies) has been best situated to capture and remobilize it.

Third, both the nationalist purpose and the Islamic discourse of the historic FLN have furnished public opinion with yardsticks by which to judge their rulers. The dominance of the successive regimes' internal life by factional conflicts between regional and parochial vested interests tarnished the regimes' nationalist credentials in the public eye. The self-interested preoccupations of these factions, and the corruption and nepotism they exhibited, eroded the state's moral authority and subverted its claim to embody the Islamic ideal of just government.

Fourth, an aspect of the revolution was Algeria's return to the wider Muslim world. Since 1962 Algeria has therefore been open to the influence of cultural and ideological currents emanating from the Middle East. It has not been an easy matter for Algeria's rulers to stigmatize these influences on exclusively nationalist grounds.

The International Context

It is generally agreed that the Arab defeat in the 1967 war with Israel was the moment of truth for Nasserism and the secularist ideology of pan-Arab nationalism in the Middle East, and as such the moment when the radical Islamist critique of this ideology began to seize the moral and political initiative from Arab nationalist regimes. The development of the Islamist movement in the Maghreb, however, has obeyed a significantly different chronology.[36]

Algerian nationalism as represented by the regime of Houari Boumediène was not discomfited by the 1967 debacle, and continued to show great vigor in pursuit of its domestic and international strategy for the next eleven years. The moment of truth for this nationalism was 1978, the year that saw the Camp David agreement between Egypt and Israel (and thus the disruption of the radical nationalist camp within which Algeria located itself in the Arab world) and the first phases of the Islamic revolution in Iran. It was also the year that ended with the death of Boumediène and the abortion of his ambitious and increasingly controversial project of socialistic nation-building.

Thereafter uncertainty and a retreat from radicalism marked the policy and political style of the Algerian government at home and abroad. In December 1979, the Soviet invasion of Afghanistan, a Muslim country, further subverted the self-confident, anti-imperialist thrust of Algeria's international stance, insofar as its non-aligned posture had been inflected under Boumediène in the direction of a tacit pro-Sovietism. By 1980 it was clear, in the mediating role Algeria played in the U.S. hostage crisis in Iran, that the government was seeking a new relationship with the West; the election of François Mitterrand to the French presidency in April 1981 led to a dramatic rapprochement between Paris and Algiers. At the same time, the reorientation of Algeria's diplomacy in the Middle East following the disruption of the radical camp led to closer ties with the Gulf states, and Saudi Arabia in particular.

The new, moderate, "businesslike" relationship which Algiers sought to develop with Western capitals proved a failure in practical terms. It did not lead to a more fruitful version of the "north-south dialogue"—let alone the "new international economic order"—which had been the objects of Algerian diplomacy in Boumediène's day. It facilitated the raising of international loans in the early 1980s, but Algiers was later to regret this move following the oil price collapse in 1986 and the crippling character its debt burden thereafter assumed.

Finally, the discrediting of Marxism-Leninism, the political collapse of the communist world in 1989, the subsequent preoccupation of Western European governments with Eastern Europe, the moves toward European economic and political union, and the corresponding relegation of the "south" to a marginal place in their concerns, reshaped Algeria's international environment in ways that favored the worldview offered by the Islamist movement. The cumulative impact of these international events made the Islamist movement seem both reasonable and realistic to people who earlier would have stoutly resisted its appeal.

The Seeds of Militancy: Islamic Dissidence in the 1970s

Algerian Islamism prior to the formation of the FIS in February 1989 was a highly variegated and nebulous movement on the fringe of political life, articulating the points of view and representing the interests of a variety of marginalized sections of the society. Islamism before 1989 posed an ideological challenge to the state's project of socialistic nation-building and to the state's supervision and monopoly of the religious sphere. During the Boumediène period, Islamic opposition was largely confined to small discussion circles, university students, and a number of exiles. With the advent of Chadli Bendjedid, however, it quickly established a far more emphatic presence, if not in the center of the political and religious stage, at least no longer in the wings.

The movement that developed so rapidly in 1980–81 had been gestating since the mid-1970s and represented the confluence of three elements. The first element was the dissident wing of the older generation of the reformist ulama, embittered by their own marginalization, hostile to the socialistic policy trend in the later Boumediène period, and increasingly critical of the regime as a whole. The second element was composed primarily of the arabisant wing of the younger generation, students who had been educated in the Arabic-language stream of the state education system and found themselves at a major disadvantage in the job market. The third element consisted of the doctrines of the radical Islamist movements of the Mashreq, especially the theories of Abul A'la Maududi and Sayyid Qutb, which were being disseminated inside Algeria during the 1970s by Middle Eastern teachers of Arabic.

Dissident ulama had already clashed with the Ben Bella regime in 1964. After a period of quiescence secured by the Boumediène regime's adroit combination of concessions and repression, their opposition surfaced again ten years later. After six years of broadly consensual policy-making, Boumediène embarked in late 1971 on a radical turn to the left with a range of controversial policies. These included the Agrarian Revolution (which nationalized large Muslim landholdings and promoted the establishment of a collective farm sector in agriculture); the introduction of free medicine at the expense of private practitioners, and "socialist management" in the state sector of industry at the expense of managerial executives; and the state takeover of the wholesaling of agricultural produce.

Muslim leaders reacted by vigorously denouncing the ideology underlying government policy and questioned the arbitrary character of Boumediène's conduct of government in general. Shaykh Abdellatif Soltani, in exile in Morocco, published a diatribe titled "Mazdaqism Is the Source of Socialism" in 1974.[37] Soltani had been one of the disciples of Ben Badis in the Association of the Reformist Ulama and had participated in the activities of the Al-Qiyam group before retreating into exile. Given the success of the Boumediène regime in identifiying its egalitarian policies with Islamic ethical traditions, Soltani did not attack these policies openly, but challenged what he saw as their underpinnings, and the extent to which they might be attributed to an unacknowledged alliance within the regime between tacit Marxists and the spokesmen for official Islam. By "Mazdaqism" Soltani was alluding to the doctrines of Mazdaq, the leader of a sect in Persia in the fifth century B.C.E reputed for its communist and libertine outlook. The essence of Soltani's attack was to stigmatize the regime's socialism as the expression of "destructive principles imported from abroad," leading to "the degradation of morals," especially in regard to the position of women. These principles, he claimed, were being encouraged in the name of "progress" by the socialistic element within the regime. He also attacked the tendency of certain left-wing intellectuals loosely associated with the regime to adopt a dismissive attitude toward Islam as a superannuated worldview.[38]

In this way, Soltani established several key themes of the later Islamist movement—opposition to socialist policies, denunciation of Marxist and other alien ideas, the identification of the former with the latter (and thus rejection of the regime's claim to practice a specifically Algerian socialism compatible with Islam), and the identification of modern and liberal attitudes on the position of women with moral decay and imported ideologies.

The second feature of the Islamic reaction was the distribution of tracts calling for a Constituent Assembly and for *shura* in Algiers in December 1974.[39] Shura, "consultation," is one of the key themes of the Sunni Islamist movement: the good government of a Muslim state involves respect for the principle of *ijmaʿ*, the consensus of the community, to be ascertained by the consultation of the authorized spokesmen of the community, the ulama, with the ruler. The principle of shura is the Islamic tradition's (superior) alternative to the Western liberal-democratic concept of "representation."

The demand for shura expressed the resentment within the middle classes at the *dirigiste* manner of Boumediène's regime. By 1974, Algeria had been subject to unconstitutional government for nine years. On taking power in 1965, Boumediène and his allies had suspended the 1963 constitution sine die and had governed without constraint by any constitutional framework whatever. After 1971 this mode of government became controversial and provided the fledgling Islamic opposition with an issue that concerned large segments of the society. Boumediène responded by announcing elections for both the presidency and a reconvened National Assembly, by introducing a new constitution, and by holding a nationwide public debate on the government's policies as embodied in a national charter in 1976. At the same time, his regime outflanked the Islamic opposition by taking measures of an Islamic character which this opposition had not been audibly demanding; notably, he outlawed gambling in March 1976 and introduced the Muslim weekend (Friday) the following August. These maneuvers enabled Boumediène to disarm the Islamic critique for the short run, and the Islamist presence consequently remained largely confined to a section of the intelligentsia and the student body until 1979. But the developments within the younger generation were to have important consequences in the long run.

By the mid-1970s a polarization had occurred between arabisants and francisants within the politicized element of the student population in Algeria's universities. At issue was the question of Algeria's national culture. Francisant students were generally inclined to a Western (and especially French) conception of modernity and progress, while arabisant students tended to reject such a conception as "un-Algerian," in that it promoted a foreign idea of civilization, and to counterpose to it a vaguely formulated conception of "Islamic civilization" in the name of authenticity. This preoccupation with "authenticity" reflected the influence of the teachings of Algeria's most important Islamic intellectual since Ben Badis, Malek Bennabi. The irony in all this was that Bennabi was a francisant, the author of several impressive books, theoretical and programmatic essays written in exquisite French.[40] His young disciples in the 1960s and early 1970s were initially drawn predominantly from francisant rather than arabisant students.[41]

Bennabi's vision was not conservative in the sense of defensive or backward looking. On the contrary, it was preoccupied with the question of the future of Muslim societies in relation to the wider world. But a central element of his vision was its emphasis on the need for moral and cultural coherence in renascent Muslim society. His writings provided a critique of twentieth-century Western (and primarily European) society on the grounds that it was lapsing into moral chaos and ceasing to be civilized even in its own terms, and a corresponding *criticism* of what he called the "modernist movement" in the Muslim world for its tendency to borrow in an eclectic and incoherent fashion from the West. But he also insisted on the limitations of the

Islamic reform movement of 'Abduh, Rida, and Ben Badis and especially its failure to address the problem of culture effectively.

Although this outlook initially appealed to a small minority of French-educated students, it eventually made considerable headway among arabisant students, who were drawn predominantly from families that had not been much influenced by French culture during the colonial period and were disposed to resent and be suspicious of the "modernist" majority of the francisant intelligentsia. But the arabisants were also drawn predominantly from the poorer, underprivileged sections of Algerian society, especially the rural population, and tended correspondingly to be suspicious of the reformist ulama, whom they saw, not without reason, as representing the social interest of the traditional urban bourgeoisie and the (closely connected) landlord class. Their attitude toward the Boumediène regime and its policies was therefore distinct from that of Shaykh Soltani and his followers.

Many of the arabisant students influenced by Bennabi's thinking tended to support Boumediène's socialism, especially its controversial centerpiece, the Agrarian Revolution of 1971–76.[42] In doing so they clashed bitterly with the clandestine Communist party (known from 1966 onward as the Socialist Vanguard party, Parti de l'Avant-Garde Socialiste or PAGS). Whereas Soltani represented a hostility to socialism as such, and a concern to discredit it by association with atheistic communism and Western licentiousness, the arabisant students approved of Boumediène's socialism but tried to dissociate it from its Marxist camp followers.[43] As such, they represented an element of the student body who were susceptible to co-optation by Boumediène when, from 1976 onward, he felt the need for a counterbalance to the PAGS and the Marxist left.[44] They also represented a popular and socially radical tendency within the embryonic Islamist movement which had high expectations of the Algerian state. On matters of culture and morals, on the other hand, their outlook was close to Soltani's, as became clear at a seminar on family law held at the University of Constantine in the spring of 1975, in which arabisant defenders of Islamic family law clashed bitterly with francisants who advocated women's rights along contemporary Western lines.[45]

Neither of these two tendencies were, as yet, Islamist in the full sense of the term during the 1970s. The fire of dissident ulama such as Soltani was concentrated on Mazdaqism rather than on the FLN state itself, and the ire of the arabisant students was directed against the more privileged francisants and the Marxist left, not the Boumediène regime. The development of these ingredients into a fully Islamist movement owed much to the influence of such Muslim thinkers as Maududi and the theoreticians of the Muslim Brotherhood in Egypt, Hasan al-Banna and Sayyid Qutb.

These thinkers described contemporary Arab society as lapsing, under the influence of the West and local secular nationalist regimes, into a state of *jahiliyya* (pre-Islamic ignorance of the Qur'anic message), and called for a missionary movement to reform society along properly Islamic lines.[46] These ideas, conspicuously absent in Boumediène's Algeria,[47] were disseminated partly by the many Arabic-language teachers recruited from the Middle East in the mid-1970s by the Algerian government to assist in its drive to Arabize the education system,[48] and partly by devout Algerians returning from pilgrimage to Mecca and from other sojourns in the Mashreq in the late 1970s. But these ideas were circulating only very discreetly, if at all, in Algeria before Boumediène's death in December 1978.

The Radical Mission: Algerian Islamism, 1979–88

By the early 1980s a qualitative change had occurred in the character of Islamic agitation in Algeria. The marginal, occasional, ideologically diverse and politically ambivalent character of this agitation during the Boumediène years had given way to a vigorous, ambitious, and self-confident movement increasingly active in the public arena and capable of mobilizing militant energies on an impressive scale. Algerian Islamism was coming into its own.

The movement remained nebulous in organizational terms.[49] It consisted of a large number of different groupings which it would be more accurate in many cases to describe as *followings*—the followers of particular celebrated preachers, such as Shaykh Sahnoun of the Bayt al-Arkan (House of the Pillars of the Faith) mosque in Algiers,[50] Shaykh Djaballah of Skikda and Shaykh Mohamed Salah Abed of Constantine,[51] not to mention Shaykh Soltani himself. There were also the followers of a younger and increasingly prominent academic at the University of Algiers, Abassi Madani, and various other networks of students of theorists such as al-Banna and Qutb and of contemporary preachers such as the highly popular Egyptian, Shaykh Kishk, whose inflammatory diatribes circulated on cassettes with increasing frequency.

Despite this nebulous character, however, Algerian Islamism was without question a *movement* by this stage, in the sense that it was oriented by definite ideas and animated by a definite sense of purpose. This growth in coherence was reflected by the fact that its adepts, whatever their differences on secondary matters, were increasingly disposed to refer to themselves in terms of two all-embracing formulae, as *islamiyyun* (Islamists) and as *ahl al-da'wa* (the people of the call). The significance of the second name is explained by Bruno Etienne:

> The Da'wa is not to be understood simply as preaching crystallized around a missionary (da'i): it is a religious reform which embraces all profane aspects capable of reinforcing the cohesion of the group. The latter feels itself therefore to be invested with a mission of reform which leads necessarily into a mission of conversion from the necessity of commanding that which is proper and forbidding that which is reprehensible. . . . This mission implies the *jihad* and this logic leads ultimately to the exercise of political power. But the taking of power is not an explicit objective, for the first duty is the censorship of morals (*hisba*) and numerous Muslim authors as well as numerous Muslims treat those who do not observe good morals as unbelievers to be combated by arms.[52]

This description of the da'wa in general applies to the Algerian Islamist movement of the early 1980s. But we can identify three main aspects of the movement's dynamism in this period, of which the censorship of morals was only one. The first was the drive to assert the autonomy of the religious sphere. The movement took up the earlier criticisms of the dissident ulama regarding the way in which the state had established its monopoly of religious life, and set about subverting this monopoly by promoting the establishment of "free mosques" outside the supervisory control of the Ministry of Religious Affairs. In doing so, it took advantage of an odd feature of the state's approach to the expansion of the country's religious establishment.

After independence, vast numbers of mosques were built in Algeria, often on the basis of initiatives of local notables and businessmen anxious to consolidate or enhance their social standing, but almost always with the eventual blessing and cooperation of the state authorities.[53] Once a mosque was completed, however, the state immediately asserted its authority in respect to the appointment of its *imam* (leader of prayer). The Ministry of Religious Affairs organized the training of imams in a network of Islamic Institutes, paid their salaries, and issued regular guidelines concerning the content of the *khutba,* the weekly sermon delivered by each imam to the faithful at Friday prayers.[54]

There were two reasons for dissatisfaction with the state's emerging role in religion. First, the massive proliferation of mosques after 1962 outpaced the state's capacity to staff them with imams of the required standard. The state-appointed imams often were not up to the job, their knowledge of scripture was superficial, the theological and spiritual content of their preaching inadequate.[55] (This criticism echoed those made of numerous other state-employed personnel outside the religious sphere, from factory managers to ambassadors.) The second criticism was that the state used the imams as agents of government propaganda, with the Friday sermons furnishing religious legitimation for government policy.[56] The more inadequate an imam's grasp of scripture and religious doctrine, the more intellectually dependent he would be on ministerial guidelines and the more liable to substitute crude political apologetics for religious preaching properly so-called.

As long as new mosques remained unfinished, however, the state claimed no authority over them, and this quirk was exploited by the Islamists to enormous effect. By the early 1980s over two thousand uncompleted mosques were functioning to all intents and purposes as mosques except that they were outside the state's control.[57] The imams who preached in them, being independent of the ministry, were able to ignore its guidelines and deliver their own sermons. These imams were dependent on local worshipers for their remuneration, and therefore had an interest in delivering lively sermons, a state of affairs which put a premium on controversy, and especially on the denunciation of corruption.

The constitution of a religious sphere outside the ambit of official Islam was a central element of the radical Islamist strategy. The long-term goal of this strategy was an Islamic state. An Islamic state, in the Islamist doctrine, is a state governed in accordance with the Shari'a, and Islamic law, being of divine origin and therefore immutable, presupposes a state in which the executive is subordinate to the judiciary and the judiciary operate within parameters defined by the ulama. In such a state the legislature has only a very secondary role, since innovative law-giving is by definition un-Islamic and ruled out. The Islamic state is thus a state in which the religious sphere has primacy over the political sphere. In Algeria, the realization of the ideal of an Islamic state thus required turning the actual relationship between political and religious spheres and their respective leaderships upside down. But in the short run it required the religious sphere to recover its independence of the political sphere as the precondition of subordinating the latter to itself.

The second aspect of the Islamist movement in the early 1980s was its vigorous engagement in the practice of *hisba,* the censoring of morals. In particular this meant mobilizing opinion and intimidating individuals to change their behavior (such as the "immodest" dress of women, and sexual behavior in general) and to give up alcohol and prostitution, "decadent" cultural imports (Western films, French pop singers, etc.), and even certain traditional Algerian practices, from ostentatious consumption at family celebrations to risqué theatrical productions, which fell foul of the canons of Islamic puritanism. By the early 1980s something of a revolution was under way in respect to women's dress, in Algiers and the other larger cities, with the heavy veils of the Middle East, including the Iranian chador, becoming widespread at the expense of not only short skirts but also the traditional, rather coquettish, Algerian veil, the *haïk.*

The third aspect of the movement was its confrontation of the Algerian left, and especially the clandestine PAGS and its followers, in their bastions in the universities and the National Union of Algerian Youth (Union Nationale de la Jeunesse Algérienne or UNJA). The left had been in the ascendant in the universities since the summer of 1972. The launch of the Agrarian Revolution in particular had been warmly supported by the PAGS, and in 1972 a student volunteer campaign in support of the Agrarian Revolution was set up with the PAGS's support, if not at its instigation. It was soon endorsed by Boumediène's left-wing minister of higher education, Mohamed Seddik Benyahia, and by Boumediène himself. Thereafter PAGS influence grew through its leading role in the Comités du Volontariat, and this influence later spread to the UNJA. At the same time, Marxist ideas enjoyed great currency in Algerian academic circles, especially in the economics and other social science departments. From 1980 onward, the Islamists challenged Marxist teaching and left-wing control of university committees and student hostels and the UNJA in particular.

Each of these activities—the constitution of free mosques, the censorship of morals, and the confrontation with the left—involved recourse to violence on occasion. The constitution of free mosques sometimes required taking over existing public premises by force, such as a prayer room at the University of Algiers which the Islamists were able to control for several years, with the authorities refusing to intervene.[58] Violent clashes sometimes accompanied such takeovers, either with other tendencies in the student body or with the police, as happened in the southern town of Laghouat, where the occupation of a mosque in September 1981 led to a pitched battle with the gendarmerie in which a policeman was killed.[59] The practice of hisba was even more prone to involve violence, as Islamists beat up men out walking with young women to whom they were unrelated by blood or marriage, attacked women "immodestly" dressed (a frequent occurrence), or descended upon establishments of which they disapproved, as when a hotel serving alcohol was burned down and the clients of a brothel in the Saharan town of El Oued were assaulted in January 1980,[60] or in similar incidents in Batna, Biskra, and El Oued again in June 1980.[61] Finally, the struggle with the left involved a number of violent clashes. On 2 November 1982, for example, a left-wing student, Kamel Amzal, was killed by blows from a sword, inflicted by Islamists at the Ben Aknoun campus of Algiers University.[62]

Up to this point, the movement had not mobilized large-scale demonstrations. It had been an affair of prayer meetings in free mosques on the one hand, and strong-arm tactics by generally small groups of militants on the other. But when the Chadli regime, in response to the Amzal killing, clamped down, arresting twenty-nine Islamists, the movement responded by organizing a prayer meeting of some five thousand supporters,[63] on 12 November 1982 at the Algiers University central faculty building. This demonstration was an unprecedented defiance of the state. When the aged Shaykh Soltani died under house arrest on 12 April 1984, his funeral in the Kouba district of Algiers, although not announced in the press, was attended by some twenty-five thousand people in what, too, was a demonstration of the movement's vitality and defiance.[64]

No further demonstrations on this scale took place thereafter, however, and no further violent incidents comparable to those of 1980–82 in which Islamists opposed the left or the police occurred between November 1982 and October 1988.[65] The exception was the Bouyali maquis, which was marginal to the mainstream movement. From 1983, the Islamist movement progressed essentially through its expanded presence in the religious sphere as a result of the increase in the number of free mosques and through the influence this generated on government policy, as reflected notably in the promulgation in May 1984 of a family code based on the Shari'a.[66]

The considerable reduction in the political activity of the Islamist movement after 1982 was not an effect of a diminution of popular discontent with the regime. On the contrary, this discontent grew steadily and gave rise to a number of demonstrations and riots, culminating in those at Constantine in November 1986. Nor can the reduction be explained purely as an effect of repression, since it was not severe.[67] Evidence strongly suggests that the political impact of the movement reached its height in 1980–82, and that it had failed to mobilize the sympathy of more than a small minority of the Algerian public. Even the impressive demonstrations of November 1982 and April 1984 were not as significant in political terms as many observers have supposed. The five thousand people mobilized on the first occasion equalled the number in the audience at the first public meeting held by al-Qiyam in January 1964, for example.[68] And while attendance at Soltani's funeral was impressive, attendance at the funeral of Messali Hadj in Tlemcen in 1974 during the heyday of Boumediène's regime and the country's prosperity had also been impressive. This funeral as well had not been announced by the official media.[69]

In short, while the change in the sociocultural climate in the country between 1979 and 1988 was striking, with Islamist ideas exercising a noticeable influence on public behavior, female dress, and government social, cultural, and educational policy, and with the Islamist denunciation of corruption finding a ready audience in public opinion, there was little reason in 1988, even after the October riots, to expect a major development of the movement.

The Mutant: The FIS, 1989–92

The FIS was, in effect, a mutation of the Islamist movement in Algeria. It obeyed the logic of the new political framework of the pluralist constitution introduced in February 1989, insofar as this constitution created the prospect of free elections. The mutation in question concerned the strategic perspective of the movement, its organization and leadership, the nature of its constituency, and the content and especially the ordering of priorities within its discourse and propaganda. In all four of these respects there were elements of continuity with the Islamist movement prior to 1989, but these elements of continuity were henceforth subsumed within, and subordinated to, the new elements.

Strategic Perspective

The strategic aim of the FIS was conquest of the political sphere as the precondition for realizing its ultimate purpose, "the establishment of an authentic Islamic society."[70] As such, the strategy of the FIS was the exact opposite of that followed by the Islamist movement prior to its foundation. The earlier strategy had been essentially a gradualist one in which the reform of society along properly Islamic lines, to be achieved by the missionary activity of the da'wa, was to precede, prepare the ground for, and receive its culmination in the eventual conquest of the political sphere with the constitution of an Islamic state, *dawla islamiyya*.

This inversion of the strategic relationship between reform of society and conquest of the political sphere partly followed from the nature of the constitutional change of February 1989. Introduction of the pluralist constitution immediately prompted the armed forces to withdraw their representatives from the Central Committee of the Party of the FLN and to announce that they would thenceforth stay out of party politics.[71] By legalizing political parties, the new constitution created a party political arena where none existed before and a political sphere which was, for the first time since 1954, clearly distinct, at least in theory, from the military sphere. It thereby created a political sphere in which it was possible to envisage conquering without having to challenge the Algerian army. But the strategic inversion was made possible, rather than necessary or inevitable, by this change. The decision to found a political party was not forced on the Islamist movement by the new constitution, and by no means did all sections of the Islamist movement approve of or participate in the FIS.[72]

Looked at in another light, however, the FIS could claim that its strategy held a degree of continuity with that of the earlier period. Because the new political sphere was a function of the freely elected local, regional, and national representative assemblies which were in prospect, it constituted a new point of contact between the society and the state, the point where the two met and merged. Thus the FIS's strategy of contesting elections could be seen as a development of the missionary enterprise of the earlier period in so far as the strategy continued to involve the canvassing of Islamist ideas among the people. But did it?

Organization and Leadership

Between its foundation in February 1989 and the elections of June 1990, the FIS developed an impressive nationwide organization which had no counterpart in the earlier movement. This organization had five clear levels.[73] At the national level was the Bureau Executif National (BEN, National Executive Bureau), also referred to as the Majlis al-Shura (Consultative Council). This body had five dependent national commissions responsible, respectively, for (1) organization and coordination; (2) education; (3) social affairs; (4) planning and programming; and (5) information. This structure was replicated at the level of the *wilaya* (administrative region) by the Bureau Executif de Wilaya (BEW) and its five commissions, and at the level of the commune by the Bureau Executif Communal (BEC) and its five commissions. Two levels existed below that of the commune. Within each commune were a number of mosques, which constituted the fourth level of organization. Each mosque was the focal point for the populations of several neighborhoods, which formed the fifth, and base, level of the FIS's organization in the *comités de quartier* (neighborhood committees).

The relations between these five levels were strictly hierarchical. The Majlis al-Shura (or BEN) appointed the BEWs, which in turn appointed the BECs, and it was the Majlis al-Shura, not the lower-level bodies, that selected the candidates which the party fielded in the communal and regional elections in 1990.[74] Information concerning the composition and functioning of the Majlis al-Shura is scarce, but the original body was presumably constituted by informal negotiation and is reported to have had between thirty and forty members. Thereafter, recruitment to it was by co-optation.

Over and above the Majlis al-Shura, however, the leadership of the FIS was closely identified with two men, Abassi Madani (b. 1931), a professor of education sciences at Algiers University, and Shaykh 'Ali Ben Hadj (b. 1956), the imam of the El Sunna mosque in the popular neighborhood of Bab El Oued in Algiers. After several weeks of uncertainty following their arrest in June 1991, the role of leader eventually devolved upon Abdelkader Hachani, who continued to exercise it until his arrest in January 1992.

Much of the media and academic commentary on the FIS leadership since 1989 has focused on the contrast between the predominantly conciliatory, reassuring, and moderate discourse of Abassi and the intransigent, inflammatory, and extremist discourse of Ben Hadj. The relationship between Abassi and Ben Hadj was essentially complementary,[75] but the preoccupation with this question has tended to obscure the three truly significant aspects of the FIS's leadership.

First, despite the notional supremacy of the Majlis al-Shura, real supremacy was enjoyed by Abassi and Ben Hadj, as demonstrated in the course of the crisis of May 1991. The decision of Abassi and Ben Hadj to launch a frontal challenge to the Hamrouche government by calling a general strike in protest against the new electoral law,[76] and then escalating the confrontation by mobilizing thousands of supporters to occupy large areas of central Algiers for over a week, was disavowed by the Majlis al-Shura, which, having already publicly reminded Abassi that he was merely its spokesman,[77] issued a further statement on 29 May denouncing the strike.[78] These statements were dismissed by Abassi, who insisted on 30 May that "the strike continues" and that only he and Ben Hadj had the authority to call it off.[79] When Abassi was at last arrested, he named his own successor,[80] and his right to do so was not contested. Thus the development of the FIS involved, inter alia, the development of a highly centralized and personalized leadership, in sharp contrast to the extremely diffuse leadership that characterized the movement before 1989.

The second significant aspect was the ascendancy of Abassi over Ben Hadj, which was not only a matter of seniority. While Ben Hadj was first and foremost a man of religion, combining the three statuses of imam, 'alim, and *da'i* (missionary preacher), Abassi was none of these things. A member of the revolutionary nationalist PPA before the war,[81] he was a member of the FLN from its inception in 1954.[82] Having spent most of the war in jail, he remained in the FLN after independence, securing, despite his involvement with the al-Qiyam group, his inclusion on the list of FLN-approved candidates to the Algiers APW for a five-year term in 1969. Abassi then broke with the FLN and concentrated on his studies, first as a doctoral student at the Institute of Education at the University of London (1975–78) and thereafter as a professor at the Institute of Education Sciences at the University of Algiers, where he played an influential role in developing the Islamist presence on campus.[83] He never underwent the specialized training of an imam or an 'alim or a da'i. Thus, the primary leader of the FIS was, first and foremost, a political activist of thirty-five years' standing.

This preeminence of the political figure over the religious figure within the FIS's leadership constituted a radical rupture with the earlier Islamist movement. While Abassi himself had been a prominent figure in that movement, and thus represented an important element of continuity with it, his role in the early 1980s had been clearly subordinate to that of the distinguished ulama, Shaykh Sahnoun and Shaykh Soltani, and this relationship was consistent with the underlying purpose of radical Islamism of subordinating the political to the religious sphere. The rise of the FIS under Abassi thus represented a reversal of the previous relationship between the religious and the political within the leadership of Algerian Islamism, and a striking departure from its original perspectives. In the process, the most dynamic element in Algerian Islamism came to resemble closely the radical Islamist movements in Egypt, of which Emmanuel Sivan has noted: "Men of religion are rare in their leadership; they are composed for the most part of university students and modern professionals, autodidacts in religious matters."[84] But whereas the timorousness and time-honored subservience to the state of the Egyptian ulama may well explain this state of affairs in Egypt,[85] in Algeria dissident ulama of authority and distinction were available to the movement and had previously led it. The FIS's approximation to the Egyptian model was the result of a change.

This change was predicated upon Abassi's personal position within the FIS. But Abassi's position was itself predicated upon the *absence* from the FIS of three other leading figures within Algerian Islamism—Shaykh Ahmed Sahnoun, Shaykh Mah-foud Nahnah, and Shaykh Abdallah Djaballah. It is unclear whether these figures declined to join the FIS or were denied the option of joining. In any case, their absence from the FIS leadership was itself a significant aspect of this leadership.

Djaballah (b. 1956) is a leader among the younger generation of Islamist ulama, and by 1989 he had already built up a considerable following in Skikda and Constantine, with ramifications in other towns of eastern Algeria.[86] He eventually formalized his following as the Movement of the Islamic Renaissance (Harakat al-Nahda al-Islamiyya, generally known, in a characteristically Algerian combination of French and Arabic, as the Mouvement de la Nahda Islamique or MNI), which was legalized in October 1990 and polled 150,093 votes on 26 December 1991.[87] The MNI represented a doctrinally sophisticated and socially progressive trend within Algerian Islamism. Both in its appeal to intellectuals and its opposition to unbridled economic liberalism, it contrasted sharply with the FIS.[88] The absence of Djaballah and his colleagues from the FIS was thus a complicating factor, one that would have blurred its populist profile and confused its economic policy outlook.

Nahnah (b. 1942), based in the large town of Blida fifty kilometers south of Algiers, is the leader of Hamas (Al-Haraka li-Mujtama' Islami, the Movement for an Islamic Society), which is an evolution of his earlier Jam'iyyat al-Irshad wa'l-Islah (Association for Guidance and Reform) and was legalized as a political party under the new name in April 1991.[89] In the legislative elections in December 1991, Hamas polled 368,697 votes (2.78 percent of votes cast) and five of its candidates got through to the second round, one of them in first place.[90] Nahnah has adhered consistently to the view that the reform of society along properly Islamic lines must precede the ultimate conquest of the political sphere; he has advocated a correspondingly gradualist approach, unreservedly accepting the new pluralist constitution and eschewing confrontation with the state.[91] The presence of Nahnah and the others in the FIS would have blunted its censure of pluralist democracy and inhibited its confrontational posture vis-à-vis the FLN, while precluding its strategic priority of conquering the political sphere.

In short, for the FIS to develop as it did in terms of profile, outlook, posture, and strategy, both Djaballah's and Nahnah's absence were necessary. Both men had substantial followings outside Algiers, in the Constantinois and Algérois. Had they participated in the FIS, these followings would have given them great influence within its leadership, enabling the Majlis al-Shura to make good its pretention to supremacy as the collective leadership of the party, at the expense of Abassi's personal authority and the primacy it gave to the political over the religious dimensions of the party's leadership. What is true of Djaballah and Nahnah in this respect is even more obviously true of Shaykh Ahmed Sahnoun.

After Shaykh Abdellatif Soltani's death in 1984, Sahnoun possessed a unique status and moral authority within the Algerian Islamist movement. A veteran of Ben Badis's Association of the Reformist Ulama of the 1930s and 1940s,[92] as well as of the al-Qiyam group of the 1960s,[93] Sahnoun personified the Badissian tradition within the contemporary Islamist movement, and with it the emphasis on da'wa. He has continued to represent that approach since 1989 in the association he leads, Rabitat al-Da'wa al-Islamiyya, the League of the Islamic Call, which has refused to operate as a political party. As such, his presence in the FIS would have implied a very different strategic perspective from the one it actually developed. He would have overshadowed Abassi, thereby preserving the primacy of the religious over the political elements in the FIS leadership. But Sahnoun's presence would have had two other crucial implications.

First, the Badissian tradition is the tradition of the Reformist Ulama, whose movement represented the outlook and interests of the long-established bourgeoisies of traditional Arab-Islamic culture of such towns as Constantine, Mila, and Tebessa in eastern Algeria, Bejaïa and Medea in central Algeria, and Tlemcen in the west. In stigmatizing the Islam of the mrabtin and turuq, the movement was combating the popular forms of Islam in Algeria, and seeking to establish the ideological hegemony of the cultured urban elite over a largely illiterate people through the medium of a scripturalist and puritanical Islam. As such, the Badissian tradition was not in the least populist. Had this tradition furnished the principal leader of the FIS, the FIS would have been badly placed to mobilize mass popular support.

Second, although the Reformist Ulama rallied to the FLN in 1956, they did so reluctantly.[94] From the point of view of Ben Badis's disciples, the FLN represented a dangerous and distasteful upsurge of popular boorishness. While its mobilization of the passions and violent energies of the people might be a regrettable necessity for securing independence, the ulama could not overlook the fact that the FLN's leaders held an essentially *instrumental* attitude toward Islam, using it to mobilize popular support for their essentially modernist project of constituting Algeria into a sovereign nation-state.[95] In addition, the revolution had catapulted thousands of men of humble origins into positions of great power, originally by virtue of the fact that they possessed guns or controlled other men who possessed guns and subsequently by virtue of the fact that they were the privileged members of networks of influence emanating from the wartime FLN.[96]

From the point of view of the bourgeois ulama, the FLN had exploited the fruits of Ben Badis's project of religious reform for its own purposes and had usurped Ben Badis's disciples as the leadership of the society. In doing so the FLN had turned the ulama's world upside down. There accordingly developed after 1962 a tendency within the Reformist Ulama to belittle the FLN's role in achieving Algeria's independence, and to suggest that the *real* revolution had been achieved by Ben Badis and his followers from the 1920s to the 1940s—the spiritual revolution which canvassed the cultural and religious aspects of the national idea in the social consciousness—and, furthermore, that the revolution of 1954–62 was a merely political sequel to Ben Badis's achievement and the FLN mere executants of the anticolonial aspect of his project.[97]

It is likely that Sahnoun shared this point of view and was seriously at odds with the FLN. A FIS under his leadership would therefore have been disabled from laying claim to the mantle of the historic FLN of 1954–62. This claim was a prominent element of FIS propaganda and an indispensable element of its popular appeal. And a large part of the conviction which it undoubtedly carried was due to the fact that the FIS was *not* led by Shaykh Sahnoun, but by one of that distinguished company of audacious men who went into action on the fateful night of 31 October–1 November 1954, Abassi Madani.[98]

With Sahnoun's absence from the FIS, and Abassi's resulting supremacy in its leadership, the subordination of the religious to the political leadership which occurred within Algerian anticolonialism in 1954–56 under the aegis of the FLN was replicated within Algerian Islamism in 1989 under the aegis of the FIS. And this same subordination of religion to politics was also apparent in the mosques under FIS control. Within the elaborate organizational structure described above, the role of the mosques was the one element of continuity with the pre-1989 Islamist movement. In effect, the FIS built up around the mosques, which its members and supporters already controlled, the apparatus appropriate to a political party competing for votes, that is, the apparatus of an electoral machine.

By building its electoral machine around the mosques, the FIS imposed on them a palpable political function and, moreover, a party-political function. As a result, the old Islamist reproach of the state-appointed imams, that their sermons tended to substitute political apologetics for their proper content of guidance in matters of faith and morals, became increasingly applicable to the imams in the FIS-controlled mosques. Furthermore, the FIS was at odds not only with those political parties that might plausibly be denounced as un-Islamic such as the Marxist PAGS, but also with an FLN possessing substantial Islamic credentials of its own and, from the autumn of 1990 onward, with other groupings within the wider Islamist movement which had refused to join or endorse it. Thus the political content of the sermons of FIS imams could not be justified in terms of the absolute dichotomy between good Muslims and unbelievers, but tended to express and aggravate explicit political differences among the former.[99]

Thus in respect of both its leadership and its use of the mosques, the FIS involved an unacknowledged but nonetheless fundamental departure from the perspectives of the earlier Islamist movement, and tended to subvert this movement's original conception of the relationship between religion and politics. It thus became reasonable to wonder whether the FIS was really canvassing Islamist ideas among the people or doing something else altogether.

Constituency

Analysis of the FIS's constituency is gravely hampered by the fact that the official vote tallies for individual candidates in the local and regional elections of 12 June 1990 and the national legislative elections of 26 December 1991 have never been published by the Algerian authorities. The only figures available are the aggregates of votes received by the various parties, and the number of seats won in each commune and wilaya assembly in 1990 and in the national assembly in 1991.

The available data nonetheless demonstrate the FIS's massive success in mobilizing the electoral support of the urban poor—the most important respect in which the constituency of the FIS differed from that of the Islamist movement before 1989. The latter had enjoyed the support of most of the arabisant wing of the Algerian intelligentsia, and of the class of small- and medium-sized traders and entrepreneurs in the private sector of the economy, traditionally inclined to piety and frustrated by and hostile to the state economic bureaucracy. These established sources of support for the Islamist movement were undoubtedly available to and mobilized by the FIS in 1989–90, although a large proportion of them likely defected to the rival parties, the MNI and Hamas, when these at last entered the lists in 1991. The decline of the FIS's aggregate electoral vote from 4,331,472 in 1990 to 3,260,222 in 1991 cannot wholly be explained by the impact of the MNI and Hamas, since between them they can have taken from the FIS at most 518,790 votes, which leaves at least 552,460 votes unaccounted for. Only part of these can be attributed to Ahmed Ben Bella's MDA (Movement for Democracy in Algeria), which, having boycotted the 1990 elections, contested the 1991 ones and polled 135,882 votes in all.[100]

But whatever the reason for the loss of over a million votes between 1990 and 1991, a loss of support among the urban poor was responsible for it. The scale of this support was demonstrated in 1990 when the FIS swept the board in the big cities, winning control of all 33 APCs in the wilaya of Algiers, all 12 in Constantine, 24 out of 26 in Oran, and all 29 in Blida.[101] Moreover, the FIS won control of 28 of the 30 most heavily populated communes in the country, securing a total of 433 seats to the FLN's 168.[102] To a large extent, this urban support was mobilized again in the legislative elections in 1991, enabling the FIS, on the first ballot, to win outright 15 of the 22 Algiers seats, 8 of the 12 Constantine seats, 11 of the 14 Oran seats, and so on.[103]

Thus, while all brands of Islamist opinion supported the FIS in 1990, it seems that much of the traditional audience for the Islamist message defected to the FIS's rivals in 1991, whereas the FIS's *popular* support remained largely intact. The FIS thus appears to have been a popular party first and foremost, a party mobilizing the enthusiasm and loyalty of "the people," *al-sha'b,* in general and the urban poor, *al mustad'afun* (the wretched, the oppressed) above all. This popular support was the largest and most constant element of the FIS's constituency, and it was the element to which the FIS leadership gave priority.

This was made graphically clear by the FIS's behavior during the crisis in the Gulf from August 1990 to April 1991, when the evolution of mass public opinion in Algeria toward militant support for Iraq and enthusiasm for Saddam Hussein obliged the FIS to choose between the Islamist movement's traditional outlook and connections (hostility toward "godless" Ba'thism, close ties with Saudi Arabia) and its own popular constituency. Put on the spot in this way, the FIS unequivocally chose the latter from January 1991 onward. While this was primarily a tactical maneuver to cope with an unforeseen and awkward situation, it fit naturally into the political strategy of the FIS.

Discourse and Program

Virtually all the main elements of the discourse of Algerian Islamism prior to 1989 were carried over into the discourse of the FIS. These included the championing of cultural authenticity, notably in relation to the demand for reform of the educational system; the role, rights, and responsibilities of Algerian women; and the related demand for the segregation of the sexes in educational establishments, offices, and other public places. The FIS discourse also stressed the puritanical censorship of morals (hisba), notably the denunciation of immodest dress, sale and consumption of alcohol, and indulgence in un-Islamic cultural activities (risqué Western music, concerts, etc.). Finally, it condemned corruption and arbitrariness in government and demanded justice and good government on the basis of the Shari'a and shura. To these elements of continuity with the pre-1989 movement, however, were added several new elements.

First, the FIS endorsed liberalism in economic policy[104]—something it suggested rather than emphasized, let alone elaborated; it certainly did not put forward any serious policy proposals under this head. But its general position was unmistakable, and while one might argue that this position merely made explicit the long-standing hostility to socialism which underlay Soltani's diatribe in 1974, it was a development, as was the definite abandonment of the "Islamic-socialist" wing of the fledgling Islamist movement of the 1970s.

Second, the FIS repeatedly proclaimed as its ultimate political objective the establishment of an Islamic state. Abassi himself declared his attachment to this objective on several occasions.[105] Although this represented the explicit statement of what had been implicit in the demand for shura as far back as 1974, and the call for Shari'a in the early 1980s, the discourse of the FIS went further by suggesting that the attainment of this objective in the short run was a practical political possibility and by emphatically counterposing this political ideal to the continued rule of the FLN and to the ideal of pluralist democracy.[106]

Third, the FIS appropriated many of the central themes of Algerian nationalism. In particular, it made itself the spokesman for the most passionate anti-French feelings in Algerian public opinion, notably in 'Ali Ben Hadj's vehement denunciation of France for the massacres of May 1945[107] and more generally in its campaign against the *antennes paraboliques* (satellite television disks), by means of which Algerian homes could receive French television channels.[108] It also proposed that French be replaced by English as the first foreign language taught in Algerian schools.[109] And, as we have noted, in taking up a militant pro-Iraq position on the Gulf Crisis, the FIS appropriated both the anti-imperialist and the pan-Arabist elements in Algerian nationalism with gusto. There was a substantial element of ambiguity in this stance, for it was unclear whether the FIS attached importance to the Algerian nation as such or whether—as Islamist doctrine unquestionably enjoined—it took second place to the supra-national community of the faithful, the *umma*. For much of the Algerian public, the FIS convincingly established its nationalist credentials, and its leaders took care to ensure this.

Finally, a major element of the FIS's propaganda was its discourse on the FLN, in which it sharply contrasted the wartime FLN of 1954–62 with the FLN since independence. The discourse on the two FLNs was a characteristic expression of the FIS's penchant for Manichean contrasts in general; the original FLN embodied good (and in particular the value of keeping faith, in several ways at once), and the post–1962 FLN embodied evil and the related idea of betrayal. As 'Ali Ben Hadj put it, immediately after the FIS's landslide victory in June 1990, "we have not given a slap to the FLN, we have given a slap to the people who have betrayed the FLN."[110]

In lauding the wartime FLN, the FIS was staking its own claim to the mantle of revolutionary legitimacy as the "true" FLN's rightful heir. While an element of this discourse was the attempt to rewrite history by ascribing to the wartime FLN an unequivocally Islamic character and purpose, the significance of this discourse was its premise that the legitimacy of the wartime FLN and its revolution could not be questioned and that the FIS had to present itself as the lineal successor if it was to win the support of the Algerian people. Various ploys were relentlessly used to this end, including the adoption of traditional FLN (anti-French, anti-imperialist, pan-Arabist, etc.) rhetoric, but also the exploitation of Abassi's personal role in 1954. The very choice of the party's name echoed the FLN in its use of the term "front"—*jabha*—and permitted a significant and characteristically Algerian play on words, in that the French acronym—FIS—is pronounced exactly as the French word for "son" (*fils*). This encouraged the Algerian public to perceive the FIS as the legitimate offspring of the original FLN and as thereby entitled to assume power as its rightful inheritance. The Islamist movement before 1989 had never presented itself as primarily an offshoot of the historic FLN in this way; its origins in both the Badisiyya and the wider Islamist movement beyond Algeria had powerfully inhibited it from doing so. The FIS had no such inhibitions and unquestionably gave priority to its filiation to the FLN over its other filiations.

Because the FIS was bidding to supplant the actual FLN in power as the rightful heir of the historic FLN, it needed to delegitimize the former and claim descent from the latter. The earlier Islamist movements made no such criticisms or claims because they had evinced no such ambitions.

The priority of the new and specifically political elements of the FIS discourse over the religious and cultural elements inherited from the pre–1989 Islamist movement was graphically illustrated in the fifteen-point platform presented as a petition to the presidency of the republic by a delegation headed by Abassi on 20 April 1990.[111] The first ten points of this platform are wholly political in content (e.g., dissolution of the National Assembly, establishment of an independent political structure to supervize the elections, rehabilitation of the Court of Accounts, revision of security policy, an end to the FLN's monopoly of press and broadcast information, dissolution of the existing trade union structure, etc.). With the exceptions of point 5 (calling on the state to guarantee public liberties), which makes a formal reference to Islam, and point 7 (calling for a system of hisba to control the independence of the judiciary), these ten points contain nothing that is necessarily, let alone peculiarly, Islamist. The call for Shari'a appears as point 11, a very moderate-sounding and unspecific proposal concerning women appears as point 12, and the demand for educational reform in line with "the preservation of the authenticity and identity of the people" appears as point 14. In short, the traditional preoccupations of the Islamist movement are veiled in the blandest possible language and introduced very low down on the list, while priority is given to demands that might have been raised by any ambitious political party maneuvering for position in an election campaign. From February 1989 to December 1991, this tendency to prioritize political concerns lacking any particular Islamist content over specifically Islamist items continued to characterize the FIS discourse.

Examples of the intolerant and menacing elements of the FIS's discourse are legion, and much ink has been spilled over them since February 1989. Virtually all the commentary has been from the standpoint of the actual or potential victims or targets of these attitudes, and this commentary has largely condemned these attitudes or argued that it was they, rather than the blandly reassuring noises made by Abassi at regular intervals, which represented the "true" nature of the FIS and thus constituted proof that it posed an unmitigated threat to the democratic constitution and the rights enshrined within it. This commentary has not reflected, however, on the *function* of these elements of the FIS's discourse. Preoccupied with the misconceived search for formal coherence in the propositions composing the FIS's discourse, most commentators have concluded that the lack of formal coherence reflected an underlying incoherence in substantial outlook—that is, the existence of contradictory elements in the discourse expressed real conflicts within the leadership between Abassi and Ben Hadj; or, that the existence of contradictory elements reflected the combination of "true" (i.e., sincere) and "false" (i.e., hypocritical) aspects of the FIS's presentation of itself. If we examine the function of both the alarming and reassuring elements of the FIS's discourse, however, we find that the two aspects were equally "true," and that the way in which they complemented each other in the FIS's political démarche expressed the underlying coherence of its outlook and strategy.

The intolerance displayed by the FIS actually combined two elements. The first was simply the continuation of the intolerance displayed by the Islamist agitation of the early 1980s and by al-Qiyam before it. This intolerance was inherent in practicing hisba, the censorship of morals, and in combating the ideological vectors of the jahiliyya, notably secularist and Marxist parties. To this the FIS added a distinct and novel element, namely, a posture of extremely aggressive intolerance of political rivals *within the Islamist movement,* from October 1990 onward.[112]

The menacing rhetoric of the FIS combined three main novel elements. The first was the repeated threat to punish members of the FLN regime guilty of wrongdoing, notably in Ben Hadj's promise in May 1991 that politicians and military men guilty of corruption would be jailed and their property confiscated.[113] The second was the repeated raising of the political temperature by means of threats to the authorities, and especially the armed forces, of dire consequences should they try to cheat the FIS of its anticipated victories. Thus at an election rally in Algiers on 4 June 1990, Abassi warned the army against attempting a coup,[114] and in a speech at Tlemcen on 14 April 1991 he again warned the army that, in the event of a general strike, "if one drop of blood is split, I swear by God that we will fight to the point of annihilation."[115] Finally, and most notoriously, there were the repeated statements expressing the FIS's fundamental hostility to the democratic constitution[116] and its intention, once elected to power, of introducing an Islamic republic without delay.[117]

All of these elements of its discourse made perfect sense given that the FIS's immediate political objective was to establish and preserve its absolute monopoly of the political representation of the popular element of the Algerian electorate. The threat to punish the corrupt merely expressed the long pent-up popular demand for justice and a settling of accounts; the fact that the Westernized middle class was visibly terrified by the prospect of the Shari'a only made this prospect more attractive to the mustadh'afun. The threats issued to the army afforded enormous psychological satisfaction to the urban poor, and especially urban youth, whose protests in October 1988 the army had drowned in blood. And the FIS's promise to establish an Islamic republic, by keeping the eyes of its mass popular constituency firmly fixed on a millenarian goal, facilitated the policing of the ranks of this constituency against infiltration of rival political agendas. Since the FIS was alone in proposing an Islamic republic in the short term, it had by doing so outflanked the entire political spectrum in radicalism, and having captured the reflexes of the urban poor by means of this radicalism it merely needed to remind all and sundry of its radical intentions at regular intervals in order to maintain its popular following. And since its commitment to economic liberalism meant that in practical economic policy terms the FIS had nothing to offer the urban poor that was distinct from what the Hamrouche government was offering (i.e., higher prices and more unemployment), it badly needed a radical *political* project to compensate for the absence of an appealing economic project if it was to evoke popular enthusiasm. The invocation of the imminent establishment of an Islamic state served this purpose admirably. Given the centrality of dawla islamiyya to the FIS's popular appeal, it became vital to block all rival tendencies *within Algerian Islamism* from access to its popular constituency. The FIS did so by an aggressive and intolerant rhetoric.

All these elements of its discourse also made perfect sense when looked at in light of the fact that the FIS was presenting itself as heir to the historic FLN.

The suggestion in both academic and media commentary on Algeria in recent years, that the Algerian public, largely composed of people under thirty, has no memory of or interest in the revolution, is mistaken. By the late 1980s Algerian public opinion had grown audibly weary of the relentless invocation of the revolution by the personnel of a regime which was clearly discredited, and that was trading ever more shamelessly on its revolutionary origins in an attempt to compensate for the incontrovertible exhaustion of all other conceivable sources of legitimacy. Moreover, in consequence of the vicissitudes of Algerian politics since 1979, the element of this personnel which had actually done anything of note in the revolution had dwindled to virtually zero by 1989,[118] and a large proportion of those trading on the revolution were men who had never so much as missed a meal, let alone fired a shot in anger, between 1954 and 1962. Official invocations of the revolution had, therefore, increasingly assumed the force of an outrageous insult to the intelligence of the public at which they were directed.[119] Because the actual brunt of the revolution had been borne by the population of the countryside, and the urban poor thirty years later were none other the sons and daughters of this same population come to town, both a vivid memory of this revolution, as transmitted directly from parents to children, and an appreciation of the historic FLN that had conducted it were alive and well in the collective consciousness of the poor and the youth of Algiers, Constantine, Oran, and every other large town in the country. The FIS acted on this assumption, and to enormous effect.

The threats to punish the corrupt elements of the regime exactly echoed the FLN's threats to punish Muslim notables who had compromised themselves and betrayed or exploited their fellow believers by serving the colonial administration. The bold, almost commanding, and deliberately bloodcurdling tone of the FIS's warnings to the army exactly echoed the FLN's promises to the French military authorities of retaliation and reprisals in the event of further massacres. The radiant vision of an Islamic republic occupied exactly the same place in the FIS's rhetoric and project as independence did in the FLN's. And the refusal to tolerate rival Islamist parties exactly echoed the FLN's intolerance of the rival nationalist organization known as the Mouvement National Algérien, MNA, which it made a point of liquidating physically,[120] and expressed the same determination to be recognized as the sole *interlocuteur valable* (valid interlocutor) by the regime it was confronting.[121]

Given that its claim to be the legitimate heir, and spiritual reincarnation, of the historic FLN was fundamental to its popular appeal, all of these elements of the FIS's discourse were not only functional but indispensable to its moral authority and political credibility.

Abassi's moderate and reassuring rhetoric provided a counterpoint to the radical and disconcerting rhetoric of the FIS, and his discourse is significant. It expressed, above all, a disposition to negotiate with the other forces in Algerian politics and, in the first instance, the Chadli regime. This disposition to negotiate, including a willingness to operate within the framework of a constitution to which the FIS was in principle opposed,[122] while formally at odds with the radical elements of the party's discourse, was not at odds with its underlying purpose. Because the FIS's chief aim was to establish its monopoly of the political representation of the popular section of the electorate, it was prepared, if necessary, to alienate other sections of public opinion. Thus the FIS knew perfectly well that it could not aspire in the short term to a total monopoly of the political representation of the Algerian people and that negotiation with other forces, at any rate as mediated by the Chadli presidency, was accordingly necessary. In adopting this approach, the FIS was once again imitating the historic FLN, which displayed absolute intransigence over its claim to be the sole interlocuteur valable with which France might deal, but which, once this point had been gained, immediately displayed a wholly pragmatic attitude, including a willingness to make important concessions, in the subsequent negotiations with the French authorities.[123]

That the FIS was sincerely prepared to negotiate with the Chadli regime is suggested by its discourse on the FLN since 1962, its support for economic liberalism, and its acceptance of Chadli's personal role and order of business in promoting political reform.

The FIS's discourse on the post-war FLN, while delegitimizing the party of which Chadli had been head since January 1979, actually comforted rather than subverted Chadli's personal position by making an issue of the FLN's post-independence rule in general, and thereby distracting attention from the performance of the Chadli regime in particular. Recall that the riots of October 1988, which were not instigated or led by the Islamists, were a very specific disavowal of Chadli and his supporters. The rioters themselves made it clear that neither the price of bread nor thirty years of FLN misrule had prompted the upheaval, but their exasperation with and contempt for the Chadli and his regime. As the rioters' slogans put it, "Ma bghina la zabda wa la felfel / Lakin bghina zaïm fhel" (We don't want butter or pepper / We want a leader we can respect).[124] The contrast in the rioters' minds was not between the post-war FLN in general and the wartime FLN, but between Chadli's regime and that of his immediate predecessor: "Boumedien, ardja' lina! / Hlima wellet tehkoum fina!" (Boumediène, come back to us! / Halima [Chadli's wife] has come to dominate us!).[125]

By blaming Algeria's economic and social crisis, not to mention its political malaise, on the FLN's rule of over thirty years, Chadli was able to evade his own (arguably enormous) responsibility for the situation the country was in after ten years of *his* rule, and to acquire credibility, at least in the eyes of Western governments, as the pioneer of the necessary process of political reform. In this context, the FIS's discourse on the FLN was a priceless endorsement of a crucial element of Chadli's post-1988 position, not only because it distracted attention from his own role but, above all, because it disqualified en bloc Chadli's critics within the FLN and preempted any efforts they might make to mobilize popular feeling against him.

That the FIS's support for economic liberalism was also grist for Chadli's mill should be evident, given the determined pursuit of economic liberalization and the introduction of a market economy by Chadli's regime from 1988 onward. The FIS's position on this issue was remarkable, given the circumstances. An opposition party bidding for political power in free elections can normally be expected to exploit every weakness of its opponent in government, and when the governing party is pursuing an economic policy that is relentlessly raising prices and throwing people out of work, an opposition party seeking to mobilize precisely that section of the electorate worst affected by such things will normally not hesitate to make an issue of the policy in question. That the FIS not only did not do so but actually went so far as to endorse in principle the policy in question cannot be adequately explained by the fact that the middle-class element of its constituency—the private sector retailers, merchants, and entrepreneurs—stood to benefit from it. On the contrary, the FIS's priority was to mobilize popular support, and it was prepared to risk losing some of its middle-class support to the more moderate Islamist parties, notably Hamas, rather than tone down the radical rhetoric on which its popular appeal depended. In short, the FIS's position on economic liberalism simply does not make sense unless its willingness at some point to come to terms with the Chadli regime is taken seriously.

Finally, it is striking that during the first two crucial years of its existence, from the spring of 1989 to the spring of 1991, the FIS actively endorsed Chadli's timetable for political reform and his role in overseeing it. At the very outset of the FIS's career, Ben Hadj called on voters to abstain in the referendum on the new constitution in February 1989,[126] but this request reflected the FIS's objections in principle to an unIslamic constitution and perhaps also its desire to measure the extent of its influence on voters' behavior at that stage. Thereafter, however, for the next two years the FIS went along with Chadli's every move. In particular, it raised no objection to the order in which Chadli proposed to hold elections—local and regional elections together first, then national assembly elections, and finally the presidential election—despite the fact that the dismantling of the discredited power structure which the FIS was in principle contesting that required elections be held in precisely the opposite order. Nor did it object to postponing the first set of elections from December 1989 to March and then to June 1990. And, following its victory on 12 June 1990, the FIS promptly repreated its call for legislative and then presidential elections in Chadli's preferred order, emphatically endorsed the elections just held as entirely fair, and paid handsome tribute to Chadli himself.[127]

In the light of its endorsement of these cardinal elements of Chadli's position, how is the FIS's massive success in mobilizing the support of the urban poor—the element of public opinion most hostile to the Chadli regime and to Chadli himself—to be explained?

The Manipulation

Had the FIS's electoral victory in June 1990 been widely anticipated, the subsequent conventional wisdom that the victory was an inevitable "punitive vote" against the FLN might be compelling.[128] However, virtually every observer and commentator on Algerian affairs had expected the FLN to win.[129] So disconcerted was the British Foreign Office by the result that its astonishment was itself a news item on British television, an admission that had no precedent in living memory.[130] The subsequently fashionable notion that the FLN was utterly discredited and therefore bound to lose was conspicuous for its absence from media and academic discussion alike before 12 June.[131]

The FLN had selected Chadli Bendjedid as its candidate for the presidency of the republic for three successive terms in 1979, 1983, and 1988. From 1979 to 1991 Chadli personally held the party's senior leadership position, as general secretary until December 1988 and as president of the party thereafter. Although from late 1985 onward he had been increasingly at odds with the party's second in command, Mohamed Cherif Messaadia, the powerful head of the Permanent Secretariat of the Central Committee from 1980 to 1988, Chadli reasserted his own control over the party after the 1988 riots by sacking Messaadia and replacing him with Abdelhamid Mehri.[132] Mehri, whose daughter had married Chadli's son in 1989, was a close political ally.[133] The connection between the two men was further demonstrated by the choice of Mouloud Hamrouche, a senior Chadli aide in the presidency and a Mehri protégé, for the post of prime minister in September 1989.

If we make the usual assumption that Chadli, Mehri, and Hamrouche wanted the party they led to win the June 1990 elections, we are faced with the problem of explaining the following: first, that the Hamrouche government, which was nominally an FLN government, insisted on proceeding more rapidly than ever with a program of economic liberalism which was bound to alienate the urban poor and disqualify the FLN from competing with the FIS for this constituency; second, that both government and party officials allowed a massive vacuum of authority to develop on the ground into which it was easy for the FIS to move; third, that both Chadli and Hamrouche, far from discouraging public opinion from taking the FIS seriously as an electoral challenger to the FLN, repeatedly did the opposite; fourth, that at crucial junctures support was given by members of the Chadli-Mehri-Hamrouche circle to the key elements of the FIS's discourse—its nationalist discourse on France, and its moralistic discourse on the FLN's corruption.

The program of economic liberalization was extremely unpopular, given the general context of extreme austerity in which it was being pursued and in view of the steep price rises it provoked as subsidies were abolished and the additional unemployment it created as enterprises made subject to capitalist criteria of efficiency cut their work forces or folded altogether. This program had been launched in 1981,[134] long before the riots of October 1988, which were indeed "a revolt against perestroïka" among other things.[135] That President Chadli should have decided to persist with this program after the riots is not as surprising as the decision both to accelerate the reforms after September 1989 and to identify the FLN alone with this unpopular policy on the eve of the first-ever freely contested elections. Immediately after succeeding Kasdi Merbah as prime minster, Mouloud Hamrouche not only promised to accelerate the economic reform program but also ruled out the question of inviting other parties to join a coalition government as "premature."[136] On 16 September (twenty-four hours after the legalization of the FIS as a political party), he announced the appointment of an exclusively FLN cabinet.

In his speech to the FLN congress on 28 November 1989, Abdelhamid Mehri called on the party to support the government's reform program.[137] Although several former associates of Boumediène known for their hostility to Chadli's economic liberalization strategy were elected to the new Central Committee, the supporters of economic reform were undeterred by this. "The return of the Old Guard in no way calls into question the reforms," an unidentified "leading reformer" was quoted as saying,[138] and Ghazi Hidouci, the new economy minister charged with supervising the reform program, declared that the economic reforms would be given priority.[139] Mehri himself declared that the congress "was a victory for Chadli's reforms,"[140] despite the fact that, as an anonymous diplomat observed, "many FLN members would be shocked if they really knew what they were supporting."[141] Senior officials subsequently insisted that "the Hamrouche government will press ahead with a range of policies to retructure the economy—no matter what resistance it faces."[142] The Hamrouche government continued to emphasize its determination to accelerate economic liberalization thereafter.[143] The FLN continued to be identified with this policy in the state broadcasting media and its own press, while offering nothing in the way of secondary items of economic or social policy to compensate the urban poor for the hardships being imposed on them.

Creating Space for the FIS

Given the decisions to press ahead with unpopular economic reforms and to oblige the FLN to take sole political responsibility for them, while allowing the FIS to function as an electoral challenger to it, one might have expected the Hamrouche government to have taken particular care to limit the opportunities available to the FIS to develop its presence at the FLN's expense, at the very least by ensuring that the FIS did not tacitly usurp the government's own functions, let alone flagrantly break the law. But Hamrouche's government did nothing of the sort.

For example, the government allowed the FIS to substitute its own apparatus for that of the state in organizing relief for the victims of the Tipasa earthquake of 29 October 1989.[144] Moreover, the government did not offer protection to the victims, notably young women, of the strong-arm methods of FIS activists zealously practicing the censorship of morals.[145] It made no attempt to deter such activities by arresting those responsible and seeing to it that they received exemplary sentences.[146] Nor did the government move to impede the party-political exploitation of mosques;[147] it even permitted fundamentalist sermons to be broadcast over state television.[148] The government even introduced a new labor law in February 1990 which facilitated setting up new trade unions at the expense of the FLN-controlled General Union of Algerian Workers (Union Générale des Travailleurs Algériens or UGTA) and thereby encouraged the formation of Islamist-inspired unions linked informally to the FIS, thereby disrupting the FLN's electoral base in the organized working class.[149] Finally, the government failed to see to it that polling stations were properly staffed on 12 June 1990 to ensure that citizens were able to cast their votes free of interference or intimidation. Numerous polling stations were left entirely unattended by state officials, and FIS militants were allowed to take them over unchallenged and supervise the voting process.[150]

Hyping the FIS's Prospects

The question of economic reforms and the disconcerting return of the old guard to the Central Committee were not the only remarkable aspects of the FLN's congress in November 1989. The third notable feature of this congress was the vigorous assertion of elements of an Islamist agenda, namely, demands for Islamic law and for the abolition of mixed schooling, by a section of the delegates.[151] The demands were glossed by official spokesmen briefing the foreign journalists who attended the congress and consequently the journalists reported them, as evidence of the FLN's alarm at the threat posed by the FIS.[152] The demands were not explained as evidence of the FLN's ability to accommodate the Islamic strain in public opinion and thus marginalize the FIS.

Senior FLN spokesmen continued to stress the threat posed by the FIS at regular intervals prior to the June 1990 elections. On 21 January 1990, Hamrouche claimed in an interview on a French radio program that the FIS would control as much as 30 percent of the vote in the forthcoming elections.[153] Shortly afterward, in an interview with the London-based daily paper *Al-Hayat,* he admitted that the FIS was "a challenge,"[154] a theme promptly taken up by the French weekly *L'Express* in an article that caused a major stir: *"Islamisme: Si l'Algérie bascule?"* (Islamism: What if Algeria totters?).[155] As the Algerian sociologist Lahouari Addi subsequently observed, "the alarmism of the French press and television, in particular, when reporting the popularity of the FIS, has served Mr. Madani's [sic] organization."[156] The alarmism of the

French media, however, merely amplified the alarmism of Hamrouche. At a press conference in Algiers on 13 March 1990, President Chadli himself admitted the possibility that the FLN might be *"mis en minorité"* (reduced to a minority) after the eventual legislative elections and obliged to share power.[157]

Two months later, the propaganda of the FIS concerning the moral bankruptcy of the FLN regime received a boost in the widely publicized declaration of ex-Prime Minister Abdelhamid Brahimi that corruption had cost the country some $26 billion—more than the total foreign debt—over the previous twenty years.[158] This declaration vindicated the FIS's description of the FLN as "thieves"[159] and provoked bitter public wrangling between spokesmen of the FLN's various factions,[160] which reinforced the widespread impression of its disarray.

Brahimi's announcement was presented as the revelation of an honest and disinterested public figure who had nourished no further personal ambitions since his own dismissal from the premiership following the 1988 riots. If that were the case, he nonetheless waited seventeen months and announced it at a moment when it was bound to greatly harm the FLN's electoral prospects and benefit those of the FIS. Moreover, his brother, Mohamed El Mili Brahimi, was the minister of education in the Hamrouche government.[161]

These incidents suggest that Chadli and his closest associates deliberately boosted the FIS's prospects in order to secure the landslide victory of the FIS and the crushing humiliation of the FLN on 12 June 1990. Indeed, evidence indicates that members of the FLN were aware of their leaders' extraordinary conspiracy against their own party, notably the report in the French daily *Libération* in the wake of the 1990 elections that several regional sections of the FLN were "in open revolt against the party leadership, and the prime minister Mouloud Hamrouche in particular, whom they accuse outright of having 'plotted' against the party."[162]

The manipulation was undertaken by Chadli and his supporters in the wake of the October 1988 riots, which provided the most spectacular and appalling demonstration of the extent to which the vast majority of the urban population, the young and the poor, had become alienated from the state. Since Chadli had been presiding over this state for the previous ten years, this demonstration gravely weakened his position by permitting major critics of the Chadli regime who had been marginalized throughout the 1980s to return to the political stage and to positions of potential influence.

This development was ominous from Chadli's point of view, for many of the critics—notably Mohamed Salah Yahiaoui,[163] Abdelaziz Bouteflika,[164] and Belaid Abdessalem[165]—had played major roles during the Boumediène years, which the rioters recalled with nostalgia, and were not themselves personally implicated in the misgovernment of the country during the 1980s. Moreover, none of them could plausibly be tarred with the brush of corruption, since highly publicized attempts to blacken their reputations in this way in the early 1980s had visibly failed.[166] They were therefore politicians who could hope to get a hearing with a populace exasperated with the Chadli regime. The return of this group boosted the position and influence of other critics of Chadli who had managed to survive inside the regime throughout the 1980s, notably the president of the National Assembly, Rabah Bitat,[167] its vice-president, Saïd Aït Messaoudène, senior military figures such as General El Hachemi Hadjerès, senior party figures such as Abderrazak Bouhara, senior ministers such as Boualem Bessaih, and the man whom Chadli had been obliged to appoint as his prime minister after the riots, Kasdi Merbah. The ranks of Chadli's critics had been further swollen after the riots by major figures from the historic FLN who had been out of politics since the 1960s and who had publicly distanced themselves from Boumediène. This group included Colonel Lakhdar Bentobbal, Colonel Tahar Zbiri, Commandant 'Ali Mendjli, and Bachir Boumaza.[168]

For Chadli, the prospect of these three groups of opponents, each of which possessed substantial historic legitimacy, joining forces and constituting a powerful opposition faction inside the FLN leadership was extremely dangerous. Unlike many of his own supporters in the army, party, and government, they could convincingly rebut charges of corruption and disclaim responsibility for both the mistaken policies and repressive measures of the 1980s. Unlike the young activists of both the Berberist and Islamist movements, they were experienced politicians with insiders' knowledge of what the Chadli regime had been up to and what its weak points were. In the circumstances that prevailed after October 1988, they could not be eliminated. They could only be outflanked.

Once this is understood, one sees the fundamental reason for the manipulation of the Islamist movement. By introducing a pluralist constitution, Chadli had temporarily made himself secure on his democratic flank, and had created the conditions within which the attempts of his critics to appeal to popular audiences could be preempted by a massive expansion of the newly legalized Islamist movement, whose discourse reinforced Chadli's position and disqualified his critics in crucial ways. But the purpose of the maneuver required it to be heavily disguised, and here, as so often in politics, timing was of the essence.

The talking up of the FIS's electoral prospects and the implicit connivance with its intimidating activism (by turning a blind eye to it) only occurred after January 1990, that is, after the extraordinary FLN congress of late November 1989, at which Yahiaoui, Bouteflika, Abdessalem, Bitat, Aït Messaoudène, Hadjerès, Bouhara, Bessaih, Kasdi, Zbiri, and Boumaza had all been voted onto the FLN Central Committee.[169] Had the nature of Chadli's maneuver been apparent in November 1989, most of these figures would have detected it and refused to be drawn into compromising positions within the party leadership. But the maneuver became apparent only in early 1990.

The striking thing about the electoral campaign in June 1990 was that the business of putting the FLN's case forward at meetings across the country was almost entirely shouldered by Chadli's critics within its leadership.[170] Thus, official spokesmen, having vigorously talked up the FIS's prospects, began after March 1990 to talk them down again, and to suggest that the FLN would fend off the challenge of Abassi and and his followers and secure a comfortable majority.

The FIS's mobilization had appeared to climax in its impressive march on the presidency on 20 April 1990, in deference to which the FLN had canceled its own march scheduled for the same day, a decision that was extremely demoralizing for the FLN supporters and greatly boosted the morale of FIS activists.[171] But the FLN's march was eventually held on 17 May and was an enormous success, with the official media claiming that it had comfortably dwarfed the FIS's demonstration four weeks earlier.[172] Immediately following the FLN march, on 18 May, the Ministry of the Interior published the results of an opinion poll which it had itself commissioned, giving the FLN 40–50 percent of the vote, the FIS 20–30 percent, with 10–20 percent going to the nine other parties then in existence.[173] From then on the climate of confidence that the FLN would win without difficulty set in, and Chadli's critics adopted a high profile in the election campaign; they too were fooled.

The point of the manipulation, of course, is that, having played such a leading role in the campaign, Chadli's critics could not easily avoid responsibility for the FLN's humiliating defeat. The effective point of their denunciation of Chadli in October 1988—"see, you are a liability, the people are against you"—could now be turned round and used against them with a vengeance, and it was. When asked by a journalist on 12 June how he would react to a possible Islamist victory, Chadli "displayed a great calmness." Did he, the journalist wondered, "intend to profit from the situation and the humiliation inflicted on the FLN to rid himself of a party which has never been very keen on him?"[174] The answer was: yes and no. What he intended, as subsequent events made clear, was to keep the party but rid it of his critics and convert it into "un parti présidentiel" under the control of his supporters,[175] which could then be given the unreserved support of the presidency and the government in contesting the elections that really mattered—those for the National Assembly—when these were finally held.

At this point Saddam Hussein invaded Kuwait and the Gulf Crisis erupted. This development forced Chadli to put his plans on hold, and placed the internal cohesion and strategies of both the Chadli regime and the FIS itself under strain. The war against Iraq gave the Algerian army much food for thought and strengthened the hand of those factions of the officer corps opposed to Chadli's risky dealings with the Islamist movement.[176] At the same time, the FIS's decision to identify itself with Iraq in order to keep a grip on its popular constituency accentuated tensions within it between adherents of the orthodox Islamist outlook and those willing to take their bearings from Algerian realities in preference to Islamist doctrine. The result within both parties were fundamental misgivings about the relationship that had existed between the FIS and the Chadli regime since February 1989; these misgivings were to surface in the aftermath of the war as the relationship went into crisis. This crisis came to a head in late May 1991 and was characterized by a significant radicalization of the FIS's positions.

The Dynamics of Radicalization and Deradicalization

The radicalization of the FIS's positions in May 1991 involved both its demands and methods. Whereas throughout the period from February 1989 to June 1990 the FIS had not challenged President Chadli's personal position and had, indeed, effectively underwritten it, in May 1991 it changed its line on this cardinal point completely.

Then it demanded not only that early presidential elections be held but that they actually be held at the same time as the planned elections for the National Assembly. In addition, while throughout the earlier period the party had carefully abstained from engaging in confrontation with the government, as opposed to strong-arm tactics against individuals and political rivals to which the authorities had turned a blind eye, in May 1991 it launched a general strike and then a campaign of mass protests on the streets of Algiers in what was clearly a major trial of strength with the Hamrouche government.

It was widely assumed by Western observers that the change in the FIS's attitude and behavior was the cause of the crisis and in particular of the two explosions of violence, on 4–5 and 25–30 June, which accompanied it. Many observers suggested that the radicalization either reflected a victory of radicals over moderates within the FIS or simply revealed at last its true, radically anticonstitutional and subversive, face. The radicalization that occurred, however, was without question the work of Abassi Madani, that is, of the "moderate" in the FIS leadership, and was opposed by most of the true radicals in the Majlis al-Shura. And its spirit was not to subvert the democratic constitution of 1989, but to take it in earnest.[177] It was the Chadli regime, not the FIS, which demonstrated its lack of commitment to democratic principles and its willingness to resort to violence during the summer of 1991.

Radical Moderates and Moderate Radicals

The decisions to call a general strike on 23 May to go into effect from 25 May and to follow this up with mass street protests in Algiers from 26 May onward were taken by Abassi Madani in defiance of a substantial minority within the Majlis al-Shura. Of the thirty-eight members of this body in May-June 1991, reportedly as many as seventeen were openly opposed to Abassi's line.[178]

In matters of doctrine, the main division within the FIS leadership was between the tendency known as the Salafiyyists and that known as the Algerianists. What was originally at issue between the two was not their degree of militancy or their attitude to the pluralist constitution, but their relationship to the international Islamist movement on the one hand and the Algerian nation on the other. The Salafiyyists, also referred to as the Hanbalists,[179] were oriented to the wider movement in the rest of the Sunni Muslim world, and in particular tended to take their bearings from Saudi Arabia (hence the designation "Hanbalist").[180] Thus they were the pan-Islamic tendency, for whom the supra-national Islamic umma was paramount and the Algerian nation of secondary concern at best, if they recognized it at all. One might say they were the purists of the party, adherents of the orthodox Islamist outlook. In the days of the one-party system, prior to Chadli's liberalization in 1989, some Salafiyyists had been perfectly prepared to engage in revolutionary action against the state, in the Islamist guerrilla movement of Mustapha Bouyali.[181] From 1989 onward, however, their attitude was to accept the new pluralist constitution and play by its rules, since it gave them space to canvass their message, while criticizing it as a matter of principle and promising to change it to a properly Islamic constitution at the first opportunity.

The Algerianists, organized in a grouping known as the Djeza'ara (from the Arabic for Algeria), advocated a specifically Algerian Islamism, one that recognized the Algerian national identity and national interest, and that might thereby more easily come to terms with other forces in Algerian society and politics and also rebut the charge of being the agents of foreign powers. The Djeza'ara initially existed as a grouping within the Islamist umbrella organization of Shaykh Ahmed Sahnoun, the League of the Islamic Call (Rabitat al-Da'wa al-Islamiyya), but it entered the FIS at Abassi's invitation in June 1990.[182] Although Abassi refrained from identifying himself with the Djeza'ara, since his role required him to mediate the differences within the FIS and his deputy, 'Ali Ben Hadj, was a confirmed Salafiyyist,[183] it is likely that his own views tended toward the Algerianist outlook.

During the Gulf Crisis, the Salafiyyists had been reluctant to embrace the pro-Iraqi position which the FIS eventually adopted. Their doctrinal orthodoxy disposed them to detest Iraqi Ba'thism and to condemn the invasion of Kuwait as a deplorable aggression by one Muslim state against another, and their links to Saudi Arabia disposed them to line up on the anti-Iraqi side in the early stages of the emerging conflict.[184] In getting the FIS to take a pro-Iraqi position, Abassi gave priority to the nationalist and populist element of its political profile over the strictly Islamist element. While the Salafiyyists had to go along with this, they were far less willing to go along with Abassi on two other issues which subsequently arose. These were the question of the FIS joining with the other Islamist parties in a broad Islamist alliance, and the question of the FIS's attitude to the new, blatantly unfair, electoral laws introduced by the National Assembly at Mouloud Hamrouche's instigation on 1–2 April.[185]

As we have seen, the FIS at its inception by no means included all groupings within Algerian Islamism. Neither the Jam'iyyat al-Irshad wa'l-Islah of Shaykh Nahnah nor the Al-Nahda group of Shaykh Djaballah had joined the new party in 1989, and they had declined the invitation to do so which Abassi had briefly addressed to them from a position of commanding strength in June 1990. They preferred to constitute themselves into rival parties as Hamas and the MNI respectively than come under Abassi's sway.[186] From the autumn of 1990 onward an overt struggle for influence was in progress, with Nahnah in particular canvassing the idea of a broad Islamic alliance and Abassi furiously denouncing these moves as divisive. But it was Abassi's attitude that was increasingly seen as sectarian and divisive, and the Salafiyyist wing of the Majlis al-Shura was powerfully attracted to the idea of sinking the differences between the various parties in one common enterprise. There was, after all, no doubting the credentials of both Nahnah and Djaballah as bona fide Islamists. Thus it became difficult for Abassi to find convincing arguments in defense of his refusal to link up with them, despite the probability that such an alliance would have compromised the FIS's ability to present itself as the historic FLN reborn and so monopolize the populist constituency in Algerian politics, while at the same time qualifying his personal ascendancy in its leadership and complicating its relationship with the reformist faction in the FLN led by Hamrouche and Mehri. But cogent as these strategic considerations were, they had nothing to do with Islamist doctrine, and it seems that Abassi was on the defensive over this issue by March 1991.[187]

In short, because the Salafiyyists were the radicals in matters of doctrine, they were inclined to give priority to the unity of the Islamist movement over the strategic aim of mobilizing the populist vote, and, as such, while more inclined than the Algerianists to denounce the 1989 constitution as un-Islamic, were actually less inclined to challenge the Chadli regime and the Hamrouche government in practice. Winning power in the short term was less important to them than remaining true to their beliefs. For this reason, they were disposed to accept the new electoral laws, despite their manifest unfairness, rather than engage in a dangerous confrontation. If the 1989 constitution was un-Islamic anyway, why quibble over a couple of cynical electoral laws? The FIS should denounce the laws by all means, but contest the elections nonetheless, since it would in any case win a substantial number of seats in the new assembly, and thus advance its cause.[188]

At the same time, because the Algerianists were comparative latecomers to the FIS, the Salafiyyists were the more strongly represented in key positions in the party's apparatus; this apparatus had blossomed and prospered since June 1990, and the men who ran it were naturally chary of putting at risk in a head-on collision with the state all they had achieved in the way of an organized presence on the ground. It is understandable, therefore, that the leaders of the Salafiyyist opposition to Abassi on the issues of Islamist unity and confrontation over the electoral laws should have been Said Guechi, the FIS leader in Setif who was also president of the national commission for organization and coordination, and Mohamed Kerrar, head of the party's national secretariat and of its financial and administrative departments.[189]

For Abassi, on the other hand, his entire political position was at stake. To concede to Guechi and his group would be to accept a drift to Islamist unity, which would undermine his own paramount leadership. At the same time he would have to abandon the high moral ground in relation to Hamrouche and the FLN, which would abort the entire FIS strategy of posturing as the "real" FLN or at least the legitimate heir of the historic FLN, on which its popular support really hinged. As we have seen, a crucial aspect of this strategy was to maintain a monopoly of political radicalism, to ensure that no other formation ever outflanked it. But in early May 1991 this monopoly was being seriously infringed.

By the spring of 1991 a number of other parties, including Kasdi Merbah's newly formed Algerian Movement for Justice and Development (Mouvement Algérien pour la Justice et le Développement or MAJD) and Ben Bella's MDA were making an issue of Chadli's position, calling for early presidential elections, and even threatening to call a one-day general strike on the issue of the electoral law.[190] Since popular hostility to Chadli ran deep, there was a real danger the FIS would be decisively outflanked by other parties unless it regained the initiative on this issue. And since neither Hamas nor the MNI were among those parties calling for presidential elections, Abassi could emphasize a major policy difference with Hamas and MNI (thereby repudiating the advocates of alliance and tactical moderation within the Majlis al-Shura), and he could simultaneously outflank all the other parties calling for presidential elections and revision of the electoral laws.

In short, in leading the FIS into a confrontation with the Hamrouche government in May 1991, Abassi was not abandoning his earlier strategy in favor of an insurrectionary adventure. On the contrary, he was fighting desperately to preserve his original strategy. This strategy was one of coming to power within the framework of the 1989 constitution by mobilizing a popular majority in elections. It presupposed that the FIS could maintain its monopoly of the mass popular vote, and that the electoral process would fairly and properly translate this vote into a legislative majority. There was no way Abassi could save the premises of his strategy without challenging Chadli over the issue of presidential elections and Hamrouche over the electoral laws.

That the resort to confrontational tactics was devoid of insurrectionary or anticonstitutional intent is further suggested by the fact that Abassi took care to negotiate with the Hamrouche government over the question of which public squares in Algiers the FIS demonstrators might occupy,[191] and ensured that the party's stewards kept discipline among the demonstrators. While it can be argued that the mass occupation of public places was technically illegal from 1 June onward, since the campaign for the National Assembly elections scheduled for 27 June officially began on that day and the FIS's demonstrations infringed the election regulations, there was no violence from the start of the protest on 26 May until the early hours of 4 June, when on orders from the presidency, riot police began clearing the streets by force, attacking demonstrators who, far from engaging in insurrection, were actually fast asleep at the time.[192] This abrupt resort to force by the authorities provoked a bitter spasm of street fighting which lasted for more than a day and in which dozens of people were killed.

From Abassi's point of view, the 1989 constitution was an acceptable framework within which to pursue his political ambitions. But from Chadli's point of view, the constitution enabled him to exploit the Islamist movement via the agency of the FIS. As an auxiliary force the FIS denied Chadli's enemies within the FLN access to popular audiences and thus preserved his own position. For as long as the FIS was developing its presence and mobilizing popular support at the expense of his enemies and at the same time tacitly underwriting Chadli's own position as president, it made sense for him to indulge it. At the moment the FIS began to call for early presidential elections, however, it ceased to be an ally of Chadli and immediately became a threat.

In May–June 1991 the latent contradiction in Chadli's strategy came dramatically to the surface. The strategy of backing the reformers led by Mehri and Hamrouche and relying on them to convert the FLN into "un parti présidentiel" involved bottling up Chadli's critics inside the FLN as a permanently frustrated minority. But the very conditions of political pluralism which Chadli had introduced gave his critics an alternative to being marginalized inside the FLN, namely, to quit the party and found new parties of their own. Once they had made this move, it was possible for them to turn the tables on Chadli—which is precisely what Kasdi Merbah did.[193]

Because Chadli's strategy of manipulating the FIS required it to monopolize the mass popular electorate by cornering the market in political radicalism, it was a comparatively easy matter for Chadli's enemies to manipulate the FIS in their turn. All they needed to do was to raise political demands that struck a chord with popular audiences—such as the demand for early presidential elections. Chadli reacted to this demand by dropping Hamrouche and the reformers. With them he abandoned the hope of converting the FLN into a presidential party, and resigned the FLN presidency on 28 June. Thereafter he backed the new government of nonparty technocrats headed by Sid Ahmed Ghozali.

This new strategy implied a new attitude toward the FIS. It was, of course, desirable from Chadli's point of view to prevent the FIS from sweeping to victory in the legislative elections when these were finally held, but he knew he could no longer rely on the FLN reformers to do this. The new strategy was therefore to work for an election result that would give rise to a hung Parliament, with neither the FLN nor the FIS securing a majority of seats. Such a result would have left Chadli free to reappoint Ghozali and the core of his cabinet of technocrats, while offering a few ministries to the FIS as well as the FLN and some of the smaller parties, in a coalition government of national union.[194] This outcome would permit Chadli to stay in business as the arbiter of the political game.

For this strategy to work, it was vital to ensure that the FIS could not win a clear majority, that is, to emasculate its electoral appeal. This appeal had depended on the FIS's credentials as the historic FLN's legitimate heir, credentials derived largely from Abassi's personal stature and charismatic authority as well as from 'Ali Ben Hadj, as the fiery tribune of deprived urban youth, who had consistently endorsed Abassi's position. It was therefore necessary to remove both Abassi and Ben Hadj from the political stage. Following the declaration of the state of siege and the sacking of Mouloud Hamrouche, however, Abassi had pronounced himself satisfied with Ghozali's assurances concerning both the revision of the electoral laws and the timing of presidential elections and had promptly called off the general strike.[195] Accordingly it was necessary to manufacture a pretext for arresting him.

On 6 June a French national, Dominique Pierron, was arrested wearing a military uniform in the FIS offices in Oran.[196] On 9 June the army began arresting Islamists belonging to violent fringe groups outside the FIS across the country, a development to which Abassi did not react.[197] On 12 June a second French national, Didier Roger Guyon, was arrested, once more in Oran, in possession of firearms and explosives.[198] Interviewed on state television, Guyon claimed to have been in touch with Abassi Madani.[199] These developments conveyed the impression that Abassi was involved in a terrorist conspiracy; associating him with French nationals tarnished his personal credentials as a patriot. He responded to this claim on 18 June by conveying his good wishes to Ghozali's new government announced the previous day and declaring that "the country is heading toward the return of peace and a way out of the political crisis";[200] decoded, this read: "if anyone is engaged in a terrorist conspiracy, it is not me; I am looking for dialogue, not trouble."

Three days later, on 21 June, the army ordered that unofficial Islamic signs on FIS-controlled town halls be removed; on 25 June special police units began enforcing this order in a heavy-handed manner and fighting flared; that evening, three leading dissidents in the Majlis al-Shura appeared on state television and explained their disagreements with Abassi, with one of them calling on FIS militants to disregard Abassi's instructions and denouncing him as "a danger for the FIS and the Muslims."[201] Abassi responded the next day that he represented the FIS and mobilized FIS militants in Algiers to demonstrate with slogans denouncing the three "traitors." Abassi also secured from the Majlis al-Shura a communiqué (co-signed by him) denouncing the conspiracy against him, blaming the authorities for the disorders, demanding the immediate lifting of the curfew, the abrogation of the state of siege, the reinstatement of employees sacked for their part in the general strike, the freeing of Islamists arrested since 4 June and the dropping of legal proceedings against them, and the publication of the new dates of the legislative and presidential elections.[202] The same day, the army issued a public warning that it would "employ all means to ensure that the rule of law and security may be assured on every last corner of the national territory."[203] Abassi responded by telling supporters at the Ibn Badis mosque at Kouba on 28 June that he was not intimidated and that "if the army does not return to its barracks, the FIS will have the right to call for a resumption of the jihad, as in November 1954."[204] On 30 June he and Ben Hadj were arrested on charges of "armed conspiracy against the security of the state," which carried the death penalty.[205] On 7 July, the man whom Abassi had named as his successor, Mohamed Saïd, had no sooner announced that he was assuming the leadership than he too was arrested without pretext.

At stake in these developments was not a genuine insurrectionary threat by the FIS, but Abassi's position as its leader and spokesman. Since Abassi and Ben Hadj did in fact enjoy majority support in the Majlis al-Shura and massive popularity at the grass-roots level, to arrest them was a dangerous move, since it involved the risk of sparking an uncontrolled and uncontrollable explosion. Thus their arrests were accompanied by an unprecedented massive wave of arrests of FIS activists: between 30 June and 10 July, many hundreds if not thousands of Islamists were arrested, including most of the FIS senior cadres in Algiers, so the organizational capacity of the FIS to react to its leaders' incarceration was destroyed.[206]

Deradicalization and the Djeza'ara

The Chadli regime's decisive surgery on the FIS leadership did not radicalize the party even further, but deradicalized it, as was intended. This result was not because, with Abassi out of the way, the regime was able to induce the Salafiyyist critics of Abassi's confrontational tactics to assume the leadership. On the contrary, in the course of July 1991, many of the leading Salafiyyists were either expelled or suspended from the Majlis al-Shura, and the special congress of the FIS held in Batna on 25–26 July saw the definitive triumph of the Algerianists within the party's leadership.[207] The congress affirmed its loyalty to Abassi and Ben Hadj by reelecting them in their absence to the presidency and vice-presidency of the party, but for practical purposes the leadership was assumed by Abdelkader Hachani as the president of a new body, the Provisional Executive Bureau. With the eviction of many Salafiyyists from key posts, members of the Djeza'ara assumed control of the party's apparatus. Abassi's loyal supporters on the Majlis al-Shura took over the party in his absence, but the FIS did not persist with its radical positions, because the radicalization of May had been tactical, not doctrinaire, in character, and the changed circumstances in late July dictated tactical caution and a moderate stance.

Thereafter debate within the party turned on the question of whether to participate in the electoral process which the Ghozali government was publicly committed to relaunching. It appears that the new FIS leadership was aware that what had been done to the party had deprived it of any serious prospect of winning a clear majority in the National Assembly elections. Hachani was by all accounts an able politician who enjoyed the confidence of his colleagues and the endorsement of the imprisoned leaders, but he was no substitute for either Abassi or Ben Hadj.[208] Because he was a young man (b. 1956) and thus had played no part in the national revolution, he was incapable of personally sustaining the FIS's pretensions as the reincarnation of the historic FLN. While he was the same age as Ben Hadj, he had been a petrochemical engineer, not an imam with a local following. He was completely unknown to the public prior to his emergence in late July/early August 1991, and possessed none of the charisma, national stature, and popular constituency of the firebrand from Bab el-Oued or the man of 1 November 1954. The FIS's new leader was an effective stopgap, adequate to the task of holding the party together and rebuilding its organization in the wake of the drubbing it had received from the military authorities. He was not a serious candidate for the office of prime minister, however, let alone someone who could plausibly challenge Chadli in a presidential election. The FIS needed to set itself far more modest objectives in the changed circumstances. And so, under the leadership of those who had loyally supported Abassi's ambitious position in May, the FIS actually reverted to the position of Abassi's critics. This view was the one defended by Saïd Guechi, namely, that the party should avoid confrontation with the state and accept whatever opportunities were offered for developing its presence on the national stage.

Yet the overall strategic position of the FIS remained unclear until mid-December. Its priority at first was to pressure the regime to release the imprisoned leaders and rank-and-file activists and lift the state of siege; this concern led it to adopt a predominantly recalcitrant stance throughout the summer of 1991. It refused to take part in the highly publicized forum Ghozali organized with the political parties from 30 July to 2 August, and the defiant tone of its journals *El Munqidh* (The savior) and *El Forkane* (The proof [Al-Furqan]) led them to be suspended by the military authorities on 15 August. When the authorities, while releasing 300 Islamists on 18 August, made it clear that the trial of Abassi and Ben Hadj would go ahead, the FIS responded by boycotting the second round of talks between Ghozali and the political parties on 22 August. Although an additional 259 Islamists were released from detention on 28 August, Hachani declared on 2 September that the FIS would not participate in elections unless the state of siege was lifted and the FIS leaders freed, and on 9 September the eight FIS leaders in prison began a hunger strike which they sustained until 20 September.

For their part, the authorities were playing a game of cat and mouse with the FIS, balancing concessions with further repressive moves. Thus, while the state of siege was finally lifted on 29 September, it was immediately preceded by the arrest of Hachani on 27 September and immediately followed by the banning of two FIS demonstrations in Algiers on 30 September. Nonetheless, the tendency to employ maximalist rhetoric remained in force throughout Hachani's absence in October. Thus a FIS rally in the Belcourt district of Algiers on 4 October demanded not only the release of the imprisoned leaders but also the installation of an Islamic republic,[209] and, despite the party's palpable lack of a plausible candidate in Abassi's absence, it continued to demand early presidential elections (although this rhetoric was promptly abandoned following Hachani's release from custody and his return to active leadership on 29 October).

Thereafter, despite the unyielding attitude of the authorities, Hachani guided the FIS toward a tacit understanding with the Ghozali government. The eight FIS leaders remained in prison, the judicial preparations for their trial went ahead, and they were not allowed to be candidates for the National Assembly when the FIS submitted its list on 3 November. Moreover, thirty-one Islamists received prison sentences at Sidi Bel Abbes on 15 November, two more were sentenced on 12 December, and several FIS journalists on 14 December. Instead of reacting vigorously to these developments, the FIS began to take part once more in the electoral process, submitting a full list of candidates for the legislative elections on 3 November and unequivocally abandoning its earlier insistence that release of the eight leaders was a precondition of its participation. Moreover, far from attacking the Ghozali government, the more aggressive activities of FIS militants were directed against Ghozali's main enemies, the Hamrouche faction in the FLN, against which Ghozali was secretly sponsoring independent candidates,[210] and Ben Bella's MDA, with which Ghozali and Chadli were determined not to have dealings. Thus the FLN's head office in Algiers was attacked by FIS activists on 31 October, two days after Hachani's return to the fray, during a press conference given by Hamrouche,[211] and a number of Ben Bella's public meetings were disrupted between 20 and 26 November.[212]

The party still had not finally made up its mind to contest the elections, however, and it appears that the Majlis al-Shura was deeply divided on the question. Hachani and his supporters argued that the party needed to demonstrate to international opinion that it was sincerely willing to play by the constitutional rules, and that they were bound to end up with a substantial number of seats and thus advance their cause, an echo of Guechi's position eight months earlier. Their opponents argued that the elections were, once again, being rigged against them and that to take part while Abassi and the others were still imprisoned was to abandon the high moral ground and confuse and disarm the party's popular following. They also appear to have felt that the party could expect to have more influence if it boycotted the elections, and thereby discredited them, than if they legitimized them by taking part.[213]

In the event, Hachani won a narrow majority for participation on 14 December, with many of the advocates of abstention absenting themselves from the meeting of the Majlis al-Shura which took this decision.[214] Hachani expected the FIS to emerge as the largest party in the new Assembly, but to fall short of a majority,[215] and that the question it would then face was whether to join a coalition government of national union or form the main constitutional opposition to this government. Instead, on 27 December he was confronted with the fact that his party was heading for a majority of the seats in the new Assembly on a scale that would virtually oblige it to form a government composed overwhelmingly, if not exclusively, of its own members.

A party leader who has just won an election cannot be expected to bemoan the fact in public. On 27 December Hachani was contemplating not an electoral triumph but a strategic disaster which spelled the downfall of Chadli and thus the collapse of the particular relationship between the state and the Islamist movement which had made the development of a "constitutional Islamism" possible. And so, within weeks of the election, Hachani was under arrest, the FIS had been dissolved, and the initiative had passed to those who, like Mustapha Bouyali in 1982–87, believed that armed struggle was the only way. How had this strategic disaster occurred?

The Second Manipulation

When the Algerian army insisted in June 1991 on forcing FIS-controlled municipalities to take down the Islamic signs and replace them with the official signs of the Algerian republic, it thereby provoked a violent confrontation with the FIS a mere fortnight after its earlier confrontation with the Hamrouche government over the electoral laws that had been resolved in its favor. Thus it appeared that the army's purpose was at the very least to cut the FIS down to size. But when it pushed this provocation to extremes, and arrested Abassi and Ben Hadj on 30 June on the gravest charges, it seemed beyond question that the army had decided to finish off the substance of the FIS once and for all, whatever formal existence it might, under new and less experienced leadership, be allowed to preserve thereafter.[216]

In the event, however, the FIS was allowed not only to survive but to win a massive majority in the first round of the legislative elections of December 1991. Only after this did the army finally move decisively against it, by inducing the new five-man High Committee of State (Haut Comité d'État or HCE) formed after Chadli's resignation to enforce the law banning the party-political use of mosques, thereby provoking the FIS to break the law and provide the pretext for its own dissolution.

Why did the army not induce President Chadli to ban the FIS outright in July or August 1991, on the same grounds on which it had arrested Abassi and Ben Hadj—that they were involved in an armed conspiracy against the security of the state? By making its move when it did, after 26 December 1991, the army incurred international opprobrium, since it left itself open to the charge that it had conducted a coup d'état and was deliberately subverting the democratic process for the simple reason that it had produced the wrong result.

There is evidence that the army leadership did indeed want the FIS banned in July but that it failed to persuade Chadli to agree.[217] Therefore, short of overthrowing Chadli in a blatant coup in July, it had no choice but to go along with the presidency's new strategy of emasculating the FIS's vote-pulling capacity in order to contrive a hung Parliament in which the FIS would pose no real threat to the constitution. Chadli's closest colleagues thought this strategy would work. Opinion polls commissioned by the government before election day showed an FIS share of between 23 and 34 percent of the vote,[218] and even using the high estimate it was reasonable to expect that these numbers would be translated into less than 50 percent of the seats.

The last thing the government expected was a FIS landslide, and Major-General Larbi Belkheir, who had taken over the interior ministry on 16 October, appeared visibly shaken by the results it was his duty to announce on 27 December.[219]

The FIS polled 3,260,222 votes on 26 December 1991, that is, 24.59 percent of the total registered electorate of 13,258,554.[220] In other words, its vote had fallen substantially since June 1990, as the government's opinion polls had forecast; even if we take the combined votes of Hamas and the MNI into account, it is clear that the aggregate Islamist vote had fallen by about 500,000. Yet, despite this decline in votes, the FIS secured 188 seats outright on the first ballot and was well placed to take the vast majority of the remaining seats on the second ballot. It was thus heading for a majority in the National Assembly, perhaps as much as 75 percent of the seats, on the basis of a quarter of the electorate.

The second striking aspect of the 1991 result was that overall turnout was only 59 percent, compared to 65.2 percent for the APC elections in June 1990. Yet this drop occurred despite the fact that the two major parties that had boycotted the 1990 elections, Hocine Aït Ahmed's Socialist Forces Front (Front des Forces Socialistes or FFS) and Ahmed Ben Bella's MDA, were both contesting the 1991 elections and polled respectively 510,661 and 135,882 votes. Not all of this aggregate of 646,543 votes can be regarded as entirely additional to the 1990 turnout, since both parties would have drawn votes away from other parties that had contested the 1990 election. But most of the FFS votes in particular may be regarded as coming from electors who had abstained in 1990, for the participation in the two Kabyle wilayat of Tizi Ouzou and Bejaïa, which had been 22.82 percent and 27.08 percent respectively in 1990, rose to 57.23 and 53.19 percent respectively in 1991. It was in these two wilayat that the FFS had the bulk of its support, winning twenty-three of its twenty-five seats there. In other words, given that the MDA and especially the FFS were contesting the 1991 elections, and that this had a demonstrable effect on participation in Tizi Ouzou and Bejaïa (and also Algiers, where turnout rose from 56.02 percent in 1990 to 61.01 percent in 1991), why should the overall turnout have fallen by 6.2 per cent, when it might rather have been expected to rise by something approaching that amount?[221] Part of the explanation is that some 900,000 polling cards were never delivered to the voters entitled to receive them.[222] In addition, the rules concerning proxy voting were very much tighter in 1991 than in 1990; as a consequence, many women did not cast their votes in 1991.[223]

The third striking feature of the 1991 election was the massive increase in spoiled ballots. There had been 381,972 blank or spoiled ballots recorded in June 1990; in December 1991 the figure rose to 924,906, 11.82 percent of votes cast.[224] The explanation lies in the fact that the 1991 ballot form was considerably more complicated than that employed in 1990 and induced many unsophisticated voters to make mistakes, to which returns officers had been instructed to show no indulgence.[225]

The FIS was able to take as many as 188 seats on the first ballot, essentially because the FLN vote collapsed. The aggregate FLN vote on 26 December was 1,612,947, a mere 12.17 percent of the electorate. This result represented a major decline since June 1990, when the FLN had polled 2,245,798 votes in the APC elections, equivalent to 17.49 percent of the then electorate of 12,841,769.[226] The loss of votes was no less than 632,851 on 26 December. Where had they gone?

In short, what happened on 26 December 1991? The explanation I propose comprises two separate elements.

The first is that President Chadli's closest supporters, and notably his long-standing ally Major-General Larbi Belkheir, who supervised the elections as minister of the interior, deliberately contrived to minimize popular participation in the 1991 elections, in order to reduce the FIS vote to manageable proportions and thereby manufacture a hung Parliament. To this end a new electoral law was enacted at Ghozali's insistence on 13 October which, while providing a fairer distribution of constituencies across the country, also severely inhibited proxy voting; a new ballot form was introduced which encouraged people to spoil their vote; and, by one means or another, 900,000 electors failed to obtain their poll cards. In this way, a major drop in turnout was engineered despite the participation of the FFS and MDA, and, while the FLN vote was adversely affected by this drop to some extent, the main loser was unquestionably the FIS, which saw its vote fall by over a million as was intended. But while all these moves went according to plan and produced their intended effects, the overall outcome was the opposite of what Belkheir and Chadli had intended and expected, which is why Belkheir appeared so shaken on 27 December.

This outcome leads us to the second element of the explanation, namely, that the opponents of President Chadli deliberately contrived to ensure that the FIS won the legislative elections. They managed this outcome by compensating for the government's sabotage of the FIS vote by themselves massively sabotaging the FLN's vote, enabling the FIS candidates to win by default in many constituencies and so reach the massive total of 188 seats. The calculation involved was that, although this maneuver would not give the FIS an immediate legislative majority, it would guarantee it for the simple reason that, no matter how well the pro-Chadli FLN leaders mobilized their supporters in the 198 seats to be contested in the second ballot, the FIS would be well placed (benefiting among other things from Hamas and MNI transfers) to win many of the remaining seats, and the damage that had already been done in 188 seats could not be undone. The sabotage of the FLN vote was essentially effected by securing a vast number of outright abstentions in some areas (which is the final factor accounting for the overall fall in turnout) and straight transfers of former FLN votes to FIS candidates in other areas. This is why, despite its share of the electorate falling to only 24.59 percent, the FIS was heading for a massive overall majority in the new Assembly.

The appendix summarizes the available information for each of Algeria's forty-eight wilayat concerning the performance of the FIS and the FLN in the 1990 APC elections, their performance in respect to seats won on the first ballot in 1991, and the change in turnout between 1990 and 1991. The table shows that turnout in the wilayat containing Algeria's major cities (Algiers, Oran, Constantine) hardly fell at all and that the FIS performed as well as in 1990; the same is true of the two largely urbanized wilayat immediately south and east of Algiers (Blida and Boumerdes). In short, the evidence suggests that the FIS's big city vote held up well. It is likely this was due to the FIS's strong organization in the cities, which enabled it to counteract the negative effects of the complex ballot (by providing clear instructions to potentially bewildered electors) and the restrictions on proxy voting (by getting the female Islamist vote out),[227] while its control of municipal offices may have enabled it to ensure delivery of poll cards. But it is also likely that the FIS's big city vote held up well due in part to a collapse, or defection, of the FLN vote in the cities.

There is, however, one exception to this pattern, and a most significant one: the city of Annaba registered the lowest fall in turnout of any wilaya. However, this success in maintaining the 1990 turnout did not entail a good performance by the FIS, but its opposite: having easily outdistanced the FLN in Annaba in 1990, the FIS failed to win a single seat on the first ballot in 1991. A hypothesis which would explain this is that, given that Annaba is the hometown of President Chadli,[228] the FLN machine in Annaba was in the hand of Chadli's supporters. They worked successfully to bring out the FLN vote and, by doing so, kept turnout up. Simply mobilizing the full FLN vote for FLN candidates was enough to force the FIS into a second ballot on every one of Annaba's seats. Elsewhere, lower turnout almost invariably denied the FLN seats or delivered them to the FIS.[229] The FIS was able to win because a significant element of the FLN vote simply was not mobilized or was mobilized against the FLN and for its rival.[230]

In many parts of the country, the FLN vote simply was not mobilized in support of FLN candidates. The conventional wisdom is that the FLN tried, but failed, to mobilize it. I believe that, as the Annaba case suggests, where local FLN bosses really tried to mobilize the vote, they succeeded and held the FIS at bay, and that where the failure to mobilize the FLN vote was palpable, it was because local FLN notables had deliberately refused to mobilize it or had mobilized it to vote for the FIS.

The leading critics of the Chadli-Mehri-Hamrouche leadership within the FLN had played a high-profile role in the 1990 election campaign. In the 1991 campaign they were invisible and inaudible; several of them had already left the FLN, notably Kasdi Merbah, who had founded his own party, and Belaïd Abdessalem, who ran as an independent.[231] In the 1991 campaign, public responsibility for presenting the FLN's case to the electorate was left almost entirely to Mehri, Hamrouche, and their supporters. Evidence strongly suggests that their opponents let them carry the whole burden and either looked on with folded arms or discreetly encouraged the voters they could influence in their local constituencies to invest in an FIS victory. In doing nothing, they were simply following the logic of Chadli's maneuver the previous year; since they were obviously regarded as a liability,[232] they would take no part.

This maneuver yielded a rich and complex political dividend. It demonstrated that Chadli and the reformers could at best claim the support of 12.17 per cent of the electorate, and that Chadli's opponents and critics within the FLN still represented a force within the society, and could not so casually be dismissed as "yesterday's men." It demonstrated, in particular to the army's officer corps as a whole, that Chadli's strategy of manipulating the FIS had come to grief, since it required Chadli to preserve his position as arbiter of the political game and this in turn required him to preserve a balance between the various political forces in this game. That balance definitively lost, Chadli had obviously outlived his usefulness from the army's point of view as the orchestrator of a political sphere congenial to it. It demonstrated to liberal and modernist opinion in the society that, with the sudden reemergence of the prospect of an Islamic republic concentrating their minds wonderfully, they had an interest in rediscovering the virtues of the Algerian military establishment. And, finally, it demonstrated to Chadli's supporters in Western capitals, especially Paris, that they could no longer justify their support for Chadli on the grounds that he was a bulwark against an Islamist takeover. On the contrary, if Paris and the West in general wanted to keep Chadli in power, they would have to tolerate the FIS in power as well; if they wanted to stop a FIS takeover, they would have to abandon Chadli and come to terms with his successors.[233]

Conclusion

The dramatic expansion of Algerian Islamism cannot be explained solely in terms of the force of economic, social, and ideological factors. The dynamic of this development has been largely political, and only an analytical approach which appreciates the details of Algeria's political history can grasp it.

This political dynamic has not been located primarily within the Islamist movement. Changes in tactics or strategy or discourse have been accompanied or mediated by struggles for influence between competing currents or factions within the movement, but they have nonetheless been in the first instance responses to changes in the attitude and behavior of the state, rather than the product of spontaneous developments within Islamist ranks, and the changes in the strategy of the state have been dictated primarily by the struggle for power between competing factions within the state apparatus itself. In other words, the divisions within the Islamist movement have been secondary to the divisions within the state apparatus and the politicomilitary elite that staffs it, and it is the latter that have largely determined the expansion and subsequent contraction of Algerian Islamism.

It may be suggested that the entire Algerian case should be classified as an instance of "pseudo-fundamentalism," but I would argue that this is the academic theorist's easy way out and does not do justice to the complexity of Algerian reality. The sincerity of the convictions of Algeria's Islamists should not be doubted. What the manipulations I have described have presupposed is that Algeria's Islamists, like the Algerian people as a whole, have been profoundly ignorant because they have been deliberately kept ignorant of the political history of the national revolution,[234] and consequently have never had the measure of the state they have been confronting, and have been easily manipulated.

The Algerian case also suggests that the nation-state in Muslim countries can hope to manage its relationship with its fundamentalist critics and, by manipulating them, harness their energies for its own changing purposes. Because of its revolutionary origins, the state the historic FLN created in Algeria has possessed an unusually large armory of political resources in this respect, and the governments of other Muslim states may well be disinclined to engage in the kind of audacious maneuvers that come naturally to the FLN.

APPENDIX

CHANGES IN FIS AND FLN FORTUNES AND TURNOUT BETWEEN 1990 AND 1991, BY WILAYA[1]

Wilaya	1990 APC Turnout (%)	APC Seats Won			1991 Turnout (%)	1990–91 Change	1991 APN Seats			2d Round
		FIS	FLN	Others			FIS	FLN	Others	
Adrar	59.39	22	177	15	42.95	−16.44	0	3	0	6
Aïn Defla	74.38	193	77	46	60.47	−13.91	8	0	0	1
Aïn Temouchent	79.01	101	88	27	70.84	−8.17	0	0	0	5
Alger	56.02	343	85	25	61.01	+4.99	16	0	0	6
Annaba	59.31	76	46	10	58.78	−0.79	0	0	0	7
Batna	66.61	233	190	62	54.83	−11.78	8	0	0	6
Bechar	74.61	30	119	14	71.24	−3.37	0	0	0	8
Bejaïa	27.08	16	179	249	53.19	+26.11	0	0	11	1
Biskra	66.11	105	121	45	57.35	−8.76	4	0	0	6
Blida	70.49	227	58	8	64.90	−5.59	9	0	0	3
Bordj Bou Arreridj	74.00	119	119	40	64.72	−5.28	4	0	0	4
Bouïra	65.06	152	119	94	54.96	−10.10	6	0	1	2
Boumerdes	62.76	230	78	28	61.38	−1.38	6	0	0	5
Chlef	69.11	216	82	33	56.56	−12.55	9	0	0	2
Constantine	66.87	98	37	3	63.45	−3.42	8	0	0	2
Djelfa	61.19	109	115	76	45.85	−15.34	5	0	0	4
El Bayadh	69.22	29	85	50	60.75	−8.56	5	0	0	5
El Oued	59.65	(11	13	6)[2]	55.69	−3.96	3	1	0	4
El Tarf	80.43	77	104	15	69.80	−10.63	0	1	0	4
Ghardaïa	76.64	(0	8	5)[2]	65.30	−11.34	1	1	3	4
Guelma	72.16	90	112	62	65.19	−6.97	0	0	0	6
Illizi	66.57	7	31	4	51.16	−15.41	0	3	0	0
Jijel	61.03	189	54	11	46.82	−14.21	7	0	0	1
Khenchela	53.53	51	78	29	48.31	−15.22	0	1	0	4
Laghouat	75.15	61	95	28	67.60	−7.55	1	1	0	3
Mascara	76.42	207	124	46	62.04	−14.38	7	0	0	3
Medea	72.78	294	152	54	54.62	−18.16	9	0	0	3
Mila	68.59	(30	1	1)[2]	56.02	−12.57	8	0	0	1
Mostaganem	67.71	(28	3	1)[2]	54.93	−12.78	1	0	0	7
M'Sila	66.01	145	148	92	52.83	−13.27	9	1	0	1
Naama	64.53	(4	5	3)[2]	57.64	−6.89	1	0	0	2
Oran	63.04	164	52	32	60.95	−2.09	11	0	0	3
Ouargla	59.45	39	114	22	54.28	−5.17	4	0	0	7
Oum El Bouaghi	70.61	112	91	36	57.33	−13.28	4	0	0	4
Relizane	66.14	(38	0	0)[2]	54.26	−11.88	8	0	0	1
Saïda	67.06	61	55	18	59.10	−7.96	1	1	0	2
Setif	73.06	260	159	113	59.34	−13.72	13	0	1	4
Sidi Bel Abbès	79.81	207	144	43	68.98	−10.83	2	0	0	6
Skikda	71.14	161	109	66	61.60	−9.54	1	0	0	9
Souk Ahras	71.19	48	111	45	56.15	−15.14	0	0	0	6
Tamanghasset	68.53	2	62	16	51.52	−17.01	0	2	0	3
Tebessa	71.32	56	107	74	55.63	−15.69	0	0	0	8
Tiaret	70.46	137	153	60	57.20	−13.26	4	0	0	6
Tindouf	71.28	1	5	10	58.01	−13.27	0	0	0	2
Tipasa	73.00	(29	10	3)[2]	68.16	−5.18	3	0	0	7
Tissemsilt	71.42	100	68	10	49.30	−22.12	0	0	0	5
Tizi Ouzou	22.82	19	211	338	57.23	+34.41	0	0	12	4
Tlemcen	78.01	277	145	25	64.73	−13.28	7	1	0	5

1. Sources: 1990 APC election: (i) turnout: *Horizons,* 17 June 1990; (ii) results: *El Moudjahid,* 18, 19, 22–23, 24, 25, 26, 27 June 1991 APN election (i) turnout: *Journal République Algérienne,* 4 January 1992; (ii) results, *El Forkane,* 21–28 January 1992.
2. Details of the distribution of APC seats in the wilayât of El Oued, Ghardaïa, Mila, Mostaganem, Naama, Relizane and Tipasa are unavailable; I have used figures for APC instead, which give a rough idea of the balance of support for the FIS and the FLN.

Notes

1. *Le Monde,* 5 November 1989; "L'exploitation d'un séisme," *El Moudjahid,* 7 November 1989.

2. Arun Kapil, "Portrait statistique des élections du 12 Juin 1990: Chiffres-clés pour une analyse," *Cahiers de l'Orient* 23 (Summer 1991): 41–63.

3. For a fuller discussion of the Bouyali affair, see Hugh Roberts, "Radical Islamism and the Dilemma of Algerian Nationalism," *Third World Quarterly* 10 (2 April 1988): 556–89; and François Burgat, *L'islamisme au Maghreb: La voix du Sud* (Paris: Éditions Karthala, 1988), pp. 164–68.

4. *Le Monde,* 11, 13, 14, 15, 16–17, and 18 November 1986; *The Guardian,* 12 and 18 November 1986.

5. Burgat, *L'islamisme au Maghreb,* p. 296.

6. *Libération,* 8–9 October 1988; *Le Monde,* 9–10 October 1988.

7. Abed Charef, *Dossier octobre* (Algiers: Éditions Laphomic, 1989), pp. 102–3, 205–310; Jean-François Kahn, "Algérie: La deuxième révolution," *Événement du jeudi,* 13–19 October 1988.

8. See *El Moudjahid,* 5 February 1989, which carried the full text of the draft constitutional revisions.

9. Notably articles 31–37.

10. *Le Monde,* 4 July 1989.

11. Notably President Chadli's declaration of 23 October 1988, published by Algérie-Presse-Service (Reuters, 25 October 1988), his subsequent rejection of the petition of eighteen well-known personalities calling for democracy (*Le Monde,* 1 November 1988), and his speech to the Sixth Party Congress on 27 November 1988, in which he insisted that his proposed political reforms did not necessarily signify the establishment of political pluralism (*Libération,* 28 November 1988).

12. *Mrabit* (pl.: *mrabtin*)—whence the French term *marabout*—literally means a holy man or saint (living or dead), possessor of *baraka* (blessing, divine grace, charisma); *sharif* (pl.: *shurfa*) means "noble" and indicates descendants of the Prophet Muhammad; many but not all mrabtin claim and are popularly credited with sharifian descent. *Tariqa* (pl.: *turuq*) literally means "a way" and by association a (Sufi) religious order or brotherhood.

13. Ali Merad, *Le réformisme musulman en Algérie de 1925 à 1940: Essai d'histoire réligieuse et sociale* (Paris: La Haye-Mouton, 1967); see also Ernest Gellner, *Muslim Society* (Cambridge: Cambridge University Press, 1981), pp. 149–73; and Fanny Colonna, "Cultural Resistance and Religious Legitimacy in Colonial Algeria," *Economy and Society* 3, no. 2 (1974): 233–52.

14. Gellner, *Muslim Society,* p. 156.

15. "Proclamation du Front de Libération Nationale, le 1er novembre 1954," in Mohammed Harbi, ed., *Les archives de la révolution algérienne* (Paris, Les Éditions Jeune Afrique, 1981), pp. 101–3; emphasis added.

16. See the testimony of Rachid Benaïssa in Burgat, *L'islamisme au Maghreb,* pp. 153–54.

17. Pierre Bourdieu, *The Algerians* (Boston: Beacon Press, 1962), chaps. 6 and 7; Pierre Bourdieu and Abdelmalek Sayad, *Le déracinement: La crise de l'agriculture traditionnelle en Algérie* (Paris: Éditions de Minuit, 1964).

18. Hugh Roberts, "The Algerian Constitution and the Restructuring of State-Capitalism," *IDS Bulletin* 18, (4 October 1987): 51–56; see also Mohammed Harbi, *Le FLN, Mirage et Réalité* (Paris: Éditions J.A., 1980), pp. 377–85.

19. Bourdieu, *Le Déracinement;* see also Mostefa Lacheraf, "Le village algérien dans l'univers insaisissable du No-Man's Land," *Terre et Progrès* (Algiers: Ministry of Agriculture, June 1973), pp. 22–39.

20. This sense of the old urban world turned upside down is admirably conveyed in fictional form by Tahar Ouettar's splendid novel, *Ez-Zilzel* (The Earthquake) (Algiers: SNED, 1981).

21. Hugh Roberts, "The Algerian Bu-

reaucracy," in Talal Asad and Roger Owen, eds., *Sociology of "Developing Societies": The Middle East* (London: Macmillan, 1983), pp. 95–114; see also Bruno Etienne, *L'islamisme radical,* pp. 91–117; and idem, "Clientelism in Algeria," in Ernest Gellner and John Waterbury, eds., *Patrons and Clients* (London: Duckworth 1977), pp. 291–308.

22. See, for example, the article "Célibataire à trente ans," in the new Algerian weekly *Le Jeune Indépendant,* no. 2, 17–23 April 1990.

23. Jean-Claude Vatin, "Popular Puritanism versus State Reformism: Islam in Algeria," in James Piscatori, ed., *Islam in the Political Process* (Cambridge: Cambridge University Press, 1983), pp. 98–121.

24. Only one candidate was nominated for each seat in the Ben Bella period, however, whereas in National Assembly elections from 1977 onward the electors had a choice among three FLN-approved candidates for each seat.

25. For a fuller discussion of the real nature of the Party of the FLN in the Algerian political system, see Roberts, "The Algerian Bureaucracy," in Asad and Owen, *Sociology of "Developing Societies"*; "The Politics of Algerian Socialism," in Richard Lawless and Allan Findlay, eds. *North Africa: Contemporary Politics and Economic Development* (London: Croom Helm, 1984), pp. 5–49; and idem, "The FLN: French Conceptions, Algerian Realities," in E. G. H. Joffé, ed., *North Africa: Nation, State and Region* (London: Routledge, 1992).

26. Roberts, "The FLN."

27. Namely, the Union Générale des Travailleurs Algériens (UGTA), the Union Générale des Commerçants Algériens (UGCA) and the Union Générale des Étudiants Musulmans Algériens (UGEMA), all founded in 1955–56.

28. Namely, the Fédération de France du FLN (FFFLN), the Fédération de Maroc du FLN and the Fédération de Tunisie du FLN.

29. The thoroughly modernist outlook of the leadership of the FLN was made clear by the platform adopted by the FLN at its first Congress in the Soummam valley in Kabylia in August 1956; the text of this platform is published in *El Moudjahid* (journal of the wartime FLN) 1, no. 4, of the republished official edition (Belgrade, 1962): 61–73.

30. See, for example, Mouloud Feraoun's account of how the FLN established its control of his own village of Tizi Hibel in Kabylia, in his *Journal 1955–1962* (Paris: Éditions du Seuil, 1962), pp. 43 and 72–73; see also the memoir of an FLN guerrilla commander, Mohamed Benyahia, *La Conjuration au Pouvoir* (Paris: Éditions de l'Arcantère, 1988), pp. 50–51.

31. Hence the use of the word *mujahidin* (fighters of the jihad, fighters for the faith) to refer to the combat troops of the FLN, not to mention numerous other uses of Islamic terminology, notably passwords, for example in the following exchange: Sentry: "Achkoun?" (Who goes there?). Answer: "Islam." Sentry: "Dini" (That's my religion). Ali Serradj, "Les combats du 24 octobre dans la région de Tigrine-Beni Mançour," in Mahfoud Kaddache, ed., *Récits de Feu* (Algiers: SNED, 1977), pp. 81–92.

32. For a fuller discussion of this point, see Roberts, "A Trial of Strength: Algerian Islamism," in James Piscatori, ed., *Islamic Fundamentalisms and the Gulf Crisis* (Chicago: The Fundamentalism Project of the American Academy of Arts and Sciences, 1991), pp. 138–39.

33. For a detailed description of the Algerian jama'a and its logic, see my article in Joffé 1992, "The FLN."

34. Roberts, "Radical Islamism."

35. Roberts, "The Algerian Bureaucracy," and "The Algerian Constitution."

36. Roberts, "Radical Islamism," pp. 562–66.

37. *El Mazdaqiyya Hiya 'Asl el Ishtirakiyya.* See Burgat, *L'Islamisme au Maghreb,* pp. 146–50.

38. Notably Kateb Yacine (1929–89), widely regarded as Algeria's greatest writer, whose left-wing views had led him to make remarks concerning Islam which scandalised the ulama: see Burgat, *L'islamisme au Maghreb.*

39. Jean-Claude Vatin, "Religion et Politique au Maghreb: le renversement des perspectives dans l'étude de l'Islam," in Ernest Gellner, Jean-Claude Vatin, et al., *Islam et politique au Maghreb* (Paris: Éditions du CNRS, 1982), pp. 15–43.

40. Malek Bennabi, *Les conditions de la renaissance Algérienne: Problème d'une civilisation* (Paris: Éditions du Seuil, 1949); *Vocation de l'islam* (Paris: Éditions du Seuil, 1954); *Mémoires d'un témoin du Ssècle* (Algiers: Éditions Nationales Algériennes, 1965).

41. See the testimony of an Algerian Islamist intellectual, Rachid Benaïssa, in Burgat, *L'Islamisme au Maghreb*, pp. 100 and 154.

42. According to Rachid Benaïssa, in Burgat, *L'islamisme au Maghreb*, p. 153.

43. Ibid.

44. On this period, see Mahfoud Bennoune and Ali El Kenz, *Le Hasard et l'Histoire: entretiens avec Belaïd Abdesselam* (Algiers: ENAG, 1990); see also Ahmed Rouadjia, *Les Frères et la Mosqué: enquête sur le mouvement islamiste en Algérie* (Paris: Éditions Karthala, 1990), pp. 34–36.

45. Rouadjia, *Les Frères et la Mosqué,* pp. 112–13, gives a description of this event but situates it in 1974, whereas both Burgat (*L'islamisme au Maghreb,* p. 155) and Etienne (*L'Algérie, cultures et révolution,* p. 181) situate it in 1975.

46. Bruno Etienne, *L'islamisme radical* (Paris: Hachette, 1987), p. 20.

47. In this connection, it is significant that when Bennabi uses the term *jahiliyya,* he does so in the traditional way, that is, *in the past tense,* whereas for the radical Islamist movement, taking its cue from Qutb especially, the jahiliyya it is preoccupied with is a contemporary reality.

48. As Etienne suggests in *L'islamisme radical,* p. 219.

49. Etienne uses the terms *marée* (wave) and *nebuleuse* (nebula) to characterize the organizational form of the radical Islamist movement in general, in *L'islamisme radical,* pp. 70, 132, 201, 214.

50. Burgat, *L'islamisme au Maghreb,*

pp. 159–64 (where the name of the mosque is given, incorrectly, as Bait el Arkam); Rouadjia, *Les frères et la mosqué,* p. 160.

51. Rouadjia, *Les frères et la mosqué,* p. 156.

52. Etienne, *L'islamisme radical,* pp. 141–42.

53. Rouadjia, *Les frères et la mosqué,* pp. 15–18, 59–69, 64–65.

54. Etienne, *L'Algérie, cultures et révolution,* pp. 135–36.

55. As was admitted in 1981 by the then Minister of Religious Affairs, Abderrahmane Chibane, himself, when he claimed that three-fifths of the imams were insufficiently qualified to do their job; see Vatin, *art.cit.,* in Piscatori, 1983, *op.cit.,* p. 112.; see also Burgat, *L'islamisme au Maghreb,* pp. 98–99; Rouadjia, *Les frères et la mosqué,* p. 90.

56. Etienne, *L'Algérie, Cultures et Révolution,* pp. 135–36 and 135n.3.

57. Burgat, *L'Islamisme au Maghreb,* p. 98.

58. Bernard Cubertafond, "Algérie," in Bernard Badie et al., *Contestations en Pays Islamiques* (Paris: CHEAM, 1984), pp. 31–62.

59. *Le Monde,* 6 October 1981.

60. Ibid.; Cubertafond, in *op.cit.,* p. 51.

61. John P. Entelis, *Algeria: The Revolution Institutionalised* (Boulder, Colo.: Westview Press; London and Sydney: Croom Helm 1986), p. 85.

62. Burgat, *L'islamisme au Maghreb,* p. 162; Rouadjia, p. 158; Cubertafond, in *op.cit.,* p. 59.

63. Burgat, *L'islamisme au Maghreb,* p. 162.

64. *Le Monde,* 15 April 1984.

65. With the exception of the Bouyali maquis, which was entirely marginal to the mainstream movement. See Burgat, *L'islamisme au Maghreb,* pp. 164–68 and especially p. 166, citing Rachid Benaïssa.

66. *Code de la Famille* (Algiers: Office des Publications Universitaires, 1984; for a discussion, see Rouadjia, *Les frères et la mosqué,* pp. 219–27.

67. Roberts, "The Algerian Constitution," pp. 579–80.

68. Jean Leca and Jean-Claude Vatin, *L'Algérie Politique: Institutions et Régime* (Paris: Presses de la Fondation Nationale des Sciences Politiques, 1975), p. 308.

69. Mohammed Harbi, *Aux Origines du FLN: Le Populisme Révolutionnaire en Algérie* (Paris: Christian Bourgois, 1975), p. 314; Benjamin Stora, *Messali Hadj (1898–1974), Pionnier du Nationalisme Algérien* (Paris: L'Harmattan, 1986), pp. 282–83.

70. *Le Monde,* 16 September 1989, citing FIS spokesmen.

71. Reuters, 6 March 1989; *Libération,* 7 March 1989; *Le Monde,* 7 March 1989.

72. *Le Monde,* 23 February 1989.

73. Ghania Samaï-Ouramdane, "Le Front Islamique du Salut à travers son organe de presse (Al Munqid)," in *Algérie: vers l'État Islamique?* (special number of *Peuples Méditerranéens* (52–53), July–December 1990, pp. 155–65.

74. Samaï-Ouramdane, "Le Front Islamique du Salut," p. 158.

75. Roberts, "A Trial of Strength," p. 136.

76. The electoral law of April 1991 involved a flagrant exercise in gerrymandering constituencies, giving an exaggerated weighting to the thinly populated rural and Saharan constituencies where the FLN was strong, at the expense of the densely populated urban constituencies where the FIS had the bulk of its support. For a discussion of this law and the ensuing confrontation between the FIS and the Hamrouche government, see Roberts, "A Trial of Strength," pp. 144–47 and *Le Monde,* 28 May 1991.

77. *Le Monde,* 28 May 1991.

78. According to a report on Radiodiffusion-Television Algérienne on 29 May 1991: BBC Summary of World Broadcasts (hereafter, *SWB*), 31 May 1991; see also *Le Monde,* 31 May 1991.

79. *SWB,* 31 May 1991.

80. This was a certain Mohamed Saïd, who was himself promptly arrested in the Kouba district of Algiers on 7 July 1991. *Middle East Economic Digest,* 19 July 1991.

81. Arun Kapil, "Les partis islamistes en Algérie: éléments de présentation," *Maghreb-Mashrek* 133 (July–September 1991): 103–11.

82. *Le Monde,* 16 June 1990; Kapil, "Les partis islamistes en Algérie."

83. Kapil, "Les partis islamistes en Algérie."

84. Emmanuel Sivan, *Radical Islam: Medieval Theology and Modern Politics* (New Haven and London: Yale University Press, 1985), p. 56.

85. Sivan, *Radical Islam,* p. 55

86. Rouadjia, *Les frères et la mosquée,* p. 156; Kapil, "Les partis islamistes en Algérie," pp. 110–11.

87. République Algérienne Démocratique et Populaire: *Journal Officiel,* 4 January 1992.

88. *Africa Confidential* 32, no. 8 (19 April 1991).

89. Kapil, "Les partis islamistes en Algérie," p. 108.

90. The names of candidates elected in the first round on 26 December 1991, and of those who went through to the second round, were published in the FIS's paper *El Forkane,* 21–28 January 1992.

91. As Nahnah made clear in his discussions with President Chadli on 29 January 1990 (*SWB,* 1 February 1990); see also Roberts, "A Trial of Strength," pp. 136–37, and Kapil, "Les partis islamistes en Algérie," pp. 108–10.

92. *Arabia* (London), July 1984, p. 15; Abed Charef, *Dossier Octobre* , pp. 205, 209; Rouadjia, op.cit., p. 156.

93. Burgat, *L'Islamisme au Maghreb,* p. 146.

94. Harbi, 1980 *op.cit.,* pp. 136–37; Mohamed Teguia, *L'Algérie en Guerre* (Algiers: OPU, 1988), pp. 169–71.

95. As clearly expressed in the Soummam platform; see note 30 above.

96. For the way in which these grievances against the wartime FLN were subsequently recycled by the radical Islamist movement, see Rouadjia, *Les frères et la mosqué,* pp. 147–49.

97. Ibid.

98. Yves Courrière, *La Guerre d'Algérie,* vol. 1: *Les Fils de la Toussaint* (Paris: Fayard, 1968), pp. 322–23.

99. Samaï-Ouramdane, in "Le Front Islamique du Salut," p. 165.

100. Details of aggregate voting figures for the major parties were published in the *Journal Officiel,* 4 January 1992.

101. Kapil, "Portrait Statistique des Élections du 12 Juin 1990," p. 50.

102. Ibid., p. 48.

103. *El Forkane,* 21–28 January 1991.

104. See "Les réformes algériennes confrontées au 'libéralisme islamique,'" *Les Échos,* 14 June 1990; and "Les ambiguités de l'islamisme algérien," *Le Monde,* 14 June 1990.

105. See Abassi's remark, on the occasion of the creation of the FIS, that "we must take the hand of the People and realize, if God wills it, the Islamic state," *Le Monde,* 23 February 1989; his statement on 15 June 1990 that the victory in the local and regional elections constituted "the keystone of the future Islamic state," *Libération,* 16–17 June 1990; and his declaration during an address to a rally at Setif that the FIS "will soon set up an Islamic state," as reported on Algerian radio on 28 March 1991. *SWB,* 1 April 1991.

106. Notably in Ben Hadj's declaration, in an interview with the Algerian daily *Horizons*: "Yes to pluralism within an Islamic framework. But if today Berbers, communists and all others are going to express themselves our country is going to become a field of competing ideologies at odds with the belief of our people" (Reuters, 7 March 1989). See also the excerpt from one of his sermons published in French translation in *L'Express,* 9 February 1990, in which he rejects democracy as an impious and un-Islamic concept, and his speech at a mosque in the Kouba district of Algiers on 15 June 1990, when he declared that "we will not barter shura for democracy . . . it is Islam which has been the victor, as always, not democracy. We did not go to the ballot boxes for democracy" (*Le Monde,* 17–18 June 1990).

107. *Le Monde,* 17–18 June 1990.

108. *L'Express,* 9 February 1990; *Nouvel Observateur,* 31 May–6 June 1990; for a discussion of the *antennes paraboliques* themselves, see Rouadjia, *Les frères et la mosque,* pp. 231–38.

109. *Le Point* 897, 27 November 1989.

110. *Libération,* 16–17 June 1990.

111. Details of the FIS platform were published in *El Moudjahid,* 20–21 April 1990.

112. Samaï-Ouramdane, "Front Islamique du Salut," pp. 165–66; see also Roberts, "A Trial of Strength," p. 137, and Ahmed Rouadjia, "Le FIS à l'épreuve des élections législatives," *Cahiers de l'Orient* 23, no. 3 (1991): 75–82.

113. *Middle East Economic Digest,* 24 May 1991.

114. *SWB,* 8 June 1990.

115. *Le Monde,* 17 April 1991; Peter Hiett, "Algeria: Pre-Election Jostling," *Middle East International,* 19 April 1991.

116. See n. 106 above.

117. For example, *Le Monde,* 14 and 30 May 1991.

118. The last senior army officers to have been drawn from the guerrilla forces of the interior were Major General Abdallah Belhouchet and General Mohamed Attaïlia; both men lost their positions in the wake of the 1988 riots.

119. A striking measure of the extent to which the Chadli regime had lost control of this source of legitimacy was the foundation in 1985 of the Association des Enfants des Chouhada (Association of the Children of the Martyrs, i.e., of those who gave their lives during the war of national liberation); this group was founded as a private initiative, in breach of the FLN's monopoly of public life, and its members immediately and most publicly contested the right of state representatives to officiate at commemorative ceremonies at war memorials.

120. For a good account of the FLN-MNA rivalry, see Harbi, *Le FLN: Mirage et Réalité,* pp. 143–62.

121. Ibid., pp. 142, 279–81, 320; Alistair Horne, *A Savage War of Peace* (London: Macmillan, 1977), pp. 135, 397.

122. As expressed by Abassi in a televized debate on 15 June 1990, immediately after the FIS's electoral triumph, in a characteristic remark, at once reassuring and vague: "We will leave the word to the people. Whether we are in power or not, democracy means a diversity, choice and freedom. We have promised this, God willing, and we will keep our promise" (Reuters, 16 June 1990).

123. Cf. Abassi's statement, on 13 June 1990, in answer to the question whether the FIS would be willing to "co-habit" with the FLN; "we are not egoists. We feel no aggressiveness toward the FLN, since in those regions where we did not present lists [of candidates], we called on people to vote for the FLN's" (*Libération,* 14 June 1990)—another classic instance of Abassi's rhetoric, in which he *suggested* a willingness to make a deal with the FLN without actually stating this.

124. Cited in Naget Khadda and Monique Gadant, "Mots et gestes de la révolte," *Peuples Méditerranéens,* nos. 52–53 (July–December 1990): 20; see also Charef, *Dossier octobre,* pp. 105–7, for a refutation of the thesis that the riots were food riots.

125. Khadda and Gadant, "Mots et gestes de la révolte."

126. Reuters, 22 February 1989.

127. *Libération,* 14 June 1990; see also *L'Opinion* (Algerian daily), 15 June 1990.

128. The FLN newspaper *El Moudjahid* used the term in its edition of 14 June 1990; see also Benjamin Stora, "Les FIS: à la recherche d'une autre nation," *Les Cahiers de l'Orient* 23, no. 3 (1991): 83.

129. Reuters and *The Independent* reported on 11 June 1990 that the FLN was expected to win the elections; the call for a boycott issued by Ahmed Ben Bella and Hocine Aït Ahmed was premised on the assumption that the elections would be rigged in the FLN's favor. According to *Le Monde* of 17–18 June 1990, FLN leading circles were led to believe by reports from the *walis* (regional governors) that the FLN would win at least 55 percent of the vote.

130. BBC Television, "Newsnight," 14 June 1990.

131. This notion was a constant, if tacit,

theme of the articles of the French historian Benjamin Stora in particular; see, for example, Stora, "Les FIS," pp. 83–90.

132. *Le Monde,* 1 November 1988.

133. *Libération,* 11 September 1989.

134. Roberts, "The Algerian Constitution."

135. Jean-François Kahn, "Algérie: La deuxième révolution," *L'Événement du Jeudi,* 13–19 October 1988.

136. *Libération,* 12 September 1989.

137. Reuters, 28 November 1989.

138. Ibid., 1 December 1989.

139. *Daily Telegraph,* 30 November 1989.

140. Reuters, 1 December 1989.

141. "Reformists Carry On Regardless," *Middle East Economic Digest,* 15 December 1989.

142. Ibid.

143. See Ghazi Hidouci's well-publicized address to a conference of public-sector managers in Algiers on 6 February 1990, *Middle East Economic Digest,* 16 February 1990.

144. See "Responsables—où êtes-vous?" *Le Monde,* 5 November 1989; see also *Le Monde,* 16 June 1990; and "La fulgurante ascensions des islamistes," *Libération,* 14 June 1990.

145. See "Algérie: Des femmes dénoncent l'intolérance," *Libération,* 26 November 1989; the article carries a photograph of Algerian women demonstrating with banners asking "Pourquoi l'inaction de l'État?" This article details the authorities' indifference to repeated acts of Islamist violence and intimidation, especially against women, including the refusal of Prime Minister Mouloud Hamrouche to receive a delegation of women on the subject.

146. Ibid.; see also "La fulgurante ascension des islamistes."

147. *Le Monde,* 25 January 1990.

148. Ibid.

149. *Middle East Economic Digest,* 2 March 1990.

150. Reports of FIS takeovers of polling stations, and of the surprising absence of

FLN personnel, were carried in *Libération*, 14, 15, and 18 June 1990.

151. Reuters, 29 November 1989; *Middle East Economic Digest*, 15 December 1989.

152. Reuters, 29 November 1989; *Daily Telegraph*, 30 November 1989.

153. *Le Monde*, 23 January 1990.

154. *Middle East Economic Digest*, 2 February 1990.

155. *L'Express*, 7 and 9 February 1990.

156. Lahouari Addi, "Le choix des algériens," *Monde Diplomatique*, June 1990.

157. *Le Monde*, 16 March 1990.

158. In the form of *pots-de-vin*, payments to state officials on foreign contracts deliberately overpriced to allow for these payments. *El Massa*, 25 March 1990; *Le Monde*, 3 April 1990.

159. *Le Monde*, 15 June 1990.

160. *El Moudjahid*, 31 March, and 3, 6, and 10 May 1990; and *Algérie-Actualité*, 3–9 May 1990.

161. *Le Monde*, 19 September 1989.

162. *Libération*, 18 June 1990.

163. Yahiaoui was born 1932; teacher before war; fought in wilaya I, 1954–62; member of the Council of the Revolution, 1965–78; director of the Cherchell Combined Services Academy, 1969–77; coordinator of the Party of the FLN, 1977–80; member of the FLN Central Committee, 1979–83, and of the Political Bureau, 1979–81.

164. Bouteflika was born 1937; staff officer at Oujda headquarters of the army of the frontiers, 1956–62; minister of foreign affairs, 1963–78; member of FLN Central Committee, 1979–83, and of the Political Bureau, 1979–81.

165. Abdessalem was born 1928; founding member of UGEMA; served in Oujda headquarters, 1957–62; member of Provisional Executive, 1962; PDG Sonatrach, 1963– 65; minister of industry and energy, 1965–77; minister of light industry, 1977–78; member of FLN Central Committee, 1979–83 and of the Political Bureau, 1979–80.

166. Economist Intelligence Unit, *Quarterly Economic Review: Algeria*, no. 4 (1983): 6, and no. 1 (1984): 7–8.

167. Bitat was born 1925; one of the "nine historic chiefs" credited with founding the FLN in 1954; colonel commanding wilaya IV (Algérois), 1954–55; in French custody, 1955–62; minister of state for transport, 1965–77; president of the National Assembly, 1977–90.

168. Bentobbal was a member of the Group of 22, 1954; commander of wilaya II, 1956–57; minister of the interior in the GPRA, 1958–61; minister of state in GPRA, 1961–62; in retirement since independence. Zbiri was commander of wilaya I, 1960–62; chief of staff of the ANP (Armeé Nationale Populaire, i.e., the army after independence), 1963–67; leader of abortive coup against Boumediène, 1967; in exile, 1967–84. Boumaza was a member of leadership of FFFLN, 1956–62; in prison, 1958–61; minister of national economy, 1962–64; minister of industry and energy, 1964–65; minister of information, 1965–66; in opposition 1966–1979. These three men were signatories, together with fifteen other historic figures, of a declaration delivered to Chadli on 29 October 1988 calling for democracy and a national conference to elaborate the necessary program of political reforms—a declaration he rejected out of hand.

169. *El Moudjahid*, 4 December 1989.

170. Apart from Mehri and Hamrouche, it was above all Yahiaoui, Bouteflika, Abdessalem, Hadjerès, Kasdi, Zbiri, and Boumaza who between them constituted the public face of the FLN's appeal to the electorate. *El Moudjahid*, 27, 29, 30, 31 May, and 1–2, 3, 5, 6 June 1990.

171. The FLN held marches in the provinces on 20 April 1990 as planned, but canceled its march in Algiers at the last moment.

172. *El Moudjahid*, 18–19 May 1990.

173. Addi, "Le choix des algériens."

174. José Garçon, "Les hypothèques d'une victoire," *Libération*, 14 June 1990.

175. *Libération*, 18 June 1990.

176. The first clear statement of the

army's general political outlook on both domestic and international affairs, as modified in light of the United Nations' war against Iraq, was an editorial in *El Djeich* (The army [al-Jaysh]), the monthly magazine published by the Political Commissariat of the army, in April 1991; this statement included a strong reaffirmation of a modernist nationalist outlook and an emphatic hostility on both modernist and nationalist grounds to the Islamist movement and the prospect of an FIS government. It thus clearly distanced the army from Chadli's strategy.

177. That the FIS had democratic principle on its side in its objections to the electoral laws and its call for presidential elections cannot be seriously disputed, and orderly demonstrations and peaceful civil disobedience certainly have their place in the political life of modern democracies. To say this, however, is not to say that the FIS was a democratic movement.

178. Jacques de Barrin, "Algérie: Les secrets du DIS," *Le Monde,* 3 January 1992.

179. Kapil, "Les partis islamistes en Algérie," p. 108.

180. Hanbalism is one of the four rites or schools of law of Sunni Islam, and the one dominant in Saudi Arabia; virtually all Sunni Muslims in the Maghreb are Malikites by tradition.

181. Kapil, "Les partis islamistes en Algérie."

182. De Barrin, "Algérie: Les secrets du DIS."

183. Ibid.

184. Roberts, "A Trial of Strength," pp. 140–41.

185. For a discussion of these laws, see ibid., p. 145; and Le Monde, 3 April 1991.

186. De Barrin, "Algérie: Les secrets du DIS."

187. A number of reports appeared in the Algerian press in late April suggesting that moves to establish an Islamist alliance involving Hamas, the MNI, and the FIS were imminent; see *SWB* 27 April 1991.

188. Aïssa Khelladi, *Les islamistes algériens face au pouvoir* (Algiers: Editions Alfa, 1992), p. 178.

189. Ibid.; Kapil, "Les partis islamistes en Algérie," p. 106.

190. For Kasdi's position on the electoral laws and the question of early presidential elections, and the threat by eight parties including the MAJD to call a general strike, see *SWB,* 4 April 1991.

191. Abassi and Ben Hadj met Hamrouche and a senior security officer Colonel Smaïn to discuss this on 29 May, and Abassi and his close colleague Abdelkader Boukhamkam met Hamrouche and Smaïn again on 31 May; see the account of the trial of Abassi and his colleagues at Blida in July 1992 by K. Ben, "Procés des dirigeants de l'ex-FIS: la défense piégée par l'accusation," *L'hebdo Libéré* (Algiers), 15–21 July 1992.

192. That the orders came from the presidency and not the prime minister's office was admitted by the former interior minister Mohamed Salah Mohammedi in his testimony at the Blida trial; see Ben, "Procés des dirigeants de l'ex-FIS."

193. Kasdi had quit the FLN and founded the MAJD in October 1990; see *The Guardian,* 8 October 1990; and *Le Monde,* 9 October 1990.

194. My hypothesis that a coalition government of national union was Chadli's preferred scenario at this juncture is strongly supported by the fact that the FLN, still led by his close friend Abdlhamid Mehri, publicly pronounced itself in favor of this at an extraordinary meeting of its Central Committee in Algiers on 21 November 1991; see "Chronologies: 4e Trimestre 1991: Pays arabes: Algérie," *Maghreb-Machrek* 135 (January–March 1992): 109.

195. *SWB,* 8 June 1991.

196. Ibid., 12 June 1991.

197. Reuters, 10 June 1991; *SWB,* 12 June 1991; *Le Monde,* 18 June 1991.

198. *Le Monde,* 16–17 and 18 June 1991; these reports gave Guyon's name incorrectly as Guillaume.

199. Ibid., 16–17 June 1991.

200. Ibid., 2 July 1991.

201. *SWB,* 27 June 1991 (which gave Bachir Fqih's name incorrectly as Bachir Stef).

202. *Le Monde,* 28 June 1991.

203. Ibid.

204. Ibid., 30 June–1 July 1991; this statement of Abassi's was widely misreported as a full-blooded call for jihad.

205. Ibid., 2 July 1991.

206. According to *Libération,* 11 July 1991, 5,870 people had been arrested since 30 June. Other sources do not confirm this figure, but speak of several thousand arrests; these certainly included most of the key figures in the FIS at grass roots level.

207. Five leading Salafiyyists—El Hachemi Sahnouni, Benazzouz Zebda, Mohamed Kerrar, Saïd Makhloufi, and Kamreddine Kherbane—were suspended from the Majlis al-Shura, and Saïd Guechi, having thus been thoroughly marginalized, walked out of the conference; Ahmed Merrani and Bachir Fqih had already been expelled from the Majlis shortly after their television broadcast on 26 June (Kapil, "Les partis islamistes en Algérie," p. 107). Key posts were assumed by Algerianists, notably Rabah Kebir and Abderrazak Redjam.

208. For details on Hachani, see Kapil, "Les partis islamistes en Algérie," pp. 106–7, de Barrin, "Algérie: Les secrets du FIS"; George Joffé, "Hidden Strength on God's Party," *The Guardian,* 15 January 1992; and especially *Le Monde,* 24 January 1992.

209. "Chronologies," p. 108.

210. *Le Monde,* 16 January 1992.

211. "Chronologies," p. 109.

212. Ibid.

213. According to information received from sources in the Algerian Islamist movement.

214. De Barrin, "Algérie: les secrets du FIS."

215. According to Algerian Islamist sources.

216. Roberts, "A Trial of Strength," pp. 148–50.

217. See José Garçon, "Comment l'armée a monté son coup," *Libération,* 27 January 1992).

218. See the interview Belkheir gave to *Algérie-Actualité,* no. 1392 (18–24 June 1992.

219. Ibid.

220. *Journal Officiel,* 4 January 1992.

221. Figures for turnout in 1990 were published in *Horizons,* 17 June 1990; for 1991, in *Journal Officiel,* 4 January 1992.

222. Jacques Fontaine, "Les élections législatives algériennes: Résultats du premier tour," *Maghreb-Machrek* 135 (January–March 1992): 155–65, 158.

223. Ibid.

224. *Journal Officiel,* 4 January 1992.

225. Fontaine, "Les élections législatives algériennes," p. 158.

226. Figures for votes by party are taken from Kapil, "Portrait statistique des élections du 12 Juin 1990," p. 45, for the 1990 elections, and from *Journal Officiel,* 4 January 1992, for the 1991 elections.

227. Private informants in Algiers interviewed in November–December 1992 affirmed that an impressive number of female FIS supporters went to the polls on 26 December 1991 and that this appeared to have been well organized. It may well be that the FLN vote in the traditionalist countryside was far more adversely affected than the FIS vote in the urban districts by the new rules restricting proxy voting by male heads of households on behalf of their womenfolk.

228. Annaba is the major town nearest his birthplace (Boutheldja, thirty miles to the east) and has been associated politically with Chadli and his followers since 1980 if not earlier.

229. The really significant cases are Djelfa, M'Sila, and Tiaret. In each of these, the FLN did better than the FIS in 1990, but turnout in 1991 was down heavily, and the FIS took respectively five, nine, and four seats on the first ballot, with only M'Sila yielding a single first-ballot FLN seat. This was an extraordinary turnaround in party fortunes, when we bear in mind that these three wilayat are in the sparsely populated High Plateaux, far from the FIS's urban bastions, and the FIS's vote, falling overall, cannot have risen here in 1991 unless mass numbers of FLN voters defected to the FIS candidates.

230. Turnout falls greatly benefited the FIS in other wilayat as well: at Medea,

where the FLN was beaten but not disgraced in 1990, and should have received a share of the 1991 seats on the 1990 showing, turnout fell by 18.16 percent and nine of the wilaya's twelve seats went to the FIS on the first ballot, and none to the FLN. The same pattern is seen at Aïn Defla, Batna, Bouïra, Chlef, Mascara, Oum El Bouaghi, Setif, and Tlemcen; in each case the FIS did far better in 1991 than 1990, and turnout was down dramatically.

Another group of wilayat tell a different story, however. In Bechar, which was an FLN bastion in 1990, turnout fell by only 3.37 percent in 1991, but this was enough to deny the FLN a single first-ballot seat; in El Oued, where the FLN had been narrowly ahead of the FIS in 1990, a turnout fall of only 3.96 percent was enough to give the FIS three first-ballot seats to the FLN's one in 1991; in Ouargla, which the FLN carried with ease in 1990, a fall of 5.17 percent gave the FIS all four seats won on the first ballot in 1991; in Bordj Bou Arreridj, where the two parties had been dead level in 1990, a fall of 5.28 percent gave the FIS all four first-ballot seats; in Naama, where the FLN was narrowly ahead in 1990, a fall of 6.89 percent gave the FIS one seat on the first ballot to the FLN's none; and in Biskra, where the FLN had also been ahead in 1990, a fall of 8.76 percent delivered all four seats decided on the first ballot to the FIS. In all of these cases, the fall in participation was modest compared with places

such as Medea or Souk Ahras or Tebessa, and cannot alone explain the changes in party fortune which occurred. The hypothesis that accounts for these results is that it was in these wilayat that large-scale defections of voters from the FLN to the FIS occurred.

231. Abdesselam was one of the members of the Central Committee who found they had been dropped from the FLN's list of candidates on the orders of Mouloud Hamrouche in the summer of 1991, when the legislative elections were originally scheduled to be held on 27 June; *Middle East Economic Digest*, 24 May 1991.

232. Other prominent figures dropped on Hamrouche's orders from the FLN list in May 1991 included Bouteflika, Yahiaoui, and Abderrazak Bouhara; ibid.

233. That the French government in particular had been giving Chadli full and vigorous support throughout his struggle with his critics was openly admitted, for example, in *Le Monde*, 15 June 1990.

234. That Algerians have been kept in ignorance of the political history of their own country is a theme Algerian commentators have been touching on with increasing frequency since 1988; see, for example, Fatiha Akeb, "Un destin à part," *Algérie-Actualité*, no. 1245 (24–30 August 1989), and especially the interview with Commandant Azzedine in *El Watan* (The nation), 28 January 1992.

Izala: The Rise of Muslim Reformism in Northern Nigeria

Ousmane Kane

Founded in Nigeria in 1978, the Izala movement has become the most important and largest reformist movement in West Africa. Its adherents tend to refer not to the local religious order but to the Qur'an and the Traditions of the Prophet Muhammad (Sunna) as the only legitimate source for the conduct of religious and, to some extent, social life.[1] Beyond their emphasis on *sola scriptura* (the primacy of the scriptures over doctrines), adherents of the Izala movement accord great importance to social morality.

Izala today is a divided movement. For different motivations and to varied degrees, many social groups identify with its teachings or associate with its reform project, making it difficult to trace an evolutionary curve that could explain the external behavior of all who have been touched by its teachings. Nevertheless, I advance the hypothesis that a good part of Izala's leadership has recently moved from a rather aggressive posture toward nonmembers to one of accommodation. Clashes between Izala preachers and Sufi Muslims during the late 1970s and early 1980s had often led to loss of life. This has led some members of the movement to distance themselves from it in order to constitute a more radical tendency, which could be called neo-Izala.

In order to understand this complex movement, we must situate it within the political, economic, and social evolution of Nigeria. In this chapter I present the social and cultural milieu of northern Nigeria and the context which favored the birth of Izala, its expansion, the moderation of a part of its leadership, and, finally, its fragmentation. Against the background of the evolution of Izala, I suggest how one can account for the behavior of these Nigerian fundamentalists toward the outside world.

By far the most populous country in Africa, Nigeria, with its 88.5 million inhabitants in 1992,[2] shelters close to a quarter of the population of the black continent. This population, composed of 350 ethnolinguistic groups,[3] is heterogeneous from all points of view. However, three important groups stand out from this mosaic: the Hausa-Fulani (based essentially in the northern part of the country, covering a large part of Hausaland), the Yoruba in western Nigeria, and the Igbo in the eastern part.[4] The center of the country (Middle Belt) shelters many ethnic groups. The confessional distribution of these groups is shared between Christianity, Islam, and traditional African religions.

To a certain extent this ethnolinguistic diversity assumes the pattern of the various religious divides in Nigeria. Hausaland is largely Muslim; Igboland is essentially Christian. Yorubaland, with its even distribution of Christians and Muslims, is dominated by Christianity and Islam and at the same time very much influenced by its traditional culture.[5] In Yorubaland more than anywhere else in Nigeria, native African tradition seems a fundamental base for religious expression.[6]

Nothing is more controversial in Nigeria than the geographical and religious distribution of its population. The last official head count mentioning the religious distribution of the population was conducted in 1963; demography used to be a criterion taken into account in the distribution of national wealth. According to the 1963 census, Muslims represented 47.2 percent of the population, Christians 34 percent, and followers of traditional religions 18.2 percent.[7] In contrast to Christianity and Islam, the traditional religions have been in constant decline and the number of their adherents has dropped since the 1963 census.

Based largely in the north and to a lesser extent in the southwest of the country, Nigerian Muslims have been influenced by the concepts and practices of the Sufi brotherhoods since the jihad of the nineteenth century. Although these brotherhoods draw their inspiration from Sufism, they also preserve some indigenous African religious practices. One of the most important objectives of the Izala movement has been to eliminate these local religious practices.

The various West African reform movements of the eighteenth and nineteenth centuries were led by men solidly anchored in the tradition of Sufi Islam and they exemplified orthodoxy par excellence. Other anti-Sufi reformist movements born in the Muslim world in the eighteenth and nineteenth centuries made little impact in Africa in general and in Nigeria in particular,[8] partly because the British colonizers, like the French, strove to isolate black Africa from the Arab world. The politics of isolation was particularly motivated, in the case of Nigeria, by the painful recollection of the Mahdist revolt in Sudan, a country not far from northern Nigeria, and by the rise of Arab nationalism in the Arab world in the early twentieth century. Until the beginning of the 1950s, Nigerians could not attend Arab universities because those universities were considered bastions of revolutionary ideas. A confidential report by an academic and former education officer, Mervyn Hiskett, on his return from Sudan, reveals the distrust of the Nigerian colonial administration of that time, which led to the isolation of northern Nigeria from the Arab world.

> This interview with the minister was one of the many indications which go to show that the new Sudanese Government has identified itself with the Egyptian-inspired crusade against colonialism. That the Egyptians see them-

selves at the head of such a crusade there is no doubt. In my opinion this is now likely to make a strong appeal to many young Sudanese of the "Effendiyya" class. It is this that is to be most feared in relation to any students of ours who may come to their orbit. This is a very heady wine for Muslim adolescents and is the more dangerous because it is closely associated with a militant "pan-Islamism." Not only might students themselves be indoctrinated. On their return to Nigeria they might well, by contacts made in Sudan, act as channels for the entry of "anti-imperialist" propaganda into this country. . . . Al-Azhar remains much the same as it has always been—medieval! From an academic point of view there would be no great harm done by sending students there. Politically it would be most unwise.[9]

Only through reinforced contacts with the Arab world, thanks notably to the zeal of the late Shaykh Abubakar Gumi, who was the inspiration of the Nigerian reformist movement, were Nigerian Muslims sensitized to the teachings of Muslim reformers of the twentieth century. Son of a *qadi* (Islamic judge), he was born in 1922 at Gumi, in Sokoto state.[10] After attending Sokoto primary and middle schools and Kano Law School (which later became the School for Arabic Studies), he went to Bukht al-Ridha Institute in Sudan, where he obtained the Higher Diploma in Arabic Studies—a qualification by no means inconsequential in northern Nigeria at the time. During his stay in Sudan, Gumi went on a pilgrimage to Mecca and reestablished contact with Ahmadu Bello, the former prime minister of Nigeria, whom he had met in Sokoto when they were young men.

On his return from Sudan, Gumi was sent to Saudi Arabia by the federal government of Nigeria as a pilgrim officer. During that assignment he made solid contacts with the political and religious authorities of Saudi Arabia. With the economic assistance he procured from Saudi religious authorities, the indefatigable Gumi, inspired by the teachings of neo-Hanbalis—notably the religious doctrines of Muhammad Ibn 'Abd al-Wahhab—began to preach religious and social reformation.[11] Appointed grand qadi (supreme judge) of northern Nigeria in 1962 and based in Kaduna, the capital of the former northern region of Nigeria, Gumi commenced his reformist actions by criticizing different aspects of the Sufi brotherhoods during the course of the Qur'anic exegesis he led at the Sultan Bello Mosque.

Gumi also was Ahmadu Bello's religious adviser. Bello had undertaken to unify northern Nigeria and made Islam the central element of his unification policy, a policy also aimed at ensuring a northern hegemony in the Nigeria federation. Bello consolidated contacts with Muslim countries, especially Saudi Arabia and Kuwait. In reaction to the rise of Nasserism, which questioned the legitimacy of the Saudi dynasty, King Faysal Ibn 'Abdul 'Aziz advocated a pan-Islamic policy aimed at curtailing Nasserism and spreading Saudi influence in the Muslim world.[12] Nigeria, with the largest Muslim population in Africa, was certainly too important to be ignored. The Saudis eventually named Bello vice-president of the Muslim World League (Rabitat al-'Alam al-Islami).

In his unification drive in Nigeria, Bello created the religious movement Jama'at

Nasr al-Islam or JNI (Society for the Victory of Islam). With Saudi and Kuwaiti financing, JNI engaged in an active conversion campaign in the north as well as the south.[13] Moreover, given the importance of the Sufi presence in Nigeria, Ahmadu Bello undertook creation of a religious community called Usmaniyya, from the name of his ancestor Usman Dan Fodio; the community would be based on common heritage and transcend the Sufi brotherhood rifts, which had been a source of profound division and hostility in the political and social life of northern Nigeria. He entrusted Gumi with elaborating the doctrinal foundations for this community, so Gumi was duty-bound not only to soften his antibrotherhood stance, but to work out a *wird* (a collection of litanies) that in many respects was identical to those of the Sufi brotherhoods.[14]

In 1966 a bloody military coup brought down the First Republic, which had been dominated by the north. Many northern leaders were assassinated, including the prime minister, Abubakar Tafawa Balewa, and Ahmadu Bello himself. The coup was intended to rid Nigeria of regionalism and tribalism, but the majority of those who took part were Igbo, and they were saved by the coup leaders. The coup d'état challenged the hegemony of the north and was a traumatic event for the northerners. The Igbo who took power, General Ironsi, obliged to appoint a Hausa Muslim to head the northern administration in order to maintain peace in the region, appointed Major Hassan Usman Katsina, a Hausa-Fulani northerner, as the miltary governor of the north. But all those appointed to important posts immediately after the coup were seen, wrongly or rightly, as accomplices. Conscious of this fact, Katsina strove to win the support of those who had been close to Ahmadu Bello, in order to clear himself from suspicion and complicity. Thus Abubakar Gumi enjoyed the favors of the governor, who allowed him access to the media—written and audio—which aided his proselytization. Moreover, the political constraints on Gumi were relaxed after Bello's death, and he resumed his attacks against the traditional Islam defended by the Sufi brotherhoods.

In 1971, Gumi published an antibrotherhood work in which he zealously set out to show the "heterodoxous nature" of the two most popular brotherhoods (the Tijaniyya and Qadiriyya),[15] triggering an unprecedented polemic between Gumi and the leaders of the brotherhoods. Immediately after the book's publication, two of the most important leaders of the brotherhoods, Nasiru Kabara, leader of the Qadiriyya movement in West Africa, and Sani Kafanga, an important Tijaniyya figure, counterattacked with a pamphlet in which they explained that Sufism is in line with Islamic teachings and demonstrated the opportunism of Gumi.[16] This period marked the beginning of the reshaping of the northern Nigerian religious landscape around two poles: the first represented by traditional Islam and the second by a reformist and fundamentalist Islam which Gumi and the JNI promoted and which culminated in the formation of the Izala movement.

At the beginning of the 1970s, Gumi's preachings were transmitted by television and published in the Hausa weekly *Gaskiya Tafi Kwabo*.[17] Most of his clientele were preachers he had trained in the JNI and members of the educated urban strata. However, the sociocultural context of Nigeria was changing. Decline of the agricultural economy and transition toward an industrial economy encouraged migration from rural to urban areas in Nigeria in the 1970s. The expansion of the urban centers and the increase in literacy which resulted created a trend toward individualism in which people hoped to extricate themselves from the tutelage of the religious and moral authorities. The simplification of religious ritual increased as well. As we shall see, the success of the Izala movement has been due to its capacity to legitimize these aspirations in religious terms.

Urbanization and the Expansion of Reformism

During the military era, the former geopolitical configuration was dismantled and in its place was created a federal structure of nine, twelve, later nineteen, twenty-one, and quite recently thirty states. This structure weakened the power of the regions to the advantage of the federal government. Petroleum revenues also served to strengthen the central government.

Throughout its history, Nigeria had had an essentially agrarian economy. However, during the first military rule (1966–79), when the price of a barrel of crude oil rose dramatically from US $2 to US $40, federal government revenues multiplied almost tenfold as a result. According to the Aboyade Revenue Allocation Commission, federally derived revenues rose from 785 million naira in 1970–71 to 6.107 billion naira in 1976–77.[18] In 1975, black gold constituted 45 percent of the gross national product, 93 percent of Nigeria's export receipts, and 87 percent of federal government revenues.

The agricultural sector did not benefit sufficiently from the resources petroleum incomes placed at the disposal of the Nigerian economy. Even though agricultural production grew in certain years, this growth was annulled by the combined effects of inflation (100 percent) and demographic growth (2.5–3.1 percent). Generally, in percentage and in absolute terms, the agricultural sector experienced a decline of the aggregate gross domestic product. In 1958–59, on the eve of independence, agriculture represented 65.9 percent of the gross national product, but it fell to 41.8 percent in 1970–71, then to 18 percent in 1980. In 1964, revenue from the agricultural sector's exports was 304 million naira, or 70.8 percent of the country's export. In 1970, on the eve of the first oil shock, the agricultural sector represented 286.8 million naira in export revenue, or 32.8 percent of the total. With export earnings of 449.5 million in 1979, agriculture represented only 4.6 percent of the country's export revenue.

In addition to the economic distortions created by petroleum revenues, the Sahelian drought of 1968–73 hit the Nigerian agro-pastoral universe very hard. In 1973, the most difficult year of the drought, the fall in agricultural production was estimated between 25 percent and 40 percent. More than 300,000 cattle died, and thousands were equally slaughtered prematurely.[19] Added to all these misfortunes of the Nigerian peasants were price distortions and the revenue gap between urban and rural dwellers, which resulted from the diffusion of oil revenue as well as discriminatory investment favoring urban over rural towns. Rural-urban discrimination was especially pronounced during the first military era (1966–79), when public and private investments were concentrated only in the urban centers. In the ensuing transition from an agricultural to a petroleum economy, there was massive migration from the countryside to urban centers. Agriculture, which employed 80 percent of the active population two decades ago, engages only 54 percent today. Observers believe that the decline in rural population is even more pronounced than official statistics suggest, but absent viable statistics, that hypothesis cannot be confirmed. Still, Nigeria offers an example of one of the most rapid diminutions of an agricultural population experienced by a country of the south.[20]

Nevertheless, without the assistance of Saudi Arabia and other Arab countries, growth of a reformist movement would have been impossible. In spite of the retreat of Nasserism after the Arab defeat of 1967, pan-Islamism remained a constant of the Saudi cultural policy toward the Muslim world, including black Africa. Saudi Arabia worked to thwart Israel, which had begun to strengthen its relations on the Africa continent. Nigeria, whose demographics and relative economic prosperity made it a hub of West Africa, became a more important player in international relations, especially in the Muslim world, in the wake of the oil boom. Saudi Arabia's pan-Islamic cultural policy was also strengthened in Nigeria after the overthrow of the Pahlavi dynasty in Iran. The Islamic Republic of Iran, which did not forgive the petro-monarchies for siding with Iraq during the Iran–Iraq War, launched a massive propaganda campaign against Saudi Arabia. The Saudis engaged in counterpropaganda and financed their local allies, notably Abubakar Gumi and the JNI. However, in contrast to the 1960s, when Saudi cultural assistance was limited, the increased price of oil gave the Saudis greater means than before. During the period following the oil boom, Saudi grants to Third World countries reached 6 percent of its gross national product.[21] Ninety-six percent of Saudi Arabian aid to Africa went to Muslim countries.[22]

Because the Saudi aid was given by official organs, nongovernmental organizations, and individuals alike, a precise breakdown of sources is difficult. However, the aid contributed enormously to the development of Islamic education and thereby prepared the ground for the expansion of reformist Islam in northern Nigeria. Arabic and Islamic education enjoyed the support of several governmental and nongovernmental Saudi Islamic societies, notably the Muslim World League, the Dar al-Ifta (the organization charged with issuing fatwas), the World Assembly of Muslim Youth, and the International Federation of Arab and Islamic Schools. Through these intermediaries, subventions were accorded not only to associations, schools, and Muslim religious leaders all over West Africa, but also to those in Europe, Asia, and America. These associations awarded scholarships to Africans to pursue their studies in Saudi Arabia, and by the beginning of the 1980s, two thousand Africans were studying there.[23] The Saudis also distributed thousands of Qur'ans and Wahhabi theological books in northern Nigeria. From these texts the reformists derived the principal elements of their preaching corpus. Due notably to the JNI, which managed a substantial part of the Saudi aid, schools were built even in the remote corners of Nigeria.

But in contrast with other schools, the JNI ones were run by reformist missionaries dedicated to the task of training new missionaries. And, as the urban centers expanded, so did modern education in northern Nigeria, which was determined to catch up with the south. (In 1972 there were only 4,225 primary schools in the north compared to 10,313 in the south; there were 854,000 primary-school pupils in the north compared to 3,536,731 in the south.) In 1976 the Universal Free Primary Education program was launched.[24]

Institutions were established for modernizing Islamic education and integrating pupils from traditional Qur'anic schools into the modern school system. Thus after 1970, modern education in one form or another was available to all northerners, regardless of social background. In this context, there emerged a new class of intellectuals who were neither truly modern nor traditionally Qur'anic. From this group Gumi's team of activists was recruited. On the strength of their officially recognized religious knowledge, these new actors nurtured legitimate ambitions if not of leadership, then at least of social mobility. However, first they encountered a religious terrain dominated by the Sufi brotherhoods, where accession to leadership was restricted to the descendants of the leaders of those movements. And their substandard secular education ensured that their opportunities for social mobility were unequal to those of their counterparts who had pursued normal courses in state or public schools. These limited opportunities in the secular sphere reinforced their new Islamic vocation.

The history of the person known as U. M. I. (Usman Muhammad Imam), vice-president of the Committee of Ulama of the Izala movement, illustrates this situation. He was born in 1948 in a village in Kano state and as a young man studied the Qur'an and religious sciences, as well as grammar, jurisprudence, and Islamic knowledge and poetry. In his youth, he studied during the dry season and worked on the farm during the rainy season. When his father died in 1969, U. M. I. went to stay with his brother in Jos. There he was admitted to a JNI school and groomed by Shaykh Muslim Khan of the Muslim World League, who transformed the young U. M. I. into an Islamic reformer. Later U. M. I. passed the Junior Secondary Examinations and went to Gombe Teachers College in Bauchi state, where he studied from 1970 to 1979. He obtained the Higher Islamic Studies Certificate and, between 1980 and 1985, studied at Bayero University in Kano. On completion, he was admitted to the University of Maiduguri in the Arabic, Islamic studies and Hausa section, where he obtained a diploma before returning to Jos. "Each time I listened to Shaykh Gumi attack the brotherhoods," he confided to me, "I asked Shaykh Muslim Khan if the criticisms were well founded and he responded in the affirmative. I started to study the books *Fath al-Majid* and *Kitab al-Tawhid*[25] from Shaykh Muslim Khan. Moreover, Shaykh Ismail gave religious talks where he too denounced the heterodoxy of the brotherhoods. I introduced myself to him and followed his courses in Arabic and theology [*tawhid*]. Then in 1978 I became a member of the constituent committee of the Izala movement. In 1979, Shaykh Ismail Idris constructed a school called Islamiyya Primary School and made me the head."[26]

U. M. I.'s biography illustrates the sociology of the leadership of the Izala movement. During the 1970s, the reformist schools resocialized many urban migrants. A large number of these migrants were responding to rural decline or to the quest for formal education, which was prestigious and accessible at the time to all social strata. Availability of formal education led in turn to the creation of a class of would-be intellectuals, who in the quest for social recognition came up against the preeminence of the Sufi brotherhoods. In the end, most of the reformist leaders did not preach in their native cities, perhaps in part because of the geographical mobility of the period, and perhaps it was far easier for these migrants to attack taboos in social spaces other than their own.

The changes in religious affiliations linked to the population's passage from rural to urban life in northern Nigeria recall the emergence of fundamentalist-like movements elsewhere. What Pablo Deiros wrote of the new class of evangelicals in Latin America in the 1960s and 1970s could be said in essence of the new reformers in Nigeria:

> Migration changed the balance of Latin America's population in these years from rural to urban: from 1950 to 1980, the share of the population living in urban areas doubled from 30 percent to approximately 60 percent. Religious patterns were dramatically affected by industrialization and the corresponding migration to the cities. . . . The weakening of traditional social controls, the sense of confusion and helplessness in the anonymity of city life, the shock of new social values sometimes accompanying the adaptation to industrial work, the absence of familiar community loyalties and of the encompassing paternalism still characteristic of rural employment: all these conditions favored the growth of an acute crisis of personal identity for the migrants. Under such conditions, the exchange of old religious values for new ones was, and remains, likely to occur. Evangelical proselytism has taken advantage of these circumstances.[27]

Passage to an Organized Movement

According to the founders, the impetus to create the Izala movement was the attempt on the life of Shaykh Gumi in 1978 by the adherents of the religious brotherhoods in Kaduna. The persecution of Ismail Idris, imprisoned for his attacks on the religious brotherhoods, also inspired the move toward organization. According to Abbas Isa, "All of us who responded to the call of Shaykh Gumi and of Shaykh Idriss have taken the decision to form a movement which will continue their work if they happen to be assassinated."[28]

Izala—Jama'at al-Izalat al-Bid'a wa Iqamat al-Sunna (Society for the Removal of Heresy and Reinstatement of Tradition)—was launched in May 1978 on the initiative of Ismail Idris and with the blessing of Shaykh Gumi. The movement's mission is to eradicate "innovative practices"—especially practices it believes are supported by the religious brotherhoods, notably the Tijaniyya and Qadiriyya[29]—and to restore the Sunna of the Prophet.

Izala was originally composed of different committees, the more important of which were the Committee of Ulama, charged with the responsibility of proselytization and headed at the national level by Ismail Idriss; the Committee of Elders, providing financial support and made up of businessmen/politicians headed at the national level by Musa Mai Gandu; and the First Aid Group, established to maintain the organization of preaching.

Religion is a powerful instrument of mobilization in northern Nigeria, and it is no surprise that ambitious politicians and local notables supported the creation of the Izala movement. While one cannot reduce the motive for this support to manipulation alone—religious conviction is also an important element of their engagement—support for a religious movement offers politicians political rewards. This is all the more so given that religious leaders mediate between politicians and civil society. Moreover, with the 1979 pledge by the Nigerian military to hand over power, and with the heightened inter- and intraparty competition, an intensification of contacts between politicians, local notables, and religious leaders has occurred.

The president of the National Committee of Elders was the prominent businessman and politician Alhaji Musa Mai Gandu, district head of Bukuru. He was an active member of the Northern People's Congress during the First Republic and of the National Party of Nigeria during the Second Republic.[30] Of Kano origin, the vice-president of the National Committee of Elders, Habibu Gado Da Masu, is also a prominent businessman and politician. During preparations for handing over power from the military to civilians in 1978, the ulama were divided between the different factions of the rival parties, the National Party of Nigeria and the People's Redemption Party. Habibu Gado Da Masu, who could not make any political headway in his native Kano, distanced himself from the Tijaniyya of which he was a member and supported the creation of the Izala.

Beyond searching for a clientele, these men joined the Izala movement to build an Islamic identity for themselves more in line with the requirements of economic and social life. For some, the movement provided access to the national and international networks of Shaykh Abubakar Gumi, the spiritual leader of the Izala movement, who was known to be in a position to introduce or recommend Nigerian middlemen to Saudi commercial partners and decisionmakers. For example, Alhaji Ahmadu Chanchange was one of the major financial backers of the Izala movement. He enriched himself by transporting beer, an illicit economic activity. When, as a result of his business dealings, he was refused the hand of a woman he had wanted to marry, he consulted Gumi, who introduced him to Theophilus Danjuma, the former chief of staff of the Nigerian army. Through Danjuma's intervention, Chanchange secured a contract to transport petrol for the Nigerian National Petroleum Corporation. This singular act transformed his business into an Islamically licit enterprise and thus cast his enormous wealth accumulated from beer transport into a better light. An interesting contact (and contract) indeed!

As for the Committee of Ulama, struggle for control of the Nigerian religious scene seems to have been a major factor in its attempt to reform Islam. However, the success of Izala preachers in mobilizing much support depended on factors other than their capacity to mobilize specific interests. Analysis of the ideas propagated by the Izala movement leaves no doubt that it legitimizes individual aspirations, individual emancipation from the control of religious authorities and elders, and a minimal emancipation of women. In short, it represents a form of modernity which responds to the aspirations of certain urban social groups.

The Preaching Corpus of the Izala Movement

In denouncing traditional Islam and legitimizing the aspirations of some urban strata, the preachers of the Izala movement draw from the stock of symbols in the Qur'an and the hadith.[31] Thus the Qur'an and the Traditions of the Prophet Muhammad are used to denounce the traditional Islamic order.[32] According to the *Tsarin ka'idojin*, "All activities of this organization respond to divine injunctions."[33] Izala focuses on preaching because Allah says in the Qur'an, "Let there arise out of you a community inviting to what is good, enjoining what is right and forbidding what is wrong. They are the ones to attain felicity" (3:104). It is their duty, Izala members claim, to sanction good and prohibit evil in carrying out God's assigned mission.

The worst sin, according to them, is that of associationism *(shirk)* because, according to the Qur'an, "Allah will not forgive associating with other than Him; but He will forgive the lesser sins to whomsoever He pleases" (4:48). One of the important traits of the Sufi brotherhoods is their capacity to adapt, an ability that helps explain their spread in sub-Saharan Africa. Following the logic of adaptation, the brotherhoods have integrated such practices as carrying charms, use of holy water, divination, excessive veneration of the founders of Sufi brotherhoods, and so on. All these practices are seen by the reformers as associationism.

The *Kitab al-Tawhid* (The Book of Oneness) of Muhammad Ibn 'Abd al-Wahhab constitutes the foundation of the preaching corpus of Izala. On the construction of mausolea, a current practice linked to an ancient worship of saints, it emphasizes: "Do not build graves within your homes; do not make any grave a place for celebration. Your prayers will reach me wherever you make them."[34] In the same vein, the *Kitab* cites an hadith transmitted by al-Tabari (d. 923) in which the Prophet is quoted as saying, "No man may seek my help, only the help of Allah is worth being sought."[35] The wearing of a talisman, which is widespread even today among the adherents of the brotherhoods and other followers of traditional Islam, is condemned by the *Kitab*: "Whosoever carries a talisman has committed a sin of associationism. Theurgy, talismans, and bewitchment are all instances of *shirk*."[36]

The manipulation of these concepts inspired by the theological work of Muhammad Ibn 'Abd al-Wahhab (1703–87) allows the preachers of Izala to show that all those who practice traditional Islam, whether or not they are followers of the Sufi brotherhoods, are associationists. Only the Ahl al-Sunna, the People of the Sunna, as they prefer to be called, are the true Muslims. Often they repeat that the numerical superiority of *ahl al-shirk* (associationists), as they degradingly call other Muslims, does not signify that they are on the right path. For the Prophet has said, "At the end of time, the Muslim community will be divided into seventy-three sects. Seventy-two of them are destined for the fires of Hell. Only the members of one sect will be saved, that of Ahl al-Sunna."

The concept of tawhid, which emphasizes the oneness of God, is a key concept of the Izala doctrine. Tawhid historically includes the notion that there is no other deity but God, that God is unique in himself, that only God has an absolute existence (thus the existence of other beings is relative). Tawhid can also have a pantheistic meaning, that is, God is the sum of that existence.[37] The preachers of Izala restrict its meaning; for them, tawhid consists of having faith, which is the first Pillar of Islam, and, above all, conforming to the creed. This implies that certain religious and social practices which, according to them, contradict the creed of tawhid must be abandoned.

A second key concept is that of *bid'a* (a condemnable innovation). Preachers often cite the hadith which quotes the Prophet Muhammad: "Every new thing is an innovation, every innovation is akin to going astray, and every going astray will lead its maker to Hell." The charge of innovation is directed against the brotherhoods because the preachers of Izala claim that the Sufi concepts and practices appeared after the death of the Prophet. They constitute innovations because God has said, "This day have I perfected your religion for you, completed my favor upon you, and have chosen Islam as your religion" (Qur'an 5:3). All that came after the Prophet Muhammad, they emphasize, is therefore an innovation. Nevertheless, their call for a return to the source does not imply a rejection of modernity. Rather, like the Algerian reformists, they try to find a middle path between Islam and modernity.[38] For example, I have observed that some Izala preachers, as distinct from the fundamentalists of the Arab countries, have accounts in non-Islamic banks and even savings accounts that generate interest, which seems contrary to the teachings of classical Islam.

The democratization of religion is also on the Izala agenda. For example, they reject the use to which the brotherhoods put the notion of *wali*, which means closeness to God and piety. In Sufi eschatology, at least in Africa, only the Sufi shaykhs tend to be considered walis. It is also believed that by the virtue of their being walis, they are capable of accomplishing miracles (*karamat*). The preachers of Izala have redefined and enlarged the notion of wali to mean quite simply a pious Muslim. The term does not confer any capacity to accomplish wonders,[39] nor does it signify sainthood in the restrictive sense of the Sufi brotherhoods. The preaching strives to deny religious bureaucracy its sources of subsistence by denouncing honoraria in exchange for prayers as another innovation. In fact, part of the revenues of the traditional religious authorities is derived from offerings or honoraria from their clientele. The latter contribute in cash or in kind in exchange for the formers' performances during naming ceremonies, marriages, and propitiatory or deprecatory prayers.

On the issue of women's education, the followers of the Izala movement have introduced a novelty. Against the Hausa tradition of secluding married women, the Izala movement has made women's education its battle cry. They argue that the seclusion of women is contrary to the teachings of the Qur'an: "Oh ye who believe protect yourselves and your families from fires which men and stones will be combustible!" (66:6). Without religious knowledge, they argue, one is destined to end in hell. Therefore women must also learn or study their religion.

Unlike the fundamentalist movements in the Arab world or the brotherhooods in Nigeria, the leaders of the Izala movement do not make political demands a priority. According to them, the "Prophet Muhammad did not attack the Meccans at the beginning of his apostolate. He was satisfied with calling on people to embrace Islam. He reacted only in self-defense after having been attacked." They emphasize that Usman Dan Fodio, who paradoxically is another of their models, "limited himself to preaching for a long time. He resorted to violence only for self-defense when he was attacked by the Habe who governed Hausaland before the jihad." However, Izala members argue that their *ultimate* goal is to transform Nigeria into an Islamic state, to be attained first by educating Muslims and second by occupying key state offices. This Izala position is explained by the fact that its preachers are generally supporters of conservative politicians and that a number of their sympathizers aspire above all to reform syncretic practices, introduce morality into social life, and eradicate certain traditional practices. Islam cannot become an effective political power in its own right, they believe, until these reforms are accomplished.

At the outset of the movement, however, the preachers of Izala won great sympathy and thus constituted a threat to the prestige and economic and symbolic power of the leaders of the brotherhoods, especially those of the Qadiriyya and the Tijaniyya. This threat forced these two otherwise bitter rivals to unite and confront a common enemy.[40] Other organizations were also created with the express aim of checking the expansion of the Izala movement. In Ilorin an organization named Jama'at al-Sufiyya Ilorin, created, with the support of the emir, by the leaders of the Tijaniyya and Qadiriyya brotherhoods, undertook to react against all attacks from the Izala movement. In Kaduna, two similar organizations were formed, Jama'at Ahl al-Sunna (Association of the Followers of Sunna) and Kungiyar Dakarun Dan Fodio.[41] These two coordinated their activities. In Kano, Fityan al-Islam (Young Muslim Congress of Nigeria) and Jundullahi (God's Soldiers) mounted a stiff resistance to the Izala followers. Skirmishes that claimed lives ensued between members of Izala and the adherents of the brotherhoods.[42]

Since the Izala movement aimed at cutting all links between its sympathizers and the traditional authorities, the latter were determined to halt its expansion. Those who converted to the movement were subjected to all sorts of pressure, but this did not effectively stop diffusion of the movement's ideas. Trying to adapt themselves to this new reality, the brotherhoods resolved to effect a doctrinal counter-reform and at the same time modernize Qur'anic and Islamic teaching. Finally, after an intense phase of diffusion, the Izala movement lost some steam at the beginning of the 1980s.

The Early 1980s: The Waning of the Izala Movement

If the 1970s were marked by intense diffusion of reformist ideas, the Iranian Islamic Revolution and the northern Nigerian Muslims' struggle for the inclusion of measures favorable to an Islamic judicial system in the constitution of the Second Republic conferred on the Nigerian religious question an unprecedented dimension. A number of educated Muslims who considered the struggle against "innovation" secondary demanded the establishment of an Islamic state. The leader of these Muslims, called Brothers or Shi'ites due to their support for the Iranian Islamic Revolution, was Ibrahim al-Zakzaki.

As this movement expanded, the young Islamic militants divided between pro-Iranian Islamists, who called for establishment of an Islamic state,[43] and pro-Saudi reformists, who made the struggle against "innovation" their priority. This new development affected Izala's capacity to recruit. When the ban on political activities was lifted and the army handed over power to civilians, Izala was weakened because its supporters as well as its leadership were split among the different political parties.

In 1980, a charismatic prophet, Maitatsine, recruited a large following from the mass of unemployed rural migrants residing in Kano. This group railed against all that represented luxury to them, declaring as non-Islamic the wearing of a watch, the riding in an automobile, and so forth. After receiving numerous complaints of attacks committed by these people, Abubakar Rimi, the governor of Kano state, ordered Maitatsine and his disciples out of the city. Maitatsine and his men reacted violently, plunging Kano into blood and fire for many days. At final count, thousands of people had died in the violence. At the end of the uprising, revenge was taken on those who challenged mainstream Islam, and many were lynched. Many Izala movement sympathizers undeservedly bore the brunt of this retaliation.

Other violent revolts in Kaduna, Yola, Gombe, and Bulunkutu which occurred between 1981 and 1985 led to strict control of religious preaching in general and the federal government's refusal to recognize the Izala movement during the regimes of Shehu Shagari (1979–83) and Buhari (1983–85). The movement, which at its peak numbered in the hundreds of thousands, waned but remained alive through its organizational momentum in urban centers.[44] After the overthrow of the Buhari regime by General Ibrahim Babangida, the movement was awarded formal status and recognition. Thus Izala had a green light to continue to proselytize, and its following increased considerably—so much so that by 1992 approximately two million Nigerian Muslims had come to identify with Izala religious teachings.

A New Lease on Life after 1985

After its official recognition by the minister of internal affairs in 1985, the Izala movement continued to expand. Its sponsors donated generously for construction of schools and large mosques, and for maintenance of the preacher corps. For religious gatherings, the preachers were and are able to mobilize thousands of men to listen to their message of "genuine Islam," which includes rejection of Sufism and certain elements of the Islamic traditions (such as kneeling to great elders) thought to inhibit individualism. Izala, despite its name and its professed goal, can thus be seen as a movement of *selective emancipation from tradition*—a movement, furthermore, which legitimizes the aspirations of urban dwellers.

The sponsors of Izala are high state functionaries and businessmen who have tried to close the gap between the organized movement and independent preachers in northern Nigeria. Notable among the state functionaries are such people as Abdul-kadir Ahmed, governor of the Central Bank of Nigeria, who comes from Bauchi, and Major General A. B. Mamman, the minister of internal affairs. As we shall see, the state used these functionaries to control the movement.[45]

After its official recognition, the movement based its headquarters in Jos and suc-ceeded in re-establishing the three central committees at the state and local govern-ment levels. It tried to absorb the independent preachers as well as their clientele by coordinating the organization of preaching. Each month, two national preachings were organized whereby representatives of the movement were dispatched all over the country. Each state and local government and section had a preacher. A section rep-resented a group of *majalis*—local mosques where followers of the movement would meet to pray, learn doctrine, and listen to the sermons of a preacher. Generally the majalis were independent of the organized Izala movement.

These public preachings and the sale of cassettes containing the sermons helped the Izala movement continue to spread throughout the north, in urban centers as well as small villages. Its influence in the south, however, including Yorubaland which has a large Muslim population, remained negligible. But the determination of the preach-ers of Izala broke the resistance of certain rural areas to the ideas of the movement, especially in the states of Bauchi, Katsina, and Kaduna as well as in certain un-Islamized rural areas. Still, its essential clientele was and is based in urban centers. In addition to the organized movement, whose hub is the Committee of Ulama, there are many independent preachers who support the religious ideology of Izala.

Like the Tablighis, in whose apostolic activities they sometimes participate, the independent preachers of the Izala movement organized their preaching from ward to ward, village to village, and also offered evening lessons at their mosques. They taught books of the Wahhabi creed such as *Kitab al-Tawhid,* the *Fath al-Majid,*[46] and the *Taysir al-Aziz al-Hamid.*[47] Also taught was the book of hadith, *Riyad al-Salihin* (Garden of the virtuous), as well as the Qur'anic commentary of Shaykh Abubakar Gumi.[48]

As of spring 1993, the Izala movement controls many primary and secondary schools which are managed by the Committee of Ulama of the cities in which they are located. There also exist a number of important schools and majalis constructed by rich sympathizers or independent preachers.

Beside scholarly textbooks imposed by the Federal Ministry of Education, basic texts on the doctrine of the movement are studied in the schools run by the Commit-tee of Ulama. The organized Izala movement runs a clinic, many hospitals, and first aid groups which help finance its activities. In its mosques every evening, preachers teach the art of Qur'anic recitation, tawhid, and the different orthodox books already mentioned. Due to northern Nigeria's intense fascination with Arabic, these classes attract many sympathizers. Beside the intense educational activity, the classes also offer free officiating at marriage and naming ceremonies. The Jos center also trains preachers. Some are trained specially to convert Christians, using the spurious Gospel according to Saint Barnabas and the highly polemical pamphlets of the South African preacher Ahmad Deedat. This new type of proselytization coincided with the rise of

Christian ecumenism, the success of charismatic movements, and the political propaganda of the Christian Association of Nigeria.

Christian Ecumenism's Influence on the Relationship between Muslims

The Pentecostal and charismatic movements founded in North America and Great Britain in the 1960s have had an enormous impact in Nigeria, especially since the beginning of the 1970s.[49] At the same time there has been an important trend toward Christian unity in the Christian population.

The Christian Association of Nigeria (CAN) works for both the unity of Christians in Nigeria and their political mobilization. Its major activists are from the far north and the Middle Belt. This organization has tried to mobilize Christians against Nigeria's membership in the Organization of the Islamic Conference and the Islamic Development Bank and against the inclusion of the Shariʿa in the constitution of the Third Republic. In a recently published book, CAN emphasized that Christians constitute more than 60 percent of the Nigerian population,[50] while political power is in the hands of northern Muslims, who manipulate religion for political ends.[51]

In 1987 a confrontation between Muslims and Christians occurred in Kafanchan, Kaduna state, which claimed many Muslim lives and resulted in the destruction of a mosque. In turn, more than one hundred churches in Zaria were destroyed. Using these events as an excuse, the Christian Association of Nigeria mounted a campaign of criticism against northern Muslims.[52]

In April 1990, a coup aimed at overthrowing the military government of General Babangida failed. This coup d'état, financed by a millionaire from the former Bendel state in southern Nigeria, was led by a Christian and undoubtedly had the sympathy of CAN. This failed attempt led to a modification of the relationship between the Izala and other Muslim movements, culminating in the renewal of alliances. The coup leaders described it as follows:

> We wish to emphasize that this not just another coup, but a well-conceived, planned, and executed revolution by the marginalised and oppressed and enslaved peoples of the Middle Belt and South, with a view of freeing ourselves and our children, yet unborn, from external slavery and colonisation by a clique of this country. . . . *Our history is replete with numerous and unaccounted instances of callous and insensitive, dominative and oppressive intrigues by those who think it is their birth right to dominate till eternity, the political and economic privileges of this great country to the exclusion of the people of the Middle Belt and the South.*
>
> Even though they contribute very little economically to the well-being of Nigerians, they have, over the years, sat and presided over, the supposedly national wealth the rights of the men of the Middle Belt and southern part of this country, while people from those parts of the country have been completely deprived from benefiting from the resources given to them by God.

In the light of the above, in the recognition of their formative aristocratic factor and the overall problem of the Nigerian state or states, a temporary decision to excise the following states, namely Sokoto, Borno, Katsina, Kano and Bauchi comes into effect immediately. . . . All citizens of the five states already mentioned are temporarily suspended from all public offices in the Middle Belt and Southern part of the country. . . . They are also required to move back to their various states within one week from today.[53]

This statement reflects the discontent of the Christian population vis-à-vis the "domination," real or presumed, of the north. It was rumored that the failed plotters had drawn up a list of northern personalities to be assassinated—a list that included Shaykh Abubakar Gumi and others. The specter of the 1966 coup d'état reappeared in 1990.

After the attempted coup, the former president of the Nigerian Federation, Shehu Shagari, along with Shehu Musa 'Yar Adua and other members of the northern establishment, met in Abuja in order to float an idea for the reconciliation of Muslims. Shortly after, Bashir Tofa, a businessman from Kano and the president of the Islamic Propagation Center; Muzammil Sani Hanga, a businessman and leader of an Islamic organization called Umma; Abdul Karim Dayyabu, president of the Committee of Elders of Izala in Kano; and Isyaku Rabi'u, a prominent businessman and an active member of the Tijaniyya, organized a reconciliation meeting between Nasiru Kabara, the leader of the Qadiriyya in West Africa, and Gumi.

Nasiru Kabara paid Gumi a historic visit in Kaduna with the blessing of preachers who had hitherto vehemently antagonized the Sufi brotherhoods. Although this reconciliation was not accepted by the radical members of Izala, others within the movement insisted that Kabara had agreed to conform to the Sunna, but that he could not openly declare it or he would risk death at the hands of his former disciples. Abubakar Gumi suggested that for the time being the reformists had accomplished their mission because the adherents of the religious brotherhoods were worn down, their silence being a form of consent.[54]

Certainly this was not the first time northern religious leaders had attempted to reconcile their differences. The history of that region is marked by the will to unite, a will dictated by economic and political imperatives. Many attempts at reconciliation between the leaders had been undertaken but had not stopped renewed antagonisms. However, this particular reconciliation seemed durable because the preachers of the Izala movement were able to win social recognition and become members of the religious establishment. They occupy some important posts in the Izala organization. Most of the Izala preachers I interviewed, including those extremely hostile to the brotherhoods, welcomed the reconciliation. Shaykh Abbas Abdul Hamid, the imam of the central mosque of Bayero University and the president of the Committee of Ulama of Kano, for example, had preoccupied himself over the past few years denouncing the brotherhoods; now he called on Muslims to unite.[55]

The financiers of Izala, who had taken effective control of the movement, knew that their interests had never been so threatened. The campaign against northern

Muslim "domination" is directed against Muslims irrespective of their religious persuasion. The elders sorely needed to close ranks in order to fashion new strategies to confront these new challenges. These new circumstances have redesigned the religious universe of the north. Of course the majority of the members of the Izala movement continue to pray in their own mosques, but antagonisms have been dramatically reduced. Furthermore, adherents of traditional Islam know that the Izala movement has become a durable component of Nigeria's social life, which has contributed to a reduction in the level of antagonism between the two groups. In short, the official recognition of the Izala movement and the waning of reciprocal antagonisms between its adherents and partisans of traditonal Islam set in motion a process of moderation within the Izala movement which led to a major split.

The Split within the Izala Movement

The co-option of the Izala movement by the authorities, as well as the moderation of some of its leaders, led to Izala's split. Co-opting Izala was part of the military government's strategy for controlling Nigeria's religious movements—a strategy based on the desire of the Nigerian military to promote national unity. The military believes it is imperative to guard against the mobilization of centrifugal forces which not only challenge national unity objectives but also threaten the military itself and therefore the survival of the regime. Religion has been and remains one of the strongest centrifugal forces in northern Nigeria.

After the riot of Kafanchan, northern Nigerian Muslims organized a demonstration in Kaduna in solidarity with the Muslim victims of the riot. According to some estimates, this demonstration brought together close to two million Muslims of all persuasions and convinced the military authorities that Islam could be a strong base for mobilization. From that moment, an effective policy for controlling religious movements was initiated. The government made use of the Minister of Internal Affairs, General A. B. Mamman, who had become a patron of the Izala movement, to control it. In exchange for the financial support and patronage of the minister, Ismail Idris, president of the National Committee of Ulama, undertook to transfer decision-making power from the Committee of Elders to the Committee of Ulama. The Minister of Internal Affairs, it seemed, pushed Ismail Idris and certain members of the Committee of Ulama to dismiss officials hostile to the government. In 1990, the composition of the movement's leadership was modified in many states; officials hostile to the military government were dismissed. The best example was dismissal of the Kano chairman of the movement. In June of the same year, Ismail Idris, in a statement at the Kano mosque which served as the movement's office, marked the beginning of the disintegration of Izala:

> It has come to my notice that here in Kano some young people are calling and parading themselves as the "youth wing of Izala." As far as I am concerned, we don't have any wings whatsoever in Izala. . . . This group of people are not

true members of Izala, rather, they are merely Shiʻites. Again, I note with dismay the circulation of publications, here in Kano, whose contents appear to be antigovernment. The authors of these publications claim that they have been sanctioned by Izala. But I want you to understand one thing: as far as the constitution of Izala is concerned, nobody has the right to issue any publication whatsoever without the approval of the National Committee of Ulama of Izala. Also, for your own information, this Committee of Ulama is the highest policy-making body or even the heart of Izala movement. In other words this committee does not receive any directive from anybody; rather, it issues commands and directives. These directives must be obeyed by every member willingly. Let me explain something to you. Izala is not a political party which could be capitalized on for the achievement of personal ambition or selfish interests. Izala is a purely religious organization whose main objective is to promote the cause of Islam by reinstating the pure tradition [of the Prophet]. Now let me issue a stern warning. From now on, we will not hesitate to dismiss any person who infringes the . . . regulations of the movement. In addition we will dissociate ourselves from any unauthorized publication, telling the world that it is not from Izala movement. In the end I would like to advise you to be more alert to the existence of this so-called Izala youth wing here in Kano, to avoid being deceived under the guise of Izala.[56]

After this declaration Abdul Karim Dayyabu, president of the Kano Council of Elders, who was known for his political activism and opposition to the military government of General Ibrahim Babangida and a main publisher of antigovernment tracts, was relieved of his office. Moreover, the National Committee of Ulama based in Jos adopted a pro-government line and dismissed members who continued to challenge the Nigerian government. These antigovernment activists were lumped together with the Shiʻites. In the northern Nigerian context, as we have seen, the term Shiʻite has no doctrinal connotation; it characterizes the radical movement which supports the Iranian Revolution.

A fight ensued between the two factions, one led by Ismail Idris and the other by the national chairman Musa Mai Gandu, who was also the national president of the Committee of Elders.[57] The faction led by Musa Mai Gandu, aware that it would be vulnerable to attack if it accused the ulama of taking a pro-government position, decided to question the sources of Ismail Idris's wealth, which they judged too great for a preacher. In June 1991 the Mai Gandu faction suspended Ismail Idriss and his deputy, U. M. I., alleging that they had embezzled funds. The faction also dissolved the committees of the movement and replaced them with a caretaker committee headed by Rabi'u Daura, former president of the Committee of Ulama of Kaduna state. In response Ismail Idris and his supporters dismissed the Mai Gandu faction from Izala and refused to hand over properties of the movement in their possession. In the summer of 1991 these two factions, each controlling part of the property of Izala (its schools, clinics, mosques, etc.), unleashed campaigns aimed at discrediting each other. The extremists among them had physical confrontations.

Conclusion

We can distinguish three phases in the evolution of reformist influence in northern Nigeria up until late 1991. The first phase coincided with the training of the first intellectuals in formal schools (as opposed to Qur'anic schools). During this period, the reformists transmitted their message through the Jama'at Nasr al-Islam. . The preachers formed within the movement served as channels of the new ideology. The urban, educated elites constituted a large number of the supporters of the reformist movement because it expressed some of their aspirations.

The second phase of the movement was triggered at the end of 1970 by a period of considerable geographical and professional mobility in Nigeria, and by development of the mass media, and telecommunications, the general availability of formal education, and the reinforcement of contacts with the larger Muslim world, especially Saudi Arabia. Because of these favorable conditions and the unrivaled zeal of Shaykh Abubakar Gumi and his group of preachers, reformist ideas had a profound impact on the youth of northern Nigeria. Although at the beginning of the 1980s the Izala movement stagnated somewhat, still the preachers of Izala succeeded in diffusing the ideas of the movement not only in the north of Nigeria but also in Niger, Cameroon, Chad, Togo, and Ghana. During this period the elders associated with the movement gave it considerable financial support; in exchange, the ulama not only accepted the tutelage of the elders but also gave them greater respectability. These elders influenced decision making in the movement. This second phase of the diffusion of the Izala movement, which had commenced with vehement opposition to traditional Islam, came to a close with a reciprocal acceptance and a considerable reduction of antagonisms between reformists and partisans of traditional Islam.

The more recent third phase corresponded with the drive by the federal military government to infiltrate the Izala movement as part of its national strategy of controlling all religious movements. In the course of this phase, the fight for effective control of the Izala leadership led to the emergence of two factions, one of which seems very close, if not subservient, to the Ministry of Internal Affairs.

The evolution of the Izala movement from radicalism to moderation can be compared in some respects with that of the Tijaniyya order. The latter had enjoyed considerable popular support, especially among Nigerian youth, partly because it incarnated opposition to the arbitrariness of the emirs and native authorities in the 1950s and 1960s. Later it was assimilated by the established order. Izala took over its protest functions for a time, but eventually lost this identity by becoming subservient to the authorities. As a result, the leadership of the movement split.

Although break up of the movement was provoked by quarrels among personalities, it was rendered possible by the fact that a large section of Izala's membership disapproved of the pro-government positions of Ismail Idris. This group I have labeled neo-Izala. Today this neo-Izala tendency, represented by those opposed to compromises with the government, is made up of not only independent preachers but also young people with a Western education and a more profound political consciousness. Engrossed in the religious doctrine of the movement, the neo-Izalas have an appreciation of national and international politics totally different from that of Ismail Idris and the majority of preachers who constitute the current Committee of Ulama.

During the Gulf War, the neo-Izala was clearly sympathetic to Saddam Hussein and sharply condemned the major powers, especially the United States. It equally condemns the current structural adjustment program imposed on Nigeria by its financial creditors as a condition for rescheduling the country's debt. Finally, the neo-Izala movement, made up primarily of educated people and some students, disapproves of the impending re-establishment of diplomatic relations with Israel.

By opting for radical demands in the face of the moderation of the religious leadership of the movement, the neo-Izala tendency immerses itself in the same waters as the movement called Brothers. The Brothers, reputed for their radicalism and their anti-Western animus, draw their legitimacy from the numerous prison terms of their leader, Ibrahim al-Zakzaki.

On the question of how to account for the fundamentalists' attitudes toward the external world, the Izala movement allows us to formulate two conclusions. First, religious ideology seems to be a constant, enshrined in the dynamics of reform which is central to the evolution of Muslim societies. The durable character of this reformism, which many movements have tried to promote in the course of this century,[58] is well defined by Ernest Gellner as a "tendency towards a more scripturalist, fundamentalist, rigorous, form of religion, which seems to be the central theme of cultural history of Muslim countries for the past century."[59] The desire to purify Islam and rid it of local influences seems to be, in the case of the Izala movement in Nigeria, a variable independent of the size of the movement and other external circumstances.

Second, the political agenda of the sympathizers of the Izala movement is a variable influenced by external circumstances. Throughout the period of the petroleum euphoria, when Nigeria received substantial manna, the sympathizers of the reformist movement insisted on the reform of religious practices and directed their efforts toward the community whose practices it wanted to reform. With the oil glut, the devaluation of national currency, the fall in living standards, the imposition of the structural adjustment program with devastating dramatic consequences, and the federal military government's support for the United Nations resolution against Iraq during the Gulf War, the target of many reformists has shifted to the political authorities, away from the traditional religious order. Now the authorities are, not the community, are perceived as responsible for the economic and social climate. The more the economic and social malaise is accentuated in Nigeria, the more probable the neo-Izala movement will bite deep into the clientele of the original Izala and link up with the Brothers in order to make political demands.

Notes

1. I consider as members all those Muslims who have come under the influence of Izala whether they are engaged in preaching or not.

2. Figure of the last census conducted in 1992.

3. See M. K. Barbour, "Nigeria in Africa," in Barbour, J. S. Oguntonyinba,

J. O. C. Onyemelukwe, and J. C. Nwafour, eds., *Nigeria in Maps* (London: Hodder and Stoughton, 1982), p. 2.

4. Despite its very large proportion of the Hausa, Hausaland, like Yorubaland, also consists of ethnic minorities.

5. According to Laitin, 40 percent of the Yoruba call themselves Muslims, 40 percent Christians, and 20 percent adherents of ancestral cults. See David Laitin, "Religion, Political Culture and the Weberian Tradition," *World Politics* 30, no. 4 (July 1978): 563–92, 589.

6. See J. A. Makinde, "L'Islam en pays Yoruba: Religion et politique" (Ph.D. diss., Institut d'Etudes Politiques, Bordeaux, 1989).

7. See A. I. Doi, *Islam in Nigeria* (Zaria: Gaskiya, 1984), p. 81.

8. For example the Wahhabi movement born in the Hijaz in the nineteenth century or the Salafi movement in Egypt.

9. See Mervyn Hiskett, *Race Relations in the Anglo-Egypt Sudan: Hiskett Report*. National Archives, Kaduna.

10. See Muhammad Sani Umar, "Sufism and Anti-sufism in Nigeria" (M.A. thesis, Bayero University Kano, 1988), p. 240.

11. From the name of Muhammad Ibn Hanbal (780–855), a famous Muslim theologian who declared war on "innovations" *(bid'a)* the intrusion of foreign influences into Islam. The neo-Hanbalis are those Muslim thinkers inspired by his thoughts, such as Ibn Taymiyya (1263–1328), Ibn Qayyim al-Jawziya (1292–1350), and Muhammad Ibn 'Abd al-Wahhab (1703–87). The neo-Hanbalis had condemned especially the Sufi orders, the cult of the saints, and spiritual concerts.

12. See James Piscatori, "Ideological Politics in Saudi Arabia," in Piscatori, *Islam in the Political Process* (Cambridge: Cambridge University Press, 1983), p. 59; Sulayman Nyang, "Saudi Arabian Foreign Policy toward Africa," *Horn of Africa* 5, no. 2 (1982): 3–17.

13. King Faysal donated a hundred thousand pounds between 1962 and 1965. See

Awwalu Anwar, "Struggle for Influence and Identity: The Ulama in Kano, 1937–1987" (M.A. thesis, University of Maiduguri, 1989), p. 140. Shaykh Sabah of Kuwait donated close to two million pounds to help Ahmadu Bello proselytize. See John Naber Paden, *Ahmadu Bello, Sardauna of Sokoto: Values and Leadership in Nigeria* (Zaria: Hudahuda Publishing, 1986), pp. 561, 578.

14. See Abubakar Gumi, "Al-Wird al-'Adhim min al-Ahadith wa'l-Qur'an al-Karim" (manuscript).

15. See Abubakar Gumi, *Al-'aqidat al-sahiha bi Muwafaqat al-Shari'a* (Beirut: Dar al-'Arabi li'l-Tiba'a wa'l-Nashr wa'l-Tawzi', 1972).

16. See Nasiru Kabara, *Kitab al-Nasiha al-sariha fi'l-Radd 'ala'l-'aqidat al-sahiha* (Kano: Zawiya Kabara, 1972); Sani Kafanga, *Al-Minah al-Hamida fi Radd 'ala Fasiq 'Aqida* (Beirut, n.d.).

17. See Umar, "Sufism and Anti-Sufism in Nigeria," p. 240.

18. See "Introduction," in Oyedele Oyed-Iran, ed., *Nigerian Government and Politics under Military Rule* (Lagos: Macmillan, 1979).

19. See Tayo Lambo, *Nigerian Economy: A Textbook of Applied Economy* (Ibadan: Ivan Brothers, 1987), pp. 32–33.

20. See Johny Egg, "La nouvelle insertion de l'agriculture nigériane dans le marché mondial," in Daniel Bach, ed., *Le Nigéria un pouvoir en puissance* (Paris: Karthala, 1988), pp. 169–70.

21. See Fouad al-Farsy, *Modernity and Tradition: The Sa'udi Equation* (London: Kegan Paul International, 1990), p. 295.

22. See Nyang, "Saudi Arabian Foreign Policy toward Africa," pp. 3–17, 11.

23. Ibid., pp. 3–17.

24. See Mark Bray, *Universal Primary Education in Nigeria* (London: Routledge and Kegan Paul, 1981), p. 17.

25. See nn. 34 and 46; these volumes constitute part of the preaching corpus of the Izala.

26. Interview with U. M. I., Jos and Kano, September 1990.

27. See Pablo Deiros, "Protestant Fundamentalism in Latin America," in Martin E. Marty and R. Scott Appleby, eds., *Fundamentalims Observed* (Chicago: University of Chicago Press, 1991), p. 155.

28. Interview with Abbas Isa Lawyer, coordinator of preachers of the Izala movement in Zaria, August 1990.

29. See *Tsarin ka'idojin kungiyar Jama'at izalatil bidi'a wa ikamatis sunnah* (Statutes of the Izala Society) (Zaria: Gaskiya, 1978), p. 2.

30. He is now a member of the National Republican Convention, a right-wing party which supports liberalism and market economy and one of the two authorized parties to which the military intended to hand over power in 1992.

31. The author worked as a participant observer during several field trips to Nigeria between 1985 and 1991. He was able to identify the concepts Izala preachers refer to in their preaching activities.

32. On the mobilizing power of Islamic political language, see Bernard Lewis, *Le langage politique de l'Islam* (Paris: Gallimard, 1988), p. 17.

33. See *Tsarin ka'idojin,* p. 2.

34. See Shaykh Muhammad Ibn 'Abd al-Wahhab, *Kitab al-Tawhid,* trans. Ismail Raji al-Faruqi (Beirut and Damascus: Holy Qur'an Publishing House, 1979), p. 70.

35. Ibid., p. 43.

36. Ibid., p. 26.

37. See H. A. R. Gibb and J. H. Krammers, eds., *Shorter Encyclopaedia of Islam* (Leiden: Brill, 1974), pp. 586–87.

38. The Association of Reformist Ulama was a reformist movement formed between the two wars in Algeria. Its preaching activities led to considerable shrinkage of the brotherhoods' following in Algeria. See Merad Ali, *Le réformisme musulman en Algérie de 1925 à 1940, Essai d'histoire religieuse et sociale* (Paris: Mouton, 1967).

39. See 'Abd al-Samad al-Kathini, *Risalat al-Da'i ila Sunna wa'l-Zajir 'an al-Bid'a* (Beirut: Dâr al-'Arabi li'l-Teba'a wa'l-Nashr wa'l-Tawzi', 1978), p. 11.

40. See Yasir Anjola Quadri, "Qadriyya and Tijaniyyah Relations in Nigeria in the 20th Century," *Orita: Ibadan Journal of Religious Studies* 6, no. 1 (June 1984): 26.

41. See Yasir Anjola Quadri, "A Study of the Izala, a Contemporary Anti-Sufi Organization in Nigeria," *Orita: Ibadan Journal of Religious Studies* (1985): 102.

42. Interviews conducted at different places in northern Nigeria. See also the detailed report of the incident in the Federal Republic of Nigeria *Report of the Commission Enquiry on Kano Disturbances* (Lagos: Federal Government Press 1981), pp. 73–77.

43. See Umar Birai, "Islamic Tajdid and the Political Process in Nigeria," in Martin E. Marty and R. Scott Appleby, eds., *Fundamentalisms and the State: Remaking Polities, Economies, and Militance* (Chicago: University of Chicago Press, 1993).

44. Even during the suppression, Izala members and unauthorized Izala preachers tried to convince others, especially from the Sufi brotherhoods, that Izala followed the true path of Islam. Nigerian youth who supported the ideas behind the Iranian Revolution of 1979 did not necessarily reject the religious teachings of Izala, but their political agenda was different from that of the ulama leading Izala. Although the number of Izala followers probably did not decrease significantly in the early 1980s, they did not openly antagonize the followers of traditional Islam during that period, as they had in the 1970s.

45. The most eminent businessmen-sponsors of the movement are Alhaji Shehu Mohammad, from Jos; and a shareholder in the largest tobacco company in Nigeria (Nigeria Tobacco Company), Ahmadi Kurfi, who owns many companies and has contributed enormous sums for the construction of schools; Alhaji Ahmadu Chanchange, mentioned earlier, who possesses one of the largest transport companies in Nigeria; and Alhaji Bukar, a millionaire from Biu but a resident of Bauchi state.

46. See Muhammad Ben 'Abd al-Rahman Ben Hassan al-Shaykh, *Fath al-Majîd sharh kitab al-tawhid* (Beirut: Dâr al-Ihyâ al-turath al-'Arabi, 1957).

47. Sulayman Ibn 'Abd Allah Ibn Muhammad Ibn 'Abd Allah, *Taysîr al-Azîz al-Hamid fi sharh kitab al-tawhîd,* n.d.

48. Al-Imam Abi Zakariya Yahya al-Nawawi, *Riyâdh al-sâlihin min kalâm Sayyid al-mursalîn* (Beirut: Mu'assassa al-tiba'at wa al-taswir al-iliktroniya, 1985). See Abubacar Gumi, *Radd al-adhhân 'ala ma'anî al-Qur'ân* (Beirut, 1979).

49. See Mathews Ojo, "The Contextual Significance of the Charismatic Movements in Independent Nigeria," *Africa* 58, no. 2 (1988): 175.

50. See Christian Association of Nigeria, *Leadership in Nigeria* (Kaduna CAN Kaduna Publicity Committee, n.d.), p. 5.

51. Ibid, pp. 6–28.

52. On the politization of religion, see Jibrin Ibrahim, "The Politics of Religon in Nigeria: The Parameters of the 1987 Crisis in Kaduna State," *Review of African Political Economy* (1989): 45–46.

53. *Today,* 29 April–5 May 1990, p. 5; emphasis mine.

54. Interview with Abubakar Gumi, September 1990.

55. See *The Pen* 3, no. 2 (31 August 1990) 16, during a conference he organized at the end of August 1990.

56. Extracts from a speech given by Ismail Idris in Kano, 6 June 1990, translated from Hausa language by the author.

57. Mai Gandu represents conservatism in all its ramifications, but he used the conflict between Ismail Idris and the radicals to get rid of Idris and control the movement.

58. On the numerous contemporary reformist movements, one can cite the Assocation of Reformist Ulama in the Maghreb, the Union Culturelle Musulmane in black Africa and Muhammadijah in Indonesia. For the first, see Ernest Gellner, *Muslim Society* (Cambridge: Cambridge University Press, 1980), p. 154; and Merad, *Le réformisme musulman en Algérie*; for the second, see J. C. Froelich, "Le réformisme de l'Islam en Afrique Noire de l'Ouest," *Revue de Défense Nationale,* January 1961, pp. 77–91; Christian Coulon, *Les musulmans et le pouvoir en Afrique noire* (Paris: Karthala, 1983), pp. 120–42; for the third, see C. Geertz, *The Religion of Java* (Chicago: University of Chicago Press, 1960), p. 138; James L. Peacock, *Muslim Puritans: Reformist Psychology in Southeast Asian Islam* (Berkeley: University of California Press, 1978), p. 23.

59. Ernest Gellner, ed., *Islamic Dilemmas: Reformers, Nationalists and Industrialization: The Southern Shore of the Mediterranean* (Berlin: Mouton, 1985), p. 1.

Authority and Community in Soviet Islam

Mark Saroyan

U<small>NTIL</small> recently it has been common, when thinking about the Islamic world, to overlook the formerly Soviet region of Central Asia. But with nearly fifty million adherents of the Muslim faith, the region has one of the world's largest Muslim populations. And it is distinctive in more than numbers. Though relegated to the geopolitical and religious periphery of the Islamic world, today's Central Asian Muslims are heirs to a once flourishing center of Islamic civilization. One need only recall such original founders of Islamic religious science as al-Bukhari (d. 870) and al-Tirmidhi (d. ca. 872)—both of whom lived in the present territory of Central Asia—or view the grandeur of the great Muslim cities of Bukhara, Khorezm, and, of course, Samarkand, which was founded as the capital of Tamerlane's medieval empire.

Most of the region's Muslims live in the five states that comprise Central Asia, but the lands stretch from the Central Asian steppes and oases to the Middle Volga region in the heart of Russia, through the northern Caucasus, and into Azerbaijan. The geographic size of this Islamic world is complemented by a diversity of populations. Turkic speakers such as Uzbeks, Kazakhs, Azerbaijanis, and Tatars predominate numerically, but the region is also home to the Iranian-speaking Tajiks and a myriad of smaller nationalities speaking a range of Turkic, Iranian, and Ibero-Caucasian languages. In terms of religion, the Muslims of Central Asia and the Middle Volga are overwhelmingly followers of the Hanafi school (*madhab*) of Sunni Islam, while the north Caucasians are primarily Shafi'i Sunnis. The majority of Azerbaijanis in the southern Caucasus are Ja'fari Shi'is, and other pockets of Shi'is can be found in the north Caucasus and in Central Asia (for example, Isma'ili Shi'is in Tajikistan).

Despite the geographic, cultural, and religious diversity of the Muslim population in Central Asia, the religious institutions of the organized Muslim community developed during the course of Soviet rule a remarkable degree of standardization and uniformity. This resulted from decades of antireligious policies and restrictions imposed by the Soviet government on organized religious activities of any kind, including, of course, Islam.

The history of the Soviet government's relation with Islam must thus be taken into account in any observation of political processes in the late Soviet period. Beginning in the mid-1920s, the Soviet government not only implemented a radical program separating religion from the state but also carried out an often violent campaign against religious institutions and religious belief more generally.[1] The Soviet Communists closed down mosques and religious schools, nationalized religious endowments *(waqfs),* and dispersed the Muslim religious officialdom through relocation, exile, imprisonment, and assassination. Mosques continued to function and religious leaders continued to preach well into the 1930s, but they did so in vastly reduced numbers and under conditions of often extreme and persistent persecution. In effect, by the 1930s the organized Muslim community had been closed down by the Soviet government.

Not until World War II, when the Soviet government sought to tap religious sentiment as a source of support against the Nazi invasion, did a new era in relations between organized religion and the state begin. Many mosques reopened, religious training for ulama was reestablished on a limited scale, and the Muslim clergy was allowed to reorganize itself. In the following decades, while antireligious propaganda waxed and waned at the whim of Soviet leaders, the clerically led Islamic religious institutions that reemerged during the war survived as vital centers for the Islamic faith—despite a widespread wave of mosque closings and other increased restrictions imposed on them during the Khrushchev years.

In a context in which Islam was a scarce presence, the religious organizations under the ulama's control were, in the post–World War II period, the sole effective arbiters of Islam. This chapter focuses on the activity of these surviving religious associations, known as Muslim Religious Boards (in Russian, *dukhovnoe upravlenie),* which until recently represented the only organized Islamic religious movement in what was the Soviet Union.[2] In the first part of this chapter, I describe the organizational structure and social composition of these leading Islamic institutions as they developed under Soviet rule. Many of the features described in this section have been amended or eliminated during the current period of political reforms following the disintegration of the Soviet Union, but the survey provides important information for understanding the context in which Islam developed in the Soviet Union leading up to the early 1990s. Then I turn my attention to the character of the religious principles espoused by the ulama who led the Muslim Boards. In both structure and beliefs, I argue, the ulama-led Muslim Boards reflected a religiopolitical orientation that moved between fundamentalist and accommodationist modes under Soviet rule. The Muslim Boards were fundamentalist in their dedication to a "return" to the scriptural foundations of Islam, from which, they argued, the Soviet Muslim community had strayed. At the same time, however, the Muslim Boards promoted a conception of a "purified" Islam which was consonant with modern social and economic development and which also encouraged loyal citizenship and political participation in the Soviet Union.

In the third part of the chapter, I examine the fate of the Muslim Boards in the years of Soviet *perestroika* (restructuring) and *glasnost* (liberalization)—years of radical reforms in politics, society, and the economy. In this account I have stressed continuities as well as changes in the structure and operation of the organized Muslim community. I propose that the character of the religious movement led by the Muslim Boards reflects a remarkable degree of consistency in their pre- and post-reform activities. However, there are important implications for Central Asian Islam in the emergence of new Muslim religious movements that operate outside the networks established by the Muslim Boards.

Structure of the Soviet Muslim Community

As in most other Muslim societies, the fundamental organizational unit of the Soviet Muslim religious community was the mosque. Given the general elimination of religious endowments and most religious schools in the Soviet Union, the mosque stood as one of the few remaining religious institutions in the region after World War II. Like other religious associations in the country, mosques were allowed to operate legally by registering with their local governments. To form a religious association, a minimum of twenty people (in Russian, the *dvatsatka*) of the same faith was required to petition the local government for registration of their religious community. Upon registration, the local government would generally provide the given religious community with a building (in the case of Islam, a mosque), but otherwise the mosque-based religious association financed itself almost entirely through the voluntary donations of its parishioners and supporters.

In principle and in practice, organized Soviet Islam was virtually confined to the activity of the mosques.[3] Soviet legislation on the operation of these religious communities defined more restrictions than rights. The most significant restrictions provided that religious associations, including of course the mosques, confined themselves to the conduct of religious rites. Thus, mosques were legally forbidden from engaging in such "nonreligious" activities as social services (including health care and housing), education (including establishment of schools or libraries), or any kind of economic or commercial enterprise. However, some of these harsh restrictions were not regularly enforced by the Soviet government. For instance, larger mosques often possessed sizable libraries of religious publications, and in Uzbekistan, religious education survived at two religious academies in Bukhara and Tashkent, where young men were trained for religious careers.

Mosques formed the foundation of the Soviet Muslim community, but they did not operate as independent religious associations. Each registered mosque was affiliated with one of four independent, regionally organized Muslim Religious Boards and was subject to the administrative jurisdiction of these boards. The largest of these organizations was (and remains) the Muslim Religious Board for Central Asia and Kazakhstan, which regulated the religious life of Muslim communities in the Central Asian republics of Uzbekistan, Tajikistan, Turkmenistan, and Kirgizia as well as Kazakhstan. The administrative headquarters of the Central Asian Board was in Tashkent, the capital of Uzbekistan. The Muslim Religious Board for the Transcaucasus, centered in Baku, supervised the Muslim communities of Azerbaijan, Armenia, and Georgia and served as the nominal religious center for Shi'i minorities outside the Board's legal jurisdiction. The North Caucasian Muslim Religious Board worked out of Makhachkala, the capital of Dagestan, and coordinated the mosques of the autonomous ethnic territories of southern Russia, including among others Dagestan, Chechen-Ingushetia, Kabardino-Balkaria, and North Ossetia as well as parts of southern Russia.

The geographically most extensive administration was the Muslim Religious Board for the European USSR and Siberia. Its center was in Ufa, and it administered the religious life of Muslims living in the Middle Volga (Tatarstan and Bashkiria) as well as communities scattered throughout the rest of the Russian republic and the European parts of the country.

The Muslim Boards, like the mosques they oversaw, administered themselves separate from the state. They registered with the state as religious associations, and, though subject to a variety of external political pressures, they nonetheless operated formally as private organizations. As hierarchically structured organizations led by self-certified Muslim religious leaders, they defined their main task as organizing and regulating the religious life of the Muslim community. As such, their existence challenged a common stereotype about Islam, according to which Islam has no church and no clergy. Moreover, unlike "Muslim" countries where "official" religious hierarchies operate under the direct auspices of the state (in Egypt, for instance), in the Soviet Union the "official" Muslim establishment was nominally independent and self-financing. The activities of the Muslim Boards were funded through voluntary contributions (*sadaqa*), and the salaries of local mosque officials were determined by contract with the given mosque's executive board.

Each of the boards was administered by an executive council and headed by a religious official. The executive councils were formally elected by periodic congresses of ulama and lay representatives of the religious communities under a particular board's jurisdiction. In a practice that parallels the operation of the Communist party, the leaders of the Muslim Board typically presented a preselected slate of candidates to the executive council, and the slate in turn would be "approved" by the congress. The executive council of the Muslim Board then selected its own chairman. These leaders were elected to positions of administrative rank but also bore titles of religious distinction. The Central Asian, European, and North Caucasian boards were led by a *mufti*, a person learned in the Islamic religious sciences. Given the Shi'i majority composition of its constituency, the Transcaucasian Board was headed by a Shi'i religious figure known as *shaykh-al-islam*. In this respect, the leadership of the Muslim Boards combined features of both "traditional" Muslim religious institutions and modern, impersonal bureaucracies.

Like other religious organizations in the postwar Soviet Union, the Muslim Boards traditionally operated under the harsh restrictions of Soviet religious legislation and political pressures, meaning that the Muslim Boards were generally restricted to meeting the purely "religious" needs of the population. Nevertheless, the internal organization and administration of the boards were generally left to Muslim religious leaders themselves.[4] For example, each Muslim Board was run according to an internally adopted set of by-laws which defined its rights and responsibilities with regard to the Muslim communities under its administration. Thus, each Muslim Board reserved the right to define the principles of the Islamic faith and decide questions of religious dogma by *fatwa* (an explanation based on religious science) if necessary. The boards also issued guidelines on the proper forms of religious conduct, from the Friday prayers to observance of various calendar rites and holidays.

The fatwa provided another example of the Muslim Boards' synthesis of traditional Muslim practices and modern bureaucratic innovations. Customarily, a fatwa is the prerogative of a mufti, who in the Soviet case also headed the Muslim Board. In the Soviet Union, however, the larger administrations had fatwa departments which were involved in researching and preparing the issuance of a fatwa. Prior to the announcement of a fatwa, the mufti discussed the research accomplished by the fatwa department with the board's executive council. Then the fatwa was issued on behalf of the Muslim Religious Board as a whole and not simply by an individual mufti.

Apart from their general supervision of religious dogma and practice, the Muslim Boards regulated the administrative operation of the mosque-based religious communities under their jurisdiction. In this role, the Muslim Boards acted in a fashion that resembled the Communist party apparatus—centralized and highly bureaucratized. Mosques and local religious officials were registered not only by government agencies; they were also certified by an appropriate Muslim Religious Board. The boards organized religious training for the ulama at all levels and provided an official certification that authorized an individual to perform religious services. Only the Muslim Boards retained the right to appoint ulama to positions of religious responsibility in the mosques, and likewise only the boards were able to transfer officials from one mosque to another. Moreover, the Muslim Boards could choose to revoke the certification of ulama under their supervision for violations of religious or administrative codes of the given Muslim Board.

The Ulama's Image of Islam and Community

One of the main concerns reflected in clerical arguments about the nature of Islam and the Muslim community in the post–World War II era was a "return" to Islam in its purest forms.[5] Thus increasingly in the 1980s, the Soviet Muslim ulama sought to mobilize the religious institutions they led in order to revitalize the religious life of the community around the textual origins of Islam—the Qur'an and the Prophetic traditions.

The ulama's argument about the need to return to the fundamentals of Islam was based, of course, on the assumption that the Muslim community has strayed from those fundamentals. Orthodoxy is constituted only in relation to heterodoxy, as Pierre Bourdieu has argued, and the ulama's depiction of a Muslim community having strayed from Islam provides the necessary contrast.[6] Given the picture the ulama painted of the religiously ignorant, indeed degenerate, state of the Muslim community, this picture established the need for religious leadership, which could best be provided, the argument went, by the educated Muslim clergy. In this way, clerical arguments about the need to return to an authentic Islam were linked with the legitimation of the activity of the Muslim Boards and the network of clerics and mosques under their jurisdiction. By painting the Muslim community as having fallen into superstitious and heretical ways, the ulama simultaneously fixed a place for themselves and their institutions in Muslim society.

For most of the 1980s the ulama's arguments about Islam and the Muslim community reflected a struggle for leadership within Soviet Muslim society. Ironically, the clergy's claim to leadership within the community was based on a theological condemnation of the community. Clerical discourse was directed, however, not only internally toward Muslim society; it was also aimed externally at the Soviet polity and society more generally. Over its decades-long development, Soviet political discourse characterized Islam, like all religions, as a social ideology which served only to hamper human progress. As a vestige of a pre-socialist era, Islam and religious beliefs more generally were thus seen as doomed in the context of building a progressive Soviet social order.

The Muslim clergy's image of Islam, however, challenged and subverted this hegemonic argument about Islam and its place in Soviet society. The Muslim community, the ulama insisted, retained its Islamic distinctiveness and actively contributed to the progress of Soviet society. In fact, these clerics pointed out, an "authentic" Islam prescribes many of the same social and economic values as did Soviet socialism. In contrast to Soviet secular propaganda's portrayal of Islam as a brake on social development, then, the Muslim clerics pointed to the benefits Islam brings to society in general and Soviet society specifically.

These were the ulama's two main arguments about the nature of Islam and the Muslim community and their relation to Soviet society. But before looking at a more detailed analysis of these arguments, it is useful to examine the ways in which the ulama drew on their religious traditions to make such arguments. How exactly did they formulate their arguments about Islam and the Muslim community?

The main discursive instrument employed by the ulama in the quest to re-center the Muslim community around an authentic Islam was *ijtihad,* or the independent interpretation of sacred texts. Soviet ulama sought to legitimate their reliance on this practice by citing historical figures as diverse as Abu Hanifa (700–767), one of the early Arab founders of Islamic religious science, and Shihabeddin Marjani (1818–99), a Tatar cleric and philosopher in whose work ijtihad was an integral part of religious thought. In a reflection of broadly accepted clerical views on the nature of ijtihad, one Soviet mufti pointed out that successive generations of Muslims have approached the sacred scriptures with equal respect, but each new generation interprets the essence of these texts in a new way and thus discovers new ideas that had previously gone unnoticed.[7]

By means of ijtihad, the ulama hoped to effect a double move. On the one hand, they emphasized the scriptural foundations of the Islamic faith and idealized the historical traditions of "authentic Islam." At the same time, their reliance on ijtihad opened the possibility for interpreting and reinterpreting these texts in ways that would allow for the construction of new religious principles to meet contemporary social, religious, and other concerns. The Soviet Muslim ulama's reconstruction of Islam through ijtihad thus reflected a synthesis of both "traditional" and "modern" elements.

The ulama's reconstructed image of Islam was legitimated by means of ijtihad, but the emphasis on the authenticity of the scriptural origins of Islam and on the centrality of the historical legacy of Islamic thought at the same time implied a devaluing of present-day Islam, that is, the range of beliefs and practices which characterizes the lived religious experiences of those people who identify themselves as Muslims.

Indeed, one main thrust of clerical arguments about the character of the contemporary Muslim community is that it has fallen into seriously un-Islamic ways. In their critique of contemporary Islam, the ulama condemned what they considered *jahiliyya*, or pre-Islamic ignorance. Jahiliyya can be understood as a general ignorance of Islam, including a lack of familiarity with the fundamental principles of the faith as expressed in the Qur'an or the Traditions of the Prophet Muhammad. More specifically, the ulama decried the widespread existence of *bidaʿ*, or heretical innovations in religious belief and practice. Such innovations include, for example, "superstitious" beliefs, saint worship, pilgrimage to local shrines, and the use of amulets for healing or other purposes.

A lead editorial in the magazine of the Central Asian Muslim Board, illustratively titled "Along the True Path of the Qur'an," provided a concise statement of these views: "In defending the principles ordained by the Holy Qur'an, we [ulama] actively fight against all negative occurrences which happen in the everyday lives of Muslims and draw them away from all kinds of superstitions and bidayat which do not correspond to instructions provided by our shariat. By doing so, we strengthen the conscience of our faithful."[8]

It is ironic that the ulama's depiction of the contemporary Muslim community underscored the community's un-Islamic ways. One of the main tasks of the Muslim clergy is not simply defining the content of an "authentic" Islam based in history and scripture and condemning the range of un-Islamic practices observed by contemporary Muslims. Rather, in its contrast of an idealized religious authenticity and a degenerate religious reality, the ulama fixed themselves as the force that could provide the leadership to bring the Muslim community back to the "true" Islam.

If Muslim leaders in the Soviet Union made somewhat abstract claims about their leadership role in bringing Islam to the Muslim community (and thus bringing the community back to Islam), these claims were concretized in the institutional mechanisms at the disposal of the ulama. In this way, the religious discourse of the Soviet Muslim clergy and the organizational structures of the religious institutions that they dominated were intimately linked. The most important of these mechanisms, all of which operated under the supervision of the regional Muslim Religious Boards, included the mosque, the religious center of the Muslim community where prayers are recited and sermons are delivered; the imam, or local religious scholar who leads the mosque-based community and provides a range of religious services; the sermon (*khutba* in Sunni tradition, *moiza* in Shi'i tradition), by which a cleric provides a general but authoritative representation of Islam; the fatwa, a formalized decision issued by a cleric trained in religious science; and the *madrasa*, the religious school which in the Soviet context provided only training and education for aspiring ulama.

The centrality of these religious institutions was frequently noted, and ulama emphasized the function of these institutions as vital instruments for re-Islamicizing the Muslim community. A clerical statement on the role of mosques in contemporary society, for example, represented the mosque as a site where Muslims could gain greater awareness and understanding of themselves as Muslims. In this process, ulama emphasize, the interconnected function of mosque, sermon, and *'alim* was the means to bring Islam to the community and to return the community of believers to an "authentic" Islam: "In our mosques, sermons are recited, fatwas are announced and elucidated and the profound humane principles of the personal behavior of Muslim society, the family and daily life are persistently propagated. Therefore, the role of mosques is immensely important in the course of solving our common important task—implanting in new generations of Muslims a consciousness and profound value of our sacred religion."[9]

In this context, then, appeals of the ulama for "strengthening" the role of the mosques in the life of the community followed from an understanding of the mosque as an instrument in the reconstruction of an authentic Islam under the "competent" guidance of the clergy.

Distinction and Integration in Religious Discourse

In their image of a reconstructed, reinvigorated Islam, postwar Soviet Muslim ulama sought to restore the authority of "tradition" among Muslims. But this reinvention of an Islamic tradition operated not only internally in the Muslim community. At the same time, Muslim officials constructed arguments that sought to recontextualize the Muslim community in relation to political, social, and economic developments in the Soviet Union. Thus, postwar clerical discourse sought not only to rewrite the "text" of Islam but also to recast the context in which Islam existed. Concomitant with their struggle to mobilize the Muslim community around their own religious institutions and instill in that community their own sense of the Islamic faith, the Muslim ulama argued that Islam and the Muslim community had a vital role to play in Soviet society. In a concrete example of this challenge, the ulama reworked the Soviet state's discursive constitution of a "new Soviet man," who lived successfully without religion. In its place, the arguments of Muslim clerics described the formation of a "new, Soviet Muslim citizen."

Clerical arguments about the nature of Islam's relation to Soviet society were made in conscious recognition of prevailing notions of the inherent incompatibility of Islam and Soviet power. The mutually exclusive character of Islam (or any religion) and Soviet-led social progress was a common theme of Soviet antireligious propaganda and academic polemics. In this sense, ulama arguments about the place of Islam in Soviet society were a counterdiscourse, a reply to the powerful challenge of external images of Islam produced in nonreligious scholarship and polemics.

The formulation of a counterdiscourse, however, did not entail a total rejection of the arguments to which it responded. Rather, the clerical projection of Islam's image subverted the state's hegemonic position by incorporating into its representation of Islam many features of that position which would seemingly negate it. Thus, numerous political, social, and economic values espoused by representatives of the Soviet state were appropriated by the ulama as traditional elements of the Islamic faith. In fact, Soviet ulama sometimes effected a reversal, by which they asserted the essentially religious underpinnings of Soviet values. This is evident in the comments made by a cleric at an Azerbaijani mosque, who declared: "I am glad and full of admiration for the genius of the prophet who foresaw the social principles of socialism. I am also glad that many socialist practices are the present-day realization of the dreams of the Prophet Muhammad."[10]

The ulama's appropriation of elements of the state's discourse served in part to reproduce that discourse. In this connection, many observers have simplistically assumed that ulama were nothing more than docile functionaries of Soviet power. But in reinterpreting state values as traditional components of Islamic thought and thereby underscoring the vitality of Islam, the ulama also revised and rejected the state's arguments concerning the religion's backwardness and obsolescence. Thus the "loyal" position of Soviet Muslim authorities was not merely a surrender to their political context; it was an attempt to subvert and reconstruct that context.

Clerical arguments positing the existence of a "Soviet Muslim citizen" relied on a combination of two distinct strategies.[11] I refer to the first as a strategy of integration, a symbolic representation of Muslims as active participants in the construction of Soviet power and integral members in the broader realm of Soviet society. I refer to a second, simultaneous tendency as a strategy of distinction. Thus, the clerics emphasized the Muslim distinctiveness of the community of believers that they led. In this way, clerical arguments posited the existence of a conscientiously Muslim community; they also promoted the integration of that community, not as a nameless collection of individuals but as emphatically Muslim citizens, into a Soviet society that the ulama envisaged as broader than perhaps it was.

One of the archetypes of the Soviet Muslim citizen presented by the clergy was Rizaetdin Fahretdinov, a Tatar 'alim and religious philosopher who was a leader of the Soviet Muslim community in the interwar period. His case was raised by the ulama to claim that adherence to the Islamic faith posed no obstacle to the social participation of devout Muslims and that Muslim piety and Soviet citizenship were in fact mutually reinforcing. In a statement that compares his religious devotion and secular activities, it was argued that "Religion in no way hampered Rizaetdin Fahretdinov from actively participating in the social and political life of our country. With a feeling of great emotion he used to speak of many things which he dared only dream of before the Great October Revolution, like general educational facilities, the emancipation of our women, the flourishing of our science, culture and art in all spheres which have nowadays become a reality."[12]

In the context of a dominant political discourse that portrayed Muslims as backward and threatening to maintenance of Soviet power, the ulama's representation of the Soviet Muslim community aimed to transform Muslims from passive victims or opponents of Soviet policy into active agents in the social and political structures in which they lived. In emphasizing a continued, even renewed, devotion to the Islamic faith in tandem with participation in Soviet society, the Soviet Muslim ulama thus established a claim for benefits from that society—as integrated but distinctly Muslim citizens. As one account put the case: "For more than 65 years Muslims of our country have been living in socialist society and they have real cause to be proud of making their contribution to the progress and prosperity of their native land while not deviating from the prescription of their holy religion of Islam."[13]

In contrast to arguments that Islam is an obsolete vestige of the past, the Soviet ulama thus subverted these notions, claiming that "without religion a person cannot be moral, since only fear of God keeps people from doing amoral, sinful deeds."[14]

The clerical strategies of distinction and integration, moreover, proved inseparable from the broader fundamentalist ideal of reorienting the community around the origins of the faith and re-centering the Muslim community around the religious institutions controlled by the clergy. Thus, in a denunciation of ignorant superstitions and practices, the former mufti of Central Asia argued that the return to the fundamentals of Islam was in fact the foundation for the positive, active contribution of the Muslim community to Central Asian society: "These superstitions cannot contribute to the progress that characterizes the contemporary era. It is only the return to the Qur'an and the Sunna that created indispensable conditions for the active participation of Muslims in the building of a new life."[15]

Unlike some Islamic ideological tendencies outside the Soviet Union, where secular and religious ideas were combined in constructions of "Islamic Marxism" or "Islamic socialism," Soviet Muslim authorities maintained the distinctiveness of each system of ideas.[16] They argued for a commonality of interests of two separate discursive traditions: one Islamic and the other Soviet/Marxist. In this respect, Soviet ulama appealed for a kind of mutually advantageous coexistence—but not synthesis—of Islam and Soviet state power.

Central Asian Islam in an Era of Change

Over the past several years, the former Soviet Union has undergone a tremendous transformation in all spheres of human life: from the political, social, and economic to the cultural and religious. These transformations are very much in process, and given the intensity of debates about the fate of reform both inside the region and beyond its borders, it would be foolhardy to predict the likely outcomes. In the case of Islam and the Muslim community, however, one can nonetheless attempt a review of the major trends and the directions in which Muslim activism in the former Soviet Union is heading.

Perhaps the most striking aspect of Islamic activism in the glasnost period of reform was not the emergence of some movement but its absence. In the 1970s and early 1980s, many Western observers of Islam (and privately, many Soviet analysts as well) interpreted a perceived persistence in Muslim-Slavic tensions, the continued adherence of the Muslim community to its faith, a rise in Muslim birthrates, and an impending socioeconomic crisis as the basis for widespread antigovernment agitation among Muslims.[17] During perestroika, however, one could argue with little exaggeration that everything *but* an Islamic revolution had taken place in the former Soviet Union: the dismantling of the Communist party's monopoly over political power, relatively free and competitive elections, unprecedented market reforms, proclamations of independence by the republics, persistent civil wars in the Caucasus, and periodic intercommunal violence.

Nonetheless, the political liberalization of the perestroika period afforded the Muslim community with expanded opportunities for religious expression, and a rise in religious activisms of all kinds, including of course Islam, is characteristic of contemporary life in Central Asia. In the survey that follows, I highlight not simply the changes that can be observed within the Muslim community but also the equally important continuities. Indeed, the main axis of political conflict emerging in Central Asian Islam is not between the Muslim community and the individual republics but within the Muslim community itself.

The most significant change in relations between Islam and the state emerged, ironically, in connection with the 1988 celebrations of one thousand years of Christianity in Russia. After 1988, a general relaxation of institutional and political restrictions on religious activity became evident, and Soviet traditions of antireligious polemics gave way to more positive evaluations of the role of religion in Soviet society. In effect, journalists and politicians increasingly adopted traditional clerical arguments concerning the beneficial role of religion in Soviet society, thus transforming the clergy's sometime oppositional discourse into a tenet of mainstream political thought. Both institutionally and ideologically, such changes in predominant attitudes toward religion had an immediate and profound impact on the scope and nature of Muslim religious life throughout the region.

The general trend toward liberalization in political life has had both quantitative and qualitative consequences for Islam. Many of the changes are thus an expansion—sometimes dramatic—of institutions and practices that characterized religious life during the period of *zastoi* or stagnation. In other cases, the activity of the Muslim Religious Boards has undergone an important "restructuring," with profound implications for the future of the Muslim community. Only the most significant and extensive of the current changes are mentioned here.

Among the quantitative changes, perhaps the most visible development has been a virtual campaign, initiated after 1988, to open new mosques throughout the Soviet Union. Various bureaucratic and political obstacles that had traditionally impeded the operation of mosques—and indeed frequently led to their illegal closure—were cleared away, allowing for a rapid increase in the building of new houses of worship and the restoration to religious communities of older mosques.[18]

The sudden expansion in the number of mosques has created a sort of personnel crisis in the Muslim community. With more mosques, a commensurate need for more religious officials, especially parish imams, has emerged. To meet these needs, two paths have been followed by the leadership of the Muslim Boards. In numerous cases, unregistered ulama who performed religious services on an informal (and nonlegal) basis have been certified by the boards and incorporated into the official structure of the organized Muslim community.

To meet the long-term needs of the community, however, new centers for religious education have been set up throughout the country. In the postwar Soviet Union, only two religious schools operated for the training of ulama: the Mir-Arab madrasa in Bukhara (a middle school in Soviet educational terms) and the al-Bukhari Islamic Institute in Tashkent (an establishment of higher education). In the late Soviet period, Islamic middle and higher schools opened in Ufa (Bashkiria), Baku (Azerbaijan), and Makhachkala (Dagestan). In Central Asia alone, schools have opened in Alma-Ata (Kazakhstan), Dushanbe (Tajikistan), and Tashauz (Turkmenistan).

The educational programs of these establishments take from two to five years to complete, and like their older counterparts, these schools are not designed to provide religious education for the general population. Rather, they provide solely for the education and training of young men who plan to enter religious service as mosque-based officials or administrators on one of the Muslim Religious Boards.

During the period of "stagnation," the Muslim Religious Boards had a limited but regular program of publications, including printing annual Muslim calendars and various religious books, such as editions of the Qur'an and authoritative collections of prophetic traditions. The Central Asian Muslim Board also published a quarterly journal, *Muslims of the Soviet East,* which was circulated only among ulama and readers abroad. By the late 1980s, these publishing activities had been expanded. In addition to more book titles with higher press runs, the Muslim Board for Central Asia has, for example, initiated publication of *Muslims of the Soviet East* in Uzbek in both Arabic and the more widely accessible modified Cyrillic script. Once difficult to obtain, the journal, with a press run of fifty thousand, is now distributed through the official state press distributor in towns and cities throughout Uzbekistan and other parts of Central Asia.

Even more significant is the creation of a mass-circulation Muslim press. In 1990, *Islam Nuri* (Light of Islam), a biweekly Uzbek-language newspaper edited by the Central Asian Muslim Board, became the first Muslim newspaper to be published in the Soviet Union since the 1920s. In 1991, another biweekly newspaper, *Islam,* joined the ranks of the Muslim press as the organ of the Muslim Religious Board for Transcaucasia.

Apart from extending their traditional activities, the Muslim Religious Boards have introduced a number of innovations with significant implications not just for the boards' activities but for the Muslim community as a whole. Among the most far-reaching of such qualitative changes is the reestablishment of *waqfs,* or religious endowments, which had been nationalized by the Soviet government in the 1920s. By the early 1990s, religious endowments had been set up under the direct supervision of the Muslim Boards or in association with mosques that operate under board supervision.

In Central Asia and parts of Azerbaijan, the waqfs typically consist of plots of land used for farming and livestock herding. Within months of the restitution of waqf, the Transcaucasian and Central Asian Muslim boards came to control at least one hundred hectares of land each. In Uzbekistan, it quickly became regular practice for the government to allocate two to three hectares of land when assigning land for construction of new mosques. The agricultural and livestock-breeding undertakings of the majority of waqfs are supplemented by other, less essential but potentially profitable activities. For example, in 1991 the Transcaucasian Muslim Board opened a well-stocked carpet and folkcraft shop in the heart of Baku's old city.

Reestablishment of the religious endowments is of immense significance in that for the first time in decades, the ulama are provided with an independent source of financing. As a consequence of their expansion and strengthening, ulama-led religious institutions are now even better positioned to mobilize the community around their notions of Islam. At the same time, however, the establishment of waqfs has lessened the ulama's financial dependence on the voluntary contributions of the faithful to fund the range of religious activities they supervised.

Both the quantitative and qualitative changes experienced by Muslim religious organizations have clearly profound institutional ramifications. But what of the political implications of these developments? The most important of these implications can be identified in two trends: first, a virtual transformation of institutional tendencies evident within the Muslim community; second, and to many perhaps most surprisingly, an essential continuity in the ulama's image of Islam in Central Asian society.

Conditioned by both externally imposed political restrictions and an internally generated clerical vision of a pristine Islam, one of the most salient tendencies within the postwar Soviet Muslim community was a trend toward unification. As a result of the concentration of religious training in only two establishments and the regulation of all religious life by the Muslim Boards, the religious life of the culturally and religiously diverse Soviet Muslim community was thus becoming more standardized and thereby more homogenized. If the tendency during zastoi (stagnation) was homogenization, then the tendency during the period of perestroika (restructuring) was toward localization and fragmentation. Following in part from a less restrictive political atmosphere, greater local autonomy of religious communities and religious organizations has led to an increasingly fragmented community where the lines of separation and conflict run along both ethnic and sectarian distinctions.

The ethnic-based fragmentation of the Muslim community is evident at the highest reaches of Muslim institutional life. Dissatisfied with the lack of decision-making autonomy, Kazakh clerics gathered in Alma-Ata in early 1990 to declare their independence from the Central Asian Muslim Board and the formation of a Muslim Religious Board for Kazakhstan. The former qadi of Kazakhstan, who had been appointed by the mufti of Central Asia, became the mufti of Kazakhstan.[19] In the North Caucasus, disputes between various nationalities resulted in a declared dissolution of the North Caucasian Muslim Religious Board. Although the North Caucasian Board continued in late 1991 to operate out of Makhachkala and claimed jurisdiction over its traditional domain, a series of mutually independent "religious centers" were set up in the autonomous ethnic territories of the North Caucasus to administer religious life there.[20]

Ethnic distinctions are more evident at the mosque level as well. Whereas in the past, restrictions on the registration of mosques meant that local Muslims of various nationalities prayed together in the same mosque, relaxation of these restrictions has now led to a kind of "every Muslim for himself" mentality. In northern Azerbaijan, for example, separate mosques have been established for ethnic minorities, including Avars, Lezghins, and Ingilois (Georgian Muslims). A similar trend is evident in the multi-ethnic North Caucasus and parts of Central Asia.

Likewise, establishment of religious training centers throughout the former Soviet Union and emergence of a local-language Islamic press have increasingly contributed to a strengthening of more localized religious practices and beliefs. Not only are local national traditions becoming increasingly salient, but sectarian differences among the Soviet Muslim populations are also becoming more marked. Azerbaijani Shi'is, for example, who were traditionally educated at Uzbek-run Sunni institutions and thus received no formal training in the fundamentals of Shi'i Islam, now have their own Islamic institute in Baku. Reflecting local traditions, the educational program of the Baku madrasa naturally is founded in Ja'fari Shi'i Islam. Commenting on the opening of a new madrasa in Makhachkala, the mufti of the North Caucasus underscored the theological differences between local Shafi'i traditions and the Hanafi traditions that predominate in Central Asia.[21]

Sectarian and ethnic distinctions are increasingly evident in the institutional structures of the ulama-led Muslim Religious Boards, but what of the religious vision that these institutions produce? Given the chaos in public life, one might expect the ulama would exploit policies to revise their traditional image of Islam and the place of the Muslim community in contemporary Central Asia.

Undoubtedly an increase in the public role of religious organizations more generally has resulted in a greater localization of religious discourse. For example, the Azerbaijani leadership of the Transcaucasian Muslim Board took an active role in opposing Armenian agitation in the political dispute over the province of Nagorno-Karabakh.[22] But despite this and other instances of the "nationalization" of Islamic discourse, what is perhaps surprising about the recent forms and content of the argumentation of the religious scholars is its essential continuity with the traditions of Soviet Islamic argument. Indeed, the image of Islam and the Muslim community produced by the ulama in the period of Gorbachev's reform was largely a reprise of postwar themes. The Muslim community, the ulama still argue, has fallen into un-Islamic ways and needs clerical leadership in order to return to the fundamentals of the faith. Not only has the dissolution of the Soviet Union afforded Muslims new opportunities for religious and secular development, the ulama argue, but Muslims are in fact active participants in the construction of a renewed social and political order.[23]

Armed with the language of glasnost, ulama continued to promote their notions of distinction and integration with regard to the Muslim community. If in the past the ulama praised Soviet power for the realization of Islamic ideals, under perestroika they praised the Soviet innovations of glasnost and perestroika for allowing restitution of religious rights and self-esteem to the pious population.[24] The innovations of glasnost, they were quick to point out, should assure freedom of religious conviction for all citizens of the former Soviet Union, including, of course, Muslims. And in a claim for greater integration of Muslims in Central Asian society, the qadi of Turkmenistan stated that "perestroika has put an end to the view that believers are narrow-minded, even backward, and that they are the carriers of a different ideology alien to the officially accepted dogmas."[25]

The essential content of Muslim religious discourse remained largely unchanged in the recent period of reform, but there have been changes in the tone and forms of the arguments of the ulama. For example, Muslim officials have exhibited a greater willingness to blame the Muslim community's religious ignorance on the political restrictions imposed during the seven decades of Soviet power.[27] The newspaper of the Transcaucasian Muslim Board in 1991 ran a serialized translation of an anti-Soviet tract published by an emigré in Germany and titled *The Kremlin Empire: The Soviet Form of Colonialism*. At the same time, the ulama appropriated the language of perestroika and glasnost to criticize themselves for lack of religious vigilance to corruption within their ranks.[27]

The emergence of a critical bent in the views voiced by the ulama, whether directed internally at developments within the Muslim community or externally against the injustices practiced against Islam during the period of Soviet rule, must be understood in context. By 1991 some political activists publicly equated communism with fascism, current and former leaders of the Communist party regularly condemned party policies in the harshest terms, and mainstream journalism commonly depicted the Soviet Union as an empire that had been held together by violence and coercion. In this sense, then, the ulama in 1991 appeared not as a radical but as a deeply conservative social force. They engaged in sometimes harsh criticisms of past Soviet policies and practices with regard to religion and religious institutions, but Muslim religious leaders did not reject the Soviet political system wholesale. Given the political context briefly described above, the tenor of clerical criticisms reflected the ulama's longstanding position as an unusually loyal opposition.

The Muslim Boards and the New Muslim Opposition

The rapidly changing political environment has not only afforded the traditional centers of Muslim religious life new opportunities but has also created conditions for new forms of Muslim religious association. In the past, the Muslim Religious Boards could rely in part on the coercive power of the Soviet state to prevent the emergence of independent Muslim religious centers. In the period of glasnost, however, a general relaxation on the formation of public organizations allowed the emergence of several new Muslim religious movements. Thus, as the Muslim Religious Boards confronted a new set of religious and political challenges, they also increasingly faced a challenge from below—from the organization of Muslim religious movements that began in the early 1990s to operate independently of the Muslim Boards.

Unlike the Muslim Boards, whose well-developed institutional reach extends across entire republics and regions, new Muslim religious movements have emerged in relatively few places and are generally highly localized. The largest and most active of such movements are to be found mainly in the North Caucasus and parts of Central Asia. The most important of these movements include the Islamic Democratic Party in Dagestan, the Turkestan Islamic Party centered in Uzbekistan's Fergana Valley, and the Islamic Renaissance Party that operates in Uzbekistan and Tajikistan.[28]

The Turkestan Islamic Party in Uzbekistan is typical of these independent opposition movements.[29] Mistakenly identified in the West as a Wahhabi movement, these Muslims in the Fergana town of Namangan began their movement in February 1989 with the takeover of a mosque being used as a storage facility for wine.[30] After renovating the building, the Namangan Muslims chose an imam and mosque council and opened the mosque for regular worship, which then became the first mosque in the postwar Soviet Union to operate outside the jurisdiction of a Muslim Religious Board. In the ensuing months, local activists began constructing a madrasa alongside the mosque. Unlike the schools affiliated with Muslim Boards, the Namangan madrasa provided religious education for young people in general, not just training for clerics.

What is significant about the Fergana Valley movement and the other independent religious movements that have emerged in recent years is the particular nature of their oppositional challenge. The chief opponent of these new Muslim movements is not primarily the state but the Muslim Religious Boards, which traditionally dominated the religious life of the Muslim community. Thus, one of the chief targets of the Muslim opposition has been the leadership of the Muslim Boards, which the opposition condemns as self-serving and corrupt.

Interestingly, one of the main thrusts of the opposition's critique of the Muslim Boards is not that they are former agents of Soviet state power, but that they are parasitic organizations exploiting the good will of the Muslim community. In this view, financial corruption among members of the Muslim Boards has impeded the members' role as religious leaders of the Muslim community. Thus it falls to the new Muslim movements to move into positions of community leadership where the Muslim Boards have failed.

That the Muslim opposition's challenge to the Muslim Boards concerns mainly the official clergy's institutional authority is highlighted by the fact that in many respects the opposition shares the stated religious values and ideals espoused by the Muslim Board. Like the Board ulama, many activists in the independent Muslim movement condemn the community's fall into degenerate ways and criticize saint worship, local pilgrimages, and the use of amulets. Likewise, they advocate a re-centering of Islam around the Qur'an and the hadith and seek to bring their own religious leadership to effect such a reorientation within the Muslim community.

In addition to the development of tensions along sectarian and ethnic lines, then, one of the main axes of political conflict in Central Asian Islam is the emergent struggle for religious and political authority in the Muslim community. In this contest, the advantages of the Muslim Boards are enormous. With several decades of institutional development behind them, the Muslim Boards have huge organizational, human, and financial resources at their disposal. The new Muslim movements, while increasingly popular within the community, nonetheless possess a significantly less developed set of resources and remain relatively localized in the scope of their activities. Moreover, the Board-affiliated ulama's campaign to reform themselves could severely undercut the power of oppositional critiques concerning the Boards' reputed internal corruption and faulty religious leadership. As the Central Asian Muslim community enters a new era, these internal conflicts over power and authority will remain central in the development of Muslim religious activism in the former Soviet Union.

Notes

1. For useful surveys and periodizations of Soviet policy toward Islam, see Nugman Ashirov, *Evoliutsiia islama v SSSR* (Moscow: Politizdat, 1973); and T. S. Saidbaev, *Islam i obshchestvo*, 2d ed. (Moscow: Nauka, 1984).

2. Some observers see the widespread persistence of informal religious practices as a "movement," but in fact there was no significant organizational coherence to these activities. See Alexandre Bennigsen and S. Enders Wimbush, *Mystics and Commissars: Sufism in the Soviet Union* (Berkeley: University of California Press, 1985).

3. For a survey of Soviet legal codes on religious organization, see G. J. Mürshüdlü, *Dini ayinlär haggïnda sovet ganunverijiliyi* (Baku, 1983).

4. For accounts of the Boards' internal structures, see Ziyauddin Khan ibn Ishan Babakhan, *Islam and Muslims in the Land of the Soviets* (Moscow: Progress, 1980); and Abdulla Vakhabov, *Muslims in the USSR* (Moscow: Novosti, 1980).

5. There are variations in the expression of purificationist tendencies among Muslim clerics. For example, a discourse of "return" to Islam was much less salient among North Caucasian and Transcaucasian Muslims.

Nevertheless, the account presented here focuses on the most general, common attributes of contemporary clerical images of Islam. On the distinctive trends in the Transcaucasus, for example, see R. Aslanova, "Shiälikdä modernizmin kharakteri," *Azärbaïjan dövlät universiteti. Elmi äsärlär. Tarikh, hügug vä fälsäfä seriyasï* 4 (1979).

6. Pierre Bourdieu, *Outline of a Theory of Practice* (Cambridge: Cambridge University Press, 1972).

7. A. Mavlankul, " More Attention to Depositories of Knowledge and Wisdom," *Muslims of the Soviet East* 4 (1984): 11.

8. "Along the True Path of the Qur'an," *Muslims of the Soviet East* 1 (1983): 1–2.

9. "At the X Session of the World Supreme Council of Mosques," *Muslims of the Soviet East* 2 (1985): 5.

10. Quoted from A. Akhmedov, *Sotsial'naia doktrina islama* (Moscow: Politizdat, 1982), p. 27. Translation mine.

11. "Soviet Muslim citizen" is my own descriptive device and not that of the Soviet Muslim ulama.

12. Talgat Tajuddin, "The Pride of the Tatar and Bashkir Peoples," *Muslims of the Soviet East* 1 (1984): 12.

13. "Muslims and Freedom of Religion in the Soviet Union," *Muslims of the Soviet East* 2 (1983): 2.

14. From a sermon quoted in Nugman Ashirov, *Nravstvennye poucheniia sovremennogo islama* (Moscow: Znanie, 1977), pp. 12–13.

15. "La mise en oeuvre des doctrines du Coran et de la Sunna, *Musulmans de l'orient Soviétique,* no. 1 (1977): 8)

16. This view is shared by some Soviet specialists of Islam. See M. A. Abdullaev and M. V. Vagabov, *Aktual'nye problemy kritiki i preodoleniia islama* (Makhachkala, 1975).

17. Alexandre Bennigsen and Marie Broxup, *The Islamic Threat to the Soviet State* (New York: St. Martin's, 1983).

18. Despite the pace of current mosque openings, nearly ninety mosques are reported to have opened in the period of "stagnation" between 1977 and 1987. "Novoe myshlenie i svoboda sovesti," *Literaturnaia gazeta,* 18 May 1988, p. 10.

19. For an account of the Kazakh mufti, see Paul Goble, "The New Mufti of Alma-Ata," *Report on the USSR,* 22 June 1990.

20. *Kommunist* (Baku), 10 March 1990.

21. Novosti press dispatch, 3 March 1989.

22. *Izvestiia,* 5 December 1988.

23. "Inexhaustible Source of Wisdom and Strength," *Muslims of the Soviet East* 1 (1989): 2.

24. For a mainstream clerical perspective, see Abdulgani Abdulla, "Musul'mane v usloviiakh glasnosti, perestroiki i novogo myshleniia," in *Na puti k svobode sovesti* (Moscow: Progress, 1989).

25. *Muslims of the Soviet East* 2–3 (1989): 10.

26. See, for example, the Central Asian mufti's critical comments as described in Paul Goble, "The Mufti on Television," *Report on the USSR,* 4 May 1990.

27. Self-criticism was a common theme at the fourth congress of the Central Asian Muslim Religious Board held in 1989. The entire issue, *Muslims of the Soviet East* 2–3 (1989), is devoted to the fourth congress.

28. For a useful survey of the Islamic Renaissance party, see Bess Brown, "The Islamic Renaissance Party in Central Asia," *Report on the USSR,* 10 May 1991.

29. This account of the positions of what I am calling a Muslim opposition is based in part on the Soviet press in addition to interviews conducted in Central Asia in 1990 and the Caucasus in 1991.

30. For a view of the Namangan movement as "Wahabbi," see James Critchlow, "Islam in the Fergana Valley: The Wahhabi 'Threat,'" *Report on the USSR,* 8 December 1989.

Two Roads to Revolutionary Shiʿite Fundamentalism in Iraq

Amatzia Baram

The two most important Islamic Shiʿi fundamentalist revolutionary movements of contemporary Iraq share essentially the same goals, but they chose two very different roads to attain them. Their common goal (as well as that of the other Iraqi Shiʿi fundamentalist opposition organizations)[1] is to topple the Baʿth regime and to replace it with an Islamic government that would impose the Islamic law (Shariʿa) in all walks of life. These organizations also seek to redress the historical imbalance in Iraq between the ruling Sunni Arabs (20 percent of the population) and the ruled Shiʿi Arabs (55 percent) by turning the latter into the hegemonic community. Beyond these goals, all the Shiʿi revolutionary movements are united in their resolve to use violence, if there is no other way to bring down the "infidel" Saddam Hussein and his regime. In this they have departed from a long Shiʿi tradition of quietism and non-involvement in political affairs. For many generations, political quietism was the prevalent (though not the exclusive) way in which the Shiʿi ulama preserved a weak Shiʿite minority in powerful, violently anti-Shiʿite Sunni states. (Only in the twentieth century, within the framework of the newly born nation-states of the Arab East, have the Shiʿa become an absolute majority in one country—Iraq.) The traditional theological tenet of *taqiyya* (precautionary dissimulation) was an important element of the quietist approach.

Other similarities stem from the common theology and activist tendency. Thus, for example, all the movements emphasize the activist, while playing down the quietist, aspects of the teachings and activities of the Shiʿi Imams, as well as historical and contemporary heroes. Finally, in varying degrees of clarity all the movements accept the legitimacy of the Iraqi nation-state and uphold the principle of Iraq's territorial integrity. By the same token, due to a combination of historical and contemporary reasons, none of these movements shows any enthusiasm toward pan-Arab unity. But here the similarity ends.

The older of the two most important movements, the Islamic Daʿwa party (Hizb al-Daʿwa al-Islamiyya), was established in the late 1950s in the Shiʿi holy city of Najaf by the most charismatic of the young Shiʿi ulama in Iraq of those days, Ayatollah Muhammad Baqir al-Sadr. The Daʿwa is an indigenous Iraqi organization, largely independent of Iranian dictates. Its counterpart, the Supreme Assembly for the Islamic Revolution in Iraq (al-Majlis Aʿla liʾl fiʾl-ʿIraq al-Islamiyya fiʾl-ʿIraq), or SAIRI, was established in November 1982 in Tehran as a front organization for the Iranian Islamic revolutionary government. Its all-powerful leader, Ayatollah Muhammad Baqir al-Hakim, has been an uninspiring bureaucrat and is one of the sons of the Supreme Authority (al-marjaʿ al-aʿla) of the Shiʿi world, Grand Ayat Allah Mushin al-Hakim of Najaf (d. 1970). SAIRI was initially designed to serve as an umbrella organization for all the fundamentalist Shiʿi opposition movements of Iraq. However, due to the perennial factionalism among those movements and their reluctance to come fully under Iranian tutelage and to recognize al-Hakim's leadership, SAIRI never fully served its purpose. Rather, it became an organization in its own right. While the Daʿwa operates from Tehran, Damascus, and London (and, to a lesser extent, from Lebanon), and thus retains some degree of independence, SAIRI operates exclusively from Iran.

In addition to the different degrees to which they depend on Iran, the two movements also differ substantially on the crucial issues of organization and leadership. While the Daʿwa is a small and elitist group at its core, organized along very strict lines of a closely knit underground party, reminiscent of the clandestine Communist party and the Baʿth in its clandestine stages, SAIRI is a mass organization, and it operates according to the old-time tradition of the Shiʿite community of mass adherence to leading ulama. Indeed, the whole issue of party organization has been a subject of bitter controversy between traditionalists and innovators within the religious university of Najaf since the first days of the existence of the Daʿwa party. While the Daʿwa activists felt that in modern-day Iraq it was necessary to emulate the organizational patterns of rival parties in order to succeed, strong circles in Najaf who saw the change as an "innovation" (*bidʿa*) and, as such, a dangerous deviation from Islamic tradition. While the Daʿwa was led by a charismatic *ʿalim* and considered charisma one of the most important requirements of its senior leadership, SAIRI was led from the outset by a bureaucrat. In the course of time, and especially after the execution of its founding leader in 1980, the Daʿwa went through a partial metamorphosis, with many laymen becoming an integral part of its most senior collective leadership, alongside their ulama counterparts. SAIRI, for its part, remained a strictly ulama-led organization, with a cult of personality around al-Hakim unmatched by any other Shiʿi opposition movement. This is one of the reasons for yet another ideological-organizational metamorphosis: while SAIRI remained committed to the principle, espoused by both Sadr and Ayatollah Ruhollah Khomeini, of the Rule of the Jurist, the Daʿwa detached itself from this principle. Finally, partly because it no longer depended on a single charismatic (or bureaucratic) leader, the Daʿwa since 1980 has made decisions in a far more diffuse and democratic fashion than has its counterpart.

On the ideological level both organizations are ostensibly pan-Islamic, but both are in fact merely pan-Shi'i. Within this general ideological commitment, however, the Da'wa, or at least those parts of it based in Europe and Damascus, short of support for pan-Arab unity, shows a deeper attachment to its Iraqi and Arab identity than does its SAIRI counterpart. This way it distances itself from the overpowering political and cultural influence of its Iranian host and patron. In that respect the Da'wa shows greater inclination to adopt modern Western concepts of language and territorial-based national identity. Similarly, it seems that the Da'wa's Western and Syrian-based cadres are less inclined than SAIRI to follow the Iranian directive of spreading the Islamic revolution into the Sunni world.

Another ideological difference is the far greater degree to which the Da'wa (or at least its Western-based parts) seems ready to consider the establishment of a Western-style liberal parliamentary democracy in Iraq once Saddam and his regime are defeated. Finally, the Da'wa is more amenable than SAIRI to forming political coalitions with forces that, until recently, had been an anathema to the fundamentalist opposition of Iraq: for example, such internal forces as Communists and ex-Ba'thists but also such external forces as the Saudis, the Gulf Emirates, and even the Western powers. This is yet another example of the Da'wa's greater freedom from Iranian dictates.

Organizational Structures

Hizb al-Da'wa al-Islamiyya

"And who so taketh Allah and His messenger and those who believe for friends [will know that], lo! the party of Allah, they are the victorious (Sura V, The Table, verse 56)."[2]

On a warm morning in early October 1957, on the occasion of the Prophet's birthday, a group of young ulama and one or two laymen assembled to celebrate this important religious occasion at the home of one of Najaf's leading young scholars, Muhammad Baqir al-Sadr, an ingenious yet controversial *mujtahid* (a senior Shi'i scholar, authorized to issue legal opinions). According to their annals, this was the genesis of the Islamic Da'wa party. As explained by al-Sadr, *da'wa*, "the call [to Islam]," was "the natural name for our action and the legitimate expression of our duty to call the people to Islam. There is no hindrance in our expressing ourselves as a party, a movement, and an organization because we are the party of God [*hizb Allah*] and the partisans of God and the partisans of Islam. And we are a movement in society and an organization in action, and in any case we are Callers [*du'at*] to Islam and our work is the Call to Islam." The occasion was chosen to create an association between the new party and "the First Caller," Muhammad, who "replaced the First Jahiliyya with Islam."[3] According to somewhat differing sources, those present at Sadr's home—the founding members of the party—were his young students (born in the 1930s), and most of them were ulama (graduates of the "University" or the "Circle of Learning" of Najaf).[4] Later, when Sadr became the moving force behind the establishment of a Da'wa party branch among the Shi'ite population of Lebanon, his Lebanese students at Najaf were its first leaders.

According to a party document, the Da'wa had an elaborate organization from the outset. The structure is defined as "pyramidal." At the head of the party is a Council of Jurists. Membership on this council is limited to well-established mujtahids (apparently ulama with the rank of at least ayatollah), who combine religious eminence with deep understanding of social and political affairs. Politically active, they decide on the broad lines of the party's political stance, solve legal issues (*fiqh*) that arise as a result of the political struggle, and provide "legal backing" to the lower echelons. One stage lower is the Council of Leadership, whose responsibilities include day-to-day ideological guidance, a more detailed planning of the party's activity, and supervision of the activity of the lower bodies, known as the Executive Committees. While the two higher bodies are international, the Executive Committees are regional, that is, they lead the activities of the movement in a particular country. The committees execute the higher body's instructions and include representatives from the various parts of the country. Each such part, or small region, elects a Central Committee. There is strict separation between the various committees in order to avoid exposure by the authorities.[5]

The Da'wa's structure developed very gradually. According to one interview, in the 1970s, during the years of underground activity in Iraq, the Da'wa's lowest echelons were five-to seven-member "rings" (*halaqat*); above them were the "committees" (*lajna*) of the "quarter" (*mahalla*), then of the "region" (*mintaqa*). A member knew only the other members in his own ring. To guarantee maximum security, and following Ba'th patterns of clandestine organization, communication among the various rings was strictly vertical, that is, through the higher body and not directly or horizontally.[6] There is no evidence that under 'Abd al-Karim (1958–63) or the 'Arif brothers, Shi'ite activists were persecuted. Indeed, Shi'ite sources are full of descriptions of public activities which apparently went unopposed by the regime. Yet Sadr took it for granted that the party's initial stage ought to be secret.[7] He argued that during this stage of the party's activity, total secrecy was essential not only to avoid an official crackdown, but also to avoid repression by powerful circles within the traditional Shi'ite religious establishment.[8]

This elaborate structure may have never been fully accomplished. There is no evidence, for example, that the body of mujtahids ever existed. Rather, it seems that Sadr himself was the embodiment of the Council of Jurists. The group that assembled that day at his home in Najaf, consisting of more junior ulama and two laymen, may have been the Council of Leadership.

Even though this description is very general, it is clear that, as a matter of principle, the party's organization derives its inspiration from the Communist and the Ba'th parties. Indeed, both supporters and opponents of the Da'wa within the religious Shi'ite community agreed that it derived its inspiration from the secular parties that were modeled after Western patterns.[9] In later years, apparently following the Communist example, one of the top institutions received the name al-Maktab al-Siyasi (the Political Office or Politburo).[10] In his treatise Sadr made great efforts to differentiate between the Islamic and non-Islamic style of party organizations, but the difference as he defined it is found in the inner spirit of the movement rather than in its formal structure: in total obedience to God and his command rather than to a human authority.

According to an account by the party's own sources, Sadr and his colleagues were prompted to establish the Da'wa in response to two developments. One was the decline of religiosity among the Iraqi public and, more importantly for the young ulama, in the Shi'ite areas. In Sadr's own words, this decline necessitated "an intellectual change" in the nation.[11] According to an Iraqi Shi'ite source, the Shi'ite areas also witnessed a major decline in the activity of the religious establishment. Thus, for example, there were no more than five ulama and fifty lower-level religious functionaries in the al-Thawra quarter of Baghdad in the late 1950s and early 1960s, while there were more than one hundred mosques in that quarter and its population exceeded one million. And in Basra, with a population of one million and about one hundred mosques, there were only fifteen ulama.[12] This organizational weakness was reflected also in the number of students in the *hawzat* (the "circles of learning" or religious universities) of Najaf, Karbala, and Kazimiyya. In 1958 this number reached 1,954, of whom only 326 were Iraqis.[13] These figures were particularly depressing for the young ulama, who must have been aware that the Iraqi centers of religion had seen better days.

Thus, for example, before the British invasion of Iraq in 1914, the number of religious students and teachers at the religious *madrasas* (schools) in Najaf was reported to have been 12,000. As noted by a visitor to southern Iraq a few years later, "the number is decreasing day by day; it is feared that religious learning might one day become extinct."[14] In 1918 a British source reported that the number of students (as opposed to teachers and other religious functionaries) in Najaf was 6,000.[15] Furthermore, in the late 1940s, the Indian government suspended contributions by the Indian kingdom of Awadh (the Oudh Bequest), which for many years had helped support students of religion. Even if the figures were inflated, and even if the 1958 figure relates to Najaf alone, the decline is still meaningful. In addition to the understandable ideological concern of young students and teachers of religion, their social and economic status also played a part in their urge to reverse the decline. After all, none of them, perhaps with the exception of Sadr himself, had yet established himself as a widely accepted authority. In Shi'ite Islam, establishing such authority is crucial not only to the religious and social standing of an 'alim but also to his economic status: in Iraq traditionally, in contrast to their Sunni counterparts, the Shi'ite ulama were supported by their followers rather than by the state. The more adherents a mujtahid had, the more contributions he was likely to receive. While well-established (and thus well-financed) "authorities"[16] could accept the shrinking of their audience with relative equanimity, ambitious lesser-known ulama found the decline in religious life in general and in the number of religious students in particular to be ominous signs. Indeed, the initiative to establish an Islamic (Shi'i) party came from the young ulama (and one young layman, al-Dakhil), who turned to Sadr for guidance.[17]

Religious circles in the Shi'ite holy cities regarded the Communists rather than the Ba'thists as the most potent enemy. As defined many years later by a source close to the Da'wa party: "The Iraqi arena suffered during the 1950s from the surge of the

Communist movement which concentrated on combatting religious belief with the intention of uprooting it from the hearts of the sons of the nation, particularly those of the youth. They made tremendous headway due to the absence of anyone who could confront them, until the martyred [Sadr] appeared. . . . He spread the light of truth and brought back many of the lost youth to its religion."[18]

Communist influence in the Shi'ite holy cities increased throughout the 1950s, but with the downfall of the monarchy, under the sympathetic regime of 'Abd al-Karim Qasim, the Communists gained a meaningful foothold in internal security, in the media, and in the state educational system. The circulation of their newspaper *Ittihad al-Sha'b* (*Union of the People*) increased from two thousand copies before the revolution to twenty-three thousand copies in March 1959. Even non-Communist newspapers started to reflect Communist views, as in the case of the Najaf-based *al-Ayyam* (*Days*). Following Qasim's revolution, the Communists also gained control over the National Teachers' Association and various peasant associations, both very active in the Shi'ite south. In the early months of the Republican rule, a number of violent clashes occurred between Communist supporters and religious circles in Kadhimayn, Karbala, and Najaf.[19] The quantum jump in Communist activity under Qasim necessitated a counteroffensive by the religious circles, aimed at "educating the public about Islam . . . as a total way of life and social order," to enable them to differentiate "between Islam and infidel ideologies."[20]

A senior lay Da'wa member explained to this author his hatred for the supercilious Communists, "who always had perfect answers to all the questions" and "whose infidelity was very extreme," and who tried to deceive the gullible masses by claiming that Shi'i and Shuyu'i (a Communist) are one and the same. His hatred for the Communists was far greater than his reservations toward the Ba'thists, who were merely secular and whom Shi'ites regarded as religious people before 1968. Indeed, many traditional Shi'ites regarded the Ba'thists as allies due to the latter's vicious animosity toward the Communists as well as their claim to religiosity.[21]

Establishment of an Islamic party modeled after modern Western parties, so different from the historic pattern of religious Shi'ite activity, met with fierce opposition from more traditional Shi'ite circles. As pointed out by a Da'wa spokesman, in those days "many of those religious people who believed in hollow religiosity accused anyone who belonged to an Islamic party, let alone anyone who established an Islamic party, of deviation from the road of correct Islam and of connection with infidel imperialism." Al-Hakim, however, did not object to the existence of an Islamic party. But Da'wa sources relate that when things came to a head, al-Hakim sent one of his sons to tell Sadr that, due to the latter's eminent position in the hawza, it was not appropriate that he belonged to a particular party or "organization" (*al-tanzim*). He had to be available equally to all the believers. Sadr accepted al-Hakim's rule and in 1962 announced that he could no longer be a member of the Da'wa, though he remained in close touch with the party.[22]

Indeed, differences between those objecting to and those defending the Western-inspired party system remained an integral part of the internal politics of the activist Shi'ite movement in later years. In the late 1980s the opponents of the party system accused al-Da'wa, Munazzamat al-'Amal, and lesser parties of borrowing "a Western idea that comes from the infidel countries" and thus deviating from Islam. They also objected to the secrecy that typified the clandestine Islamic parties as incompatible with the traditional openness of the *marja'iyya* (the supreme religious authority). In addition, the party system was competing with the ulama or, as they put it, "opposed [the principle of] the Rule of the Jurist." Sadr's participation in establishing the Da'wa was denied or ignored, and he reportedly forbade Muslims to belong to it. Paradoxically, Muhammad Baqir al-Hakim was, according to some sources, one of the founders of the Da'wa (he left it a few years later). A student of Sadr's, he became a torchbearer in the struggle against the party system after establishment of the Supreme Council in 1982.

Muhammad Baqir al-Hakim and his followers in the Supreme Assembly regarded such parties with "collective leaderships that are represented by leading committees" as "incompatible with the Islamic theory of leadership." To legitimize this stance, the Assembly's chief ideologue presented it as a central theme in Sadr's thought. Sadr is reported to have forbidden "all those who love him and believe in his line and all the students of religion from belonging to a party, however Islamic, clean and dedicated it may be." In a contradictory way, in the same source Sadr is also reported to have allowed the existence of Islamic parties, provided they remain loyal to the principle of the Guardianship of the Jurist (*wilayat al-faqih*) and accept totally "the line of the marja'iyya." In the last analysis, however, al-Hakim and his followers on the Assembly were highly suspicious of any party and felt that it was bound either to ignore completely the Rule of the Jurist or to pretend to accept it but only in a purely formal fashion, switching from one *faqih* (jurist) to another according to their immediate political needs.[23]

The Da'wa resorted to the same method in basing its legitimacy on Sadr's authority; the party never tired stressing that it was established by Sadr himself. Quoting an article he published in the early 1960s, the Da'wa wrote in a publication commemorating the first anniversary of his martyrdom:

> The organizational form which we chose for our Da'wa is a development of the widespread form [typical of] modern organizations, together with consideration for the interest of the Da'wa to Islam. . . . Since the Islamic Shari'a did not enforce a specific way for spreading the message . . . we are free to chose whatever useful way to spread the meanings of Islam and its rules and to change society . . . as long as this way does not include anything forbidden by the Shari'a. . . .
>
> The Prophet-leader had he lived in our age would have used in his great wisdom the modern and suitable means of communications and of spreading the message. Indeed, his way in the Da'wa was not far from the cell organization [*al-tanzim al-halaqi*]. . . . Concentrating [all] efforts for Islam and coordinating them wisely and choosing the best way for organization . . . in our age . . . is a duty. . . . The practice of the various world organizations has proved that the organization is the successful way in changing society whether toward good or evil.[24]

In this article, Sadr legitimizes the principle of a small, well-organized, and closely knit group as flag-bearer of the Islamic message by quoting a hadith: "There are three things which a Muslim man's heart should not give up: devotion to Allah, guiding and counseling the Muslims, and adherence to their community. It was said: and who are the community of Muslims? Said [the Prophet]: the people of truth even if they are but few."[25]

Sadr's dissociation from the party in the early 1960s is explained in terms of his bowing to conservative pressure from the hawza. His 1974 decision to make a clean break between the party and the hawza was explained in terms of hawza security, for fear of Ba'th reprisals; it was defined as unavoidable taqiyya.[26] The Da'wa also made special efforts to emphasize its allegiance to the *fuqaha* (jurists) as the legitimate interpreters of the rules of the Shari'a, but made no secret of its independence in the more practical, day-to-day conduct of political affairs.[27]

The Da'wa in Action: The Early Years

Even though its leadership in its initial stages consisted almost exclusively of young ulama, the Da'wa's main thrust was in the realm of lay intellectuals, chiefly in Baghdad but also in other Shi'ite concentrations, starting with the holy cities. This fact emerges from explicit assertions by Da'wa spokesmen, but it can also be deduced from lists of martyrs. One list, prepared from thirty-eight biographies that appear in *Al-Da'wa Chronicle* between May 1980 and May 1983, shows that 61 percent of the martyrs were university educated—many with scientific education, or university students. Thirteen percent had a high school education, 13 percent were small businessmen, and 13 percent were students of religion. According to another list based on 178 martyrs from all the Shi'i religious activist movements until the end of 1980, most of whom were Da'wa or ex-Da'wa members, 52 percent were students and graduates of secular universities. (Of this group, 42 percent had studied the sciences and engineering, 9 percent medicine, and 33 percent teaching.) Fourteen percent of the total were in the army, and only 10 percent were students of religion. Ten percent were small businessmen, 6 percent had a secular high school education, 4 percent had less than a high school education, and 3 percent were unknown.[28] From a study of 61 martyrs who died in all the organizations during the war between Iraq and Iran, it emerges that the level of education of the recruits fell sharply between 1980 and 1988. This was no doubt due to SAIRI's mass mobilization policy.[29] The limited information available indicates that the draftees came from the city's lower-middle class, but it is unclear whether their inclination to join the Da'wa (and after 1979 al-Mujahidin) should be ascribed to their social strata; after all, the regime had given many of them the opportunity to improve their social status through education. However, many may have felt that the regime did not treat them as well as their Sunni counterparts, as they were deeply aware of their Shi'ite identity. And they had other reasons for joining a fundamentalist activist movement: some came from traditional families; others were influenced by a charismatic *da'iya* or "caller"; others were simply dissatisfied with their secular way of life and were looking for something more satisfying spiritually, sometimes without even being fully aware of it.[30]

On the intellectual level, Sadr, the Da'wa's founder, made a major contribution toward combatting Marxism (and, to a lesser extent, other Western theories) when in 1959 he wrote his now well-known *Falsafatuna* (Our philosophy), aimed chiefly at secular youth. In 1961 Sadr published his second such book, *Iqtisaduna* (Our economics).

The party's first nonclergy members came from the weekly religion study circles organized by Sadr and others. The participants were chiefly Shi‘ite students of Baghdad University and young intellectuals, mostly from the professions, to whom Sadr and other Da‘wa activists taught the interpretation of the Qur'an. To those few who could spare more time and make the effort they taught *usul al-fiqh* (the principles of jurisprudence). According to the Da‘wa manual, a new recruit has to memorize the Qur'an and understand its interpretations; he has to acquaint himself with Islamic philosophy and ideology, the latter through Sadr's book *Al-madrasa al-islamiyya* (the Islamic school) and Sayyid Qutb's *Al-tasawwur al-islami* (the Islamic imagination); he must acquire basic knowledge of the life history *(al-sira)* of the Prophet, the Prophet's important "companions" *(sahaba)*, and the twelve Shi‘ite Imams; he must be versed in the rules of the Qur'an insofar as everyday life is concerned; and he must study the Da‘wa line on political, social, and organizational methods. At an advanced level, a member must be able to select and present sophisticated ideas about politics and society and "to develop original thoughts and concepts from their original Islamic sources," the Qur'an and the Sunna.[31]

These meetings took place, at first, in a number of mosques around Baghdad (in later years some educational activities for lay religious youth were conducted in various parts of the Shi‘ite south, including tribal areas) and were very unusual. Not only did they demonstrate Sadr's appreciation for the capacity of lay intellectuals to grasp complicated religious issues, but they demonstrated his readiness to share such knowledge with laymen and thus relinquish the ulama's monopoly. Indeed, Sadr complemented his study circles with a book designed to simplify the study of usul al-fiqh, replacing the textbook from the Qajari period. The book was organized in three parts, in a way similar to modern Arab textbooks, and was aimed at students of religion and lay intellectuals. In these circles Sadr also discussed economics and politics, dedicating a part of the discussions to refuting Marxist dialectical materialism. Both of these aspects—the religious and the political—were new to the young lay intellectuals. Nor were they used to being regarded by ulama as worthy of being taught high-level religious studies. A mujtahid talking authoritatively about economics and Marxism was a shock. One of the reasons for these students' detachment from religious life was their low view of the "turbaned ones as reactionaries who know little about real life."[32] These fiqh study groups involved only very small numbers of students, however, due to the great complexity of the subject. For busy university students and professionals, membership in one of these groups was indeed a heavy burden.[33]

The day-to-day work of the Da‘wa included a variety of activities. During religious festivals, and especially during the months of Muharram (when the Shi‘ite community commemorates the death of their third Imam, Husayn, in 680 C.E.) and Ramadan, Da‘wa activists hung Islamic flags at Baghdad University and spread Islamic slogans urging believers to abide by the rules of Islam. Though the party's name was never mentioned, everyone knew who was behind the activity. During the mid-1960s the party (or at least its young ulama leadership, notably Muhammad Baqir al-Hakim and Nuri Tu'ma) organized university students' 'Ashura processions. Instead of self-flagellation and other traditional violent expressions of grief, the university youth marched in a "mass procession that had also an air of tranquility and organization." Reportedly, university students from Mosul and Basra participated as well.[34]

Every day the party organized a public noon prayer in which many of the teachers participated. Under 'Abd al-Rahman 'Arif (1966–68) the party also ran for election to the student union under its own banner. On the personal level, each member of the Da'wa party was expected to win new members. Between 1966 and 1969 the party managed to recruit "hundreds" of new members from among Baghdad University students. Recruiting students, especially from the more prestigious departments of the university, fit Sadr's demand to "prepare the believing, struggling, conscious group," or "the changing group," namely, the cadre, or the hard core.[35]

Another method of recruiting new members, practiced by 'Arif al-Basri in Baghdad, was sending agents to high schools and university graduation parties. The agent would seek out the brightest students, giving them an expensive Schaefer fountain pen in the name of the Da'wa. This was the first step toward co-opting those endowed with "the most outstanding potential and the most intelligent to serve Islam." Yet another way was taking names of doctors and engineers from a telephone book and sending them letters, in the name of a senior religious authority, asking them to contribute money for Islamic activities and institutions.[36] If a candidate replied and sent money, the movement won both financial support and a new member.

The three stages to actual recruitment began with the "familiarity stage" (*marhalat al-ta'aruf*), which involved collecting information about the new candidate, his family, social and political background, problems, inclinations, and so forth. If it were found that he was not clearly "committed" to an already existing political body, and if he were "suitable material" (i.e., both intelligent and impressionable), the "caller" (*da'iya*) entered the second phase—the "friendship phase" (*marhalat al-sadaqa*). The intention was to forge a strong personal friendship with the new recruit and influence him through manipulating his emotions. The third was the "targeting phase" (*marhalat al-iltizam,* literally "engagement"), during which the new recruit was gradually influenced by the da'iya to behave in an Islamic way. If he drank alcohol, he was encouraged to stop. If he never prayed or attended a mosque, he was encouraged to start praying. And if he met these conditions, he was encouraged to join the party, become an active member, and work toward recruiting others. The party also tried to recruit Sunni students, but with limited success: only about 5 percent of the total membership were Sunnis. No efforts were made to convert Sunnis, but when some Christian students joined the party and then converted to (Shi'i) Islam, the party's leadership rejoiced and saw in it a great promise.

The fact that the veteran party members were university students at more advanced stages of study was an important mobilization tool. Recruitment was mostly carried out through personal contact within each member's own faculty. Upon the arrival of a new class, the more senior students were in the position to offer the freshmen assistance with their studies (books, tuition). This tutorial assistance proved a powerful recruitment tool.[37] (However, as soon as the Ba'th regime started to persecute the party, and membership in the Da'wa could mean torture, even death, such small favors no longer made any difference, and new recruits had to be made of far sterner stuff.) Reflecting the party's incremental approach to recruitment, one of its historians noted that every week, every member was interrogated as to "how many people he introduced himself to, and established with them ties of friendship and brotherhood; how many did he manage to convince to return to Islam; how many did he impress with the corruption of the situation; and . . . with the need to work for Islam, . . . and how many persons did he prepare for jihad for Allah."[38]

The Da'wa has no initiation ceremony, but each new recruit goes through an informal period of candidacy to show that he is a pious Muslim and a committed activist. He also has to believe that the best way to serve Islam is through an organized body, like a party (*hizb*), rather than through the old system of the Shi'ite religious networks. During his candidacy a member enters a "one-way system" in which he is only giving—spending time and money, risking his and his family's life—without getting anything in return. Following this test period the candidate receives political and ideological guidance (religious guidance comes, of course, from the start). He is never told explicitly that he has become a member. Rather, he senses it through his superior's attitude and can be sure of it when he is promoted within the ranks of the organization. "Wherever he is, the da'iya is a soldier in the Da'wa party and a leader in his community." He must strive to become a central figure in his community and use this influential position to mobilize others.

An additional dimension to the party's work is recruitment of *ansar* ("supporters," a term used also by the Communists and the Ba'th) from among the lower and less-educated classes. As instructed by Sadr, members, and in particular the ulama among them, were bent on social and religious activities designed to create around the party a protective shield of people "with some degree of consciousness" who would provide mass support and make it more difficult for a hostile regime to crack down.[39]

Da'wa Organization and Activities in the 1980s

In its new, post-1980 incarnation, the Da'wa's organizational structure is changed, at least at the top. Its founder and main inspiration, Sadr, was executed by the Ba'th regime in April 1980. Other ulama who led the movement in its early stages were executed as well (including 'Arif al-Basri). One of the leading ulama, Mahdi al-Hakim, was assassinated by Ba'th agents in the Sudan in January 1988.[40] According to one internal source, in 1990 the top echelon of the Da'wa party, the General Leadership (al-Qiyada al-'Amma, sometimes the Central Committee), consisting of seven to twelve people, included a few laymen, even though the majority were ulama. In the lower body, the General Congress or the Politbureau, of some one hundred representatives from various regions of Iraq and exiles abroad only 10 percent were "turbaned" while more than 60 percent were lay professionals. The supreme body was responsible only for delineating the broadest lines and ensuring that activity would not contradict the Shari'a, while the second body made the day-to-day political decisions.[41]

Bearing in mind the great secrecy surrounding the party, these claims are difficult to corroborate. However, the party's public records bear evidence that laymen are indeed conspicuous among people who represent the party in its external contacts and who speak at public party gatherings (mostly on political, but sometimes on religious occasions).[42]

There is no clear information about the organization of the party's lower levels, but evidence suggests that the strict secrecy and compartmentalization have been substantially relaxed in Iran and Europe, where the party can operate openly. Reportedly, the party operates on the basis of democratically made decisions. The General Congress is elected on a regional basis. It, in turn, elects the smaller body above it. Important decisions are made by a majority vote in the Congress. Special strategic decisions, like the Da'wa's position on the invasion of Kuwait, are adopted by a two-thirds majority. The highest body, too, makes its decisions by majority vote, and since the Da'wa lost its mentor, Sadr, no single figure has replaced him. The party has a two-way system of communication: from the top to the grass roots, *al-nazar al-nazil* (the descending view), and vice versa, *al-nazar al-sa'id* (the ascending view). The latter finds its main expression in written policy recommendations.

Islamic scholarship is one criterion for electing a member of a regional branch to the higher bodies, but other no less important criteria include religious piety, charisma, social status, and influence that translates into mass support among party members and sympathizers. Still, Da'wa members admit that the accusations of intellectual elitism aimed at them have more than a grain of truth. "The party's natural direction was to co-opt intellectuals, university graduates and professionals, because we preached for new Islamic thinking, and such a credo is not effective with peasants."[43] A party historian noted, with undisguised satisfaction: "[People] were whispering: they [the Da'wa] managed to win over the intellectual stratum, leaving for us the illiterates and the ignorant."[44]

"However," noted a Da'wa activist, "through the ulama and the 'agents' [*wukala*] we were able to influence many simple people in various parts of Iraq, particularly in Saddam's City [the al-Thawra quarter of Baghdad where more than one million poor Shi'ites live]." Indeed, according to the Da'wa weekly, some 80 percent of Sadr's agents in 1979 were members of the party.[45] The same, it seems, applies to present activities in Iran among the Iraqi expatriates. According to *Al-Jihad*, the Da'wa weekly issued in Tehran since December 1981,[46] the party conducts a great variety of activities among the Iraqi ex-patriates through a plethora of organizations associated with it. Such organizations include the Society of the Muslim Woman in Iraq; the Institute of the Martyred Sadr; Partisans of Husayn; the Association of the Procession of the Pious Students (organizing processions in memory of Husayn on the fortieth day of his death); the Association of the Martyred Bint al-Huda, a cultural women's organization; the Jihad Office of the Da'wa party; the Islamic Cultural Center; the Committee of Ceremonies and Celebrations; the Committee of the Iraqi Union of Islamic Students; and the Islamic Union of Iraqi Workers. There is also a medical society and an Islamic Union of Iraqi Engineers.

All of these organizations are primarily intended to indoctrinate through cultural and religious activities. The latter four also serve more practical purposes. The student organization assists students with their particular problems, and the workers' organization, established in 1980, helps Iraqi workers find jobs and communicate with Iranian institutions; it also looks after needy and poor members. The engineers' union organizes professional courses like computer programming and graphics classes. Finally, there is a Jihad Bureau in more than one center which coordinates armed activities inside Iraq.[47] The party has branches in a number of countries where there is a large Shi'ite community, chiefly in England, Lebanon, Syria, and Afghanistan.[48]

The number of Da'wa's active members (and members of similar organizations) inside Iraq was fairly large before the Ba'th crackdown of 1979–80, but the regime executed several hundred of them and jailed some ten thousand. After the crackdown that included the exile of at least 250,000 supporters and potential supporters to Iran, its numbers declined substantially.[49]

One organizational aspect that came up in interviews, and that could be gleaned from contrasting party sources in Tehran and those in the West, is the division between party activists who operated out of Iran and those who operated out of Europe. In 1990–91 the latter showed more ideological flexibility on a number of issues, apparently due to their relative independence of Iranian tutelage. Even more intriguing is a claim that the Arab Shi'ites of Iraq, due to their long-standing contacts with the Arab Sunnis there, have developed a more moderate approach to the Shi'ite-Sunni divide in particular, and to politics in general, than their Iranian counterparts have. This radicalism found expression in less accommodating positions vis-à-vis the Sunnis as well as in deep fascination with the "international dimension of the movement," namely, with export of the revolution and eradication of the international borders between Muslim countries. Sadr, according to this analysis, was a moderate along the Iraqi-Arab tradition, as was the party. His last communiqué to the Iraqi people called for Shi'ite-Sunni equality and cooperation within Iraq. When he died, and his disciples went to Khomeini's Iran, "they were radicalized from a Shi'ite point of view." Those who continued to adhere to the original party ideology were suspected of "becoming somewhat Sunni."[50] Sadr did call for cooperating with the Sunnis of Iraq and even paid tribute to two historical heroes upheld by the Sunna but traditionally despised by the Shi'ites, the Caliphs Abu Bakr and 'Umar.[51] Due to their historical ties to Sunnis and their long history of living under Sunni rule, the Shi'ites of Iraq are more ecumenical (or more accustomed to taqiyya).

The Da'wa's Armed Activity

According to Da'wa sources, even though it preached fundamental revolution in society rather than mere reforms, the party operated openly and peacefully as long as the authorities allowed it to do so. In other words: revolution did not necessarily mean violence. Sadr demanded a revolution (*al-inqilab*) because he believed that all the regimes to rule Iraq after the disintegration of the Ottoman Empire were so hopelessly and totally removed from Islam and influenced by the Christian West that they were beyond remedy.[52] However, until 1969–70 the party's activity was tolerated, and thus it could spread its message effectively, without resorting to violence or undue secrecy (although the party has always retained a certain degree of secrecy).[53]

In June 1969 the Ba'th regime clashed head-on, for the first time, with the Shi'ite religious establishment, and thereafter things went from bad to worse. At first, new students were warned by the Ba'thi Students' Union to keep a distance from Da'wa activists. The latter were later warned to cease all Islamic political activity, and then they were arrested and tortured. In 1972, one of the party's founding members 'Abd al-Sahib Dakhil was executed. In 1974, five more activists were executed. As reported by party sources, this prompted the party to establish an armed organization and to engage in violent activities. In the mid-1980s the party established a regular army unit (The Forces of the Martyred Sadr), which fought with the Iranian army during the Iran-Iraq War.[54] These activities became noticeable following Khomeini's rise to power in Tehran, when party members started attacking police stations, government and Ba'th offices, and Ba'th officials. The severe crackdown in 1979–80 crippled the Da'wa, but its armed activities continued within and outside Iraq throughout the 1980s.[55]

The number of regular soldiers and underground Da'wa activists was probably in the hundreds. Most served in the party's regular unit. Some operated inside Iraq, and some in other countries of the Middle East and, occasionally, in Europe. Inside Iraq their activities were aimed at Ba'th party offices in the Shi'ite areas, and in Baghdad at government buildings, senior government officials, ammunition dumps, and military facilities. Their most lethal weapons were car bombs, but they also tossed hand grenades and sprayed Ba'th facilities with submachine guns, sometimes from a passing motorcycle.

These armed activities came in waves. For example, in April and early May 1987 the party killed the head of the Ba'th branch in the Shi'ite Baghdad quarter of al-Shu'la (29 April), attacked a party office in the Mansur quarter of Baghdad (3 May), and attacked a few Ba'th personnel in the Shi'ite quarter of al-Thawra. All this, apparently, was in response to a call by a SAIRI conference of December 1986 to escalate the war from within Iraq. On 9 April 1987 the Da'wa attempted to assassinate Saddam Hussein, who was driving in his motorcade on a central street in Mosul. In the shoot-out, twenty people were killed but Saddam emerged unscathed. In August 1987, four car bombs exploded in Baghdad, and a number of people were killed. During early September 1987, the party attempted to assassinate Muhammad Samir al-Shaykhali, the minister of the interior. His driver and two of his escorts died but he was unhurt. The assassins may have thought they were shooting at Saddam's car. On 7 September 1987, at an official ceremony in Ba'quba, east of Baghdad, they attacked local guests and foreign diplomats who were sitting on the stage and managed to kill a number of Iraqi dignitaries. No diplomats were hurt. This attack was an attempt by the Da'wa to prove to the foreign diplomatic corps that Saddam did not control Iraq. On 4 December 1988 they exploded a car bomb to destroy the Social Security building in central Baghdad, which was also used by Iraqi intelligence. There were dozens of casualties.

The regime, for its part, acted just as ruthlessly and executed people for mere membership in the party, even if they did not participate in any terrorist activity. In a few cases the executions were public. For example, on 12 October 1987, four Da'wa members were executed for sabotage, by a firing squad in the Sunni Baghdad quarter of al-A'zamiyya, in the presence of a throng of local citizens.[56] Most of these Da'wa activities seemed typified by great courage and reasonably good planning up to the point of the actual attack. In the case of shoot-outs, as opposed to car bombings, the planning of escape routes was clearly deficient, so Da'wa members were actually acting as suicide squads.

As for activities outside of Iraq, Kuwait became an important target due to its substantial financial support for Iraq and its strategic contribution to the Iraqi war effort through its extensive port services. On 12 December 1983, a suicide car bomb driven by a member of the Da'wa exploded near the U.S. embassy, causing extensive damage. This explosion was one of six that day in Kuwait City. A few other car bombs were dismantled before they could explode near official buildings. The Kuwaiti authorities apprehended nineteen people: Lebanese, Iraqis, and Iranians belonging to the Da'wa.[57] In later years the Da'wa warned the Kuwaiti government against extraditing the terrorists to Iraq and even tried to get them released by taking Kuwaiti hostages. There were a few other cases of Da'wa terrorist activities in Kuwait, the last of which was an attempt on the life of the emir in 1989, as well as in other countries, particularly Turkey and Lebanon, against Iraqi targets. They all demonstrated the members' dedication and courage as well as their complete lack of respect for international codes of conduct. In 1989, however, the organization felt it would need Western support to topple Saddam, so the Da'wa suspended all terrorist activities abroad.[58]

Jama'at al-Ulama

A few months after the establishment of the Da'wa party, sometime in 1958 following Qasim's Republican Revolution and the upsurge of "Communist terrorism," a somewhat different organization came into being. Unlike its predecessor it was much less closely knit, smaller, and included only ulama. But its goal was essentially the same, namely "combating atheism and its numerous trends . . . building bridges between Islam and the various sections of the [Islamic] nation, particularly the educated classes and university students." The new body called itself Jama'at al-Ulama (the Group of Ulama, henceforth Jama'a). Even though the Jama'a was clearly separate from the Da'wa, there were many contacts and some of their leading personalities were closely connected.[59] While Sadr and his generation could not become full-fledged members of the Najaf-based Jama'a, which consisted of more elderly and better-established ulama, they were active in a younger Jama'a established a little later in Baghdad and Kazimayn. Between 1964 and 1969, when he had to flee Iraq, Mahdi al-Hakim was a central member in the latter Jama'a. Indeed, both the Da'wa and the Jama'a enjoyed the financial and spiritual support of Mahdi's father, Iraq's chief mujtahid, Grand Ayatollah Muhsin al-Hakim. Other active members in the Jama'a of Baghdad were also members of the Da'wa.[60]

Examination of the activities of one of the leading members, Isma'il al-Sadr, provides insight into the typical activities of Jama'a members. Sadr used to give weekly lectures on the interpretation of the Qur'an to Baghdad University students in "a new style" (namely, a more modern, less complicated style of teaching) at the Hashimi Mosque in Kazimayn. He made religious educational speeches at various celebrations as well as at memorial ceremonies. He lectured after the noon and afternoon prayers every Friday, and he used to hold open meetings in the months of Ramadan, Muharram, and Safar. Once a day, at the holy tomb at Kazimayn or the Hashimi Mosque, he held a special session "to look into people's problems and answer their inquiries" on religious and personal matters. He used to supervise a few cultural and welfare institutions. "To protect the youth from deviation," he also sponsored a football team in Kazimayn.[61]

Even if this report idealizes Sadr's activities somewhat, all the same, it indicates the nature of the Jama'a's activities. Members met occasionally in each other's homes to discuss their activities. Most members of the Baghdad Jama'a were, in fact, agents sent by senior ulama to conduct Islamic activity. While lay Islamic activists were limited to the Da'wa, young activist ulama could work for the Da'wa, the Jama'a, or individual mujtahids, and differentiating among them is impossible. Al-Hakim's agents and the members of the Jama'a, helped by al-Hakim's funds, initiated Islamic activities aimed to attract Shi'ite youth in general and young intellectuals in particular. Apparently the first major activity organized by the Najaf-based Jama'a was a 1959 mass gathering in al-Hindi Mosque to celebrate the birthday of 'Ali, the first Shi'ite Imam. Thereafter religious and other occasions served as rallying points in the Shi'ite cities and in Baghdad. Such occasions included the birthdays of the twelve Imams, the nights of Ramadan, the Prophet's birthday, and the first ten days of the month of Muharram leading to the Ashura, but also funerals and memorial services on the fortieth day in honor of deceased Shi'ite ulama and other personalities. On such occasions, speeches were made, poems read, and the public was called on to follow the rules of Islam. Similar activities were organized by other organizations.

The 1950s saw the growing identification of a traditional ceremony with the Shi'ite revivalist movement; after 1977 this ceremony served as the movement's most important anti-Ba'th rallying point. Every year, on 18 Safar, mass Husayni processions would emerge from Najaf on a three-day, fifty-mile-long march to Karbala. On 20 Safar, the fortieth day of the Imam's martyrdom, the masses would enter the city in which Imam Husayn is buried to pray at his tomb. In February 1977 the Ba'th regime tried to prevent the march, but the activist leadership and the masses resisted in a series of violent clashes dubbed by the Shi'a *intifadat safar* (the Safar uprising). That Sadr and his activist students were involved is evident from the report he sent his student Muhammad Baqir al-Hakim, instructing the marchers to refrain from provoking the authorities unnecessarily. According to Da'wa sources, Sadr and the party were behind the march. In the Iranian exile, the Iraqi community adapted and continued this particular ceremony, thus forcefully demonstrating both its Shi'ite and Iraqi identification.[62]

The 1960s saw the establishment of a great number of institutions, many sponsored by al-Hakim. One such institution, a library with reportedly more than sixty branches throughout the Shi'ite population centers, was established and maintained by al-Hakim's wukala. Baghdad saw the establishment in the early 1960s of Kuliyyat Usul al-Din, a modern faculty meant to serve as the first example of a modern Islamic university, modeled after Cairo's al-Azhar. The faculty issued an important magazine, *Risalat al-Islam* (Islam's message), that objected to secularism, but it was shut down by the Ba'th regime in 1972, together with the kuliyya. Yet another institution, established by al-Hakim in 1965, was Madrasat al-'Ulum al-Islamiyya (the College of Islamic Sciences) at Najaf. Here too Sadr's students were paramount among the teachers, and Sadr's *Falsafatuna* was taught. Following al-Hakim's death in 1970, Sadr himself took over responsibility for continuing the madrasa.[63]

The revivalist movement, encouraged by al-Hakim (but also by other senior ulama, including Abu al-Qasim al-Kho'i), also established during these years a number of kindergartens and schools for boys and girls in various Shi'ite centers, as well as a great number of welfare institutions.[64]

The most surprising aspect of all these activities was that, even though the Shi'ite community developed a whole genre of horror-and-redemption stories about Sunni regimes thirsty for Shi'ite blood,[65] from 1958 through 1969 the regimes allowed activities to continue without much interference. Within certain limitations they even enabled revivalist Shi'ite preachers to use the state-owned media to spread their message.[66] Indeed as the Da'wa's Tehran-based weekly puts it, under 'Abd al-Rahman 'Arif, "the Islamic movement reached . . . the peak of its power . . . which forced the international superpowers to change its plans," namely, to replace 'Arif with the Ba'th.[67]

The Supreme Assembly for the Islamic Revolution in Iraq (SAIRI)

Following the death in 1970 of the chief mujtahid, Muhsin al-Hakim, Sadr started to contemplate establishing a body of leadership consisting of senior ulama. This collective leadership was meant to serve as a supporting body for the chief marja' (the man widely recognized as the supreme religious authority). It was to consist of a great number of Shi'ite ulama throughout the world and to function through an elaborate committee system. Such an organization could guarantee continuity and consistency of leadership in the event of the death of the chief marja'.[68]

Sadr's organizational idea has never been put into practice in Iraq, let alone in the wider Shi'ite world. Following Khomeini's return to Tehran in February 1979, and with the growing tension between the Shi'ite leadership and the Ba'th in Iraq, Sadr came to believe that his martyrdom was close at hand.[69] This, according to SAIRI sources, induced him to start planning for the organization's survival after his death. He was fully aware that there was not one single activist mujtahid who could replace him. The most senior one, Abu al-Qasim al-Kho'i, was a far older and better established mujtahid than Sadr, but unlike al-Hakim, he was much closer to the quietist pole and kept the activist ulama at arm's length. Thus, according to his student and the head of SAIRI, Muhammad Baqir al-Hakim, Sadr suggested establishing an alternate leadership that would replace him after his martyrdom. A few days after Sadr's martyrdom in April 1980, a group of ulama established the Council of Ulama of the Islamic Revolution in Iraq, apparently in conformity with Sadr's wish. This body dissolved after a short while, for it did not include outstanding ulama and, more importantly, it failed to win Khomeini's recognition.

The next body to be established, Jama'at al-'Ulama al-Mujahidin fi'l-'Iraq (the

Group of the Struggling Ulama in Iraq), began in November 1980, with Muhammad Baqir al-Hakim as its secretary general. This time the Iraqi ulama learned from the experience of their predecessors and declared their complete loyalty to Khomeini. Members were supposed to be elected to the leadership on the basis of their competence, effort in the jihad struggle, and religious scholarship. Jama'at al-'Ulama al-Mujahidin never became an important center among the Iraqi exiles in Iran, but it continued to function.[70] By the late 1980s an organization of the same name was politically very close to the Da'wa, and its members were frequent guests and lecturers at Da'wa events; today it serves as the body of ulama legitimizing the Da'wa without being involved in the day-to-day running of the movement.[71]

The next phase was marked by establishment of the short-lived Bureau of the Islamic Revolution in Iraq, led again by ulama and with al-Hakim as its supervisor. The last phase began in Tehran under the close supervision of the Iranian Supreme Council for Iraq Affairs. This body was composed of various Iranian government representatives and was fully controlled by Hojjatulislam 'Ali Khamene'i, then Iran's president and, according to some Shi'i Iraqi sources, a distant relative of al-Hakim. Also at this time, the Supreme Assembly for the Islamic Revolution in Iraq (SAIRI) was established on 17 November 1982 in Tehran, with Muhammad Baqir al-Hakim as its first spokesman. Al-Hakim remained the leading figure in SAIRI and, since the mid-1980s, its chairman. His deputy in the mid-1980s (and later SAIRI's secretary) was Abu Amad al-Ja'fari. SAIRI's chief ideologue from the outset has been Hojjatulislam Sadr al-Din Qabanji.[72] SAIRI's leadership has consisted of both ulama and lay intellectuals—"intellectual bearers of the message of Islam." However, as a SAIRI publication has it, "the line of the ulama is the leading line . . . and the presence of the ulama is a real one in so far as numbers and influence are concerned."

For all practical purposes this body was (and still is) run by ulama.[73] As reflected in its organ *Liwa al-Sadr,* SAIRI is effectively controlled and run by Muhammad Baqir al-Hakim, who in 1982 was merely a *hojjatulislam* (the "authority" or "proof" of Islam; one step below an ayatollah) but, by the mid-1980s was elevated by the Iranian leadership to ayatollah. SAIRI publications make no secret of the fact that they regard al-Hakim as the future leader of the Iraqi nation (he is defined, for example, as "the commander in chief of the Islamic Armed Forces of Iraq"), and they imply that he was Khomeini's choice as well.[74] It is significant that both the Da'wa and its rival, SAIRI, have traced their origins to Sadr, using different parts of his legacy to legitimize their existence.[75]

In the beginning SAIRI was an umbrella organization encompassing chiefly Jama'at al-'Ulama, al-Da'wa, Munazzamat al-'Amal, and al-Mujahidin.[76] At the end of the Iraq–Iran War, however, it began to be regarded, at least by the Da'wa and Amal, as an organization in itself, even as one competing with their own. SAIRI was too close to the Iranian leadership to truly represent all the Iraqi groups following the cease-fire between Iraq and Iran. At that time Iran started to follow its political interests as a "state" rather than as a "revolution," while the Iraqi opposition was still adamant on continuing its revolution by fighting Saddam and his regime until it was toppled.[77] Al-Hakim's growing self-aggrandizement, which made cooperation with other movements difficult, found expression in the introduction during the late 1980s of a traditional ceremony in which delegations "renew an oath of allegiance" to him by giving him the traditional Islamic *bay'a* (a commitment to accept and obey him).[78] The same practice had been adopted by Sadr during the 1979–80 confrontation with the Ba'th regime; there is little doubt that al-Hakim was thus trying to establish himself as Sadr's heir. SAIRI reportedly depends for its financing almost entirely on the Iranian government and follows Iranian dictates to the letter.[79]

Beneath SAIRI's highest body, the Central Committee, is the General Assembly consisting of some two hundred members. Between the two institutions is the Majlis al-Shura al-Markazi (the Central Advisory Council), but its size and function are unknown.[80] There are a number of committees: a political committee, a military one, committees for information and internal security, and a more general executive committee. On the military level SAIRI has a regular army corps called Badr (after the 624 C.E. battle in which the Prophet and his troops won the day against the Meccan idol worshipers), also sometimes called Army Corps Number Nine. As reported by SAIRI sources, in 1986–87 this corps consisted of between ten thousand to fifty thousand fighters, recruited from among Iraqi expatriates and prisoners of war. Independent sources claim that the Badr corps consists of no more than three thousand to four thousand soldiers. During the Iran-Iraq War the group participated in battles against the Iraqi army mainly on the fronts in the south and in the Kurdish north. The corps has been placed under the supervision of the Iranian Revolutionary Guards. In a speech made after the Iraqi invasion of Kuwait, Muhammad Baqir al-Hakim implied that he did not have fifty thousand fighters ready at hand when he declared that SAIRI could mobilize inside and outside Iraq fifty thousand warriors and, if necessary, even one hundred thousand.[81] While both claims seem inflated, no doubt all the Shi'ite movements managed to field between four thousand and ten thousand fighters. In the battles between the regime and the Shi'ite rebels following the Iraqi defeat in the war against the allied forces in February 1991, reports from Basra confirmed that between four thousand and five thousand civilians and army deserters were fighting there against Saddam's troops. Major revolts also occurred in Najaf, Karbala, Diwaniyya, Samawa, Nasiriyya, Suq al-Shuyukh, Kut, Kumayt, Amara, and a few other smaller towns. While it is difficult to assess how many of Muhammad Baqir al-Hakim's people (either those operating inside Iraq or those who crossed over from Iran) were involved in the fighting, evidence shows that at least a few hundred were involved.[82]

The Badr Army Corps Number Nine consists of a few divisions organized in turn into brigades and then battalions. The corps also has a heavy artillery brigade. Each unit bears the name of a historical Shi'ite hero (Shi'ite Imams and lesser figures and such contemporary heros as Sadr). The commander of the army corps is "Brother Shams," and the command post is situated in Bakhtoran. Near the commander's headquarters a special religious indoctrination unit sponsors lectures and other cultural activities, like an army theater group which stages religious and popular plays apparently in the Iraqi colloquial dialect. The corps is also bent on commemorating all the martyrs who died during the war and after it. The corps has eight football teams, and takes care of the social needs of its soldiers and their families.[83] SAIRI also has a women's fighting division, Fawj al-Shahida Bint al-Huda, named after Sadr's martyred sister, who train with live ammunition, but there is no evidence that they have participated in actual military operations.[84]

On the civilian side, SAIRI sponsors Husayni committees, each of which is in charge of the activities at one mosque where Iraqi expatriates gather and pray. Their activities range from the religious and cultural to the social. On special religious occasions there are Qur'an readings, speeches (*khutab*) and "Husayni poems," processions commemorating Husayn, and various other religious activities. Often meals are served and contributions collected. The Husayni committees also issue cooking oil, meat, sugar, and other commodities which they receive from SAIRI's Unit of Social Services. The committees also contribute money, equipment, and food to the Badr corps. They visit bereaved families and try to help them spiritually and economically.[85] A central indoctrination institution of SAIRI is the Husayni pulpit. The *minbar* (pulpit) prepares preachers who bring the Husayni message to the masses. It also collects donations for the warriors, conducts Qur'an lessons, and even engages in some military training. Another SAIRI institution, the Bureau for Message Bearers, specializes in sending senior ulama on Husayni occasions as well as collecting money for such occasions. In 1990 the bureau reportedly managed to collect two and a half million riyals.[86] SAIRI also runs clinics and centers for high school examinations.[87] As befitting an organization run by the Hakim family, it has established a special center for collecting documents on the members of the family who were executed by the Ba'th regime.[88]

Between 1983 and 1988, SAIRI organized several general congresses in Tehran. Participants came from most of the Iraqi Islamic movements, the main Kurdish movement and some secular Iraqi Arab movements (except the Communists). The participants, whose numbers oscillated between three hundred and six hundred, discussed human rights, political cooperation between the movements, and the future regime in liberated Iraq.[89]

The existing evidence indicates that inside Iraq, the Da'wa and SAIRI are forced to operate in much the same way: membership is secret, and great efforts are made to compartmentalize information and severely limit horizontal interaction between members. In Iran, and possibly in Syria, where large numbers of Iraqi expatriates live and may be co-opted, on the public level both movements operate in the same way. They both work openly to attract the largest numbers of followers through their religiocultural and socioeconomic activities.

Yet there are five main differences between the two organizations. First, while SAIRI depends heavily on Iranian financial support, the Da'wa is self-funded. This may be explained by the great disparity in the size of the two movements: the Da'wa numbers in the hundreds, perhaps a thousand, while SAIRI's regular armed unit alone numbers a few thousand. It seems that the Da'wa's financial and organizational independence (having branches outside Iran) renders it more independent of Iranian political dictates, but this independence is found almost exclusively outside Iran. Second, SAIRI is a mass organization. The Da'wa, by comparison, while not averse to mass support, puts heavy emphasis on the education of high-level cadres. Third, while SAIRI is controlled by one family, with a blatant personality cult revolving around Muhammad Baqir al-Hakim, the Da'wa is led by a collective body and is somewhat more democratic. Fourth, while SAIRI is fully controlled by ulama, the Da'wa's leadership is a mix of ulama and laymen, with the latter very active on the political level (religious guidance is still the domain of the former). Finally, in the case of the Da'wa in Europe, its members fear Saddam's assassins, so the party is still highly secretive. The party may also be keeping some of its organization in Iran and Syria under cover for fear of internal Iraqi rivalries and the repercussions of political differences with the host regimes.[90] This would be in keeping with Sadr's legacy.

The Shi'ite Opposition Movements and the Invasion of Kuwait

Even before Saddam invaded Kuwait on 2 August 1990, the Shi'ite opposition movements showed signs of realizing the need for cooperation with Iraqi Arab secular movements (cooperation with the Kurds has been fairly extensive since 1980). Thus, in February 1990 the first document signed by individuals belonging to fundamentalist and secular movements was issued. It called upon the sons of the Iraqi people to topple the Ba'th regime and to establish on its ruins a liberal democracy that would guarantee full freedom for the press and for political organization and activity. The new regime, it said, would be based on free elections to a parliament and a new, democratic permanent constitution that would guarantee the separation of the three authorities—the judicial, the executive, and the lawmaking branches. This communiqué was not signed by movements as such, and more importantly, no one who was officially a member of a Shi'ite fundamentalist movement signed it.[91] Yet people who were close to these movements did sign it, and the principles laid down in this document later became the basis for documents on which the fundamentalist movements were ready to affix their signatures.

Twelve days after the invasion the important political movements of the Iraqi opposition signed a joint program denouncing the occupation of Kuwait and calling for the downfall of Saddam Hussein and his regime. The communiqué steered clear of any fundamentalist Islamic vocabulary and demands.[92] In mid-December 1990 these and other movements from the Islamic fundamentalist and secular camps met at a conference in Damascus, emerging with a more detailed program that included some concessions to the Islamic parties (for example, the Iraqi people were defined as "an Islamic people, that includes religious minorities"). Yet the program called for establishing an interim coalition government that would supervise the following: elimination of all vestiges of Saddam's dictatorship; establishment of freedom of political and social activity and freedom of expression, including freedom of the press and of political organization; secret and direct free elections for a Constituent Assembly, which would compose a permanent constitution within one to two years. The communiqué denounced the invasion of Kuwait and the atrocities committed there by the Iraqi forces and demanded its evacuation.[93]

These and later documents were brought to the attention of the Western media in order to attract support for the opposition movements and present the opposition as a viable alternative to Saddam's regime. These documents were also meant to encourage active opposition to Saddam's rule. Shi'ite opposition personalities in Damascus, Tehran, and London made themselves widely available to the Western media, something they had not done before for fear of the regime's long arm. The Congress in Damascus established the National Action Committee for the Opposition Forces to coordinate the opposition's activity. On 11 March 1991, a few days after the eruption of mass revolts in the Shi'ite south and Kurdish north, more than twenty opposition parties met again in Beirut to discuss ways to help the revolt. The General Conference of the Iraqi Opposition Forces established five committees (information, political, financial, ideological, and field support), but there was little they could do to bring Saddam Hussein down.[94] This was left to the revolutionaries inside Iraq.

On 2 March, following the Iraqi defeat at the hands of the allied forces in late February 1991 and their withdrawal from Kuwait, a series of local revolts erupted in a number of towns in the Shi'ite south of Iraq. Within a few days the south was ablaze. In the annals of the Shi'ite movements this came to be called the 15 Sha'ban Intifada. According to eyewitness reports, in Basra alone between four thousand and five thousand people, civilians and army deserters, fought against government troops. Because the city was effectively cut off from the main body of Iraq by U.S. troops, the central government's control over Basra was substantially weakened. This revolt, aided to an extent with small arms, ammunition, Iraqi expatriates, and, apparently, Iranian Revolutionary Guards who crossed over from Iran,[95] demonstrated Shi'ite resentment and anti-Ba'thi sentiment. Yet it is impossible to tell how many of the fighters were members of the activist organizations' underground inside Iraq, how many crossed over, and how many of the revolutionaries were disaffected soldiers and nonaffiliated Shi'ite civilians.[96] SAIRI claimed responsibility for the whole revolt: on 3 March 1991, Ayatollah al-Hakim implied that he was directing the revolt in Basra and elsewhere.[97] The Da'wa, for its part, claimed that it started it.[98] However, by late March, the Republican Guard and other government troops reconquered all the main Shi'ite cities at a horrendous cost of human lives and property.[99]

Some early signs of disquiet notwithstanding, the revolt started soon after it became clear that the Iraqi army had suffered a decisive and humiliating defeat, and that many believed it had been rendered inoperative.[100] The first sign the coast was clear occurred when many party and internal security officials fled the south; the police stations too were abandoned. This created a power vacuum.[101]

A typical example of the way things developed in most parts of the south may be found in the description of events in Rumaytha. The first anti-Ba'th demonstrations started when people realized that the regime was under tremendous pressure from the allied attack, but these demonstrations and occasional armed activities were quickly suppressed. Following the retreat from Kuwait, people again tested the water by starting a commerce strike and gathering in the main street and other public places. When the security forces did not respond, the protesters marched to the local police station, shouting anti-Ba'thist slogans. Still there was no response from the authorities. The police stations were deserted. So, the demonstrators went in, equipped themselves with arms, and released the prisoners, some of them Kuwaiti citizens kidnapped after the invasion. They then marched on the internal security and party centers, where they met sporadic resistance that lasted less than one day. The revolutionaries established various committees to run the community—a provisions committee, a committee for services and electricity, and a military committee to mobilize the population. The military commander was a retired army major.[102] According to an interview with a Da'wa activist in the West, many people joined the revolt because the food distribution system had broken down, and they were hungry and frustrated.

In Najaf and Karbala the command posts were housed in the tombs of 'Ali and Husayn and in the adjacent buildings. In Karbala the arms cache, field hospital, and prisoners' interrogation center were also in this compound, which explains the tremendous damage sustained by the two holy places during the fighting that led to the suppression of the revolt.[103] The revolt's two centers were Basra, where it started, and Najaf, the focal point in the Middle Euphrates. As reported by participants, Karbala rose only three days after Najaf, when the latter's success was apparent. Later Karbala asked Najaf to send them a commander to run the military campaign. Najaf also sent them one hundred fighters, including people who had come to Najaf from other towns, as well as other kinds of help and guidance. Likewise, Najaf was asked by Rumaytha to send them a clergy to act as a supreme arbiter, and Grand Ayatollah Abu al-Qasim al-Kho'i dispatched one of his agents. Rumaytha, for its part, placed a large force at Kho'i's command once Najaf came under siege.[104] The revolt encompassed all of the governorates of the south.[105]

The role of individual tribes is unclear, but we know that tribes fought on both sides, although mostly they supported the regime. In al-Madina district near Basra, forty-five tribes supported the revolt with an army of two thousand men. At the same time in Rumaytha there was need for an 'alim to intervene to bring the citymen and the tribes together. The Shi'ite sources themselves admit that some tribal shaykhs and their men were "traitors" who helped the regime.[106] The regime's media, too, shows evidence that a number of tribes collaborated with the regime.[107]

Putting down the revolt was easy, however. In hindsight Saddam disclosed that, in his view, "such a [devastating] event has not happened in Iraq for the last two or three centuries."[108] The governor of Karbala reported that the number of rebels (apparently throughout the south) reached fifty thousand and admitted that they fought bravely. Some three thousand of them, he said, made their last stand in Karbala at the two shrines and were dislodged only with heavy artillery fire.[109] The opposition sources, too, describe massive artillery, tank-gun, and helicopter gun-ship bombardments against various parts of the revolting towns, but mostly against the shrines' area.[110] A visiting journalist reported later from Karbala: "Hussein's artillery has reduced to rubble the entire neighborhood around the two great mosques [of al-Husayn and al-'Abbas] . . . and the army has uprooted hundreds of date palms for miles in every direction."[111] The Shi'ite opposition reported some thirty thousand casualties.[112]

Indeed, in the second half of March, Saddam and his generals managed to reorganize the Republican Guard at tremendous speed, mainly because it had not been affected by the war as seriously as the opposition believed. In addition, possibly upon the request of the Saudis, who feared a fundamentalist and pro-Iranian Shiʿite victory in Iraq, the United States and Britain did not limit Saddam's use of helicopter gunships. The Shiʿite rebels who faced the Republican Guard (composed largely of Sunni Arabs) were thus badly out-gunned. As it emerges from participants' reports, they were lightly armed, lacked ammunition, were poorly trained and organized, were without an effective central command and strategic plan, and had no communication system. There is also evidence of internal rivalry that split their ranks.[113] Finally, the revolutionaries admit that, when they tried to win over disaffected regular army officers whose units were deployed in the south, the latter were reluctant to give their support because they were put off by the radical Islamic nature of the uprising.[114] Saddam, for his part, is reported to have managed to recruit Yazidis (a Kurdish tribe) and Palestinians who participated in the fighting.[115] Saddam's tactics were also to prove decisive. He concentrated all his force against the Shiʿite rebels, who posed a much greater danger, and left the Kurdish north for later. In the south, the Guard quelled the revolt in the various Shiʿite cities one by one, starting with Basra. This tactic of concentrating firepower gave the government another obvious advantage.

In addition, as a result of statements of a particularly influential religious leader, the revolt may have suffered from a collapse of morale. On 5 March 1991, at the height of the revolt, Grand Ayatollah al-Kho'i, the senior religious authority in the Shiʿite world and traditionally a political quietist who refused staunchly to get involved in antiregime activities throughout his career, published a surprising legal opinion *(fatwa)* in which he called on believers to preserve the holy places and uphold Islamic values by abiding meticulously by the Islamic Shariʿa. He urged his flock to guard people's private property and their honor and not to damage the public institutions which are the property of all the people. He also demanded burial of all corpses in the street. In itself this fatwa was nothing more than a call to preserve law and order. Under the circumstances, however, it was nothing short of seizing control. Two days later al-Kho'i published another fatwa stating that "the country these days is going through a difficult phase that necessitates the preservation of order and the return of security . . . and the supervision over the public, social and religious affairs. . . . The common good of society necessitates that we appoint a Supreme Committee" that would supervise all these affairs. "Its view will represent our view, and its instructions will represent our instructions." Al-Kho'i appointed nine ulama to this committee, including his son Muhammad Taqi.[116]

Al-Kho'i waited three days after eruption of the revolt in Najaf before issuing his first fatwa, so one may infer that he had concluded public order was disintegrating and the Baʿth regime was doomed, and thus he had to assume responsibility for the Shiʿite community. From the description of the attitude of the revolutionaries of Rumaytha toward him (asking him to send them one of his deputies), one may conclude that he was under pressure from his community to lead them. That he did not initiate the revolt (or did not wish to be directly identified with it at first) may be concluded from another internal report to the effect that when the masses started the revolt in Najaf, al-Kho'i was, in fact, in Karbala. He had gone there on a pilgrimage to Husayn's tomb to celebrate the birthday of the Imam Mahdi on 15 Shaʿban.[117] Indeed, according to a few interviews with Shi'i activists, he refused to talk to the masses in Karbala, who ran after his car in despair and bewilderment, pleading that he address them. Back in Najaf, he was surprised to find that the revolt had started and that the revolutionaries regarded him as their leader. Once he became involved, however, there was no way back, which explains his efforts at coordinating the military and civilian activities in the central Euphrates area. Al-Kho'i also sent his son Majid to ask for U.S. help, but he was turned down.

The Ba'th regime, however, was not interested in nuance. They saw the revolt as a straightforward attempt to establish an independent Shi'ite government in the southern part of Iraq. Two weeks later, as soon as government troops had re-conquered Najaf, al-Kho'i appeared on Iraqi television with Saddam Hussein, and he denounced the "mobs" for acts of arson, looting, and vandalism. He admitted had he issued a statement forbidding murder, destruction, and rape and ordering the burial of corpses, but he presented this act as one designed to secure public order. Al-Kho'i also prayed that "God would exalt President Saddam in this world and the hereafter."[118] After he returned from Baghdad al-Kho'i stayed at his modest home in Kufa in what seemed to be semi-house arrest: he was allowed to see foreign reporters occasionally, but he was watched very carefully until his death in August 1991. All the same, he managed to tell Milton Viorst that his son (apparently Muhammad Taqi), son-in-law, and four other family members were in jail, and he demanded their release.[119]

Both the Da'wa and Ayatollah Muhammad Husayn Fadl Allah in Lebanon, who has been very close to the Da'wa since the 1960s, as well as the Iranian leader Ayatollah Khamene'i, interpreted the tone of this interview as the result of al-Kho'i's kidnapping and detention.[120] This claim seems valid, but whatever the circumstances of al-Kho'i's announcement, one can not refrain from comparing him to his young colleague Muhammad Baqir al-Sadr, who in 1980 flatly refused to make any announcement that would play into the hands of the authorities. Clearly, once he realized the battle was lost, Kho'i was trying to save himself and the hawzat of Najaf and Karbala and to prevent the Shi'ite community of southern Iraq in general from undue suffering. There is no better example to demonstrate the tremendous tension between the two poles inside the Shi'ite political community, between activist and quietist. Dialectically, however, it was al-Kho'i, of all mujtahids, who, when conditions changed, established himself as the supreme political authority, an act apparently interpreted by the Ba'th regime as establishing the Rule of the Jurist. This is evidence of the ease with which the borderline in Shi'ite Islam between quietism and activism may be crossed.

Discourse

Shi'ite Martyrdom and Eschatology

In most aspects of their public discourse the two main movements of the Iraqi Shi'ite opposition, SAIRI and the Da'wa (and other movements, to the extent that their writings are available) differ little. In such matters as group identity and Shi'ite history, as well as theological matters such as millennium and martyrdom, the differences are practically nonexistent. Both movements regard themselves as the committed disciples of a long line of Shi'ite thinkers including the twelve Shi'ite Imams. Not all twelve, however, receive the same share of attention, and not all are seen equally as examples to be followed. Actively and openly defiant in their attitude toward the various secular ruling regimes in Iraq, the two major Shi'ite resistance organizations adopt as their main source of inspiration the third Shi'ite Imam, Husayn, who died in 680 C.E. in Karbala, fighting a lost battle against the Umayyad army.

With Husayn's martyrdom, the Shi'ites became a religiopolitical sect that challenged the Sunni order because it believed the three caliphs who preceded 'Ali, and who are regarded by Sunnis as exemplary figures, were immoral and despotic nonbelievers who adopted Islam only externally to serve their personal ambitions.[121] Furthermore, in Shi'ite eyes, all the caliphs who came after 'Ali, starting with Mu'awiya and through the 'Abbasid dynasty that ruled from Baghdad, were illegitimate rulers, and some are believed to have murdered Shi'ite Imams. Indeed, as some scholars see it, even Shi'ite rulers enjoyed only limited legitimacy because, with the disappearance of the Twelfth Imam, the only source of both spiritual and temporal authority had vanished.[122]

Throughout the ages the Shi'ite community has mourned al-Husayn and awaited the return of the Mahdi. The oppression to which they occasionally were subjected only served to heighten their sense of having been wronged by the Sunni majority. The Shi'a have a rich literature of martyrdom and suffering, but more important in terms of popular sentiment are the various religious occasions on which the Shi'ite masses mourn their saints. Most conspicuous among these are the occasions connected with Husayn's martyrdom: the tenth day of Muharram (the *'ashura*) and the fortieth day of his death (*al-arba'in*). This does not mean that the Shi'ite community was always ready to resort to the sword to put an end to Sunni rule. Due to their relative weakness, the Shi'ites adopted taqiyya. The tension between rage and grief, between the urge to revolt and to correct the historical wrong, and the need to act cautiously in order to preserve the community and prevent its annihilation accompanied the Shi'ites throughout their history. Thus, some Shi'ite thinkers, notably al-Shaykh al-Mufid (d. 1022 C.E.), ruled that in cases of extreme danger, taqiyya is a duty, and that there are no situations in which it is strictly forbidden. Others, like Muhammad Husayn Kashif al-Ghita (d. 1954), felt that under certain circumstances, taqiyya is in fact forbidden.[123] Shi'ite history provides examples on both sides of the divide. Thus, the Imams Hasan, Muhammad al-Baqir (d. 732), and his son, Imam Ja'far al-Sadiq (d. 765), the second, fifth, and sixth Imams, behaved politically in a passive way and may be perceived as quietists. 'Ali and Husayn, on the other hand, as well as other famous Shi'ite revolutionaries, rose against the ruling Umayyad and 'Abbasid dynasties (661–750 C.E. and 750–1258 C.E., respectively) whom the Shi'ites saw as oppressive and deviating from the correct path of Islam.

Political Activism and Sacrifice

All the activist Shi'ite movements elevate Imam Husayn's martyrdom; it is their highest ideal and the most important example to be followed. It is also the most important historical moment through which they define their identity. The most important religious ritual adopted by the activist ulama of Najaf at the beginning of their revivalist activity in the 1950s was the *arba'in* Husayni processions—the three-day march from Najaf to Karbala. Under the Ba'th these marches generated so much hostility the regime decided to clamp down on them. The tension came to a head at the February 1977 march, during which the masses chanted religious slogans. Some slogans were fairly innocent, for example, "By Allah! We shall never forget our Husayn." Others were more defiant: "Allah's hand above their hands; Allah is great, oh 'Ali! They hit us with machine guns. If they cut off our legs and hands we shall reach you crawling, Master Husayn. Oh Saddam, take your hands off the army and the people do not want you." During the march, after a few participants were killed by police bullets, the marchers took their bloody shirts and used them as Husayni flags, chanting "al-Husayn! al-Husayn!" In Karbala the masses renewed their oath of allegiance to Imam Husayn.[124]

The Husayni processions on the arba'in remained the most important religiopolitical occasion for the Iraqi expatriates in Iran during and after the Iraq-Iran War. On the eve of the celebration, many Iraqi exiles would gather in every large city in Iran near a central mosque that serves the Iraqi diaspora. A typical example was the Da'wa-sponsored arba'in in Qum in September 1990. The various groups filled the city and set up tent camps in it. As pointed out by the Iraqi magazine *Al-Jihad*, Iraqi identity was borne out by the participants' special head gear (a white *kufiya* with black crossed lines) and other folkloric outfits. One camp was named after 'Ali ibn al-Husayn, another after those who died in the battle of Karbala. After the night prayers, the participants marched from their camps to the martyred Sadr's Mosque, carrying religious banners as well as the names of the cities in Iraq from which the marchers originated. They chanted "revolutionary and Husayni slogans in which the rejection of the tyrants and the yearnings for the Iraqi homeland were inseparably mixed."[125] At around nine o'clock the evening program started. It included a speech by the Da'wa-affiliated Shaykh Mahdi al-'Attar in which he discussed some of Husayn's sayings urging people to sacrifice themselves for Allah *(al-istishhad)* and the interpretations given to those sayings. Al-'Attar also turned to current political events, denouncing both the U.S. presence in the "Islamic area" and the Iraqi invasion of Kuwait. A poet read a Husayni poem about the battle of Karbala and how mothers used to educate their children to love al-Husayn, and a preacher then discussed the political events following the invasion of Kuwait. He called on all Iraqis to rise to the occasion. Husayn was then lamented by a few poets.

At nine o'clock in the morning on the arba'in day the united procession left Sadr's Mosque carrying banners with slogans, black and red flags, and three large pictures of Khomeini, Sadr, and Khamene'i. The most important slogan was probably the one by Sadr calling on the believers to launch a jihad against the oppressors. The procession was led by a group of ulama and by others, starting with a group that had originated in Najaf. Some groups marched under the names of their present homes in Iran. There were also a few women's groups. The chants were anti-American and anti-Ba'thist, but there were also traditional Husayni slogans. The common denominator was the need for sacrifice. The procession ended at the tomb of the Sayyida Fatima, al-Imam al-Rida's sister. Inside the tomb the Da'wa spokesman, Shaykh Asifi, addressed the participants on the need to continue the jihad against Saddam until his downfall. He denounced again the U.S. presence in the area but did not call for jihad in that context. Rather, he politely asked the American people to withdraw their forces. He warned the Muslim masses (referring to many Sunni-Islamic activists) not to fall into the trap of admiring Saddam, who is the sole reason for the "Crusader" Christian presence in the Gulf. After the speech the demonstrators returned in a procession to Sadr's Mosque, where they prayed together the noon and afternoon prayers and then dispersed.

Since the early 1980s these Husayni processions have been a powerful expression of a fusion between Shi'ism, revolutionary spirit, and national Iraqi identity. The marchers express all three identities with equal enthusiasm. As pointed out by the Da'wa magazine *Al-Jihad,* the street in Qum assumed "a countenance close to an Iraqi street and an Iraqi mosque and an Iraqi quarter. The Iraqi identity here is not just a place. Rather it is all the feelings and emotions and yearnings which transform everything [around us] which is not Iraqi into Iraqi."[126]

The most common theme in the opposition literature relating the tragedy in Karbala is that even though Husayn was defeated militarily, "in the divine account" he won. Through his total devotion and readiness for sacrifice, Islam was saved because the Muslim community was shown the right path and given a sublime example. The Shi'ite sources are careful not to define Sunnism explicitly as deviation, but it is clear from their discourse that Shi'ite Islam is the only true Islam, and that its continued existence, even though it is followed by only a small part of the Islamic community, is the only guarantee against the deviation of the whole Islamic community. Husayn's sacrifice guaranteed the continuity of Shi'ism.[127]

Husayn is present in almost all other religiocultural activities of the movements. His birthday and day of martyrdom serve as occasions for mass rallies and processions and, together with the fortieth day, have been the most important occasions the year round. Husayn's martyrdom is also presented as the single most important source of inspiration of those who died in the battle against Saddam Hussein and the Ba'th party. In that context, immediately following Khomeini's rise to power in Iran, Sadr realized that the Iraqi masses were slow to follow the Iranian example; he is reported to have said to his disciples, "not all people are moved by ideas. Indeed, there are people who can be moved only by blood." To move the masses he planned to go to 'Ali's tomb in Najaf to speak openly against the Ba'th. He would escalate his attacks "until the regime will be forced to kill me at the tomb." As his disciples understood it, what he had in mind was that "when thousands of the children of Iraq will see [him] . . . murdered at his grandfather's [i.e., 'Ali's] tomb with blood streaming from his noble body, they will be impressed at the level wished by Sayyid [Sadr]."[128] As Sadr himself is reported to have put it, the 1979 situation in Iraq was "similar to the situation of the nation at the time when the Umayyad rule was preparing to kill Imam Husayn." The people were numb and unable to act against the oppressors. Thus his jihad should be sealed with martyrdom, for "its influence will be like the influence of the blood of Imam Husayn."[129] When he was arrested by the authorities, tortured, and threatened with execution, he flatly refused to make even the slightest concession, thus refusing to practice the slightest degree of taqiyya and assuring his martyrdom.[130]

The most interesting religious innovation introduced by the Shi'ite activists was also connected with Husayn's legend. Sometime between the 1950s and 1980s the marchers in the 'ashura stopped chaining themselves and carrying axes. Instead, guns and blood donations were introduced. "The chains that were supplanted by guns had symbolized the acceptance of agony and pain, and the ax that was exchanged for blood donations had symbolized the readiness for sacrifice for Islam." This, the opposition magazine *Liwa al-Sadr* implied, was a contribution to modernizing the movement.[131] A similar change was introduced in Iraq in the 1960s, when Da'wa activists organized university youth to march quietly and in a dignified way during the 'ashura processions. Although this change was the result of the authorities' intervention (the Sunni authorities were traditionally wary of the great excitement caused by the 'ashura processions), the movement has apparently internalized it and has ascribed it to its own initiative.

Close to Husayn's example of martyrdom is that of his sister Zaynab, who showed great courage in Karbala. Sadr's sister, Bint al-Huda, who unlike Zaynab was executed by her enemies, "stood as if she were Zaynab," facing the Ba'thi criminals and reproaching them in very strong words for arresting her brother. She, too, reached the conclusion that "the time for quietism has passed, and there is no escape from opening a new leaf of jihad." "By Allah!" she exclaimed, "I am craving for martyrdom for Allah."[132]

Another part of the movement's endeavor to define participants' identity through Shi'ite mythology is its definition of the enemy. Here the choices are not surprising. Saddam is worse than Nimrod, the mythological idol-worshiper tyrant king, because he tortures his prisoners before he kills them and he tortures their families. He is also worse than Pharaoh because Pharaoh only killed the male children, and he never executed the leaders of the Israeli community, Moses and Aaron. Saddam is torturing and killing women, and he executed Sadr and his sister. Saddam is compared to al-Hajjaj ibn Yusuf, the notorious Umayyad ruler of Iraq (694–714), and to the Mongol Hulagu, who conquered Baghdad in 1258, demolished it, and beheaded all its educated people.[133]

Taqiyya and Millennium

From the previous section it is clear that the activist movements reject the concept of taqiyya, at least as their present modus operandi. This rejection is mostly implicit and only rarely explicit. In addition to examples of activist Shi'ite saints the activist movements also make use of Qur'anic verses to legitimize their approach. Thus, when mourning their martyrs they refer to the verse "Think not of those who were killed in the way of Allah as dead. Nay, they are living. With their Lord they have provision" (Sura III, 169).[134] Even more explicitly, the need for activism and sacrifice is expressed in the verse "Lo! Allah changes not the condition of a folk until they [first] change that which is in their hearts" (Sura XIII, 11). And, "Man has only that for which he makes efforts" (Sura LIII, 39).[135] And quoting a hadith of the Prophet, "the best of my nation's actions is expecting redemption." The conclusion derived from this hadith is that the Prophet saw the waiting period for the Mahdi as positive action rather than as a passive interval.[136]

Even though the radical Shi'ite movements belong to a community that holds waiting for the Messiah as one of the most central tenets of its faith, they keep millennial expectations strictly within the realm of theological theory and never allow them to permeate into everyday political thinking. Preaching for immediate activism means, in effect, total rejection of passive waiting for the return of the Imam Mahdi. The Da'wa party and its founder, Sadr, met with severe criticism from traditional quarters in Najaf in the 1950s and 1960s over this precise issue. "Many of the believers in empty religiosity there accused [us] . . . of deviating from correct Islam and of tying [ourselves] to *kafir* imperialism. Everybody who called for the establishment of an Islamic rule was accused of such crimes, because the establishment of Islamic rule was, in their view, [to materialize] only after the appearance [*al-zuhur*] of the Imam, the master of time [*sahib al-zaman*], may God hasten his elevated redemption."[137] Indeed, the Da'wa is clear in what it says to its members on this issue:

> We believe that the idea of waiting quietly and peacefully in the expectation that the Imam Mahdi [would appear] is not based on realistic or Shari'a foundations. If we are looking for the origin of this idea, we find that these people believe that Allah decided that Islamic rule will be in force only in that period [after the Return of the Imam]. Thus, [as they see it,] any effort to resurrect the Islamic entity . . . is hopeless. . . . [Indeed it is even harmful] because it exposes the Muslims . . . to danger.

As the Da'wa ideologues see it, the Prophet was very active in his effort to spread his ideas:

> There are people who say that his victory stems from divine, supernatural reasons. But we are telling them: the Islamic Da'wa, even though it was supported by Allah, did not win and succeed due to supernatural reasons. Rather it won in perfectly natural and mundane ways, and this is why some were martyred and others were oppressed. The Prophet lived in a continuous struggle and war and we can repeat this history . . . and revive his struggle and his jihad.[138]

I found explicit mention of the return of the Imam Mahdi, in a way that is not purely theological, in only two places. In an article discussing Khomeini's contribution to the history of Shi'ism and Islam, the writer points out that Khomeini has changed the human equation, and thus made a major contribution toward preparing for the return of the Imam. But the writer makes it clear that he does not expect the Mahdi to come soon and that, in any case, a precondition for his arrival is human action.[139]

It took the momentous events of 1989–91 to induce a SAIRI writer to suggest that perhaps the messianic age is approaching. As he understands the changes in Eastern Europe, the world has reached the point in which "all the theories that were brought up to solve human problems," meaning both communism and capitalism, have failed. Human civilization has reached a point at which "the strong devour the weak," and colossal events are following each other at such a "fantastic speed" that it is beyond anyone's ability to predict or analyze them. Finally, huge Christian armies are massed "under the leadership of the Greater Satan [the United States] in Islam's holiest land and they are desecrating Mecca . . . in response to an invitation from those who pretend to defend the holy land." The writer's conclusion is that "the banners of the Promised Saviour's journey . . . are already fluttering in the distant horizon." However, he makes it clear that one should not indulge in "negative waiting," but rather shoulder the "responsibility of man" and work toward preparing the world for the Mahdi's arrival.[140]

Latter-Day Saints

All the movements emphasize cultivation of a cult of contemporary martyrs, hoping to create an emotional reservoir that will serve to educate the next generation of activists and imbue them with enthusiasm for the cause. While there is no reason to doubt the effect that Husayn's legend has on contemporary Shi'ites, a generation of contemporary martyrs is seen as essential to help bridge the gap of over thirteen hundred years. After these contemporary martyrs are intertwined with the memories of Husayn, 'Ali, and Zaynab, a whole genre of saints' stories is developed around them. The most conspicuous martyrs are Muhammad Baqir al-Sadr and his sister, Bint al-Huda. Then come Mahdi al-Hakim, Hasan al-Shirazi, and any other Islamic activist who found death in Saddam's torture chambers or on the battlefront.

A great variety of institutions were named after Sadr, and the day of his death is commemorated religiously. But around Sadr there is also a rich literature of saint stories. For example, we are told by his disciples that he never took a penny of his followers' donations for himself. Rather he always spread it among his needy students, which consequently left his family penniless at his death. In one case, we are told, Khomeini donated a large sum of money to him. So as not to offend his senior colleague, he accepted the donation, but immediately afterward he gave it out to Najaf's poor.[141] Sadr's elder brother, Isma'il, is reported to have been extremely poor since childhood, and he died without owning a home.[142] The same applies to other young ulama and laymen who joined the activist movements. Thus, for example, a clergyman from the Hakim family had to be forced to accept a refrigerator after he married.[143]

Another proverbial quality of ulama martyrs is their lack of pomp and total devotion to their community. Sadr and 'Arif al-Basri are described as showing an extreme degree of modesty. Unlike most other ulama, they took great interest in everyone who came to see them. Another example of extreme modesty is that of al-Sadr's elder brother, a well-known scholar. When people asked him to "allow them to follow him" as a religious authority, he said, "as long as my teachers are alive I shall not allow anyone to follow me."[144]

Brave behavior in the face of a ruler's threats and tenacity under torture are yet other characteristics of a latter-day saint. Sadr's courageous confrontation with Saddam and his internal security apparatus has been discussed above.[145] Sadr is also reported to have kept from the masses information about his torture in the Ba'thist prison in 1977 so as not to intimidate them.[146] Honorable behavior in prison in spite of torture, including refusal to disclose any information about the party, and fatherly help to younger party members who are imprisoned with them, are also some of the features of a *shahid* (martyr).[147]

Sufi elements are prominent in these exemplary biographies: idealization of poverty; total devotion to Allah; readiness for martyrdom but also profound piety as expressed by frequent mention of Allah's name; and frequent prayers. Most extreme is the case of one of the lesser saints, a shahid by the name of Abu Dhurr al-Hasan of whom it was said that the two things he hated most were eating and sleeping. His victory was achieved when he died on the battlefield.[148] Judging by the literary style of many of these stories, this genre's traditional form is found not only in its content but also in the way the story is related; it is similar to a hadith in which those who relay the story are as important as the story itself.

Occasionally the activist movements drive the Husayni principle of sacrifice to its illogical conclusion, as in their approach to the cease-fire between Iraq and Iran. Stranded in Iran without hope that Iran would liberate Baghdad for them, but not giving up hope for a victorious return to their homeland, they write, "When the Free will see death as victory there will be no despondency afterward . . . and when the noble ones will understand death as honor and triumph, there will be no meaning to defeat and retreat . . . and when the children of Iraq understand today that their victory is in their perseverance on the path of al-Husayn's religion and practice [we shall be victorious] . . . we are fundamentalists [*usuliyyun*] from this pure origin and from this sacred extremism."[149]

Sadr's martyrdom, too, qualifies as death that is better than life. This we saw in the account of his decision to challenge the Ba'th and thus assure his martyrdom. This approach is also reflected in a speech by al-Hakim, who mourns Sadr but implies that, in the case of such an outstanding figure, his death was preferable to his life, in view of the tremendous contribution he made to the movement by dying the way he did.[150] Even though there is no apparent organizational connection between the Shi'ite fundamentalist groups and Sufi orders, this notion of martyrdom is evidence of the influence of Sufi tradition, in which death is seen as salvation, life is death, and death is life.[151] Another Sufi (but also traditional Shi'i) characteristic is ascribing to some great martyrs superhuman qualities. This is done sparingly, but it seems to be a trend. Thus, for example, Sadr is said to have foreseen his own death in a dream in which he saw his late brother and uncle sitting on chairs, with his own empty chair, awaiting him, between them.[152]

Tradition and Modernity

Sadr had no qualms about borrowing ideas from the successful examples of Western civilization. He modeled the Da'wa after the Ba'th and Communist parties, for example, and he used modern terminology in his discourse and discussed modern economics and social affairs in order to approach lay intellectuals. Sadr also believed that had the Prophet lived in our day he would have used modern means of communication to his movement's advantage. Sadr's "agents" followed in his footsteps in trying to appeal to secular youth: 'Arif al-Basri's soccer team in Kazimayn, and similar soccer teams recruited by SAIRI and matches it organized in the Iranian exile are the most obvious examples. Since the Da'wa has recruited university students primarily, it could ill afford to deviate from this path.

A typical article in *Al-Jihad* dealing with this subject and written by a lay intellectual is titled "Science in the Service of Religion." Advanced science and technology are essential for the development of any nation, the author writes; a nation has to develop a great variety of scientific fields and educate its youth beyond religious studies. Religion and science are not mutually exclusive. In fact they are mutually supportive.[153]

In an official platform delineating its future educational policy once Iraq is liberated, the Da'wa states that, in addition to Islamic studies and Arabic language, it intends to develop secular fields. In primary school this would include foreign languages, mathematics, sports, and agriculture. Vocational training would get a major push. In high school and university, students would study mathematics, medicine, and literature—Islamic and non-Islamic—and would continue to study a foreign language of choice. Just as 'Abbasid caliph al-Ma'mum did in his time, the modern Islamic regime in Bagdad too would make a major effort to translate scientific and other works into Arabic. All this, of course, in addition to religious studies.[154]

In the same vein Hojjatulislam Muhammad Taqi al-Mudarrisi, 'Amal's leader, explains that the Muslims should "interact with the reality of [Western] civilization but not with its history," or with the "means" and not with its "aims," because Western aims are "materialistic jahiliyya in most part." The West too, at the beginning of its renaissance, interacted with the reality of the Islamic civilization but not with its history and cultural roots. The West has accepted the scientific heritage of Islam but rejected the characteristics of its personality. The Muslims should do the same today. The two cultures are wide apart, and that of the West emanates from Greek culture, which is very different from the Islamic one (al-Mudarrisi forgets to mention that the Muslims in their own turn had borrowed from Greek sources). In summary, Muslims should not submerge themselves in Western civilization, but neither should they reject it altogether. The Qur'an criticizes those unwilling to learn new things: "Nay, for they say only: lo! we found our father's following a religion and we are guided by their footprints" (Sura XLIII, 22). To relinquish technology would mean to retreat into the past. After all, technology is "the result of the proper interaction between man and the capabilities of nature." In addition to technical aspects of its civilization, Muslims should take from the West its concept of "rejecting determinism," namely, Muslims should reject all the concepts that limit "man's endeavor." They should be rational. Inspiration (*al-wahy*) should never come instead of rationalism (*al-'aql*). Rather, it should "invigorate rationalism." Muslims need only return to their true legacy which was corrupted throughout the ages. Mudarrisi stops short of wholeheartedly embracing Western knowledge: the Iraqi scholars and scientists who studied in the West are not fully trustworthy. Leadership should be placed in the hands of people with less exposure to the West. In the future, however, all these scholars and scientists will be fully integrated into society.[155]

Islamic activists went far beyond borrowing technology or rationalism from the

West, however. One major concept they borrowed does not fit well with pan-Islam, namely, European-style territorial nationalism. In almost every newspaper article, the Iraqi identity is played up no less than the Islamic identity of the members of these movements. While, according to al-Mudarrisi, the majority of the Iraqi expatriates in Iran tend to assimilate there,[156] the activist movements (the Da'wa and 'Amal more than SAIRI, but the latter too) are working in the opposite direction. And while talk about pan-Islamic unity is vague and noncommittal, preoccupation with Iraqi identity and the Iraqi state is overwhelming.

Thus, for example, in its two most important documents, one issued in the early 1980s, the other in early 1992, the Da'wa works out in great detail its future policy in Iraq once it is liberated—from economic and social affairs, through the introduction of Islamic law, to foreign and defense policy. In terms of the future of the Iraqi nation-state the Da'wa promises "to turn the unsuitable relations between the Islamic regions into good relations" and to "guard Iraq's independence and guarantee its national [*al-wataniyya*] sovereignty and territorial integrity"; there is no intention to unite all the Islamic countries into one.[157] In the same vein, 'Amal, too, while not counting out the possibility of pan-Islamic unity in the distant future, makes it clear that unity will take a long time and that it must be the result of free choice.[158] Indeed, in this respect both al-Da'wa and Amal continue the line delineated by Sadr himself.[159]

Note that SAIRI, while turning to the Iraqi people as often and as clearly as the others do, refrains from discussing the future of the Iraqi nation-state after it is liberated. This is at least partially the result of its great dependence on its Iranian patrons.

While all the movements reject explicitly the Ba'th secular European-style language-and-ethnicity-based Arab nationalism, their approach to the Arab identity of the Iraqi Shi'a is far more complex. Rejection of secular Arab nationalism (and, by implication, of pan-Arabism)[160] is explained, in the first place, in terms of the need to distance the Muslim community from Ba'th paganism, as the latter are turning Arab nationalism into a new idol, to replace Islam. Somehow, the party does not feel that territorial Iraqi nationalism harbors the same danger. Arab nationalism is also seen as racist, because it treats as inferior, and thus leaves out, many Iraqis, chiefly Kurds, Persians, and Turkomans.

By implication, the special relations with Iran, too, as well as the fact that many an Iraqi 'alim are of Persian stock, play a role in the rejection of Arab nationalism. This rejection seems to reflect also the traditional reservations of many (though clearly not all) Iraqi Shi'ites vis-à-vis pan-Arabism, which has been fostered by the Sunni regimes since the 1920s. In a united (Sunni) Arab state stretching from the Atlantic Ocean to the Gulf, the Shi'a are certain to be marginalized even further than they are in the Iraqi nation-state.[161] However, the written sources do not mention these traditional reservations explicitly, and thus they remain a matter of speculation.

As for their Arab identity, during the first years of the Iraq–Iran War it, too, was ignored, as the Iraqi people were almost as a rule defined as merely a "Muslim people" (*al-sh'ab al-'iraqi al-muslim*). Sometimes the Arab identity was even rejected: more often than not, when the Da'wa used the word "Arab" in its literature, it had a derogative connotation.[162] Since the late 1980s, however, the Da'wa approach has changed in both respects: the Arabs have no longer appeared necessarily in negative connotations, and the Arab connection of the Iraqi people has surfaced in the party's central documents. This has been balanced by an emphasis on its Islamic identity and values, and by warnings against "sectarian and ethnic discrimination."[163] The change was, partly, the result of the growing need for cooperation with Arab regimes, especially following the invasion of Kuwait, and partly due to the wish to distance the party somewhat from Iran and hit a middle course between it and the Arab world.[164]

Just as one should not be surprised by the Iraqi Shi'is' reservations vis-à-vis integrative pan-Arab unification, one should not be surprised by their attachment to their Arab identities. Many Iraqi Shi'ites descended from Sunni Arab tribes who had become sedentary during the eighteenth and nineteenth centuries. Many such tribes split apart during this process, with part of the tribe moving north and remaining Sunni, and part settling in the south and becoming Shi'i. This split between the two (or more) tribal groups still exists, with the Shi'i segments seeing themselves as no less Arab than their Sunni brothers. SAIRI's criticism of all the Arab regimes, too, has disappeared, but by mid-1993, they had not yet endorsed the Arab identity of the majority of the Iraqi people as did the Da'wa, let alone the Kho'i Foundation.[165]

Foe and Friend

Arranged around the fundamentalist organizations are a number of concentric circles of rivals and enemies. The first such circle involves the other Shi'ite radical organizations. Inter-Shi'ite rivalry has typified the development of the fundamentalist movement from the outset. Initially there was bitter rivalry between the activist circles in Najaf and the more traditional forces, with Muhsin al-Hakim playing arbiter. At a later stage—sometime during the 1970s—the Da'wa became estranged from a number of activist ulama, Muhammad Baqir al-Hakim chief among them. In the controversy over whether the Islamic movement is a structured organization or a spiritual movement, Sadr's writings and Qur'anic verses are used on both sides. From the constant talk of the need to bridge the gaps between the various Islamic (Shi'ite) movements it is evident that such gaps do exist.[166]

Throughout the writings of Muhammad Baqir al-Sadr one notices the tension between his ecumenical drive and his Shi'ite particularism. In his youth Sadr managed to keep the gap between the two poles narrow. Immediately before his death this gap assumed unprecedented proportions in theological Shi'ite thinking. On the one hand, Sadr called for Sunni-Shi'ite cooperation on the basis of equality, even implying Shi'ite readiness to accept Sunni hegemony provided that Islamic law would be enforced in Iraq. (The differences between the Sunna and the Shi'a in terms of substantive law are marginal.) In the process he bestowed de facto legitimacy on two of the three first caliphs, 'Umar and Abu-Bakr. On the other hand, Sadr rendered Sunni-Shi'ite cooperation unworkable when, in early 1979, he legitimized the rule of the Shi'ite jurist and presented it as the only legitimate system of government.[167]

His disciples remain locked in this dilemma today. On the one hand, they call for

Sunni-Shi'ite cooperation against the Ba'th regime as well as against all other enemies of Islam. A typical example of this apparent ecumenical approach may be found in the communiqué issued by the Da'wa, 'Amal, the Mujahidin, and three other smaller Shi'ite movements in September 1990, calling on the movements "to work toward the achievement of unity and cooperation between all the Muslims on the basis of faith in Allah and the common destiny and the common interests, and confronting the haughty [powers] and Zionism, and the support for the liberation movements in the area . . . and in its forefront the movement of the Palestinian people and all the Islamic people for self-determination."

The communiqué is addressed to the "Islamic Iraqi People" and seems to treat both Islamic sects equally. But in the same document one can also find unmistakable evidence of Shi'ite particularism, bordering on delegitimization of the Sunna as a whole. When the document asserts the need for mobilization and sacrifice in order to achieve the movements' goals, it reminds readers of "the sense of tremendous responsibility that rests on the shoulders of the dedicated sons of the Iraqi people. Defending dear Islam and the heritage of the Prophet's pure family . . . in Iraq, this is a tremendous responsibility which Allah has laid upon the shoulders of our generation in preparing the road for the establishment of the rule of heavenly truth and total justice."[168]

The Shi'ite-centered approach in these sentences gives priority to the Shi'ite concept of the special place of the Prophet's family in Islam, and they refer to the arrival of the Imam Mahdi. In the same way Shi'ite sources present the Shi'ite interpretation of the events that occurred at Ghadir Khumm in the seventh century as the only acceptable interpretation; they also make it clear that on that occasion the Prophet appointed 'Ali as his successor.[169] Indeed, Shi'ite publications are full of anti-Sunni allusions—the intellectual climate whenever the suffering of the Shi'ite imams at the hands of Sunni rulers is discussed and whenever the issue of legitimacy comes up. On occasions, under the guise of a demand that the Islamic movements will play the hegemonic role in liberated Iraq, there is an implied message that, once the Ba'th regime is toppled, the Shi'ite majority of Iraq will turn the tables on their Sunni counterparts.[170]

Severe criticism is leveled against the Arab regimes that do not impose the rules of Islam in their countries, including those regimes that impose Islamic law in a half-hearted way, accompanying their hypocrisy with acceptance of Western Christian domination. The Shi'ite fundamentalists' most ferocious attacks are aimed at the Ba'th regime of Iraq. They exploit the fact that one of Saddam Hussein's chief lieutenants, Tariq 'Aziz, is Christian. Indeed, Christian penetration into the Muslim lands has been an extremely sensitive issue in Islamic politics since the nineteenth century and is used as a potent weapon against the Ba'th party. The Ba'th regime is accused of being anti-Islamic; as such, the Shi'ite fundamentalists insist, it should be uprooted. They write that the Ba'th is "a satanic 'Aflaqite party" that excels in its "Crusader-Masonic hatred toward the Islamic peoples of Iraq and Iran alike."[171] Occasionally the Shi'ite fundamentalists indulge in anti-Christian diatribes, as when they accuse the Catholic church of attempts to advance at the expense of Islam through active missionary work.[172]

Occasionally this fear of missionary work turns into paranoia: "The hatred of Christianity and Zionism and their master, the world haughty forces, against Islam and the Muslims is no secret; neither is it new. This hatred and what it entails, namely, wars and plots on the part of a number of international forces, repeated themselves throughout history and especially in modern history."[173] For the most part, however, their attitude toward the Christian world has been more relaxed.

Ba'th-style pan-Arabism is unacceptable to Shi'ite fundamentalists because they believe it is based on secular European nationalism and, in fact, is meant to replace Islam in the hearts of Arabic-speaking Muslims.[174] According to the Shi'ites, the Ba'th regime is doing everything in its power to corrupt the Iraqi armed forces and youth in general by inducing them to drink alcohol and to participate in immoral and promiscuous parties. At the same time, it prevents pious youths from going to mosques, and it censures preachers.[175] Saddam Hussein is defined as an "enemy of religion and the Qur'an."[176] In short, eliminating the Ba'th regime is the Iraqi Muslim's foremost duty.

The attitude toward the secular regimes of the Arab world as well as toward the religious yet pro-U.S. regimes such as Saudi Arabia, or even toward an anti-U.S. regime such as Libya, is somewhat less hostile. But they, too, were regarded explicitly or implicitly as illegitimate until the end of the Iran-Iraq War.[177]

Change between 1979 and 1991

Due to changing political conditions in the Middle Eastern and international arenas, and organizational changes in both al-Da'wa and, to a lesser extent, 'Amal, the movements under study have gradually changed their political line on a number of key issues. These changes are not radical, but they are meaningful. Some are meaningful on both the ideological and the practical level; others are purely ideological and must still go through the test of political practice and time. Whatever the case, these modifications mean that the activist Shi'ite movements are not immune to political change and that they behave in a realistic and practical way: they are not prisoners of their own radical ideology.

The Attitude toward Syria

Upon Khomeini's rise to power, Shi'ite masses started demonstrating against the Ba'th regime in the al-Thawra Shi'ite quarter of Baghdad and in major Shi'ite population centers in the south. The regime cracked down on the demonstrators, and by the beginning of the war against Iran, in September 1980, it had executed hundreds of activists and imprisoned thousands. During these months, relations between the Ba'th regimes of Baghdad and Damascus deteriorated, and in the summer of 1980 they almost ceased to exist. At the same time, Syrian-Iranian relations improved steadily. Indeed, this improvement was one of the reasons for the deterioration of Iraqi-Syrian relations. It seems possible that the opportunistic Muhammad Baqir al-Hakim was moving in the same direction as Iran, but SAIRI was not then in existence.

The Da'wa, for its part, was slow to react. Its English-language publication was hostile toward Damascus. As late as February 1982 it had written:

> Syria is ruled by a rival faction of the Ba'th party and displays all the characteristics of its twin in Iraq. Based on Arab nationalism and originating from Christian and secular ideologies, the Ba'th is dedicated to the elimination of Islam as a political force. . . . The events in Hama have shown what can happen in any city under Ba'thist control. With proper coordination Ba'thism can be purged from Damascus and Baghdad by the Muslim people in no time. . . . Moves must be made to make it plain to Ba'thists of all colorations that the Ba'th per se is unacceptable to the Muslim peoples of Iraq. Furthermore, [it has to be made] clear to the Arabs as a whole that the neo-Jahili concept of Arabism has no place in the hearts of Muslim peoples of Iraq.[178]

By the late 1980s, however, the Da'wa branch in Damascus was active in organizing religious and intellectual activities and won prominence through the Da'wa magazine.[179] In the mid-1980s SAIRI, too, established close ties with Damascus, even though it never established a permanent branch there: SAIRI was an Iranian creation, and Iranian and Syrian interests were never in total harmony.[180] In view of the need to preserve their relative independence, it is not surprising that the fundamentalist and secular opposition organizations that united in a common front following the Iraqi invasion of Kuwait met in Damascus and Beirut, rather than in Tehran, between December 1990 and February 1991.[181]

Saudi Arabia and the West

The same constraints that forced the fundamentalist movements to change their position over Ba'thist Syria forced their hand in terms of their approach to Saudi Arabia, the other Arab monarchies of the Gulf, and the West. The watershed is much more easily identified than in the case of Syria. Immediately following the Iraqi invasion of Kuwait in 1990, the Islamic movements issued a forceful denunciation of the invasion. They played down their differences with the Kuwaiti regime and treated Kuwait as a perfectly legitimate Arab "people" (*sha'b*) who were oppressed and wronged by a criminal regime. The invasion, they claimed, violated Islamic principles, contradicted the Shari'a, and united the oppressed Iraqi people and its Kuwaiti brother in a crucible of suffering; Kuwait would be liberated when Saddam's regime was toppled.[182]

The movements' approach toward Saudi Arabia is more ambivalent, but it marks a major change from the previous hostile approach. Playing to a radical anti-U.S. audience, the Shi'ite fundamentalists could not resist the temptation to denounce the Western military presence on the holy soil of the Arabian peninsula. Occasionally they even demanded the evacuation of troops so that the whole affair would be left to the Muslim people to settle. Thus, for example, in a joint communiqué with non-Islamic movements, they called for "applying pressure on the regime to force it to withdraw from Kuwait unconditionally"; at the same time, they pledged "to mobilize all forces for the withdrawal of the foreign armies from the region."[183] The Western armies in Saudi Arabia, "under the leadership of the Big Satan in the holiest of all lands of the

Islamic world," were "defiling Mecca . . . at the request of those who claim to be defending the sacred land."[184] Regarding Saudi Arabia, the Shiʿite movements satisfied themselves with merely pointing out that "the huge military presence on our Islamic land in the Arab peninsula . . . draws that area into a dangerous situation." The blame for this presence, they reminded their followers, should be laid squarely on the shoulders of the Baʿth regime of Iraq, which invaded Kuwait.[185]

Occasionally the Shiʿite opposition announced it would demand the evacuation of the foreign troops from the area only after Kuwait was liberated.[186] On one occasion al-Hakim turned down an appeal from an Islamic Sunni pro-Saddam delegation in Tehran to join forces in fighting the Western forces in the Gulf. Al-Hakim pointed out, with obvious frustration, that the Muslims of the world must "refrain from any mistake," as in taking sides in the conflict. Supporting the wrong side, he warned, "endangers the very existence of the Islamic nation."[187] Indeed, the fact that many Sunni Muslim fundamentalist movements adopted Saddam as their hero, seeing in him a latter-day Saladin, was an extremely annoying phenomenon in the eyes of the Shiʿite fundamentalists, who argue that Saddam and his regime are criminal, atheistic, and inimical to Islam. Not only does Saddam refuse to apply the Shariʿa in Iraq and allow drinking of alcohol in public and sexual corruption, he also has murdered thousands of pure, devout Muslims for their beliefs.[188] The Daʿwa warned that the "false glitter of the Iraqi regime" should not deceive the Sunni Muslim Brothers. Saddam "did Zionism the greatest service when he destroyed the unity of the nation" and when he sacrificed "hundreds of thousands of Iraqi youth" in his aggressive wars. Indeed, as they saw it, the atrocities he committed against other Muslims, especially against his own Iraqi people, by far surpassed even what the Zionists had done to the Palestinians.[189] By comparison, the Saudi regime, even though imperfect and previously supportive of Saddam Hussein, was regarded as an ally due to its fierce opposition to the Iraqi invasion of Kuwait. Thus, despite ideological differences, the Daʿwa was the first of the Shiʿite movements to engage in political ties with the Saudis. This news was reported by its magazine in early December 1990, even though the party's spokesman made it clear that so far these talks were without results.[190]

In late February 1991 it was reported from Damascus that four representatives of the various movements of the Iraqi opposition, including a representative of SAIRI, met in Riyadh with one of King Fahd's sons and with another senior official. As reported by a Communist and by the Kurdish leader Jallal Talabani, who participated in this delegation, these discussions were "very friendly and fruitful." The Iraqi opposition asked for Saudi recognition, and the Saudis were open and forthcoming, though they said they needed time to become better acquainted with the various opposition groups. The reason for the delay in establishing more formal relations was Saudi, not Iraqi, opposition and hesitance.[191] In early April, a representative of the Daʿwa went to Riyadh to talk to Saudi officials, but again with no results The same practice was repeated by SAIRI's al-Hakim in June 1992.[192]

The Shiʿite opposition's approach to the West and particularly to the United States is the epitome of ambivalence. While objecting as a matter of principle to the presence of Western troops in the Gulf area, and while stressing that this invasion was carried out by the "imperialist . . . arrogant, haughty forces" for their own exploitative and expansionist ends,[193] the Shi'ite opposition nevertheless blamed Saddam for providing U.S. imperialism with an excuse to establish itself in the Gulf area.[194] Moreover, the Shi'ite opposition recognized that the new developments hold great promise. The economic embargo on Iraq was seen, at least by the Da'wa, as a useful means of applying pressure on the regime. Even though they were reluctant publicly to condone a food and medicines embargo, let alone a war that would destroy Iraq's infrastructure and cause suffering to the Iraqi people, they did endorse a partial embargo, limited to technology, spare parts, and military hardware.[195]

During the waiting period following the invasion, the Shi'ite opposition turned to the "international community" or to "world public opinion" or to "those who take interest in the future of Iraq." These were inoffensive ways of addressing the West, asking it to come to the aid of the Iraqi people. The fundamentalists even complained often that they were being ignored by the world media, which again could only mean Western media.[196] Indeed, one of the most noticeable changes in the Shi'ite opposition's modus operandi following the Iraqi invasion of Kuwait was its great effort to mobilize the Western media to support its cause. SAIRI, the Da'wa, and 'Amal leaders gave ample interviews to the press and to the electronic media, telling the Western public about their struggle against the hated Saddam and trying to convince this public of their democratic inclinations.[197]

One day before the UN ultimatum expired, the Da'wa spokesman warned the United States against any attempt to "play with fire," because "the Islamic peoples . . . can force the Iraqi regime to withdraw from Kuwait" if and when they decide to do so.[198] As soon as the Western offensive began, the Da'wa unleashed a vitriolic attack against the United States for launching "the widest aggression in history on our land and people and its institutions and armed forces." Echoing Saddam's own media, the party defined the coalition forces as "the columns of evil and foreign aggression," and the United States was dubbed "a haughty, treacherous and corrupting power that will stop at nothing in its quest to satisfy its desires." They do not wish to liberate Kuwait but, rather, to "destroy Iraq, crush its people, annihilate its army and capabilities . . . and deprive it of . . . progress and prosperity." The United States, which made Saddam, is punishing him now for breaking loose, but its main aim is to weaken Iraq. The Americans were warned: "We cannot stand idle in the face of this treacherous aggression." The fire with which the Americans were playing would "burn their fingers," warned Shaykh Asifi.

When it came to a plan of action, however, there was precious little the party had to tell its membership. Those inside Iraq were instructed to "join the forces of the mobilization to defend our homeland against the Western plots" and "to prepare for confronting the American invasion of Iraq." Yet this was not a call to join Saddam's forces. Indeed, the most important message was concealed in the party's lengthy communiqué when the activists were advised "to be on the alert so as to fill any political vacuum that will be created in Iraq." Unlike the regime's media, there was no mention of jihad in the Shi'ite opposition press, and there were no calls for terrorist activities against Western interests. The only immediate action recommended was to put political pressure on the United Nations, the American and British people, and on world public opinion in general to influence President Bush to stop the war.[199]

Following suppression of the March 1991 "intifada," the Da'wa accused the United States of "following a twisted, deceitful road in Iraq." The United States "freed [Saddam's] hand to suppress the intifada of our revolutionary people." Saddam understood how much the United States needed him, and thus turned with impunity to exterminate the Iraqi people.[200] The United States, the Da'wa pointed out rather convincingly, wants Saddam out, but not at all cost. To them, "the Shi'a are extremists, and the Kurds are secessionists." Thus they want "a military coup d'état that will produce a pro-American regime."[201] The Da'wa also accused the United States of helping to defeat the popular (Shi'ite) uprising in order to protect "the Zionist occupation of Palestine . . . fortifying its cancerous existence."[202]

Despite such rhetoric, the Shi'ite fundamentalists' traditional position of unmitigated hostility toward the West was somewhat softened by the Western action against Saddam. This change was not deep enough, however, for the opposition to go on record expressing its support for the Western presence in the area, or to make any explicit friendly comments in regard to the West. In its quest for public support inside Iraq it could not condone a shooting war, and once it started it had to denounce it. Like the Iranians, the opposition denounced it but expected to benefit from it. Fighting the coalition forces was out of the question. As late as the fall of 1991, ambivalence and pragmatism remained the hallmarks of its attitude toward the United States. Despite its disillusionment, its delegations still kept seeking U.S. help in toppling Saddam.[203]

Here, as in the case of other political changes, the Da'wa led the way. The party's relative independence from Tehran and its greater exposure to the West—a part of its leadership stays in the West or visits often—contributed to its more pragmatic approach.

The Rule of the Jurist

Before the late 1970s, in its approach to the issue of national leadership, the Da'wa oscillated between two concepts: that of *shura* (namely, a collective leadership consisting chiefly, if not entirely, of ulama, which takes decisions by a majority vote), and the principle that later became identified with Ayatollah Khomeini, that of the Rule of the Jurist.[204] In February 1979, Muhammad Baqir al-Sadr presented the Iranian government with a document designed to provide the principle of the Rule of the Jurist (*wilayat al-faqih*) with Shari'a legitimacy. In it he wrote, "the rightly-guided religious authority is the legitimate expression of Islam, and the marja' is the general representative of the imam. . . . Based on this he should take upon himself the following: firstly, the marja' is the supreme representative of the state and the commander in chief of the army. Secondly, the marja' is the one who appoints . . . the individual or individuals who would assume the presidency of the executive power." The marja' was also charged with enforcing the Shari'a and controlling all other important aspects of the state.[205]

During the next few years al-Da'wa followed Sadr's, and Khomeini's, line religiously. Thus, for example, in a document published in 1981, the party presented the Shi'ite approach to government as one in which "the person in charge [of the state ought] to be a faqih . . . and it does not accept a non-faqih to take charge merely because the majority of the nation votes for him." The Da'wa argues that while according to Sunni Islam a ruler does not necessarily have to be a faqih, neither does it require that under no circumstances should he be a faqih. In other words, while to the Sunnis this whole issue is of little concern, to the Shi'a this issue is an important tenet of faith. Thus Sunni Muslims should bow to the Shi'ite dictate on this issue because a faqih-ruler can serve as a common denominator.[206]

The mid- and late 1980s saw a major development that may be responsible for a subtle yet important change in the Da'wa's position. The development was a shift in the actual circumstances of Shi'ite fundamentalist leadership, which led to a subtle ideological shift on the role of the leader. In April 1980 Sadr was executed. Nine years later Khomeini's death removed from the scene the second faqih who was regarded by all movements as an undisputed religious as well as political authority. With Khomeini's death and his replacement by Ayatollah Khamene'i, the political rules changed in Iran itself, and more power went into the hands of the political leaders. (Even though President Rafsanjani is an 'alim, he is first and foremost a politician rather than a man of religion, and he is perceived as such by the majority in Iran.) Under such circumstances, a modification in the position of the Iraqi movements was no longer seen as a major deviation from the Iranian line. In addition, during the 1980s Ayatollah Muhammad Baqir al-Hakim became the most conspicuous contender among the Shi'ite activist movements for the leadership of Iraq. Continued and unreserved support by al-Hakim's rivals, the Da'wa and 'Amal, that the principle of the Rule of the Jurist be applied in Iraq as soon as Saddam was toppled was, thus, counterproductive: it would have legitimized al-Hakim's claim to leadership. Finally, between 1979 and the mid-1980s the Da'wa lost many of its ulama leaders, and even though some prominent ulama were still connected with the party, their relative weight decreased substantially. If the information regarding the role of lay intellectuals in the party is accurate, then this is an additional reason for the decline of support for the principle of the Rule of the Jurist within the Da'wa. Thus, while SAIRI, under one uncontested senior 'alim, remained religiously loyal to this principle,[207] al-Da'wa steered clear of explicit support for it.

As early as 1986, when Khomeini was still at the height of his authority, Da'wa's leading ideologue, Hojjatulislam Muhammad Baqir al-Nasiri, gave a lecture in London which served to pull the carpet out from underneath this theory. On the one hand, he declared that "our belief in the marja'iyya is an extension of our belief in the imams" and that "the marja'iyya has already solved the problem of leadership by relying on the jurists in the government and elsewhere." On the other, however, he pointed out that "the marja'iyya is an intellectual, not a political issue." Despite the close ties between the Islamic movement of Iraq and the Iranian regime, when it comes to "the form of government [in Iraq] we shall turn to the people [to get their opinion]."[208] Similar vagueness typifies a long account of Sadr's political and intellectual history in which the principle of the political Rule of the Jurist is blurred beyond recognition.[209] On occasions when one might expect the principle of the Rule of the Jurist to be reiterated, Daʿwa spokesmen have refrained from doing so.[210] Indeed, at least since 1988, the present author could not find a single case where this principle was upheld by Daʿwa spokesmen, including their "program" (*barnamijuna*) of March 1992.[211]

This omission by the Daʿwa of a central principle in Sadr's legacy as well as in Khomeini's theory was clarified in an interview with a senior Daʿwa activist in Europe in 1990. When asked about his party's attitude toward the principle of the Rule of the Jurist he said, "Khomeini's mistake was that he acted from above. He tried to impose Islam from the top and to force people to follow its rules. Khomeini ruled for ten years and people haven't changed in depth! They fast and pray, but they have not changed inside. . . . We are working from the bottom up. We believe in a democratic rule. This is very different from the Rule of the Jurist."[212] In another interview he disclosed that following Khomeini's death, the party went through a process of ideological "rehabilitation" and now this principle "is no longer an issue."[213] It seems, then, that the traditional Shiʿite principle, according to which a believer should follow a living marjaʿ, was the most important reason behind the party's change of heart: when Khomeini died, and with Sadr long dead, adherence to the controversial principle that was so closely identified with them started to wane. Yet because the decline of this principle in party ideology began even before Khomeini's death, there were likely additional reasons for it—reasons pertaining to organization and political environment.

The Daʿwa's retreat from the principle of the Rule of the Jurist is not unique among the Islamic movements. Even before Khomeini's death, Muhammad Taqi al-Mudarrisi, effectively the leader of ʿAmal and a religious scholar himself, was equally vague and noncommittal. As he sees it, only a jurist who combines all the qualifications—religious *ijtihad* (independent reasoning or interpretation), political involvement, and leadership competence (*al-tawjih*)—has the right and the ability to become a political leader. A faqih like that should dedicate all his time to political leadership. However, given the 1993 situation in Iraq and in the Iraqi community outside of it, the ulama cannot dedicate enough time to political activity; accordingly, leadership should be given to others. These leaders ought be as close as possible to the religious authorities (but not necessarily identical with them). When asked specifically about his attitude toward the Rule of the Jurist, al-Mudarrisi refused to commit himself: "if [the Iraqi people] will know the jurist ruler directly, it is possible they will accept him." He pointed out that the people of Iran had accepted this principle only after they had become acquainted with it, and in the past the Iraqi people had fought under ulama like Muhammad Taqi al-Shirazi in 1920. It depends on the personality of the faqih.[214]

Democracy and Islamic Rule

As pointed out by the Daʿwa activists, the issue of the Rule of the Jurist is intimately connected with internal democracy in the Islamic state. If a government is placed in the hands of an eminent jurist as a matter of a sacred tenet of faith, not much is left for people who disagree with him, be they lay Shi'ite intellectuals, even religiously pious ones, let alone anyone else. Until the second half of the 1980s all the Islamic activist movements regarded both the imposition of the Islamic Shari'a in every walk of life in post-Ba'th Iraq and the Rule of the Jurist as inseparable and indisputable principles. In the early years of the Iraq–Iran War, the present author did not come across even one document in which these principles were questioned. Following the cease-fire between Iraq and Iran in August 1988, new thinking permeated the movements' publications with the growing realization that Khomeini could no longer be expected to liberate Baghdad and thus win the war for the Iraqi expatriates. Under the new circumstances there was need for closer cooperation not only between the Islamic movements (or, as was the case since the early 1980s, between the Islamic and the secular Kurdish movements) but also between the Islamic and the Arab secular movements. These included ex-Ba'thists, Nasserites, pro-Syrian Ba'thists, liberal intellectuals, and Communists.

Coming to terms with the idea that they would have to establish a common front with the Communists was difficult, particularly for the Da'wa rank and file. And being a more democratic organization than SAIRI, they were faced with an even greater difficulty. In addition, establishing a common front with non-Islamic (or, more accurately, nonfundamentalist) movements meant the political platform had to be changed. The change was introduced on two mutually enforcing levels: the approach to democracy, and the approach to Islam. As for the former, the Da'wa and 'Amal accepted the principle that once the Ba'th regime was removed, an interim coalition government would be established. After a preparatory period of six months to two years in which an interim constitution would be promulgated, free elections would be held. Whatever government and regime the Iraqi people choose would be respected. As the author was told by the senior Da'wa activist:

> We shall accept everything that the public will accept. Even if they choose a perfectly non-Islamic regime. If they do not choose Islam, this means that they are not prepared for it. If Islam is imposed, it will become an Islamic dictatorship and this would alienate the public. The Sunni [fundamentalists] are saying that the Shari'a should be imposed everywhere—that the drinking [of alcohol] should be stopped. We, the Da'wa, [and] Najaf, do not cling to the Shari'a like [Sudan's] Numeiri. The main thing is—and this is contrary to Khomeini, who said you should impose [Islam] from above—that you should change society [through education from below]. This is different from [Khomeini's] school of Qom. . . . And this is why we accept the multiparty system.[215]

Muhammad Mahdi al-Asifi, the party's official spokesman, in an interview with a Lebanese fundamentalist Shi'ite magazine said, "we reject strongly without any hesitation the imposition of solutions for the future on these people from the outside. The future of Iraq will be decided by the Iraqi people." In March 1992, the party committed itself to the separation of the three authorities; to "free and direct" as well as secret parliamentary elections in which women as well as men may vote; establishment of a system in which "the government is responsible to the Parliament"; and to complete freedom of political activity, within a multiparty system.[216] 'Amal, too, is ready to allow the Iraqi people to determine their own future. Al-Mudarrisi writes that fighting with arms can only be justified when there are "idols" (*asnam*) like Saddam who prevent a free call to Allah. If the majority of the people choose a non-Islamic regime, "then we start with positive opposition, within the framework of the law. We shall lay down our arms and start to spread the message among the masses. . . . We shall present our ideas and call [the public] to join us. . . . We do not see ourselves as guardians of the people . . . in the way they choose the regime of their life. Islam gave all the people the freedom of choice as it says in the Qur'an, *afa'anta tukrihu al-nas hatta yakunu mu'minin* [Will you compel people until they become believers?]"[217]

All this, while important, remains a theoretical matter; no movement has yet had the chance to prove they can carry out these promises. Some of the movements, however, have proved their readiness to cooperate with nonfundamentalist forces, a practical political matter of some importance. The first document, which was signed by both fundamentalist and nonfundamentalist organizations and which necessitated a more democratic approach than before, was published twelve days after the invasion of Kuwait. It had no Islamic content. Instead, it denounced the foreign presence in the Gulf area, but more importantly, it called for "the rescue of our homeland and the destruction of Saddam Hussein's regime."[218] By late December the same parties were joined by a few other opposition parties in a communiqué that was clearly designed to compensate the Islamic movements but which, all the same, remained relatively free of religious content. It did mention that the Iraqi people are "a Muslim people while it includes also religious minorities," but the communique's main thrust was denouncement of the invasion of Kuwait, of the dictatorial and murderous nature of Saddam's regime, and of the presence of foreign armies in the Gulf zone. It called for a peaceful settlement of the crisis, but it also called for increasing the pressure on the Ba'th regime so that it would withdraw from Kuwait unconditionally. Finally, it called for establishment of an interim coalition government that would pave the way for a liberal parliamentary democracy. The agreement guaranteed the rights of national minorities and a meaningful autonomy for the Kurds according to the 11 March 1970 Kurdish-Ba'th agreement that never materialized.[219]

SAIRI's views about democracy have never been elaborated in the same way the Da'wa and 'Amal elaborated theirs.[220] When the issue was mentioned by SAIRI, it was done in an unconvincing way that left the reader wondering about the group's real intentions. Still the Da'wa and 'Amal sometimes speak in conflicting voices of a less liberal fashion, in a way reminiscent of the early 1980s.[221] But their commitment to democracy seems much deeper than SAIRI's.

Whatever the case, the Islamic movements' readiness to issue joint communiqués with secular parties and groups, and to establish a de facto joint front with them, as well as their overtures toward the West and pro-Western Arab regimes, provides evidence of the movements' great flexibility. This is clearly the result of the extraordinary situation that evolved following the invasion of Kuwait and their realization that, probably for the first time since the cease-fire between Iraq and Iran, they had a chance to topple the Ba'th regime. To achieve this, cooperation with pro-Western, secular, and even atheistic forces was deemed necessary and unavoidable.

Conclusion

By far the most important organizational aspect of the Da'wa, and to an extent other Shi'ite fundamentalist organizations, involves its approach to modernity. The fact that Sadr and, following him, the Da'wa party admitted explicitly that they were following the organizational patterns of the Communist party and the Ba'th, whom they accused of atheism and enmity toward Islam, is no less important than the actual fact that they followed such patterns. By doing so they were sending a powerful message to their membership: if modernity could benefit the party and Islam, it should not be rejected out of hand. The same approach is implied by their lack of inhibitions in regard to Western sciences and by many other practices of the various movements, ranging from efforts at recruiting secularly educated intellectuals through sanctioning soccer and other Western sports. More important, it extends to an explicit adherence to the alien concept of Western-style territorial nationalism, democracy, and the sovereignty of the people (in principle, at least).

As we have seen, there is also a growing readiness to cooperate with secular parties and groups. In the case of the Da'wa, the process of integrating Western political and social modes was certainly facilitated by the fact that lay intellectuals rose to positions of leadership, and that a fairly large number of Da'wa activists have been living in the West since the late 1970s. But they had a very unusual mentor, Sadr, who set this process in motion. As he saw it, only by talking to the secular youth in their own language, and by fighting the secular and atheistic movements with their own intellectual and organizational weapons, could Shi'ite Islam, and Islam in general, in Iraq be saved. At the same time, however, it must be stressed that these adaptations to the modern age have by no means diluted the strength of Da'wa's religiosity. In 1993, as in the early 1960s, party Da'wa members are ardent Muslims dedicated to the cause of spreading their message.

How deep and lasting is the democratic transformation of the Islamic movements of Iraq? It is impossible to answer this crucial question in a satisfactory way before these movements come to power and are in the position to practice their preaching or relinquish it. While it is important to note that these movements are theoretically committed to democracy, one must also bear in mind that the democratic principles are newly adopted by the Da'wa and 'Amal, and only vaguely adopted by SAIRI, if that. Furthermore, democratic principles have been adopted under tremendous duress, and, as pointed out, they have so far not been practiced. Sadr's approach in the early years of Da'wa could be interpreted as democratic because he preached an educational rather than a military road to Islam. His treatise on the Rule of the Jurist, however, was as far from "liberal democracy" as one could imagine.

It seems, then, that the democratic trend is still tenuous and easily reversible. The very principle of the people's sovereignty, which lies at the foundation of modern democracy, goes contrary to the fundamentalists' belief in the absolute and total sovereignty of God. Indeed, theirs is an absolutist vision, according to which Islam is as much a social and political order as it is a divine message, and thus mosque and state cannot and should not be separated. If they have the power to do so, even if a democratic opinion poll, or democratic elections, rule otherwise, the Shiʻite fundamentalists may still try to impose the Shariʻa, in the service of what they believe to be a higher authority.

As evidenced by the fundamentalists' ambivalence on this question, their pragmatic approach toward the West in general and the United States in particular is also likely to be of a transient nature. In both cases—their approaches to democracy and the West—the Shiʻite fundamentalists, especially SAIRI, may be expected to be greatly influenced by political expediency. If they depend heavily on the Islamic Republic of Iran, they may be expected to tow its political line. Even in the case of the Daʻwa—the majority of whose leadership, membership, and supporters are staying in Iran, some independent voices in the West notwithstanding—the Iranian influence may still be expected to be overwhelming as long as the organizational ties are as strong as they are. If, however, the Shiʻite fundamentalists come to constitute only one, and not the most powerful, component in a much wider national coalition in Iraq, and if Western rather than Iranian influence is paramount, if their past practice is any indication, then they may be expected to show a great deal of adaptability.

Acknowledgments

In addition to the American Academy of Arts and Sciences, I am indebted to the Harry S. Truman Research Institute for the Advancement of Peace and to its director, Professor Moshe Maoz, and to Mr. Irving Young of London for supporting this study.

Notes

1. There are a few other, albeit minor, Shiʻi fundamentalist opposition organizations that work to topple the Baʻth regime in Baghdad. The single most important of those is the Islamic Action Organization (Hizb al-ʻAmal al-Islami), established in Karbala in the early 1960s, with armed activity in 1975 after the executions of a few Daʻwa activists by the Baʻth regime. In the 1980s ʻAmal went underground in the form of revolutionary Shiʻite movements in Saudi Arabia, Kuwait, Oman, and Bahrain. The organization is very small but close-knit and militant, carrying out a relatively large number of sabotage and assassination activities in Iraq and occasional terrorist activities abroad.

2. This verse appears at the top of the front page of many issues of the Daʻwa party's weekly magazine *Al-Jihad*. It is designed to legitimize the concept of a political party in Islam. In this chapter, all translations from the Qurʼan are based on that of Marmaduke Pickthall, *The Glorious Koran* (London: George Allen and Unwin, 1969).

3. *Al-Jihad, Sawt al-Haraka al-Islamiyya fiʼl-ʻIraq* (The weekly magazine of the Daʻwa

party), issued in Tehran since 1981 (henceforth *Al-Jihad*), 9 October 1989, pp. 10–11. Sadr thus implied, in the tradition of Abu al-A'la al-Maududi, Sayyid Qutb, and others, that the present should be seen as the Second Jahiliyya. See also Hizb al-Da'wa al-Islamiyya fi'l-'Iraq, Maktab Lubnan (Islamic Da'wa party, Bureau of Lebanon), *Istishhad al-imam muhammad baqir al-sadr min manzur hadari* (The martyrdom of Imam, Sadr from a civizational perspective) (Lebanon, 1981), pp. 49–51.

4. The party was also called al-Hizb al-Fatimi, after Fatima-al-Zahra', the Prophet's daughter, 'Ali's wife, and Hasan and Husayn's mother (interview with a senior Da'wa activist, Europe, 10 September 1990). The founding members comprised also the first leadership of the party.

5. *Al-Da'wa Chronicle* (henceforth *DCh*); the Da'wa monthly issued in London since May 1980), no. 4 (August 1980): 3.

6. Interview with a senior party member, Europe, 27 September 1992. For a somewhat different account, see R. H. Dekmejian, *Islam in Revolution: Fundamentalism in the Arab World* (Syracuse, N.Y.: Syracuse University Press, 1985), p. 130. According to another, more junior, member who joined the party in the early 1970s, secrecy was such that he was not aware that he was attending party meetings until told so by the Ba'th security. Interview, Europe, 29 September 1992).

7. Al-Sayyid Kazim al-Husayni al-Hairi, *Mabahith al-usul: Taqriran li-abhath samahat ayat Allah al-'uzma al-shahid al-Sayyid Muhammad Baqir al-Sadr,* pt. 1 of vol. 2 (Qomm, 1986), pp. 90–91.

8. See *Istishhad al-imam*, pp. 65–66.

9. For the opponents' view, according to which membership in political parties *(al-hizbiyya)* conflicts with the principle of the Rule of the Jurist *(wiliayat al-faqih),* see Ahmad al-Katib, *Tajribat al-thawra al-islamiyya fi al-'iraq mundhu 1920 hatta 1980* (Tehran: Dar al-Qabas al-Islami, 1981), pp. 178–82. And see Hairi, *Mabahith,* pp. 87–88. And for defense of the party system, see Muhammad Baqir al-Sadr as quoted in *Al-Jihad,* 9 October 1989, p. 11; *Istishhad al-imam,* pp. 44–51; and see below.

10. See, for example, *Al-Jihad,* 10 December 1990, p. 5.

11. Hairi, *Mabahith,* p. 90.

12. Katib, *Tajribat al-thawra,* pp. 192–93. For description of declining religiosity, see *DCh,* no. 4 (August 1980): 3. Interview with Mahdi al-Hakim, *Impact International,* 25 April–8 May 1980, p. 5.

13. Based on statistics that appeared in *Majallat al-'Alam al-Islami* in 1960 as reported in Katib, *Tajribat al-thawra,* pp. 172–73.

14. Muhsin al-Amin, *Rihlat al-sayyid muhsin al-amin,* as reproduced in Fuad Ajami, *The Vanished Imam: Musa al-Sadr and the Shia of Lebanon* (Ithaca, N.Y.: Cornell University Press, 1986), p. 40.

15. Hanna Batatu, "Shi'i Organizations in Iraq: Al-Da'wa al-Islamiyah and al-Mujahideen," in Juan R. I. Cole and Nikki R. Keddie, *Shi'ism and Social Protest* (New Haven: Yale University Press, 1986), p. 189.

16. According to Shi'i tradition, one-fifth *(khums)* of every believer's net income is to be given to the senior ulama to be shared with people who are descendants of the Prophet's family through the offspring of 'Ali and Fatima, the Prophet's daughter (single: *sayyid;* plural: *sadah).* See, for example, Moojan Momen, *An Introduction to Shi'i Islam* (New Haven: Yale University Press, 1985), pp. 179–80, 190. Many of the senior ulama were also sadah (for example, both al-Hakim's and al-Sadr's families are believed to be descendants of the Prophet's family). Senior mujtahids traditionally received other substantial donations from rich muqallidun as well as many small donations from their less affluent followers. Such mujtahids managed to accumulate great wealth. Grand Ayatollah Kho'i from Najaf established a number of large centers of Shi'i learning and missionary activity in the West, notably in Queens, New York, London, and in India.

17. Interview, Europe, 27 September 1992.

18. 'A. Najaf, *Al-Shahed al-shahid* (Tehran: Jama'at al-'ulama al-Mujahidin fi al-'Iraq, 1981), p. 15.

19. Uriel Dann, *Iraq under Qassem: A Political History, 1958–1963* (Tel Aviv, 1969), pp. 110–13, 125–26, 144; Hanna Batatu, *The Old Social Classes and the Revolutionary Movements of Iraq* (Princeton: Princeton University Press, 1978), pp. 858, 895–97, 950–53.

20. Interview with Mahdi al-Hakim, *Impact International*, 25 April–8 May 1980, p. 5. Interview with Muhammad Baqir al-Hakim, *Imam* (a magazine issued by the Iranian embassy in London) 3, no. 1 (January 1983): 29–30. See also, *DCh*, no. 4 (August 1980): 3, 6.

21. Interview, Europe, 9 October 1990. See also al-Khatib ibn al-Najaf, *Ta’rikh al-haraka al-islamiyya al-mu‘asira fi al-‘iraq* (Tehran, 1981), p. 14.

22. Hairi, *Mabahith*, pp. 87–89.

23. Sadr al-Din al-Qabanji, in an introduction to the Supreme Assembly's publication *Al-‘ulama al-shuhada, fi tariq al-thawra al-islamiyya fi al-‘iraq* (Tehran, 1990), pp. 17–18, 25–26. See also Qabanji in another publication of the Supreme Assembly, *Buhuth fi fikr al-shahid al-Sadr, no. 2: Al-tanzim fi khatt al-marja‘iyya* (Tehran, n.d.), pp. 17–31. Musa al-Tamimi in the Supreme Assembly's *Dama al-‘ulama fi tariq al-jihad* (Tehran, 1984), pp. 98–99.

24. *Istishhad al-imam*, pp. 49–50; *Al-Jihad*, 9 October 1989, p. 11.

25. *Istishhad al-imam*, p. 51.

26. See an account in a classical hadith style quoting Sadr, in Hairi, *Mabahithl*, pp. 100–103.

27. See, for example, *Al-Massar*, 28 October 1987. For a detailed discussion of the Da‘wa's attitude toward the principle of *wilayat al-faqih*, see the section headed "The Rule of the Jurist."

28. *Al-Zahf al-Akhdar*, 20 January 1981, p. 15.

29. The same may have happened to Da‘wa draftees, but the numbers are not large enough to draw meaningful conclusions. Based on *Liwa al-Sadr* and *Al-Jihad*, 1988–89.

30. Based on conversations with a senior Da‘wa activist, Europe, 10 September 1990 and 14 July 1991; with a Shi‘i religious but liberal intellectual and political activist who does not belong to any of the organized groups, London, 9 March 1990; and with a Shi‘i political activist who belongs to a well-known ulama family in Iraq but who never joined any of the fundamentalist organizations, Europe, 13 September 1990.

31. *DCh*, no. 37 (May 1983): 7; interviews with a senior Da‘wa member, Europe, 10 September 1990 and 14 July 1991. For fiqh classes given by one of Sadr's students in Baghdad's al-Tamimi Mosque, see Khatib, *Ta’rikh*, p. 76. For a member's duty to be regularly present at the *halaqa* (the party's circle of learning and its basic unit) and "to absorb the studies of fiqh," see *Istishhad al-imam*, p. 63. Still, the number of lay fiqh students was very small due to the great complexity of the subject.

32. Interview with a senior Da‘wa member, Europe, 10 September 1990. For educational activities in the tribal areas and in the countryside in general, see *al-‘Ulama al-shuhada*, pp. 42, 76, 100–101, 106–7, 161–62.

33. In an interview with the Da‘wa activist in Europe, 14 July 1991, I was told that his circle with Sadr included only himself and two other lay intellectuals.

34. Khatib, *Ta’rikh*, pp. 37–38; interview with a senior Da‘wa member, Europe, 10 September 1990.

35. *Istishhad al-imam*, pp. 63–65.

36. *Al-Jihad*, 6 September 1982, pp. 6, 11.

37. Interview with a senior Da‘wa activist, Europe, 10 September 1990 and 27 September 1992.

38. *Al-Jihad*, 24 September 1990.

39. *Istishhad al-imam*, pp. 64–65. Interview with a central party activist, Europe, 10 September 1990; for these activities, see the section "Da‘wa Organization and Activities in the 1980s."

40. *Al-‘Ahd* (Lebanon), 21 January 1988; *Al-Tayar al-Jadid*, 29 February 1988.

41. Three interviews with the same Da‘wa activist, Europe, 10 September 1990, 14 July 1991, and 27 September 1992. And see interview with Shaykh ‘Ali ibn ‘Abd ‘Aziz, a member of the politburo of the

(Shi'i Iraqi) Kurdish Islamic Movement, who was also influenced by Sadr's political thought, in *Al-Bilad* (Beirut), 30 November 1991, according to which the movement hierarchy consists of the general adviser, Shaykh 'Uthman ibn 'Abd al-'Aziz. He heads the politburo, which is elected, in its own turn, by the twenty-one-strong Majlis Shura (Consultative Council). The latter consists of "ulama, engineers, and lawyers."

42. In the late 1980s and early 1990s the more outstanding laymen were in Iran and Syria. For examples of interviews with laymen and clergy, see *Liwa al-Sadr,* 21 October 1990; *Al-Jihad,* 23 October, 25 September, 11 December and 20 November, 1989; 30 April and 3 December 1990; and 14 November 1991; *Al-Tayyar al-Jadid* (London), 8 June 1987; BBC World Service, 4 April 1991; *al-Ahram,* 4 September 1991.

43. Interview with a senior Da'wa member, Europe, 10 September 1990.

44. Professor Abu Ahmad al-Khaliji, *Al-Jihad,* 24 September 1990. This observation is corroborated by the leader of a competing movement, Munazzamat al-'Amal, who confirmed that the Da'wa are the leaders within the Islamic movement in terms of educating intellectual cadres. See Muhammad Taqi al-Mudarrisi, *'An al-'iraq wal-harakat al-islamiyya* (London: al-Safa, 1988), p. 51.

45. Interview with a senior Da'wa member, Europe, 10 September 1990. *Al-Jihad,* 2 April 1990, p. 8. For the influence of Sadr's wukala on the masses in al-Thawra quarter, see also *Liwa al-Sadr,* 9 February 1983.

46. *Al-Jihad,* 18 December 1989, p. 7. The weekly was first issued as a monthly magazine. A Kurdish version was issued first in 1982. See *Al-Jihad,* 14 May 1990, p. 4.

47. See, for example, *Al-Jihad,* 25 July 1988, p. 10; 23 October 1989; 6 November 1989; 4 December 1989, pp. 2, 3; 29 January 1990, p. 3; 12 February 1990, p. 2; 19 February 1990, p. 3; 26 February 1990, p. 3; 19 March 1990, p. 3; 23 April 1990, p. 2; 28 May 1990, p. 2; 10 September 1990.

48. For example, *Al-'Ahd* (Beirut), 21 Jan-

uary 1988, p. 10; *Al-Jihad,* 6 November 1989; 1 January, 25 June, and 3 December 1990.

49. For details about repression see Tariq 'Aziz, in the *New York Times,* 11 January 1981; *New York Times,* 3 April 1984; Najaf, *Al-Shahed al-shahid,* pp. 63–64; Amnesty International, *Report and Recommendations: To the Government of the Republic of Iraq,* 22–28 January 1983, pp. 21, 39; Amnesty International news release, London, 10 March and 12 June 1980; *Imam,* April–May 1982, pp. 60–61; *Tehran Times,* 28 February 1989.

50. Interview, Europe, 14 July 1991. For more, see the section "The Rule of the Jurist."

51. Najaf, *Al-Shahed al-shahid,* pp. 135–38.

52. Muhammad Baqir al-Sadr, "Da'watuna ila al-islam yajibu an takuna inqilabiyya," in Hizb al-Da'wa al-Islamiyya (Central Communication Bureau), *Min fikr al-Da'wa al-islamiyya,* no. 13 (Tehran, n.d.), pp. 35–38.

53. Sadr decided that the party should begin as a clandestine organization, and, conditions permitting, it would "start a stage of overt political activity." Hairi, *Mubahith,* pp. 90–91.

54. Interview with Mahdi al-Hakim, *Impact International;* and in the same direction, see Sadr, "Da'wa tuna ila al-islam," pp. 35–38.

55. *Al-Jihad,* 10 September 1990. Reports of armed activities have appeared in the party's publications since 1980.

56. Most of this information is based on interviews with Western diplomats and officials in Europe and in Washington, D.C., between September 1988 and March 1990. See also *Ma'ariv,* 11 May 1987, and *Al-Wahda al-Islamiyya* (Lebanon), 4 December 1988.

57. Reuter, AP, 13 December 1983; *HaAretz,* 14 December 1983; *New York Times,* 14 and 15 December 1983.

58. See interview with a central party activist in the Saudi newspaper *Al-Sharq al-Awsat,* 3 March 1991.

59. For example, the Jama'a was headed

by Ayat Allah Murtada Aal Yasin, a relative of Muhammad Baqir al-Sadr on his mother's side. A central member in the Jama'a was Sadr's elder brother, Isma'il. Sadr himself, while too young to be officially a founding member, was very active within the group, especially as the driving force behind its magazine, *Majallat al-Adwa al-Islamiyya* (The Islamic lights), which appeared in the early 1960s. (Sadr wrote a controversial column titled "Risalatuna," "Our Message.")

60. Khatib, *Ta'rikh,* pp. 16–17.

61. *Al-Jihad,* 25 June 1990, p. 7.

62. See, for example, *Liwa al-Sadr,* 11 September and 2 October 1988; *Al-Shahada,* issued by SAIRI's Unit for Information, 22 November 1983; *Al-Tayyar al-Jadid,* 21 October 1987; *Al-Jihad,* 17 September 1990. According to *Al-Jihad,* 2 April 1990, Sadr and the Da'wa were the forces behind the Intifada.

63. Khatib, *Ta'rikh,* pp. 57–58.

64. Sadr's sister, Bint al-Huda, and the wives of some of Sadr's colleagues taught in and supervised a system of such Shi'ite religious schools for girls. This system was nationalized by the Ba'th regime in the mid-1970s and apparently closed down in 1979.

65. See, for example, in *Liwa al-Sadr,* 15 January 1989, p. 6, the reminiscences of Ayat Allah al-'Askari of his work with the martyred Mahdi al-Hakim in which he tells how 'Abd al-Salam 'Arif planned "to strike at the followers of the school of the Prophet's family" and how they were saved.

66. Khatib, *Ta'rikh,* pp. 20–37, 54, 57–58, 61–62. For activities in Karbala and Kufa, see pp. 65–68. For the media, especially the radio and television, see pp. 70, 81, 83, 88, 93.

67. *Al-Jihad,* 2 April 1990, p. 8.

68. Hairi, *Mabahith,* pp. 91–100; Qabanji, in *Buhuth fi fikr al-shahid al-Sadr,* pp. 10–16.

69. *Dama al-'ulama,* p. 98.

70. *Dama al-'ulama,* pp. 97–104; Tehran Radio (in Arabic), 13 November 1980; BBC, 15 November 1980; *DCh,* no. 8 (December 1980): 1.

71. See, for example, *Al-Jihad,* 11 June 1990, p. 2. See there, also, a speech by Ayat Allah Muhammad Husayn Fadlallah, the most senior Shi'i clergyman of Lebanon, who was himself very close to the Da'wa in its early stages and who remained close to it and to the Jama'a afterward.

72. For Ja'fari, see Damascus Radio, 6 August 1985. Qabanji is also responsible for the education and culture of SAIRI's regular army; see *Liwa al-Sadr,* 25 September 1988 and 22 April 1990.

73. *Dama al-'ulama,* pp. 103–8.

74. For example, *Liwa al-Sadr,* 24 February 1991, p. 2; *Dama al-'ulama,* pp. 111–13. In order to prove that al-Hakim is indeed the leader of the opposition, this source reports Saddam Hussein's attacks against al-Hakim and his challenge to the latter to compete with him for popularity among the Iraqis. The Ba'th, for their part, announced, mockingly, that Khomeini appointed al-Hakim the future president of Iraq (Baghdad Radio, 21 November 1982, in *FBIS-Daily Report,* 2 December 1982).

75. See, for example, *Al-'ulama al-shuhada,* pp. 13–14.

76. Associated Press, Nicosia, 17 November 1982; *Liwa al-Sadr,* 9 February 1983, pp. 1, 8; 16 June 1982, p. 2; *Imam* 3, no. 1 (January 1983): 29; *DCh,* no. 49 (May 1984): 6; *Jeune Afrique,* 25 January 1984, pp. 48–51.

77. See "Abu Bilal," *Al-Jihad,* 3 December 1990. One example of a clash of interests, in addition to the obvious wish of the Iraqi revolutionaries that Iran would continue the war until Saddam's downfall, was the issue of the return of the Iraqi exiles in Iran to their homeland. The Da'wa demanded that this be one of the Iranian preconditions for peace with Iraq. Iran refused to raise the issue, and SAIRI was reluctant to antagonize the Iranian regime over this issue. Interview with a senior Da'wa member, Europe, 10 September 1990. For criticism of SAIRI over its failure to cooperate with the movements and to mobilize underground activity inside Iraq, see Mudarrisi, *'An al-'iraq,* pp. 53–56.

78. For example, *Liwa al-Sadr,* 14 August 1988 and 22 April 1990.

79. Interview with a senior Da'wa member, Europe, 10 September 1990.

80. Iranian News Agency (Tehran), 5 January 1988; *Liwa al-Sadr,* 11 December 1988.

81. *Ettela'at* (Tehran), 18 November 1982; *Kayhan* (Tehran), 27 November 1982; *Dama al-'ulama,* pp. 106–7, 113–14. Tehran Radio, November 1986, reported ten thousand. Al-Hakim reported fifty thousand in and outside Iraq. See Tehran Radio, 17 November 1987, in BBC-SWB-ME, 18 November 1987. Also Amatzia Baram, "The Impact of Khomeini's Revolution on the Radical Shi'i Movement of Iraq," in David Menashri, ed., *The Iranian Revolution and the Muslim World* (Boulder, Colo.: Westview, 1990), p. 147. *Liwa al-Sadr,* 19 August 1990.

82. See, for example, *Time Magazine,* 18 March 1991, pp. 27, 28.

83. *Liwa al-Sadr,* 11 and 25 September, 2 and 23 October, 13 and 20 November, and 4, 11, and 25 December 1988, and 22 April 1990.

84. Ibid., 14 August 1988.

85. Ibid., 12 August, 4 and 11 September 1988.

86. Ibid., 11 September 1988, 12 August 1990.

87. Ibid., 28 November 1988, 29 April 1990.

88. Ibid., 10 December 1989.

89. For example, French News Agency from Tehran, 24 December 1986; Tehran Radio, 6 January 1988.

90. In an interview in November 1990 with a Western official, I was told that the Iranian authorities are wary of the Da'wa's independence.

91. *Nida min ajli al-dimuqratiyya wa huquq al-insan fi al-'Iraq* (A call for democracy and human rights in Iran) (London), February 1990.

92. *Bayan al-haraka al-wataniyya wal-islamiyya al-'iraqiyya hawla al-ijtiyah al-'askari al-'iraqi lil-Kuwait wa makhatir al-tadakhkhul al-ajnabi fi al-mintaqa* (A communiqué by the patriotic and Islamic Iraqi movement regarding the military Iraqi suppression of Kuwait and the dangers of foreign intervention in the area) (London), 14 August 1990. Signatories: the pro-Syrian Ba'th, the major Kurdish parties, the Iraqi Communist party, Iraqi Nasirites, SAIRI, the Da'wa (under the pseudonym al-Haraka al-islamiyya al-'iraqiyya), and others.

93. *Bayan quwa al-mu'arada al-'iraqiyya* (A communiqué of the force of the Iraqi opposition) (Damascus), 27 December 1990. Signed by: SAIRI, the Da'wa, 'Amal, Jama'at al-'Ulama al-Mujahidin fi al-'Iraq, Jund al-Imam, the Islamic bloc, the Communist party, the main Kurdish parties, ex-Ba'thists, and others.

94. Syrian Arab News Agencies (SANA), 12 March 1991; BBC, 14 March 1991, pp. A1, A2; Radio Lebanon, 11 March 1991; BBC, 13 March 1991, p. A3; *Liwa al-Sadr,* 6 October 1991.

95. The Ba'th regime accused Iran of sending a large number of Pasdoran into Iraq. See Milton Viorst, *The New Yorker,* 24 June 1991, p. 72, quoting the governor of Karbala to the effect that he had captured fifty of them. And Saddam Hussein in a speech in Najaf, *al-Thawra* (Bagdad), 28 July 1991. The participation of Iranians was confirmed to me in an interview with a Da'wa activist, Europe, 14 July 1991. Yet the number of Iranians was no more than a few hundred.

96. See, for example, *Newsweek,* 18 March 1991; *Time,* 18 March 1991; Saddam Hussein's speech, Radio Baghdad, 16 March 1991; *Al-Jihad,* 10 June 1991. The Shi'i press that comes out in Tehran ignores the issue of the infiltrators all together, but they have an ulterior motive—the need to exonerate Iran from any charge of helping the U.S. war effort and to present the revolt as an autonomous Iraqi-Shi'i event.

97. See France Inter Radio (Paris), 6 March 1991, and Syrian Arab Republic Radio, 5 March 1991, in BBC, 7 March 1991, pp. A6, A7.

98. *Al-Jihad,* 2 September 1991.

99. Great devastation and much loss of life have been admitted by both sides, though each side blamed the other for caus-

ing it. The government admitted massive riots in all eight governorates of the Shi'i south (Basra, Maysan, Dhiqar, Qadisiyya, Karbala, Najaf, Muthanna, and Babil). It also admitted huge destruction and many dead lying unburied in the streets. See Iraqi News Agency (Bagdad), 22 March 1991; BBC, 23 March 1991, p. A1.

100. See al-Hakim's account, *Liwa al-Sadr*, 27 October 1991.

101. Interview with a Da'wa activist, Europe, 14 July 1991.

102. *Al-Jihad*, 10 June 1991.

103. Ibid., 22 April and 5 May 1991.

104. Ibid., 22 April, 6 May and 10 June 1991.

105. Indeed, fourteen out of the eighteen governorates of Iraq revolted. Those that did not were Baghdad and the three Sunni areas: Anbar, Salah al-Din, and most of Nineveh. The opposition sources report details about revolts in Basra (1 March); Najaf, Talha, al-Mudayana (2 March); al-Hira, Mishkhab (3 March); 'Amara (4 March); Karbala, al-Kifl (5 March); and in the following days, in Kut, Qurna, Nasiriyya, Samawa, Rumaytha, al-Hayy, al-Kahla, Qal'at Salih, Hilla, Diwaniyya, al-Warka, and Safwan. See, for example, *Liwa al-Sadr*, 28 July; 18, 25 August; 1, 15, 22, 29 September; and 6, 27 October 1991; *Al-Jihad*, 22 April, 10 June, and 30 September 1991.

106. *Al-Jihad*, 10 June and 30 September 1991; *Liwa al-Sadr*, 28 July 1991.

107. See on the Basra area *al-Thawra*, 6 August 1991. And on the Najaf area, ibid., 28 July and 16 August 1991.

108. *Al-Thawra*, 28 July 1991.

109. Milton Viorst interviewing Khalid 'Abd al-'Aziz Sayyid, *The New Yorker*, 24 June 1991, p. 72. Sayyid reported only six hundred casualties, an unlikely figure, but also, and much more credibly, three thousand prisoners.

110. For example, *Al-Jihad*, 22 April 1991.

111. Louise Lief, *U.S. News and World Report*, 30 September 1991, p. 54.

112. *Al-Jihad*, 22 April 1991.

113. Dr. Abu Huda al-Khaza'i to *Al-Jihad*, 2 September 1991.

114. *Al-Jihad*, 6 May 1991.

115. Ibid., 22 April 1991.

116. Ibid., 25 March 1991.

117. Ibid., 22 April 1991.

118. Iraqi News Agency, 20 March 1991; BBC, 22 March 1991, p. A2. For Kho'i's son accusing the rebels of storming the holy places and thus violating them, see Baghdad Radio, 21 March 1991; BBC, 23 March 1991, pp. A1, A2. He carefully refrained, however, from demanding punishment for the rebels or from defining what kind of punishment they deserved. For information on Kho'i's activities during the Intifada: interviews with Shi'i activists in Europe, 27 September 1992; New York, 10 February 1992. Also see *The Observer*, 19 May 1991.

119. Viorst, *The New Yorker*, 24 June 1991. And see a French reporter quoted in *Al-Jihad*, 22 April 1991.

120. Lebanese Pro-Hizbullah Radio, 21 March 1991; BBC, 22 March 1991, p. A2. And see *Al-Jihad*, 25 March 1991.

121. Etan Kohlberg, "The Evolution of the Shi'a," *Jerusalem Quarterly*, no. 27 (Spring 1983): 116–17.

122. See, for example, Hamid Algar, *Religion and State in Iran, 1785–1906* (Berkeley: University of California Press, 1960), pp. 4, 8–9, 21. A. K. S. Lambton, "A Reconsideration of the Position of the Marja al-Taqlid and the Religious Institution," *Studia Islamica* 20 (1964): 116–17. See also Roger M. Savory, "The Problem of Sovereignty in an Ithna Ashari ("Twelver") Shi'i State," in M. Curtis, ed., *Religion and Politics in the Middle East* (Boulder, Colo.: Westview, 1981), p. 131.

123. For an extensive discussion of this issue, see Eitan Kohlberg, "Some Imami Shi'i Views on Taqiyya," *JAOS* 95, no. 3 (July–September 1975): 395–402.

124. *Al-Shahada*, 22 November 1983; *Al-Jihad*, 10 September 1990.

125. *Al-Jihad*, 17 September 1990.

126. Ibid. See also, for example, ibid.,

25 September 1989; for a procession leaving from al-Sadr's Mosque to the tomb of Zaynab, al-Husayn's sister, in Damascus, see Ibid., 2 October 1989; *Liwa al-Sadr,* 4, 11, and 25 September; 2 and 16 October 1988. The motif of al-Husayn is also very prominent in love poems to Iraq.

127. See, for example, *Liwa al-Sadr,* 14 August, 4 and 25 September, and 16 October 1988. A communiqué of Harakat al-Jamahir al-Islamiyya for Muharram, *Tariq al-Thawra,* no. 28 (Rabi' al-Awwal 1403 [1982]): 44.

128. Hairi, *Mabahith,* pp. 160, 162.

129. *Al-Jihad,* 2 April 1990.

130. Hairi, *Mabahith,* pp. 161–63.

131. ˆ*Liwa al-Sadr,* 14 August 1988.

132. Hairi, *Mabahith,* pp. 127–28. See also pp. 129–31.

133. For example, *Al-Jihad al-Duwali,* 7 and 14 May 1990.

134. See, for example, in a publication of the small Harakat al-Jamahir, *Al-Afkar al-salbiyya, isti'rad wataqyim* (Tehran, 1982?), pp. 52–68.

135. Mudarrisi, '*An al-'iraq,* pp. 60–61.

136. *Tariq al-Thawra,* no. 30 (Rajab-Sha'ban 1403): 8–11. The choice of the hadith is arbitrary. For a very different hadith that actually emphasizes the passive waiting, see al-Shaykh al-Mufid, *Kitab al-irshad* (n.p., 1360H), p. 142.

137. Hairi, *Mabahith,* pp. 87–88.

138. *Al-Jihad,* 3 October 1983.

139. Ibid., 18 September 1989.

140. See Ahmad al-Katib, *Tajribat al-thawra al-islamiyya fi al-'iraq, mundhu 1920 hatta 1980* (Tehran, 1981), pp. 181–204. For competition between the Da'wa, 'Amal, and SAIRI over which is more active inside Iraq, see Mudarrisi, '*An al-'iraq,* pp. 51–56. See claims by SAIRI that Muhsin al-Hakim, despite his advanced age, was a Husayni activist, confronting the Ba'th regime openly and bravely, while the Da'wa party proved unwilling to engage in any real action. *Liwa al-Sadr,* 6 and 13 November 1988.

141. *Liwa al-Sadr,* 15 April 1990; *Al-*

Jihad, 23 October 1989, and 26 March and 30 October 1990.

142. *Al-Jihad,* 25 June 1990. For another shahid, see *Al-Jihad,* 13 August 1990, p. 4. For a dentist from the Hakim family who gave his own money to needy patients even though he had just started a private practice and was in great need of every penny, see *Al-Jihad,* 30 April 1990.

143. *Al-Jihad,* 25 September and 23 October 1989.

144. *Al-Jihad,* 25 June 1990.

145. Hairi, *Mabahith,* pp. 162–63. For his sister, ibid., p. 127–30. In *Al-Jihad,* 25 June 1990, see Sadr's brother demanding of 'Arif to turn the whole nation into practicing Muslims.

146. Hairi, *Mubahith,* p. 109.

147. See, for example, about Shawky, *Al-Jihad,* 2 and 23 October 1989. See also a poem in his memory, ibid., 23 October 1989.

148. *Liwa al-Sadr,* 22 January 1989. And for Shawky's devotion to Allah and frequent prayers, see *Al-Jihad,* 25 September 1989.

149. *Liwa al-Sadr,* 5 August 1990.

150. Ibid., 15 April 1990.

151. See, for example, Abu 'Abd Allah Ahmad ibn Muhammad ibn Hanbal al-Shaybani, *Kitab al-zuhd* (Beirut, 1988), pp. 13–18.

152. Hairi, *Mabahith,* pp. 164–65.

153. *Al-Jihad al-Duwali,* 8 January 1990.

154. *Bayan al-Tafahum al-Sadir min Hizb al-Da'wa al-Islamiyya ila al-Umma fi al-'Iraq,* publication no. 7 (Da'wa's Central Information Bureau, ca. 1982), pp. 53–55.

155. Mudarrisi, '*An al-'iraq,* pp. 124–40.

156. Ibid., p. 72–73.

157. *Bayan al-Tafahum,* pp. 29–58. See in particular, pp. 55–58. See also, *DCh,* no. 21 (January 1982): 6. And expressions of competition with Iran, *DCh,* no. 19 (November 1981): 4, 6; no. 22 (February 1982): 4. Also see *Barnamijuna: Al-bayan wa al-barnamij al-siyasi lil hizb al-da'wa al-islamiyya* (Our program: The communiqué and political program of the . . . Da'wa)

(London, March 1992), pp. 44–45, 62–64, 84.

158. Mudarrisi, *'An al-'iraq*, p. 25.

159. Translated from Sadr's communiqué in Hairi, *Mabahith*, pp. 151–53. For an English version, see also *DCh*, no. 3 (July 1980): 2.

160. For example, the Da'wa *barnamij* of March 1992 steers clear of the pan-Arab expression "Arab unity" when foreign policy is discussed. Instead it uses more limited expressions like "the unity of the Arab and Islamic rank" and "political, cultural, and economic integration [*takamul*] among the Arab and Islamic countries" (p. 85).

161. For a discussion of these reservations, see Amatzia Baram, Culture, History, and Ideology in the Formation of Ba'thi Iraq (New York: St. Martin's Press, 1991), pp. 5–7.

162. For example, the party's program of March 1992, *Barnamijuna*, pp. 48, 50, 52, 61, 76, 82, 84–85.

163. Layth Kubba, *Al-Hayat* (London, Beirut), 7 September 1992.

164. See, for example, Hakim's speeches in *Liwa al-Sadr*, 28 June 1992, upon returning to Tehran from Saudi Arabia; 5 July 1992, following his visit to Kuwait; 19 July 1992, his speech on the *'ashura;* 2 May 1993, a speech to exiled Iraqi tribesmen and their chiefs at Dezful (Khozestan).

165. See, for example, al-Mujahidin in *Al-Kayhan al-'Arabi* as quoted in Joint Publication Research Services (Near East and North Africa), Washington, D.C., 23 June 1981, p. 37. SAIRI's spokesman, quoted in *Imam*, January 1983, p. 30; *Al-Tayar al-Jadid*, 23 July 1983; *Jeune Afrique*, 25 January 1984, pp. 48–51, reports that there is competition over members and that activists of each movement are trying to win over members from other movements. For the latest account of rivalries among the various movements, see Mudarrisi, *'An al-'iraq*, pp. 41–56.

166. Mudarrisi, *'An al-'iraq*, p. 49.

167. Muhammad Baqir al-Sadr, *Lamha tamhidiyya 'an mashru' dustur al-jumhuriyya al-Islamiyya* (Beirut, 1979), pp. 13, 20. For

more details, see Baram, "The Radical Shi'ite Opposition Movements in Iraq," pp. 107–23.

168. "Bayan al-quwa al-mu'arada al-islamiyya al-'iraqiyya," published in *Al-Jihad*, 17 September 1990. See also Muhammad Baqir al-Hakim, emphasizing that the future rule in Iraq would be "neither Shi'i nor Sunni nor sectarian," *Liwa al-Sadr*, 28 October 1990, p. 1.

169. See, for example, *Al-Jihad*, 9 July 1990.

170. Bear in mind that practically all the Islamic parties within the opposition are Shi'ite ones. There is no meaningful Sunni fundamentalist movement in Iraq. See, for example, al-Hakim's speech to his soldiers, *Liwa al-Sadr*, 24 February 1991.

171. *Sawt al-'Iraq*, July 1982, p. 3; *DCh*, no. 16 (August 1981): 3; see also *DCh*, no. 5 (September 1980): 2; no. 17 (September 1981): 7; no. 37 (August 1983): 3.

172. See, on the pope's visit to Indonesia, *Al-Jihad*, 23 October 1989.

173. Al-Shaykh 'Abd al-Karim al-Shukri, one of the Da'wa's leading ideologues, *Al-Jihad*, 18 September 1989.

174. For example, *DCh*, no. 37 (August 1983): 6. See also no. 22 (February 1982): 1, 6; no. 4 (August 1982): 1.

175. *Sawt al-'Iraq*, July 1982, p. 3; *Al-Jihad*, no. 52, p. 5; *Jami'at al-Rafidayn*, no. 9, 1982; *DCh*, no. 17 (September 1981): 8.

176. *DCh*, no. 2 (June 1980): 1.

177. See, for example, *DCh*, no. 6 (October 1980): 5; no. 24 (April 1982): 2; no. 25 (May 1982): 2–3; no. 29 (September 1982): 3; no. 30 (October 1982): 1; no. 40 (August 1983): 4; *Sawt al-'Iraq*, no. 42 (1 December 1983): 1. For support of the antigovernment Islamic demonstrations in Egypt, see *Liwa al-Sadr*, 2 October 1988. For severe criticism of the corrupt life of the Saudi family, its wine parties, sexual orgies, rape, and other pastimes, see, for example, *Liwa al-Sadr*, 11 September 1988. For a Saudi fatwa allowing the killing of all opponents of the Saudi regime and especially the true Muslims, see *Liwa al-Sadr*, 2 October 1988.

178. *DCh*, no. 22 (February 1982): 1.

179. See, for example, an interview with Professor Abu Bilal, the senior Da'wa representative in Damascus, *Al-Jihad*, 3 December 1990, p. 5.

180. See for example, *Liwa al-Sadr*, no. 18 (30 October 1988) for an extensive report of a few days' visit of Muhammad Baqir al-Hakim to Damascus in which he met Syrian officials all the way up to President Asad.

181. The first such meeting took place in Damascus in December and produced a joint communiqué on 27 December 1990. See "Bayan al-quwa al-mu'arada al-islamiyya al-'iraqiyya" (A communiqué of the forces of the Iraqi opposition). And see news agency reports about continuous discussions between the various opposition groups in Damascus and a special interview with 'Amal's leader, Muhammad Taqi al-Mudarrisi, in *HaAretz*, 4 February 1991. See also a report in *Le Monde*, as translated in *HaAretz*, 25 February 1991. And also a report from London on the establishment on 27 December 1990 of a joint action committee for all the opposition movements in Damascus, *HaAretz*, 1 March 1991.

182. 'Abd al-'Aziz al-Hakim, head of the Mujahidin, *Liwa al-Sadr*, 11 November 1990; Muhammad Baqir al-Hakim speaking for all the Shi'i opposition movements, *Liwa al-Sadr*, 11 November 1990. And see the joint communiqué of six fundamentalist Shi'i movements including al-Da'wa, 'Amal, and Mujahidin, "Bayan al-quwa al-mu'arada al-islamiyya al-'iraqiyya."

183. *Bayan* (Damascus), 27 December 1990; see also al-Hakim, *Liwa al-Sadr*, 19 August 1990.

184. *Liwa al-Sadr*, 16 September 1990, p. 15.

185. Communiqué of the Islamic opposition forces of Iraq, *Al-Jihad*, 17 September 1990.

186. Muhammad Baqir al-Hakim to a Japanese television station, *Liwa al-Sadr*, 10 December 1990.

187. *Liwa al-Sadr*, 7 October 1990, p. 1.

188. For example, "A Communiqué by the Forces of the Islamic Opposition," *Liwa al-Sadr*, 23 September 1990; al-Hakim, *Liwa al-Sadr*, 9 December 1990. Also *Al-Jihad*, 27 August 1990.

189. The Da'wa politburo, a communiqué addressed to the Muslim Brothers in Jordan, *Al-Jihad*, 8 April 1991.

190. "Abu Bilal," *Al-Jihad*, 3 December 1990.

191. *Le Monde*, as reproduced in *HaAretz*, 25 February 1991. And see report from London, *HaAretz*, 1 March 1991.

192. Muwaffaq al-Rubay'i, in an interview with the BBC World Service, 5 April 1991; *Liwa al-Sadr*, 28 June 1992.

193. See, for example, *Liwa al-Sadr*, 28 October 1990; and objection to war because it may destroy the Iraq army that is "the property of the people before it is the property of the regime and the hatred of the West against the Iraqi people, *Liwa al-Sadr*, 4 November 1990; and for President Bush and the United States defined as "Satan," *Al-Jihad*, 13 August 1990; and for the U.S. presence in the Gulf being a greater danger to the Muslims than Saddam's invasion of Kuwait, *Liwa al-Sadr*, 12 August 1990.

194. See, for example, a joint communiqué of Islamic and secular forces, *Bayan al-haraka al-wataniyya wal-islamiyya al-'iraqiyya hawla al-ijtiyah al-'askari al-'iraqi lil-kuwayt wa makhatir al-tadakhkhul al-ajnabi fi al-mintaqa* (London), 14 August 1990.

195. An interview with a senior Da'wa activist, Europe, 10 September 1990; see also a Da'wa communiqué, *Al-Jihad*, 6 August 1990. "Abu Bilal," *Al-Jihad*, 10 December 1990; al-Aasifi, *Al-Jihad*, 17 September 1990. See implied support for international struggle against Saddam, provided it is not against the Iraqi people, in SAIRI's view on UN resolution 678, *Liwa al-Sadr*, 9 December 1990; and see *Al-Jihad*, 27 August 1990.

196. See, for example, al-Aasifi, *Al-Jihad*, 6 August 1990; al-Hakim, *Liwa al-Sadr*, 19 August 1990.

197. See, for example, Hujjat al-Islam Husayn al-Sadr, *The Guardian*, 15 January 1991; a SAIRI representative to *Le Monde*, as quoted in *HaAretz*, 25 February 1991.

"Abu 'Ali," representative of al-Da'wa in London to *Le Monde*, as quoted in *HaAretz*, 24 October 1990; an interview to Sawt al-Kuwait, given in Damascus by Muhammad Taqi al-Mudarrisi of 'Amal, *HaAretz*, 4 February 1991. The interview given to the present author by a senior Da'wa activist in Europe, 10 September 1990, was a part of this media campaign. Al-Hakim to the French News Agency, *Liwa al-Sadr*, 4 November 1990.

198. *Al-Jihad*, 14 January 1991.

199. Ibid., 21 January 1991. And see a call to the "presidents and kings of the Arab countries": "Use your influence to stop this devastating war," ibid., 9 February 1991.

200. Ibid., 3 June 1991.

201. Ibid., 22 April 1991.

202. Ibid., 3 June 1991.

203. In August 1991 a large and mixed delegation of opposition leaders, including Da'wa representatives, met in Washington with fairly senior officials from the Department of State. They sought practical help but were promised none. See a report in the Da'wa weekly of a three-day sit-in strike of opposition activists in front of the U.S. embassy in London, "in protest of the world's silence over Saddam's slaughter of our people, Arabs and Kurds," *Al-Jihad*, 22 April 1991. This protest sounds more like a plea and bears evidence that the opposition recognizes the United States as the sole power that can save the Iraqi people and expect it to behave in a moral way. There is no recourse to "Satan" terminology.

204. Interview, Europe, 14 July 1991.

205. *Al-Jihad*, 27 September 1982, p. 5. And see Ayatollah Muhammad Husayn Fadlallah from Lebanon, who is closely associated with the Da'wa, about the faqih who is "the commander who supervises . . . the theory and the practice," *Al-Kashif*, no. 45 (Muharram 1403H [1982]): 10.

206. *Liwa al-Sadr*, 9 February 1983, p. 11.

207. See, for example, the introduction by SAIRI's leading ideologue, Hujjat al-Islam Sadr al-Din Qabanji, in *Al-'ulama al-shuhada*, pp. 17–18. See also pp. 12–13;

and see *Dama al-'ulama*, pp. 98–112; Sadr al-Din Qabanji, in *Buhuth fi fikr al-shahid al-Sadr*, pp. 17–32. And see Qabanji in *Al-Tayar al-Jadid*, 8 June 1987, p. 10.

208. See report in *Al-Masar* (London), 4 September 1986, back page.

209. *Al-Jihad*, 2 and 9 April 1990.

210. See, for example, Muhammad Mahdi al-Aasifi, *Al-Jihad*, 11 December 1989, and more. In a joint communiqué for the Mujahidin, 'Amal, al-Da'wa, Jund al-Imam, and the Islamic movement of Iraqi Kurdistan, the issue of the Rule of the Jurist is completely missing, even though the political system of a post-Saddam Iraq is being discussed. See, *Al-Jihad*, 17 September 1990.

211. Interview, Europe, 10 September 1990.

212. Interview, Europe, 14 July 1991.

213. Mudarrisi, *'An al-'iraq*, pp. 62–65.

214. Interview, Europe, 10 September 1990. And see Hujjat al-Islam Husayn al-Sadr who is close to the Da'wa in London, *The Guardian*, 15 January 1991.

215. *Al-Jihad*, 3 December 1990, p. 5.

216. *Barnamijuna*, pp. 19–52.

217. Mudarrisi, *'An al-'iraq*, pp. 23–24, 43 (Sura X, 99).

218. *Bayan* (London), 14 August 1990. Signed by the Da'wa, SAIRI, the pro-Syrian Ba'th (*qiyadat qutr al-'iraq*), the Talabani and Barazani Kurdish parties, the Communist party, and others.

219. *Bayan* (Damascus), 27 December 1990. See also the news agencies from London, *HaAretz*, 1 March 1991; and from Riyadh, *HaAretz*, 4 February 1991.

220. The closest a SAIRI spokesman came was al-Hakim's interview with a Lebanese newspaper in which he explains that "a democratic regime should be established in the state that will adopt a policy of non-alignment but at the same time it will oppose Israel," *Al-Dunya*, 27 October 1988. And in another place, "we want that the will of the Iraqi people will prevail so that it can choose the regime it wants and so that the Iraqi citizens will have all the rights and so that their Islamic identity will be emphasized." *Liwa al-Sadr*, 28 October 1990.

221. See, for example, the joint communiqué by the Mujahidin, 'Amal, the Da'wa, and three lesser movements in which, after they promise "freedom of religious faith . . . freedom of political, social and professional organization, freedom of press, association and expression and the protection of human rights," they also promise that "faith and the Islamic Shar'i rules in the planning of the basis of the Iraqi state and society" will serve as their guiding line. Even though they promise that this will be "in harmony with the choice of the people," the ring of this whole clause is totalitarian. *Bayan,* 11 September, as quoted in *Al-Jihad,* 17 September 1990.

4

Accounting for South Asian Fundamentalisms

CHAPTER 21

Accounting for Fundamentalisms in South Asia: Ideologies and Institutions in Historical Perspective

Robert Eric Frykenberg

For introducing the essays on South Asia, I have combined a broad and simple definition of fundamentalism with a more elaborate construction. Together, the two strategies serve not only to identify essential elements and functional features of fundamentalist movements in general but also to enable the marking and measuring of peculiarities unique to any particular fundamentalist movement. In general terms, then, we are seeking to account for a distinctive and extreme kind of religious reaction to modernism—a reaction that is conservative and separatist but that also possesses modern and radical features. As a radical reaction to modernism, fundamentalism is at once reductive and adaptive. As a reaction to ideological or institutional changes which are perceived as threats to ultimate "Truth," or as enshrining "Falsehood" or "Impurity," it is militantly defensive, even though some militantly defensive forms of fundamentalism have been manifestly inward-looking, quietistic, and otherworldly, if not spiritual.

How this twentieth-century American concept describing militantly antimodernist elements and forces within American evangelicalism can help explain historical events in South Asia is our central concern.[1] The cultural context in which religious fundamentalism originally arose was so markedly different from the cultural contexts of similar movements in South Asia that some may doubt whether any useful cross-cultural analysis is possible or even desirable. Yet, in their metaphorical and rhetorical militancy, in their extreme opposition to perceived changes within their own traditions, in their hostility to selected elements of cultural secularization, and in their drawing of severe lines or boundaries between the "changeless" and the "changeable," one can discern real points of comparison between the South Asian movements under consideration here and the American case. The South Asian movements also insist on maintaining that which is considered absolutely essential for any "true religion" or

591

"true faith," that is, they too insist on "fundamentals"—fundamental verities and values embodied within or revealed by some sacred (eternally valid) institution (including a "text").

The American case has never been as coherent, simple, or uniform as popularly portrayed.[2] There were three historically different kinds of events: the original, strongly intellectual, rationalistic, scientific, and theological movement which first coined the term; the strongly moralistic and pietistic, if not emotional, anti-intellectual, and political movement against "godlessness" and "worldliness" which marked the struggles between modernity and more orthodox tradition which culminated in, and became epitomized by, the public humiliation of William Jennings Bryan in the Monkey Trial of 1925; and, finally, the "fundamentalism" constructed by the countermovement of cultural modernists from the secular media, the academy, and theologically liberal, modernist, or "mainline" branches of religion in the West. The cultural modernists used the term as a device for branding, caricaturing, and labeling all whom they saw as "know-nothing" religious obscurantists or archaic relics of medieval superstition. Finally, these American versions of fundamentalism must be distinguished from the "globalizing" movement which, beginning roughly in 1979, applied the negative stereotyping of the cultural modernist as an epithet to similar phenomena almost everywhere in the world, or to any time in the present or past. For the present analysis, the original intellectual and anti-intellectual kinds of fundamentalism mentioned above serve as useful models.

Obviously, the concept has long departed from its American, Christian, Protestant, and evangelical roots. Essays produced for the Fundamentalism Project bear strong testimony to this process of enlargement, not only in conceptual and theoretical terms but in empirical or historical terms as well. Emptying the concept of culture-specific and tradition-specific content or context, Marty E. Marty and R. Scott Appleby have constructed a metaphysical or "pure" fundamentalism—an abstraction referring to one specific form of religious idealism.[3] This model marked out "an irreducible [and immutable] basis for communal and personal identity" which, being "intentionally scandalous" in its extremist positions, acted as a "stumbling-block" which separated insiders from outsiders, true believers from nonbelievers. This model also noted how fundamentalisms possess a "dramatic eschatology" by which moments of time and space (history) could be uncannily "matched" to sacred truths, texts, and traditions. From a slightly different perspective, Gabriel A. Almond and Emmanuel Sivan have produced a grid, combining salient features of ideas put forward by members of the project.[4]

Of course, no abstract grid, model, or template marking essential features of a "pure fundamentalism" can ever perfectly reflect (or be found replicated) in phenomena actually found in any particular instance of fundamentalism.[5] In one way or another, the pure form is deconstructed historically. Over and over again, in varying degrees, its parts are found, identified, and accounted for within a specific ideological/institutional complex or movement. By building upon previous attempts, one may identify and account for phenomena in South Asia, manifested either in beliefs or behaviors that exhibit some of the elements or features particular to fundamentalism.

Certain key features or ingredients are always found to be present. Five of these features are "foundational" and three other features can be characterized as "functional." All are common to a fundamentalist movement. In determining the degree, marking the exact measure, or accounting for specific roots of any given fundamentalist movement, this template of features provides a convenient way of identifying how fundamentalistic a movement is and also of accounting for or charting its development. It is a procedure to determine how extreme and militant or moderate a movement is, how benign or malignant, how nonviolent or violent, how quietistic or aggressive, how authoritarian or egalitarian its ideologies or institutional structures are (as "fundamentals"), how "this-worldly" or "otherworldly." Of course a given movement, at a given moment, may be changing its attitudes toward perceived threats, whether internal or external.

A fundamentalist movement, in short, consists of a conjunction of the following "fundamentals."

1. *The Truth*. The Truth is a central doctrine or set of doctrines, ideology, message, or worldview. As objectified in sacred text[6] or sacred code,[7] its role is definitive and its authority profound, if not final. As objectified in sacred tradition and sacred heritage,[8] or in hallowed custom, its demands are determined and all-encompassing. This truth is variously described as the Law, the Gospel, the Word, the Ideology, the Revelation, the Science, the Succession. Its certitude is, for its holders, altogether compelling. It possesses an imperative voice and a sacred, supreme, and transcendent status. As a transforming vision, pointing to a hallowed past and to a golden future, either immediately or ultimately, its message is contagious. As a metaphysical system, as a worldview internally consistent, it claims grounding in ultimate reality. As an ideology, it simplifies complexities, defines concepts, and sets doctrines, values and goals, along with practical methods and procedures for attaining those goals. If nothing else, it clearly demarcates the lines between falsehood and truth, darkness and light, evil and good, impurity and purity, black and white. No fundamentalism can exist without this most basic of "fundamentals."

2. *The Messenger*. The Messenger is one who embodies or personifies the Truth and is the original person who conveyed it: the Teacher, the Preacher, the Prophet, the Guru, the Leader, the Master, the Enlightened One. Message and messenger are so closely identified that when combined, they are the Living Word. This charismatic person brings a sense of excitement, expectation, and urgency. The contagion ignited by his influence brings about radical conversion. New fires are kindled, spread, and merged, and in a radical movement it happens over and over again. This person inspires awe, if not devotion, reverence, and submission. The Prophet breathes the Word and brings Wisdom from on high. Among some fundamentalisms, what is authority in the Word can become authoritarian in the Prophet. This conjunction has usually required that, under no circumstances, should such authority be granted to any other person or persons. Only a pure lineage of successors will do. Yet, in the absence of any living Prophet or successor here and now, the ground of ultimate authority is level, and intrinsically egalitarian.[9]

3. *The Community.* Select and special are Born-Again or Twice-Born *(Dvija),* the Chosen, the Elect, or, quite simply, the People. In their collective and corporate existences, they can go by many other names: the Abode-of-Peace *(Dar-ul-Islam),* the Believers, the Brotherhood, the Church, the Community; [10] the Congregation, the Faithful, the Family; [11] the Lineage *(vaṃṣa),* the Class *(varṇa:* color), the Elite (or Elect), the Fellowship, the Folk (or *volk*), the Nation *(rashtra),* or the Working Class. Many indeed are the "insider" names and self-definitions by which those "who belong" distinguish between themselves and those who are the "outsiders" or "others." Those who define themselves by "fundamentals," by whatever code words they use, draw sharp and stark lines. Between the True and the False, the Believers and the Unbelievers, the Children of God and the Heathen (or Pagan), the Clean and the Unclean, the Good and the Evil, the Natives and Aliens, the Civilized and the Barbarians, the Noble *(arya)* and the Servile *(dasya),* there can be no compromise. Distinctions are made by those who are discriminating. Outsiders, aliens, and foreigners are assigned labels which are negative and pejorative: barbarians, Gentiles *(goyim),* heathens, idolaters, pagans, unbelievers, *kafirs, mlechchas, panchamas, farangis,* or worse. A hundred epithets mark the line between those who are accepted and those who are not. Those who are insiders find ways, subtle or crude, to avoid or shun outsiders. Whatever cultural or ideological or rational or scientific reasons may be given (or excuses used), those with powers of discrimination know just how and where to draw lines, how to justify distinctions. Not to know the right hand from the left is the essence of obscenity. For all who lie within the circle, however, relationships can be comparatively and qualitatively different.

4. *The Destiny.* One feature common to all fundamentalists is their certainty of a utopian future. The future belongs, ultimately, to them. It can be seen as imminent, immediate, and attainable, or it may be delayed inexplicably or mysteriously. Yet certainty of reaching the Land of Promise is absolute. It may not come until after the Holocaust or Armageddon; or after the Apocalypse or the Return or Rescue (the Rapture or Second Coming of the Messiah or Mahdi). But it will come. This is the Great Expectation ("the Blessed Hope"). Heaven on earth—or even a New Heaven and a New Earth—is coming, perhaps soon. This certainty has a hundred metaphors and names: Albion, Celestial City, Classless Society, Dar-ul-Islam, Fatherland, Golden Shores, Independence, Liberation, Motherland, New Jerusalem, Promised Land, Purple Mountain Majesty, Green and Pleasant Lands, Ram Rajiya, Zion. Its metaphors and visions seem limitless. But, whatever its name, it is *that perfect place*—where all is well, where harmony and peace prevail, where joy and light never cease, where relationships never break or fail, where truth triumphs and evil is vanquished, where "lion and lamb lie down together," and where "swords are beaten into plowshares."

The wonders evoked by such rhetoric touch deep yearnings. Epic poems, anthems, buildings, monuments, paintings, and sculptures celebrate its promise. Terrible are the wars and struggles invoked in its name. Whether the vision has been theistic or nontheistic (nationalist, socialist, or Marxist), chauvinistic and irredentist claims have been made on its behalf. When apocalyptic or chiliastic *and* malignant, some visions have led its blinded followers to doom and destruction. It is in this sense that some fundamentalisms, but by no means all, are prone to cling to historicist certainties and dreams. Others, building their ideologies and institutions carefully and solidly, have seen dreams turn into things more substantial, into kingdoms on earth. Yet others, seeing how hopeless, how corrupt beyond redemption, the world really is and seeing themselves overwhelmed and surrounded by forces of evil they are, have given up, withdrawing and spiritualizing that Future Day. Not all fundamentalisms strive for power dominion in this world.

5. *The Evil*. Corruption and danger and pollution come from outside, from out there, in the world. That is expected. But there is often a danger more deadly. It comes from within. Like a serpent, it is insidious and insinuating. Betrayal and deception lurk inside the shadows of the best of societies. Hidden warfare by secret foes in the ranks of the faithful never ends. Those who compromise truth and negotiate with the enemy or with falsehood are especially sinister. The godless and faithless are not just or only "out there" in the world. They are also concealed "in here," among those claiming to be true—*within* the Church, the Elite, the Establishment, the Nation, the Party (or the Proletariat), the Ruling Class, or the System. Master deceivers they are, cleverly disguising their designs, their indecency, and their "worldliness." The faithful must wage a holy war (Crusade, Mission, Jihad, Rath Yatra) against obvious external enemies. But they must also be on guard against stealthy internal evils, watching out for covert betrayals and devilish conspiracies and "knavish tricks." Such evils can slither into any good House. Good people must be vigilant, ready to fight, and, if necessary, to suffer. "The System" of evil is profoundly deceptive, sinister, and subtle.

In functional terms, three further features characterize any fundamentalist movement. Along with the five kinds of fundamentals described above, they make up the template used to account for fundamentalisms in South Asia. Each fundamentalist movement actively advocates and pursues courses of action leading to radical conversion, revivalism (radical reconversion), and radical separatism. The first two are essentially internal. They may actually also be seen, in some measure, as intrinsically the same—like opposite sides of the same coin. The third has had to do with enhancing and preserving purity, ensuring isolation from contaminants, and with attaining some sort of utopian destiny, or perhaps more modest sociopolitical objectives.

1. *Radical Conversion*. Each movement seen as truly fundamentalistic lies within a tradition of radical conversion—one that calls for a drastic and complete reaction against evil. Awareness of evil is seen within the person or persons who become converted and also within society at large. Radical conversion is a transformation from one condition or state of being, from one outlook, worldview or way of life, to another; from one set of beliefs to another; from one ideology, party, religion, or condition (psychological, spiritual, metaphysical) to another; and/or from one institutional affiliation to another. In one way or another, it involves a thorough metamorphosis of belief and, therewith, of behavior (or, at least, of ideals and norms). Radical conversion normally involves the experience of a single person or, in corporate terms, the shared experience of a single community of persons (whether a family or group outside the family). Conversion involves changes in identity and personality, changes in ideology and institutional identification, and changes in social or political actions.

Conversion brings about a complete reorientation of emotional life and intellectual outlook. While such an event can occur within one or two zones of life—for example, economic, social, political, philosophical, or other—radical conversion brings total and often sudden changes in "religious" life. This leads to a new persuasion, a new doctrinal-ideological position, and a new institutional framework. Moreover, within its wider context, conversion usually leads to social and political reactions from the unconverted, often in the form of persecution, social segregation, and outright oppression.

Each radical conversion movement examined in this section has rested on a bedrock of fundamentalism. Moreover, it has been accompanied by a proliferation of additional conversions, which in turn have led to increasing numbers of conversions still. It has involved converts (or like-minded and converted groups) working together to bring about more and more conversions. The result of each such movement has been an increasing proliferation of conversions among more and more groups of converts, which in turn have embodied an expanding community of true believers.

In terms of ideal types, another name for a radical and expanding conversion movement is a revolution. Each true revolution has consisted at its core of those who were attempting to radically transform an entire society or culture, if not the whole world order. True or total revolutions are radical revolutions. When any revolution has been described as in some way conservative (as in the case of the American Revolution), this rhetorical device has served to describe an event or process that was less than a radical event. India's independence, despite the trauma of the Partition, was such an event. Pakistan's birth, as an event, was in many respects more problematic and radical.

2. *Revivalism*. Another name for an ideological and institutionalized tradition in which revival movements occur is "reconversion." This is a strategy for restoring vitality to what has become moribund. Implicit in each tradition of revivalism has been a worldview that holds, despite all illusions of permanence, that there can be no guarantee of permanence for anything in this world. It has been obligatory for each generation to fan the flames anew.

3. *Separatism*. Finally, studies of fundamentalist movements in South Asia, as elsewhere, show the movements to be by nature separatistic (if not exclusivistic). Each has held an attitude of alienation toward the outside world and toward all "outsiders," even those within the same tradition who have become "outsiders" by having abandoned or betrayed or compromised the Truth. Outsiders are seen as attacking, undermining, or threatening "things that matter." If radical conversion has enabled commitment or entry into a particular conversionist or fundamentalist perspective and into the tradition it was generating, and if revivalism pertained to renewal *within* such a tradition, *militant* alienation and separatism (for example, secession from membership in some larger community or even withdrawal) have been a stance toward all those forces perceived to be outside that tradition, forces that have been seen as dangerous or subversive.

Militant fundamentalism in South Asia, as shown in each chapter in this section, has raised a standard of separatism against all that is alien and evil. It has called for a rhetoric of warfare and a strategy of opposition against an outside Other. It has consisted of attempts to make sure that the purity and vitality of the community could not be compromised. Separation from the world—from backsliders, from betrayers, from unbelievers, from foreigners, from other communities: in short, from any and all dangerous elements of apostasy and worldliness—has been a prime reactive strategy. It is a device for holding onto "fundamentals." As a device, it has become a standard organizational technique for trying to accent true identity and for building or perpetuating the strength of the movement. In pejorative terms, as seen in descriptions of some American forms of fundamentalism, it has been called "empire building." Still, the metaphors employed are those of implacable and perpetual warfare—and, when necessary, of martyrdom. The struggle of each fundamentalism, rhetorically speaking, is against "the world, the flesh, and the devil." It consists of confrontations with actual communities, forces, or institutions.

How does one account for the distinctive features of such radical movements? Having tried to account for distinctive features, how can one account for and assess the human worth, in qualitative and quantitative terms, of different fundamentalist movements? Quite obviously, not all fundamentalist movements in South Asia, nor in the world, have been the same. Some have been benign, some grand in vision and in accomplishment. Others have been malignant and have brought untold human suffering, or are threatening to do so. Distinctions of human worth can hardly be avoided. In short, can one find ways to determine the character of each movement so as to judge its worth?

Obviously, here one comes upon matters of personal belief. It makes a great difference, for example, whether one holds to a positivistic (verificationist) theory of meaning or to a theory of ethical relativism which holds that no moral principle is true or false. By looking at the content of different ideologies and institutions of fundamentalist movements in South Asia—at the sinews of their belief structures (worldviews) and the methods of operation advocated and employed by their members and organizations—one can, indeed, discover exactly how beneficent or malevolent, in human terms or in social terms, each movement has been or how it evolved into what it now is. Movements that have preached and practiced hatred, sometimes toward special groups, advocating extreme violence and terrorism, can be seen for what they have become. Movements advocating the use of violence (to the point of self-destruction), even if only for their own self-defense, have provided clues as to what might be expected. For some of the most extreme, mass self-destruction (or suicide) has been preferable to compromise. Extreme pacifists, on the other hand, have been prepared to suffer, whatever the cost, rather than advocate or participate in any form of violence.[12] In short, analysis of words and deeds enables judgments about how humane each movement has been. Only paucity of records need hamper such investigation.

Another question that might be raised is the possibility of some sort of genetic connection between various forms of radical conversion, revivalism, and fundamentalisms. One can posit, for example, the possibility of a common, single origin—a common "genetic" root out of which sprang several radical conversion movements, in their forms of institutional proliferation if not in their specific ideological content. Did any such genome arise out of one single tradition or set of traditions? This question is worth asking, not because it can be answered, but rather because its very asking prompts closer comparative analysis and suggests startling possibilities.

As offering a functional model of opposition to secular modernity, all radical (conversion) movements—and, therewith, all fundamentalisms—are by nature highly contagious, regardless of the actual content or the internal quality of any given movement. I suggest, as a corollary, that all such movements are contagious in direct proportion to the presence and intensity of the essential features found in the template described above.

Following this line of thinking, asking whether or not it is possible that many radical conversion and fundamentalist movements can be traced back to some single common root, one might posit the possibility of a culturally generic root. Historical investigation may show, for example, that many of the movements in South Asia, as elsewhere in the world, have indeed been influenced, in one way or another, by contact with one branch or another of some cultural movement that stemmed out of such a common root centuries ago. It might be possible to find a common tradition—or branches or sub-branches of a tradition—which might be traced back, in one form or another, to the "seed of Abraham." If that were so, then maybe it would be possible to suggest "generic" or "Abrahamic" connections based on various forms of cultural contact and to trace connections between branches of different movements, so that all such movements may be found to have possessed some common ancestry. By this line of speculating, it may be possible to find that, from the Law of Moses down to the Law of Marx, there have been and still are movements which, in one way or another, have been connected genetically at a functional level, and that there have been chain reactions of cultural influence stemming from a single generic cultural strain (or from several such strains arising in different contexts). And yet not until all the various fine distinctions between different kinds of fundamentalist movements have been clarified, not until their intrinsic characteristics have been separated and sorted out, and not until each has been measured, numbered, and weighed in the context of other movements, can one hope to establish possible connections of any significance and subject them to comparative analysis.

In constructing some sort of taxonomy or typology of radical conversionist or revivalist movements, the first division to recognize is between religious or ideological systems that are theistic and those that are nontheistic in their foundations. The possibility that certain radical theistic movements have descended from Judaic, Christian, or Islamic movements—or that other movements, even those that were nontheistic, were also reactions to such movements, may seem startling, if not outrageous. Yet any single cultural influence may have little or nothing to do with ideological or institutional substance. The actual fundamentals of what was believed or practiced within any given movement may be so different, indeed, that they are diametrically opposed. Rather, the cultural gene strain inherited, in the metaphor suggested here, may be a peculiar form of functioning. It may be a kind of behavior, something having much more to do with the ways in which particular ideological and institutional substances react to threats. A fundamentalist movement, in short, exhibits certain typical ways of acting and reacting. The kinds of fundamentals which are engendered, and the functional means by which any particular fundamentalism has handled itself in relation to other groups against which it was reacting, may follow similar patterns in all fundamentalistic movements.

As one looks closely at the fundamentalisms considered here, it may be possible to suggest some further kinds of connections. Movements outside the West, in Asia and Africa, have often been reactions to previous movements. Interestingly, almost all of the nontheistic movements are of modern or relatively recent origin. Some of the most radical and revolutionary of modern conversion movements, stemming from the same kinds of theistic roots and sharing many common traits of their theistic progenitors, have themselves been the most vehemently nontheistic and antitheistic. Most forms of nationalism, socialism, and Marxism, not to mention atheism and secular humanism, one may even surmise, stem from the radically nontheistic (even antitheistic) spirit of the Enlightenment;[13] this spirit itself may be traced back, in turn, to cultural radical progenitive energies released by the Reformation. As secular religions or civil religions, these types of movements have often possessed and then passed on to others, including subject peoples in the colonial worlds over which Europeans ruled, some of the flames they themselves had ignited. And these various kinds of fiery blazes—radical ideologies both sacred and profane—can then be seen as having generated such heat as to have affected large parts of the world outside Europe.

There have also always been conversion movements that were never radical in character and hence never able to generate revivalistic, reconversionistic, or fundamentalistic features. Among such, there is a possibility that, shorn of political or royalist or statist overtones, various kinds of pre-modern Buddhism, Confucianism, Jainism, or Taoism—to name just a few examples—would tend to fall almost completely outside the scope of this analysis.

Fundamentalisms in South Asia might then be accounted for in terms of the degrees to which elements in the theoretical template (described above) can be isolated and identified within actual historical events. As this point, we move from theoretical to historical analysis. Specifically, historical information found in these chapters on South Asia can provide clues concerning generic relationships: each essay directly attempts to account for one or another specific "fundamentalism," each demonstrates the ways in which the fundamentalism in question is related to institutional and ideological factors, and each examines the interaction of historical events and contexts. These two kinds of perspectives, one theoretical and the other empirical, come together within each essay. Each essay also enhances and informs our understanding of the other essays. A synthesis of perspectives enables us to see recent events in ways that help us better appreciate the roots from whence all of the manifold forms of fundamentalism have sprung. It enables us to see the contexts within which different manifestations of fundamentalism now apparent in South Asia have come into being.

Fundamentalisms in South Asia can be accounted for by looking at a trajectory of events that go back through several centuries. At their heart is a dialectical process (if not several sets of parallel processes). We can identify the processes by which modern Hinduism came into being. From out of this Hinduism emerged those movements we now group together under the rubric "Hindu fundamentalism." On the one hand was that amazingly complex and extremely pluralistic environment in which thousands of distinctly separate and separatistic ethnicities ("birth-groups" or *jatis:* caste communities) had for so long coexisted. On the other hand were a succession of intellectual, organizational, and sociopolitical attempts to rationalize and synthesize everything within the subcontinent. Both kinds of phenomena—one "native" or "natural" and the other "constructed" or "man-made"—came to be called Hinduism in the nineteenth century. Hinduism, in both senses, became institutionalized during, if not actually under the approving eye of, the Indian Empire. Hinduism inadvertently became, for practical purposes, the unpublicized de facto official (or Establishment) religion of the Raj. Nothing suited or supported the imperial Raj better than the construction of such an imperialistic Hinduism. This officially reinforced system, with its supporting pillars of eclectic, syncretistic, and tolerant doctrines, ideologies, and philosophies, provided a wonderfully "neutral," "secular," and tolerant environment within which to rule over so many cultures and communities. Any and all communities and religions, by this vision, could flourish and grow, separately. And they could do so without fear. Tampering with things native to any community or any locality was to be avoided, or kept to a minimum. The brahmanical norms of Varnashramadharma reigned supreme. They became enshrined within the imperial Mahachhakra of the Raj.[14]

This structural arrangement was all too neat and convenient. It was the sort of thing that might have continued indefinitely had it not been disturbed by radical conversion movements. Mass movements, such as those that began to occur in the late eighteenth and early nineteenth centuries, did not have to be massive.[15] Precedents for conversion movements go back at least two and a half millennia—perhaps as far as the Buddha. But, in measurable terms, we know little about how radical or how massive pre-eighteenth-century movements were. It is inconceivable, nevertheless, that some of the events that accompanied the establishment of early Jewish, Christian, and Islamic communities in India did not possess some radical features, at least in their initial stages and in those localities in which they established their settlements. Moreover, it is difficult to believe that there were not strong local reactions to some of the events that did occur. In due course, however, all such movements became indigenized: they lost their original impetus and momentum, settled down as separate encapsulated communities, and came to terms with the requirements for survival within the cultural environment of India. Within the complexities of local culture within the subcontinent, they had come to a modus vivendi with the social environment within each locality; and the radicality of conversion movements had diminished, or stopped, as each community had gained for itself a relatively more comfortable and secure place within the bounds of its own separate, enclosed living-quarters (alongside the *agraharams* of Brahmans and the *muhallahs* of Muslim princes, the *cheris* for pariahs, and countless other uniquely distinct enclaves). Thus, as Susan Bayly has so well shown,[16] the massive turning of seafaring Paravas to a local form of

Roman Catholic Christianity (ostensibly under the influence of Xavier) seems to have been as much conservative as radical, as much a means of securing help against Muslim (Arab) sea power as a radical transformation of personal convictions, ideologies, or institutions. Various Christian and Muslim communities in South India had long since, on Bayly's reckoning, become as indigenous (or "native" or "Hindu") as any other community.

Whatever the historical circumstances of earlier movements, by the middle of the nineteenth century, the consequences of radical conversion movements, both theistic and secularistic, triggered radical reactions and led to the rise of reactive movements. These possessed the seeds of new forms of radical conversion, which in turn gave rise to a wholly new kind of Hinduism. This new Hinduism became increasingly self-conscious, "organized" or "syndicated."[17] Its proponents saw themselves as belonging to a single religion. This newly reifying religion had never before existed. In its various manifestations and movements, it copied the forms and substances and techniques of the radical conversion movements against which its proponents were reacting. Reacting to what they saw as militantly aggressive forms of Christianity and Islam, if not later also against radical forms of secularism and modernism, these newly organized movements were not only "nativist," but fundamentalistic in their nativism. Indeed, each new movement became more and more fundamentalistic with each new generation, earlier movements successively spawning movements each of which was more extreme and fundamentalistic than what have gone on before. There is a lineage of descent from the Brahmo Samaj, founded by Raja Ram Mohan Roy and built around a rediscovered and reconstituted religion of a universal "Brahma" as based upon the original Smriti and Sruti texts of the Vedas, down through the Dharma Sabha, Vibuti Sangam, Prarthana Samaj, and Nagari Pracharini Sabha to the founding of the Arya Samaj by Dayanand, the Ramakrishna (Vedanta) Society by Vivekananda, the Hindu Mahasabha by Savarkar, and the Rashtriya Swayamsevak Sangh (RSS) by Hedgewar. In each of these, research would show how important were our five essential and three functional categories; and in each, these would be found in a more explicit and in an increasingly more extreme form.

What occurred was a complex synthesis. The two older forms of Hinduism—one rooted in manifold nativistic impulses and another arising, however inadvertently, within imperial structures and official institutions—were exploited and expropriated by partisans of the New Hinduism. This New Hinduism was itself a product of modernity. It was itself also a reaction to radical conversions being generated by modern movements which, in their ideologies and institutions, had come out of "Abrahamic" roots. Western movements, whether theistic (missionary) or nontheistic (nationalist, socialist, Marxist, or scientistic), drew from similar kinds of traditions. The New Hinduism blended together and drew inspiration from the cultural seeds of fundamentals found in radical movements coming from Europe.[18]

In this case, however, the text for a new matrix of fundamentals was different. It, too, was genetic and it was *desi* (that is, indigenous, rooted in the sacred earth). It was defined by "sacred birth" and "sacred earth." Its textual inerrancy lay in genomes, in "pure blood" and "holy soil," in race and place. The earth was the Divine Mother, and Vandé Mata stood for all that was and is most truly native to India. Thus configured and transfigured, *desi* (native or local) fundamentals were blended with brahmanical, classical, and *margi* (cosmic or universal) structures. Both the ideological and institutional elements already integrated under the Raj, largely under brahmanical energy, inspiration, and enterprise, were brought together, codified, and synthesized. They combined the ingredients necessary for an incipient religious and political nationalism.

This, as it turned out, would be a Hindu nationalism. One has but to follow publications by Dayananda, Vivekananda, and Aurobindo, leading to Tilak, Savarkar, and Hedgewar, to see their direction. It was a nationalistic Hinduism, mobilizing and reacting defensively against radical conversion movements (with their monocentric, monotheistic Abrahamic roots: Jewish, Christian, Islamic theologies; or, nationalist, socialist, secular humanist, Marxist ideologies). As such this new kind of Hinduism became ever more stridently fundamentalistic as the twentieth century unfolded. Its message emphasized the "timeless" foundations of Truth as found in sacred birth and sacred earth. The message of new nationalism, resting on the newly restored foundations of sacred texts and sacred myths, linking itself to a heroic past, called for radical conversion. Or, perhaps as precisely, it also called for what its proponents envisioned, namely, a "radical purification/reconversion" *(shuddi)*. All who were born of "Aryan blood" and born on "Aryan land" (Aryavartha or Bharatvarsha) should awaken themselves from their deathlike sleep of centuries, from centuries of slavery and "foreign" rule. "Radical reaction" against all that was alien for the sake of the hallowed and sacred Motherland was seen as essential.

Like all true believers, like participants in radical conversion movements, those who now march under the saffron banners of Hindu fundamentalism seem to possess those kinds of convictions and to conform, in varying degrees, to virtually all of those features of the template by which fundamentalisms can be identified. They have the Truth—Hindutva. It is revealed in an inerrant text genetically codified in "sacred birth" and "sacred earth." The Truth bringer or messenger is Savarkar, followed by Hedgewar and Golwalkar. The Community is the Hindu Nation (Rashtra). The Destiny, an inevitable return of Ram Rajiya, will happen as soon as all impurities are removed. Finally, there is Evil, as embodied in all those "alien" and "malignant" impurities, elements not native to the "sacred blood" or "sacred soil" of India. Only after these have been completely eradicated or made permanently subservient will the Hindu Nation reach its true destiny.

Thus understood, the essays presented here by Ainslie T. Embree (chap. 22) and Peter van der Veer (chap. 23) focus on ideologies and institutions of two fundamentalistic organizations. Taken together, however, these can be seen as two branches of a single movement. Both institutions lie at the heart of contemporary Hindu fundamentalism. Drawing upon some forty years of experience and scholarship as a historian,[19] Embree describes the means by which the RSS, the "parent" organization, built upon traditions of the Hindu Mahasabha and earlier movements. It has been able to bring about the radical conversion and indoctrination of many "true believers," to inspire leaders and train cadres, and to form echelons of committed *sevaks* (workers). For his part, drawing upon fieldwork as an anthropologist in Uttar Pradesh

(Ayodhya) and Gujarat,[20] Peter van der Veer describes the strengths of one of the main "offspring" of the RSS "family." The VHP (Vishva Hindu Parishad), staffed at the top level by *pracharaks* (staff leaders) of the RSS and served at bottom levels by battalions of disciplined *kar sevaks* (volunteer laborers) and other frontline "shock troops" of the movement, has formed "missionary" organizations. It has mounted campaigns aimed at the radical conversion ("purification" or "reconversion") of converts to Buddhism and Islam. It has aimed its attention at peoples who, in reaction against caste, deprivation, and perpetual thralldom, now call themselves *Dalits* ("oppressed")—peoples from Backward Castes, Other Backward Castes (OBCs), Scheduled Castes (Untouchables), and Tribes.

But Hindu fundamentalism is clearly not confined to these two organizations. As a movement (or complex of movements), it tends to embrace more than the sum of the organizations that fly saffron flags or wave tridents (*trishuls,* symbols of Shiva) in its name. These include the RSS, VHP, the Bharitiya Janata Party (BJP), the Shiv Sena (Shiva's Army), and the Bajrang Dal. Together these allied and related groups are known as the *Sangh Parivar.* When examined together, these institutions can be seen as a broad movement among people of the highest, purest, "twice-born" castes; those who already possess the greatest cultural and material resources of India are the newly converted. They are those who fear the vast masses of "impure" or "polluted" communities who suffer from malnourishment and thralldom. They seek to hallow and legitimize a system of intrinsic social inequality. They are being won to the Hindu cause. By their reckoning, all who are "born" in India should be fitted into the places and ranks for which they were born. All who are "pure-born" or "twice-born" are entitled thereby to rule over the land and its peoples. Despite all protests to the contrary, by proponents of Hindu fundamentalism, about the special places the "low-born" are destined to occupy in the Hindu Rashtra of Ram Rajiya, many who are less than "twice-born" are not convinced. No amount of persuasion from champions of Hindutva has been able to assuage such fears. Hindu fundamentalism is thus perceived by all in South Asia who fear and oppose this kind of thinking.

Taken together, the studies by Embree and van der Veer provide us with a foundation for the other studies of different fundamentalisms in South Asia. The various manifestations of militant Hinduism have produced the chain reactions of fear that have largely accounted for counterfundamentalisms. From elements within all communities which have felt threatened have come such rumblings. As our other authors show, all communities, whether religious or ethnic, who have been deemed as "non-Hindu" or who have designated themselves as "non-Hindu" (due to socioeconomic thralldom or ritual exclusion), for whatever reason, are among the peoples who are reacting and organizing. By reacting and by resorting to actions, either directly or indirectly, in defense of what they have deemed their own most sacred interests, if not their very survival, such movements have been engendered by the threats of Hindu fundamentalism. Fear and desperation, inspired by Hindu extremism and militancy, have spurred reactions by Muslims, Sikhs, Christians, and Buddhists.

Thus, no study of fundamentalism in South Asia can avoid or ignore the pervasive presence of Hindu fundamentalism. The essays by Barbara Metcalf (chap. 25) and

Rafiuddin Ahmed (chap. 24) on quietistic and militantly defensive Muslims of South Asia; by James Manor (chap. 27) on militantly defensive Sinhala Buddhists of Sri Lanka; and by Susan Bayly (chap. 26) on militantly defensive Christians of India: each in its turn revolves around acute anxieties aroused by the various kinds of totalistic claims and demands of militant Hindus who are calling for submission to the Hindutva Motherland.[21] The very enormity of Hindu India in the minds of those on whose behalf such claims and demands are being made has played a role in generating fundamentalistic fears by those who feel threatened by an aggressive, all-encompassing Hindutva. Consequent activities, assertions, counterclaims, counter-demands, and defenses have been raised. Told that they can no longer consider themselves truly Indian, or native to South Asia, elements in many communities in South Asia are torn by anxiety.

Anxiety of Sinhala Buddhists in Sri Lanka comes from the very proximity of that enormous elephantine entity that is India, from whence the Tamils have come. The ubiquitous presence of Tamils in Sri Lanka goes back a thousand years. Tamils on the Jaffna Peninsula, on more recent migrant-labor tea plantations, and, until recently, in disproportionate predominance in high- and middle-level bureaucratic and professional positions have evoked Sinhala fears and resentments. But many more communities on the mainland feel threatened by "Hindu India." Finding themselves defined, by fiat, as minorities, aliens, or outsiders; finding that they may be obliged to submit to claims respecting a "divinely" inspired ideology of "Hindu" dominance; and finding that both the world and its public media have swallowed the notion (if not tautology) that "Hindus" form a "permanent majority community" in India, it is hardly surprising that communities such as the Sinhala Buddhists have generated fundamentalistic ideologies of their own and organized to defend themselves.[22] Each of those communities which now feels excluded "by definition" have taken steps, gathering all possible resources at their disposal, to discover "fundamentals" of their own and to organize themselves in self-defense. In the cacophonous and discordant din of clashing fundamentalisms, the old imperial and national vision of an eclectic, syncretistic, and tolerant Hinduism, such as was first generated under the Raj and then fostered by Ghokhale and Nehru, has begun to disappear. The dreams and visions of a constitutionally balanced polity—a state structure within which democratic and constitutional and liberal and secular ideals would continue to grow so as to bring increasing social equality and harmony—are being lost in the clamor of communal conflict.

Muslim fundamentalisms have emerged in at least two forms. The more overtly political, ambitious, and highly organized form, described in chapter 24 on the Jama'at-i-Islami by Rafiuddin Ahmed, has been especially influential in Pakistan (and Bangladesh); the other has been more loosely organized, inward looking, quietistic, and pietistic in its appeals to the simple rank and file among Muslim communities everywhere. From the pens of Mumtaz Ahmad, Rafiuddin Ahmad, Mushirul Hasan, Riaz Hassan, and others have come a number of insightful analyses and vivid descriptions of both the Jama'at-i-Islami and the Tablighi Jamaat in South Asia. Hitherto, however, much more attention has been focused on the former movement founded by Maulana Maududi, with its dramatic appeals and more drastic attempts, mainly by political means, to enforce the ideals of a purely Islamic state, especially in Pakistan.

Much less attention has been focused on the far less publicized spread of the far more profoundly radical movement, the Tabligh. Founded by Maulana Muhammad Ilyas, this movement, with its populist appeal to private conscience, attempts to reach and radically reconvert every nominal Muslim. Mainly through face-to-face contacts between individuals and small groups, the movement is working to establish a true "Abode of Peace" (*Dar-ul-Islam*) where the "rule of God" enters the heart and mind of each and every person. In some measure bypassing professional clerics and religious experts, its members are striving to eradicate corruption and restore the original and pure "fundamentals" of the faith to their proper and rightful place in the hearts and minds of all "true believers." In chapter 25 Barbara Metcalf has examined the ideological and institutional origins and growth of this latter movement.

Drawing on her gifts as a historian and Islamicist, Metcalf brings us to an outwardly quietist, inwardly (or spiritually) militant movement. She and others may argue that her work is not strictly about a fundamentalist movement. Yet, in terms of the template of features laid down above, the Tablighi movement manifests the same kinds of fundamentals and functional traits—radical conversion, or reconversion of Muslims to Islam; separation of "true believers" from elements of unbelief and corruption and worldliness found in modern secular cultures; and a call for extremist pietism so as to heed all five kinds of essential fundamentals found in our template: the Truth (God's Word), the Prophet (only Muhammad qualifies), the Community (only those who pray and strictly practice all five essential pillars of the faith), the Evil (unbelief is seen as having come mainly from a corruption of the Truth by clerics), and the Destiny (only true godliness will bring God's rule to earth; better to withdraw than to attempt transformations which only God can accomplish). These are key features of the Tablighi Jamaat. A fundamentalist insistence that "heaven be brought to earth" is not necessarily an insistence that this must be brought about by human agency so much as an insistence that, one way or another and mainly by divine agency (and by divine timetables), there will inevitably be a reign of Allah's "paradise and peace on earth."

The differences are well worth noting, however. In the case of the Tabligh, corporate authority is carried "lightly": the rhetoric and structures of leadership are strikingly egalitarian, especially when compared with the heavy-handed ways of the Jama'at-i-Islami. As Rafiuddin Ahmed argues, the Jama'at-i-Islami has evolved into a political pressure movement that has periodically committed violent acts and incited riots. By such means it has put pressure on regimes precisely because it has been unable to amass enough popular support to win elections. The ideological and tactical evolution of Tablighi, furthermore, has undermined Maududi's original hope for an "Islamic order" which, he once declared, is a necessary prerequisite for an authentic Islamic state. The Islamic state, as an ideal, has itself become the Jama'at-i-Islami's controlling fundamental. Meanwhile the politically quietist Tablighi Jamaat has again emphasized what it holds as the much more important Islamic "fundamental" of utter reliance upon divine agency and divine authority for the accomplishment of divine purposes. Tablighi Jamaat, in short, represents an ideal model of quietistic fundamentalism.

A movement, any movement, is always more than the sum of its organization(s).

Movements may bring about organizations which work to implement the purposes of the movement. But organizations are, especially in their purposes, defined and discrete structures with elements carefully fitted together, like those of a machine, for the accomplishment of clear and definite and more immediate goals and objectives. In contrast, movements are larger and more diffuse, more jagged around the edges, with degrees of commitment and membership varying from time to time (as the movement waxes and wanes). The old maxim that "movements generate machines" (organizational structures) and that, as they ossify, "machines turn into monuments of dead movements" can be seen, in this respect, as having some validity. The institutionalization of a movement and the institutionalization of an organization (as with any corporate structure, from a small family or business to a large state or empire) need not, on such accounts, be confused. Thus, while both the Jama'at and the Tablighi movements have fundamentalistic features, there are grounds for arguing that the Tablighi represents, in the long term, the more truly fundamentalist *movement;* moreover, by its very quietistic emphasis it may prove to have been the more powerful. The Jama'at, on the other hand, has the features of a special-interest *organization.* This is all the more evident as a result of its ideological shift after the trouncing it suffered in the 1971 elections. Consequently, its impact on Pakistan, on India and on Bangladesh, all of which Ahmed surveys, has proven to be politically significant but culturally equivocal. For that reason, as its organizational fortunes wax and wane, the Jama'at's long-term influence may be less profound.

Viewed in simple demographic terms, the forces of Hindu and Muslim fundamentalism are evenly matched in South Asia. South Asia contains over one billion people.[23] If each substratum (*varna*) of "twice-born" communities were roughly calculated at 5 percent of India's total population of roughly 840 million, such communities would account for 126 million people. And even if other powerful communities in India which are neither Muslim, Sikh, Parsee, Jewish, Jain, Christian, or Buddhist were added so as to double, or even triple, this number—so that those "Hindus" once labeled "Sat-Shudras" by Brahman/British Census officials were now lumped together with the "twice-born"—the total of all such peoples still would not amount to half of India's population. On the other hand, if Muslims in India were seen as accounting for at least 12 percent of the same base population, their numbers would roughly come to at least 110 million. If the numbers of Muslims in India (110 million), Pakistan (roughly 110 million), and Bangladesh (over 120 million) were added together, the total number of Muslims in South Asia, not counting those in Afghanistan (16 million?) or Sri Lanka (2 million?), would far surpass the numbers in "twice-born" strata and would perhaps come close to a parity with all dominant "Hindu" communities in India. Moreover, if Sikhs in India (25 million) are counted as distinct from "Hindus," which they demand, and if Christians in India (17 million) were also counted as non-Hindus (despite their "Hindu" cultures and customs), the combined numbers of Muslims, Sikhs, and Christians in India alone can be seen as far exceeding the numbers of "twice-born." Finally, without even counting such tiny communities as Jains, Jews, Parsees, and "Old" (non-Mahar) Buddhists, there are hundreds of separate communities of Backward, Dalit (Scheduled, or Untouchable), and Tribal peoples. Of these, Untouchables are usually thought to amount to at least 20 percent of India's total population, or about 170 million people.

Of course, despite their blatant exploitation for partisan purposes, communal "vote banks" have been increasingly evident during the past two decades, and such rough figures as these do not come close to translating themselves into reliable estimates of the numbers of fundamentalists who might exist within any given community or set of communities. Indeed, all the inflated rhetoric of partisan journalism notwithstanding, we now know that the so-called mass movements of the 1920s and 1930s, as well as even the massive rallies of the 1980s, were comparatively small in proportion to demographic figures taken as a whole. Yet, no matter what one wishes to make of these figures or what kinds of empirical data one may use to estimate numbers of communal extremists, fundamentalists, or revivalists within any given community, neither South Asia as a whole nor India in particular has ever possessed anything resembling a "permanent majority community." Nor is there anything comparable to such a majority, from which one could make long-term political predictions as to possible future alignments or behavior. India, as the whole of South Asia, can be seen as little more than a "mosaic of minorities," a kaleidoscopic array of ever-changing combinations.

What has exacerbated fears, and rubbed communal nerves to the raw, has been the blatant and continual exploitation of caste or "communal" blocs, known as "vote banks." While competing political parties, each promising more than the next, have striven to secure the support of such "vote banks," the report of the Mandal Commission, recommending affirmative action on behalf of "birth-groups" so long backward and downtrodden that there seemed no escape from the perpetual thralldoms they have always known, terrified high-born people in the middle and upper classes. Promises by the Janata government of V. P. Singh to implement the Mandal Commission recommendations provoked vociferous public demonstrations and protests, including some public immolations by middle-class college students who saw their chances for professional education and employment being given, as "reserved places," to aspirants from disadvantaged communities.

When seen in such a light, analysis of Sikh, Christian, or Buddhist fundamentalisms in South Asia becomes even more challenging. The essays presented here give strong indications of a rising ideological and institutional revivalism which has led to forms of defensive extremism among certain segments of each community. Yet, questions about whether any of them exactly fit the fundamentalist grid or template described cannot be understood without reference to the historical circumstances out of which recent movements have emerged. In each case, the record of communal identity has not been altogether clear. Indeed, in all three cases, revival or "reconversion" movements led to a sharpening of communal identities and to extremist activities in which fundamentalist-like claims have been made.

The Sikh case, for example, covered in detail in earlier volumes in this series, offers its own complexities. Like Mormonism in the United States, Sikhism is one of the younger religious systems in India. In many ways, it is still in the process of being formed and reified. Coming out of the extremely volatile frontier zone, it has continued to change and grow in that cultural environment. Its birth in the Punjab occurred at roughly the same time as the arrival of Babur and the rise of Mughal hegemony. Out of the *sant* tradition came Guru Nanak (1469–1539) and his community (*panth*, or "Path"). This tradition, stressing formless divinity, disciplined inner devotion, and congregational singing instead of many "empty" trappings of religion, gradually added other elements over time, including the sacred place *(tirtha)* and sacred tank, on land granted by the Mughal emperor Akbar in 1577, at what became Amritsar.[24] In addition there occurred the codifying of hymns within the "canonical" scriptures now known as the Sri Guru Granth Sahib (1604); the consecration of the warrior *rahat* (code of discipline) and the distinctive *panj kakke* (the "five k's") emphasizing the "all steel" *kirpan* (sword), *kara* (bangle), and *kangha* (comb), plus the *kesh* (uncut hair) and *kachch* (shorts), during sojourns as persecuted wanderers in the Siwalik jungles. Among the formative experiences of the tradition were the execution (or martyrdom) of the ninth guru, Tegh Bahadur (1675); the founding of the warrior elite of the Khalsa (1699), with its "death vow" and "baptism" (*pahul*) for "warrior heroes," after which each warrior acquired the title Singh (Lion); the establishing of war-bands (*jathas*), each under its own warlord; and the forming of the twelve *misls* (brigades or regiments). After the rise of Ranjit Singh and the creation a Sikh kingdom, with its political seat at Lahore (1799) and spiritual seat at Amritsar, and reinvestment of ultimate authority in the Granth Sahib, there has never been a final closure putting a definite end to Sikh ideological and institutional evolution.

The annexation of Punjab by the Raj (1849) and recruitment of disbanded battalions (*misls*) of the Khalsa Dal into the Indian army led to the increasing identification of Sikhs with the *keshdhari* (hair-uncut) warriors of the Khalsa, as distinct from the more numerous *sahajdhari* (relaxed) elements of the Panth. Thereafter, a steady progression of fresh innovations marked each new development of Sikhism: the rise of militantly revivalist Singh Sabhas (120 by 1900), local "lion societies" which advocated return to such "fundamentals" as the Rahat and the Gurmukhi; the formation of *gurdwaras* (courts of the Guru), serving as a place for worship and for adjudicating disputes within the community; the reform agitations for reform in administration of religious properties which brought passage of the Sikh Gurdwara and Shrines Act (1925) and subsequent community-wide elections of the Shiromani Gurdwara Prabandhak Committee (SGPC); the emergence of the Akali Dal as a dominant political force within Sikh institutions, together with constant factional struggles and turmoils within the community; and, finally, the movement to achieve a territorially distinct "destiny" in the form of either an autonomous Punjabi Subha or a completely independent and sovereign Khalistan (Land of Purity).

The intensity of continuous struggles to defend Sikh survival and separate identity—before, during, and after the Partition—is too easily forgotten. Sikh revivalist protests (*morchas*) and fasts-to-death, begun by Master Tara Singh and taken over by Sant Fateh Singh in 1960, focused on creation of a Punjabi Subha (in 1966). The Andandpur Sahib Resolution (16–17 October 1973) demanded greater constitutional recognition and state autonomy. Further failures of compromises with Congress regimes and with the Government of India frequently led to a sense of manipulation, betrayal, and frustration. Ensuing frustrations, partially due to a breakdown in Sikh leadership structures which had been so carefully nurtured since 1925, eventually provided an opportunity for extremists of the militant Damdami Taksal and All-India Sikh Students' Federation, under Sant Jarnail Singh Bhindranwale and Amrik Singh, to turn to terrorist violence.[25]

Sir Penderel Moon, in his volume *Divide and Quit*,[26] gave acute observations of how, during all the blood and smoke of Partition violence in 1947, Sikh leaders organized their community so as both to rescue it from annihilation and to establish a separate sovereign state. A mandarin of the Government of India, stationed in the princely state of Bahawalpur to smooth the transfer of power and the flow of refugees, Moon was strongly sympathetic to the new India and stayed on until after Nehru's death in 1964. His books, covering two centuries of events from Warren Hastings down to the slaying of Indira Gandhi, also won lasting respect. His twilight years were devoted (under Nicholas Mansergh) to the publication of *India: The Transfer of Power, 1942–47*.[27] These twelve huge volumes of hitherto unpublished documents on constitutional relations between Britain and India, drawn from the official archives and private papers, are loaded with petitions from representatives of the Sikh community, then led by Master Tara Singh, urging recognition of a separate Sikh national identity and state. Sikh hopes were dashed even more when section 25 of the new Constitution of India (1951) incorporated Sikhism, Buddhism, and Jainism within its definition of the "Hindu" religion.

Misunderstandings over Sikh separatism which have arisen since India achieved its independence and suffered the Partition in 1947 are hardly surprising. By 1947, the path of fundamentalistic-type political action was already well worn. Indeed, actions by Tilak and Gandhi had paved the way. If "selective retrieval, picking out from [one's] religious traditions certain elements of high symbolic significance with a view to mobilizing coreligionists for action"[28] can be seen as characteristically "fundamentalist," Gandhi's own *satyagrahas* (campaigns of nonviolent civil disobedience) had demonstrated how this could be done. Less than forty years after Gandhi himself was assassinated by an irate Hindu fundamentalist,[29] Indira Gandhi was assassinated by Sikh members of her Household Guard. Her slayers, outraged at the defiling of the Golden Temple by the Indian Army (in Operation Bluestar) and the slaying within the sacred precincts of the Akal Takht itself of their latest martyr-hero, Jarnail Singh Bhindranwale, were merely defending what they saw as sacrosanct "fundamentals" of the panth. Thereafter, struggles within factions of the Akali Dal, the SGPC, and the All-India Sikh Students' Federation continued both before and after the Rajiv-Longowal Accord of 1985, abated briefly after the assassination of Sant Harcharan Singh Longowal, but were never resolved.

The history of the rise and reification of Sikh religion has been marked by the spirit of frontier turbulence.[30] In accounting for Sikh radicalism and this frontier spirit, there is considerable scholarly debate about Sikh "fundamentalism." On the one hand, W. H. McLeod has argued, by means of exegetical (and philological) exposition, that the ways in which Sikh terms and texts are handled do not permit us to confuse Sikh revivalism and extremism with Western stereotypes of fundamentalism. By focusing mainly on definitional problems and texts rather than upon the historical development of ideologies and institutions, however, McLeod has not addressed the question of how or why "forms of Sikh extremism or Sikh revivalism"—whether or not one sees these movements as Western-style fundamentalism—came into being.[31] On the other hand, H. S. Oberoi and T. N. Madan show us how, within events arising out of the ideological and institutional constraints of the Sikh religious development, features of fundamentalism can be discerned. J. C. Heesterman has also stressed the role of frontier turbulence within Sikh culture, the importance of a "transcendental impulse embodied in its canonical scriptures that speak another language than that of the berserk warrior," and the open and full potentialities for development which still remain within "the present crisis" for "the unfinished Sikh community."[32]

And, as other historians argue, pressures of Sikh insecurity have led to extremism and fundamentalism, producing a contradiction between long-term strivings for a separate religious identity, secure from the dangers of being Hindutva, and opportunistic strivings for immediate political power.[33] Yet none of these arguments make sense apart from the context of a self-confident modern Hinduism and the rise of a more strident form of Hindu fundamentalism, as embodied in the doctrines and institutions of the Sangh Parivar, as embodied in the RSS, VHP, BJP, Bajrang Dal, and Shiv Sena.

The same generalization is true of the relationship between Sinhalese Buddhism, Sinhala nationalism, and Buddhist extremism in Sri Lanka on the one hand, and the looming shadow of India, with its ever growing sense of Hindutva, on the other. In historical terms, Sinhalas have had to face many, if not all, of the same threats as the Sikhs: imperial rule, missionary expansion, secular modernity, and, no less importantly, the rise of the very same Hindu fundamentalism. Sri Lanka, with a total population of about 17 million, is smaller than most of the major regional cultures (and states) of India. The Tamil presence across the Palk Strait is huge: Tamils of India (Hindu, Muslim, Christian) outnumber Sinhala Buddhists of Sri Lanka by approximately six to one—over 75 million Tamils in Tamil Nadu overshadow about 12 million Sinhalese (Buddhists) in Sri Lanka.[34]

Among those who have studied recent Sinhalese history and religion, there is as much variety of perspective as among those who have studied Hindu, Muslim, or Sikh history and religion in South Asia. Yet, when these perspectives are taken together, a composite view of modern Sinhala Buddhist nationalism emerges which, whether designated as extremist, revivalist, or fundamentalist, is not only clearly marked but also seems, from a historical perspective, to conform to the features of the fundamentalist template described in the first part of this chapter.[35]

What emerges from the literature is a modern Sinhala Buddhist fundamentalism—a cultural-linguistic-religious nationalism—in which ideological and institutional components have come to correspond to and share many of the characteristics of all such "fundamentalist-like" movements in South Asia. In historical terms, each of the fundamentalisms in South Asia—whether Buddhist, Christian, Hindu, Muslim, or Sikh—is as an extreme reaction to modern secularism. In each, some form of radical conversion, sometimes manifest as a "revivalism" or a "reconversion," has become institutionalized within a movement. As the following chapters demonstrate, each such fundamentalism has embodied a compulsive attachment to a single sacred Truth (or set of Truths); each has found such Truth embedded within sacred texts, either doctrinal or historical; each has awakened (or radically converted) a charismatic or prophetic embodiment of that Truth; each such movement has seen itself as embodying a sacred (select or special) community or Nation, emphasizing the sharp line between insiders and outsiders; each has discovered a sinister evil (both within and without the community) against which members of the community must wage a "holy war" and, if necessary, suffer martyrdom; and each awaits the fulfillment of its mission and sacred destiny.

Fundamentalisms in South Asia are a phenomenon unto themselves because they share a common historical experience shaped by the impact of a common imperial (and/or colonial) rule under an Indo-British Raj which, except for that of Sri Lanka, was initially constructed by the East India Company upon foundations laid by the Mughal Empire.[36] That common experience, accounting for fundamentalisms in each of the traditions, was also shaped by the profoundly intrusive forms of radical conversion movements exported to South Asia from Europe by Christian (Catholic and Protestant) missionaries and by the fiercely antitheistic forces of the Enlightenment, with the various Eurocentric strains of radical atheism, nationalism, socialism, and Marxism following in their train.

Finally, fundamentalisms arose in South Asia in conjunction with the "rescue," preservation, and reconstruction of some of the priceless legacies, some of the "remnants of purity" from the past, by means of an Indological Orientalism. This Orientalism was a collaborative achievement, staffed both by "interested" local scholars (from indigenous elites) and by Europeans whose work reflected biases of the Enlightenment and/or of the Evangelical Awakening. This combination of influences produced virulent forms of radical conversion and radical reaction to such conversion in the form of indigenous revivalisms. Either way, in generic terms, the "seed of Abraham," in its most radical forms, came to South Asia. In generic terms, the indigenous fundamentalisms which were engendered eventually (if not inevitably) led to various forms of fundamentalism, some militant and some quietistic. All sorts of these can now be found in South Asia. Each of these fundamentalisms can be seen as an extreme reaction against threats of profane modernity as perceived to be aided and abetted, if not embodied and empowered, by structures of the modern state.

It seems that every form of fundamentalism imaginable arose within Sri Lanka itself. There were both theistic and nontheistic forms: linguistic and ethnic, nationalistic, socialistic, and Marxian which found lodging on the island. Just as fears of Hindu fundamentalism—Hindutva and Hindu Rashtra—have awakened "minority" communities in India (Buddhist, Christian, Muslim, Sikh, Tribal, Untouchable), so also a very similar chain reaction of consequences seems to have occurred in Sri Lanka. Some Sinhala Buddhists, reacting against colonial rule and loss of official state support for Buddhist institutions, and resentful of Christian missionary influence, were open to the appeal of radical anti-Christian countermovements coming from the West in the wake of the Enlightenment. Such Buddhists were more than ready for a "contagion of change" and for the organizing reaction against impending dangers to the Sinhala Buddhist Sasana.

Since the late eighteenth century, in the wake of learning pursued by Indologists and Orientalists in the eighteenth century and the romantic fervor of Unitarians and Theosophists, no sacred text was more persuasive than the Mahavamsa. This most hallowed of historical traditions emphasized, like no other work, the role of the Buddha, of Asoka, and of Sinhala kings in preserving the "purest race" (of the most noble "Lion People") and "purest remnant" of Theravada *vamsha* in Sri Lanka.

It was in Sri Lanka that the most heroic efforts had been made to keep this Theravada remnant pure. It was here, on this sacred soil, thrice blessed by mythic visits from the Buddha himself, that sacred wars of resistance, rebellion, and reconquest had been waged against the alien Tamils, their Chola monarchs, and their Saiva deities. It was here, in Sri Lanka, that *bhikkus* (monks) had urged upon King Dutugamanu, the Asokan ideals of Righteous Rulership notwithstanding, that killing millions of Tamils was necessary: the killing of barbarians and heretics was justified as comparable to exterminating dogs and mice. Only by such action had it been possible to restore the Sinhala (Buddhist) *sasana* (order/religion) and *saddharmakanaka* (community/nation) to its rightful ascendancy and glory.[37] It was here also that, during the nineteenth century, this same mythic heritage of sacred narrative, drawn from the Mahavamsa and from other stories and tales in Sinhala traditions again enjoyed a resurgence. This revivalism came with the publication, both in Pali and in English, of these sacred texts (and, perhaps no less, with the hallowing of a Sinhala/Buddhist genetic code). The prophets of this revival, Mohuttivatte Gunanand and Angarika Dharmapala, had approved the publication of Henry Olcott's *The Buddhist Catechism* (1881). Yet this revival would have been bloodless without the pietistic passion generated by the myth of Sinhala separation from evil, as represented by India; and the integration of virtue, as represented by Sri Lanka.

The Sinhala Buddhist "movement" began with the establishment of the Society for the Propagation of Buddhism (SPB) in 1862 and the Buddhist Theosophical Society (BTS) in 1879. These early developments led, step by step, to the publication of All-Ceylon Buddhist Congress Resolutions of 1951, as embodied in the English pamphlet *Buddhism and the State,* and the report of the All-Ceylon Buddhist Congress's Commission of Enquiry, *The Betrayal of Buddhism*, on 4 February 1956—the year of the great Buddha Jayanthi, celebrating the 2500th year of the Buddha's death. In this context, *The Betrayal of Buddhism* evoked eschatological fervor. That was the year that Bandaranaike, riding a whirlwind of bhikku activism and expectations, came to power. The Official Language Act ("Sinhala only") became law, effectively altering the old (Seabury) constitution's protections for minorities by a simple majority vote. The mid-1959 report of Prime Minister Bandaranaike's officially appointed Buddha Sasana Commission (February 1957) advocated reform of the Buddhist Sangha and appointment of a Ministry of Cultural Affairs. While these recommendations did not really begin to produce results until after Bandaranaike's assassination (26 September 1959), the triumph of Sinhala Buddhist nationalism was clearly in sight. As James

Manor explains, further battles have been fought and victories won over the past thirty years, first against Christian (mainly Catholic) influence and then against Tamil ("Hindu") separatism. Yet, despite the killings that have occurred in struggles with Tamil Tigers and with the Janata Vimukhti Peramuna (JVP) and the Indian army, the destiny of the Sasana Restoration within the Sinhala State of Sri Lanka—assuring rulership for Sinhalese-speaking Buddhists and/or their eventual role in bringing "Universal Peace" (Nirvana)—hardly seems in doubt. Only a further intrusion from India, that Great Elephant across the Palk Strait, could alter this equation. As with other "fundamentalisms" in South Asia, in the Sri Lankan case a great deal depends on developments in Hindu (or Tamil) fundamentalism in India.

Susan Bayly's essay (chap. 26) on Christian fundamentalism in India also demonstrates, eloquently and persuasively, the centrality of "Hinduism" and of Hindu fundamentalism in generating countermovements. Hindu fundamentalism has impinged upon some Christian communities with such force that it has inspired a Christian self-definition in these communities, which resembles hardline evangelicalism or fundamentalism. In short, they, like Hindus, Muslims, Buddhists, and Sikhs, can be understood by the ways in which they have defined themselves. Yet, ironically, in the very efforts to revive themselves and to marshal fundamentals—those features which make Christians in India distinctive—Christian movements of reaction have also taken to themselves elements which are clearly "Hindu." With a remarkable array of descriptive detail and a powerfully argued logic, Bayly shows us just how profoundly Hindu and distinctively "Indian" are various Christian denominations within the subcontinent. This Hindu-ness, while setting itself apart from the great and threatening Evil and Darkness of Aryan Hindutva, reaches beyond the inerrancy of biblical texts by also appealing to the inerrancy of "sacred blood" and "sacred soil." The Shoreline Movement is striving to defend the sacred precincts of shrines, ready to shed blood with eucharistic zeal for the sake of sacred domains. Their crusade evokes the blood of martyrs.

The militancy of Christians in the jungled hill-country of Nagaland and Mizoram, like that of the Sinhala Buddhists of Sri Lanka, reflects fears of further incursion from forces of Hindu fundamentalism rising out of the plains of Assam. The Pentecostal fundamentalists in South India, while adhering to most features found in any pattern of Christian fundamentalism, see themselves in a titanic struggle with the forces of darkness and evil. This darkness and evil is not only epitomized in local demons but also, on a large scale, in an all-encompassing, all-pervasive presence of a threatening Hindu fundamentalism. Echoes of the ever louder cries of Hindu Rashtra and Ram Rajiya, along with the ever increasing din of Rath Yatras, have awakened fears and stirred up movements of militant reaction. Wherever the Christian presence is sufficiently strong—as in Kerala, Tamil Nadu, and Nagaland—a bewildering number and variety of fundamentalist movements have arisen. The ideological and institutional roots of these movements, on one level, may be Syrian, Catholic, Protestant, or Pentecostal. But beneath them all is a substratum of indigenous culture which, whatever its particular local flavors, may nonetheless be seen as Hindu. No fundamentalist movement in South Asia, whether Hindu, Muslim, Sikh, Buddhist, or Christian, is able to escape from its Hindu/Indian matrix.

Notes

1. George Marsden, *Fundamentalism and American Culture* (New York: Oxford University Press, 1980), pp. 4–5.

2. Jeffrey Hadden's cutting analysis and carefully drawn insights found in "Global Fundamentalism: Concept or Battle Cry?" (Paper presented at the Public Conference of the Fundamentalism Project, Chicago, 2–4 November 1991), have skillfully deconstructed early complexities and distinctions, showing how subtle biases and barely concealed contumely supported the pejorative presuppositions behind many supposedly intellectual responses to fundamentalism. The work serves as a cautionary signal.

3. Martin E. Marty and R. Scott Appleby, "Conclusion: An Interim Report on a Hypothetical Family," in Marty and Appleby, eds., *Fundamentalisms Observed* (Chicago: University of Chicago Press, 1991), pp. 814–42.

4. Gabriel A. Almond and Emmanual Sivan, "Fundamentalism: Genus and Species" (Paper for the Fundamentalism Project, 16 October 1991).

5. See Lionel Caplan, ed., *Studies in Religious Fundamentalism* (Albany: State University of New York Press, 1987); and Bruce Lawrence, *Defenders of God: The Fundamentalist Revolt against the Modern Age* (San Francisco: Harper and Row, 1989).

6. For example, the Bible (Sacred Writ); the Qur'an, the Vedas, Manu (Smriti versus Sruti texts) or the Bhagavad Gita (as a hallowed part of the Mahabharata), the Adi Granth or Granth Sahib (and Dasam Granth), and the Mahavamsa (or some Pali or Sinhala text).

7. The Sacred Blood and the Sacred Soil (sacred birth/lineage [Jati/Vamsha] and sacred earth/land [Desh, e.g., Vande Mata]); and the Sacred Order or Color Code (Varnashramadharma). For exposition on "genetic code" as inerrant text, see Walter K. Andersen, and Sridhar D. Damlé, *The Brotherhood in Saffron: The Rashtriya Swayamsevak Sandh and Hindu Revivalism* (Boulder, Colo.: Westview Press, 1987), pp. 75–77.

8. For example, the "Faith" ("Once Delivered to the Saints"), the "Tradition" (Hadith) or the "Faith" *(din),* the proper or right "Order" *(dharma* and *karma),* the (Cosmic) "Breath" or "Sound" (brahma, e.g., Om), and the "True Order" or Buddha Sasana.

9. For those members of that community which is bound by such authority, this is so. In communities where, on principle, there has been no preordained succession, no guru, no *tabarrakat,* no *imam,* nor pope, as in Protestant Christianity (especially on its radical Anabaptist, congregationalist, dissenter, leveler, or separatist fringes), and in Sunni Islam, this has been especially so.

10. The *Khalsa* or the *Panth,* the *Umma,* the Saddharmakanaka, the Sasana or the Sangha.

11. *Kulam* or *Jati:* People of "the Birth," "the Born," "the Blood," "the Race" or "the Seed."

12. Such movements, for example, have had historical analogues in certain Anabaptist/Brethren, Mennonite, or Friends/Quaker movements—although not all such groups have always, or necessarily, been fundamentalistic (except in certain of the generic features).

13. James H. Billington, *Fire in the Minds of Men: Origins of the Revolutionary Faith* (New York: Basic Books, 1980), traces the development of some of these elements of the Enlightenment, especially in their political manifestations.

14. For details of this argument, see Robert Eric Frykenberg, "Constructions and Deconstructions of Modern Hinduism: In-

teractions of History and Religion in South Asia," *Journal of Interdisciplinary History* 23, no. 3 (Winter 1993): 523–50.

15. If "mass" movements were measurable with empirical instruments, one might come to more accurate assessments of these events. Even Gandhi's "mass movements" were, in demographic terms, relatively limited. Their significance lies in the fact that no movements so massive had ever before been mobilized.

16. Susan Bayly, *Saints, Goddesses and Kings: Muslims and Christians in South Indian Society, 1700–1900* (Cambridge: Cambridge University Press, 1989).

17. Romila Thapar, the distinguished dean of India's historians, first coined this term in "Syndicated Moksha?" *Seminar* 313 (1985): 14–22, a special issue on the Hindus and Their Isms: A Symposium on the Complexities of a Dominant Religion.

18. See Robert Eric Frykenberg, "The Impact of Conversion and Social Reform upon Society in South India during the Late Company Period: Questions Concerning Hindu-Christian Encounters," in C. H. Philips and M. D. Wainwright, eds., *Indian Society and the Beginnings of Modernization, c. 1830–1850* (London: School of Oriental and African Studies, 1976), pp. 187–243; Frykenberg, "Conversion and Crises of Conscience under Company Raj in South India," in Marc Gaboreieau and Alice Thorner, eds., *Asie du Sud, Traditions et changements: VIth European Conference on South Asian Studies, Sevres: 8–13 juillet 1978* (Paris: Colloques Internationaux du Centre National de la Recherche Scientifique, 1979), pp. 311–21; idem, "On Roads and Riots in Tinnevelly: Radical Change and Ideology in Madras Presidency during the 19th Century," *South Asia* 4, no. 2 (December 1982): 34–52.

19. See Ainslee T. Embree, *Utopias in Conflict: Religion and Nationalism in Modern India* (Berkeley: University of California Press, 1990).

20. See Peter van der Veer, *Gods on Earth: The Management of Religious Experience and Identity in a North Indian Pilgrimage Centre* (London: Athlone Press, 1988).

21. Elsewhere in volumes of this series, T. N. Madan, Harjot Oberoi, and Hew McLeod have produced essays which similarly describe the militantly defensive actions and attitudes of extremist Sikhs.

22. This tautology is somewhat comparable to saying that "Indians form a majority in India." For analysis of this issue, see Robert Eric Frykenberg, "The Concept of 'Majority' as a Devilish Force in the Politics of Modern Indian History," *Journal of Commonwealth and Comparative Politics* 25, no. 3 (November 1987): 267–74.

23. India alone is now roughly estimated to have more that 840 million people; Pakistan and Bangladesh, 110 to 120 million people each; Sri Lanka, roughly 17 to 18 million (making it smaller than all major states of both North India and South India, so that it is dwarfed even by the presence of Tamil Nadu, across the Palk Strait); Nepal and Afghanistan each being somewhat comparable to Sri Lanka in numbers of people.

24. Cf. *Amritsar Gazetteer*, 1883–84.

25. Narrative details are found in Kushwant Singh, *A History of the Sikhs*, 2 vols. (Princeton: Princeton University Press, 1963, 1966); Rajiv A. Kapur, *Sikh Separatism: The Politics of Faith* (New Delhi: Vikas, 1986); and T. N. Madan, "The Double-Edged Sword: Fundamentalism and Sikh Religious Tradition," in Marty and Appleby, *Fundamentalisms Observed*, pp. 594–627.

26. Sir Penderel Moon, *Divide and Quit* (London: Chatto and Windus, 1961; Berkeley: University of California Press, 1962).

27. Sir Penderel Moon, *India: The Transfer of Power, 1942–47* (London: H.M.S.O., 1970–83).

28. Madan, "Double-Edged Sword," p. 596.

29. Nathuram V. Godse, a Chitpavan Brahman member of the RSS from Puné, fired the fatal bullet on 30 January 1948.

30. This can be seen in scholarly work done by W. H. McLeod, Harjot Oberoi, T. N. Madan, J. C. Heesterman, and others. Essays by the first three have become parts of the Fundamentalism Project.

31. See his essay, "The Meanings and

Origins of Sikh Fundamentalism," in Martin E. Marty and R. Scott Appleby, eds., *Fundamentalisms Compared* (Chicago: University of Chicago Press, forthcoming).

32. I am grateful to J. C. Heesterman for a draft copy of "The Sikh Problem: Some Reflections on History and Tradition" (Lecture/Paper delivered at the University of Wisconsin-Madison, 9 April 1990).

33. Paul Wallace, "The Dilemma of Sikh Revivalism: Identity versus Political Power," in James Warner Bjorkman, ed., *Fundamentalism, Revivalists, and Violence in South Asia* (New Delhi: Manohor, 1988), pp. 57–74.

34. In crude terms, the total population of Sri Lanka, roughly 17–18 million, also has about 2 million Old (or Jaffna) Tamils (who came a thousand years ago and, being Tamil speakers, can be seen as Sri Lanka "Hindus"—worshipers of Minakshi, Murugan, etc.); under 2 million Muslims (virtually all of whom, while claiming Arab descent, also speak Tamil); over 1 million Christians (mostly Catholic, with varied ethnic roots, going back to Portuguese times); more recently arrived Indian Tamils (also "Hindu" laborers, etc., from lower castes); and other ethnic groups (Malay, Veddah, etc.). The definitions used for these statistics are themselves subject to political controversy and open to dispute.

35. See S. Amunagama, "Anagarika Dharmapala (1864–1933) and the Transformation of Sinhala Buddhist Organization in a Colonial Setting," *Social Science Information (SSI)* 24, no. 4 (1985): 697–730; idem, "A Sinhala Buddhist 'Babu': Anagarika Dharmapala (1864–1933) and the Bengali Collection," *SSI* 30, no. 3 (1991): 555–91. See M. K. de Silva, "Buddhist Revivalism, Nationalism and Politics in Modern Sri Lanka," in J. W. Bjorkmann, ed., *Fundamentalism, Revivalism and Violence in South Asia* (New Delhi: Manohar, 1988), pp. 107–58; and idem, "Religion and the State," in M. K. de Silva, ed., *The Governance of Sri Lanka* (New Delhi, 1992). See also G. Obeyesekere, "The Problem of Fundamentalism in a Non-Monotheistic Religion: A Case of Theravada Buddhism," in Marty and Appleby, *Fundamentalisms Compare,* forthcoming.

36. In the case of Sinhala Buddhist Sri Lanka, this heritage is more indirect, more second hand. Sri Lanka could have been ruled by the Colonial Office had not resources of the East India Company's Raj, succeeded by the resources of the India Office, held sway across the Palk Strait.

37. Obeyesekere, "The Problem of Fundamentalism in a Non-Monotheistic Religion," as drawn from the Saddharmalamkara, a work written some eight centuries after the Mahavamsa.

The Function of the Rashtriya Swayamsevak Sangh: To Define the Hindu Nation

Ainslie T. Embree

"The Rashtriya Swayamsevak Sangh is hot news today," an official publication of the organization declared in 1985; "the public discuss it in buses and trains. Politicians dilate upon its political impact. Religious leaders of every hue and color are drawn to it. . . . The popular wave is rising all over in favour of its thought and activities. . . . The whole world has come to recognize it as a most potent force in shaping the future destiny of this great and vast country" of India.[1] Twenty years earlier, even the most ardent supporter of the RSS would have hesitated to make such claims for it, and outsiders thought of it mainly as a small, though malign and sinister, organization that had been accused of involvement in the assassination of Mahatma Gandhi in 1948. At the time the organization was banned, but when the charges remained unproven and it was allowed to function once more, the general public was mainly aware of it through the faintly comic spectacle of its members, ranging in age from little boys to old men, dressed in khaki shorts and carrying long sticks, engaged in not very well coordinated gymnastic exercises.

By the time of the 1991 national elections, however, the RSS was seen in a very different light. The international press reported that the disciplined youth cadres of the RSS, who were playing a crucial role in electing of the candidates of "the right-wing, pro-Hindu, Bharatiya Janata Party" (BJP), were "bright, clean-cut," "brisk and efficient." These young, middle-class RSS workers might be religious zealots, but they presented a marked contrast to "the mobs of unkempt ruffians" surrounding the candidates of the Indian National Congress, the party of Mahatma Gandhi and Nehru, that had led India to independence.[2]

The attribution of influence to the RSS by both its friends and enemies seemed verified by the BJP's performance in the election's of June 1991, when it won 122 seats in the national legislature, in contrast to the 2 it had won in 1984. This stunning result was not, of course, simply due to the RSS support the party acknowledged receiving, or even to the leadership of people like L. K. Advani and Atal Behari Vajpayee, whose skills had been honed in the movement. Rather, it indicated acceptance by a large group of the electorate of the ideological positions formulated by the RSS as valid statements of the Indian national interest.

While the RSS claims that its positions have always been congruent with the national interest, a series of events in the 1980s created a climate that made those positions seem reasonable and attractive to many people. These events can only be listed here, but their general impact was to raise questions about the past, about the directions in which Indian society had moved since the coming of independence in 1947, and about new directions for the future. In the 1980s, separatist movements of Muslims in Kashmir (and to a lesser extent in Assam) and Sikhs in Punjab raised fundamental questions about the basis of the political unity of India. In other geographic areas, sporadic violence defined in ethnic and religious terms challenged the ability of the state to maintain public order and protect its citizens. The murders of Prime Minister Indira Gandhi and later, in 1991, of her son Rajiv Gandhi were not random acts committed by mentally unbalanced individuals, but calculated political statements that declared the Indian state did not have a monopoly on the use of force. On a quite different level, the celebrated Shah Bano case, which on the face of it was only concerned with the right of an elderly Muslim woman to an alimony settlement, led to a passionate debate, and considerable violence, over the right of Muslims to have their religious laws enforced by the state rather than following laws applicable to all citizens. Furthermore, the attempt by the V. P. Singh administration to provide special educational and employment benefits through affirmative action for what had become known as the "backward classes" aroused a storm of protest from those who argued that establishing quotas for certain groups in society would lead to further fragmentation and bitterness in an already divided social order. Finally, in 1985, an extraordinary controversy erupted over the Babri Masjid, a mosque that had been built in the sixteenth century on the site of what was alleged to be the birthplace of Lord Ram, a deity held in great veneration throughout India.

Against the background of these debates, demonstrations, and violence the elections of 1991 were held with their evidence that the RSS had become an important national movement. The RSS leaders would, however, frame that statement differently: they would say that their articulation of a Hindu worldview had at last been recognized as a fundamental part of the main political discourse of India. That worldview, they argued, explained what had been mistaken about the directions taken by India in the past and provided a blueprint for a future in which her glory would be restored.

Both Indian and Western commentators tend to use such terms as "militant Hinduism," "Hindu fundamentalism," "religious revivalism," or "reactionary Hinduism" to describe the ideology of the movement, although these terms may seem an inappropriate category for the study of Hindu religious phenomena. Hinduism is without the foundation texts, defined dogmas, and institutional structures that are characteristic of most varieties of fundamentalism in other belief systems. This point of view finds frequent expression in modern Indian thinking, with its emphasis on the Hindu view of life as grounded in a spiritual experience that is essentially rational and humanistic. Hinduism is free, according to S. Radhakrishnan, a leading exponent of this interpretation, of the intellectually debilitating exclusiveness of the Semitic religions, with their tendencies to form alliances with political powers in order to enforce their dogmas.[3] And yet, rereading these familiar irenic statements one is struck by the possibility that insistence on majority rule by liberal politicians like Nehru, and Radhakrishnan's belief in the inclusion of all religions under the overarching umbrella of Truth as understood within the Hindu tradition, is not contrary to RSS ideology. The RSS insists that it wholeheartedly supports democracy, with its basic premise that the majority will rule, enforcing what it believes to be true.

Leaders of the RSS themselves have frequently denied that the movement is either religious or political, asserting instead that it is a cultural organization that eschews political involvement, with its membership open to people of all religious persuasions or none. This argument must be taken seriously, and not just dismissed as a subterfuge, for it involves the whole usage of such terms as religion, culture, and politics. The title of one of the movement's recent pamphlets, *RSS: Spearheading National Renaissance,* summarizes its stated goals and speaks of the "light and warmth" it has given in crucial national situations through the fulfillment of its function since its founding in 1925, of defining and defending the Hindu nation.[4]

The Hindu nation, it should be noted, not the Indian state—the distinction is important, if not always clear, in RSS writings. A distinction is made between *raj* and *rashtra,* with *raj* including, in RSS usage, not much more than the law-and-order functions of the state, while *rashtra* is the all-inclusive term for society in all its aspects.[5] "Nation," "religion," and "culture" are used interchangeably in RSS literature, and since the function of the state is to serve society, it is plausible for the RSS to claim that it is a cultural, not a religious or political, organization. At the same time, to outsiders it appears as the quintessential example of the involvement of religion in politics.

While critics describe RSS members as fanatics and extremists, the group's formal constitutional aims are mild enough: "To eradicate differences among Hindus; to make them realize the greatness of their past; to inculcate in them a spirit of self-sacrifice and selfless devotion to Hindu society as a whole; to build up an organized and well-disciplined corporate life; and to bring about the regeneration of Hindu society."[6] One could substitute Christian, Jewish, or Muslim for Hindu in this statement and get a rather commonplace example of religious rhetoric, but behind each phrase can be read, as many people in India do, the sinister agenda for domination of the nation by a religious faction that excludes those who reject its vision of the good society as a Hindu society.

The general thesis of the present chapter is that the goals of the RSS indeed place it in the mainstream of Indian nationalist aspirations, which is, of course, in accordance with the stated positions of the RSS itself. Both Indian and foreign observers of the movement criticize this image, however, charging that the RSS is a fascist organization intent on the destruction of parliamentary democracy, that it encourages violence and terrorism, and that its bitter antagonism to the adherents of non-Hindu religious groups, particularly Muslims and Christians, has created an atmosphere of

hatred and suspicion. All of these aims, its critics allege, arise from its perverted interpretation of Hinduism and Indian history. These charges have been made in numerous publications and are continually heard in private conversations with members of
the non-Hindu religions as well as from many well-informed Hindus. The content of
these attacks has been quite accurately summed up by Nana Deshmukh, a prominent
RSS leader, in a pamphlet titled *RSS: Victim of Slander*. The members of the RSS have
been accused, he wrote, of being "fascist, obscurantist, chauvinistic, supporters of
dictatorship, a secret organization, enemies of socialism, opposed to the minorities,
believers in violence," and of collecting arms and giving training in their use.[7] The
most famous charge against the RSS, and one that was certainly widely believed at
the time, was that the RSS was responsible for the assassination of Mahatma Gandhi
because of his support for Muslims. Jawaharlal Nehru was undoubtedly expressing
the view of many Indians when he wrote to the leader of the RSS in 1948 that the
activities of the movement were "anti-national and often subversive and violent."[8]

What can only be described as the growing respectability and acceptance of the
RSS can be explained in terms of both changes within Indian politics and adjustments
in ideology and modes of action by the RSS to accommodate itself to these changes.
This accommodation is not denied by its leaders, but they insist, however, and the
evidence seems to support them, that in its organizational structure and ideology
there has been no real shift.[9] For the RSS, organization is not separable from ideology, but both reflect the fundamental nature of Indian religion and culture, or Hindutva, the term that has long been used by RSS ideologues but that has only in recent
years gained wider currency. The concept of Hindutva, the idea that the Hindus constituted a nation, was elaborated by Vinayak Damodar Savarkar (1883–1966), the
famous nationalist leader, in a book written while he was in prison in 1922 for sedition.[10] Its argument, which greatly influenced the leaders of the RSS, is that Hindus
are those whose ancestors have lived in India from the most ancient times and who
acknowledge that their religion, their culture, and their language originated in India
and not outside it. Some RSS publicists suggest that the only real analogy to this
understanding of nationhood is found in Zionism.

Quite clearly, the RSS has become a phenomenon to be reckoned with in the
interaction of religion and politics in contemporary India. The RSS has achieved this
status because four closely related aspects of the movement enabled its leaders to take
advantage of social and political changes after 1975. One of these aspects is the nature
of its leadership, including both the national leader, known as the *sarsanghchalak,* or
supreme guide, as well as the regional leaders, the *sanghchalaks* and *pracharaks*. The
second is the organization of the movement, with its network of local groups known
as *shakhas,* consisting of members known as *swayamsevaks,* or volunteers dedicated to
the service of the movement. The third aspect is an ideology which, by fusing religion
and nationalism, appeals to a wide spectrum of Indian society. The fourth aspect of
the movement is the kind of activities in which it is engaged. Some of these activities
are carried out directly by the shakhas, some by swayamsevaks, or members, as expressions of individual commitment, and, of great importance, especially at the present time, through numerous structures outside the actual RSS organization, but to
which the RSS supplies organizers and leaders. These range from journals, like the

Organiser, to political parties, like the Jana Sangh and the Bharatiya Janata party, and to large, amorphous cultural organizations like the Vishva Hindu Parishad. There is also a women's organization, the Rashtra Sevika Samiti, which is parallel to the RSS, shares its ideology and structure, but is independent of it. These organizations and activities are referred to in RSS literature as "the family."[11]

It is impossible to give an exact date for the RSS's emergence as an important actor in Indian political life, but its spokesmen are probably correct in seeing the years of the Emergency, 1975–77, when Prime Minister Indira Gandhi curtailed civil liberties and jailed many of her opponents, as a crucial period for both gaining public support and perfecting their operational techniques. After Mrs. Gandhi's defeat in the national elections in the spring of 1977, the RSS claimed, for example, that much of the success and popularity of the Jaya Prakash Narayan's message of "total revolution" was due to the work of its local cadres, and Narayan himself said the RSS was "the most potent and idealistic instrument for total transformation of the country."[12] The evidence seems clear that the RSS leaders at the national, regional, and local level were active in organizing opposition in India. RSS members and sympathizers in foreign countries, especially in the United States and England, also helped financially to support antigovernment activities in India and helped spread information about the alleged excesses of the Gandhi government.[13]

Leadership: Alienations and Affirmations

This period of growth associated with the Emergency was facilitated to a considerable extent by a change in leadership which had taken place in 1973. The RSS was founded in 1925 by Keshav Baliram Hedgewar (1889–1940), who on his death was succeeded by Madhava Sadashiv Golwalkar (1906–73), who in turn was succeeded on his death in 1973 by Madhhukar Dattatraya Deoras (1917–), who had been secretary-general of the organization. Both Hedgewar and Golwalkar had insisted that the RSS was strictly a cultural organization, concerned with national renewal through character building, and that it should not engage in politics. Deoras was one of a group within the leadership who had begun to demand the movement take an active political role, so he was well positioned to make use of the RSS cadres for antigovernment work during the Emergency. While changes in the policies of the RSS undoubtedly took place during this period in response to changing social and political conditions, the claim of its publicists seems to be essentially correct that the movement has not deviated from its original vision.

Neither the RSS's apologists nor its critics deny the centrality of the leadership and its responsibility for the organization's achievements, but no one agrees on how the leaders function and what their motivations are. For critics, the leader is a dictator, demanding blind obedience, suffering no independent judgments on the part of the members, encouraging a cult of personality, and operating in secrecy. RSS spokesmen dismiss these characterizations as the product of ignorance and malice, arguing that the role of the leader is misunderstood by their critics, who, as Westernized Indians, are unaware that Indian culture has its own traditions of leadership which are different from those of the West. What they have in mind is that pervasive concept of the spiritual guide, the guru, the one who possesses knowledge that is imparted to followers.

The concept of the leader receives considerable attention in RSS literature, partly because its opponents' charge that the movement is utterly undemocratic, partly because the concept undergirds both the functioning of the movement as an organization and its ideology. The leader, in RSS understanding, is not a representative of the people, but one who plans, implements the plans, determines policy, rewards good workers, and punishes poor ones; "he brings his comrades around to his point of view." Discipline is maintained by a "skilled and efficient leadership" who are not only obeyed but revered.[14] This reflects not, the RSS insists, a cult of personality, but the true nature of Indian society in its recognition of moral and spiritual worth. Leaders are thus able to gain the unswerving loyalty of a band of followers on all levels, down to the basic unit, the shakha. From such leadership comes the discipline, it is argued, that explains the success of the Sangh in gaining influence in the lives of its followers and in the many organizations in which they work.

Unlike other traditions, RSS spokesmen are fond of pointing out, Hinduism is not based on the historicity of an individual or on the authority of a book. "The tragedy of movements which revolved solely around individuals for their inspiration and ideals," M. S. Golwalkar, the second leader of the RSS declared, "is there for all to see." Instead of a founder and texts, at the heart of Hinduism is the overarching concept of *dharma*. The definition the RSS gives to this word suggests what the function of the leader will be. Dharma has two aspects: the first is the "proper rehabilitation of the mind," and the second is "adjustment of individuals for a harmonious corporate existence." The RSS leader, in the true Indian tradition of leadership, he argues, would work for these two ideals and would not stress his own role. To emphasize an individual leader would show that Hindus "were no better than Muslims and Christians."[15]

The founder of the RSS gave to the Hindu nation as a symbol of leadership instead of a person or a book a banner, a holy flag, the Bhagva Dhwaj. It is a reddish orange color, the traditional saffron associated with both Hindu holy men and Sivaji, the seventeenth-century Maharashtrian warrior who rebelled against the Mughals, thus symbolizing at once the spiritual and military greatness of the Hindu people. More specifically, the color symbolizes the holy sacrificial fire that dissolves the egoism of the individual.[16] In other words, the leaders as spiritual guides, as dictators, disappear behind the symbol, but the potency of their power remains.

Much is obscure about the early years of the Rashtriya Swayamsevak Sangh, partly because of the myths of origin that grow up around organizations, particularly religious ones not open to public scrutiny, but also because it was not accorded much importance by outsiders. Hedgewar, the founder, himself wrote nothing and seems to have actively discouraged writing about his work and ideas. The name of the organization is usually translated as National Volunteer Organization, but this does not quite give the emphasis of the original, which is meant to convey a spirit of self-service to the nation, with "nation" defined as the Hindu people of India. That the word

"Hindu" is not in the name of the organization is of great significance for its members. "Rashtriya," or nationality, they insist, means Hindu. As Hedgewar put it, "If we use the word Hindu it will mean that we consider ourselves only as one of the innumerable communities in this land and that we do not realize our natural status as nationals of the country."[17] By this he meant that the Hindus were the only true nationals; members of other religions, if they denied that they were Hindus, were also denying that they were Indians.

This interpretation of Hinduism is a radical fundamentalism because of its implications for India with its immense Muslim population of nearly one hundred million, not to mention such other Indian groups as Sikhs, Christians, and Buddhists. While claimed as Hindus by the RSS, Sikhs and Buddhists, of course, regard themselves as distinct religions. The RSS's insistence on identifying Hindu with India is central to the whole issue of the relation of religion to politics in India. Although outwardly very different from the manifestations of fundamentalism in the Semitic religions, the RSS view is analogous to the attitudes toward other religious communities of Christian fundamentalists in the United States, Jewish ones in Israel, and Islamic ones in Pakistan.

Keshav Baliram Hedgewar is said to have shown extraordinary brilliance as a child and, after graduating from medical school, had opportunities for a comfortable life. As an admiring biographer puts it, he had "a bed of roses waiting for him—what with matrimonial offers from rich families," but, in the classic pattern of Indian spirituality, he renounced it all for a life of poverty dedicated to the search for truth.[18] There was, however, a divergence from the pattern. He refused to marry so that instead he could offer himself with complete devotion on the "altar of the motherland"; furthermore, his search was not for personal enlightenment, as it had been for the great sages of the past, but for a way to serve India. Nothing so clearly identifies him and the RSS as belonging to the domain of modernity as this concern for the social order. One could argue that his was a purely secular quest, but, as in the case of Gandhi, the vocabulary is that of religion. Less clear is the meaning of his rejection of family life, for lifelong celibacy is not part of normative Indian spirituality, although it remains a prominent feature of the lives of many contemporary RSS workers.

Other biographical details, fictional or not, provide models for behavior and give insights into RSS thinking. As a little child, Hedgewar refused to celebrate Queen Victoria's Diamond Jubilee, and he is said to have asked his elders the question that became the frame for his life and for the RSS: "How could a handful of foreigners coming from six thousand miles away become our masters?"[19] Such precocious questioning drew him into the radical wing of the Indian National Congress, led by Bal Gangadhar Tilak, who by the end of the nineteenth century had enunciated a militant anti-British nationalist rhetoric that exalted the glory of the Hindu past. In this atmosphere Hedgewar revised his childhood queries to ask a series of questions that have almost startling relevance for India in 1991. Is it true that British rule was really the cause of India's degradation? What about the eight hundred years of Muslim rule—were they not even more responsible for the present condition of the land of the Hindus? And, above all, was it not the disunity of the Hindus themselves that made possible the conquest of India, the homeland of the Hindu race? Hedgewar's answers to these questions were embodied in both the ideology and the organization of the RSS: its worldview is rooted in understanding the history behind these questions, and the organization was structured to change the mental and moral attitudes of Hindus to end the degradation brought about by centuries of foreign rule.

India, according to the vision of history attributed to Hedgewar, was the homeland of the Hindus, the people of India. It was subjected to successive waves of invaders, but these had always been absorbed into Hindu society until the coming of the Muslims, who, refusing to follow the path taken by other invaders, maintained their separation and persecuted the Hindus. In return, the Hindus "waged a relentless struggle for eight hundred long years." Why, then, since the Hindus were so much more numerous, did they not drive out the Muslims? Hedgewar's answer to this query is at the heart of RSS thought: despite their courage and valor, the Hindus, because of their internal disunity and dissension, were responsible for the fate of the Hindu nation.[20] Then came a more subtle invader, the British, who, knowing the physical courage of the Hindus, set out to destroy the Hindu spirit. They used various stratagems, but the most successful one was to convince the Westernized elite that India had never been a nation, that Hinduism was only a conglomeration of superstitious practices, and that all the varied groups of India, including the Muslims and Christians, were equally part of the new political entity that had been created by the British. Out of this misperception, according to Golwalkar, Hedgewar's successor, came the emphasis of the nationalism movement led by the Indian National Congress on the creation of a new sense of nationality. The Congress leaders had forgotten that "here was already a full-fledged ancient nation of the Hindus" and that other communities, such as the Jews and Parsis, were there as guests or, in the case of the Muslims and Christians, as invaders.[21] In pursuit of "the phantom of unity," the Congress denied the essential reality of India as a Hindu nation.

Hedgewar came to believe that the leaders of the Indian National Congress were mainly motivated by the desire to be rid of the British so that they could take their place and that they had no positive vision of the Hindu nation. What was needed, he concluded, according to a disciple, was an organization whose members would be wholly devoted to the Hindu nation, who would have "a passionate devotion to the motherland, a feeling of fraternity, a sense of sharing in national work, a deeply felt reverence for the nation's ideals, discipline, heroism, manliness and other noble virtues."[22] These rhetorical phrases are a quite exact summary of the organization and the ideology of the RSS as it was founded by Hedgewar in the provincial city of Nagpur in 1925.

To understand leadership of a movement, it has been suggested, one needs to know both the personality of the leader and the "alienations and affirmations" of the followers,[23] and in the case of the RSS, the clue to both is surely to be found in a passionate assertion of the glory of Hindu culture before it was degraded by its enemies. These enemies are frequently identified: foreign invaders, especially the Muslims, and, to a lesser extent, the British; Hindu elites who have been, so to speak, de-

Hinduized; after they became a recognizable force in India, the Communists; and, above all, those Indians who fail to recognize that the basic enemy of Hindu culture is its own disunity. The leaders and followers of the RSS proclaim their alienation from India as it exists but assert that they find a meaning and purpose for their lives in the affirmation that the greatness of Hindu culture can be restored through the strength of their characters. The mechanism that Hedgewar devised for this task was the shakha, the youth corps.

Organization: Renewal through Discipline

The formal organization of the RSS has developed through the years, but it did not have a constitution until forced to make one in 1949 as the price of freedom from the ban placed on it after being suspected of involvement in the assassination of Mahatma Gandhi. The structure as it exists at the present time has been in place, however, throughout most of its history, although RSS literature insists that what is important is the quality of leadership, dedicated to the ideals of the movement, and participation in the shakhas by those in sympathy with those ideals. This view reflects the fact, made clear in many interviews, that it is relatively easy to participate in RSS activities without making any long-term commitments. While this is no doubt true, article 6 of the RSS constitution speaks of members taking the Sangh's pledge and subscribing to its rules and regulations, and it provides for their expulsion for misconduct or indiscipline.[24]

The organization of the RSS, as detailed in its constitution, is quite elaborate, with various seemingly overlapping jurisdictions, but essentially it is a pyramid of geographically defined groups with leaders at every level. In the organizational chart given in the constitution, the officials and the groups are given in one listing, a reminder of the centrality of leadership. The organization is similar to that of the Indian National Congress and no doubt drew upon it for a model. There is an all-India assembly (the Akhil Bharatiya Pratinidhi Sabha), and then the country is divided into zones, states, divisions, districts, cities, and groups of villages. In both theory and practice, it is the leaders who are the dynamic centers of the organization, and they are in no sense executives or representatives of their groups; the measure of their success is in carrying out the aims of the movement. These aims, as succinctly summarized in the constitution, are to weld together the diverse groups within Hindu society, and to revitalize it on the basis of its religion and culture (*dharma* and *sanskriti* in the original); the methods for achieving them are devised by the leadership and carried out by the members under the instruction of the leaders. The emphasis is on Hindu society, not at all on religious doctrine.

At the national level, there is a director or sarsangchalak, referred to in the literature as the supreme guide or philosopher of the movement. While in theory the office is elective, in practice the sarsangchalak has chosen his own successor. Hedgewar, the first who held the office, was unambiguous about its authority. It was essential, he said, that the swayamsevaks, the members, obey implicitly the commands of the sarsangchalak. There was no question of challenging his decisions. "The tail should not wag the body. That is the secret of the success of the Sangh."[25] This complete authority given the leader has led to the criticism that the RSS is a fascist body, but the answer the leaders give is that the Sangh had no need to derive its inspiration from "a perverted foreign model; it modelled itself on an ideal Hindu family." The members are like children, working for the welfare of all, with the sarsangchalak as head of the family. He has a central working committee to carry out the day-to-day business of the movement and to pass on decisions to the various regional groups. Each of these regional groups has an official known as the sanghchalak, or guide, but this post seems largely ceremonial. The most important work at all levels in the various regional groups is done by the pracharaks, whom the constitution defines as unpaid, full-time workers whose "mission is to serve the society through the Sangh, and who, of their own free will, dedicate themselves to the Cause."[26] As an authoritative RSS spokesman phrases it, the pracharak system "is the bedrock on which the Sangh stands," noting that there are now "a few thousands" spread all over the country.[27] They are given no independent authority and have no control over funds; they are appointed by the secretary-general, and serve where they are sent. The source of their influence comes, as the constitution has it, because they are dedicated to a cause, to something that integrates their lives and gives them a sense of purpose.

Any generalization about the caste and class of the pracharaks involves asking why young men join the RSS in the first place. The RSS insists that it appeals across caste and class lines, but it is not at all clear that it does so. As to motivation, the answer, or variants of it, that RSS members themselves give when questioned is probably not far from the truth. The RSS attracts people, it is argued, who are dissatisfied with the condition of India and see in the organization and ideology of the RSS a way of bringing about change. Most commentators agree that members tend to belong to upper castes and to the urban middle class, which means they are college-educated, although seldom, it would appear, at one of the prestigious colleges. Many now come from families where the father or other relatives have been members of the RSS, so no longer do families oppose, as they once did, commitment to a movement that demands great personal sacrifice in terms of lifestyle.

Although the RSS constitution does not require celibacy of the pracharaks, most have in fact been unmarried. With the tremendous value placed on marriage and family life in India, and by all religious communities, not just by Hindus, self-chosen celibacy is as dramatic a statement of commitment to a cause as one can make. The stated reason for celibacy in the literature is that family life inevitably makes demands that would prevent the pracharak from giving his full time and energy to the work of the movement. No denigration of family life is found in RSS writing, nor are there expressions of the danger of the seductive wiles of women which is common in much Indian literature, but the pracharaks, as well as other young workers, live austere and self-denying lives. It is reported with admiration that Babasaheb Apte, one of the well-known pracharaks, refused to see his sister when he was working in the city in which she lived. "This may appear hard-hearted," the writer comments, "but severance of family ties to enable single-minded devotion to the Sangh has become standard practice for the workers aspiring to become pracharaks."[28] For many RSS workers, the fact that Atal Behari Vajpayee, who was foreign minister in the Janata government from 1978 to 1980, and one of the ablest of the many politicians in the BJP with an RSS background, has remained a bachelor, is indication of his loyalty to the cause.

"The real spirit of our work," M. S. Golwalkar declared, "will be understood when one comes in contact with the shakha." By way of explication he painted a word-picture, at once romantic and factual, of what goes on in these local meetings of the RSS. The picture touches upon so many aspects of leadership, organization, and ideology that it is worth quoting:

> There is an open playground. Under a saffron flag (the *bhagva dhwaj*) groups of youths and boys are absorbed in a variety of Bharatiya (Indian) games. Resounding shouts of joyous enthusiasm fill the air. . . . The leader's whistle or order has a magical effect on them; there is instant perfect order or silence. Then exercises follow—wielding the lathi, marching, etc. The spirit of collective effort and discipline pervades every programme. Then they sit down and sing songs charged with patriotism. Discussions follow. They delve deep into problems affecting national life. And finally they stand in rows before the flag and recite the prayer, "Many salutations to Thee, O loving Motherland."[29]

Reading this account of the shakhas, it is hard not to see analogies to two other movements. One is Hitler Youth. Golwalkar was frequently reminded that Hitler had started in a similar manner—gathering young people and instilling in them discipline, unity, and love of the national culture—but that then he later used his power to suppress all other political parties. Golwalkar did not deny the outward similarity, but said the difference was that Hitler was interested in politics, whereas the RSS tried to build a new life of moral character without being dependent upon political power.[30] The shakhas were begun in 1925, so there cannot be any direct imitation, but the comparison is suggestive.

The other movement that makes use of similar techniques is, somewhat incongruously, the Boy Scouts, founded in 1908 by General Baden-Powell, with its emphasis on quasi-military discipline as the foundation of character for a life of service to the nation. The movement had spread to India, but it was condemned by the nationalists as a thinly disguised prop of British imperialism, and various indigenous scout movements were organized, so its organization might have influenced Hedgewar.

Some of the outward forms of the shakhas might have been influenced by Western-style schools in Nagpur, where the RSS originated, but in fact there is little in their concepts or practices that cannot be shown to belong to India. The emphasis on physical exercise, for example, has its roots in an indigenous tradition that combined "martial arts" with spiritual discipline and character building.[31] Swami Dayananda Saraswati, founder of the Arya Samaj, and Swami Vivekananda, the immensely popular speaker and writer at the end of the nineteenth century, both had stressed physical culture as an essential element in rebuilding the Indian nation.

Accounts of the origins of the RSS make the point that when Hedgewar became critical of the Indian National Congress for its refusal to take an uncompromising stand in asserting Indian values, he might have spent his time trying to reform it from within, but instead he abandoned it. Moving in an entirely different direction, he began to work with boys aged eleven to thirteen, in whom he saw "potential to develop into great instruments of national service."[32] He joined in the games of a group of boys, got them interested in his ideas, and then organized them into a shakha or training group. The daily meetings were followed by setting up a training camp, where the boys were taught to use such Indian weapons as the lathi, or wooden stave, dagger, javelin, and sword. Lectures were given on Hindu nationalism, the main burden of which, according to a former member, was that "the Hindus were unorganized, liberal, generous, and peaceable, because of which the Hindu society had suffered at the hands of non-Hindus."[33] This is a reading of history that many Indians, who have no sympathy with the RSS as an organization, would accept, which, of course, is a reason such ideas find a receptive audience when they are given political expression in the discourse of modern Indian politics.

In the shakhas the RSS is struggling with the necessity, given the social and political situation of India in the twentieth century, to make a public statement about cultural identity. The purpose of the shakha, in a very important sense, is to train the members to answer the question "Who am I?" with the affirmation, "I am Hindu." In earlier times, the answer would probably have been given in some much narrower frame of reference of region and family. In this respect, the RSS represents the most unequivocal public statement of Hinduism as a form of social identity. It does not contradict traditional forms of self-identity but goes far beyond them in asserting that to say "I am an Indian" is also to say "I am a Hindu." H. V. Seshadri, a prominent RSS leader, tells of speaking to people in Karnataka, who had been accustomed to thinking of themselves as Brahmins, Lingayats, or Untouchables, about a larger identity, that of being Hindu, which encompasses other identities. People's enthusiastic reception of this idea came, he said, as a joyous surprise. "We never imagined that the word Hindu held such a magic spell even for those hearing it for the first time."[34]

In the late nineteenth and early twentieth century, as a result of the development of modern electoral politics, people began to identify themselves, and to be identified by others, as Hindus and Muslims in a way that would not have been true a hundred years before. This is a complicated and controversial subject, but much modern scholarship provides support for what has been called "the construction of an authentic and defensible Hindu identity" in the nineteenth and twentieth centuries.[35] Hedgewar's romantic description of a meeting of a shakha is, then, a portrait of a nation in the making, to use the title of the autobiography of S. N. Bannerjee, the famous nationalist. Bannerjee tells how he tried, although in a different way, to inspire young Indians with a sense that they belonged to a great, if fallen, nation.[36]

Ideology: Hindu Nationalism

To get its members to answer a question about personal identity with the affirmation "I am a Hindu," the RSS follows the rigorous indoctrination procedures of the shakhas. Giving content to the word "Hindu, " however, is a harder task. The leaders are aware, of course, that many people, both within and without the Hindu world, argue that the word cannot be used to denote a structure of religious beliefs in the sense that "Christianity," "Islam," or "Judaism" is used. They are also aware that the word derives from the usage of the Muslim conquerors for the people of the land, a fact that suggests it is a term of opprobrium. That "Hinduism" and "Hindu" cannot be defined does not, however, deter the RSS leaders from using the terms, for the very good reason that they are not talking about a religious system one joins by subscribing to a set of beliefs, but to membership in a nation, the Hindu nation. The ideology of the RSS, as well as its concept of leadership and its organization, is based on the centrality of the nation that had its origin in the land now known as India. RSS literature says remarkably little about religious beliefs; instead it seeks to define that nation which has existed from time immemorial in India. It is to this point that RSS writers return constantly, and they insist that the name and its origin are of no real concern, nor is the fact that the religion designated as Hinduism includes a bewildering multitude of beliefs and practices. These can be defined, but not the larger entity that encompasses them. What is important is the existence of the nation to which the name "Hindu" has been given in the land of India. Words that are repeated very frequently in one form or another in the literature define patriotism as "identification with the mainstream of our country, unalloyed devotion to the Motherland, a spirit of fraternity . . . with all the rest of the countrymen and an attitude of adoration towards the great nation-builders and the values of life bequeathed to us by them."[37]

This definition sounds like conventional patriotism, but the nation builders include Ram, Shiva, and the other deities of popular Hinduism, and neither they nor the values they represent will find ready acceptance by many Indians, especially Muslims and Christians. The RSS leaders are aware of this, but they are also aware that both Christianity and Islam have made their way through versions of that enigmatic Christian text, "Compel them to come in."

That the explication of ideology in RSS literature does not lead to a systematic statement of political theory does not, then, in the leaders' understanding, point to a deficiency in the movement, but rather underlines what they regard as its essential function, namely, the definition of a Hindu nation. Such a definition is not built on the elaboration of a political theory of the state but is grounded in what the movement claims to be the Hindu worldview, by which is meant a view of society in which the state is one component but not necessarily the most important. Nor in RSS literature is there much attention given to the use of proof texts and the assertion of canonical authority for scriptures—something one finds in other religious movements. RSS ideology appears to give as much, or more, attention to such aspects of the movement as organization, mechanisms for instructing the membership, physical disciplines, and the position of the leaders in a complex, carefully articulated hierarchical structure, as it does to religion. The RSS leaders point out, however, that Hindus base every aspect of their existence on the Ultimate Reality called God, so that, properly understood, everything is an expression of religion. Religions like Christianity and Islam can be defined because they are partial expressions of the truth, but Hinduism and the Hindu nation cannot be defined because they come from the Ultimate. M. S. Golwalkar gave rather poetic expression to this idea of the Hindu nation when he wrote:

> The origins of our people, the date from which we have been living here as a civilized entity, is unknown to the scholars of history. . . . We existed when there was no necessity for any name. We were the good, the enlightened people. We were the people who knew about the laws of nature and the laws of the Spirit. We built a great civilization, a great culture, and a unique social order. We had brought into life almost everything that was beneficial to man. Then the rest of mankind were just bipeds and so no distinctive name was given to us. . . . The name "Hindu," derived from the river Sindhu, has been associated with us in our history and tradition for so long that it has now become our universally accepted and adored name.[38]

This is heady stuff, and it is not hard to see why it would make a special appeal to the young, the idealistic, the patriotic, and those who felt disinherited and marginalized. It is an expression of religious fundamentalism, but it uses the vocabulary, as the RSS would argue, of Hindu culture, not of a religion concerned with a personal relationship to a deity.

Not only is there little reference to specific Hindu religious beliefs in RSS literature, but in private conversations its members frequently emphasize that they are not religious. When pressed as to the meaning of this statement, they tend to say that they do not do *puja,* the making of an offering to a deity's image or symbol. Daniel Gold has observed that in modern India many varieties of what may be thought of as new religious phenomena have emerged, such as gurus as leaders of cults, yogic centers, and devotional movements.[39] Many modern Indian movements appear to encourage a purely personal inward devotion, without social reference. Such movements have, of course, their analogues in the well-established *bhakti* and *sant* traditions. But, Gold suggests, Hindu fundamentalism has emerged as an alternative path for personal religion that does not demand devotion to a deity, but rather concentrates on the identification of the individual with the Hindu nation, which for many may "appear more immediately visible and attainable than the ritual cosmos of traditional Hinduism" and "offer the most viable personal religion available." Members of the RSS, however, perhaps more in conversation than in their literature, stress their adherence to the ancient practice of *karmayoga,* that discipline which attempts to combine two central Hindu constructs, *dharma,* the path of action in this world, with *moksha,* the way of liberation or salvation. RSS thinkers thus stress the necessity of a life of action without denying the efficacy of the devotional way.

The oath a candidate takes when he becomes a member of RSS is a summary of its ideology and links the way of disciplined action with religious belief and dedication to the nation. The candidate swears before the God of All Power and his ancestors that his reason for joining the movement is to achieve the greatness and unity of India (Bharatvarsh) by fostering the growth of the sacred Hindu religion, Hindu culture, and Hindu society.[40] This stress on the centrality of Hindu culture as the defining element of both religion and the nation is often made in RSS writings, but it was given wide currency by M. S. Golwalkar, in the pamphlet *We or Our Nationhood Defined*, first published in 1939 and reprinted many times.[41] By "nation," he means the Hindu nation, the only usage that has meaning in the Indian context, and not the Indian state as it exists, although he admits the possibility of a Hindu state coming into being. What he is insisting upon is the distinction the RSS makes between rashtra, nation, and raj, or state.

The nation is a compound of what Golwalkar calls the "famous five unities": geography, race, religion, culture, and language.[42] The definitions of these terms are not very precise, but they occupy a large place in RSS thinking. Of the five, geography is very important for the concept of the Hindu nation, for the concept depends on the congruence of the nation with the physical reality of India. "A nation without its country is unthinkable." The Jews had race, religion, culture, and language, but were driven out of their land and could not be a nation until they returned to it. As for race, it is the basis of a hereditary society, with common origins and culture. India is both motherland and fatherland in RSS usage, and the words are more than metaphors: they indicate actual biological links between the people who live in India today and whose most remote ancestors lived there. Culture and religion are part of that biological inheritance.

Religion, the RSS ideologues admit, is not easily defined, except, they insist, it is essentially the Spirit of Race. There is no very close analogue to this phrase in the India tradition, and as many Indian intellectuals admired nineteenth-century German thought, the Hegelian echo is probably not accidental. For the Hindu, they insist, every action of life is a command of religion. "We make war or peace, engage in arts and crafts, amass wealth and give it away—indeed we are born and die—all in accord with religious injunctions."[43] These injunctions are not, however, like the laws of Jews and Muslims; they are matters of Spirit, to be discovered by the seeker. At the same time, the RSS rejects utterly the idea that religion is a private matter, without a role in public life. Nor is it otherworldly—it is intensely concerned with society. What is being explicitly rejected in this definition of religion is the Indian secular state, the ideal that guided Nehru and other nationalist leaders before and after independence.

Culture, another of the components of the nation in RSS literature, is usually a translation of the Hindi word *sanskriti*. In explaining what is meant by the term, however, none of the RSS ideologues get much beyond a circular definition: "Culture, being the cumulative effects of age-long customs, most particularly of religious beliefs . . . planting on the Race consciousness its own particular stamp."[44] The listing of language as the fifth of the "famous five unities" may come as a surprise to anyone familiar with the linguistic complexity of India, but the explanation given is that all the languages of India have been enriched and inspired by "that queen of languages, the language of the gods—Sanskrit."[45] The purported division between the Indo-European and Dravidian languages is an attempt by foreigners and their dupes in India itself to spread disunity, for the only un-Indian languages, such as Persian and English, are those brought in by conquerors.

Perhaps every nationalism needs an enemy, and certainly for Hindu nationalism, as articulated by the RSS, its enemies are essential to many of its ideological positions.

They are a disparate group, but what they have in common, according to the RSS, is their denial, in some fashion, of one or all of the five components—geography, race, religion, culture, language—of the Hindu nation. From the RSS point of view the groups are not just enemies of the RSS but of India. They can be conveniently placed in four categories: Indian adherents to foreign religions; Communist party members and their sympathizers; Westernized members of the Indian intelligentsia; and foreign powers. The first three of these groups willingly admit they are enemies of the RSS, although they do not admit, of course, to being anti-India or anti-Hindu. The fourth group, foreign powers, is more nebulous and does not occupy so prominent a place as the others in RSS discourse; in the literature they are often characterized as acting through agents of one or another of the first three groups.

In the period from 1985 to 1990, the RSS attitude toward Indian Muslims was dramatized by the savage controversy over the Babri Masjid, a mosque allegedly built by the Mughal emperor Babar (1526–30) after he destroyed a Hindu temple on the site of the birthplace of Lord Ram. It is generally acknowledged that the extraordinary excitement generated by the issue owed much to the skilled leadership of RSS cadres in the Vishva Hindu Parishad, a broad-based alliance of many groups, and the BJP.[46] For the RSS leadership, the movement was recognition of the argument it had made since its founding—that India was a Hindu nation which had been despoiled and contaminated by the Muslim invaders.

Nor was Babri Masjid the only mosque that could be used to symbolize past defeats of Hinduism by Islam: a list has been compiled of over two thousand mosques that had been erected on the ruins of Hindu temples.[47] Such destruction, it was alleged, was not accidental, but rooted in Islamic teaching, theology, and law. As Arun Shourie, a well-known and respected journalist put it, the destruction of Hindu temples by the Muslim invaders "was the way to announce hegemony. . . . This was the way to strike at the heart of the conquered . . . for the temple was not just a place of worship; it was the hub of the community's life, of its learning, of its social life."[48]

But the great symbol that proves, for the RSS, the enmity of Islam for the Hindu nation is the partition of India in 1947. For Indian nationalists at the time and since, the creation of Pakistan is seen as a tragedy, and RSS rhetoric, when it speaks of the monstrous crime of dividing the sacred Motherland, is expressing a view that is probably held by the overwhelming majority of the people of India. Unlike most Indian nationalists, however, the RSS leaders stress that partition was not due so much to British machinations as to Hindu weakness. According to an authoritative statement, the RSS had tried, unsuccessfully, both before and after partition, to convince the Indian National Congress that "the Muslims could be made to give up their aggressive and anti-national postures only when the Hindus became organized and powerful enough to make them realize that their interests were best served in joining the Hindu mainstream."[49]

Islam still threatens India, according to the RSS. Externally, Pakistan, it is alleged by many, gives aid and comfort to the potential fifth column of the one hundred million Muslims in India while they arm the rebels in Kashmir. Saudi Arabia and other wealthy Muslim states send money and missionaries to convert the Untouchables and other low castes. In addition to practicing a foreign religion, and having extraterritorial loyalties, Muslims are seen as a drag on the nation because they are ignorant and illiterate, resist education, and, unlike Hindus, refuse to practice birth control, so they will soon be in the majority.[50]

This insistence that Muslims and other minorities must be brought into the mainstream raises the complex issue of the place of violence in RSS ideology and practice. There is no doubt, as one writer puts it, that when one mentions the name of the RSS, many people's reaction is, "They do violence in the name of religion and commit outrages against humanity."[51] The grounds for this public image of the RSS, aside from suspicion that it was implicated in Mahatma Gandhi's assassination, is the charge that it has incited many of the communal riots between Hindus and Muslims which have taken a fearful toll of life and property in India. The anatomy of communal riots has been much studied. While they differ from place to place, common provocations are often such things as a religious procession by one community through an area heavily inhabited by another, rumors that a woman from one community has been attacked by a man from the other, or charges that offensive remarks have been made against the other's religious tradition. Violence breaks out, very often guided, it is alleged, by members of the RSS shakhas, who are armed and disciplined.

The RSS leaders' answer to these charges is unequivocal: "Nowhere in India, by any judicial commission, has the RSS been found guilty or responsible for the outbreak of any communal riot."[52] They are equally unequivocal, however, in asserting that the disasters that have befallen Hindu society are due to its failure to fight the invaders, particularly the Muslims. There is no place in their ideology for Gandhi's nonviolence, for which they find no sanction in the Hindu tradition, and the swayamsevaks are encouraged to defend Hindus when they are attacked. Here, they argue, is where misunderstanding about the role of the RSS in riots arises—the cadres simply go to the rescue of Hindus threatened by Muslim mobs.

The RSS attitude toward India's Muslims has involved an attack on secularism, that distinctive policy devised by the Indian National Congress as a solution to the religious divisions and antagonisms that threatened Indian independence. The Indian usage of "secularism" does not mean rejection of the transcendental values of religion; on the contrary, there is an insistence that all religions are true and that all have an equally valid place within the nation. Religion, however, is not a component in defining nationality. All of these points are resonant with the history of the Indian nationalist struggle and with the complex mosaic of India's religious pluralism.

The RSS insists that the public rhetoric of secularism conceals the reality of Indian life, which is deeply and irrevocably grounded in Hindu culture, and that the political practice distorts and corrupts the social order, by the official pretense that Hinduism is one religious sect among many. Only Hinduism, the RSS leaders insist, can create a meaningful secular society, for only Hinduism genuinely believes in tolerance. This message was, ironically, the one Deoras, the RSS leader, gave in 1979 in the industrial city of Jamshedpur on the eve of a communal riot. The commission investigating the riots noted that, in his speech, Deoras had extolled the tolerance of Hinduism, contrasting it with the fanaticism of Islam. This was coupled with an exhortation to

Hindus not to yield to Muslim demands out of a misplaced tolerance for the intolerant. When his speech was followed by a display of martial arts by one thousand swayamsevaks, the climate, the commission remarked, became "most propitious for the outbreak of the communal disturbance."[53]

Some of the most virulent criticism of the RSS comes from the Communist party of India, which accuses the RSS of being a fascist movement, stirring discord between sections of the working classes, and promoting violence. The Communist party in India seldom attacks religion as an opiate of the people or as false ideology. Instead, it often denounces the RSS for giving a false impression of Hinduism, making it appear obscurantist, a champion of the caste system, and, in general, the oppressor of the poor and downtrodden, whereas true Hindus are the champions of the poor.[54] RSS writing, in contrast to Christian apologetics, rarely criticizes communism or Marxism as atheistic or godless. The accusation they make more frequently is that it is committed to internationalism, by which is meant that its Indian adherents place the interests of the Russians and Chinese above those of India.

In common with other groups in India, the RSS frequently names "foreign powers" as enemies of India without always identifying them. The RSS list is fairly extensive, including the USSR (before 1991), the United States, Pakistan, Saudi Arabia, and other Islamic countries in the Middle East. The general accusation made against them all is that, with the assistance of their dupes in India, they are introducing alien elements into Indian society. From the Marxist countries come "unassimilated, crude, class-war ridden, monolithic social structures" that threaten the harmonious ideals of Hindu society."[55] Some RSS spokesmen, in common with representatives of other political parties, accuse the United States, with Pakistan its willing ally, of wanting to keep India poverty-stricken and subservient so she will not challenge their hegemony.[56] Also criticized is the morally corrupting influence of American culture, in the form of movies, music, and dress, but there is not as much criticism as one might expect. What does bulk very large in RSS literature is the organization's condemnation of foreign missionaries for their activities in converting tribal peoples and untouchables. The RSS was allegedly instrumental, for example, in having a commission appointed in Madhya Pradesh in 1954 to investigate Christian activities. One of its conclusions, that "conversion muddles the convert's sense of unity and solidarity with his society," echoes a frequent theme in RSS ideology.[57] In recent years, Islamic missionary activity has been the subject of similar criticism, especially because the RSS charges that Islamic governments are supplying money for the conversion of untouchables and other outcaste groups. The RSS was especially active in publicizing mass conversions of untouchables to Islam which took place in the village of Meenakshipuram in South India in 1981, allegedly because the Muslims offered financial assistance to them. As with Christian conversions, these were seen as a threat to the unity and cultural identity of India.[58]

The fourth group identified in RSS literature as an enemy, and the one that is perhaps the most important for the future, is succinctly described as "sections of the intelligentsia who are influenced by Western education and culture and who are ashamed to call their culture their own."[59] The members of this group are traitors to their class in the eyes of the RSS, for they have accepted interpretations about Indian history and culture from their British overlords, including the false views that Hinduism does not constitute a definable religion and that the Indian nation is a modern construct. The leaders of the RSS and these opponents come, in fact, from the same Hindu upper castes, have much the same Western-style education, are engaged in similar professional activities, and in their private lives have quite similar commitments to Hindu social customs and traditions. The differences between them lie ultimately in their understanding of the meaning of Hindu culture and its relationship to political practice. The RSS perceives, no doubt correctly, that many members of this "de-Hinduized intelligentsia," principally made up of journalists, academics, lawyers, and writers, view the modern state and its function as basically antagonistic to the RSS vision of a Hindu nation, and that they have used their influential platforms to propagate this viewpoint.

For the RSS, Jawaharlal Nehru is a ready symbol of this intelligentsia. Mahatma Gandhi, they acknowledge, introduced into the Indian nationalist movement many elements drawn from the Hindu cultural heritage, but he made two major errors that have worked against the realization of a Hindu social order in India. One was his support for Muslims; the other was choosing Nehru as his major lieutenant, a person who had nothing in common with his ideas of man, nation, and God. "The Nehru Mind is made mostly abroad . . . and Nehru never succeeded in catching the spirit of Indian culture at its best." His blueprint for independent India was drawn from Russian, American, and British sources, not from the genius of India. Nehru, and those who followed him, rejected the very things that might have created a new society, "the foundational ideas of the past."[60]

The RSS ideology fits remarkably well, therefore, with suitable adjustments for the particularities of Indian society, into a definition of fundamentalism as given by Robert Frykenberg. Fundamentalism, he suggests, is "an extreme kind of militantly religious conservatism and separatism which is at once both radical and reductive in its reaction against 'modernism' and against ideological or institutional changes which are perceived as threats to ultimate 'Truths' or 'Verities,' changes which are perceived enshrining 'Falsehood.'"[61]

Activities: The RSS—A Vision in Action

The subtitle of this section, "The RSS—A Vision in Action," comes from the title of a book by H. V. Seshadri, who has served the RSS as secretary-general and as the pracharak, or regional leader, in the southern zone. He is often referred to by members of the RSS as their leading ideologue, and his writings are cited by rank-and-file swayamsevaks as giving authoritative statements of the movement's positions on matters of public policy. His book, published at the centenary of the birth of K. B. Hedgewar, founder of the movement, sets out to do precisely what Hedgewar apparently always discouraged during his lifetime, namely, to publicize the activities of the RSS. The claim of the book—and it is made in many others, although with less detail—is that the active members of the RSS, the swayamsevaks, "have built up powerful movements which have had remarkable impact on millions of our countrymen."[62]

Over 150 organizations of various kinds are listed in Seshadri's book, and many more are mentioned in the text.[63] However, the list is a conflation of at least four separate categories of activities which may be broken down as follows: organizations wholly unconnected with the RSS but in which its members have influential positions; organizations which have aims somewhat congenial to RSS ideology but which are in fact independent; political parties in which RSS members have been dominant; and groups that have been organized by the RSS for its own purposes.

Organizations in the first category, ones in which RSS members have played fairly important roles in decision making, are probably not of much concern to the RSS. There have been, for example, former members of the RSS in the World Bank and International Monetary Fund, but there is no indication of RSS ideology influencing these organizations' work. Other organizations such as the International Labor Organization and Amnesty International are cited as having made favorable comments on the RSS, but they refer to the humanitarian work of RSS affiliates or individual members.[64] On the other hand, organizations that have not found their way onto Seshadri's list but in which the RSS does have some influence include national journals, radio, and television, where individual members have an opportunity as writers and editors to express views reflecting positions favored by the RSS. The same is even more true of schools and colleges, where teachers often interpret their subjects, especially Indian history, in ways that are sympathetic to RSS ideology. The influence of this kind of activity is no doubt considerable, but it is difficult to measure or, at times, even to identify it with certainty as influenced by the RSS, since, as this essay has emphasized, the RSS shares many of its positions with the mainstream of Indian nationalism.

The impact of the RSS as "a vision in action" on the other three categories of organizations is more easily tracked. The second category consists of groups that, although established prior to the RSS or independently of it, share its ideological positions. RSS members have been active in these groups yet the organizations cannot be seen as joint enterprises. The best-known example of a group in this category is the Hindu Mahasabha. The RSS and the Arya Samaj are also linked, through membership and political positions.[65]

The relationship between the RSS and Hindu Mahasabha is curious and, to outsiders, confusing, as the two organizations have much ideology in common, for which both draw heavily on the concept of Hindutva in the writings of V. D. Savarkar.[66] The Mahasabha was founded as a political party in 1913 to oppose what appeared to a group of Hindu leaders as the increasing influence of the Muslim League and to safeguard the interests of the Hindu community. After the RSS was founded, the leaders of the Mahasabha tried to persuade its leaders to join with them, but the RSS insisted that it was a cultural organization, not a political party, and refused a formal alliance. The differences between the two were to some extent based on personalities, but the perception of the RSS leaders was that the Mahasabha was more interested in political power than in creating a Hindu nation of the kind the RSS envisioned. In pursuit of this long-range goal, the RSS wanted to create disciplined cadres that would be able to provide leadership when the time was opportune for a major shift in power, rather than to become involved in the shifting alliances and compromises of the Mahasabha. The leadership of the RSS was also younger and more single-minded, some would say more fanatical, in its devotion to the Hindu nation.[67] That the RSS read the future correctly is suggested by the fact that by the 1980s, the Mahasabha had ceased to be of any national importance, while the RSS had become a formidable political presence.

The third category of organizations that display the RSS "vision in action" includes political parties, most notably the Jana Sangh and the Bharatiya Janata party (BJP). Neither can be correctly characterized as a creation of the RSS, but both represent, as the RSS claims, the result of a growing awareness of a Hindu national identity and disenchantment with the policies of the ruling Congress party in general, especially in respect to what many people regarded as favoritism shown to the Muslim population in order to get its votes, and a weak military response to Pakistan.

While the RSS contributed organization skills through its local cadres as well as effective national leadership to the parties, it is misleading to consider either the Jana Sangh or its successor, the BJP, as mainly a "religious" party. In most respects, they function in much the same fashion as the Indian National Congress or the regional parties. In normal public discourse, their leaders like Atal Behari Vajpayee and L. K. Advani make no more specific references to Hinduism than American leaders do to Christianity, and much fewer than Pakistani leaders do to Islam or Israeli ones to Judaism. But in India the rhetoric of the nationalist movement has stressed its religious neutrality, and in the concept of secularism has denied that religious belief is a component of national identity. The RSS attacks this position with vigor, arguing that in order to get the Muslims and other minorities to support them, the Congress leaders have betrayed Hindu culture, the only genuine basis of an Indian identity. Since the ideological commitment of the major leaders and many of the party functionaries of the Jana Sangh and the BJP to the RSS vision of a Hindu nation is well-known, people assumed the parties would seek to make it a reality. Since no religious establishment in Hinduism is comparable to that of the Semitic traditions, the RSS takes the place of such an establishment in the minds of Indians, both those who dislike what it stands for and those who accept it. Critics of the movement often, in fact, refer to it as "Semitized Hinduism." Those who dislike the RSS, assume the party leaders are subservient to it in much the same way as old-fashioned American Protestants assumed a Roman Catholic president would follow the dictates of the pope.

The Jana Sangh was founded in Delhi in 1951 under the leadership of S. P. Mukerjee, who was not a member of the RSS, and, while known to be a Hindu nationalist, he was generally moderate in his views and was interested in gaining political power through compromises with the urban elites of North India. The inner circle of the new party, however, included such able swayamsevaks as Balraj Madhok, Deendayal Upadhyaya, and P. N. Oke, whose unswerving commitment to the concept of the creation of a Hindu nation followed the lines so often stated in RSS ideology. The manifestos of the party played down these commitments to some extent, but policy references to the need for an aggressive stance toward Pakistan and the importance of supporting the national culture were heard as statements of the RSS positions on the place of Muslims and other minorities in India. The Jana Sangh polled 3.06 percent of the vote in the 1951 elections and 7.4 percent in 1971, the last election in which it acted as an independent party.[68] What these raw figures conceal is the strength of the party in North India and its weakness in the south, and the fact that to a considerable extent the party's constituency matched that of the RSS. A party identified as standing for a Hindu nation seemed to draw support from urban middle-class white-collar workers, professionals, shopkeepers, and government workers.

The Jana Sangh dissolved itself in 1977 to merge along with other parties into a national front, the Janata, to defeat the Congress under Mrs. Gandhi. In 1980 its leaders reformed it into an independent party, the Bharatiya Janata party (BJP). The success of the BJP in making the positions of the RSS central to the Indian political process is noted above, and it appears that a large number of Indian voters, although not the majority, find these positions increasingly attractive.

An important factor in the electoral success of the BJP and other parties that espouse the ideology and positions of the RSS has been the activities of groups and movements in the fourth category, that is, those which quite clearly owe their origin to RSS members and have the full approval of the central leadership. These are the groups of affiliates referred to as the "RSS family." Some of them, known under such names as Virat Hindu Samaj, Vishal Hindu Sammelan, or simply Provincial Hindu Conference, are regional groups of an ad hoc nature, used to organize crowds for the great rallies which are such a spectacular feature of Indian public life. The purpose of such gatherings, according to the RSS, is to give the people a sense of Hindu solidarity and to show politicians that there is a Hindu vote that must be taken into account. A kind of subtext in the speeches, which is easily understood, reminds Muslims and Christians that India is a Hindu country in which they live by courtesy of the Hindu majority.

The important national organization Vishva Hindu Parishad (VHP) was established under RSS sponsorship in 1964 to bring together the various Hindu religious leaders. Peter van der Veer has examined the work of the VHP in detail in the chapter following this one, noting its goals of consolidating Hindu society, spreading Hindu values, and establishing links with Hindus abroad.[69] These goals reflect the stated aims of the RSS, as did the VHP's special concern in its early years to oppose the efforts of Christian and Muslim missionaries to convert tribal groups and untouchables. For the RSS, it was a moment for special celebration when a mammoth VHP gathering at Allahabad in 1966, despite long-standing opposition from orthodox Hindu leaders, resolved to re-admit into the Hindu fold those who had been converted to other faiths, no matter how many generations before. The word popularized by the VHP for this process, *paravartan,* was especially pleasing to the RSS, for it can be translated as "turning around" or "coming home," a recognition that all true Indians see themselves as Hindus.[70]

Cow protection, which in effect meant that the government should ban the slaughter of cows, was one of the causes the RSS supported with great effect after independence. In RSS literature there is not much emphasis on cows as objects of special religious veneration, but simply a declaration that they have a unique place in Hindu culture and in the economy, a place that has been obscured with the passage of time. As Mushirul Hasan has said, for the articulation of a Hindu identity, "high-caste Hindus discovered in the cow a powerful symbol of common identification."[71] As in so many instances, the RSS leaders were building on an attitude from the mainstream of Indian life to strengthen their own positions and to gain a wider hearing for what they saw as one of the fundamentals of Hindu culture.

There is, then, great emphasis placed on past cow slaughter as a symbol of the evil practices of foreign invaders, especially the Muslims, and on its continuance in the present as a sign of the government of independent India's failure to respond to the demands of the majority of the people. Golwalkar had once been asked how and when cow slaughter had begun in India, and his answer is an example of the way RSS thinking can combine history and ideology in a call for specific action that will appeal to large numbers of people: "It began with the coming of the foreign invaders. In order to reduce the population to slavery, they thought that the best way was to stamp out every vestige of self-respect in Hindus. They took to various types of barbarism such as conversion, demolishing our temples and . . . cow-slaughter."[72] In those phrases he summed up three specific grievances of the RSS against the Muslims which from 1950 on were to become popular rallying points for the convergence of religion and politics. In 1952, reasonably certain of a popular response, the RSS issued a call for mass demonstrations against the central government to demand a total ban on cow slaughter as "a point of cultural sanctity and a symbol of national oneness."[73]

Those who opposed the ban were those usually identified by the RSS as the enemies of Hindu culture: the Muslims, the Communists, the Westernized elites, and the Americans. The Americans were included because they wanted to buy Indian hides and beef to save their own cows, and, if bullocks were killed, Indian farmers would have to buy American tractors.[74] In the following years there were many mass demonstrations, which often led to Hindu-Muslim riots; as noted earlier, accusations were made that the RSS was involved in the riots, but these charges were never proved in court.

Less dramatic than the cow protection groups are those organized by the RSS for special constituencies or specific issues, for example, two groups organized for college and university communities—the Akhil Bharatiya Vidyarthi Parishad (ABVP) and the Students' National Association. The ABVP illustrates how the RSS works through its organizations. Few of the students involved in it are actual members of the RSS, and not more than a third have ever taken part in other RSS activities, such as the meetings of the shakhas.[75] The ABVP emphasizes work among the tribal peoples, partly to prevent them, as the RSS puts it, from falling into the clutches of the Christians, but also to demonstrate the unity of all sections and classes of Hindu society. It also goes in for what has been called the RSS penchant for "organizing shows, minding the details and mobilizing trained workers," and vast gatherings of ABVP students, where their cleanliness, order, and perfect silence are contrasted with the unruly, messy, and noisy meetings of other students.[76] "Discipline" and "order" are words used continually in RSS literature to describe the most desirable qualities in the young.

The Students' National Association was a much more regional group founded by swayamsevaks who were students in Jammu, that part of the state of Jammu and Kashmir where Hindus are in the majority. According to the RSS record, in 1948 the association, moved by patriotism, led a demonstration and went on a hunger strike demanding that the Indian national flag be flown over the government buildings.[77] But in fact much more than simple patriotism was involved. Golwalkar, the head of the RSS, was carrying out secret negotiations, on behalf of the government of India, with the maharajah of Kashmir, described in RSS literature as "a devout and patriotic Hindu," although he is characterized elsewhere as a debauched eccentric. The RSS version of events is that Golwalkar persuaded the maharajah to join India, even though the Muslim population, which made up 85 percent of the population, wanted to join Pakistan. The local Muslims, according to RSS accounts, joined hands with the invaders and "butchered thousands of Hindus and abducted thousands of Hindu women." The young swayamsevaks, who had formed the Students' National Association, were responsible for holding Jammu until the Indian army arrived.[78] While there is no independent verification of this event, it exemplifies the ideals of the RSS in a striking manner, with its combination of the devout Hindu ruler, the barbarous Muslims, and the brave young Hindu fighters protecting the honor of women.

Another special constituency to which the RSS turned its attention was labor. In India, trade unions had largely been formed by organizers from the political parties as a means of mobilizing the workers to support independence. After 1947, the two most prominent parties involved in the trade union movement were the Indian National Congress and the Communist party of India, both of which, but especially the Communists, the RSS regarded as enemies of the India of its dreams. Both sets of trade unions, to the RSS, were built on foreign models, stressing confrontation and struggle between the worker and the employer. What was needed was the introduction of Indian values and models of social behavior. Thus in 1955 the RSS sponsored the founding of a new union in Bombay, the Bharatiya Mazdoor Sangh. In the new union, the familiar ideas of RSS ideology were to be realized: the goals would be harmony, not struggle; spirituality, not materialism; and the building of individual character, not dependence upon the government.[79] The symbol of the union was the saffron flag, the Bhagva Dhwaj, which for the RSS was "the traditional national symbol representing universal welfare."[80]

The Indianization, or Hinduization, of the labor movement was further indicated by the adoption of the festival of Vishwakarma, the architect of the universe, in place of May Day as a holiday. RSS organizational strength was combined with its ideological appeal to give the Mazdoor Sangh a considerable measure of success. Its one million members, drawn not so much from the factory workers as from the usual constituency of the RSS, were white-collar workers in banking, municipal services, and the retail trade.[81]

One of the most interesting of the RSS-related organizations with a special con-

stituency is the Rashtra Sevika Samiti, which describes itself simply as "an organization of Hindu women." It was founded in 1936 on the initiative of a remarkable
woman, Lakshmi Bai Kelkar. Like so many of the early leaders of the RSS, she was a
Maharashtrian Brahman. A biographical sketch in an official publication, intended to
be an inspirational guide to the members of the Samiti and to appeal to middle-class
women, provides insight into the tensions caused by social change which lead people
into the RSS and its affiliated organizations.[82] A patriotic and socially conscious
woman, Mrs. Kelkar was not content with running a prosperous household, so she
turned toward the nationalist movement. She found, however, that its leaders were
only intent on gaining power to drive out the British, not to build a new India. Other
women of her class were attracted to the ideas of equal rights and economic independence for women, but she was aware that "this unnatural change in the attitude of
women might have led to the disintegration of the family."[83] She found the answer
to her dilemma through her sons, who were in the RSS: it was possible through an
organization that stressed discipline and patriotism for women to serve the nation
through the deepest tradition of the role of women in Hindu society.

Mrs. Kelkar met Hedgewar, who encouraged her to begin a women's organization
modeled on the RSS. All the techniques of the RSS were to be used, including the
meetings of the shakhas, with their emphasis on physical training, study, obedience
to the leader, and complete dedication to the ideals of restoring the Hindu nation.
The two organizations were, however, to be entirely separate, since, as the Samiti
literature puts it, the basic principles and philosophy of women's life in India are quite
different from those of men. The refusal to let women join the RSS was not, as has
been suggested, the result of Hedgewar's fear that men would be seduced by proximity to women; rather separate education for women was the norm at the time in
India, and Hindu families probably would not have permitted their womenfolk to
participate in mixed athletic activities. Among the innovations of the Samiti was the
worship of what seems to be a new manifestation of divinity, a goddess known as
Devi Ashtabhuja, who represents the realization of true Hindu womanhood. She is a
symbol, according to the Samiti, of "integrated society, woman's chastity, purity,
boldness, affection, alertness." While the primary role of women is that of wife and
mother, fulfilling their own special organic function, this does not preclude a role as
fearless leader in all areas of nation building. History and ideology are combined by
the Samiti to provide examples of heroic women from the Maharashtrian world: Ji-
jabai, who trained her son Sivaji to fight the Muslims; the Rani of Jhansi, who fought
to the death against the British; Ahalyabai of Indore, who encouraged trade. "Moth-
erhood, leadership, and efficient administration, are the qualities to be followed from
these great lives."[84]

The Samiti places great emphasis on calling oneself a Hindu, arguing that those
who say "Hindu" is a modern, un-Indian term have been brainwashed by foreigners.
Thus in small ways, it tries to give women a sense of pride in the Hindu nation, but
like the RSS, the Samiti does not aspire to be a mass organization. The leaders argue
that it demands too much by way of complete dedication of time and self-discipline

to attract many to full-time service, so it expends its energies and resources on summer training camps for *sevikas,* the potential leaders. It also runs schools to develop the qualities of Hindu womanhood. In addition to these formal activities aimed at its inner circle, the Samiti sponsors the celebration of Hindu festivals, arranges exhibitions on the lives of Hindu heroes and heroines, and publishes works in Hindi, Marathi, and Gujarati of interest to women. There are no reliable figures on membership, but the greatest impact of the Samiti seems to be in Gujarat, Maharashtra, and the Delhi area.

Overseas Indians are another special constituency of the RSS, and they are frequently mentioned in RSS literature and in conversation as playing an important role in the work of the organization. As already noted in reference to the activity of the RSS during the so-called Emergency from 1975 to 1977, overseas Indians supported opposition movements within India. Wherever there are numbers of Indian immigrants, former swayamsevaks form the nuclei for gatherings to discuss current events in India and to strengthen each other's devotion to the motherland. In New York, for example, a group known as the Hindu Swayamsewaks has weekly meetings and a three-day training camp in the summer. Many of its members also belong to one called Friends of the BJP.

Among the most important of the activities associated with the RSS are more than thirty newspapers and journals published in twelve languages. Use of the print media by the RSS is primarily a post-independence phenomenon, as in its early days the central leadership discouraged publicity on the grounds that the material would be used by RSS enemies, including the government, against it. The appearance of journals interpreting the news from an RSS point of view marks the growing influence of the more activist elements in the leadership as well as the growing self-confidence engendered by the coming of independence. The activists, of whom the present leader of the RSS, Deoras, was one, believed that the time had come to enlighten the public on the need for building a Hindu nation rather than a secular state on the Western model. These journals are not published directly under the RSS but through various trusts set up by workers in different areas. Two are national newspapers, the *Organiser,* an English-language weekly, and *Panchjanya,* a Hindi weekly. The editorials in both are regarded by RSS workers as well as outsiders as expressing the views of the central leadership.

Conclusion: A Reaction to Failure?

Fundamentalist movements of all kinds have been called "a reaction to failure," the argument being not that the particular movement has failed in its goals, but that it arises because of failures in the larger society.[85] This is indeed the way the RSS understands its position in the life of modern India. The exultant quotation on RSS success at the beginning of this chapter has as its obverse an insistence that the defeats India has suffered at the hands of conquerors were due to disunity within Hindu culture. That the Muslims ruled parts of India for a thousand years and then the British ruled parts of it for nearly two hundred years is a measure of this disunity. The history of the nationalist movement as represented by the Indian National Congress is also, for the RSS, a record of failure because of its attempts to create a nationalism that failed to take into account Hindu culture, the only possible basis of an Indian nation. The message of Gandhi, so appealing to a generation fighting for independence, drew on the resources of Hindu culture, but erred in his persistent concessions to Muslims. After independence, Nehru and the Congress party failed to build a new society through their allegiance to the false dogma of secularism, which was used to win the electoral support of minorities, especially the Muslims and Christians. It is in this situation of repeated failure, according to its leaders, that the RSS offers the people of India a message that can be truly called "fundamentalism" since it draws on the timeless message of Hinduism. K. R. Malkani, one of the most persuasive of the RSS writers, summarizes the record of failure by declaring, "it was Gandhism yesterday, and it can only be the redoubtable RSS tomorrow."[86]

There is another kind of failure to which the RSS is a reaction, namely, the sense of personal and psychic failure experienced by many people, especially young men from the middle class. They feel they have not shared in the sweeping changes that have taken place in India since 1947, and that, in terms of opportunities for advancement and influence in the country, they have been marginalized by the urban elites. These elites have deserted the old values of Hindu society and have become Westernized. The message of the RSS is not a call to reject science, technology, and all the other fruits of modernity, but rather to use them in the service of the Hindu nation: this can only be done by those who are truly dedicated, who have seen the vision of a Hindu India.

The pathway to this RSS future is well mapped out for its adherents through its leadership, its organization, its ideology, and its activities. To the outside world, the leaders of the RSS, at the central, regional, and local levels, appear to be dictators, demanding and receiving blind obedience. This, the RSS argues, is a misreading of their nature and function. Their concept of leadership comes from the deepest level of the Hindu tradition, with the leader being one who translates dharma, that most fundamental of Hindu concepts, into actions that lead individuals to a harmonious corporate existence.[87] From this will come a renewal of the Hindu nation through the character of its people, for individual character is the basis of the nation. The leaders offer a way of disciplined activity that the members gladly accept. The true symbol of the RSS, its followers insist, is not the leader, but its saffron-colored flag, the Bhagva Dhwaja, which speaks at once of the spiritual and military greatness of the Hindu past.

The organization of the RSS follows from this understanding of leadership, and the most distinctive aspect of the movement is the shakha, the gathering where the members engage in strenuous physical exercise that disciplines both mind and body, in study, and in acts of devotion to the motherland. The leaders insist that there are no members in the ordinary sense, in that there is no payment of dues, no membership rolls, no formal initiation. The test of membership is participation in the shakhas and in the activities of the local units. Many take part for a short time and then drop out, so the turnover is high, which the leaders accept as part of the process of winnowing the chaff from the wheat. For this reason, it is difficult to estimate the actual numbers of the movement, but a million seems a reasonable figure for members at any one time, bearing in mind that many do little more than take part in the exercises. At the heart of the movement are the trained and disciplined cadres, mainly made up of young men, who come out of the shakhas and are available for the many activities sponsored in one way or another by the RSS.

The ideology of the RSS is summed up in the concept of Hindutva, the word that has become increasingly popular in recent years both within and without the movement. The concept defines the goals of the RSS in terms of the revitalization of the Hindu nation, of identifying who is a Hindu, and the place of non-Hindus within the Hindu national polity. More than anything else, it is the position assigned to non-Hindus, especially the Muslims, that they are not true nationals, which has aroused fear of the RSS and its power. People remember Golwalkar's chilling promise that "they may stay in the country wholly subordinated to the Hindu nation, claiming nothing, deserving no privileges, far less any preferential treatment, not even citizens' rights."[88]

The RSS leaders have always insisted that their organization is not a political movement, but a cultural one. Technically this is correct. In the dozens of organizations and activities associated with the RSS, it is the dedicated members, the swayamsevaks, who, acting as individuals, provide dynamic leadership. The parallel women's organization, the Rashtra Sevika Sangh, has also supplied leadership in much the same fashion. The skill of the RSS leadership has been shown most dramatically in the successes of two political parties, first the Jana Sangh and then the Bharatiya Janata party, but it has also been the backbone of student organizations and a labor union.

If one asks about the future of this movement that drew so much attention at the beginning of the 1990s, the answers are varied and contradictory. The RSS leaders themselves probably did not expect to gain political power at the center in 1991, but what they set out to do they almost certainly achieved, namely, to put the issue of the place of Hindu culture on the national agenda and to weaken the commitment to Nehru's dream of a secular India. Some well-informed observers, however, believe that the passions of the 1980s over the assertion of Hindu rights were short-lived and will have no enduring appeal. Others believe that the RSS, having achieved considerable electoral success through the BJP, including control of Uttar Pradesh, the largest state in the union, will not be able to deal with success, having depended too long on exploiting failure. Others, including knowledgeable scholars, see a parallel between the ideas and tactics of the RSS and those of the Nazis in Germany of the 1930s, with the Muslims taking the place of the Jews. This group of observers can no doubt be identified as players in what Paul Brass has called "one of the great enduring games of political analysts to assert the tacit dominance and to predict the ultimate emergence of a militant Hindu nationalist political category which will overwhelm the Indian state and establish mastery over the Indian population."[89] For many, this prospect is exceedingly unattractive, but it is also pejoratively stated. For believers, the RSS states it in an attractive form—as the promise of rebirth of the Hindu nation.

Postscript: December 1992

On 6 December 1992 an event in India seemed to confirm, both to the supporters of the RSS and to its enemies, its proud boast, quoted at the opening of this chapter, that the RSS had become "a most potent force in shaping the future destiny of this great and vast country." That event, the destruction of the Babri Masjid in Ayodhya, a Muslim mosque of no particular architectural merit and virtually unknown in historical records, created such a reaction that many thoughtful observers saw it as presaging the triumph of the militant Hindu nationalist ideology of the RSS over the modern democratic state that had been the inheritance of the long struggle for Indian independence. This reaction was due partly to the violence and bloodshed that followed the event, but on a deeper level there was a sense that the destruction of the mosque symbolized a fundamental shift in Indian social and political life. This shift was away from the fragile political consensus of religious neutrality, known as the "secular state," that had held together the diverse ethnic, religious, and social communities since independence, toward the new configuration of a Hindu nation, which the RSS had defined through its ideology, leadership, and organization. Whether such a change had indeed taken place will be known in the future; this postscript attempts only to suggest why, at the end of 1992 and the beginning of 1993, the RSS was so confident of the hegemony of the dominant Hindu majority.[90]

That the implications of such a shift were a cause of great anxiety to many people in India, especially among India's vast Muslim population, was made clear in the news media; what is not so well documented, but which many careful observers assert is true, is that probably a larger number of people felt that the destruction of the mosque, and the emotions that had led up to it, were accurate representations of the reality of Indian cultural life. Opinion polls on such matters are not very reliable, but one taken in North India, by a reliable organization, indicated that 54 percent of those questioned approved of the demolition,[91] giving credence to the claim by H. V. Seshadri, the secretary-general of the RSS, that it was "undoubtedly a tremendous morale booster to the Hindu psyche" that the "standing monument to a foreign invader's insult to the nation's honor and independence has itself been erased."[92]

While the news of the demolition of Babri Masjid on 6 December was received with pleasure, or at least with equanimity, by large numbers of the population, nevertheless, almost no event since the coming of independence in 1947 had evoked such soul-searching in a quest for causes and such deep anxieties about what the destruction of the mosque and the bloodshed that followed meant for the future of the nation. Other acts of violence would seem to have been far more momentous, such as the assassination of Mahatma Gandhi in 1948 or of Prime Minister Indira Gandhi in 1984, but the public's reaction at the end of 1992 was qualitatively different than it was after those incidents. Perhaps this is because in the case of both assassinations, individuals with specific grievances were known to be directly responsible and were quickly identified, even though, as noted above, it was widely believed although never proven that the RSS was implicated in Mahatma Gandhi's death. His death was, furthermore, a form of shock treatment which seemed to draw people into a close national unity. In the case of Mrs. Gandhi, one religious community, the Sikhs, was blamed by elements in Indian society for her death, and fearful vengeance was taken upon them; in Delhi alone, four thousand Sikhs were said to have been killed in a wave of violence. But while Sikhs in the Punjab and elsewhere were undoubtedly deeply alienated by the massacre and the failure of the government to punish the guilty, there seems to have been no widespread feeling, as in December 1992, that the fabric of the political order was changing. Especially for those who feared the change, the RSS was seen as the activating element.

For over seven years, the RSS and its skilled cadres in its "family" organizations such as the Hindu Vishwa Parishad, the Bajrang Dal, and, the most important, the BJP, had been involved in a massive campaign regarding the Babri Masjid. The BJP was of critical importance in this campaign, since many of its leaders, such as Lal Advani, Atal Behari Vajpayee, and its president, Murli Manohar Joshi, were former or current members of the RSS, and it was the second largest party in the central legislature, where the ruling party, the Indian National Congress, was in the minority and so depended upon its support. The BJP had come to power in three large states, Uttar Pradesh, Madhya Pradesh, and Rajasthan, where the influence of RSS cadres was strong, and where there was probably more anti-Muslim sentiment than elsewhere as well as more emphasis on the glories of the Hindu past in school textbooks and in political rhetoric.

Because of the activity of all these groups, Babri Masjid had become a symbol for a large number of Hindus of the defeat of Hindu India by the Muslim Turks in centuries past, although many of these Hindus would have expressed antagonism toward the wider aims of the RSS. And equally for Muslims the mosque was a symbol not so much of the greatness of their past but of their precarious position in modern India. They read the demand for the destruction of the Masjid as a code word for the RSS assertion that they were an alien element in India, surviving on Hindu tolerance and goodwill, not on their rights as people of the land. The agitation for removal of the mosque and, in its place, reconstruction of the Hindu temple was based on the belief, assiduously promoted by the RSS and its affiliates, that a temple commemorating the birth place of the god Ram had been destroyed in 1528 by the Muslim invader Babar, in order to build the mosque on its site.

The date of 6 December had been set by the various Hindu groups for beginning construction of the temple, and great excitement had been created throughout North India. Groups of mainly young men, under leaders clearly inspired by RSS ideology, began to move toward Ayodhya, the site of the Masjid. While the crowd appears to have been overwhelmingly male, an RSS reporter claimed there were five thousand women *kar sevaks,* or volunteers for work on the temple and mosque, at Ayodhya.

Although they did not take part in the actual demolition, they cheered as the male kar sevaks began their work.

Two women, Sadhvi Rithambara and Uma Bharati, were among the most passionate speakers for the movement against the mosque. They had extraordinary success in both public speeches and widely circulated cassette recordings that were so inflammatory in their anti-Muslim sentiments that they were banned by the government. Cultural ethnic cleansing, a getting rid of Islamic influences, was the burden of the tapes, and while they made no direct incitement to violence against the Muslims, they stressed that Hindu men who would not shed their own blood for Hindu India had water, not blood, in their veins. The memory of great Hindu heroines of the past was also invoked, such as the Rani of Jhansi, who had died leading her men into battle in the great uprising against the British in 1857–58. As noted above, the role of women in militant Hindu nationalism as represented by the RSS has been little studied, but observing the response of crowds of men to the fiery appeal of women orators like Rithambara and Bhatati, it is hard to resist a connection with the great goddesses, such as Durga, Bhavani, and Kali, especially remembering that great patriotic song of Indian nationalism, "Vande Mataram," which in its original version had the lines

> Mother, to thee I bow,
> Who hath said thou art weak in thy lands,
> When the swords flash out in twice seventy million hands
> And seventy million voices roar
> Thy dreadful name from shore to shore.

Many heard that "dreadful name," some with rejoicing, some with fear, in December 1992.

The leaders of the crowd at Ayodhya were kar sevaks, volunteer workers, numbering about sixty thousand, who were committed to building a temple to Ram on the disputed site, and many of whom, it was generally believed, were members of RSS shakas. The others who converged on Ayodhya were, as most Indian newspapers described them, "a motley crew"—*sadhus* (holy men), shopkeepers, peasants, students. The crowd was in a holiday mood reminiscent of religious pilgrimages, but that mood was colored by the sense that they were engaged in a great work that would benefit them and the country through the spread of Hindutva, that once arcane word, now widely used, which summarizes RSS nationalist ideology.

Before the crowd arrived at Ayodhya, the Supreme Court, responding to a plea from Muslim leaders, had issued an order that no damage was to be done to the Masjid, and the BJP government of Uttar Pradesh, where the temple was located, agreed to see that the order was obeyed. But on 6 December, a few kar sevaks broke without resistance through the police lines, climbed to the domes of the mosque, and began the work of demolition. They were followed by hundreds more, armed with the necessary tools, and in a few hours the four-hundred-year-old building had been demolished. According to newspaper reports, as the domes collapsed at the end of the day, a holy man saw a favorable omen in the setting sun. Because of the dust and haze, it had taken on a saffron hue, the traditional color of the robes of holy men, and he exclaimed, "The sun sets on Babar at last. The taint has been removed forever."[93]

In the next few days, a wave of violence swept through many towns and cities, with at least a thousand people killed by the end of December. The culmination came in early January 1993, when riots in Bombay left at least two hundred dead, many hundreds injured, and hundreds of homes and businesses destroyed. The common explanation for such outbreaks is that they are communal riots, the product of Hindu-Muslim hatred, in this case triggered by the rage of Muslims at the destruction of the mosque. In fact, most of the people killed were Muslims, their property suffered the most damage, and it was Muslims who crowded the train stations trying to flee from what they saw as a planned attack against them in the city's immense slums. It was believed, at least by many journalists, that not Muslim outrage but planned attacks, fueled by the anti-Muslim, pro-Hindu ideology of the RSS, acquiesced in by political authorities and actively promoted by the police, were behind the rioting. "It is a pogrom of Muslims, it is a nightmare," said Alyque Padamsee, a well-known Muslim actor in Bombay.[94] The central government gave credence to this belief when they banned the RSS and its related organizations, including the VHP and the Barang Dal, and arresting Advani and other BJP leaders. The Jama'at-i-Islami, usually identified as the voice of Islamic fundamentalism, was also banned. In addition, the BJP governments of the three states in which it ruled were dismissed by the central government.

"Banning" of organizations, like so much else in the Indian legal system, is an inheritance from British administrative practice. Devised to control groups regarded as a threat to law and order, the ban means that a group can no longer hold meetings, publish, or distribute its literature, collect money, or have bank accounts, and often its prominent leaders are arrested. The most famous incident of banning before 1947 was at the time of the Quit India movement in 1942, and it is likely the leaders of the RSS were aware of the parallels as the Babri Masjid crisis reached its climax. In 1942 the Congress had been deeply divided over what course of action to pursue, ranging from those who were sympathetic to the British war aims against the fascists to those who saw the weakness of the British as India's opportunity. Gandhi was aware that the British would take strong measures to prevent disruption of the war effort at a time when their power had been greatly eroded by the Germans and the Japanese, but he was also aware that a radical action such as beginning a movement aimed at forcing the British to leave India, however little chance it might have of success, would unify the Congress. The result was the decision to launch the Quit India movement, and the British did indeed take swift action. The Indian National Congress was banned and all its prominent leaders were jailed, including Nehru and Gandhi. But while the banning and the arrests gave the British control, two other results followed. One was widespread sympathy for the nationalist cause throughout India, as well as in the United States and Great Britain. The second was that, with the moderate leaders in jail, power passed to others who, freed from the moderation of the leadership, could harass the British in a multitude of uncoordinated attacks.

Whether it was deliberate or not, something of this 1942 model can be seen in RSS activities in the period before and after the events at Ayodhya. While there seems to have been agreement within the organization that the mosque must come down and a temple replace it, some members of the RSS leadership wanted to postpone the date of demolition because of the Supreme Court order. Kar sevaks were detailed to prevent an attack on the mosque, and H. V. Seshadri, the general secretary of the RSS, and other leaders, after the demolition had begun, appealed to the kar sevaks to stop. But, Seshadri said afterward, they had misjudged the passion burning in the hearts of the kar sevaks. Uma Bharati, the fiery orator who had won many to the cause, said she and others had made careful plans to prevent the demolition that day, but that she had forgotten "God too plans things and what ultimately happened was His will."[95]

As for the ban on the RSS, the government's action prevented the leaders from enforcing discipline among their followers. The decision was taken in a panic, Vajpayee declared, and the government would pay for it, for "if nationalist and patriotic organizations like the RSS, imbued with a sense of service are stifled, then the situation will worsen. The government will be responsible." More bluntly, another RSS spokesman pointed out that the ban on the RSS and the arrest of its top leaders would have little effect, because it is "a huge family supported by the Hindu society which will not take this stupid onslaught lying down." The leaders had time enough to draw up contingency plans, and these will be carried out, he argued, by thirty-five thousand branches of the RSS, with their two and a half million dedicated members. In addition, there are all the members of the family of organizations with their RSS-trained cadre of leaders: the VHP; the Bajrang Dal; the labor union, the Bharatiya Mazdoor Sangh, with its three hundred thousand members; and, of course, the BJP. Beyond members of those organizations, H. V. Seshadri appealed to all patriotic Indians "to come forward in this hour of trial to uphold the causes of Hindutva and democratic values of life."[96]

In the turmoil and violence of December 1992 and January 1993, many opponents of the RSS compared its tactics and its agenda to that of the Nazis in Germany in the 1930s. Rejecting this comparison as the product of the thinking of an English-speaking, denationalized elite, some RSS members preferred a comparison with the early Christians in their struggle with the Roman Empire. Whether or not their confidence in victory over the secular, neutral state is misplaced, one can conclude with a fair degree of certainty that they have put their vision of a Hindu society on the national agenda and it will not be easily removed.

Acknowledgments

I gratefully acknowledge the assistance given me during a visit to India in January–February 1991 by Walter Andersen. Dozens of others, during this period and through the years, have discussed the work of the RSS with me. The sources used in this chapter are, whenever possible, writings by recognized spokesmen for the RSS and discussions with people who readily acknowledge their adherence to its teachings or who have been members of the shakhas. For a variety of reasons, many of them do not wish to be identified.

Notes

1. *RSS: Spearheading National Renaissance* (Bangalore: Prakashan Vibhag, 1985), p. 5.

2. Barbara Crossette, *New York Times,* 8 May 1991.

3. S. Radhakrishnan, *Eastern Religions and Western Thought* (New York: Oxford University Press, 1960), pp. 20–22, 283–90.

4. *RSS: Spearheading National Renaissance,* p. 5.

5. D. R. Goyal, *Rashtriya Swayamsewak Sangh* (New Delhi: Radha Krishna, 1979), p. 195.

6. Translation of Hindi original, ibid., p. 206.

7. Nana Deshmukh, *RSS: Victim of Slander* (New Delhi: Vision Books, 1979), p. 12.

8. Jawaharlal Nehru to M. S. Golwalkar, 10 November 1948, in *Justice on Trial: A Collection of the Historic Letters between Shri Guruji and the Government* (Bangalore: Prakashan Vibhag, 1969), p. 16.

9. *Balasaheb Deoras Answers Questions* (Bangalaore: Sahitya Sindhu, 1984), pp. 1–4.

10. These ideas are found in Vinayak Damodar Savarkar, *Hindutva: Who Is a Hindu?* (Bombay: Veer Savarkar Prakashan, 1969); and idem, *Hindu Rashtra Darshan* (Bombay: Veer Savarkar Prakashan, 1984).

11. Walter Andersen and Sridhar D. Damle, *Brotherhood in Saffron* (Boulder, Colo.: Westview, 1987), p. 2.

12. Quoted in H. V. Seshadri, ed., *Dr. Hedgewar, The Epoch Maker* (Bangalore: Sahitya Sindu, 1981), p. v.

13. Andersen and Damle, *Brotherhood in Saffron,* p. 212. Deshmukh, in *RSS: Victim of Slander* gives what appears to be a reliable account, confirmed by personal interviews at the time, of RSS activities at home and abroad during this period. Conversations in New York with former members of RSS youth groups suggest that considerable support came from the United States, but no reliable figures are available.

14. Dina Nath Mishra, *RSS: Myth and Reality* (New Delhi: Vikas, 1980), p. 73.

15. M. S. Golwalkar, *Bunch of Thoughts* (Bangalore: Jagarana Prakashan, 1980), pp. 515, 59, 516.

16. Ibid., p. 514.

17. Quoted in ibid., p. 177.

18. *RSS: Spearheading National Renaissance,* p. 7.

19. A somewhat different version, placed in 1901, is given in Seshadri, *Dr. Hedgewar, The Epoch Maker,* p. 6. Seshadri is one of the leading ideologues of the RSS.

20. *RSS: Spearheading National Renaissance,* p. 8.

21. Golwalkar, *Bunch of Thoughts,* p. 182.

22. Ibid., p. 511.

23. Eric C. Sharpe, "Study of Religion: Methodological Issues," in *The Encyclopedia of Religion* (New York: Macmillan, 1987), vol. 14, p. 87.

24. An English translation of the original Hindi version is found in Mishra, *RSS: Myth and Reality,* pp. 207–19. M. S. Golwalkar, the then leader, commented somewhat enigmatically: "The Government of India wanted us to put down our constitution in writing. We have done so. People might call it clarification if they chose." He insisted, however, that nothing had been given up of the original principles of the RSS. Quoted in *Justice on Trial,* p. 102.

25. Seshadri, *Dr. Hedgewar,* pp. 112–13.

26. Article 17, RSS Constitution, as in Mishra, *RSS: Myth and Reality,* p. 214.

27. Mishra, *RSS: Myth and Reality*, p. 63.

28. Ibid.

29. Golwalkar, *Bunch of Thoughts*, pp. 511–12.

30. Ibid., p. 675.

31. Andree F. Sjoberg, "The Dravidian Contribution to the Development of Civilization," in *Comparative Civilizations Review*, no. 23 (Fall 1990): 64–65.

32. S. Gurumurthy, *Dr. Hedgewar: His Life and Mission* (Madras: Vigil, 1988), p. 4.

33. D. R. Goyal, *Rashtriya Swayamsewak Sangh*, p. 63.

34. H. V. Seshadri, *Hindu Renaissance under Way* (Bangalore: Jagarana Prakashana, 1984), p. 42.

35. Brian K. Smith, "Defining Hinduism" (Paper, 1990); and Robert Frykenberg, "The Emergence of Modern 'Hinduism' as a Concept and as an Institution," in Gunther Sontheimer and Hermann Kulke, eds., *Hinduism Reconsidered* (New Delhi: Manohar, 1989), pp. 29–49.

36. S. N. Banerjee, *A Nation in Making* (Bombay: Oxford University Press, 1963).

37. H. V. Seshadri, comp. and ed., *RSS: A Vision in Action* (Bangalore: Jagarana Prakashana, 1988), p. 11.

38. Golwalkar, *Bunch of Thoughts*, pp. 73–74.

39. Daniel Gold, "Organized Hinduism: From Vedic Truth to Hindu Nation," in Martin E. Marty and R. Scott Appleby, eds., *Fundamentalisms Observed* (Chicago: University of Chicago Press, 1991), pp. 531–93.

40. Hindi text in Goyal, *Rashtriya Swayamsewak Sangh*, p. 200.

41. M. S. Golwalkar, *We or Our Nation Defined* (Nagpur: M. N. Kale, 1947). This pamphlet was based on a longer work of Hindu nationalism, *Rashtra Mimansa*, by G. D. Savarkar, the brother of V. D. Savarkar, whose discussion of Hindu culture in *Hindutva: Who is Hindu?* greatly influenced the formulation of RSS thought.

42. Golwalkar, *Our Nation Defined*, pp. 23–34.

43. Ibid., p. 28.

44. Ibid., p. 27.

45. Golwalkar, *Bunch of Thoughts*, p. 148.

46. Sushil Srivastava, *The Disputed Mosque: A Historical Inquiry* (New Delhi: Vistaar, 1991), summarizes the history of the controversy. An account of the Vishva Hindu Parishad is given by Peter van der Veer in "Hindi Nationalism and the Discourse of Modernity: The Vishva Hindu Parishad," chap. 23 of this volume. An analysis of its cultural significance is found in Sumanata Banerjee, "'Hindutva'—Ideology and Social Psychology," *Economic and Political Weekly*, 19 January 1991, pp. 97–101.

47. *Hindu Temples: What Happened to Them* (New Delhi: Voice of India, 1990).

48. Arun Shourie, "Hideaway Communalism," in *Hindu Temples*, p. 10.

49. Seshadri, *RSS: A Vision in Action*, p. 3.

50. For statements of this kind, see H. V. Seshadri, *Warning of Meenakshipuram* (Bangalore: Jagarana Prakashana, 1981), but they were made very frequently in interviews and in conversation in 1991.

51. Goyal, *Rashtriya Swayamsewak Sangh*, p. 151.

52. Evidence before Jamshedpur Riot Inquiry Commission, quoted in *RSS—The Guilty: Jamshedpur Riot Commission Findings* (New Delhi: Communist Party of India, 1981), p. 6.

53. Ibid., pp. 8–9.

54. K. L. Mahendra, *Defeat the RSS Fascist Designs* (New Delhi: Communist Party of India, 1973), pp. 75–79.

55. M. A. Venkata Rao, "Introduction," in Golwalkar, *Bunch of Thoughts*, p. xxxvii.

56. Deshmukh, *RSS: Victim of Slander*, p. 12

57. *Report of the Christian Missionary Activities Enquiry Committee, Madhya Pradesh* (Brindavan: Baba Madhavdas, n.d.), p. 79.

58. Seshadri, *Warning of Meenakshipuram*, p. 1.

59. Deshmukh, *RSS: Victim of Slander*, p. 12.

60. Rao, "Introduction," p. xxxiii.

61. Robert Frykenberg, "Accounting for Fundamentalisms in South Asia," chap. 21 in this volume.

62. Seshadri, *RSS: A Vision in Action,* p. 1.

63. Ibid., pp. 321–26.

64. Ibid., pp. 169, 295.

65. Gold, "Organized Hinduisms."

66. See n. 10.

67. J. A. Curran, *Militant Hinduism in Indian Politics* (New York: Institute of Political Relations, 1951), p. 64.

68. These figures are based on the reports of the Elections Commission of India.

69. See n. 46.

70. Seshadri, *RSS: A Vision in Action,* pp. 74–75.

71. Mushirul Hasan, *Nationalism and Communal Politics in India, 1885–1930* (New Delhi: Manohar, 1991), pp. 217–18.

72. Golwalkar, *Bunch of Thoughts,* p. 648.

73. *RSS Resolves: Full Text of Resolutions from 1950 to 1983* (Bangalore: Prakashan Vibhag, 1983), pp. 4–5.

74. Golwalkar, *Bunch of Thoughts,* p. 650, and Deendayal Upadhyaya, *Political Diary* (Bombay: Jaico, 1968), p. 154.

75. Andersen and Damle, *Brotherhood in Saffron,* p. 148, n. 31.

76. Seshadri, *RSS: A Vision in Action,* pp. 156–57.

77. Ibid., p. 250.

78. Ibid, pp. 25–29.

79. D. B. Thengadi, *Focus on the Socio-Economic Problems* (New Delhi: Suruchi Sahitya, 1972).

80. Seshadri, *RSS: A Vision in Action,* p. 265.

81. Vishwanathan Venkatachalam and Rajiv K. Singh, *The Political, Economic, and Labor Climate in India* (Philadelphia: Wharton School Industrial Research Unit, 1982), p. 84.

82. "Preface," in *Rashtra Sevika Samiti: An Organisation of Hindu Women* (Nagpur: Sevika Prakashan, n.d.). I am grateful to Paula Bacchetta of the Sorbonne for information about the Samiti.

83. Ibid., p. 13.

84. Ibid., p. 4.

85. Pervez Hoodbhoy, "Islamic Science" (Paper, Quaid-i-Azam University, 1991).

86. K. R. Malkani, *The RSS Story* (New Delhi: Impex India, 1980), p. 197.

87. Mishra, *RSS: Myth and Reality,* p. 100, commenting on the RSS constitution.

88. Quoted in Goyal, *Rashtra Swayamsewak Sangh,* p. 157.

89. Paul Brass, *The Politics of India since Independence,* in *The New Cambridge History of India* series (Cambridge: Cambridge Univesity Press, 1990), p. 15.

90. This postscript on events in India in December 1992 and January 1993 is based on reports in Indian newspapers and journals and private communications from Indian and foreign observers.

91. Reported in *India Today,* 15 January 1993, p. 14.

92. *Organiser* (New Delhi), 20 December 1992.

93. *India Today,* 31 December 1992, p. 25.

94. *International Herald Tribune,* 16 January 1993.

95. *Organiser,* 20 December 1992.

96. Ibid.

Hindu Nationalism and the Discourse of Modernity: The Vishva Hindu Parishad

Peter van der Veer

In 1983 India witnessed an interesting mass-scale ritual intended to promote Hindu nationalism. Several processions traversed the country in what was called Ekatmatayajna, a procession for national unity, which reached, according to the organizers' own estimate, some sixty million people. In 1984 this was followed up by the Ramjanmabhumi-muktiyajna, a procession to liberate the birthplace of Lord Rama. This ritual action, which still continues in 1992, aims at removing the Muslim mosque from the site alleged to be the birthplace of the god Rama. This cause has developed into one of the hottest issues in Indian politics over the last five years. Hundreds of people have died in riots connected to these processions. A major political party has very successfully embraced the issue of Rama's birthplace in its electoral campaign, and in 1990, the Indian government fell over it. In this chapter I describe the organizational structure and ideology of the Vishva Hindu Parishad or World Hindu Council which has organized these mass cultural performances. Attention is given to the dynamics of ritual/political action in the movement, since the VHP achieves through them an appeal which goes beyond that of its official doctrine.

The Vishva Hindu Parishad (VHP) was founded in Bombay on an auspicious day, the birthday of Lord Krishna, 29 August 1964. One hundred and fifty religious leaders were invited to Sandeepany Sadhanalaya, the center of a Hindu missionary movement headed by Swami Chinmayanand. The host had been instrumental in organizing the conference and became its president. Shivram Shankar Apte, a worker for the Rashtriya Swayamsevak Sangh (RSS) or National Volunteer Corps,[1] was elected its general secretary. In the meeting it was decided that the organization would have the following objectives:

(1) To take steps to arouse consciousness, to consolidate and strengthen the Hindu Society. (2) To protect, develop and spread the Hindu values of

Some ideas in this essay are further developed in my book *Religious Nationalism: Hindus and Muslims in India,* published by the University of California Press.

life—ethical and spiritual. (3) To establish and reinforce contacts with and help all Hindus living abroad. (4) To welcome back all who had gone out of the Hindu fold and to rehabilitate them as part and parcel of the Universal Hindu Society. (5) To render social services to humanity at large. It has initiated Welfare Projects for the 170 million down trodden brethren, who have been suffering for centuries. These projects include schools, hospitals, libraries etc. (6) Vishva Hindu Parishad, the World Organization of six hundred million at present residing in 80 countries, aspire [*sic*] to revitalize the eternal Hindu Society by rearranging the code of conduct of our age old Dharma to meet the needs of the changed times. (7) To eradicate the concept of untouchability from the Hindu Society.[2]

The conference also decided to organize a World Hindu Convention on the occasion of the Kumbh Mela festival, 22 January 1966, in Allahabad. Kumbh and Magh Melas are important bathing festivals held at regular intervals in holy places. They are visited by millions of Hindus and provide a crucial occasion for the laity to meet monk-mendicants (*sadhus*). A second World Hindu Conference was held in 1979, also in Allahabad, with the Dalai Lama as its chief guest. It is hard to know from the existing documentation what kind of decisions were taken at these conferences, but one may infer that it was there the VHP decided to start work both in tribal areas and among overseas Hindus.

It is important to note here that Hinduism does not know any overarching church-like organization. It is rather a field of related religious discourses and practices, organized by a great number of diverse types of religious specialists. An important form of organization in Hinduism is the religious community, whose core is a group of religious specialists—often celibate monks (*sadhus*)—who act as "spiritual" leaders (gurus) for a community of lay followers. The main division between these religious communities is between the Vaishnavas, who have taken the god Vishnu—with his main incarnations, Rama and Krishna—as their "chosen deity," and the Shaivas, who have taken the god Shiva as their "chosen deity." The Shaiva monks appear to be the best organized under a number of regional leaders, called Shankaracharyas. Even here, however, these leaders have only limited authority over the Hindu community. Since the relation between lay devotee and guru depends on personal choice, one can understand the fragmented nature of this kind of organization. Moreover, one has to appreciate that various gurus within one region compete with each other for support from the laity. This competition sometimes occurs not only between individual leaders, but also between larger units of organization, such as ascetic orders. Those leaders able to gain large followings through this competition are considered "big men" with considerable power and authority. The main feat of the VHP is that it has brought a great number of the main religious leaders (gurus) under the banner of Hindu nationalism.

A meeting of important religious leaders on 20 June 1982 in Delhi gave the VHP organization its final shape. It was to have two levels: "an assembly of religion" (*dharmsansad*) as a central body, and on the state level, "advisory committees" (*marg-*

darshak mandal) whose members were leaders of the various participating religious communities. While the VHP prefers being not too specific about the way it operates, we can infer from data I have gathered that a relatively small number of high-powered industrialists—such as Jaidayal Dalmia, high officials such as justices of regional High Courts, aristocrats like VHP President Maharana Bhagwat Singh Mewar, and high office-bearers of the RSS—work together with influential gurus in a kind of informal management structure that makes the main policy decisions. The RSS always supplies the general secretary, the main executive officer in the VHP. For the rest, the VHP is organizationally independent of the RSS.

It has recently been argued that the VHP was founded on the initiative of the leader of the RSS, M. S. Golwalkar, to give RSS an opportunity to work with leaders of Hindu religious movements.[3] There is probably a good deal of truth in this statement. As we see later in this chapter, there is no doubt the RSS was actively involved in organizing the political rituals staged by the VHP in the 1980s. However, it is important for understanding the success of the VHP to see the crucial differences between the RSS and the VHP. To see the VHP as simply an instrument of the RSS, part of the so-called RSS family of organizations, as is routinely done in India, is to underestimate the extent to which the VHP goes beyond the RSS in its articulation of what I call "modern Hinduism."

The RSS focuses on the physical culture of young men in a way reminiscent of Baden-Powell's Boy Scouts or the fascist youth groups of pre-war Germany and Italy. Such features as military discipline and physical exercise feed on the well-established culture of wrestling among young men in North India. This culture has strong religious roots in asceticism and celebrates masculinity and age-grade bonding. Its discourse connects the healthy body with the healthy nation. Related to its disciplinary aspect is the members' unquestioning attitude toward their leader, making the RSS one of the best functioning organizations in India. Religious ritual and doctrine are absolutely minimal.

The VHP, on the other hand, is an organization in which religious leaders play a major role. These leaders are united in their wish to promote a certain kind of "spiritual" Hinduism through ritual propaganda, but, otherwise, each has his own followers and agenda. Because Hinduism does not have a central authority or a churchlike organization, it is almost miraculous to see the extent to which the VHP is able to keep all these independent leaders on one platform, without major conflicts and breakups.[4] This unity is due to the extent the discourse of Modern Hinduism has come to be shared by these leaders and the extent to which the VHP has been able to focus on issues with great unifying potential. These differences in organizational structure and discursive style between RSS and VHP are important and explain, at least partly, the greater success of the VHP in comparison to the RSS.

Still it is difficult to assess the VHP's following among the general population, although the following is probably as broad as that of the constituent religious communities. These communities have emerged from a wide cross-section of the urbanized middle class and the middle peasants, with the notable exclusion of tribals and untouchables. It is to them that the VHP tries to reach out. In the 1970s the VHP focused on missionary work in tribal areas and on the organization of Hindus overseas. In 1982 it claimed to have 302 district units under which there were 2,700 branches, and outside of India, to have 3,000 branches in twenty-three countries. Its total membership at that point was 118,522, with 233 full-time workers;[5] no doubt the organization has grown considerably in the decade since then. Only in the 1980s did it gain prominence on the Indian political scene by the creative use of political ritual on a grand scale.

Before turning to the two political rituals that boosted the VHP into prominence in the 1980s, we must examine the VHP's ideology. In short, the VHP strives to create a modern Hinduism as the national religion of India, and in this way nationalism embraces religion as the defining characteristic of the nation. The VHP is certainly not an "antimodernist" movement. In fact if nationalism is the discourse of modernity, the VHP's project is fundamentally modernist. It articulates certain long-term transformations in Hindu discourse and practice which largely feed on Orientalist understandings of India and are thus deeply implicated in Western conceptions of modernity. Rather than rejecting capitalist development, science, and technology, the VHP attempts to nationalize these signs of modernity. What it does reject is the secular state, but its argument is based on the modern democratic principle of majority rule.[6] It argues that the "majority community" should rule the country, while the "minority communities," such as Muslims and Christians, should accept that rule as a political reality.

If we take fundamentalism as antimodern, as Bruce Lawrence does in his book *Defenders of God*, we lose sight of the fact that many fundamentalist movements are not only implicated in modernity as a material structure but that, as a countertext, fundamentalisms may share some basic discursive premises with the modernist text.[7] This is certainly the case with the VHP. What we might consider are the ways in which indigenous discursive traditions are transformed through their encounter with colonizing discourses from the West.

Modern Hinduism, as defined by the VHP, is the religion of the Indian nation. The term "Hindu" embraces all people who believe in, respect, or follow the eternal values of life—ethical and spiritual—that have evolved in Bharat (India). This is remarkably similar to Robert Frykenberg's definition of Hinduism as "nativism," and it shows the collusion of the VHP's definition of Hinduism and the scholarly discourse which portrays Hinduism as a civilization rather than as a religion.[8] This very broad definition transcends internal differences of a doctrinal, organizational, or regional nature. While it might appear that Indian Islam and Christianity could also be included in such a definition, one of the VHP's key themes holds that Hindu society is threatened by Islam and Christianity, which are forces of disintegration. Hindu civilization is seen as originating from the Indian soil, while Islam and Christianity are "foreign" despite their long presence in India. Muslims and Christians can thus redeem themselves when they realize that they are in fact converted Hindus and return to the Hindu fold.

A recurring theme in VHP ideology is Hindu weakness. Hindu society has to be defended against "external" weakness, caused by conversions to "foreign" religion, and against its "internal" weakness caused by differences and conflicts among Hindus. Unity is the remedy of weakness, and unity is accomplished through the rhetoric of "nativism." However, this is not to exclude nonresident Indians. On the contrary. At the founding session of the VHP there were delegates from Nairobi and Trinidad, and in 1992 the VHP was probably the strongest transnational movement among Hindus all over the world. Thus there is an interesting interplay of "foreignness" and "nativeness," of "nationalism" and "transnationalism" in the VHP which seems germane to many of the movements we are discussing in this project under the rubric of fundamentalism. The marginality felt by migrants to other parts of the world makes them into important agents of innovation at home. The "foreign" experience of innovators like the Hindu leader Vivekananda or the Sri Lankan Buddhist leader Dharmapala thus has a kind of paradigmatic value for the millions of South Asians who, by reconstructing their religion abroad, have a decisive influence on its transformation in their places of origin.

The theme of Hindu weakness derives from nineteenth-century discourse on "foreign rule." The VHP perpetuates an argument of decline from a golden age in which a just society based on Hindu dharma (moral law) gave way to a long period of barbaric oppression, first by Muslim rulers (from 1200) and then by the British (from 1800). While this argument is related to a more common Hindu belief that we live in the worst of times, *kali-yuga,* there is a strong activist element here which demands that this decline be reversed and Hindu society redeemed. One way of doing this is through religious reform.

This theme has been most eloquently elaborated by the Arya Samaj, a reformist movement that originated in the nineteenth century and focused on a return to the ancient religious standards of the Vedas, which could be retrieved through reconstruction of texts. The very "foreignness" of this discourse, with its emphasis on textual purity rather than on the purity of its interpreters and its repudiation of practices such as image worship, greatly limited the appeal of the Arya Samaj. Due to its Western fundamentalist-style scripturalism the Arya Samaj remained a marginal movement rather than the popular Hindu answer to modern challenges. Therefore I argue that its major importance is not found in its message or appeal, but in its impact on Hindu discourse in general. For example, the Arya Samaj shared with its "orthodox" detractors the notion of the sacredness of Mother Cow. By organizing cow protection societies it shaped the defense of Hinduism against British and Muslim "butchers." Even more importantly, it set a model for the communication of Hindu nationalism. The cow protection movement, though initiated by Arya Samaj reformists, had nothing to do with reform, but much to do with religious nationalism. The Arya Samaj thus demonstrated the ability of organized activism to stop Hindu weakness and decline.

This message was received by those who strongly opposed reformism. While reformism is historically at the roots of Hindu nationalism, it is not synonymous with it. There is certainly scope for activism without reform, and this is explored and exploited by the VHP, a salient feature of which is its propagation of Hindu unity by obliterating differences in doctrine and practice. This strategy is indeed antithetical to the one taken by reformism.[9]

The VHP is therefore not a scripturalist movement. It avoids disputes on "fundamental scriptures," since its aim is to unite Reformism and "orthodoxy" (sometimes called Sanatana Dharma) in all its manifold forms. The VHP even wants to include Jainism, Buddhism, and Sikhism by defining them as part of an all-embracing Hindu civilization in which "Hindu" refers to the sacred soil from which all these religions spring. This strategy is often presented as part of the "tolerance" that characterizes Hinduism in the eyes of both Hindus and outsiders.

Yet this characterization has a specific orientalist history. "Religious tolerance" as an ideal in the West derives from an abstraction and universalization of religion which is part of the Western discourse of "modernity." The move in seventeenth-century Europe to produce a universal definition of natural religion as existing in all societies shows a fragmentation of the unity and authority of the Roman Catholic Church, but also the rise of new discourses and practices connected to modern nation-states.[10] A growing emphasis on religious tolerance as a positive value is thus related to the marginalization of religious institutions in Europe. At the same time it replaces the violence between religious groups with the violence between nation-states. This discourse is brought to bear on the Muslim and Hindu populations incorporated in the modern world-system. Muslims, the old rivals of the Christian West, are labeled "fanatics" and "bigoted," while Hindus are seen in a more positive light as "tolerant." At the same time, this labeling explains why Muslims have ruled Hindu India and why Hindus have to be "protected" by the British. In short, I contend that the attribution of "tolerance" to Hinduism is a product of a specific orientalist history of ideas. As such, it has also come to dominate Hindu discourse on Hinduism to the extent that tolerance is now one of the most important characteristics of Hinduism, despite the fact that, as a doctrinal notion, it had no specific place in Hindu discursive traditions.[11]

As observed by the German Indologist Paul Hacker, "tolerance" is a poor translation for what is in fact Hindu "inclusivism," a form of hierarchical relativism.[12] There is the Hindu idea—often repeated by the VHP—that there are many paths leading to God as well as many gods. An important underlying conception here is "hierarchy." The many gods and paths are manifestations of the One who is formless. Some of these manifestations are higher than others. Moreover, they perform different functions in a hierarchical order. The general idea seems to be that other paths do not have to be denied as heretical, but that they are inferior and thus cater to inferior beings. This relation between the devotee and his chosen god is thus one of co-substantiality. This might be one of the reasons Hindus visit Muslim shrines for rituals of healing, since Muslim saints are said to control the powers of darkness. At least in some contexts this attribution associates Muslims with those very powers. Some Muslim practices are thus included in a Hindu cosmological framework, but given an inferior position. At the same time this inferiority precludes Muslim participation in practices at higher Brahmanical temples. The point is that modern Hindu thinkers have combined hierarchical relativism with orientalist discourse on "tolerance" to include all religions in the Vedanta, the spiritual "essence" of Hinduism in its philosophical form, as in Sarvepalli Radhakrishnan's famous formula: "The Vedanta is not a religion, but religion itself in its most universal and deepest significance."[13]

Much of what I have just said about "tolerance" could also be applied to a concept such as Gandhi's "nonviolence." It is sometimes difficult for Westerners to grasp violence perpetuated by Hindu monks who speak and act militantly, since there is the persistent notion of "nonviolent" otherworldliness attributed to Hindu "spirituality." Again, while nonviolence had a place in Hindu discursive traditions as a rejection of the violence of animal sacrifice, which has resulted in vegetarianism among some groups, the idea that Hindus would always choose nonviolent means because of their religion is Gandhi's construction of Hindu spirituality. Hindu monks have a long and interesting history of warfare related to trading which continues to the present day.[14] There is considerable historical evidence of violent struggle between different Hindu religious groups as well as between Hindus and Buddhists, Hindus and Jains, and Hindus and Muslims. It is modern Hinduism that ignores these traditions in its self-presentation through the mirror of the West, while at the same time manifesting a behavior that is not nonviolent by any stretch of the imagination. The construction of tolerance as a Hindu virtue is used by the VHP not only to unite competing Hindu groups, but also to complain about the intolerance of those who do not want to be included, such as Muslims.

In my view, the VHP's ideas are directly derived from the discourse of modern, spiritual Hinduism, and the organization takes a kind of "Oriental spiritualism," which it offered as a package to Western audiences, and brings it back to India. On the level of discourse, therefore, there is little difference between VHP propaganda and the sayings of the founder of the Ramakrishna Mission, Vivekananda (1863–1902). Moreover, Vivekananda had the same audience as the VHP. The difference lies in the historical development of that audience, the modern middle class.

What is striking in the VHP is the extent to which the leadership of a modern guru like Chinmayananda, who has a middle-class following in urban India and in the United States, is accepted. As a disciple of Shivanand and a co-disciple of Chidanand, the founder of the Divine Life Society, he belongs squarely in modern Hinduism. After a period of living in the Himalayas with his second guru Tapovanam, Chinmayananda began in the 1950s to give lectures which he called "sacrifices of learning" (*jnanayajna*, no pun intended on the Sanskrit word). At that time he was opposed by the "orthodox" because of his position against caste and gender differentiation in spiritual education. Gradually he became a well-known guru, and today his schedule includes annual stops in India, Malaysia, Africa, and summer camps in the United States. His movement is similar to the Ramakrishna Mission, and one can see a direct link between his teachings and those of Vivekanand.

This kind of teaching has moved from the margin to the center of "monastic" Hinduism. Even gurus with a much longer pedigree and a firm footing in established high-caste communities, like some of the Shankaracharyas, have begun to use the discourse of modern Hinduism. For example, the influential Shankaracharya of Kanchipuram in Tamil Nadu makes extensive tours throughout India to express the need for renewal of the Hindu spirit, which he feels is threatened from all sides.[15] He is involved in the "uplift" of Untouchables and in the construction of Hindu mission hospitals, social matters of no concern at all to his immediate predecessor. Moreover, all modern religious leaders seem to follow Chinmayananda's lead in that they are interested in the Indians overseas. All this suggests that the flow of daily experience of an important constituency in India, the middle class, has caught up with its Western counterparts and that, as such, modern Hinduism caters to similar needs. This is reflected in VHP discourse on "individual growth," "social concerns," and religion as "a code of conduct for every man to make life a success," which sounds like the credo of a success-oriented Western middle class. If there is a "mainstream" constituency for the VHP's discourse on spiritual Hinduism as India's "national identity," it is the middle class, together with those who aspire to its status.

However, the attempt to "mainstream" India is not without its problems and contradictions. Inclusion and exclusion are aspects of the historical processes of identity formation which have to be understood in terms of their internal dynamics as well as their changing context. The Sikhs are an interesting case in point. Two of their important leaders in the early 1960s, Master Tara Singh and Ghyani Bhupendra Singh (president of the Shiromani Akali Dal), were among the founders of the VHP. Tara Singh addressed the 1964 conference in Bombay as follows: "I am confident that once the Hindus and Sikhs embrace each other, it will send a new current of revitalization all over the country and the movement shall flood the hearts of even those who live abroad."[16] This was not exactly what happened in the 1980s. Clearly, separatism has a greater importance on the Sikh agenda today than does Hindu unity.

Another important example of the politics of inclusion rather than tolerance of difference is the VHP's program to bring tribals and untouchables within the Hindu fold. The VHP has worked continuously to bring these groups within the Hindu nation, since their marginality makes them in the VHP view easy victims of "foreign" conversion by Christian and Muslim missions. These communities are beyond the pale in the Hindu view, but the mere fact that they live on "Hindu" territory means, in the logic of nationalism, that they should be part of the Hindu nation.

The VHP rhetoric on this point is simultaneously one of Gandhian development ideology (the so-called uplift of the tribals) and battle against competing missionary efforts. On the one hand VHP discourse feeds on Gandhian concepts of social reform in its attacks on the "evils of caste society." On the other hand, the missionary activities of the VHP among tribals can be interpreted as a continuation of the expansion of Hindu monastic groups in frontier areas. This long-term expansion has been reframed in terms of social welfare and nation building. The VHP sees conversion to Christianity in the northeastern parts of India as the cause of the separatist movements in those areas.[17] Similarly, VHP activities among untouchables gained an enormous boost in late 1982 after an untouchable subcaste in Tamil Nadu was converted to Islam. In the VHP rhetoric, "petro-dollars" became the master-trope not only to make Muslim missionary efforts suspect, but to demonstrate that the Hindu nation was threatened by world Islam. The Meenakshipuram conversions have been the most publicized issue in the VHP's "defense of Hinduism," which gained momentum with the Procession for Unity in 1983 and continued with the movement for liberating Hindu sites in 1984.

In short, VHP tries to formulate a modern Hinduism that can serve as the basis of a Hindu nation. This goal brings it into conflict with the self-proclaimed secularism of the Indian state and with Muslims and Christians who cannot be included in its idea of the nation.

Nationalist Ritual in Modern Hinduism

Modern Hinduism cannot be made into the religion of the Indian nation through the spread of pamphlets by VHP workers. In fact, I argue, the VHP would have remained a fringe organization if it had not captured worldwide attention by staging mass performances of political ritual. The homogenization of religious identity in nationalism requires symbolic action which constructs and confirms the need for unity against the threatening Muslim Other. In this way the VHP develops a tradition in Hindu nationalism of which the several cow protection movements in the nineteenth and twentieth centuries are the best examples.

The first successful ritual of Hindu nationalism, organized by the VHP, was the Sacrifice for Unity (Ekatmatayajna) of November and December 1983, in which three large processions (*yatra*) traversed India.[18] One went from Hardwar to Kanyakumari, the second from Gangasagar to Somnath, and the third from Kathmandu (Nepal) to Rameshwaram, inaugurated by the king of Nepal. At least forty-seven smaller processions (*upayatra*) of five days traversed other parts of the country and connected at appointed places with one of the three large processions. The routes taken by the processions were well-known pilgrimage routes connecting major religious centers, suggesting a geographical unity of India (Bharatvarsha) as a sacred area (*kshetra*) of Hindus.

In this event, pilgrimage was effectively transformed into a ritual of national integration. Processions of temple-chariots (*rathas*) are an important part of temple festivals in India. An image of the god is taken for a ride in his domain, confirming his territorial sovereignty and extending his blessings. The processions of the VHP made use of two "chariots," rathas in the modern form of new trucks, and so the symbolism of the temple-chariot was perpetuated, as was the militant symbolism of the "war-chariot" of Arjuna in the Bhagavad Gita.[19]

On one of the two chariots of the VHP an image of Bharat Mata, Mother India, was carried. The Mother Goddess is worshiped in many forms in India, some of which are new. Santoshi Mata, Satisfying Mother, for example, conquered India in the 1960s under the influence of a very successful movie. The political use of mother symbolism is also nothing new in India. In Andhra Pradesh the regional party Telugu Desam has introduced a Telugu Mother Goddess, and the late prime minister Mrs. Indira Gandhi tried to use goddess symbolism for her own glorification. The connection between worship of the Mother Goddess and Mother India has been most forcefully made in Bengal, where the cult of the goddess is exceptionally strong. The Indian National Congress has chosen "Bande Mataram" ("Hail Mother"), a poem by nineteenth-century Bengali nationalist Bankim Chandra Chatterjee, as the national anthem, despite the strong Hindu emphasis of this poem. Creation of an image representing Bharat Mata is the VHP's contribution to this nationalist tradition. The other chariot contained an enormous waterpot (*kalasha*) filled with water from the Ganges and a smaller waterpot filled with local sacred water. This chariot was followed by a truck which sold Ganges water in small bottles. The Ganges is seen as a deity, and her water contains the power to purify from sin and to grant salvation. All the sacred water in the rest of India is a secondary derivation of the Ganges. In this way all rivers and temple-tanks are symbolically connected with the Ganges as the unifying symbol of Hindu India. The waterpot is one of the most important objects in Hindu ritual. It symbolizes power and auspiciousness.

Thus the processions of the Sacrifice for Unity made very effective use of an existing ritual repertoire which includes the Mother Goddess, the sacredness of Ganges water, and Lord Ram; the processions transformed this repertoire to communicate the message of Hindu unity. The VHP effected this transformation by using a ritual repertoire which engages generally accepted Hindu conceptions without running into conflict with specific doctrines espoused by one of the many religious movements represented in the VHP. It was also made perfectly clear that those who did not participate in this Hindu ritual could not be seen as part of the nation. Effectively, the message was as much about Hindu unity as about the Muslim Other.

The processions gained enormous publicity and enabled the VHP to start local branches in all parts of the country, forming the basis for a VHP movement to rebuild Hindu temples allegedly demolished by Muslim rulers and replaced by mosques. In 1984 the VHP made a strategic choice by starting with a "sacrifice to liberate the birthplace of Lord Ram" (Ramjanma-bhumimuktiyajna), an ancient mosque in the North Indian pilgrimage center Ayodhya which was built in 1528 by a general of Babar, founder of the Mughal dynasty. The following details and other "historical facts" are disputed at present, with public debate in India occurring in such diverse places as university publications and newspapers.[20] According to local tradition which is followed by the VHP, the mosque was built to replace an even more ancient Hindu temple of the god Ram which had occupied the spot from the eleventh century C.E.[21] The temple commemorated the place where Ram, the god-hero of the Ramayana, had been born. After destroying the temple the general used some of its materials, such as the carved pillars, to build his mosque. After annexing of the regional realm to which Ayodhya had given his name (Awadh) in 1856, the British decided to put a railing around the mosque and to raise a platform outside on which Hindus could worship, while Muslims were allowed to continue their prayers inside. After the partition of India and Pakistan in 1947, the Indian government placed a guard outside the mosque, which was now declared out of bounds for both communities. However, on the eve of 23 December 1949 an image of Ram was placed in the mosque by a group of young Hindus who were never caught. The next day a rumor spread quickly that Lord Ram had appeared in the form of an image to claim the mosque as His temple. The ensuing riots were quelled by the army, but the image was never removed. Leaders of Hindu and Muslim groups filed suit to claim the place as theirs.

In 1984 the VHP began to demand that the lock on Ram's birthplace be opened.[22] A procession, starting in Sitamarhi (the birthplace of Sita, Ram's wife), reached Ayodhya on Saturday, 6 October 1984. It consisted of not more than a few private cars carrying monks and trucks carrying large statues of Ram and his wife Sita under a banner with the slogan "Bharat Mata ki Jay" (Hail to Mother India). The next day, speeches were given in Ayodhya by VHP leaders and local abbots. None of these activities was very impressive. When the procession moved on to the state capital Lucknow, however, it gained considerably more attention. And when it moved on from Lucknow to Delhi, where the VHP intended to stage a huge rally, it was caught in the aftermath of the assassination of Mrs. Gandhi by her Sikh bodyguards, which turned national attention away from the Ayodhya issue. Nevertheless, in the following years the VHP continued to pressure politicians, resulting in a decision by the district and session judge of Faizabad on 14 February 1986 that the disputed site should be opened immediately to the public. This decision triggered communal violence all over North India, and on 30 March 1987 in New Delhi, Muslims staged their biggest protest since independence.

Today the mosque is open to the Hindu public, but its future is still contested. The VHP demands that the mosque be demolished and a Hindu temple built in its place. The Muslim Babri Masjid Action Committee demands the opening of the mosque for prayer and removal of the image. It argues that the Babri Masjid should be regarded as an unalienable place of Islamic worship under the authority of the Waqf Board (as overseer of religious endowments), whose sanctity should be protected by the state.

After the Faizabad judge's 1986 decision, the temple-mosque issue has been taken up increasingly by Indian political parties, and it played an important role in the 1989 elections. Although even the leader of the Congress Party, Rajiv Gandhi, insisted at a rally in Faizabad/Ayodhya that he supported the VHP case, the issue was made central by the Bharatiya Janata party (BJP), a party with a long history of Hindu nationalism and direct ties with the RSS, and it gained considerably in the elections.

From this point onward—and probably as far back as 1986—the political agenda of the BJP was tied to the agenda of the VHP. We see a direct coordination of rituals, agitation, and political maneuvering by a high command made up of BJP, RSS, and VHP leaders and in fact an important overlap of functions. In 1992 Vijaye Raje Scindia was a vice-president of the BJP and a leader of the VHP; L. K. Advani and A. B. Vajpayee were leaders of the BJP, with a background in the RSS; an important leader of the RSS, Manohar Pingle, had the VHP in his portfolio. To a considerable extent the VHP leadership drew on the experience of retired members of the higher echelons of the Indian bureaucracy, such as former director-generals of police, former chief judges, former ministers, and so on.

After September 1989 the VHP engaged in the worship of "bricks of Lord Ram" (*ramshila*) in villages in North India and organized processions to bring these sacred bricks to Ayodhya for building a temple at Ram's birthplace in place of the mosque of Babar. It is estimated that some three hundred lives have been lost in connection with these "building processions." The heaviest casualties occurred in Bhagalpur in Bihar, where the Muslim population was almost wiped out. Eventually, the VHP was allowed to lay its foundation stones in a pit outside the mosque on so-called undisputed lands. Some of the stones prominently exhibited come from the United States, Canada, the Caribbean, and South Africa, as if to emphasize the transnational character of this nationalist enterprise.

In 1990 two major political developments affected the course of action regarding Ayodhya. First, the issue of Kashmir, where Muslim separatists seek to secede from India, flared up, with Muslims inflicting unprecedented violence against the Hindu population, causing many to leave that part of the country. The BJP took a strong anti-Pakistan stance toward this crisis, and in India this stance is always related to an anti-Muslim stance. Second, in September 1990, V. P. Singh's government decided to implement an earlier report of the Mandal Commission, which had suggested increasing considerably the number of reservations for members of the so-called Backward Classes in educational institutions and government service. This action resulted in widespread antireservation riots in which a number of students immolated themselves in a new form of protest.

Since the agitation around reservation imperiled the Hindu agenda of the VHP/ BJP/RSS, L. K. Advani, the leader of the BJP, began a procession from Somnath in Gujarat to Ayodhya, again a rath yatra, through ten states, with its goal the construction of the temple on 30 October 1990. This initiative met with great enthusiasm all over the country. Members of a recently established youth branch of the VHP, the Bajrang Dal, offered a cup of their blood to their leader to show their determination. All this set a kind of time bomb, which ticked with every mile taken in the direction of Ayodhya. Mulayam Singh Yadav, the chief minister of Uttar Pradesh, in which state Ayodhya is located, took a vow that he would not allow Advani to enter Ayodhya, and indeed, before 30 October, Advani was arrested. This did not prevent Advani's followers from marching to the mosque, but they were stopped by police gunfire. To appreciate Mulayam Singh Yadav's firm stance, backed by V. P. Singh's central government, one has to remember that he is the leader of an upwardly mobile Backward caste which would benefit considerably from implementation of the Mandal Report. Nevertheless, the government's action resulted in its loss of the BJP's support in Parliament and its subsequent fall on 16 November 1990.

Since 1990 the VHP has continued its agitation with a highly effective video and audio cassette campaign on the happenings in Ayodhya on 30 October. It claims that thousands have been killed by the police and that the evidence was suppressed. Martyrs have been cremated, and their bones and ashes taken in ritual pots (*asthi-kalashas*) through the country before immersion in sacred water. In Ayodhya itself a major ritual sacrifice has been sponsored by the VHP, with Vijaye Raje Scindia as the principal sacrificer.

Religious issues, such as the mosque-temple controversy, involve passionate feelings and violent action. A common fallacy is that these passions are "natural" and that the violent struggle is an explosion of pent-up feelings. Passions are certainly involved, but their "naturalness" is produced in a political process. The mosque-temple controversy did not evoke strong feelings between 1949, when the image was installed, and 1984, when the VHP started its agitations. The VHP had been instrumental in homogenizing a "national" Hinduism by transforming the mosque in Ayodhya from a local shrine into a symbol of a "threatened" Hindu majority. This is not to say that this kind of religious controversy is only a smoke screen behind which we find the "real" clash of material interests of social groups. Nor is it simply a political trick conjured by leaders for their own benefit. Such arguments overlook the importance of religious meaning and practice in the construction of identity. What we have to understand is how certain issues are being promoted as "naturally" crucial to the "self-respect" of a collectivity which is portrayed as a homogeneous whole, as if it were an "individual." If we want to penetrate the very real passions and violence evoked by the mosque-temple controversy, we must see how it is related to fundamental, orienting conceptions of the world and of personhood which are made sacrosanct. This implies that we have to analyze not only ideologies that produce these conceptions, but also the historical context in which they are produced.

The growing significance of the middle class is central to this context. Before the VHP started its campaign, Ayodhya had already been adopted in a scheme to promote indigenous tourism which included building tourist hotels and publishing tourist information available in the many travel offices throughout the country. The nature of pilgrimage has not changed into one of state-sponsored tourism, but it has become important enough that politicians have decided the state should provide for middle-class needs on pilgrimage. In 1985 the state government of Uttar Pradesh embarked on an ambitious and extremely expensive scheme to beautify the waterfront of Ayodhya's sacred river. In the middle of the stream a platform was raised which can be reached from the bank of the river, in imitation of a similar platform in the Ganges at Haridwar and called "Ram's footstep." The Faizabad judge's decision to "unlock" the mosque can clearly be interpreted as a move in the struggle for control over Hindu places of pilgrimage which are increasingly included in middle-class tourist itineraries.

A parallel development has been the success of religious stories in Indian cinema and, more recently, on Indian television. In South India movie actors have for some time acted as leading politicians and set the stage for a cinematic populism with use of religious imagery. This trend is now emerging throughout the rest of the country. Playing a saint or a god in a movie qualifies a person for saintliness or godliness on the stage of political populism, and the public has a clear penchant for the struggle between good and bad on the screen. While in principle this interest could be satisfied with nonreligious themes, the Indian entertainment industry has recently discovered the popularity of dramatized religious tales. Undoubtedly a major event in the history of Indian television was the serial dramatization of the Ramayana, starting in late January 1987. This event made a standardized version of the Ramayana known and popular among the Indian middle class. And indirectly, it enhanced the general television-viewing public's knowledge of Ayodhya as Ram's birthplace and therefore as one of the most important places of pilgrimage in Uttar Pradesh. In this way the controversy concerning the mosque "on Ram's birthplace" has become an issue loaded with affect in popular imagination.

Telecasting the Ram story also subtly changed Ram's iconography from the pose of a detached god (*shanta*) to that of an active warrior (of course for the Hindu cause).[23] The goddess Sita, Ram's wife, clearly takes a secondary place, as exemplified by the fact that the devotional greeting SitaRam or SiyaRam is no longer allowed in Ayodhya; one must now use Jay SriRam. This is not to say there is nothing militant in the Ram tradition, but that the historical move in the tradition from warrior-asceticism to sweet devotion has received an interesting twist. What we see is an adoption of militant devotionalism by a middle-class laity—an adoption supported by media images rather than traditional instruction in beliefs and practices.

Concluding Remarks

In arguing that the VHP can be considered a movement that tries to make modern Hinduism the national religion of India, we must clarify the terms "modern Hinduism," "national religion," and "India." "Modern Hinduism" does not refer to a definite set of authoritative doctrines and practices based on a body of scriptures. The term "Hinduism" as used by the VHP is ambiguous because it is used to create a "Hindu unity" rather than a "unified religion." That is, the VHP's project is primarily a nationalist rather than a scripturalist one.

Nevertheless, we have to acknowledge that religious nationalism and fundamentalism resemble each other in terms of discourse and practice. The Hinduism of the VHP is a selection of religious features from disparate traditions. The selected features are then employed in a discourse on the continuity of a national religious identity. This is a "modern" Hinduism, because, although it denies the significance of historical discontinuities, it is part of the search for the Indian nation in terms of the nationalism that has been the universally accepted discourse of modernity since the nineteenth century. Moreover, it is "modern" in the sense that it builds on Orientalist understandings of Indian religious traditions, which are themselves part of a discourse of modernity. The term "national religion" implies that the VHP tries to define national identity in terms of religion. This may sound "traditionalist" to those who equate "modern" with "secular" and "tradition" with "religion," but in fact it is only a variation within the discourse of modernity. In India "secular nationalism" is often portrayed as the enemy of "religious nationalism" (for which the derogatory term "communalism" is used). I suggest, however, that they are strands in the same search for national identity. Nationalism makes "nation" and "national history" into objects of religious worship. In that sense a "secular" nationalism is not less religious than a Hindu or Muslim one.[24] The nationalism of Nehru's Congress derived much of its rhetoric from Gandhi's construction of "Indian spirituality." As far as I can see, the main issue here is not "secularism" but Gandhi's vision of pluralism, over against the VHP's vision of a "Hindu majority."

Finally, the term "India" itself is contested, since the VHP has a vision of a "Greater India," as argued in one pamphlet: "History has witnessed vivesection [*sic*] of India from time to time and with each division part of our motherland has gone away together with number of Hindu sacred places and gems of our culture. Afghanistan was first to go, followed by Burma, Ceylon, Pakistan and Bangladesh. Yet a further division of the motherland is being silently planned by foreign powers and a situation like Lebanon is slowly developing in India."[25]

This statement by the VHP shows the extent to which nationalist politics in South Asia has international implications. This was already clear in the case of Partition, which required the breakup of British India into two nation-states, India and Pakistan, to provide a "homeland" for Indian Muslims. This demand for a separate homeland has served as a blueprint for Indian Sikhs to demand their own Khalistan. The VHP answers these separatisms with a counterdemand for the defense of the "integrity" of the Motherland, based on a mixture of colonial realities and Hindu conceptions of sacred space. It effectively establishes a link between internal tensions among Hindus and Muslims and the international relations between India, Pakistan, and Bangladesh.

Acknowledgments

This chapter was completed before the demolition of the mosque in Ayodhya on 6 December 1992. I wish to acknowledge the comments made on an earlier draft of this chapter by Arjun Appadurai, Robert Frykenberg, Philip Lutgendorf, and Lisa McKean. I thank my research assistant in India, Sanjay Joshi. Versions of this chapter were delivered at the Philadelphia Anthropological Society, Harvard University, Columbia University, and El Colegio de Mexico. I thank Ashutosh Varsney, John Hawley, and David Lorenzen for inviting me and my audience for their response.

Notes

1. For a discussion of this organization, see chapter 22 of this volume, Ainslee Embree, "The Function of the Rashtriya Swayamsevak Sangh."

2. Quoted from a VHP publication, *Message and Activities* (New Delhi, 1982).

3. Walter Anderson and S. Damle, *The Brotherhood in Saffron* (Boulder, Colo.: Westview Press, 1987), p. 133.

4. For example in May 1990 a religious leader, the Dwarka Shankaracharya, who is alleged to have ties with the Congress (I) party, started a campaign independent of the VHP because of a disagreement over astrological issues. By seeking an authoritative statement of Brahman scholars on those issues, the VHP contained the damage.

5. See *Message and Activities.*

6. See Robert E. Frykenberg, "The Concept of 'Majority' as a Devilish Force in the Politics of Modern India: A Historiographic Comment," *Journal of Commonwealth History and Comparative Politics* 25, no. 3 (1987): 267–74.

7. Bruce Lawrence, *Defenders of God* (San Francisco: Harper and Row, 1989).

8. See Robert E. Frykenberg, "The Emergence of Modern 'Hinduism' as a Concept and as an Institution: A Reappraisal with Special Reference to South India," in Gunther D. Sontheimer and Hermann Kulke, eds., *Hinduism Reconsidered* (New Delhi: Manohar, 1989), pp. 67–81.

9. For a thorough discussion of the relation between the Arya Samaj and Hindu nationalism, see Daniel Gold, "Organized Hinduisms: From Vedic Truth to Hindu Nation," in Martin E. Marty and R. Scott Appleby, eds., *Fundamentalisms Observed* (Chicago: University of Chicago Press, 1991), pp. 531–93.

10. Talal Asad, "Anthropological Conceptions of Religion: Reflections on Geertz," *Man* 18, no. 2 (1983): 237–60.

11. In an unpublished paper titled, "Cul-

tural Collusion in Ethnography: The Religious Tolerance of Hindus," Richard Burghart argues convincingly that we do not find the direct equivalent for the English term "tolerance" in Hindi/Nepali.

12. For a thorough discussion of Hacker's argument, which is found in a number of articles written between 1957 and 1977, see Wilhelm Halbfass, *India and Europe* (Albany, N.Y.: SUNY Press, 1988), pp. 403–18.

13. Quoted in Halbfass, *India and Europe*, p. 409. Radhakrishnan's distinction between various "religions" and "religion" as the unifying essence of them makes the important move to equate "religion" with Hinduism as the spirit of India. See Robert N. Minor, "Sarvepalli Radhakrishnan and Hinduism," in Robert Baird, ed., *Religion in Modern India* (Delhi: Manohar, 1989), pp. 421–55.

14. Peter van der Veer, *Gods on Earth: The Management of Religious Experience and Identity in a North Indian Pilgrimage Center*, London School of Economics Monographs on Social Anthropology, no. 59 (London: Athlone Press, 1988).

15. Mattison Mines and Vijayalakshmi Gourishankar, "Leadership and Individuality in South Asia: The Case of the South Indian Big-Man," *Journal of Asian Studies* 49, no. 4 (1991): 781.

16. *Hindu Vishwa* (Pamphlet, 1980), p. 5.

17. It is unclear how successful the VHP is in regions like Assam, but evidence indicates it has made inroads into the tribal population of Gujarat, leading to a newly developed tension between tribals and Muslims in the area.

18. See *Ekatmata Yajna*, a publication of the VHP.

19. Arjuna's chariot is a recurring symbol in VHP pamphlets, and the story of the Bhagavad Gita, made into the fundamental text of Hinduism in the nineteenth century and later by Gandhi, emphasizes the duty of the warrior to fight when war is inevitable.

20. An important statement has been issued by members of the Center for Historical Studies, Jawaharlal Nehru University, New Delhi: "The Political Abuse of History: Babri Masjid-Rama Janmabhumi Dispute," *India Alert-Special Bulletin* 2, no. 3 (December 1983). See also Sushil Srivastava, *The Disputed Mosque: A Historical Inquiry* (New Delhi: Vistaar Publications, 1991). The BJP/VHP has published a response to the argument of the JNU historians, by a Belgian author, Koenraad Elst, *Ram Janmabhoomi vs. Babri Masjid: A Case Study in Hindu-Muslim Conflict* (New Delhi: Voice of India, 1990). It has also published a study of "Hindu Temples Destoyed and Desecrated and Converted into Mosques," written by a number of important Indian journalists. See Arun Shourie and Jay Dubashi, *Hindu Temples: What Happened to Them: A Preliminary Survey* (New Delhi: Voice of India, 1990). An important role in the current debate is played by B. B. Lal, former director general of the Archeological Survey of India and currently director of the archeological survey of the Ramayana sites. He has conducted excavations in Ayodhya and claims to have found evidence in the mosque area of "brick built bases which evidently carried pillars thereon" (see VHP newsletter, *Sri Janmabhoomi*, Special Anniversary Issue 5, nos. 3 and 4 (March and April 1990).

21. For the local tradition, see van der Veer, *Gods on Earth,* pp. 19–21.

22. For a description of how this movement was perceived at the local level in Ayodhya, see Peter van der Veer, "God Must Be Liberated! A Hindu Liberation Movement in Ayodhya," *Modern Asian Studies* 21 (1987): 283–303.

23. See Anuradha Kapur, "Militant Images of a Tranquil God," *Times of India,* 10 January 1991.

24. This argument has been recently developed in Bruce Kapferer, *Legends of People, Myths of State* (Washington, D.C.: Smithsonian, 1988), p. 5.

25. Anandshankar Pandya, *Defence of Hindu Society* (Delhi: VHP, n. d.), p. 10.

Redefining Muslim Identity in South Asia:
The Transformation of the Jama'at-i-Islami

Rafiuddin Ahmed

The minority Ahmadi Muslims in Pakistan were declared "non-Muslims" by an act of Parliament in 1974 and have since been subjected to systematic discrimination and persecution for their religious views.[1] Ironically, even Maulana Sayyid Abul 'Ala Maududi (1903–79), the founder and ideologue of the fundamentalist organization Jama'at-i-Islami, who was largely responsible for keeping alive the tension on the status of the Ahmadis in Pakistan, was himself declared a *kafir* (infidel) by the Sunni Deoband school on charges of distorting Islam.[2]

Islamic fundamentalism on the Indian subcontinent became so preoccupied with the controversy over the boundaries of "authentic Islam" that the ideology, programs, and activities of the Jama'at-i-Islami, the major fundamentalist organization, were eventually transformed by this preoccupation. This represented a fundamental shift in strategy for the Jama'at, from its proclaimed commitment to a revolutionary and absolutist ideology to a collaborative stance requiring participation in the existing secular political institutions.

The Jama'at recognized that without a certain measure of support from the entrenched interests, notably, the conservative ulama, the army, and the bureaucracy, its desired goal of realizing an Islamic polity may not be achieved. In consequence, the Jama'at had to reconsider its political strategy, making compromises with those who, theoretically at least, espoused the idea of an Islamic system. Thus, although its commitment to an absolutist ideology was not necessarily modified in favor of a more moderate approach, its immediate political objective, that is, gaining control of the state apparatus, was considered so crucial in transforming the Muslim polity into a "truly" Islamic one that it has on occasion purposely "deviated" from its stated principles for political gain. In effect, the evolving political strategy of the Jama'at—especially since the anti-Ahmadiya riots of 1952—induced it to modify some of its programs and strategies, making it function more like a political party, along the lines of communist and fascist parties, than a movement of religious revival. Its immediate concern since then has been to gain access to political power as a means of effecting fundamental changes in society. The themes of an "ideal Islamic community" and a "true Islamic identity," which have dominated its discourse in recent years should be judged in the context of this changed political strategy.

In this chapter I argue that the absolutist tendencies of the Jama'at moved the organization away from its self-description, contained in its original constitution, as the builder of an Islamic order and toward a radical fundamentalist position of exclusivity that has led to increased social and religious unrest and political tension in the Muslim societies. Furthermore, as a result of an ideological shift precipitated by its failure to usher in a "theo-democracy" at the polls, the organization has tailored itself to become a political pressure group that employs various tactics, including violence, to achieve a measure of influence with regimes that it has been unable to achieve with the general Muslim population of Pakistan.

For the past four decades the Jama'at has played an important role in the sociopolitical life of the Muslims in this region. Since the 1970s, it has emerged as the most powerful radical Islamic organization in Pakistan and Bangladesh. The Jama'at has been equally active in India, which is home to the largest religious minority in the world—almost a hundred million Muslims in a total population of over seven hundred million. India also offers a key example of a complex cultural setting where Islam is placed in a larger non-Islamic environment.

Setting the Boundaries of "Authentic Islam"

Why are certain groups categorized as "fundamentalist" while others are excluded from its scope? Can fundamentalism be commensurate with possessing political power? Should we consider the state-sponsored programs of Islamization to be part of the fundamentalist phenomenon? In this chapter the term *fundamentalism* is "shorthand to gain entry into some more compelling and discrete reality."[3] What is essential, however, is to define its scope and delimit its boundaries by making a distinction between the activist ideology of the Islamic movements, on the one hand, and the efforts of those who also seek a return to the laws of Islam but reject the militant views and programs of the movements. The "conservative" *ulama* and the traditional leaders of popular Islam, namely, the *pirs* and *mullahs*, may be grouped in this second category.

The fundamentalist ideologues openly distance themselves from the programs and activities of the conservatives, look upon themselves as the sole champion of true Islam, and dismiss the role of others as inadequate in realizing the goal of an Islamic order. While they acknowledge the "significant contributions" made by others, such as the members of the Tabligh movement, in promoting Islam among Muslims, fundamentalists argue that these are not enough to alter the character of the society.[4] A Jama'at leader, for example, has cautioned that the Tabligh movement might indeed be damaging the cause of Islam by projecting a "wrong" image of the Prophet "merely as a religious leader."[5] Maulana Maududi even dismissed the mission of Shah Waliullah (1703–62), the Islamic ideologue from Delhi who inspired a number of puritanical reform movements in India in the nineteenth century,[6] as irrelevant for modern-day situations. He wrote:

> The insight and power of interpretation displayed by Shah Waliullah and the earlier mujtahids and mujaddids cannot cope with the present day situations. The new age accompanied by new means and powers has brought with it new evils and produced countless new problems of life, which could not even have crossed the mind of the Shah Sahib and the early doctors. . . . Therefore, the only source of guidance and inspiration for an ideological movement for the renaissance of Islam in this age are the Book of Allah and the Sunna of His Prophet.[7]

By challenging the validity of the religious views of the early reformers, including the medieval schools of Islamic law and theology, Maududi was ostensibly emphasizing the irrefutability of divinely inspired sources. But the significance attached to "the independent power of ijtihad," which he described as "the disciplined judgment of jurists" on the basis of "the general principles and precepts of the Shari'a," allowed Maududi and his movement the freedom to interpret the laws and principles of Islam without reference to the views of other Islamic scholars. This is evident from Maududi's expressed repugnance for the ulama who "are tied to the intellectual atmosphere of the fifth century A.H. [eleventh and twelfth century A.D.], as a consequence of which they have not been able to produce such leaders of Islamic thought and action as could be capable of administering the affairs of a modern state in the light of Islamic principles."[8]

What clearly sets the fundamentalists apart from their "orthodox" coreligionists is the notion of institutional change. While fundamentalists are very specific and categorical—like the Marxists—about the changes they would like to make in the structure of the polity, the ulama and the pirs either do not have a definite program in this regard or have generally failed to offer a concrete plan of change and Islamization. Furthermore, while the fundamentalists are forthright in their denunciations of the existing institutions and the "modernizing" influences of the West, the conservatives have not proven so unequivocal in their condemnations and have traditionally allied themselves with the state.[9]

At the ideological level, the fundamentalist position on the existing state apparatus and the secular elites who run it has been one of extreme hostility. Maududi was clearly indignant of the role of secular Muslim leadership, whom he considered "ignorant of even the ABCs of the Islamic Shari'a."[10] The "mentality" of this elite, he argued, had been so deeply "affected by the poisonous content and the thoroughly materialistic bias of modern secular education" as to render them unsuitable to lead a truly Islamic society. "Can an irreligious state, with Westernized people at its helm," build an Islamic society? "Will the persons well-versed only in running bars and night clubs and movie-houses spend their energies in constructing and maintaining mosques?" asked Maududi. "If the answer is in the affirmative, it will indeed be a unique experiment of its kind in human history: ungodliness fostering godliness so that it might ultimately be supplanted by the latter!"[11]

Maududi's ideal Islamic polity, which he called theo-democracy, prescribes the establishment of a "divine democratic government" which repudiates the "theory of popular sovereignty and rears its polity on the foundations of the sovereignty of God and the vicegerency [*khilafat*] of man."[12] "A true Muslim" under this divinely ordained system "regards himself subject to the Law of God in all that he does and exercises his will to regulate his affairs only to the extent he has been permitted to do so by Allah."[13] Every aspect of life of the Muslims would be governed by the laws of the all-embracing Shari'a and nothing could be considered "personal" and "private."[14] Maududi thought that the Islamic state "bears a kind of resemblance to the Fascist and Communist states" in this regard, although, unlike the latter, it does not have room for dictatorship.[15] Moreover, "the vicegerency of God (i.e., the authority of the Muslim ruler) is not the exclusive right of any individual or clan or class of people; it is the collective right of all those who accept and admit God's absolute sovereignty over themselves."[16] "All men enjoy equal status and position in such a society. The only criterion of superiority in this social order is personal ability and character."[17]

Maududi articulated his notion of an ideal Islamic order in explicitly rigid terms. There could be no compromise on the fundamental principles that should guide the conduct of the faithful. The choice was not simply between Islam and another system, but between Islam and *kufr* (infidelity). There could be no alternative.[18] In essence, this rigidity reflects how fundamentalists seek to delimit the boundaries of "authentic Islam." In this sense Bruce Lawrence's definition of fundamentalism as "the affirmation of religious authority as holistic and absolute, admitting of neither criticism nor reduction" seems appropriate[19] but does not suggest fundamentalists have consistently opposed cooperation with others. Despite the differing approaches to questions of Islamic law and theology between the fundamentalists and the ulama and the pirs, for example, there exists certain agreement between them on the key issue that "Islam must continue to provide the purpose of the Ummah for the future."[20] This has, indeed, induced them on a number of occasions to collaborate with each other, especially in political matters. In recent elections in Pakistan, the Jama'at-i-Islami joined the ulama and the *Islam-pasand* (Islam-loving) political groups in destablizing the governments of Zulfiqar Ali Bhutto (1972–78) and his daughter, Benazir Bhutto (1989–90).[21] Similar political motivation induced the Jama'at-i-Islami to lend its total support to the centrist Bangladesh Nationalist party in a bid to contain the power of the left-oriented Awami League and its allies. Such collaboration has its own problems nevertheless. The differing approaches of the fundamentalists and other Islam-oriented groups, including the conservative ulama, and lack of trust make it impossible for them to forge a genuine alliance with each other based on common programs and strategies.

Thus, although the quintessence of fundamentalism is its opposition to the status quo, any attempt to describe it as unceasingly oppositional to the prevailing political ethos is somewhat restrictive.[22] In fact, the Jama'at-i-Islami has consistently argued in favor of participating in democratic elections as a means of gaining access to political power, although in principle it is opposed to the concept of representative government. "For unless one possesses necessary power and authority to enforce one's programme," wrote Maududi, "the proposed system can not possibly take root in the world of reality."[23]

Despite their uncompromising ideological stance, not all fundamentalist movements are revolutionary in character. Some adhere to their own rigid interpretations of the Islamic Shari'a, generally rejecting all other views as unacceptable, yet politically assuming a collaborative stance rather than a revolutionary one. Such collaborative fundamentalism may assume oppositional qualities or equate the existing social, economic, and political order with approximations of colonialism, secularism, or Westernism which historically coincided with the concurrent decline or "corruption" of Islam. Similarly, it is possible that collaborative fundamentalism may desire political power without seeking to preserve or legitimize the existing political order and thus is willing to adjust its political program to serve as a vehicle for the ultimate realization of ideological goals. The Jama'at-i-Islami fits more closely within the context of this collaborative definition rather than in a framework of revolutionary movements. The movement's imperative for an "Islamic order" manifests itself in a language necessitating the restructuring of the Muslim society according to its own interpretation of the Shari'a. Its proclaimed goals resulted in a perception of the organization as a fundamentalist movement oppositional in character and desirous of replacing the existing political, social, and economic order with an Islamic system as defined by its principal ideologue. Implicit in this characterization of the Jama'at is its underlying revolutionary intent. Yet goals and programs aside, the Jama'at-i-Islami on the Indian subcontinent, rather than distinguishing itself as a "revolutionary" fundamentalist movement as suggested by the natural progression of its rhetoric, demonstrated itself instead to be a "collaborative" movement, as we shall see.

For the fundamentalist as well as for his opponent, the heart of the problem is to determine the parameters of "true Islam." But can one objectively define "true Islam?" The court of inquiry constituted to inquire into the anti-Ahmadi riots in Punjab (Pakistan) in 1953, otherwise known as the Munir Commission, interviewed some of the leading ulama of Pakistan, including Maududi, on the definition of a Muslim. The ulama so differed with each other on this fundamental question that they failed to come up with a definitive model of a "true believer." The commission, which included no Ahmadi, felt constrained to point out:

> If we attempt our own definition as each learned divine has done and that definition differs from that given by all others, we unanimously go out of the fold of Islam. And if we adopt the definition given by any one of the ulama, we remain Muslims according to the view of that alim but kafirs according to the definition of everyone else. . . .
>
> If the constituents of each of the definitions given by the *ulama* are given effect, . . . the grounds on which a person may be indicted for apostasy will be too numerous to count.[24]

In sum, then, the term "fundamentalism" is generally used restrictively to define the role of the activist groups and movements that have a more definitive and militant

Islamic agenda than the latter. Although equally puritanical in orientation, orthodox ideology has generally tended to be less politicized than fundamentalism. Fundamentalism is characterized by a heightened sense of exclusivity and intolerance; it is strongly assertive and is determined to impose its own behavioral norms on others. Despite a certain similarity in their goals—supposedly the establishment of an ideal Islamic system—the fundamentalists and the orthodox do not necessarily hold similar views on the scope and definition of the Shari'a which forms the core of the Islamic system.[25] In effect, their differing approaches to doctrinal and mundane matters and the vehemence with which they reject each others' views on questions of Islamic law and theology inevitably give rise to tension in the society.[26]

The Emergence of the Jama'at: Ideology and Politics

The Jama'at-i-Islami was launched on 25 August 1941 by Maulana Maududi with the declared aim of establishing the rule of the Shari'a. No mention was made in its constitution of an Islamic state as such or the methods to be employed to bring about such a state. Rather, the emphasis was on personal righteousness at the individual rather than the social or collective level. Despite this constitutionally projected image of an Islamic reform movement directed at evolving the religious self, the Jama'at soon emerged as a fundamentalist Muslim organization concerned with the evolution of the Muslim society of the subcontinent into an Islamic one based on its own interpretation of the Shari'a. Maududi later argued that an Islamic state with its accompanying Qur'anic implications could not be established until an Islamic revolution had first taken place in the society.[27] Like the Ikhwan al-Muslimin (Muslim Brotherhood) in Egypt, the Jama'at became less concerned at this stage with realizing an Islamic state than with establishing an Islamic order.

Since the declared goal of the Jama'at was to transform the life of Muslims in its totality, it could not remain unconcerned about the political problems of the time—a period of rising tension in Indian politics. The end of World War I and the emergence of Mahatma Gandhi as the leader of the Indian National Congress had infused a new vigor to the nationalist movement. Meanwhile the tone and temper of Muslim politics were increasingly becoming more aggressive and uncompromising, especially in so far as their demands to special privileges and political rights. The collaborative stance of the elitist leaders, which was the dominant theme of Muslim politics until after the War, was soon discredited. The defeat and humiliation of Ottoman Turkey—considered the seat of the Islamic Khilafat by large numbers of Sunni Muslims in India—by the Allied Powers raised concerns among the Indian Muslims about the future of Turkey. A younger generation of Western-educated Muslim leadership and sections of the ulama soon emerged as champions of Islam, and the Muslim interests, and launched the Khilafat Movement (1920–23) ostensibly to protect the integrity of the Turkish Empire.[28] Gandhi lent his total support to the Muslim cause hoping to achieve a broad-based unity of Muslims and Hindus against the colonial regime. But Hindu-Muslim relations had already so soured that it was difficult to coordinate Gandhi's programs of non-cooperation with the Khilafat Movement of the Muslims. In consequence, communal violence erupted in different parts of the country disrupting peace and shattering Gandhi's hopes.

The disastrous end of the Khilafat and the Non-Cooperation movements further exacerbated Hindu-Muslim tensions. In the emotionally charged atmosphere of communal mistrust, issues like the Hindu agitation against cow slaughter by the Muslims, the playing of music before mosques by Hindu processionists, competition for jobs and other middle-class opportunities, and illegal levy of taxes by Hindu landlords excited sentiments and created conditions for communal violence. The new sense of Muslim political consciousness articulated by the new Bourgeoisie, including the ulama, proved decisive in shaping the future of Indian politics, ultimately resulting in the partition of India in 1947 ostensibly on the basis of Muslim claims to separate nationhood.

Reacting to this political situation, Maududi wrote a series of articles in Urdu between 1937 and 1939, arguing against the Congress and its nationalist Muslim allies—and against the Muslim League as well.[29] For Maududi, who envisioned Islam as a worldwide revolutionary movement led by pious Muslims, both positions were equally un-Islamic. Assailing the nationalist ulama of Deoband and the Jamiyat-i-ulema-i Hind for their support of the Congress view of a composite Indian nationalism, Maududi accused them of "drinking Jawaharlal's *suddhi* like sweet syrup" and thus misguiding the Muslims.[30] He was equally vehement in his denunciation of the Muslim League. The political problems of the Indian Muslims, he contended, could not be resolved by creating a separate state for them. What was required was establishment of an Islamic order based on the Shari'a:

> As a Muslim I do not believe in "the government of the people." . . . For me the most important question is whether in your Pakistan the system of government will be based on the sovereignty of God or on popular sovereignty based on Western democratic theories. In the case of the former, it will certainly be Pakistan [i.e., holy land], otherwise it will be as "na-Pakistan" [unholy land] as the other areas where, according to your scheme, non-Muslims will rule. But in the eyes of God it will be much more reprehensible and unholy than even that. Muslim nationalism is as reprehensible in the Shari'a of God as Indian nationalism.[31]

Pakistan, as envisaged by Jinnah and the Muslim League, could be no better than a pagan state, Maududi held, because "not a single leader of the Muslim League from Jinnah himself to the rank and file has an Islamic mentality or Islamic habits of thought."[32] The Jama'at, therefore, could not be a party to such an un-Islamic movement.

In March 1940 the Muslim League passed its momentous resolution at Lahore demanding establishment of a separate state for Muslims. Maududi and the Jama'at remained steadfast in their opposition to both the Congress and the Muslim League until mid-1947. This stance seemed logical from their ideological point of view: Muslims did not constitute a national entity but an organized community of believers (*umma*); therefore, the concept of territorial nationalism was inimical to Islam. However, once the creation of Pakistan became inevitable, Maududi softened his stand against it. He subsequently stated: "I honestly believed, and still believe, that it was my duty to remind the Muslims that their objective should not be just the setting up of a Muslim national state but of setting up an Islamic state, and that they should try to build up the personal qualities and character which were essential for the tasks involved."[33]

After partition, Maududi and other leaders of the Jama'at moved to Pakistan and became the most active voices supporting the Islamic cause. Their belated support for the new state and their somewhat reconciliatory acceptance of the leadership of Jinnah were apparently designed to placate the Muslim League leadership, which in 1947 assumed the reins of government in Pakistan, and to make themselves acceptable to the people as leaders of the community. They also sought to repair the damage done to the Jama'at by its opposition to the Pakistan movement. Thus the Jama'at embarked on an agenda that would demonstrate its pro-Pakistan stance by illustrating how it worked for the establishment of Pakistan "from a different perspective" during the period 1941–47.[34] The Jama'at portrayed itself as an ideological movement concerned with the idea of a "total Islamic revolution" "which could be brought about in both India and Pakistan." Maududi was not interested in a simple solution to the Muslim problem. "He did not want to change the rulers only but wanted to change the system as well. . . . He was [Pakistan's] staunch supporter if the purpose of Pakistan was to bring about an Islamic revolution."[35]

Despite the apparent inconsistency in Jama'at's position on nationalism generally and the Pakistan movement in particular, there was a certain logic in Maududi's stand: he wanted a total transformation in the system, not a partial solution. His concern was for realizing his Islamic goals, not for solving immediate political problems. For similar reasons, he later refused to characterize the Kashmir War (1947–48) as a jihad. He argued that armed intervention in the state by frontier tribesmen and elements of the Pakistan army in an attempt to force its accession to Pakistan could not be called Islamic as long as the declared policy of the government was to negotiate the dispute.

The Jama'at in Pakistan: Confrontation and Collaboration

Pakistan was created on the assumption that the Muslims of India constituted a separate "nation" and, as such, were entitled to a separate homeland. The leadership came mostly from among the ranks of the English-educated, liberal Muslims like Jinnah who demonstrated little or no interest in an "Islamic system" and conceived of a society based generally on the ideals of Western democracy where one is free to go to his temple, to his mosque, or "to any other places of worship" because "that has nothing to do with the business of the state."[36] Although Islamic symbols and slogans helped unite Muslims of different social and cultural background under a common banner, "the irony of the argument that Pakistan was founded on religious ideology lies in the fact that practically every Muslim group and organization in the Indian subcontinent that was specifically religious—Islamic—was hostile to Jinnah and the Muslim League, and strongly opposed the Pakistan movement."[37]

Despite its earlier opposition, after independence the Jamaʿat emerged as a strong proponent of an Islamic Pakistan. "If, now, after all these sacrifices," Maududi stated in 1948, "we fail to achieve the real and ultimate object of making Islam a practical, constitutional reality which inspired us to fight for Pakistan, our entire struggle becomes meaningless."[38] Since then, the Jamaʿat has been persistent in its demand for the establishment of an Islamic order in Pakistan and has made it the principal agenda in its program. In an effort to make its argument for an Islamic system more appealing, Maududi even invoked the name of Jinnah, whom he had earlier described as "ignorant of Islam's goals and missions," claiming that Jinnah "had categorically stated that Pakistan's constitution would be the Qur'an."[39]

The Jamaʿat's revision of its Pakistan position did not mean the movement won automatic political recognition or legitimation in the new state. Its opponents continued to raise questions about the Jamaʿat's role during the independence movement, forcing Maududi to defend his party on several occasions.[40] Maududi was aware of the massive obstacles facing his mission. The most important step in overcoming these obstacles was to create a dedicated, well-trained cadre of young leaders "in every locality, every village and every street" who, "with the support of the general public," should be "in a position to suppress the bad element of the society."[41] Since true Islam enjoined a struggle against the inward perversities, creation of such a cadre was considered essential for the success of the movement.

The Jamaʿat thus embarked on a program of reorganizing the party, founding branches all over the country, and enlisting the support of college youth and the various professional groups. Maududi now appeared more pragmatic than before and agreed that it was not possible to launch an Islamic revolution in Pakistan immediately; the changes had to be achieved in gradual stages. The most important stage in this gradual process was to Islamize the state structure by repealing all un-Islamic laws and restoring the sovereignty of God over the sovereignty of the people. Although democratic elections are considered un-Islamic by the Jamaʿat, Maududi accepted them "because this is at present the only peaceful course for changing the system and rulers."[42] He argued that legislation in the normal sense was possible in an Islamic state, at least on issues not covered by the Qur'an and the Sunna, but that this could occur only within the framework of the Shariʿa by people qualified by reason of their piety and knowledge of Islam.

Alongside its organizational activities, the Jamaʿat soon started an ambitious program of publishing Islamic literature, including editing and republishing Maududi's pre-Partition speeches and writings in an effort to project a favorable image of his role in the Pakistan movement. One tactic used by the Jamaʿat was to have books containing more or less the same material published by numerous publishers under the names of different editors. The object was to create a wider readership for its publications. Although the membership of the party remained almost static throughout the 1950s (partly because of its rigorous policy of scrutinizing would-be members), its influence increased considerably, which became evident from its role in drafting the ill-fated

Islamic directives in the report of the Basic Principles Committee of the first Constituent Assembly of Pakistan in 1954.[43] The Jama'at's involvement in constitutional politics technically meant abandoning its programs for an Islamic revolution, though, in reality, it never modified its commitment to a radical program of change, i.e., a revolutionary ideology. The shift in favor of constitutional politics was primarily designed to molify public opinion and create a favorable atmosphere for its Islamic agenda.[44]

In the absence of any significant popular support for its programs, participation in the existing political process was considered a rational choice which, it was thought, would give it a certain measure of flexibility in propagating its ideas and enable it to function as a legitimate political forum, unhindered by governmental action or ban, as has often been the case with its more revolutionary counterpart in Egypt, the Muslim Brotherhood. "Whether we like it or not," Maududi stated in 1978, "the elections shall have to be a starting point, because this is at present the only peaceful course for changing the system of government and rulers."[45]

Violence and the Changing Ideology of the Jama'at-i-Islami

At the same time, the use of force as a factor in the "Islamization" program continued to be emphasized,[46] and periodically resorted to, alongside its policy of participation in constitutional politics. Although Maududi interpreted jihad in a very broad sense to include a wide spectrum of activities such as writing in defense of Islam, propagating Islam, or donating for the cause of Islam, the use of force for a "just cause" (meaning the cause of Islam), and suffer martyrdom for this, remained the ultimate and highest form of jihad.[47]

Broadly, Jama'at's evolving strategy after the riots of 1952 consisted of (1) participation in electoral politics, while not rejecting the option of using force whenever the need arose; (2) recourse to democratic institutions and forums to popularize its Islamic agenda; (3) a massive propaganda campaign to "educate" and mobilize public opinion in favor of an Islamic system; and, (4) recruitment and training of more and more young members, "the soldiers of Islam," to act as vanguards of the Islamic movement, particularly by helping to contain the power of the secular-socialist groups and parties. The primary goal of this modified strategy was to ensure "the transference of the reins of power to the [righteous] people."[48] Although the revolutionary rhetoric of Maududi was softened considerably over time, in practical terms this only meant abandoning the idea of the organized armed struggle against the state, not a rejection of jihad. Its commitment to constitutional politics could thus only be a strategic move and not a genuine shift in ideology.

Although article ten of the Jama'at's constitution forbids the use of violence to achieve its objectives, jihad, according to Maududi, can be used for both offensive and defensive purposes and is theoretically meant to establish the supremacy and sovereignty of God over man. Those who want an end to the kingdom of *jahiliyya* (pre-Islamic ignorance) and hope to revive the Islamic umma are obliged to wage war against the infidels. A true Muslim must first fight the internal enemy, that is, the secularist-socialist state, and then the external enemy, the larger non-Muslim world.[49] This ideology was clearly reflected in the growing emphasis on the recruitment and training of younger members drawn mostly from colleges and universities. This resulted in the creation of a highly structured, cadre-based, political movement organized along the lines of communist and the fascist movements. It geared up its efforts to establish party offices in towns and cities, recruited thousands of young members over time, trained them as a disciplined force, and used them as a support base for its politics.

In time, these cadres played decisive roles in organizing and leading street protests and demonstrations against the regimes of Ayub Khan (1958–69) and Z. A. Bhutto (1972–77) in Pakistan, and that of Ershad (1982–90) in Bangladesh. Their presence has been particularly felt in university campuses, which became the focal point of political mobilization against unfriendly regimes. They also succeeded over time in driving the socialist cadres underground in most campuses. Despite a rigorous selection process, the number of young recruits increased phenomenally in the 1970s and 1980s, making it the most organized and disciplined political force in both Pakistan and Bangladesh.[50] Growing financial support from the oil-rich Arab countries helped significantly in strengthening the organizational bases of the Jama'at and making possible the publication of numerous books, tracts, and pamphlets in the local languages designed to appeal to the religious sentiments of the young and the middle aged.

The first indication of how violence could be used against those whom the Jama'at considered enemies came in 1953, when the Jama'at joined forces with the extremist Majlis-i-Ahrar, a Muslim religiopolitical party founded in Punjab in 1930, which, like the Jama'at had opposed the creation of Pakistan.[51]

The Ahmadis have been the object of great controversy in Sunni Islam since the late nineteenth century, especially because of their pronouncements on the question of *khatm-i-nabuwwat* (the finality of Prophethood).[52] Although the actual meaning of the Qur'anic term *khatam al-nabiyin* (Seal of the Prophets) remains far from clear, the ulama have long contended that the Ahmadis, by repudiating the finality of the Prophethood of Muhammad, ceased to be Muslims. Mirza Ghulam Ahmad (d. 1908), the founder of the Ahmadiya movement, did claim to be a "prophet," but only "in a shadowy and manifestational sense," while making it clear that "no law-bearing prophet can come [again]."[53]

The Ahmadi issue initiated a bitter debate in South Asian Islam after the 1890s when the claims of Ahmad to be the promised messiah and mahdi of the age were made public. The controversy took on a political connotation with the involvement of the Majlis-i-Ahrar in the mid-1930s. Its persistent demand that the Ahmadis be declared "non-Muslims" created widespread tension in northern India.[54] The politicization of the Ahmadi question was so complete in the Punjab as to convince the provincial branch of the All-India Muslim League to declare the Ahmadis non-Muslims in early 1941, barring them from membership of the party.[55] The issue was resurrected soon after independence at the insistence of the Majlis-i-Ahrar, which started a determined campaign to exclude Ahmadis from the Muslim community. The issue did not involve theological disputes alone; it was "transformed into a constitutional problem of the first order, having far-reaching implications for the civil rights of the Ahmadi community."[56]

The controversy also revealed the prejudices associated with the fundamentalist conception of a theocratic state. Theoretically, the Jama'at's position on the Ahmadiyas could be linked to its ideological commitment to the establishment of an "authentic" Islamic system in which rigid conformity with the dictates of the Shari'a was considered essential. The Ahmadiyas, by bestowing a "prophethood" on the founder of the sect, were ostensibly challenging an established view on the finality of the Prophethood of Muhammad, and thus raised legitimate questions about their links with Sunni Islam. But the vehemence with which the Jama'at campaigned against the community and questioned their status as Muslims, especially during the anti-Bhutto demonstrations of 1977, demonstrated the political importance of the subject to the Jama'at in popularizing its own particularist notion of an Islamic polity.

Apparently the Jama'at was not involved at the initial stage of the campaign against the Ahmadis, but it soon joined others (the Majlis-i-Ahrar and numerous other ulama organizations) after Maududi issued a highly inflammatory pamphlet, titled *Qadiani Masala* (The Qadiani Problem), likening the Ahmadis to "a cancer eating up and gradually consuming the vitals of the Muslim society." His argument was based on the construction of Ahmadiyas as "non-Muslims" because of their "heretical" views on the finality of Prophethood. "The Qadianis have," he wrote, ". . . evinced some dangerous political trends which must receive prompt attention. . . . They are planning to establish a Qadiani State within the State of Pakistan."[57]

Maududi's efforts to portray the Ahmadis as a threat to the political and economic status of the majority Sunnis in Pakistan were ill conceived. A persecuted minority, consisting of less than one-fiftieth of the total Muslim population of the country, they could never have threatened the political and economic prospects of the larger community. While there is a certain ideological consistency in Maududi's stand on the Ahmadiya question, which was relevant to his expressed desire of defining the boundaries of "authentic Islam," the issue became so overtly politicized that doctrinal arguments quickly were submerged under emotion-charged slogans. His *Qadiani Masala* inflamed the passions of the mob rather than initiating debate on the subject. It is possible the Jama'at perceived the Ahmadiya issue as a popular and crucial subject for the Muslim population of Pakistan. As such, assuming the vanguard of an anti-Ahmadi position would perhaps legitimize the Jama'at with those who still viewed its pre-Partition anti-Pakistan/anti-Muslim League stance with suspicion. Maududi's strong dislike for the Ahmadi Muslims perhaps made it easier for him to convince himself to join the controversy. Consequently, the Jama'at joined an all-Pakistan Muslim parties convention on the Ahmadi question in January 1953. When the convention decided on "direct action" against the latter, Maududi thought it prudent to disassociate the Jama'at from the agitation. Nonetheless, he chose to publish the *Qadiani Masala* in March 1953 inciting the mob to violence. Widespread rioting in Punjab in the following months cost hundreds of lives, mostly Ahmadis. A government inquiry commission under the chairmanship of the chief justice of the Supreme Court of Pakistan later castigated the Jama'at for its unruly conduct, charging that "its founder flung the *Qadiani Masala* in the midst of a colossal conflagration," showing little respect for human life.[58]

If the Jama'at's position in the anti-Ahmadiya violence was deliberate, then it was a calculated risk that failed. Rather than garnering national support, the Jama'at found itself involved in a fiasco. Publicly the Jama'at damaged its credibility and was viewed with even more suspicion than before by its opponents. The activity of the Jama'at during the riots made people apprehensive about its future political role. From the point of view of the government, Jama'at's resort to violence could mean only one thing: it would not hesitate to use force for political purposes when force was necessary and available.

Indeed, despite its initial setback, the Jama'at did gain insight into the psychology of mob violence: symbols and targets, if carefully chosen and articulated, could make a fundamental difference in mobilizing public support in favor of an Islamic system, if not in favor of the Jama'at itself. The Jama'at hoped that once the public was made aware of the Islamic alternative, the party would benefit the most in view of its leading role in the Islamic movement. Its organizational strength, persistent use of the media to propagate, and the limited use of force, as and when necessary, would ensure the eventual success of its mission.

Thus I would argue that the anti-Ahmadiya riots and the events following the riots, including the appointment of a high-powered judicial commission of enquiry, proved decisive in transforming the Jama'at into an openly aggressive political organization. The riots inspired a critical policy shift in the Jama'at from open hostility and criticism of other Islamic groups to a meaningful cooperation for realizing the ultimate goal of an Islamic order. It also demonstrated to the Jama'at the power of urban mobilization, specifically the use of violence, as a means of exerting pressure on the ruling elites, and brought into the fore the symbolic importance of certain religious issues in mobilizing support from a wide spectrum of Muslim public opinion. For the Jama'at, which had played no role in public life to that point, these were critical lessons in politics from which it was destined to benefit in the future.

These lessons were applied, for example, when the Jama'at exerted pressure on the Bhutto government in 1974 and 1977. The issues and targets were chosen so carefully as to garner support from a cross section of the Islam-oriented parties and groups. The Finality of the Prophethood thus became the premise for a well-orchestrated campaign in 1974, designed to create political instability in the country and force the ouster of the pseudo-socialist regime of Bhutto. Although the immediate target of the movement was the Ahmadiya community, the ultimate goal was to create confusion in the minds of the public about the Islamic nature of Bhutto's regime. Organized under the umbrella of the student front of the Jama'at, the IJU (Islami Jamiat-i-Tulaba), the campaign was pursued with so much vigor and aggressiveness that the ensuing violence practically disrupted the functioning of the government.[59] This was a clear victory for the Jama'at and demonstrative of its ability to manipulate emotive symbols and slogans for political gain.

In the Jama'at ideology, justification for violence found its fullest expression in 1971 during the war in (former) East Pakistan, which resulted in the creation of

Bangladesh. The national elections of 1970 had given the secular-oriented Awami League of Shaykh Mujibur Rahman an overall majority in the Pakistan Parliament. The refusal by the military junta to hand over power to the elected majority and attempts to suppress the autonomy movement in (former) East Pakistan led to a popular uprising in March 1971 under secularist-socialist leadership. The Jamaʿat, along with the other Islam-oriented parties, joined the pro-Chinese People's Party of Z. A. Bhutto in supporting the Pakistan army in its brutal armed crackdown on civilians, causing the death of millions of innocent lives, the destruction of property, and the rape of hundreds of thousands of Bengali women.

The Jamaʿat actively helped the army in its war effort in (former) East Pakistan by taking partial responsibility for internal policing. It helped organize "peace committees" all over the country, consisting of persons sympathetic to the notion of a united Pakistan, and was also responsible for creating a militia, known as the Razaqars, in efforts to intimidate opponents and help restore "law and order." In the process, it encouraged hoodlums and street gangs to indulge in reckless looting and plundering of property and abduction of women. It organized its youth cadres into volunteer forces, named al-Badr, trained them in the use of firearms, and deployed them against the "enemies of Islamic Pakistan."[60] As a result, this group committed murders of scores of innocent Bengalis—students, members of the intelligentsia, factory workers, politicians, and professionals—who were sympathetic to Bangladesh. The Jamaʿat cadres often abducted their victims, brutally tortured and maimed them, extracting their eyes and cutting off their limbs, before putting them to death. They systematically burned "un-Islamic" and "anti-Pakistani" literature and created terror on university campuses, making it impossible for others to function.[61]

The Jamaʿat hoped, through its violent activities against the civilian population of East Pakistan, to force them to abandon their nationalistic aspirations. The Jamaʿat felt responsible for countering the growing strength of the Bengali nationalists, most of whom were inspired by the ideals of secularism and socialism, and saw in the army action an opportunity to reassert its position. In May 1970, on the occasion of the birthday of the Prophet, the Jamaʿat responded to a call by General Yahya Khan, the military dictator of Pakistan, "to defend the ideology of Pakistan." A week later, the movement announced its own Shaukat-i-Islam (Glory of Islam) day denouncing socialism, secularism, and provincialism.[62] This was quite consistent with its militant ideology of jihad, which permitted the use of force in defense of a "righteous cause." The Jamaʿat has since never wavered from its commitment to using force to ensure the defeat of secular-socialist ideologies. Its involvement in the Afghanistan conflict in the aftermath of the Communist takeover, and the subsequent Soviet intervention on behalf of the Communist regime was, in large measure, dictated by the Jamaʿat's commitment to jihad.

Since the separation of Bangladesh from Pakistan in 1971, the Jamaʿat in Pakistan has pursued a generally collaborative policy toward the army, while trying to ensure its place in the mainstream of politics with a varying degree of success. Given the powerful role played by the army in the sharply polarized Pakistani politics, between the left-oriented Pakistani People's Party and the right-wing Islamic groups, it is not difficult to see why it has succeeded in keeping its place as a major player in politics, despite limited popular support. The Jama'at's strategy of violence has been consistently directed against secular-socialist parties, principally the PPP (in Bangladesh, principally against the Awami League, which gave leadership to the freedom movement in 1971); this was in keeping with the programs and policies of the right-wing political parties as well as of the army. As long as the actions of the Jama'at did not disturb the status quo in favor of the latter, there was little chance that the army would act against it, especially, in view of its desire to maintain an "Islamic image" for itself. The Jama'at has thus been particularly careful not to antagonize the army. Even when General Zia hurt it by some of his actions in 1984, it did not take to the streets demanding his ouster.

Perhaps this partly explains why violence has not isolated the Jama'at from the "mainstream" of politics in the country. Indeed, violence has been one of the means of wielding power in Pakistani politics; the repeated seizures of political power by the army, and its efforts to suppress political opposition and dissidence, which in turn occasioned violent reactions at different times (in 1968–69 against the quasi-military regime of General Ayub Khan; in 1970–71, against the military regime of General Yahya Khan, and against General Zia ul-Huq's regime throughout the 1980s until his death in 1988), have served to legitimize the use of force in politics.[63]

In sum, the Jama'at's strategy involved strengthening the party organization through recruiting new members and aligning itself with other Islam-oriented parties. Its cadres began infiltrating the ranks of the opposition parties, the army, and the bureaucracy. It had already acquired a powerful base of support among the Urdu-speaking migrants from east Punjab and central India, who had emerged as a dominant entrepreneurial class in the aftermath of partition. Concentrated in the cities, especially in Karachi, Hyderabad, and Lahore, the migrants were in a position to play a disproportionately larger role in public life than their numbers justified, partly because of the weakness of the local leadership.[64] Members of this "community" initially proved receptive to the idea of an "Islamic" Pakistan and provided unwavering support to the party. Not until the 1984 formation of the MQM (Muhajir Qaumi Mahaj), an umbrella organization of migrant Muslims in Sind, was there any major erosion in Jama'at's support among the latter.

The Jama'at could use this powerful constituency to exert pressure on the indigenous elite, even in East Pakistan, and make itself increasingly visible in politics despite the smallness of its organization and lack of popular support. Recourse to violence increasingly became entwined with its political agenda and proved far more effective than the ideological propaganda. This was a sure way of exerting pressure on the secularists and socialists, who lacked similar organizational strength. The issues were chosen carefully so as to create the maximum impact on educated society. For example, the political tug-of-war was presented as a confrontation between Islam and kufr (infidelity), a theme bound to gain support even from the ulama, who were generally opposed to the Jama'at.

This strategy proved useful in 1973 when a new constitution was promulgated in Pakistan. Although the People's Party of Z. A. Bhutto, with its commitment to an

"Islamic" socialist system, had an absolute majority in Parliament, the Islamic Alliance was able to exert enough pressure to force inclusion of a unique declaration in the president's and prime minister's oath of office: the oath asserted the finality of the Prophethood of Muhammad, on the basis that such a declaration was a prerequisite for establishing of an ideal Islamic system.[65] While this change may have had some relevance to the persistent call of the Jama'at to set the boundaries of "authentic Islam," the real intention was to demonstrate the group's political strength by focusing on issues that not even the socialist Bhutto could ignore.

The political motivation became further evident in 1974 when the Ahmadi issue was raised again following an incident at the railway station at Rabwa, a small town in the district of Jhang in Punjab where the Ahmadiya movement has its world headquarters. On May 29 some members of the IJT, the student wing of the Jama'at in Pakistan, were involved in violent clashes with the local Ahmadis, raising the specter of a nationwide witch-hunt against the latter. Unlike the riots of 1953, when the Jama'at seemed to play the role of a "reluctant" participant and even disavowed any part in the violence, it was now at the forefront of a "holy war" known as the Khatm-i-Nabuwat movement. This movement demanded that the Ahmadis be declared a "non-Muslim" minority.[66] Then the Saudis interfered in the matter; they had earlier declared Ahmadi belief "incompatible with Islam."[67] Bhutto hoped to diffuse the tension against his government by conceding to this demand and, sensing greater trouble, gave way. A unique measure appropriating to itself the right to define a "true Muslim" was passed by Parliament on 19 September 1974. Thus the Ahmadis were constitutionally "excluded" from the fold of Islam by an act of a secular institution—the Parliament—which, according to Maulana Maududi himself, had no role in the System of the Prophet![68] Bhutto succumbed to the pressure politics of the Islamic right led by the Jama'at.

This victory was interpreted by the Jama'at as the consequence of its engaging in political violence. Emboldened, the Jama'at embarked on a policy of destablizing the government of Bhutto.

Maududi harbored a strong dislike for Bhutto, principally because of the success of his socialist appeal to the ordinary voters in (West) Pakistan in the elections of 1971, which all but eclipsed the Islamic appeal of the Jama'at, so assiduously propagated since 1948. Maududi had been so irritated and disturbed at the sudden rise of Bhutto that he appeared ready to support the Bengali nationalist leader Shaykh Mujib during the constitutional crisis of 1971 until the situation spun out of control.[69] Pakistan's military defeat in the Bangladesh war in December 1971 propelled Bhutto to the center of power politics in "new" Pakistan. His populist rhetoric, and the skill with which he handled the post-war situation, helped rebuild the confidence of a shattered nation and brought it closer to the oil-rich Arab countries. By projecting the Islamic image of Pakistan even while maintaining his socialist stance, Bhutto became the undisputed leader of his people. For a while, he made efforts to neutralize the religious appeal of the right wing by recourse to Islamic symbols and slogans.[70] It seemed unlikely Bhutto's government could be unseated in the foreseeable future through constitutional means.

The Jama'at and its allies were not, however, willing to sit it out and see the country take the road to socialism. The surest way of discrediting Bhutto was to question his allegiance to Islam and force him into a defensive posture. The fight over the Ahmadi issue in 1974 was, in all probability, intended as a dress rehearsal for a much bigger episode, directed specifically against the Bhutto regime and generally against the secular-socialist leadership. The Jama'at would no longer tolerate a leadership that might "deviate in any matter from the Islamic System." "If we suppose," warned Maududi in 1978, "that once a majority of wrong persons is elected [to the Parliament] it would manipulate the elections a second time, they will be faced with a similar movement which uprooted a dictator like Bhutto."[71]

National elections scheduled for March 1977 gave the Jama'at the opportunity to mobilize opposition to Bhutto's socialist programs. An alliance of nine Islam-oriented parties, consisting of the Jama'at, two conservative ulama organizations, and six other right-wing parties was forged with the avowed object of discrediting Bhutto on the issue of the "Islamic system," also known as the Nizam-i-Mustafa (the System of the Prophet). From the ideological point of view, this move, demanding the imposition from above of an "Islamic system," without recourse to structural changes in society through a program of reform, was the very antithesis of Maududi's proclaimed goal of an Islamic revolution.[72]

Bhutto began to feel the pressure from a mounting attack on his Islamic credibility. He offered concessions to narrow Islamic interests, such as a ban on alcohol consumption, gambling, horse racing, and nightclubs, and in deference to the sentiments of the Muslims he changed the weekly holiday from Sunday to Friday.[73] But this was not enough to satisfy the political ambition of the Jama'at; it was bent on destroying the credibility of Bhutto. The concessions merely exposed the vulnerability of the regime to pressure politics, making the Jama'at even more aggressive. Thus, although Bhutto won election overwhelmingly, the Jama'at-led alliance—backed by business interests that had been adversely affected by Bhutto's nationalization policy, and with the tacit approval of the army—mobilized enough political support to paralyze the government. A desperate Bhutto offered to enforce the Shari'a within six months,[74] but this offer failed to stop the violence in urban areas; the army intervened within less than four months of the elections and assumed control of the government.

Although organized under the aegis of the combined opposition, the Pakistan National Alliance (PNA), the student wing of the Jama'at (Islami Jamiat-i-Talaba) played a decisive role in organizing and leading the demonstrations against Bhutto's government. It had already emerged as the dominant force in campus politics by winning elections to a majority of student councils in the colleges and universities.[75] These victories gave them virtual control over campus politics and thus ensured them a powerful role in national politics. When the PNA launched its campaign against Bhutto in 1977, the IJT logically emerged as the voice of urban youth and were in a position to articulate the grievances of the middle class. With cooperation from madrasa (Islamic religious seminary) students, who have been traditionally loyal to the conservative ulama, the Jama'at cadres were instrumental in mobilizing a wide coalition of groups against the government. Through paralyzing strikes—which severely affected the communication system, urban business, educational institutions, and even government offices—street demonstrations, and violent confrontations with the police, the major cities were virtually brought to a standstill.[76]

Arguably, Bhutto had to blame himself for much of the political tension in Pakistan at this time. He had raised high hopes and expectations among different groups by his slogans and rhetoric; in power he acted otherwise. He put restrictions on civil liberties, suppressed the press, used the highly politicized paramilitary force, the Federal Security Force, to intimidate his opponents, antagonizing even members of his own party who did not agree with him, and let loose a reign of terror in Baluchistan, forcing the powerful autonomy movement there to degenerate into a full scale guerilla war.[77] On the economic front, his half-hearted measures of nationalization and land reform created widespread discontent both among those who were adversely affected and those who expected to gain. Finally, as Omar Noman puts it, when he "began to suppress those groups who genuinely believed in the rhetoric of the party, they became the most hostile enemies of Bhutto's PPP."[78] Although the PPP still had widespread support among the lower classes, especially in rural areas, the erosion of support from the urban middle classes proved too expensive to him and equally advantageous for the Jama'at and its allies in the PNA. As the only cadre-based party in existence, it could provide effective leadership to the disenchanted by articulating their economic grievances and religious sentiments. Subsequent developments left no doubt that the Jama'at was ready for the occasion.

If Jama'at's support for the military regime of Yahya Khan and the group's subsequent attempts to force out the Bhutto government in collaboration with its "Islam-pasand" allies seem paradoxical from an ideological viewpoint, so was its unquestioned support for the new military dictatorship that overthrew Bhutto in 1977. With the rise of General Zia ul-Haq (d. 1988), the political situation in Pakistan suddenly became so favorable for the Jama'at that Maududi came out in support of the military regime and offered, in a series of interviews broadcast on state-controlled radio, to provide the basic guidelines for an Islamic system for Pakistan.[79] To the Jama'at, Zia's Islamic agenda was an affirmation of the worldview that had helped create Pakistan; thus, the regime certainly deserved support. As many as four members of the Jama'at party were later inducted into the military government in a demonstration of support for Zia's programs and in order to help him consolidate his political position.

Zia began emphasizing the political role of Islam in Pakistan immediately after assuming power. In 1978 he initiated a move to bring the Jama'at and the other Islam-oriented parties, like the Muslim League (Pagaro) and the Jamia't-i-Ulama-i-Islam (JUI), under a common platform in an unsuccessful attempt to create an Islamic Front. The initiative failed due primarily to interparty rivalry and the conflicting political ambitions of their leaders, but the Jama'at continued to maintain close links with the military regime.[80] Zia's interest in an Islamic political alliance and his zeal for Islamization had direct relevance to his political survival. Though the Islamization program lacked significant grass-roots support, some of the measures, such as reform of the legal system, had substantial institutional impact which profoundly affected the structure of the state. (Thus, even secularist Benazir Bhutto, when elected prime minister in 1989, had to acquiesce to many of these changes. A 1990 election poster, showing Benazir in *shalwar* and *kamiz* (the traditional North Indian dress for women), with her head fully covered, reading the Holy Qur'an, reflected the social transformation that had taken place in Pakistan under Zia.[81]

Zia's concept of an Islamic order, the Nizam-i-Mustafa (literally, the System of the Prophet), bore the clear imprint of Maududi's thought.[82] Zia took up the Ahmadi question—a strategy frequently used by the Jama'at to make its Islamic appeal more attractive to the ulama and others loyal to the idea of an Islamic polity—and vowed to "persevere in our efforts to ensure that the cancer of Qadianism is exterminated."[83] In April 1984, he issued a decree prohibiting the Ahmadis from calling themselves Muslims, from calling their mosques "mosques," and from chanting the call to prayer.[84] An immediate objective of this move was to remove all Ahmadis from senior positions in the armed forces and the civil service. Many were brutalized by "mullah-inspired mobs in collusion with government officials, for no other reason than professing and practicing their personal faith as Muslims." Others fled the country.[85]

The Jama'at's cooperation with Zia lasted through 1984, when it decided to distance itself from the military regime for a variety of reasons. Open identification and collaboration with a military regime had created apprehensions among many in the Jama'at about the danger of isolating the party from the political movement that was taking shape against the military regime, under the leadership of the Movement for the Restoration of Democracy (MRD), an alliance of some major political parties, in which the Jama'at was not represented. Open collaboration with the military regime had already created confusion about its commitment to democratic change. It was essential for it to make a move to restore public confidence in its credibility as a political party. The Jama'at political party's poor showings in the elections of 1985, held under the auspices of the military regime with which it had close rapport,[86] made the leadership particularly wary.

It is also possible that the Jama'at grew restive with the slow pace of Islamization under Zia and decided in favor of exerting pressure on the regime by being openly critical of its programs, and the pace of Islamization. The Jama'at had welcomed the imposition of martial law in 1977 because it "rid the nation of the rule of socialist despotism" and promised to inaugurate "a truly Islamic era in the life of this country."[87] Like many other political parties which had resisted the Bhutto regime, the Jama'at had possibly hoped that Zia's regime would serve as an interim government, eventually handing over power to the "Islamic Alliance" through some mechanism, but there were no indications that this was going to happen.[88] The Jama'at became particularly restive after the referendum of 1984, which purportedly confirmed Zia's programs of Islamization and solidified his position. Henceforth, Zia became increasingly less dependent on the Jama'at and, in the Jama'at's view, began appropriating to himself the authority to define the Shari'a, which rightfully belonged to the elected Majlis-i-Shura, or an Islamic Assembly of pious people.[89] The tension surfaced when Zia made a number of sweeping amendments to the constitution of 1973, giving himself arbitrary power, without consulting the newly constituted Parliament.[90] It does not seem, though, that the rupture in relations between the two sides was ever complete. The Jama'at remained apprehensive of the possibility of a return to power by Bhutto's People's Party and would support any measure to keep that from happening.

After Zia's death in an unexplained plane crash in 1988, free elections were held again in Pakistan. The Jama'at and its Islam-pasand allies mounted a determined campaign against the People's Party (then led by Bhutto's daughter, Benazir, and his wife, Nusrat Bhutto) and other secular-oriented parties. Alongside its campaign for an Islamic polity, it tried to undermine the public image of the People's Party by a smear campaign against its leadership. An old photograph of Nusrat Bhutto dancing with the former U.S. president Gerald Ford was reproduced on hundreds of thousands of handbills and posters to shock Muslim voters.[91] Questions were also raised about the appropriateness of a woman leading a Muslim state; this position was a total reversal of the Jama'at's stand in 1965, when it supported the candidacy of Miss Fatima Jinnah for the presidency of Pakistan against the incumbent military president General Ayub Khan (1958–69). But such propaganda failed, and the candidates of the Jama'at and its allies were routed nationwide by the secular-oriented parties. The People's Party won the largest number of seats. In a 237-seat Parliament, the Jama'at's share was limited to 5, demonstrating the lack of popular enthusiasm for Zia's programs of Islamization from above.

But in less than two years, circumstances changed. The Islam-pasand groups soon regrouped under the banner of an Islamic alliance issuing *fatwas* against the "un-Islamic" government of Benazir Bhutto. Eventually they succeeded in removing her troubled government from office through a "constitutional coup" by the president, acting in collusion with the Islamic groups.[92] Subsequent elections in October 1990, though "certified" by foreign observers as "generally open, orderly, and well-administered,"[93] were held under circumstances that left little room for the People's Party to maneuver, forcing its defeat. Two close advisers to the newly elected prime minister Nawaz Sharif later resigned from the government and claimed in August 1991 that "election cells" had been set up during the 1990 elections to manipulate the results of the elections to "see that Ms. Bhutto did not return to power."[94]

Although the Jama'at aligned itself closely with the new government formed after the elections of 1990, there were immediate signs of tension. In its efforts to exert the maximum pressure for Islamization on its allies, the Jama'at has consistently pursued a policy of keeping alive the debate on ideological issues. It is aware that without that debate, or in the absence of a target, the momentum in favor of an Islamic polity, in which it expects to be the principal beneficiary, might be lost.

One such debate was on the question of *riba'*. Although riba' is often defined by the fundamentalists and the ulama as "interest" charged on loans, the concept of interest, which forms the basis of the modern economic system, is singularly different from riba', or usury, which is exploitative in character. But it is not exactly the merit of the system with which the fundamentalists are concerned. To them, the issue is essential to the question of Islamization of the institutions to which the government is theoretically committed. The ideological importance attached to riba' is too great to be ignored, but of equal importance to the Jama'at is the question of possible political advantage. A senior official, representing Prime Minister Sharif, argued that "there's a fear psychosis, and they [the fundamentalists] create it. And the more we're squeezed, the stronger these guys get." He insisted it was not simply a matter of interpreting the implications of riba' but of "whether we want to go towards the fanatical, obscurantist Islam of the mullahs or whether we want Islam of Iqbal and Jinnah."[95] It seems the question will not be resolved easily, and the consequent tension is bound to aggravate the tenuous relations between the fundamentalists and others who earlier had formed an electoral alliance based on an ambivalent program of Islamization in their bid to defeat Benazir Bhutto. In 1992 there were signs of disagreement within the alliance on important policy matters. The Jama'at appeared determined to use its manipulative power to force the government to come to terms with it.[96]

As we have seen, the manipulative power of the Jama'at rests mostly on its ability to use Islamic rhetoric, symbols and slogans in articulating the social and economic grievances of the urban middle and lower middles classes. Effective support comes from the Jama'at's youth cadres, which no other political party in Pakistan can match. The Jam'at, furthermore, is practically assured of the support of most of their Islamic allies, including the conservative ulama, when faced by an "enemy" like the PPP; the flimsy nature of their own organizations leaves little scope for them to make any move independently of the Jama'at, putting the latter in a leadership role in their fight against the secular-socialist parties. In the same way, the government of Nawaz Sharif, despite obvious support from the army, did not wish to alienate the Jama'at as long as the PPP of Benazir Bhutto held ground.

The Jama'at, aware of this predicament of the Sharif government, did not waste any opportunity to advance its own agenda. Its urban street power, coupled with the uncertain political situation in Pakistan, resulting partly from the dismissal of Benazir Bhutto in 1990, and the latter's continued challenge to the regime, and partly from the unwillingness of the army-bureaucratic establishment to hand over effective power to an elected government headed by the PPP, has elevated the Jama'at to a position of undue influence in national politics, which is not obvious from the electoral support it has enjoyed, especially in the countryside. It may not be in a position to take over the reins of power in Pakistan in the near future, but it has mustered enough strength to exert pressure on any government that may not take it seriously.

The Jama'at in Bangladesh: Fundamentalism in a Hostile Environment

Although the Jama'at in Bangladesh is functionally a separate organization, it works in close concert with its world headquarters in Mansura (Punjab), Pakistan. The importance of this link should not be underestimated; the Jama'at itself has never considered political and physical separation of Bangladesh from the rest of the Muslim world significant for its Islamic goals, and has consistently emphasized the unitary character of the movement in the Indian subcontinent.[97] Somewhat like the Communist International, which promoted the idea of a worldwide workers' revolution against their class enemies, the fundamentalist Jama'at-i-Islami believes in waging war against all "un-Islamic" regimes as an essential condition for an Islamic revolution. In this scheme, geographical boundaries are considered irrelevant, and nation-states artificial constructs. The inescapable fact that nation-states do exist, and there are boundaries separating them from each other, made it necessary for the Jama'at to limit its formal operation within the boundaries of each state, but with the ultimate goal of uniting all Muslims under one divinely ordained Islamic government.[98] This made Maududi's and his party's acceptance of the principle of nationality in the context of the division of India in 1947, and of Pakistan in 1971, conditional. Thus, although the Jama'at in Bangladesh may not have any organic links with the parent organizations in Pakistan, it is bound by inseparable ties with the latter, and is directly influenced by its decisions and policies.[99]

But the new state of Bangladesh offered a strikingly different context for Jama'at's programs of Islamization than Pakistan. Not only was its creation a challenge to the professed Islamic ideology, which provided the raison d'etre for the establishment of Pakistan, Bengali Muslims have also resisted the imposition of nonindigenous cultural values on them to a marked degree, as exemplified by their resistance to the Arabic script, and equally by a loyalty to the Bengali language.[100] While allegiance to the Islamic religion has impinged "in some ways" upon their "patriotic and civic commitment," their ethnic identity as Bengalis has equally influenced their commitment and worldview.

The Jama'at invariably perceived this allegiance to indigenous culture as un-Islamic and has sought to counter this by imposing rigid rules of conduct on its own members, and by opposing Bengali culture oriented festivals and celebrations, many of which attracted the participation of both Muslims and Hindus. Bangladesh's forced separation from Pakistan in 1971—with military support from India, considered a Hindu state—further reinforced Jama'at's opposition to the Bengali ideology, which proved critical in the creation of Bangladesh.[101]

Unlike Pakistan, where the Jama'at found strong allies in the army, the bureaucracy, and the conservative ulama in its battle against the PPP, the situation in Bangladesh has been quite different. Even though the army has exercised effective control over the government for a considerable period of time, and has used Islamic rhetoric as a means of legitimizing its authority, on occasions even allying itself with the Jama'at, it has hardly subscribed to the idea of a fundamentalist Islamic state. And, unlike Pakistan, where an alliance between the conservative ulama and the Jama'at has generally worked to the advantage of the latter, the ulama in Bangladesh have refused to support the Jama'at, thus denying the latter a much-needed larger platform for its Islamization programs. Finally, the secular-socialist parties in Bangladesh have proved far more articulate and determined in opposing the Jama'at, particularly for its open hostility to the Bangladesh movement in 1971, than their counterparts in Pakistan. In this, they have been aggressively supported by the dominant members of the intelligentsia and public opinion, thus creating a hostile environment for the Jama'at.[102]

This partly explains why fundamentalist ideology has had a limited appeal for the Muslims of this region.[103] Although developments in Bangladesh since 1975 might indicate a greater recourse to religious symbolism, there is no reason to suppose that Bengali culture has lost its relevance for the society or that fundamentalist Islam has emerged as the dominant theme in the life of the people. The vigor and enthusiasm with which the fundamentalist Jama'at-i-Islami has pursued its Islamic agenda in recent years should be ascribed more to the failure of the secular elites in addressing the social, economic, and political problems of the country, and to external influences, especially Middle Eastern money and political support for Islamization, than to any radical change in the attitudes and perceptions of the average Bengali Muslim.[104] It is not the masses who determine the role of the fundamentalists; the fundamentalists' organizational structure, power of propaganda, and increased militancy all point to their growing power in national life.

After independence (16 December 1971), the Jama'at-i-Islami along with other religious-oriented parties were legally banned in Bangladesh for their notorious collaboration with the Pakistan army. The government was concerned that ordinary people could be "misled easily [more] in the name of religion than by any other means."[105] The new leadership in Bangladesh, including Shaykh Mujib, could not have been under any illusion about the strength and appeal of Islam in a predominantly Muslim country. Mujib had asserted, however, that Islam should not be abused for political purposes: "Our position is very clear. We are not believers in the label of Islam. We believe in the Islam of justice. Our Islam is the Islam of the holy and merciful Prophet."[106] The policy of secularization that the new government pursued, however, created misgivings among many of the people about its real intentions. The government's close ties with India (in popular perception a "Hindu" country) and the communist bloc (symbolic of Godlessness) were exploited by its opponents to portray an un-Islamic image of the government which was bound to affect its credibility in the public eye.

During and after the war in 1971, the Jama'at, with support from the Saudi establishment and the Pakistan government, launched a powerful propaganda campaign against the "un-Islamic" character of the Bangladesh movement, thereby alienating Bangladesh from the oil-rich Arab countries. The propaganda was further reinforced with the declaration of Bangladesh as a "secular" state in 1973. The Jama'at and its allies were now in an advantageous position, despite the ban on their political activities, to undermine the Islamic credibility of the new leadership. For Mujib and his government, it was essential to win recognition from the Arab countries to obtain funding for the war-ravaged economy. It was thus desirable to deflate domestic tension on the question of secularism. This relaxation resulted in a gradual softening of tone of the Mujib government (1972–75), especially during the last phase of its rule, toward certain issues—government support for religious institutions, inclusion of Islamic themes in school curriculum, support of pilgrims bound for Mecca—but such support had merely a cosmetic value.[107]

This policy of "reconciliation" encouraged the Islam-oriented groups to reassert themselves gradually. The Jama'at, though still under a legal ban, joined others opposed to the regime and initiated a hate campaign against the secularist and socialist programs of the government, successfully capitalizing on a growing anti-Indian and anti-communist sentiment among the people.[108] A near-famine condition in several regions of the country in 1974 was aggravated further by the inefficiency of the government, the degenerating law-and-order situation, and the high-handedness of the highly politicized paramilitary force, the hated Rakshi Bahini. Finally, introduction of a single-party system, the BAKSAL, created widespread resentment against the ruling party, even causing erosion in the personal popularity of Shaykh Mujib, the country's founding father.[109] Favorable conditions were thus created for the renewed use of religious symbols.

The assassination of Shaykh Mujib on 15 August 1975 signaled the formal reemergence of confessional politics in Bangladesh and consequently the revival of the fundamentalist Jama'at-i-Islami. The political disorder and confusion that followed Mujib's death as well as the urgent need for forging closer ties with the Muslim Middle East induced the military regime of General Ziaur Rahman (d. 1981) to take an overtly pro-Islamic stance in public affairs, encouraging the renewed use of religious symbols in politics. Taking advantage of the situation, the Jama'at began playing an increasingly active role in the political life of the nation. Efforts to strengthen the party organization through recruitment of new members, publication of party literature, and collaboration with the new regime were matched by its powerful campaign of propaganda against secularism and socialism.

By the mid-1980s, the Jama'at reemerged as a sold political force in Bangladesh, despite lingering public memories about its negative role, including the massacre of civilians by its cadres, during the liberation war. It set up active branches in all districts, towns, and cities, reorganized its cadres, and successfully integrated itself into the political life of the country. This was a remarkable achievement for a party which seemed dead at independence. Its full membership rose to over a thousand, while the strength of its associate members rose to more than a hundred thousand active participants. The numbers continued to increase phenomenally in the years ahead due partly to its successful drives and transformed it into the largest cadre-based political organization in the country. The recruits came mostly from the urban educated classes with roots in rural areas, and included, among others, teachers of secondary schools, colleges and universities, mid and lower grade employees of the government and autonomous bodies, attorneys, doctors, members of small business, and a few from the traditional religious seminaries. Wary of the uncertain and hostile political environment, the Jama'at leadership paid particular attention to younger recruits, ensuring the creation of a disciplined and highly motivated youth force. It succeeded in attracting hundreds of university and college students to its student organization, the Islami Chatra Shibir (ICS), which, like the Islami Jamiat-i-Tulaba in Pakistan, subsequently led a successful campaign against their secular-oriented student opponents in several campuses, especially in Chittagong and Rajshahi divisions. The Jama'at, however, failed to win any large measure of support from among the madrasa students, who have mostly remained loyal to the conservative ulama and supportive of military regimes.[110]

The Jama'at successfully established a network of organizations throughout the country, consolidating its political strength. Through a well-coordinated program, its cadres infiltrated the ranks of the army, the bureaucracy, and other vital public and private institutions and made conscious attempts to influence the decision-making process.

Better employment opportunities for the Jama'at cadres ensured financial security of its members and induced others to join the organization. Its numerous covert operations, which include private trusts, schools, medical facilities, publishing firms, banking and business institutions, and a large number of "sociocultural" forums, considerably enhanced its organizational strength and support base, which no other party or movement could rival.[111]

A significant portion of the funding for these institutions seemed to have come from outside the country, although the Jama'at would not acknowledge it. Individuals and institutions in Saudi Arabia and the Gulf States are known to have donated millions of dollars to the Jama'at in support of its programs of Islamization. Support also came from the migrant workers in the Middle East, many of whom have been openly loyal to its ideology and donated a portion of their income to its official fund, the Bait al-Mal. Other than this, members of the Jama'at are required to make an obligatory monthly contribution to its fund; donations from "supporters and sympathizers," and investments in Islamic banks and trusts equally help in beefing up its funds.[112] The money is collected and spent through a well-coordinated program designed to promote its programs and attract newer support. Unlike the secular-oriented parties and organization, which often lack similar discipline and commitment to a cause, the Jama'at's organizational structure, ensuring strict discipline within the movement is a guarantee to the proper use of this fund.

Even a cursory glance at the daily newspapers in Bangladesh, especially between 1985 and 1993, would reveal the extent and frequency of violence used by the Jama'at. There have thus been widespread reports of maiming and killing of their political opponents, using gruesome methods such as chopping off of hands and extraction of eyes.[113] Its opponents have been guilty of similar outrages in several places against the Jama'at; they have recently mobilized a considerable amount of public opinion against the latter, especially on the issue of a public trial of Ghulam Azam, for his alleged role during the liberation war, aggravating the tension further.[114]

The inaction of the current government, which forged a fragile alliance with the Jama'at in 1990, and the ambivalence of the secular parties in dealing with the problem,[115] have further emboldened the Jama'at. By a combination of anti-Indian rhetoric—which has a strong appeal to many, including the army and the urban middle and lower middle classes—Islamic slogans and organized violence against chosen targets, the Jama'at cadres have put the secular opponents on the defensive, despite the latter's widespread electoral support. The army has always stood in the sidelines in this conflict; its strong dislike for the Awami League, the leading secular-oriented political party in the country and a desire to seize power virtually made it a silent instigator of violence.

The success of the Jama'at-i-Islami in Bangladesh, like its counterpart in Pakistan, has been particularly spectacular in educational institutions. Its student wing, the Islami Chatra Sibir (the Islamic Students' League), has emerged as the most organized and determined student organization in the country and has been responsible for much intimidation and violence on campus. In a clear demonstration of its brute force, armed cadres of the Sibir took control of the university campus in Chittagong in 1986 (where this author was then located), terrorizing their opponents, including faculty and staff, and cruelly maiming several of them.[116] Since then, while retaining their firm hold on that campus, they have further extended their control over several other institutions.

The organizational strength of the Jama'at cadres has not, however, been matched by similar successes in national elections. Since its formal revival in 1979, it has generally pursued a policy of containing the power of the secularists and the socialists and promoting the idea of an "Islamic" Bangladesh as an integral part of an indivisible Islamic umma.[117] The assassination of General Zia in 1981, and the subsequent military takeover under General Ershad, after a brief civilian interlude, changed the political environment of the country so dramatically that the Jama'at found itself fighting alongside its enemies (as well as friends) for the "restoration of democracy." Even its archenemy, the secularist Awami League, maintained an ambivalent silence about the Jama'at's past and established close liaison with it for furthering the "cause" of democracy.[118]

While fully participating in the campaign for the "restoration of democracy," the Jama'at never abandoned its commitment to a militant Islamic ideology. It thus consistently demanded the implementation of Shari'a and declared Bangladesh an "Islamic" state.[119] It held rallies, organized meetings, and published a stream of literature to popularize the idea. Its techniques of political mobilization were so impressive that neither the secularists nor the military-led government could ignore its role in national politics. General Ershad admitted that his decision to proclaim Islam as the state religion in 1988 was induced largely by a desire to "take the wind out of the sail of the Jama'at."

The power of the Jama'at owed more to its organizational strength and the militant role of its youth cadres than to any appreciable increase in the popularity of its Islamic agenda. In the national elections of 1991, its electoral support still stood at 6 percent.[120] This result was not significantly different from its performance in earlier elections. Its 18 seats in the 300-seat Parliament (another 30 seats are reserved for women, who are subsequently "elected" by the members of the House), however, enabled it to ensure the formation of a center-right government, led by Khaleda Zia, widow of the assassinated military ruler General Ziaur Rahman.[121]

The position of the Jama'at in Bangladesh is seemingly a paradox. While its popular support remains virtually unchanged, it has certainly emerged as a dominant force, able to exert powerful influence on the political process of the country. Furthermore, it has succeeded in creating momentum in favor of an Islamic agenda (however ill-defined) which secularist opponents find hard to ignore. The violence and terror associated with the activities of its student and youth cadres have so unnerved the student population that a minor incident involving a strike call at a university campus can create widespread fear and apprehension among them. The tensions provoked by the recent election of Ghulam Azam, notorious for his collaboration with the Pakistan army during the Bangladesh war in 1971, and who still retains a Pakistani passport, as the amir of the Bangladesh Jama'at-i-Islami further demonstrate the depth of unease, and a certain degree of helplessness, among those opposed to the militant ideology of the Jama'at.[122]

Fundamentalism, Extremism, and Political Transformation

What do we learn from our discussion of the shifting ideology, programs, and activities of the Jama'at-i-Islami in Pakistan? Does the growing appeal of the Jama'at, and its increasing involvement in politics, indicate the existence of a causal relationship between the fundamentalist ideology and state power? Is fundamentalism a specific answer for present-day problems, as often suggested?

We have looked at two different and somewhat distinct phases in the history of the Jama'at and have witnessed its evolution from a movement of "religious revival" to a radical religiopolitical organization. In each stage, loyalty to an inflexible, absolutist Islamic ideology provided the sine qua non for its actions. The formative phase of its existence, spanning roughly between 1940 and 1952, was marked by a certain idealism emphasizing its commitment to an Islamic revolution. Since the fundamentalist conception of an Islamic polity makes no distinction between the religious and political life of the individual, this commitment to an Islamic revolution also required participation in political activities. At the initial stage, however, this participation was minimal, and basically limited its opposition to the Muslim nationalist ideology: it did not function as a political party at that time and, instead, concentrated on activities related to its quest for a religious revival. With Partition and independence in 1947, circumstances changed and the Jama'at became increasingly active in formal politics in Pakistan (and later, in Bangladesh and India), gradually transforming itself into a political pressure movement with the declared goal of attaining state power as a necessary condition for realizing its Islamic goals. From the ideology of an Islamic revolution, which promised to transform the society almost logically, the emphasis shifted to political goals and strategies, thus undermining Maududi's original hope for an "Islamic order" which he once declared a necessary prerequisite for an authentic Islamic state.

The shifting ideological concern of the Jama'at manifested itself in its willingness to participate in secular political institutions and forums, like the constituent assemblies, and its ad hoc acceptance of the principle of popular sovereignty, which forms the basis of modern democratic systems. It also adopted a policy of "gradual" implementation of its Islamic ideals through constitutional means. It thus voted in support of enacting the first constitution of Pakistan in 1956, which was no more than a revised version of the Government of India Act, 1935 (including subsequent amendments), proclaiming the establishment of a parliamentary system of government modeled along the Westminster style. A pledge, incorporated in that constitution, that no law should be enacted that was repugnant to the injunctions of Islam had only an academic value in the absence of any fundamental change in the constitutional and legal sphere. And yet the Jama'at greeted the constitution as a success for Islam.[123] Although it never abandoned the ideology of jihad and would invariably describe itself as a revolutionary Islamic movement,[124] it unlike the latter, often compromised on matters of fundamental principle, raising questions about its revolutionary credential.

But the loss of revolutionary fervor affected neither its organizational discipline nor its political progress. As a carefully structured and regimented movement, it set down rigid rules of conduct for its members, making ideological indoctrination a basic theme of its training and education, thus guaranteeing almost a total unity in all important matters. It thus restricts "individual freedom" and "freedom of expression" of its members for the sake of the common good of the Jama'at. "If an individual fails to make these small sacrifices, he will eventually end up losing all his freedom [as a result of the possible victory of his enemies due to inaction and lack of sacrifice on his part]," stressed a Jama'at document.[125] Ghulam Azam even discouraged spiritually "weak" people from joining the organization, as the sacrifices required of them would be too great and the dangers they would encounter too great.[126] However, dissensions do exist within its ranks, as manifested in a leadership contest in the Bangladesh Jama'at in 1983,[127] but the kind of vicious factionalism that has continually dogged the secular, socialist, and communist parties in these countries, are practically unknown to it. This has allowed the Jama'at to operate as a solid force in resisting the secular opposition.

What particularly helped the Jama'at and certain other fundamentalist movements in other regions (such as the Brotherhood of Egypt), in gaining organizational and political strength during the 1970s and 1980s is debatable. It is, however, possible to discern a number of common factors that have caused growing social and political unrest in many Muslim countries in the post-colonial period which added strength to radical movements, either on the Left or on the Right. Of particular significance has been the failure of the postcolonial elites in dealing with basic social and economic problems; mismanaged economic growth, rampant corruption, and authoritarianism thus often resulted in political instability and violence. The 1950s, it may be remembered, was a period of great optimism in the subcontinent. By the 1960s, however, political stagnation had set in, especially in Pakistan, resulting in erosion of political authority. Repeated army takeovers (since 1975, especially in Bangladesh), and the consequent political repression and counter violence led to a crisis of legitimacy in both Pakistan and Bangladesh, radicalizing the political behavior of large sections of the population, especially the younger generation. An initial surge in popularity of the leftist movements, which characterized the political ethos of the younger generation in these countries in the 1960s and 1970s, and an aggravated emphasis on ethnic, linguistic, and regional identities, were some of the characteristics of the early protest movements against the dominant elites. Although the situation in India was far more complex for the Muslims, consequent upon the partition of India in 1947, a similar process of alienation—accentuated by the hostility of the right-wing Hindu-oriented parties, and the ambivalence of the ruling Congress party—gradually turned many inward. Given the fact that Islamic symbols and slogans played seminal roles in the Muslim separatist movement in colonial India, it was only natural that the emotional appeal of religion—which remained alive in mosques, religious seminaries, and in religiously oriented individuals and groups—would resurface again. The Jama'at, as the most fanatical and organized Islamic group in the subcontinent, was certain to play a significant role in revitalizing the momentum in favor of Islam.

The factors which caused the erosion of political authority, especially in Pakistan and Bangladesh, worked to the advantage of the Jama'at. Despite limitation of resources, and the failure of the nationalist elites, political independence had opened up new opportunities of education and employment for many, especially in the rural areas, inducing them to migrate to towns and cities.[128] It was primarily from these classes that most members of the Jama'at have been recruited. They felt that they have been denied legitimate privileges by the entrenched elites, and they were appalled by the Westernized lifestyle of the urban rich, which appeared to them as vulgar and un-Islamic. In desperation, and out of genuine repugnance for what they saw, many turned to radical Islam.[129]

Most of those who thus joined the Jama'at came from the younger generation. The induction of more and more younger members considerably affected the organizational structure and programs of the Jama'at, with the former increasingly taking the lead in political movements. It is no wonder that the party gradually moved toward a more militant ideology than had been apparent in the 1950s and early 1960s. The perception that Islam was in danger, and that it was the young cadres of the Jama'at alone who would successfully resist the secular-socialist enemies, emboldened the younger members and allowed them a certain measure of latitude within the party in pushing forward their militant goals.

It is vain to search for evidence of historical continuity in the fundamentalist ideology, although this does not negate certain linkages between Islam's historical past and the modern-day fundamentalist movements. The fundamentalist notion of Islamic history itself negates the theory of continuity. Appealing to a perceived purity of the first Islamic century, the fundamentalist vision short-circuits time, seeking to "come full circle" and claim finality. It is all too obvious these movements are searching for a new paradigm in response to present-day experience, while ideologically conforming to the perceived Islamic model of the first century. The changes and adjustments in the programs and idioms of the Jama'at indicate a certain pattern in the fundamentalist response to the "problems" encountered by them which has little relevance either to the reformist or to the nationalist Muslim notions of Islamic history of an earlier era. What is of crucial significance is that the Jama'at first came into being basically as a reaction to the nineteenth- and early twentieth-century Muslim reformist and nationalist ideologies which made little mention of the Shari'a or an Islamic government. The Jama'at failed to popularize its ideology then, partly because of its inability to offer a viable alternative to the nationalist ideology. But the circumstances changed after independence, and it was able to put forward a coherent theme of Islamization which no other movement or organization in the region could rival. Indeed, it goes to the credit of the Jama'at that through its efforts alone, Islam has become a consistent theme in the political discourse of Pakistan, Bangladesh, and to a certain extent, the Indian Muslims.

The religious ideology of the Jama'at gained legitimacy partly due to its increased appeal to the authoritarian, military regimes in Pakistan and Bangladesh, seeking to legitimize their illegal seizure of power. Each time a military regime appeared on the scene, the Jama'at became one of the principle beneficiaries. While the regimes of Zia in Pakistan openly courted the support of the party, thus encouraging it to popularize its Islamic themes, the regime of Ershad (ousted in 1990) in Bangladesh, though openly hostile to the Jama'at, helped create favorable conditions for it, first, by declaring the country an "Islamic state" and, more importantly, by making possible its entry into the democratic movement launched jointly by all opposition parties. Despite reservations about the Jama'at, even the communist and secular parties, including the Awami League, maintained close liaison with the latter, thus giving it a much-needed political legitimacy in post-independent Bangladesh. The religious ideology attracted particular attention partly due to its increasing appeal to the authoritarian regimes in Pakistan and Bangladesh seeking to legitimize their illegal seizure of power.[130]

But developments in other Muslim countries created an equally favorable environment in popularizing Islamic themes among large numbers of Muslims in the subcontinent. The Islamic Revolution in Iran in 1979 was particularly inspiring to many, despite the Shi'ite basis of that upheaval. I interviewed scores of Muslims from these countries from 1988 to 1992 and was amazed to discover that Khomeini had become a symbol of Islamic revival to many. The Jama'at, despite its close links with Iran's number one enemy in the Muslim world, the Saudis, has never failed to acknowledge this fact.[131] Ghulam Azam saw Khomeini's revolution as the first victory of Islam against a secular, un-Islamic regime and hoped that this victory would inspire confidence among Muslims all over the world in seeking similar changes in their conditions.

The oil wealth of the Arabs has had a similar impact on the activist movements. Cheap religious tracts proclaiming God's special mercy on the Muslims in the form of oil could be seen circulating even in poverty-ridden Bangladesh, whose people have little benefited from the wealth of their Arab coreligionists. Despite a recent denial by the Saudi king,[132] evidence suggests that the Saudis and the Gulf states have pumped millions of dollars into these countries to support the fundamentalist Jama'at-i-Islami through formal and informal channels.[133] This has enabled the Jama'at to invest money in banking and charitable institutions, to indulge in an ambitious program of publishing propaganda literature, and to pay a regular allowance to its cadres, attracting support from some of the brightest members of the younger generation in colleges and universities.[134] Consequently, the Jama'at, as we have seen, succeeded in organizing a highly disciplined youth cadre which has spearheaded movements against the Bhuttos in Pakistan and the Ershad regime (1981–90) in Bangladesh.

Despite all incentives, propaganda, and organizational discipline, however, the Jama'at has not been successful in popularizing its Islamic programs among the majority of Muslims in any of these countries. Other than its secular and socialist enemies, the Jama'at also faces an uphill battle against the traditional clergy, the "conservative" ulama, pirs and mullahs, who have traditionally exerted great influence over the masses and who have remained opposed to the Jama'at.[135] Although the perceived fear of Benazir Bhutto's return to power has served to unite the Jama'at and the traditional clergy in Pakistan in a close electoral alliance, their conflicting interests and programs make it impossible for them to work together indefinitely. In Bangladesh such a marriage of convenience has not even taken place, nor does it seem likely. Numerically speaking, the Jama'at is thus a marginal force with limited support primarily among sections of lower-middle and middle-class Muslims mostly concentrated in urban areas. The masses remain indifferent to the ideological discourses of the Jama'at and are more concerned with the problem of how to keep themselves alive. Still, the numbers do not undermine the argument that the Jama'at has emerged as a powerful force in these countries through the use of emotive symbols and slogans, discipline, hard work, and the use of violence. The result is that although it holds basically an ideology of the lower middle and middle classes, the Jama'at has succeeded in making Islam the subject of an intense debate, creating an atmosphere whereby even the secularists, socialists, traditionalists, and modernists equally find it necessary to look upon Islam as a potential force and can hardly ignore the Jama'at. Even socialist Bhutto in Pakistan had to reformulate the goal of his party to affirm that his idea of a classless society was derived from the political and social ethics of Islam.

The growing militancy of the Jama'at has long-term social and political consequences for South Asia. Since violence has become inextricably linked with their ideology, they might influence the lives of others by sheer application of force, as has already happened on a number of occasions. The growing disenchantment and frustrations of the educated youth with their existing conditions are likely to make the fundamentalist appeal increasingly more attractive over time. Trouble for the established order might come even from unknown sources: the violent demonstrations against Salman Rushdie and against Western involvement in the Gulf Crisis demonstrated the emotional appeal of symbolic issues that could be conveniently used by the Jama'at to rally support in its favor when circumstances appear favorable.

The Jama'at is not going to be a spent force in the near future; it has an ability to survive adverse conditions. Since its ultimate goal is to gain control of state power and establish the dictatorship of the party in order to implement its own version of the Islamic state, even its allies may find themselves abandoned when the time comes. The Jama'at does not have a charismatic leader, a Khomeini; it does not seem to need one. Maududi was an uncharismatic leader and ideologue. He laid the basis of the Jama'at and was responsible for articulating the ideological basis of the movement, but excited little emotion among people by his highly technical discourses. Jama'at members are fanatically dedicated to a cause, however, which they believe to be the ultimate solution for all mundane and spiritual problems of Muslims; they are determined to achieve their goal, no matter what the price may be. They have the manipulative power, the money, and the organizational strength and discipline needed to wage a long-term battle; the hopeless divisions and rivalries within the ranks of their opponents serve to encourage them further in pursuit of their goals. Whether they have the ability to expand their base of support and take control of the state, in Pakistan or Bangladesh, is a hypothetical question and depends largely on the changes in objective conditions in these countries. No one would dispute the fact, however, that the Jama'at has emerged as a major force in the life of the Muslims in the subcontinent over the last two decades and is certain to play an important role in the social and political life of these countries for an indefinite period. Whether this represents a "resurgence of Islam" is debatable, but it certainly points to the growing appeal of Islamic symbols and slogans to the Muslim peoples, the implications of which cannot be measured in terms of actual support for specific movements or programs.

Acknowledgments

I am indebted to Bruce B. Lawrence and Barbara D. Metcalf for their useful comments on an early draft of this chapter, and to Marta Nicholas and Ralph W. Nicholas for their unfailing support of the project.

Notes

1. See Antonio R. Gualtieri, *Conscience and Coercion: Ahmadi Muslims and Orthodoxy in Pakistan* (Montreal: Guernica, 1989), chap. 3 and *passim;* also *Review of Religions* 83, no. 3 (March 1988): 27–28; no. 5 (May 1988): 15–21; no. 10 (October 1988): 38–39.

2. See Abul Hasan 'Ali Nadwi, *'Asri hazir men din ki tafhim-tashrik* (Lucknow: Dar-i 'Arafat, 1978), pp. 13, 15–16, 112, and *passim;* also Gualtieri, *Conscience and Coercion,* p. 27.

3. Bruce B. Lawrence, pers. comm., 12 November 1990; see also Lawrence, *Defenders of God* (San Francisco: Harper & Row, 1989), p. 190.

4. Ghulam Azam, *Jama'at-i-Islamir Vaisishtya,* 3d ed. (Dhaka: Jama'at-i-Islami Bangladesh, 1988), p. 10.

5. Ghulam Azam, *Ikamat-i Din* (1988), p. 45.

6. M. Mujeeb (1967), pp. 277–82, 445–54; also Barbara Daly Metcalf, *Islamic Revival in British India: Deoband, 1860–1900* (Princeton: Princeton University Press, 1982), chaps. 1 and 2.

7. Sayyid Abul A'la Maududi, *A Short History of the Revivalist Movement in Islam,* trans. Al-Ash'ari (Lahore: Islamic Publications, 1972), pp. 114–15.

8. Sayyid Abul A'la Maududi, *The Islamic Law and Constitution,* trans. and ed. Khurshid Ahmad (Lahore: Islamic Publications, 1960), p. 10.

9. See Riaz Hassan, "Religion, Society, and the State in Pakistan," *Asian Survey* 28, no. 5 (May 1987): 558–65.

10. Maududi, *Islamic Law,* pp. 9, 46.

11. Ibid., pp. 44–45; Sayyid Qutb of the Ikhwan al-Muslimin was similarly hostile to secular leadership and went to the extent of denouncing Mustafa Kemal Atatürk, father of modern Turkey, as an agent of world Zionism and Christianity.

12. Maududi, *Islamic Law,* p. 147.

13. Ibid., p. 194.

14. Ibid., p. 154.

15. Ibid., p. 155.

16. Ibid., p. 235.

17. Ibid., p. 158; Maulana Maududi thus categorically dismissed the notion of Arab superiority over non-Arab Muslims.

18. Sayyid Abul A'la Maududi, *Towards Understanding Islam,* trans. Khurshid Ahmad, 14th ed. (Lahore: Idara Tarjumanul Quran, 1970), p. 13.

19. Lawrence, *Defenders of God,* p. 27.

20. Yvonne Yazbeck Haddad, *Contemporary Islam and the Challenge of History* (Al-

bany: State University of New York Press, 1982), p. 71.

21. See John L. Esposito, "Islam: Ideology and Politics in Pakistan," in Ali Banuazizi and Myron Weiner, eds., *The State, Religion, and Ethnic Politics: Afghanistan, Iran, and Pakistan* (Syracuse, N.Y.: Syracuse University Press, 1986), pp. 338–43; also Omar Noman, *Pakistan: Political and Economic History since 1947* (London: Kegan Paul, 1990), pp. 108–10.

22. Bruce Lawrence seeks to explain the "oppositional" stance of fundamentalism by putting it within a broad politicohistorical context: "Only movements in direct contact with the dominant world order, itself reflecting ascendent European capitalism, could and did spark the beginning of what emerged as Islamic fundamentalism." Lawrence, *Defenders of God*, p. 193.

23. Maududi, *Revivalist Movement*, p. 36.

24. Report of the court of inquiry constituted under Punjab Act II of 1954 to enquire into the Punjab Disturbances of 1953 (hereinafter the *Munir Commission Report*) (Lahore: Government Printing, 1954), pp. 218–19.

25. Sayyid Abul A'la Maududi, *The Islamic Law and Its Introduction in Pakistan*, trans. and ed. Khurshid Ahmad (Lahore: Islamic Publications, 1960), p. 10; see also Ghulam Azam, *Ikamat-i Din* (Dhaka: Adhunik Prokashani, 1988), pp. 41, 46, 64–65, 81–82, 94.

26. For an interesting discussion of the question, see Gopal Krishna, "Piety and Politics in Indian Islam," *Contributions to Indian Sociology*, n.s., 6 (December 1972): 143–44; and Christian W. Troll, "The Meaning of Din: Recent Views of Three Eminent Indian Ulama," in Troll, ed., *Islam in India: Studies and Commentaries* (New Delhi: Vikas Publishing House, 1982), pp. 168–77.

27. Lawrence, *Defenders of God*, p. 37.

28. See Gail Minault, *The Khilafat Movement: Religious Symbolism and Political Mobilization in India* (New York: Columbia University Press, 1982), esp. chaps. 1–3.

29. Sayyid Abul A'la Maududi, *Musalman awr maujuda siyassi kasmakash* (Muslims and the present political struggle), vols. 1–3 (Pathankote: Maktab-i-Jama'at-i-Islami, 1937–39). After independence, the first two volumes were reprinted in one volume under the title *Tehrik-i-azad-i-Hind awr Musalman* (The freedom movement of India and the Muslims) as part of the Jama'at's massive effort to redefine its role in the freedom struggle. See Kalim Bahadur, *The Jamaat-i-Islami of Pakistan: Political Thought and Political Action* (New Delhi: Chetna Publications, 1977), pp. 41–46.

30. Ibid., pp. 37–46; also Asad Gilani, *Quaid-i-Azam, Maududi awr Tashkil-i-Pakistan* (Lahore: Maktaba Tamir-i-Fikr, 1977), p. 112.

31. *Siyassi Kasmakash*, vol. 3, pp. 86–87.

32. Ibid., p. 25.

33. Quoted in Sayed Riaz Ahmad, *Maulana Maududi and the Islamic State* (Lahore: People's Publishing House, 1976), p. 26.

34. Gilani, *Maududi awr Tashkil-i-Pakistan*, p. 92.

35. Sarwat Swalat, *Maulana Maududi* (Karachi: International Islamic Publishers, 1979), p. 14.

36. Quaid-i-Azam Muhammad Ali Jinnah, *Speeches as Governor-General of Pakistan, 1947–1948* (Karachi: Pakistan Publications, n.†.), pp. 8–9.

37. Hamza Alavi, "Ethnicity, Muslim Society, and the Pakistan Ideology," in Anita M. Weiss, ed., *Islamic Reassertion in Pakistan* (Syracuse, N.Y.: Syracuse University Press, 1986), p. 20.

38. Maududi, *Islamic Law*, p. 10

39. See Gilani, *Maududi awr Tashkil-i-Pakistan*, p. 140.

40. "There is nothing in the activities of the Jama'at between 1941 and 1947 to show that it had opposed the creation of Pakistan." Quoted ibid., p. 140.

41. Sayyid Abul A'la Maududi, *System of Government under the Holy Prophet (PBUH)* (Lahore: Islamic Publications, 1978), p. 19.

42. Ibid., p. 21.

43. Freeland Abbot, "The Jama'at-i-

Islami of Pakistan," *Middle East Journal* 20 (1957): 47.

44. See Maududi, *System of Government under the Holy Prophet* (PBUH), 1978, pp. 17–18, 19, 25.

45. Ibid., p. 21; also *The Islamic Law and Its Introduction in Pakistan* (1960), p. 41–49.

46. Ibid., p. 20.

47. For a fuller discussion on the concept of jihad, see Abul 'Ala Maududi, *Jihad in Islam* (Lahore: Islamic Publications, 1976), pp. 5–12.

48. Maududi, *The Islamic Law,* pp. 48–49.

49. See Sayyid Abul A'la Maududi, *Jihad in Islam* (Lahore: Islamic Publications, 1976) for a discussion of the fundamentalist conception of jihad, or holy war.

50. See "Annual Report of the Islami Jamiat-i-Tulaba Pakistan" (Lahore: Islami Jamiat-i-Tulaba, 1988), pp. 4–10; *Islami Jamiat-i-Talaba Pakistan: A Panoramic View* (Karachi: Islami Jamiat-i-Talaba, 1981), pp. 12–14; Talukder Maniruzzaman, "Bangladesh Politics: Secular and Islamic Trends," in Rafiuddin Ahmed, ed., *Religion, Nationalism, and Politics in Bangladesh* (Delhi: South Asian Publishers, 1990), pp. 84–87; also his *Bangladesh Revolution and Its Aftermath* (Dacca: Bangladesh Books International, 1980), pp. 30–33.

51. For details, see Wilfred Cantwell Smith, *Modern Islam in India* (Lahore: Minerva Books, 1943), pp. 260–64.

52. For details of the controversies surrounding the Ahmadi Muslims, see Yoanan Friedman, *Prophecy Continuous: Aspects of Ahmadi Religious Thought and Its Medieval Background* (Berkeley: University of California Press, 1989), pt. 3; Gualtieri, *Conscience and Coercion, passim*; S. Abul Hasan Ali Nadwi, *Qadianism: A Critical Study* (Lucknow: Academy of Islamic Research, 1967); and Mohammad Wali Ra'zi, *Qadianism on Trial* (Karachi: Maktaba Darul Uloom, n.d.).

53. See Mirza Ghulam Ahmad, *Tajalliyat-i ilahiyya,* in *Ruhani Khaza'in,* vol. 20 (Rabwa: Anjuman-i-Ahmadiyia, 1967),

pp. 411–12; also idem, *Tuhfat al-nadwa,* in *Ruhani Khaza'in,* vol. 19 (Rabwa: Anjuman-i-Ahmadiyia, 1966), p. 95; for an illuminating discussion of the issue, see Friedman, *Prophecy Continuous,* pp. 49–93, 119–46.

54. Spencer Lavan, *The Ahmadiya Movement: A History and Perspective* (New Delhi: Monohar Books, 1975), pp. 176–82.

55. Friedmann, *Prophecy Continuous,* p. 37.

56. Ibid., p. 39.

57. Sayyid Abul A'la Maududi, *The Qadiani Problem,* 1st English ed. (Lahore: Islamic Publications, 1979), p. 40.

58. *Munir Commission Report,* p. 252.

59. See weekly *Lail-o-Nahar,* Lahore, August and September 1974; also *The Morning News* (daily), Karachi, August and September 1974.

60. See *Dainik Pakistan* (Dhaka), 25 July, 16 August, 26 September 1971; also *Dainik Azad,* 3 November 1971.

61. The much feared and hated al-Badr killed ten professors of Dhaka University, five leading journalists, two prominent litterateurs, and twenty-six doctors in Dhaka alone. See *Dainik Pakistan,* 22 December 1971, for a list of the victims.

62. *Pakistan Observer* (Dhaka), 1 and 2 June 1970; also *The Morning News* (Dhaka), 1 June 1970.

63. For an overview of the tensions and conflict in Pakistani politics, see Omar Noman, *Pakistan: Political and Economic History since 1947* (London: Kegan Paul International, 1990), esp. pp. 3–47, 57–70, 117–38, 192–206; also Ali Banuazizi and Myron Weiner, eds., *The State, Religion, and Ethnic Politics: Afghanistan, Iran, and Pakistan* (Syracuse, N.Y.: Syracuse University Press, 1986), caps. 10 and 12.

64. See Tariq Ali, *Can Pakistan Survive?* (London: Pelican, 1982), pp. 139–40; also Noman, *Pakistan,* pp. 151–52.

65. See *The Constitution of the Islamic Republic of Pakistan* (as modified up to 18 February 1975) (Karachi: Government of Pakistan Press, 1975), pp. 102–3; also Fazlur Rahman, "Islam and the New Con-

stitution of Pakistan," in J. H. Korson, ed., *Contemporary Problems of Pakistan* (Leiden: E. J. Brill, 1974), pp. 30–44.

66. See Bahadur, *Jamaat-i-Islami of Pakistan,* p. 213; also *The National Assembly of Pakistan Debates,* 31 May, 1–4 June 1974.

67. Bhutto's position became particularly delicate because of Saudi involvement in the controversy. See Noman, *Pakistan,* pp. 109, 113.

68. Maududi, *System of Government,* pp. 12–13.

69. For Maududi's statement, see *Dainik Pakistan,* 17 and 27 February, and 28 November 1971.

70. For an overall view of the summit, see Zahid Malik, *Reemerging Muslim World* (Lahore: Pakistan National Centre, 1974).

71. Maududi, *System of Government,* p. 25.

72. Ibid., pp. 20–21.

73. *Pakistan Times,* 18 April 1977; Lahore daily, *The Sun,* observed: "Reaffirming his faith in Islam and reiterating his determination to introduce complete Islamic order in Pakistan, Prime Minister Zulfikar Ali Bhutto yesterday announced major steps designed to make Pakistan a true Islamic state." *The Sun,* 18 April 1977.

74. *Pakistan Times,* 18 April 1977.

75. See *The Jasarat* (Karachi), 28 March 1976, and subsequent issues.

76. Based on information from the daily *Pakistan Times,* various issues in June 1977.

77. See Selig S. Harrison, "Ethnicity and Political Stalemate in Pakistan," in Ali Banuazizi and Myron Weiner, *The State, Religion, and Ethnic Politics,* 1986, pp. 274–76; also Omar Noman, 1990, pp. 64–67.

78. Omar Niman, 1990, p. 69.

79. The interviews were later published as Maududi, *System of Government under the Holy Prophet (PBUH).*

80. *Pakistan Times,* 26 October 1978, press conference by the pir of Pagaro.

81. For the election poster of Benazir Bhotto, see Shalid Javed Burki, *Pakistan: The Continuing Search for Nationhood* (Boulder, Colo.: Westview Press, 1991), p. 105.

82. See for example, Maududi, *Islamic Law;* and idem, *The Process of Islamic Revolution* (Lahore: Jama'at-i-Islami Publications, 1955); also C. J. Adams, "The Ideology of Maududi," in P. E. Jones, ed., *South Asian Politics and Religion* (Princeton: Princeton University Press, 1972).

83. General Zia ul-Huq's message to the Khatm-i-Nabuwat conference in London, 4 August 1984. *The Times* (London), 5 September 1985.

84. Ordinance No. 20 of 1984, *Gazette of Pakistan* (Islamabad), 26 April 1984.

85. Gualtieri, *Conscience and Coercion,* pp. 12–13; also C. H. Kennedy, "Towards the Definition of a Muslim in an Islamic State: The Case of the Ahmadiyya in Pakistan," in Dhirendra Vajpeyi and Yogendra Malik, eds., *Religious and Ethnic Minorities in South Asia* (Riverdale: Riverdale Press, 1989), pp. 71–108.

86. Even though political parties were not officially permitted to contest the elections, they did support specific candidates: the Jama'at won only nine seats out of fifty it supported. Noman, *Pakistan,* pp. 143, n. 80; also Burki, *Pakistan,* p. 78.

87. *An Introduction to the Jamaat-i-Islami Pakistan* (Lahore: Jamaat-i-Islami, 1978), p. 10.

88. See Leonard Binder, "Islam, Ethnicity, and the State in Pakistan," in Ali Banuazizi and Myron Weiner, eds., *The State, Religion, and Ethnic Politics,* 1986, p. 262 and 345.

89. See John L. Esposito, ibid., p. 345.

90. See *The Muslim* (Islamabad), 6 March 1985.

91. *India Today,* 15 December 1988, p. 45.

92. See *The Muslim,* 7 August 1990, and *The Dawn* (Karachi), 7 August 1990, for President Ishaq Khan's reasons for dismissal of the Benazir ministry.

93. See *Pakistan Affairs* (Embassy of Pakistan, Washington, D.C.), 7 November 1990, pp. 1–2, for a summary of these views.

94. *New York Times,* 5 August 1991.

95. Ibid., 23 February 1992.

96. Ibid., 19 November 1991; also *The*

Dawn, 29 January, 23 February, 30 March, 8 April 1992.

97. See Ghulam Azam, *Jama'at-i-Islamir Vaisishtya,* 1982, p. 6.

98. For a fuller discussion, see Maududi, *Jihad,* pp. 6–33.

99. Based on conversations with several young members of the Jama'at in Bangladesh in 1986–87.

100. For a discussion on this theme, see my earlier work on the Bengali Muslims, *The Bengali Muslims, 1871–1906: A Quest for Identity* (New Delhi: Oxford University Press, 1981 and 1988), esp. chaps 3, 4, and 5.

101. Professor Ghulam Azam, the controversial chief (amir) of the Bangladesh Jama'at-i-Islami has characterized the Bengali nationalists as "secularist, pro-Indian, and socialist" agents of world imperialism. See his *Ikamat-i-Din,* pp. 37–39, 95.

102. The Jama'at's point of view has been adequately explained by Ghulam Azam in *Ikamat-i-Din,* pp. 19, 21–24, 94.

103. See Asim Roy, *Islamic Syncretistic Tradition in Bengal* (Princeton: Princeton University Press, 1983); M. R. Tarafdar, *Hussain Shahi Bengal, 1494–1538* (Dacca: Asiatic Society of Pakistan, 1965).

104. See Syed Anwar Husain, "Islamic Fundamentalism in Bangladesh: Internal Variables and External Inputs," in R. Ahmed, ed., *Religion, Nationalism, and Politics in Bangladesh* (New Delhi: South Asian Publishers, 1991), pp. 137–52.

105. Speech by Shaykh Mujibur Rahman, 18 January 1974 (Dacca Dept. of Publications, Ministry of Information, 1974).

106. *Mujibarer Rachana Sangraha* (Calcutta: Reflect Publications, 1971), p. 65.

107. See Aftabuddin Ahmed, "The Mujib Regime in Bangladesh, 1972–75: An Analysis of Its Problems and Performances" (Ph.D. diss., University of London, 1983), pp. 254–91; also Shaykh Akhter Hussain, *Sarajantrer Shikar Golam Azam* (Dacca: Mahbub Prokashani, 1986), pp. 12–13.

108. See Badruddin Umar, "On Muslim Bengal," *The Holiday* (Dacca weekly), 27 May, 3 and 10 June 1973.

109. For details, M. M. Khan and H. M. Zafarullah, eds., *Politics and Bureaucracy in a New Nation: Bangladesh* (Dacca: Centre for Administrative Studies, 1980), esp. pp. 149–75, 198–219; Robert S. Anderson, "Impressions of Bangladesh: The Rule of Arms and the Politics of Exhortation," *Pacific Affairs* 49, no. 3 (1976): 551–64.

110. Based on information supplied to the author by members of the ICS (who preferred not to be identified) during 1985–87. Ghulam Azam identifies the fundamental problems confronting the Jama'at in Bangladesh in his *Jama'at-i-Islamir Vaisistya,* pp. 17–18, and Ikamat-i-Din (1988), and then argues in favor of creating a highly structured and disciplined Islamic force to counter its secular opponents. (pp. 19, 31–35, 47); see also Talukder Maniruzzaman, "Bangladesh Politics: Secular and Islamic Trends," in R. Ahmed, ed., *Religion, Nationalism, and Politics in Bangladesh,* pp. 84–87.

111. See Emajuddin Ahmed and D. R. J. A. Nazneen, "Islam in Bangladesh: Revivalism or Power Politics," *Asian Survey* 30, no. 8 (August 1990); also *Weekly Bichitra,* 26 June 1987.

112. See Ghlan Azam, *Jama'at-i-Islamir Vaisistya,* p. 21; Syed Anwar Husain, "Islamic Fundamentalism in Bangladesh: Internal Variables and External Inputs," and also Talukder Maniruzzaman, in R. Ahmed, ed., *Religion, Nationalism, and Politics in Bangladesh* (1990), pp. 87, 144–47; also weekly *Bichitra,* 13 March 1987.

113. See the *Azadi,* various issues in February, November, and December 1987; the daily *Sangbad,* various issues, November–December 1992 and January–March 1993; and weekly *Bichitra,* issues in March 1987, December 1992, and January–March 1993.

114. See the *Bichitra,* October–December 1992 and January–May 1993; also *The Bangladesh Observer,* various issues in the same period.

115. For a time, during the anti-Ershad movement between 1982 and 1989, the secular parties are known to have secretly cooperated with the Jama'at for political reasons. See the *Bichitra,* 13 March 1987, pp. 36–37.

116. See *Weekly Bichitra,* 13 March 1987; also *Daily Azadi* (Chittagong), 28 and 29 November 1987.

117. Azam, *Vaisistya,* pp. 6, 8–9.

118. See *Weekly Bichitra,* 27 April 1984 and 13 March 1987; also *Jama'at-i-Islamir Sadasya Sammelaner Prostab* (Dacca: Abul Kalam Muhammad Yusuf for Jama'at-i-Islami, 1983).

119. See, for example, *Jama'at-i-Islamir Udatta Ahban: Islami Biplob Sadhaner Lakshey Durbar Gano Andolon Gorey Tulun* (Pamphlet calling for an Islamic revolution)(Dacca: Jama'at-i-Islami Publications, 1984); *Arab News,* 5 January 1985.

120. *India Abroad,* 8 March 1991.

121. Craig Baxter and S. Rahman, "Bangladesh Votes–1991: Building Democratic Institutions," *Asian Survey* 31, no. 8 (August 1991): 683.

122. See *Bangladesh Observer,* April and May issues, 1992.

123. See Sarwat Saulat, *Maulana Maududi* (Karachi: International Islamic Publishers, 1979), p. 46.

124. See Ghulamn Azam, Jama'at-i-Islamir Vaisistya, 1988, pp. 6–7.

125. *Jama'at-Islamir Kayrja Vivarani,* vol. 2, translated by Abdul Mannan Talib, being a translation of the proceedings of the annual conference of the Jama'at-i-Islami, held in 1945 (Dhaka: Jama'at-i-Islami Bangladesh, 1985), pp. 105–6.

126. Ghulam Azam, *Ikamat-i-Din,* 1988, p. 73.

127. See B. M. Monoar Kabir, "Jamaat-i-Islami and Student Politics," unpublished paper, Bangladesh Political Science Conference, 1985, passim.

128. See Willem van Schendel, *Peasant Mobility: The Odds of Life in Rural Bangladesh* (Van Gorcum: Assen, 1981), passim; Omar Noman, Pakistan, 1988, pp. 74–100, 157–79; Atul Kohli, *The State and Poverty in India: The Politics of Reform* (Cambridge: Cambridge University Press, 1991), passim; also Alan Richards and John Waterbury, *A Political Economy of the Middle East: State, Class, and Economic Development* (Boulder: Westview Press, 1990), passim)

129. Based on notes from discussions with members of the Jama'at and other Islamic groups, in Dhaka, Chittagong, and Calcutta in January–June 1987 and May–August 1989.

130. Kemal A. Faruki, "Pakistan: Islamic Government and Society," in John L. Esposito, ed., *Islam in Asia: Religion, Politics and Society* (New York: Oxford University Press, 1987), pp. 53–78; and Kabir, "Politics of Religion," pp. 129–31.

131. Azam, *Vaisistya,* p. 7; also Agwani, "Islamic Fundamentalism in India," p. 105.

132. See *New York Times,* 9 and 30 March 1992.

133. Husain, "Islamic Fundamentalism in Bangladesh," pp. 144–49; *Weekly Bichitra,* 1 June 1984; and Hyman, *Muslim Fundamentalism,* pp. 11, 19–20.

134. Based on fieldwork in the region in 1985, 1989, and 1990.

135. Hassan, "Religion, Society, and the State in Pakistan," pp. 560–65.

CHAPTER 25

"Remaking Ourselves":
Islamic Self-Fashioning in a Global Movement
of Spiritual Renewal

Barbara D. Metcalf

Outside observers of modern Islamic movements have tended to see in them occasional glimmers of liberalism (influenced by contact with Europeans) and a great deal of persistent, even obstinant, rigidity and intransigence.[1] Understanding the origins and nature of those judgments about Islamic movements is, of course, a subject of considerable interest. Not least deserving of attention is the term "fundamentalism" as applied to Islam—a term constituted less in scientific observation than in political encounter. "Islamic fundamentalist" has been understood to mean medieval, reactionary, militant, and oppressive of women; by implication it has identified those using the term as having the opposite characteristics—modern, liberal, peaceable, egalitarian, and so forth. That the term "fundamentalism" has occasionally been utilized by some Muslims to describe themselves is not surprising. One reason may be suggested by Gananath Obeysekere's observation that so-called cannibals rapidly realized the utility of deploying this self-identification, given the fear and horror it evoked in Europeans.[2]

"Fundamentalism" has been applied as a blanket term to describe virtually all modern Islamic movements that use a religious vocabulary and encourage fidelity to Islamic practice. This imprecision, coupled with the term's pejorative connotations, makes its use in relation to Islam particularly problematic. The movement studied in this chapter is distinguishable because its behavior is not typical of that imputed to Islamic movements today. Nonetheless, to describe this movement as "not fundamentalist" would imply that "fundamentalism" accurately describes a range of other—presumably, most—Islamic movements, a position I judge to be misleading.

The subject of this chapter, the Tablighi Jama'at, does indeed call our "common sense" about Islamic movements into question.[3] This movement is rooted in a century-long tradition of religious reform, stimulated by colonial rule in India, but articulating goals and utilizing modes of argumentation from within the historic tradition. It is a movement intended to recover pristine revelation and as such creates what might be called a "counterculture" movement that implicitly stands against both the practices of consumer culture and of local, customary religious life. Nonetheless, it is a movement that withdraws completely from the realm of explicit political activity and engagements. It is, moreover, a movement in which not only men but many women as well find a significant range of autonomous, meaningful action. Sociologically, it appears to engage people of very diverse backgrounds, from members of families of government servants, academics, and traders to those of humble shopkeepers and rural workers. It has flourished in a variety of twentieth-century contexts. Meetings in the subcontinent today can attract a million people. Tablighis are active in Malaysia, several countries in Africa, continental Europe and Britain—and places like Detroit, Los Angeles, and Toronto as well.[4] The most distinctive feature of the Tablighi Jama'at, and the source of its effectiveness, is its organization—the main subject of this essay. The teachings of the movement cannot be isolated from its modus operandi: this movement could not, for example, propagate its message through electronic media in the interests of efficiency. The teachings are the practice and vice versa.

Muhammaad Ilyas and the Six Points

In the mid-1920s, a period of dashed hopes, aggressive Hindu proselytization, and communal violence in northern India, Maulana Muhammad Ilyas (1885–1944), a saintly scholar linked by education and spiritual initiation to the reformers associated with a seminary located at Deoband, became convinced of the limitations of conventional academic teaching and began a process of seeking out ordinary Muslims and inviting them to undertake missionary work, *da'wa* or *tabligh*. This was a radical teaching, for it assumed that any sincere Muslim could, in effect, engage in what had heretofore been the province of men distinguished by education, saintly achievement, and, often, notable birth.[5] In this the movement was one of many in the twentieth century that redefined the qualifications of those exercising religious leadership among South Asian Muslims. Ilyas' movement was quickly labeled by others as the Tablighi Jama'at because of its central activity. The movement was very much a part of its time—a period of intense religious competition, conflicting missionary movements, and grass-roots mobilization, including that of Gandhi and the Congress party.

As presented by Ilyas and remembered by followers today, however, his effort sprang full blown from a perfect moment of insight into what was deemed the core activity of the Companions of the Prophet, namely *tabligh*—conveying or communicating divine guidance—the source of their worldly triumphs and spiritual reward. In Tabligh lore, it was not military prowess but preaching that took Muslims from Sind to Spain within sixty years of the Prophet's death. Tabligh effectiveness in stimulating participation is intimately linked to its organization, explained by Prophetic example, and intended to produce a range of personal characteristics—hence, the "self-fashioning" in my chapter title. It is the reciprocal interaction of organization, personal qualities, and—informing both—dogma that I examine here. I do not attempt to investigate the degree of implementation of Tabligh strategies or their variation over time and place; I assume, however, substantial continuity.

Drawing on core themes in the Islamic tradition that stress complete humility before God and resultant respect among humans, the Tabligh seeks to transform human character away from habits of false hierarchy and pride. The movement's six basic points *(che baten),*[6] published separately as well as in the members' ever-present book the *Faza'il-i A'mal,*[7] which they cherish and recite, work toward that transformation. All of the points posit active behavior, implicitly utilizing the pervasive Islamic theory of the power of habits and consistent practice to work on and transform the inner self.[8] Individuals thus shaped are presumed to interact in accordance with divine precepts.

The basic teaching of Tablighis is faithful adherence to ritual—above all, performance of the canonical prayer. (Indeed their critics often fault them for not going beyond this emphasis.) The first two points are precisely two of the so-called Islamic "pillars" of ritual observance, the attestation of faith and the prayer. Neither should be understood as a primarily intellectual activity. The *kalima,* the attestation, not only affirms doctrine but is a powerful phrase that one must repeat endlessly—so often that a person will find "its spirit permeates all his being, his spirit is filled with the burden of its music and all his actions are performed with the total submission of his will to Allah."[9] Its repetition, moreover, is believed to be the channel of God's grace in answer to one's needs. The Tablighis cherish stories of how the repetition of the kalima secures a goal or turns away opposition. The second point invokes the great act of worship in Islam, the five times' daily canonical prayer, *salat* or *namaz,* preceded as it is by ablution, marked by physical postures, and preferably performed congregationally, an emphasis cultivated by the Tabligh. Many people know of the Tablighis because they have encountered them in airports, on buses, in neighborhoods, or in college hostels going on rounds to invite other men to join them for congregational prayer.

The third point is that of knowledge, *'ilm,* whose acquisition is again ideally done in public, with the cherished texts shared and read outloud. Knowledge is focused on fundamental teachings, especially as modeled on the lives of great Muslims of the past: 'ilm in this context does not define unbounded intellectual pursuits, but instruction and examples meant to be enacted. It is coupled with *zikr,* the recollection of God, understood as the physical act of repeating phrases and prayers of praise, penitence, and so forth. These first three points are the foundation of individual piety and morality, yet in every case best realized in community as *ijtima'i a'mal,* corporate acts. Together they affirm, above all, human dependence on God.

On this foundation, the participant bases the final set of three points, all of which turn his actions outward to forge respectful and humble relations to other people. The fourth point is *ikram,* respect for Muslims, most evidently manifest in the pervasive attempt to transcend concern with worldly status. In the movement, moreover, the goal is to ignore each other's shortcomings and faults in favor of cherishing whatever glimmer of worth can be found. The fifth point, *ikhlas,* calls for sincerity of intention, that all one does is for the sake of God and his favor: one thus acts with no concern for public opinion, to secure any personal reputation, or to seek one's own aggrandizement. These two points are meant to transform relations to other people. The final point is the freeing up of one's time, *tafrigh-i waqt,* the sacrifice critical to the missionary tours which are the heart of both self-reformation and proselytization.[10]

It is in the tour that the points as a whole can be realized. The movement functions primarily by sending out teams (*jama'ats*) of some ten to twelve men to call on all Muslims not simply to live righteously but actually to join them in going out to invite, persuade, and cajole still more Muslims to do the same. An active male worker continues his work-a-day and familial responsibilities, but ideally absents himself for tabligh one night a week, three days a month, forty days a year—a *chilla,* in a transvaluation of the Sufi term[11]—and for three continuous chilla, 120 days, once in a lifetime. The Tablighi is (minimally) marked by his dress and by these withdrawals for missions; he is also likely to be aloof from political activity or discussion, as well as from the activities and behavior of consumer culture.

Whether for an evening, a few days, or a prolonged journey, the tour is meant to represent a radical break with all enmeshments, including the intense face-to-face hierarchies of family and work typical for most people. At the simplest and most explicit level, travel, like a retreat, allows for focused worship and attention to spiritual life and obligations. Undertaken in the company of fellow believers, it encourages mutual example and the enthusiasm inspired by the group. Because the withdrawal from society ideally involves travel, it also encourages a state of permanent vulnerability and uncertainty in which, outside one's normal moorings, one learns to be dependent on God. The humility which is the movement's goal is further encouraged by the priority given to face to face communication so that each participant places himself continually in a situation that risks rebuff. He learns his own limits. Articulating a message also serves to clarify and strengthen the participant's own faith, particularly when it is joined, as it apparently was during the 1940s and 1950s, with the injunction to write frequent letters home describing the mission tour.

Tours as enjoined by Maulana Ilyas were to be directed toward either the populace generally (the *'awam*) or the educated ulama and spiritual leaders (the *khawas*), whose favor was always to be solicited, even as their unique role in teaching was now to be shared. Jama'ats, particularly since the 1960s, cover the world. In Dewsbury, England, which is the European center of the movement, I met a group of South Africans of Indian origin, fresh from the hajj and en route to an American *ijtima'a* or meeting in Los Angeles. Elsewhere I met North Indians who had spent three months in Malaysia. I heard from Pakistanis about a tour to Alaska. I met a group of West Bengalis who had frequently crossed into Bangladesh and included members who had toured to South India as well.

In major cities in Pakistan, men gather to spend all Thursday night in a central mosque so they can experience concentration in worship and, ideally, plan for future tours.[12] At the Madani Masjid in north central Karachi—a mosque that is still being built and whose land apparently was given by a single individual—several thousand men (estimates I heard varied from seven thousand to fifteen thousand) gather every week. Even in this brief experience they are meant to have a taste of the blessings derived from "going out in the path of God." These blessings were described to me by a jama'at of young women, accompanied by their husbands and staying in a private home, whom I met in the course of a forty-day tour. They minimized the importance of their sacrifices of time, money, and leaving their children in comparison to the opportunity they now had for uninterrupted obedience to Allah. Words with the same root as *tafrigh,* the sixth point, suggest being free from work for recreation: here one frees up one's time precisely for work, *mehnat,* a word often used by Tablighis in this context. Yet this mehnat, *mehnat-i din* (religion), is understood to yield happiness just as more conventional freedom is assumed to do.

Although individuals volunteer to go out on tour, voluntary councils review the jama'at's proposed composition and plans. In Pakistan, for example, international tours are first approved at the local level, then at the national level council. In the summer of 1991, over one hundred international jama'ats were approved at Raiwind; at the annual meeting in November, their participants hear instructions, *rawangi ki hidayat,* and are embraced by the countrywide *amir* or his deputy in farewell. A summary of instructions was recently published by an individual participant who felt that the increased numbers and geographic spread of the movement made a printed version desirable.[13]

A concern in forming groups has been the nature of the target audience of the tour. Thus, for example, in the Indian setting, Aligarh—a center of Western-style education—has been the source of many jama'ats proceeding abroad. When I went to Dewsbury in Britain at the time of the annual meeting in 1991, simply arriving with an English colleague, I was shortly taken off to meet a fellow American woman, a convert (uncannily from my own hometown), and my colleague was led off to meet a recent university graduate, a young fellow Englishman. To some extent, this concern to bring Tablighis into contact with people like themselves is deliberately planned. I was told, however, that that approach, while necessary, is second best. "Our real desire is to send out people of *iman* [faith], whatever their language or occupation."

Practice and the Self

The movement's goals are not to "remake the world" by reorganizing social and political institutions, but to remake individual lives, to create faithful Muslims who undertake action in this life only because of the hope and promise of sure reward in the next. The phrase "self-fashioning" points to the conviction that it is not belief, discussion, or persuasion that transforms a person, but practice—action, repetitive behavior, and physical habits. It also points to a process, an on-going practice, the fulfillment of which in this life is impossible. Tabligh members emulate the Companions and turn toward them as models. A gap between ideal and reality results, making the long-term goal of a separate utopia even more elusive. Thus, it follows that this emphasis on individual transformation is not viewed instrumentally, that is, by the expectation that the transformation of individuals will ultimately produce a just society. On the contrary, the concern is wholly with orienting Muslims toward an Islamic pattern in individual lives, the one dimension of life over which one appears to have full control. The shape of the larger world is simply left to God. The movement therefore cannot falter because of worldly "failure."

The process of tabligh is thus the end. If not a single Muslim is persuaded by the Tablighi's preaching, his goal might still be achieved. As one young chemist in Karachi explained to me, the Prophet's charge to his followers was "not to convince but to convey," trusting to God for whatever impact his words might have. While outsiders marvel at the Tablighi's apparent increased influence, participants insist on its marginality and distance from its goals.

As conceived by Maulana Ilyas, beyond formal preaching, the time spent on tour was to be an opportunity for Muslims to immerse themselves in worship and proper behavior in a way that the constraints of time and custom in the home and community did not allow. Maulana Ilyas's own dictum was: "We have left our homes to reform ourselves, before we reform others. Our real aim and object during the journey is that being in the atmosphere of the pious, and the God fearing, we should strengthen our relationship with Him, should perform our Prayers in the best possible manner. Thus we should remember Allah as much as possible, should serve one another sincerely, and should devote ourselves to all good deeds."[14] These social obligations are significant only as they enhance a participant's own behavior and accrual of reward: the focus on individual salvation is the movement's motivating force.

Before every act the group is assembled for instruction on the *adab* or precise rules of behavior derived from Prophetic example, which are seen as appropriate to eating, sleeping, traveling together, and so forth; thus ordinary acts become occasions of profound signficance. Muslims acting jointly also offer each other a mutual correction both implicit and explicit. Life on the road contrasts sharply with definitions of status and hierarchy central to life at home. Maulana Ilyas said that the jama'at was to be a moving *madrasa* or *khanaqa*, a school or hospice, educating the teachers above all. In all this, Tablighis could expect to be recipients of grace rained down on Muslims acting jointly "in the way of God," that is, precisely because they were engaged in tabligh.

At the heart of a whole range of seemingly disparate practices is the goal of encouraging participants to "unlearn" the socialization of hierarchic stratified societies. To have any sense of how radical are the principles of human relations within the Tabligh, one must recall the fundamental principles of Indo-Muslim society in which the Tabligh took shape and continues to flourish.[15] The society is defined above all by structures of subordination and hierarchy. From the earliest age both boys and girls learn the careful calibrations of age, gender, and birth, all displayed in a range of obligations, manifestations of deference, and expectations of respect in virtually every daily interaction. Children must learn forms of proper address and precise discriminations of grammar and diction in order to be considered well bred.[16] Boys are not only subject to the authority of elders within the family, but as they move into the public world they are expected to respond without question to the authority of teachers and spiritual leaders, an authority not uncommonly exercised through displays of corporal punishment and humiliation. Ultimately, the male moves into a role where these habits shape relations to superiors and inferiors in the workplace, where markers of status abound.[17] In the public realm, no gap has been greater than that between the Western-educated elite and the majority of the population. Men moreover expect and are expected to exercise authority over women in their household, at least over those their junior.

Tablighi practice ideally ignores these forms of rank and power. A critically important aspect of the functioning of the movement, in marked contrast, for example, to a political group like the Jama'at-i-Islami, is its openness to all Muslims. Each person by virtue of being born a Muslim is assumed to be a potential participant worthy of respect. Indeed, the movement lays distinct stress on human fallibility or brokenness. Yet a critical distinction remains: gender. Men go on missionary tours; women offer guidance to their families, meet with other women, and, occasionally accompany their menfolk on tours. Maulana Yusuf, son of and successor to Maulana Ilyas, stressed the necessity of Tabligh among women, but warned of the "delicacy" and risk of *fitna* (disorder) should they go alone.[18]

Countless anecdotes describe, however, the uncritical welcome accorded other men. A Delhi-based sociologist of Muslim background diffidently approached members of the movement to express his interest in studying them; their response was to welcome him with open arms even though he was not a practicing Muslim. "You are an educated man, you are better than us," they assured him. A Pakistani jama'at invited a habitual drinker to join them and were astonished when he agreed. What to do about the drink? They agreed on a compromise: he would entrust his bottle to the amir, the group's leader, who would provide him a drink whenever he asked—the amir, for whom drink was virtually unthinkable. The story as told to me was that all went as expected, with the drink being regularly provided, until one night the drinker awoke to find all the Tablighis engaged in earnest supplication on his behalf. He said nothing, but never asked for the bottle again. Another anecdote: a simple villager who himself could not even repeat the kalima (the attestation of faith) was credited with remarkable influence by the impact of his heartfelt and sincere request to others, as he haplessly traveled from place to place, to say the kalima for him in order to help him, if they could, to master it. Participants do not earn their way in.

Tablighi ideally do not assert their authority by engaging in conflict. A jama'at from one of the national universities in Delhi which encountered stone throwing in a mosque in south Delhi, even damaging the sight of a member, refused to press police charges as they were urged to do. The ur-story for this humility comes from Muhammad Ilyas's first visit to Mewat, the area whose inhabitants are conflated in Tabligh lore with the pre-Muslim bedouins of Arabia. Maulana Ilyas put his hand on the shoulder of a Mewati peasant, who protested and struck him. Ilyas responded by touching the peasant's feet: "You did not forbid me to touch your feet," he said. These stories are invoked to illustrate the goal of withdrawal from all conflict, but they suggest a withdrawal from conventional social practices as well.

Moreover, the injunction to follow Prophetic models of behavior means that members dress alike, have with them the same minimal possessions, and in basic ways even act alike despite their varied backgrounds. Normative behavior is a marker of social respectability, so participation in Tabligh becomes a route to behaving like the well-born.[19] This is particularly significant when one considers that the first target of the Tablighi Jama'at was the simple peasant Mewatis from the countryside nearby Delhi, and everywhere the movement has worked at least in part among the dispossessed. Shared behavioral norms contribute to a more egalitarian social milieu.

Of similar import is Tablighi simplicity in language. Urdu speakers delight in eloquence and hierarchic language, and regard linguistic facility as a mark of high breeding and birth. A Tablighi, however, as more than one person pointed out to me, will say, for example, such and such *bayan karega*," will give a talk," avoiding such expressions as *taqrir farma'enge*," will issue a discourse," using the more formal plural form. At the weekly women's meeting I attended at the Makki Masjid in Karachi in the summer of 1991, where perhaps a thousand women had gathered for the hours between the noon and the midafternoon prayer, the warmth, gentleness, and simplicity of the speaker, whose voice reached us over a loudspeaker, was palpable. He encouraged women to be pious, to use their position to guide their family in proper behavior, and to support those going out on mission; he implored God for guidance, forgiveness, and mercy in a low-key, conversational style. Tabligh preachers avoid an eloquent or bombastic style that would set up a hierarchy between speaker and audience.

Tabligh organization does not, in principle, provide an alternate hierarchy of its own. Decisions are supposed to be made through a process of consultation known as *mashwara*. The amir himself is chosen by the group. He ideally should be distinguished by the quality of his faith (*iman*), not by worldly rank: a peon can be an amir. Indeed one person, himself involved in government, laughingly suggested to me that it was better that a senior civil servant not be an amir because then anyone of a higher grade would have difficulty accepting his leadership! There are echoes of Sufi notions in the conviction that the least likely person may be one of the spiritual elect. In part it is for participants a lesson in humility to accept as leader an unlikely person understood to be the recipient of God's grace.

The authority invested in collective opinion embodies roles that in classic Sufism are carried out by the shaykh; here, charisma is attributed to the body as a whole. Even the amir himself is advised by mashwara. Participants jointly make choices for the group's destination, direct the behavior of individuals, and consult on such issues as securing leave. There is, to be sure, an amir, but authority is diffused in the collectivity acting together. This is not to say that authority is less: on the contrary, the power of a collective "sense" (one thinks of Quakers) can be relentlessly compelling. A further practice to obviate false self-confidence is *muzakira*, discussion with others to review three central principles upon undertaking any activity. Review of these principles—the intention (*maqsad*) of the undertaking, the blessings or reward (*fazilat*) incumbent on it, and the manner of acting (*adab*) while carrying it out—also fosters humility. Relentless attention to these considerations is part of the "work" or mehnat of iman.

In yet another practice related to status, different roles are assigned all members of a mission. There is, in principle, no hierarchy of roles, no ladder of achievement to climb. Ideally, roles are shifted, and a single person may act as teacher or preacher on one occasion but humble cook or cleaner on another. Maulana Ilyas preserved in his papers the letter of a university graduate describing the service or *khidmat* of one jama'at's amir:

> He looked after everyone's comfort throughout the journey, carried the luggage of others on his shoulders, in addition to his own, in spite of old age, filled the glasses with water at mealtimes and refrained from sitting down to eat until everybody had been seated comfortably, helped others to perform *wuzu* [ablution] on the train and drew their attention to its rules and proprieties, kept watch while the others slept and exhorted the members to remember God much and often, and did all this most willingly. . . . For a person who was superior to all of us in age, social status and wealth to behave as the servant of everyone was the most unforgettable experience of the tour.[20]

The concept of khidmat is clearly key to the relationships among each group.

A particularly poignant example of this behavior was recounted to me by a Pakistani academic concerning an East Bengali jama'at he had encountered while a graduate student at Harvard in the mid-1960s. The jama'at was staying in a condemned house in a black neighborhood, seriously constrained, as he saw it, by the presence of a sick elderly man for whom they had to provide continuous care. When he expressed his astonishment that they had brought the old man along, they replied that they only felt gratitude toward him, for through him they learned to give service.[21]

Participants in a group are meant to be interdependent. One concern in forming jama'ats has been the balance of experienced and inexperienced members. As one old worker explained to me, the inexperienced members cannot now take an active part as quickly as they once did because the net for participation is spread so much more widely. Another concern has been for balance of skills among members: one strategy today, for example, is always to have someone with linguistic virtuosity and someone with expertise in Islamic Shari'a, as issues requiring guidance arise. Thus a person may go on a mission to a country where he does not even speak the language: one person I spoke with had encountered members offering da'wat in Urdu in Nigeria. Many different explanations might be given, but the main emphasis of the mission is always on the participant himself; that Tablighis feel they communicate not through words but through their whole being, which must radiate the strength of iman. "Our *bayan* [discourse] is not mouth to ear but heart to heart." Another explanation would focus on the variety of roles among participants; one person's presence may be critical simply because he engages in supplication, *du'a*, that implores God's grace, while another can serve as translator as needed.

Related to this corporate sense, and a further key to the kind of experience evident in the jama'at, is the practice of always keeping silent while the person chosen to speak performs his role. The silent are showing that they trust their companions: "If you trust someone," one Tablighi explained to me, "he will never betray you." And even more important, I was told, Tablighis are learning to trust in God, to be dependent on him, to absorb themselves in prayer and meditation, seeking God's grace and not depending on their own intervention, their own superior knowlege or status, to guide the person who speaks. Humans are not meant to be all knowing or always in control.

Two other aspects of Tabligh practice, usually noted only in relation to the modest institutional profile of the movement, are significant in terms of what might be called re-socialization. First, each person must provide for his own expenses. This means that the finances of the organization could not be simpler; everything from fund raising to audits is eliminated since even during a mission tour, money is not pooled. Beyond the deeply valued simplicity this kind of financing allows, the impact of self-financing, for both the participant and those he meets, is significant. For people living on modest incomes the ability to control disposable income is profoundly empowering. Tablighi spoke to me of how others were astonished that they were able to undertake trips: believers see these trips as not only a matter of careful management but also of divine blessing. Self-financing also enhances commitment: one recalls the brilliance of Gandhi's four anna membership for Congress, initiated shortly before Maulana Ilyas organized tabligh.

Most important, the impact of self-financing shapes relations by eliminating the bonds of patron and dependent, minimizing the reciprocity and exchange true of so many dimensions of everyday social interaction. If Tablighis stay in a mosque, they are scrupulous about not using resources that are not theirs. One of the first comments a non-Tablighi is likely to make is that "They ask nothing from you"—not even a cup of tea. In this they present a contrast even with the Sufis who accept unsolicited gifts or *futuhat*. They implicitly stand apart from all the elaborate transactional arrangements that organize so much of subcontinental societies. This scrupulosity in material goods is a central theme of one pattern of guidance given those leaving on a tour. "Points to be shunned" include asking for help (*zaban ka sawal*), or even thinking of such help (*dil ka sawal*), spending frivolously, and using something belonging to anyone else without permission.[22] A person I interviewed for the better part of a morning at his office explained that he would make up the time spent with me so that his earnings would not be *haram* and adversely affect both himself and his family.

Second, those going on tour, even for several months or a year, take along only what they can carry on their back. For those accustomed to deferential service in hierarchic societies, this is a radical transition. One participant from a large and prosperous family spoke to me of his sudden realization of how little one needed for survival: he experienced the freedom promised in many religious traditions for those who forsake riches.

As norms for men and relations among men change, so too do relations between women and men, since gender is part of a larger hierarchic pattern. The Tablighis, like the Deobandis generally, espouse an ideal of human behavior, understood as that exemplified by the Prophet, which is gentle, self-effacing, and dedicated to serving others.[23] Men engaged in Tabligh activity are expected to develop a new way of relating to others and a new standard of humility. They also, rich and poor alike, learn to cook, wash their clothes, and look after each other. In that sense, the Tabligh encourages, particularly in the experience of the missions, a certain reconfiguring of gender roles.

Does it follow then that life within the family and women's roles change? Generally speaking, it appears that women, although expected to conform to rules of modesty and seclusion, are included in a common model of personal style as well as in a shared commitment to tabligh, and that patterns of domestic life may indeed be modified.

Just as men in the course of travel on missions experience some redrawing of gender roles as they cook and wash, in the same way women left at home are likely to take on a range of previously male responsibilities. Similarly, as in the reformist movement generally, women in this tradition are expected to become educated in religious teachings, to sustain the household so that men can go out (thus earning themselves equal reward), and to engage in da'wa in their own sphere of women and members of their family.[24] Women's jama'ats occasionally go out, accompanying their menfolk, but this is largely the exception. More common are neighborhood meetings for women which are occasions for the committed to assemble and for others to be drawn in. In some places these meetings are daily; in others they are less frequent.

Two aspects of these activities are striking. One is that they offer an unusual opportunity for women to congregate. Among South Asian Muslims, women are discouraged from even going to the mosque; now in the Tabligh, they have occasions for congregational gatherings and common worship. In Karachi, for example, women meet on Fridays at the Makki Masjid in the heart of the city for the hours between the noon and late afternoon prayer; when I attended a meeting there in July 1991, perhaps a thousand women were present. Second, certain women take on roles of leadership and guidance for others. In a sense differential opportunities for men are less in this movement than in more politically oriented movements because no one, neither men nor women, seeks out public roles in the society at large.

Several men I spoke to credited women either directly or indirectly for involving them in the movement. One touching story, told to me by the person involved, will suffice as example. This man serves as the president of his local union as well as of his national federation. For several years, his mother, to whom he was devoted, had faithfully attended a weekly women's *bayan* (discourse) in one of the city's central mosques and had frequently volunteered his name (as women are asked to do for their relatives) to go out with a jama'at. Because of the heavy demands and unpredictable hours of his job, he never went. In 1984 she died, a loss he took very hard. His brother, a very young man in his early twenties, was equally stricken, to the extent that his health declined and within the year he too was dead. At that point, this person, who had never been involved in the Tabligh before (and was known, other people told me, as secular and a "leftist"), committed himself on the spot to go out for four months—and has never looked back, sustaining a full schedule of Tabligh activities including leadership in the city council (*shura*) of the Tabligh, responsibilities for a large family, and a successful career as a labor leader. Women I met took pride in their role and in the stories of the Prophet's female companions, which they know from the *Faza'il-i A'mal*.

As for relations among women and men, two people spoke to me of how the atmosphere in their household had improved. One young man, the father of two young children, criticized his society generally for widespread harshness, including physical punishment, toward children, and even suggested that in this respect behavior in the West was more humane. In his own case, he felt that the personal traits he was honing in the Tabligh had made his family life far more cooperative and harmonious. Another person recalled hearing someone explain how he had come to sympathize with his wife's household problems once he realized how easy it was to ruin his cooking!

The standard set for women's seclusion is, to be sure, rigorous. In the limited circle of people I met, however, this did not preclude university-level education or marriage of daughters to husbands settled in the West. "Seclusion" can thus be part of widely varying patterns of personal and family life.

Thus both in relations based on status and those based on gender, participants in the Tabligh learn new patterns of behavior. Critics of the Tabligh insist that members neglect and mistreat their families (and their jobs), but participants present a very different interpretation of their behavior, behavior which clearly challenges mainstream expectations about individual personality, behavior within the family, and attitudes to society as a whole. The very image of the simply dressed, non-instrumental itinerant preacher implicitly devalues the wealth, success, and rootedness, that most of the society desperately seeks.

Practice and Doctrine

The scripted, patterned behavior enjoined by Tabligh creates a distinctive personal style, above all a disposition to humility that serves as well to confirm theological doctrine. It is in the context of lived experience that Tabligh beliefs become plausible. Participants believe above all that God in his time will effect perfect justice, rewarding good and punishing evil. What is the source of this belief in ultimate justice and an afterlife which, by definition, cannot be seen? At least part of an answer is that the visible world created by participation in Tabligh, above all the shared experience of travel in the missionary tour of the jama'at, becomes nothing less than an analog of the invisible world to come. The conviction that despite human brokenness God is merciful and just, and will reward his faithful, is ideally foretold and confirmed by the mutuality and corporate identity constituted in the experience of missionary travel, and so marked a contrast from mundane life. The jama'at offers acceptance, purpose, and community. Again, my interlocutors explicitly point the way. Tabligh provides, one active participant told me, nothing less than *jannat ka namuna,* a model of heaven itself. Muhammad Ilyas wrote, "[the servant of God] will find, in this world, the pleasures of paradise."[25] Doctrine ideally confirms, even as it is confirmed by, life in the Tabligh.

Tablighis immerse themselves in exemplary texts. The stories of the Companions, read and recited daily from Tabligh compilations, become stories about oneself. The stone-throwing incident cited above echoes the story of the Prophet at Ta'if, the first story in the movement's vade mecum, the *Faza'il-i A'mal,* which is regularly read out loud and retold. Virtually every Tablighi has a "Ta'if story" of his own. Since the text lives, its promises become promises believed.

The experience of the jama'at community seems to offer the empirical evidence, the lived confirmation, that the Tabligh vision is true. Tablighis have "seen" the power of their prayers; they report that they immediately receive the "openings" (*kashf*) a seeker on the Sufi path may struggle years to attain. They have *tasted* the paradise to which they aspire. In the experience of nonjudgmental, nonhierarchic, and interdependent relationships, the community provides a person engaged in Tabligh in a lived and vital way some sense of what is to be his final reward: the assurance of God's forgiveness and the realization of divine justice. Whatever confidence there is in the ultimate reckoning, it is this likeness of paradise, realized in the jama'at, that gives the movement its strength.

The emphasis participants often place on concrete improvements in material life— cure of an illness, the flourishing of business when one returns from a mission—can be seen as a metaphor for the deep sense of well-being engendered by the simplicity, commonality, and purposefulness of the Tabligh experience at its best. One Tablighi's sense of well-being was evident as he listed for me what he had gained in his eight years of participation: first, peace of a kind that simply cannot be explained; second, love and respect from Muslims and non-Muslims because of giving and expecting nothing in return, bringing comfort, and, through Allah, guidance (*hidayat*); third, power in du'a (supplication) for himself and for others so that prayer is answered at least through granting peace; and, finally, abundance, *baraka,* so that food and money are always enough. People marvel, he explained, at how we are able to do so much more than they on the same salary.

It is little wonder that expectations about the afterlife are so concrete. Calculations about benefits from righteous acts can only be called arithmetical. The concrete *faza'il,* or merits for prayer, for example, is astronomically inflated depending on where one is: one must perform the canonical prayer, but in a mosque its value is enhanced 27 times; in Medina 50,000 times; in Mecca, 100,000 times; in the path of God, that is, on a jihad including a Tabligh mission, 490,000,000! More poetically, Tablighis remind you, all creation prays for those who do such works—animals, birds, the fish in the water. They pray for you, one Tabligh worker explained to me, because they feel God's mercy that descends on those doing his work; some people, he added, have even heard this zikr of the creatures.

Practice as Ritual

Tablighis catagorize their activities, perhaps surprisingly, as *'ibadat,* a word commonly translated in English as "ritual." Tabligh emphasis on the priority of action, and the dialectic between experience and doctrine in fact strongly recall classic Islamic theories of the effect of Islamic ritual like salat (the canonical prayer) in transforming human life. Tabligh can be seen as a prolonged example of what students of religion call "ritual time," time that is bounded, extricated from the usual tangles of everyday life, time which one understands as a particularly intense opportunity for encountering the sacred. Discussion of what we call "Islamic rituals" is usually limited to the Five Pillars or 'ibadat that Muslims define as required acts of obedience, which are human transactions with the divine (in contrast to human actions among other humans), yet clearly 'ibadat, in this case "going out in the way of God," includes more than the so-called Five Pillars.[26]

While participating in Tabligh, as in other 'ibadat, Tablighis are meant to live in an intense awareness of fulfilling divine commands and earning divine pleasure, an emphasis in 'ibadat, one might note, characteristic of Sufism, *tasawwuf*. They are, when engaged in tabligh, wholly separate from the constraints of everyday life as required by the fundamental premise that they move out from their usual home and employments. Tablighis on a mission do not sightsee or even visit family: a Pakistani participant told me, when I inquired, that he preferred not to volunteer for missions to Britain because he would want to see his family members living in London and could not. Those on a mission seek, as Muslims are required to do, for example, within the ritual bounds of hajj, to avoid conflict or disputation of any kind. Participants in annual meetings, whether at a national or city level, speak of the extraordinary discipline that prevails. In one case, a participant at Raiwind criticized the chaotic departures that followed the final prayer or du'a, comparing the event to the discipline of the Ramadan fast followed by a vulture-like attack on food (note the comparison to ritual). People often compare annual meetings to the hajj—in numbers involved, in the variety of national and ethnic representation, at times in the depth of spiritual experience equivalent only to that at Mecca. Realizing that tabligh is 'ibadat suggests that our English term "ritual" does not do justice to what is included in Islamic 'ibadat overall. 'Ibadat are nonsacramental acts of obedience directed to God and thus form a continuum of required and meritorious acts.

Indeed, seeing Tabligh as ritual raises questions about seeing it as a "movement." As "ritual," many aspects of Tabligh practice become clear—not least its inclusiveness and its self-conscious distance from formal hierarchies, paid staff, official journals, and so forth. Being a "movement" is to some extent forced on Tablighis by opponents, while Tablighis have preferred to be seen, if possible given their distinctive protocols of behavior and the organization that in fact exists, simply as people who cultivate and communicate a correct standard of faith within the worldwide community of Muslims as a whole. While participants use the word *tabligh* and mean 'ibadat, outsiders may register "the Tabligh" and understand "movement," an ambiguity made possible since Urdu has no definite article or capitals to distinguish the two possible implications of the Urdu term.

Accounting for Tabligh

The Tabligh's overall continuity is in part explained by the movement's aloofness from direct interaction with political or social institutions that would inevitably produce change. In this, Tabligh stands apart from the other movements charted in this volume whose ideology and organizational structures have changed over time as they engage with a range of social and political institutions. The organizational network of the Tablighi Jama'at is, moreover, condicive to expansion, not consolidation. The simple process of voluntary groups forming and re-forming to conduct missionary tours has remained the same. Any single community could function alone: the movement is thus infinitely resilient, able to persist even were the center to disappear. Leadership is not only fluid and based on consultation, but is highly local, again a striking contrast to more politically oriented groups.

Even without a paid staff or formal bureaucracy, however, Tablighi Jama'at has full-time workers and now a considerable organization. In India, for example, zones are subsumed under districts, which in turn are under provinces, all focused on the center, the *markaz* at Nizamu'd-din, headed by the amir, who is chosen for life, and a council (*shura*). Jama'ats come to the markaz from all over; ten years ago a five-story building was erected to accommodate foreign jama'ats. Delhi itself, for example, is divided into five zones. In addition to a weekly mashwara in each locality, there is a monthly mashwara for the leaders. The leaders, or *zimmedar,* of all the zones gather four times a year for an ijtima', using the occasion also to call ordinary people for a discourse. An annual meeting also occurs, in India, now largely for the leaders; recent meetings have been held in Bhopal. The last large ijtima' in India was in 1983; apparently the leadership has moved away from such meetings because of the intensity of anti-Muslim feeling in the country. In Pakistan, annual meetings have been held in Raiwind; in Bangladesh, in Tongi.

With the increased scale and worldwide spread of the movement, particularly after the 1960s, there is now more emphasis on organization. Names or first names of core participants are listed with their phone numbers in small directories to aid in planning and contacts. Local groups, moreover, increasingly keep written records of tours and contacts in order to provide appropriate follow-up. There are now, at least in the diaspora, explicitly Tabligh institutions, for example, madrasas in Dewsbury and Toronto—a mark that the movement's lack of institutions is in the process of decline and that at least in some contexts the Tablighi Jama'at is emerging as a formal affiliation. Even so, the institutional profile of the movement remains low.

For all its continuity of form and program, the movement has been able to engage strikingly diverse populations. Thus while at some level it may be appropriate to say that the movement is not dynamic, it has, nonetheless, proven salient to remarkably divergent populations. In its origin, Maulana Ilyas set out to find an answer to the question "What is the cause of Muslim decline?" This question, very much a question of this century in its conceptualization of Muslims as a census-based community, was the question at the heart of every subcontinental Islamic movement at that time and thereafter. In focusing on tabligh, Maulana Ilyas identified in "ritual" a program of compelling individual action and community creation seen as sanctioned in every detail by tradition; that program, the subject of this essay, has proved the thread of continuity throughout the movement's history.

If we look at only two contexts of Tabligh, we can see something of its range of meanings. For Maulana Ilyas and other ulama at the core of the initial movement, the Tabligh allowed a program of active endeavor that responded to the two most dramatic events affecting Muslim political life in the 1920s: the collapse of the Khilafat Movement, and the intensification of aggressive Hindu proselytization and communal riots. The Khilafat Movement had proven a chimera, a cause disavowed by the very people it purported to defend; it had, moreover, entailed cooperation with the nationalist movement, whose goals were not necessarily those of the ulama.

By turning into a movement of popular participation, Tabligh shared elements of the new mass movement of the Indian National Congress without the risks of a political participation that spilled into alien activities and that, clearly, was vulnerable to disappointment. By foreswearing controversy and confrontation of every kind, Tabligh participants withdrew from the triangular relationship in which Muslims and Hindus competed with each other for favors from the British, including competition that lit the fuse for riots. Following from this quietism, the texts of the movement and the lore of its participants put virtually no emphasis on the contemporaneous history of religious competition but only on what one might call an internal genealogy of Muslim decline. To read Tablighi texts, one would barely know that Hindus exist, for the story is told wholly in terms of a Muslim historiography.[27] Focusing on Muslim error alone, Tabligh fostered a movement of boundary maintenance and bonding.

To turn briefly to the postcolonial states of Pakistan and India, we may wonder why the movement has persisted after independence. Tabligh participants have seen the new states, like the old, as alien, corrupt, and arbitrary, much as the colonial state was. Tabligh in this context continues to create social solidarities in ways that are beyond the reach of state control or intervention, much as they did at the beginning. At least two new themes, however, are evident today. One is that Tabligh helps create, even as it offers a way of participating in, the new transnationalism of the world today. Even humble Tablighi see themselves as part of the contemporary world of passports and migration. For them, one dimension of the Tabligh is its "contemporaneity." When I rather unacademically expressed dismay to a Bengali shopkeeper who had left his family behind for a year, he retorted that I would have uttered no such comment had he gone to the Gulf to work—a reminder of my worldliness and his participation with guest workers in today's mobile world. National boundaries are ignored. In this Tablighis are like the Mexican workers studied by Roger Rouse, who speaks of the "social space of postmodernism," at least in so far as "nationality" is no longer unambiguously a self-evident aspect of identity and the multiple sites of people's activities are not necessarily assimilated to the immediate geographic context.[28] Dewsbury, the Tabligh center for Europe, looks more like Pakistan than does Pakistan itself. In Tabligh participants are part of this contemporary world of movement even as they transcend cultural pluralism by the re-lived Medina their actions create.

A second theme, particularly salient to those Westernized and educated participants for whom "contemporaneity" is all too present, is "authenticity." In Tabligh the elite English-speaking classes, the upper stratum in what one person described to me as the real "apartheid" of subcontinental societies, identify with the humble as they can in no other way: a brigadier dons a lungi to serve others, a scientist in a prosperous family travels with a pack by foot and by road, a professor educated in English literature in Britain finds the simplest language he can to invite riksha drivers to pray.

In all of this, members take pride in the way the movement seems to replicate pristine example. In a letter purportedly written to an official investigating the group, who was suspicious, as many people are, of the claim that there is no formal organization, a Tablighi juxtaposed the historic precedent to the English words set off in quotes: "You have studied history . . . did the founders of *hindu dharm* or Mahatma Gautam Budhh or Hazrat 'Isa or the Prophet of Islam . . . form a 'party' or *anjuman,* were there 'members,' a 'chairman,' a 'secretary'? Did they establish a 'fund' for subscriptions?"[29] Moreover, a handful of intellectuals go beyond such descriptions to articulate an "authentic" Islam of practice rather than "system," seeing political movements like the Jama'at-i-Islami and others that focus on "Islamic systems" as participating in a derivative, modern discourse that Tabligh alone defies. For urban Muslims in the homeland or immigrant Muslims in the West, participating in Tabligh may be part of a very conscious—and very contemporary—quest for authenticity and roots. That quest asserts a "sub-altern" distinctiveness apart from the "hegemonic" narratives of the times.[30]

In different times and countries, and among individuals of different classes and personalities, the meaning of Tabligh varies widely. Yet certain themes persist: a radical focus on individual self-fashioning, a sense of community and communal boundedness, a withdrawal from political action, and, above all, a resistance to hegemonic narratives of our times, like those that implicate their participants in the projects of economic development and the nation-state. In their contribution to a de-nationalized communal solidarity in particular, Tablighis participate in a central theme of emerging social patterns in the world today.

For the humble and the sophisticates, for women and men, the Tabligh has the potential of significantly reconfiguring human relationships and breaking old patterns of religious authority and religious style. As it supplants old relationships of patron and client, it also supplants dependent relationships in the spiritual realm of the holy dead and their living representatives. Dependence is meant to be dependence wholly on God. But the Tablighi, far from being left humanly alone, finds at best human bonds in the relatively egalitarian and interdependent—and replicable, not enduring—relationships of the jama'at. Tablighis seek to relive Medina, honing a faith of radical monotheism and relishing the life of communities in motion, where temporary uprootedness from mundane existence allows a taste of something like heaven. The Tablighi Jama'at is a remarkable example of "medium as message," in this case of organizational practices as the key to the dissemination and embodiment of doctrinal and personal teachings. In all this the Tabligh, to its participants at once contemporary and authentic, offers a powerful alternative to inaction on the one hand and the frustrations and corruption of political life and formal organizations on the other.

A final vignette sums up the salient characteristics of Tabligh mentality in India, where Muslims recently have been subject to virulent communal propaganda and violence, much of it focused on a sixteenth-century mosque in Ayodhya, alleged to be the site of the birthplace of the Hindu god, Ram. The mosque, known as the Babri

Masjid, was destroyed on 6 December 1992; this conversation took place some two years before its destruction. I sat with a Bengali jama'at comprised of shopkeepers and small businessmen in New Delhi's Kalan Masjid, a mosque which is, as it happens, older and architecturally more interesting than the "late" Babri mosque. I asked them their opinion about Ayodhya. The gist of the answer, in which a number of people participated, was this: "We do not care about that mosque because it is not being used for prayer [having been closed by government order because of the contestation]. All we care about is whether people pray. An unused mosque is like a forgotten sweet that is left out; the ants come and it is eaten away." So the mosque, a symbol of Hindu resurgence and a powerful cause embraced by Muslim defenders of their rights, was reduced in their analysis to an ant-eaten sweet.

No one linked this response to the story of where we sat—a site that until a decade or so ago had been inhabited by low-caste squatters, when Muslims began to pray there and gradually took over the space for a small religious school for boys, lodgings for jama'ats like this one, as well as a place for prayer. Thus Tabligh, in this case as in others, had fostered adherence to original textual truths and implicitly challenged dominant cultural values, including those of consumer society on the one hand and communal politics on the other. In acting this way, Tabligh is, to be sure, ultimately political in drawing group boundaries and directing activity away from the common public sphere. Yet to call it "fundamentalist" obscures more than it reveals.

Notes

1. I am grateful to many people, above all participants in the Tablighi Jama'at, for discussions that have contributed to this chapter. I have benefited from three recent workshops: on the Tablighi Jama'at organized by the Joint Committee on the Comparative Study of Muslim Societies of the Social Science Research Council/American Council of Learned Societies (convened by James Piscatori at the Royal Commonwealth Society, London, June 1990); Making Space for Islam, also under the auspices of the Joint Committee (held at the Center for Middle East Studies, Harvard University, November 1990); and Local Interpretations of Islamic Scripture in the Twentieth Century (convened by John Bowen at Washington University, St. Louis, 31 May–1 June 1991). I have also presented, to my benefit, material on the Tabligh to three seminars: at a graduate student seminar at the University of Chicago (organized by Susanne Rudolph, November 1991); at the Nehru Memorial Library, New Delhi (organized by Ravinder Kumar, August 1990); and at the National Center for Pakistan Studies, Quaid-e-Azam University, Islamabad (organized by Fateh Muhammad Malik, July 1991). I am grateful to the Fundamentalism Project for supporting travel to Britain (including Dewsbury) and Pakistan in the summer of 1991. Scott Appleby, David Gilmartin, Nasser Husain, Khalid Mas'ud, and Mark Woodward provided helpful comments on earlier drafts of this chapter.

2. Gananath Obeyesekere, "British Cannibals: Contemplation of an Event in the Death and Resurrection of James Cook, Explorer," *Critical Inquiry* 18, no. 4 (Summer 1992): 630–54.

3. For a general background to the movement, see Mumtaz Ahmed, "The Jamaat-i-Islami and the Tablighi Jamaat of South Asia," in Martin E. Marty and R. Scott Appleby, eds., *Fundamentalisms Observed* (Chi-

cago: University of Chicago Press, 1990), pp. 457–530.

4. Published work on the Tabligh in Europe and North America includes Felice Dassetto, "The Tabligh Organization in Belguim," in Tomas Gerholm and Y. G. Lithman, eds., *The New Islamic Presence in Western Europe* (London: Mansell Publishing, 1988); Gilles Kepel, *Les banlieux de l'Islam* (Paris: Éditions du Seuil, 1987); S. H. Azmi, "An Analysis of Religious Divisions in the Muslim Community of Toronto," *Al-Basirah* 1, no. 1 (January 1989): 2–9; and Philip Lewis, "Being Muslim and British: The Challenge to Bradford Muslims," in Roger Ballard, ed., *Desh Pardesh* (London: C. Hurst, forthcoming).

5. For the Indian origins of the movement, see M. Anwarul Haq, *The Faith Movement of Maulana Muhammad Ilyas* (London: George Allen and Unwin, 1972), which is based on S. Abul Hasan Ali Nadwi, *Life and Mission of Maulana Mohammad Ilyas*, 2d English ed. (Lucknow: Academy of Islamic Research and Publications, 1983). The Urdu original was written ca. 1948 and published as *Maulana muhammad ilyas aur un ki dini da'wat*. See also Christian W. Troll, "Five Letters of Maulana Ilyas (1885– 1944), the Founder of the Tablighi Jama'at, Translated, Annotated, and Introduced," in Troll, ed., *Islam in India: Studies and Commentaries 2: Religion and Religious Education* (Delhi: Vikas Publishing House, 1985), pp. 138–76. See this article for references to important Urdu sources. For the late nineteenth-century origin of the Deoband movement, see Barbara D. Metcalf, *Islamic Revival in British India: Deoband, 1860–1900* (Princeton: Princeton University Press, 1982).

6. Apparently the points are now often referred to as "qualities," the *sifat*, specifically the *sifat* of the Companions.

7. The author of this work, Maulana Muhammad Zakariyya Kandhlawi, while not himself engaged in missions, was a supporter and close associate of the Tablighi Jama'at. This book, a compendium of several of his writings, was probably first collected in 1958. Published in many editions, it is available in Urdu, Arabic, English, and French. For a more detailed study of this text, see Barbara D. Metcalf, "Living Hadith in the Tablighi Jama'at," *Journal of Asian Studies* 52 (August 1993).

8. For a collection of essays on this subject, see Barbara Daly Metcalf, ed., *Moral Conduct and Authority: The Place of Adab in South Asian Islam* (Berkeley: University of California Press, 1984.)

9. Faruqi, "The Tablighi Jama'at," p. 64.

10. According to one participant, point five is now spoken of as *tashih-i niyat*, rectification of intention, putting the emphasis on practice rather than on ikhlas, the desired outcome. The sixth point is now spoken of as *da'wat aur tabligh*, the activity for which one frees up time; here the change is partly an urge to include in the list these basic and familiar terms.

11. Among Sufis, the chilla was a forty-day period of meditation, spiritual excercises, etc.

12. As described to me by one active participant in Karachi, the address or *bayan* following the *maghrib* prayer, which explains proselytization, *da'wa*, culminates in *tashkil*, the volunteering of names for missions. If the people have come prepared to go out that very day, he said, "we call it *naqd*, cash, but if it is for next month we call it intention, *irada*."

13. For a description of conducting *Jama'at* behavior, see Miyanji Muhammad 'Isa Firozpuri, *Tabliqhi Jama'at ke li'e rawanaqi ki hidayat* (Guidance for setting out for the Tablighi Jama'at) (Karachi: Maktaba-yi 'arifin, n.d.). See pp. 29ff. of that volume on inviting different classes of the *khwas*, the *'awam*, etc.

14. "Six Fundamentals," in Mohammad Zakariyya, *Teachinqs of Islam* (New Delhi: Ishaat-e-Islam, n.d.), p. 23.

15. I am grateful to Lisa Pollard (Department of History, University of California, Berkeley) for sharing with me her work in progress on the meaning of religious reform, particularly for gender roles, in a society dominated by themes of subordination.

16. See the text translated as *Perfecting*

Women: Maulana Ashraf 'Ali Thanawi's Bih-ishti Zewar, trans. and ed. Barbara Daly Metcalf (Berkeley: University of California Press, 1991). First published at the turn of the century as a guide for girls and women to the reformist Islam that also produced the Tabligh, the book is an excellent source for understanding hierarchy.

17. For a brilliant evocation of this hierarchic culture among the privileged ashraf, see David S. Lelyveld, *Aligarh's First Generation: Muslim Solidarity in British India* (Princeton: Princeton University Press, 1978), chap. 2.

18. Muhammad Sani Hasani, *Sawanih Hazrat Maulana Muhammad Yusuf* (Lucknow: Nadwatu'l-'ulama, n.d.), pp. 761–62.

19. For the link between the spread of normative religious practice and a quest for social mobility, see the text widely used by women in this century in India by Maulana Ashraf 'Ali Thanawi, *Bihishti Zewar,* in Metcalf, *Perfecting Women.*

20. Quoted in Nadwi, *Life and Mission of Maulana* Mohammad Ilyas, p. 150.

21. I met a jama'at in Delhi (during the summer of 1991) who also had settled into a mosque and interrrupted their travel to care for a member who was ill. This may be a common pattern.

22. These points were reviewed for me by a Tabligh activist. They are also available in written form in Muhammad 'Isa, *Rawan-agi ki hidayat,* pp. 78–94.

23. See the essay on the Prophet's character, given as a preface to a hundred tales of model women—in itself significant that the Prophet is a model for women as well as for men—in Metcalf, *Perfecting Women,* pp. 255–58.

24. See my introduction to *Perfecting Women* where I contrast this inclusive conception of women with the discussion of women by the Jama'at-i-Islami, which elaborates a more differentiated view of women as "complementary to men" or even the "opposite sex."

25. Troll, "Five Letters of Maulana Ilyas," p. 171.

26. See, for example, Muhammad 'Isa, *Rawanaqi ki hidayat,* p. 7.

27. This continues true today in an era of "Hindu fundamentalism," when one can almost speak of "pogroms" against Muslims rather than of "Hindu–Muslim riots," given the tremendous imbalance in suffering. See, for example, the report of the People's Union for Democratic Rights, "Bhagalpur Riots" (Delhi, April 1990); the document is chilling but is also a reminder of the good will of many non-Muslims. See also reports on riots following destruction of the Ayodhya Mosque, December 1992.

28. Roger Rouse, "Mexican Migration and the Social Space of Postmodernism," in *Diaspora* 1, no. 1 (1991): 8–23.

29. Muhammad Manzur No'mani, *Tab-lighi Jama'at, Jama'at-i islami, aur barelwi hazrat* (Lucknow: Al-Furqan Book Depot, 1980), pp. 17–18.

30. The locus classicus for these terms in the South Asian context is the series of publications edited by Ranajit Guha. See Ranajit Guha and Guyatri Spivak, eds., *Selected Subaltern Studies* (New York: Oxford University Press, 1988).

Christians and Competing Fundamentalisms in South Indian Society

Susan Bayly

The Fundamentalism Project's task for the Indian subcontinent team has been to explore the regions and societies we know best in South Asia so as to identify and "account for" fundamentalism in our complex and religiously plural environment. Ours are societies in which self-declared defenders of pure faith have become increasingly dynamic in the last ten to twenty years, and we have all had experience of militants who seek to promote and reclaim what they define as true religion. For all their diversities, such groups and their causes are readily recognized across the four countries of India, Pakistan, Bangladesh, and Sri Lanka. Activists who claim to speak for revitalized or aggressively separatist Hinduism, Sikhism, Islam, and Buddhism command much popular attention, receive wide media publicity, inspire and cultivate fear among their declared enemies, and set new standards for public debate and state policy within their homelands.

South Asia's distinctive manifestations of Christianity, however, have been overlooked in debates about the rise of large-scale fundamentalist movements in the nations of the subcontinent. Furthermore, much of the drama associated with South Asia's organized fundamentalisms appears to be centered at the two extremities of the subcontinent, where there is much scope to investigate militant Islamizing movements in Pakistan, Bangladesh, and north India; Sikh separatism in the Punjab; the assertive promotion of Hinduism in northern and western India; and the role of armed and politicized Buddhists in Sri Lanka's current conflicts. By contrast, India's southernmost states have generally been left out of the reckoning, even though they contain 25 percent of India's population and have recently become the scene of assertive religious revival campaigns which have added important new zones to the domain of South Asia's competing fundamentalisms. Indeed, as this chapter shows, south India has been brought unexpectedly close to the mainstream of the country's fundamentalist activism. The four states of the region, Tamil Nadu, Kerala, Karnataka, and

Andhra Pradesh, have become a crucial reference point in large-scale pan-Indian campaigns of assertive Hindu nation-building involving spokesmen and affiliates of the RSS and the VHP (the Rashtriya Swayamsevak Sangh and the Visva Hindu Parishad, two of the powerful Hindu militant groups examined by other members of the team). The south has also been a focus for expansive Islamizing campaigns. And again unexpectedly, these developments have had a profound effect on the numerous and dynamic forms of Christianity which have their home in the southern states, especially in Tamil Nadu and Kerala, which contain a disproportionately large number of India's fifteen million professing Christians.[1]

Thus south India and its large populations of indigenous Christians form the centerpiece of this study. The groups discussed include the elite Saint Thomas Christians of Kerala, whose ancestors embraced Christianity as early as the first or second century C.E., as well as maritime and hinterland Roman Catholics and Protestants descended from more recent periods of indigenous Christian cult worship and European missionary activity throughout the south. Here, organized fundamentalisms have gained much power as bearers of political and economic resources at a time of exceptional upheaval in a delicately balanced social order. As set out in the guidelines for this volume, the aim is to relate these movements' organizational characteristics to their changing worldviews, ideologies, and programs. But in south India as in all other parts of the subcontinent, the "dynamics" of movements that can be classed as fundamentalist may not be discussed simply as the mobilization of fellow believers against one fixed enemy or opposition group. It does not matter whether this supposed enemy is called "modernity," "imperialism," or just "the outside world." In South Asia, no such terminology can approximate the subtleties and the rapidly changing calculations which continually define and redefine those whom "fundamentalists" perceive as friend or foe.

Instead, two points should be made. First, contrary to some conceptions of a worldwide fundamentalist phenomenon, South Asia's experience of contemporary fundamentalist movements can only be understood as a product of conflicts emanating from within its own complex regional societies. As in many other parts of the world, those who take part in such disputes often borrow the tactics and language of fundamentalist activists as they are portrayed in reports of conflict beyond their regional homelands and beyond the borders of individual South Asian nation states. But this has not produced anything resembling a single monolithic "South Asian fundamentalism." Second, because the nation-states of South Asia are heterogeneous societies containing large numbers of interacting religious communities, confessional groupings, and caste groups, it is a mistake to look for "outsiders" as the prime organizers or inspiration for fundamentalist movements. It is true that a notion of external conspiracy, the agency Indians call "the foreign hand," is constantly cited to explain the rise of militant religious activism among those defined as opponents in such conflicts. But despite the claims of the conspiracy theorists, what really exists in South Asia is a multitude of interlocked and mutually enhancing assertions of militancy and purist religion across the subcontinent's states and subregions. And certainly in south India, this internal dimension and the phenomenon of mutual interaction and reaction between organized home-grown fundamentalisms must be paramount in any account of the dynamics of individual fundamentalist groups or movements.

What then of south India and its Christian communities? Here we must first identify the features that characterize organized fundamentalism in its south Indian manifestations. No single movement has gained paramountcy as an all-embracing fundamentalist force in the region. What has emerged instead is a wide range of loosely organized groups and movements which can all be described as fundamentalist in their behavior and ideology. But while many of these are short-lived and evanescent in structure and organization, they possess certain key characteristics that have come increasingly to color the language of religious life and political agitation across the entire region. These characteristics may be set out as follows:

1. Militancy. For Christians as well as other groups in south India, the leading hallmark of the new fundamentalism is a commitment to campaigns of public activism which are generated out of local disputes and then recast to take on a larger pan-regional and pan-Indian dimension.

2. Scripture and Charismatic Authority. The new assertiveness embodies a concern for the literal interpretation of scripture; also pervasive is an emphasis on the supernaturally derived charismatic authority of individual leaders and spiritual adepts.

3. Solidarity and Exclusiveness. This has involved an emotive move toward the heightening of corporate identity. In the case of Christian populations in the south, fellow believers are encouraged to rally around symbols of "true" Christianity, and to repudiate emblems and forms of worship which express common ground with Hindus and Muslims in the same densely populated sacred landscape. In this shift toward exclusiveness and a strengthening of previously loose and fluid communal boundaries, the fact of interaction, of being spurred to assertive behavior by the example of others, has been a crucial element in the rise of organized fundamentalism in the southern states.

Two final points follow from this. First, while fundamentalism has become a powerful organized force in south India, each individual movement does not necessarily possess every one of the identifying features which characterize fundamentalist expression in the region. Thus at any given moment, one group of Christians may be activist but not scriptural literalists; others will emphasize scripture without an equally strong focus on charismatic guru-figures. All, however, observe and borrow from one another's example; greater standardization and mutual interconnection may be in prospect. Second, Christians and other south Indians who adhere to the new fundamentalist movements should not be seen as persons who have become less "Indian" or "South Asian" in culture and belief. Such assumptions are often made in discussions of contemporary religious activism around the world; for example, when Asian and African Muslims adopt new scriptural and puritan forms of faith, these have been taken as a sign of "Arabization" or conformity to dominant standards emanating from the west Asian Muslim "heartland." This kind of oversimplification has no place in the study of South Asian societies. The expansion of fundamentalist Christianity does not make believers more "Western" or "Americanized" in ideology or behavior. As this study shows, while south Indian fundamentalists may withdraw from sharing shrines and sacred territory with Hindus or Muslims, they continue to behave toward their fellow believers in ways that are still recognizably "South Asian" or "south Indian." This would be true of many societies in Asia, from Sri Lanka and Burma to Indonesia and the Philippines, where "fundamentalism" must emanate from traditions of religious pluralism and "syncretic" culture.

Radical Religion in a Volatile Society

Christianity has been an active force in south Indian society from as early as the first or second century C.E. For hundreds of years before the era of European colonial hegemony, Christian clerics and traders from west Asia implanted traditions of cult worship which attracted adherents from powerful commercial and military communities based in the cosmopolitan maritime localities of the southern coastline.[2] In southwestern India the elite Malayalam-speaking Saint Thomas Christian community still retains links with this indigenous heritage of precolonial Christianity.[3] Most of south India's other Christians, however, are perceived as the descendants of more recent converts from Hinduism, or from the so-called animist religions of the region's forest tribal peoples. Today such Christians are often regarded as people of degraded or suspect origin. Unlike the many South Asian Muslims who claim descent from "true" Muslim migrants of Arab, Persian, or central Asian origin, the forebears of most Indian Christians are presumed to descend from "mass converts" of the colonial era. At the time of Portuguese colonial expansion in the sixteenth century, and then under British rule in the nineteenth and early twentieth centuries, sizable groups of Tamil-, Telugu-, Malayalam-, and Kannada-speaking "untouchables" (or Harijans), "tribals," and low-ranking Hindu groups became identified as professing Christians and were claimed as adherents by European Roman Catholic and Protestant missionaries.[4]

Throughout India these matters of history and origin are still being debated because minority groups, including south India's Christians, are constantly held up to scrutiny as a possible threat to the country's security and national integrity. This is not just a result of uncertainty about the loyalties of India's one hundred million Muslim citizens at a time of growing tension with the country's Muslim neighbor states, Pakistan and Bangladesh. Since the early 1970s, India's rapid but uneven economic growth has helped to engender movements of social protest among a wide range of disadvantaged populations. These include many "untouchable" or Harijan populists calling themselves Dalits and campaigning on behalf of landless laborers and other groups who fall into this large Harijan classification. (Members of the Harijan or "scheduled" castes constitute some 15 percent of India's population. In the southern states a sizable proportion of ex-"untouchable" and lower-caste groups are descended from converts who embraced Christianity and Islam during the era of colonial rule in the nineteenth and early twentieth centuries.)

There are also comparable movements among the country's sixty million tribals.

(The so-called tribals, numbering about 7 percent of the Indian population, come from a variety of small population groups including societies of hunter-gatherers and slash-and-burn agriculturalists; again, in the northeast of India and in the forest and hill tracts of Kerala and Tamil Nadu, many have become Christian converts.) Among these tribal groups, protests against deforestation and intrusion by land-hungry peasant settlers into the tribals' hill and forest tracts have included campaigns for a separate autonomous "homeland" (referred to as Jharkhand).[5]

To many who fear the breakup of India's delicately poised ethnic and political unity, it is particularly alarming that agrarian radicalism and other forms of protest by poor and low-caste militants and separatists have frequently been associated with adherence to Islam and Christianity. In south India, especially in Kerala state where Marxist political parties have had significant electoral successes since the late 1950s, Christian activists have acquired considerable renown as leaders of confrontational "social justice" campaigns. Many of these have been based in maritime areas containing large populations of impoverished Christian fisherfolk; like Hindu and Muslim fishing groups, such people have low status in local schemes of caste rank and ritual precedence. Among these maritime communities, it is well known that agitations, boycotts, and strikes are often led by radical Roman Catholic priests and nuns who have renounced formal church affiliation in the name of Latin American-style liberation theology. Many south Indians ascribe sinister motives to Christian activists such as the self-styled Beach Blossom movement (a network of maritime "people's associations" founded by Christians in Calicut in the late 1970s). The assertive campaign tactics of these groups have evoked fears that their portrayal of Christ as a millenarian social liberator may provide a revolutionary rallying force for any low-caste or economically disadvantaged group with a reason to challenge India's existing social and political order. Their language is often intentionally provocative: "A Christian can not be neutral. He must enter into the struggle for justice. The Indian masses can achieve liberation only through a total revolution, consisting in a restructuring of society with a new ideology. Fidelity to Christ demands an option in favour of the poor and oppressed. The liberation groups [in contemporary Kerala] consist of prophetic individuals who articulate the revolts against the unjust society."[6]

Such protests in both north and south India tend to be directed against the power and assertiveness of India's rapidly growing Hindu middle class. Especially since the lifting of Indira Gandhi's twenty-one-month authoritarian "Emergency" regime in 1977, this disparate population of newly prosperous entrepreneurs, substantial cash crop farmers, and urban professional people has been free to communicate disquiet about the real and imagined links between social unrest and the spread of "foreign" faiths and religious adherences. For a large proportion of this uneasy middle class, such uncertainties have been translated into the idiom of defensive or "fundamentalist" Hindu religious activism.[7]

All this has set the stage for the proliferation of fundamentalist religious movements in the country's southern states. As elsewhere in India, volatile energy and commodity prices and other rapid changes in the economy have overturned existing social relationships and have provoked intense conflicts in many rural and urban localities. Since the late 1970s large hinterland and coastal tracts in the states of Tamil Nadu, Karnataka, and Andhra Pradesh have been subject to intermittent drought and crop failures, leading to waves of short- and long-term migration by displaced cultivators to the packed slum colonies of Madras and other large cities.[8] Such shifts in regional political geography have paved the way for violent clashes initiated by self-styled "sons of the soil." These are militants who have organized themselves to resist threats to employment and control of regional political institutions at the hands of those identified as "aliens" or incomers. One of the many manifestations of this new unrest was a series of riots in Karnataka state in 1982 and 1984, when speakers of the state's majority Kannada language proclaimed themselves "defenders of the Kannada nation" and induced the state's administration to close off educational and employment opportunities to locally settled speakers of Tamil, Telugu, and Urdu.[9]

Conflicts like this which express supposed injustice in the idiom of threatened nationhood or linguistic and communal solidarities have become increasingly widespread in south India, as in many other parts of the subcontinent. For those singled out as enemies or outsiders, this has been a stimulus to new and unaccustomed attempts to firm up communal boundaries or to project an equally assertive sense of corporate solidarity. And often it is at this point that the defenders of "threatened nationhood" have organized themselves beneath the banner of religious fundamentalism. For example, the Karnataka Urdu-speakers who were hit by the 1982 agitation were all Muslims. But it was only at this point, when they were denounced as aliens and job-stealers by "sons of the soil," who were predominantly Hindu, that the region's Muslims began to respond in unprecedented numbers to the appeal of militant organizations expressing an ideology of Islamization and exclusive Muslim religious identity.[10] These events were equally alarming to the large Christian populations in Karnataka and the three neighboring southern states. They, too, were caught up in the disruption of social ties which has accompanied the southern states' economic uncertainties.

In Kerala state, too, there has been widespread social dislocation, beginning with a particularly high rate of migration to the Gulf; exceptional standards of literacy and professional training made the area a fertile recruiting ground for labor-hungry Gulf enterprises. Also, the state has exceptionally large Christian and Muslim populations (4.5 million Christians and 4.2 million Muslims out of a total of 21 million, according to the 1971 Census of India). Both of these Keralan minority groups have been disproportionately well represented in the emigrant Gulf work force; Arab recruiters have sought both Christian and Muslim workers from Asian countries and certainly prefer them to Indian Hindus, and the state's high population density and severe unemployment among graduates and other qualified job-seekers had pushed nearly half a million Keralans into emigrating to the oil-producing countries by the late 1970s. In the 1970s the inflow of Gulf remittances to the state helped create the kind of uneven economic growth that has heightened social tensions elsewhere in India. With the collapse of the oil boom in the early 1980s and the current decline in employment prospects for Indians in many Arab countries, even greater tension was unleashed in Kerala. The mid- to late 1980s saw a rapid upsurge in the numbers of returning Gulf migrants; the majority of these were young, male, and unable to find employment at home. All this has greatly enhanced the volatility of social relations in the state.[11]

One further factor has been widespread publicity about south India's demographic trends. Compared to other parts of the country, the southern states contain relatively high populations of "untouchable" or Harijan groups; for example, such groups account for over 25 percent of the population in large areas of Tamil Nadu, and Kerala contains proportionately high Harijan and tribal populations. It is widely held that social and economic unrest among these groups is inducing them to turn in large numbers to Islam and Christianity. These claims gained greater substance when the 1971 Census of India (published in 1978) found that in the southern states, population growth among Muslims and Christians had occurred at a rate as much as 10 percent higher than the rate of increase for the population as a whole.[12] The result of all this is that as other groups have turned to the simplistic new vocabulary of exclusion and defensive nationhood, Muslims and Christians have had little choice but to respond in kind. Here, moves toward organized fundamentalism have had more to do with a closing of options than a positive decision to embrace a new ideology of purist or fundamentalist faith.

Christian Fundamentalisms in Southern India

South India's many manifestations of social instability form the backdrop to the growth of organized fundamentalism in the southern states. Today a high proportion of those in the area who would be classed as professing Christians have become associated with churches and charismatic, guru-like individuals whose teachings and observances can be classed as fundamentalist. Their forms of worship emphasize miraculous healing and other supernatural intercessions in everyday life, as well as exorcism, prophetic utterance, the infallibility of scripture and expressions of contact with the divine such as glossolalia (speaking in tongues). This is activist religion which challenges the authority of conventional church hierarchies. Insofar as it possesses lasting formal structures, these tend to be small in scale and to be built up around individual laypeoples' assemblies, lay confraternities, supernatural healing and exorcism circles, and ad hoc campaigns for the physical reoccupation or "conquest" of contested religious precincts, especially along the south Indian coastline in the localities around Kanniyakumari. The adherents of this activist Christianity seek to cleanse and invigorate, to impose new behavioral codes on fellow believers, to communicate an urgent personalized religion of blood, power, and living accessible divinity, and, in certain highly publicized cases, to defend and attack where danger is perceived from within a landscape of heightened communal boundaries.[13]

Far from being the exclusive preserve of lower-class urban Protestant Christians, or any other minority subdivision within the region, radical forms of millenarian and revivalist adherence have appeared among virtually all the populations now identified as Christian in south India. For example, hundreds of Pentecostal or "holy spirit" churches now flourish in centers such as Kottayam, Tiruvella, and Mavelikara in southern Kerala. Many proclaim at least nominal affiliation to worldwide churches and evangelizing agencies of Western origin such as the largest of the North American Pentecostal denominations, the Assemblies of God.

This confederation of millenarian Protestant churches maintains a global missionary network offering a loose structure of adhesion to like-minded Christians in many Third World countries. In Kerala the eschatological urgency of the Assemblies of God and its affiliates and the region's many other comparable Pentecostalist church organizations now attracts thousands of English-speaking professional and commercial people of the Saint Thomas Christian community. Women, especially those with menfolk working in the Gulf or other distant places, are especially prominent in these congregations. This pattern reflects the pressures faced by women from divided Malayali Christian families who run households and often take outside employment, while still subject to the rigorous norms of propriety which prevail even among educated middle-class Christians in this conservative society. Thus significant numbers of Saint Thomas Christian women have been replacing or supplementing their adherence to conventional churches and denominations. They find in the small, independent "holy spirit" churches an emphasis on healing, on the relief of affliction, and on the accord of power and prestige given to inspired lay adepts (often female). This is a welcome contrast to the constraints of the established Saint Thomas Christian churches with their formal rituals and male priestly hierarchies.[14]

Among Roman Catholic Tamils, an assertive new puritanism and social activism now emanate from the men's lay confraternities of such sea-going port towns as Manapad and Tuticorin. Like the Tamil Christian fishermen of Kanniyakumari, who have fought pitched battles against invading devotees of the Hindu goddess Bhagavati, these believers perceive themselves as defenders of faith and terrain in a milieu where the threats come as much from lax fellow Christians as from the newly aggressive proponents of heightened Hindu and Muslim solidarities. As we have seen, fundamentalist organization has involved a strong trend of assertiveness among lay Christians who have felt the need to distance themselves from conventional churches and clerical authorities. As in many other parts of the world, however, the established churches have been quick to recognize the power of the new Pentecostal and charismatic religion that has been manifesting itself among professing Christians in the West as well as in India.

In the southern Indian states, this domestication of radical or fundamentalist Christianity by the hierarchy of the Roman Catholic church has been focused most conspicuously on one of the region's best-known pilgrimage sites, the shrine complex of Our Lady of Health at Velankanni, two hundred miles south of Madras. Devotees of all communities and religious traditions have frequented this shoreline holy place from as early as the seventeenth century. From the late nineteenth century, elaborate schemes were undertaken to popularize the site as a center of formally recognized mass pilgrimage under the sponsorship of south India's Roman Catholic ecclesiastical hierarchy. Even greater growth has occurred since the mid-1970s; the episcopal authorities in Tamil Nadu have used large sums from the Vatican and from pious lay benefactors in a massive program of expansion and rebuilding at the site. Like comparable Roman Catholic healing shrines such as Lourdes in southern France and Knock in Ireland, this basilican shrine has been a beneficiary of the Vatican's current commitment to manifestations of emotionally charged lay piety; such traditions provide a counterweight to the challenge of anti-authoritarian liberation theology. At Velankanni, pilgrims undergo exorcisms and experience instantaneous cures, which they attribute to the power of the basilica's miracle-working statue of the Virgin Mary. The priests who preside over the site have built up a "museum" of cast-off crutches and gilded kidney stones donated by grateful devotees whose afflictions have been healed by the power of the Velankanni Virgin. These authorities also disseminate publications containing accounts of the Virgin's powers and miraculous intercessions in a style which parallels that of the region's Hindu and Muslim shrine chronicles and other popular devotional lore.[15]

Velankanni is an established south Indian holy place which has grown up over the last three hundred years in close relationship with the region's indigenous Hindu and Muslim cult traditions. Now, however, its building and publicity campaigns have attracted more pilgrims than ever before to the site and have linked the official Roman Catholic church hierarchy to a tradition of worship focusing on miracles, demonic exorcisms, and ecstatic healing experiences. Even professing Hindus, especially women from the southern states, declare themselves in large numbers as cult devotees and disciples (*bhaktas*) of the all-powerful Velankanni Virgin. Thus the church authorities' policy of supporting the shrine has broadened the appeal of a literal, intercessory, and charismatic tradition of Christianity which has gained increasing popularity in south India.

This manifestation of Christianity can legitimately be called fundamentalist since it focuses on expressions of faith and enthusiasm which deny rational, intellectualized theologies and insist on the literal presence of the supernatural in everyday life. In structure it has combined the formality of official church sponsorship with the element of personal cult-centered adherence which is typical of south Indian religious life. Affiliation takes the form of loose and spontaneous cult adhesion around the person of the Velankanni Virgin, and this gives the cult its dynamism as an expression of indigenous "fundamentalist" Christianity.[16]

South India's Contested Religious Landscape

South India's indigenous Christians comprise a disparate population of many different castes and regional backgrounds. Its most powerful constituent community is the body of just over two million Malayalam-speaking Saint Thomas Christians who still preserve traditions of elite rank dating from their privileged status as warriors, traders, and landholders within the precolonial Hindu kingdoms of what is now Kerala. This population is divided into twenty or more distinct denominations and confessional groupings; some are affiliated with the ancient Christian patriarchates of western Asia, while others acknowledge the authority of locally based church hierarchies, including

Roman Catholic and Protestant denominations with their own regional ecclesiastical organizations. South India's Christians also include two to three million Roman Catholics belonging to the Tamil and Malayali maritime groups whose ancestors embraced Christianity in the sixteenth century, at a time when Portuguese imperial expansion fostered large-scale missionary activity among such strategic groups as sea-farers and trading people. About half of this group consists of poor and often illiterate fishers and manual laborers such as the Tamil- and Malayalam-speaking Mukkuvas of the Keralan and southwestern Tamil Nadu coastline. These are the people among whom the Beach Blossoms and similar campaigns of radical "liberation" have been organized by Christian activists. In such areas the Christian "people's organizations" have encouraged Tamil and Malayali fishing communities to organize cooperatives as a means of reducing dependence on local entrepreneurs (some Hindu, some higher-caste Christians) who keep fish prices low and charge high rates of interest on loans for vital equipment purchases.[17] Such people have had an ambivalent relationship with the local ecclesiastical hierarchies because bishops and other senior church authorities are widely thought to be hostile to social activists like the Beach Blossoms. This has helped to confirm the appeal of more individualized cult traditions like that of Velan-kanni, which embody "fundamentalist" forms of enthusiasm and lay power. Farther east along the Tamil Nadu coastline, these poor maritime fishermen have a powerful set of Christian neighbors, the Tamil-speaking Catholic Paravas. This population in-cludes a dominant commercial elite who play a leading role in the region's southern fishing and trading ports. They too are ardent supporters of the Velankanni shrine and are also active in the lay confraternity movement.[18]

South India's agrarian hinterland has also acquired sizable Christian populations over the last three hundred years. Some of these date from the seventeenth and eigh-teenth centuries, when new adherents were attracted by the supernatural powers ascribed to isolated rural saint-cult shrines and touring holy men. By the nineteenth century such people had been brought into contact with formal European-run mission churches. Other indigenous Christian groups were formed at the time of nineteenth-century "mass conversions" among lower caste, "untouchable," and forest tribal people; these were claimed as affiliates by the Protestant and Catholic missions and confessional groupings that had become active in the territories constituting the Ma-dras Presidency of British India.[19]

The moves many of these Christians have been making toward Pentecostal, mille-narian, and charismatic religious organizations should not be seen as an implanting of Western religion within an alien South Asian culture. New adherents of teachings that can reasonably be called fundamentalist are not a marginal underclass hungering for contact with "modernity" or "uplift" or repudiation of a constraining cultural inheritance. Both the missionaries of the past and many of the foreign clerics who make contact with the region's Pentecostals and charismatics today have made this mistake. With its massive and well-endowed Hindu temples and monastic foundations and its ancient centers of Hindu dynastic power, south India has been seen by many outsiders as a bastion of Hinduism in an exceptionally rigid and hierarchical form. The south's substantial Christian and Muslim minorities have therefore been portrayed as a class of internal refugees, as people who embraced the egalitarian and monotheist world religions so as to opt out of a social order defined by concepts of ritual purity and Brahman-centered caste ranking schemes.

As elsewhere in India, however, exclusive boundaries defining distinct and opposing communities of Hindus, Muslims, and Christians are far from being a universal "ethnographic fact" of south Indian life. The Hinduism of Brahmanical ritual and vegetarian all-India "high" gods came relatively late to much of the south. In many areas, especially in those which are now centers of fundamentalist Christian activism in its many different manifestations, formal Vaishnavite and Shaivite Hinduism came into prominence in a partial and qualified form, and certainly not as a universal model for correct observance and social behavior. The forms and institutions of this sort of Hinduism still overlap and coexist with south India's characteristic traditions of cult worship. This second version of Hinduism focuses on the healing and destructive powers of deified warrior heroes, on ferocious blood-taking goddesses, and on other divinities of power and active intercessory force.[20]

Given their centrality in local religious life, it is not surprising that these fierce power divinities and supernatural royal conquerors provided the context in which both Christianity and Islam were received and made intelligible in the region. The result, over many centuries, was the creation of strongly rooted south Indian manifestations of the two formally monotheist world religions. In both cases the emphasis has been on the literal presence of the supernatural in everyday life. This is made manifest through the transforming and intercessory powers of Christian saints and Muslim *pirs* (divinely empowered beings from the tradition of Muslim Sufism). These figures of the Christian and Muslim pantheon still share the features of indigenous south Indian divinity.[21] They inhabit a shared religious landscape of pilgrimage sites, parallel shrine complexes, and overlapping festival observance in which believers address one another's cult beings with the same titles, offerings, and conceptions of activated power or *sakti*. Velankanni is one of many such sites in south India: even today the shrine's official literature portrays the Velankanni Virgin as a supernaturally endowed counterpart of the region's heroic Hindu warrior goddesses.[22]

Furthermore, at shrines that date back over many centuries such as the Parava church of Our Lady of Snows at Tuticorin, and the shoreline cult shrines of Saint Francis Xavier, the veneration of the goddess-like Virgin Mary and cult saints has allowed professing Christians to contend for tokens of ritual precedence and honor like those of south Indians who would be classed as Hindu or Muslim. Under colonial rule and also in more recent times, ecclesiastical authorities of all denominations have sought to root out these indigenous concepts of divinity. But throughout the south, Christians still participate in local goddess and spirit cults, and clash over ceremonial ranking schemes in ways that have readjusted the traditions of conventional scriptural Christianity to fit the local religious environment. Here figures of the Christian pantheon—including the saints of Roman Catholicism, and even Christ and the Virgin—are still perceived as rulers of supernatural domains in which their devotees contend as subjects and standard-bearers seeking tokens of precedence within the terrain marked out as the kingdom of their reigning lord. This emphasis on power, precedence, and command within and between local Christian populations has also tended to set limits on the power of ordained clerics and formal ecclesiastical hierarchies.[23]

All this has shaped the dynamics of fundamentalist religion in the region. Organized expressions of fundamentalism have been appearing with increasing persistence among professing Christians at a time when adherents of the region's indigenous churches and confessional groupings have reason to feel bombarded by the language, the slogans, and the contentious activism of a whole host of regional and pan-Indian propagandists and militant organizations.

One major sequence of events stands out for Christians who have acquired a commitment to fundamentalism in their dealings with groups whom they identify as menacing outsiders. These conflicts began in February 1981 with the now-infamous story of six hundred rural Harijans, or "untouchables," from the poor, barren cultivating village of Minakshipuram in hinterland Tamil Nadu. These people, who would have been classed as Hindus within the loose meaning of the term in south Indian society, became the center of heated controversy throughout India when it was announced that they had undergone a public conversion to Islam as a consequence of their "social oppression" at the hands of higher-caste local Hindus, mostly local landholders of the Tamil Marava caste group.[24]

Almost immediately these Minakshipuram "converts" were seized upon as symbols of lost and degraded Hindu nationhood by publicists of the RSS and the newly assertive VHP operating from as far away as Madras, Bombay, and Delhi. This occurred at a time of heightened ethnic and communal activism all over the subcontinent. Minakshipuram is situated in a typical Tamil Nadu drought district; the area was characteristic of the country's many contentious social milieux in which economic differentials had been widening with increased bitterness in relationships between groups of insecure landholders, laborers, and tenant farmers. Across the country as a whole, the new buying power of a "middle class" of professional, commercial, and farming people had generated new forms of conspicuous consumption that included the taste for a distinctively Indian form of tourism. The appeal of this kind of journeying is still evident to any traveler on the country's overcrowded trains and long-distance buses. It combines the secular pleasures of holiday making with notions of *Bharat darshan,* the patriotic and religiously meritorious visitation of holy places. For Hindus this phenomenon has helped to generate a more coherent vision of India as a unified land of interlinked Hindu shrines, temples, and pilgrimage sites.

All this helped to make intelligible the outcry that focused attention on a hitherto obscure hamlet in the barren Tamil Nadu countryside in 1981. Sensationalized press coverage of Minakshipuram showed no awareness of the fluidity of religious boundaries and confessional allegiances which has prevailed for many centuries in the south, particularly among the distinctly un-Brahmanical ex-predator groups like the Maravas of the Minakshipuram area. Here reality has been adjusted to present a picture of competing monolithic religious communities rather than shadings of mixed and overlapping cult adherence. Hindus "shall not tolerate any further loss of their own brothers and sisters from the Hindu fold to the Christian faith or Islam," declared defenders of the "Hindu nation."[25] This cry of religion in danger provided an unexpected rallying point for Tamil Christian fishing people in maritime communities one hundred miles from Minkashipuram.

It was here in a zone of powerful sanctity to Tamils of all communal affiliations that a new movement of organized fundamentalism took shape among Christians. This has been described as the "shoreline revival movement," which organized its adherents to reclaim sites of shared supernatural significance along the contested Kanniyakumari coastline. Immediately after the Minakshipuram conversions, the RSS and its local affiliates launched campaigns proclaiming the restoration of what was called "Hindu supremacy" in south India. Recruitment drives and noisy public rallies brought the threatening martial style of the Hindu solidarity cause to localities around Colachel, Pudur, Muttam, and other centers in Kanniyakumari district which had relatively little experience of the banners, posters, and pamphleteering of contemporary Hindu fundamentalism.

In campaigns such as this one, invective against Christians has been as prevalent as anti-Muslim themes. As elsewhere in India, attempts to foster consciousness of Hindu solidarity ascribe a high level of cohesiveness to the rival "community." It is frequently asserted by supporters of the VHP, for example, that Hinduism as the true faith of Indians is now in danger of obliteration in its homeland. This, they insist, is because the so-called conversion religions possess supposed strengths such as a talent for proselytizing, and a propensity to high birthrates among their adherents. The claim is that the two "alien" faiths are endowed with centralized institutional structures and systems of belief which are less diffuse and pluralistic than South Asian Hindu belief. Thus for all its exaggeration of the "enemy's" solidarities and resources, the so-called lesson of Minakshipuram was applied with little difficulty to the delicately balanced schemes of social order which prevail in the Kanniyakumari area. From the beginning of this conflict, representatives of the RSS and its local allies (e.g., a group calling itself the Hindu Seva Sangham or Hindu Service Association) denounced local Christians as pawns of foreign churches and subversive missionary organizations.[26] As receivers of foreign finance they were accused of seeking out converts in order to rob them of their "true" nationhood through the exploitation of alien resources and un-Indian techniques of organization. Such accusations sprang from a peculiar synthesis of ideas about dynamic forms of minority religious adherence in the region. On the one hand, the lavish building program at Velankanni and recent Saudi-backed campaigns to erect opulent Arab-style mosques in south Indian Muslim localities have confirmed a general view of both Christians and Muslims as big spenders and recipients of outside benefactions. On the other hand, there is the notion of both Christianity and Islam as faiths of social protest. Groups such as the RSS have long held that Christians and Muslims attract new converts by offering low-caste and tribal people cash handouts and by championing them against landlords, creditors and other figures of authority. This conspiratorial view bears little relation to reality; in response, however, populations such as the Christian fishermen of the Kanniyakumari region forged a tighter and more exclusive level of organization than they had previously possessed.

Beginning in March 1982, this new organized activism expressed itself in the form of riots which swept the region over a period of several months. The focus was the annual festival of the goddess Bhagavati, which attracts tens of thousands of pilgrims every year to elaborate processional rites around the goddess's seafront temple in the village of Mandaikadu. This area, from the modern border of Kerala state to the southern tip of Tamil Nadu at Kanniyakumari, is an area containing countless shrines to Tamil goddesses and other power divinities. Along the shoreline and its immediate hinterland there are shrines and pilgrimage places to Muslim pirs, "high" and blood-taking Hindu divinities, and potent Christian cult figures such as Saint Francis Xavier, the sixteenth-century European missionary who is now revered as a supernaturally endowed hero and healer in south India. Sporadic violence has been occurring in villages across the region ever since the staging in mid-February 1982, at the nearby town of Nagercoil, of a Hindu Unity and Resurgence Conference featuring widely publicized speeches by representatives of the VHP, the RSS, and another of the many evanescent locally based militant organizations, the Hindu Munnani Kazhagam or Hindu Front. Printed wall posters appeared throughout the coastal region calling for Hindu Raj, that is, the assertion of political power by Hindus in a Hindu homeland; newly sworn-in recruits to the RSS gathered to stage the organization's characteristic displays of military-style drilling and slogan-chanting.[27] Those targeted by these displays and by charges of subversive organizational links were principally Roman Catholics of the shoreline fishing communities.

For these Tamil Christians, manifestations of fundamentalism with a new basis of public agitation began sporadically. They were primarily a response to the Hindu Raj campaign. The earliest organized activism came from ad hoc associations of young Christian laymen in villages with a long tradition of delicate and often combative relationships between Shanars (Nadars) and Tamil maritime people who were linked in complex schemes of local honor and ceremonial precedence. (In Brahmanical terms the Shanars are a relatively low-ranking population of cultivators and brewers of country liquor or "toddy.")[28] This whole region, including Mandaikadu, Colachel, and neighboring localities, is especially sensitive because of the special potency ascribed to its auspicious seafront bathing sites; it is no surprise that it should be marked out as a key zone in the new confrontation to redefine concepts of nationhood in terms of exclusion and primacy in a contested sacred landscape.

Among the first expressions of the new Christian activism were outbreaks in which young Tamil Christian fishermen organized attacks on stalls kept by Hindu shopkeepers, destroying the stallholders' stocks of colored oleographs depicting Hindu gods and goddesses.[29] These pictures of popular deities are of a type displayed in homes, vehicles, shops, and offices throughout India; in the south it is common to find similar conventionalized renderings of Gandhi, Jesus, and a wide array of other human and supernatural personalities displayed side by side with the high gods and power divinities of the Hindu pantheon.[30] These attacks expressed a new "fundamentalist" consciousness among Christians. Its adherents were repudiating emblems from a shared sacred landscape which is populated by saints and divinities who possess the capacity to act both as allied and mutually interacting power divinities, and as beings of confrontation and divinely mandated earthly warfare.

It was at this point that self-professed Hindu militants made moves to turn the annual Bhagavati festival at Mandaikadu into an assertion of Hindu solidarity and "resurgence" in the region. Such attempts to use big temple festivals as arenas in which "to preserve and foster Hindu culture" have become standard practice in many parts of India.[31] Here most of the activists were men of the Shanar (Nadar) caste group. Their new tactic was to shepherd an unusually large body of pilgrims from adjacent districts of Kerala and Tamil Nadu to the holy site at Mandaikadu in preparation for the annual mass sea-bathing ritual scheduled for the auspicious time of the goddesses's chief festival day. Bhagavati is not a "pure" vegetarian deity, but a typical south Indian goddess of fierce aspect, a blood-taker and avenger; she is worshiped with blood sacrifice by devotees from many south Indian caste groups. The sacred significance of shore-shrines is a potent theme in virtually all manifestations of south Indian religion. Even the local Roman Catholic bishop admitted at the time of the riots that the Mandaikadu bathing rite, through which worshipers make contact with the awesome power or sakti of this avowedly Hindu goddess, has been "much frequented" by local Christians.[32] Indeed Bhagavati is one of many south Indian power divinities whose cults have served for many centuries as a common focus for professing Christians and Hindus; the elite Malayali Christians of Kerala, for example, still preserve legends in which their cult hero Saint Thomas contends as an equal in a great cosmic struggle with this same female warrior deity Bhagavati.[33]

Now, however, assertion of an enhanced Hindu solidarity was excluding Christians from terrain in which they had previously shared in schemes of devotion and ranked ceremonial precedence directed toward the goddess. These clashes did not represent an expression of borrowed Western "fundamentalism" which would deny the authenticity of local "heathen" religion and its divinities. On the contrary, there was still common ground between Hindus and Christians in their perception of the shrine's power and sanctity. The dynamic face of "fundamentalism" in this case, then, was an organized response to exclusion from a shared sacred territory. In the eyes of professing Christians and Hindus alike, Bhagavati is the sovereign of her shorefront domain, and she radiates supernatural energies which may heal and succor those who submit to her as subject-devotees at the shrine and its adjacent bathing place. Now, however, the organized manifestations of Hindu fundamentalism were using this familiar idiom of conquest and divine sovereignty to transmit claims of supremacy for a revitalized "Hindu nation." In the words of a local politician, addressing yet another Hindu "resurgence" conference which took place in nearby central Kerala in the wake of these clashes: "While having goodwill for all religions as enjoined in its scriptures, Hinduism will no longer remain a passive spectator to hostile incursions upon it."[34]

Such references to incursions and activated, defensive Hinduism explain the next move in the conflict, which was the formation of the Kanniyakumari area's Christian "defense of the shoreline" (or "shoreline revival") movement. Coming at a time of mutual challenges and attacks, the exceptionally large numbers of pilgrims brought to the Mandaikadu festival by the RSS and its supporters could only be perceived as an incursion of exactly the sort referred to by the defenders of "Hindu nation" and "Hindu homeland." As was seen above, once accused of being suspiciously centralized and subversive, these rather fragmented local Christian populations began to form small-scale militant lay action committees. Then, when the annual goddess festival was transformed into a territorial invasion with strong supernatural overtones, a new and more coherent level of fundamentalist activism was organized. This seems to have been entirely a campaign of lay people; its structural features were rudimentary. Rallies were held, church bells were rung to summon self-styled "defense committees," and with little apparent planning or external support, several thousand villagers of the shoreline fishing communities gathered at Mandaikadu to blockade the seafront and repel the pilgrims who had been transported to the locality to take their ceremonial sea-baths.[35]

As the universally recognized domain of the goddess, this terrain had long been accessible to members of all communities and confessional groupings who sought incorporation within her domain. Now it had been claimed as the exclusive province of "aliens," intruders who were using the well-known terminology of indigenous religious honors disputes to exclude Christians from their delicately balanced positions of power and ceremonial standing within the locality.[36] Thus the response of the new Christian activist movement was to stage a reclamation of their own, to assert primacy in a sacred precinct which was as potent for them as for the militant preservers of "Hindu homeland" who were ranged against them. At the same time, however, the newly adopted tactics of these groups were directed against symbols of the activist and exclusive Hinduism which had manifested itself in their midst. The Christian action committees began with the destruction of Hindu sacred images; they went on to expel avowedly Hindu intruders from what they now claimed as "their" precincts on the shoreline. The action committees then began to build up stronger village-to-village links; weapons were distributed, and there were arson attacks on Hindu temples in a twenty-mile radius around Mandaikadu.

Accounts of these clashes were spread through detailed reports in the vernacular and English-language press and by word of mouth. Where initially this heightening of Christian solidarities had been confined to communities of Tamil Catholic fishermen, signs of organized militancy appeared in localities hundreds of miles away. In such cases the supposed lessons of Minakshipuram and Mandaikadu were cited in attacks and counterattacks involving Christians of many different caste groups and confessional affiliations.[37] Anti-Christian posters were particularly widespread across the old Marava heartland, that is, in the Ramnad country around the great temple center at Ramesveram.[38] For hundreds of years, populations like the Paravas and Saint Thomas Christians have preserved their own distinct traditions of identity which focus on endogamous descent patterns, complex internal ranking schemes, and the veneration of tutelary cult saints. But they are also conscious that outside opinion, especially that of militant Hindu and Muslim organizations, has sought to lump all Christians together as a single supercommunity with suspect foreign links and un-Indian belief systems. The result, then, has been a call for a more disciplined and assertive public face for Christianity in south India; its organized expressions have acquired a wider territorial span and a new search for ways to instill greater dynamism and cohesiveness into "Christian" life in the south.

Nationhood and Fundamentalist Adherence

Naturally the delicate electoral maneuverings of regional and national politics have played a role in these events. The 1982 Kanniyakumari clashes occurred at a time when the electoral significance of Hindu Raj campaigns and heightened communal consciousness movements was becoming ever more visible in Indian public life. At the time of these riots in the south, the Tamil Nadu press was full of stories about gestures being made by the ruling Indian Congress party under the then prime minister Rajiv Gandhi to propitiate supporters of Hindu activist campaigns. For example, in March 1982 Rajiv Gandhi promised that his government would tighten laws to restrict the slaughter of cows for meat and leather in every state in the country.[39] This issue, the protection of sacred Mother Cow, had been a favorite theme of self-proclaimed defenders of Hindu moral and spiritual integrity (known as *sanatan dharm* or "orthodox religion" societies) since the late nineteenth century. With its old overtones of anti-Muslim and anti-Christian militancy, the cow protection issue was now being revived by activists who included prominent Hindu *acaryas* (the spiritual heads of important Hindu monastic institutions known as *maths*).[40]

This was not a time, then, when the elected chief ministers of Indian states could afford to use their powers to restrain activists who spoke for the defense of India's Hindu moral and spiritual order. Tamil Nadu's chief minister, the late film-star and politician M. G. Ramachandran, was at this time leader of a regionally based political party that had entered into a fragile tactical alliance with the dominant All-India Congress party. Key opposition members of the state's Legislative Assembly were gaining political ground by associating themselves with the cause of Hindu Raj and religious paramountcy for Hindus at Mandaikadu.[41] As violence spread across Tamil Nadu, left-wing legislators in both the state assembly and the national parliament accused unnamed "imperialist forces" of using both Christian and Hindu militants as a front to penetrate and destabilize the country's strategic coastal areas.[42] Again Christians came off the worst in these attacks: for once, Communist politicians and the assertive "Hindu right" (as personified by the VHP's political partner, the Bharatiya Janata or Indian People's party, founded in 1980) joined in denouncing the minority "convert" groups as subverters of the nation and dupes of the "foreign hand." The Tamil Nadu chief minister uttered veiled denunciations of "a certain *math*-head," meaning the prestigious acarya (or "pontiff" in local English usage) of south India's most famous monastic foundation.[43] But the state's political authorities made no serious move to undercut the Hindu Front, the RSS, the VHP, and the other locally active "fundamentalist" organizations. Thus the conclusion for the many Christian communities who had organized or had been caught up in these attacks, or who feared that they too would be targeted by militant organizations, was that heightened consciousness and organized defense campaigns were necessary safeguards in times of uncertainty and aggressive fundamentalist activism.

Of course, the context for these organized assertions of fundamentalism was the local economic and social tension in regions of dense population and sparse material resources. With the rise of assertive Hindu militant organizations in the southern states, existing tensions within such localities have been reformulated under the banner of "religion in danger" and demands to exclude the "alien." For example, Tamil Christian maritime people from this same Kanniyakumari region have been involved in disputes at the site of the great offshore memorial to the nineteenth-century Hindu sage and religious reformer Swami Vivekananda. This site is both a tourist attraction and a pan-Indian holy place. Because it is situated just off the southernmost tip of the subcontinent, at the confluence of two seas and many mutually enhancing *tirthas* or holy bathing places, including an important goddess temple and several Christian saint cult shrines, the memorial is a place of special sanctity.

Here, too, clashes over primacy and status between Christian Paravas and rival low-caste Hindus have acquired new force in the last ten years. The major stimulus was the initiative taken by activist Hindu organizations to build an extension to the shrine. During the 1890s Vivekananda became a worldwide celebrity who promoted a vision of revivalist Hinduism linked with newly asserted Indian nationalist themes. This makes him an obvious hero for today's militant Hindu organizations, and attempts to memorialize him have stressed a vision of India's physical terrain as a vast interlocking grid of shrines and landmarks associated with the sacred Hindu homeland. Because the building program for the Vivekananda rock-shrine is a means of asserting Hindu paramountcy, it has threatened the local Christian fishermen's monopoly of transport boats carrying pilgrims to the site. And in organizing strikes and boycotts to isolate the shrine and to cut the pilgrimage traffic, yet another set of locally based lay activists has constituted themselves into ad hoc defense committees whose concerns have united economic uncertainties with the new militant issues of religious exclusion and contested sovereignty.

Thus the lesson for Christians in south India has been that in uncertain times it is best to conform to the stereotype that ascribes a high level of organization to "People of the Book," which in the subcontinent is a term embracing Muslims as well as Christians. The region's locally based Hindu Front organizations have issued statements blaming events such as the 1982 riots in Tamil Nadu on bodies of lay Christians, who are held up as a threat to Hindu "nationhood" because they use their resources to stage mass meetings and conferences during which Christian speakers "make remarks" against Hindu gods and goddesses.[44] The Christianity which is identified in such statements as a source and inspiration for confrontation between "communities" does exist as a manifestation of fundamentalist urgings within Christian populations in south India. Such organized expressions of Christian affiliation have indeed become a conspicuous feature of Christian life in the south. They are seen in the Christianity of charismatic witness and Pentecostalism, among the Holy Spirit churches and lay organizations which actually do stage rallies and conferences articulating themes of urgent piety, millenarianism, and Puritan consciousness.[45] Such activism is often explicitly modeled on the challenging moves being made by the region's fundamentalist Hindu and Muslim organizations; it has already been seen that militant Hindu "unity" and "resurgence" conferences are also a permanent feature of the region's contested religious landscape, as they are in most other parts of India.

Along the south Indian coastline between Madras and Kanniyakumari, the powerful lay confraternities that control cult festivals within important Roman Catholic Parava localities have now become conspicuous standard-bearers of this fundamentalism. This movement took organized form in the mid-1970s by transforming existing institutions, the men's confraternities, to meet a need for expressions of faith and affiliation which emphasized pride, strength, and confidence in the eyes of the "outside" or non-Christian world. Since the Paravas' original conversion to Christianity in the sixteenth century, the group's Catholicism has functioned as a caste lifestyle for its members, that is, as a tradition of shared corporate morality and worship which has marked off the Paravas as a distinctive *jati* or ritual community like those of the "traditional" Hindu social order.[46]

During the era of colonial rule, Jesuit missionaries operating in important Parava port centers such as Manapad founded lay confraternities in imitation of the sixteenth- and seventeenth-century pious urban laymen's societies of southern Europe. Today some of the same confraternities still flourish as an arena for displays of power and ceremonial primacy. In Manapad, for example, the Confraternity of the Five Wounds of Our Lord takes a commanding role in the locality's annual processional festival in honor of the town's best-known sacred relic, a fragment of the True Cross which has been housed in this much-frequented site of indigenous Christian piety since 1583.[47]

These rituals still retain their long-standing role in allowing Parava worshipers to share in the power and sanctity which emanate from the Holy Cross shrine, and to rank themselves within the community's contentious internal schemes of ritual precedence. But since the mid-1970s, such confraternities have taken an increasingly forceful role as shapers and defenders of a more public, externally directed identity for Paravas in particular, and for "Christians" as a more general category within the Tamil country. It is now the presiding laymen of the confraternities who claim the right to articulate standards of correct morality within their communities. They tend to come from Parava families with an old tradition of honor and ceremonial office within the caste group.[48] Their young men are often English-speakers with professional qualifications and close links to the industrial and commercial concerns of the major Tamil port towns. In this new guise the confraternities have been quick to update the old concerns which emphasized punishment of sexual misconduct, marital misalliances (i.e., marriage outside the caste), and other deviations from the Paravas' code of corporate morality (*dharma*) which were perceived as threatening the "blood purity" of the caste. Today, too, the confraternities concern themselves with standards of morality in ways that correspond elsewhere in the world to the linking of activist fundamentalist religion with the definition of strict codes of honor and rectitude for fellow believers. Now that the Parava confraternities see themselves as organized defenders of corporate morality among Roman Catholics, there is a similar insistence on disciplining the lax and guarding against an appearance of weakness or moral deviance in the eyes of the wider world.

This trend is occurring in light of what "outsiders" are expected to perceive and acknowledge about those who fall within the region's new and more rigid boundaries of community and confessional allegiance. Since the mid- to late 1970s, the processions of the confraternities at events such as the Manapad Holy Cross festival have become occasions when symbols of militancy and territorial sovereignty are deployed: the robes and crowns worn by members, the quasi-martial regalia, the brandishing of crucifixes and "kingly" scepters are received now as part of an assertion of something militant, active, even aggressive from within the world of indigenous Christian communities. One feature of this assertiveness is the emphasis on laymen's power. When Manapad's annual Holy Cross festival ends, the family whose male leader has been chosen to preside over the confraternity for that year feasts local Catholic priests as well as bishops and other clerics brought in specially for the occasion. This gesture of public munificence allows these leading lay families to "capture" the priesthood and hold it up to view as receivers of kingly favor like the dependent Brahman ritualists of a "traditional" Hindu court. The declarations in favor of purist behavioral standards are another side of the vigorous public face which is still being cultivated for the Paravas and for Catholics in general by the confraternities. Once again, we see a religious group defining itself in new ways, deploying symbols of assertion and supremacy, and acting according to stereotypes of unity and disciplined activism which are generating both action and reaction in the wider society. Thus throughout south India, there has been a competitive hardening of confessional boundaries which has transformed outsiders' stereotypes into a model for new forms of activism and organization among previously fragmented Christian populations.

A Christianity of Lay Power and Public Activism

What else is at stake, then, in this turn toward activist forms of Christianity featuring unity conferences, lay action committees, and confraternities presenting themselves as moral exemplars and guardians of corporate discipline? The emphasis on lay power has been a widespread feature of fundamentalism in its different manifestations among Christians. This, too, has involved a reassertion of indigenous themes and devotional traditions which have given south Indian Christianity its distinctive character across the region for many centuries. When the confraternities assert their primacy in relations with the region's Roman Catholic ecclesiastical authorities, they have had much in common with the many Pentecostal and charismatic groups that have sprung up all over the southern states. In these movements of religious enthusiasm, adherents commonly reject conventional church affiliation in favor of informal personal attachments to individuals who are recognized as bearers of divine gifts.[49] Such people are to be found all over south India. They act as exorcists, healers, prayer leaders, and guru-like millenarian teachers and spiritual adepts, often attracting sizable bodies of adherents. In all these roles they are directly comparable to the inspired male and female adepts or Christian gurus of past centuries; these historic guru figures are still widely revered as founders of important precolonial cult shrines, and as leaders of the many small hinterland devotional circles that were eventually placed under the authority of the European missionary churches.[50] In some parts of south India, especially in Kerala, modern lay adepts or gurus have been identified by their followers with famous charismatic cult leaders of the past, most notably with the late nineteenth-century Malayali Christian prophet known as Justus Joseph or Vidwan Kutti ("the learned youth"). At a time when the Saint Thomas Christians' old ecclesiastical structures had been thrown into disarray by a series of crises over leadership and episcopal succession,[51] this ordained Malayali Brahman convert broke with his Anglican missionary sponsors and proclaimed the imminence of Christ's Second Coming. Beginning in 1875, he acquired a following of ten thousand to fifteen thousand Malayalis, mostly Saint Thomas Christians who danced and sang in a secret Celestial Language, revering their self-professed messiah as a composite incarnation of Jehovah, the Hindu Ram, the biblical Joseph, the Muslim imam and martyr Ali, and the nineteenth-century Anglican evangelical bishop of Calcutta, Daniel Wilson.[52]

There are still families in Kerala who preserve a tradition of former adherence to this sect, which was typical of the region's tendency to generate wildfire millenarian groups and breakaway churches in a period of widespread religious enthusiasm and revivalist activity among its large Christian populations. For many south Indians, the return to expressions of guru-centred revivalist Christianity over the last fifteen years or so has linked this consciousness of an individualized lay guru tradition in the past with the new concern to present a strong public face for Christianity as the faith of the Paravas, the Saint Thomas Christians, and other professing Christian groups. Thus when south Indian believers have organized themselves around the informal, guru-like authority of a lay prayer leader or charismatic healer who exorcises demons and makes utterances in unknown tongues (still a widespread feature of Pentecostal Christianity across the world), they have often done so in repudiation of conventional ecclesiastical hierarchies.

To these believers, ordained churchmen are figures of weakness and uncertainty in the contested terrain of Hindu Raj and militant communalism. The followers of radical breakaway churches and Pentecostal lay leaders condemn the liberal, ecumenical Christianity of the modern south Indian churches; there is much hostility toward liberation theology and even toward the churches' more modest concerns with charity ventures and the implementation of a living "social Gospel." Equally deplored are moves toward interfaith "dialogue" among the Protestant affiliates of the Church of South India and within the region's Roman Catholic dioceses. To those imbued with the imperatives of Pentecostal or charismatic teaching, a Christianity centered on humanitarian "social work" is a weak-kneed evasion of God's call to witness, save souls, and contend with the devil. Similarly, as for many evangelical Christians outside India, ecumenical "dialogue," the search for common ground between the teachings of formal theological Hinduism and Christianity (and sometimes Islam as well), is a Satanic invitation to "syncretism" and the abandonment of Christian revelation as absolute truth.[53] Furthermore, if south Indian Christians fail to embrace a commitment to Christ, the Virgin, and the pantheon of saints as embodiments of assertive power with a literal presence in everyday life, they are at risk of conceding to those other purveyors of Christianity as a religion of force and assertion. These are the organizations that conceive of Christ as a secular liberator and social activist; there is a strong view among "fundamentalist" Christians of Pentecostal and charismatic affiliation that this type of Christianity must be stopped from holding the high ground as south India's leading embodiment of Christian activism.

Modern followers of the divinely endowed Christian gurus and like-minded affiliates of south India's many small-scale Pentecostal churches have in common a vision of their everyday environment as a landscape of the supernatural. Hindu deities, demons, Christian saints, and Muslim pirs are real living presences, not fictions or abstractions. Professing Christians attend exorcisms in which adepts who may be of either Hindu or Christian affiliation relieve sufferers from demonic afflictions visited upon them by blood-taking goddesses, ghosts, and malign spirits (*peys*), as well as devils and demons from the Christian pantheon.[54] In south India's "indigenized" manifestations of Christianity, with their emphasis on demonic cult personalities and visitations of divinity in fierce anthropomorphic forms, such overlapping of communal and confessional boundaries is a normal feature of everyday worship. Liberal modern clerics who are visibly out of step with this lay sectarian Christianity are condemned as purveyors of a bloodless religion offering "love and peace" in place of the active intercessory powers deployed by the charismatic healers and gurus.[55]

The southern Indian states now contain thousands of active millenarian and Pentecostal churches, some wholly independent and some linked to U.S. and other Western evangelizing agencies. Typical of these are the thousands of churches in Kerala which identify themselves as offshoots of the U.S. Assemblies of God. The first of these began to attract adherents from among established Christian populations and the so-called "untouchable" communities of the Malabar coast in the 1920s. In the late 1970s their membership was said to have reached as much as a quarter of a million, with believers moving in and out of affiliation to loosely structured fellowships of Pentecostal Christians, including the U.S.-backed Assemblies of God, the Apostolic United Pentecostal Gospel Society, the Philadelphia Pentecostalists, and the so-called Backward Pentecostalists (who recruit among Harijan or ex-"untouchable" groups). The largest of these informal networks in Kerala, the Indian Pentecostal church, which has bases in over twenty localities around Tiruvella, is reported to have acquired some fifty thousand members in the state by the late 1970s. The others report memberships ranging from under one thousand to as many as twenty thousand or thirty thousand, but these figures must all be regarded as approximations, since adhesion to Holy Spirit churches is primarily a matter of loose, spontaneous, and often short-lived personal links with local prayer leaders, healers, and adepts, rather than formal confessional attachments.[56]

Some of the organizational characteristics of these fundamentalist churches are consistent with those of Protestant Pentecostal churches in the West and in the many non-European societies where Pentecostal missionaries now operate. Although they are far from being pawns of the "foreign hand" as the Hindu campaigners claim, many of the lay leaders who have played a central role in creating independent Pentecostal churches and prayer circles go on to seek affiliation to prominent overseas Pentecostal and millenarian church organizations. This is consistent with the trend elsewhere in India for groups such as purist Muslims to seek outside connections and finance as a means of enhancing their appeal and stature among local adherents. For the same reasons, many south Indian Christians have accepted sponsorship from the missionary agencies of groups such as the U.S. Assemblies of God and its British offshoot, the Assemblies of God of Great Britain and Ireland. For literate adherents, the spontaneous personal appeal of prayer meetings and the ministrations of healers and exorcists are supplemented by vernacular and English-language gospel tracts and journals. These include internationally disseminated Assemblies of God publications such as the *Pentecostal Evangel, Redemption Tidings,* and the *Missionary Messenger* as well as locally produced pamphlets and magazines such as the English-medium *Pentecostal Witness* and the Malayalam journal *Messenger.*

This trend is comparable to the one noted above among Roman Catholics, for whom the dissemination of devotional texts and journals has confirmed adherence among devotees of the spontaneous cult-centered worship found at sites such as Velankanni. These large-scale international Christian agencies and their local affiliates also make systematic contact across south Indian society through their networks of hospitals, schools, orphanages, and other humanitarian aid and work. But in Kerala as in other parts of south India, the organizational features of these religious groups are still extremely fluid. Adherence and corporate institutions are highly volatile, and their dynamism still comes from charismatic individual leadership rather than formalized structures of affiliation and recruitment.[57]

The Tamil country also contains organized Pentecostal groups of this sort. Some, like the Zion Sangham Church at Neyyattinkara, ten miles southeast of Trivandrum (in Kerala's Tamil-speaking southern border zone) have a core of affiliates dating back over several generations, but with a more recent upsurge of activity stimulated by the appeal of the church's charismatic lay preaching and healing sessions.[58] Other Tamil Pentecostal groups like the Open Bible Church of God are of more recent origin. This church is based among low-caste Tamil weavers in a factory workers' housing complex in Coimbatore. Here, too, we see the characteristic features of radical Pentecostal Christianity with its emphasis on visions, miraculous healing, ecstatic prophesy, and speaking in tongues.[59] Many other Christian bodies in the south trace their origins to Britain's nineteenth-century Plymouth Brethren movement, whose Brahman lay messengers attracted many adherents in the Tamil country, and among the Saint Thomas Christians of what is now Kerala. Its contemporary version is found among groups who use titles such as the Open Brethren, the Syrian Brethren,[60] and the Separatist Brethren; these believers, too, practice an eschatological Christianity which rejects formal church leadership and emphasizes forms of ecstatic religious experience based solely on "witness" and the authority of Scripture. Like other fundamentalist groups in the region, it has only rudimentary institutional forms. Andhra Pradesh contains what are probably its most highly developed organizational manifestations to date: in the western part of this state, the Brethren's insistence on "the universal priesthood of believers" has engendered a more lasting scheme of operations by building on the region's existing traditions of guru-style itinerant preaching and autonomous church formation. Thus lay adepts have built up permanent "gospel circles" among thousands of ex-"untouchables," Harijans, in remote hinterland villages northwest of Anantapur by attracting adherents to ecstatic salvation meetings and inviting initiates to undergo dramatically staged public baptisms.[61]

In fact all of these groups, even those with international connections, give primacy to lay prayer leaders and other inspired adepts; they deny the validity of formal ecclesiastical hierarchies and organize instead around networks of small-scale gospel halls and preaching centers. More and more, these churches are recapturing the prophetic individualism of the region's nineteenth-century sectarian revivalists and breakaway churches. In Kerala especially, some of the most active groups are those which have stripped away all features of recognizable Western-style church organization. One in particular, a body of Tamil Sri Lankan origin called the Ceylon Pentecostal Church, now operates in southern Kerala adjacent to Kanniyakumari district. It appears to have much in common with the nineteenth-century Justus Joseph sect, with adherence to the charismatic authority of celibate lay elders who call on their adherents (as Justus Joseph did) to sell their possessions and live together in a network of communal "faith homes."[62]

In these loosely organized Pentecostal churches, and among the followers of the lay spirit diviners and millenarian gurus of Tamil Nadu and Kerala, attempts are being made to reclaim an activated Christianity of power and dynamism from the conventional churches. These believers want to reassert their primacy over the rich supernatural terrain of south India with its living pantheons of divinities, warrior heroes, and cult saints. For them, Jesus, the Virgin, and the Christian saints must be made known to the wider world as fierce figures of power with the capacity to contend as warriors in the crowded and menacing supernatural landscape of contemporary south India. Among the confraternities, the Pentecostal organizations, and the other activist organizations of the south, it is a matter of concern that other Indians—Sikhs, Muslims, professing Hindus—have access to divinity in this awesome martial form. Whether personified in the form of Hindu power divinities, Muslim warrior cult saints, or the fighting supernaturally endowed historical gurus of Sikhism, this is the divine in a form that gives believers access to dynamic supernatural resources. To be known as adherents of such divinity gives a community stature in contemporary India, which is why there is now extra urgency for many Christians in the moves being made to cultivate comparable manifestations of the divine. Such conceptions have long been available within the traditions of south Indian Christianity, which have portrayed Christian cult saints as bringers and healers of affliction and as sovereigns and heroes locked in combat with demonic antagonists.[63] But now that south India has become yet another of the country's contested religious domains, there is enhanced scope for organized activists to proclaim themselves in terms that identify them with this Christianity of power and dynamism. It is a Christianity that is "fundamentalist" in the sense of being organized around militancy, puritan values, and cults of activated, fearful divinity.

The New Challenge of Hindu Raj in Southern India

The call for an assertive public voice among Christians has become more persuasive because of south India's new and unaccustomed prominence in the country's fundamentalist Hindu Raj campaigns. Repeatedly in the 1980s, confrontations involving rival religious "communities" were pursued in the idiom of territorial invasion and contested sovereignty. This made them alarmingly intelligible to the south Indian Christian population. Even thousands of miles from the southern states, Hindu activists cited the Muslim conversions at Minakshipuram as a violation of the common Hindu homeland, an intrusion by "aliens" into the culture and terrain of the Hindu patriot. For example, in the early 1980s, Minakshipuram was repeatedly held up as an evil example by spokesmen of the militant Hindu VHP in Assam, that is, in India's far northeast, where indigenous "sons of the soil" have been seeking since the 1970s to expel land-hungry migrants from adjacent Bangladesh.[64] Most, though not all, of these intruding "aliens" are Muslims; they are an obvious target for the conveners of large-scale "Hindu supremacy" marches and congresses in the key towns of the region. But here, too, as in south India, opposition to Muslim "intruders" has also acquired anti-Christian overtones. In this same area, especially around Shillong near the Burma border, up to 70 percent of the large ethnic minority groups who are described as "tribals" have become professing Christians; the decade 1961–71 has been identified as a period of sensational growth in the numbers of tribal people adhering to Christianity in northeastern India.[65] Hindu militants have been outraged: "It has been time and again stated that conversion to the Christian faith leads to degeneration and demoralization."[66] The VHP's avowed aim of "reclaiming" such people for Hinduism, and its commitment to fight off further "incursions" by the churches among tribal and lower-caste groups, has also been a source of conflict in the northeast, and has been observed with alarm in south India, the country's only other zone of large-scale Christian populations.[67]

As a counterblast to these supposed despoliations of the Hindu homeland in the early 1980s, the VHP organized the first of its well-known series of "unity processions."[68] These were widely publicized tours in which decorated chariots (*raths*) modeled on those used in Hindu temple festivals were borne from town to town bearing vessels of holy Ganges water and other sacred items. The chariots' triumphal progresses were conceived as a reclamation of the threatened domain of Hinduism. In south Indian localities, as in other regions of the country, their arrival aroused an intense emotional response.[69] But in the southern states the message of the chariot processions was particularly galvanizing because it evoked themes of power and sanctity which have been a dynamic feature of indigenous religious tradition for many centuries, making the processions a potent reference point for activist Christian and Muslim groups in the region.

In the precolonial period, would-be rulers of south India's competing chiefdoms and warrior-controlled principalities constituted their claims of sovereignty around the concept of an activated sacred landscape. Whether these aspiring rulers were professing Hindus or Muslims, their assertions of political dominance were closely bound up with the deep-rooted south Indian perception of divinity as a manifestation of sovereign power. In order to assert dominion, a ruler had to map his domain onto a physical landscape which was portrayed as being marked out for him by the shrines and holy places in which the region's fierce martial power divinities held their sway. These key sites could include the dargahs of Muslim *pirs* (cult saints) as well as the

shrines of Hindu gods and goddesses and even of Christian saints; these were all lords
and conquerors with an endowment of the power or sakti that could create and perpetuate the authority of kings.[70] Much of this is still familiar in south India, where
observers of the Hindu Raj campaign and the VHP chariot processions can readily
recognize the parallels in a modernized twentieth-century move to constitute India's
polity around the "reconquest" of sacred terrain. It is no accident that some of the
most violent clashes at the time of the Minakshipuram conversion controversy occurred in localities in the Marava-dominated Tirunelveli hinterland, near the centers
of some of the old Marava chiefdoms, where the VHP had been staging chariot processions of Hindu images to rally "untouchable" Harijans against the call of activist
Muslim proselytizing bodies.[71]

Thus despite its heritage of shared cult religion and the comparatively small size
of its Muslim minority, south India has become a zone of special prominence in these
appeals in the name of a revived fundamentalist Hinduism. In addition to the controversies aroused over the conversions at Minakshipuram, the south has been thrust into
the limelight through the activism of the region's campaigning Hindu ascetics, most
notably the presiding acaryas of the powerful monastic foundations located at major
Hindu temple centers such as Kanchi (also known as Kanchipuram or Conjeeveram).
During the 1980s the most celebrated of these south Indian acarya ascetics became
national celebrities whose utterances added prestigious new support to the agitations
of the VHP. This had important consequences for the rise of organized confrontational fundamentalism among all three major religious groupings in the southern
states, which is why this study must turn again to the wider north Indian context of
these developments in the south.

The best known of the Hindu Raj campaigners' recent causes was once again
constituted around a territorial scheme of conquest.[72] Looked at from the south Indian perspective, the battle to assert exclusive control over the contested site (the
birthplace of the god Ram, according to Hindus; the Babri mosque, for Muslims)
acquired new visibility through appeals issued by Hindu VHP campaigners in 1989.
Devotees all over the country were called on to rebuild their "lost" holy shrine by
consecrating bricks and sending them on yet another strategically designed itinerary
of territorial reclamation across the "Hindu heartland" to the contested shrine site at
Ayodhya.[73]

Prominent acaryas (Hindu spiritual preceptors) from the south Indian math foundations have been ardent supporters of this cause. The most active of them have
stepped onto a public stage reaching far beyond the regional constituency of their
shrines. Addressing their hearers uncharacteristically in Hindi as well as in their accustomed native Tamil, these widely revered acaryas have expressed commitment to
the concept of patriotic exclusive Hinduism which has been articulated around the
Ayodhya conflict. (Since Independence, Tamils and other south Indians have sought
to resist the contention that Hindi, the tongue of most north Indians, is the true
language of the united Indian "nation"; use of Hindi by a south Indian acarya is thus
a powerful gesture signifying belief in an overarching nationhood defined around
shared language as well as Hindu religious conformity.)

Such declarations by the south Indian Hindu acaryas have had particular power when issued from the platform of public religious congresses organized in the late 1980s and early 1990s by groups such as the VHP and held at the giant bathing festivals which attract millions of worshipers every year to auspicious sites along the river Ganges. In 1989 at one of the largest such gatherings, the Kumbh Mela at Prayag (Allahabad) in Uttar Pradesh, the presiding acarya of south India's Kanchi-puram Kamakoti math was widely acclaimed for his presidential address to the VHP's congress of sages and Hindu notables. One speaker described the aim of the congress as an attempt to encourage Hindus "to unite to win over the forces who are trying to disintegrate Hindu society."[74] The Kanchi acarya's contribution was to declare that "the time has come to mobilize Hindus through dharma (right moral conduct) which never created disturbances, but brought order in public life."[75] Other speakers at this congress called on holy men like the Kanchi acarya to organize bodies of ascetics (sadhus) to travel the country "and strengthen the religion."[76] The Kanchi "pontiff" himself may have been the inspiration for this proposal to constitute India's highly individualistic holy men into a force of itinerant exemplars traversing India to generate "unity," "strength," and "mobilization" among Hindus. His own journey to that year's Kumbh Mela festival (February 1989) was itself an exercise in the marking of terrain across a sacred "Hindu" homeland. For his "pontifical" progress to the north, he was installed in an expensive, headline-grabbing imitation "pope-mobile." Key stages of his nine-week journey to the Mela site were filmed for posterity, and in speeches and interviews at this time he returned continually to the theme of a sacred itinerary with the power to unite the Hindu nation as a people of one blood and one heritage. In these declarations the beating of physical boundaries by pilgrims and their ascetic exemplars was portrayed as an act with the power to constitute and defend the domain of an all-embracing Hindu community as the true nation of India.

> From time immemorial Indians have been going on pilgrimage and have been blessed by holy men. It is in their blood. Kumbh Mela [the pilgrim's convoca-tion at Allahabad] maintains this custom. It is natural. It is in their blood. . . .
> Even though India is politically divided, this pilgrimage [to the Kumbh Mela] creates spiritual unity. From the southernmost tip to the north, and from the east to the west, the entire country is unified by people traveling around on pilgrimage. What is now called national unity has always been in the blood of Hindus and Indians since time immemorial. Despite all our differences, we are one and the Kumbh Mela is the perfect example of this.[77]

Since this picture of community and nationhood equates an invigorated Hindu identity with Indian nationhood, it must therefore exclude Christians and Muslims. These "communities" have no place in what the acarya defined as the function of the Kumbh Mela as a celebration of Hindu blood and Hindu devotion.[78] As the Kanchi "pontiff" and his fellow acaryas have continued to seek out platforms from which to proclaim the principles of Hindu primacy in the Indian sacred homeland, south In-dians of Christian and Muslim affiliation have increasingly found themselves with no option but to define themselves in correspondingly stark terms as people of one blood, one "fundamentalist" affinity, which excludes outsiders and incorporates all those who can be identified as fellow believers.[79]

These events have helped place south India in the forefront of the debate about the nature of Indian "community" and religious affiliation at a time when organized fundamentalisms have become increasingly assertive in Indian public life. Significant changes have occurred now that key southerners like the Kanchi acarya have shown their sympathy for the claims of the Hindu Raj campaigners. Their moves have over-turned many of the old stereotypes which once portrayed the southern states as back-waters and places of irrelevance to the heightened Hindu consciousness of the northern and western Indian "cow belt" regions. On the Hindu side, the proselytizing of notables like the Kanchi acarya has helped to reclaim south India as a bastion of the "pure" or high theological Hinduism which the organized militant groups have sought to articulate as the true culture of India. Once again, therefore, the goddess Bhagavati has been in the limelight. In their attempts to implement the vision of a shared universal Hinduism with the power to stave off low-caste "defections" to Islam and Christianity, campaigners of Kerala's Hindu Unity Front have staged their own blockades at an important Bhagavati festival at a temple in the town of Kodungallur. Here no Christians were involved; the targets of the agitation were low-caste profess-ing Hindus who have traditionally cultivated the violent "demonic" power of the goddess by engaging in "impure" acts which channel this same violent energy on their behalf. At the time of the goddess's annual festival, the Hindu Unity Front trans-ported scores of Hindu ascetics to the site to stop the customary hurling of filth at the shrine because, they said, such acts "were not graceful," that is, not proper and acceptable as expressions of Hindu faith in a Hindu homeland.[80]

This incident exemplifies the way in which affiliates of the fundamentalist Hindu organizations have been attempting to assert discipline and primacy over south Indi-ans whom they now claim as fellow believers, while simultaneously beating out the boundaries of a revitalized Hindu homeland reclaimed from rival Christian and Mus-lim "communities." It is not surprising, then, that this assertiveness on all sides of the region's hardening communal boundaries has generated a vigorous organized re-sponse among the self-styled defenders of activated Christian divinity. Often the mod-els for these moves appear to come from well-publicized conflicts which are occurring far outside the region. For example, attempts to expel "aliens" at the Ayodhya shrine are said by Hindus to have been divinely mandated by the miraculous discovery of a sacred image of the deified Ram.[81] Comparable "discoveries" of sacred items have also occurred in south India, most notably at Kottayam in southern Kerala, where the locality's large Saint Thomas Christian population has lived for centuries in a densely populated zone containing a wide range of different communities and caste groups. Here, too, the unearthing of a cross, supposedly an item of great antiquity, became a widely publicized wonder in south India. For local Christians the find was put for-ward as a means of declaring territorial primacy, a "proof" of rights over the region dating back to an unidentifiable point in the prehistoric past. Since the mid-1980s, Keralan Hindu militants described as "RSS men" have fought back with the same tactic, proclaiming their miraculous "discovery" of *lingas* [emblems of the god Shiva] and other sacred idols in the forest," that is, in disputed forest tracts that have been claimed as farmland (in defiance of local conservation laws) by Saint Thomas Christian settlers.[82]

Such exclusive claims would once have been unusual in a domain of shared pilgrimage networks and overlapping divinity. Now, though, when religious "rights" are being expressed in the language of territorial incursion and reclaimed sovereignty, it is no wonder that Christians and Muslims in the south are organizing in new ways and deploying new modes of communication. Once again, long-standing conceptions of divinity are being merged with more modern fundamentalist themes, some drawn from international sources. In Kerala, for example, where teachers in state schools often belong to the Christian caste groups, Malayali Christian children have been told by their science teachers, "The government tells us to teach you about Darwin and evolution and the geological formation of the Earth, but we all know that the truth is what Genesis says."[83] This familiar assertion of Christian fundamentalist ideology, the principle of scientific creationism, has apparently been influenced by accounts in U.S. missionary magazines of Monkey Trial–type controversies over science teaching in U.S. schools in the 1970s and 1980s. In its recent south Indian manifestation, however, this issue also bears the hallmark of debates about Hindu political activism and the identification of state and national governments in India with the cause of a patriotic exclusive Hinduism.

In Tamil Nadu as well, conflict is becoming increasingly common in localities that were once distinguished by the sharing of devotional observance in a sacred terrain frequented by Hindus, Christians, and Muslims. Thus in July 1990 there was rioting between Hindus and Muslims in and around one of south India's most popular pilgrimage places, the celebrated *dargah* (tomb shrine) at Nagore.[84] This complex is endowed with the miraculous intercessory power of its entombed Muslim pir, Shahul Hamid Naguri, whose annual commemoration festival attracts hundreds of thousands of Hindus, Muslims, and Christians from all over south India. Since at least the eighteenth century the shrine has been part of the same shoreline pilgrimage network that includes the nearby Velankanni Virgin shrine and a number of Tamil Hindu goddess temples in a common terrain of activated curative power or sakti. On this occasion, however, the local press publicized accounts of a visiting Muslim holy man (*fakir*) who made speeches at the festival describing bloody rioting four months earlier in Bombay. These riots had begun with marches protesting the U.K. publication of Salman Rushdie's *The Satanic Verses;* thus the "fakir" was conveying a message of "religion in danger" and "vengeance for our brothers."[85] This story was picked up by local newspapers, which reported the unnamed Muslim as "making derogatory remarks against the Hindus and the Indian nation." At the same time a poster and graffiti campaign occurred in the area, organized by Hindu Raj activists who were seeking to rouse public indignation about yet another alleged case of mass conversion to Islam among Harijan "untouchables" in a nearby village.[86]

In this case, as in others, the organized manifestation of fundamentalism was the loosely coordinated recruitment of young men into ad hoc local "defense committees." When the police banned a public appearance by the speech-making fakir, vanloads of young men from the Muslim shoreline towns surged into Nagore to fight pitched battles in defense of "their" sacred shrine town against Shanars and other Hindus identified with the anti-Muslim slogan campaign. The cry of religion in danger rallied opposing forces from among groups with a common stake in the same sacred landscape. In a sense, this was an expression of a fundamentalism of insider against alien "outsider." As in the case of the Mandaikadu and Kanniyakumari disputes, it was activist, and it demanded exclusive command of sovereign territory. With its focus on the Nagore shrine and its festival, however, this "fundamentalist" assertion was rooted in the sort of popular cult religion usually thought of as the chief target for hostile Islamizing fundamentalists. Here these categories have little relevance; as in many other parts of south India, fundamentalism appeared as a mutually reinforced competition over homeland and sacred terrain.

Conclusion

As an organized force in south India, fundamentalism does not emanate from rigidly defined groups, movements, or communities with sharp boundaries and clear-cut recruitment processes. Among those identified as Christians as well as Muslims and Hindus in the four southern states, the growth of fundamentalist affiliation has been stimulated in the last fifteen to twenty years by widespread social dislocation, by the upheavals associated with uneven economic growth, by ecological instability, and by the sensationalism of the region's English and vernacular press. Even lowering the voting age from twenty-one to eighteen in 1984 has been a factor, since this change led virtually all of the country's political parties and activist organizations to present their aims in a more emotive and populist style.

Who, then, are the people who have become "available" to the fashioners of fundamentalism? Neither in south India nor in any other part of the subcontinent are there Machiavellian outsiders fashioning or imposing alien "fundamentalist" creeds to be transmitted to "vulnerable" segments of the population. Even when its adherents make tactical alliances with foreign sponsors or religious agencies, organized fundamentalism in India is a home-grown phenomenon that has gained ground in a period of profound social and political uncertainty. While some of its finance, literature, idiom, and organizational models may come from outside, its dynamism comes entirely from within the society.

In the southern states, fundamentalism has its roots in indigenous religious culture. Two elements are paramount here. First are the distinctive manifestations of Christianity and Islam which have taken root in the southern region over many centuries. Second is the interaction between the many forms of Hinduism actually practiced in south India and the simplified propaganda of the Hindu Raj campaigns, representing Hinduism as a monolithic culture of the nation. Thus the expansion of fundamentalism has been stimulated among south India's religious minority populations by a mutually reinforcing language of nationhood and exclusion which has conveyed increasingly threatening messages to people who share the same perception of their environment as a terrain of politically charged supernatural landmarks. Among Christians, fundamentalism has taken the form of militant activism, the assertion of a puritanical and dynamic public face for one's fellow believers, and the embrace of religious affiliations which emphasize the power of Christian divinity and the active intercessory presence of the divine in everyday life. For those who have been drawn to the new fundamentalist traditions, institutional forms have been rudimentary. Although some prayer circles and church groups are affiliated with prominent foreign churches and missionary agencies, adherents have their primary attachment to fluid, small-scale groups formed around the evanescent and personalized authority of tiny, loosely structured Holy Spirit churches and individual guru-like adepts.

We have seen that such groups have been driven by hostility to what they see as the bloodless Christianity of ecumenical dialogue, Social Gospel, and the liberal or rationalized "modern" theologies of the established churches. In the case of the Roman Catholic Parava confraternities and the Protestant Pentecostal assemblies of Kerala and Tamil Nadu, for example, the emphasis has been on local lay power at the expense of formalized networks of leadership and authority. This reaction has been sharpened by the identification of many ordained clerics with liberation theology and campaigns on behalf of poor and low-caste victims of alleged social injustice. Large numbers of south Indian Christians have repudiated this campaigning, quasi-revolutionary Christianity in favor of an equally activist faith that refuses to see Christ as a millenarian liberator. Such people embrace Christ and the pantheon of saints, demons, and other related divinities as supernatural beings who fight, heal, and vanquish and who therefore command a sacred terrain as well endowed with intercessory power or sakti as that of the society's Hindu and Muslim believers. These indigenous Christian enemies of Social Gospel and liberation theology are not motivated by some kind of generalized ideological reaction against the influence of revolutionary Marxism on the world stage. In south India these organized "fundamentalists" are part of a specifically Indian reaction against movements that threaten those with a stake in the existing social order, however fragile and contested their place may be within that order.

It follows, then, that the extreme volatility in Indian social relationships has been the strongest driving force behind organized fundamentalism in south India. The principal catalyst has been the experience of confrontation across increasingly contentious religious and communal boundaries. These assertions of territorially based exclusiveness, the battles with Hindu Raj campaigners, the accusations of sedition and illegitimacy within the sacred terrain of the Hindu homeland, have been reforming the religion of the Christian Pentecostals and charismatics into a vehicle for defense and self-assertion. Conflicts such as the Kanniyakumari riots and the Kottayam cross controversy have kept fundamentalist manifestations of Christianity in the public eye and attract increasing numbers of adherents and disciples to the Holy Spirit churches, the revival conferences, and the assertive territorial reclamation campaigns such as those of the Tamil maritime districts.

All this prompts a more general question about the possible evolution of fundamentalist activism in Indian society over the next few decades. South India's Christian fundamentalism has grown up around traditions of indigenous cult worship focusing on demonic exorcism, miraculous intercession, and a terrain of supernaturally charged local shrines and holy places. These fundamentalists may renounce symbols and forms of worship which imply links with local Hindus and Muslims, but their contested sacred landscape is still full of local landmarks and localized perceptions of the divine as a force that possesses individuals and resides in cult shrines and holy places. In contrast, other fundamentalisms in South Asia, particularly among Muslims (and Sikhs as well), are usually portrayed as repudiations of a religiously plural terrain containing "syncretic" local shrines and cult divinities. But is it possible that in their South Asian manifestation, purist Islam and some of the subcontinent's other organized fundamentalisms may move in the same direction? Will they eventually renounce the cosmopolitan, the cultivation of links with the wider world, including that of Arab Islam, for example, and focus more insistently on the contested South Asian terrain which has provided south Indians with their most powerful expression of organized religious activism?

Postscript

The preceding was written before the destruction of the Babri Masjid at Ayodhya on 6 December 1992. This act of widely applauded public vandalism was undoubtedly a landmark in the history of South Asia's organized fundamentalisms, and so some additional reflections are clearly called for here. The Ayodyha attack and its aftermath gave India's Hindu majority, as well as the subcontinent's Muslim, Sikh, and Christian populations, a dramatic display of the power of activist religion, allied to claims of territorial exclusion and conquest. Yet these events do not mean that India and its neighboring states are in the grip of some worldwide or monolithic fundamentalist menace. Even within India, much of the violence that followed the Ayodhya attack was only indirectly related to the spread of purist religious ideologies and the claims of confessional supremacists. For example, although Muslims are thought to have been the chief victims of the 1992–93 rioting, there is evidence that in cities such as Calcutta, Surat, and Bombay, much of the carnage was caused by criminal gangs, many of them Muslim-dominated, who used the outbreaks as cover for looting and illicit property takeovers.

But the victory of the Hindu militants at the Babri Masjid is still likely to encourage self-styled purifiers and holy warriors in many other parts of South Asia, where local conflicts over territory and resources have interlocked with wider campaigns to seize shrines and expel those of rival faiths from contested terrain. As most readers will know, the demolition of this 450–year-old mosque by two hundred thousand self-professed "servants" or *kar sevaks* of the Hindu god Ram provoked Hindu-Muslim rioting in almost every region in the subcontinent. These are thought to have been South Asia's worst intercommunal riots since the violence that accompanied the Partition of India in 1947–48. There were also wholesale police shootings, mass arrests, and terrorist bombings in at least two major Indian cities.

The months following the demolition of the Ayodhya mosque brought an intensification of the propaganda war between the subcontinent's competing fundamentalists. Thus while India's Congress government struggled to restore the credibility of the country's so-called secular constitution, which guarantees equal civic rights to those of all religious and ethnic communities, the would-be champions of endangered Hindu and Muslim faith drew predictable lessons from the crisis. In Muslim-dominated Pakistan and Bangladesh, there were attacks on temples and churches belonging to the countries' small Hindu and Christian minority communities. The burning of Hindu shrines was seen by militant Muslims in all three countries as revenge for Ayodhya. Those who attacked temples in Pakistan and Bangladesh were praised for ridding their home terrain of sites that were holy to Hindus and that had therefore come to be associated with India's expansionist proponents of Hindu Raj. But the inclusion of Christian targets in these outbreaks suggests a more generalized vision of patriotic territorial cleansing. It appears that the very small and hitherto uncontroversial Christian convert populations of Pakistan and Bangladesh were being equated with Hindus by activist Muslims within these countries. Ironically they too were being treated as enemy aliens whose churches could no longer be tolerated on the soil of a Muslim nation, just as India's Hindu supremacists have tended to bracket together Muslims and Christians as seditious internal enemies of the Hindu "nation."

For Hindu supremacist organizations within India, the destruction of the Babri Masjid was hailed as a conquest in its own right, and also as a foretaste of future triumphs at thousands of similar sites across the country, where Muslim, Hindu, and sometimes Sikh or Christian holy places have all occupied adjoining sites for many centuries. To the VHP and its allies, these are all places where former Muslim conquerors desecrated the shrines of their defeated Hindu enemies and allegedly built mosques over the ruins of Hindu temples they had looted and despoiled.

The goal throughout the Ayodhya agitations was and still is expressed as the achievements of Hindutva, that is, the remaking of India as a polity defined by Hinduism in the assertive and expansionist form proclaimed by organizations such as the VHP. This would reduce the country's diverse and regionally dispersed population of one hundred million Muslims, that is, 15 percent of its citizens, to the status of suspect aliens, an enemy within to be assimilated, expelled, or annihilated by those of so-called Hindu blood. To this end, Hindu organizations have called on their followers to "liberate" all the shared shrine sites they have identified as intolerable challenges to Hindu pride and piety.

Such places are particularly abundant in the so-called heartland of Hinduism in Gangetic north India, as, for example, at the important pilgrimage centers of Mathura and Benares. Like Ayodhya, Mathura is sacred to an important *avatar* or personification of the god Vishnu, who is represented throughout India as an all-powerful king in majesty. Benares is the terrain of the second great pan-Indian deity, Shiva. Both of these centers have been singled out as localities where Mughal mosques were allegedly erected on the sites of former Hindu temples, and where "true" sons of the Indian motherland must therefore wipe out the inherited humiliations of centuries by repeating the "victory" of the Ayodhya kar sevak warriors. Once again, there are striking parallels with the conflicts in south India which were described in the main body of this chapter. These north Indian localities too have become zones of combat where Hindus are being called on to extend the domain in which their deities rule as sovereigns. Whether he is personified as Ram at Ayodhya, as the sovereign Krishna of Mathura, or as the trident-bearing Shiva of Benares, the god-king must be "liberated." His "servants" or holy warriors are being told they must relieve their god of the shame of ancient defeats and desecrations. His divine rule will then be made absolute, no longer to be diluted and compromised by the sharing of shrine sites with seats of Muslim power.

These interconnected themes of vengeance, conquest, and exclusion were invoked yet again in March 1993, following a series of devastating terrorist attacks in Bombay, the country's commercial capital, as well as a number of smaller-scale bombings in Calcutta. Once more, it was said, the Hindu homeland had been betrayed and despoiled. Indeed the Hindutva campaigners have consistently portrayed India's history as a sequence of atrocities against the Hindu "nation," beginning with Muslim invasions and conquests in the distant past, and continuing through the more recent intercommunal massacres of the 1947 Partition, and the current separatist struggles in Kashmir and the Punjab.

Although these painful episodes have all involved atrocities against Sikhs, Muslims, and Christians as well as Hindus, they have been depicted by the Hindu Raj propagandists as one-sided outbreaks of violence against Hindus and their holy places. This supposed victimization is seen to be of a piece with the failures of successive Congress governments to suppress the agitations of Sikh and Kashmiri Muslim militants. Most Hindutva campaigners denounce the Congress party's commitment to so-called secularism as an unpatriotic sham under which self-serving politicians are said to have undermined the country's security by conciliating refractory and "seditious" minorities. Predictably, then, many commentators jumped to the conclusion that the 1993 Bombay and Calcutta bombings were further assertions of this supposedly eternal Muslim enmity, insisting that they were organized as additional acts of Muslim "revenge" for the events at Ayodhya. Thus the leader of the Bharatiya Janata party (BJP), Lal Krishna Advani, immediately demanded the international proscription of Pakistan as a "terrorist state," and Hindu activists issued statements calling for the mass expulsion of Muslims from India once it was "proved" that the country's Muslim enemies had organized the bomb attacks.

The speed and deftness with which the chief spokesmen for the Hindutva cause responded to each development in the Ayodhya crisis was typical. While the Congress government was widely criticized for indecisiveness and impotence in the months after the attack, the BJP was notably successful in presenting itself as a moderate force, ever willing to compromise with "obdurate" opponents, a body of valiant patriots seeking to protect the country from internal and foreign enemies. One consequence of this portrayal of the Hindu Raj campaign as a response to shared national danger was to confirm the role of south Indians in the organized pan-Indian activism of the

Hindu supremacists. Thus it was a matter of great pride in the south that one of the largest contingents of kar sevak "liberators" to take part in the assault on the Babri Masjid were recruits from the southernmost states.

In other parts of India, too, the Ayodhya campaign stimulated comparable struggles involving assertions of heightened Hindu consciousness, and contests over terrain and national identity. In the state of Bihar, for example, Hindutva militants launched a campaign against ex-"untouchables" who follow the example of the pre-Independence leader Ambedkar, renouncing Hinduism for the egalitarian spiritual teachings of the Buddha. These neo-Buddhists have sought to expel Hindus from the ancient Bodhgaya shrine which is revered as the site where the Buddha attained enlightenment. Thus, once again, two contending groups have been struggling for supremacy within the same shared landscape of power and divinity, and both showed a keen awareness of the wider national ramifications of their conflict.

So why have the Hindutva organizations broken through from the extremist margins of political life to establish themselves at the center of the electoral mainstream? And in a country with all the legal and constitutional trappings of a pluralistic parliamentary democracy, why have so many Hindus from both north and south India expressed approval for the attack on the Ayodhya mosque? In part, the answer is that the Hindutva campaigners have used tactics which are comprehensible in virtually every region of the subcontinent. In both the north and the south, the example of dynamic Christian and Muslim activists has convinced many believers that Hinduism can thrive only if it is remade as another religion of centralized and exclusive authority, even to the extent of insisting that the religion's Vedic scriptures be made a fundamental religious document for all Hindus. This was the goal of the Arya Samaj and the many other so-called Hindu revivalist organizations that flourished in colonial India during the late nineteenth and early twentieth centuries. Such groups urged Hindus to renounce pluralism and "syncretic" accommodations, and to unite instead around a new version of the faith defined by the Vedic scriptures. On both of these counts, devotees of the country's regional cult divinities can easily grasp the idea of a Hindu homeland preserved and sanctified by a god-king. It is not difficult then to understand the appeal of activists from all religious communities and confessions who have portrayed themselves in recent years as defenders of a god's terrain.

The activities of such groups have therefore been organized around attempts to remap local landscapes as zones of exclusive dominion for faiths which their adherents now conceive of as monolithic communities of Christians, Muslims, Sikhs, Hindus, and Buddhists. This has made the proponents of Hindu Raj both intelligible and attractive to the very large numbers of Indians who have lost confidence in both the Indian National Congress and its disorganized leftist political rivals.

Thus it is not only in south India that such clashes have been closely tied to rapid economic change and social dislocation. These changes have been especially rapid in the years since the lifting of Mrs. Gandhi's authoritarian "Emergency" regime in 1977. It took a mere eleven years for the BJP to become the second largest party in India's national legislature. In the 1991 elections, the BJP also gained power in the most important of the country's provincial assemblies. These gains have helped to undercut and fragment the Congress party, which has held power almost uninterruptedly since Independence. Like its counterparts in Algeria and other ex-colonial countries, the Congress is now widely reviled as the tool of a corrupt elite and is no longer associated with the triumphs of the anticolonial freedom struggle.

The electoral successes of the BJP have been further attributed to the uncertainties of India's newly prosperous entrepreneurs, substantial cash crop farmers, and urban professional families. Such people would once have been a part of the fluid alliance of regional interest groups on which the Congress has built its political strength since the 1930s. In recent years much of the support for Hindutva has come from this disparate but assertive Hindu middle class. Its members are now clinging uncertainly to the gains they made during the mid-1980s under Rajiv Gandhi's policies of economic liberalization. Gandhi's administration embraced modern technology and free market principles, promising to liberate the country from its Nehruvian legacy of centralized planning and swollen public sector monopolies. More recently, middle-class Indians have been gripped by fears about the growing urban and rural unrest that has accompanied the international credit squeeze, rapid price inflation, and the militancy of disadvantaged groups. In south India this unrest has involved many followers of Christian "liberation" movements, as described in the initial sections of this chapter. Elsewhere, however, in northern and western India, similar campaigns have been waged by a disproportionately large number of the country's Muslims, who have been badly hit by cuts in government spending and diminished levels of state employment.

In 1986, when the VHP and its allies began to orchestrate the campaign for the "liberation" of Ayodhya and the construction of a temple, the so-called Ram Janmabhoomi, on the site of the Babri Masjid, members of the aspiring middle classes, who came primarily from the middling and upper Hindu castes, were generally sympathetic to these agitations. Thus many college campuses have become bastions of the Hindutva cause. This is largely because middle-class Hindu students tend to see the BJP and its affiliates as allies in their fight against reservation of scarce university places for students of low caste, long a contentious feature of the country's schemes of positive discrimination for the disadvantaged.

After the destruction of the Babri Masjid, such students and their families were among those who praised both the BJP leaders, and the kar sevaks who stormed the mosque, as model patriots and spiritual exemplars. Prime Minister Narasimha Rao and his Congress government made little attempt to counter this with a revitalized vision of "secularism." Instead, representatives of central authority made gestures of support for the Hindutva cause. Soldiers and policemen were filmed praying to the images of Ram which were enshrined at the demolished mosque site. Newspapers carried pictures of police officers kneeling in reverence to the *sants* and *sadhus* (holy men) gathered at the site. These ascetics had blessed the demolition of the mosque and were openly defying a short-lived ban on Hindu worship at the site. They also constituted themselves as a *dharma sansad,* or quasi-parliament, and were asserting that this assembly had divine authority to flout rulings by "mere" judges and politicians.

But although these symbols and gestures refer to distinctively Indian ideas of kingship and sacred dominion, the Hindutva campaign has also had much in common with organized fundamentalisms in many other parts of the world. The Hindu Raj organizations have used twentieth-century publicity techniques in their attempts to inspire and threaten Indians with the vision of a supernatural warrior-king claiming his dominion. These Hindutva campaigners seek to endow their claims with a self-consciously "scientific" authenticity. For example, the self-styled champions of the god Ram have sought since the late 1980s to persuade that most august scholarly body, the Archaeological Survey of India, to declare as a matter of literal scientific fact that their deity was indeed born on the disputed Ayodhya site. Hindu activists have therefore made much of items which they say they have "excavated" from the site of the demolished mosque.

The language used here is that of contemporary science and scholarship. What the activists want is for the "modern" disciplines of archaeology and history to endorse the claim that the Ayodhya site (like those in Mathura and elsewhere) was first occupied by Hindus and then "desecrated" by Muslim usurpers. The same tactic has been widely used elsewhere in India, for example, at the site claimed by neo-Buddhists in Bihar, where the Hindu supremacists say they have "discovered" ancient Hindu relics which disprove their rivals' claims.

This suggests something very notable about the role of history and religiously defined landscape in Indian political life today. It was once the case that pious Hindus deified human beings. Heroes and kings became gods, and even ordinary people could become divinities if they died by violence or otherwise came into contact with powerful cosmic energies. What has happened in recent years, however, is that Ram and some of the country's other divinities are being removed from their remote and ahistorical supernatural domains. Their adherents and paramilitary servants want the gods to be recognized as historical personalities who lived real lives in a real historical landscape. Academics are being called on to certify that the locale of the divine Ram's birthplace belongs in the realm of literal fact, not mythology. If Ram is "real" in this precise and literal sense, his cause attains a new reality too, and so his followers will acquire a powerful new weapon in the war for Hindu political supremacy. The Hindu activists thus seek to make Ram into a counterpart of Jesus, Muhammad, and the historic saints and martyrs of Islam and Christianity. They think that Muslims and Christians have special strengths because their divinities fought real wars and possess historically attested genealogies: Hinduism's champions are now being endowed with similar credentials.

This focus on modernity, science, and scholarship has given a new "scientific" gloss to the racial claims made by many nineteenth- and early twentieth-century Hindu revivalists. Today Muslims are said by many Hindu supremacists to be people of alien, "Semitic" blood. Such blood, they say, bears a taint of guilt from past crimes against Hindus. To the more extreme Hindutva campaigners, "true" Indians inherit the blood of a demonstrably real historic Ram and are therefore the only authentic sons of the Indian motherland. In order to reinforce this appeal to what are supposedly the literal facts of history and biological descent, the kar sevaks have reportedly offered up cups of their own blood in dedication to the cause. This may be intended as a gesture of modernity. There seems to be an idea that the offerings will be pooled in technologically advanced Hindu blood banks to protect Ram's followers from AIDS and other contaminations which supposedly come from hospitals where blood from Hindus is mixed with that of "unclean" Muslim donors.

A deep ambivalence exists here about the power of Western-style science and technology, and this is characteristic of many so-called fundamentalists around the world. One might expect groups like the BJP and its allies to be hostile toward anything that appears to conflict with their vision of faith and divinely ordered sacred landscape. But the Hindutva cause is emphatically not the preserve of mystics and holy men. Its adherents may cherish god-kings and deified warriors, but they also have much in common with Islamic militants and other defenders of "pure" religion around the world who strive to make their faith a force built on divine scripture and the supernatural, while also deploying the technical skills and resources once monopolized by "godless" infidels. Thus the Hindutva campaigners clearly crave the prestige of computer-age publicity coups. And as they are beginning to persuade professors from reputable universities as well as institutions such as the Archaeological Survey to endorse the cause, the claims of the Hindu Raj campaigners have certainly gained force by being linked to the domain of science and "modernity."

In keeping with their enthusiasm for moral uprightness and "scientific" probity, the BJP and its allies have sidetracked many of their opponents into sterile disputes over which historic mosques may or may not have been built on demolished Hindu shrine sites. Only a few would-be defenders of India's "secular" heritage have pointed out that in past centuries, rulers throughout Asia committed such acts of religious triumphalism because these constituted a universally recognized declaration of suzerainty. It may therefore be difficult, though not impossible, for professional historians and others who oppose the Hindutva cause to persuade patriotic Indians that conflicts between Mughal emperors and their subjects four hundred years ago are not crimes demanding redress in the twentieth and twenty-first centuries.

The 1992–93 upheavals in India certainly raise serious questions about whether secular nation-states as they are understood today have much of a future outside of a handful of contemporary Western countries. But there is no sign yet that the country is prepared to accept the rule of an ayatollah, a military dictatorship, or any other alternative to pluralistic parliamentary rule. Thus even if Congress fails to regain its position as India's dominant pan-Indian political party, it is still far from clear that the country's only alternative is the triumph of Hindu supremacists, together with equally aggressive demands for solidarity and supremacy among the subcontinent's other faiths and communities. The organized fundamentalisms that have taken such an assertive role in India's public life in recent years have flourished only because of the very distinctive circumstances of the country's current economic and social dislocations. It is not true that the subcontinent is engulfed in some one-way process of unstoppable fundamentalist "transformation." India is still a constitutional democracy with an established history of resilience in times of crisis. Thus far even the upheaval and bloodletting of the Ayodhya crisis do not seem to have done irreparable damage to this heritage of pluralistic "secular" nationhood.

Notes

1. The VHP became active in the 1960s. The RSS was founded in 1923, at a time of intense Hindu-Muslim communal conflict in north India. Both organizations have expanded dramatically since the early 1980s.

2. Ancient travelers' accounts of Christianity on the Malabar and Tamilnad coasts include, for example, *The Christian Topography of Cosmas, an Egyptian Monk,* trans. J. W. McCrindle (London, 1897). See also L. W. Brown, *The Indian Christians of St. Thomas* (Cambridge, 1956), pp. 11–91.

3. They are also known as "Syrian" Christians, in reference to the group's use of Syriac as a liturgical language. They claim descent from Brahmans who are supposed to have embraced Christianity at a time of mythical apostolic mission by the biblical Saint Thomas. Further details are found in Brown, *Indian Christians;* and Susan Bayly, *Saints, Goddesses and Kings: Muslims and Christians in South Indian Society, 1700–1900* (Cambridge, 1989), pp. 241–320.

4. See Stephen Neill, *A History of Christianity in India, I: The Beginnings to A.D. 1707* (Cambridge, 1984); and idem, *A History of Christianity in India, II: 1707–1858* (Cambridge, 1985). Also R. Frykenberg, "On the Study of Conversion Movements," *Indian Economic and Social History Review* 17 (1981):121–38.

5. This is analogous to the goal of a separate "Khalistan" among militant Sikh separatists. On tribal agitations, see, for example, *Economic and Political Weekly* 17, no. 34 (21 August 1982): 1376–84; on Dalits, *India Today,* 1–15 March 1981, pp. 39–41. Population figures from 1971 Census of India.

Since the early 1980s, northern Andhra Pradesh state has been a center of violent agitation involving Gond "tribals" belonging (allegedly) to an underground revolutionary or "Naxalite" organization. These so-called People's War Group activists seek to expel peasant cultivators who are charged with expropriating the tribals' ancestral lands. *India Today,* 30 April 1984, p. 24; 30 September 1985, pp. 46–47. Hindu activists of the RSS have championed the tribals' peasant-caste opponents, claiming to be acting as superpatriots and defenders of Indian nationhood against the threat of revolutionary "extremists." *The Week* (Kerala newsmagazine, published by *Malayala Manorama* press, Cochin), 25–31 March 1984, p. 35.

6. Extract from a report by an activist nun in Kerala, in D. S. Amalorpavadass, ed., *The Indian Church in the Struggle for a New Society* (Bangalore, 1981). Comparable agitations in southern Kerala began in 1981 under the leadership of militant nuns and a crusading Redemptorist priest; around Alleppey, mass marches and hunger strikes have been organized to press for restrictions on motorized trawling vessels which have depleted fish stocks and damaged the livelihoods of nonmechanized Christian and Muslim fishermen. My fieldwork in south India, 1980, 1983, 1985, 1988–89. Also see *India Today,* 15 September 1985, p. 32.

7. The decade 1975–85 has been identified as the decisive period in the emergence of what Rajiv Gandhi identified as the "new middle class" of one hundred million Indians. Gandhi's Congress party government (in power 1985–90) sought to confirm this trend by enacting tax provisions and other measures favoring private enterprise. Hallmarks of this unevenly distributed prosperity have been the growth of private investment in trade and industry, rapid urbanization, a boom in consumer spending, an enhanced demand for educational qualifications, and a massive increase in factory employment. See *India Today,* 31 December 1985, pp. 69–85.

8. From 1982 to 1987, drought and monsoon failure have been especially severe in areas where up to 80 percent of agriculture depends on rain rather than man-made water sources. In some drought regions, state governments provide facilities for Hindu, Muslim, and Christian rituals to be performed to summon divine aid against monsoon failure. *India Today,* 15 November 1982, p. 17; 31 January 1986, p. 20; *Hindu* (newspaper, published in Madras), 5 March 1988, p. 4.

9. *Hindu,* 24 April 1982, p. 16; *India To-day,* 31 March 1984, p. 28.

10. *Hindu,* 24 April 1982, p. 16; field-work carried out by author in Tamil Nadu and Karnataka; *The Week,* 25–31 March 1984, p. 30. The 1984 riots in Karnataka again targeted Urdu-speaking Muslims as well as Tamils.

11. On the collapse of Gulf employment, see *India Today,* 15 November 1985, pp. 32–33. On Kerala's returning migrants, see *Hindu,* 5 March 1988, p. 15. Tamil Nadu also had difficulty absorbing repatriated Tamils fleeing ethnic violence in Sri Lanka; half a million were resettled in the state between 1981 and 1983. *India Today,* 15 December 1983, pp. 56–57. For Kerala's large Muslim minority, employment in the Gulf has brought new resources to militant Islamizing bodies which have sought to impose rigorous standards of propriety and religious practice on fellow believers. See *Frontline* (newsmagazine published by the *Hindu* newspaper group, Madras), 29 June–12 July 1985, pp. 92–95.

12. For example, Tamil Nadu state (population forty-one million according to the 1971 Census of India) was reported to be 89 percent Hindu, 5.75 percent Christian, and 5.11 percent Muslim. Overall the population had grown by 22.3 percent since the 1961 Census, while the Muslim population had increased by 34.8 percent and the Christian population by 34.3 percent. Census of India 1971, series 19, Tamil Nadu, Table C—VII, Pt. II-C (i), p. 3. The state of Andhra Pradesh was equally volatile over the same period, as reflected in the rise of yet another movement of linguistic "nationhood," the populist Telugu Desam (Telugu speakers' homeland) party. The party won a sensational election victory in the state in 1983, under the leadership of the spellbinding film-star politician N. T. Rama Rao.

13. Although these are distinctively Indian manifestations of fundamentalism, they can usefully be compared with accounts of radical millenarian and Pentecostal Christianity in other parts of the world. See, for example, James Barr, *Fundamentalism,* 2d ed. (London, 1981).

14. Compare Lionel Caplan's study of Protestant Pentecostalism among city dwellers in Madras: *Class and Culture in Urban India: Fundamentalism in a Christian Community* (Oxford, 1987). On the Assemblies of God, see D. B. Barrett, "The Twentieth-Century Pentecostal/Charismatic Renewal," *International Bulletin of Missionary Research* 12, no. 3 (1988): 119–24; G. B. McGee, "Assemblies of God Mission Theology: A Historical Perspective," *IBMR* 10, no. 4 (1986): 166–70. The Saint Thomas Christians include an exceptionally high proportion of graduates and qualified professional people. In the nineteenth century their landholding and commercial families were quick to gain a foothold in the region's expanding export economy; the group is still prominent in trade, banking, and plantation agriculture in the state. Kerala's distinctive cultural traditions are related to the experience of economic change and class formation in Genevieve Lemercinier, *Religion and Ideology in Kerala,* trans. Y. Rendel (New Delhi, 1984).

15. The shrine's early history is discussed in A. Meersman, *The Franciscans in Tamilnad* (Schoneck-Beckenried, 1962), pp. 71–81. A typical pamphlet issued by the shrine is S. R. Santos, "The Shrine Basilica of Our Lady of Health Vailankanni" (Tanjore, 1980).

16. From interviews with devotees at Velankanni, 1983. See also M. Egnore, "On the Meaning of 'Sakti' to Women in Tamil Nadu," in S. S. Wadley, ed., *The Power of Tamil Women* (Syracuse, N.Y., 1980), pp. 1–34. Personal testimonies indicate the spontaneous nature of devotees' adherence to the cult and the role of local publicity about the shrine.

17. Amalorpavadass, *The Indian Church,* pp. 473–80. There were violent clashes in 1981 when radical priests and nuns joined marches of catamaran fishermen protesting competition from better-equipped trawlermen. Conservative local bishops and other representatives of the ecclesiastical hierarchy have been identified as opponents of these militant groups. *India Today,* 15 September 1985, p. 32.

18. Bayly, *Saints, Goddesses and Kings*, pp. 321–78; P. A. Roche, *Fishermen of the Coromandel Coast* (New Delhi, 1984). See also Kalpana Ram, *Mukkuvar Women: Gender, Hegemony, and Capitalist Transformation in a South Indian Fishing Community* (London, 1991).

19. R. Frykenberg, "The Impact of Conversion and Social Reform upon Society in South India," in C. H. Philips and M. D. Wainwright, eds., *Indian Society and the Beginnings of Modernization* (London, 1976), pp. 187–243; Neill, *History of Christianity in India*, II.

20. M. L. Reiniche, *Les dieux et les hommes: Étude des cultes d'un village du Tirunelveli Inde du Sud* (Paris, 1976); F. W. Clothey, *The Many Faces of Murugan* (The Hague, 1978); B. Stein, "Temples in Tamil Country," *IESHR* 14, no. 1 (1977): 11–45; B. Beck, "The Goddess and the Demon," in M. Biardeau, ed., *Autour de la déesse hindou* (Paris, 1981), pp. 83–136.

21. Christians and Muslims certainly recognize the transcendence of the one God, but this notion of remote and abstract divinity is easily reconciled with the physical reality of saints, demonic spirits, and other cult beings who take a direct role in everyday human affairs; such beings possess the living, and are bringers and lifters of affliction.

22. Santos, *The Shrine Basilica*.

23. Bayly, *Saints, Goddesses and Kings*, pp. 321–452; cf. C. D. F. Mosse, "Caste, Christianity and Hinduism: A Study of Social Organisation and Religion in Rural Ramnad" (Ph.D. diss., University of Oxford, 1986). Historically south Indian Christians have often reduced their priests to a status like that of dependent ritualists among Hindus.

24. *Hindu*, 3 July 1982, p. 10; *EPW* 17, no. 25 (1982): 1027ff.; no. 26 (1982): 1068ff. And see A. M. Mujahid, *Conversion to Islam. Untouchables' Strategy for Protest in India* (Chambersburg, Pa., 1989).

25. B. N. Banerjee, "A Hindu Attitude to Conversion," *International Review of Mission* 62, no. 287 (1983): 393–97. Stereotypes of caste and community as monolithic entities derive in part from the inheritance of Indian colonial ethnography. They are also fostered by militant fundamentalists like the VHP who seek to portray the country as a land in which religious boundaries are clear and unambiguous.

26. *Hindu*, 13 March 1982, p. 15; local fieldwork by author.

27. *Hindu*, 3 April 1982, p. 3; and 10 April 1982, p. 15. It was no accident that the conference was held at Nagercoil. Since the nineteenth century the town has been a major center of Christian-run missionary hospitals as well as Christian schools, colleges, and publishing houses. To groups like the RSS it is thus a symbol of "alien" intrusion into the crowded landscape of "Hindu" south India.

28. A significant proportion of the region's Shanars are Roman Catholics and Protestants whose ancestors embraced Christianity between the seventeenth and late nineteenth centuries.

29. *Hindu*, 13 March 1982, p. 15; local interviews by author.

30. Occasionally one finds these intermingled with pictorial representations of Islamic themes, including pictures of popular local pir cult shrines *(dargahs)* or Qur'anic verses. Their display by professing Hindus or Christians expresses reverence for the supernatural power which Tamils recognize as inherent in a divine Islamic "Allahswami," or in the pirs of the Sufi mystical tradition.

31. *Hindu*, 3 April 1982, p. 3. In light of these clashes, Hindu militants proposed that organizations such as the VHP take a more prominent part in running established panregional festivals such as Kerala's Onam celebrations. The goal was to draw tribal people and Harijans into such events and exclude the indigenous Christians, particularly Malayali Saint Thomas Christians, who held prestigious rights ("shares") in these ceremonies for many centuries. *Hindu*, 24 April 1982, p. 15.

32. *Hindu*, 3 April 1982, p. 2.

33. Interviews by author; L. K. Anantha Krishna Iyer, *The Cochin Tribes and Castes*, 2 vols. (Madras, 1909–12), vol. 1, p. 239.

34. *Hindu,* 24 April 1982, p. 15. He then called for exclusion of all but "true Hindu believers" from the management committees of Hindu temples and festivals.

35. Ibid., 20 March 1982, p. 15.

36. Bayly, *Saints, Goddesses and Kings,* pp. 348–78, 420–52.

37. *Hindu,* 27 March 1982, pp. 3, 15.

38. Ibid., 17 April 1982, p. 4.

39. Ibid., 13 March 1982, p. 16.

40. On the history of Indian cow protection campaigns, see J. R. McLane, *Indian Nationalism and the Early Congress* (Princeton, 1977), pp. 271–331; G. Pandey, "Rallying round the Cow," in R. Guha, ed., *Subaltern Studies* II (Delhi, 1983).

41. *Hindu,* 20 March 1982, p. 15. Ramachandran's party claimed to have inherited a populist ideology opposing the supposed domination of Brahmanical religion in south India.

42. Ibid., 27 March 1982, p. 3.

43. Ibid., 10 April 1982, p. 15.

44. Ibid., 27 March 1982, p. 15, quoting members of the Hindu Munnani Kazhagam. This article referred to more riots between Hindus and Christians in a locality near Arcot, nine hundred miles north of Kanniyakumari, where such a conference is supposed to have been held. The rioting mobs are reported to have shouted slogans relating to the Mandaikadu clashes, an indication that heightened communal consciousness is often enhanced by the reporting of threats to fellow believers in distant locales.

45. See Caplan, *Class and Culture,* chap. 8.

46. Bayly, *Saints, Goddesses and Kings,* pp. 321–78.

47. Ibid., p. 348.

48. Like some (but not all) Hindu caste groups, the Paravas (population roughly 500,000 to 750,000 in 1990) possess their own hereditary caste notables and ritualists who have acted as preservers and enforcers of this unusually precise code of conduct. The notion of a shared caste dharma or corporate morality is still invoked to underscore regulations governing marriage, descent, sexual morality, and other aspects of corporate identity and honor amongst the Paravas.

49. These "gifts" of the Holy Spirit include the power to exorcise, heal, and speak in tongues. See Caplan, *Class and Culture;* Barrett, "Twentieth Century Renewal," p. 124.

50. Historic Christian gurus are memorialized in south Indian hagiographical literature, for example, A. S. Durairaj, P. Kaithanal, and S. Jeyabalan, *Directory of the Diocese of Palaiyamkottai* (Palaiyamkottai, 1973), p. 7.

51. Bayly, *Saints, Goddesses and Kings,* pp. 281–320.

52. *Church Missionary Record* (journal of the Church Missionary Society, London, 1877), pp. 29–33; *Kerala Mitram* (newspaper), 15 October 1881, quoted in *Reports on Native Newspapers,* Madras, India Office Library, London.

53. Compare Caplan, *Class and Culture,* chap. 7. Typical targets for fundamentalist Christian critique are the many ordained Protestant and Catholic clerics (and some Saint Thomas Christians) who seek to "integrate" the values and practices of "Sanskritic" high Hinduism with Indian Christian observance. See, for example, "Abhishiktananda" (pseudonym of an Indian-based priest), *Towards the Renewal of the Indian Church* (Cochin, 1970), pp. 43–47, proposing adoption by Indian Christians of a Brahmanical Hindu vegetarian diet and calling for the use of Sanskrit as a Christian liturgical language.

54. Observed during fieldwork in south Indian Christian localities; compare Caplan, *Class and Culture,* chaps. 7–8.

55. Caplan, *Class and Culture.*

56. M. A. Thomas, *An Outline History of Christian Churches and Denominations in Kerala* (Trivandrum, 1977), pp. 155–62.

57. Ibid.; C. E. Jones, *Guide to the Study of the Pentecostal Movement,* 2 vols. (Metuchen, N.J., 1983), vol. 1, p. 581; F. A. Tatford, *The Challenge of India* (Bath, 1983) (a popular account of missionary work by Christians attached to the Plymouth Brethren movement).

58. The church was founded in about 1940; its hybrid title with the use of the Indian term *sangham* (assembly or association) is typical for such Indian Christian groups. Information on modern-day activities from personal communication to author; see also 1971 Census of India, series 9, part VI-B, "Special Survey Reports," pp. 217–18.

59. Jones, *Guide to the Study of the Pentecostal Movement,* vol. 1, p. 581.

60. Again, "Syrian" is an alternative title for the Malayalam-speaking Saint Thomas Christians.

61. On modern Brethren churches, see V. C. George, *The Church in India before and after the Synod of Diamper* (Alleppey, 1977), p. 196; and Tatford, *The Challenge of India,* pp. 129–37. See also *Church Missionary Record 1869,* pp. 304–5; *1870,* p. 329; *1873,* pp. 164–66.

62. This group claimed ten thousand adherents in the late 1970s. Thomas, *Outline History,* pp. 159–60.

63. See, for example, Mosse, "Caste, Christianity and Hinduism," pp. 428–33.

64. *EPW* 17, no. 19 (8 May 1982): 765–66.

65. *EPW* 17, no. 34 (21 August 1982): 1376–78.

66. Banerjee, "Hindu Attitude to Conversion," p. 397.

67. *EPW* 17, no. 19 (8 May 1982): 766. There are close parallels with campaigns of *shuddhi* or "reconversion" of Christians by militant Hindus in north India in the late nineteenth century. See K. Jones, *Arya Dharm: Hindu Consciousness in 19th-Century Punjab* (Berkeley, 1976), pp. 202–15. The pope's tour of India in 1986 was portrayed by Hindu militant organizations as yet another incursion into the "Hindu homeland." They claimed that *darshan* (the Hindu concept of sanctified sighting) of the pope would "induce" Hindus to convert to Christianity. In Kerala, Hindu organizations protested against the erection of a temporary papal rostrum on a site that was claimed as a place of Hindu sanctity. Muslims, too, used this idiom of territorial defense: in 1985, Muslim fishermen in a village in southern Kerala claimed that an ill-conceived scheme of slum clearance was targeting their hutments rather than those of neighboring Christians "because the Pope is coming next year." *India Today,* 30 November 1985, p. 19; *Guardian* (newspaper), 14 January 1986.

68. Daniel Gold, "Organized Hinduisms," in Marty E. Marty and R. Scott Appleby, eds., *Fundamentalisms Observed* (Chicago: University of Chicago Press, 1991), pp. 531–93.

69. *Hindu,* 26 June 1982, p. 3.

70. Bayly, *Saints, Goddesses and Kings.*

71. *Hindu,* 3 July 1982, p. 10. Rioting occurred in and around Sokampatti and Kadayanallur after rallies addressed by representatives of the All India Muslim League and a self-styled Muslim "service organization" which declared itself to be working for "unity" among Harijans and Muslims.

72. See Peter van der Veer, "Hindu Nationalism and the Discourse of Modernity," chap. 23 in this volume. Also, see Gold, "Organized Hinduisms."

73. Gold, "Organized Hinduisms"; *EPW* 24, no. 40 (7 October 1989): 2219.

74. *Hindu,* 11 February 1989, p. 16.

75. Ibid.

76. Ibid.

77. Transcribed from interviews given by the Kanchi acarya for the BBC television film "Dust and Ashes" (1989), made at the February 1989 Kumbh Mela.

78. In 1988 this Kanchi acarya, Sri Jayendra Saraswati, proclaimed the Hindu cause at a World Hindu Congress in Nepal. Here he took part in ceremonies designed to widen the span of Hindu Raj by glorifying the spiritual lordship claimed by the reigning Hindu king of Nepal. *Hindu,* 2 April 1988, p. 16. Soon after the 1989 Kumbh Mela festival, this same acarya participated in celebrations commemorating the centenary of the founder of the RSS. This event was strategically sited in Jammu, close to the zone of conflict between India and Pakistan over yet another contested part of the "homeland," Kashmir. *Hindu,* 13 May 1989, p. 5.

79. The recent adoption of Western titles like "pope" and "pontiff" for the south Indian acarya ascetics suggests an attempt to elevate them to the standing many Hindus identify with Western Christian primates. This is part of the attempt to take over the institutional structures of the non-Hindu "enemy" so as to remake Hinduism as a unified vehicle of nationhood and supremacy.

80. *Hindu,* 15 April 1989, p. 2.

81. This "discovery" actually occurred in 1949, but was in the forefront of debate about the site during the 1980s. Gold, "Organized Hinduisms."

82. This parallel display of rival sacred items has occurred in a forest zone where, in 1984, the government of India superseded the cultivation ban, granting titles to sixty thousand families on land that had been cleared and cultivated illegally since the 1950s. Most of these settlers were Saint Thomas Christians. By building churches and erecting standing wood and stone crosses in their settlements, they had sought to mark out claims of primacy in the disputed tracts. Their opponents were land-hungry Hindus who adopted the idiom of exclusion and sacred symbolism, affiliating themselves with the RSS to gain organized backing for their campaign. *India Today,* 31 May 1984, pp. 22–23.

83. Local informant, 1990.

84. *Hindu,* 28 July 1990. On the historical significance of the Nagore shrine, see Bayly, *Saints, Goddesses and Kings,* pp. 91–94, 134–35, 146–47, 216–21.

85. *Hindu,* 28 July 1990.

86. Ibid., 13 May 1990, p. 5.

Organizational Weakness and the Rise of Sinhalese Buddhist Extremism

James Manor

Many of the other chapters in this book analyze movements with strong organizations whose strength plays an important role in fueling fundamentalism or extremism. This chapter deals with a movement where—unusually, but not uniquely—the opposite is true. The growth and the great destructive power of Sinhalese Buddhist extremism in Sri Lanka are substantially explained by the existence of various kinds of organizational weakness.

To establish this central point, I assess several structures and groups: the formal institutions of the state, political parties, the Buddhist clergy or Sangha, the wider community of Buddhist believers, avowedly extremist groups, and the broader extremist movement. Organizationally, all of these tend to be fragmented, truncated, and insubstantial. Before we consider all of that, however, it is necessary to explain what Sinhalese Buddhist extremism is and how it fits into a project on fundamentalism.

Let us begin with a few essentials. Buddhism is theoretically capable of generating "fundamentalism" inasmuch as it provides sources from which it is possible to divine certain "fundamentals." It is a univocal tradition in that the faithful can turn to the codified Pali canon and a few postcanonical texts which, taken together, constitute a reasonably coherent set of textural sources.[1] It also traces its origins to a single historical figure. It shares this status as a univocal tradition with Judaism, Christianity, and Islam but not with the predominant religious and cultural tradition of South Asia, Hinduism. Hinduism is so heterogeneous that it is immensely difficult to derive "fundamentals" and therefore "fundamentalism" from it, but Buddhism does not pose such a serious problem for its adherents.

Why then the phrase "Sinhalese Buddhist extremism" used to describe the movement under discussion here, rather than "Buddhist fundamentalism?" This form of words is not meant to imply that our Buddhist extremists utterly fail to qualify as fundamentalists, but rather that the situation is complicated, in two ways.

First, there is another group of Buddhists in Sri Lanka to whom the "fundamentalist" label might more plausibly be attached—although no group on the island has ever sought to be called that. Second, while the extremists see themselves as upholders of a set of Buddhist fundamentals, others have doubts about (1) whether some of the religious practices in which many extremists engage are consistent with the fundamentals of Buddhism, and (2) whether some of the political means that the extremists use conform to the way of the Buddha.

Let us begin with the alternative group that might be labeled Buddhist "fundamentalists," and for the sake of clarity, let us call them Buddhist "purists." Most (though not all) of them have kept their distance from the Buddhist extremist movement, but the main thing that distinguishes them is their attitude to the tenets of the faith.

The purists take exception to the widespread tendency in Sri Lanka to incorporate non-Buddhist elements into Buddhist religious practice. The elements in question include Hindu ideas, gods, and modes of worship, which have achieved considerable currency. Indeed, even the preeminent place of Buddhist worship on the island—the Dalada Maligawa or Temple of the Tooth in Kandy—has shrines to four deities of Hindu origin standing before it. The purists further object to the widespread involvement of Buddhists—often at places of worship and with the assistance of the Buddhist clergy—with spirit religion, black magic, demons, astrology, sorcery, trancelike states, and so forth. They would like to see these things cast aside so that worshipers could focus on what might be called the "fundamentals" of the Buddha's teachings.[2]

This chapter assesses the Sinhalese Buddhist extremists rather than the purists mainly because the latter have had only a limited impact on Sri Lanka's recent history. The purists have had to sit by, dismayed, as the popularity of Hindu elements and especially of things magical and demonic has grown enormously in Sinhalese Buddhism since World War II. They have also seen people turn increasingly to Sinhalese extremism and the extremists turn increasingly to violence, which the purists regard as contrary to Buddhist principles.[3] These trends have reduced the purists to a marginal force.

Sinhalese Buddhist extremism, by contrast, has had enormous influence. Donald Swearer has discussed this phenomenon at length in the first volume of this series, so it is unnecessary to cover that ground again in exhaustive detail here. But it should be noted that the movement surfaced as a potent force in national politics during the mid-1950s and was exploited by leaders of both major political parties so that it has remained an important element in the island's politics. If we were only writing about the years up to 1977, we might call it Sinhalese Buddhist "revivalism" or "chauvinism," but in recent times it has become far more extreme. After a partial eclipse during the late 1960s and early 1970s, it reemerged in the severe anti-Tamil riots of 1977. Since another, more ghastly pogrom in 1983, extremism of a more virulent and often hysterical kind has become the central preoccupation of nearly every important group in Sinhalese politics.

The immense influence extremism has achieved is the main justification for our concern with it here, but there are also ways in which it resembles "fundamentalist" movements elsewhere. The extremists believe—indeed, their "identity has been grounded in the belief"—that their Therevada Buddhism is the pure form of the faith, that the Mahayana tradition is "tantamount to heresy," and that it is they, the Sinhalese, who have preserved the Therevada tradition in its purest form.[4] They derive these views in part from a chauvinistic interpretation of a text, the Mahavamsa. They argue that the text provides evidence that the Buddha bestowed the island of Lanka on the Sinhalese and charged them with the mission of preserving it as a citadel of pure Buddhism. They are thus, to a degree, textually oriented, but they refer to this text rather cursorily and mainly as a justification for their pursuit of political and social dominance in the island rather than as a guide to correct living. Indeed, the Sinhalese Buddhist extremists have paid little heed since the mid-1950s to promoting orthodox or appropriate religious practices—that is left to the purists. Instead, they presume that such practices have always prevailed among the Sinhalese masses, and their predominant concern is to ensure that the state serves the cause of Buddhism and that the Sinhalese enjoy dominance in Sri Lanka. As a result, this movement tends to resemble the Algerian movement discussed elsewhere in this book by Hugh Roberts, in that the poverty of its language on matters religious is matched by the richness of its language on matters political.

This set of characteristics is bound up with the belief that the Buddha bestowed the island of Lanka upon the Sinhalese—upon the "lion race," as they see themselves—and charged them with the mission of preserving the island as a sacred redoubt where Buddhism in this pure form might survive. This mission is seen as the fundamental basis for their collective identity, indeed for their very existence as a collectivity. It is a short step from that idea to their assertions that Sinhalese Buddhism is the only thing that can hold them and the island together, and thus that it necessarily provides the only reliable fundamentals on which state structures can be built.

Their preoccupation with this set of fundamentals might make it possible to describe them as "fundamentalists," but if we consider their ideas and doings more fully, the reasons for regarding them as "extremists" rather than "fundamentalists" will become clearer. It is not just that they focus more on things political (dominating the island, maintaining the Sinhalese Buddhist nation) and social (the fate of the "lion race") than on what most people see as the teachings of the Buddha. When faced with the choice between their political and social concerns and the Buddha's opposition to violence, they have *increasingly* turned to the former. In the 1980s they did so wantonly and on a massive scale. They would not, however, recognize this distinction between their political and social concerns on the one hand and the Buddhist way on the other. They regard political and social concerns as important because the Buddha charged them with special responsibilities.

They perceive their history as a succession of struggles, continuing to the present, to fulfill those responsibilities, to accomplish that mission. Those struggles are seen to have occurred within the broad arena of South Asia, which includes not only their island but the Indian subcontinent as well. In that wider context, the Sinhalese see themselves as a tiny Buddhist minority vastly outnumbered by the Hindus of India, and especially by the Dravidian masses of South India which stands just twenty-five miles away across the Palk Straits. The struggle to accomplish their mission was made particularly difficult by the large-scale immigration of Tamil Hindus hundreds of years ago into the northern and eastern areas of the island, where they are still found in large numbers today. We know that for long periods of Sri Lanka's history, Tamil kingdoms in the north coexisted peacefully with Sinhalese Buddhist kingdoms in the rest of the island. But Sinhalese extremists tend to ignore this history and instead stress, first, the attempts by certain Sinhalese kings to conquer the predominantly Tamil areas and, second, the periods after such conquests when appropriately Buddhist regimes held sway throughout the island.

That sort of Buddhist dominance was rendered impossible by the coming of the Western powers—first the Portugese, then the Dutch, and finally the British, who defeated the last of the Buddhist Kandyan kings in 1815. After independence was achieved in 1948, Sinhalese extremists hoped once again for some sort of "reconquest" or fulfillment of their mission,[5] and successive governments got themselves elected by suggesting that they would pursue that end. Once in power, however, most of them have felt compelled to show at least minimal consideration to the Tamil minority, which has repeatedly displeased the extremists. The emergence, from the late 1970s onward, of an armed Tamil separatist movement and its success at controlling large portions of the Tamil majority areas for much of the 1980s have naturally inflamed feelings still further.

The political agenda of the Sinhalese Buddhist movement has grown more extreme over time. Because they have never been tightly organized, there have always been differences of view on what the agenda was, but until the late 1950s, they sought to persuade the state to restore Buddhism to its rightful place as the core around which the nation might be forged. For most of them, this meant making Buddhism the state religion, but all were agreed that Buddhist institutions and the Sinhalese language and cultural heritage should be provided with resources and patronage. Indeed, in that early period, the need to assist the language at the expense of English and Tamil was a more urgent concern than was religion.

The 1960s saw Sri Lankan governments make substantial concessions to Sinhalese Buddhists, partly because of their widespread popular support and partly because concessions were seen as a way to make the group less extreme. This tactic probably had some effect since no anti-Tamil riots occurred between 1958 and 1977. But by the latter date, the failure of the government that had ruled since 1970 to heed Sinhalese Buddhist concerns and the sad state of the economy, which inspired widespread anger, contributed to the outbreak of anti-Tamil rioting after a change of government at the 1977 election.

We have noted that Sinhalese Buddhist extremists are preoccupied with political and social issues, but they have not developed a thoroughgoing political and social ideology as becomes vividly apparent if we try to place them on a conventional right-left spectrum. There is in fact no position on this spectrum which extremists have not occupied at one time or another. Conservatives of the right or center-right who wish to thwart or restrain social reform have made use of these sentiments, and so have more radical rightists, free marketeers. So have reformers on the center-left and Gue-varist insurrectionaries on the far left. Sinhalese Buddhist extremism leaves enough questions unanswered that it can be and has been exploited by virtually everyone—so long as he or she is Sinhalese and at least nominally (in the case of the Guevarists) Buddhist.

Extremism has similarly been used both to bolster incumbent regimes in Sri Lanka and to undermine them. Indeed, it is hard to think of a time since the emergence in the mid-1950s of something close to a two-party system when both the ruling party and the opposition did not claim to be more attentive to Sinhalese Buddhist concerns than their opponents. Comparatively liberal regimes have sought to establish their credentials by making concessions to Sinhalese Buddhist interests, while their rivals in the other main Sinhalese party have called for their ouster because these concessions were insufficient. In more recent times, repressively statist regimes have deployed le-thal force on the grounds that it was necessary to protect Sinhalese Buddhist ideals from nefarious forces. The present regime (1991) has slaughtered thousands on this pretext. Their victims include not only Tamils but those on the far left who share the romantic Guevarist belief in the possibility that the existing political order can be overthrown with relative ease. Extremism has come to pervade the politics of the island's linguistic majority.

The movement is shot through with ironies and incongruities that are more acute than in most fundamentalist movements. Indeed, it is possible that some extremists have become more vehement and uncompromising precisely because they sense that these incongruities may undermine the purity of their cause. But that proposition is difficult to prove, so let us simply identify the incongruities in question.

First, the extremists' claim that they are defending Buddhism in its purist form overlooks the extensive role Hindu beliefs and practices and various forms of spirit religion and magic play in their daily lives and in the "Buddhism" they practice. Some of these things—such as the Sinhalese caste system—have been present for a very long time. But many other non-Buddhist elements—such as the involvement with gods of Hindu origin and with demons, and the use of *huniyam* (black magic)—have clearly been gaining ground during the period in which Sinhalese Buddhist extremism has achieved such prominence.[6]

Second, the Sinhalese linguistic group, which the extremists like to describe as the "lion race," imperiled by the Dravidian menace, is not a distinct and homogeneous "race" at all. It is well known that a large minority of this "race" consists of Dravidian immigrants who settled long ago in southern Sri Lanka and abandoned their original languages, Tamil and Malayalam, for Sinhalese, and abandoned Hinduism for Bud-dhism. Indeed, anthropologists have identified sizable settlements which spoke Tamil a generation ago but which have recently gained admission to this "race" by adopting the Sinhalese language.

Third, the anxieties Sinhalese extremists so often express about the dangers they face as a minority within the South Asian region sit oddly alongside one of the basic realities of life on the island—that they have made the Sinhalese majority in Sri Lanka dangerously intolerant of the Tamil minority.

A fourth difficulty concerns the belief that only Sinhalese Buddhism can hold Sri Lanka together and preserve it as a nation. This notion has, not surprisingly, served to integrate the Sinhalese linguistic group, for example, by making the "race" more salient than Sinhalese caste divisions and the division between Kandyan and Low Country Sinhalese, which once were important. But this belief clashes mightily with the plain fact that the excesses of Sinhalese Buddhist extremists have come very close to tearing the island apart and have made it impossible for huge numbers of the island's residents to accept the notion of Sri Lanka as a nation. Put slightly differently, the extremists' habit of equating the "nation" with the Sinhalese "race" has raised great difficulties on an island where roughly a quarter of the population is non-Sinhalese.

Finally, there is the problem of the political means. Sinhalese Buddhist extremists have often and increasingly resorted to violence to promote their cause. Extremists in the civilian population have indulged in murderous rioting against the Tamil minority in 1956, 1958, 1977, 1981, and 1983—and on that last and most appalling occasion, they were assisted and to some extent directed by agents of the state. Extremists in Sri Lanka's security forces have been responsible for massacres of unarmed Tamil noncombatants on several dozen occasions since 1983. Some of these actions occurred after Tamil terrorists had committed atrocities against Sinhalese, but the principal source of terrorism on the island in recent years is nonetheless the state.

The security forces and shadowy death squads (most of which were associated with the security forces) were also responsible for the murders of approximately forty thousand young Sinhalese people between 1987 and 1990. Many of the dead were participants in the Janatha Vimukthi Peramuna (JVP) insurgency, but a great many were also victims of indiscriminate killing. These acts of violence were often undertaken in reaction to murders and acts of terrorism by the JVP which were themselves often inspired by Sinhalese Buddhist extremists—in the belief that the government, although heavily influenced by Sinhalese Buddhist extremists, was insufficiently extreme.[7]

The use of even a little violence would suffice to raise doubts about the commitment of such people to the fundamental teachings of the Buddha, and Sri Lanka since 1983 has experienced not one but a succession of massive slaughters. Although these people see themselves as adhering to the fundamentals of Buddhism, it is more accurate to describe them as Sinhalese Buddhist "extremists" rather than "fundamentalists."

Accounting for Sinhalese Buddhist Extremism

The process by which Sinhalese Buddhist extremism became such a pervasive and destructive force is complex. Various types of organizational weakness have played an important part, and we consider them presently. Before we do so, however, let us briefly consider seven other factors which also had some impact.

There is, first, the content of extremists' perceptions of themselves. Their stories of past struggles, of heroic conquests, and of bitter grievances from more recent times, and the goal of a "reconquest" of the island are exceedingly difficult to interpret in ways that might make even modest compromise possible.

A second difficulty is posed by the distinctive role in Sinhalese Buddhism of monks (*bhikkhus*) who often articulate the extremists' perceptions. The monks are not merely religious leaders; they are objects of worship. This means that it is virtually impossible for a believer to dissent from comments offered by a monk when he is speaking for homiletic purposes—as he generally is when articulating these views. And yet many Buddhist monks—especially the extremists—are young men with little education in anything other than the faith. Their comments on matters political therefore tend often to be naïve in the extreme. A survey of the island's newspapers since the 1940s would reveal hundreds of political pronouncements by monks which are extreme, even hysterical, and naive. And yet since they are objects of worship, these men never encounter questions or dissent which might temper their extremism.

A third factor is the tendency of elite politicians to manipulate extremist sentiments in order to advance their own narrow, short-term interests. This tendency was most vividly apparent in the long, brazenly short-sighted career of S. W. R. D. Bandaranaike, the island's fourth prime minister and the man who brought Sinhalese extremism onto center stage, but many others have behaved similarly.[8] Leaders have had great latitude for such manipulation because of the absence or weakness of organizational structures that might have linked the elites and the masses. The lack of such links has effectively meant that elites are free to indulge themselves without worrying about being called to account by underlings. Tamil leaders have been as unbridled in this as have Sinhalese. Of course, elite misbehavior occurs everywhere and Sinhalese leaders are no worse than some others, but the record suggests that they are also no better.

Fourth, the existence of something like a two-party system after 1956, which produced much that was of value, also tended to sustain Sinhalese Buddhist extremism. The predominant pattern, with some exceptions and variations, was for those in opposition to foment Sinhalese resentments against the ruling party for failing to deliver on their promises to attend to those very resentments.

This pattern paid off because of a fifth factor. Until 1978, most power was vested in a Westminster-style Parliament whose members were elected on a first-past-the-post system. That, and the spatial distribution of Sinhalese and Tamils on the island, meant that control of Parliament always went to the party that captured the most Sinhalese votes, creating an incentive for the two main parties to compete in Tamil bashing. The switch to a strong presidency in 1978 was intended by moderates to make Tamil votes count more and thus to discourage Sinhalese extremism. But electoral chicanery[9] and bloody conflict between Sinhalese and Tamils have prevented this change from having any effect.

Sinhalese Buddhist extremism was also sustained by economic difficulties, a sixth element in the story. Until the late 1970s, the problem was slow (or no) growth. Thus Sinhalese youths, whose expectations of employment and prosperity had been stimulated by the promises of assertively Sinhalese politicians, experienced bitter disappointment which was in turn exploited by still more extreme leaders. Since the late 1970s, free market policies have produced periods of rapid growth, but they have disrupted status hierarchies and produced considerable social dislocation. The resulting confusion and anxiety have fueled extremism still further. Since 1983 the two ghastly conflicts—the Sinhalese versus Tamils, and the government versus the JVP—have wrought economic havoc.

The seventh factor is the tendency for polarization, once it begins, to develop a momentum of its own and escalate. Sri Lanka since 1983 has repeatedly been scarred by the politics of vendetta and reprisal, of massacre and countermassacre, of terrorist acts that beget terrorist responses.[10]

These seven factors, while important, do not provide an adequate explanation for the emergence of Sinhalese Buddhist extremism. More important than any of these is the problem of organizational weakness. Daniel Gold hypothesized in his essay in *Fundamentalisms Observed* that "fundamentalist Hinduism is pre-eminently organized Hinduism." Sinhalese Buddhist extremism, however, has become virulent and has endured primarily because of several sorts of insubstantial, incomplete organizational structures—not only within the extremist movement but also in the larger sociopolitical context in which they exist.

Perhaps the most important reason that several types of organizations in Sri Lanka tend to be weak and truncated is that the island's political institutions have always been that way themselves. This is true of both political parties and the formal institutions of state. Both have suffered from a national political elite which has long concentrated power in their own hands at the apex of the political system. The apex and the base have been poorly integrated because institutions at intermediate and local levels have been given too little power to develop much substance.

Local councils have always suffered from three problems, any one of which alone would have nearly crippled them: (1) responsibility for most important services in local arenas is assigned to bureaucratic agencies of the central government; (2) inadequate funding is the general rule; and (3) in rural areas there is an absence of genuinely local boards. The failure of intermediate-level councils to link local boards to the national level might be included as a fourth affliction, but we will come to that in a moment.[11]

The tendency to entrust the delivery of services in local arenas to agencies of the central government derives in part from the pre-independence period when elected politicians controlled ministries. To maximize their leverage in the unequal contest with British colonial authorities, they refused to share power either with district-level civil servants (who were agents of the colonial regime) or with local-level councils. This eventually had the effect of shifting power from the districts to the national level, and although it originated as an anticolonial (and hence "progressive") tactic, it was maintained after independence to bolster the dominance which a tiny elite then came to exercise (so that it ceased to be quite so "progressive").

As a consequence, local authorities—city, town, and village councils—were left with a severely limited range of activities, and those they were allowed to perform were the kind that notoriously fail to stimulate local enthusiasm. The local councils were also made inordinately dependent on a central ministry for local government, as was to be expected from the radically centralizing elite at the apex of the system. These problems have survived in their essentials until the present day.

More crucial were the inadequate finances provided for local councils—a well-recognized reality for decades, as enquiries in 1928, 1962, 1969–70, and 1974–75 have demonstrated. And yet leaders at the national level have steadfastly refused to do anything about it. Even after a 500 percent increase in central grants to local boards in 1959, the money available to them was too modest to perform even a minimal set of functions. And their funds have always come mainly from central grants rather than from their own tax-raising powers since an increase in the latter might undercut their utter dependence on the national level. A perusal of official documents over the years reveals something close to contempt for local government in Sri Lanka.[12]

If local councils were to be effective at integrating people in villages (where most Sri Lankans live) into the national political system, the area each covered had to be sufficiently small to permit local residents to regard it as a geographical and social entity with which they could identify. This has not been the case, and it constitutes a third impediment to the effectiveness of these institutions. In 1971 the average number of people living within a village committee's jurisdiction was 18,225[13]—a number too large to draw local people in effectively, but too small to serve as an intermediate-level link between the local and national levels.

Since about 1972 the difficulties of local institutions have been compounded by a tendency of successive governments to manipulate them in a wantonly illiberal manner for their own partisan advantage. Governments have gone to the extent of abolishing whole categories of local committees and councils because the previous regime had packed them with its own backers. New institutions were created by the new regime (just as new, partisan constitutions have been introduced after the last two changes of government), and they in turn have been packed with loyalists who operate as the minions of the central authorities rather than as representatives of the local populace.[14] The bullying, extortionate behavior of the ruling party's members of Parliament since 1977, including use of private armies of toughs to intimidate people and to thwart free exercise of the franchise, has caused further damage to local institutions.

Elected intermediate-level councils, which were eventually created to link the local and national levels, have also failed. Until 1981 no such institutions existed, mainly because of the centralist inclinations of leading politicians, but also because of the deterioration of relations between Sinhalese and Tamils. After that occurred in the mid-1950s, proposals to create elected councils at either the provincial or district (that is, subprovincial) level appeared to many Sinhalese politicians to be dangerous concessions to the Tamil minority's appeals for greater autonomy—concessions that could threaten national unity and hence the Sinhalese "race" itself. As a result, such councils were not created, and both Sinhalese and Tamils living at the local level continued to be deprived of any participatory link with official institutions other than by way of their votes every few years for a member of a rather remote Parliament in Colombo.[15]

During the 1980s, elected councils were established first at the district level and then at the provincial level, but in practice little changed. In 1981 moderates in the ruling party managed to establish district councils as part of an effort to build bridges to moderate Tamils. But the councils were quickly stripped of most of their power by President Jayewardene under intense pressure from Sinhalese chauvinists, so Tamil opinion grew more embittered, not less. Later, provincial councils were created, partly to undermine the most extreme Tamil groups. They have been overtaken, however, by the ghastly civil strife of the late 1980s, and it appears unlikely at this writing that they will play a significant role in the political system.

Thus at the local level the great mass of Sri Lankans still have no functioning intermediate institution to link them with the national level. And the use, since 1982, of intimidation and chicanery on a massive scale at national elections raises doubts about whether they any longer offer people a chance to make meaningful political choices. The elite and the masses, the apex and base of the political system, are thus very poorly integrated, producing feelings of impotence and alienation among the masses. In Sri Lanka these feelings have fed extremism among both Tamils and Sinhalese.

Party building has never been easy in Sri Lanka. Until independence in 1948, the structures of the colonial political system severely impeded the development of political parties. Since 1948, the nonexistence of a framework of formal institutions linking the national and local levels created major problems for those who wished to forge party organizations that penetrated down from the national level, through intermediate levels toward the grass roots.

To make matters far worse, most party leaders at the apex of the system sought systematically to avoid creating strong parties. However much the existence of a strong organization might have assisted them in gaining or retaining power, it would also have curbed the immense freedom of maneuver which they enjoyed in the absence of such organization, and they consistently chose the latter over the former. (One exception to this pattern occurred briefly in the United National Party, but it was short-lived and need not detain us here.) As a result, Sri Lanka's major political parties have been as organizationally weak and truncated as the formal institutions of the state. They offer Sinhalese extremists (and everyone else outside the tiny national elite) no significant opportunity for influence or participation.[16]

We also find organizational fragmentation among the Buddhist clergy, or Sangha, in Sri Lanka. The Sangha is divided into three fraternities or *nikayas,* which operate independently from one another and differ somewhat in their social composition and religious emphases: the Siyam Nikaya, which is the oldest and largest, and two others which developed out of reformist efforts in the nineteenth century, the Amarapura and Ramanna nikayas. This fragmentation should not be taken to mean, however, that Sinhalese Buddhism is divided into three relatively cohesive "denominations." Individual temples and individuals or small groups among the monks (*bhikkhus*) tend to have only tenuous links to the great temples and their incumbents. As a consequence, little discipline is exercised within the nikayas to hold monks to any sort of orthodoxy. Most monks, especially those in the vast number of small and widely scattered villages temples, have relatively little formal training in the faith—the sort of training that might inculcate such an orthodoxy.

Most monks therefore have considerable autonomy to engage in whatever religious practices and political activities they prefer. In the 1950s, this meant that huge numbers of village monks felt free to participate in public campaigns for political parties that sought to promote Buddhism and the Sinhalese language, even though many (not all) senior figures in the clergy preferred that monks not become politically active.[17] In recent years, it has meant that senior figures, such as the incumbents of important temples, who regard the use of violence as anathema, have been unable to restrain many village monks from lending support to the revolt of the Guevarist JVP. The JVP engaged in widespread acts of terrorism and ritualized murder until its destruction by police and death squads in 1988–89.[18] The Sangha is so loosely organized that the great mass of the clergy tends to be carried along by whatever prevailing winds happen to be blowing. In recent years, a stiff breeze has been blowing in the direction of extremism.

The groups and associations that have arisen to promote Sinhalese Buddhist revivalism and extremism over the years have—with one exception—been extremely ill organized. This is true of both associations composed entirely of monks and those that contain clergy as well as laity, but it is not apparent from every study of Sri Lankan politics. Some scholars have presumed that because an association with a plausible-sounding name is frequently mentioned in the press, it must necessarily possess organizational substance. (They tend to make the same mistake about political parties.) But careful analyses of these associations reveal that there is far less substance to them than press reports suggest.[19] We will examine the implications of this in due course, but let us first briefly consider the one exception to this generalization.

The only Sinhalese extremist group to have a tight organization was the JVP in the late 1980s. It had a core leadership of no more than a few dozen persons, with perhaps as many as two thousand people substantially involved in the group. Activists in these cells were in intermittent contact with many thousands of JVP sympathizers. The activists were often linked with JVP front organizations that recruited university students, other youths, and women. Several thousand people were involved in this second ring of JVP fronts.[20]

Unfortunately for the JVP, the period in which it qualified as a "Sinhalese extremist" group coincided precisely with the period that the government brutally suppressed it. (After 1987, "exterminate" would be a more accurate word than "suppress.") Even in its early phase as a Guevarist or Maoist leftist movement, when it mounted an abortive insurrection in 1971, the JVP's message contained anti-Indian sentiments consistent with Sinhalese chauvinism, but this theme was relatively unimportant until the 1980s. Then, after the severe anti-Tamil riots of 1983, which the government falsely blamed on the JVP, relations between the linguistic groups were so polarized that the JVP leaders took up Sinhalese extremism as their main theme. The year 1983 also brought a government ban against them, however, so they were driven underground and subjected to severe harassment.

As a result, they were prevented from building up their organization during the very time they began to achieve wide popularity, especially among Sinhalese youths. Their popularity particularly grew after mid-1987, when Rajiv Gandhi forced the Sri Lankan government to accept the presence of Indian troops in the predominantly Tamil areas, on the pretense that they had been invited in. The presence of Indian forces fulfilled the paranoid fantasies of Sinhalese extremists, many of whom turned to the JVP in revulsion at their own government. This surge in JVP membership, coupled with the ruthless effectiveness of JVP assassins and terrorists, posed a grave threat to the regime, which responded by slaughtering approximately forty thousand youths, mainly in the two provinces where the JVP was strongest. This horrific campaign destroyed the JVP, but most of those who were killed had no connection to the organization.

The fragmentation among Sri Lanka's Buddhists is further compounded by the nature of the religious practices engaged in by two important groups of believers. The first and less important of these are the "Protestant" Buddhists, a subset of the purists mentioned earlier. These are usually middle-class people who, in the manner of Protestant Christians, are not prepared to leave religion to specialized priests. Theirs is a highly rationalistic and individualized faith based on their own study, often in isolation, of scriptures and written commentaries on the Buddha's teachings. They tend not to involve themselves much in temple worship or other collective activities. Thus they contribute to the atomization of the body of Buddhist believers.

The second of these groups, far larger and far more given to extremism, is made up of those who engage in spirit religion, encounters with demons, black magic, sorcery, and the like. Such people tend to become involved in one-on-one relationships with teachers, mediums, and so forth, that is, with persons who provide access to these practices. Neither these persons nor the devotees who turn to them are "supervised by a public body" such as the Buddhist Sangha. Obviously the presence of this group also leads to "the fragmentation and mystification of the tradition."[21]

The Consequences of Organizational Weakness

Several consequences follow from the extremists' organizational weakness. First, these weaknesses make it difficult for extremist organizations to achieve their purposes. The absence of solid structures within most extremist groups has left them prey to self-indulgent behavior by group leaders, which has repeatedly prevented the groups from accomplishing their goals. This was made apparent, for example, when Bandaranaike, once in office, proved unwilling to accede to many extremist demands. A high-ranking Buddhist monk in Bandaranaike's party, who, with sufficient organizational discipline, might have led extremist protests against this perceived betrayal, turned instead to profiteering. (When the prime minister thwarted his ambitions, the monk conspired to have Bandaranaike murdered.) Subsequent leaders who rode Sinhalese extremism to power also tended to ignore the extremists after attaining power, in favor of factional intrigue and/or nepotism. Politicians to whom extremist groups appeal for action are often reluctant to take the groups seriously because they can see that their poor organization makes it impossible for them to mobilize effectively for or against those in power.

Organizational weakness has also made it difficult for extremist groups to provide their members with a sense of reinforcement or community, with the reassurance that they are effectively linked to others of like mind. This problem and the persistent failure of such groups to achieve goals have frequently left members of extremist groups feeling betrayed either by their own leaders or by politicians or both—and that feeling has fueled still more extreme views and still more organizational fragmentation in an already fragmented extremist movement. (There are certain parallels here with some of the Muslim fundamentalist movements discussed elsewhere in this book.)

Organizational weakness has also often prevented elites within organizations from persuading members to accept common sets of ideas or programs of action. Nor can they effectively impose these things from above. Nor are members or constituent units of organization able to participate effectively in the development of a consensus view to which they might therefore adhere. The result is that there is precious little restraint on the behavior of those who—in any organization—tend toward extremism. There are exceptions to these generalizations, but not enough of them to undermine the basic point.

When organizational weakness is such a serious problem, people often look for substitutes to compensate for it. It is sometimes possible for strong, effective leadership to compensate—at least to a limited degree—for organizational inadequacy, but this has not happened in Sri Lanka. None of the senior politicians who have come to power in part because they appealed to Sinhalese extremist sentiments has ever succeeded for long in controlling or restraining the movement. The main reason is obvious and tautological—it is well nigh impossible for a single person standing at the apex of the political system to lead such a fragmented, chaotic, amorphous movement. But the specific failings of successive leaders also partly explain it.

Contrary to some reports, independent Sri Lanka has never had a leader who exercised a "charismatic" hold over his or her followers.[22] S. W. R. D. Bandaranaike turned out to be recklessly overgenerous with power and quickly squandered his authority. His widow, Sirimavo Bandaranaike, and Dudley Senanayake made enough concessions to Buddhist interests to win broad sympathy from them for a time. But the latter was again insufficiently canny and forceful, and while the former was tough enough to curb some of the more extravagantly destructive extremists, her governments so damaged the economy that extremism was fueled in another way. J. R. Jayewardene was the only leader to attempt to build a party organization, between 1973 and 1977, but for reasons that are still unclear, the organization fell apart after he assumed power in 1977. He drew extremists into his government in order to control them, but found in 1983 that he was too weak even to criticize their slaughter of unarmed Tamils. Since then, the movement has got quite beyond him and his successor, despite the latter's systematic brutalization of politics, which has even entailed threats of physical harm against cabinet ministers who express dissent on major issues.

The second possible substitute for good organization—though it is even less promising than the first—is rhetoric, which has a long history of use in Sri Lanka. Indeed it is the main means by which Sinhalese extremists have sought to recruit, inspire, and retain members and to structure their actions.

It succeeds well enough at the first three of these tasks but does little to structure these actions—indeed, it is remarkable how little the extremist movement demands of its members. It foments and focuses their grievances, but it does not ask that they restrain or discipline themselves in the interests of the movement. Indeed, incandescent and frequently hysterical extremist rhetoric invites people to indulge themselves, to let their anger take over. And since it is difficult to see how the extremist goal of Sinhalese Buddhist domination of the island can be realized without massive use of lethal force against the Tamil minority, this rhetoric impels people to self-indulgence of an exceedingly intolerant and violent kind.

Had better organizational structures been forged—structures like those several Indian parties have built up since independence, and which Jayewardene showed to be possible in Sri Lanka between 1973 and 1977—this movement might have relied less on rhetoric and thus been less extreme. A stronger organization might have made it possible for followers to restrain leaders from wayward, selfish, or extreme acts, for followers to feel less alienated, and for leaders to discipline followers who became destructive. The consensus building that tends to occur within strong organizational structures might have compelled people to compromise and given them a realistic understanding of what was politically feasible, what the limits were. In the absence of such structures, wildly unrealistic expectations tended to develop and persist. These inevitably produced frustration, which fed further extremism. Had stronger organizational structures existed, this movement might not have destroyed liberal political institutions, along with every hope of accommodation and minimally civilized social relations. It might not have encouraged people to resort to massacres as a matter of routine, at the cost of tens of thousands of lives. But that is what happened.

Notes

1. I am grateful to S. J. Tambiah and Richard Gombrich for clarifications on this point.

2. This "purist" category includes most of the people Gananath Obeyesekere refers to as "Protestant" Buddhists, but it would include others as well. See Obeyesekere, "Theodicy, Sin, and Salvation in a Sociology of Buddhism," in E. R. Leach, ed., *Dialectic in Practical Religion* (Cambridge, 1968), pp. 7–40.

3. R. Gombrich and G. Obeyesekere, *Buddhism Transformed: Religious Change in Sri Lanka* (Princeton, 1988); G. Obeyesekere, "Social Change among the Deities: The Rise of the Kataragama Cult in Sri Lanka," *Man,* December 1977, pp. 377–96; and G. Obeyesekere, *The Cult of the Goddess Patini* (Chicago, 1984).

4. Gombrich and Obeyesekere, *Buddhism Transformed,* p. 460. See also M. Roberts, ed., *Collective Identities, Nationalisms and Protest in Modern Sri Lanka* (Columbo, Sri Lanka, 1979).

5. See in this connection, D. E. Smith, "Religion, Politics, and the Myth of Reconquest," in R. N. Kearney and T. Fernando, eds., *Modern Sri Lanka* (Syracuse, 1979), pp. 83–99.

6. See Gombrich and Obeyesekere, *Bud-*

dhism Transformed; Obeyesekere, "Social Change among the Deities"; idem, *The Cult of the Goddess Patini.*

7. The estimate of the number of youths killed in the anti-JVP campaign emerges from careful calculations by a respected Sinhalese journalist who, for his own safety, cannot be identified. Evidence of the massacres of Tamil noncombatants by the security forces has appeared on numerous occasions since 1983 in the BBC World Service, *The Economist,* and the highly regarded Indian newspaper *The Hindu.* These and other sources have also documented terrorist actions by Tamils, most especially the Liberation Tigers of Tamil Eelam (LTTE), many of which have been spectacularly grotesque. But those actions and the politically insane assassination of Rajiv Gandhi by the LTTE should not distract us from the fact that the main source of terrorism in the period since 1983 has been the state.

8. J. Manor, *The Expedient Utopian: Bandaranaike and Ceylon* (Cambridge, 1989), and G. Obeyesekere, "The Origins and Institutionalization of Political Violence," in J. Manor, ed., *Sri Lanka in Change and Crisis* (London, 1984), pp. 153–75.

9. Fair elections have not occurred in Sri Lanka since malpractice by leaders of the ruling United National Party became the norm in late 1982. See P. Samarakone, "The Conduct of the Referendum," in J. Manor, *Sri Lanka in Change and Crisis,* pp. 84–117.

10. There was a brief decline in the frequency of Sinhalese-Tamil atrocities in the late 1980s, while the security forces and death squads concentrated on the slaughter of tens of thousands of Sinhalese in the JVP suspected of plotting insurrection. In the first three years of the 1990s, however, the previous vile pattern of Sinhalese-Tamil conflict has been revived, especially along the island's eastern coast.

11. The arguments presented in this section are set out in much greater detail in J. Manor, "The Failure of Political Integration in Sri Lanka," *Journal of Commonwealth*

and Comparative Politics 17 (March 1979): 21–46.

12. Ibid., pp. 24–27.

13. This figure is extrapolated from V. Kanesalingam, *A Hundred Years of Local Government in Ceylon* (Columbo, Sri Lanka, 1971), p. 195; and M. W. J. G. Mendis, *Local Government in Sri Lanka* (Columbo, Sri Lanka, 1976), Appendix 3 (j).

14. T. Gunasekera, "The Impact of National Level Politics on Regional and Local Level Politics in Sri Lanka" (Paper, London School of Economics, 1989).

15. Manor, "The Failure of Political Integration in Sri Lanka," pp. 28–29.

16. For more detail, see ibid., pp. 29–37. For evidence of the same trends in recent times, see Gunasekera, "The Impact of National Level Politics."

17. D. E. Smith, ed., *South Asian Politics and Religion* (Princeton, 1966); W. H. Wriggens, *Ceylon: Dilemmas of a New Nation* (Princeton, 1960); Manor, *The Expedient Utopian.*

18. See, for example, B. Matthews, "The Janata Vimukthi Peramuna and the Politics of the Underground in Sri Lanka," *Round Table* 312 (1982): 428.

19. See, for example, the case of the Eksath Bhikkhu Peramuna in Manor, *The Expedient Utopian,* chaps. 7 and 8.

20. Matthews, "Janata Vimukthi Peramuna," pp. 425–39; C. A. Chandraprema, "Putchism, Ethnic Chauvinism and Social Revolution" (Independent Studies Union, Colombo, Sri Lanka, 1989. I have also benefited from discussions on this and related matters with Eric Meyer of the Centre d'Etudes de l'Inde et de l'Asie du Sud, Paris, and with Jan Filipsky of the Oriental Institute, Prague.

21. Gombrich and Obeyesekere, *Buddhism Transformed,* p. 462.

22. In volume 2 of this series, Donald Swearer attributes charisma to S. W. R. D. Bandaranaike. After writing a biography of the man, however, I am strongly convinced that this is not true.

Movement Dynamics and Social Change: Transforming Fundamentalist Ideology and Organizations

Rhys H. Williams

The general purpose of volume 4 of the Fundamentalism Project is to examine and illuminate the relationships between the organizational characteristics of fundamentalist movements around the world and their changing worldviews, ideologies, and programs. Implicit is the assumption that "movements" are embodied, however imperfectly, in some type of "organization," however seemingly disorganized. More explicitly stated is the assumption that the ideological commitments of fundamentalist movements are not static, but evolve over time in relationship to organizational demands and changes. Tying these two points together is the understanding that both movement ideology and organization must respond to their societal environment—that fundamentalist movements are shaped by, even as they attempt to shape, their social, political, and religious contexts.

The twenty-seven chapters preceding this conclusion explore fundamentalist movements in many parts of the world, among most of the world's major religions. The wealth of detail and the immense variety within the religious impulses we term "fundamentalist" are almost intimidating. But paradoxically, this very variety is also testimony to the remarkable innovative capacity of religion and ultimately says something about the general human condition. It may well be that within the context of the modern world, fundamentalist religion appears as a generic human reaction. The task of this chapter is to distill some of the commonalities from these disparate cases and place them within an analytic framework that offers some generalized understandings. Thinking of the fundamentalisms examined here as "movements" is the point of departure. This essay treats fundamentalist movements as a specific type of social movement and examines their dynamic interactions among ideology, organization, and environment.

Thinking about Social Movements

What exactly is a "social movement?" As one might well imagine, that deceptively simple question is a matter of on-going dispute among the field's scholars. Depending on the analytic question at hand, definitional choices range from the broad: social movements are "socially shared activities and beliefs directed toward the demand for change in some aspect of the social order,"[1] to the narrow: "A social movement is a formally organized group that acts consciously and with some continuity to promote or resist change through collective action."[2] In the first approach, a social movement could be a collection of preferences, shared but largely inchoate; in such cases a social movement would be difficult to distinguish from public opinion or from a collective behavior such as a crowd or mob. Under the narrow definition, social movements must be formally organized—and are not essentially different from such organizations as interest groups or lobbying efforts. Further, the narrow definition leaves groups focused on *personal* rather than *social* transformation out of the definitional umbrella. This defintion is obviously less helpful for the study of religious movements.[3]

A useful middle ground is to refer to a movement as a social collectivity that "opposes the dominant institutional order and proposes alternative structural [and cultural] arrangements."[4] Social movements usually arise among groups who are (or feel) somewhat marginal to a society's sources of institutional power; they often use extra-institutional means (tactics, strategies) to try to accomplish their goals. Thus social movements are attempts by outsiders to affect changes in "the system," often by unconventional means. The system in question can be societal, political, religious, or cultural and can include the necessity of personal transformation. As the foregoing chapters show, most fundamentalist movements are interested in both personal and social transformation.

At the least, however, the term "movement" implies that something "moves." For religious movements, it connotes a sense of development and change, whether in the lives of individual believers, the faith tradition and its organizational forms, or the wider society and culture. Fundamentalist movements, first and foremost, are about change. To that extent, fundamentalist movements are built on dissatisfaction with what is perceived to be the predominant social order. In recent years, however, movement scholars have been careful not to overinterpret the status of that dissatisfaction. A consistent theme in this chapter is that movements generally, and fundamentalist movements in particular, are not irrational, reactionary convulsions by people who are suffering from falling social status (or perceive themselves to be). The "deprivation" and "compensation" models of movement genesis and activism have not held up empirically.[5] Rather, social, political, and religious movements are widely varying social phenomena that embody certain commonalities but must also be understood in their own terms. They can be both instrumental and expressive modes of collective action, have multiple "goals" of movement activity, and contain coalitions of different social groups as members.

A useful distinction is that between a social movement as a general collectivity and social movement *organizations*[6] as collectivities with consciously conceived goals and programs for achieving those goals. Social movement organizations (SMOs) are usually accompanied by the accoutrements of "formal" organization, such as a recognized leadership, a formal name, and a set of routinized, coordinated activities, some of which are designed to distinguish members from nonmembers. Many, if not most, empirical studies of social movements are in fact studies of social movement organizations. Indeed, social *movements* are reasonably thought of as fairly loose coalitions of social movement *organizations*.[7]

Social movement organizations should be kept distinct from other types of organizations, however. They are not as institutionalized, with regular access to established power, as are interest groups.[8] And unlike voluntary associations such as fraternal groups or church congregations, SMOs exist explicitly for the purpose of sponsoring some type of change, and are thus usually ideologically and instrumentally driven.[9] But SMOs within one movement can be very different from each other. Specific SMOs within the same overall social movement may in fact be competitors as they vie with each other for members, financial resources, and legitimacy with the public or the government. The problems confronting fundamentalist movement organizations, as they try to balance the demands of their theology and their societal environments, is one of the central foci of this volume.

This chapter discusses fundamentalist movements as a type of social movement in terms of three distinct, but necessarily overlapping, levels of analysis. First, movement *ideology* is discussed as having both "internal" and "external" roles. Internally, ideology is important in both recruiting new adherents to the movement and then mobilizing them to become active in movement activities. Externally, ideology is a resource that movements wield in their attempts at affecting institutional change; it is part of a movement's strategic "tool kit."[10] Second, the importance of the movement *environment* is examined. The wider social contexts in which movements are located are crucial in both constraining and facilitating their activities. For the purposes of this essay I divide the social environment into the political-economic environment and the cultural-religious environment. Third, I focus directly on movement *organizations* as the collectivities that mediate between the social environment and the ideological impulses that are the heart of fundamentalism. In particular, I focus on aspects of organizational membership, leadership, and institutionalization.

The distinctions used here are analytic levels of analysis; the empirical world is not so neatly divided. Indeed it is the *interactions* among ideology, organization, and environment that are most interesting. But analytic distinctions are useful ways to see various dimensions in movements that might otherwise go unnoticed. Within each analytic level I use the rich empirical descriptions of the previous chapters to illustrate the usefulness of a social movement approach and to learn something about fundamentalism as a general religious phenomenon.

Movement Ideology: Recruitment, Mobilization, and Strategy

Social movements are distinguished by the central role ideology plays in their purposes, programs, and operations. By definition, movements are attempts at some type of change, often articulated with a great degree of clarity.

Yet change happens to movements as well as to society. SMOs are transformed by their interactions with the world even as they attempt to transform their surroundings. Many organizations can undergo substantial ideological change and yet remain viable as organizations. For example, the need to win elections—a political party's raison d'être—often requires that the party's ideological positions be adjusted to take into account changes in the electorate. And many colleges and universities have changed their statements of purpose and mission, adjusting both their philosophies of education as well as the types of people they seek to educate. Such changes accompany dramatic shifts in organization.

Ideological change is a more delicate task for social movements and their organizations. Social movements' ideological appeals are central to their existence: to recruitment strategies that attract new members; to members' loyalty through the fostering of distinct identities; to mobilizing the membership for activities aimed at accomplishing change; and, as tools for waging struggles with other organizations or governments. The centrality of ideological appeals is particularly salient for fundamentalist ideologies that rest upon an unalterable truth. The need to be both timeless and timely results in considerable "ideological work."[11] And the extent to which a movement organization can experience ideological development and remain fundamentalist is an important conceptual question.[12]

In addressing the varied roles ideology plays in movements' lives, and its centrality to fundamentalism, scholars have made distinctions between ideology's internal processes of recruitment and mobilization, and external dimensions of strategy.

Recruitment

While it is accurate to observe that movements recruit members through ideological appeals, it is important to understand how this is done. Two common views misunderstand this process, one by slighting individuals' reasons for participation, the other by granting individuals more discretion than is warranted. The first approach comes from the "mass society" or "collective behavior" traditions.[13] Briefly, this approach asserts that with the rise of modernity, individuals are increasingly cut off from traditional social attachments such as religion and extended families. Such rootless individuals experience "anomie" or a state of normlessness and are thus susceptible to the recruitment appeals of demagogues and social movements. Collective behavior thus becomes a mass expression of individualized discontents. The growth of many "totalizing" movements, from the Nazis to religious fundamentalists, has been attributed to the effects of mass society.

At the other end of the spectrum, a school of thought generally termed "rational choice" theory treats individuals as "ideological consumers," picking and choosing among competing movement ideologies until they find one in accord with their personal preferences, then joining that movement. In this view, individuals are hyperrational, weighing the costs and benefits of participation and acting only when they obtain a "good deal." Participation that does not yield obvious benefits is thus "irrational." And the biggest challenge for social movements is to control the "free rider" problem; that is, if individuals can benefit from a movement's success without having to participate in its activities, they will do so. Movements must control free riders by offering "selective incentives" for participants.[14]

Both the mass society and rational choice approaches to movements lead to a focus on the psychological makeup of individuals and the structure of their preferences. Recruitment and participation are understood as essentially individualized behaviors. Accordingly, extremist social movements are thought to be the expression of the (often irrational) dissatisfaction or maladjustment of the individuals composing them.

More sociological perspectives on movement recruitment offer a different understanding. Lone individuals are less likely targets of recruitment than are persons tied into some social network.[15] With regard to religion, this seems obvious in societies where identification is tied strongly to ethnic, clan, or family identities. But it also holds for societies where religion is marked by an ethos of voluntarism, such as the United States and parts of Europe.[16] And it is true for voluntary associations other than religion. Friends and friends of friends are the social pathways through which a movement's appeal is carried, interpreted, and made to seem reasonable. Face-to-face interactions are what sociologists call the "micro-context"[17] of movement recruitment—where movement messages are passed along, and the movement's activities are made to seem plausible, reasonable, and even necessary.

Some insights into the nature and process of movement recruitment can be generated by thinking of the process as a form of conversion.[18] There is an entire literature on conversion that can only be touched upon here, but the dynamic quality that ideology adds to the process is worth mentioning. Conversion is basically a process of constructing a new identity, not just adopting new beliefs; for movements the new identity must be disposed toward some type of activism and is thus usefully termed "collective identity."[19] The process is both psychological and interpersonal as bridges to an older life are burned and new bridges built to those persons and groups who reinforce the new identity.

The fact that movement recruitment travels along social pathways explains why recruitment tends to happen among similarly situated people. While stories of Damascus-road-type personal transformations are dramatic (and in accord with American cultural tendencies to understand the world in individualist and psychological categories), more often recruitment and conversion happen through more gradual processes such as "role learning" and the transformation of the "universe of discourse."[20] Persons do not adopt new identities wholesale, but learn their roles as movement members—and the appropriate beliefs that go with membership—as they become progressively more affiliated with a group. Beliefs generally require social supports;[21] thus persons with social networks to support their emerging beliefs (and social roles) are more likely to make a longer-term commitment to a new movement. Thus, far from working out their personal problems, people become active in movements that provide them and their peers with a critical understanding of a social problem and a plausible accounting of how to change it. Ideology articulated by movement leaders, and among movement members, offers recruits and converts the interpretive tools to make sense of their change of identity and to justify it.

The extent to which recruitment is tied to social networks is evident in the consistent success fundamentalist movements have recruiting among students, as Dario Zadra's chapter on Comunione e Liberazione in Italy demonstrates. This movement is not the product of normlessness among students, but just the reverse: student subcultures develop distinct ways of understanding the world, based on students' status as only partially integrated into adult society, but keenly aware of its problems. The message of change offered by fundamentalist movements thus has both a network to carry it and a "resonance" with students' lives that makes it plausible to whole groups, not individuals deciding in isolation.[22] That student subcultures are fertile places for fundamentalist movements is also demonstrated dramatically by the fact that Jewish fundamentalism is based in yeshivas—religious academies.

Tod Swanson (chap. 4) discusses patterns of conversion in Ecuador and demonstrates how village and clan ties are the pathways along which the new religious spirit has traveled. The Puruha's social life, organized around the fiestas that transferred *suerte* (religious power), could not be completely abandoned, even with the conversion to teetotaling Protestantism. Rather, conversion has transformed fiestas into *conferencias,* while the important roles of ritual kinship affirmation and communication of social status remain intact. Thus conversions are necessarily connected to clan and village social networks. Swanson notes that Puruha conversion testimonies even have a corporate character—relating to Puruha history, not just personal biography.

Mobilization

Recruitment and conversion are processes of the reconstruction of identity, both personal and social. Movements have a particular interest in ensuring that the new identities of recruits are couched in group terms and are accompanied by an imperative for participation in movement activities. In that sense, the crucial test for movement ideology is whether it can successfully mobilize members to struggle for social change. Mobilization starts by providing movement members with a clear understanding of the conditions the movement is committed to change.

In many ways movement ideology helps to *create* the problems that the movement itself proposes to solve. Of course, the fundamentalist religious movements discussed in this volume "create" neither the secularism nor the modern culture to which they are opposed. But they do create "secular modern culture" *as a problem* that requires the answers they provide. The dynamics of problem construction and movement mobilization are currently understood as a matter of "framing activities."[23]

Frames are the "schemata of interpretation" that people use "to locate, perceive, identify, and label"[24] events and occurrences in their world. That is, frames give meaning to events, organize experiences, and provide guides for actions. To use slightly different metaphors, they are "templates" that provide "models of" and "models for" thinking about the world.[25] Framing is important and necessary ideological work, for movements must define and explain the social world within which they operate to current and potential members, onlookers, and opponents. This process is often thought of as "frame alignment"—"the linkage of individual and social movement interpretive orientations, such that some set of individual interests, values and beliefs and SMO activities, goals, and ideology are congruent and complementary."[26]

Implied in the concept of "alignment" is the idea that both *movement* frames and *individuals* must go through processes of adjustment and development if mobilization is to occur. Individuals must be able, to some significant extent, to align their personal frameworks of meaning with the ideological orientations offered by the movement. Concomitantly, movements adapt their symbolic appeals to take account of members' frames (e.g., beliefs, values, or understandings) even as they offer persuasive reasons why individuals should adapt their personal frames to accommodate the movement's ideology.

Given that movements are collectivities in pursuit of change, their framing is often done in terms of a social, religious, or political "problem" that requires action. Movements rhetorically construct social problems through frames that define what the problem *is* ("diagnostic frames"), what should be *done* about it ("prescriptive frames"), who has the *responsibility* for doing it, and why action is *imperative* ("motivational frames").[27] That is, as a problem is named and its dimensions identified, a movement's frames are simultaneously establishing those responsible for causing the situation and advancing their own credentials for solving the problem. Or in other terms, movement frames first establish the "ownership" and then the "responsibility" for a social problem.[28] The problem, the solution, and the social groups responsible are all contained, at least implicitly, in the movement's frames.

Once a social problem is identified and the appropriate victims, villains, and heros located, movements must still motivate people to act. The mere existence of grievances is not enough. Many people will agree with any given movement frame; the more difficult task is to prompt significant numbers of those people to activism. The "motivational frame" must identify both who should act and why they should do so. This calls for an "injustice frame."[29]

Injustice frames are ideological and symbolic constructions that locate a social movement's identified problems and proposed solutions in a moral order, with an accompanying imperative toward action. Grievances that are understood as involving "fate" or "private troubles" are transformed into grievances involving issues of public justice: "what was previously seen as an unfortunate but tolerable situation is now defined as inexcusable, unjust or immoral."[30] And just as importantly, while blame for the problem is externalized, responsibility for the solution is internalized. Thus there is a moral dimension to almost every social movement: things are wrong; they can and should be changed; my involvement will help produce that change.

Religion readily produces the injustice frames needed to problematize social arrangements and organize the motivations that induce people to act on the perceived injustice: "The members of [religious] institutions tend to feel their cause is not only advantageous but just, [so] their sense of injustice can be far greater than that of antagonists in a purely economic relationship."[31] Religious worldviews that are particularly moralistic and have well-articulated boundaries between the moral and the immoral—such as fundamentalisms—are thus particularly well suited to producing injustice frames and activist movements.

There is a long history of attributing religion's main political impact to the fostering of submission, resignation, and quiescence to "worldly" power arrangements.[32]

As this multivolume series makes unmistakably clear, there is nothing intrinsically necessary about that relationship. When the conditions warrant, religion has provided the impetus for many politically charged movements, from fundamentalism to liberation theology. For religious people the stakes are high—often nothing less than God's will and their immortal souls are at issue. When movement mobilization requires the moral outrage necessary to power an "injustice frame" the vocabularies and social networks of religion are especially well suited as carriers.

At the same time one must not overestimate how smoothly movements can be mobilized through ideological framing. Frames are just that—frameworks offered by movement actors in the hope that others will understand them as they are intended. But there is always room for considerable interpretation. There are certain limitations imposed by the logic of framing itself that may keep any given frame from being as effective as intended.

For example, it is often the case that the more persuasive a "diagnostic frame" ("things really are terrible because the world is in the grip of a powerful evil"), the more difficult it is for the accompanying "motivational frame" to be persuasive ("what can I do about a problem so overwhelming, even if I want to?"). Many types of movements have faced this dilemma—whether they are revolutionary movements against the entire "system," movements attempting to end the threat of nuclear war, or movements fighting Satan-inspired evil to restore an entire nation to its moral senses.

Susan Harding (chap. 3) offers a valuable analysis of the ideological work American fundamentalist clergy performed in the late 1970s and 1980s to transform premillennial resignation and political withdrawal into an activist concern with the affairs of this world. Protestants convinced by premillennial theology held a vision of the ultimate fruitlessness of human activity before the Second Coming and were less concerned with conventional politics.[33] But, as Harding documents, Jerry Falwell, Hal Lindsey, and others drew on distinctly fundamentalist understandings of history and human action to portray the absolute necessity of participating in God's plans for the world, including reform of human institutions. The logic of dispensational history is a timeless struggle between good and evil in which humans participate. During the Last Days, Christians must respond through holy living and political action if the nation is to be saved from its sins. Dispensationalism became a frame that mobilized fundamentalists into urgent engagement with the world, for, as Harding tells us, it "renarrated the pattern of history and the place of born-again believers in that history."

Strategy

Movement frames are external, strategic resources as well as tools of recruitment and mobilization. When used in their strategic capacity they are directed less at current and potential members than at onlookers and opponents—and they become "public" properties. Frames are the weapons with which movements fight their battles; they function at several levels of political struggle.

First, frames are designed to capture the terms of the public political debate. Every political issue is talked about with particular terms and not with others—the terms with which an issue is discussed are what constitute the issue, as, for example, an "economic" or a "moral" issue.[34] In that sense every issue has a "culture," a set of terms, symbols, or general understandings that surround the issue, making it what it is. But issue cultures are not pre-given; they are products of the various frames offered by the groups competing for influence on the issue.

The various frames connected to an issue define what the issue is, how it could be solved, and who should do it. So frames legitimate both the involvement of groups as well as their proposals. Thus, when a fundamentalist movement frames the question of women's voting rights as a backsliding from adherence to Shari'a, it is identifying a social or political problem and proposing a solution to it. But simultaneously the frame explains why it is appropriate for the movement to speak out on this issue, and why it is uniquely qualified to offer its solution. In this case, the movement's frame establishes the movement itself as the guardian and interpreter of religion in the society. The frame establishes women's votes as a "religious" issue, qualifying the movement to speak to it.

That frames function in this way often seems so natural that it is hard to notice. When Christian fundamentalists protest the absence of school prayer, or Jewish fundamentalists object to automobile traffic on the Sabbath, or Islamic fundamentalists demonstrate against popular literature with revealing photographs, they are seen as protecting their core values, their "turf" as it were. In many societies the "naturally" religious turf has become the areas of private life and personal morality. And indeed, fundamentalist groups have had powerful impacts in those areas, as demonstrated by the series's second volume, *Fundamentalisms and Society.*[35] It seems natural that religious groups should have attitudes toward, and a legitimate right to speak to, issues that touch their beliefs directly. Thus "defensive" actions by fundamentalist groups are often quite effective in defending the group from outside incursions. If necessary, of course, fundamentalist movements establish alternative institutions, such as religious schools, to keep the secular world at bay.

But fundamentalism often entails "wholistic" worldviews, leading to struggles over issues less "naturally" in religion's home domain. Indeed, the separation of the world into public and private spheres, with the relegation of religion to the latter, is a particular bête noire of fundamentalist movement organizations (an issue engaged below). Fundamentalists have contested issues of political representation (for example, the Moral Majority in the United States), foreign policy (the Gush Emunim in Israel), and economic development (e.g., contenders in Iran's Islamic Republic). In those cases, fundamentalists must make a case as to why their frames should be privileged. The debate over public political issues is primarily a series of efforts by various groups to win acceptance for their particular categorizations of the issues in the face of competing efforts by other groups on behalf of different ones.

That religious groups have been so successful in gaining a platform in contemporary public politics is testimony to what has been termed "cultural power."[36] Several dimensions of cultural power are particularly relevant to the study of religion and deserve explanation here. First is the power and authority attached to the social status of religiously credentialed people—the *symbolics* of clergy and faith generally. This phenomenon is particularly evident where the manifestations of religious status, such as clerical collars, yamulkes, or untrimmed beards, are important. The symbols signify that the promoter of the ideological frame is connected to religious knowledge and authority. The moral imperative of the frame is reinforced with signs of institutional authority, personal devotion, and sacrifice. This form of cultural power is particularly powerful for people connected to organized religious groups. Their public discourse is immediately recognizable as religiously legitimate because they wear the signs of organizational authority—a form of power.[37]

The use of visual symbols of religious authority to substantiate one's claim to public space is particularly valuable for fundamentalist movements. Fundamentalist groups place a premium on boundaries between themselves and others. These boundaries are often marked by distinctive patterns of dress for members. They become clear symbols in public politics as well. Political actors are immediately identifiable as Sikhs, or Hasidim, or ulama. To the extent that their religious identification has any cultural legitimacy, their recognizable identity gives their political positions instant credibility. In contrast, liberal-secular political actors have much less visual flair, and their religious-political symbolism is concomitantly more difficult to communicate.

Ousmane Kane's analysis (chap. 18) of the personal authority carried by Islamic ulama in Nigeria is another example of the power of status symbolics. While the Izala movement has gone through several organizational manifestations, including schisms, it continues to produce reformist-minded preachers who take its message into Nigeria's urban centers and parts of rural northern Nigeria. Even the government's crackdown on neo-Izala SMOs, and prison terms for movement leaders, contributed to movement legitimacy within non-Izala populations. Kane notes that visible symbols, such as the common practice of wearing talismans by traditionalist Muslims (non-Izala), became a focal point for religious tension.

The second dimension of cultural power important here is the *moral authority* that appends to religion as a general cultural system. This authority is distinct from the direct symbols of institutional or organized religious authority; it is a matter of general cultural legitimacy. It is not the institutional location of the carrier of the ideological frame that is decisive, but rather the receptivity of the cultural "field" into which the frame is entered. Direct connections to recognized organizations are secondary.

In a cultural setting in which religion has a generalized legitimacy, moral authority and the cultural power that goes with it may be available to non-"clergy" as well as to those institutionally credentialed. Since the authority is in the frame itself, and not the individual's connection to an organization, laity can activate cultural power. The inherently egalitarian component in religion leaves some room for new interpretations (if not revelations) that are based in the believers' relationship to the divine, not on the credential-granting functions of institutions. Personal religious experiences provide a space between the individual and institutionalized hierarchical systems.

There are many clear examples of this "populist" dynamic in Christianity where new revelations have led to new churches and new "religions." Particularly among

Protestants, the institutionalized church has had difficulty holding a monopoly on religious authority—sectarianism and schism are rife. But Dario Zadra's account of the predominantly lay movement Comunione e Liberazione (CL) also demonstrates this effect in Roman Catholicism; while the locus of authority remains in the organization, it is laity—not the clerical hierarchy—who directs the movement's organizations. Even in Islam, where revelation ended with the Prophet, the practice of *ijtihad* has offered new religious voices the opportunity to assume the mantle of religious and moral authority.

Thus, many forms of fundamentalism have used the space between the subjective experience of religious truth and institutional credentials to gain autonomy from established religious organizations. In turn it is important to note how movements then use religion's attendant cultural power in battles with secular and ecclesiastical organizational structures. The many "special purpose groups"—organizational coalitions across denominational or faith boundaries that pursue religiously inspired political agendas—stand as evidence for this form of cultural power.[38]

Perhaps the clearest example of fundamentalist groups attempting to draw on a general cultural legitimacy for their particularistic frames is the coalition of the Rashtriya Swayamsevak Sangh (RSS) and Vishva Hindu Parishad (VHP) in India. Historically Hinduism has lacked the organized institutional structures, clear clerical authority, and established scriptural canon that Islam or Christianity has. The RSS-VHP are establishing an organized Hinduism even as they call for a return to the foundations of the faith. As the chapters by Ainslie Embree (chap. 22) and Peter van der Veer (chap. 23) demonstrate, these groups are taking the heretofore generalized association between Hindu practices and Indian culture as the legitimating basis for regularizing a set of religious and political beliefs, and firmly locating religion's cultural power under their organizational umbrella. Whereas many Western fundamentalist movements have de-centered institutional religious authority, these Hindu nationalist groups are attempting the reverse. Van der Veer mentions the irony of the attempt at producing a homogenized, national Hinduism to give form to the traditional cultural association—even as that form is tied to the political interests of particular groups of Hindus. It is a clear expression of cultural power—movement frames activating cultural symbols for clear political impact.

That religion is so clearly identified with moral authority is a historical phenomenon that varies from culture to culture. The strength of the association is an aspect of the "cultural environment" in which a religious tradition exists. But it is important to note the efficacy that the aura of moral authority lends to the ideological frames used by fundamentalist movements. By basing their appeals in religion, fundamentalist movements automatically align themselves with what is framed as good and valuable and worth preserving in the culture. Further, movement representatives can present themselves as *disinterested* participants, involved with public politics out of a sense of duty and righteousness, not personal gain. The fact that many movement members have made significant personal sacrifices for their beliefs only reinforces their claims. And of course, fundamentalist ideology is premised on a transcendent standard of right and wrong, good and evil. By their own accounting, fundamentalist frames are beyond the vagaries of human life; they call society to a place where all humankind stands to benefit from divine favor. Whatever the divisiveness of their actions, fundamentalist movements have an ideological cultural power with the moral authority to speak to all who hear it.

That fundamentalist movement ideology can so easily activate religion's moral authority within the wider culture is another of the ironies of fundamentalisms and modernity. A de-sectarianized respect for religion—a "civic religious" sentiment in the United States [39]—provides a cultural space available to fundamentalist appeals. Religion has a widespread public legitimacy even among many of those not personally religious. Yet that very generalized cultural religion is something that fundamentalist religion opposes. Where cultural religion blurs boundaries, fundamentalism focuses on them. Where cultural religion downplays divisive sectarian identities, fundamentalist religion often promotes them. Even so, the legitimacy of religion generally extends to fundamentalism. A paradox of the cultural power of moral authority is that it is particularly available as a resource to movements that oppose the conditions of its existence.

There is, of course, a dark side to the cultural power of the interpretive frames used by religious movements. The power of the frames is not always something that can be controlled completely by the groups who enter them into public discourse. Once symbols are loosed into the public arena, they can take on a vitality of their own—a Pandora's box phenomenon in which the power of the symbols is such that no group truly "owns" them. James Manor's chapter on Sri Lanka (chap. 27) demonstrates a tragic consequence of this type of symbolic autonomy: no matter who enters public politics and with what intentions, the powerful symbolic constructions of Sinhalese extremism sweep the society toward violence. It is a cultural cycle that seems unbreakable.

In a less violent but still instructive example, studies of the Islamization campaign in Pakistan have illuminated how the symbolic importance of Islamization has a life independent of the interests of the fundamentalist groups who would presumably stand to gain from it.[40] While many people do not fully support Islamization, few public figures dare oppose the goal. As a result, the call for Islamization is more powerful than the groups promoting it. Even the Jama'at-i-Islami itself has suffered organizationally, as Rafiuddin Ahmed notes in this volume (chap. 24). Not only has the Jama'at-i-Islami failed to realize all its goals (even within Muslim Pakistan) and been forced into collaborative actions with groups whom it distrusts ideologically, but Maududi (Jama'at's founder) was declared a *kafir* on charges of distorting Islam. Thus can a revolution devour its own.

It is common, in both popular wisdom and scholarly commentary, to treat movement ideology as a whole. There is an assumption that movements (or movement organizations) have *an* ideology and that it is relatively uniform in its meaning and interpretation. But contemporary anthropological and sociological work on symbolism takes the opposite view. That is, symbols and their meanings are understood as "constructed"—people create and interpret meanings in the process of interaction. In this case, symbol ambiguity (or "multivocality") is regarded as a virtue, allowing many people to rally around shared symbols even if their meaning is only partially shared.[41] Certainly the extent to which a movement's ideology is coherent and uniform varies, but the important point is that ideology is by nature internally complex, adaptive, and multivocal. That is precisely why it is such a valuable resource to all types of social movements. By dividing ideology into dimensions of recruitment, mobilization, and strategy, I have made analytical distinctions among processes that overlap in the lives of actual movements—an interaction shown clearly in the preceding chapters.

Movement Environment: The Societal and Cultural Contexts

The environment in which a religious, political, or social movement exists plays a crucial role in shaping the timing, nature, direction, and to some extent even the content of the movement itself. As Robert Wuthnow and Matthew Lawson demonstrate in this volume (chap. 2), taking the "environment" seriously has many analytic benefits. "Organizational ecology" is a way of thinking about the lifecycles and characteristics of organizations by understanding them as responding to the social climate in the same ways as organisms respond to the natural world. Movements' lifecycles and success are influenced by such factors as competition for resources (e.g., members or money), population density, functional specialization, and structural niche. The overall population of organizations becomes the level of analysis; its dynamics shape individual SMOs. Several chapters illustrate this principle by chronicling the rise and fall of various movement organizations: Kane notes that the Izala movement prospered and then declined as its itinerant preachers tried to expand beyond its geographic base in the north; and Legrain's organizational chronology documents the extent to which the competition among SMOs within Palestinian populations has led to a fragmented, rather than coherent, movement agenda.

Yet the organizational ecology perspective does not place much importance on understanding human agency. One can be an "ecologist" without having to be concerned with why people act as they do, and indeed, without giving human actions much credence for movement success or failure. Ecologists treat the fate of individual movements more as an aspect of the impersonal laws of the organizational environment than of the decisions, meanings, and struggles of actors themselves. As a result, organizational ecology is more useful in describing the general "population" of organizations than it is in explaining the fate of any given SMO.

Concepts associated with ecological thinking are most useful in providing an understanding of the relative *opportunities* social environments provide to specific movement organizations. If social movements are to exist, let alone succeed, they must mobilize organizational and symbolic resources. The societal environment is the source of most of those necessary resources. But it is essential to keep in mind that the social, cultural, and organizational environment itself is not static; it changes to accommodate movement dynamics just as movements respond to environmental "demands." Thus understanding environments, as well as considering movements' own understanding of their contexts, is a necessary complement to ideological analysis.

The overriding context for fundamentalist religion is "modernity." While debates as to what exactly constitutes the modern world are too lengthy to engage here, there is no denying that there have been basic shifts in social organization in most of the world's societies in the last two centuries. Whatever the cause or pace of these changes, three dimensions of modern social organization are both common and particularly worthy of note.

The first dimension is an "institutional differentiation" in which the polity, the economy, religion, and the family (as well as other institutions) are distinct spheres of life, with distinct norms of behavior and appropriate forms of knowledge. This has led to a "disarticulation of statuses" in that personal or group status in one institution is not automatically transferable—or related—to status in other institutions (of course, this has been more true for men than for women and is true to varying degrees in different societies). Finally, the result is a "compartmentalization" of everyday life, in which persons must use institution-specific norms, ideas, and behaviors to negotiate daily living, bracketing other identities.[42]

In societies where the development of modernity has been justified by norms connected to classical liberalism, capitalism, and governmental democracy, the processes of differentiation, disarticulation, and compartmentalization have resulted in a distinction between "public" and "private" life. Such a distinction leads increasingly to an understanding of religion as more relevant to the private sphere (i.e., family life and voluntary expressive relationships). Ironically, both secularists and fundamentalists agree that modern societies are necessarily marked by a public-private distinction, although they clearly evaluate the situation differently. John Garvey accurately analyzes most contemporary fundamentalist *political* challenges as attempts at reconfiguring the public/private separation.[43]

Some groups, like the Jewish haredi, attempt to maintain a way of life that antedates the development of the modern world. This tends to produce what Samuel Heilman (chap. 8), Haym Soloveitchik (chap. 9), and others in this volume call a "defensive" fundamentalism, striving to keep the modern world out of its temple (both literally and figuratively). In contrast, other groups are creating new worlds, either through a selective merger of "traditional" values with contemporary technology (such as American televangelists) or newly fusing religious, ethnic, and national identities (such as the RSS-VHP in India or the Sinhalese in Sri Lanka). In these cases the public-private distinction calls for an aggressive activism, where public institutions are made accountable to religious standards and private lives are understood to be relevant to the moral health of the entire community.

While the public-private distinction may be anathema to many fundamentalist movements, the stance taken toward these three dimensions of modern social organization illuminates the paradoxical relationships between fundamentalism and modernity: fundamentalisms reject modernity ideologically even as modernity provides the necessary context for fundamentalist movements. Further, fundamentalist movements often use modernity to their strategic advantage, even as it is a foil in their ideological constructions of the good society. A few brief examples make this point.

Because religion has legitimacy within the private sphere, and as an institution is distinct from governmental polity, fundamentalist groups have a relatively easy time constructing a world distinct from the incursions of either the state or other institutions. "Defensive" fundamentalism is common; movements keep their own terrain religiously pure by claiming that they are free from any obligation to allow public institutions or norms into their world. Thus fundamentalist ideological frames are "privileged" in that the language of liberal secularism constrains the state from interfering with their community. They can use the compartmentalization of religion into the private realm as a cultural "free space" to create alternative institutions and lives.

Relatedly, institutional differentiation has often given religious organizations an advantage in the use of political rhetoric. As carriers of the "moral" in society, religious groups are uniquely positioned to make authoritative pronouncements on the moral acceptability of certain public issues. Moral authority becomes a form of "expertise" that is useful in the struggle to define the terms of political discourse.[44] And when reform of the secular world fails to meet utopian religious expectations, the compartmentalization of life makes possible the return to a "private" sphere of religious purity. The tendency for contemporary fundamentalists to build alternative institutions in order to institutionalize their commitments makes this option viable, but further reinforces the distinction between public and private life.

Thus modernity is the "macro-context" for contemporary fundamentalism, and many of the present chapters document attempts at challenging or reversing aspects of the three dimensions described above. For our present purposes in understanding the dynamics of movements, I consider the modern world's movement environment to be distinguishable into two broad contexts: political-economic and cultural-religious.

Political-Economic Contexts

Consider first the political environment in which movements exist. "Political" here has two different connotations. First, it calls to mind the important and often central role of the state in modern societies. Second, the political is the entire collection of activities involved as competing social groups struggle for power and rewards.

One of the hallmarks of the "modern world" has been the increasing size, centralization, and authority of the central state apparatus. In the industrialized capitalist world, the so-called liberal welfare state has reached into health, education, and family life in a manner unprecedented a century ago, virtually creating many of the church-state tensions that appear in many countries.[45] Socialist states, to the extent they still exist, explicitly use the state to remake civil society to accord with centralized political principles. And in much of the developing world the heritage of colonialism has too often left precarious states astride fractious civil societies; such states are forced to cling tenaciously to all the power and authority they can muster, often at the expense of democracy and human rights.

In keeping with the general trend in which societal power increasingly resides in a centralizing state, the nature of social movement action has also changed. As Charles Tilly has noted, it is only against the backdrop of the modern state that the "national social movement" has arisen. In feudal and semifeudal societies, collective actions were local and more fragmented. With the creation of nation-states came national opposition movements.[46] Since movements often tend to be "politics by other [i.e., noninstitutionalized] means,"[47] as states have become the locus of power, those wanting to either gain or protect power have had to tangle with the state.

That the modern state plays a role in the creation and nature of contemporary fundamentalism is undeniable. An entire volume of the Fundamentalism Project[48] is devoted to the important topic of the relationships between fundamentalisms and states. Without recapitulating the entire argument here, it is important to note that in many cases it is *actions by the state itself* that provide the precipitating incident for fundamentalist activism. Attempts at regulating aspects of civil society heretofore unregulated (such as family law), or changing the legal status of certain salient practices (such as the legalization of abortion), or changing the definition of the state's legitimate sphere (such as the annexation of territory) have been rallying points for Islamic, Christian, and Jewish fundamentalisms.

Repression directed by the state has also kept fundamentalist movements intrinsically intertwined with the center of secular power. Repression can mean direct coercion against an entire group, such as India's current campaign against the RSS, or Israel's stance toward the Palestinian group Hamas. More commonly, states suppress only those activities that threaten social order, as when they cracked down on Operation Rescue's abortion clinic blockades,[49] Gush Emunim's deliberately provocative settlements, or Egypt's Muslim Brotherhood.[50] Less direct forms of repression, such as surveillance or administrative harassment, often control movement actions without raising the specter of violence or religious civil war.

Within democratic polities, states seeking to neutralize fundamentalisms may choose a policy of co-optation or symbolic appeasement rather than direct confrontation. Occasionally the symbols of democratization serve such a purpose by giving fundamentalist groups a stake in the government (through, for example, portfolios in the cabinet) and a popular identification with it.[51] In this volume, for example, Gehad Auda (chap. 15) documents the attempt at "normalization" between Egypt's state and the "Islamic movement." Alternating selective repression with concessions and attempts at co-optation, including the occasional de facto recognition of the Muslim Brotherhood, three different Egyptian regimes tried to contain Islamic radicalism while simultaneously benefiting from Islam's political legitimacy. As a result, Islamic political principles are well established in Egypt's political culture (but less well in its governmental bureaucracies), while radical violence is pushed to the edges of the Islamic movement. In a similar manner, SMOs within the Islamic movement, particularly the Muslim Brotherhood, have also tried alternating strategies of cooperation and militance. Continued economic crises, of course, may make the state's manipulations moot.

Several chapters in this volume offer examples of societies where the state is the *reward* of political action rather than the adversary of fundamentalist movement struggles. James Manor's analysis of Sri Lanka is one such case. The weakness of the Sri Lankan state vis-à-vis its larger neighbor or its competing ethnopolitical groups gives it little autonomy of action. David Stoll's chapter on Guatemala (chap. 5) illustrates a similar dynamic. While Ríos Montt did not institutionalize evangelical Protestantism within the state apparatus, his reign nonetheless made it clear how fragile the government's handle is on Guatemalan society. Traditional governmental practices are being challenged by a new religious ethos, and the close identification of the government with the interests of Catholic elites or secular militarists is now disrupted.

Analysis of the political environment that spawns fundamentalist movements cannot be limited to just the state. The institutions and organizations of "civil society" are often the most important political context. Any given fundamentalist movement must compete or (perhaps) cooperate with other social groups. A point made consistently by many contributors to the Fundamentalism Project is that fundamentalisms are products of nonhomogeneous societies. Only in societies where there are competing options is it necessary to declare so vigorously that there can be one and only one correct choice. Pluralism, with its threat of an easy tolerance that weakens religious commitment itself, is the yeast of many a fundamentalist movement.[52]

Heterogeneity need not be at the national level and is ideologically "constructed" as much as it is a social structural "fact." As demonstrated in the section on Judaism in this volume, the encroachment of pluralism on a subculture can have fundamentalism-producing effects. The taken-for-granted life of the Eastern European shtetl, with its tradition-bound Judaism-as-a-way-of-life, was disrupted and dispersed. One could no longer observe religious life as it had always been observed—that way of life was gone. Instead, Jews found themselves comprising subcultures in several rapidly changing and modernizing countries. The condition was ripe for the rise of a text-based fundamentalism that could provide the certainty of interpretation once offered by a tradition-bound culture.

The South Asian subcontinent is perhaps the clearest example of a pluralistic political context creating the conditions for fundamentalist activism. As Robert Frykenberg notes (in chap. 21), in a setting where the population is divided among several distinct major religions, the gains of any one religious group are readily interpreted as losses for other groups. Particularly for fundamentalist groups with "totalizing" worldviews, rival movements' successes become almost intolerable. Certainly in India the state is a major political actor, but it is hardly the only one against which fundamentalist movements strive. Further, it has become impossible for the state to play an "honest broker" role any longer. To try to do so violates the ideological frames of the Hindu nationalist VHP-RSS, while state actions not aimed at protecting minority rights further convince Muslims of Jama'at-i-Islami or Christians in Kerala that the state is their enemy as well.[53] The clashes of December 1992 in Ayodhya were a cacophony of violence, with Muslim, Hindu, and state forces all fighting each other. And the violence draining Kashmir between Muslim fundamentalists aligned with Pakistan, Kashmiri independence guerrillas, and the state security forces, has made everyone into everyone else's enemy.

The Indian state is not alone, of course, in its inability to play the role of honest broker among competing societal groups. Hugh Roberts's analysis of Algeria (chap. 17) documents the extent to which the state was deliberately manipulative regarding Islamist movements. Indeed the 1992 national elections were cancelled after Algeria's Islamist parties demonstrated their popularity, further eroding the government's legitimacy. And Northern Ireland remains caught in a circular web of violence among Catholics, Ulster Protestants, and the British security forces.[54] The Ulster government cannot mediate between Protestant and Catholic demands, and its consequent reliance on London leads to its identification with Protestant interests by the Catholic minority. And completing the circle is the Protestant radicals' distrust of the British, concerned that Ulster will be abandoned to the shifting sands of international political expediency.

The environment of political opportunities is a shifting collage of groups at various levels of power. The rise of politicized Christian fundamentalist groups in the United States in the late 1970s became possible as the influence of a more liberal religiopolitical coalition began to wane. In many ways the Christian Right groups that came to the fore had less to do with the demise of the liberal consensus than did factors such as economic difficulties and social unrest resulting from some of the liberals' victories.[55] Nonetheless, the public tide clearly turned from religiously based campaigns for peace, disarmament, and civil rights to religious movements concerned with school prayer, abortion, pornography, and "family values." The emerging fundamentalist movements helped seal their claim to the new era by creating a dramatic sense of cultural crisis for which they offered solutions simultaneously "new" and "traditional."

There are times when increased leverage for a particular challenger group does not affect the overall distribution of power in a political system. This is less likely, however, when the movements at issue are religious fundamentalist movements. First, fundamentalist movements, however much they may eventually have to accommodate themselves to political realities, have ideological programs that encompass many aspects of life; as noted above, they are "totalizing." Fundamentalists who actively engage public politics seldom approach it with modest, partial agendas. The attack on the distinction between the public and the private in social life is often explicit in fundamentalist programs for change. Other group subcultures are implicated in such sweeping challenges, whether economically, politically, or culturally. Explicit pluralism is not an option; when the political environment is open to challenges—either through open political systems or state weakness—fundamentalist movements and their political opponents are inextricably drawn into the public political arena together.

For these reasons periods of large-scale fundamentalist political activity coincide with periods of generalized political instability often leading to "regime crises." When a regime's very existence is in doubt, the stakes for winners—and losers—become that much higher. The loss of regime legitimacy is a consistent problem, even though states have grown in power. This relationship is not difficult to understand. The more the state intervenes in previously unregulated aspects of social life, the more opportunities it has to fail in its programs or antagonize constituents. As a consequence the state needs legitimacy from other social institutions all the more.

From Central America to Central Asia, regime change has tremendous implications for fundamentalist movements. Ríos Montt came to office in Guatemala during a period in which the basic nature of the state and direction of the country were at issue. A majority of the population did not support Ríos Montt's specific vision of cultural revolution, but the instability itself was both the political opportunity for his rise to power and the sense of crisis that made a call for change generally appealing.

Similarly, Mark Saroyan (chap. 19) demonstrates how Islamic fundamentalists in Central Asia took advantage of the waning strength of the Soviet state's bureaucratic apparatus to establish their own organizations. The Soviet demise not only decreased the threat of political repression from the state, but also discredited the state's bureaucratic model of organization, a form of organization the conservative ulama used as their power base.

The increasing needs modern states have for legitimacy have led to what many observers term a "legitimation crisis."[56] As contemporary national economies find themselves competing within an increasingly integrated world economy, the state must assume an increasingly larger role in its national domestic economy. Laissez-faire policies are outmoded so the state must act as an economic regulator, developing industrial policies, protecting national industries from foreign competition, and even managing some issues of internal economic distribution. States have taken on "steering functions" in the economy and are judged in part on their performance in that arena. Indeed, modern industrial states have created something of a new "social contract" wherein the state guarantees a certain level of consumption and lifestyle comfort in return for legitimacy and the loyalty of the citizenry. In place of the direct class-based struggles of the nineteenth century have developed the legitimacy crises of the post–World War II period (an argument with considerable application to the state socialist regimes of the former Eastern bloc).

A historically important prop through which states have legitimated themselves has been organized religion. The content of legitimation needed by modern states in the contemporary world has changed, however, and seldom do religious ideologies connect secular power directly to some sort of divine right. But legitimacy itself is an ever more important resource. The expanded state has more steering crises, needs credibility in more areas of human endeavor, and is responsible more directly to larger numbers of social groups. It is this economic context that makes the political dilemmas leading to regime crises so acute. Thus, generalized political instability is an environmental condition that is fertile soil for fundamentalism, whether such movements are offering their moral authority in support of or to challenge an embattled state.

However, it is overly simplistic to associate the performance of the economy with the frequency or intensity of collective action challenges. Social movements occur when the economy is doing well, doing poorly, or stagnant. It has been repeatedly demonstrated that revolutions do *not* always occur at the point of greatest emiseration. Revolutions are products of complicated interactions among the actual material circumstances in which people find themselves, and those same people's perceptions about and understandings of their situation. Revolutions are social movements *in extremis* and are coalitions of groups, not all of whom share the same economic situations.[57]

Thus in the modern world the political and the economic are deeply intertwined. Crisis in one arena has consequences for conditions in the other. This very interrelatedness is the environmental basis for the state's legitimacy needs and the political context for the types of political activities currently associated with fundamentalist movements around the world. But lest this discussion give the impression that fundamentalism is only a political expression of macro-material interests, let us consider the very important cultural and religious environments that are also spawning grounds for movements.

Cultural-Religious Contexts

So far the discussions of movement culture have treated any given movement's culture, including its ideological frames, as though it stood clearly and cleanly on its own. Of course, that is not the case. As fundamentalist movements exist in political and economic contexts, so they exist both in wider cultural contexts and within specifically religious traditions. Movements must simultaneously borrow from and distance themselves from their cultural-religious setting. They must demonstrate that they are different and better—rejecting the existing wider culture as corrupt—without falling so far beyond the pale that their beliefs and practices appear to be madness.

And of course the frames offered by a given fundamentalist movement are not the sole ideological appeals in members' or potential members' lives. Movement frames must compete with the many demands of everyday life, the frames of rival movement organizations, and the frames promoted by existing political and social powers that encourage stability and inaction. The competition among change-oriented movements, including those that are religiously fundamentalist, is for attention, members, and legitimacy. How effectively movements compete is largely a matter of "frame resonance."[58]

Movement frames resonate to the extent that they cohere with frames already existing in the wider culture and in the lives of members, recruits, and onlookers. The wider culture thus acts as a constraint on framing—movement frames must not vary too far from the cultural context if they are to be effective.[59] This limit to the distance of frames from dominant cultural patterns is thus internal to the logic of frame resonance itself. To make sense, movement frames must accord with wider worldviews and meanings; they must achieve "narrative fidelity." Narrative fidelity for movement frames is the "degree to which proffered framings resonate with cultural narrations, that is, with the stories, myths and folk tales that are part and parcel of one's cultural heritage."[60]

In terms of their narrative fidelity, fundamentalist frames have both an advantage and a corresponding disadvantage. They are disadvantaged by their status as countercultural constructions, often drawing on the experiences and understandings of marginal societal groups. And the importance of boundaries in fundamentalist ideology—between good and evil, the elect and the damned, members and nonmembers—lead movements to play up (or rhetorically create) distance where many might not perceive it. Fundamentalist movements are always in danger of offering frames that are too "different" to make sense to people they are trying to persuade. While this discussion has focused primarily on the "worldview" frames that movements offer members for making sense of the world, the same logic holds for "action" frames that orient movement strategy and tactics.[61] In this volume Gehad Auda points out, for example, that the escalating use of violence by the radical Jama'at served ultimately to isolate the militant groups from the larger Muslim populace, which was not willing to justify such levels of violence.

But reflecting the paradoxical nature of fundamentalisms generally, their frames often have a great advantage in terms of their narrative fidelity. They draw upon symbol systems rooted in tradition. They call for reconnection to a glorious past within terms that allow it to be meaningful to a "fallen" present. What fundamentalist movements are saying makes a great deal of sense to many of those hearing it; it resonates by tying what is already constructed as good and valuable to a coherent explanation of what has gone wrong—all within a narrative that offers an eventual return to a state of grace.

While it is true that fundamentalisms are marked by their selective reinterpretations of traditions, it is just as true that by grounding interpretations in "tradition" the resulting frames are easily accessible and intuitively appealing to many people. The power of tradition is great, and religion can plausibly claim to be preserving many of its most important virtues. There is a religious dimension to the myths with which most peoples explain their origins. Fundamentalisms take advantage of that fact, and their ideological appeals have a tremendous sense of fidelity with the tradition. Thus, for example, while both religious fundamentalism and economic socialism offer critiques of the rampant individualism in North American culture, the United States has had consistent waves of fundamentalist revivals, and rarely a significant socialist movement.

Along with the interaction and alignments between movement frames and cultural traditions, there appear to be more general cultural cycles that are more or less receptive to socioreligious movement activity. These cycles may well be grounded in the political and economic fluctuations described above. But once a cultural cycle is launched, it bears no necessary resemblance to social structural conditions. In the parlance of sociological theory, the cultural dimension of movement environment is at least partly "autonomous."

Several movement scholars have developed ideas about what they term the "cycles of protest."[62] Movements develop in historic clusters, when grievances in the population are accompanied by the resources and opportunities for collective action. And once collective action is seen as possible—and even desirable or imperative—the protest cycle is perpetuated whether the "objective" opportunities exist or not. The new interpretive frames generated by movements become common wisdom, yielding a "master frame"[63] and have an impact outside the people directly mobilized. A "general climate of insurgency" shapes new actions.[64]

That a master frame develops to interpret and inspire movements in a variety of cultural settings draws together the disparate insights of many of the chapters in this volume. The international reality of Western colonialism and the language of a cross-national *umma* gave Islamic fundamentalists a readily available way to interpret events in many different settings. Thus the Iranian revolution—a Shi'ite uprising among a Persian people—could be a template for Arab Sunni aspirations. Or fire the imagination of Malaysians or Nigerians.

Similarly, the antisecularist language of Islamic fundamentalism, combined with

India's experience with colonial rule, provided elements of a master frame for rival religious fundamentalisms—Hindu, Muslim, Sikh, and Christian—within India. Each fundamentalist movement can legitimate itself with both nationalists and co-religionists by equating colonialism with secularism and opposing them both. This presents obvious problems for the Indian state, which has tried to manage religious pluralism through an officially secular government.[65] And of course the use of a similar master frame by different movements does not imply cooperation among them. As another example, the cyclical dynamic plays itself out within one religious tradition in one national setting. Kane's exploration of reformist Islamic activity connected with the Nigerian Izala movement demonstrates cycles of activity that have shifting bases of popular support, and different organizational manifestations, but overlapping and related rhetorical frames.

Fundamentalism is as much a rebellion against conventional ecclesiastical authority (and authorities) as it is a protest against modern secular culture. That is, fundamentalism is a campaign for religious as well as cultural change. In the United States, the movement that coined the term "fundamentalism" began as a protest within Protestant Christianity against liberal forms of theology and biblical criticism that were appearing in the early twentieth century, generally termed "modernism."[66] It was the accommodation to modernity by sectors of organized religion, rather than modernity itself, that prompted the fundamentalist reaction and was its first target. Similar examples can be drawn from other religions. Fundamentalist ulama in Central Asia were disenchanted with the de facto accommodations the established mullahs had made with the Soviet bureaucracy. They began rival religious organizations as a form of religious as well as political protest. And Menachem Friedman (chap. 13) and Aviezer Ravitzky (chap. 12) describe developments among the Lubavitcher Hasidim in which they have moved to the extreme position of not considering other expressions of Judaism authentic—the Lubavitch's defensive actions are defending the true faith against the weakened commitment of "liberal" Judaism. Its activist positions are directed against the influence of established non-Hasidic Jews in both religious and wider cultural circles.

For fundamentalist activists, actions directed at conventional religious authorities are not entirely "internal" matters or civil wars. The movement has a purity of vision, and often of organizational expression, that permits a firm judgment as to who is religiously proper and who is not. Nonfundamentalist co-religionists are in many ways the biggest threat to fundamentalisms, as they provide a possible organizational and ideological alternative to people who find the movement's demands too great. Israel's haredim offer a clear example of such a critique; or consider that much of Randall Terry's book-length programmatic statement for Operation Rescue is a jeremiad aimed more at pro-life Christians who are not activists than at the secular humanists who are the organization's easily identified opponents.[67]

Thus a fundamentalist movement must emphasize the slippery slope of compromise, the fatal attraction of accommodation. Established religious authorities are to be particularly castigated. Their pact with "the world"—their exchange of ideological purity for worldly acceptance and influence—is a type of Faustian bargain and often emerges as a "temptation mythology" in religious worldviews. Veering from the way, even if to another religious orientation, signals the death of a fundamentalist movement. Fundamentalism must be about a challenge to religious authority, just as it must be realized within a context of heterogeneity.

This leads to perhaps the greatest paradox of fundamentalist religious movements. To survive, movements must embody themselves in some type of organization. The message of the charismatic leaders must be systematically preserved. And yet, establishing stable organizations seems to be a recipe for the "veering from the way" that dilutes fundamentalism's intensity and diffuses activist energies. The dynamics of movement organizations is the next concern.

Movement Organizations: Structuring Boundaries and Authority

In examining various dimensions of social movement ideology and social movement environments, the connections and interplay between them are apparent. Movement ideology is understood as a series of "frames" that must "resonate"—or in Wuthnow and Lawson's terms "articulate"—with the movement environment; that is, the frames must connect the movement's purposes and programs with established cultural themes. The frames must make sense internally to movement members and externally within the cultural environment.

In the life of specific social movements, ideological-contextual connections are mediated through social movement organizations, the formally organized embodiments of the collective impulses for change that are a social movement. SMOs can be analyzed like any formal organization, but in movements where requirements for ideological fidelity are important—such as fundamentalisms—ideology, organization, and environment are caught in a particularly intricate web. At one level, fundamentalist organizations must be ideologically "static" in that they have captured a truth beyond human transience. And yet societies and cultures change as do the movements in them. Fundamentalist SMOs must develop organizational mechanisms to negotiate the tension between stasis and change, avoiding the Scylla of stagnation and the Charybdis of accommodation. No matter how "generic" the fundamentalist response to modernity may seem, the fact that so many fundamentalist movement organizations have successfully managed organizational flexibility without sacrificing ideological distinctiveness is testimony to the creative capacity of human innovation.

Explanation for this success rests on the observation that, unlike discussions of the nature of fundamentalist ideology, there is no characteristic or intrinsic "fundamentalist" mode of organization. Fundamentalism embodies no particular structure, nor does it dictate specific organizational principles. Certainly fundamentalism is a rebellion against established ecclesiastical authority, but that rebellion does not mandate a particular form of ecclesiastical polity. It could be participatory and egalitarian in the face of religious bureaucracy, or hierarchical and authoritarian in the face of an unacceptable diffusion of religious authority. Or even some combination of those characteristics, as in American Protestantism, where congregational polity and a focus on the individual's relationship to God coexist with a strong pastor tradition and an emphasis on obedience and conformity.

In sum, fundamentalist movements can draw on a variety of organizational forms and polity traditions. As Hadden and Shupe put it, "there is a reclamation of moral/ spiritual authority in the name but not necessarily in the form of the older tradition."[68] The cultural resources available to a movement organization may predispose it toward certain authority patterns rather than others, or facilitate "loosely coupled" rather than "tightly coupled" internal structures.[69] But they are tendencies and possibilities, not inevitably determined.

The assertion that fundamentalism does not require a specific polity form is not shared by all who study fundamentalism. John Garvey, for example, states that fundamentalism is intrinsically populist in that it embraces simplicity and a nonhierarchical style: "This in turn is connected to a characteristic form of ecclesiastical polity. Believers in a system of this kind have no need of a hierarchy of religious ministers to mediate between them and God. Churches create complex ecclesiastical structures when they have to enforce doctrinal orthodoxy and provide religious services to their members. But these are not concerns for fundamentalist movements, which tend to assume a populist, loosely connected, nonhierarchical aspect."[70]

While some organizational styles do show up consistently in fundamentalist movement organizations, Garvey overstates the case. First, his concern is specifically limited to fundamentalist organizations involved in public politics, leading him to miss the extent to which more "defensively" oriented movement organizations do provide religious, and nonreligious, services to their members. He then conflates the fundamentalist conviction in the *immanence* of religious authority with the idea of *democratic* access to that authority, and its embodiment in particular ecclesiastical forms. And there is an implication that "movements" are qualitatively distinct from "organizations," when in fact both are modes of organizing behavior. Embodying a movement in formal organizational structures can take a variety of forms.

These relationships are contingent, not logically necessary, and the empirical variety offered in this volume is testimony to the organizational elasticity—and complexity—of the world's fundamentalisms. Many fundamentalist movements have been responses to what are perceived to be ossified religious organizations. North American Protestantism is the classic case in point.[71] But some, such as Italy's Comunione e Liberazione, are motivated by a desire to refocus religious authority in the hierarchical structures of the polity. Secularism has threatened authority through diffusion, and the social movement *organization* itself is part of the answer to that problem.

Two particular characteristics of the generic fundamentalist ideology—the clear separation of the elect/believer from the nonelect/outsider, and the firmly delineated articulation of religious (and social) authority—have unavoidable organizational implications. A movement organization cannot be termed "fundamentalist" unless organizational principles are worked out to preserve the coherence of these ideological stances. Nonetheless, the specific structural form these principles take is indeterminate, shaped largely by the cultural and religious context in which a fundamentalist movement is emerging.

I order my observations of fundamentalist movement organizations by examining the organizational problems associated with the ideological commitments to clearly marked boundaries and clearly understood authority. In organizational terms, this involves dimensions of membership, leadership, and movement institutionalization. For each dimension, the discussion focuses on processes of interaction among movement ideology, movement environment, and the practical requirements of organizational maintenance. I begin with the received sociological wisdom on religious organizations.

Church-Sect Theory

At one time the sociology of religious organizations was dominated by the terms of "church-sect theory."[72] The terms have generally died out in the sociology of religion as concern with religious organizations is now subsumed under more general conceptual frameworks that address issues found in secular, social movement, and parachurch organizations as well. However, the church-sect literature offers some revealing insights about fundamentalist movement organizations and deserves a brief review.

While there may be no inherently "fundamentalist" organizational forms or structures, most of the fundamentalist movements discussed in this volume fall more or less under the "sect" distinction. Examples from U.S. Protestantism and Jewish haredim jump quickly to mind. Traditionally, "sects" are thought of as small, exclusive collectivities, centered around experiential approaches to religion and eschewing more elaborated organizational structures. Formed as reactions to the world-accommodating practices of more universalistic "churches," sectarian groups have well-defined ideological and organizational boundaries demarcating members; they form pockets of *gemeinschaft* communalism within a larger impersonal society.[73]

As is readily apparent, this traditional typology is of religious "collectivities," not organizations per se. "Church" and "sect" are analytic ideal-types that mix doctrine, social practices, and organizational forms, based on both internal structures (clergy status, membership requirements) and external, societal functions ("accommodation" with the world). But when examining actual religious groups these matters are revealed as variables that can vary independently, undermining the usefulness of the general categories. For example, many fundamentalist movement organizations are world-rejecting and demand some type of conversion experience, usually considered sectlike attributes. But simultaneously, a group may well be ideologically "universalistic" in that it has the truth considered relevant for all people, and organizationally "rationalized" with an educated, hierarchically organized clergy (churchlike attributes).

More recent social scientific perspectives have forsaken church-sect typologizing for the more general conceptual tools used in organizational analysis. Thus insights into business, political, fraternal, and nonprofit organizations are also applied to religious organization;[74] this has expanded our understanding of the "sectarian" ideal-type and led to an examination of religious organizations, including those in fundamentalist movements, in terms of salient organizational variables.

All is not lost from the church-sect legacy, however. Some important observations have emerged that focus on properties that distinguish religious organizations from other types. For example, religious organizations are particularly sensitive to, and driven by, ideology. At least some dimensions of that ideology concern the organization itself. Thus to an extent not found in many organizations, religious movement organizations treat *the organizational form itself* as embodying some of its ideological goals.[75] "Organization" is expressive, not just instrumental. But because formal organizations are in a dynamic interaction with their societal environments, processes of adaptation—and justification of that adaptation—are necessarily ongoing. Thus the role of ideology as an *organizational* variable is tremendously important for religious organizations and even more so when those organizations are part of emerging movements. The yeshivot of the Israeli haredim, for example, are focused tightly around the authority and leadership of the rebbe; each yeshiva is organized on traditional principles that are clearly understood as religious ends in themselves. As Menachem Friedman illustrates in his discussion of the Lubavitch Habad, the religious centers are very much dependent on the authority and personalities of their leaders. And, of course, Protestant fundamentalists are Protestants at least in part because of religious commitments to certain forms of polity; while the strong pastor model of North American fundamentalism is not necessarily democratic, it is decidedly not an episcopal form of organizational governance.

For groups that have totalizing understandings of how believers should live in the world—this obviously includes fundamentalists—significant ideological work is necessary to maintain the on-going life of the organization. Organizational adaptations to the movement environment, such as the search for new members or cooperation with nonfundamentalist organizations, must be justified ideologically; concomitantly, certain ideological commitments demand organizational expression whether they are directly functional for movement maintenance or not. For these reasons the intimate interaction of fundamentalist ideological commitments and organizational structures can be seen in the areas of membership, leadership, and institutionalization.

Organizational Membership

The basic building block of any religious movement is the people who compose the membership. Movement spokespersons and organizational leaders may get the publicity, but without a following they are ultimately self-limited. Thus the question of what constitutes—and who qualifies as—a member is crucial.

As a social movement becomes embodied in more elaborated formal organizations, the distinction between the movement and the environment becomes sharper. Specifically, the process creates more precise distinctions between adherents, constituents, neutral onlookers, and opponents. Generally, *adherents* are people who are sympathetic to and supportive of the movement's goals or program, while movement *constituents* are people who stand to benefit if the movement is successful. Often, but not always, these people are the same. People not "with" the movement in one of these capacities are either more or less neutral, often termed *"bystander publics,"*[76] or *opponents*. While the boundaries between these categories can be fluid, it is generally in the interest of movement organizations to make the lines between members and nonmembers as significant as possible. Indeed, the more oppositional a movement is, the more likely it is to reduce member categories to a bi-polar dualism—one is either with the movement or against it.

The boundaries between those inside and outside the organization must be drawn clearly and then reinforced, often with dramatic symbols. External signs are established to demarcate members from "others." Clothing, habits of speech, ritualized behaviors, various forms of dues, and attendance at meetings are some of the organizational mechanisms that denote membership. The more involved these signs are, the more attachments members have to the organization and the correspondingly fewer ties they can nurture with the outside world.

If movements become increasingly interested in achieving the stability that comes with formal organization, signs of membership become increasingly established. Thus was conservative evangelical Christianity embodied into "fundamentalism" with the publishing of books that specified a set of beliefs; thus was the definition of what it means to be a Sikh narrowed to particular practices and personal accoutrements; thus was "Hinduism" created as a set of sacred texts and a separate national identity. New "traditions" become established in order to separate the followers of the light from those left in the darkness. The earlier discussion of recruitment and conversion indicated that member distinctions are aspects of a movement's ideological work; the consequences of that work become manifest in internal organizational signs of status.

For example, it is with the clarification of what constitutes membership that ideological hegemony is often established—that is, ideological purity among rank-and-file members often *follows* organizational membership as an effect of that membership, rather than preceding it as a cause of recruitment. People join movement organizations for a variety of reasons, and often with only a minimum of ideological "frame alignment." But as people become more fully socialized into their roles as "members," they take on more completely the appropriate ideological frames. One cannot be unaffected by the practice of wearing distinctive religious clothing day after day. Organizational behaviors develop *with* ideological frames. A strong movement culture is essential to the formation and survival of fundamentalist movement organizations. But such a culture develops interactively among members and leaders; it is not a prerequisite to membership.

The more group members are separated from the world, either symbolically or physically, the more they must have their material interests as well as spiritual needs met by the organization. Fundamentalisms draw dramatic lines between the elect and the unsaved; one cannot cross those lines too often without peril. Thus the ideological conviction of "election" leads to organizational practices marking "membership," and eventually to organizational structures providing member services.

Lofland and Richardson posit a continuum of *corporateness* for religious movement organizations, running from "clinics" that provide only "cognitive orientations" and no other significant social services or interactions, to "colonies," which are more or less "full-round" distinct societies.[77] At the most corporate end of the spectrum, a completely self-contained movement organization (a colony) would have to provide income, shelter, food, family-like supports, collective belief systems, and the belief that the organization itself is ideal. Fundamentalist organizations vary to the extent that their members live separate from the secular world; this volume offers examples of fundamentalist movements at almost every point on the clinic-to-colony continuum.

For all their variety, fundamentalist movement organizations are generally pushed to offer more rather than less corporateness (within the context of their social and cultural environments). Sharply demarcated boundaries and more corporate subcultures offer both disadvantages and corresponding advantages to movement organizations. Fundamentalists' disenchantment with their surrounding society pushes them toward separatism (and paradoxically, toward reformism as well). Due to the very totalness of their theology, belief systems, and behavioral ethos, fundamentalist movements offer more or less complete substitutions for their existing cultural contexts. Their ideological frames have the salience, scope, intensity, and internal coherence necessary so that those people willing to leave the broader culture can find a fully formed substitute. Movement organizations must often follow suit.

Certainly this totalness is an obstacle to attracting some prospective members—movements demanding fewer requirements for membership have wider numbers of potential recruits to draw upon.[78] But those who do join fundamentalist movements tend to become more completely committed, and thus member activism is high. In this sense the very totalness of the movement culture, and the concomitant organizational commitment, reinforces member/nonmember distinctions. Movement culture and organizational demands are significant boundaries, giving membership significant costs—those willing to pay the costs hold the membership dear.[79]

Ironically, because fundamentalist organizations offer totalizing worldviews, and exist as reactions to the compartmentalization of modern life, they are often forced to provide their members with a broader range of services than do less separatist religious organizations. Many of these services are decidedly this-worldly, such as economic rewards or social status, but they are nonetheless necessary. As increasingly intense or long-lived membership in the SMO increases the believer's ideological commitment and pulls him or her farther out of secular society, it leaves the believer with fewer non-SMO options. Thus the organization's commitment to the member necessarily increases along with the member's commitment to the organization.

For highly corporate fundamentalist organizations, the demands associated with participation, along with the relatively insular social world containing the membership, help account for both internal ideological hegemony and the recruitment of similarly situated individuals. This is a slightly different way of accounting for the fact that many fundamentalist organizations rely on distinct social bases for their memberships. It is less a matter of individuals from a particular social class or status all thinking alike, or all perceiving the world's problems in identical terms, than it is an organizational consequence of significant membership demands. Maintaining one's position as a member in good standing requires commitment; those persons having social supports for such commitment are most likely to persevere.

Fundamentalist ideological frames are often "universalist" and include an imperative to proselytize beyond group boundaries. This tendency is so pronounced that even Judaism has developed a fundamentalist evangelical ideology, embodied in the

Lubavitcher Habad described in part 2. And it certainly makes organizational sense to increase the membership pool. But there are intrinsic organizational difficulties with realizing this ideological strategy. Incorporating different social groups into the membership is often ideologically impossible, and even when possible has the potential to undermine organizational commitment. Persons from different social groups may have different interests, motivations, worldviews, and competing loyalties and identities. Every movement organization will of course attempt to socialize new members into the extant roles and beliefs it has established. But socialization is costly to an organization, and often incomplete.

Incompletely socialized members thus continue to experience "cross-pressures" from the various demands placed on them by the religious organization and their own competing identities. One result of such cross-pressure is the diminished ability of any one organization to demand high commitment or activism. The organization's control over members is attenuated, and its capacity to act independently becomes constrained by members' commitments to other organizations or institutions. Thus, for organizations there is a hydraulic interplay between dependence and diversity: the vulnerability associated with the former is offset by the latter; but the stability offered by the latter diminishes the capacity for focused, coordinated action available from the former. In less abstract terms, for fundamentalist movements there is a tension between the imperative to proselytize, convert, and capture part of the societal public sphere on one hand, and the ability to keep movement membership distinct, separate, and highly committed, on the other.

One solution to the dilemma is suggested by several of the studies in this volume. While individual SMOs may vary in their degree of corporateness, in terms of the overall fundamentalist movement a de facto differentiation of functions develops. Movement members can live more or less completely within a fundamentalist social world, but that entails involvement with several SMOs. Societies with large "movement sectors" demonstrate this well: Egypt and India are prime examples. Gehad Auda notes how internally differentiated the Egyptian Islamist movement is, containing SMOs that run the gamut of organizational corporateness, from rural communal societies to the Muslim Brotherhood's political arm, which is basically a political party. Similarly the triangle of the VHP-RSS-BJP in India gives Hindu fundamentalists an organizational expression for almost all modes of social life. Significantly, the Bharatiya Janata Party is the most instrumental and publicly political of the three organizations, and thus involves the most ideological compromise and collaboration with nonfundamentalists. In all these societal settings, however, managing environmental and ideological demands is a prime dilemma for the leaders of fundamentalist movement organizations.

Organizational Leadership

Noting that fundamentalist movement organizations tend to rely on particular social strata for members does not mean that such organizations are socially homogeneous. Organizations that span geographic regions may draw on different populations in different areas. Highly elaborated organizations with distinct organizational subsidi-

aries (such as schools or proselytizing societies) may incorporate different social groupings within the organization's overall control. Different historical periods may change
an SMO's recruiting frames so that they resonate with different elements of the societal population; what was at one point an organization of students may be an organization of small shopkeepers at another time.

Importantly, the distinctions between the organizational leadership and rank-and-
file members may well develop along lines marked by other social cleavages. In other
words, while fundamentalism is a response to a sense of crisis, it is not always those
people most threatened by the crisis who lead the fundamentalist movement. People
with more resources—including "human capital" resources such as education or organizational experience—with which to fight the movement's battles are drawn into
organizational leadership. To use the United States as an example, the fundamentalist
rank-and-file has been traditionally drawn from parts of the population who are often
less educated and employed in working-class-level occupations; but the leaders of the
movement organizations—particularly those who have become active in public politics—are usually middle-class college graduates.[80]

For fundamentalist organizations, leadership involves an important interaction
with the ideological commitments toward authority. Leaders are those who can direct
followers, so one can only understand leadership through an understanding of the
nature of the leader-follower authority relationship—why subordinates view the
leaders' directives as authoritative and legitimate demands on them. In fundamentalist
movements, religious authority and organizational authority are intimately intertwined. Framed in these terms, the problem recalls sociologist Max Weber's typology
of authority. Weber described three ideal types: charismatic, traditional, and legal-
rational authority.

According to Weber, the term *charisma* "will be applied to a certain quality of
an individual personality by virtue of which he is set apart from ordinary men and
treated as endowed with supernatural, super-human, or at least specifically exceptional
powers or qualities."[81] These qualities are generally thought to be inaccessible to
others—more like "gifts" than achievements. Thus followers view directives as authoritative because they are deemed to originate in some special—perhaps transcendent—source. Note, however, that Weber was less concerned with charisma as such
than with charismatic authority. His focus was on the relationship between leaders
and led; sociologically, charisma is less the property of the person than of the relationship. In that sense, it is an "organizational" variable.

The extent to which charismatic organizational leaders are legitimate is the extent
to which they are seen as authentically representing the transcendent source of religious and social authority. When leaders are successful, the connection of their leadership with divine authority is a powerful tool for mobilization and action. For these
reasons, charismatic authority was integral to one of Weber's conceptions of social
change, often providing the "breakthrough" that would challenge traditional relationships and reshape the world.

The relevance of charismatic authority to fundamentalist movements is obvious.
Many chapters in this volume examine movements whose spark lay in the charisma of

a founder, from Hasan al-Banna of the Muslim Brotherhood, to Maulana Sayid Abul 'Ala Maududi of Jama'at-i-Islami, to Luigi Giussani of Comunione e Liberazione, to Rabbi Menachem Mendel Schneerson of the Lubavitcher Habad. Religious insight reframes the problems and possibilities of the world, offering new ways of thinking and promoting new ways of acting. Fundamentalism's drive to remake the world finds its inspiration in some gift of the spirit.[82]

However, as an organizational principle, charismatic authority can be unstable.[83] Organizational directives that are the product of a single person, however inspired, are subject to his or her (in fundamentalist movements, "his" is overwhelmingly the case) whims. Authority may be difficult to delegate, putting too much administrative burden on the founder—or forcing subordinates to justify all decisions on the leader's perceived desires. Organizational forms based on revelation may be reinterpreted as illegitimate by future revelations and thus need over-haul. And societal authorities may become suspicious of the influence a charismatic leader amasses and make life more difficult for the movement.

But most important for movement and organizational survival, there must be some method to transfer the charisma to a new generation of leadership once the leader/founder dies. Thus a generic organizational problem for movements marked by charismatic authority is the "routinization" of charisma. The organization must continue to embody mobilizing authority in someone—or something—other than the leader. The difficulty of the task is evident in the high "death rates" among religious and political movements. Providing an orderly routinization of the founding charisma has eluded many groups, produced schisms in others, and left others vulnerable to co-optation, repression, or stagnation.

"Derivative" charisma is one common response to problems of transference and succession. Organizational members who were among the initial membership cohort, or who had a special relationship with the leader/founder, assume the mantle of organizational power, but legitimate their position on the founder's charisma. Written texts are often reexamined in search of more generalized or abstract legitimating organizational principles. Or the issue of organization is ignored in public; other teachings and writings are given special attention while the organization evolves its practices from a distinct source of authority.[84]

Certain activities are necessary in order for organizations to maintain and reproduce themselves. At a minimum, organizations must gain and keep members, facilitate communication among members and with leaders, and coordinate the actions that justify the organization's existence. But organizations are not self-sustaining; they must obtain the resources necessary to survive by drawing upon their societal environments. The more regularized the access to necessary resources, the greater the chance of organizational survival and growth. Thus as a general rule, organizations tend to develop routines rather than rely on spontaneity. And if one examines entire "organizational fields" as opposed to isolated organizations, there is a marked tendency for the organizations within a field to perform necessary maintenance tasks in remarkably similar ways.[85]

Given the nature of these maintenance activities, charismatic authority has both advantages and disadvantages. Its instability, as noted, makes charismatic authority difficult to transfer and difficult to rely on consistently. On the other hand, its very flexibility often permits organizational leaders to meet a variety of environmental demands with legitimate ideological frames. The central point for leadership is that it must in some way, over time and in a variety of situations, tame the religious charisma that inspires the movement and marshal the charismatic mobilizing power to promote the movement's organizational as well as ideological agenda. For that reason, leadership in religious movement organizations can be understood largely as a matter of aligning ideological frames with organizational necessities; leaders are defined by their ability to align ideological frames with actions that obtain organizational resources.

Organizational Institutionalization

Fundamentalism, as a religious impulse and a particular type of religious movement, is not necessarily dependent on a leader's charismatic authority. While fundamentalism is built on an unshakable commitment to transcendent authority for social, political, and religious life, there are fundamentalist movements that outlive their charismatic founders without losing their distinctive call and identity.

Dario Zadra demonstrates the extent to which the CL, as a representative of Catholic fundamentalism, focuses authority in the Church organization, not individual charisma. Barbara Metcalf's exploration of the Tablighi Jama'at Islamic movement in India (chap. 25) reveals implicit patterns of participatory democracy in its embodiment of both spiritual and organizational authority (particularly when contrasted to the Jama'at-i-Islami). This can be quite self-conscious, as Ousmane Kane reports in his chapter on Nigeria; followers of two shaykhs made a decision "to form a movement that will continue their work if they happen to be assassinated." Thus justificatory rationales other than personalized charismatic authority may be available.

However, all legitimating rationales designed to perpetuate a movement beyond its founding charisma involve some aspect of *institutionalization,* defined as the "processes by which social processes, obligations, or actualities come to take on a rule-like status in social thought and action."[86] These processes become embodied in elaborated formal organizational structures. Importantly, the formal structures are a "blueprint" of the organization; the degree to which they reflect accurately day-to-day practices by organizational members is an empirical question—one tellingly dependent upon the intersections with ideology and environmental conditions.

Several institutionalizing processes are common, however, particularly among religious organizations, and particularly among organizations that emerge on societal margins and must fight for social legitimacy.[87] One option for keeping internal authority intact is through developing a "charisma of office." In this aspect of routinization, the special charismatic qualities become attributed properties of the holder of an organizational position, rather than of the actual individual. The Catholic papacy and the presidency of the Church of Jesus Christ of Latter-Day Saints are clear examples. In the view of some scholars, routinizing charisma in an office is a stage in the transition from charismatic to "traditional" authority. That is, leaders are granted authority based on their relationship to past precedent and traditional modes of action or belief.[88]

The last of Weber's ideal-types of authority, "legal-rational" authority, represents a significantly different approach to organizing the relationships within an organization. Unlike charismatic relationships, legal-rational authority is based on formal, impersonal, rationalized rules and regulations. Persons hold positions of authority based on their occupation of recognized organizational positions and adherence to legitimate operational guidelines.[89] The organizational structure is "rational" in that it is designed for efficiency, predictability, and stability, and the positions within it exist in a framework of legal empowerment, sanctions, and constraints.

Legal-rational authority's most common organizational manifestation is *bureaucracy,* even though neither phenomenon actually exists in pure ideal-typical form.[90] But as an organizational form, bureaucracies have become prevalent in religious organizations, just as they have in political, governmental, and other nonprofit organizations.[91] Whether bureaucratic forms of organization conform to particular theological postulates is an open empirical question. But particularly in Western countries, even fundamentalist movement organizations have developed bureaucratic structures; they play a major role in orienting movements to their changing environments.

Bureaucratic forms of organization are criticized for many reasons, but two critiques are especially relevant here. First, bureaucracies are designed for stability—the entire purpose is to regularize and depersonalize decision making—and often have difficulty adapting to changing circumstances. They may cost a movement some flexibility in dealing with its environment even as they seem to be rationalizing much of the affective religious ferment out of movement organizations. Second, bureaucracy is often a means of centralizing power in an organization, even as it legitimates or disguises that centralization;[92] bureaucracy can be legitimated through forms of democratic ideology, since in theory it removes arbitrariness and favoritism from decision making, even as it centralizes power in the hands of the few.

Both of these criticisms are consistent with themes found in fundamentalist objections to the modern secular and the modern religious world. Fundamentalism is a rebellion against conventional ecclesiastical authority, and in many traditions conventional organized religion is thoroughly bureaucratized. While fundamentalism is not first and foremost a rejection of bureaucracy per se, it is by nature a response to the compartmentalization of the modern world. In the industrial West, bureaucratic forms have expanded to the point where most people live in a "society of organizations"[93] and bureaucracies are seen as the embodiments of the modern world gone wrong. In the societies of Africa, Latin America, and Asia, many people see bureaucracy as an unwelcome legacy of Western colonialism—a foreign mode of social organization that represents a lingering aspect of domination.

In either societal situation, fundamentalist reactions to modernity play upon that distaste of bureaucratic structures. As noted above, that response often has taken advantage of religion's intrinsically egalitarian component—that religious truth is available to those outside the ecclesiastical hierarchy. Thus fundamentalist movements may be aimed significantly against the formal bureaucracy in established religious institutions and the legal-rational authority that supports it. Of course that does not exempt fundamentalist SMOs from the environmental pressures for which bureaucracy is one answer (such as the regularization of leadership authority). Rather, it means that fundamentalist organizations face yet another situation in which tension with the societal context requires continual ideological work in order to insure membership commitment and justify organizational decision-making.

Another common institutionalizing process in movement organizations is *professionalization;* this is distinct from the development of bureaucracies. Professionalization is the development of expectations that representatives of the religious organization, including but not restricted to the clergy, will accept their vocation as a full-time occupation and will have the training necessary to perform organizational roles.[94] With professionalization develop standards, ethics, behaviors, and knowledge deemed appropriate to—and the more or less exclusive property of—the profession. Charles Selengut's chapter on the rise and expansion of the yeshiva organizational form (chap. 10) is almost a case study of the development of a religious hierarchy along these lines.

Professionalization and bureaucracy are not necessarily compatible or coterminous organizational arrangements. They are guided by different modes of internal discipline (hierarchical vs. collegial) and different understandings of authority (legal-rational procedures vs. educational expertise). Thus while professional modes of organization are often embedded within bureaucracies, the two principles do not necessarily synchronize smoothly.[95] But both are factors in the elaboration and formalization of movement organization. As movements grow, managing internal relationships is an increasingly complex task. This is all the more true for "second generation" movements attempting to carry on after a charismatic authority has passed. To the extent that movement leadership wants to control internal processes, bureaucracies and professionalism develop.[96]

The importance of both professionalized and bureaucratic organizational forms for the volume at hand is the impact they have on movement organizations' ability to pursue their goals. An organization cannot pursue its goals if it cannot consistently regenerate the resources it needs to maintain itself. In that way, SMOs are the conduits through which movements draw resources from their societal environments. Resources such as members, money, buildings, and social legitimacy must be consistently generated and renewed. Only the most corporate and secluded of movements can do so without relying to some degree on the nonfundamentalist world. But the needs of organizational maintenance can result in subtle and not so subtle transformation of ideological goals in unanticipated ways.

One of the most frequently documented of these transformations is termed "goal displacement."[97] In these cases, organizational processes, structures, or objectives that began as means to a greater end become ends in themselves. For religious organizations this is a particular challenge because so often their ultimate ends are difficult to measure in worldly terms. More measurable aspects of organizational growth, such as financial contributions, attendance at religious services, or social status in the wider society become the operative goals. Or organizational maintenance alone becomes the driving force, even if it means submerging less crystallized or more precarious group goals. Given that many religious organizations exist as expressive ends in themselves, this type of transformation may be completely unrecognized.

Having laid out a tripartite scheme for the analysis of fundamentalist movements, it is necessary to suggest the ways that ideology, environment, and organization interact to shape the dynamic quality of movements. Given that fundamentalist movements are about the transformation of the modern world, movement dynamism is also a perspective on social change. But the following section, however, is not meant to be predictive of movement development and is certainly not exhaustive of the interactive possibilities. Rather, it is meant as an example of the complex ways in which ideology, environment, and organization are intertwined, the multiplicity of possibilities for their analysis, and a suggestion as to why particular interactions are specific problems for fundamentalisms.

Movement Dynamics and Social Change

Traditionally the study of the "dynamics" of religious movements has meant the exploration of some type of developmental continuum wherein the charisma of the first generation is institutionalized and the movement's inherent rebellion is "accommodated" to the world.[98] There is an implicit antinomy between "movement" and "structure."

Such a perspective is now generally recognized by scholars of both religious and social movements as only a partial story. There is not an univariate continuum, the transformation from "sect" or "movement" to "church" or "structure" happens only occasionally and not always in the same manner. While in some cases the white-hot ideology of rebellion becomes cooled in ossifying processes of bureaucratization and accommodation, there are other possibilities. For example, often organizational forms emerge with—and as a dimension of—ideological frames. In other cases, the elaboration of formal organizational structures promotes rather than retards world-rejecting or politically radical tendencies. Recent research on specifically political movements demonstrates that "some movement organizations may be comparatively immune to pressures to adapt to the existing institutional environment. . . . Processes of conservative organizational transformation are conditioned by both the social identity of those organized and the character of existing . . . institutions."[99] That is, some models of organizing are more susceptible to co-optation than others just as some ideological frames are more susceptible to transformation than others. But for all movements, organizational forms and ideological frames have important influences on each other.

Since fundamentalism does not demand a particular organizational form, fundamentalist SMOs may draw on a wider organizational "repertoire" than do established religious institutions. Religious movements have a variety of ideological and organizational tools, often in inchoate form, with them from their beginnings. Some tools are more conducive to successful institutionalizing practices in particular societal contexts. Other tools may help a movement institutionalize itself without abandoning its call for social and personal change. In this regard, the importance of the organizational form as one expression of a movement's ideological ends may prevent movement-destroying adaptations. It is not a two-way dynamic of ideological purity and organizational constraint, but a delicate dance of actions and reactions. In Nancy Ammerman's words in chapter 7 of this volume, "the creation of a fundamentalist movement is a dynamic social process in which the raw materials of culture and discontent are shaped by the particular ideological and social resources of the movement itself." That dynamic is endlessly interesting but ultimately undetermined.

Organizational adaptation is unquestionably a significant social and ideological process in the development of all types of social movements. Adaptation allows movements to pull resources from their environment even as they are dedicated to remaking it. And many "developmental" theoretical approaches contain ideology, organization, and environment (particularly a religious culture of "denominationalism") as implicit analytic elements. But I propose examining each element explicitly, recognizing that influences run in every direction and that consequences for particular movements are contingent. A general example illustrates how ideological impulses of reformism and separatism, environmental conditions of pluralism within a nation-state, and organizational principles of boundary-maintenance and bureaucratic elaboration, necessarily impinge upon and partially transform each other.

Fundamentalist ideological and organizational frames, I have noted repeatedly, tend to be totalizing. They are predicated on a rejection of the differentiation and compartmentalization of life in the modern world, and as such push toward some form of de-differentiation. The challenge to liberal capitalism's public-private distinction is part of that push. Thus the basic ideological impulse of fundamentalism is toward engagement with the public sphere, including some type of involvement in public politics.

At some point, however, this involvement will engage pluralism. In the United States and India, pluralism is obviously a major aspect of the religious culture, but even in societies such as Israel, Iran, or Pakistan, a certain amount of ideological pluralism is inevitable. Indeed, this is almost true by definition, since fundamentalism uses a rejection of pluralism as one of its defining and mobilizing features. So where social structural pluralism does not exist, fundamentalist movements create some. This can be done rhetorically by playing up the danger of religious minorities (as Iran has done with the Baha'is) or drawing ever stricter lines around legitimate textual interpretation (as the chapters on Israeli yeshivot or Protestant dispensationalist theology demonstrate). Organizationally, this is manifested in heightened signs of membership status and increased distancing from the nonelect.

And yet if movement organizations are to have any control over the public sphere, they will necessarily encounter the demonized ideologies or practices of nonfundamentalist groups. If they are unable to persuade others to abandon their ways, fundamentalist SMOs will be forced to struggle for some aspect of state power and its legitimate coercive powers. In countries from the United States to Egypt to Sri Lanka, this struggle has involved fundamentalist movements in organizational coalitions with "others." Auda notes that Egypt's Muslim Brotherhood had to make common cause with the Labor party; Don-Yehiya reports (chap. 11) that religious Zionist groups had to cooperate with non-observant Jews (indeed, material in this volume implies that Gush Emunim is more an expression of secular Zionism than religious fundamentalism); and Operation Rescue had to pull Protestants, Catholics, and nonfundamentalist (though militant) pro-lifers together.

If such political activism is pushed far enough, commitment to the *agenda* becomes the effective entrance requirement to the movement organization. In effect, organizational goals—and instrumental ones at that—replace religious values as the marker between adherents and opponents. A form of "value displacement" develops as expressive values are displaced by instrumental goals. Personal transformation and righteous lifestyles are downplayed and movements begin affirming in practice things to which, in principle, they once objected. The instrumental goals of a reformed and godly community are then in turn rendered vulnerable to compromise politics or the type of quantifiable goal displacement discussed above.[100]

Yet the potential threat from ideological and organizational pollution caused by lowering boundaries leads many movements to develop organizational auxiliaries or subsidiaries to manage just such organizational coalitions. Organizational elaboration, even if it entails the development of bureaucracies and hierarchies, is preferable to lowering group boundaries or standards. Political lobbying groups, militias, or business ventures may develop. The important point is that reigning ideological frames may be dictating organizational developments rather than being inevitably debased by them.

The irony is that organizational elaboration and specialization are forms of separation and compartmentalization that are familiar in the modern world. And they separate an aspect of organizational decision-making from the immediate source of religious authority. Thus, North American fundamentalists preserve the purity of their religious vision by not "fellowshipping" religiously with those not sharing their theology. At the same time, their cooperation with others in issue-based political participation begins to look much like conventional interest-group politics. Compromise on some ideological principles becomes the ticket for organizational influence. Ideological reformism and separatism interact to push the movement into gaining some shaping power over the world while still retaining a cohesive community; the differentiating effects are unintentional but real nonetheless.

In the public arena, however, fundamentalist movements have proven to be effective players. As political movements they have cadres of committed activist members, an unrelenting focus on issues important to them, and cultural legitimacy resting on the rhetorics and symbols of tradition. Indeed in many polities, social movement politics is the prime impetus for instigating change; as effective purveyors of movement politics, fundamentalist organizations have taken major roles in shaping public policies. States, political parties, administrative bureaucracies, and other sociopolitical movements have had to respond to fundamentalisms, and have sometimes been politically defeated by them.

But that very success in shaping the public realm has meant that fundamentalist movements become less oppositional. The societal environment is less hostile; they have less to protest. And if fundamentalist SMOs at all routinize their access to conventional politics (in a sense becoming less like "movement" organizations and more like an interest group or political party), they then have a stake in the status quo. This stake can cost the movement a degree of militant activism (motivational frames are less persuasive) due to a self-satisfied retreat from public affairs by portions of the membership, but it also means further accommodation with other elements of the pluralist mix (even Iran's Islamic Republic must deal with the accommodating realities of international politics).

That fundamentalist organizations have developed the ability to defend their own turf successfully is noted in several empirical chapters in this volume. The organizations always have the option of retreating to the enclave and absorbing themselves with internal affairs. This can be a tempting response to either political defeat or political victory. The general dynamics of religion and power in contemporary society offer religious movements ready access to "negative power," that is, the capacity to effectively block change within a delineated sphere of social life. The concomitant "positive power" to shape the nature and direction of change, particularly as it effects other enclaves, is a more precarious and partial achievement, and perhaps more frustrating for those whose vision is encompassing.[101]

Perhaps it is the ambiguous and partial character of fundamentalists' public political "victories" in combination with the changes subsequently wrought to the movements themselves which has led many observers to predict an inevitably secularized ending to even the most vehement fundamentalist movements. Alternately, some scholars posit that only "defensive" fundamentalism is "true" fundamentalism since defensive movements so often manage to keep the outside world out of their affairs and slow the clock of social change. And it certainly seems to be the case that movement dynamics differ between publicly activist movements and their separatist counterparts. In particular, political engagement has movement-transforming consequences whatever its outcome.

Yet here again is the irony in fundamentalism's dynamic relations with modernity; fundamentalisms use modernity's forms, both ideological and organizational, as part of their critique of it. The differentiation that allows fundamentalists to create their own enclaves and preserve a way of life by organizing churches, clubs, schools, and families according to their own vision also constrains them from being able to export their vision easily. The dialectical impulse to separate themselves from the world even as they attempt to transform it gives fundamentalisms an ambivalent position on public life—denying its differentiations even as they stand astride them.

Despite these obstacles, examples of complex, multilayered fundamentalist organizations and diverse organizational coalitions abound in most of the world's societies. The selectivity of fundamentalist "tradition" is important in this respect. Fundamentalist frames can allow for what might seem unlikely coalitions, and totalizing theology is an impulse that can be resisted within particular contexts. As Marty and Appleby noted in volume 1 of this series, fundamentalists are not traditionalists—they seek to best modernists at their own game without sacrificing the essential fundamentalist identity.[102]

Fundamentalism's intrinsically modern situation also helps explain why public fundamentalism is so often led by a younger, socially rising stratum of leadership even when religious traditions and authority may still be invested in community elders. The college-educated middle class leads U.S. fundamentalist churches and political organizations; Western-educated Indians using Western organizational models populate South Asian fundamentalisms; young men form the backbone of the itinerant preachers from the Izala in Nigeria to the Tablighi in India; students are successfully recruited by a variety of fundamentalist movements. These are people who understand the modern society they so oppose. They have the resources, personally and ideologically, to participate outside their own enclave. In Don-Yehiya's apt phrase, they combine "traditional particularism and modern activism."

Thus while fundamentalism is clearly a "reaction" to modernity, it is not necessarily reactionary.[103] It is a tool for groups reacting to what is perceived as their marginal place in society. Yet fundamentalist activism is often conducted by newly empowered people using whatever ideological or organizational resources they have available. The "language of return" is particularly useful for groups in these situations since it has a built-in legitimacy their social statuses may not automatically provide. In a similar manner, charismatic authority powers most fundamentalist organizations at some point not because of any intrinsically necessary connection between fundamentalism and an organizational form, but because the traditional rebbe or preacher or guru happens to be the organizing resource available to those movements.

It may be that Laurence Moore's insights into religion on the societal margins are less specifically American than his title proclaims.[104] Fundamentalism is a valuable resource for outsiders all over the world. It offers a simultaneous certainty with flexibility; it can be defensive and activist, rigid and selective, separatist and reformist. Fundamentalist religion is part of a dynamic of reaction and opposition that makes its carrier movements both challengers and potential establishment. Fundamentalism is formed by, even as it attempts to reform, the modern world.

Conclusion

Synthetic chapters such as this one are ultimately frustrating to those looking for generalized "laws" of social life. I have spoken of conditions that lead to tendencies, giving rise to more possibilities, rather than offering predictive inevitabilities. Such is the balancing act between the historically particular and the generically social. If we are to understand the curious modern-medieval hybrid that is fundamentalism, we must sacrifice some specificity in order to get a handle on its central tendencies. At the same time, if we ignore too much of the world's religious diversity—not to mention the self-understandings of many of the world's "fundamentalists"—we risk producing logically coherent categories empty of empirical content.

The perspective on fundamentalism obtained through the lenses of social movement thinking offers several benefits. Fundamentalist religion is often understood as monolithic, at least within a specific religious tradition. It is often viewed as static, an oasis of stability in an ever-changing—and ever-secularizing—world. Neither understanding is complete, and disentangling the various dimensions of ideological framing and organizational adaptation illustrates the variation clearly. As we have seen, ideological frames are interpretive and flexible, allowing fundamentalist religion to speak to its context (often drawing on culturally resonant "master frames") even as it resists certain aspects of that context. And the "cultural power" that appends to fundamentalist frames is a significant political and social resource that must be considered independently of the numbers of believers or the strength of organizations and political parties.

In organizational terms, fundamentalist movements show even more diversity. They resist easy categorization and fit uneasily into developmental schema that posit uniform or inevitable outcomes. Fundamentalist SMOs often exhibit an "institutional isomorphism" with many organizations in contemporary society: they often adapt to their context by drawing organizational practices from other religious—and sometimes secular—organizations. Yet the importance of ideology to religious movements generally and fundamentalist religion specifically puts certain conditions on institutionalization and organizational adaptation. Power, hierarchy, formal elaboration, and routinization, may all exist within fundamentalist SMOs but they typically do so in ways that preserve the ideological uniqueness that makes them fundamentalist. Fundamentalist movements are not impervious to change but neither are they captives of it; they are fascinating variations of human organization which deserve systematic and comparative attention.

In turn, social movement theory and research would benefit from more systematic consideration of fundamentalist movements. In many ways, fundamentalisms portray the archetype of social movements. They are ideologically driven forces for social change, often fluid, and draw many varied issues, social groups, and historical periods under their rhetorical umbrellas. At the same time, fundamentalist movements are committed to embodying timeless truths, institutionalizing "proper" ways of living, and instrumental and secular action combined with their expressive forms. The potential internal tensions within fundamentalist movements as they attempt to manage ideological fidelity and organizational survival offer a clear picture of the roles of ideology, organization, and power in movement dynamics. The relations between movements and their environments also reveal insights into the nature of contemporary politics and the limits of "social order" in the modern world.

Fundamentalism is not a unified whole, either around the world or within any given society. Fundamentalist movements are collections of different groups with only partially shared interests—totalizing ideologies that leave crucial organizational practices with significant latitude for adaptation. This volume has grouped together many different movements in many different contexts, not in order to offer a "theory of fundamentalism" but rather to illuminate a social endeavor that is both particularly specific and generically human.

Acknowledgments

My understanding of fundamentalism has been enhanced through conversations and interactions with Nancy Ammerman, Gabriel Almond, D. Scott Cormode, Jay Demerath, and Terry Schmitt. Special thanks to Scott Appleby, whose incisive editorial pen is exceeded only by his abilities at academic diplomacy.

Notes

1. Joseph R. Gusfield, "Introduction," in Gusfield, ed., *Protest, Reform and Revolt: A Reader in Social Movements* (New York: John Wiley and Sons, 1970), p. 2. To be fair, Gusfield's empirical work clearly recognizes the need for a cognizant collectivity to form around the desire to change. Using his definition out of context serves an heuristic purpose here.

2. Robert A. Goldberg, *Grassroots Resistance: Social Movements in Twentieth Century America* (Belmont, Calif.: Wadsworth Publishing, 1991), p. 2.

3. Robert Wuthnow and Matthew P. Lawson's chapter 2 in this volume criticizes the "resource mobilization" approach to social movements on just these grounds: they are too "organizational" in focus, and underplay the role of ideas and personal agency in understanding social dynamics. Obviously, I am convinced there are perspectives in social movement theory that do not have these difficulties and can help illuminate fundamentalist movements.

4. John Lofland and James T. Richardson, "Religious Movement Organizations: Elemental Forms and Dynamics," *Research in Social Movements, Conflict and Change* 7 (1984): 30.

5. Reviews of the empirical failings of analytic approaches relying on some form of "deprivation" or "social breakdown" explanations are numerous. See, for example, James A. Beckford, "Explaining Religious Movements," *International Social Science Journal* 29 (1977): 235–49; George M. Thomas, *Revivalism and Cultural Change* (Chicago: University of Chicago Press, 1989); Jeffrey K. Hadden and Anson Shupe, eds., *Secularization and Fundamentalism Reconsidered* (New York: Paragon House, 1989).

6. The phrase "social movement organization" is generally credited to Mayer N. Zald and Roberta Ash (Gardner), "Social Movement Organizations: Growth, Decay and Change," *Social Forces* 44 (1966): 327–41. It is a fully developed theme in Mayer N. Zald and John D. McCarthy, *Social Movements in an Organizational Society: A Collection of Essays* (New Brunswick, N.J.: Transaction Books, 1990, 1987). Some scholars, however, have been critical of the overly "organizational" slant in McCarthy's and Zald's work; see Steven M. Buechler, "Beyond Resource Mobilization? Emerging Trends in Social Movement Theory," *Sociological Quarterly* 34 (1993): 217–35.

7. Faye Ginsburg's analysis of the antiabortion group Operation Rescue illustrates this point with the "pro-life" movement: Ginsburg, "Saving America's Souls: Operation Rescue's Crusade against Abortion," in Martin E. Marty and R. Scott Appleby, eds., *Fundamentalisms and the State: Remaking Politics, Economies, and Militance* (Chicago: University of Chicago Press, 1993), pp. 557–88.

8. See Bert Useem and Mayer N. Zald, "From Pressure Group to Social Movement: Organizational Dilemmas of the Effort to Promote Nuclear Power," *Social Problems* 30 (1982): 144–56. They distinguish interest groups by their routine access to accepted institutionalized channels of political influence.

9. A solid exploration of voluntary associations as an organizational type is in David Knoke and David Prensky, "What Relevance Do Organizational Theories Have for Voluntary Associations?" *Social Science Quarterly* 65 (1984): 3–20.

10. Ann Swidler, "Culture in Action: Strategies and Symbols," *American Sociological Review* 51 (April 1986): 273–86. See also the overview offered by Michael Schudson, "How Culture Works: Perspectives from Media Studies on the Efficacy of Symbols," *Theory and Society* 18 (March 1989): 153–80.

11. A phrase generally credited to Bennett M. Berger, *The Survival of a Counterculture* (Berkeley: University of California Press, 1981).

12. The classic study of *organizational* transformation in a social movement is Mayer N. Zald, *Organizational Change: Political Economy of the YMCA* (Chicago: University of Chicago Press, 1970).

13. There are many more lengthy critiques of this approach. See, for example, Goldberg, *Grassroots Resistance,* chap. 1; or Doug McAdam, *Political Process and the Development of Black Insurgency, 1930–1970* (Chicago: University of Chicago Press, 1982), chap. 1. In this volume Wuthnow and Lawson (chap. 2) criticize approaches to fundamentalism that are based on mass society assumptions. For a sensitive delineation of the collective behavior approach without the ideological overtones, see Ralph H. Turner and Lewis M. Killian, *Collective Behavior,* 3d ed. (Englewood Cliffs, N.J.: Prentice-Hall, 1987).

14. The most definitive statement of the rational choice approach to movement recruitment is in Mancur Olson, Jr., *The Logic of Collective Action* (Cambridge: Harvard University Press, 1965). The rational choice approach is spreading in social science generally. A recent journal, *Rationality and Society,* was founded to promote the perspective, and one of the journal's founders recently published a major theoretical exposition, James S. Coleman, *Foundations of Social Theory* (Cambridge: Harvard Belknap Press, 1990). For a good critical overview of the rational choice and other perspectives in the contemporary study of organizations, see the introductory review in Walter W. Powell and Paul J. DiMaggio, eds., *The New Institutionalism in Organizational Analysis* (Chicago: University of Chicago Press, 1991).

15. See, for example, Luther P. Gerlach and Virginia H. Hine, *People, Power, and Change: Movements of Social Transformation* (Indianapolis: Bobbs-Merrill, 1970); and Beckford, "Explaining Religious Movements."

16. The sense of voluntarism in contemporary U.S. religion is documented in Wade Clark Roof and William A. McKinney, *American Mainline Religion: Its Changing Shape and Future* (New Brunswick, N.J.: Rutgers University Press, 1987). While Roof and McKinney examine the "mainline" explicitly, the interesting empirical question here is the extent to which that argument applies to fundamentalist-style religious commitments.

17. On the micro-context of recruitment, see David A. Snow, Louis Z. Zurcher, Jr., and Sheldon Ekland-Olson, "Social Networks and Social Movements: A Microstructural Approach to Differential Recruitment," *American Sociological Review* 45 (October 1980): 787–801; also Doug McAdam, John D. McCarthy, and Mayer N. Zald, "Social Movements," in Neil J. Smelser, ed., *Handbook of Sociology* (Newbury Park, Calif.: Sage, 1988), pp. 695–737.

18. See David A. Snow and Richard Machalek, "The Sociology of Conversion," *Annual Review of Sociology* 10 (1984): 167–90.

19. The phrase "collective identity" is currently associated with Italian sociologist Alberto Melucci, "The Symbolic Challenge of Contemporary Movements," *Social Research* 52 (Winter 1985): 789–815. It has been elaborated by many scholars: see Aldon D. Morris and Carol McClurg Mueller, eds., *Frontiers in Social Movement Theory* (New Haven: Yale University Press, 1992).

20. See Snow and Machalek, "The Sociology of Conversion." Thomas Robbins, *Cults, Converts, and Charisma* (Newbury Park, Calif.: Sage, 1988), offers a thorough review and critique of scholarly work on the "new religious movements" of the 1960s and 1970s. He makes the important point that recruitment, as joining a movement, and conversion, as a transformation of personal and social identity, are not the same thing.

21. Peter L. Berger's famed "plausibility structures," in *The Sacred Canopy* (New York: Anchor/Doubleday, 1967).

22. An insightful discussion of the fundamentalist appeal to students is in Zulkarnaina M. Mess and W. Barnett Pearce,

"*Dakwah Islamiah:* Revivalism in the Politics of Race and Religion in Malaysia," in J. Hadden and A. Shupe, eds., *Prophetic Religions and Politics* (New York: Paragon House, 1986), pp. 196–220.

23. In social science literature, the term "framing" is generally attributed to sociologist Erving Goffman in his classic *Frame Analysis: An Essay on the Organization of Understanding* (New York: Harper, 1974). Leaders in adapting the concept to problems in contemporary politics and social movement ideology are William Gamson and David Snow, many of whose works are cited here.

24. Goffman, *Frame Analysis*, p. 21.

25. These metaphors appear in one of the most influential works in contemporary culture theory, Clifford Geertz, *The Interpretation of Cultures* (New York: Basic Books, 1973). See in particular his essay "Religion as a Cultural System" in that volume.

26. David A. Snow, E. Burke Rochford, Jr., Steven K. Worden, and Robert D. Benford, "Frame Alignment Processes, Micromobilization and Movement Participation," *American Sociological Review* 51 (August 1986): 464.

27. David A. Snow and Robert D. Benford, "Ideology, Frame Resonance, and Participant Mobilization," *International Social Movement Research* 1 (1988): 197–217.

28. Joseph R. Gusfield, *The Culture of Public Problems: Drinking-Driving and the Symbolic Order* (Chicago: University of Chicago Press, 1981), p. 10.

29. The term originated in William A. Gamson, Bruce Fireman, and Steven Rytina, *Encounters with Unjust Authority* (Homewood, Ill.: Dorsey Press, 1982). The role of religion in creating an injustice frame is detailed in Christian Smith, *The Emergence of Liberation Theology: Radical Religion and Social Movement Theory* (Chicago: University of Chicago Press, 1991).

30. Snow et al., "Frame Alignment Processes," p. 474.

31. Sidney Tarrow, "Old Movements in New Cycles of Protest: The Career of an Italian Religious Community," *International Social Movement Research* 1 (1988): 281–304.

32. Excellent empirical examples of religion promoting resignation and rebellion are Liston Pope's classic study of religion's involvement with a labor dispute, *Millhands and Preachers: A Study of Gastonia* (New Haven: Yale University Press, 1970); and Dwight B. Billings, "Religion as Opposition: A Gramscian Analysis," *American Journal of Sociology* 96 (July 1990): 1–31.

33. While it may be that secular social scientists made too much of this "quiescence," there was nonetheless a significant change in conventional political participation by evangelical and fundamentalist Protestants between the mid-1950s and mid-1970s. See Robert Wuthnow, "The Political Rebirth of American Evangelicals," in R. Liebman and R. Wuthnow, eds., *The New Christian Right* (New York: Aldine Publishing, 1983).

34. In Rhys H. Williams and N. J. Demerath III, "Religion and Political Process in an American City," *American Sociological Review* 56 (August 1991): 417–31, the authors offer an example of a political debate about jobs and economic development between a city political establishment and an activist group of clergy. The latter consistently framed the issue as a moral dilemma, while the former responded by stressing the "economic" dimensions.

35. Martin E. Marty and R. Scott Appleby, eds., *Fundamentalisms and Society: Reclaiming the Sciences, the Family, and Education* (Chicago: University of Chicago Press, 1993).

36. The phrase "cultural power" has been used by several authors, each with a slightly different definition. The understanding of cultural power offered here is developed more systematically in a series of publications. See N. J. Demerath III and Rhys H. Williams, *A Bridging of Faiths: Religion and Politics in a New England City* (Princeton: Princeton University Press, 1992); Williams and Demerath, "Religion and Political Process in an American City"; and Rhys H. Williams and N. J. Demerath III, "Cultural Power and Empowered Culture: Conver-

gent Notes on a Theory of Politics, Religion, and Social Movements" (Manuscript in press, 1993).

37. Edelman links the symbolics of personal status to the cultural power of an ideological frame. See J. Murray Edelman, *Political Language: Words That Succeed and Policies That Fail* (New York: Academic Press, 1977), p. 25.

38. On this development in the United States, see Robert Wuthnow, *The Restructuring of American Religion: Society and Faith since World War II* (Princeton: Princeton University Press, 1988).

39. Williams and Demerath, "Religion and Political Process in an American City"; see also N. J. Demerath III and Rhys H. Williams, "Civil Religion in an Uncivil Society," *Annals of the American Academy of Political and Social Science* 480 (July 1985): 154–66.

40. Along with the chapter by Rafiuddin Ahmed on Jama'at-i-Islami in this volume (chap. 24), see N. J. Demerath III, "Religious Capital and Capital Religions: Cross-Cultural and Non-Legal Factors in the Separation of Church and State," *Daedalus* 120 (Summer 1991): 21–40.

41. Innovative reviews of this thinking can be found in David I. Kertzer, *Ritual, Politics, and Power* (New Haven: Yale University Press, 1988); Schudson, "How Culture Works."

42. Frank Lechner has posited similar developments as modernity's context for fundamentalism: institutional differentiation, compartmentalization, and cultural pluralism. Clearly I am sympathetic to much of his analysis, although I think the problem of cultural pluralism is most applicable in the American case and less so elsewhere. Lechner also offers his analysis from a neofunctionalist theoretical perspective with which I am less comfortable. However, he makes the valuable point that whatever the fundamentalist stance toward modernity, it has unintended modernizing consequences. See Frank J. Lechner, "Fundamentalism and Sociocultural Revitalization in America: A Sociological Interpretation," *Sociological Analysis* 46 (1985): 243–60; also, idem, "Fundamentalism Revisited," in T. Robbins

and D. Anthony, eds., *In Gods We Trust,* 2d ed. (New Brunswick, N.J.: Transaction Books, 1990), pp. 77–97.

Shupe and Hadden consider institutional differentiation the most important development to which fundamentalisms react, but they consider it as intrinsically connected to the process of "secularization"—a point that produces another conceptual argument too lengthy to engage here. See Anson Shupe and Jeffrey K. Hadden, "Is There Such a Thing as Global Fundamentalism?" in Hadden and Shupe, eds., *Secularization and Fundamentalism Reconsidered,* pp. 109–22.

43. John H. Garvey, "Introduction: Fundamentalism and Politics" and "Fundamentalism and the Law," in Marty and Appleby, *Fundamentalisms and the State,* pp. 13–27, 28–49. For a general consideration of the intersection between liberal political theory and the nature of religion, see Clarke E. Cochran, *Religion in Public and Private Life* (New York: Routledge, Chapman and Hall, 1990). Also, Barbara Epstein notes that the "religious" wings of the contemporary peace and environmentalist movements also challenge the public-private separation of modern life. Epstein, *Political Protest and Cultural Revolution* (Berkeley: University of California Press, 1991).

44. Williams and Demerath, "Religion and Political Process in an American City."

45. A good overview is Thomas Robbins and Roland Robertson, eds., *Church-State Relations: Tensions and Transitions* (New Brunswick, N.J.: Transaction Books, 1987).

46. Charles Tilly, *From Mobilization to Revolution* (Reading, Mass.: Addison-Wesley, 1978). For a similar argument, see also Charles Bright and Susan Harding, eds., *State Making and Social Movements* (Ann Arbor: University of Michigan Press, 1984).

47. McAdam, McCarthy, and Zald, "Social Movements," p. 699.

48. Marty and Appleby, *Fundamentalisms and the State.*

49. As Faye Ginsburg notes, the fines levied against Operation Rescue have forced dramatic reorganization, even if the group itself was not banned. Ginsburg, "Saving America's Souls."

50. Whether the Brotherhood is actually

fundamentalist is a point of contention. And the relative level of state hostility has shifted with changes in regime (Nasser, Sadat, Mubarek) and Brotherhood tactics. Nonetheless, the role of state repression in shaping the movement is discussed by both Gehad Auda (chap. 15) in this volume, and Raymond William Baker, "Afraid for Islam: Egypt's Muslim Centrists between Pharaohs and Fundamentalists," *Daedalus* 120, 3 (Summer 1991): 41–68.

51. This is precisely how King Hussein of Jordan attempted to defuse fundamentalist pro-Iraqi agitation during the recent Gulf War; see Beverly Milton-Edwards, "A Temporary Alliance with the Crown: The Islamic Response In Jordan," in James Piscatori, ed., *Islamic Fundamentalisms and the Gulf Crisis* (Chicago: American Academy of Arts and Sciences, 1991), pp. 88–108.

52. Of course what constitutes a "homogenous" society is at least in part a social construction. Israel's haredim do not see Israel as homogenous, but rather as containing dangerous amounts of variation from the true expression of Judaism they embody. However, there are societies where social structural heterogeneity cannot be ignored, and these are often situations of tremendous violence, as the section on South Asia illustrates.

53. Susan Bayly convincingly demonstrates the extent to which Christian fundamentalism in South India is both a rhetorical and organizational reaction to Hindu and (to a lesser extent) Muslim movements. See Bayly, "Christians and Competing Fundamentalisms in South Indian Society," chap. 26, in this volume.

54. Steve Bruce, "Fundamentalism, Ethnicity, and Enclave," in Marty and Appleby, *Fundamentalisms and the State*, pp. 50–67.

55. Several commentators trace these developments in both the political and religious spheres. See Wuthnow, *The Restructuring of American Religion;* E. J. Dionne, Jr., *Why Americans Hate Politics* (New York: Simon and Schuster, 1991); Jeffrey C. Goldfarb, *The Cynical Society: The Politics of Culture and the Culture of Politics in American Life* (Chicago: University of Chicago Press, 1991).

56. The idea is associated most clearly with Jürgen Habermas, *Legitimation Crisis* (Boston: Beacon Press, 1975). See also, William Connolly, ed., *Legitimacy and the State* (New York: New York University Press, 1984).

57. For analyses of the complicated realities that are revolutions, see Gerald M. Platt, "The Psychoanalytic Sociology of Collective Behavior: Material Interests, Cultural Factors, and Emotional Responses in Revolution," in J. Rabow, G. Platt, and M. Goldman, eds., *Advances in Psychoanalytic Sociology* (Malabar, Fla.: Robert E. Krieger Publishing, 1987), pp. 215–38; and Fred Weinstein, *The Dynamics of Nazism: Leadership, Ideology and the Holocaust* (New York: Academic Press, 1980).

58. Snow and Benford, "Ideology, Frame Resonance, and Participant Mobilization"; see also William A. Gamson, "Political Discourse and Collective Action," *International Social Movement Research* 1 (1988): 219–44.

59. Michael Schudson ("How Culture Works") provides a model of the properties necessary for any given cultural symbol to have political meaning. For change-oriented symbols there is clearly a balancing act between having enough resonance with existing interpretations to be comprehensible, while offering a different enough interpretation of the world so that existing power arrangements do not appear immutable.

60. Ibid., p. 210.

61. Klandermans uses similar ideas in discussing the differences between "consensus" and "action" mobilization in social movements. I am uncomfortable with the implications of "consensus" for understanding ideological mobilization, but the distinction between the diagnostic frames contained in a worldview, and strategies for action contained in prescriptive frames is valuable. Of course, it is more an analytic distinction than an empirical difference. See Bert Klandermans, "Mobilization and Participation: Social-Psychological Expansions of Resource Mobilization Theory," *American Sociological Review* 49 (1984): 583–600; idem, "The Formation and Mobilization of Consensus," *International Social Movement Research* 1 (1988): 173–97.

62. The "cycles of protest" concept has been developed most clearly in relation to social movements by political scientist Sidney Tarrow. See, for example, Tarrow, "Old Movements in New Cycles of Protest"; and idem, "Mentalities, Political Cultures, and Collective Action Frames," in Morris and Mueller, *Frontiers in Social Movement Theory*, pp. 174–202; David Snow and Robert Benford also contribute to the notion in "Master Frames and Cycles of Protest," pp. 133–55, in the same volume. The related notion that United States history is marked by cycles of revivalist and activist religion is much debated: see William McLoughlin, *Revivals, Awakenings and Reform: An Essay on Religion and Social Change in America, 1607–1977* (Chicago: University of Chicago Press, 1978); Samuel P. Huntington, *American Politics: The Promise of Disharmony* (Cambridge: Harvard Belknap Press, 1981); the journal *Sociological Analysis* 44, no. 2 (1983), devoted an issue to the question of revivalist cycles.

63. Snow and Benford, "Master Frames and Cycles of Protest."

64. Tarrow, "Old Movements in New Cycles of Protest," p. 284.

65. See the analysis in Ralph Buultjens, "India: Religion, Political Legitimacy, and the Secular State," *Annals of the American Academy of Political and Social Science* 483 (January 1986): 93–109.

66. For a concise accounting, see Nancy T. Ammerman, "North American Protestant Fundamentalism," in Martin E. Marty and R. Scott Appleby, eds., *Fundamentalisms Observed* (Chicago: University of Chicago Press, 1991), pp. 1–65.

67. Randall A. Terry, *Operation Rescue* (Springdale, Pa.: Whitaker House, 1988).

68. Hadden and Shupe, *Secularization and Fundamentalism Reconsidered*, p. xxiii.

69. There is a variety of solid work on social movement organizations. See, for example, Zald and McCarthy, *Social Movements in an Organizational Society*, especially the chapter "Religious Groups as Crucibles of Social Movements"; Ralph H. Turner and Lewis M. Killian, "Movement Organization," in Turner and Killian, *Collective Behavior*; Lofland and Richardson, "Religious Movement Organizations"; J. Kenneth Benson and James H. Dorsett, "Toward a Theory of Religious Organizations," *Journal for the Scientific Study of Religion* 10 (1971): 138–51; Zald and Ash, "Social Movement Organizations."

70. Garvey, "Introduction: Fundamentalism and Politics," p. 16.

71. Ammerman, "North American Protestant Fundamentalism"; Lechner, "Fundamentalism and Sociocultural Revitalization in America."

72. Church-sect theory as an organizational perspective was first elaborated systematically by Ernest Troeltsch in his classic *The Social Teachings of the Christian Churches* (London: George Allen and Unwin, 1931). Other classic statements include H. Richard Niebuhr, *The Social Sources of Denominationalism* (New York: Henry Holt, 1929); J. Milton Yinger, *Religion, Society and the Individual* (New York: Macmillan, 1957); and Benton Johnson, "On Church and Sect," *American Sociological Review* 28 (1963): 539–49. A recent review and critique is Rodney Stark, "Church and Sect," in P. Hammond, ed., *The Sacred in a Secular Age* (Berkeley: University of California Press, 1985), pp. 139–49.

73. The terms *gemeinschaft* and *gesellschaft* come originally from the sociology of Ferdinand Toennies. Loosely translated as "communal" and "associational," they are ideal-typical descriptions of two types of relationships (and the societies that contain them). The former are close, intimate, and more encompassing; the latter are formal, affectively neutral, and partial. My use here is not meant to call on Toennies's theory of social change, but merely to characterize a type of relationship often found in families, religious groups, and other closely knit collectivities. Thomas Bender casts a critical eye on the theory of social change connected to Toennies's work and maintains that the concepts work best when thought of as forms of social relations. He notes in particular that some of the developments associated with modernity might invigorate traditional relational patterns of communalism—an insight

clearly applicable to fundamentalism. See Bender, *Community and Social Change in America* (Baltimore: Johns Hopkins University Press, 1982).

74. See, for a sample of conceptual and empirical work on religious organizations, not confined to fundamentalism: James A. Beckford, *Religious Organization: A Trend Report and Bibliography* (The Hague: Mouton, 1975); idem, "Religious Organizations," in Hammond, *The Sacred in a Secular Age*, pp. 125–38; Ross P. Scherer, ed., *American Denominational Organization: A Sociological View* (Pasadena, Calif.: William Carey Library, 1980); and John Seidler and Katherine Meyer, *Conflict and Change in the Catholic Church* (New Brunswick, N.J.: Rutgers University Press, 1989). Important articles on general organizational theory with relevance to religion include John W. Meyer and Brian Rowan, "Institutionalized Organizations: Formal Structure as Myth and Ceremony," *American Journal of Sociology* 83 (September 1977): 440–63; Paul J. DiMaggio, "The Relevance of Organization Theory to the Study of Religion" (Program on Non-Profit Organizations, Working Paper No. 174, Yale University, 1992); and N. J. Demerath III and Terry Schmitt, "Transcending Sacred and Secular: Mutual Benefits in Analyzing Religious and Nonreligious Organizations" (Program on Non-Profit Organizations, Working Paper No. 187, Yale University, 1993).

75. Beckford, *Religious Organization;* also, Lofland and Richardson, "Religious Movement Organizations."

76. Turner and Killian, *Collective Behavior,* p. 217.

77. Lofland and Richardson, "Religious Movement Organizations."

78. It is not necessarily the case, however, that a movement organization can increase its membership or its appeal by dropping requirements or broadening its program (by, for example, adding new political issues to its list of concerns). Such tactics often add "cross-pressures" that end up diminishing the SMO's hold on its membership. See Debra Friedman and Doug McAdam, "Collective Identity and Activism: Networks, Choices, and the Life of a Social Movement," in Morris and Mueller, *Frontiers in Social Movement Theory,* pp. 156–73.

79. Laurence R. Iannaccone, "A Formal Model of Church and Sect," *American Journal of Sociology* 94 (Supplement, 1988): S241–68, provides a rational choice approach to sectarian religious behavior. His approach offers keen insights into the intense commitments produced by "high cost" religious organizations and has implications for thinking about many types of "sectarian" groups. It is not an organizational analysis per se.

80. More thorough analysis of the social bases of U.S. fundamentalism is in Ammerman, "North American Protestant Fundamentalism"; and James Davison Hunter, *American Evangelicalism: Conservative Religion and the Quandary of Modernity* (New Brunswick, N.J.: Rutgers University Press, 1983).

81. Max Weber, *The Theory of Social and Economic Organization,* ed. T. Parsons (New York: Oxford University Press, 1947), p. 358.

82. Fundamentalisms are not, however, as reliant on charismatic authority as some other types of religious movements. Fundamentalisms are generally rooted in the traditions of the societies in which they emerge. What scholars call "new religious movements" are usually cultural imports (and often labeled "cults"). Without the legitimating resonance of traditional authority, it may be that new religious movements are actually more reliant on charisma than are fundamentalisms. For a concise summary, see Jeffrey K. Hadden, "Religious Movements," in E. F. and M. L. Borgatta, eds., *Encyclopedia of Sociology* (New York: Macmillan, 1992), pp. 1642–46.

83. Thomas Robbins thoroughly discussed charismatic leadership and group stability among "new religious movements" in *Cults, Converts, and Charisma,* chap. 4. A classic functionalist perspective on institutionalization is Thomas F. O'Dea, "Five Dilemmas in the Institutionalization of Religion," *Journal for the Scientific Study of Religion* 1 (1961): 30–41.

84. A classic case study of this process is Paul M. Harrison, *Authority and Power in the Free Church Tradition* (Princeton: Princeton University Press, 1959). Harrison documents the development of "rational pragmatic" authority by Baptist denominational officials given responsibilities without attendant legitimacy.

85. A lucid textbook treatment of the sociological approach to organizations is W. Richard Scott, *Organizations: Rational, Natural, and Open Systems* (Englewood Cliffs: Prentice-Hall, 1981). Current approaches to concepts such as "organizational field" and "neo-institutionalism" can be found in Powell and DiMaggio, *The New Institutionalism in Organizational Analysis*.

86. John W. Meyer and Brian Rowan, "Institutionalized Organizations: Formal Structure as Myth and Ceremony," p. 341.

87. Robbins, *Cults, Converts, and Charisma*.

88. N. J. Demerath III and Phillip E. Hammond, *Religion in Social Context: Tradition and Transition* (New York: Random House, 1969), offer the textbook treatment of this perspective; it remains a standard in the sociology of religious organizations.

89. As an ideal-type, Weber explores legal-rational authority most thoroughly in his essay "Bureaucracy," in H. Gerth and C. W. Mills, eds., *From Max Weber: Essays in Sociology* (New York: Oxford University Press, 1958), pp. 196–244.

90. Charles Perrow, *Complex Organizations: A Critical Essay*, 3d ed. (New York: McGraw-Hill, 1986), offers a book-length critique of this and other theories of organization.

91. Paul J. DiMaggio and Walter W. Powell, "The Iron Cage Revisited: Institutional Isomorphism and Collective Rationality in Organizational Fields," *American Sociological Review* 48 (April 1983): 147–60; see also Charles Perrow, "A Society of Organizations," *Theory and Society* 20 (December 1991): 725–62.

92. Perrow, *Complex Organizations*, chap. 1.

93. Perrow, "A Society of Organizations."

94. This is a modification of the approach offered by Benson and Dorsett, "Toward a Theory of Religious Organizations."

95. See Perrow, *Complex Organizations*, pp. 42–46, for another perspective on the professional-bureaucrat tension.

96. The relationship between the existence of a large sector of social movement activity within a society and the development of social movement professionals is a central theme of Zald and McCarthy, *Social Movements in an Organizational Society*.

97. Demerath and Hammond, *Religion in Social Context*.

98. The classic study of the U.S. religious scene from this perspective is Niebuhr, *The Social Sources of Denominationalism*. It is also common in the study of new religious movements, as Robbins documents in *Cults, Converts, and Charisma*.

99. Elisabeth S. Clemens, "Organizational Repertoires and Institutional Change: Women's Groups and the Transformation of U.S. Politics, 1890–1920," *American Journal of Sociology* 98 (January 1993): 756–57; see also, idem, "Organizational Form as Frame: Collective Identity and Political Strategy in the American Labor Movement, 1880–1920" (Paper presented to the Conference on European/American Perspectives on Social Movements, Washington, D.C., August 1992). Attempts at understanding the interactions between emergent ideological and organizational frames in religious movements are discussed in Rhys H. Williams, "Social Movement Theory and the Sociology of Religion: 'Cultural Resources' in Strategy and Organization" (Program on Non-Profit Organizations, Working Paper No. 180, Yale University, 1992).

100. Thanks to Nancy Ammerman and Jay Demerath for the conversation in which musings about "value displacement" emerged.

101. For a typology of religious influence in political power arrangements see N. J. Demerath III and Rhys H. Williams, "Religion and Power in the American Experience," in Robbins and Anthony, *In Gods We Trust*, pp. 427–48.

102. Martin E. Marty and R. Scott Ap-

pleby, "Conclusion: An Interim Report on a Hypothetical Family," in Marty and Appleby, *Fundamentalisms Observed,* pp. 814–42.

103. It may not even be necessarily conservative in the political sense; see Shupe and Hadden, "Is There Such a Thing as Global Fundamentalism?" pp. 109–22.

104. R. Laurence Moore, *Religious Outsiders and the Making of Americans* (New York: Oxford University Press, 1986).

CONTRIBUTORS

RAFIUDDIN AHMED, an expert on Islam in South Asia, is a visiting professor of history at Cornell University. He is the author of several studies of religion and politics in the Indian subcontinent.

R. SCOTT APPLEBY is associate professor of history at the University of Notre Dame where he also directs the Cushwa Center for the Study of American Catholicism. His latest book is *Church and Age Unite! The Modernist Impulse in American Catholicism*.

NANCY T. AMMERMAN is associate professor of the sociology of religion at the Candler School of Theology, Emory University. Her most recent books include *Southern Baptists Observed* (ed.) and *Baptist Battles*.

GEHAD AUDA is director of the Center for Political and International Development Studies, Cairo. He has written extensively in Arabic and English on contemporary political affairs in Egypt.

AMATZIA BARAM is lecturer in Islamic history at the University of Haifa and the author of numerous works on Iraq and Shi'ite movements within Iraq. His most recent book is *Culture, History, and Ideology in the Formation of Ba'thist Iraq*.

SUSAN BAYLY is fellow and tutor at Christ's College, Cambridge and author of *Saints, Goddesses and Kings: Muslims and Christians in South Indian Society, 1700–1900* (Cambridge University Press, 1989).

ELIEZER DON-YEHIYA, the author of numerous works on Jewish radicalism and the Jewish political tradition, is an instructor in the political studies department, Bar-Ilan University.

AINSLEE EMBREE is professor emeritus of history at Columbia University, where he was chairman of the department of history, director of the Southern Asian Institute, and associate dean of the School of International and Public Affairs. He taught in India at Indore Christian College from 1948 to 1958, and at Duke University from 1969 to 1972. He was Cultural Counsellor in the American Embassy in Delhi, 1978 to 1980. His books include *India's Search for National Identity, Imagining India*, and *Utopias in Conflict: Religion and Nationalism in India*. He edited *The Hindu Tradition. Encyclopedia of Asian History*, and the revised edition of *Sources of Indian Tradition*.

MENACHEM FRIEDMAN is professor of the sociology of religion at the department of sociology at Bar-Ilan University and senior research fellow at the Jerusalem Institute for Israel Studies. He recently published *Haredi (Ultra-Orthodox) Society: Sources, Trends and Processes* (in Hebrew).

ROBERT ERIC FRYKENBERG is professor of history and South Asian studies at the University of Wisconsin at Madison. He is the author of *Guntur District, 1788–1848: A History of Local Influence and Central Authority in South India*, has published numerous articles, and is the editor of several volumes on India, including *Land Tenure and Peasant in South Asia, Delhi through the Ages,* and *Studies of South India.*

SUSAN HARDING is professor of anthropology at the University of California, Santa Cruz, and author of *Remaking Ibieca: Agrarian Reform under Franco* and co-editor of *Statemaking and Social Movements: Essays in Theory and History.* She is currently completing *Miraculous Discourse,* an ethnography of narrative politics in Jerry Falwell's community during the 1980s.

SAMUEL C. HEILMAN is professor of sociology at Queens College and the Graduate Center of the City University of New York. His most recent works include *The Gate Behind the Wall* (winner of the *Present Tense* Award), *A Walker in Jerusalem* (winner of the National Jewish Book Award), and *Defenders of the Faith: Inside Ultra-Orthodox Jewry.*

OUSMANE KANE holds degrees in Arabic and Islamic studies from the Sorbonne. An expert on Islam in Black Africa, he is the author of several studies of sub-Saharan Islam.

MATTHEW P. LAWSON is a sociologist studying at Princeton University. He is the author of several articles on American religion and society in the twentieth century.

JEAN-FRANÇOIS LEGRAIN is Researcher in political sciences at the Centre d'Etudes et de Documentation Economiques, Juridiques et Sociales (CEDEJ), Cairo. Formerly professor of Islamology in the Institut Catholique de Paris, he was written extensively on Islamic movements and communities in Europe and the Middle East.

JAMES MANOR is a professorial fellow of the Institute of Development Studies, University of Sussex, and director of the Institute of Commonwealth Studies, University of London. He has written and edited seven books on South Asian politics including most recently, *The Expedient Utopian: Bandaranaike and Ceylon* and *Power, Poverty and Poison: Disaster and Response in an Indian City.* He has taught at Yale, Harvard, and Leicester Universities.

MARTIN E. MARTY is the Fairfax M. Cone Distinguished Service Professor of the History of Modern Christianity at the University of Chicago, the director of the Fundamentalism Project, and a senior editor of *Christian Century.* A fellow of the American Academy of Arts and Sciences, Marty is the author of over forty books, including the four-volume history, *Modern American Religion.*

BARBARA METCALF is a professor in the department of history at the University of California at Davis. She is the author of several works on Islam in South Asia, including the translation and commentary, *Perfecting Women: Maulana Ashraf 'Ali Thanawi's Bihishti Zewar.*

JAMES PISCATORI teaches at the University of Wales and is an associate fellow of the Royal Institute of International Affairs in London. He is the author of *Islam in a World of Nation-States* (1986) and the editor of *Islam in the Political Process* (1982) and (with Dale Eickelman) *Muslim Travellers: Pilgrimage, Migration, and the Religious Imagination* (1990).

AVIEZER RAVITZKY is professor of Jewish philosophy and chair of the Institute of Jewish Studies, The Hebrew University, Jerusalem. He is the editor of *Sanctity of Life and Martyrdom* (Zalman Shazar Center, 1992) and author of *Messianism, Zionism, and Jewish Religious Radicalism* (Am Oved, 1993).

HUGH ROBERTS is an associate of the Geopolitics and International Boundaries Research Centre at the School of Oriental and African Studies, University of London, and an honorary fellow of the School of Development Studies at the University of East Anglia. He is the author of *Northern Ireland and the Algerian Analogy* (1986) and *Revolution and Resistance: Algerian Politics and the Kabyle Question* (forthcoming) as well as numerous articles on Algerian politics and history.

MARK SAROYAN taught government at Harvard University and has been a visiting scholar at the Faculties of History and Philogy at Azerbaijan State University. He has published several articles on politics and ethnic conflict in the Caucasus. He currently resides in Oakland, California.

CHARLES SELENGUT is on the faculties of Drew University and County College of Morris in Randolph, New Jersey. The author of various scholarly works on new religious movements, he is currently conducting research on the relationship between modernity and contemporary theology. Professor Selengut's recent works include "American Jewish Converts to New Religious Movements" in the *Jewish Journal of Sociology* (December 1988) and *Seeing Society: Perspectives on Social Life* (Allyn and Bacon), 1990.

HAYM SOLOVEITCHIK is professor of Jewish history and literature at Yeshiva University, Bernard Revel Graduate School. A critical historian specializing in medieval Jewish history, his publications include *Pawnbroking: A Study in the Inter-Relationship Between Halakhah, Economic Activity and Communal Self-Image* (Magnes Press) and *Studies in the Halakhah in Exile* (forthcoming).

DAVID STOLL is an anthropologist who has written several articles and books on Latin American religion and political culture, including *Is Latin America Turning Protestant? The Politics of Evangelical Growth* (1990).

TOD D. SWANSON is assistant professor in the department of religious studies at Arizona State University and an expert in tribal religions of South America.

PETER VAN DER VEER is director of the Research Center for Religion and Society and professor of comparative religion at the University of Amsterdam. He is the author of *Gods on Earth* (1988) and *Religious Nationalism* (Berkeley, 1984). He is co-editor of *Orientalism and the Postcolonial Predicament* (Philadelphia, 1993) and editor of *Nation and Migration* (Philadelphia, 1994).

RHYS WILLIAMS is a visiting fellow at Yale University's Program on Non-Profit Organizations and a visiting professor in the department of sociology, Yale University. His most recent publication (with N. J. Demerath III) is *A Bridging of Faiths: Religion and Politics in a New England City* (Princeton University Press, 1992).

ROBERT WUTHNOW is the Gerhard R. Andlinger Professor of Social Sciences at Princeton University and author of numerous books, including *The Restructuring of American Religion: Society and Faith Since World War II* (Princeton University Press).

DARIO ZADRA is currently director of the Istituto Europeo delle Regioni/Europaeisches Institut der Regionen, Trent, Italy. He holds degrees in theology and political science from Trent and Milan and a Ph.D. from the Committee on Social Thought, University of Chicago. Dario Zadra has taught at the Universities of Trent, Rome, Chicago, and Northwestern. His latest book is the forthcoming *New Horizons of European Democracy*.

INDEX

ʿAbduh, Muhammad, 433, 442
Abed, Mohamed Salah, 443
Abu Bakr, 542, 565
Adam, Karl, 128
Adua, Shehu Musa ʿYar, 505
Advani, L. K., 618, 663, 664, 759
al-Afghani, Jamal al-Din, 433
Afghanistan, Islamic movements in, 398
Agha, Amin, 427n.18
Agudat Yisrael party, 298; schism in, 354
Ahmadi Muslims, 669; as controversial, 679
Ahmed, Hocine Ait, 475
Ahmed, Ishtiaq, 370
AIDS, 41, 60
Akhil Bharatiya Pratinidhi Sabha, 625
Akhil Bharatiya Vidyarthi Parishad (ABVP), 639
Al-Daʿwa, magazine of the Muslim Brotherhood, 380
Algeria, Islamic movements in, 365, 368, 369–70. *See also* FIS; FLN
ʿAli, Imam Husayn, 553, 556, 558, 561
ʿAli, Muhammad, 383
Alkalai, Yehuda, 273
All-Ceylon Buddhist Congress Resolutions of 1951, 612
Allegemeiner Journal, 345
All-India Congress party, 742
All-India Muslim League, 679
All-India Sikh Students' Federation, 609
Alon Shvut, 289–90
AMAL (Afwaj al-Muqawama al-Lubnaniyya, the Lebanese Resistance Brigades), 365
Ambedkar, 760
American Association of Lubavitcher Hasidim, 339
American Coalition for Traditional Values, 167
"American Millennium, The," 59–61
Amin, Husayn Ahmad, 407n.10
Amital, Rabbi Yehuda, 290
Amrik Singh, 609
Amritsar, 608
Andandpur Sahib Resolution, 608

Andean Catholicism, 79; conversion to, 80
Andean religion, 79; role of rum in, 82
Andhra Pradesh, 727, 748
anti-Ahmadiyas riots of 1852, 669
anti-British Jewish underground, 281–84
Antichrist, 61, 64
Anti-Intellectualism in American Life, 20
anti-Tamil riots of 1977, in Sri Lanka, 771, 780
Apostolic United Pentecostal Gospel Society, in south India, 747
Approaching Hoofbeats: The Four Horsemen of the Apocalypse, 69
Apte, Babasaheb, 626
Apte, Shivram Shankar, 653
Aqsa mosque, 419, 423
Aquilo, Father Federico, 90
Arafat, Yassir, 73, 364, 372n.6, 418, 423, 426. *See also* Palestine Liberation Organization
Ariel, Rav Yisrael, rabbi of Yamit, 278, 290; support of Jewish underground, 280
ʿArif, ʿAbd al-Rahman, 540, 547
Armageddon, 72, 74; battle of, 57, 61, 64
Armageddon, Oil and the Middle East Crisis, 72
Arukh ha-Shulhan, 198, 226n.4, 350
Arya Samaj, 627, 636, 657, 760
Asher, Rabbi of Stolin, 309
al-Ashmawi, Muhammad Saʿid, 407n.10
Ashur, Faraq al-Sayyid, 411n.64
al-Asifi, Muhammad Mahdi, 558, 570, 574
Assemblies of God, 37, 733; in south India, 748
Associazioni Cristiane Lavoratori Italiani, 125
Asyut, riots at, 397, 398, 400, 403
Atatürk, Mustafa Kemal, 700n.11
Ateret Cohanim Yeshiva, 188
Aviner, Rabbi Shlomo, 188, 290, 293, 302n.76; influence within the Mercaz Harav community, 277; criticism of Gush Emunim, 278
Awami League, 672, 682, 694, 698
Ayish, Hasan, 427n.18
Ayodhya, crisis of, 645, 646, 662–63, 723, 763. *See also* Babri Masjid
Ayub Khan, 679